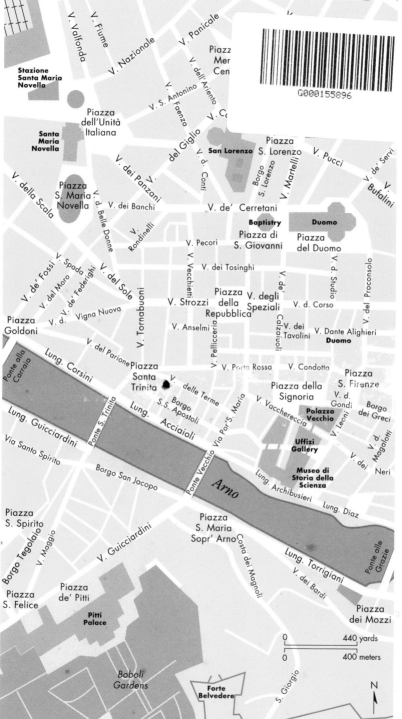

BB £1.99 ex display copy

G000155896

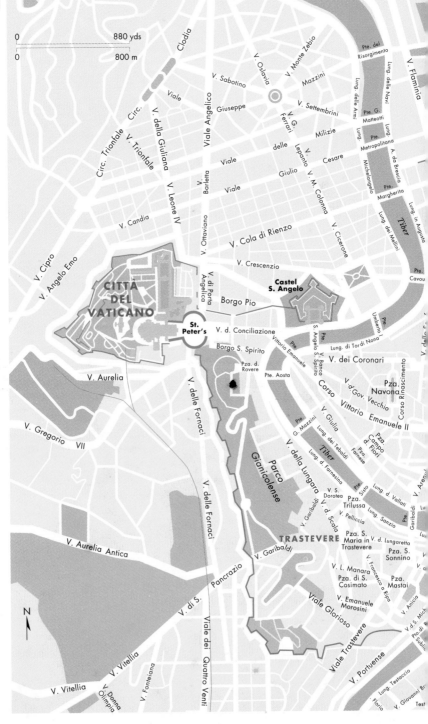

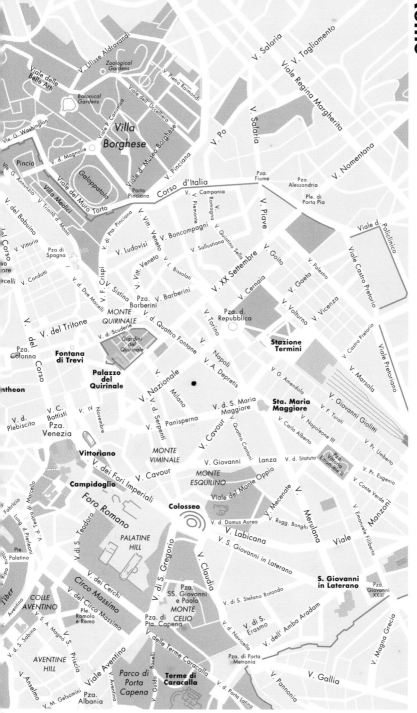

Rome

Venice

Sacca Fisola

Isola della Giudecca

Canale della Giudecca

Can. d. Lauraneri

Rio d. S. Biagio

Fond. S. Biagio

Fondamenta delle Zattere

Rio d. Oznissanti

Calle Avogaria

Campo S. Barnaba

Rio d. S. Barnaba

Rio d. S. Margherita

Campo di S. Margherita

Rio d. S. Nicola

Rio terra dei Pensieri

Rio d. S. Andrea

Canale di S. Chiara

Canaledi S. Chiara

Bus Station
Piazzale Roma

Stazione Santa Lucia

Rio Nuovo

F. Minotto

S. Simeon Piccolo

Lista di Spagna

Canal Grande

Riva di Biasio

Lista di Bari

Riva d. Biasio

Riva d. S. Martin

R. di S. Zan Degola

Corte Canal

C. d. Lacca

Rio della Frescada

Rio Frescada

Rio terra Canal

C. Larga

Inton C. d.

Ca' d'Oro

R. di Mala

C. Larga

R. di S. Cassiano

Campo S. Polo

Campo d. Pescheria

Rio d. Santi Apostoli

Strada Nuova

Rio S. Caterina

R. d. Gesuiti

R.d. Mala

Campo S. Stefano

C. d. Carrozze

C. Morosini

22 Marzo

Campo S. Angelo

C. Larga

C.d. Mandola

Canal Grande

Rio d. S. Luca

Campo Manin

Riva del Carbon

Riva del Vin

Ponte Rialto

R. d. S. Marina

Rio d. S. Fava

Campo Santa Marina

Campo Santa Maria Formosa

Ruga Giuffa

C. d. Testa

C. d. Squero

R. dei Mendicanti

Campo Santi Giovanni e Paolo

Barbaria delle Tole

R. d. S.

Rio della Panada

Canale delle Navi

Campo della Carità

Calle de Toletta

Rio d. S. Vio

Rio d. Fornace

Rio d. Fornace

Campo S. Maurizio

S. Moisè

R. d. Moisè

Frezzeria

C. Fabbri

Piazza San Marco

Basilica di San Marco

R. d. Palazzo

Palazzo Ducale

Molo

C.d. Bande

Sal. di S.

C. d. Lion

R. d. Greci

R.d. S. Severo

R.d.S. Lorenzo

R. d. Pietà

C. d. Furlani

R. d. S. Guistina

R. d. S.

Riva degli Schiavoni

Isola di S. Giorgio Maggiore

Canale di S. Marco

Fond. delle Zitelle

R.d. Arsenale

Canale d. Galeazze

Rio della Tana

Arsenale

Riva d. Sette Martiri

Riva V. Garibaldi

R. d. Scudi

R. d. Gorne

R. d. S.

TO LIDO

▲ Vaporetto stop

N

0 440 yards
0 400 meters

the BERKELEY guides

CRITICAL ACCLAIM FOR THE BERKELEY GUIDES

"Planet-wise instruction for [the] cash conscious . . . for the price, the time of your life." **—Details**

"[The Berkeley Guides are] brimming with useful information for the low-budget traveler—material delivered in a fresh, funny, and often irreverent way." **—The Philadelphia Inquirer**

"The [Berkeley Guides] are deservedly popular because of their extensive coverage, entertaining style of writing, and heavy emphasis on budget travel . . . If you are looking for tips on hostels, vegetarian food, and hitchhiking, there are no books finer." **—San Diego Union-Tribune**

"[The Berkeley Guides] offer straight dirt on everything from hostels to look for and beaches to avoid to museums least likely to attract your parents . . . they're fresher than Harvard's Let's Go series." **—Seventeen**

"The [Berkeley Guides] give a rare glimpse into the real cultures of Europe, Canada, Mexico, and the United States . . . with in-depth historical backgrounds on each place and a creative, often poetical style of prose." **—Eugene Weekly**

"The new On the Loose guides are more comprehensive, informative and witty than Let's Go." **—Glamour**

"The Berkeley Guides have more and better maps, and on average, the nuts and bolts descriptions of such things as hotels and restaurants tend to be more illuminating than the often terse and sometimes vague entries in the 'Let's Go' guides." **— San José Mercury News**

"The well-organized guides list can't miss sights, offbeat attractions and cheap thrills, such as festivals and walks. And they're fun to read." **— New York Newsday**

"Reading (these guides) is a lot like listening to a first-hand report from a friend...They're also just plain fun to read." **— Greensboro News & Record**

"Written for the young and young at heart...you'll find this thick, fact-filled guide makes entertaining reading." **— St. Louis Dispatch**

"...bright articulate guidebooks. The irreverent yet straightforward prose is easy to read and offers a sense of the adventures awaiting travelers off the beaten path." **— Portland Oregonian**

THE BERKELEY GUIDES are printed using soy-based ink on 100% recycled paper, including 50% post-consumer fiber and 100% de-inked newspapers, magazines and catalogs. What's the use of traveling if there's nothing left to see?

THE BERKELEY GUIDES

the BERKELEY guides

italy '96

On the Loose
On the Cheap
Off the Beaten
Path

WRITTEN BY BERKELEY STUDENTS IN COOPERATION WITH
THE ASSOCIATED STUDENTS OF THE UNIVERSITY OF CALIFORNIA

ISBN 0-679-02985-0

BERKELEY GUIDE TO ITALY

Editors: Tara Duggan, Elisabeth Schriber
Managing Editors: Nicole Harb, Kristina Malsberger, Sharron Wood
Executive Editor: Scott McNeely
Map Editor: Bob Blake
Cartographers: David Lindroth, Inc.; Eureka Cartography
Creative Director: Fabrizio La Rocca
Text Design: Tigist Getachew
Cover Design: Fabrizio La Rocca
Cover Art: Poul Lange (3-D Art), Bob Krist (photo in frame), Paul D'Innocenzo (still life and digital imaging)

SPECIAL SALES

Contents

WHAT THE BERKELEY GUIDES ARE ALL ABOUT *x*

THANKS TO YOU *xi*

BERKELEY BIOS *xii*

INTRODUCTION *xv*

MAP OF ITALY *xviii–xix*

1 BASICS *1*

Planning Your Trip *1*
Useful Organizations *1*
Student and Teacher ID Cards *5*
How Much It Will Cost *5*
When to Go *6*
Passports, Visas, and Red Tape *7*
Rail Passes *8*
Money *11*
What to Pack *14*
Protecting Your Valuables *15*
Customs and Duties *15*
Staying Healthy *16*
Resources for Women Travelers *17*
Resources for Gay and Lesbian Travelers *17*

Resources for Travelers with Disabilities *18*
Working in Italy *19*
Studying in Italy *19*
Coming and Going *20*
By Air *20*
Staying in Italy *23*
Getting Around *23*
Phones *24*
Mail *25*
Business Hours *25*
Language *26*
Where to Sleep *26*
Food *27*
After Dark *31*
Further Reading *31*

2 VENICE AND THE VENETO *33*

Venice *33*
Map of Venice 38–39
Near Venice *59*
The Veneto *60*
Padova *60*
Map of the Veneto 61

Vicenza *66*
Verona *68*
Map of Verona 69
Bassano del Grappa *72*
Treviso *75*

3 THE DOLOMITES AND THE NORTHEAST *77*

Trentino-Alto Adige *77*
Map of Trentino-Alto Adige 78
Trento *79*
Bolzano *84*
Map of Bolzano 85
Merano *87*

Friuli-Venezia Giulia *89*
Udine *89*
Aquileia *91*
Trieste *92*
Map of Trieste 93

4 MILAN, LOMBARDY, AND THE LAKES 97

Map of Lombardy and the Lakes 98–99
Milan *100*
Map of Milan 101
Lombardy *111*
Pavia *111*
Cremona *113*
Bergamo *115*
Brescia *117*

Mantova *119*
The Lakes *123*
Lago di Garda *124*
Lago d'Iseo *126*
Lago di Como *129*
Lago Maggiore *131*
Lago di Orta *133*

5 PIEMONTE AND THE VALLE D'AOSTA 135

Map of Piemonte and the Valle d'Aosta 136–137
Piemonte *138*
Torino *138*
Map of Torino 139
Asti *146*

Northern Piemonte *147*
Valle d'Aosta *148*
Aosta *148*
Parco Nazionale del Gran Paradiso *150*
Courmayeur and Mont Blanc *153*

6 THE ITALIAN RIVIERA 155

Genova *155*
Map of Genova 157
Near Genova *162*
Riviera di Ponente *162*
Finale Ligure *162*
Map of the Italian Riviera 163

San Remo *166*
Riviera di Levante *169*
Camogli *169*
Santa Margherita Ligure *170*
Cinque Terre *172*

7 BOLOGNA AND EMILIA-ROMAGNA 175

Map of Emilia-Romagna 176
Bologna *177*
Map of Bologna 178
Emilia-Romagna *184*
Modena *185*

Parma *188*
Piacenza *192*
Ferrara *193*
Ravenna *197*
Rimini *203*

8 FLORENCE AND TUSCANY 209

Map of Tuscany 210–211
Florence *212*
Map of Florence 214–215
Near Florence *239*
Tuscany *245*
Lucca *245*
Map of Lucca 247
Pisa *248*
Livorno *252*

San Gimignano *254*
Volterra *256*
Siena *258*
Map of Siena 259
Arezzo *264*
Cortona *267*
Southern Tuscany *269*
Elba *273*

9 UMBRIA AND MARCHE 277

Umbria *277*
Map of Umbria and Marche 278–279
Perugia *280*
Map of Perugia 281
Lake Trasimeno *285*
Gubbio *286*
Assisi *288*
Map of Assisi 289

Spoleto *293*
Todi *295*
Orvieto *296*
Marche *298*
Urbino *298*
Pesaro *300*
Ancona *302*
Ascoli Piceno *303*

10 ROME 305

Basics 306
Where to Sleep 311
Map of Rome Lodging 312–313
Food 319
Exploring Rome 324
Map of Rome Sights 326–327
Shopping 348
After Dark 349
Near Rome 352
Frascati 352

Map of Lazio 353
Tivoli 353
Subiaco 354
Rieti and Monte Terminillo 355
Cerveteri 356
Ostia Antica 356
Civitavecchia 358
Viterbo 358
Monte Rufeno Wildlife Reserve 359

11 ABRUZZI AND MOLISE 361

Abruzzi 361
L'Aquila 361
Map of Abruzzi and Molise 362
Sulmona 364
Parco Nazionale d'Abruzzo 365

The Abruzzi Coast 367
Molise 368
Isernia 368
Campobasso 369
Termoli 370

12 NAPLES AND CAMPANIA 371

Naples 371
Map of Campania 372
Map of Naples 376–377
Near Naples 384
Bay of Naples 385
Pozzuoli 385
Herculaneum 386
Pompeii 387

Map of Pompeii 389
The Islands 390
Sorrento 394
The Amalfi Coast 396
Amalfi 397
Salerno 400
Paestum 401

13 PUGLIA, BASILICATA, AND CALABRIA 405

Puglia 406
Map of Puglia 407
Foggia 408
Lucera 409
Gargano Promontory 410
Tremiti Islands 415
Bari 416
Map of Bari 417
Taranto 421
Brindisi 423

Lecce 424
Basilicata 427
Map of Basilicata and Calabria 428
Matera 429
Metaponto 431
Maratea 432
Calabria 433
Cosenza 434
Near Cosenza 435
Reggio di Calabria 439

14 SICILY 443

Map of Sicily 444–445
The Ionian Coast 447
Messina 447
Taormina 449
Catania 452
Mt. Etna 457
Siracusa 459
Southern Sicily 463
Noto 463
Ragusa 464
Agrigento 465

Western Sicily 468
Marsala 468
Trapani 470
Egadi Islands 474
Palermo 475
Map of Palermo 476
The Tyrrhenian Coast 484
Cefalù 484
Milazzo 486
Aeolian Islands 487

15 SARDINIA *491*

Map of Sardinia 492
Cagliari *494*
Map of Cagliari 495
The West Coast *498*
Oristano *498*
Alghero *501*

The Northern Coast *504*
Sassari *504*
Santa Teresa di Gallura *507*
The East Coast *510*
Olbia *511*
Nuoro *511*

ITALIAN GLOSSARY *515*

ARCHITECTURAL PRIMER *521*

INDEX *529*

What the Berkeley Guides Are All About

Four years ago, a motley bunch of U.C. Berkeley students launched a new series of guidebooks—*The Berkeley Guides*. Since then, we've been busy writing and editing 13 books to destinations across the globe, from California, Mexico, and Central America to Europe and Eastern Europe. Along the way our writers have weathered bus plunges, rabies, and guerrilla attacks, landed bush planes above the Arctic Circle, gotten lost in the woods (proverbially and literally), and broken bread with all sorts of peculiar characters—from Mafia dons and Hell's Angel bikers to Capuchin monks and anarchist squatters. And don't forget about the train station sleep-ins, voodoo bus schedules, and, of course, Italy's "Gilligan-had-a-better-chance-of-getting-off-the-isle-than-I-do-of-escaping-this-town" train strikes.

Coordinating the efforts of 65 U.C. Berkeley writers back at the office is an equally daunting task (have you ever tried to track manuscript from Morocco?). But that's the whole point of *The Berkeley Guides*: to bring you the most up-to-date info on prices, the latest budget-travel trends, the newest restaurants and hostels, where to catch your next train—all written and edited by people who know what cheap travel is all about.

You see, it's one of life's weird truisms that the more cheaply you travel, the more you inevitably experience. If you're looking for five-star meals, air-conditioned tour buses, and reviews of the same old tourist traps, you're holding the wrong guidebook. Instead, *The Berkeley Guides* give you an in-depth look at local culture, detailed coverage of small towns and off-beat sights, bars and cafés where tourists rarely tread, plus no-nonsense practical info that deals with the real problems of real people (where to get aspirin at 3 AM, where to launder those dirty socks).

Coming from a community as diverse as Berkeley, we also wanted our guides to be useful to everyone, so we tell you if a place is wheelchair accessible, if it provides resources for gay and lesbian travelers, and if it's safe for women traveling solo. Many of us are Californians, which means most of us like trees and mountain trails. It also means we emphasize the outdoors in every *Berkeley Guide* and include lots of info about hiking and tips on protecting the environment. To minimize our impact on the environment, we print our books on recycled paper using soy-based inks.

Most important, these guides are for travelers who want to see more than just the main sights. We find out what local people do for fun, where they go to eat, drink, or just hang out. Most guidebooks lead you down the tourist trail, ignoring important local issues, events, and culture. In *The Berkeley Guides* we give you the information you need to understand what's going on around you—whether it's yet another government scandal in Rome or a Mafia-related bombing in Palermo.

We've done our best to make sure the information in *The Berkeley Guides* is accurate, but time doesn't stand still: prices change, places go out of business, currencies get devalued. Call ahead when it's really important, and try not to get too stressed out.

Thanks to You

Hundreds of people helped us put together *The Berkeley Guide to Italy 1996.* Some are listed below, but many others—whom our writers met briefly in hostels, piazze, train stations, and gelaterias—also pitched in. We'd like you to help us update this guide by giving us feedback from the road. Drop us a line—a postcard, a scrawled note on a piece of toilet paper, whatever—and we'll be happy to acknowledge your contribution. Our address is 515 Eshleman Hall, University of California, Berkeley, CA 94720.

Special thanks go to the Altafini family (Savigliano), Barbara (Rome), Chiara Barbieri (Venice), Sergio Bertoni (Elba), Francesca Biondi (Rimini), Lauren Brandt (Venice), Tommy Brooks (Venice), Katherine Burke (London), Michelangelo Cinaglia (Taranto), Simon Dang (San Francisco), Jane and Michael Duggan (Naples), Ben Duggan (San Francisco), Umberto Gentilioni (Rome), the folks at the Peggy Guggenheim Collection (Venice), Lucia Hwang (Berkeley), Karimo (Sardinia), Jen Ketring (San Francisco), Kathy Krause (Los Angeles), the Landis Family (New Orleans), Baty Landis (New Orleans), Andrea Lazzoni (Bologna), Kristine Marcovich (Venice), Maurizio and Mauro (Rome), Jullian Mettler (Basel), Andrea De Michelis and family (Padua), Melanie Moss (Venice), Sakura Ozaki (Torino), Willy Palin (Venice), Ben Plant (London), Chica Preda (Merano), the Editrix Quintet (Berkeley and San Francisco), Reef (Rome), Elena Rinaldi (Bologna), John Ronan (Merano), Roberto, Paolo, Angela e tutti at Ostello Archi Rossi (Firenze), Alex Rubin (Las Vegas), Stephanie and Robert Schriber (Dayton), Rebecca Schwaner (Los Angeles), the Sowden family (Milan), Tabby Sowden (Freiburg), Morgan Sowden (Prague), Matteo Sperling (Montepulciano), Arthur and Dorothy Sprague (Castro Valley, CA), Jutta Springer (Emilia), Filippo Staiano (Bologna), Marco Steinberg (Rome and Helsinki), Tania (Rome), Ciccio Toscana (Bologna), Elin Towler (Berkeley), Angelique Tremble (Berkeley), Liz Willette (Impruneta), Steve Yung (São Paulo), and Sammy Zaher (Venice).

We'd also like to thank the Random House folks who helped us with cartography, page design, and production: Bob Blake, Ellen Browne, Mike Costa, Fionn Davenport, Denise DeGennaro, Janet Foley, Tigist Getachew, Laura M. Kidder, Fabrizio La Rocca, Linda Schmidt, and Tracy Patruno.

Berkeley Bios

Behind every lodging review, restaurant blurb, and introduction in this book lurks a student writer. You might recognize the type—perpetually short on time, money, and clean underwear. Six Berkeley students spent the summer traveling around Italy to research and write this book. Every few weeks, they sent their manuscript back to a two-person editorial team in Berkeley, who pushed, pummeled, and squashed it into shape.

The Writers

While recording the sights, sounds, smells, and tastes of Emilia-Romagna, Marche, Umbria, Abruzzi, and Molise, **Laura Altieri** had to contend with more than her fair share of wild sheep, squirrels (oh my!), and heat stroke. Having successfully refused all those tempting green-card-hopeful marriage proposals, she has returned to the United States to finish her degree in History and Italian at the University of California, Berkeley; unless, of course, an offer from *Gourmet* magazine comes first.

During her travels in Tuscany and on the Riviera, **Sara Fisher** was hounded by well-meaning Italians to remain *sempre tranquilla* (always calm). She strove to remain tranquilla when her Ligurian bus driver descended from the bus in the middle of nowhere to take a one-hour nap, when dealing with an offer she couldn't refuse (she managed to anyway) from a persistent Sicilian, and when hitching a midnight ride across Florence on the handlebars of a bicycle whose owner failed to stop for red lights and speeding buses. Sara now plans to become the first truly tranquilla journalist in U.S. history.

Paul Kottman covered a lot of ground, including mountains, lakes, coastline, and congested cities while writing Naples and Campania, Piemonte, the Valle D'Aosta, and the Northeast. He was able to practice French, German, *napolitano*, and on occasion even Italian. Surprisingly, Paul came away from his Italian odyssey relatively unscathed. A *moto* in Sorrento gave him a little trouble, but after a two-minute lesson (and a shameful episode he wishes to forget) he was riding along the Amalfi coast on cliffs 500 feet above water.

Having just earned her bachelor's in Political Science and Italian, **Janet Morris** plans to continue studying, either for a Ph.D. in poli sci, or an infinitely more practical degree in the culinary arts. Traveling through Calabria, Basilicata, Puglia, Lombardy, and parts of Piemonte, she learned that a country's beauty lies not in its monuments, not even in its pasta, but in its people. Janet's modest long-term aspirations are to become a world traveler, gourmet chef, woman of culture, and philandering philanthropist.

All that studying of art history paid off for **Oliver Schwaner-Albright** in Sicily and the Veneto, especially when he accurately guessed the date of the Palazzo Balibi-Valier based solely on the style of its three arches, which he viewed as he fell from the palazzo's terrace into the Grand Canal (it's much saltier than he had imagined). After schmucking through the world for the

Berkeley Guides off-and-on for three years, Oliver's mommy is making him graduate from the University of California this May.

Erin Williams escaped a double major in English and Italian to travel in Rome and Sardinia. With the help of several outrageous Roman friends, she discovered the secrets of the Eternal City at dawn, and mastered the subtleties of cursing in Romano—"alle mortacci tua!" Searching Sardinia's coastline for the perfect beach, she ran out of expletives and synonyms for azure and turquoise and wished she'd brought that 10-pound thesaurus after all. At the moment she is contemplating the writer's life in the south of France for an indefinite period of time.

The Editors

Despite emotionally draining phone conversations with writers, totally manic commutes from The City, and some serious jitters from hourly trips to the local espresso bar, editor **Tara Duggan** managed to complete her editing duties without loosing too much gray matter—though it's true that her little noises ("urwmph de do") and facial contortions worsened as the summer progressed. While her plans for the future are loose, and her morals loosening every day (sorry Grandma), Tara looks forward to a long, grueling, and ultimately fulfilling career in some kind of literary field or other.

Editor **Elisabeth Schriber** (commonly known as Bip, Bipissima, or Sasquatch) had some troubles with mathematics, on occasion finding herself having to cut a few pages too many (Oh well . . . nobody goes to Calabria, right?). Other than that, she thrived over the summer, armed with an extensive background in Roman caffè and carciofi. Many months with her nose buried in *The Berkeley Guides* helped Elisabeth to cast her humble Ohio origins aside and blossom as a full-fledged Bay Area person. And, of course, almost every San Francisco resident on the *Berkeley Guides* staff owes her thanks for the many times she crossed the Bay Bridge in the Bipmobile.

What to do when your *money* is done traveling before you are.

Don't worry. With **MoneyGram**,^{SM} your parents can send

you money in usually 10 minutes or less to more than

19,000 locations in 80 countries. So if the money you

need to see history becomes history, call us and we'll

direct you to a **MoneyGram**^{SM} agent closest to you.

USA: **1-800-MONEYGRAM**   Canada: **1-800-933-3278**   France: **05-905311**
Germany: **0130-8-16629**   England: **0800-89-7198**   Spain: **900-96-1218**

or call collect **303-980-3340**

MoneyGram
INTERNATIONAL MONEY TRANSFER
_{SM}

Introduction

By Tara Duggan and Elisabeth Schriber

The turmoil that characterizes life in Italy may not be apparent when you first arrive. In fact it's pretty easy to be seduced by the country's beautiful and varied scenery, incredible food and wine, warm people and climate, and stunning architecture and fashion— not to mention the most concentrated collection of artistic masterpieces in the world. Like countless others who have "discovered" Italy through the centuries, you'll take your first lick of gelato or your first peek inside the Pantheon and realize, suddenly, what you've been missing all your life. But there's more to "the most sensuous country in Europe" than meets the eye. You'll probably be introduced to the downside of Italy on a sweltering summer afternoon, thirsty and tired, as you consider the many contrasts of 20th-century life here: traffic jams, Roman ruins, pollution, baroque cathedrals, and Vespa drivers swerving through narrow streets as they chat on cellular phones. These kinds of contradictions have led many Italians to raise some difficult questions. Can the clash between past and present ever be resolved? When subway construction hits underground ruins, does digging stop or continue through? How will the information revolution fare in a country where it takes six months to install a phone line? And should a country accept, or even exploit, its role as a cultural theme park? One response to these dilemmas came early in this century, from the futurist poet Filippo Tommaso Marinetti, who advocated blowing up Italy's museums and giving Venice a helpful shove into its lagoon. Not everyone has taken such a radical posture, though someone did set off a bomb in Florence's Uffizi Gallery in 1993. Still, even the more traditional Italians have begun to wonder whether their country is prepared to cope with its many problems or if it's doomed to become a third-world museum of antiquity.

A study of Italy's past provides some major clues as to how the country's problems first arose. In a period spanning 3,000 years, the narrow peninsula and its islands have supported a series of sophisticated peoples from a nearly endless variety of ethnic, religious, and philosophical backgrounds. These invasions kept the country permanently in flux, encouraging Italy's inability to maintain political and social security.

Excavations have uncovered evidence of prehistoric societies from as early as 2400 BC, though much more is known about the Carthaginian, Etruscan, and Greek civilizations that gained influence in the 8th and 7th centuries BC. These more advanced cultures built magnificent cities throughout Italy, edging out indigenous tribes. In the 6th century BC, Italy's most advanced and indefatigable conqueror, the Roman Republic, laid claim to the land. But even after the founding of the nearly impenetrable Roman Empire in 509 BC, invasions from north, south, east, and west continued to pummel the land, leaving behind new languages, religions, and hair styles. Roman territory expanded nonetheless, and a succession of ambitious, often maniacal emperors put together the largest, most powerful force in the west. It was not without reason, and definitely *with* arrogance, that the Romans referred to everyone else as "barbarians."

Eventually even the Romans spread themselves too thin, and a schism between the eastern and western sides of the empire developed. Constantinople succeeded Rome as the "in" place to be, and Christianity, once it was accepted by Constantine in AD 313, strengthened its hold on the continent. A power struggle between emperors and the papacy ensued almost immediately thereafter, setting off a series of smaller-scale conflicts that lasted for centuries. This clash between secular and ecclesiastical Italy remains even today: Many modern-day Italians tend to hold ambivalent, if not antagonistic feelings toward their church and *il Papa* (the pope).

As if the situation weren't already a complete mess, semiautonomous city-states emerged in Italy in the 1300s, ruled by inbred autocrats and dominating dynasties. Art and literature thrived in this secular, commercialized environment, but fighting between the states made life in the early Renaissance not as idyllic as it's made out to be in Art History 101. In the centuries that followed, dynasties such as the Austrian Hapsburgs and the Spanish Bourbons laid claim to parts of Italy, leaving behind a mixture of languages, architectural styles, religious heroes, and culinary treats. It wasn't until 1810 that Italy achieved a sense of unity, and even then it was at the hands of a foreign power, namely Napoleon, who ruled the peninsula with his puppet government until Waterloo. Finally, in 1861, an idealistic rabble-rouser by the name of Giuseppe Garibaldi, with the help of his thousand-man army (the "Red Shirts"), succeeded in unifying the Kingdom of Italy.

When asked if it was difficult to govern the Italians, Mussolini reportedly answered, "No, it's not difficult. But it is useless."

Naturally, the *Risorgimento* (unification) didn't bring cohesion and order to Italy. It would seem that confusion is the state most comfortable to the Italians, having existed amidst chaos for so many years. Fortunately, Italy's inability to organize itself paid off for the Allies in World War II. The Italian Fascist party under *Il Duce*, Benito Mussolini, entered the war completely unprepared (surprise, surprise), and with dated equipment. For four years the Italians found themselves enmeshed in countless bloody battles, first against the Allied powers, then against the Axis powers, *and* finally against partisan revolutionaries. In the end Mussolini was overthrown by his own compatriots and brutally assassinated.

The void left at the end of the war was filled by a government consisting of a series of coalitions, with the majority alternating between the right-wing *Democrazia Cristiana* party, and the left-wing *Partito Socialista Italiano*. What was a largely underdeveloped agricultural country before the war was on its way to becoming a prominent industrialized nation. But as money poured into the north through companies such as Olivetti and Fiat, industry in the *mezzogiorno* (the provinces south of Rome) stagnated. This disparity continues to affect Italians today: Many northerners consider those from the south to be ignorant and southerners often complain of the northerners' coldness and obsession with money, accusing them of having their *nasi in sù*, or noses in the air.

In the last 49 years, 54 Italian governments have come and gone. Just in the past decade, Italy has seen a left-of-center majority, a center-right majority, a growing neo-fascist contingent, a northern separatist movement, and a virulent capitalist force personified by the recently ousted Silvio Berlusconi.

Northerners may jump at the chance to blame all their problems on the southern half of the boot, but political disorder and corruption have recently been found to be nation-wide afflictions. When former judge Antonio Di Pietro took charge of uncovering the *Tangentopoli* (literally, Bribesville) scandals in 1992, he exposed corruption in nearly every nook and cranny of Italian politics: Within a year, a huge percentage of Italian politicians—from the socialists to the neo-fascists—were behind bars. The Christian Democrat Party lost its hold on a relative majority in Parliament, and there hasn't really been a functioning government since. The last nearly successful attempt at a cohesive governing party, headed by media mogul Silvio Berlusconi, resulted in more investigations and consequently, more arrests. This political intrigue would not be surprising from many of the so-called third-world nations of Africa, Asia, or Central America, where food is scarce, political freedom unheard of, or where poverty and illiteracy is rampant. But people in Italy are not hungry. They are free to argue, criticize, and publish any manner of things regarding their country and government. Almost everyone manages to afford a nice pair of shoes and a holiday by the sea. Still, for a country producing such luxuries as Ferrari automobiles, Valentino fashions, and nearly priceless black truffles, much of Italy retains a rustic atmosphere and provincial attitude that may seem primitive to foreigners.

Ironically, the best organized thing in Italy is crime. Known as the *'ndragheta* in Calabria, *la camorra* in Naples, and just plain *mafia* in Sicily, organized crime has been the subject of graphic movies, novels, and news reports for decades. Whether Mafia bosses are a holdover from the time of feudal lords or a surrogate power for a country whose elected politicians seem perpetually paralyzed by red, white, and green tape will never be known. For whatever reason, the Mafia continues to flourish in Italy, and the scandals of 1993 prove that its contacts penetrate to the highest offices of Italian government and finance.

The Italy of the 1990s may not have a clear direction or purpose, but even the most jaded cynic cannot mistake Rome, Florence, Naples, or Venice for anything other than what they are—at once extravagant, dilapidated, and quintessentially Italian. Even those who complain of lecherous men and chronically late trains agree: The time-honored reasons for traveling here are as compelling as ever. To appreciate Italy, one has only to open one's eyes (or mouth), and live for each moment, each new sensation—just as the Italians do. Seemingly oblivious to the political and economical woes of their homeland, they know how to make the most of everything—and lucky for us, their passion and appetite for life is contagious.

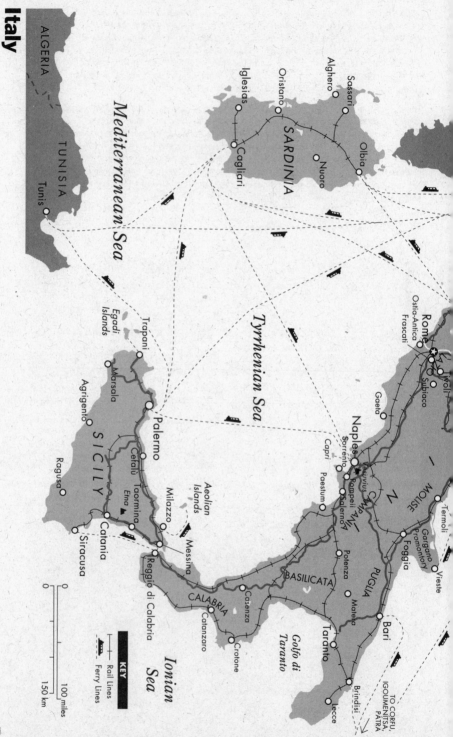

Italy

ALGERIA

TUNISIA

Tunis

Mediterranean Sea

Tyrrhenian Sea

SARDINIA

Sassari
Alghero
Oristano
Iglesias
Nuoro
Cagliari
Olbia

Egadi Islands
Trapani
Marsala
Agrigento
Ragusa

SICILY
Cefalù
Palermo
Taormina
Etna
Milazzo
Catania
Siracusa
Aeolian Islands
Messina
Reggio di Calabria

Rome
Ostia-Antica
Frascati
Tivoli
Subiaco
Gaeta
Naples
Capri
Sorrento
Pompeii
Vesuvius
Salerno
Paestum

CAMPANIA
MOLISE
Termoli
Vieste
Gargano Promontory
Foggia
Potenza
Matera
PUGLIA
BASILICATA
CALABRIA
Cosenza
Catanzaro
Crotone
Taranto
Golfo di Taranto
Bari
Brindisi
Lecce

Ionian Sea

TO CORFU,
IGOUMENITSA,
PATRA

KEY

—|— Rail lines
--- Ferry Lines

0   100 miles
0   150 km

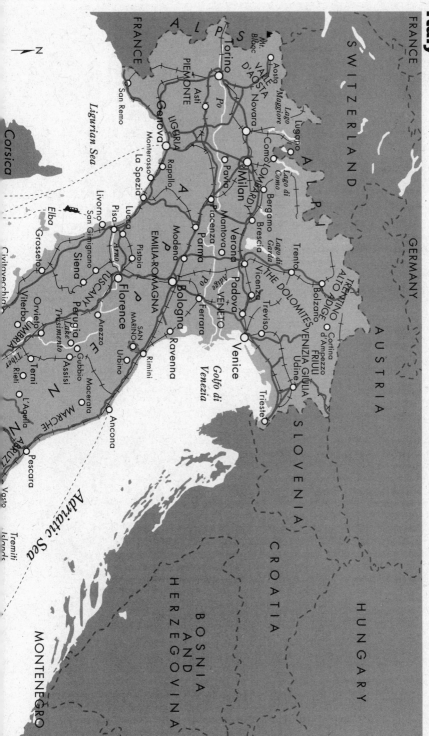

Italy

STUDENT TRAVEL.

Two ways to spend $1000:

A. 10 CDs, trendy boots, two surfwear T-shirts, wild haircut, navel ring, a new tattoo, party all week, one bottle of aspirin.

B. Air ticket to somewhere exciting, rail pass, backpack, meet people, experience new cultures, learn about the world.

Education is expensive. Spend wisely.

STA Travel: 800-777-0112 • http://www.sta-travel.com

New York: 212-627-3111
Boston: 617-266-6014
Philadelphia: 215-382-2928
Washington DC: 202-887-0912
Chicago: 312-786-9050
San Francisco: 415-391-8407
Los Angeles: 213-934-8722
Seattle: 206-633-5000

STA TRAVEL
We've been there.

BASICS 1

If you've ever traveled with anyone, you know there are two types of people in the world: the planners and the nonplanners. You also know that travel brings out the very worst in both groups: Left to their own devices, the planners will have you goose-stepping from attraction to attraction on a cultural blitzkrieg, while the nonplanners will invariably miss the flight, the bus, and the point. This Basics chapter offers you a middle ground, providing enough information to help plan your trip without saddling you with a strict itinerary. Keep in mind that companies go out of business, prices inevitably go up, and at some point a *sciopero* (strike) will cancel buses or a *chiuso per restauro* (closed for restoration) sign will be posted on the museum you were dying to visit. Such are the joys of traveling in Italy.

Planning Your Trip

USEFUL ORGANIZATIONS

GOVERNMENT TOURIST OFFICES You'll find **Italian Government Tourist Offices** (**ENIT**) in the United States, the United Kingdom, and Canada, as well as in Rome (Via Marghera 2, 00185 Rome, tel. 06/49711). The **Azienda di Promozione Turismo** (**APT**) and **Ente Provinciale per il Turismo** (**EPT**) offices you see all over Italy are run by this organization.

➢ **IN THE UNITED STATES** • The folks at ENIT (630 5th Ave., Suite 1655, New York, NY 10111, tel. 212/245–4822, fax 212/586–9249; 12400 Wilshire Blvd., Suite 550, Los Angeles, CA 90025, tel. 310/820–0098, fax 310/820–6357) have information on lodging and outdoor activities, and will send you brochures with useful maps upon request.

➢ **IN CANADA** • In Montréal, ENIT (1 Pl. Ville Marie, Suite 1914, Montréal, Qué, H3B 3M9, tel. 514/866–7667, fax 514/392–1429) has helpful, trilingual staffers.

➢ **IN THE UNITED KINGDOM** • ENIT in London (Princes St. 1, London WIR 8AY, tel. 171/408–1254, fax 171/493–6695) is called the Italian State Tourist Office.

➢ **IN AUSTRALIA AND NEW ZEALAND** • These countries don't have ENIT offices, so residents should contact one of the above branches.

STUDENT TRAVEL ORGANIZATIONS **Student Travel Agency** (**STA**) has 120 offices worldwide and offers low-price airfares to destinations around the globe. STA offers the **American Youth Hostels** (**AYH**) card (*see below*), the **International Student Identity Card** (**ISIC**), the **International Youth Card** (**IYC**), and the **International Teacher Card** (**ITIC**), as well as their own **Go Card** (for

TOP 5 Ways to Save Money While Traveling

5. Ship yourself in a crate marked "Livestock." Remember to poke holes in the crate.

4. Board a train dressed as Elvis and sneer and say "The King rides for free."

3. Ask if you can walk through the Channel Tunnel.

2. Board the plane dressed as an airline pilot, nod to the flight attendants, and hide in the rest room until the plane lands.

1. Bring a balloon to the airline ticket counter, kneel, breathe in the helium, and ask for the kiddie fare.

But if you're serious about saving money while you're traveling abroad, just get an ISIC--the International Student Identity Card. Discounts for students on international airfares, hotels and motels, car rentals, international phone calls, financial services, and more.

The International Student Identity Card

For more information call:

1-800-GET-AN-ID

Available at Council Travel offices (see ad in this book) and universities nationwide.

CIEE: Council on International Educational Exchange
205 East 42nd Street, New York, NY 10017-5706

about $10) for recent graduates; all of these cards prove your eligibility for travel discounts. Write or call one of the following offices for a slew of free pamphlets on services and rates, or info on the STA nearest you. *United States: 5900 Wilshire Blvd., Suite 2100, Los Angeles, CA 90036, tel. 213/937–1150. United Kingdom: Priory House, 6 Wrights Ln., London W8 6TA, tel. 171/ 938–4711. Australia: 224 Faraday St., Carlton, Melbourne Victoria 3053, tel. 3/347–6911. New Zealand: 10 High St., Box 4156, Auckland, tel. 9/309–9723.*

Council on International Educational Exchange (**Council** or **CIEE**) is a private, nonprofit organization that administers work, volunteer, academic, and professional programs worldwide. Its travel division, **Council Travel**, is a full-service travel agency specializing in student, youth, and budget travel. They offer discounted airfares, rail passes, accommodations info, guidebooks, budget tours, and travel gear. They also issue the ISIC, GO25, and ITIC identity cards (*see* Student and Teacher ID Cards, *below*), as well as Hostelling International cards. Forty-one Council Travel offices serve the budget traveler in the United States, and there are about a dozen overseas (including ones in Britain, France, and Germany). Council also puts out a variety of publications, including the free *Student Travels* magazine, a gold mine of travel tips (with information on work- and study-abroad opportunities). *205 E. 42nd St., New York, NY 10017, tel. 212/661–1414.*

Educational Travel Center (**ETC**) books low-cost flights to destinations within the continental United States and around the world. Their best deals are on flights leaving the Midwest, especially Chicago. ETC also issues Hostelling International cards. For more details, request their free brochure, *Taking Off. 438 N. Frances St., Madison, WI 53703, tel. 608/256–5551.*

STA Travel, the world's largest travel organization catering to students and young people, has over 100 offices worldwide and offers low-price airfares to destinations around the globe, as well as rail passes, car rentals, tours, and more. The Italian equivalent of STA is **Centro Turistico Studentesco** (**CTS**), with offices in all the major cities (*see box*, STA Offices, *below*, for

Council Travel Offices in the United States

ARIZONA: Tempe (tel. 602/966–3544). CALIFORNIA: Berkeley (tel. 510/848–8604), Davis (tel. 916/752–2285), La Jolla (tel. 619/452–0630), Long Beach (tel. 310/598–3338), Los Angeles (tel. 310/208–3551), Palo Alto (tel. 415/325–3888), San Diego (tel. 619/270–6401), San Francisco (tel. 415/421–3473 or 415/566–6222), Santa Barbara (tel. 805/562–8080). COLORADO: Boulder (tel. 303/447–8101), Denver (tel. 303/571–0630). CONNECTICUT: New Haven (tel. 203/562–5335). FLORIDA: Miami (tel. 305/670–9261). GEORGIA: Atlanta (tel. 404/377–9997). ILLINOIS: Chicago (tel. 312/951–0585), Evanston (tel. 708/475–5070). INDIANA: Bloomington (tel. 812/330–1600). LOUISIANA: New Orleans (tel. 504/866–1767). MASSACHUSETTS: Amherst (tel. 413/256–1261), Boston (tel. 617/266–1926), Cambridge (tel. 617/497–1497 or 617/225–2555). MICHIGAN: Ann Arbor (tel. 313/998–0200). MINNESOTA: Minneapolis (tel. 612/379–2323). NEW YORK: New York (tel. 212/661–1450, 212/666–4177, or 212/254–2525). NORTH CAROLINA: Chapel Hill (tel. 919/942–2334). OHIO: Columbus (tel. 614/294–8696). OREGON: Portland (tel. 503/228–1900). PENNSYLVANIA: Philadelphia (tel. 215/382–0343), Pittsburgh (tel. 412/683–1881). RHODE ISLAND: Providence (tel. 401/331–5810). TEXAS: Austin (tel. 512/472–4931), Dallas (tel. 214/363–9941). UTAH: Salt Lake City (tel. 801/582–5840). WASHINGTON: Seattle (tel. 206/632–2448 or 206/329–4567). WASHINGTON, D.C. (tel. 202/337–6464). For U.S. cities not listed, call tel. 800/2–COUNCIL.

their phone numbers). STA issues the ISIC and the GO25 youth cards (*see* Student and Teacher ID Cards, *below*), both of which prove eligibility for student airfares and other travel discounts. Call 800/777–0122 or the nearest STA office for more information.

Student Flights, Inc. specializes in student and faculty airfares and sells rail passes, ISE cards (*see* Student and Teacher ID Cards, *below*), and travel guidebooks. *5010 E. Shea Blvd., Scottsdale, AZ 85254, tel. 602/951–1177 or 800/255–8000.*

Travel CUTS is a full-service travel agency that sells discounted airline tickets to Canadian students and issues the ISIC, GO25, ITIC, and HI cards. Their 25 offices are on or near college campuses. Call weekdays 9–5 for information and reservations. *187 College St., Toronto, Ont. M5T 1P7, tel. 416/979–2406.*

Hostelling International (**HI**), formerly IYHF, is the umbrella group for a number of national youth hostel associations. HI offers single-sex dorm-style beds ("couples" rooms and family accommodations are available at certain hostels) and self-service kitchen facilities at nearly 5,000 locations in more than 70 countries around the world. Membership in any HI national hostel association, open to travelers of all ages, allows you to stay in HI-affiliated hostels at member rates (about $10–$25 a night). Members also have priority if the hostel is full, and are eligible for discounts on rail and bus travel around the world. A one-year membership runs about $25 for adults (renewal $20) and $10 for those under 18. A one-night guest membership is about $3. Family memberships are available for $35, and a lifetime membership will set you back $250. Handbooks listing all current hostels and special discount opportunities (like budget cycling and hiking tours) are available from the national branches listed below; one covers Europe and the Mediterranean, while the other covers Africa, the Americas, Asia, and Australasia ($13.95 each). *733 15th St. NW, Suite 840, Washington, D.C. 20005, tel. 202/783–6161 or 800/444–6111.*

National branches of Hostelling International include **Hostelling International–American Youth Hostels** (**HI–AYH**): 733 15th St. NW, Suite 840, Washington, D.C. 20005, tel. 202/783–6161 or 800/444–6111; **Hostelling International–Canada** (**HI–C**): 400-205 Catherine St., Ottawa, Ont. K2P 1C3, tel. 613/237–7884 or 800/663–5777; **Youth Hostel Association of**

STA Offices

- **UNITED STATES. CALIFORNIA:** Berkeley (tel. 510/642–3000), Los Angeles (tel. 213/934–8722), San Francisco (tel. 415/391–8407), Santa Monica (tel. 310/394–5126), Westwood (tel. 310/824–1574). **MASSACHUSETTS:** Boston (tel. 617/266–6014), Cambridge (tel. 617/576–4623). **NEW YORK:** Columbia University (tel. 212/854–2224), West Village (tel. 212/627–3111). **PENNSYLVANIA:** Philadelphia (tel. 215/382–2928). **WASHINGTON:** Seattle (tel. 206/633–5000). **WASHINGTON D.C.** (tel. 202/887–0912).

- **INTERNATIONAL. AUSTRALIA:** Adelaide (tel. 08/223–2426), Brisbane (tel. 07/221–9388), Cairns (tel. 070/314199), Darwin (tel. 089/412955), Melbourne (tel. 03/349–2411), Perth (tel. 09/227–7569), Sydney (tel. 02/212–1255). **ITALY:** Bologna (tel. 051/261802), Florence (tel. 055/289721), Genoa (tel. 010/564366), Milan (tel. 02/5830–4121), Naples (tel. 081/552–7960), Rome (tel. 06/467–9291), Venice (tel. 041/520–5660). **NEW ZEALAND:** Auckland (tel. 09/309–9995), Christchurch (tel. 03/379–9098), Wellington (tel. 04/385–0561). **UNITED KINGDOM:** London (tel. 0171/937–9962).

England and Wales (YHA): Trevelyan House, 8 St. Stephen's Hill, St. Albans, Herts AL1 2DY, England, tel. 01727/855–215; **Australian Youth Hostels Association (YHA):** Level 3, 10 Mallett St., Camperdown, New South Wales 2050, tel. 02/565–1699; and **Youth Hostels Association of New Zealand (YHA):** Box 436, Christchurch 1, tel. 03/379–9970.

➤ **IN ITALY** • **Informagiovani** or **Informa Giovane** offices provide the usual tourist office fare with a slant toward students, and they distribute a handout called *Informagiovani!* Don't let the goofy backpacking youths on the cover fool you; there's some good information inside. These offices are scattered all over Italy; look for their addresses in the Visitor Information section of specific cities in this book.

Transalpino is a major Italian bucket shop with offices all over the country, usually near a university. Inquire here for student discounts on air and ferry travel, as well as Billet International de Jeunesse (BIJ) discount international train tickets (*see* Getting Around by Train, *below*).

Touring Club Italia (TCI) offers tours all over Italy, mostly in Italian and for Italians. Still, look for their centers in major cities; they usually have excellent bookstores that offer maps and travel books in both English and Italian.

STUDENT AND TEACHER ID CARDS

The **International Student Identity Card (ISIC)** entitles students to special fares on local transportation and discounts at museums, theaters, sports events, and many other attractions. If purchased in the United States, the $18 cost for the popular ISIC card also buys you $3,000 in emergency medical coverage and limited hospital coverage, and access to a 24-hour international, toll-free hotline for assistance in medical, legal, and financial emergencies. In the United States, apply through Council Travel or STA (*see above*); in Canada, the ISIC is available for C$15 from Travel CUTS (*see above*). In the United Kingdom, students with valid university IDs can purchase the ISIC at any student union or student-travel company. Applicants must submit a photo as well as proof of current full-time student status, age, and nationality. Upon request, purchase of the ISIC card includes the *International Student Identity Card Handbook*, which details the discounts and benefits available to cardholders.

The **Go 25: International Youth Travel Card (GO25)** is issued to travelers (students and non-students) between the ages of 12 and 25, and provides services and benefits similar to those given by the ISIC card. The $10 card is available from the same organizations that sell the ISIC. When applying, bring a passport-size photo and your passport as proof of your age.

The **International Student Exchange Card (ISE)**, available to students and faculty members, offers benefits similar to those for the two previous cards, in addition to giving you a $10 discount on flights within the United States and a $50 discount on many international flights. Write or call for more information or to enroll over the phone. You pay $18 for the card. *5010 E. Shea Blvd., Suite A104, Scottsdale, AZ 85254, tel. 602/951–1177 or 800/255–8000, fax 602/951–1216.*

The $19 **International Teacher Identity Card (ITIC)**, sponsored by the International Student Travel Confederation, is available to teachers of all grade levels, from kindergarten to graduate school. The services and benefits you get when buying the card are similar to those for the three cards mentioned above. For member benefits, ask for the *International Teacher Identity Card Handbook* when you buy the card.

HOW MUCH IT WILL COST

Thanks to its unsteady economy, Italy has become cheaper in the last few years, though it's still not as good a deal as Eastern Europe or Spain. At press time, the exchange rate was about L1600 to the dollar, making it easy to travel cheaply. Don't deprive yourself, though: Hostels are inexpensive, but a hotel will seem mighty nice should your hostel be overtaken by a pack of preteens; pizza for dinner is tasty, but so is a three-course meal; and admission to churches is free, but you'll still want to check out the many excellent museums here, despite steep entrance fees.

For the most part, the north is more expensive than the south. If you're strapped for cash, stay in smaller, less-touristed towns near the cities you wish to visit (e.g., Padova instead of Venice). You can travel in Italy on about $40–$50 a day if you're careful—and on even less if you're really frugal.

WHEN TO GO

Anytime is a good time to visit, except during *ferragosto*, the holiday in August when almost all Italians take their big vacation. At that time, large cities and inland villages suddenly resemble ghost towns, while beach, mountain, and lake retreats are filled to the till. Not surprisingly, many foreigners also vacation in Italy during the summer, so prices along the coast and on the islands are at their highest. The winter features prime skiing in the Alps and amazingly empty streets even in Florence and Venice (except during Venice's *Carnevale* in February). Most experienced travelers to Italy will tell you that late fall and early spring—when you can usually find relative solitude and mild weather—are the best times to go.

HOLIDAYS Most businesses and sometimes entire towns close for the following dates: January 1 (New Year's Day), January 6 (Epiphany), Easter, April 25 (Liberation Day), May 1 (Labor Day), August 15 (Assumption of the Virgin), November 1 (All Saints' Day), December 8 (Feast of the Immaculate Conception), December 25 (Christmas Day), and December 26 (St. Stephen's Day). Many towns also close down on the day of their patron saint.

FESTIVALS Each big city and tiny town has its share of traditional festivals. Details are sometimes covered in the individual chapters, but here is a list of some of the biggies. It's worth making the effort to attend these festivals; just be sure to book a hotel far in advance.

On May 1 in **Cagliari**, the costumed procession of Sagra di Sant'Efisio (Feast of St. Efisio) features an effigy of Christ on the cross. In **Florence**, the Scoppio del Carro (Explosion of the Cart) celebrates Easter Sunday with fireworks and a mechanical dove. In **Genova**, the Palio Marinaro dei Rioni (Maritime Race of the Districts) is a traditional rowing race held each June 29. The Festa di San Gennaro (Festival of St. Gennaro) on September 19 celebrates the patron saint of **Naples**. In **Pisa**, the Gioco del Ponte (Battle of the Bridge), in which costumed participants reenact a medieval battle, takes place on the first Sunday in June. Every January 6 in Piazza Navona, the citizens of **Rome** celebrate Befana (Epiphany) with sweets, toys, and presents. **Siena**'s Il Palio, a highly competitive, bareback horse race dating from the Middle Ages, hap-

The Highs and the Lows

The following are average maximum and minimum temperatures in degrees Fahrenheit and Celsius:

	Jan.	Mar.	May	July	Sept.	Nov.
Milan	40F/5C	56F/13C	74F/23C	84F/29C	75F/24C	51F/10C
	32F/0C	35F/2C	57F/14C	67F/20C	61F/16C	43F/6C
Rome	52F/11C	59F/15C	74F/23C	87F/30C	79F/26C	61F/16C
	40F/5C	42F/6C	56F/13C	67F/20C	62F/17C	49F/10C
Venice	42F/6C	53F/12C	70F/21C	87F/30C	75F/24C	53F/12C
	33F/1C	41F/5C	56F/13C	66F/19F	61F/16C	44F/7C

pens every July 2 and August 16. **Venice** is a festival capital, with its Carnevale, regattas, and celebrations of the Virgin, all covered in detail in Chapter 2, Venice and the Veneto.

PASSPORTS, VISAS, AND RED TAPE

Citizens of the United States, the United Kingdom, Canada, Australia, and New Zealand don't need a visa to visit Italy for less than three months, but everyone needs a passport. If you plan to work or study in Italy, or to stay for more than three months, apply for a visa at your nearest Italian consulate several weeks before you leave home; it's usually easier to do it from a consulate than at an office in Italy.

Once in Italy, you are required by law to register with the nearest *questura* (police headquarters) within 10 days. Bring a passport and address information and be prepared to wait. If you stay at a hotel, hostel, or campground, you're relieved of this duty by the proprietors, who take passports at check-in and return them after having copied the information to be passed along to the police.

OBTAINING A PASSPORT

➤ **U.S. CITIZENS** • Those who must apply for a passport in person include: first-time applicants; travelers whose most recent passport was issued more than 12 years ago or before they were 18; those whose passports have been lost or stolen; and travelers between the ages of 13 and 17 (a parent must also accompany them). Otherwise, renewals can be taken care of by mail. Apply at one of the 13 U.S. Passport Agency offices a *minimum* of five weeks before your departure. For fastest processing, apply between August and December. Johnny-come-latelys can have passports issued within five days of departure only if they have a plane ticket in hand and pay an additional $30 processing fee. This method will probably work, but if there's one little glitch in the system, you're out of luck. Local county courthouses, many state and probate courts, and some post offices also accept passport applications. The following items are required: (1) a completed passport application (Form DSP-11), available at courthouses, some post offices, and passport agencies; (2) proof of citizenship (certified copy of birth certificate, naturalization papers, or previous passport issued in the past 12 years); (3) proof of identity with your photograph and signature (for example, a valid driver's license, employee ID card, military ID, student ID); (4) two recent, identical, two-inch-square photographs (black-and-white or color head shots); (5) a $55 application fee for a 10-year passport ($30 for those under 18 for a five-year passport). First-time applicants are also hit with a $10 surcharge. If you're paying cash, exact change is necessary; checks or money orders should be made out to Passport Services.

Those lucky enough to renew their passports by mail must send a completed Form DSP-82 (available from a Passport Agency); two recent, identical passport photos; their current passport (less than 12 years old); and a check or money order for $55 ($30 if under 18). Send everything to the nearest Passport Agency. Renewals take from three to four weeks. For more information or an application, contact the **Department of State Office of Passport Services** (tel. 202/647–0518) and dial your way through their message maze.

➤ **CANADIAN CITIZENS** • Canadians should send a completed passport application (available at any post office, passport office, and many travel agencies) to the **Bureau of Passports** (Suite 215, West Tower, Guy Favreau Complex, 200 René Levesque Boulevard West, Montréal, Qué H2Z 1X4, tel. 514/283–2152). Include C$35; two recent, identical passport photographs; the signature of a guarantor (a Canadian citizen who has known you for at least two years and is a mayor, practicing lawyer, notary public, judge, magistrate, police officer, signing officer at a bank, medical doctor, or dentist); and proof of Canadian citizenship (original birth certificate or other official document as specified). You can also apply in person at regional passport offices in many locations, including Edmonton, Halifax, Montréal, Toronto, Vancouver, and Winnipeg. Passports have a shelf life of five years and are not renewable. Processing takes about two weeks by mail and five working days for in-person applications.

➤ **U.K. CITIZENS** • Passport applications are available through travel agencies, a main post office, or one of six regional passport offices (London, Liverpool, Peterborough, Belfast,

Glasgow, and Newport). The application and photos must be countersigned by your bank manager or by a solicitor, barrister, doctor, clergyman, or justice of the peace who knows you personally. Send or drop off the completed form; two recent, identical passport photos; and a £25 fee to a regional passport office (address is on the form). Passports are valid for 10 years (five years for those under 16) and take a minimum of four weeks to process.

➣ **AUSTRALIAN CITIZENS** • Australians must visit a post office or passport office to complete the passport application process. A 10-year passport for those over 18 costs AUS$77. The under-18 crowd can get a five-year passport for AUS$38. For more information, call 008/026022 toll-free in Australia weekdays during regular business hours.

➣ **NEW ZEALAND CITIZENS** • Passport applications can be found at any post office or consulate. Completed applications must be accompanied by proof of citizenship, two passport-size photos, and a letter from an attorney, employer, school registrar, etc. The fee is NZ$56 for a 10-year passport. Processing takes about three weeks.

LOST PASSPORTS If your passport is lost or stolen while traveling, you should immediately notify the local police and nearest embassy or consulate (see Basics, Rome, in Chapter 10). A consular officer should be able to wade through some red tape and issue you a new one, or at least get you back into your country of origin without one. The process will be slowed up considerably if you don't have other forms of identification on you, so you're well advised to carry alternative forms of ID—a driver's license, a copy of your birth certificate, a student ID—separate from your passport, and tuck a few photocopies of the front page of your passport in your luggage and your traveling companion's pockets.

A United States embassy or consulate will only issue a new passport in emergencies. In non-emergency situations, the staff will affirm your affidavit swearing to U.S. citizenship, and this paper will get you back to the United States. The British embassy or consulate requires a police report, any form of identification, and three passport-size photos. They will replace the passport in four working days. Canadian citizens face the same requirements as the Brits, but must have a guarantor with them. Since most travelers don't know a local guarantor (see Obtaining a Passport, Canadian Citizens, above, for requirements), there is also the option of paying an officer of the consulate/embassy to act in that capacity—proving once again that throwing enough money at a problem usually makes it go away. A replacement passport usually takes five working days. New Zealand officials ask for two passport-size photos, while the Australians require three, but both can usually replace a passport in 24 hours.

RAIL PASSES

Italian trains are so cheap that it might not be worth your while to buy a rail pass. If, however, you're popping into other countries, you should give rail passes a thought. But before plunking down hundreds of dollars, there are several issues to consider. First, add up the prices of the rail trips you plan; some travel agents have a manual that lists ticket prices, or you can call **Rail Europe** (tel. 800/438–7245), **Railpass Express** (tel. 800/722–7151), or **DER Tours** (tel. 800/782–2424), three agencies that sell rail passes over the phone. If you're under 26, subtract about 30% from the prices quoted by Rail Europe or your travel agent; that's how much you can save by purchasing a BIJ ticket in Europe (see Getting Around, below). If you're under 26 years of age on your first day of travel, it's always a better deal to get a youth pass of some sort (Europass Youth, Eurail Youth Flexipass, or Eurail Youthpass). Youth passes are always valid for second-class travel only. If you're 26 or over on your first day of travel, you're not eligible for a youth pass and have to buy one of the (much more expensive) passes valid for first-class travel.

Be sure to buy your rail pass *before* leaving home. Eurail passes are not available in Europe (although you might be able to buy one for a slightly inflated price at some questionable European travel agencies). Also, if you have firm plans to visit Europe next year, consider buying your pass *this* year. Prices for Eurail passes generally rise on December 31, and your pass is valid as long as you start traveling within six months of the purchase date. The upshot is that a pass bought on December 30, 1995, can be activated as late as June 30, 1996. Prices listed below are valid through December 30, 1995.

Fortunately, when you travel on Rail Europe, there are some sights you'll miss.

No goofy hats. No big sunglasses. No plaid shirts with striped shorts. Instead, on Rail Europe, you'll experience Europe the way Europeans do. You'll enjoy scenic countryside no one else can show you. And meet unique and interesting people. In short, you'll explore Europe the way it was meant to be explored. When it comes to visiting 33 European countries, get real. Go Rail Europe. Because traveling any other way could end up showing you some pretty dreadful sights. To learn more, call your travel agent or 1-800-4-EURAIL. (1-800-438-7245)

Rail Europe

Last warnings: Don't assume that your rail pass guarantees you a seat on every train. Seat reservations are required on some express and overnight trains. Also note that many rail passes entitle you to free or reduced fares on some ferries (though you should still make seat reservations in advance).

ITALIAN PASSES The Italian train system offers three main types of passes available at train stations throughout Italy or through the **Italian State Railway Representative** (in Los Angeles, tel. 310/338–8618, fax 310/670–4269; in New York, tel. 212/697–2100, fax 212/697–1394; in Montréal, tel. 514/845–9101, fax 514/845–9137; in Toronto, tel. 416/927–7712, fax 416/927–7206). The **Italy Flexi Railcard** costs $126 for four days of second-class travel taken within nine days; $174 for eight days of travel within 21 days; and $220 for 12 days of travel within 30 days. The **Italian Tourist Ticket**, or **BTLC**, allows unlimited use of all second-class trains for eight days ($236), 15 days ($284), 21 days ($330), and 30 days ($406). The **Italian Kilometric Ticket** is valid for up to two months and can be used by as many as five people to travel a total of 3,000 kilometers for up to 20 trips in a two-month period (you'll have a hard time using it up unless you're traveling with at least two companions). This pass costs $171 for second class (plus $10 per person), or L190,000 if bought in Italy (plus $16 a person). The **Cartaverde** for youths under 26 and the **Cartargento** for seniors over 60 save you 20%–30% on first- or second-class travel, but they aren't really worthwhile for short-term travel. Both cost about L40,000 and are good for one year. You must purchase these cards in Italy, and the discount is not applicable June 26–August 14 and December 18–28.

EURAIL The **EurailPass** is valid for unlimited first-class train travel through 17 countries—Austria, Belgium, Denmark, Finland, France, Germany, Greece, Hungary, Italy, Luxembourg, Netherlands, Norway, Portugal, Republic of Ireland, Spain, Sweden, and Switzerland. It's available for periods of 15 days ($498), 21 days ($648), one month ($798), two months ($1,098), and three months ($1,398). If you're under 26, the **Eurail Youthpass** is a much better deal. One or two months of unlimited second-class train travel costs $578 and $768, respectively. For 15 consecutive days of travel you pay $398.

A **Eurail Saverpass**, which costs a little less than a comparable EurailPass, is intended for couples and small groups. A pass good for 15 days of first-class travel is $430, for 21 days $550, for one month $687. The pass requires that a minimum of two people each buy a Saverpass and travel together at all times. Between April 1 and September 30 there is a three-person minimum.

Unlike the EurailPass and Eurail Youthpass, which are good for unlimited travel for a certain period of time, the **Eurail Flexipass** allows you to travel for five, 10, or 15 days within a two-month period. The Flexipass is valid in the same 17 countries as the EurailPass and costs $348 for five days of travel, $560 for 10 days, and $740 for 15 days. If you're under 26, the second-class **Eurail Youth Flexipass** is a better deal. Within a two-month period it entitles you to five days ($255), 10 days ($398), or 15 days ($540) of travel.

For travel in France, Germany, Italy, Spain, and Switzerland, consider the **Europass** (first class) or **Europass Youth** (second class). The basic Europass is good for five, six, or seven days of travel in any three of the above-named countries, as long as they border one another. The five-day pass costs $280 (first class) or $198 (second class). The eight-, nine- and 10-day passes are good in four of the five countries. The eight-day pass costs $394 (first class) or $282 (second class). A pass good for 11–15 days and valid in all five countries costs $508 (first class) or $366 (second class). In all cases, the days of travel can be spread out over two calendar months. Call Rail Europe or ask a travel agent for the brochures "1995 Europe On Track" or "EurailPass and Europass" for details on adding extra travel days, buying a discounted pass for your companion, or expanding the reach of your pass to Austria, Belgium, Greece, Luxembourg, and Portugal.

INTERRAIL European citizens and anyone who has lived in the EU for at least six months can purchase an **InterRail Pass**, valid for one month's travel in Austria, Belgium, Bulgaria, Croatia, the Czech Republic, Denmark, Finland, France, Germany, Great Britain, Greece, Hungary, Italy, Luxembourg, Morocco, the Netherlands, Norway, Poland, Portugal, Republic of Ireland, Romania, Slovakia, Slovenia, Spain, Sweden, Switzerland, and Turkey. It works much like

Eurail, except that you only get a 50% reduction on train travel in the country where it was purchased. Be prepared to prove EU citizenship or six months of continuous residency. InterRail can only be purchased in Europe at rail stations and some budget travel agencies; try the European branches of STA or Council Travel.

MONEY

ITALIAN CURRENCY The unit of currency in Italy is the lira. Lire (plural) come in notes of 1000, 2000, 5000, 10,000, 50,000, and 100,000. Coins come in denominations of 50, 100, 200, and 500. Throughout the text, lire are noted with a capital *L* preceding the number (for example, L5000). At press time, the exchange rate was about L1600 to the U.S. dollar, L2500 to the pound sterling, and L1230 to the Canadian dollar.

TRAVELING WITH MONEY Cash never goes out of style, but traveler's checks and a major U.S. credit card are usually the safest and most convenient way to pay for goods and services on the road. Depending on the length of your trip, strike a balance among these three forms of currency, and protect yourself by carrying cash in a money belt, necklace pouch (available at luggage or camping stores), or a front pocket. Also, keep accurate records of traveler's checks' serial numbers and record credit-card numbers and an emergency number for reporting their loss or theft. Carrying at least some cash (hard currency) is wise; most budget establishments will accept cash only, and outside urban areas, changing traveler's checks may prove difficult. Carry about $100 (in as many single bills as possible) in cash; changing dollars will generally be easier than cashing traveler's checks.

CHANGING MONEY When you think you've found a fabulous exchange rate, ask if they charge a commission; some places take up to 5% off the top, though 2%–3% is more common. It helps to exchange money during regular business hours when you have the greatest number of options.

It's almost always cheaper to buy a country's currency in that country, rather than from home. In other words, you'll get a better deal buying Italian lire in Italy than at your bank in the United States. However, it's still a good idea to change $20–$50 into foreign currency before you arrive in a country in case the exchange booth at the train station or airport is closed or has an unbearably long line.

TRAVELER'S CHECKS Traveler's checks may look like play money, but they work much better. They can be used for purchases in the same way as cash (always ask first), or they can be exchanged for cash at banks, some hotels, tourist offices, American Express offices, or currency-exchange offices. American Express checks are the most widely accepted; other brands are sometimes refused. Some banks and credit unions will issue checks free to established customers, but most charge a 1%–2% commission fee. The reward for paying this commission is being able to get your money back if some nimble-fingered thief takes off with your checks (*see* Lost and Stolen Checks, *below*).

American Express cardholders can order traveler's checks in U.S. dollars and six foreign currencies by phone free of charge (with a gold card) or for a 1% commission (with your basic green card). In three to five business days you'll receive your checks—up to $1,000 can be ordered in a seven-day period. Checks can also be purchased through many banks, in which case both gold and green cardholders pay a 1% commission. AmEx also issues **Traveler's Cheques for Two**, checks that can be signed and used by either you or your traveling companion. True to Karl Malden's repeated pledges, if you lose your checks or are ripped off, American Express has the resources to provide you with a speedy refund—often within 24 hours. At their Travel Services offices (about 1,500 around the world) you can usually buy and cash traveler's checks, write a personal check in exchange for traveler's checks, report lost or stolen checks, exchange foreign currency, and pick up mail. Ask for the *American Express Traveler's Companion*, a handy little directory of their offices, to find out more about particular services at different locations. *Tel. 800/221–7282 in the U.S. and Canada.*

Citicorp (tel. 800/645–6556 in the U.S. or 813/623–1709 collect outside the U.S.) traveler's checks give you access to the 24-hour International S.O.S. Assistance Hotline. **Mas-**

terCard International (tel. 800/223–7373 in the U.S., 609/987–7300 collect from outside the U.S.) traveler's checks are issued in U.S. dollars only. **Thomas Cook** traveler's checks are available in U.S. dollars and foreign currencies; for more info, contact MasterCard (*see above*). **Visa** (tel. 800/227–6811 in the U.S. and Canada; otherwise 813/623–1709 collect) traveler's checks are available in various currencies.

If you don't have an Am Ex gold card, you can still get American Express traveler's checks free with an AAA membership. Talk to the cashier at your local AAA office.

➤ **LOST AND STOLEN CHECKS** • Unlike cash, lost or stolen traveler's checks can be replaced or refunded *if* you can produce the purchase agreement and a record of the checks' serial numbers. Common sense dictates that you keep the purchase agreement separate from your checks. Caution-happy travelers will even give a copy of the purchase agreement and checks' serial numbers to someone back home. Most issuers of traveler's checks promise to refund or replace lost or stolen checks in 24 hours, but you can practically see them crossing their fingers behind their backs. If you are traveling in a remote area, expect this process to take longer. Keep the toll-free or collect telephone number to call in case of emergencies (*see above*) in a safe place.

GETTING MONEY FROM HOME Provided there is money at home to be had, there are at least four ways to get it: (1) If you're an **American Express** cardholder, you can cash a personal check at an American Express office for up to $1,000 ($2,500 for gold cardholders) every 21 days; you'll be paid in U.S. traveler's checks or, in some instances, in foreign currency. Express Cash further allows American Express cardholders to withdraw cash from their personal checking accounts via ATMs (*see* Cash Machines, *below*). The **American Express MoneyGram** service can be a dream come true if you can convince someone back home to go to an American Express MoneyGram agent and fill out the necessary forms. You don't have to be an AmEx cardholder to use this service: Simply have them pay up to $1,000 with a credit card or cash (and anything over that in cash) and, as quick as 10 minutes later, it's ready to be picked up. Fees vary according to the amount of money sent but average about 5%–10% to send money from the United States to Europe. You have to show ID when picking up the money. For locations of American Express MoneyGram agents call 800/926–9400; from overseas call 303/980–3340 collect or contact the nearest AmEx agent. (2) **MasterCard** and **Visa** cardholders can get cash advances from many banks, even in small towns. The commission for this handy-dandy service varies from nothing to almost 10%, so ask your credit-card company about it before you leave. If you get a PIN number for your card before you leave home, you might even be able to make the transaction with an ATM machine. For more info on this handy trick, *see* Cash Machines, *below*. (3) Have funds sent through **Western Union** (tel. 800/325–6000). If you have a MasterCard or Visa, you can have money sent up to your card's credit limit. If not, have someone take cash, a certified cashier's check, or a healthy MasterCard or Visa to a Western Union office. The money will reach the requested destination in minutes but may not be available for several more hours or days, depending on the whim of the local authorities. Fees range from about 5% to 15% depending on the amount sent. (4) In extreme emergencies (arrest, hospitalization, or worse) there is one more way American citizens can receive money overseas: by setting up a **Department of State Trust Fund**. A friend or family member sends money to the Department of State, which then transfers the money to the U.S. embassy or consulate in the city in which you're stranded. Once this account is established, you can send and receive money through Western Union, bank wire, or mail, all payable to the Department of State. For information, talk to the Department of State's Citizens' Emergency Center (tel. 202/647–5225).

➤ **CASH MACHINES** • Most banks in Italy now have cash machines—the only problem is getting one to give you money. If your card is heartlessly rejected by an Italian machine, persist in your search and you'll probably find a taker. On the plus side, you get local currency instantly, at a generally excellent rate of exchange. That said, some banks do charge a 1%–3% fee per ATM transaction, so consider withdrawing larger chunks of cash rather than small bundles on a daily basis. To find out if there are any cash machines in a given city, call your bank's department of international banking. A **Visa** or **MasterCard** can also be used to access cash through certain ATMs (provided you have a PIN for it), but the fees for this service are usually

You can't eat pasta without bread.

When in Rome, it's not a problem if your cash supply runs dry. Because with Western Union, you can receive money from the States within minutes, in case the situation arises. Plus, it's already converted into lire.

Just call our number in Italy, 039 6 16701 6840, or in the United States, 1 800 325 6000,* and then hop on a gondola to the nearest Western Union location.

Oh, and enjoy your dinner.

WESTERN UNION | MONEY TRANSFER®
*The fastest way to send money worldwide.*ᴿᴹ

through certain ATMs (provided you have a PIN for it), but the fees for this service are usually higher than bank-card fees.

Express Cash allows American Express cardholders to withdraw up to $1,000 in a seven-day period (21 days overseas) from their personal checking accounts via a worldwide network of ATMs. Gold cardholders can receive up to $2,500 in a seven-day period (21 days overseas). Each transaction carries a 2% fee, with a minimum charge of $2.50 and a maximum of $10. Apply for a PIN and set up the linking of your accounts at least two to three weeks before departure. Call 800/CASH–NOW for an application.

WHAT TO PACK

It is impossible to overemphasize the importance of packing lightly: If you can't tote your bag all the way around the block at home, it's going to be worse than a ball and chain in Italy. Backpacks are the most manageable way to lug belongings; try to get one with a waist strap or external frame for back support. Outside pockets on backpacks are especially vulnerable to pickpockets, though, so don't store any valuables there. If you want to blend in more with the local population, bring a duffel or large shoulder bag.

Besides packing the essentials, bring along a day pack; this will come in handy not only for day excursions but also for places in which you plan to spend only a day or two. When you put on both straps, small backpacks are also almost impossible to rip off. You can check cumbersome bags at train or bus stations and just carry the essentials with you while you look for lodging.

BEDDING If you're planning to stay in hotels, you won't need to bring any bedding. Most hostels provide sheets for free, and others rent them to you (around L3000). If you plan to stay in a lot of hostels, you might save money by taking a sleep sheet. A sleeping mat will make train- and bus-station floors a tad more comfortable, and you can roll it tightly and strap it onto the bottom of your pack.

THE SLEEP SHEET DEFINED:

Take a big sheet. Fold it in half the long way. Sew one short side and then the long, open side. Turn the whole thing inside out. Get in. Sleep.

CLOTHING If you're traveling to Italy in summer, you can get away with packing very lightly. Bring comfortable, light, and easy-to-clean clothes. Artificial fabrics don't breathe and will make you hotter than you ever thought possible, so go with light cotton instead. Bring several T-shirts, a sweatshirt or sweater for cool nights, and a light anorak for rainy weather. If you come during winter—it gets surprisingly cold throughout Italy—bring a coat and an extra sweater or two. A good pair of hiking boots or tennis shoes (broken in before your trip) will keep your feet happy. But be forewarned—hiking boots are cumbersome and often too hot to wear in the summer, and wearing them in Italy displays an unrefined fashion sense (if you care about that sort of thing). A sturdy pair of walking shoes weighs less and may help you blend in with the locals. Plastic thongs protect feet from hostile shower floors.

TOILETRIES Use a separate, waterproof bag for anything gooey; the pressure on airplanes can cause lids to pop off and create instant moisturizer slicks inside your luggage. Don't weigh down your pack with gallons of shampoo, because you can find almost any toiletry item you need in Italy. Do consider coming prepared with a good supply of such essentials as contact lens solution, tampons, and condoms, because you probably won't be able to find the brands or quality that you rely on at home. Also don't forget sunscreen and lip balm.

LAUNDRY Coin-ops are hard to come by and cleaners cost a bundle; the cheapest way to clean clothes is in your hotel room. A bring-your-own laundry service includes: a plastic bottle of liquid detergent or soap (powder doesn't break down as well), a rubber drain cover, about six feet of clothesline (enough to tie to two stable objects), and some plastic clips (bobby pins or paper clips can substitute). In hot areas, your clothes will dry overnight. Be sure to bring an extra plastic bag or two for still-damp laundry and dirty clothes.

CAMERAS AND FILM Keep film as cool as possible, away from direct sunlight or blazing campfires. On a plane trip, unprocessed film is safest in your carry-on luggage—ask security to inspect it by hand. Inspectors at American airports are required by law to honor requests for hand inspection. All airport scanning machines used in U.S. airports are safe for any number of scans from five to 500, depending on the speed of your film. The higher the speed, the more susceptible it is to damage.

MISCELLANEOUS Stuff you might not think to pack but will be glad to have: (1) extra day pack for valuables or short jaunts; (2) small flashlight; (3) Walkman; (4) pocketknife; (5) Band-Aids; (6) sunglasses; (7) several large zip-type plastic bags (useful for wet swimsuits, towels, leaky bottles, and stinky socks); (8) travel alarm clock; (9) needle and small spool of thread; (10) aspirin or Tylenol; (11) batteries; and (12) some interesting books to trade with other travelers along the way.

PROTECTING YOUR VALUABLES

Money belts may be dorky and bulky, but wouldn't you rather be embarrassed than broke? You'd be wise to carry all cash, traveler's checks, credit cards, and your passport in a money belt or similarly inaccessible place: a front or inner pocket, a pouch that fits underneath your clothes, or even in your shoes. Neck pouches and money belts are sold in luggage or camping-supply stores. Fanny packs (small, zippered nylon bags that are strapped around your waist) are safe if your keep the pack part in front of your body, safer still if your shirt or sweater hangs over the pack. If someone approaches you closely, thrusting a sign or a baby in your face, it's more than likely there's an accomplice ready to pick your pockets while you're distracted. Stay alert, especially in Rome and Florence.

When is it safe to take your valuables off your body? Hostels and even hotel rooms are not necessarily safe; don't leave anything valuable out in the open. When sleeping or when leaving your room, keep what you cherish on your body or at least inside your sleep sheet (if you're in it). On night trains, lock your bag onto the racks or sleep with your arms around it. And it may go without saying, but *never* leave your pack unguarded or with a total stranger in a train or bus station or any other public place—not even if you're only planning to be gone for a minute. It's not worth the risk.

Tipping: never obligatory but expected for hairdressers, taxi drivers, and baggage porters. Don't bother in food places. Bars and restaurants charge a "servizio" (service fee) just for seating you.

CUSTOMS AND DUTIES

ARRIVING IN ITALY Unless the customs officials take a disliking to you for some reason, going through customs upon entering Italy is so painless that you won't even know you did it. Big dogs might sniff you, officers may ask you a couple questions, and then you're in. Tourists arriving in Italy after visiting other countries are allowed to bring in souvenirs with a total value of $500 duty-free. To avoid hassles, don't even *think* about drugs. Being cited for drug possession is no joke, and embassies and consulates often can't or won't do much to persuade country officials to release accused drug traffickers or users.

RETURNING HOME It's probably best to have all the souvenirs and gifts you're bringing home in an easily accessible place, just in case the officials would like to have a peek.

➤ **U.S. CUSTOMS** • You won't have to pay duty unless you come home with more than $400 worth of foreign goods, including items bought in duty-free stores. Each member of a family is entitled to the same exemption, regardless of age, and exemptions may be pooled. Duty-free allowances are as follows: 1 liter of alcohol or wine (for travelers 21 or older), 100 cigars (non-Cuban), 200 cigarettes, and one bottle of perfume. Anything above and beyond these limits will be taxed at the port of entry and may also be taxed in the traveler's home state. Gifts valued at under $50 may be mailed duty-free to friends or relatives at home, but the limit is one package per day to a single addressee, and you may not send perfume, tobacco, or liquor. Mailing may not be the safest route—you're probably better off paying the custom tax. For more information, write to the U.S. Customs Service (Box 7407, Washington, D.C. 20044, tel. 202/927-6724).

➤ **CANADIAN CUSTOMS** • Exemptions for returning Canadians range from $20 to $500, depending on how long they've been out of the country: For two days out, you're allowed to return with C$200 worth of goods; for one week out, you're allowed C$500 worth. Above these limits, you'll be taxed about 15%. Duty-free limits are: up to 50 cigars, 200 cigarettes, 400 grams of tobacco, and 1.14 liters of liquor—all must be declared in writing upon arrival at customs and must be with you or in your checked baggage. To mail back gifts, label the package: "Unsolicited Gift–Value Under C$60." For more details, call the automated information line of the Revenue Canada Customs, Excise and Taxation Department (2265 St. Laurent Blvd. S, Ottawa, Ont. K1G 4K3, tel. 613/993–0534 or 991–3881), where you may request a copy of the Canadian Customs brochure "I Declare/Je Déclare."

➤ **U.K. CUSTOMS** • Travelers age 17 or over who return to the United Kingdom may bring back the following duty-free goods: 200 cigarettes or 100 cigarillos or 50 cigars or 250 grams of tobacco; 1 liter of alcohol over 22% volume or 2 liters of alcohol under 22% volume, plus 2 liters of still table wine; 60 ml of perfume and 250 ml of toilet water; and other goods worth up to £136. If returning from another EU country, you can choose, instead, to bring in the following, provided they were *not* bought in a duty-free shop: 300 cigarettes or 150 cigarillos or 75 cigars or 400 grams of tobacco; 1.5 liters of alcohol over 22% volume or 3 liters of alcohol under 22% volume, plus 5 liters of still table wine; 75 grams of perfume and ⅜ liter of toilet water; and other goods worth up to £250. For further information, contact HM Customs and Excise (Dorset House, Stamford St., London SE1 9PY, tel. 0171/928–3344).

➤ **AUSTRALIAN CUSTOMS** • Australian travelers 18 and over may bring back, duty free: 1 liter of alcohol; 250 grams of tobacco products (equivalent to 250 cigarettes or cigars); and other articles worth up to AUS$400. If you're under 18, your duty-free allowance is AUS$200. For more rules and regulations, request the pamphlet "Customs Information for Travellers" from a local Collector of Customs (GPO Box 8, Sydney NSW 2001, tel. 02/226–5997).

➤ **NEW ZEALAND CUSTOMS** • Travelers over age 17 are allowed, duty-free: 200 cigarettes or 250 grams of tobacco or 50 cigars or a combo of all three up to 250 grams; 4.5 liters of wine or beer and one 1,125-ml. bottle of spirits; and goods with a combined value up to NZ$700. For more details, ask for the pamphlet "Customs Guide for Travellers" from a New Zealand consulate.

STAYING HEALTHY

There are no serious health risks associated with travel in Italy, and no inoculations are needed to enter the country. For up-to-the-minute information about health risks and disease precautions in all parts of the world, you can call the U.S. Centers for Disease Control's 24-hour **International Travelers' Hotline** (tel. 404/332–4559). In general, common sense prevails. Get plenty of rest, watch out for sun exposure, don't drink unpasteurized milk or water from a river, and eat balanced meals—do we sound like your mother yet?

FIRST-AID KIT Packing a few first-aid supplies could save you from physical and financial pain during your travels. The rugged individualist should round up some bandages, waterproof surgical tape and gauze pads, antiseptic, cortisone cream, tweezers, a thermometer in a sturdy case, an antacid such as Alka-Seltzer, something for diarrhea (Pepto-Bismol or Imodium), and, of course, aspirin. Depending on your health situation, you might also ask your doctor for a general antibiotic. If you're prone to motion sickness or are planning to use particularly rough modes of transportation during your travels, take along some Dramamine. No matter what your race or coloring, pack sunscreen to protect against cancer-causing rays. Women: Bring tampons. Even those sold under familiar name brands are not the same quality in Italy.

HEALTH AND ACCIDENT INSURANCE Some general health-insurance plans cover health expenses incurred while traveling, so review your existing health policies (or a parent's policy, if you're a dependent) before leaving home. Most university health-insurance plans stop and start with the school year, so don't count on school spirit to pull you through. Canadian travelers should check with their provincial ministry of health to see if their resident health-insurance plan covers them on the road. Organizations such as STA and Council include health-and-accident coverage with the purchase of an ID or credit card. For more details, contact your favorite student travel organization or one of the agencies listed below.

Carefree Travel Insurance is, in fact, pretty serious about providing coverage for emergency medical evacuation and accidental death or dismemberment. It also offers 24-hour medical phone advice. Basic coverage for an individual ranges from $86 for a 30-day trip to $180 for a 90-day trip. 100 Garden City Plaza, Box 9366, Garden City, NY 11530, tel. 516/294–0220 or 800/323–3149.

Travel Guard offers an excellent variety of insurance plans, including coverage for sickness, injury, lost baggage, and trip cancellation. You can choose from an advance purchase ($19), super-advance purchase ($39), or a megaplan for trips up to 180 days (8% of your travel costs). 1145 Clark St., Stevens Point, WI 54481, tel. 715/345–0505 or 800/782–5151.

MEDICAL ASSISTANCE International Association for Medical Assistance to Travellers **(IAMAT)** offers free membership and entitles you to a worldwide directory of qualified English-speaking physicians who are on 24-hour call. United States: 417 Center St., Lewiston, NY 14092, tel. 716/754–4883. Canada: 40 Regal Rd., Guelph, Ont. N1K 1B5, tel. 519/836–0102. Switzerland: 57 Voirets, 1212 Grand-Lancy-Geneva. New Zealand: Box 5049, Christchurch 5.

British travelers can join **Europe Assistance Worldwide Services** (252 High St., Croyden, Surrey CRO 1NF, tel. 0181/680–1234) to gain access to a 24-hour telephone hotline. The American branch of this organization is **Worldwide Assistance Incorporated** (1133 15th St. NW, Suite 400, Washington, D.C. 20005, tel. 800/821–2828), which offers emergency evacuation services and 24-hour medical referrals. An individual membership costs $62 for up to 15 days, $164 for 60 days.

PRESCRIPTIONS Bring as much as you need of any prescription drugs as well as your prescription (packed separately). Ask your doctor to type prescriptions and include the following information: dosage, the generic name, and the manufacturer's name. Luckily, prescriptions are often much cheaper in Italy than at home. To avoid problems clearing customs, diabetic travelers carrying needles and syringes should have handy a letter from their physician confirming their need for insulin injections. Italian pharmacies are everywhere and have regular business hours. In big cities, 24-hour pharmacies are on a rotating schedule, which is usually published in the newspaper.

CONTRACEPTIVES AND SAFE SEX AIDS and other STDs (sexually transmitted diseases) do not respect national boundaries. Protection when you travel takes the same forms as it does at home. If you are contemplating an exchange of bodily fluids, condoms (*preservativi* in Italian) or dental dams (oral condoms) are the best forms of protection against sexually transmitted diseases. For the unplanned liason, or if you feel uncomfortable saying "ultra-ribbed" in Italian, most pharmacies have a coin-operated condom machine just outside the door.

RESOURCES FOR WOMEN TRAVELERS

Though Italian men can be obnoxious, especially to blondes and women of color, annoying behavior is usually limited to the verbal realm. Take the same precautions in Italy as you would take at home: Avoid dangerous situations like hitchhiking and walking around empty city streets at night. Confront unwanted male attention as Italian women do: by feigning deafness.

ORGANIZATIONS Domani Donna in Venice (tel. 041/405370) and Padova (tel. 049/875–4296) is an organization that promotes women's causes, activities, and well-being. **ISIS** (Via Santa Saba 5, 00153 Rome, tel. 06/574–6479) is a gathering place for women. **Associazione Cattolica Internazionale al Servizio della Giovane** (Via Urbana 159, 00184 Rome, tel. 06/482–7989; and Corso Garibaldi 121–123, 20121 Milan, tel. 02/659–5206 or 02/659–9668) is a Catholic organization involved in women's issues.

RESOURCES FOR GAY AND LESBIAN TRAVELERS

Because Italians are affectionate in general, some same-sex hand-holding and hugging won't attract attention. But Italy is also a Catholic country with a strong dose of machismo, and obvious displays of homosexual affection could get you in big trouble—with the police in some places. Be subtle in small towns and in the south, and live it up in Bologna, Milan, Florence, Riccione, and Rome, where the gay scene thrives.

ORGANIZATIONS Bologna is the headquarters of the national gay organization **ARCI-Gay** (Piazza di Porta Saragozza 2, Box 691, 40100 Bologna, tel. 051/436700). Their organization for lesbians, **ARCI-Co-ordinamento Donne** (Via F. Carrara 24, Rome, tel. 06/35791), publishes the newsletter *Bolletino del Confessione Lesbiche Italiane*. A national lesbian hot line (tel. 0565/240384) in Florence takes calls Wednesday and Saturday 8:30 AM–10 PM. The monthly gay magazine *Babilonia*, available in all big towns, comes out of Milan (Babilonia Edizioni, Box 11224, 20110 Milan).

International Gay Travel Association (IGTA) (Box 4974, Key West, FL 33041, tel. 800/448–8550) is a nonprofit organization of 387 members worldwide that provides listings of member agencies.

International Lesbian and Gay Association (ILGA) (81 Rue Marché au Charbon, 1000 Brussels 1, Belgium, tel. 32/2–502–2471) is a good source of info about conditions, resources, and hot spots in any given country.

Are You Two...Together? is the best-known, and perhaps the most detailed, guide to traveling in Europe. *Spartacus* bills itself as *the* guide for the gay traveler, with practical tips and reviews of hotels and agencies in over 160 countries.

RESOURCES FOR TRAVELERS WITH DISABILITIES

Italy has only recently begun to provide for travelers with disabilities, and facilities such as ramps and appropriately equipped bathrooms and telephones are still the exception rather than the rule. Throughout your trip, cobblestone streets, old buildings, and winding staircases will present constant challenges. ENIT offices (*see* Useful Organizations, *above*) can provide lists of accessible hotels as well as addresses of Italian associations for people with disabilities. They also distribute a fantastic book called *Roma Accessibile: Turismo e Barriere Architettoniche* (Accessible Rome: Tourism and Structural Obstacles), with extensive information on the accessibility of public transport, hotels, restaurants, museums, and tons of other places in Rome. Unfortunately, similar books don't currently exist for other cities in Italy.

ACCOMMODATIONS Whenever possible, reviews in this book will indicate whether rooms are wheelchair accessible. Unfortunately, due to the number of hotels in centuries-old buildings, these are few and far between. Though not often reviewed in this book, large three- and four-star hotels are much more likely to have elevators and wheelchair-accessible bathrooms.

GETTING AROUND Most major airlines are happy to help travelers with disabilities make flight arrangements, provided they receive notification 48 hours in advance. Some airlines offer a discounted "companion fare" if a passenger with disabilities needs attendant help or medical attention. Ask about discounts and check-in protocol when making reservations.

Most **Intercity (IC)** trains (*see box* The Trains Explained, *below*) have wheelchair access. When you arrive at a train station, check the schedule for your destination, and look for either a lowercase *h* in a circle or the universal sign of the little wheelchair to determine which trains are accessible. Call Rail Europe (tel. 800/438–7245) for more information about accessibility where you will be traveling.

PUBLICATIONS Twin Peaks Press specializes in books for the disabled, such as *Travel for the Disabled*, which offers helpful hints as well as a comprehensive list of guidebooks and facilities geared to the disabled. Their *Directory of Travel Agencies for the Disabled* lists more than 350 agencies throughout the world. Each is $19.95 plus $3 ($4.50 for both) shipping and handling. *Box 129, Vancouver, WA 98666, tel. 360/694–2462 or 800/637–2256 for orders only.*

ORGANIZATIONS Mobility International USA (MIUSA) is a nonprofit organization that coordinates exchange programs for people with disabilities around the world. MIUSA also offers information on accommodations and organized study programs for members ($20 annually). Nonmembers may subscribe to the newsletter for $10. *Box 10767, Eugene, OR 97440, tel. 503/343-1284, fax 503/343-6812.*

Moss Rehabilitation Hospital's Travel Information Service provides information on tourist sights, transportation, accommodations, and accessibility in destinations around the world. You can request free information by phone only. *1200 W. Tabor Rd., Philadelphia, PA 19141, tel. 215/456-9900, TYY 215/456-9602.*

WORKING IN ITALY

Students interested in working abroad should contact **CIEE**'s Work Abroad and Voluntary Service departments (205 E. 42nd St., New York, NY 10017, tel. 212/661-1414, ext. 1130 and 1139 respectively). CIEE has work- and study-abroad programs in Europe, Latin America, Asia, and Australia, *and* it publishes several resource books on work and travel opportunities, including *Work, Study, and Travel Abroad: The Whole World Handbook* ($13.95); *Volunteer! The Comprehensive Guide to Voluntary Service in the U.S. and Abroad* ($8.95); and *Going Places: The High School Student's Guide to Travel, Study, and Adventure Abroad* ($13.95). When ordering, add $1.50 book-rate postage or $3 first-class postage for each book.

If you just come to Italy hoping to get hired, your best bet is teaching English either as an independent tutor or at one of the many private schools, since Italians need not be hired for these jobs. For those particularly interested in teaching, the **Institute of International Education (IIE)** (809 U.N. Plaza, New York, NY 10017, tel. 212/984-5413) offers *Academic Year Abroad* ($42.95 plus $3.80 shipping), a listing of available education positions all over the world. In addition, their information center allows free access to a wide selection of reference materials, weekdays 10 AM–4 PM. The **Italian Cultural Institute** (686 Park Ave., New York, NY 10021, tel. 212/879-4242; 1601 Fuller St. NW, Washington, D.C. 20009, tel. 202/328-5556; 12400 Wilshire Blvd., Suite 310, Los Angeles, CA 90025, tel. 213/207-4737) publishes a similar directory called *Schools for English-Speaking Students in Italy*, which lists job openings throughout the country. If you're interested in doing private tutoring on your own, your best bet is to post fliers around universities and bookstores.

The easiest way to arrange work in Europe is through Council's **Work Abroad Department** (205 E. 42nd St., New York, NY 10017, tel. 212/661-1414, ext. 1130). Participants must be U.S. citizens, 18 years or older, and full-time students for the semester preceding their stay overseas. **YMCA** oversees the **International Camp Counselor Program (ICCP)**, which entails teaching English, building houses, and hanging out with local kids. Write for a detailed brochure. *71 W. 23rd St., Suite 1904, New York, NY 10010, tel. 212/727-8800.*

LEGAL REQUIREMENTS Before coming to Italy to work in most jobs, Americans must acquire a work permit from their prospective employer and a work visa from the Italian consulate. However, it is also possible to get a permit in Italy from your employer once you've been hired. To get the work permit, your prospective employer must claim that you would fill a position that Italian citizens aren't qualified or available for, and must clear you with the provincial employment office. With a work permit from your employer, you can apply for an entry visa. With your valid Italian visa and work permit, go to the questura upon arrival to apply for residence in Italy. Residents of EU countries can work in Italy without these bureaucratic hassles.

STUDYING IN ITALY

The **CIEE**'s *Work, Study, and Travel Abroad: The Whole World Handbook* and the **IIE**'s *Academic Year Abroad* (*see above*) are great sources of information, as are the Italian departments and foreign-studies offices of local universities. Additional information is available from the Italian Cultural Institute (*see above*), especially in its pamphlets "Schools for Foreigners in Italy" and "The Italian Educational System: A Brief Outline."

If you want to study in Italy, pick up an application for a student visa from the nearest Italian consulate. Once in Italy, you'll need to check in at the *ufficio stranieri* (foreigners' office) at the questura in the city you'll call home, and request a *permesso di soggiorno* (residence permit) for the length of your stay.

Coming and Going

Flights into Milan and Rome often cost a few hundred dollars more than flights into European travel hubs such as Zurich, Frankfurt, Brussels, or Paris. Consider flying into one of these cities and taking the train down. A round-trip, second-class train ticket from Paris to Florence is about $110, and the trip takes about eight hours one-way.

BY AIR

Flexibility is the key to getting a serious bargain on airfare. If you can play around with your departure date, destination, amount of luggage carried, and return date, you'll probably save money. On your fateful departure day, remember that check-in time for international flights is two hours before the scheduled departure.

Italy's main airports are **Linate** (tel. 02/738–0233) and **Malpensa** (tel. 02/4009–9111) in Milan and Leonardo da Vinci, better known as **Fiumicino** (tel. 06/65951) in Rome. If you want to end up elsewhere in the country, you can fly to one of these hubs and hop a train or bus to your final destination.

BUYING A TICKET Although airline tickets may be your single biggest expense, planning ahead can save you hundreds. Options include charter flights, flying standby, student discounts, courier flights, and APEX (Advance Purchase Excursion) and Super APEX fares; read on to learn how to navigate this maze.

When your travel plans are still in the fantasy stage, start studying the travel sections of major Sunday newspapers: Courier companies, charter flight companies, and fare brokers often list incredibly cheap flights. Travel agents are another obvious resource, as they have access to computer networks that show the lowest fares before they're advertised.

Hot tips when making reservations: If the reservation clerk tells you that the least expensive seats are no longer available on a certain flight, ask to be put on a waiting list. If the airline doesn't keep waiting lists for the lowest fares, call them on subsequent mornings and ask about cancellations and last-minute openings—airlines trying to fill all their seats sometimes add additional cut-rate tickets at the last moment. When setting travel dates, remember that off-season fares can be as much as 50% lower. Ask which days of the week are the cheapest to fly on (weekends are often the most expensive). If you end up biting the bullet and paying more than you'd like for a ticket, keep scanning the ads in newspaper travel sections for last-minute ticket deals or a lower fare offered by desperate airlines. If you've already bought your ticket, some airlines will refund the difference in ticket price when they lower fares.

➤ **APEX TICKETS** • If you're not a student—or the kind of person who will spend days scouring newspapers for the lowest fare—APEX tickets bought directly from the airlines or from your travel agent are the simplest way to go. If you know exactly when you want to leave and it's not right away, ask for the APEX fare when making your reservation—it'll save you a bundle and guarantee you a seat. Regular APEX fares normally apply to tickets bought at least 21 days in advance; you can get SuperAPEX fares one month in advance. Here's the catch: If you cancel or change your plans, you pay a penalty of $50 to $100.

➤ **CONSOLIDATORS AND BUCKET SHOPS** • Consolidator companies, also known as bucket shops, buy blocks of tickets at wholesale prices from airlines trying to fill flights. Check out any consolidator's reputation with the Better Business Bureau before starting; most are perfectly reliable, but better safe than sorry. If everything works as planned, you'll save 10%–40% on the published APEX fare.

It goes without saying that you can't be too choosy about which city you fly into. Other drawbacks: Consolidator tickets are often not refundable, and the flights to choose from often feature indirect routes, long layovers in connecting cities, and undesirable seating assignments.

If your flight is delayed or canceled, you'll also have a tough time switching airlines. As with charter flights, you risk taking a huge loss if you change your travel plans. If possible, pay with a credit card, so that if your ticket never arrives you don't have to pay. Bucket shops generally advertise in newspapers—be sure to check restrictions, refund possibilities, and payment conditions. One last suggestion: Confirm your reservation with the airline both before and after you buy a consolidated ticket. This not only decreases the chance of fraud, but also ensures that you won't be the first to get bumped if the airline overbooks.

Well-known consolidators are **Globe Travel** (507 5th Ave., Suite 606, New York, NY 10017, tel. 800/969–4562), **UniTravel** (1177 N. Warson Rd., Box 12485, St. Louis, MO 63132, tel. 314/569–2501 or 800/325–2222), and **Up & Away Travel** (347 5th Ave., Suite 202, New York, NY 10016, tel. 212/889–2345).

➤ **STANDBY AND THREE-DAY-ADVANCE-PURCHASE FARES** • Flying standby is almost a thing of the past. The idea is to purchase an open ticket and wait for the next available seat on the next available flight to your chosen destination. However, most airlines have dumped standby policies in favor of three-day-advance-purchase youth fares, which are open only to people under 25 and (as the name states) can only be purchased within three days of departure. Return flights must also be booked no more than three days prior to departure. If you meet the above criteria, expect 10%–50% savings on published APEX fares.

➤ **CHARTER FLIGHTS** • Different charter flights have vastly disparate characteristics, depending on the company you're dealing with. Generally speaking, a charter company either buys a block of tickets on a regularly scheduled commercial flight and sells them at a discount (the prevalent form in the United States), or it leases the whole plane and then offers relatively cheap fares to the public (most common in the United Kingdom). Despite a few potential drawbacks—among them infrequent flights, restrictive return-date requirements, lickety-split payment demands, frequent bankruptcies—charter companies often offer the cheapest tickets around, especially during high season, when APEX fares are most expensive. Make sure you find out a company's policy on refunds should a flight be canceled by either yourself or the airline. Summer charter flights fill up fast and should be booked a couple of months in advance.

You're in much better shape when the company is offering tickets on a regular commercial flight. After you've bought the ticket from the charter folks, you generally deal with the airline directly. When a charter company has chartered the whole plane, things get a little sketchier: Bankrupt operators, long delays at check-in, overcrowding, and flight cancellation are fairly common. You can minimize risks by checking the company's reputation with the Better Business Bureau and taking out enough trip-cancellation insurance to cover the operator's potential failure.

The following list of charter companies is by no means exhaustive; check newpaper travel sections for more extensive listings. **DER Tours** (Box 1606, Des Plains, IL 60017, tel. 800/782–2424), **Tower Air** (tel. 800/34–TOWER), **Travel Charter** (1301 W. Long Lake Rd., Troy, MI 48098, tel. 810/641–9677 or 800/521–5267), and **Travel CUTS** (187 College St., Toronto, Ont. M5T 1P7, tel. 416/979–2406).

➤ **STUDENT DISCOUNTS** • Student discounts on airline tickets are offered through **CIEE**, the **Educational Travel Center**, **STA Travel**, and **Travel CUTS** (*see* Student Travel Organizations, *above*). Keep in mind that you will *not* receive frequent-flier mileage for discounted student, youth, or teacher tickets. For discounted tickets based on your status as a student, youth, or teacher, have your ISIC, IYC, or ITIC in hand when you buy your tickets and when you check in at the airport.

➤ **COURIER FLIGHTS** • A few restrictions and inconveniences are the price you'll pay for the colossal savings of being an air courier, accompanying packages between designated points. Restrictions include luggage limitations (check-in luggage space is used for the freight you're transporting, so you take carry-ons only), limited stays of a week or two, and often a limit of one courier on any given flight.

Check newspaper travel sections for courier companies, look in the yellow pages of your phone directory, or send away for a directory that lists companies by destination city. One of the better publications is the **International Association of Air Travel Couriers'** *Air Courier Bulletin* (8

S. J St., Box 1349, Lake Worth, FL 33460, tel. 407/582–8320); for an annual $35 fee, you'll receive updates every two months. Another good resource is the newsletter published by **Travel Unlimited** (Box 1058, Allston, MA 02134), which costs $25 for 12 issues. **Discount Travel International** (169 W. 81st St., New York, NY 10024, tel. 212/362–3636) has courier flights, but some restrictions apply so call at least two weeks in advance. Couriers must be over 18. **Now Voyager** (74 Varick St., Suite 307, New York, NY 10013, tel. 212/431–1616) arranges courier flights from New York, Newark, or Miami; book two months in advance.

Most courier flights are one week in length, with round-trip fares ranging from $150 and up. Their quoted prices do not include a $28 airport tax, which is due when you arrive at the airport. A nonrefundable $50 registration fee, good for one year, is also required.

➢ **TAKING LUGGAGE ABOARD** • U.S. airlines allow passengers to check two pieces of luggage, neither of which can exceed 62 inches (length + width + height) or weigh more than 70 pounds. If your airline accepts excess baggage, it will probably charge you for it. Foreign airline policies vary, so call or check with a travel agent before you show up at the airport with one bag too many.

FROM NORTH AMERICA **Delta** (tel. 800/325–2000) has the best average round-trip fares (standard APEX prices are given here) from New York to Rome or Milan: $568 low season, $1,000 high season. **TWA** (tel. 800/892–4141) is the most convenient airline, flying daily out of almost any city in the United States (with an international airport) to Milan and Rome. They also offer a student discount card ($15 for one year, $25 for two years) good for a flat 10% discount on any fare, including three-day youth tickets. **American Airlines** (tel. 800/543–0460) flies daily from Chicago's O'Hare airport into Milan. **United** (tel. 800/521–0810) flies daily from Washington to Rome and Milan. **Alitalia** (tel. 800/223–5730) flies from major U.S. cities into Milan and Rome. Their high-season fares run $1,266 from Los Angeles, $978 from New York; low-season $1,168 from Los Angeles, $778 from New York. **Canadian Air** (tel. 800/426–7000) flies from Toronto into both Milan and Rome. Low-season tickets cost around C$799, high-season C$1,428.

The average nonstop flight from New York to Rome lasts eight or nine hours; from Chicago, 10–11 hours; from Los Angeles, 12–13 hours. From Toronto to Rome, it's about nine hours.

FROM THE UNITED KINGDOM **British Airways** (tel. 800/247–9297) and **Alitalia** (tel. 800/223–5730) both fly frequently from London's Heathrow airport to Milan's Linate airport and into Rome (British Airways also flies from Gatwick to Rome). To travel to either Rome or Milan, both airlines charge about $250–$300 round-trip in the low season, $350–$450 round-trip in the high season. The flight takes three hours to Milan, 3½ hours to Rome.

FROM AUSTRALIA AND NEW ZEALAND **Qantas** (tel. 02/957–0111) flies from Melbourne to Rome, stopping in Sydney and Bangkok. From Auckland, you must fly first to Sydney. The current round-trip, low-season fare from Melbourne is AUS$2,099, from Auckland NZ$2,699. High-season fares rise AUS$100–AUS$200. **Alitalia** (02/271308) also flies from Sydney to Rome at similar rates. The flight from Sydney to Rome takes about 21 hours, including stopovers.

Bikes in Flight

Most airlines will ship bicycles as luggage, provided bikes are dismantled and packed in a box. Call to see if your airline sells bike boxes (around $10); alternately, you might be able to pick one up for free at your local bike shop. International travelers can often substitute a bike for a piece of checked luggage at no extra charge (as long as it does not weigh more than 75 lbs); otherwise, it will cost $100 extra. The same applies to domestic flights: Your boxed bike can act as your second piece of luggage, or you can pay a $50 fee.

Staying in Italy

GETTING AROUND

BY TRAIN   In general, Italian trains are clean, affordable, and run on schedule. Be watchful of your bags and your body on overnight trains, though, especially south of Rome. You might want to padlock your bag to the overhead rack. Always make a reservation for long rides or you may end up sitting in the aisle for several grueling hours.

Most stations have a *biglietteria* (ticket office) where you buy your ticket. Some have separate lines for reservations and *couchettes* (bunk beds for overnight trains). If a station is so small it has no biglietteria, you can buy your ticket on the train. Tickets are quite reasonable; a trip from Florence to Rome costs only about L20,000 (less than $15). First-class tickets usually cost at least 50% more and are not worth the money. Round-trip fares cost as much as two one-way tickets; the only penalty for not buying a round-trip ticket is having to wait in line twice at the ticket counters. Many stations now have computerized ticket sellers (but they're usually broken) and trip planners (also usually broken) that will tell you when the next train is coming and where to change trains. The state railway offers a variety of discounted train tickets (*see* Train Passes, *above*).

Every decent-size train station has a place to store luggage. Plop that puppy down and forget about it for L1500 per piece, per day.

An often-overlooked option for budget travelers without a rail pass is the **Billet International de Jeunesse** (International Youth Ticket), usually known as a **BIJ** or **BIGE** ticket. Travelers under the age of 26 can buy an international train ticket for about 30% off the regular second-class fare and make unlimited stops along the way for up to two months. BIJ tickets are available at budget travel agencies in major cities. Look under the heading "Discount Travel Agencies" in various chapters of this book for likely candidates. Also, ask about the **Cartaverde**, good for 20% off most train trips and valid for one year (*see* Train Passes, *above*).

BY BUS   Taking a long-distance bus can be incredibly complicated; you'll often have to get off in an obscure town to switch lines, and sometimes you'll have to suffer an ungodly long wait. But buses often cost less, run more frequently, and go more places than trains. Towns in the hills and mountains, especially, are likely to be served by bus only. Buy tickets at *tabacchi* (tobacco shops), at bars near bus stops, at the bus station (if the town has one), or on the bus. If you buy a ticket before you board, you're expected to punch the ticket on the bus. Occasionally, conductors will get on board and check tickets, and if you don't have one or haven't punched it, you face massive fines. The word to be afraid of is *sciopero* (strike), which you'll see posted at bus stops quite often. Drivers go on strike nearly every couple of weeks.

BY PLANE   Between getting to the airport, waiting for the plane, flying, and getting to the center of town, flying within the country saves you little time and costs a lot of money. **Alitalia** is the main domestic airline, but there are several others. If you must book a flight within the country, go to a travel agent, who might be able to find you a better deal than the airlines' quoted fares.

The Trains Explained

The fastest Italian train, the "Pendolino," runs between major cities only and is prohibitively expensive. Intercity (IC) is next in terms of speed, followed by "Rapido." You pay a "supplemento" (extra charge) of up to 50% for IC and Rapido service, although the supplement is waived for EurailPass holders. "Espresso" trains make a few more stops and are usually a little slower, but you don't have to pay a supplemento. "Diretto" trains make even more stops, and "Locale" trains are slow as molasses, stopping in every little podunk station along the way.

23

BY FERRY In recent years, hydrofoils have become more prevalent—making boat travel faster and more expensive—but ferries are still the primary mode of transport to Italian islands. Ferries are usually priced according to day of week and time of year; weekends in July or August are generally the most expensive. Ferries to Corsica and Sardinia leave from Genova, Livorno, and Civitavecchia; those to Greece leave from Ancona, Bari, and Brindisi. Ferries to islands closer to the mainland are less troublesome and leave more often; usually just showing up and waiting for the next one is the best idea.

BY CAR, MOPED, AND BIKE You've probably heard rumors about Italian drivers and their reckless, maniacal ways: It's all true. If you drive on Italian roads, expect a barrage of tailgaters and people who pass on impossibly narrow roads. And that's just in the country. In the city, you'll face hellish roundabouts where you'll be sitting all year if you wait for someone to yield the right of way. Defensive driving is a nice idea, but your caution will be met by shrill horn blasts and dirty looks. It's not a fun experience. If all this sounds not too intimidating, consider renting a bike. Mountain-bike touring is becoming increasingly popular, but it's very arduous in some areas. Make sure you know your limits before signing up for a 10-day tour of Tuscany—some of the hills are killers.

Still, there may be times when you'll really want a car, especially in parts of southern Italy and the mountainous north where trains and buses rarely dare to tread. With a group of three or four people, renting a car isn't such a big expense. You'll still have to deal with exorbitant tolls on the highways (L8500 per 100 km) and some of the highest gas prices in Europe (over L1700 per liter, or L6000 per gallon). Carrying a map is a prerequisite when navigating poorly marked roads. A red sign with a horizontal white stripe through it means do not enter; a red sign with a blue *X* means no parking.

If you plan to rent or buy a car abroad, you should probably get an **International Driver's Permit (IDP)** before leaving home. To qualify for an IDP you must be 18 years old and hold a valid U.S. driver's license. The IDP is available from the American Automobile Association (AAA) for $10 if you bring two of your own passport-size photos. Some offices can take photos for you ($6 for AAA members; $8 cash for nonmembers). Certain offices will issue an IDP in about 15 minutes, but be sure to call ahead; during the busy season IDPs can take a week or more. **Automobile Club D'Italia (ACI)** (Via Marsala 8, 00185 Roma, tel. 06/49981) is affiliated with AAA and provides a varying range of services to members. There is a fee for emergency auto services and maps, though tour information is free.

➤ **CAR RENTALS** • Rental rates vary widely and usually include unlimited free mileage and standard liability coverage. Most major car-rental companies are represented in Europe, including **Avis** (tel. 800/331–1212, 800/879–2847 in Canada, 0181/848–8765 in the U.K.); **Budget** (tel. 800/527–0700, 800/268–8900 in Canada); **Hertz** (tel. 800/654–3131, 800/263–0600 in Canada, 0181/679–1799 in the U.K.); **National** (tel. 800/227–7368, 0113/242–2233 in the U.K.). You can expect a discount of about 15%–30% if you call ahead and reserve a car.

HITCHING *L'autostop* (hitchhiking) in Italy is as risky as anywhere else, so always exercise extreme caution. Hitching in a group is safer, but you're less likely to get picked up. Holding a sign with your intended destination and standing near the entrance to an autostrada increases your chances of getting picked up.

Sharing a ride is safer than hitching, and it could save you money and help you meet Italians (and possibly learn some Italian show tunes). Many cities now have **ride-sharing organizations**: Rome (Via Quattro Fontane 2, tel. 06/474–6525; or Via dei Falisei 10, tel. 06/493241); Milan (Via Col di Lana 14, tel. 02/839–1763); and Florence (Corso Tintori 39, tel. 055/247–8626; or Via Guelfa 64, tel. 055/283395).

PHONES

One Berkeley Guides writer decided SIP (the official Italian pay phones) stands for "Sucky Italian Phones." He wasn't kidding. Possibly half the pay phones in Italy are out of order. And if you have a phone card, the phone only accepts coins, and vice-versa. The best place to make a call is from a quiet, cool booth in a phone office. These offices are often in big train stations and/or in the middle of town. Here you can buy *carte telefoniche*—phone cards in denominations of L5000 and L10,000. Since phones that accept coins are being phased out, you should pick up a phone card if you plan on being in the country for a while.

IRITEL, ASST, and SIP are in the process of merging to create TELECOM Italia, the new national phone company. Once the process is completed, all phone offices should be open daily 8 AM–10:30 PM and telephone credit cards will theoretically be uniformly accepted.

LOCAL CALLS A local call costs L200, and can be made at booths and in bars with either change or a phone card. Sometimes merchants will give you a phone *gettone* (token) in place of a L200 coin when making change; use them just like the L200 piece.

INTERNATIONAL CALLS Since hotels tend to overcharge —sometimes exorbitantly—for long-distance calls, it's best to make such calls from telephone offices, usually labeled SIP, ASST, or TELECOM. Here operators will assign you a booth, help you place your call, and collect payment when you're done. In some towns, you can use an AT&T or similar phone card to charge your call.

To make a direct international call from a phone booth, insert a phone card, dial 00, then the country code, area code, and phone number. The country code for the United States and Canada is 1, for Great Britain 44, for Ireland 353, for Australia 61, and for New Zealand 64. A L10,000 card will keep you on the line with the United States for about three minutes.

To use a credit card or to call collect from a pay phone, you have to deposit L200, which you get back when you finish the call. To call collect you can dial 170 to get an English-speaking operator. For AT&T USA Direct, call 172–1011; for MCI, call 172–1022.

MAIL

SENDING MAIL HOME Italian mail is slow (letters to the U.S. take about 10 days to arrive) and not too reliable, so don't send valuables in the mail. Postcards are low priority and take longer than letters. Stamps, which are available at post offices and tabacchi everywhere, cost L1250 for an average letter or postcard.

➤ **TELEGRAMS AND FAXES** • A city's main post office will either have telegram and fax facilities onsite, or there will be a telegram office nearby. Faxing to or from Italy is extremely expensive.

RECEIVING MAIL Letters from the United States will take 10–15 days to arrive; packages take a little longer. The main post offices in cities and major towns all accept *fermo posta* (held mail). Have your pen pals address correspondence to you c/o Palazzo delle Poste, with the name of the city, postal code, and the words "fermo posta." When you pick up mail, bring your passport and expect to pay about L250 per piece. The post offices can be very unreliable, however; have your mail held at the nearest American Express office if you are a cardholder.

BUSINESS HOURS

Business hours in Italy will inevitably irritate and confound you. The average business is open Monday–Friday or Monday–Saturday from around 9 AM to about 7:30 PM. But many businesses shut down for a few hours between noon and 4—right when you wanted to go out and buy/eat/see something. Be aware that many museums, except in major tourist cities like Florence, Venice, or Rome, only open in the mornings from about 9 AM to about 12:30 PM, and sometimes close on Mondays. Restaurants are open for lunch and dinner with siesta in between (*see* Food, *below*). All shops close down on Sunday, so go to the market the day before unless you want to end up at a touristy trattoria or an overpriced convenience store. Italian banks have the most absurd hours of all: weekdays 9–noon and around 3:30–4:15. Businesses will often post both *feriale* (workday) and *festivo* (weekend/holiday) hours. *Ferragosto* refers to the weeks around August 15, when most Italians take their vacation.

25

LANGUAGE

Italians are not French and therefore will be impressed by and receptive to, your attempts to speak their language. While most people who work in the tourist industry (hotels, tourist offices) speak English, the average person on the street probably does not. Italians all speak Italian—developed in Tuscany and officially sanctioned as the national language by Mussolini—as well as diverse regional dialects and languages. Signs and menus in the Valle d'Aosta, for example, are written in French and Italian, while in Alto-Adige, you'll see Italian and German. The glossary in the back of this book will help you with basic communication.

WHERE TO SLEEP

Whenever possible, reserve a room in advance when visiting a big city, a popular tourist town, or anywhere in high season. If you arrive somewhere without a reservation, tourist offices will provide lists of hotels and will sometimes call for you or recommend one.

HOTELS Hotels in Italy are classified by the government in categories ranging from one to five stars. Most hotels reviewed in this book are one- and two-star establishments. One-star hotels vary from gross to charming, with most falling into the "clean-but-generic" category. Two-star establishments are usually a little nicer and have more rooms with private baths. In small or out-of-the-way towns, a two-star hotel can be affordable. Budget hotels are almost always clustered around the train station. The words *albergo*, *pensione*, and *locanda* all basically mean hotel and are interchangeable for our purposes. Unless specified, prices listed in this book are for double rooms without bath.

The price for a single hotel room—even in a dive—starts at around L30,000, but if you're traveling in a group, hotels become more appealing. Doubles without bath cost L40,000–L90,000, with bath L60,000–L100,000. In reviews, "full pension" means you get full room and board, and "half pension" means you get a room, breakfast, and either lunch or dinner. When checking into a hotel, always ask if breakfast is included in the price (often hotels charge L6000 or so for a watery coffee and a packaged croissant). If it is included, see if you can get them to deduct the cost of breakfast; you're almost always better off going to a café down the street.

HOSTELS Italy's hostels are generally nice, but they have the usual inconveniences—daytime lockout, nighttime curfew, and terrifying hordes of kids on school trips. However, hostels are usually the best budget choice if you're traveling alone—beds cost L15,000–L20,000 and they're also a good place to meet traveling companions. The **Associazione Italiana Alberghi per la Gioventù** (Via Cavour 44, Rome 00184, tel. 06/487–1152, fax 06/474–1256), the official Italian hostel organization, puts out a complete guide to HI hostels in the country. Some are in castles or villas, and some have special facilities like a restaurants or laundry rooms. Many hostels don't take reservations more than a day in advance, but some of the bigger ones now have a computer system (called the IBN network) that allows you to reserve in advance from one hostel to the next.

Independent (sometimes "nun-run") hostels offer alternatives to expensive hotels and full hostels, but they're usually single-sex and have a score of rules to follow. If you're Catholic or Catholic-friendly and plan to stay in one town for an extended period, you can often contact the local parish either directly or through the tourist office to find a very cheap bed in the rectory.

CAMPING Campgrounds near cities are often big, ugly affairs—a large piece of roadside dirt with tents. Camping is usually the cheapest option at L7000–L15,000 per person, though some big campgrounds charge as much as L20,000 for a site. Be prepared for long bus rides in and out of town. The best places to camp are in nature areas like the Valle d'Aosta and the Dolomites. The various campgrounds range from simple, green areas to recreation parks replete with camper vans, water slides, and a full bar. **Federazione Italiana del Campeggio**, a.k.a Federcampeggio (Calenzano, Florence 50041, tel. 055/882391), issues a free, complete list of campgrounds and a map.

LODGING ALTERNATIVES Hotels and hostels are not the only way to stay in Italy. You may find that the options listed below provide more opportunities to meet Italians.

➤ **AFFITACAMERA** • *Affitacamera* means "rent a room," and lots of Italians do exactly that, especially during high season. Sometimes affitacamere are listed in the lodging pamphlets at tourist offices; otherwise, look for signs around town that say AFFITACAMERA, or ask around. These accommodations cost about L50,000–L70,000 for a double; you might be able to negotiate in the off-season.

➤ **AGRITURISMO** • *Agriturismo* is the practice of renting out rooms in rural homes. This is an excellent way to get an unusual taste of Italy. Prices are about the same as a cheap hotel (L40,000 a night), but you may get to eat farm-fresh food cooked in an Italian kitchen by somebody's mamma. Getting to the farms on public transportation may be difficult—having a car will help a lot. The best places for agriturismo are out-of-the-way locales like Puglia and inland Sardinia. Inquire at the main office, **Agriturist** (Corso Vittorio Emanuele 101, 00186 Rome, tel. 06/685–2342, fax 06/685–2424), open weekdays 8:30–11 and 3–6. Or check out the local tourist office for comprehensive lists of participating farms. Some agriturismo stays are reviewed in the following chapters.

➤ **CONVENTS AND MONASTERIES** • For those in search of peaceful surroundings, convents and monasteries provide a unique lodging experience and are often less expensive than hotels. Though guests are often expected to make their own beds, the cleanliness and beauty of the buildings usually make up for any inconvenience. Some places house only Catholics, but many are flexible. A letter from your priest, pastor, or rabbi may be helpful. Inquire at the tourist offices in major towns for availability.

➤ **RIFUGI** • The Dolomites and other mountain groups are scattered with huts called *rifugi*. Rifugi are sometimes free; most, however, cost about the same as a hostel or a cheap hotel (L20,000–L40,000). Amenities are generally few. Some have cots rather than beds, although running water is almost always provided. Definitely inquire about availability in your prospective rifugio before trudging up a mountain to find no beds available—though in many cases they will make space, especially in those very out-of-the-way rifugi. Tourist boards in towns at the base of the mountains will provide you with a list of rifugi and usually call them for you. **Club Alpino Italiano** (Via Ugo Foscolo 3, 20122 Milan, tel. 02/805–6971) owns hundreds of these huts and publishes an annual guide with information on access, prices, and equipment. The **Touring Club Italiano** (Corso Italia 10, 20122 Milan, tel. 02/85261) also publishes guides describing hikes that pass by these mountain huts.

➤ **ROUGHING IT** • Pitching your tent anywhere other than an official campground is technically illegal and usually frowned upon. Inconspicuousness is the key to roughing it; within the chapters, we give tips on where and where not to try it. Sleeping in urban public places is especially unappreciated; you probably won't be arrested, but you may be hassled and kicked off your turf by the local police. The best places to rough it are in the mountains, remote meadows, and forests.

➤ **SERVAS** • Formed in the aftermath of World War II, Servas is a membership organization that enables you to arrange a stay with host families. It's dedicated to promoting peace and understanding around the globe. Becoming a member makes you eligible for their host-list directory for various countries. Servas is not for tourists or weekend travelers; peace-minded individuals over 18 who want more than a free bed can write or call for an application and an interview. You can arrange a stay with a Servas host or host family in advance or just try your luck when you arrive. Membership is $55 per year, and a deposit of $25 is required for each five lists you receive. *In the U.S.: 11 John St., Suite 407, New York, NY 10038, tel. 212/267–0252. Canada: 229 Hilcrest Ave., Willowdale, Ont. M2N 3P3, tel. 416/221–6434. U.K.: 4 Southfield Rd., Burley-in-Wharfedale, Ilkley, West Yorks LS29 7PA. Australia: 1 Moonyah Ct., Cooma, NSW 2630, tel. 6452–5981. New Zealand: 24 Rahiri Rd., Mt. Eden, Auckland 4, tel. 9/630–6279.*

FOOD

Italian food is all about yummy plates of pasta, cheap local wine, and potent cappuccino—a delectable triumvirate that even backpackers can enjoy without breaking the bank. However, think twice before entering a *ristorante* (restaurant), which is often more expensive and stuffy than a family-run, neighborhood *trattoria*, or the even cheaper alternative, a *tavola calda* (Italy's version of fast food). For a fast, cheap, and tasty meal, there are places which sell squares of pizza to be eaten while standing; look for signs saying pizza *a taglio* or *rustica*. A true osteria is a nothing more than a basic food-serving wine shop; some conniving places call themselves *osterie*, but they're likely costly restaurants competing for your tourist dollars. *Paninoteche* serve simple sandwiches. *Gastronomie* dish-out prepared food to be taken home with you. *Panifici* and *fornai* sell bread, while *pasticcerie* provide pastries and sweets. There are also *rosticcerie* that roast and sell meat and poultry. An even cheaper way to eat is to cook for yourself. Italy has incredible fish, meat, and vegetable markets.

Vegetarians need not fear Italian food: Pasta, tomatoes, and vegetables are staples. But hardcore veggies should be aware that red sauce and risotto are often made with chicken or meat broth. Also, make sure to specify "magro" or "senza carne" when ordering a dish to avoid surprise appearances of flesh.

Breakfast in Italy will never include hash browns and pancakes; more likely you'll find yourself standing at a coffee bar with a pastry and cappuccino in hand. The *cornetto* (croissant) is one of the more popular breakfast treats. Be aware that sitting at a table may double the price of your order. When it comes to lunch and dinner, the easiest way to keep costs down is by *not* ordering a full, three-course meal. The *primi piatti*, or *primi* (first courses), are plates of pasta, risotto, or soup. They're so filling you may not need to order the more expensive *secondi* (second courses), usually chicken, beef, or fish accompanied by a *contorno* (side dish) of vegetables or salad. Of course, don't skip out on a pre-dinner trip to the *antipasti* table for appetizers. Bread is usually included in the cover charge, and bottled water costs L2000–L3000. If you don't want to pay extra for water, ask for tap water, called *acqua semplice*, *acqua di Roma*, or *acqua di Milano*, depending on the region. Wine by the bottle can double your bill, so stick with the house red or white, which is usually decent. The high price of desserts, espresso, and after-dinner drinks will surprise you, especially in tourist-oriented restaurants. It's almost always cheaper to go to a bar or a gelateria for dessert and coffee.

Throughout Italy, lunch is served roughly 1–3, dinner 8–10, sometimes later in summer months. Both meals are meant to be lingered over with wine, coffee, and conversation. Italians don't like to rush a meal. This attitude often transforms an evening bite into a full-blown feast. Most restaurants serve the same menu for lunch and dinner, so don't expect lunch to be much cheaper. At lunch, though, waiters are less likely to sneer at you for not ordering a secondo.

COVER CHARGES Restaurant throughout Italy charge a *coperto* (cover charge) in addition to the *servizio* (service charge). Cover charges range from L1000 to L5000 per person, the service charge from 10% to 15% of the bill. Be careful in tourist traps, as the prices are often low but are offset by high servizio and coperto charges. Unless you limit yourself to coffee bars and pizzerias, there's no way around the coperto, but the price of a restaurant's *menu turistico* (tourist menu) typically includes tax and service.

SPECIALTIES In northern Italy, menus are loaded with creamy pastas and thick slabs of meat. As you move south, menus lighten up a bit with the addition of fresh fish, simple tomato-based pasta sauces, and a lot fewer cholesterol-laden dishes. Even so, Italian cuisine is highly regional. Restaurants in the **Dolomites** serve a killer *knoedel* (dumplings with wine or tomato sauce), which is almost as heavy as *speck* (a cured ham) with hot sauerkraut. **Lombard** specialties include baked pike and trout, *risotto alla milanese* (risotto with chicken broth and saffron), *ossobucco alla milanese* (veal knuckles with risotto milanese), and *tortelli di zucca* (pumpkin-stuffed pasta), a typical Mantovan dish. Also try *gorgonzola* (a rich, veined cheese) and *panettone* (cake with raisins and candied fruit), both of which come from Milan. The cuisine of the French-influenced **Valle d'Aosta** features sausage, mountain cheese, and venison. The favorite form of pasta here is *agnolotti*, yet another stuffed pasta. Also try *fonduta* (fondue made with local cheeses, eggs, and grated truffles) and *cardi in bagna cauda* (edible thistles bathed in a spicy sauce of cream, olive oil, anchovies, garlic, and butter).

In the **Veneto** you'll see plenty of polenta—often as an accompaniment to *fegato alla veneziana* (liver with onion)—as well as *baccalà* (dried salt cod). Another Venetian specialty is *bigoli* (a thick spaghetti-shaped pasta) with a tangy *tonno* (tuna) sauce. The best dessert is *tiramisù*, a decadent dessert from Treviso made with ladyfingers, liqueur, espresso, and creamy mascarpone cheese. In **Trentino Alto-Adige** you'll be knee-deep in strudel and wurst, whether you like it or not. **Emilia-Romagna** is considered the food capital of Italy, especially renowned for its *tortellini* (filled pasta said to be inspired by a goddess's belly button), and pasta *al ragù* (heavy sauces made of meat and cream). The city of Parma is famous for *prosciutto* (cured pork) and the king of Italian cheeses: *parmiggiano reggiano*. **Umbria** and **Marche** are known for truffles— try *ciriole al tartufo* (pasta with olive oil and truffles)—and all sorts of fresh fish; in the latter category, *brodetto* is a rich, hearty fish chowder. Dishes typical of **Lazio** include *gnocchi alla romana* (potato dumplings sliced and slathered with butter), and *stracciatella* (egg-drop soup). **Tuscan** delicacies include *bistecca alla fiorentina* (steak served very rare); thick soups; pastas spiced with tarragon, sage, and rosemary; and tasty bean dishes (Tuscans are known as *mangiafagioli* or bean-eaters). Naples in **Campania** is famous for *pizza*; while you can find this staple in every little town, nowhere is it made better than here, in its reputed home. **Sicily** benefits from its island status with tuna, *pesce spada* (swordfish), and *pasta con le sarde* (pasta with sardines, olive oil, anchovies, raisins, and pine nuts). Both couscous and *bistecca falso magro* (beef rolled around sausage, onion, bacon, and egg) are not unheard of in Sicily, though they can be expensive. Try instead the more common *caponata*, an antipasto of eggplant, capers, and olives.

WINE Roman poets once called Italy *Oenotria Tellus* (The Land of Wine), and with good reason. If you're an undemanding *vino* consumer, Italy certainly has plenty of bargain-priced reds and whites. But if you've made the jump to amateur connoisseur, prepare yourself for quality vintages at bargain prices.

In Italy, wine comes in *bianco* (white), *rosato* (rosé), and *rosso* (red), and even the cheap stuff is good by American standards. House wine can be ordered by the ¼ liter (slightly more than a

Caffè Culture

Even if you're a seasoned coffee drinker back home, you'll find both the selection of coffee drinks and the etiquette of imbibing them a bit different in Italy. First off, the word "bar" is used to indicate a place to drink coffee. Although alcoholic beverages are available, most folks come to a bar for a boost of caffeine. Secondly, coffee is not something to savor; it is sucked down quickly, in a standing position. If you do choose to sit at one of the tables sometimes provided in larger bars, you can expect to pay up to twice as much for your drink. At most places, it is customary to pay the cashier first, then bring your "scontrino" (receipt) to the counter and repeat your order. It's also a good idea to leave a L100–L200 tip when you return the receipt. Here are a few of the most commonly ordered drinks, though the possibilities are nearly endless.

- *Caffè: a single espresso. A good choice any time of day.*

- *Cappuccino: espresso topped with steamed whole milk and foam. Considered a morning drink in Italy.*

- *Caffè Macchiato: "stained" espresso, or espresso with a drop of steamed milk.*

- *Caffè Corretto: espresso "corrected" with a healthy dose of liquor.*

- *Caffè Latte: not as popular in Italy as you might think, this morning drink is mostly steamed milk, with the addition of a shot of espresso.*

Italian History Cheat Sheet

With a history going back at least 3,000 years, it's no wonder many people feel overwhelmed in cities like Rome, Florence, and Ravenna—and, well, nearly every other town in Italy. Influenced by powerful pagan dieties, eccentric emperors, and pompous popes, Italy has gone through more phases than Bowie. Surprisingly, it became a unified republic 72 years after the United States declared independence. Not surprisingly, Italy is still struggling to achieve an organized governing power. Though you may not be able to make sense of Italy's history, with the key dates below you'll at least know who came first—Jesus or Julius.

- *1000 BC: Etruscan civilizations form in central Italy.*
- *753: Traditional date for the founding of Rome.*
- *750: Greek city-states begin to colonize southern Italy.*
- *510: Foundation of Roman republic.*
- *45: Julius Caesar becomes sole ruler of Roman Empire. He's assassinated one year later.*
- *27: Rome's Imperial Age begins. Augustus named emperor.*
- *AD 29: Jesus Christ crucified in Roman colony of Judea.*
- *238: First wave of Germanic invasions penetrates Italy.*
- *313: The Edict of Milan grants toleration of Christianity within the Empire.*
- *330: Imperial capital is moved from Rome to Constantinople.*
- *476: Last Roman Emperor deposed.*
- *774: Charlemagne invades Italy and is crowned Holy Roman Emperor by Pope Leo III.*
- *800–900: Rise of Italian city-states.*
- *1290–1375: Works by Tuscan literary giants Dante, Petrarch, and Boccaccio form the basis of literature in modern Italian language.*
- *1447: Religious status of papacy begins to be devalued and is replaced by an enriched artistic patronage of the Holy City. Artists such as da Vinci, Michelangelo, and Raphael embellish churches and palazzi throughout Italy.*
- *1563: Council of Trent marks the beginning of Counter-Reformation.*
- *1796: Napoleon begins his Italian campaigns.*
- *1848: Risorgimento troops establish the republic of Italy.*
- *1922: Mussolini and his "black shirts" take control.*
- *1944: Italy is captured by Allied troops.*
- *1993: Bribe scandals expose widespread political corruption.*

glass), ½ liter, and full liter, priced at about L5000, L7000, and L10,000 respectively. *Vini della casa* (house wines) usually arrive in an open decanter, though occasionally they do come in bottles, so don't be alarmed if one lands on the table. Expect to pay L5000–L8000 for a decent bottle in a wine shop. A good rule of thumb for the budget traveler is to stick to drinking local regional wines. You not only get the best *vino* for the buck, but regional cuisine is best accompanied by regional wine.

The northwest is best known for its full-bodied reds, such as Barbaresco and Barolo of **Piemonte**. If you prefer a lighter wine, try Dolcetto or Grignolino. Asti Spumante, a semi-sweet sparkling wine, is also common in the north. In **Trentino Alto-Adige**, German varieties such as Riesling, Gewürztraminer, and Müller-Thurgau offer a crisp taste at a low price. **Tuscany** is famous for full-bodied Chianti Classico and prohibitively priced Brunello. **Lazio** is better known for its light whites, Colli Albani and Frascati. Also notable among Italy's dry white wines is **Umbria**'s Orvieto Secco. The deep south is not as well-known for wines, but those for a taste for sweeter, fruitier vino will appreciate **Sicily**'s Corvo and Regeleali, **Campania**'s Lacryma Christi (tears of Christ), and **Puglia**'s Malvasia, a dessert wine.

AFTER DARK

Dancing outside on a sultry Mediterreanean night with passionately strutting, beautiful young Italians may be one of the most exhilarating experiences of your life—but otherwise, nightlife in Italy can be surprisingly sedate. A typical night on the town for young Italians probably entails a pizza and beer with friends at around 9–10 PM, a *gelato* and a *passeggiata* (social stroll) until around midnight–1 AM, and then bed. Going out to discos, movies, or live music performances is usually just too expensive. Entry to dance clubs costs a ridiculous L15,000–L30,000, and sometimes requires a "membership" fee of around L20,000. Movie tickets cost L9000–L12,000, and it's hard to find a cinema with films shown in the original language. Opera and theater tickets are also expensive, but many theaters have student tickets for as little as L10,000; details are covered in the relevant sections within each chapter.

In the summer, look for advertisements for open-air discos—which open up in the suburbs of large cities and in beach resort towns—and for film showings à la "Cinema Paradiso" in town squares. At night, many Roman amphitheaters are still utilized for open-air theater and concerts during the summer months.

FURTHER READING

Books about Italy tend to be predictable sigh-fests by some professor who happened to spend six months in Tuscany with his wife and dog Boccaccio. In nonfiction, the tired but true *The Italians* by Luigi Barzini leads the social-history pack. For fiction, you can't go wrong with E. M. Forster's *A Room With a View*, Tommaso di Lampedusa's *The Leopard*, or anything by Giovanni Verga. For quality travel writing, read Mary Taylor Simeti's *On Persephone's Island: A Sicilian Journal* (North Point Press), and *Sea and Sardinia* by D. H. Lawrence. Good, modern nonfiction includes Joseph Brodsky's *The Watermark* (about Venice), Vincent Cronin's *The Honeycomb* (about Italy in general), Ann Cornelisen's *Women of the Shadows*, Carlo Levi's *Christ Stopped at Eboli*, and *Italian Days* by Barbara Grizzuti-Harrison.

Escape to ancient cities and

journey to  *exotic islands with*

CNN Travel Guide, a wealth of valuable advice.

Host Valerie Voss will take you

to all of your favorite destinations,

including those off the beaten path.

Tune-in to your passport to the world.

CNN TRAVEL GUIDE

SATURDAY 12:30 PMET   SUNDAY 4:30 PMET

VENICE AND THE VENETO

2

By Oliver Schwaner-Albright

For hundreds of years, the cities of the Veneto came when Venice whistled. The region's architectural styles, the many statues of the winged lion (the symbol of Venice) in every city, and the echo of the nasal Venetian dialect in the "vowelly" Veneto accents are all remnants of Venetian dominance of the region. This stretch of land, which sprawls east–west between Venice and Verona and reaches far north to the edge of the Dolomites, is much more than just a suburb of The Canaled One, though. While the Venetian Republic was looking to the East, with its eyes on the prize of Constantinople, the rest of the Veneto was developing under the thumb of more traditional medieval dynasties: The evil landlord Ezzelino da Romano and his progeny snagged prime land in the areas around Padova and Bassano del Grappa, and the Scaglieri family dominated Verona, while the Milanese Visconti family were conquering towns all over northern Italy. The hundreds of castles and monuments to themselves that these families left behind give the Veneto an appearance different from Venice, its big sister, which was ruled as a republic for a thousand years. When Venice finally decided it was time to take over the nearby mainland at the end of the 14th century, most cities, including Verona, Vicenza, Padova, and Treviso, had already formed civic centers, a university, and discrete personalities.

The biggest share of land in the Veneto is used for agriculture; farmers grow a lot of corn (which is used in polenta) and grapes (which are used to make wines such as valpolicella and Soave, as well as grappa brandy). Today the region is among the most expensive places to live in Italy, and it is populated primarily by dress-for-excess members of the upper-middle class. Residents are notoriously closed to outsiders: Don't expect a local to immediately invite you to Sunday dinner, and do expect judgmental stares. But none of this deflects the annual flood of travelers, who come to ponder Palladian villas, peaceful green hill towns, and paintings by locals Titian, Tintoretto, and Giorgione. The extensive hostel network, the allure of Venice, and the all-around cultural appeal of the Veneto make it the most touristed province in Italy.

Venice

Pink palazzi, green canals, the blue Adriatic Sea, yellow signs pointing to the city center (Piazza San Marco), and far too many red-faced tourists swirl together to form Venice (Venezia) —no wonder the city's artists were into color over form. Ethereally beautiful, culturally vigorous, grossly overpriced, and infuriatingly crowded, Venice prods you into forming a strong opinion. The city is simultaneously a smelly stew of tourists and the most enchantingly beautiful place you've ever seen. Part of how you see Venice, though, depends on your travel savvy. Don't plan on seeing everything in a day; you'll wind up seeing nothing instead. Also try to avoid visiting Venice in July or August, when the trails to Piazza San Marco start looking like human conveyor belts and the only available food and lodging may be a Styrofoam sandwich and a legally iffy sleeping bag on the train station steps.

Due to the Great Tourist Takeover, there is little local flavor left in Venice. Most travelers come instead to absorb high culture, as the city is home to some stupendous art as well as to diverse churches. Beyond the striking structures and found artworks, the city itself is a visual master-piece: Built on 100-something islands crisscrossed by palazzo-lined canals, Venice's echoey, tiny walkways in the more remote areas are so tranquil and easy on the eye that even after an afternoon desperate for elbow room, you can see why the Republic of Venice was dubbed *La Serenissima* (The Most Serene).

Venice was formed in the 5th and 6th centuries by mainlanders trying to avoid marauding Huns and Lombards. By the 8th century, when the rest of Europe was snoozing through the Dark Ages, Venice had become a port town, dominated at first by the Byzantine Empire. You can see the Byzantine thumbprint everywhere, especially in the onion domes and opulent gold mosaics in the Basilica di San Marco. After a couple hundred years of foreign rule, the city's residents decided that while they liked being rich, they would like self-government even better. They elected the first doge (chief administrator), and in 828 the symbolic and kooky theft of the body of St. Mark (*see* Worth Seeing Venice, *below*) severed Venice's ties to anything but filthy lucre. In the following centuries, the city traded with and conquered much of the East, and it's still peppered with war spoils, most notably in the gold-dripping, jewel-encrusted basilica. Venice hit its peak in the 13th–15th centuries, when merchants commissioned scores of ostentatious Venetian-Gothic palazzi, visible today along the Canale Grande (Grand Canal).

The rise of Spanish and Portuguese naval power and the discovery of the New World during the 15th century marked the end of Venice's power. In 1508, during the War of the League of Cam-

Come Hell or High Water

Get out those rubber hip boots; the "acque alte" (high waters) that periodically flood parts of the city are getting higher and coming more often every year. The factories in Marghera have created a substantial economic base for the province, but they've also dredged up channels to the ocean and pumped raw sewage into the lagoon. The facto-ries, with a little help from natural causes, have basically stopped up the lagoon and backed up the tides, which rise higher every year during the flood season, from Novem-ber through April.

The lowest part of the city, sadly enough, is Piazza San Marco, whose buildings usually see about 1 meter of water every time it floods. When the water rises higher than that (in 1966 it rose to 2 meters), the artwork and the foundations of the buildings them-selves are in danger.

The most absurd solution to the flooding yet proposed was a series of 80 massive water walls set into the sludge of the lagoon between the islands and the mainland—during exceptionally high tides, these slabs of orange metal would have mechanically popped up and literally stopped the flow of the Adriatic. Appropriately named "Mose" (Moses), the project was shelved when the government realized—after 19 years of develop-ment—that it is just too darn difficult for humans to stop the sea. Until a new plan arises, Venetians must content themselves with carrying their work shoes in their hands and balancing on the planks the city lays across the flooded city squares.

brai, jealous Milanese, Austrians, and Turks ganged up on Venice and emptied its coffers. The city's trade with the East stayed profitable for another century or two, but the eastern market eventually bottomed out in favor of the West. When Napoleon came through at the end of the 18th century, slicing up Venice's territory, the city was lost. It was batted around by the major powers for a couple of decades before it finally (and not without reservations) joined the new nation of Italy in 1866.

So what's a landless, very beautiful city with a reputation for debauchery to do to make a little money? Desperate, Venice turned to tourism in the late 19th century. The Lido island became the hot spot for the pre-jet set, glamorized by Byron long before Thomas Mann. The city is now largely dependent on tourism, and you're just going to have to adjust to paying L35,000 or more per person to sleep, and not much less for an edible dinner. Tourism alone doesn't sustain Venice's economy, but it has helped raise the cost of living enough to force many locals to leave. Most moved across the lagoon to **Mestre**, a brutal industrial complex founded in the 20th century to boost the regional economy. The factories and the tourist industry are now more or less in direct competition, and the loss of either one would probably kill the city. Some speculate that Venice will sink into the lagoon before the tension between the two is resolved— such an ironic end to the city whose riches, glory, and beauty all depend on the water.

BASICS

AMERICAN EXPRESS The busy office close to Piazza San Marco performs all the usual money magic, exchanging at bad rates but without commission. Cardholder services include holding mail and cashing personal checks. *San Marco 1471, on Salizzada San Moisè, tel. 041/520–0844. From Piazza San Marco, a 2-min walk on Ponte dell'Accademia route. Currency exchange open Mon.–Sat. 8–8; cardmember services open weekdays 9–5:30.*

CHANGING MONEY Try to use a little foresight and change your money in Padova or wherever else you came from—Venice's rates suck. Banks windows that catch your eye with reasonable rates charge as much as 9.8% commission, and those that advertise "no commission" have sorry, sorry rates. Banks cluster on the San Marco side of the Ponte di Rialto and on Calle Larga 22 Marzo on the route from Piazza San Marco to the Ponte dell'Accademia. At either of these spots you'll find cash machines that are Cirrus- and Plus-friendly. The info office at the train station changes money at a poor rate, but at least it doesn't charge commission and has short lines.

CONSULATES The **U.K.** consulate (Dorsoduro 1051, tel. 041/522–7207) is on the Canale Grande immediately west of the Ponte dell'Accademia. U.S., Australian, and Canadian citizens should contact their consulate in Milan; the closest consulate for New Zealanders is in Rome.

DISCOUNT TRAVEL AGENCIES **Centro Turistico Studentesco (CTS).** This student travel center is the easiest place in the Veneto to get youth and student discount tickets for boat, plane, and international train rides. *Dorsoduro 3252, on Fondamenta Tagliapietra across from university, tel. 041/520–5660. From I Frari, walk down Scalater San Rocco, turn left on Crosera San Pantalon, and right on Calle Lunga Foscari, immediately after bridge. Open weekdays 9–12:30 and 3:30–7.*

Transalpino. The little booth at the train station specializes in tours and has good deals on rail trips to the rest of Europe. *Stazione Santa Lucia, to your right as you exit, tel. 041/716600. Open Mon.–Sat. 8–8.*

EMERGENCIES The general panic number is 113; **local police** (041/270–8200); **fire** (115); **ambulance** (041/523–0000); **emergency care** (041/529–4516).

ENGLISH BOOKS AND NEWSPAPERS You can find the *International Herald Tribune* and other English-language periodicals at the kiosks by the train station, the Gallerie dell'Accademia, and Piazza San Marco. **Cafoscarina**, a well-stocked foreign language branch of the university bookshop, is the best place in Venice to find a paperback novel in your mother tongue, albeit at inflated import prices. Luckily they'll give you a Rolling Venice discount (*see box, below*). *Dorsoduro 3258, tel. 041/522–9602. On Campiello degli Squelini, behind Ca' Foscari. Open weekdays 9–7, Sat. 9–noon. MC, V.*

LAUNDRY **Lavaget.** The only do-it-yourself laundromat in the Veneto, this place charges L15,000 per 5-kilo load, soap included. What can you do? You stink, and they have a monopoly. *Cannareggio 1269, on Fondamenta Pescaria, tel. 041/715976. From train station, take Piazza San Marco route across first bridge, turn left onto Fondamenta Pescaria. Open weekdays 8–1 and 3–7.*

MAIL Several satellite post offices throughout the city sell stamps and send packages weekdays 8:15–1:30. The central **Poste e Telecommunicazioni** is in the airy 16th-century Fontego dei Tedeschi, the onetime center for Germanic merchants in Venice. You can buy *francobolli* (stamps) weekdays 8:15–7, pick up *fermo posta* (held mail) weekdays 8:15–1:30, and send faxes or telegrams 24 hours a day, seven days a week. The postal code is 30100. *San Marco 5554, tel. 041/528–9317. Facing Canale Grande just north of Ponte di Rialto.*

MEDICAL AID Try to avoid falling ill in Venice—the **Ospedale Civica di Venezia** was installed in the 15th-century Scuola di San Marco by Napoleon, and astonishingly little has been done to modernize the hospital since. You might have to pantomime, because very few people on staff speak English. *Tel. 041/529–4517. On Fondamenta Nuova east of Ponte di Rialto, next to Chiesa Santi Giovanni e Paolo.*

➢ **PHARMACIES** • Call 192 to find out which **pharmacies** are open all night, as they rotate on a biweekly basis. All pharmacies have the address of the closest night pharmacy posted on their door. The folks at **Farmacia Italo-Inglese** (San Marco 3717, tel. 041/522–4837; open weekdays 8:15–1:30 and 4–7:30) speak some English; they're on Calle de la Cortesa, across the bridge from Campo Manin on the Ponte di Rialto–Ponte dell'Accademia route.

PHONES You can pay after you call at the **Telecom** office in the central post office building (open weekdays 8:30–12:30 and 4–7). Buy *carte telefoniche* (phone cards) at this office, at *tabacchi* (smoke shops), or from vending machines in the semi-soundproof pay-phone room in the train station.

VISITOR INFORMATION The APT runs two offices in Venice. The first is a small, hectic desk at the train station (tel. 041/719078), open June–September, daily 10–5; October–May, Tuesday–Sunday 11–4. The more mellow and roomy **main office** is in a building on Piazza San Marco. Both offices give out maps and the invaluable Italian–English biweekly *Un Ospite di Venezia*, with exhaustive museum, train, gondola, and concert listings. The station office also makes hotel reservations. *Main office: San Marco 71/G, tel. 041/522–6356. At end of Procuratie Nuove on Piazza San Marco. Open June–Sept., Tues.–Sun. 9:30–12:30 and 2–5; Oct.–May, weekdays 9:30–12:30.*

Like a Rolling Venetian

Make no mistake, the best deal in town is the curiously named Rolling Venice card. For those between the ages of 14 and 29, a L5000 fee entitles you to reduced entries to all major museums (some of which don't give student discounts), half-price tickets for the symphony, and discounts on restaurants, hotels, bike rentals, and even Benetton. The information that comes with the card is itself worth the L5000 price: a decent map marked with all places that give discounts; a book with some interesting walking tours; and another booklet of useful phone numbers. From June to September, Rolling Venice sets up two temporary offices where you can buy the card: one in the train station (tel. 041/521–2904; open daily 8 AM–8 PM), and one at the southwest corner of Piazza San Marco (tel. 041/521–2904; open daily 10 AM–4 PM). The rest of the year you have to hunt for their central office (the APT will give you a map).

COMING AND GOING

BY TRAIN The main **Venezia-Santa Lucia station** is named after the church that was sacrificed so visitors could step off of their trains and practically into the Canale Grande. Remember to stay on board at Venezia-Mestre, the stop before, unless you want to explore the dull streets of Venice's mainland stepsister. Ticket windows at the Santa Lucia station are open daily 5:50 AM–9:30 PM; the reservation windows, where you can book couchettes and international trains, are open daily 7:30 AM–8:30 PM; and the train information office (tel. 041/715–5555) is open daily 7:30 AM–9:30 PM. The station itself, including luggage storage (L1500 per bag), is open 24 hours, and more than a few people take advantage of the safe, clean (for a train station) lobby to save the cost of a night's lodging. When you're trying to find your way back to the station, look for the yellow signs that say FERROVIA or FS.

Every half hour, trains head to Bologna (2 hrs, L13,700), Milan (3 hrs, L20,800), Padova (30 min, L3400), Vicenza (50 min, L6800), Verona (1½ hrs, L9600), and Treviso (30 min, L3800). Less-frequent trains go to Florence (8 daily, 2¾ hrs, L20,800), Rome (7 daily, 5 hrs, L44,200), Bassano del Grappa (hourly, 1⅓ hrs, L5700), Vienna (5 daily, 10 hrs, L100,000), Geneva (2 daily, 8 hrs, L132,000), and Paris (2 daily, 12½ hrs, L156,500).

BY BUS There is no real reason to travel to Venice by bus, but if you do, you'll be deposited at **Piazzale Roma** (the city's only parking lot), which is just across the Canale Grande from the train station. You can take **ACTV** (tel. 041/528–7886) Bus 2, 4, or 7 from here to Mestre, if you decide to stay there. Buy your ticket (L1200) from the kiosks on the piazzale.

BY PLANE International and domestic flights go through the tiny mainland **Aeroporto Marco Polo** (041/260–9260), which is on the lagoon to the north of the city. If you're coming from the United States, a flight to Venice doesn't always cost that much more than one to Milan or Rome (though you will probably have to change planes in Milan). In the airport, a **luggage storage desk** (open daily 6 AM–9 PM) will stow stuff for L3500 per day.

➤ **AIRPORT TRANSIT** • To get from the airport to Piazzale Roma in Venice, your two cheapest options are to ride on the functional **ATVO** blue bus (20 min, L5000) or on the pokey orange **ATV** Bus 5 (50 min, L1200). A more stylish way of arriving in town is to take a seat on a **Cooperativa San Marco** (tel. 041/522–3303) boat, which make the one-hour trip from the airport to Piazza San Marco 15 times daily (L15,000 per person, baggage included).

GETTING AROUND

There has been only a single attempt in Venice's history to reorganize and simplify the city's meandering narrow streets, and that was when the Austrians plowed right through houses in Cannaregio and Castello, creating the arrow-straight Strada Nova and Via Garibaldi, respectively, in order to move troops and artillery through town quicker. But what the Hapsburgs did in the early 19th century isn't going to make your tromping through Venice any easier—this is essentially a medieval metropolis, where the only nods to modernity are electric lights and paved streets. A map is essential in orienting yourself, though you should remember that there is no such thing as a good map of Venice, since even a 1:5000-scale cartographer's wet dream would still leave half of the streets unnamed. After picking up a map (the tourist office freebie is just fine), the best thing you can do is wander about and pay attention to landmarks—just try to enjoy getting lost.

The 4 palazzi-saturated kilometers that are the Canale Grande—Venice's center stage, Main Street, loading dock, and open sewer all rolled into one—make up the world's grandest thoroughfare. After dark, treat yourself to a leisurely half-hour tour of the canal on Vaporetto 1 or 82.

The names for streets and passages are different in Venice that in every other city in Italy: A street is a *calle*, a covered passage a *sotoportego*, a filled canal a *rio terrà*, a street running along a canal a *fondamenta*, and a square is called a *campo* (the only piazza in Venice is San Marco). The city's alleyways are usually so short and narrow that you rarely have a chance to look more than 10 meters in front of you (unless you have the ability to see around corners), making it difficult to get your

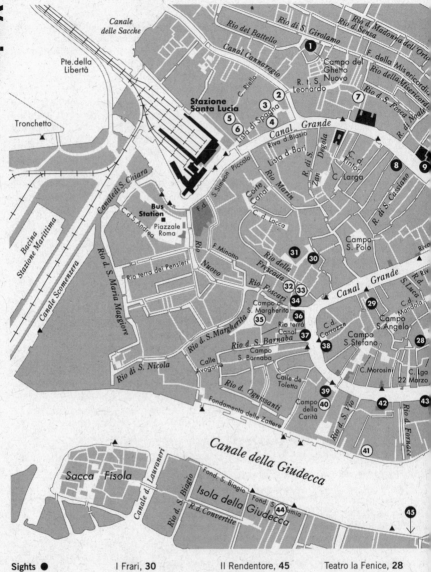

Canale delle Sacche

Pte.della Libertà

Tronchetto

Canal Cannaregio

Rio del Battello

Rio di S. Girolamo

Rio d. Sensa

Rio d. Madonna dell'Orto

F. della Misericordia

Campo del Ghetto Nuovo

Rio della Misericordia

1

R. t. S. Leonardo

7

Rio d. S. Fosca

R. di Noal

C. Riella

2

3

5

Stazione Santa Lucia

6

4

Lista di Spagna

Canal Grande

Riva d.Biasio

8

9

Lista d. Bari

R. di Dagola

C. d. Tintor

C. Larga

Canale di S. Chiara

C. d. S. Andrea

Bus Station

Piazzale Roma

Rio Marin

R. di S. Cassiano

R. di S. Cassiano

F. d. S. Simeon Piccolo

Corte Canal

C. d. Lacca

Campo S. Polo

Bacino Stazione Marittima

Canale Scomenzera

Rio d. S. Maria Maggiore

Rio terra dei Pensieri

Rio Nuovo

F. Minotto

Rio della Frescada

31

30

Canal Grande

S. Luca

R. d.

Riva

Rio Foscari

32

33

34

29

C. d. Mandola

Campo S.Angelo

28

Rio d. S. Margherita

Campo di S. Margherita

35

Rio terra Canal

36

C. d. Carrozze

37

Campo S. Stefano

C. Morosini

C. Lgo 22 Marzo

Rio d. S. Barnaba

Campo S. Barnaba

38

Calle Avogaria

Calle de Toletta

Rio d. Ognissanti

Rio di S. Nicola

39

Campo della Carità

40

Rio d. S. Vio

42

Rio d. Fornace

43

Fondamenta delle Zattere

Canale della Giudecca

41

Sacca Fisola

Canale d. Lavraneri

Rio d. S. Biagio

Fond. S. Biagio

Fond. S. Eufemia

Isola della Giudecca

R.d.Convertite

R. d. Convertite

44

45

Sights ●
Arsenale, **20**
Basilica di
San Marco, **24**
Ca' d'Oro, **9**
Ca' Foscari, **36**
Ca' Pesaro, **8**
Ca' Rezzonico, **37**
Campanile di
San Marco, **25**
Chiesa di San
Pantalon, **34**
Collezione Peggy
Guggenheim, **42**

I Frari, **30**
Gallerie
dell'Accademia, **39**
Libreria
Sansoviniana, **26**
Museo Civico
Correr, **27**
Museo Ebraico, **1**
Museo Storico
Navale, **22**
Palazzo Ducale, **23**
Palazzo Fortuny, **29**
Palazzo Grassi, **38**
Ponte di Rialto, **11**

Il Rendentore, **45**
San Giorgio
Maggiore, **48**
Santa Maria dei
Miracoli, **13**
Santa Maria della
Salute, **43**
Santi Giovanni e
Paolo, **14**
Scuola di San
Giorgio degli
Schiavoni, **19**
Scuola Grande di
San Rocco, **31**

Teatro la Fenice, **28**
Zitelle, **47**

TO MURANO,
BURANO,
TORCELLO

Sacca
della
Misericordia

San
Michele

Venice

0 _____ 440 yards
0 _____ 400 meters

N

Canale delle Navi

Racchetta
Fondamenta Nuove
Rio S. Caterina

C.

Rio d. Santi Apostoli
R. d. Gesuiti

C.d'Esia
C.d.Squero
Rio della Panada

10

Campo d.
Pescheria

dei Mendicanti

13

14

Campo Santi
Giovanni e Paolo

R. Barbaria delle Tole

Gustina

S.p.k.

TO ISOLA DI
SAN PIETRO
DI CASTELLO

Erberia

Rio d. S. Marina

Campo Santa
Maria Formosa

Ruga Giuffa

R. d. S. Lorenzo

R. d. S.
Francesco

Canale
d. Galeazze

d. Vin

11

Rio d. Fava

C.d.Bande

15

R. d. Severo

C. Lion

19

C.d.
Furlani

R. d. Scudi

R. d. Corna

Arsenale

20

Rio d. Vergini

di S. Pietro

d. Ca' Macerola

12

16

17

18

Fond.
Osmarin

R. d. Greci

R. d. Pietà

R. d. S. Daniele

Campo
Manin

Fabbri

Palazzo

Riva degli

Schiavoni

R. d. Arsenale

Rio della Tana

21

Frezzaria

27

24

25 23

22

V. Garibaldi

Rio d. S. Anna

Can.

R. d.
Molo
26

Piazza
San Marco

R. d. Moisè

Riva dei Sette Martiri

R. d. S. Giuseppe

Canale di S. Marco

48

Isola di
S. Giorgio
Maggiore

TO GIARDINI
PUBBLICI

46

Fond.
delle Zitelle

47

Calle
Michelangelo

Riva dei Partigiani

Rio dei Giardini

TO LIDO

▲ Vaporetto stop

Lodging ○
Albergo Bernardi-
Semenzato, **10**
Albergo Rossi, **3**
Albergo Santa
Lucia, **6**
Alloggi Trattoria
Nuova, **4**
Antico Capon, **35**
Archie's House, **7**
La Calcina, **41**
Caneva, **12**
Casa Bettina, **18**

Foresteria Domus
Cavanis, **40**
Foresteria
Valdese, **15**
Hotel da Pino, **32**
Hotel Marte, **2**
Hotel Villa Rosa, **5**
Istituto
Canossiano, **44**
Locanda Ca'
Foscari, **33**
Locanda Canal, **17**
Locanda
Sant'Anna, **21**

Locanda Silva, **16**
Ostello della
Gioventù, **46**

bearings. To complicate things further, Venice's essential reference point, the **Canale Grande**, cuts through the city in a backwards "S" from the train station to Piazza San Marco, which means that the canal can lie on three sides of you at once. And if that wasn't enough, the numbers painted above each door are useless as guides since they are assigned according to their district and not in a strict numerical progression—in other words, "6867 Dorsoduro" means that it is the 6867th doorway in Dorsoduro, and No. 8738 is just around the corner.

That said, there is a slight method to the madness. First, the Canale Grande is bridged in only three places: the **Ponte di Scalzi** in front of the train station, the **Ponte di Rialto** in the dead center of the city and canal, and the **Ponte dell'Accademia** to the southeast. Second, the six *sestieri* (districts) can help you to get oriented a bit: **Santa Croce**, **San Polo**, and **Dorsoduro** lie southwest of the Canale Grande, and **Cannaregio**, **San Marco**, and **Castello** are to the northeast. Third, if you know some of the major city landmarks and their relation to each neighborhood, you'll start to get a grip: **Campo San Polo** and **I Frari** are in San Polo; **Campo Santa Margherita** and the **Gallerie dell'Accademia** building (not the bridge) are in Dorsoduro; **Strada Nova** and **Lista di Spagna** lie in Cannaregio; **Campo Sant'Angelo**, **Campo San Stefano**, and **Piazza San Marco** are the hot spots of San Marco; and **Via Garibaldi** slices through the Castello district.

BY FOOT The easiest and quickest way to get around Venice is on foot. Several well-traveled routes cut through the city, which are sometimes marked by large yellow signs with arrows— these are helpful until you miss a turn and can't find any more signs. The trail through Cannaregio, along the Lista di Spagna and the Strada Nouva, starts to the left of the train station and leads to Piazza San Marco. From the train station, the trail to Dorsoduro (which passes I Frari and Campo Santa Margherita) starts over the Ponte di Scalzi and turns left before reaching the green-domed Chiesa di San Simone Piccolo before wandering manically through the back streets. The trail going through San Polo and Santa Croce continues staight across the Ponte di Scalzi. If you stray from one of these routes, follow a knowledgeable-looking person in the hopes of ending up at a large campo or the Canale Grande (hint: folks with T-shirts and backpacks don't know where they're going; lanky boys with huge bread carts do).

While wandering through Venice, you should remember that what you are walking on are streets, even though they may look like cute village paths. Pausing in the middle of a bridge to consult your map is like jerking a car to a stop in a busy intersection to read a street sign.

BY VAPORETTO The vaporetto (something like a boat-bus) is an easy and scenic way to transverse the city (and certainly the quickest way to reach Piazza San Marco), even if it's pricey and sometimes crowded. Besides getting to watch the vaporetto dudes do their work without mussing their gelled hair, you can use the vaporetti 24 hours. **Vaporetto 1** is called the *accelerato* (accelerated) though it makes almost every stop along the Canale Grande from Piazzale Roma to the Lido. **Vaporetto 82** covers essentially the same route, but makes about one-third the number of stops. If you are in a hurry, the *direttissimo* (very direct) **Vaporetto 3** runs from San Zaccaria to the train station, making only three stops on the way; **Vaporetto 4** does the same thing in the opposite direction. The other line you are likely to use is **Vaporetto 52**, which makes a huge loop around the city. Note: If a vaporetto has a sign marked LIMITATO, it only makes a loop between two major stops.

You can buy tickets for the vaporetti at the kiosks by the *fermate* (stops) or on board if the kiosk is closed. A one-way ticket is L4000, round-trip L7200. You can also get 24-hour tickets (L15,500), 72-hour tickets (L30,000, L20,000 for Rolling Venice cardholders—*see box* Like a Rolling Venetian, *above*), and one-week tickets (L55,000). Be sure to stamp your ticket in the yellow boxes by the stops before boarding. The boats are rarely controlled, but if you're caught without a validated ticket, be prepared to pay at least the ticket price plus a L1000 fee, not to mention a possible L30,000 fine.

BY TRAGHETTO Only three bridges span the Canale Grande, but another eight *traghetti* (stripped-down gondolas used as ferries) take people—mostly Venetians reading their papers on their morning commutes—across at points in between. The idea is simple: Board a traghetto at a designated station (usually noted by a yellow sign with a little gondola and an arrow), pay the guy L600, walk to the back of the gondola, and turn around so that you have your back to the water. (This will show you're in the know, because the gondola will swing out of the dock and turn 180°, giving you a proper forward-facing view.) The traghetti run from about 8 AM until 7 PM, except for when it's rainy, breezy, chilly, lunchtime, or the gondaliers are too busy gossiping.

BY GONDOLA The reality of the gondola is fat men passionlessly belting out Naples's greatest hits into a Mister Microphone to a crowd of thirty clapping and sweating strangers herded up and down a stumpy stretch of the Canale Grande. All this for the low, low price of L100,000 (about $65) per gondola for 50 minutes. If you do in fact decide to take a ride, drive a hard bargain with your gondolier before boarding—make sure the ride is a full 50 minutes and that the price is set. Don't take a gondola from San Marco, because you might end up spending all your time in boat traffic. It's better to leave from the less-congested Trinità station (tel. 041/523–1837), next to Campo San Mosiè on the San Marco–Ponte dell'Accademia route.

The job of a gondolier is a coveted thing. The ridiculously lucrative position is open only to the descendents of gondoliers, and their union is one of the most powerful in Venice. Not surprisingly, the gondoliers seem to spend more time manning their telefonini (portable telephones) than their oars.

BY WATER TAXI The wooden-hulled beauties you see cruising by as you chug along in a vaporetto are water taxis, Venice's expensive, modern-day answer to the gondola. The official rate isn't terrible—L35,000 from the Lido to San Marco—especially if you split it with friends, but the rate you actually get can be two or three times the official one, so be very careful. If you decide to go for it, it's best to either flag a taxi down or call 041/522–2303 or 041/522–8538. There are taxi stations at Piazza San Marco, the train station, and Ponte di Rialto.

WHERE TO SLEEP

Staying in Venice is going to cost you. Every other building in this city is a hotel, but rooms in the cheap ones need to be reserved at least two weeks in advance. Reservations are especially important from June to September—if your Italian isn't so hot, take advantage of the **hotel reservation desk** at the train station (tel. 041/715288), open June–September, daily 8 AM–10 PM, October–May, 8 AM–9 PM, where for L15,000 (cash only), they'll make a reservation for you in a one-star hotel and then apply the fee to the price of your room. But be warned: They don't cater to the budget crowd and may try to bump you up a price class. Since there is almost no crime in Venice, the worst thing that a budget hotel will be is smelly—no prostitutes, drugs, or bumps in the night. Inexpensive hotels are clustered around the train station in Cannaregio and way out in Castello, but it is worth the effort to hunt down a sweet place in San Polo or Dorsoduro, especially if you plan to stay for more than a few days. If you're a Rolling Venice holder, check on the map that comes with the card for a list of hotels—many of which are listed below—that will offer you a discount. Be sure to show the hotel proprietor your card when you register.

During the summer, you'll need a miracle to find a cheap place to stay in Venice without reservations. Pray to St. Christopher (patron saint of travelers) and St. Anthony (patron saint of finding things), cross your fingers, and get ready to pay.

Almost all budget hotels are family-run, which means two things: 1) they will lock the door sometime between midnight and 2 AM (you can usually ask for a key), and 2) they will close for a few weeks in November for minor repairs and for the end of December and most of January for the holidays (in other words, call ahead). Hostels and other dorm accommodations are the cheapest sleeps within the city limits, but many do not take phone reservations and have early curfews; those run by nuns often accept only women. Much is said about the benefits of staying in the nearby town of Padova, but though it is only 30 minutes away by train, it's bound to take an additional 45 minutes to get to the train station in Venice and another 30 minutes from Padova's train station to your hotel in Padova. If Venice is absolutely full, venture out into the soulless heart of Mestre for a L70,000 double at **Al Veronese** (Via Cappuccina 94, tel. 041/926275); it's on the street to the right of the train station.

CANNAREGIO This neighborhood is conveniently located close to the train station, but inconveniently situated across town from most sights. Still, there are plenty of cheap, clean rooms to be found in the area.

➤ **UNDER L55,000** • **Alloggi Trattoria Nuova.** Clean (but ugly) L50,000 doubles are a bargain, if you don't mind "showering" with a hose attached to the tub in the communal bathroom. Register downstairs at the trattoria with the same name. *Cannaregio 189, on Lista di Spagna before Campo San Geremia, tel. 041/716005. AE, MC, V.*

➤ **UNDER L70,000** • **Albergo Bernardi-Semenzato.** The hotel itself is unremarkable, but its *dipendenza* (annex) is a bizarre old palazzo with canal and garden views. The L65,000 doubles are a great deal, but you need to book in advance to ensure a place in the dipendenza. *Cannaregio 4363/66, on Calle dell'Oca, tel. 041/522–7257. At east end of Strada Nuova, turn left at church of Santi Apostoli onto Campiello Salizzada Pistor, and then left on Calle dell'Oca. 15 rooms, some with bath. Luggage storage. MC, V.*

Hotel Marte. The lobby is deceitfully schmancy, but the rooms are comfortable in an antiseptic chain-motel way. If they're full, they'll send you to the similarly priced **Biasin** across the canal. Doubles are L60,000. *Cannaregio 388, tel. 041/716351. From Lista di Spagna, follow San Marco signs to Ponte delle Guglie and turn right just before bridge. 27 rooms, 21 with bath. AE.*

➤ **UNDER L85,000** • **Albergo Rossi.** In an alley just off Lista di Spagna, Rossi gets its share of street noise. But the rooms are impeccably clean, the manager friendly, and it's close to the train station. Doubles cost L80,000. *Cannaregio 262, tel. 041/715164. From Lista di Spagna, turn left on Calle delle Procuratie. 14 rooms, 9 with bath. AE, MC, V.*

Albergo Santa Lucia. This hotel is thoroughly unexciting—bland, modern rooms, a dull staff, etc.—but the thick walls make it one of the quieter places around. For L80,000 you get a double with breakfast. *Cannaregio 358, tel. 041/715180. From Lista di Spagna, turn left on Calle della Misericordia. 13 rooms, 8 with bath. MC, V.*

Hotel Villa Rosa. You don't get ambience, just mass-produced furniture and bare walls. But L80,000 does buy you hot water under high pressure, clean bathrooms, and breakfast. *Cannaregio 389, tel. 041/716569. From Lista di Spagna, turn left on Calle della Misericordia. 28 rooms, 16 with bath. Wheelchair access. MC, V.*

DORSODURO The presence of the university means you'll find students and casual cafés and trattorie here. It's a great area if you want to be slightly off the tourist track and stay a while.

➤ **UNDER L85,000** • **Antico Capon.** The views from this hotel right on Campo Santa Margherita make for some great people-watching—at the very least, you can catch the hipsters at Bar Rosso checking you out. If you think you'll get to sleep before the trattoria downstairs empties out at 11:30 PM, think again. Call ahead to get the double without a shower (L80,000). *Dorsoduro 3004/B, on Campo Santa Margherita, tel. 041/528–5292. 7 rooms, 6 with bath.*

Locanda Ca' Foscari. In a good location near the university, this sunny, spacious hotel has rooftop views. Every room has a Venetian glass chandelier—a point of pride with the English-speaking owner. The L75,000 doubles include breakfast, but the best deal is to split the four-person room with a shower for L130,000. *Dorsoduro 3887/B, on Calle della Frescada, tel. 041/522–5817. From I Frari, go down Scalater San Rocco (which begins at Salizzada San Rocco), and turn left on Crosera San Pantalon; Calle Frescada is at the end of the street. 10 rooms, 4 with bath.*

➤ **UNDER L100,000** • **La Calcina.** A spacious hotel that manages to be both comfortable and funky, this is the place to splurge if you're feeling rich. The building was once the residence of English critic John Ruskin, and it's right on the Giudecca Canal. If you add L15,000 onto the L90,000 price of a double (breakfast included), you can have a perfect view

Wondering why every window in Venice has a box of geraniums? Besides being pretty, they repel the many mosquitoes that emerge from the city's murky canals. Geranium oil is a pleasant, nontoxic repellent that you can buy in any erboristeria (herb store); there's a good one in Campo Santa Margherita.

of Il Redentore across the water. *Dorsoduro 780, tel. 041/520–6466. From Zattere vaporetto stop, walk down Fondamenta delle Zattere. 23 rooms, 14 with shower. MC, V.*

CASTELLO The edge of the Castello closest to Piazza San Marco is predictably expensive, but you'll find good deals farther into the district.

➢ **UNDER L50,000** • **Casa Bettina.** The rooms in this tiny, haphazard place are large, and the showers are big enough that you can wash your hair without bumping your head. Doubles are only L45,000. *Castello 4388, on Campo San Giovanni Nuovo, tel. 041/523–9084. From Fondamenta Canonica (behind Basilica di San Marco), cross bridge to Rugagiuffa Sant' Apolonia, turn left at Campo San Filippo e Giacomo onto Calle Chiesa, left at Campo San Giovanni Nuovo. 5 rooms, 3 with shower.*

➢ **UNDER L90,000** • **Caneva.** This place has airy rooms, an overgrown courtyard, and a lackluster staff. At L85,000 for a double (breakfast included), it's the cheapest place you'll find close to San Marco, and prices fall to L55,000 in the off-season (November–March). *Castello 5515, on Ramo della Fava, tel. 041/522–8118. From Ponte di Rialto, walk through Campo San Bartolomeo to Calle Stagnieri, cross bridge to Campo della Fava; Ramo della Fava starts on the right. 23 rooms, 10 with bath.*

Locanda Canal. The big rooms with rickety furniture are light and not at all dank (something to consider in watery Venice). The L75,000 doubles include breakfast. *Castello 4422/C, on Fondamenta Remedio, tel. 041/523–4538. From Campo Santa Maria Formosa, walk behind church to Campiello Querini and veer to the right to Fondamenta Remedio. 7 rooms, 3 with bath.*

Locanda Sant'Anna. Way out in the *populare* (working class) section of Castello past the Arsenale, this is more like a strange old apartment than a hotel. The common areas have worn, old furniture, and the courtyard is a good place to relax. The L86,000 price for doubles includes breakfast. *Castello 269, on Corte del Bianco, tel. 041/528–6466. From west end of Via Garibaldi, veer right on Fondamenta Sant'Anna, turn left onto the second bridge, then right into Corte del Bianco. 8 rooms, 7 with bath. Curfew 12:30.*

Locanda Silva. Popular with Italian travelers, Silva has some rooms with canal views, and is run by helpful people with a happy cat. The L80,000 doubles are tiny but comfortable. *Castello 4423, on Fondamenta Remedio, tel. 041/522–7643. From Campo Santa Maria Formosa, walk behind church to Campiello Querini and veer right to Fondamenta Remedio. 25 rooms, 13 with bath. Curfew 2 AM.*

HOSTELS Venice only has one perennially packed HI hostel, but there are enough dormlike places (often called *foresterie*) to ensure that you get a cheap bed for the night. If the places below are full, try **L. Murialdo** (Cannaregio 3512, tel. 041/719933), **Patronato Salesiano Leone XIII** (Castello 1281, tel. 041/528–7299), or **Ostello Santa Fosca** (Cannaregio 2372, tel. 041/715775). The APT office has a list of other hostels, as does the Rolling Venice map (*see box* Like a Rolling Venetian, *above*).

Archie's House. As you'd expect from the name, this isn't a slice of Italy, but Archie is good-natured, multilingual, and very tolerant of the backpacker crowd. The building is in a bombed-out palazzo (and looks it), but it's a good place to stay for a few nights while picking Archie's brain on what to do in Venice. Beds cost L25,000 in three- or four-bed rooms, but you can strike a deal for long-term visits. The minimum stay is two nights. *Cannaregio 1814/B, on Rio Terrà del Cristo, tel. 041/720884. Take train station–Ponte di Rialto route over 1st bridge, turn right onto Rio Terrà del Cristo. Check-in before 9 AM or after 8 PM. Cold showers free; hot showers: L1500.*

Foresteria Domus Cavanis. Well situated between the Accademia and the Zattere, this nicer-than-most foresteria is run by a stern but warm woman. Doubles are L70,000 (L50,000 with Rolling Venice card). *Dorsoduro 912, tel. 041/528–7374. From Ponte dell'Accademia, turn right on Rio Terrà Foscarini. 59 rooms, 29 with bath. Midnight curfew. Closed Oct.–May.*

Foresteria Valdese. The dorms in this foresteria are as basic as you can get, but the room with a kitchen is a good deal if you pack it with six people. Dorm beds cost L25,000 the first night, L23,000 thereafter, breakfast included. *Castello 5170, tel. 041/528–6797. From Campo*

VENICE

Santa Maria Formosa, walk down Calle Lunga Santa Maria Formosa until it ends, then cross bridge to Protestant church; it's on the right. 47 beds. Midnight curfew, lockout 1 PM–6 PM. Reception open Mon.–Sat. 9–1 and 6–8.

Istituto Canossiano. This nun-run place is practically defined by all the no's: no men, no smoking, no eating, no coming or going after 10 PM. No wonder there's always room even though it costs only L21,000 for a bed. If you dare risk divine disapproval, play on the swings in the courtyard. *Giudecca 428, off Ponte Piccolo, tel. 041/522–2157. From train station, take Vaporetto 82 to Sant'Eufemia stop and turn left. 35 beds. Curfew 10 PM, lockout 9 AM–4 PM.*

Ostello della Gioventù Venezia (HI). Good luck trying to get a bed here in summer; this hostel only accepts phone reservations October–May. You can try to ensure a place by paying in advance at another hostel on the IBN network; otherwise show up very early and stand in line. Beds are L21,000 a night with breakfast. You can register and buy mandatory HI cards (L35,000) anytime, and the common room opens at 2 PM. *Giudecca 86, on Fondamenta della Croce, tel. 041/523–8211. Take Vaporetto 82 to Zitelle/Ostello stop and turn right. 273 beds. Curfew 1 AM, lockout 9–6.*

CAMPING Trying to camp in Venice is a little like trying to camp in downtown Los Angeles. There are no campgrounds in Venice proper, unless you count the Lido, which is actually one of the more beautiful, quiet, and convenient camping areas in all of Italy. You'll find **Europa Cavallino** (tel. 041/968069; closed Oct.–Easter) on the Adriatic side of the Lido on the Litorale del Cavallino island. Camping costs L9500 per tent, L3700 per person. Take Vaporetto 14 to Punta Sabbioni. **Camping Jolly delle Querche** (Via A. Di Marchi 7, Marghera, tel. 041/920312), a mainland site, is well equipped and only costs about L8000 per person with tent, but it's a pain to reach and none too scenic. From Piazzale Roma, take Bus 6, get off at Piazza Foscori, and follow the signs.

ROUGHING IT The gentle summer climate and almost complete lack of crime should make Venice a great city for roughing it, but the police are hip to this and patrol all the obvious public places (Piazza San Marco, the Giardini, etc.) to keep their city from becoming one big crash pad. You can always "wait for a train" at the train station, but a more pleasant, if distant option is to head out to the beaches on the Lido (avoid the ones with cabanas, which are patrolled); the Adriatic side of San Nicolò is a good choice.

FOOD

It's just not fair that the pigeons eat better than you do, but there's not much you can do about it. Even when Venice is at its cheapest, it's still not cheap—remember, all your little gnocchi, eggplants, and cappuccino cups had to get here by boat. Venice's reputation for having the least satisfactory food in Italy is especially justified if you can't pull yourself out of the quagmires of San Marco and Cannaregio, where quadralingual menus and compact disc–sized pizzas are the rule. But if you take a deep breath and wander through the back streets of Dorsoduro and San Polo, you can find excellent meals at relatively low prices.

While in town you should try the unofficial dish of Venice, *seppia con polenta* or *seppia alla veneziana* (tender pieces of squid smothered in a rich sauce made from its own black ink and served with grilled polenta). Other local specialties include spaghetti *alle vongole* (with clams in a butter-herb sauce), and *risotto alle vongole nere* (rice with black clams). Some bars have decent *panini* (sandwiches on a roll) but the square pizza slices and inexplicable triangular *tramezzini* (mayonnaise mush on white bread) are nutritionally unsound. Avoid the bars around San Marco and Cannaregio, which tend to design their sandwiches based on how long they will last in the window rather than how they will taste. Restaurants generally charge a "coperto" (cover) of L1000–L3000 plus a service charge; look for the exact amounts at the bottom of the menu. The Rolling Venice card gets you a discount of 10%–20% (sometimes a free drink, too) at many of the restaurants reviewed below; see your Rolling Venice map for a list of applicable restaurants and be sure to ask about the discount at the restaurant, or you might miss out.

If you want to construct a meal of your own, you'll find that fruits and vegetables aren't as expensive as you'd think as long as you stay away from the tiny stalls on the streets between the Ponte

Reality check. Call home.

— *AT&T USADirect® and World Connect.® The fast, easy way to call most anywhere.* —

Take out AT&T Calling Card or your local calling card.** Lift phone. Dial AT&T Access Number for country you're calling from. Connect to English-speaking operator or voice prompt. Reach the States or over 205 countries. Talk. Say goodbye. Hang up. Resume vacation. Relax with AT&T. *That's Your True Choice.ᴿᴹ AT&T.*

Austria*†††............**022-903-011**	Luxembourg......................0-800-0111	**Turkey***......................**00-800-12277**
Belgium*..................**0-800-100-10**	**Netherlands***..............**06-022-9111**	**United Kingdom**...........**0500-89-0011**
Czech Republic*..........**00-420-00101**	**Norway**..........................**800-190-11**	**0800-89-0011**
Denmark..........................**8001-0010**	**Poland**†¹.............**0◊010-480-0111**	
Finland........................**9800-100-10**	**Portugal**†....................**05017-1-288**	
France................................**19-0011**	**Romania***....................**01-800-4288**	
Germany........................**0130-0010**	**Russia***†**(Moscow)**............**155-5042**	
Greece..........................**00-800-1311**	**Slovak Rep.***..............**00-420-00101**	
Hungary*..................**00◊-800-01111**	**Spain**●......................**900-99-00-11**	
Ireland..................**1-800-550-000**	**Sweden**......................**020-795-611**	
Italy*................................**172-1011**	**Switzerland***....................**155-00-11**	

AT&T
Your True Choice

**You can also call collect or use most U.S. local calling cards. Countries in bold face permit country-to-country calling in addition to calls to the U.S. World Connect® prices consist of USADirect® rates plus an additional charge based on the country you are calling. Collect calling available to the U.S. only. *Public phones require coin or card. †Limited availability. †††Public phones require local coin payment during call. ◊Await second dial tone. ¹Dial 010-480-0111 from major Warsaw hotels. ●Calling available to most European countries.©1995 AT&T.

For a free wallet sized card of all AT&T Access Numbers, call: 1-800-241-5555.

All the best trips start with **Fodor's**.

EXPLORING GUIDES

At last, the color of an art book combined with the usefulness of a complete guide.

"As stylish and attractive as any guide published."
—*The New York Times*

"Worth reading before, during, and after a trip."
—*The Philadelphia Inquirer*

29 destinations available worldwide, priced between $19.95 - $21.00.

BERKELEY GUIDES

The budget traveler's handbook

"Berkeley's scribes put the funk back in travel." —*Time*

"Fresh, funny, and funky as well as useful."
—*The Boston Globe*

"Well-organized, clear and very easy to read."
—*America Online*

13 destinations worldwide, priced between $13.00 - $19.50.
($17.95 - $27.00 Canada)

AFFORDABLES

"All the maps and itinerary ideas of Fodor's established Gold Guides with a bonus—shortcuts to savings."
—*USA TODAY*

"Travelers with champagne tastes and beer budgets will welcome this series from Fodor's."
—*Hartford Courant*

"It's obvious these Fodor's folk have secrets we civilians don't." —*New York Daily News*

9 destinations worldwide, priced between $11.00 - $18.00.
($14.50 - $24.00 Canada)

At bookstores, or call **1-800-533-6478**

Fodor's
The name that means smart travel.™

dell'Accademia, the Ponte di Rialto, and the train station. The largest market is the daily **Mercato di Rialto**, which begins at the tourist stalls on the San Polo side of the Ponte di Rialto. To the left, past the butcher shops and cafés, is the **Erberia** (fruit and vegetable market), the largest and perhaps the cheapest place to buy fresh produce. The two-story arcaded building at the end of the Erberia holds the **Pescheria**, or fish market. Otherwise the most thrilling place in Venice to buy your tomatoes is from the vegetable boat next to Campo San Barnaba, on the route from the Ponte dell'Accademia to Campo Santa Margherita. It stays afloat Monday to Saturday. Finally, **Standa** (Cannaregio 3669, on Strada Nuova, tel. 041/520–4454; open daily 8:30 AM–7:20 PM; closed Mon. morning and all day Sun. in winter), a combination supermarket/department store, sells everything from Q-Tips to chocolate.

Rule of thumb: Panifici (bakeries), salumerie (delis), and all other food stores and stands are closed all day Sunday and Wednesday afternoons.

CANNAREGIO Avoid eating anywhere near the train station and push on into the narrow streets north of Strada Nuova—you'll thank yourself later.

➤ **UNDER L20,000 • Iguana.** Sometimes you forgo exploring a new culture in favor of something you know and need, like a burrito. This is the only place for hundreds of miles where you can get a chicken chimichanga (L8000) smothered in fresh guacamole (L3000) and wash it down with a Corona (L4000)—you have to admire that they make their own salsa and tortillas, even if neither is quite right (must be the low altitude). *Cannaregio 2515, on Fondamenta della Misericordia, tel. 041/716722. From west end of Strada Nuova, turn right on Fondamenta di San Felice and left on Fondamenta della Misericordia. Open Wed.–Mon. 11–3 and 7–1.*

➤ **UNDER L35,000 • Ristorante L'Arca di Noè.** Imagine, a macrobiotic restaurant in Venice. They serve all kinds of healthy versions of already healthy Italian dishes, like tagliatelle with *seitan* (gluten) for L9000. On Tuesday nights, there's an Indian menu (L30,000) with course after course of the real thing. *Cannaregio 5401, at Castello border on Calle Larga Giacinto Gallina, tel. 041/523–8153. From Campo San Giovanni e Paolo, cross bridge to the left, which runs into Calle Larga Giacinto Gallina. Open weekdays 11–3 and 7–11, Sat. 7 PM–11 PM.*

SAN POLO AND SANTA CROCE Not many tourists make it into the winding streets of San Polo and Santa Croce—good news for you since food tends to be better and cheaper here, but bad news since you'll have to do some tricky navigating. Be persistent.

➤ **UNDER L8000 • Mensa Universitaria.** The most bang for your lire in town—a filling four-course meal (pasta, meat, fruit, and drink) will cost you only L7700 and a glance at your student ID (ISIC or Rolling Venice cards work fine). *San Polo 2840, on Calle Magazen, tel 041/520–4496. From Campo dei Frari, cross bridge, turn left on Fondamenta dei Frari, cross another bridge, turn left on Rio Terrà San Tomà, and right on Calle Magazen. Open Mon.–Sat. 11:45–2:30 and 6:30–9, Sun. 11:45–2:30. Closed Aug.*

➤ **UNDER L20,000 • Alle Oche.** A menu with annoying cartoon birds on the cover offers over 50 different kinds of huge pizzas, such as the Inferno (L9000), with spicy salami, hot peppers, and mozzarella. If you don't see *exactly* what you want, ask nicely if you can mix and match ingredients. *Santa Croce 1552/A, tel 041/524–1161. From Campo San Polo, go up Calle Bernardo, cross bridge and continue until you can take 1st left on Rio Terrà Secondo, then right on Rio Terrà Primo Perrucchetta, and cross bridge to Calle della Madonna. Open Tues.–Sun. 11:30–3 and 7–11. MC, V.*

Due Colonne. The best pizzeria in Venice is not named after the site of executions (next to the Palazzo Ducale), but after the two interior stone pillars that purportedly hold the place up. The pizzas are large, fresh, and good—look for seasonal specials like buffalo mozzarella and tomatoes topped with fresh *rucola* (arugula) for L11,000. The tables out on the campo make for beautiful summer meals; be sure to give them a call in the morning to reserve a table. *San Polo 2343, on Campo San Agostin, tel. 041/524–0686. From Campo San Polo, walk up Corso Bernardo, cross bridge, turn left on Rio Terrà Secondo, and continue straight to Campo San Agostin. Open Mon.–Sat. noon–3 and 7–11. MC, V.*

La Perla d'Oriente. This place would do San Francisco's Chinatown proud, with tasty hot-and-sour soup (L3000) and tofu in chili sauce (L6000). It's the only restaurant on the Campo dei Frari, and the outdoor tables have views of the church's profile. *San Polo 3004, Campo dei Frari, tel. 041/523–7229. Open daily 11–2 and 7–11. AE, MC, V.*

DORSODURO Many restaurants here have gardens in back or tables out on quiet campi, making this one of Venice's more pleasant places to dine. The presence of a university means a lot of cheap, honest food, though a few places do cater to tourists.

➤ **UNDER L10,000 • Crepizza.** There isn't much atmosphere, service, or air-conditioning, but this place does offer quick and dirty pizzas on the cheap—you can get a simple *margherita* (with tomato sauce, basil, and mozzarella) made to order for L4500. They claim to specialize in crepes (get it, both crepes *and* pizzas), but you're better off keeping your taste buds virgin until you manage a trip to Paris. *Dorsoduro 3757–3761, on Calle San Pantalon, tel. 041/522–9189. Along Campo Santa Margherita–I Frari route. Open Thurs.–Tues. 11:30–3 and 7–10:30.*

Mensa Universitaria. This mensa offers the same deal as the one in San Polo (*see above*)—a four-course meal for L7700. You must show an ISIC or Rolling Venice card when you pay. *Dorsoduro 3264, on Fondamenta del Rio Novo, tel. 041/713907. From NE cnr of Campo Santa Margherita, turn left on Calle Forno, cross bridge and turn right on Fondamenta Malcanton, which dead-ends on Fondamenta del Rio Novo. Open Mon.–Sat. 11:45–2:30 and 6:30–9, Sun. 11:45–2:30. Closed Aug.*

➤ **UNDER L25,000 • Iguana.** A second branch of Venice's only Mexican restaurant (*see* Cannaregio, *above*), this one has tables by the Giudecca Canal. *Giudecca 68–71, on Fondamenta della Croce, tel. 041/523–0004. Open Thurs.–Tues. noon–3 and 7:30–11.*

Al Profeta. There are several similarly priced pizzerias scattered around the Dorsoduro, but the pies at this place tend to taste better than most, especially when eaten in the back garden. The menu is a catalog of pizzas that start at L6000 and make their way up to L24,000 for the huge, densely topped, and completely share-able "Maxipizza." *Dorsoduro 2671, tel. 041/523–7466. From SE cnr of Campo San Barnaba, take Calle Lunga San Barnaba. Open Tues.–Sun. noon–3 and 7–10:30. MC, V.*

Taverna San Trovaso. This is the best modestly priced restaurant in all of Venice, where the seppia alla veneziana (L14,000) and spaghetti alle vongole (L10,000) are both exquisite. Side orders of either *spinaci* (spinach) or zucchini (L4500 each) will make you realize how boringly vegetables are usually prepared. Reservations are paramount, especially if you want a table in the brick-vaulted rooms downstairs. *Dorsoduro 1016, on Fondamenta Priuli, tel. 041/520–3703. From Gallerie dell'Accademia, take Corso Corfù Gambara and turn left on Fondamenta Priuli. Open Tues.–Sun. noon–3 and 7:30–10. MC, V.*

Trattoria Antico Capon. Placed in one of the greatest people-watching spots in all of Venice, this joint has a large selection of pastas and pizzas within crawling distance of Campo Santa Margherita's bars. The spaghetti with salmon and cream sauce (L12,000) is their best dish. *Dorsoduro 5004, on Campo Santa Margherita, tel. 041/528–5252. Open Thurs.–Tues. noon–3 and 7–10:30. MC, V.*

➤ **UNDER L35,000 • L'Incontro.** This is a good place to treat yourself—the dishes are creative, fresh, and uniformly excellent. Primi (L10,000) include some interesting variations on the pasta theme, like *gnocchi al sugo d'anatra*, hand-made gnocchi with a duck sauce. The selection of secondi (around L20,000) depends on which fish were brought in that morning. Make reservations in advance, especially if you want a table on the campo. *Dorsoduro 3062/A, Rio Terrà Canal, tel. 041/5222–2404. On edge of Campo Santa Margherita towards Ponte dell'Accademia. Open Tues.–Sun. noon–3 and 7:30–10:30. MC, V.*

SAN MARCO As a rule, stay away from the restaurants in San Marco, unless you *want* to sample the most expensive and tasteless food in town.

➤ **UNDER L20,000 • Le Bistrot de Venise.** This place is a self-styled replica of a French bistro almost to a fault, with crepes (L5000–L15,000), pizzas with creme fraîche, café-art on the walls, and a book of poetry by the door. But the food is good, the crowd is way hip, and they stay open until 1 AM, sometimes with live music. *San Marco 4685/4686, on Calle Fabbri, tel. 041/523–6651. From San Marco, take middle alle that cuts through Procuratie Vecchie over bridge and to left where it intersects Calle Fabbri. Open Wed.–Mon. noon–3 and 7–1.*

Vino, Vino. If you happen to be in San Marco and you need a simple pasta dish in a pinch, this tiny wine bar–cum–restaurant is your best bet. The menu changes often, but you can always find staples like gnocchi with rucola sauce (L9000). And of course, there are plenty of wines to be had—engage in a little tasting during your (inevitable) wait for a table. *San Marco 2007/A, Ponte delle Veste, tel. 041/523–7027. Near Teatro la Fenice on San Marco–Ponte dell'Accademia route. Open Thurs.–Tues. 10:30 AM–midnight. MC, V.*

CASTELLO Just stay away from the backside of San Marco and you'll do fine in Castello. Via Garibaldi has all kinds of cheap, decent pizzerias and trattorias.

➤ **UNDER L20,000 • Trattoria alla Fonte.** If you're starving in San Marco, take a short walk to this trattoria for pizza or pasta, like the gnocchi *ai quattro formaggi* (with four cheeses; L8000). *Castello 3820, on Campo Bandiera e Moro, tel. 041/523–8698. From San Marco, turn left on Riva degli Schiavoni; after Chiesa della Pietà, turn left onto Calle di Dose, which becomes Campo Bandiera e Moro. Open Thurs.–Tues. noon–3 and 7–10.*

GELATERIAS When you're running out of energy, a sugar boost is in order, and gelato is probably the best way of getting one. (We thought we'd help you rationalize it.) Whatever you do, avoid *all* ice cream joints around San Marco—you might as well give a stranger some money and suck on an ice cube rather than order the tasteless junk they dare to call gelato.

Il Doge. This is the best gelateria in Venice for several reasons: It's on Campo Santa Margherita, it's open late, and the folks who do the scooping are sweethearts. Besides, the gelati (L2000 for a double) are exquisite, especially the fruity flavors like *fragola* (strawberry) and *pesca* (peach). Try their *tiramisù semifreddo* (chilled tiramisù mousse; L4500). *Dorsoduro 5058/A, on Campo Santa Margherita, tel. 041/523–4607. Open daily 11 AM–midnight; later in summer.*

Mille Voglie. Gelato pundits will argue whether this place or Il Doge is Venice's best—and it must be said that the creams here, like *baccio* (chocolate and hazelnut), are outstanding. But there's no need to fight, since each gelateria is about a double cone's (L2000) walk away from the other. *San Polo 3033/3034, Salizzada San Rocco, tel 041/524–4667. Behind the apse of I Frari. Open daily 10 AM–midnight.*

WORTH SEEING

With dazzling architecture, narrow shady streets, and art as colorful as the peeling paint on the buildings, you can easily make the argument that Venice is the most beautiful city in the world. It's also one of the most amiable: Without marathon distances or unmanageable traffic, almost every inch of the city is open to exploration, and the only thing you'll have to overcome is the propensity toward getting lost. Craming everything into one day just means visual overload and sore feet; allow yourself time to really look at the buildings surrounding you and to savor the spectacular art in the dark, cool churches.

Museums in Venice can be very expensive, but many places that no longer give discounts to students will honor Rolling Venice cards. Museum opening hours and admission costs change all the time; be sure to check *Un Ospite di Venezia* for the latest updates. During the madness of summer, it's not a bad idea to visit a museum during lunchtime (all the biggies are practically open round the clock), when most of the stores will be closed and the crowded streets are at their most miserable. Relatively few people venture out to the islands of the **Lagoon** (*see Near Venice, below*), but it's worth it for the chance to see a slightly different, and perhaps more complete, side of Venice.

PIAZZA SAN MARCO The heart of Venice, Piazza San Marco is the single-most visited spot in Italy and is always teeming with tourists. Prepare to be overwhelmed, both by the almost gaudy majesty of the buildings and the definitely gaudy tourist fanfare: Where else can you watch people pay hard-earned money to feed, touch, and take pictures of scads of disgusting pigeons, all the while listening to string quartet versions of "How Deep is Your Love" issuing from the ridiculously priced cafés. If you can, avoid the piazza until evening, when the true spirit of the place almost returns to the square.

The doge's backyard from the 9th century to the 19th century, the piazza has historically been the seat of the municipal government. The **Procuratie**, the two long buildings stretching out from the basilica, were the offices of the procurators, who tended to the more mundane aspects of running the city while the doge was out a-conquering. The Procuratie Vecchie starts at the **Torre dell'Orologio** (Clock Tower), where bronze "Moors" strike the hour on the roof; the Procuratie Nuove stands opposite. The two famous cafés, **Quadri** on the Vecchie and **Florian** on the Nuove, also played a part in history. During the Risorgimento of the 18th and 19th centuries, those who backed Italy conspired in Florian, while supporters of Austria plotted in Quadri. Now they plot together to ream tourists (L8500 for caffè when the bands are playing). The segment connecting the two Procuratie was commissioned as a ballroom for Napoleon, who used the buildings as his palace before he turned Venice over to Austria. Directly across from the Palazzo Ducale (*see below*) is the **Libreria Sansoviniana**, which Jacopo Sansovino, Venice's greatest Renaissance architect, designed to hold the doge's enormous collection of Greek and Latin texts. Though it's supposedly one of the city's architectural masterpieces, the building is closed to the public indefinitely.

➢ **BASILICA DI SAN MARCO** • This huge hallucination of a basilica has a history as bizarre as its architecture. Originally, Venice's patron saint was Teodoro, the saint of the ruling Byzantine Empire. In 828 however, two Venetian merchants on business in Alexandria stole St. Mark's body and placed it in a shipment of pork (so the Muslim customs officials wouldn't inspect it) bound for Venice. As the story goes, an angel had appeared to St. Mark while he was visiting the lagoon, saying, "Peace to you, Mark, my messenger. Your body will rest here"—a likely embellishment so the city of Venice and the sneaky merchants could rest easy believing that their Great Corpse Robbery was divinely ordained. Though the angel's greeting is written in Latin on every statue of the winged lion of St. Mark, more secular reasons lurked behind the theft. By declaring a new patron saint for the city, the increasingly powerful doges symbolically proclaimed their independence from Constantinople. In fact, Mark's remains were handed directly to the doge of the day, who erected the first basilica in 829. In 932, the basilica was

A Duke by Any Other Name is a Doge

The Republic of Venice took the nickname "La Serenissima" or the Most Serene, because of its stunning history of political stability—only once in the the republic's 13 centuries was there anything close to a popular uprising. This unusual respect Venetians had for their government came from the practice of voting for each and every one of the dukes, or doges. To avoid ballot stuffing, the Signoria (the state council) devised a complicated process to elect the doge. After praying in the basilica, the youngest member of the council took the first boy he saw with him to the Palazzo Ducale to become the ballot counter, in the hopes that the selection would be as random as possible. In the end, becoming the doge was more of an honorable burden than anything else—the tradition of tossing coins to the citizens gathered in Piazza San Marco on inauguration day almost bankrupted a few dukes. The "democratic" election, rather than "divine right," of the doge is why the Palazzo Ducale is more of a public building than a formidable noble residence, why no single family has dominated Venice's history like Florence's Medici, and why Venice was the world's longest-running "republic."

burned to the ground in an uprising against this new power; the structure you see today dates from 1094. Used as the doge's private church for centuries, it didn't become the official cathedral of Venice until 1807, when the doges were phased out.

As opposed as they were to Byzantine rule, the builders of the church were still smitten with Byzantine architecture; domes and gold mosaics abound. But the Venetians couldn't leave the thing alone, so the interior is a confusing and wonderful jambalaya of Byzantine, Gothic, and Renaissance styles, mixed with booty from around the world. Inside the basilica, sunlight is scarce in the naves and copious under the domes to enhance the feeling of divine enlightenment. On the Ascension dome in the very middle, Christ gives the blessing while borne toward the light by four angels; on the left side of the basilica's exterior is a 12th-century depiction of the corpse theft story (it was under restoration at press time). Take a free guided tour of the basilica, with explanations of the mosaics' biblical significance, at 11 AM or 3 PM weekdays; tours start at the entrance hall.

Don't bother paying to see the treasury, but by all means pay the L3000 admission (L1500 students and Rolling Venice holders) to the **Pala d'Oro**; this altar screen is covered with more than two thousand jewels and, needless to say, lots of gold. Much of the treasure was stolen from less fortunate cities and is more proof of Venetian dominance in the 12th–14th centuries. You have to share the **loggia** (a.k.a the Marciano Museum) with a swarm of tourists, but it's the only way to get up close and personal with any of the mosaics. Admission to the loggia is L2000. The four merry-go-roundish horses inside (the ones outside are copies) were stolen by Constantine from Chios, and swiped by Venice during the Fourth Crusade in 1204. Napoleon took them to Paris in 1797, where they stayed until finally being returned to the basilica. *Piazza San Marco, tel. 041/522–5205. Follow yellow signs from train station; or take Vaporetto 1, 82, or 2. Basilica and Loggia open daily 9:30–5. Treasury and Pala d'Oro open Mon.–Sat. 9– 4:30, Sun. 2–4:30.*

➤ **PALAZZO DUCALE** • The doges' private home and the site of courts, prisons, and political intrigues, the pink-checkerboard Palazzo Ducale is a perfect example of Venetian-Gothic architecture. The building was a moat-surrounded fortress in 810, and in 1340 it took on the delicate form it has today. Thick columns support the portico, but arcades, pastel marble, and the intricate crenellation on the roof alleviate any heaviness. The new design also created an inside courtyard, where anybody in Venice could drink from the wells or crash under the porticoes at night.

The main entrance, called the **Porta della Carta** (Door of the Charter) because public notices used to be posted there, contains sculptures of the four virtues, St. Mark, and Justice, all by the Bon family. The **Scala dei Giganti** (Giants' Staircase) leads up to two statues by Jacopo Sansovino: Mars (the god of war) and Neptune (the god of the sea), both symbols of the Venetian Republic. New doges would swear their loyalty to Venice standing between the two. Continue up the Sansovinian **Scala d'Oro** (Golden Staircase) to the major rooms of the palazzo; almost all are covered with paintings by Tintoretto, Veronese, Tiepolo, Titian, and other Venetian masters. The best paintings hang in the Sala di Maggior Consiglio: Veronese's virile *Apotheosis of Venice* stoked the doge's ego every time he looked up, and one whole wall is covered with a *Paradiso* by Tintoretto. From the Great Council Hall, walk down to the **Ponte di Sospiri** (Bridge of Sighs), which leads to part of the prisons. To see the best prisons, including the torture chamber and the maximum-security cells, take the tour called **Itinerari Segreti del Palazzo Ducale** (Secret Intineraries of the Doge's Palace). The L5000 tour (at 10 AM and noon) is in Italian only, but it's the only way to see Venice's most sinister side. Call 041/520–4287 a day in advance to place tour reservations. *Piazza San Marco, next to basilica, tel. 041/522–4951. Admission: L10,000, L6000 students and Rolling Venice holders. Open daily 9–7 (winter until 4).*

➤ **MUSEO CIVICO CORRER** • Venice's civic museum provides a thorough history of the city and helps put all those paintings, palazzi, and canals into context. The fascinating galleries hold a bounty of treasures, from Ottoman banners captured centuries ago as war booty to a sinister but functional-looking chastity belt. On the way out is a display of everyday objects through the ages, including board games, tarot cards, and 2-foot-high platform shoes (and you thought the '70s were bad). *San Marco, on Piazza San Marco, tel. 041/522–5625. Admission: L8000, L5000 students and Rolling Venice holders. Open Wed.–Mon. 10–5.*

➤ **CAMPANILE DI SAN MARCO** • Oddly enough, Italy's second-most recognizable tower (after that leaning thing in Pisa), is a reconstruction. After 11 centuries of standing strong as a watchtower and lighthouse, the 100-meter tower suddenly and unexplicably collapsed into a pile of rubble in 1902. The city quickly decided to rebuild it using as many of the old bricks as possible, and the tower you see today looks and functions exactly like its ancient predecessor in every way—right down to its five bells. Take an elevator to the top (admission: L5000, L2500 students and Rolling Venice holders) for an unrivaled view of Venice's canals, terraces, and winding calli. *Open daily 10–7:30.*

➤ **PIAZZETTA AND THE DUE COLONNE** • The small open area surrounded by the Palazzo Ducale, Piazza San Marco, and the lagoon is known as the Piazzetta. The most dominating elements here are the *Due Colonne*, two red Egyptian granite columns errected next to the fondamenta by the lagoon. The columns were raised in the 12th century, and symbols of the two patron saints of Venice were plopped on top. The replica statue on the right (facing the canal) portrays San Teodoro—who was worshipped when Venice still took its orders from Constantinople—as a dragon slayer (no, that's not a crocodile he's standing on). The original statue stands in the Palazzo Ducale. The more famous bronze statue, dating from between the 5th and 4th centuries BC, is of a winged lion—the symbol of St. Mark.

Two major activities took place between the columns in the Piazzetta: gambling and executions. Because of the latter, it's still considered bad luck to walk between the columns.

GALLERIE DELL'ACCADEMIA Possibly the only good to have come from Napoleon's repression of churches and schools in Venice is the Gallerie dell'Accademia, a collection founded in 1807 to preserve salvaged canvases for the scrutiny of the Accademia's art students. The collection quickly grew into the single most stunning and extensive gathering of Venetian art. In the 1940s, Carlo Scarpa arranged the 24 rooms to display the collection in roughly chronological order— from 14th-century gold-gilt altarpieces to 18th-century bucolic fantasies. It takes an hour to give the place a once-over, though you'll have to stay three times that to give the paintings their due.

The first stunning room you stumble into is **Room 4**, where several Madonnas by 15th-century artist Gentile Bellini look too elegant to have been painted by a human. **Room 5** has the tiny, enigmatic *Tempest*, by the equally enigmatic Giorgione—nobody can tell what's going on in the canvas, and scholars have decided that several additional figures were covered up soon after they were painted. The grandest is **Room 10**, with some of the greatest works by Veronese and Tintoretto. Veronese's massive *Feast at the House of Levi* was too long to fit on the gallery wall, so Scarpa carved out a few accommodating inches of the building. The painting was originally intended to be of the Last Supper, but outraged church officials threatened to excommunicate Veronese for depicting Christ in the company of African slaves, dwarves, a monkey, and a guy with a bloody nose. The artist responded by simply changing the painting's name. On the adjacent wall is Tintoretto's cycle narrating the abduction of St. Mark's body from Alexandria. Here the painter is at his nightmarish best, perversely depicting what is mythically Venice's greatest moment as something psychedelic and dark. **Room 17** has some portraits by Rosalba Carriera (1675–1757), known as one of the first independent women artists. A cycle of paintings by Vittore Carapaccio tells one of the stranger tales in Catholic lore: A beautiful Breton princess agrees to marry an English prince only after he converts to Christianity and travels with her to Rome with 10,000 virgins in tow, only everybody is slaughtered on the way home. Just goes to show you. *Dorsoduro, tel. 041/522–2247. Admission: L12,000. Open Sun. and Mon. 9–2, Tues.–Sat. 9–7.*

COLLEZIONE PEGGY GUGGENHEIM In 1949 American heiress Peggy Guggenheim (not to be confused with her uncle Solomon in Manhattan) came to Venice to avoid the NYC scene. She died 30 years later, leaving behind her 18th-century, canalside palazzo and 300 or so works that now make up Italy's most important collection of modern art. Beautifully arranged pieces by Pollock, Klee, Picasso, Man Ray, Giacometti, and Kandinsky cover the walls; a few works have personal significance, such as Max Ernst's *The Antipope*, said to be a partial portrait of Peggy (they were once married), and the silver headboard sculpted for her by Alexander

Calder. You may have seen these artists before, but you have never seen this collection, and Peggy had a hell of a nose for art. On top of it all, there's a sculpture garden, a café, the tomb of Peggy's dead dogs (twistedly called "babies"), and a staff of chatty English-speaking students. *Dorsoduro 701, on Fonda-menta Venier dai Leoni, tel. 041/520–6288. From Ponte dell'Accademia, turn left on Rio Terrà Foscarini, take 1st left on unnamed street and cross bridge; continue on Calle Chiesa, which turns into Fondamenta Venier dai Leoni. Admis-sion: L10,000, L5000 students and Rolling Venice holders. Open Wed.–Mon. 11–6.*

The best cappuccino in Venice comes from Bar Da Gino, the sidewalk café on the Accademia–Guggenheim route. The reigning froth-master is a darling man with a fantastic belly, who serves everybody—octagenerians, art students, and tourists—with astonishing grace. A cappuccino costs L1800 at the bar or L2400 at an outside table.

SCUOLA GRANDE DI SAN ROCCO As story goes, back in the mid-16th century the wealthy patrons of the Scuola Grande di San Rocco called on the greatest Venetian painters of their time to submit proposals for a cycle of canvases exalt-ing both San Rocco (a saint popular with the antiplague crowd) and the *scuola* (school) itself. Most artists, including the favored Veronese, duly prepared detailed drawings. But obsessive Jacobo Tintoretto outshone them all by frantically painting an actual canvas, sneaking into the building, and installing his works in the middle of the night—a gutsy move that was entirely against the rules. The fathers of the scuola were impressed enough to offer him the commission over the objections of the other painters. For the next 23 years, Tintoretto kept busy producing over 50 canvases, and the result is stunning. Here you see the full range of Tintoretto's abilities, such as his pulling of figures out of apocalyptic backgrounds composed of a dozen shades of black and highlighting the folds of their clothes with quick brushlines of bright white paint. *San Polo 3052, Campo San Rocco, tel. 041/523–4864. Behind I Frari's apse. Admission: L8000, L6000 with Rolling Venice. Open daily 9–5:30.*

PONTE DI RIALTO Large, clunky, and white, the 16th-century Ponte di Rialto is one of Venice's most recognizable structures. There has been a bridge between San Marco and San Polo at this spot since 1172—in fact this was the only place to cross the Canale Grande up until the last century. The original bridge was a wooden drawbridge, which was replaced by a larger wooden bridge. By 1551 the wood was dangerously rotted, so a competition was held to decide who would design a replacement (the structure you see today); the proposals of Palladio, Sanso-vino, and Michelangelo were rejected (you can hear the architecture historians groan) in favor of the single-arch scheme by a nobody named Da Ponte (which means, of all things, "of the bridge"). To his credit, the bridge was a bit of an engineering feat, since it needed to be high enough for galleys to pass under it, but not so steep as to make crossing on foot difficult—and all this out of stone. Today the Ponte di Rialto is crowded with sunglass stands and gawking tourists; if you're just trying to cross the Canale Grande, be prepared to use force.

DISTRICTS

Besides the major sights, there are a number of lesser-known museums, churches, and palazzi strewn through Venice's sestieri (districts), which you could spend weeks perusing. Many of these attractions are not on the main tourist circuit, which means you can get to know Venice without being forced to get to know those folks visiting from Tokyo or Minneapolis.

CANNAREGIO Unless you decide to head straight from the train onto a vaporetto (actually not a bad choice), the neon signs and fierce tourist traffic of the Cannaregio district will be your introduction to what is really a clean and gracious city. However once you retreat to the side streets away from the Canale Grande, the story changes dramatically. Here you'll find the **Ghetto Ebreo** (Jewish Ghetto; *see below*), still-functioning convents, and the wide, straight canals that are characteristic of Cannaregio.

➤ **CA' D'ORO** • The finest surviving example of Venetian-Gothic palatial architecture, this ornate early-15th-century house earned its name "House of Gold" from the gold gilt that once covered its lacy front. The building was brutally renovated in 1847, and only the nongold part of the facade escaped complete dismemberment. The rooms are filled with minor art, with the exception of a stunning full-size fresco of San Sebastian by Mantegna and a *Venus* by Titian. If you don't feel compelled to see every Titian in town, settle for gazing at the elaborate facade as you chug by on a vaporetto. *Cannaregio 3932, tel. 041/523–8790. From train station, follow San Marco trail; or, take Vaporetto 1 to Ca' d'Oro stop. Admission: L4000. Open daily 9–2.*

➤ **CHIESA DELLA MADONNA DELL'ORTO** • Marble Gothic tracery and statues of the apostles make for a fine facade, but the point of this 15th-century church is the Tintorettos you'll find inside. Not only are there are some striking earlier works, like the *Vision of the Holy Cross to St. Peter*, but the painter himself (or rather his remains) are in the chapel to the right of the choir. *Campo Madonna Dell'Orto. Open Mon.–Sat. 10–noon and 2–5, Sun. 1–5.*

➤ **GHETTO EBREO** • A symbol of oppression, and at times, tolerance, the Jewish Ghetto holds an uneasy place in Venice's history. Jews were first allowed to live in the city in 1381, when the policy-makers in the Palazzo Ducale ignored the objections of priests and welcomed the merchants and their money, which was badly needed to defend the lagoon against an invading navy from Pisa. The opposition never fully ceased however, and in 1516 all Jews were moved into an area called the Ghetto—actually an island separated from the rest of Cannaregio by canals. (The word *ghetto* is Venetian in origin—it comes from the *ghetti*, or metal foundries, that once stood in the area.) The neighborhood was locked at night as much to keep the Jews in as to keep looters out: Before you cross the bridge into the Campo Ghetto Nuovo, look for the holes cut into the paving stones for the old gates. The neighborhood was allowed to expand twice, but with the densest population in the city, there still wasn't room for everyone (notice the nine-story buildings—the tallest apartment blocks in Venice). In 1797 the gates were finally torn down by Napoleon, but the Jews didn't move out—partially because of habit, partially because nobody would sell them property anywhere else—until the fascists deported them to Germany during World War II. A series of bas-relief plaques in the Campo del Ghetto Nuovo is dedicated to the Venetian Jews who died in concentration camps.

The **Museo Communità Ebraico** (admission: L4000, L3000 with Rolling Venice card) houses a small collection of Torah screens and the like; more interesting is the hourly guided tour (L10,000, L8000 with Rolling Venice card) of the five beautiful synagogues still in use. *Cannaregio 2902/B, on Campo del Ghetto Nuovo, tel. 041/715359. On train station–Ponte di Rialto route, cross first bridge, turn left on Fondamenta di Cannaregio, right on Calle del Ghetto Vecchio, and continue over bridge into Campo Ghetto Nuovo. Open Sun.–Fri. 10–7. Closed Jewish holidays.*

➤ **SANTA MARIA DEI MIRACOLI** • This little church is famous throughout the Catholic world for its unspectacular painting of the Madonna, which is supposedly endowed with the power to raise the dead and perform other sundry divine acts. The building itself, a riot of color and detail designed by the father-and-sons Lombardo team in the 15th century, far outshines the painting. The roof of the church is a curious barrel vault; every square centimeter of the exterior is inlaid with pink, green, yellow, and white marble; and the interior is crammed with intricate carvings. *Cannaregio, on Campo dei Miracoli. From Ponte di Rialto, walk towards train station, turn right after 2nd bridge, continue along Salizzada San Canciano, turn right into Campo Santa Maria Nova, and cross bridge to Campo dei Miracoli. Open Mon.–Sat. 10–noon and 2–6.*

During the centuries in which Venice enjoyed the most power—from the 1400s to the 1600s—over 10% of the city's population of 150,000 were prostitutes.

SANTA CROCE This mostly working-class neighborhood was eaten up in the last century by the nasty necessities of modernity: Santa Croce is home to the city's only car park, the railroad service yard, the **Stazione Marittima** (the commercial and cruise-ship port), and a lot of touristy hotels and restaurants. Perhaps things were more interesting here a decade ago, before the police cleaned up Venice's only red-light district. Today the only reason to come here is to visit the neglected stepsister of the Collezione Peggy Guggenheim, **Ca' Pesaro** (Fondamenta Pesaro, tel. 041/721127; admission: L5000), Venice's *other* museum of modern art. It's a fairly dull place except for a few good pieces and the occasional traveling exhibiton.

SAN POLO Separated by the Canale Grande, the districts of San Polo and San Marco have always felt an intense rivalry. In fact, until the Ponte di Rialto was rebuilt, the drawbridge of the old wooden structure was raised at night to prevent easy comings and goings between the two districts. Although the lesser-known San Polo doesn't have the spectacle of its haughty neighbor across the canal, it does have fewer tourists, a handful of palazzi on **Campo San Polo**, and some of the city's greatest works of art in the **Scuola Grande di San Rocco** (*see* Worth Seeing, *above*). The **Mercato di Rialto** (*see* Food, *above*) has been Venice's marketplace since the first hardy Italians forsook the mainland for the lagoon. Before you leave San Polo, stick your head into the 17th-century **Chiesa di San Pantalon** (Campo San Pantalon, across bridge from Campo Santa Margherita). Look up at the ceiling and you'll see the largest canvas painting ever, an over-the-top tromp l'oeil masterpiece that took 24 years to paint. The artist, Fumiani, had just finished the painting when he fell off the scaffoldings to his death.

➤ **I FRARI** • The bulky brick frame of Venice's largest church is balanced by the delicate art inside: The interior walls are covered by countless canvases and panels, including some works by Titian, Bellini, and the Florentine Donatello. This is also where Titian, Cannova, Monteverdi (who composed Orfeo, the world's first opera), and a handful of doges are fully engaged in their big sleeps. The present incarnation of the Santa Maria Gloriosa dei Frari (the church's full name) dates to the early 15th century, when the gargantuan church was erected in a campo so small that it's impossible to get a full view of the church from the outside. *Campo dei Frari, tel. 041/522-2637. From San Polo side of Ponte di Scalzi, walk down Fondamenta San Simeon Piccolo to Chisea di San Simone Piccolo and then follow San Marco trail. Admission: L1000, free Sun. Open Mon.–Sat. 9–noon and 2:30–6, Sun. 3–6.*

DORSODURO Everybody likes to make comparisons, and the Dorsoduro is often called "the Greenwich Village of Venice." True, the Dorsoduro has the bulk of students and student-types, galleries, trinket stores, and bookshops, mostly thanks to the presence of the 15th-century **Ca' Foscari**, the main building of the **Università Venezia** (the NYU of Venice, so to speak). More importantly, Dorsoduro has fewer palazzi and tall buildings than the San Marco side of Rialto (the midtown Manhattan of Venice) and fewer tourists than Piazza San Marco (time to stop the joke). Despite the big-name **Gallerie dell'Accademia** and the **Collezione Peggy Guggenheim** (*see* Worth Seeing, *above*), the streets here tend to be populated more by Venetians than anybody else. You can catch most of the locals in the triangular **Campo Santa Margherita**, which holds outdoor cafés, book stalls, wine shops, restaurants, and two trees. The campo comes into its own at dusk, when everybody comes to drink an *aperitivo* (apertif), get in some shopping before the stores close, and watch little kids practicing the futile (in Venice) art of biking.

➤ **CA' REZZONICO** • The home of Venice's museum of the *setecento* (1700s) is an ornate late 17th-century palazzo, jammed with so many whirling moldings, carved tables, and fluttery sconces that you'd think they didn't know how to draw a straight line back then. Tiepolo, Venice's last great painter, is well represented here, though after viewing his swirly paintings in their equally fluffy context, you may need to head to the Guggenheim for a strong dose of cubism. *Dorsoduro 3136, on Fondamenta Rezzonico, tel. 041/522-4543. From Campo San Barnaba, cross bridge closest to Canale Grande and turn immediately right on Fondamenta Rezzonico. Admission: L8000, L5000 students and Rolling Venice holders. Open Sat.–Thurs. 10–5 (winter 1.–4).*

➤ **GIUDECCA** • Though officially a part of the Dorsoduro, the islands of the Giudecca, with their working-class populations and public housing, feel as if they should be out of sight in the lagoon. The islands were first inhabited by noble families who were dishonored enough to be banished but important enough to stay in Venice. These nobles-in-exile developed a sort of upper-class suburb, complete with villas and gardens, where they entertained the likes of Michelangelo and comissioned two churches by Palladio. The 16th-century **Zitelle** (Fondamenta delle Zitelle; open daily 8–noon and 4–6) has been converted into a contemporary culture factory with enough galleries to mount several exhibitions simultaneously; most shows are fairly interesting and free (look for posters around town). **Il Redentore** (on Fondamenta San Giacomo; open daily 8–noon and 4–7:30), also designed by Palladio, was built in 1577 to hold all the people the government promised to bring before God each year to commemorate the city's redemption from the plague. Little did Palladio know that the event would be the excuse for some seriously secular partying in the **Festa del Redentore** (*see* Festivals, *below*).

➤ **SANTA MARIA DELLA SALUTE** • Despite everybody's preoccupation with the Basilica di San Marco, this church's soaring domes and twirling buttresses will probably make a longer-lasting impression on you. Santa Maria della Salute (St. Mary of Health) was built over the course of the 17th century as a thank-you to the Virgin Mary for saving Venice from yet another plague (although half of the city's population died anyway). The half of Venice still around spared no expense, tirelessly hammering into the lagoon sludge 1,156,627 timber piles for the church's foundation and lavishly decorating the building both inside and out. It was dedicated in 1687, and every November 21 the city lights candles and organizes a boat-bridge to the church (*see* Festivals, *below*). The highlight of any visit is the **sacristy**, home to some of Titian's major works. *Campo della Salute. Take Vaporetto 1 to Campo della Salute; or, from the Dorsoduro side of Ponte dell'Accademia, go around Gallerie dell'Accademia to the left, turn left on Calle Larga Pisani, and follow it past Collezione Peggy Guggenheim all the way to the campo. Suggested donation: L2000. Open daily 9–noon and 3–6:30.*

SAN MARCO The Piazza San Marco (*see* Worth Seeing, *above*) is an unavoidable must-see, but if you have the energy (*see* Gelaterias, *above*), spend some time wandering the more subdued parts of the district.

➤ **PALAZZO FORTUNY** • Mariano Fortuny y Madrazo, painter, photographer, architect, engraver, and filthy rich fabric designer, bought the early 15th-century Palazzo Pesaro in 1889 and turned the place into a school of design, with stores and workshops on the first floor, a chemist studio on the second, silks on all the walls, and artsy people doing artsy things in every nook and cranny. The products produced here demanded an amazing amount of craftwork: Some of the fabrics were sewn with Murano glass beads and some embroidered with gold thread, while unbleached velvets were brushed with rare pigments. The bizarre and luxurious stuff he came up with is all on display, but the palazzo is at its finest when a traveling exhibition—usually photography—passes through. At press time, the museum was closed for restoration. *San Marco 3780, on Campo San Benedetto, tel. 041/520–0995. On Ponte dell' Accademia–Ponte di Rialto route, take first left after Campo San Angelo on Rio Terrà Mandola, which spills into Campo San Benedetto.*

➤ **PALAZZO GRASSI** • The last palazzo ever built on the Canale Grande, Palazzo Grassi was converted into a gallery for traveling shows in 1986 by Gae Aulenti (architect of the Musee d'Orsay in Paris). The massive 18th-century palazzo is now *the* premier space for temporary exhibitions in all of Italy—whatever is inside is not only worth your time but will probably blow you away. *San Marco 3231, on Campo San Samuele, tel. 041/523–1680. Take Vaporetto 3, 4, or 82 to San Samuele; or, from north end of Campo San Stefano, walk west on Calle Lungo Botteghe, which becomes Calle Lungo Crosera, and turn left on Salizzada San Samuele, which leads to Campo San Samuele.*

➤ **SAN GIORGIO MAGGIORE** • The best example of the Palladian "harmony" and "purity" that everyone talks about is the facade of this church on the Isola di San Giorgio (just east of Giudecca). During the 1400s, the highly intellectual architects of Florence had decided on the perfect proportions for the interior of a church, but what looked good on the inside looked like a blocky square set on a squat rectangle on the outside. Palladio succeeded not only in synthesizing the two awkward parts of the exterior but in unifying the facade with the interior. If all that doesn't float your boat, the church has some great Tintorettos, a far-reaching view of the lagoon from the tower, and a quiet old monk who sells jars of honey next to the transept. *Isola di San Giorgio Maggiore, tel. 041/538–9900. From San Zaccaria, take Vaporetto 82 to San Giorgio. Open daily 9–1 and 2–6.*

➤ **TEATRO LA FENICE** • Tucked away to the side of the small Campo San Fantin, La Fenice—one of the world's great opera houses—is surprisingly easy to walk right by without noticing it. The present snowy white and gilt-gold incarnation of La Fenice dates to 1837, when it rose out of the ashes of the first opera house built on Campo San Fantin. Along with La Scala in Milano, La Fenice was the fulcrum of 19th-century Italian opera, premiering some of Verdi's works (Rossini, Bellini, and Donizetti had all composed operas for the first Fenice).

But as Venice declined with the rise of the Italian state, the importance of La Fenice diminished, and it now produces responsible and uninspired operas to local devotees. Even if you don't see a performance (*see* After Dark, *below*), the steps of the opera house are a fine place to hang out and enjoy the campo.

CASTELLO The Castello has two distinct faces—one of which expresses the glamourous artistic and political traditions of Venice, while the other is calm and almost without history. The first part of Castello, comprising the streets and canals extending eastward out of San Marco, is home to stunning churches like the 15th-century **San Zaccaria** (just off the Riva degli Schiavoni, not far from the San Marco border), grand palazzi, and the overpriced pizza joints and ashtray stands that cater to tourists. By the time you've wandered out by the **Aresenale** (*see below*) however, anybody who isn't Venetian is either lost or a serious explorer. On **Via Garibaldi** you can find fruit stalls, low-budget trattorias, and old men and women who do nothing but smoke, chat, shop, and drink wine all day.

The best pane d'olive (bread with olives) in all of Italy is at Rizzo Pane on Via Garibaldi (at the end of the street on the left, before it turns into a canal). Warm, moist, and packed with more olives than a Greek isle, a loaf costs L6000; or you can get it by the piece.

➤ **ARSENALE** • In the 12th century, the Venetian state constructed a walled port and a drydock in order to build the navy's war galleys. Called the Arsenale, it became the most important ship factory in Europe: Dante raved about it in Canto XXI of *L'Inferno*, and one of Columbus's ships was built here. The Arsenale hit its peak in the 14th and 15th centuries, when it was producing at least one ship per day, and the Venetian navy was the world's most powerful. Because it's still a base for the Italian navy, most of the Arsenale is closed to the public, but the facade is still worth checking out for the best lion sculptures in Venice (and that's saying something). *Take Vaporetto 1 to Arsenale; or, from Piazza San Marco, turn left on Riva degli Schiavoni, cross 5 bridges, and turn left on Fondamenta dell'Arsenale.*

➤ **MUSEO STORICO NAVALE** • Venice is a watery place, so the history of the navy and the city coincide quite a bit. Come here to see model warships and re-creations of the Republic's major naval battles, not to mention the gondola of Peggy Guggenheim (she was the last person in Venice to have a private gondolier). *Castello 2148, on Riva degli Schiavoni, tel. 041/520–0276. Take Vaporetto 1 to Arsenale; or, from Piazza San Marco, walk east on Riva degli Schiavoni. Admission: L2000. Open Mon.–Sat. 9–1.*

➤ **SAN GIOVANNI E PAOLO** • This enormous, dusty, Gothic creation is not just a church, but a warehouse of death. Its collection of corpses and sundry body parts includes the foot of Santa Caterina of Siena; the skin of Marcantonio Bragdin, a war hero flayed alive by the Turks in 1571 (the urn is in the right aisle just after the entrance); and the remains of no less than 25 doges. Like its fraternal twin I Frari across the Canale Grande, this church has a mess of both schlock and masterpieces strewn across its walls—some of the more interesting pieces are Giovanni Bellini's elegant *Polyptych of San Vicenzo* and a New Testament cycle by Veronese. *Campo San Giovanni e Paolo. From train station–Ponte di Rialto route, walk to Chiesa di Santi Apostoli and follow the blue "Ospedale" signs. Open daily 9–12:30 and 2:30–7.*

➤ **SCUOLA DI SAN GIORGIO DEGLI SCHIAVONI** • In 1451 the Senate granted the Venetian *Schiavoni* (Slavs) the right to build their own *scuola* (a kind of guild). At the time, Venice, Hungary, and the Ottomans were all coveting the Dalmatian coast (yes, as in the dog), the eastern part of the Adriatic in former Yugoslavia. By bringing the Slavs into the fold, Venice hoped to gain their voluntary subjugation; they responded favorably, commissioning Carapaccio to paint a cycle of paintings about St. George and the Dragon and St. Jerome and the Lion. The building hasn't been touched since the 1600s, and the dark, hushed downstairs room helps you imagine what the meetings of the scuola must have been like. *Castello, on Ponte dei Greci, tel. 041/522–8828. From Piazza San Marco, walk east on Fondamenta degli Schiavoni, cross 4 bridges, take first left, cross Campo Bandiera e Moro to Salizzada San Antonin, veer left, and continue straight ahead. Admission: L5000, L3000 students and Rolling Venice holders. Open Tues.–Sat. 10–12:30 and 3–6, Sun. 10–12:30.*

CHEAP THRILLS

When little man Bonaparte took possession of Venice, he decided that what the city really needed was a proper, bourgeois, psuedo-Parisian park. He ordered some buildings destroyed (the fact that they were the very monestaries, churches, and scuole that most resisted his rule didn't hurt), and in 1810 Venice sprouted the **Giardini Pubblici**, a good place to rediscover what a tree looks like after too many days spent wandering through the glories of the Renaissance. Every other year, the Giardini host the **Biennale** (*see* Festivals, *below*). To get here, take Vaporetto 1, 52, or 82 to the Giardini stop, or from Piazza San Marco, turn left on Riva degli Schiavoni and keep on walking.

If you're feeling a little broke but very suave, skip the clunky vaporetti and cruise over to the Giudecca on the private launch with the HOTEL CIPRIANI sign next to the Giardini Ex Reali on the fondamenta behind Piazza San Marco. Just be somewhat well dressed and coiffed, a little arrogant, and act like you do this all the time. Along the same lines, you can catch a glimpse of Venice's former grandeur by popping into the 14th-century Palazzo Dandolo, now the four-star Hotel Danieli (Fondamenta degli Schiavoni, 1 bridge east of Piazza San Marco). Take a gander at the elegant Gothic staircase and its marble paneling, then leave quietly.

FESTIVALS

Every other summer for the last 100 years, everybody in the art world has been coming to the **Biennale di Venezia**, a huge schmooze fest where some 30 nations display the works of fairly avant-garde artists, each in their own little pavilions in the back of the Giardini Pubblici (the American one looks like Jefferson's Montecello on a bad hair day). While artsy insiders lament the dearth of creativity, the unique pavilions and their bucolic setting make it worth the vaporetto ride and the L16,000 ticket (L12,000 with Rolling Venice card). The next Biennale is scheduled for 1997, though there is talk of an architecture Biennale in 1996. Call one of the tourist offices for details, or check the posters in town from around May to October.

FEBRUARY/MARCH **Carnevale** in Venice is a week-long costume party featuring drunken revelers in outfits that have been planned for months. Parades and performances incorporating the traditional Venetian versions of *Commedia dell'Arte* masks and costumes are held more or less daily. Though the costumes are traditional, the modern Carnevale has only been celebrated for about 15 years. The more cynical see it as a ploy to lure tourists here in the off-season, but the locals seem to enjoy themselves anyway. The date varies, but it's always at the end of February or beginning of March, right before the start of Lent.

MAY Also a recently cultivated event, the **volgalonga** is a 32-kilometer rowing marathon open to anyone with a boat. Participants—some in wildly decorated craft, some in sleek, high-tech machines, and others in tubs that barely float—row their way from San Marco to Burano and back. The event usually falls on Ascension Sunday in May or June, when the mayor performs the ritual of La Sensa. Formerly a solemn, symbolic procession during which the doge would toss a ring into the water to celebrate Venice's "marriage" to the sea, it's now a tourist mess that's better avoided.

JULY On the third Sunday in July, Venice holds the **Festa del Redentore**, an offer of thanks to Jesus for ending a plague back in the 1500s. A makeshift pontoon bridge is built from Venice to the church of Il Redentore on Giudecca island (*see* Districts, in Worth Seeing, *above*). The real fun comes at night, when an unbelievable fireworks display explodes over the tens of thousands of Venetians clamoring drunkenly from streamer-covered cargo launches and trash barges turned into floating dinner parties; it starts at about 11:15 PM and lasts until midnight. If you can't finagle a spot on a local's boat, the best place to watch is from the fondamento on the Giudecca.

AUGUST/SEPTEMBER In late August and September, Venice's **International Film Festival** is held at the Lido. The best of foreign and Italian films are shown at the **Palazzo del Cinema** (tel. 041/526–0188) and the **Asta** (Via Cortù, tel. 041/526–0289). Admission is the same as for a normal movie (around L10,000), unless it's the opening-night gala (about L25,000); expect long lines. On the first Sunday in September, Venice holds the **Regatta Storica**—half boat race, half waterborne parade—with a procession of historically evocative boats containing people dressed as the doge and his entourage. The race is only for experts—usually burly gondoliers—so it's a lot more exciting to watch than the "everyone wins" Volgalonga. In the middle of September, the Communist party holds a big fete, the **Festa dell'Unità**. For around two weeks, Campo Santa Margherita is packed every night with live music, cheap food, and dancing. Occasionally the festival happens in another large campo, but ask anyone under 30 and they'll know where it is.

NOVEMBER Yet another plague festival, the **Salute** on November 21 is a more somber event than the Redentore (i.e., no party). The pious light candles and pray, and a string of boats cross the Canale Grande from San Marco to the church of Santa Maria della Salute (*see* Districts, in Worth Seeing, *above*).

SHOPPING

The likelihood of having any money left over after paying to sleep, eat, and be culturally enriched is very slim, but good deals can be ferreted out. The most blatantly commercial area is the **Mercerie**, which starts just behind the Torre dell'Orologio in Piazza San Marco; stores here sell mostly clothing and expensive crafts. On **Strada Nuova**, in Cannaregio, the shops are cheaper. Venice is famous for its glass and masks, both of which range from cheap schlock to astoundingly expensive art. Almost anyone who sells these things will ship them home for you or package them so that you can get them home in your backpack with a little care.

SPECIALTY STORES Artisiano Vetraio. Of the kabillion glass stores on Murano, this is the coolest. Stuff ranges from unusual L10,000 rings to beautiful L100,000 jars. *Fondamenta Manin 56, Murano, tel. 041/739454.*

Casa Mattiazzi Vini e Spumanti. Three of these shops scattered around the city sell good, cheap wines by the liter. Just walk in with an empty water bottle, wine bottle, or laundry tub, and they'll fill you up with red, white, or sparkling wines from various vats. A liter of merlot costs L2100, and cabernet sauvignon runs L2200—an amazing bargain. There's a shop in Campo Santa Margherita (tel. 041/523–1979), one on Via Garibaldi in the Castello hinterlands (tel. 041/522–4893), and one near Campo Santa Maria Formosa (Castello 5179, on Calle Lunga, tel. 041/523–7592); from Campo Santa Maria Formosa, walk down Calle Lunga until just before the first bridge. *All open Mon.–Sat. 9–1 and 5–8; closed Wed. afternoons.*

Mondo Novo Maschere. Masks can cost up to several hundred thousand lire, but you might want to spend next year's lunch money on these amazing pieces; they really blur the line between art and craft. Even if you can't buy anything, you're welcome to come in and browse. *Dorsoduro 3063, tel. 041/528344. On Rio Terrà Canal, across bridge from Campo San Barnabà.*

AFTER DARK

When the sun sets over the canals and the tourists return to their hotel rooms, Venice gets *very* quiet. If you want to go clubbing in summer, you have to go to Mestre or the Lido, but if you're looking to get quietly tipsy while listening to music, you won't be too disappointed. The free APT guide *Un Ospite di Venezia* comes out every two weeks and lists upcoming (usually classical) concerts.

The most happening *passeggiata* (evening social stroll) locations are Campo San Polo, the Żattere, and Campo Santa Margherita. Esterno Notte puts on **outdoor films** at night in the summer in Campo Sant'Angelo. Call the Comune di Venezia (tel. 041/270–7650) or Esterno Notte (tel. 041/524–1320) for info. Films are mostly Italian-dubbed Hollywood blockbusters that cost around L9000, but watching them from the campo you'll be reminded more of *Cinema Paradiso*.

BARS The Venetian version of a pub crawl is called a *giro di ombra*. An *ombra* is a tiny glass of wine, drunk in a gulp, and you're not supposed to drink more than one in any one place (ombre cost L1000–L2000, depending on the type of wine). The name comes from the traditional way that wine was sold—big vats of the stuff were sold outdoors in the *ombra* (shade) of buildings. *See box* Cocktails, Venetian Style, *below* for an explanation of other traditional Venetian drinks and the bars where you can sample them.

Most bars in Venice close between 10 PM and midnight, though the ones listed below stay open a little later. Bars cluster along Fondamenta della Misericordia in Cannaregio and Campo Santa Margherita in Dorsoduro. **Da Codroma** (Dorsoduro 2540, on Fondamenta del Corso, tel. 041/520–4161; closed Thurs.) has board games and a mellow atmosphere (it's also open during the day), and **The Fiddler's Elbow** (Cannaregio 3847, on Corte dei Pali Gia Testori off Strada Nuova, tel. 041/523–9930; closed Wed.) is an "Irish pub" with Guinness on tap (L3500 a half pint, L6000 a pint). Both are swarming with backpackers and neither one is anything special, but they're always around if you need them.

Ai Canottieri. This bar tolerates much less artsy bullshit than Paradiso (*see below*): It plays rock instead of jazz, serves more basic food, and has posters of "I Fratelli Blues" (The Blues Brothers) on the wall. A liter of wine is L9000, and beer is L3500–L10,500. Prices rise on Thursday and Saturday, when they host live music. *Cannaregio 690, on Fondamenta di San Giobbe, tel. 041/715408. From the train station, take San Marco route that starts to the left, turn right on Fondamenta Venier just before Ponte delle Guglie; Venier turns into Fondamenta di San Giobbe. Open Mon.–Sat. 6:30 PM–2 AM.*

Paradiso Perduto. The most popular bar on the Misericordia is home base for traveling hipsters, though things are much more low-key in winter. The package includes occasional live jazz (call for the next performance), a funky clientele, and gruff, pony-tailed bartenders who are almost too cool for their own good. The food here is excellent and not too expensive: Antipasti are L7000–L35,000, primi are about L10,000, and bread and *coperto* (cover) is L2000. Drinks run L2000–L7000, but the price goes up when the band plays. *Cannaregio 2540, on Fondamenta della Misericordia, tel. 041/720581. From Ghetto, cross Rio di San Girolamo and turn right. Open Thurs.–Tues. 6:30 PM–1:30 AM or longer; kitchen open until 10:30 PM.*

MUSIC Venice has little to offer in the way of rock music; check the ubiquitous posters for concerts that are staged on the Lido and in Mestre. For jazz, you'll have to call Paradiso Per-

---

Cocktails, Venetian Style

The drinks in Venice can be found virtually no where else in the world, not even as close as Verona or Florence. Your standard drink is prosecco, a dry sparkling wine produced in the vineyards to the north. The late afternoon drink is fragolino, a sweet nectar-like wine made from strawberry grapes. But the true Venetian drink is the spritz (white wine and seltzer water), which you can order "bitter" (with a splash of Campari) or "all' Aperol" (with a splash of orange bitters). Don't forget the after-dinner drink, the sgropino, a frothy mix of lemon sorbet and vodka whipped up in a blender and served in a wine glass (sgropini are available at restaurants or at Haig's Bar on Campo Santa Maria del Giglio).

At Bar La Fenice (Campo San Fantin), you can get a glass of prosecco (L2000) and walk it over to the steps of Teatro La Fenice. They stay open Monday–Saturday until 2 AM, and it's the only legal place in Venice to buy cigarettes after 8 PM. Venice's greatest wine bar is À Schiavi (Dorsoduro 992, just off the Zattere); order a fragolino (L2500) and take it out to the wall by the water. From its tiny fire engine-red facade on the west side of Campo Santa Margherita, Bar Rosso serves the best spritz all'Aperol (L2000) ever. It's also probably Venice's coolest bar.

duto (*see above*) to see when the next weekly performance is. You're supposed to be a members to get into the jazz club **'Round Midnight** (Dorsoduro 3102, on Fondamenta dello Squero, tel. 041/522–2376), but you might be able to get in anyway. The real music scene in Venice is **classical**. Many churches, especially I Frari (*see* Districts, *above*) hold classical concerts, though the choice of music tends toward the solemn; and **Santa Maria della Pietà** (called "Chiesa Vivaldi") on Riva degli Schiavoni holds frequent concerts with music by Vivaldi and others. **Teatro La Fenice** (San Marco 1965, down Salizzada San Moisè/Via 22 Marzo behind Piazza San Marco, tel. 041/521–0161) is famous for its opera and concerts, but tickets start at L25,000. The Rolling Venice card saves you a whopping 50% on symphony concerts. If you want to see opera, you have to pay full price, but the beautiful baroque theater is so small that you get a good view even in the nosebleed seats (*see* Worth Seeing, *above*, for a full description of La Fenice). **Teatro Goldoni** (San Marco 4650/B, tel. 041/520–5422) hosts a range of concerts and dance, and puts on several Italian plays. Check the posters or *Un Ospite di Venezia* for upcoming events.

Near Venice

The tourist office tries to sell the islands of Venice's lagoon as just another shopping venue, but in reality they're uncrowded, cool little places to explore—just a short, relaxing boat ride from Venice. The Lido is its own multi-island entity, but Murano, Burano, and Torcello together make an excellent day trip. Vaporetto 12 stops in Murano and Burano; Vaporetto 14 goes to Punta Sabbioni and Treporti on the Lido, Burano, and Torcello; and Vaporetti 23 and 52 go between San Zaccaria and Murano, sometimes stopping at the Lido and San Michele. Most tickets to the lagoon are the standard price (L4000 one-way, L7200 round-trip).

MURANO This island, most famous for its glassworks, really has little else to offer: Glass factories just aren't all that scenic. From the vaporetto stop, walk over the bridge to the Fondamenta Venier to get the best deals on glass goods. At the **Museo Vetrario Antica di Murano** (Fondamenta Giustinian 8, tel. 041/739586; open Thurs.–Tues. 10 AM–5 PM), pay L8000 to see a nifty exhibit of glass through the ages. The church of **Santi Maria e Donato** (behind the Fondamenta Venier, tel. 041/739056; open daily 8–noon and 4–7) has an old, prime example of a mosaic floor. The intricate floor was assembled in the 12th century, when the Byzantine church was rebuilt after a fire. If your stomach calls, Murano's working-class population means that there are a lot of easy-to-find, cheap, authentic restaurants here.

BURANO "The lace island" probably isn't a compelling enough description of Burano to make you want to visit, but this old fishing community is extremely pretty and tranquil. The island's ridiculously colorful houses look like they were conjured up in somebody's dream (you'll see a bright pink house next to a red one with yellow shutters), and the delicate cookies baked here make Burano everyone's favorite lagoon island. The tradition of lace-making has been revived for the tourists, so you'll see a lot of stout old women making lace by hand in chairs in front of their houses. The **Scuola di Merletti di Burano** (Piazza Galuppi, tel. 041/730034; open Tues.–Sat. 9–6, Sun. 10–4) has lace dating back to the 16th century. Admission is L3000 (L1500 with an ISIC or Rolling Venice card), and you can see workers making lace 9–1 and 2:30–6. Burano's main street leads to a grassy, tree-shaded area facing the sea. Bring a picnic lunch to avoid having to buy food in the overpriced restaurants and *alimentari* (small grocery stores). If you do decide to spring for a meal here, the restaurants along Fondamenta Galuppi have consistently good seafood for L15,000–L20,000.

TORCELLO You'd never know it from seeing it now, but this deserted, swampy island was once the most populated in the lagoon—about 200,000 people lived here in its heyday, though only a handful remain. One of the only remnants of Torcello's heyday is the **Cattedrale di Torcello**, a.k.a. Santa Maria Assunta (follow the route from the vaporetto stop, tel. 041/730084; admission: L1500). Built in the 7th century and rebuilt in the 9th, the church has astonishing 11th- and 12th-century mosaics that are simpler than those in San Marco. Especially beautiful is the 12th-century *Madonna col Bambino* on the apse. The hulking **Chair of Attila** in the square belonged to the notorious Hun. If you have time, walk down to the swampy parts of the island (off the main walkway) and look for pottery shards dating from who knows when, or get

According to legend, Lucifer himself can be seen at the banisterless Devil's Bridge on Torcello. The bridge received its name when people fell off of it, later claiming, "the devil made me do it!"

prepackaged shards from the archaeological museum, **Museo dell'Estuario** (in the Palazzo dell'Consiglio, tel. 041/730761; open Tues.–Sun. 10:30–12:30 and 2–6), which costs L3000 (L1500 students) to enter.

SAN MICHELE Even when you're dead, it's tough to find a place to stay in Venice; San Michele, the cemetery island for Venice since the Napoleonic era, is packed with bureau-drawer crypts, with bodies stacked five high in some places. Even so, the price of resting your body here is so high that most Venetian families buy leases for their deceased, whose bones are moved to an ossuary years later. Igor Stravinsky and Ezra Pound get to stay, though. The cemetary is overgrown and decrepit, and the spookiest part is the old caretaker who lives here amongst all the tombstones. If you come during a funeral procession, be respectful as you watch the ferries travel to the land of the dead. The first Renaissance church in Venice, **San Michele in Isola**, and its baptistry stand alone here. The cemetery is open 8:15 AM–4 PM.

THE LIDO The tragic elegance of the Lido (Litorale di Lido) in Thomas Mann's *Death in Venice* is now the tragic scuzziness of too much pollution and not enough sand. Nevertheless, many Venetians still come here in summer to escape all the tourists. If looking at water all day has also made you desperate for a swim, the free public beach (down Viale Santa Maria Elizabetta from the vaporetto stop) is less toxic than the canals. You can rent bikes at **Lazzari Bruno** (Gran Viale Santa Maria Elisabetta 21/B, tel. 041/526–8019) Tuesday–Sunday 8–8 for about L3000 an hour. Near San Nicolò, on Via Cipro (go left from the vaporetto stop and right on Via Cipro) is the **Cimitero Ebraico** (Jewish cemetery), a quiet, green place on the grounds of the church of San Nicolò. The gravestones tell the history of the Venetian Jewish community since the cemetery's founding in 1386. To the northeast of the Litorale di Lido, the island **Litorale di Cavallino** is full of cheap hotels that might have space in the summer (ask at the APT office in the train station), but the resorty **Lido di Jesolo** island, to the east of Cavallino, has much better public beaches. To reach the main Lido island, take **ACVO** buses (L5500) from Piazzale Roma (they get ferried to the Lido), or take Vaporetto 14 to Punta Sabbioni on Litorale del Cavallino and catch the bus from there.

The Veneto

Venice has influenced every town in the region, but each of the comfortable, relatively conventional cities of the Veneto has an appeal of its own. Verona has an excess of charisma and architecture dating back to the Romans; the university city of Padova has a Giotto masterpiece (the Cappella degli Scrovegni), as well as a schizophrenic mix of Veneto snobbery and university worldliness; slick Vicenza had Andrea Palladio in charge of its 16th-century urban renewal; and Treviso is the home of great food and frescoes. The northern part of the Veneto, from Bassano del Grappa on, sees fewer travelers on its hilly terrain and also puts on fewer airs. This is the place to go for outstanding hiking and skiing. Although the Veneto Dolomites may sound equally appealing, *don't* be tempted to visit—the snazzy resort of Cortina d'Ampezzo has a monopoly on hotels in the area, and the place is full of wealthy Veneti on vacation.

Padova

Most people use Padova (Padua) as a place to stay while visiting Venice—they see Giotto's beautiful Cappella degli Scrovegni and then skedaddle. If you come in August, when it's hotter than hell and twice as humid, this course of action might be justified. Otherwise, take some time and stay in Padova for a while. A city of both high-rises and history, it's definitely not beautiful, but it's cheaper, more convenient, and a little more mellow than its counterparts in the Veneto.

The main reason for the city's laid-back attitude is its university, the second oldest in Italy. Built in the 13th century, it was frequented by brainy types like Dante and Galileo. Most of the students commute to school, so you won't see them July–September or on weekends, but they leave

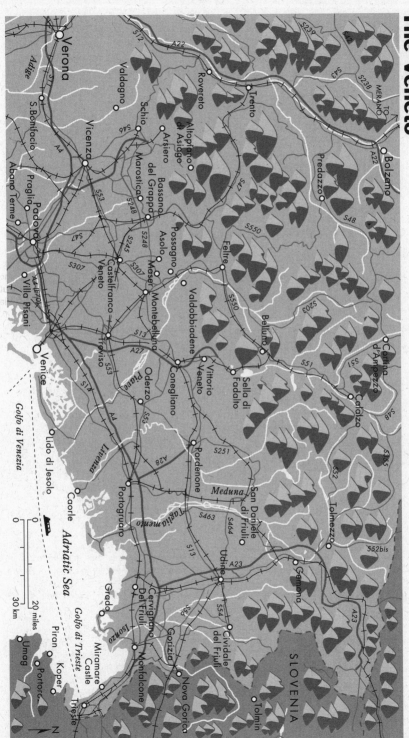

Verona

Adige

S12

A22

TO MERANO

S239

S42

S43

S238

S238

A22

Bolzano

Valdagno

Rovereto

Allopiano di Asiago

Arsiero

Schio

Trento

Predazzo

S48

Vicenza

Maróstica

Bassano del Grappa

Asolo

Possagno

S46

S45

S47

S247

S550

S48

S. Bonifacio

A4

Padova

Praglia

Abano Terme

S53

Castelfranco Veneto

S248

Maser

Montebelluna

Feltre

S550

S203

S51

Cadore d'Ampezzo

S51

A4 - A70X

Villa Pisani

S47

S307

S13

Treviso

Oderzo

Valdobbiadene

Vittorio Veneto

Belluno

Sella di Fadalto

Catalzo

S48

Venice

A13

Piave

Conegliano

S51

S52

S365

Golfo di Venezia

Lido di Jesolo

Livenza

A4

S53

Portogruaro

Pordenone

S251

San Daniele di Friuli

Meduna

S203

Tolmezzo

S52bis

Caorle

A28

S463

S464

S52

Adriatic Sea

Tagliamento

S13

Udine

A23

Gemona

A23

0

20 miles

30 km

N

Grado

Cervignano Del Friuli

Cividale del Friuli

Golfo di Trieste

Miramare Castle

Piran

Koper

Portoro.

Umag

Isonzo

Gorizia

Monfalcone

Nova Gorica

Trieste

Tolmin

SLOVENIA

Golfo di Venezia

Look carefully at the astrological signs on the clock in Piazza di Signori. When the clock was almost finished, the lord who commissioned it paid the builder less than the agreed-upon price. The builder finished his work without saying a word, but a monster Scorpio hogs up two spaces, and the sign that should be next to it, Libra, is missing. Guess what sign the lord was.

their legacy behind in cheap restaurants, bizarre theme bars, and English-language bookstores. Because of its university, Padova was a target for bombs during World War II; for the next 20-odd years, the government gave developers free rein to smash churches and replace them with ugly-but-functional buildings. Still, the heart of the city remains dominated by arcaded walkways and Gothic buildings. Here you'll find the snooty shopping-bag-and-scooter set—the sons and daughters of Padova's nouveaux-riches. They don't do much to make sweaty travelers feel welcome, but you will find more hospitality in the city's cheap hotels.

BASICS The ATP office in the train station stocks the most comprehensive source of info, the free "Padova Today." It's a toned-down version of the booklet they want money for. *Tel. 049/875–2077. Open Mon.–Sat. 9–5, Sun. 9–noon.*

➤ **CHANGING MONEY** • The best place to change your money is **Banca Antoniana** (tel. 049/839111), where you get the highest rates anywhere without paying a commission. The most central branch is on Piazza Frutte 39, next to the Palazzo della Ragione (open weekdays 8:20–1:20 and 2:35–3:35). The **American Express** representative is at Tiarè Viaggi (Via Risorgimento 20, tel. 049/666133; open weekdays 9–1 and 3–7). They won't change money, but if you're a cardholder and need an advance of up to $1,000 on a personal check, write it here, and they'll give you a slip to take to the bank for cash.

COMING AND GOING The large **train station** (Piazzale Stazione Ferrovia, tel. 049/875–1800) has trains to Venice (every 15–30 min, 30 min, L3400), Milan (hourly, 3 hrs, L18,200), Rome (9 daily, 5 hrs, L37,600), Florence (every 2 hrs, 3 hrs, L16,000), Bologna (every 1½ hrs, 2¾ hrs, L9800), and Bassano del Grappa (8 daily, 1 hr, L4200).

The **SITA** station (Via Trieste 42, tel. 049/820–6811) has buses to Bassano del Grappa (every 30 min, L5700), Montagnana (hourly, L4400), and Venice (Mestre station; every 30 min, L5700). Buses also go to Treviso every half hour. To get here from the train station, walk up Corso del Popolo and turn left on Via Trieste.

GETTING AROUND Tiny one-way streets, piazza after piazza, and all those arcaded walkways that look eerily alike—welcome to Padova. The wall-encircled city center can be covered on foot in about an hour. There's only one main street through the center, but it changes names frequently, starting at the train station as **Corso del Popolo**, becoming Corso Garibaldi, Via Cavour, Via VIII Febbraio, Via Roma, and finally, Via Umberto I. Via Umberto I runs to the gigantic ugly oval at the south end of the center, Prato della Valle (which you should avoid at night). The three main piazze (Erbe, Frutte, and Signori) are west of this main street. The best map of Padova is free at the bar **Lucifer Young** (*see* After Dark, *below*).

Though it's walkable, the 20-minute tromp from the train station into town is dull and a little taxing—save yourself and take the bus. The main **ACAP** bus station (Via Risomondo 28) is a little outside the city walls past the *fiera* (fairgrounds), but most buses stop at the train station. They don't offer information by phone, so you have to visit their office. To reach the center of town or Prato della Valle from the bus station, take Bus 3, 8, or 18 (L1300); you can buy tickets from the *biglietteria* (ticket office) in front of the station.

WHERE TO SLEEP The hostel is definitely the best deal in Padova. Hotels fill up fast in July in August as people looking for hotels in Venice become quickly disillusioned. The day of Saint Anthony, June 13, also sees a lot of traffic. If the following are full, the ATP office in the station (*see* Basics, *above*) has a list of hotels and prices. "Holiday houses" (rooming houses) pop up July–September; try **Antonianum** (Via Donatello 24, tel. 049/651444), which has doubles with bath for L20,000 per person. Most cheap hotels lie southeast of the university.

Al Santo. Walk down the street from the basilica to get a tiny but meticulously scrubbed room (the manager is in the bar next door). Ask for one away from the piazza to avoid vehicle/miracle noise. Doubles with bath are L70,000. *Via del Santo 147, ½ block north of basilica, tel. 049/875–2131. 16 rooms, 15 with bath.*

Turismo. It doesn't make any claims to greatness, but it's clean and the rooms are bigger than usual for the price. Doubles with bath are L60,000, but some of the rooms "without bath" include a shower. Deal with sharing the WC for L45,000. The manager doesn't accept phone reservations. *Via Santa Chiara 49, tel. 049/651276. From basilica, walk north on Via del Santo, turn left on Via Rudena, and right on Via Santa Chiara. 14 rooms, 5 with bath.*

➤ **HOSTELS** • **Ostello Città di Padova.** So it's not the most scenic of Italian hostels, but the price, convenience, cleanliness, and extremely altruistic staff more than make up for the less than stunning architecture. The price of L18,000 (reduced if you make a reservation for three or more nights) includes a better-than-average breakfast. The friendly staff has tons of info on things to do in Padova and Venice. *Via Aleardi 30, tel. 049/875–2219. From Piazza Signori, walk south down Piazza Duomo/Via Barbarigo, turn left on Via Camposampiero, and left on Via Aleardi. 122 beds. Curfew 11 PM, lockout 9:30 AM–5 PM. Check-in 5 PM–11 PM. Bar, luggage storage.*

FOOD Unlike in the rest of the Veneto, your food budget goes pretty far in Padova. Student mensas are easily the best bargain, but most close from mid-June to mid-September. Another money stretcher is the daily morning market in twin piazze Erbe (which means vegetables) and Frutte (which means fruit); both are sold in each piazza.

Brek. This link in a chain of self-serve restaurants is not a hidden local treasure, but it does have very cheap, very filling food. Primi are L3500–L4300, secondi L5300–L6500. *Via Piazzetta Cavour 9, tel. 049/875–3788. From station, walk down Corso del Popolo until it becomes Corso Cavour; turn left onto Via Piazzetta Cavour. Open noon–3 and 6:30–10:30.*

Mensa Universitaria. This is the main mensa and the only one open year-round. Good, filling meals, which include primi and secondi, go for around L5000. The menu changes daily, and it's a good place to meet Italian students. *Via San Francesco 122, tel. 049/660903. From Palazzo Bò, walk east on Via San Francesco. Open Mon.–Sat. 11:45–2 and 6:45–9.*

Trattoria Al Pero. Serving typical Veneto food at atypically low prices, this trattoria is usually full of old, emphysemic-looking local men. Some of the food may be a little *too* authentic (*trippa* means tripe), but the adventurous or the omnivorous will have a field day. You can't go wrong with pasta *al pomodoro* (with tomato sauce; L4500) or the polenta. *Via Santa Lucia 72, tel. 049/875–8794. 1 block north of Piazza dei Signori. Open Mon.–Sat. noon–3 and 7:30–10. Closed Aug.*

WORTH SEEING The APT Office (*see Basics, above*) sells an all-inclusive ticket to Padova's sights; it costs L15,000, is valid for a year, and will get you into the Capella degli Scrovegni, the baptistry, the botanical gardens, the Chiesa degli Eremitani, Museo Greco, and the Palazzo della Ragione. If you don't have time for all those places, save your money and just go to the sights reviewed below.

➤ **BASILICA DEL SANTO** • People come from all over the world to request help or give thanks to St. Anthony (Sant'Antonio, the patron saint of lost and found objects) in this enormous, grab-bag Gothic/Byzantine/Renaissance basilica. The most absorbing aspect isn't the artwork by Donatello (which includes the statues on the main altar and the equestrian monument to *Gattamelata* outside) or the morbid remains of the saint's tongue and jaw in the apse. It's the devotion and personal connection people have to "Il Santo," apparent in the display of votive offerings, which range from locks of hair to firearms. *Piazza del Santo, tel. 049/663944. Admission free. Open daily 6:30 AM–7:45 PM (until 7 PM in winter).*

➤ **CAFFE PEDROCCHI** • The most elaborate place in Padova to sip a L1200 coffee, Pedrocchi used to be more than just a four-star java joint. During the Risorgimento it was a haven for students and intellectuals. On February 8, 1848, it was the seat of a nationalist insurrection—hence the red, white, and green rooms, and the commemorative street name outside its door, none of which have changed a drop in the last 15 decades. *Piazzetta Pedrocchi. From station, walk down Corso del Popolo until it becomes Via VIII Febbraio; it's on the right. Open daily 7 AM–11 PM.*

➤ **CAPELLA DEGLI SCROVEGNI** • This tiny chapel harbors one of the greatest masterpieces in the history of art: Giotto's fresco cycle depicting the New Testament, which is regarded as marking the end of medieval art and the beginning of the Renaissance. A brilliant, groundbreaking artist, Giotto was one of the first painters to conceive of depth existing in pictures—his heady jobs at perspective may seem clumsy today, but this was sexy stuff in the 14th century. Giotto set expressive characters in dynamic compositions, drawing out the drama of the story of the lives of Christ and the Virgin Mary. The patron, Scrovegni, commissioned the chapel to atone for sins of his father, a usurer; you can see a portrait of Scrovegni giving the chapel to Padova on the front wall. The ticket also admits you into the other museums in the Eremitani complex, including the **Museo del Arte Medievale e Moderna** (closed Mon.), which should probably be called "Mediocre e Moderna." The nearby **Chiesa degli Eremitani** (Church of the Hermits) used to have spectacular Mantegna frescoes, but they were destroyed by bombing in World War II. *Piazza Eremitani, tel. 049/875–0975. From station, walk down Corso del Popolo, and turn left on Piazza Eremitani. Admission: L10,000, L7000 students. Open daily 9–7 (until 6 in winter).*

In the Capella degli Scrovegni, look for the fresco depicting the kiss of Judas. The torches and weapons in the air create a feeling for the anger and excitement of the crowd, while in the center, the quiet figures of Christ and Judas seem to calmly accept their fate.

➤ **PALAZZO BO** • This palazzo, which used to be part of an ox market, is now the university's main building. *Bò* means ox in the local dialect, and the critters were chained by their nose rings to the iron loops where students now lock their bikes. The steep marble balconies encircling the *teatro anatomico* (anatomy theater) are incredible, and most of the rooms are frescoed or lavishly furnished. Call the **Associazione Guida** (tel. 049/820–9711) for guided tours (L5000, L2000 students); they're usually held Wednesday and Thursday at 9, 10, 11, 3, 4, and 5, and Friday at 3, 4, and 5. Meet at the university door. *Via VIII Febbraio 2. Catercorner from Palazzo della Ragione.*

➤ **PALAZZO DELLA RAGIONE** • The "Palace of Reason" used to hold more of Giotto's masterpieces, but his frescoes were badly damaged by fire in 1420. They were reconstructed by a lesser-known artist but are still worth gazing at (especially the astrological ones). The palazzo used to be the town courthouse but is now surrounded by the market area. Its arcades and halls are filled with vendors sellling cheese and extremely pungent salami. Temporary art displays pass through occasionally, which can alter the price of admission. *Via VIII Febbraio 3, tel. 049/820–5006. Admission: L7000, L4000 students. Open Tues.–Sun. 9–7 (until 6 in winter).*

CHEAP THRILLS The **Giardini Arcella** (off Via Jacopo da Montagna) hosts free concerts and open-air films in summer. The crew that hangs out here is the most eclectic in Padova—a mix of groupies and hippie types, who may or may not have mind-altering contraband to share or sell. It's a welcome respite from the gilded city center. The movie schedule is listed in "Padova Today," and you can pick up a schedule of concerts at the garden. Take the Arcella exit from the train station (opposite the main exit), go up Via Tiziano, and turn right on Via Jacopo da Montagna.

Not Exactly Pomp and Circumstance

During graduation from the University of Padova (mid-June), strange things happen: Ribald, graphic, and anatomically correct posters depicting the graduates' academic and erotic histories pop up around Palazzo Bò. Males get a wreath of laurel to wear around their neck (Italian for "to graduate" is "laurearsi"). They then get stripped to their underwear, bawdily serenaded, and seriously hazed. Women graduates usually keep their clothes on and their dignity intact—though they do get the wreath, the chant, and a slightly less prurient poster.

AFTER DARK Though Padova's students aren't exactly get-sloshed-and-dance-all-night types, most places where you can have a beer or two stay open until 1 or 2 AM. **La Miniera** (Via San Francesco 144, tel. 049/650348; closed Wed.) has neon, gem-encrusted walls and a faux-mine motif, but the atmosphere is surprisingly low-key. A beer costs L3500–L8000. From the station, walk down the main street (Corso del Popolo) and turn left just after the university onto Via San Francesco. **Lucifer Young** (Via Altinate 89, tel. 049/875–2251) is a twisted, imaginative bar based on Dante's *Inferno*. Beers cost L4000 or more, but the food is really from hell—eat before you go. To get here, walk down Corso del Popolo and turn left on Via Altinate, just after Piazza Garibaldi. Next to Padova's snazzy pubs, the basic beer joint **Le Clochard** (Riviera Tito Livio 15–17, tel. 049/876–1146) looks like a dive, but the beer is cheap (L2500–L6000) and the place attracts an interesting, mixed straight/gay male crowd. From the station, walk down Corso del Popolo, make a left onto Via San Francesco after the university, and an immediate right onto Riviera Tito Livio.

NEAR PADOVA

MONSELICE This unassuming, somewhat barren small town with a main street and little mom-and-pop places transforms into "Super Medieval Town" once you walk up from the tiny orange train station. Even if you're just taking the train to Montagnana (*see below*) for a night, spend a little time in Monsèlice on the way. When you get here, walk up the road over the bridge, turn right when the street ends, and you'll come to **Piazza Mazzini**. Behind the piazza is a long road that winds uphill; turn left and you're at **Ca' Marcello** (Castello di Ezzelino, tel. 0429/72931), a strange cross between a medieval castle and a Renaissance villa. They usually only admit visitors Tuesday–Sunday at 9, 11, 3, 4, and 5 (admission: L8000, L5000 students), and they're serious about making you wait.

About a 10-minute walk farther up the same street leads you to the arch that marks the beginning of Via Sette Chiese, where six little chapels lead to **Chiesa San Giorgio** and the private Villa Duodo next door. The friendly groundskeeper opens the church when he feels like it (and all day Sunday). He's more than happy to tell you all about the church, but he speaks *no* English, and you might get pinched if you're a woman alone. The inside of the church is full of the skeletons of Christian martyrs clothed in Renaissance outfits, peering at you from behind glass. They were all transferred from the Roman catacombs on the orders of Signore Duodo to add a little spiritual weight to his estate. The most famous corpse is of San Valentino (St. Valentine), who is visited every February 14 by grateful lovers. The **Rocca Citadel** on the top of the hill has been closed to the public since 1960, and looks it; but you can hike up to see deer and an incredible view if Carlo opens the iron gate for you.

Near Monsèlice is the sleepy little town of **Arquà Petrarca**, where Petrarch lived. You can only get here if you have a car or manage to beg a ride off commuters or school buses in the parking lot behind the train station. If you make it to Arquà Petrarca, **Casa Petrarca** (Via Vallesele, tel. 0429/718294; admission: L6000), the poet's house, is open February–September, daily 9–noon and 3–6:30; October–January, daily 9–noon and 2:30–5.

➤ **COMING AND GOING** • Trains from Monsèlice's **train station** (tel. 0429/74383) run every half hour to Padova (20 min, L2700) and Venice (1 hr, L5000); nine daily trains go to Mantova (1½ hrs, L6200; last train at 7:30 PM). Ask at the information office, **Pro Loco** (Via Roma 2, behind Piazza Mazzini, tel. 0429/72380; open Mon.–Sat. 10–noon and 3–6:30, Sun. 10–noon) for information on buses or maps for biking.

MONTAGNANA Wall-encircled Montagnana blasts you to the medieval past—especially during the *palio* on September 13, a small but authentic equestrian tournament inspired by the one in Siena. The town is also home to two castles: **Rocca degli Alberi** and **San Zeno**, with crenellated battlements and all. Other than that, though, there isn't much to see here. **Big Ben** (Viale Spalato 2, tel. 0429/81501; closed Wed.), just outside the walls on the road from the station, serves filling pizzas for L4500–L9500, as well as *risotto agli asparagi* (risotto with asparagus) for L6000. The information office, **Pro Loco** (Piazza Vittorio Emanuele Maggiore, tel. 0429/81320), is none too helpful. From Padova, you have to change trains at Monsèlice to reach Montagnana; take the Legnano or Mantova line (10 daily; last train at 7:36 PM). The entire trip, not counting the wait at Monsèlice, takes 45 minutes.

➢ **WHERE TO SLEEP** • **Ostello Rocca degli Alberi.** If you've always wanted to sleep alone in a spooky, deserted castle, here's your chance. Prepare to be the only one here besides the owls, the (benign) scorpions, and the director. The showers are clean and hot, the castle itself is interesting (ask the director to show you around), and the price is right (L14,000). *Castello degli Alberi, tel. 0429/81076. Walk down road from station, turn left when it ends. 70 beds. Curfew 11 PM, lockout 8:30–3. Luggage storage, HI cards issued. Closed Nov.–Mar.*

Vicenza

A yuppied-out, tony city whose nouveaux became riche mainly from the textile industry, Vicenza would be completely uninspiring if it weren't for its most illustrious citizen, Andrea di Pietra della Gondola, a.k.a. Palladio. This famous Renaissance architect spewed out dozens of designs for the city's residents, who were wealthy mainland relatives of Venice's more powerful families. The buildings range from opulent palazzi in the city to comfortable villas in the surrounding area, including **La Rotonda**, known to first-year architecture students worldwide. The buildings make Vicenza visually amazing, and you can get a pretty good idea of the Palladian style just walking down the street without paying a dime. Sleeping and eating here won't break you, but unless you're really, really into Palladio, stay in Padova or Verona and make Vincenza a day trip.

Local legend has it that the Vicentines are "cat eaters." Supposedly, during the 18th century, the city was overrun by mice. Desperate, the Vicentines asked for help from Venice, who sent them 100 cats—and a tasty recipe.

BASICS **APT.** *Piazza Matteotti 12, tel. 0444/320854. Next to Teatro Olimpico at end of Corso Palladio. Open Mon.–Sat. 9–12:30 and 2–6, Sun. and holidays 9–1.*

COMING AND GOING The **Vicenza Station** (Piazzale Stazione, south of center at end of Viale Roma, tel. 0444/326046) sends hourly trains to Padova (20 min, L3200), Verona (30 min, L4300), and Milan (2 hrs 10 min, L13,800). Trains to Venice leave every half hour (50 min, L6800). Air-conditioned **FTV** (Ferrotramvie Vicentine) buses go to Padova, Treviso, Marostica, Bassano del Grappa, and Asiago. They leave from the **bus station** (Viale Milano 7, tel. 0444/323130) next to the train station; call for prices and schedules. To reach the city center from the train station, follow Viale Roma and take a right on **Corso Palladio.**

WHERE TO SLEEP Vicenza periodically hosts showy exhibitions of its posh crafts, at which time hotels fill up and travelers are out of luck. The biggies are the two international goldsmith displays in January and June and the architecture show in September. The campground **Campeggio Vicenza** (Strada Pelosa 241, tel. 0444/582311; closed Oct.–Mar.) is way out of town, but you can almost always find a space. Sites cost L8800, plus L6800 per person. To get here, take Bus 1 from the train station and get off at Torre di Quartesolo.

Affitacamere di Marchiori Rosina. A very nice older woman who speaks no English runs this tiny, little-known hotel near the train station. The cheapest rooms in the city (L45,000 for a double with bath) have all been recently remodeled. They're clean and have matching furniture. Call for reservations and check in at Bar Trombon next door. *Contra Santa Caterina 88, tel. 0444/323717. From station, turn right on Viale Venezia to Ponte Santa Liberia, left on Contra San Silvestro, and right on Contra Santa Caterina. 12 rooms, 4 with bath.*

Hotel Vicenza. The cheapest place in the center has small, clean rooms that are usually occupied—make reservations in advance. If noise bothers you, ask for a room in the back. Doubles cost L65,000. *Stradella dei Nodari 5, tel. 0444/321512. From Piazza Signori, take Contra Cavour toward Corso Palladio, and turn left on Stradella dei Nodari.*

FOOD You probably can't even afford bread in most of the restaurants near the center, but if you're in town on Thursday morning, go to the monster **market**, which oozes through half the city (including Piazza Signori and Piazza del Duomo). There is also a daily fruit and vegetable market on Piazza delle Erbe. The **Giardino Salvi** (up Viale Roma from the train station) is a shady place to picnic and feed your leftovers to the swans. For a huge cheap pizza (about L7000), head past the maroon post office to **Al Paradiso** (Contra Pescherie Vecchie 5, tel. 0444/322320). It looks like a German beer hall and smells funky, but the **Righetti Self Restaurant** (Piazza del Duomo 3, tel. 0444/543135; closed weekends) is the best deal around; serve yourself *pasta con fagioli* (pasta with beans) for L5500 or meat dishes for L6000.

WORTH SEEING Vicenza and the surrounding area are strewn with major works by the immensely influential neoclassical architect Andrea Palladio. Many of his palazzi here now house ritzy shops, cafés, and restaurants, providing a sumptuous backdrop for Vicentine daily life. The center of the city is marked by the new(er) and improved basilica, which sits across from the elegant but unfinished pink Palladian shoebox, **La Loggia del Capitaniato**. North on Corso Palladio is **Santa Maria Corona** (tel. 0444/323644), open daily 8:30–noon and 2:30–10. This one's not by Palladio, but it contains a double whammy of Renaissance superstars: paintings by Giovanni Bellini and Paolo Veronese.

The **Basilica Palladiana** made Palladio famous within his lifetime as someone who could impose Renaissance harmony on absolutely anything. The building was originally a monstrous architectural remnant of the unstable medieval style, which had defied prior attempts to make it symmetrical. Palladio's design regularized the facade by placing pilasters of different widths at strategic points so they all looked the same, creating an effective optical illusion. *Piazza Signori, tel. 0444/323681. Admission free. Open daily 9–6 (Thurs. until 8).*

The **Palazzo Chiericati** was commissioned by local bigwig Girolamo Chiericati, but in 1838 the city acquired the palazzo and made it home to the **Museo Civico**, which contains works by Veronese, Tintoretto, and van Dyck. The paintings are kept in rooms with mythological names like "Firmament," "Hercules," and "Council of the Gods." *South side of Piazza Matteotti, tel. 0444/325071. Admission: L3000, L2000 students. Open Mon.–Sat. 9–12:30 and 2:15–5, Sun. 9:30–12:30.*

The **Teatro Olimpico**'s design was based on Roman indoor theaters. The plan is Palladian, but the permanent stage decoration was done by someone else, who went a little overboard on the perspective thing. The street in the miniature "town" under the main arch is only 12 meters long, but angled to deceive. The Vincentines also placed so many sculptures around the stage that it would be impossible to pay attention to a plot while watching a play here. The cheapest tickets for performances here go for L15,000. *North side of Piazza Matteotti, tel. 0444/323781. Admission: L5000, L3000 students. Open Mon.–Sat. 9–12:15 and 2:15–4:45, Sun. 9–12:15.*

NEAR VICENZA

VILLA ROTONDA Much hullabaloo has been made of Palladio's most famous villa, and not just by the tourist board: It has been copied around the world, by everyone from Christopher Wren to Thomas Jefferson. Technically it's called the Villa Valmarana-Capri, but the perfectly symmetrical villa based on a circle-in-a-square design is nicknamed the Rotonda, which means "round." You can see the villa fine from the road—you don't have to bother paying to go inside or even to enter the grounds (though jumping over the low stone wall by the road is always an option). *Via della Rotonda 25, tel. 0444/321793. From station, take AIM Bus 8 or walk east on Viale Venezia, cross Ponte Santa Libera and head east on Viale Risorgimento, then along the pedestrian/bicycle path (10-min walk). Admission: L10,000 interior, L5000 grounds only. Grounds open daily 10–noon and 3–6; interior open Wed. 10–noon and 3–6.*

VILLA VALMARANA The non-Palladian Villa Valmarana, also known as Ai Nani, or the House of Dwarves, is just up Stradella Valmarana from Villa Rotonda. It isn't as inspired as the Villa Rotonda, but the frescoes in the house were painted by Tiepolo, those in the guest house by his son, Gian Domenico. Check out the Alice-in-Wonderland-like statues of dwarves while you're here. *Via dei Nani 9, tel. 0444/543976. Admission: L8000. Open year-round, Wed.–Sat. 10–noon; also Mar. 15–Apr. 30, Wed.–Sat. 2:30–5:30; May–Sept., Wed.–Sat. 3–6; Oct.–Nov., Wed.–Sat. 2–5.*

Verona

A collection of stone-lined streets, stagelike piazze, and sidewalks paved with the characteristic pale-pink marble, Verona is one of the oldest, best-preserved, and most beautiful cities in Italy. The town hit its first peak way back in the 1st century BC, when the Romans used it as a pit stop on the trade route to the rest of Europe, leaving behind some serious monuments (including the Arena in Piazza Brà). In the Middle Ages, the slightly bizarre and very rich Scaglieri built the city up as the prestigious family domain. Later, in the 15th century, Venice came west and sucked the city up into its empire. Instead of challenging Venice's power, Verona decided to turn all its aspirations inward, building up its cultural cache (Shakespeare placed Romeo, Juliet, and a couple of gentlemen here) and restoring the already-ancient Roman ruins. Verona still knows what a good thing it's got going: Tourism is very big, and most of the residents are wealthy, status conscious, and a little snide. But unlike its big sister, Venice, Verona doesn't feel like a tourist town; some of the people in the streets actually *live* here.

BASICS **APT** has offices on Piazza Brà (Via Leoncino 61, tel. 045/592828; open Mon.–Sat. 8–8) and Piazza delle Erbe (tel. 045/803–0087; open Mon.–Sat. 9–7:30). Ask for the "Infor-magiovani" brochure, which lists cheap hotels and restaurants, and has an excellent map of the center of town. The "Passport Verona" brochure is also helpful.

➤ **CHANGING MONEY • Fabretto Viaggi e Turismo.** This branch of **American Express** changes traveler's checks for free, but they're closed most of the weekend, as are the banks, which charge outlandish commissions. The 24-hour exchange machines are often broken, so plan ahead. If you need the services of a bank, there are several on Piazza Brà. *Corso Porto Nuovo 11, tel. 045/800–9045. 2 blocks south of Piazza Brà on the left. Open weekdays 8:30–7:30, Sat. 9–noon.*

➤ **MAIL •** The **post office** (Piazza Viviani 7, tel. 045/803–0568) is in a four-story palazzo. The office is open Monday–Saturday from 8:15 AM until somewhere between 6:50 PM and 7:40 PM.

COMING AND GOING The main train station is **Verona Porta Nuova** (Piazza XXV Aprile, tel. 045/590688), a clean, well-lit stop on the Milan–Venice line. It offers service to international, national, and regional destinations, including Milan (1¾ hrs, L11,700), Rome (5 hrs, L40,500; change at Bologna), Florence (2¾ hrs, L17,200; change at Bologna), and Venice (every 30 min, 1½ hrs, L9600). Luggage storage is open 24 hours. The "Biglietteria Self-Service" ticket machine speaks English and takes foreign credit cards and lire; if you're not technophobic, it's a good way to avoid long lines. To reach the center of town from the station, walk down Corso Porta Nuova to Piazza Brà.

The **APT** station (Piazza XXV Aprile, next to the train station, tel. 045/800–4129) sends buses through the region around Verona as well as to Milan and Venice. Trains are faster and more convenient, but buses are often the only public transportation serving the smaller, less-visited towns of the region.

GETTING AROUND The Adige River runs through Verona, separating the center from outlying neighborhoods. Most sights are in or near the center, which is full of confusing little *vicoli* (alleys) and piazzas at every turn. **Corso Porta Nuova** leads north from the train station to **Piazza Brà**, the social heart of the center. From here, **Via Roma** leads west to **Castelvecchio**, where **Corso Cavour** begins; the latter turns into Corso Porta Borsari and finally Corso Sant' Anastasia. From Piazza Brà, **Via Mazzini** stretches northeast to **Piazze delle Erbe** and **Dante**, also centers of civic activity. The **youth hostel**—as well as the university and most budget restaurants—is on the east side of the Adige in the Veronetta district; cross the Ponte Nuovo to reach this blessedly untouristed neighborhood. Walking is the best way to get around Verona, as buses and cars aren't allowed in the center. If you do need to use a bus, schedules and routes are listed at the train station, and half of the buses stop at Piazza Brà. Buy the L1300 ticket at the machines before you board.

WHERE TO SLEEP Well, you could spend L495,000 a night for a room at the Due Torri, but it might cut into your coffee budget. Luckily, it's not the only choice in town. The cen-

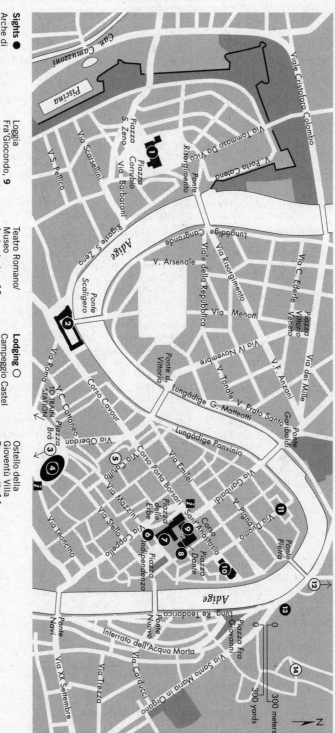

Sights ●

Arche di
Scaligere, **8**

Arena, **4**

Casa di Giulietta, **6**

Castelvecchio, **2**

Duomo, **11**

Loggia
Fra'Giocondo, **9**

Palazzo della
Ragione, **7**

San Zeno
Maggiore, **1**

Sant'Anastasia, **10**

Teatro Romano/
Museo
Archeologico, **13**

Lodging ○

Campeggio Castel
San Pietro, **12**

Locanda Catullo, **5**

Ostello della
Gioventù Villa
Francescati, **14**

Volto Cittadella, **3**

0   300 meters
0   300 yards

N

ter has a few budget hotels, and if you're not allergic to curfews or preteen travelers, the hostel isn't a bad deal.

Locanda Catullo. This nice, sunny hotel is a good value—you can't get any closer to the center unless you sleep in Piazza Brà (which, by the way, will get you promptly drummed out of town). Rooms are big, and some even have balconies for those Romeo and Juliet wanna-bes. The bathrooms are compulsively clean. Doubles (L65,000) go quickly. If you make reservations, there's a two-night minimum. *Via Valerio Catullo 1, tel. 045/800–2786. From Piazza Brà, walk up Via Mazzini and turn left on Via Catullo. 12 rooms, 4 with bath.*

Volto Cittadella. It's not in the most scenic part of the center (rooms have views of bus traffic along Corso Porta Nuova), but it's clean, rooms are usually available, and you can't argue with the price (L55,000 per double). The employees obviously aren't used to foreign travelers: They're actually nice. *Via Volto Cittadella 8, tel. 045/800–0077. From train station, walk up Corso Porta Nuova, turn right on Via Volta Cittadella. 11 rooms, none with bath.*

➤ **HOSTELS** • **Ostello della Gioventù Villa Francescati.** Housed in a 16th-century villa adorned with frescoes (look up as you're eating breakfast), the hostel is clean and well run by the laid-back employees. Both the showers and the coffee are hot, strong, and free. Beds are L15,000; camping in the garden is L8000 with a tent, L5000 without (breakfast included). *Salita Fontana del Ferro 15, tel. 045/590360. From center, cross Ponte Nuovo, turn left on Lungadige Re Teodorico, right on Ponte Pignolo, and follow signs; or take Bus 72 from train station and ask driver where to get off. 170 beds. Curfew 11 PM. Luggage storage.*

➤ **CAMPING** • The cheapest and easiest place to camp is the hostel garden, but **Campeggio Castel San Pietro** (Via Castel San Pietro, tel. 045/592037) is a pleasant alternative between mid-June and mid-August. One night, including tent, costs L12,000. From the town center, cross Ponte Pietra and follow the signs. Otherwise, you're stuck with the touristy **Campeggio Giulietta e Romeo** (Via Bresciana 54, tel. 045/851–0243), west of the center, in the San Massimo suburb. It comes equipped with modern amenities such as bathrooms, showers, a swimming pool, a supermarket, and a bar—which might justify the price (L15,000 per person). From Corso Porta Nuova in Verona's center, take the blue bus heading toward Sirmione/Brescia and get off at the campground.

FOOD Unless you're willing to hawk all your worldly possessions or are craving greasy fries with mayo for dinner, stay out of the overpriced center. The one exception is a plate at the cafeteria-style **Brek** (Piazza Brà 20, tel. 045/800–4561), where L4500 gets you some penne with ricotto and a view of the piazza. Cross the river into the Veronetta (university) district, and you'll find better food at better prices. For a cheap lunch at a student hangout, **Nuova Grottina** (Via Interrato dell'Acqua Morta 38, tel. 045/803–0152; closed Thurs.) serves two-person pizzas starting at L5000. **Gelateria Melody** on Piazza Brà scoops the best gelato in town (L1000). Also on Piazza Brà, **Caffè Motta**, a local gathering spot, has outdoor seating and excellent coffee (at L2600 for an espresso, it better be good). Delicious red valpolicella wine is a Veronese specialty; L3000 a liter is a reasonable price at most restaurants.

Il Grillo Parlante. Under construction until who knows when, this vegetarian restaurant is a favorite of a small anarchist/alternative crowd. The filling secondi are extremely cheap (L7000–L7500); try the spinach croquettes (L7500). *Vicolo Seghe San Tommaso 10, tel. 045/591156. Behind old bus station off Piazza Isolo. Open Tues., Wed., Fri.–Sun. noon–2:30 and 7:30–10, Thurs. noon–2:30.*

Trattoria dal Ropeton. Just down the street from the hostel, this place serves delicious pasta and meaty secondi to the locals, who crowd the outside tables. Pasta with artichokes is L7000, as are the rest of the primi; secondi are L12,000, and a good *verdura mista* (salad) with bitter greens is L5000. *Via San Giovanni 46, tel. 045/803–0040. From hostel, walk down Salita Fontana del Ferro and turn left on Via San Giovanni. Reservations advised for outdoor area. Open Wed.–Mon. 6:30 PM–10:30 PM.*

Trattoria Perbacco. This little-known trattoria features stupendous food, nice owners, and a pretty garden. Try the polenta with fontina and radicchio (L7000) or the pasta *con panna e peperoni* (with cream and peppers; L6000), but avoid the pricey wines. *Via Carducci 481/A, tel.*

045/594193. From Ponte Nuovo, walk on Veronetta side through Piazza San Tommaso down Via Carducci almost to Piazza Bernardi. Open Mon., Tues., Thurs.–Sat. 12:30–3 and 7:30–11.

WORTH SEEING The center is jammed with Austrian, Venetian, and Roman buildings, all within easy walking distance of each other. Go to the major sights listed below, but save some time just to walk through the small alleyways. Roman arches mark the entrances to Piazze Brà and Dante and the beginning of Corso Porta Borsari. Verona is now cashing in on its churches by charging a L4000 admission fee, but you can buy a pass in any church for all the churches for L9000 (L7000 students). One other reminder—Verona gets going earlier than the rest of Italy—most of the sights open at 8 AM. If you're an early bird, you may be able to beat some of the crowds.

➢ **ARCHE DI SCAGLIERI** • Okay, every family has a wacky rich uncle, but apparently the Scaglieri had nothing but. Consider the peculiar habit they had of naming themselves after dogs: Mastino (Mastiff) I and II, Cangrande (Big Dog), and Cansignorio (Lord Dog). Their statued Gothic tombs lie next to the Church of Santa Maria Antica, the Scaglieri's personal house of worship. Notice the dorky expression on Cangrande's face (he's the one on the horse); the statue on his tomb is a copy of the original, which is in Castelvecchio. *Via Arche Scagliere. Walk through arch at north end of Piazza Dante.*

➢ **ARENA** • Ancient, cavernous, and pink, this huge Roman amphitheater smack in the middle of Piazza Brà dominates the city. Built in the 1st century AD, it's Verona's best example of 1) the ingenuity of the Romans and 2) the meticulousness of the Veronese, who have been keeping it shipshape since the Renaissance. Big-name rock stars occasionally play here (although graffiti and damage to the building have discouraged the city from allowing concerts of this sort), and it's famous for its opera (*see* After Dark, *below*). *Piazza Brà, tel. 045/800– 3204. Admission: L6000, L4000 students; free 1st Sun. of the month. Open Tues.–Sun. 8–7.*

➢ **CASA DI GIULIETTA** • Avoid the touristy houses and tombs of Romeo and Juliet. They're architecturally boring, as well as totally spurious; the Cappuletti (Capulet) and Montecchi (Montague) families did live in Verona, but the protagonists are fictitious. If you still feel a need to see a testament to teenage love, save your money and go to the entrance of the Casa di Giulietta (Juliet's House), visible from the street. The walls are covered with layers of proclamatory graffiti of the "R + J" variety, written by modern-day lovebirds. *Via Cappello 23, tel. 045/803–4303.*

➢ **CASTELVECCHIO** • Built by the Scaglieri in 1354 as a last-ditch attempt to ward off invaders, Castelvecchio is a seriously fortified castle next to a dramatic bridge that crosses the Adige River. The castle was redesigned by local boy Carlo Scarpa and is widely considered to be one of his best works, if not one of the more interesting modern Italian buildings. The museum inside features works by Titian, Veronese, Tintoretto, Pisanello, and Rubens, as well as a startling number of breast-feeding Madonnas. *Corso Cavour 2, tel. 045/594734. From Piazza Brà, walk to end of Via Roma. Admission: L5000, free 1st Sun. of the month. Open Tues.–Sun. 8–6:30.*

➢ **DUOMO** • This candy-cane-striped Romanesque-Gothic cathedral was built on an ancient spa site, where early Christian architectural remnants have been found. A fresco by Titian, *The Assumption*, is in the first chapel on the left. It's not the most compelling sight in Verona, but it's a quiet, soothing place to spend some time. *Piazza Duomo, tel. 045/595627. From Piazza delle Erbe, turn right on Corso Sant'Anastasia and turn left on Via Duomo. Admission free. Open daily 7–noon and 3–7.*

➢ **PIAZZA DELLE ERBE/PIAZZA DANTE** • Piazza Erbe has been an open-air market since antiquity, though it's doubtful they sold Romeo and Juliet coloring books back then. The frescoed **Casa dei Mazzanti**, on the northwest side, is the antidote to all the tackiness, as is the cool, silent Piazza Dante (a.k.a. Piazza dei Signori). Separated from Erbe by the Arco della Costa, Piazza Dante sports the red-and-white-striped **Palazzo della Ragione**, as well as the prettily frescoed **Loggia Fra'Giocondo**. The **Torre dei Lamberti** (tel. 045/8032726; open Tues.–Sun. 9:30–6:30) to the right of the piazza has, for a price, a good view of the city. Take the elevator for L4000, or the stairs for L3000.

➤ **SANT'ANASTASIA** • This gloomy Gothic church looms large over the Adige on the north end of the town center. As you enter, look on each side of the door for the holy water basins; *gobbi* (hunchbacks) support the sacred liquid on their humps. In the Giusti Chapel (all the way down to the left) is *St. George and the Princess*, a fresco by Pisanello. *Piazza Sant' Anastasia, tel. 045/800–4235. From Piazza delle Erbe, turn right on Corso Sant'Anastasia. Admission: L4000. Open daily 7–noon and 3:30–7.*

➤ **SAN ZENO MAGGIORE** • A big and beautiful Romanesque basilica with a rose window, San Zeno would be perfect if it weren't for all the Viewmaster-like machines explaining its history. The bronze doors with scenes from the Bible were cast in the 12th and 13th centuries, and Mantegna's triptych, *Madonna and Saints*, on the high altar, is glorious. The arch-lined 12th-century cloister of the adjoining Benedictine abbey is so thick with atmosphere that, if you squint hard, the German tourists in Megadeth T-shirts become pious medieval monks. *Piazza San Zeno, tel. 045/800–6120. From Castelvecchio, walk along Rigaste San Zeno and turn left on Via Barbarani. Admission: L4000. Open daily 8:30–noon and 3–8.*

➤ **TEATRO ROMANO/MUSEO ARCHEOLOGICO** • So it looks a little crumbly even after all that restoration work—you would too if you had been around since the 1st century BC. Though you can feel the millennia seeping from the cracks of this flowery, open-air theater, the thrill doesn't last more than a few minutes. Go upstairs and wait forever for the elevator to the Museo Archeologico, in which the fragments of ancient sculptures (Greek, Etruscan, and Roman) give the disturbing impression that someone was dismembered here. Don't forget to look down on Verona from the balcony. *Rigaste Redentore 2, tel. 045/800–0360. Walk across Ponte Pietra and turn right. Admission: L5000, free 1st Sun. of month. Open Tues.– Sun. 8–1.*

CHEAP THRILLS The pastel buildings lining Piazza Brà watch in amusement as Verona does its daily thing. Buy an expensive coffee (consider it rent) and see if you can spot young couples dry-humping on the benches, older people in wool sweaters complaining about the heat, and kids trying unsuccessfully to scare away the stolid pigeons. For a more beatific experience, buy a cheap bottle of grappa, cross the Ponte Pietra, and walk up the steps to **Castel San Pietro**, near the hostel. It's a serene, untrafficked place to watch the setting sun turn the sky as pink as the rest of Verona.

AFTER DARK Even if you really want to do what the Veronese do at night, you can't—unless, of course, you brought two suitcases of expensive Euroclothing with you. The passeggiata down **Via Mazzini** goes on until about 2 AM on weekend evenings, and status-consciousness is the password. But there are plenty more edifying ways to spend your time and money in Verona: Both the Arena (*see below*) and the Teatro Romano (*see* Worth Seeing, *above*) host **plays**, **opera**, and **concerts** in summer. The plays, often Shakespeare in Italian, aren't worth it, but if you can catch a jazz concert, pay the L17,000 (students L14,000) for the cheapest seat.

➤ **OPERA AT THE ARENA** • The Arena is famous for its opera, which is definitely worth the cost of the ticket. The season is late June–August, and they usually stage biggies like *Aïda* and *Tosca* (check out the "Passport Verona" brochure for program schedules). A general admission seat costs L30,000 (plus 15% if you buy it more than one day in advance); reserved spots start at L120,000 and go up from there. Shows begin at 9 PM and the gates open at 7 PM. You are allowed to bring a picnic but no cans or glass (pour your wine into plastic water bottles), and be subtle about your Swiss army knife. Do bring a candle—everybody lights one up when the show starts. *Box office: Via Dietro Anfiteatro 6/B, tel. 045/800–5151. AE, MC, V.*

Bassano del Grappa

Lying low in the Valsugana Valley and crossed by the green Brenta River, Bassano del Grappa is a muggy, wealthy little town. People come to enjoy the scenery; eat fresh porcini mushrooms, white asparagus, and radicchio; buy hand-painted ceramics; and get sloshed on grappa, a local brain-kill specialty made from the last-pressed dregs of brandy. The town was founded around AD 1000 and originally just called "Bassano." It didn't take its surname from the alcoholic drink, but adopted it from neighboring Mont Grappa as a testament to the World War I soldiers slain there.

You'll find Bassano is a really cool little town that offers little to do but see the few sights and have a gelato at one of the twin piazze in the center, **Garibaldi** and **Libertà**. English-speaking travelers don't make it here all that often, but the summer sees enough vacationing Germans and Italians to jack hotel prices up. If you're planning to stay the night, make a reservation in advance or you'll get stuck paying a bundle for a room.

BASICS **APT office.** *Largo Corona d'Italia 35, tel. 0424/524351. Just inside city walls left of train station. Open weekdays 9–12:30 and 2–5, Sat. 9–12:30.*

COMING AND GOING The **train station** (tel. 0424/525034) is in Piazzale Stazione. Trains travel to Trento (5 daily, 2 hrs, L8000), Venice (via Castelfranco; hourly, 1⅓ hrs, L5000), and Padova (via Castelfranco; 10 daily, 1 hr, L4200). The town is easily covered on foot; everything of interest lies between the station and the Brenta River. To reach the town center from the station, walk up Via Chilesotti, make a right on the wide Viale delle Fosse, and turn left on Via Jacopo del Ponte.

Bus service is much more convenient and comprehensive than train service. The main stop is **Piazzale Trento** (from the train station, go down Via Chilesotti and turn left on Viale delle Fosse). The station doesn't have its own ticket counter, but **Bar Trevisiani** (Piazzale Trento 13, tel. 0424/525025; open daily 8–noon and 3–7) serves as a combined bar/restaurant/bus-ticket booth. **FTV** (tel. 0424/30850) buses to Asiago (7 daily, 1½ hrs, L5600) and Vicenza (hourly, 1 hr, L4800), and **ACTM** (tel. 0424/22201) buses to Asolo (7 daily, 30 min, L2800), Maser (10 daily, 30 min, L3800), and Possagno (7 daily, 40 min, L3600) all leave from in front of Bar Trevisiani. To catch **La Marca** (tel. 0424/227154) buses to Treviso (6 daily, 1 hr 20 min, L5700), go to **Osteria la Pergola** (Piazzale Trento 7, tel. 0424/27154) across the piazza.

WHERE TO SLEEP Most of Bassano's hotel prices hover near a hundred dollars for a double, and the cheapest rooms fill up fast. If you're here in the summer, the best deal is the **Instituto Cremona** (Via Chini 6, tel. 0424/522032). It's an elementary school/makeshift hostel June 21–September 5. If you're arriving on a weekend, you have to call during the work week 9–noon or 6–8, or they'll take the weekend off. This place is a dorm just like any other, except for the totally nonfunctional showers, kid-size sinks, and pasta mosaics in the dining room. Bed-and-breakfast costs L16,000. From the bus station at Piazzale Trento, follow Via Remondini (which becomes Salita Brocchi); turn left at the post office onto Via Emiliani, then right onto Via Chini. The **Nuovo Mondo** (Via Vitorelli 45, tel. 0424/522010) charges only L55,000 for a double, and it's right in the center; turn right from Piazza Garibaldi coming from the station. The family-run hotel/restaurant, **Al Bassanello** (Via P. Fontana 2, tel. 0424/35347), has decent doubles for L85,000 with bath. There are just 15 rooms and only a few singles, so make a reservation. Al Bassanello is on the other side of the train station from the center: Walk up Via Chilesotti, turn right on Viale delle Fosse, right again on Via Venezia, left on Via Boinucci, right on Via Trozetti, and your first left is Via P. Fontana.

FOOD The food situation is also difficult to manage in Bassano; pizza is by far the cheapest choice. The best pizzeria is **Al Saraceno** (Via Museo 60, tel. 0424/522513; open Tues.–Sun. 10–3:30 and 5:30–1), down the street that starts behind the museum (*see* Worth Seeing, *below*). Disregard the cheesy sign and the English/Italian menu; this place is all local and whips up the tastiest pizza in northern Italy. The *vegetariana* (L7000) is a work of art, decorated with loads of mozzarella, spinach, white asparagus (for which Bassano is famous), and radicchio. Primi run L6000–L8000. Get the best grappa at **Nardini** (Ponte Vecchio 2, tel. 0424/527741), a distillery whose look hasn't changed since 1776. Enjoy a glass of juniper, plum, peach, pear, or grape grappa for L2000 and look out at the Ponte degli Alpini. If you don't know which flavor you fancy, ask and they'll bring out a tray with glasses of each to sample. It's open daily 8–8.

WORTH SEEING Bassano's most famous landmark, the picnic-table brown **Ponte degli Alpini**, is a covered, wooden bridge over the Brenta. Also called the Ponte Vecchio, it's been in the same place since 1209, but it keeps getting destroyed (seven times to date) and rebuilt—once by Palladio in 1570. The view of the hills and the river is arcadian, and the bridge is a local passeggiata spot and refuge from the frequent rain. At the end farthest from the town center, look for the VEDUTA PANORAMICA sign; from here, Via Marcello leads down to the water to a prime spot for viewing the bridge and consuming more grappa. The sign next to the river is Italian for "no swimming," so if you can't resist stepping into the clean, green water, try to pass as one of the hip-deep anglers. The **Museo Civico** (Via Museo 12, tel. 0424/522235), just off Piazza Garibaldi, is best known for its works by 16th-century local yokel Jacopo da Ponte, a.k.a. Bassano. His work shares the gallery with pieces by Tiepolo, Dürer, and Canova as well as Bassanese artists you've never heard of. The museum is open Tuesday–Saturday 9–12:30 and 3:30–6:30, Sunday 3:30–6:30, and admission costs L5000 (L2500 students).

NEAR BASSANO DEL GRAPPA

ASOLO The small streets, crumbling medieval buildings, and stunning views that make up tiny Asolo have prompted writers throughout history to practically coo. In *Asolando*, Robert Browning gushed pages about this place, where he was but one of many pedigreed expatriates. The hilltop city lives up to its description. At sunset, pick a horizon, and you'll be sighing wistfully before the stars come out. Asolo's **APT** (Via Santa Caterina 258, tel. 0423/529046) is open Tuesday–Saturday 9–1 and 2:30–6 (closed Friday afternoon). It's housed in a villa with gardens, possibly the nicest tourist office in Italy. From the center, turn left on Via Canova; follow it up until it turns into Santa Caterina (past Hotel Cipriani). The **duomo**, just behind Piazza Garibaldi on Via Browning, is a severe, three-naved affair containing two *Assumptions*, one by Bassano and one by Lorenzo Lotto. The **Museo Civico** (Piazza Garibaldi, Loggia del Capitano, tel. 0423/952313) has been "temporarily" closed for two years and probably won't reopen until 1998. The museum displays some minor Venetian paintings and the personal effects of Eleonora Duse, a silent-film actress who came to Asolo to forget love troubles and the hounding press in 1924. Only the clock tower of **Castello Cornaro** (up from Piazza Garibaldi and left at the town hall) is original; the reconstructed building itself is interesting mostly for being the onetime home of Caterina Cornaro, a Venetian woman who married the king of Cyprus. When the king died, Caterina was placed in the position of having to choose between her homeland and her new subjects. Venice wanted control of Cyprus to boost its naval power. Principled Caterina said no to the hungry Venetians for nearly 10 years, but she was backed into a corner when Venice refused to help Cyprus fend off an attack by the invading Turks. In 1498, she gave up control of the island, and the Venetians gave her Asolo as a consolation prize.

➤ **COMING AND GOING** • Buses run daily from Bassano (7 daily, 30 min, L2800; last bus at 7:33 PM). The bus drops you off at the bottom of the hill, where you wait for a minibus (which looks like a Tonka toy) to take you up to the center.

VILLA BARBARO Close to Asolo in Maser, Villa Barbaro is the only villa in Italy to feature the dynamic duo of Palladian architecture and Paolo Veronese frescoes. The building was commissioned in 1550 by the Barbaro boys, Daniele and Marcantonio, educated gentlemen who contributed to the work. The middle section of the villa, stern on the exterior but breezy and comfortable inside, is still inhabited by a lucky, lucky family. Veronese's frescoes inside are characteristically colorful and playful, probably some of the most beautiful in Italy. The grounds contain a Palladian temple and a somewhat impressive museum of carriages. From Asolo, buses go to Maser five times daily (10 min, L1200). *Via Cornuda 2, tel. 0423/923004. Admission: L8000. Open Tues., Sat., Sun., holidays 3 PM–6 PM.*

TOMBE BRIONI The Brioni tombs in San Vito, designed by Italy's greatest postwar architect, Carlo Scarpa, in 1970–73, are diametrically opposed to the Villa Barbaro (*see above*) in style, purpose, and effect. This severe cement construction adjacent to an old graveyard combines right angles, geometric patterns, and obscure symbolism about crossing from one world into the next. Every angle and step of the chapel, pond, and spacecraftlike tombs was precisely planned by Scarpa and is heavily wrought with obscure significance. Try to hunt down Scarpa's remains, which are in the public cemetery and hidden next to the walls of the tombs. Admission is free, and the tombs are open daily 8–7 in summer; 9–3:30 in winter. To get here, take the bus from Asolo (8 daily, 20 min, L1500), get off near Via Castellana in San Vito (tell the driver you're going to the Tombe Brioni), and walk down the cypress-lined street that leads to the tombs (cypresses are traditional symbols of death).

POSSAGNO At the foot of Monte Grappa, Possagno is an unassuming, tree-covered town, famous in certain circles for being the home of neoclassical pioneer Antonio Canova (1757–1822). The sculptor and architect managed to breathe life into the neoclassical movement with his weighty, expressive interpretations of mythological subjects. One part of **Gipsoteca Canova** (Piazza Canova 1, tel. 0423/544323) is the house where the artist was born, and the other part is a white-walled building designed by Carlo Scarpa (who *lived* to juxtapose his work with old stuff). It contains all of Canova's most important pieces in clay, plaster cast, and marble. Some of the best are the touchy-feely *Three Graces*, the sleeping lion and angel in *Dolente Genio*, and the playful lovers *Venus and Adonis*. The museum is open Tuesday–Sunday 9–noon and 3–6, and admission costs L5000. On the other side of the Stradale del Tempio stands the **Tempio** (open daily 8–6), which Canova both designed and paid to have built. The imposing, nouveau-pantheon church with its zippy mosaic piazza makes a great photo moment with Monte Grappa hovering in the distance. For food, you can buy supplies at one of the numerous alimentari on Viale Canova and picnic in the rustic area outside the crumbling church of **Santa Giustina** (follow the signs from Via Cunial, off Viale Canova). Possagno is accessible from Bassano by ACTM buses (11 daily, 30 min, L3600). If you decide to stay, a double in the modern, spotless **Albergo Stella d'Oro** (Viale Canova 46, tel. 0423/544107), above the café/restaurant of the same name, costs L58,000.

Treviso

Don't come to Treviso because you heard that it was a "little Venice." Yes, the city has frescoes, channels of water, and some Venetian-style buildings, but the effect is more or less spoiled by the modern glass buildings built after World War II and the exhaust-spewing cars that run through most of the town. Don't come because you heard Treviso is the home of Benetton and you wanted to do some outlet shopping either: Benetton's hometown prices are the same as everywhere else. And don't come because you didn't want to deal with lodging in Venice. Treviso has only three cheapish hotels; two are dingy, and the other is more expensive and often full.

The best reason to come to Treviso, half an hour north of Venice on the train line to Udine, is for a really good splurge meal, complete with *tiramisù* (literally, "pick-me-up"), the creamy, sinful concoction of cake, liqueur, espresso, mascarpone cheese, and cocoa. Once you're stuffed, work off some of those calories with a walk through the town's galleries and churches to catch Tomaso da Modena's charismatic frescoes. Pick up the *Treviso Città Dipinta* brochure from **APT** (Via Toniolo 41, tel. 0422/547632; open weekdays 8:30–12:30 and 3–6, Sat. 8:30–noon) for a map and detailed descriptions of frescoes by other artists that you'll see around town.

COMING AND GOING The **train station** (Piazzale Duca d'Aosta, tel. 0422/541352) is on the south edge of the center. From here, trains run to Udine (hourly, 1 hr 40 min, L8800), Venice (every 30 min, 30 min, L3800), and Vicenza (hourly, 1 hr 10 min, L4300).

Treviso's **bus station** (Lungosile Mattei 29) is used by the **La Marca** bus line (tel. 0422/412222), which runs throughout the province and beyond. La Marca goes to Bassano del Grappa (every 2 hrs, 1 hr 20 min, L5700) and Padova (every 30 min, 1 hr 10 min, L5000). **ACTV** (tel. 0422/541821) runs from the station to Venice (2 per hr, 30 min, L2800). To reach the bus station from the train depot, walk up Via Roma and turn left just before the bridge.

GETTING AROUND From the station, Via Roma/Corso del Popolo leads north and forks at Piazza Borsa. To the left is Via XX Settembre, which leads straight to **Piazza dei Signori**, home of the Palazzo di Trecento (Treviso's town hall) and the city center. **Via Calmaggiore** is the town's pedestrian area, channeling a slew of well-heeled shoppers under boutique-lined porticoes northeast to Piazza Duomo. Luckily the city is small enough to walk through, as ACT buses charge L1000 to drop you off in inconvenient locations. If you must, buy tickets and get more info from the bar in the train station.

WHERE TO SLEEP Treviso specializes in luxury lodgings, which start around L95,000 for a double. The following places are no great shakes, but they're the only cheap offerings and you'd be wise to reserve in advance. The best budget hotel in Treviso, **Le Becchiere** (Piazza Ancillotto 10, just behind Palazzo di Trecento, tel. 0422/540871) has airy rooms (doubles

L50,000) decorated in suburban pastels. The excellent restaurant downstairs is popular with locals, which means that the noise won't die down until midnight. Your best option is to join in the din and pay L20,000 or so for a convenient, delicious meal (notify the management beforehand that you plan to eat). **Al Cuor** (Piazzale Duca d'Aosta 1, tel. 0422/410929) is near the train station and under the freeway, so it trembles every time a vehicle passes. The rooms verge on the ramshackle, and the common bathrooms have no showers at all. Spring for the doubles with bath (L60,000); doubles without bath cost L52,000. Turn right and go under freeway from the station.

FOOD Treviso is known for its radicchio, cherries, desserts, and sky-high prices for all of the above. Get a taste of the good life with tiramisù and caffè at **Nascimben** (Via Calmaggiore 32, tel. 0422/542325; closed Mon.), the best pasticceria in town. The price of tiramisù depends on the ambition of your tummy (about L2000 for a medium hunk). For an indulgent dinner, try **Le Becchiere's** restaurant (*see* Where to Sleep, *above*).

Al Bersagliere. It hurts to pay as much for a meal as for a hotel room, but Al Bersagliere has meals you won't soon forget. The L12,000–L13,000 primi range from pasta e fagioli to gnocchi. *Baccalà* (dried cod) with polenta and other secondi run L20,000–L35,000. *Via Barbiera 21, tel. 0422/541988. From Piazza Duomo, walk down Via Calmaggiore and turn right on Via Barbiera. Reservations advised. Open weekdays 10:30–4 and 6–1, Sat. 6 AM–1 AM; closed Aug. 5–25 and Jan. 1–7. AE, MC, V.*

All'Oca Bianca. This Trevisan fixture serves delicious, affordable food. Primi are L7000–L10,000; secondi are L9000–L13,000. Much of the menu changes daily. *Vicolo della Torre 7, off Via Calmaggiore, tel. 0422/541850. Open Thurs.–Tues. noon–3 and 6–11.*

Menu Verde. This vegetarian restaurant has no ambience, but it does have the best prices for good, green eating, with assorted pasta and vegetable treats for L4500–L7000. Best of all, it sells whole-wheat pizza by the slice (L3000). *Vicolo Avogari 6, tel. 0422/544659. Open Mon. and Wed.–Sat. noon–3 and 7:30–10, Tues. noon–3.*

WORTH SEEING The eclectic works of Tomaso da Modena, 14th-century fresco painter and artistic heir to Giotto, cover Treviso like a rash. Start in the **Capitolo dei Dominicani** (in the Seminario Vescovile, on Via San Nicolò next door to the huge church, tel. 0422/412010). Da Modena painted 40 extraordinary portraits of Dominican monks at their desks, managing to express the personality of each. Some write furiously, some stare sternly at the viewer, and some look seized with divine beatitude. Admission is free, and the Capitolo is open daily 9–12:30 and 3–7:30 in summer; it closes at 5:30 in winter.

The **Museo Civico** (Borgo Cavour 24, tel. 0422/51337; admission: L3000) houses a *Crucifixion* by Bassano and a fresco of *San Antonio Abate* by Pordenone. The strangest painting here is *Il Castragatti* (The Cat Fixer) by Sebastiano Florigero. The big, ugly, yellow **duomo** (Piazza del Duomo) is charmless except for the Cappella Malchiostro, which contains Pordenone frescoes and yet another *Annunciation* by Titian, in which an angel breaks the news to a trembling Mary.

The decanonized **Chiesa di Santa Caterina** (Piazzetta Mario Botter; call the Museo Civico for information) holds da Modena's other masterpiece, the *Ursula Cycle*, a depiction of one of the more bizzare Christian legends. Eleven thousand virgins makes for great subject matter, and Da Modena's skill shines through in the pale, crumbly, unrestored frescoes. The frescoes in the newly restored **Cappella degli Innocenti** (admission: L3000; open Apr.–Oct., Tues.–Sun. 10–12:30 and 3–6; Nov.–Mar., Tues.–Sun. 3–6), to the left as you enter, were once thought to have been painted by Tomaso as well, but now they're attributed to two unknown masters. The bright, spanking-clean frescoes look like an unfinished jigsaw puzzle, but what you can see is expressive and in glowing color. To get here from the station, walk up Via Roma/Corso del Popolo, go straight on Via Martin di Libertà, and turn right at Piazza San Leonardo.

THE DOLOMITES AND THE NORTHEAST

3

By Paul Kottman

Many travelers to northern Italy aren't aware that the country stretches east and north of Venice. Perhaps that's because the provinces of Trentino-Alto Adige (north of the Veneto) and Friuli-Venezia Giulia (northeast of Venice) are the least "Italian" regions in the country. Before the 20th century, neither even belonged to Italy. Trentino-Alto Adige was part of Austria's South Tyrol region for centuries, and its inhabitants generally prefer German to Italian and schnitzel to pasta. In Friuli, you can still find friuliani who speak their own bizarre language, and many of the residents of Trieste, the main city in Venezia Giulia, are Slavic in origin, whether they have a Macedonian great-grandmother or are recent refugees from Zagreb.

In some ways, Trentino-Alto Adige and Friuli-Venezia Giulia have more in common with each other than with the rest of the country. Besides sharing a schizoid cultural identity and a history of foreign domination, both regions are renowned for their natural beauty and offer an astounding variety of activities, from cliff diving on the Adriatic coast to rock climbing in the jagged limestone peaks of the Dolomites. In Friuli-Venezia Giulia, the white cliffs overlooking the deep blue Adriatic near Trieste inspired poet Rainer Maria Rilke to write his famous *Duino Elegies*, which rapturously describe the landscape.

If you've come for a quintessential Italian experience, get back on the train. But if you want to try new types of food, learn alternative words for "train station" and "bathroom," and see a part of Italy that is very different than the one you've seen in Florence and Rome, then this rugged region featuring a dynamic, hybrid culture is the place for you.

Trentino-Alto Adige

The two parts of Trentino-Alto Adige may share the same landscape—mountains crisscrossed by a series of lush valleys—but they couldn't be further apart culturally. Alto Adige (alias Südtirol) was Austrian most of its long life; though it was handed over to Italy as a spoil of World War I, Germanic traditions die hard. As a foreigner to the area, locals will habitually address you in German first, and you're just as likely to see sausage and sauerkraut on restaurant menus as pasta and pizza. Today Trentino-Alto Adige is looked upon as a model state—it's cleaner, wealthier, and better organized than other areas in Italy.

Nonetheless, many Alto Adige inhabitants resent their outsider status and are willing to fight for their ethnic rights—some say even to secede from Italy. Mussolini, with his aggressive nationalist campaign, only aggravated the problem by insisting that all German place-names in

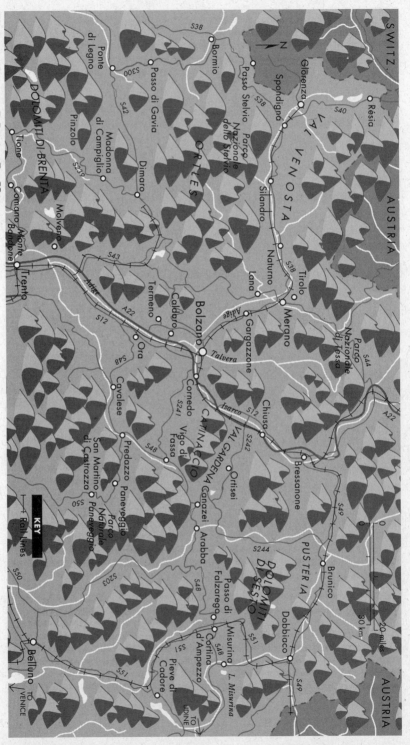

Trentino-Alto Adige

KEY

⊢ Rail lines

78

the region be paired with Italian equivalents—a task that busied official linguists for years. This is why Bozen is also known as Bolzano, Brixen as Bressanone, and why you'll encounter strange names like Piazza Walther and Castello Runkelstein. One thing everyone *does* agree on, though, is the importance of tourism, which brings a lot of money (and Germans) to the area every year. Most visitors flock here for one thing: the Dolomites. These pale, severe mountains rise from the sloping green foothills like giant stalagmites, offering everything from great post-card material and easy strolls to expert climbs over smooth faces.

BASICS To make heads or tails of the region's hiking trails, lodging options, and transport system, be sure to visit the **regional APT offices** in Trento and Bolzano (*see below*). You'll also see lots of yellow "i" signs that signify smaller offices specializing in rifugi arrangements and more specific trail maps. Tourist offices throughout the region are uniformly open Monday–Saturday 9–noon and 3–6, Sunday 9–noon. Trail maps called "Kompass Wanderkarte" (L8000), available in bookstores and some tourist offices, are a godsend.

WHERE TO SLEEP Many pensions require a minimum stay of two or three nights and expect you to pay a rate that includes all three meals ("full pension"); when you call to reserve a room, be sure to ask about all the stipulations. *Rifugi* (mountain huts) shelter hikers in remote, modest facilities for about L15,000–L25,000 a night. Some have kitchens you can use if you arrange it ahead of time with the manager. Tourist offices can tell you which trails lead to rifugi and sometimes help you contact them, which you should always do before starting off.

OUTDOOR ACTIVITIES Hiking is a big deal in the Dolomites, and both Trento and Bolzano have loads of supply stores. In summer you won't need much warm clothing unless you're planning on doing some serious climbing. In winter, **skiing** is the region's raison d'être—it's good, but not cheap. The **Centro Turistico Studentesco** in Trento (Via Cavour 21, tel. 0461/981549) sells the **Settimana Bianca** package for L500,000–L700,000 to students. It's valid for one week in one area and includes a ski pass, accommodations, and some meals.

Trento

The breezy, frescoed town of Trento is the northernmost outpost of "real" Italy. People generally know German but prefer Italian; wurst appears on menus, but you'll have a better selection of risotto and gnocchi. In the Piazza Duomo, an ornate birthday cake of a fountain topped with a statue of Neptune is an 18th-century tribute to Trento's history, which goes back to Roman times when the town was called Tridentum. Trento's biggest claim to fame is that it hosted the momentous 16th-century Counter Reformation showdown, the **Council of Trent** (*see box*, The Council of Trent, *below*). The council may not have stopped the spread of Protestantism in Europe, but it did wonders for the city of Trento. The duomo was spruced up to impress church bigwigs, and most of the palazzi, porticoes, and frescoes date from this era. **Piazza Dante**'s brilliant flowers, shaded benches, and stunning mountain views have derailed many a visitor's best laid travel plans. Trento is also the bus hub for trips into the surrounding mountains and a good place to relax (and shower) before tackling the Brenta mountain range, the Parco Naturale Paneveggio, and nearby Monte Bondone (*see* Near Trento, *below*).

Italia Irredenta

The Irredentist movement of the early 20th century was Italy's attempt to regain the control of areas—especially Trento and Trieste—that were inhabited mostly by Italians but ruled by Austria. These regions, called "Italia irredenta" (unredeemed Italy), were, depending on your interpretation, either seized from Austria or returned to Mamma Italia with the 1919 Treaty of Versailles.

BASICS The **APT** provides oodles of helpful info on Trento and Monte Bondone. *Via Alfieri 4, tel. 0461/983880. From train station, walk through Piazza Dante and turn right on Via Alfieri. Open Sept.–June, weekdays 9–noon and 3–6, Sat. 9–noon; July and Aug., Mon.–Sat. 9–noon and 3–6, Sun. 9–noon.*

For a map of the Trentino province and a list of rifugi, head for **APT Trentino**. *Corso III Novembre 132, tel. 0461/980000. From behind Piazza Duomo, walk up Via San Vigilio until it turns into Corso III Novembre. Open Mon.–Sat. 8:30–12:30 and 2:30–6.*

Don't change money at the booth in the train station; their rates make a pound of flesh and a pint of blood sound reasonable. Right next to APT Trentino is the **Cassa di Risparmio di Trento e Rovereto** (Corso III Novembre 130, tel. 0461/915700; open weekdays 8:20–1:20 and 2:35–3:35), which has good rates and a 3% commission. The **SIP phone office** (Via Belenzani 30; open Mon.–Sat. 8:30–7:30, Sun. 8–2) sits across from the duomo in a frescoed building. The **post office** (Piazza Vittoria 16–20, tel. 0461/983106; open weekdays 8:10–7:40, Sat. 8:10–1) is north of Piazza Duomo.

COMING AND GOING The **Stazione di Trento** (Piazza Dante, tel. 0461/234545) sends trains to Verona (hourly, 1 hr, L8000), Bolzano (hourly, 40 min, L4500), Venice (5 daily, 1½ hrs, L12,900), and Bassano del Grappa (4 daily, 2 hrs, L7500). Luggage storage is L1500 per piece per day. To the right of the train station, the **bus station** (Via Pozzo 6, tel. 0461/983627) sends buses to every itsy-bitsy mountain town. **Atesina** (tel. 0461/821000) runs hourly buses to Riva del Garda (1½ hrs, L5000) and Paneveggio (3 hrs, L8800).

Ferrovia Trento–Malè (Via Secondo da Trento 7, tel. 0461/822725) runs buses and electric trains to strategic mountain destinations. Trains go to Malè (4 daily, 1 hr, L5800) and buses to Molveno (6 daily, 1½ hrs, L5000). To reach the station from Stazione di Trento, turn left onto Via Dogana, veer left around the curve to Via Segantini, and walk straight ahead; the station is at the end of the street and to the left.

GETTING AROUND The muddy Adige River gurgles its way south a few blocks west of Trento's center, the Piazza Duomo. From the train station, turn right onto Via A. Pozzo; it becomes Via Orfane and then Via Cavour before it reaches the duomo. Turn left on Via Garibaldi, north of the duomo, and you'll find yourself on Via San Vigilio, the busy shopping street that changes its name many times as it leads northeast of the center. Local **buses** (L1000) all pass in front of the train station. If you want to **bike** around, ask at the tourist office. They will sometimes loan out bikes for free for a few hours, if you leave your passport and a small deposit.

WHERE TO SLEEP Trento is short on budget hotels; those listed below are *it*, and they all cost at least L80,000 for doubles. The cheapest deals are at the hostels or the campgrounds on Monte Bondone (*see* Near Trento, *below*).

Al Cavallino Bianco. The coolest thing about this hotel is the living room: The skylight, white picnic tables, and green-and-brown nature murals are straight out of a YMCA circa 1976. The rooms have passable though undependable showers and sinks, but most have no toilet. Doubles cost L80,000. *Via Cavour 29, tel. 0461/231542. From train station, turn right on Via Pozzo, which becomes Via Cavour. 24 rooms. Curfew 11:30 PM. AE, MC, V.*

Hotel Venezia. All of the dark, cramped rooms here are clean, but the mattresses are beyond lumpy. Doubles in the main building (L90,000; some with views of the duomo) all include bath, but in the annex you can get a double without (L80,000). *Piazza Duomo 45, tel. 0461/234114. From train station, turn right on Via Pozzo and left at Piazza Duomo. 48 rooms, 20 with bath. MC, V.*

➤ **HOSTELS • Ostello Città di Rovereto.** This spotless hostel is worth the 15-minute train ride south on the Verona line (last train 11:50 PM). It's run by a multilingual family that bends over backward to accommodate you. Rooms have two to six beds and bath, and a few have a terrace. Good, nourishing meals are served at lunch and dinner (L13,000 each), and they'll whip up a veggie specialty if you ask. Beds are L20,000, including breakfast. *Viale delle Scuole 16, Rovereto, tel. 0464/433707. From Rovereto train station, cross street through*

Piazza Corsi and take street on your right that starts with stairs; continue past Via Dante and turn left on Viale delle Scuole. 90 beds. Curfew 11:30 PM, lockout 9:30–5:30.

Ostello Giovane Europa. This is your basic hostel with large, institutional rooms, mostly doubles or quads with bath. Beds cost L22,000, including a meager breakfast. *Via Manzoni 17, tel. 0461/234567. From train station, turn left on Via Dogana, right on Via Romagnosi, and left on Via Manzoni. 140 beds. Lockout 9–5:30. Reception open 7:15–9 and 5:30–midnight.*

FOOD Schnitzel and Strudel sneak onto Trento's menus, but it's best to stick with the Italian dishes; highly recommended is *strangolapreti* (strangle the priests), made with spinach gnocchi, Gorgonzola, tomatoes, and basil. The busiest place for lunch, and home of the best salad bar for miles, is **Ristorante Al Giulia** (Via Gazzoletti 15, tel. 0461/984752), in an alley behind Piazza Dante's Banco di Roma. Thursday is the big **market** day in the area behind the duomo.

La Cantinota. The piano bar is cheesy, but the food is delicious and innovative. Risotto with apples and chardonnay for two people is L16,000. *Secondi* (second courses), costing L13,000–L25,000, include veal scaloppine with lemon, asparagus, whiskey, and much, much more. *Via San Marco 22, tel. 0461/238561. From train station, go right on Via Pozzo and left on Via Roma, which turns into Via San Marco. Open Fri.–Wed. 10–4 and 6–midnight.*

Ristorante Locale Tipico Antica Trattoria Due Mori. Gnocchi, polenta, and all sorts of risotto (L10,000–L14,000) are whipped up in this place. It's a bit more expensive than a pizzeria, but don't let that stop you—the polenta with porcini and cheese (L12,000) is *da morire* (to die for). *Via San Marco 11, tel. 0461/984251. Catercorner from La Cantinota (see above). Open Tues.–Sun. noon–2:30 and 7–10:30.*

Trattoria al Volt. The cheapest full meals in Trento are hidden away in this hole-in-the-wall, where the portions are generous and made with love. Typical *primi* (first courses) include tagliatelle *al pomodoro* (with tomato sauce; L5500). Secondi, like roasted chicken, are a mere L7500. *Via Santa Croce 16, tel. 0461/983776. From Piazza Duomo, turn right on Via Garibaldi and follow it to Via Santa Croce. Open Mon.–Sat. noon–2 and 7–9:30. Closed 2 weeks in Aug.*

WORTH SEEING The **duomo**, site of most of the Council of Trent meetings, is a dark cathedral made gloomier by the ridiculously huge *baldachin* (ornate canopy) on the altar. Under the cathedral are the remains of the **Basilica Paleocristiana**, a musty pre-Christian basilica turned into a crypt for bishops. *Piazza Duomo. Open daily 6:45–1:15 and 2:30–8. Basilica admission: L1500. Open Mon.–Sat. 10–noon and 2:30–6.*

Another meeting place for the Council of Trent was the **Castello di Buonconsiglio**, which is made up of two buildings: the **Castelvecchio**, a 14th-century hunk of stone renovated in the 15th century to give it that trendy Venetian-Gothic look, and the **Magno Palazzo**, a 16th-century Renaissance palace. The result is a huge maze in which you're sure to get lost. The real reason to visit (and pay the L12,000 admission) is to see the **Aquila Tower**, which houses the wonderful Gothic fresco *Cycle of the Months*, detailing everyday life for both the plebes and the aristocrats. Not surprisingly, life is all work for the peasants and all play for the lords—they're even having a snowball fight. Off the elaborate courtyard are the cells where Irredentist (*see box*, Italia Irredenta, *above*) Cesare Battisti and company were jailed. Bat-

The Council of Trent

The Council of Trent (1545–1563) marked the beginning of the Counter Reformation and the reestablishment of the Vatican's control, especially in Italy, after Luther's reforms. It was by far one of the most important events ever to take place in Trentino-Alto Adige, not to mention the entire continent, as it helped to prevent Italy's northern regions from adopting the "radical" doctrines of European countries to the north.

A fresco in the cathedral tells the legend of San Giuliano Ospitaliere, a sort of tragic cross between Oedipus and Othello: After hearing a prophecy that he would kill his parents, Giuliano left his home for Spain, where he married. His parents searched for him and finally arrived at his house, where his wife let them sleep in her bed while she went to church. Giuliano, returning to see two bodies in his bed, assumed his wife was fooling around and stabbed the two forms through the sheets.

tisti is deified in the small **Museo del Risorgimento**, next to the castle ticket office. *Via Bernardo Clesio 5, tel. 0461/ 233770. From train station, turn right on Via Pozzo and left on Via Roma; follow it to end and turn left on Via B. Clesio. Admission: L12,000, free 1st and 3rd Sun. of the month. Open Apr.–Sept., Tues.–Sun. 9–noon and 2–5:30; Oct.– Mar., Tues.–Sun. 9–noon and 2–5.*

NEAR TRENTO

Buses run from Trento to practically everywhere; even places closer to Bolzano are more easily reached by a bus from Trento. Monte Bondone is a good day or overnight trip, but the Brenta mountain range and the Parco Naturale Paneveggio all require at least two days. A number of rifugi and scattered campgrounds make finding a place to sleep no problem.

MONTE BONDONE Trento's very own overgrown pet rock, Monte Bondone, hovers over the Adige River. It rates as the locals' preferred site for picnics, ski trips, and afternoon strolls. Three towns are carved into the side of Monte Bondone: Sardagna, Vaneze, and Vason.

➢ **SARDAGNA** • Sardagna is the closest town to ground level with a spectacular view of the mountain above it—a tiny, peaceful settlement where the streets really have no names. Try the signposted bed-and-breakfast **Depedri Luciano** (tel. 0461/235438), which charges L33,000 per person and L16,000 for meals. A spectacular **funicular** (tel. 0461/232154) travels to Sardagna every 15–30 minutes (20 min, L1000) from Trento. To reach the funicular from the train station, turn right on Via Pozzo, right on Cavalcavia San Lorenzo, and left on Lung'Adige Monte Grappa. Buses from Trento's station also travel up Monte Bondone; they'll stop in Sardagna if you ask, but they won't stop for passengers on the way back down.

➢ **VANEZE** • Vaneze is larger than Sardagna, but it offers little of interest except the **tourist office** (across from bus stop, tel. 0461/947128), which gives out info on trails and ski conditions. To reach Vaneze, hop on the bus (45 min, L4000) at the station in Trento or pick up Trail 645 from the main road near the funicular stop in Sardagna; it's a two-hour hike. The cheapest place to sleep is **Albergo Vaneze** (tel. 0461/947113), with doubles with bath for L65,000. From Vaneze it's an easy two-hour hike on Trail 607 to **Malga Mezzavia** (tel. 0461/948178), a year-round campground with all the trimmings: showers, a restaurant, laundry, and greenery. Sites cost L5000 per person and L7000 per tent.

➢ **VASON** • The ski fun starts in Vason; maps of all the *piste* (ski runs) are available from **Sport Nicolussi** (tel. 0461/948163), which rents skis and boots for L35,000 a day and mountain bikes for L12,000 an hour or L35,000 a day. Eat at **Pizzeria/Pasticceria Alaska** (Via Bondone 15, tel. 0461/948061) and sleep at **Al Caminetto** (Via Bondone 15, tel. 0461/948122), with doubles for L74,000. No trails run from Vaneze to Vason, but you can walk the 5 kilometers along the main road, catch the bus, or take the **Telecabina Vaneze–Vason** (tel. 0461/ 947451) for L4000 in summer and winter. If you're coming straight from Trento, buses make the one-hour, L4000 trip.

If you're still raring to go, make the easy, one-hour hike on Trail 607 to **Rifugio Tambosi** at Viote (Viote 105, tel. 0461/948162), which serves meals but has only six beds—be sure to reserve ahead. Trail 607 continues to the Tre Cime (Three Peaks), a five-hour climb of medium difficulty; the hike is well worth it for the spectacular views atop each peak. Also at Viote is the **Alpine Botanic Garden** (tel. 0461/948050; closed Oct.–May). For a small donation, you can walk around its bright flowers and medicinal herbs.

MOLVENO All the signs in German may make you nervous that a big, fat tourist bus might descend upon the town any minute, but don't let that stop you from enjoying Molveno's beautiful location between Lago di Molveno and the Brenta Dolomites. The town really is peaceful and a good base for further hiking or skiing. The **APT** (Piazza Marconi 7, tel. 0461/586924) doesn't have much hiking info, but the folks there can help you find a room in one of the atrociously expensive Molveno hotels. Buses make the trip to Molveno from Trento five times a day (1 hr 45 min, L5000).

➤ **WHERE TO SLEEP AND EAT** • Despite its misleading name, **Gani Camping** (Via Lungolago, just before the campgrounds, tel. 0461/586169) is a hotel with large, bland rooms for L80,000 a double. RVs go to **Camping Spiagga Lago di Molveno** (Via Lungolago 27, tel. 0461/586978) to breed and die. In July, August, and December–March the cost for campers is a whopping L10,000 per person and L15,000 per tent; prices go down exponentially other times of year.

➤ **OUTDOOR ACTIVITIES** • The **Dolomiti di Brenta** are jagged, stark peaks that look— and are—forbidding. Hiking on their trails sometimes entails climbing metal ladders placed on rock (as prominently featured in Sylvester Stallone's *Cliffhanger*, in which the Dolomites stood in for the Rockies); you'll need a lot of Alpine know-how (as well as climbing equipment) to get through. The trails listed below are hikable, though often steep, and they're all mapped out on the "Kompass Wanderkarte" (L8000), available in bookstores and some visitor centers. To start off, take the funicular from Molveno to Pradel, where you catch Trail 12 and take it up to Trail 340, which leads to **Rifugio Croz dell'Altissimo** (tel. 0461/586191)— it's an easy, one-hour hike, but the rifugio is often full (L26,000 per person). From the rifugio, you have a choice: Trail 319 is more challenging, taking two and a half hours to reach the **Rifugio Selvata** (they have no phone, but the funicular operators can radio them). The easier, less scenic Trail 340 to Selvata only takes an hour. From Selvata, take the moderate 319 for three hours to **Rifugio Tosa** (tel. 0461/948115), which charges L16,000 per person. To head back to Molveno, turn around from here. Otherwise, climb moderate Trail 318 for a one and a half-hour hike to **Rifugio Brentei** (tel. 0465/41244), where you can catch Trail 323 to Trail 391 for a moderate, two and a half-hour hike to **Rifugio Vallesinella** (tel. 0465/42883). From Vallesinella, hitch or walk the 7 kilometers on Trail 391 to **Madonna di Campiglio**, the ritzy resort town where you can take one of three daily buses to Trento via Tione (2 hrs, L8000).

If you'd rather not hoof it, hire a bike for L30,000 a day from **Sala Giochi** (Via Lungolago 17) and ride down Via Lungolago past the campgrounds to the other end of the lake. In winter, skiers pack this area; the best slopes are on **Monte Paganella**, which is accessible by chairlift from Andalo, a stop on the Trento–Molveno line. Rent skis at the campground or inquire at the **Skipass Paganella-Brenta** office (Via Paganella, Andalo, tel. 0461/585869).

PARCO NATURALE PANEVEGGIO The Paneveggio Natural Park, three hours northeast of Trento, gallops over 15,703 hectares of diverse land, ranging from bushy woods to lakes and flowery meadows. You can stop in Paneveggio's **visitor center** (S.S. Passo di Rolle, tel. 0462/56283), or head straight to **San Martino di Castrozza**, which is more scenic than Paneveggio and has tons of lodging. The **APT** (tel. 0439/768867) in San Martino is impossible to miss as you get off the bus. **Hotel Suiss** (Via Dolomiti 1, tel. 0439/68087) has doubles for L55,000–L65,000. **Fratazza** (tel. 0439/68170) and **Villa Marina** (tel. 0439/68166) offer the same deal, just down the street. From San Martino, take Trail 702–24 up, up, and away; it hits **Rifugio Pedrotti alla Rosetta** (tel. 0439/68308) after two to three hours. Unless you're an experienced climber, you'll have to go back the way you came.

Before hiking in Paneveggio Natural Park, register with the visitor center so that someone knows to look for you if you get hurt, stuck, or attacked by a yak.

➤ **COMING AND GOING** • Buses run from Trento to Cavalese, where you change to the Paneveggio–San Martino bus. Two buses per day run to Paneveggio from Bolzano via Predazzo (2 hrs 40 min, L12,000). In addition, six buses run from Trento to Cavalese daily (70 min). From there you have four chances a day to catch a bus from Cavalese to Paneveggio (70 min) or San Martino (2¼ hrs). The whole Trento–Paneveggio trip costs L10,500.

Bolzano

If you travel 40 minutes northeast of Trento to Alto Adige's major town, Bolzano, you might suddenly feel like you've crossed into Austria without noticing the border station. Sure, the map *says* it's Italy, but after walking through the centuries-old market at Piazza Erbe (Obstplatz) filled with suspiciously Teutonic-looking locals, you might not be so sure. Bolzano was part of Austria for most of its history and is proud of its roots; the language of choice is German, and the food, unfortunately, is not Italian. You'll find few historic sights in Bolzano, but it's an attractive town with welcoming citizens and a happening street market scene. German and Austrian tourists, who see Bolzano as a little piece of home, crowd the city in summer and winter, and all sorts of visitors use it as a base for visiting the spectacular mountain ranges in the nearby **Val Isarco**, near Bressanone (*see* Near Bolzano, *below*).

BASICS Bolzano's **APT** (Piazza Walther 8, tel. 0471/975656; open weekdays 8:30–6, Sat. 9–12:30) gives out info on accommodations and local hikes. Walk toward the duomo on Via Posta from Piazza Walther to reach the Alto Adige **APT** (Piazza Parrocchia 11, tel. 0471/993808; open weekdays 9–noon and 2–5:30). The office has an **Alpine desk**, where English speakers will give you explicit info on hiking, skiing, climbing, and rifugi.

The convenient **Banco Nazionale del Lavoro** (Piazza Walther 10, tel. 0471/999511; open weekdays 8:20–1:20 and 3–4:30) has good rates but charges a L2200 commission. The **SIP phone office** (Piazza Domenicani 19, tel. 0471/314111; open daily 8–8) and the **post office** (Piazza Domenicani 3, tel. 0471/978679; open Mon.–Sat. 9–noon and 3–6) are next door to each other behind the duomo.

COMING AND GOING The **train station** (Piazza Stazione, tel. 0471/974292) serves Trento (hourly, 40 min, L5000), Bressanone (hourly, 30 min, L3600), Verona (hourly, 2 hrs, L13,200), Merano (every 30 min, 30 min, L3500), and Milano (twice daily, 3½ hrs, L21,500). From the station, walk up Viale Stazione and make your first left to reach the **bus station** (Via Perathoner 4). **SAD** buses (tel. 0471/971259) run everywhere, including Merano (every 30 min, 40 min, L4500) and Trento (hourly, 45 min, L5000).

GETTING AROUND Bolzano's center, Piazza Walther, is 100 meters from the train station up Viale Stazione. From Piazza Walther, a left on Via Posta (near the duomo) takes you to Via Goethe, where another right will get you to the oh-so-quaint market at Piazza Erbe. Much of Bolzano's quotidian life goes on across the Talvera River, which runs southwest of the city. Local **buses** run for L1200 a go; buy tickets at the bus station on Via Perathoner.

There are several *funivia* (cable cars) just outside Bolzano that can take you (and your bike) up into the mountains for L7000–L35,000 each way, depending on how far you go. To reach **Funivia del Colle** (Via Campiglio, tel. 0471/978545) or **Funivia del Renon** (tel. 0471/978479), turn right from in front of the train station. *See* Outdoor Activities, *below* for information on hikes that lead from the funivia.

WHERE TO SLEEP The Bolzano APT has an up-to-date list of places and prices, but it's wise to make reservations in advance, especially in high season. The **Unterhuber Hubert** (Via Garibaldi 6, tel. 0471/973439), half a block from the train station, is the cheapest place to sleep (L56,000), but has only four ugly doubles. At **Camping Moosbauer** (Via San Maurizio 30, tel. 0471/918482), camping will cost you L7500 per person and L6000 per tent. The place is more like an outdoor hotel than the great outdoors, but even the swarms of Winnebagos can't monopolize the extensive facilities. Take Bus 10A or 10B from the station, and tell the driver you're going to the *campeggio* (campground).

Agriturismo Kandlerhof. It's a sweaty uphill hike to this small house—you're doomed if you have a heavy backpack. But those who make the trek will be amply rewarded by this cozy, rustic place with an amazing view of the city. Doubles are L70,000–L80,000. If it's full, try the similar **Agriturismo Maddalena Weinstube** (Via Santa Maddalena di Sotto 22, tel. 0471/974380), a short ways down the hill, which has doubles for L60,000, breakfast included. *Via Santa Maddalena di Sotto 30, tel. 0471/973033. From train station, turn right on Via Renon; make a left on Via Brennero, a right onto alleylike Santa Maddalena di Sotto. 6 rooms, all with bath.*

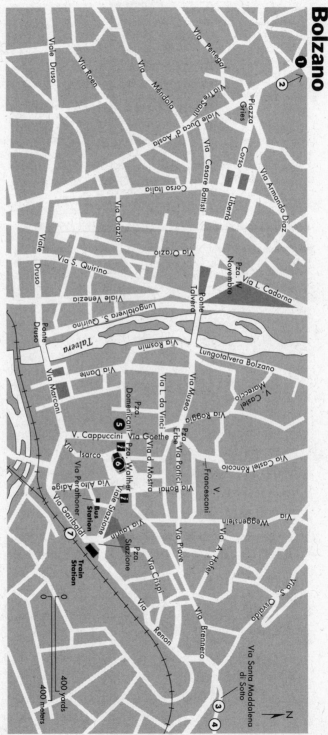

Bolzano

Sights ●
Chiesa dei
Dominicani, **5**
Chiesa Parrocchiale
di Gries, **1**
Duomo, **6**

Lodging ○
Agriturismo
Kandlerhof, **4**
Agriturismo
Maddalena
Weinstube, **3**

Camping
Moosbauer, **2**
Unterhuber
Hubert, **7**

400 yards
400 meters

85

FOOD Cruise Piazza Erbe's daily markets for produce stands, cheese stalls, honey and nut tables, or metal carts with sizzling Wurstel for L4000. Bolzano's specialty is *Knödel*, stick-to-your-ribs dumplings served in a creamy onion sauce. You can eat elbow to elbow with the locals at the cheap **Zum Bogen Weinstube** (Via Dr. Streiter 31, tel. 0471/978003; closed Sun.). From Piazza Erbe, turn left on Via Goethe and right on Via Streiter.

Birreria Forsterbrän. The outdoor patio is a prime people-watching spot, and the ravioli with radicchio, cheese, and butter (L8000) is a vegetarian's dream. *Via Goethe 6, tel. 0471/977243. From Piazza Walther, walk up Via della Mostra and turn right on Via Goethe. Open Mon.–Sat. 9 AM–midnight; dinner served 7–11.*

Cavallino Bianco. The atmosphere is on the German side at this dark beer hall; if you speak German, you're in like Flynn. Primi (L6000–L7000) are mostly Italian pasta affairs, but Wiener schnitzel dominates the secondi menu (L7500–L18,000). *Via Bottai 6, tel. 0471/973267. From Piazza Erbe, go down Via Portici and left on Via Bottai. Open Mon.–Sat. 11–3 and 6:30–9:30.*

WORTH SEEING Only the exterior of Bolzano's **duomo** (Piazza Parrocchia; open weekdays 9:30–6, Sat. 9:30–noon) is worth a look; the roof and tower are adorned with what the tourist brochure describes (accurately for once) as "stone embroidery." In the **Chiesa dei Domenicani** on Piazza Domenicani, the **Capella di San Giovanni** (Chapel of St. John) features astounding frescoes: *The Martyrdom of St. Matthew* shows the poor guy being sliced open like a hot sausage by a blue-faced heathen. Across the river is the **Chiesa Parrocchiale di Gries** (Via Martin Knoller). Walk up the stairs through a junkyard of tombstones to the little 9th-century Romanesque church, which features the painted woodwork of Michael Pacher. *The Coronation of Mary* is so intricately carved it looks like it's moving. It's worth the 20-minute walk, especially if you continue your *passeggiata* (stroll) up the hill behind the church for a picnic.

Bolzano locals celebrate the coming of spring and its Alpine flowers by hosting a series of jazz concerts in late April and early May; many are free and most are outdoors.

OUTDOOR ACTIVITIES A few well-marked, well-touristed passeggiate start in Bolzano's center. The nicest, the **Gucina**, starts above the Chiesa Parrocchiale di Gries and takes you 2½ kilometers uphill on a sunny path with an incredible view of the Dolomites. A hearty three-hour hike starts from the end of the **Funivia del Colle** (*see* Getting Around, *above*). Take the funicular to the top (L7000 round-trip) and then Trail 1; at the crucifix on the rock (after Schneidemeisen, about 45 minutes), walk straight down and hang a left at the rock with the black arrow to reach a photogenic view of the Dolomites. Walk back up to Trail 1, which intersects Trail 4 (or E5), to return to the funicular.

NEAR BOLZANO

BRESSANONE Commonly known by its German name Brixen, Bressanone is located in the region north of Bolzano, where the terrain just gets greener and more mountainous. In the heart of the Val d'Isarco, Bressanone was relatively isolated and protected from political domination by either Italy or Tyrol; for a thousand years it was ruled by its own set of prince-bishops. Today the town is more peaceful and subdued than Bolzano—a tidy, tiny place loaded with pastel buildings, shady porticoes, and Alpine hotels. Nearby Monte Plose isn't as imposing as the mountains near Trento or Merano but attracts fewer hikers in summer and has great skiing in winter. Head to the **tourist office** (Viale Stazione 9, tel. 0472/36401; open weekdays 8:30–12:30 and 2:30–6, Sat. 9–12:30), where a very kind staff will give you maps.

Bressanone's **duomo** (Piazza Duomo; open daily 8–noon and 3–6) is modeled after the one in Bolzano, with a cavernous interior covered in golden, baroque decor. The star of the show is a set of late-Gothic frescoes in the cloisters, with scenes of bodies falling into hell, grave diggers, monsters, and a truckload of bishops. Bressanone's other cultural showstoppers are the amber-scented rooms of the **Palazzo Vescovile**. The Gothic art collection on the first floor is the highlight, with painted-wood sculptures of stiff and bloody Christs, gnomelike bishops, and smiling Madonnas. To the left of the entrance, take a gander at the *presepi*, an extensive collection of tiny, 3-D Bible scenes. *Piazza Palazzo Vescovile 2, tel. 0472/30505. Admission: L5000. Museum and presepi open Mar. 15– Oct., Mon.–Sat. 10–5; presepi also open Dec. 15–Feb. 10, Mon.–Sat. 2–5.*

One of the best frescoes in Bressanone's duomo depicts Adam and Eve not yet expelled from Eden, surrounded by monstrous, multicolored incubi—each carrying a different garden tool.

➤ **COMING AND GOING** • Bressanone's **train station** (Piazza Stazione, tel. 0472/33368) has service to Bolzano (hourly, 30 min, L3600). The station is south of the center; walk for 15 minutes up Via Stazione to the tourist office. **SAD buses** (tel. 0471/971259 in Bolzano) depart from in front of the train station; you can buy tickets on board. They run to Bolzano (hourly, 50 min, L4800) and Sant'Andrea three times daily, except during ski season, when they run every half hour (20 min, L3000).

➤ **WHERE TO SLEEP AND EAT** • The **Albergo Cremona** (Via Vittorio Veneto 26, tel. 0472/35602) has large doubles with feather beds for L70,000; breakfast included; walk up Viale Mozart from the station and turn right on Via Vittorio Veneto. **Youth Hostel Gatscherhof** (San Leonardo 112, tel. 0472/35227) offers beds for L25,000, including breakfast. Take the bus to nearby Sant'Andrea and call for someone to pick you up. Under the porticoes of Bressanone's center lie scores of overpriced hotel-restaurants. One exception is the inexpensive **Fink Arcada** (Via Portici Minori 4, tel. 0472/834883), where the gulash is *real* tasty.

➤ **OUTDOOR ACTIVITIES** • **Skiing** is the most popular sport on Monte Plose. During ski season, a bus runs every half hour from the Bressanone station to the Sant'Andrea **funicular** (tel. 0472/30595), which takes you to a slew of slopes. Inside the station, you can rent skis and boots for about L20,000 per day or L75,000 per week at **Skiservice Erwin Stricker** (tel. 0472/850077) or buy ski passes at **Nuova Plose SPA** (tel. 0472/30595).

The best **hike** is the Alta Via 2, a long footpath that winds up and down Monte Plose. It's not too strenuous and provides great photo opportunities of the valley. Take the bus from Bressanone to Sant'Andrea and catch the funicular to Valcroce (L4500 each way); the trail runs past the funicular stop. About a three-hour hike uphill is **Rifugio Plose** (tel. 0472/51333); from here it's a three-hour trek along Trail 6 to **Rifugio Rossalm**, where you can catch Trail 17 back to the funicular.

Merano

A half-hour train ride west of Bolzano is Merano, where the streets are padded with glitzy boutiques. At the turn of the century, Merano attracted a handful of royals and movie-star glitterati, who left in their wake some good art nouveau architecture. The glamour is now gone, but the air of money remains: The *centro storico* (historic center) is pleasant, with a classy main boulevard, **Corso Libertà**, and most visitors still come for the **Centro Terme** spa (Via Piave 9, tel. 0473/33236), where a dip will run you L15,000. Some of the town's actual "attractions" disappoint, such as the cheesy **Castello Principesio**—it's the only thing that pretends to be ancient. But don't miss the highly original **La Donna nel Tempo** (Via Portici 68, tel. 0473/231216; open weekdays 3–7, Sat. 9:30–noon), a collection of women's fashion over the past 100 years, presented with a sense of humor you don't find in your average museum. The main reason to come to Merano however, is to use the town as a base for excursions into the small Parco Nazionale di Tessa nearby and the much larger Parco Nazionale dello Stelvio to the west (*see Near Merano, below*). The **Club Alpino Italiano** (Corso Libertà 188, tel. 0473/48944; open weekdays 6:30 PM–8:30 PM) will help you plan your hikes.

COMING AND GOING Trains from Merano's **train station** (Piazza Stazione, tel. 0473/47500) head only to Bolzano (hourly, 30 min, L3500). **Buses**, which leave from the front of the train station, are much more comprehensive. The **SAD** window in the train station (tel. 0473/221702) sells bus tickets to Naturno (hourly, 30 min, L2600), Silandro (hourly, 1 hr, L4500), and Passo Stelvio (4 daily, 2 hrs, L12,600). To the right of the station, Via Europa leads to Piazza Mazzini, where the main drag, Corso Libertà, slices through town. Take **ACT** Bus 3 (L1000) to the center or make the 15-minute walk.

WHERE TO SLEEP AND EAT The coolest places to sleep in Merano are pensions and *garni* (rooms in private homes). Both are cheap, but usually require a two-night minimum stay. **Garni Domus Mea** (Via Piave 8, across river from Piazza Teatro, tel. 0473/236777) is your best bet: The rooms (doubles L70,000) are spacious, the bathrooms clean, and the owner can recommend a good place to eat. **Villa Pax** (Via Leichter 3, tel. 0473/236290) suffers from mushy mattresses but has cooking facilities and airy rooms (about L60,000 per double). From Corso Libertà, walk east into Piazza di Rena and cross Ponte Posta, turn left on Via Cavour, right on Via Dante, and left on Via Leichter (about a 15-minute walk). Your cheapest option is setting up your tent among the RVs at **Camping Merau** (Via Piave 20, tel. 0473/31249; closed Nov.–Mar.) for L8000. It's near the racetrack past Garni Domus Mea on Via Piave.

Pizzeria Conca d'Oro (Corso Libertà 54, tel. 0473/30308; closed Thurs.) serves up yummy pizza (L6000–L10,000) on a shady outdoor patio. **Sportplatz-Weinstube** (Via Piave 50, tel. 0473/233443) overcomes its sporty name with heavenly pasta and the best homemade tiramisù north of Trento; a meal goes for about L15,000.

NEAR MERANO

PARCO NAZIONALE DELLO STELVIO The huge, mountainous Stelvio National Park lumbers through both Trentino and Alto Adige; it's so big that it has 10 visitor information offices. The park's vibrant green valleys nurture small Alpine villages, while the serrated **Ortles Mountains**, the park's main range, loom authoritatively in the distance. Skiing lasts well into the summer, and many hikes will take you through the snow—bring warm clothes. The park's wildlife still thrives, especially in Val Zebrù near Bormio, where deer, elk, chamoix, and ibex roam in remarkable numbers.

Basically, the park starts in the Val Venosta, a valley two hours east of Merano and home to an information office in the town of Silandro. The park swoops south to the Val Martello, where the Ortles mountains start, and runs to Malè in the province of Trentino. Though each region offers great hiking and communing with nature, it's best to pick one region and stay there, since distances can be great, and buses don't connect the Trentino and Alto Adige sections.

You can begin your adventure in the main town of Silandro, where you should stop by the **tourist office** (Via dei Cappuccini 2, tel. 0473/70443) for maps and accommodation listings. If you don't want to sleep in a rifugio, the office can make reservations for you at pensions throughout the park. Silandro also offers the park's only supermarket, **Standa** (open daily 9–1 and 3–7), right at the bus stop. Ask the tourist office for trail maps to the nearby rifugi **Corsi** (tel. 0473/82421) and **Casati** (0473/84301) or hike to **Rifugio Manzoni** (tel. 0473/82430) by following Trail 32 north of town for three hours, with views of all three of the park's valleys along the way. From Silandro, follow Val di Martello west by bus, passing Castello Montani, the largest of the park's castles, and you'll arrive at **Paradiso del Cevedale**, a base for exploring Monte Cevedale. If you venture farther into the park, there is also a tourist office in **Bormio** (Via Monte Braulio 56, tel. 0342/905151).

➤ **COMING AND GOING** • From Merano, take a bus to Silandro (hourly, 1 hr, L5000) or Passo dello Stelvio (July–Oct., 4 daily; 2 hrs, L10,500), near the Ortles. The electric train **Ferrovia Trento–Malè** (tel. 0461/822725) runs between Malè and Trento four times daily (1 hr 10 min, L6000). Buses run between the villages in the province of Bolzano regularly; check with the park visitor office in Silandro for a bus schedule and current prices. You can also try your luck hitching if you're in a group; passing cars often take pity on pedestrians, knowing how difficult it is to get around the park.

PARCO NAZIONALE DI TESSA The grassy, flowery Tessa park is practically in Merano's backyard, making it more accessible to panting hiker wanna-bes in summer than Stelvio. The Tessa range for which the park is named is a series of baby mountains with grassy meadows. The park's visitor center is in **Naturno** (tel. 0473/74029), where the bus lets you off. Buses from Merano's station (30 min, L3000) run here hourly.

The main trail through the park is the **Meraner Höhonweg** (Trail 24), which has a high road and a low road. The low one runs through Naturno and is speckled with overpriced hotels and restaurants that prey on exhausted hikers. The high road is steeper, less traveled, and has a few three- to six-hour stretches between rifugi. Several steeper trails cut through the circle made by Trail 24; they're less crowded and just as scenic, often taking you well above the snow line. Follow the signs for rifugi **Schnalsburg** (tel. 0473/89145) or **Panorama** (tel. 0473/85727). **Rifugio Stettiner** is the last rifugio at this altitude; after this the trails follow some extremely tricky ledges above 1000-foot drops, and the temperature is apt to drop suddenly when the wind changes course—be prepared.

Friuli-Venezia Giulia

Friuli-Venezia Giulia is one of those Let's-Make-a-Deal Italian states created when Europe was recarved after World War II, combining relatively poor, agricultural Friuli and beachy, beautiful Venezia Giulia. Until the early 16th century when Austria began its move into modern-day Friuli, most of the region owed allegiance to Venice, and before that to the former Roman city Aquileia; the area continued to change hands up until 1947. Like Alto Adige, the result is that most of Friuli-Venezia Guilia hardly even seems "Italian"; in Trieste, the region's largest city, you may have a hard time figuring out whether you're in Austria, Slovenia, or Italy. The continued fighting in Bosnia has brought a flood of refugees to the region, causing tension and frustration—particularly in Trieste, which is becoming ever more Slavic. The only part of the region that remains mostly Italian is the coast: Aquileia has a distinctly Roman flair that stems from its history as an outpost for the empire.

Udine

Don't believe the tourist brochure's tired spiel about Udine being a "little Venice." Udine's bourgeois feel, humid inland setting, and Venetian architecture are about as convincing as Venice, California. Let go of the illusion and take Udine for what it is: the pleasant, fairly untouristed capital of the Friuli region, where old-timers still speak the *friuliano* dialect, and the food is unlike any other in Italy. Udine is also home to some great art museums that include paintings by Venetian baroque master, Giambattista Tiepolo.

BASICS The **APT** (Piazza 1 Maggio 7, tel. 0432/295972; open Mon.–Sat. 9–1 and 3–6) gives out a great city map, but the abrupt staff won't field questions with any enthusiasm.

COMING AND GOING Udine's **train station** (Viale Europa Unità, tel. 0432/503656) has trains to Venice (hourly, 2 hrs, L12,000), Cividale del Friuli (hourly, 30 min, L3400), and Trieste (hourly, 1½ hrs, L7600). Luggage storage is open 7:30 AM–10:30 PM. Across the street is the **bus station** (tel. 0432/506941), from which **SAITA** (tel. 0432/208742) and **Autolinee Triestine** (tel. 0432/602211) buses run to Trieste (L7600), Cividale del Friuli (L2600), and Venice (L12,000).

GETTING AROUND The train and bus stations are on the edge of town on Viale Europa Unità. To the right as you exit the train station is Piazzale d'Annunzio, out of which runs Via Aquileia, which turns into Via Vittorio Veneto and terminates in the center at Piazza Libertà. From here you can cover everything on foot.

WHERE TO SLEEP Udine's one-star hotels tend to offer doubles only, but if you're alone you can get a nice room with bath for under L25,000 at **Pensione al Fari** (Via Melegnano 41, tel. 0432/520732). An older hotel in the city center, the quiet **Hotel al Vecchio Tram** (Via Brenari 32, tel. 0432/502516) offers clean doubles with antique beds for L50,000. To reach Vecchio Tram from the train station, turn left on Viale Europa Unità and right on Via de Rubeis, which eventually becomes Via Brenari. It's worth shelling out a little more money for **Piccolo Friuli** (Via Magrini 9, tel. 0432/507817), where doubles with dainty decor, hardwood floors, and absurdly large bathrooms go for L70,000. To get here, take Bus 5 from opposite the train station to Via Poscolle and turn right on Via Magrini.

FOOD Many of Udine's restaurants are charming places that bill themselves as home-style trattorias. Local dishes include "hearty peasant fare" like rabbit and turnips. Try *prosciutto crudo*, raw, thinly sliced ham from nearby San Daniele—locals claim it's the best prosciutto in the world.

Trattoria Al Giardino. The bewildered-looking owner whips up terrific pasta in this casual place, which is filled with the aroma of basil. The ravioli in nut sauce (L8000) is good, as are the omelets (L6000–L8000). *Via Paolo Sarpi 8, tel. 0432/604253. From Piazza Libertà, walk up Via Mercatovecchio and turn left onto Via P. Sarpi. Open Tues.–Sun. 10–3 and 7–10:30.*

Trattoria Bar Glanda. This student hangout has good, cheap food and a bleak, barlike atmosphere. The *piatti unici* (combination plates) are filling, and the many salads (L5000–L8000) will satisfy your craving for leafy greens. *Via Gemona 7, tel. 0432/507807. From Piazza Libertà, walk up Via Mercatovecchio to Riva Bartolinì to Via Gemona. Open Mon.–Sat. 8 AM–11 PM; meals served noon–3 and 6:30–9:30.*

WORTH SEEING **Piazza Libertà**, a Venetian-style square, features a rip-off of Venice's grander Palazzo Ducale. Behind the square (walk through the Palladian Arco Bollani and up the stairs) is the 16th-century castello, which houses the **Museo Civico** (tel. 0432/501824; open daily 9:30–12:30 and 3–6). The picture gallery is surprisingly good, with a painting by Carpaccio of Christ, whose blood shoots in vector-straight lines into the Holy Grail. The real draw is the Tiepolo painting *Consilium in Arena*, with swirling skies, tumbling cherubs, and voluptuous allegorical babes. It's absolutely worth the L3500 admission (L2000 for students). More of Tiepolo's works line a side of the nave in the **duomo**; the closed oratory contains more pieces—ask the sacristan if it's open yet. The largest collection of Tiepolo's works however, is in **Palazzo Arcivescovile** (Via Loxaria 14; open weekdays 9–noon), including his frescoes of scenes from the Old Testament. The Tiepoloed-out can get a dose of modernity at the **Museo d'Arte Moderna** (Piazzale Diacono 22, tel. 0432/29581). The collection is uneven but has flashes of greatness, and the knowledgeable staff is incredibly outgoing. Admission is L3200, L1600 for students, and the museum is open Tuesday–Saturday 9:30–12:30 and 3–6, Sunday 9:30–12:30.

NEAR UDINE

CIVIDALE DEL FRIULI It's a shame that most tourists never venture to Cividale—the town can easily be covered in a short day trip from Udine and has an interesting, distinctly medieval atmosphere. In the 6th century the Lombards captured Cividale, starting a building frenzy that Aquileia carried on when they conquered the town in the 8th century. Despite its history of foreign intrusion, Cividale is proudly Friuli, and friuliano remains the language of choice.

Most of the buildings left from the Lombards and Aquileians are so diminutive that they would seem cutesy if they weren't so perfectly constructed and preserved. The dark **duomo** is uninspiring, except for the stained-glass windows over the high altar, but off the right side of the nave, the **Museo Cristiano** (open daily 9:30–noon and 3–6) contains two Lombard masterpieces: Callisto's bas-relief baptistery and the cryptlike altar of Duke Ratchis carved in a wonderful, cartoonish style. The **Museo Archeologico** (Piazza Duomo, tel. 0432/731119; open Mon. 9–2, Tues.–Sun. 9–7) elaborates on the Lombard motif with a beautiful collection of ornate jewelry, tools, and religious artifacts. Admission is L4000. A trail of signs from the duomo leads through Cividale's alleys to the tiny **Tempietto Longobardo** (admission: L2500, L1500 students; closed Mon.), where the Lombards once huddled in worship. The view of the river and foliage outside this cozy temple perched over the Natisone River is spectacular. At the **tourist office** (Largo Boiani 4, tel. 0432/731398), get the key to the **Ipogeo Celtico** (Via d'Aquileia; open Tues.–Sat. 8–1 and 3:30–5:40), an eerie, possibly pre-Roman catacomb for Celtic military personnel.

➤ **COMING AND GOING** • **Trains** run to Cividale's station (Viale Libertà, tel. 0432/731032) from Udine every 45 minutes (30 min, L3400). **Buses** also run between the station next door (Viale Libertà, tel. 0432/731046) and Udine (hourly, 1 hr, L3000); buy tickets at the train station. From the stations, walk up Via Marconi and turn left on Borgo San Pietro

through a number of piazze. Turn right on Via Tomadini, and left on Largo Boiani, which ends
at the central Piazza Duomo (a 10-minute walk).

Aquileia

Before Venice was even a twinkle in anybody's eye, Aquileia was *the* Roman outpost of northern Italy (AD 400). Today, it's an unbelievably well-preserved Roman ghost town, with some of
the most impressive ruins in all of Italy. The **Basilica Patriarcale** (Piazza Capitolo; open daily
8:30–7:30) is inlaid with incredible, bright mosaic floors that look almost new because the
medieval covering wasn't removed until this century. As you enter the basilica, look for the
mosaic depicting the fight between a rooster and a turtle: It's thought to be an allegory for the
battle between good and evil, starring Christ as the rooster and the Antichrist as the turtle. In
the **Excavations Crypt** underneath the basilica, lobsters swim over peacocks while goats graze
nearby; the symbolism of the design stumps even scholars. Entrance to the basilica is free (it's
still a functioning church) and L2500 gets you into the crypts.

From the back of the basilica, a gravel road (look for the yellow sign) takes you to **Porto Flu-
viale**, the cypress-lined, fragment-studded road that ran along the river back when there was a
river. The shady walk ends at Via Gemina; a right turn leads to the **Museo Paleocristiano**
(Monastero, tel. 0431/91131), a dumpy but free barnful of worn mosaics and tombstones. The
Museo Archeologico (Via Roma 1, tel. 0431/91016; open daily 9–7) is more impressive, but
costs L6000 to enter. It features a huge display of gems and tiny bronzes of Priapus, a Roman
god who doesn't leave any doubts about his manhood.

COMING AND GOING To reach Aquileia, take a **Gradese bus** from Trieste (5 daily, 2 hrs,
L6000) or Udine (every 30 min, 1 hr 20 min, L4000) to Grado and then transfer to the
Aquileia-bound bus (every 30 min, 15 min, L2000). From Trieste, ferries also head to Grado
(1 hr, L8500) for a bus connection to Aquileia.

WHERE TO SLEEP AND EAT Aquileia itself may not have many budget lodgings to offer,
but you can always try the nearby beach town of Grado (*see below*), where there are more cheap
hotels than you can shake a stick at. Aquileia's best hotel is the **Aquila Nera** (Piazza Garibaldi
5, tel. 0431/91045), with friendly proprietors and clean L50,000 doubles. If it's full, consider
heading to **Corallo** (Via Beligna 3, tel. 0431/91065), which has doubles for L70,000. Buy food
at **Despar** (Via Giulia Augusta 17) and have a picnic at the **sepulchres** at the end of Via XXIV
Maggio, which connects Piazza Garibaldi with Via Giulia Augusta. The sunken tombs are surrounded by peaceful farms.

NEAR AQUILEIA

GRADO It may seem like a backpacking faux pax to visit a cheesy beach town, but there are
several reasons to head to Grado, a tiny resort on a peninsula stretching out into the Bay of Trieste. First of all, Grado is a good place to find affordable lodging while visiting Aquileia. Second, Grado's shallow, warm waters offer infinite frolicking possibilities, though they're
monopolized by resorts. Even Grado's historical center has something to offer: The **duomo** and
Chiesa di of Santa Maria date from the 6th century, when Grado was a powerful seaport. Buses
run to Grado every half hour from Aquileia (15 min, L2000) and Udine (45 min, L4000). You
can also take a ferry to Trieste (1 hr, L8500).

➤ **WHERE TO SLEEP AND EAT** • Despite its resort status, Grado has some affordable
one-star hotels. **Casa del Pellegrino** (Isola Barbana, tel. 0431/80453) has doubles with bath
for a mere L30,000, while **Hotel Desiree** (Viale Argine dei Moreri 83, tel. 0431/80629) rents
rooms with garden views (doubles L40,000–L50,000), including breakfast. Or try your luck at
Villa ai Fiori (Via G. Papini 4, tel. 0431/81485) where clean doubles, all with bath, go for
L60,000. Via Dante Alighieri is where the budget-conscious dine: **Isola D'Oro** (Via Dante
Alighieri 66, tel. 0431/81045) and **Onda Blu** (Via Dante Alighieri 3, tel. 0431/81036) serve
up no-frills pizza and pasta at around L15,000 per person.

Trieste

Squashed between the Adriatic and Slovenia in the eastern corner of Italy, Friuli-Venezia Giulia's largest city will surprise any traveler curious enough to venture east from Venice. Trieste just doesn't *seem* Italian. First of all, there's the sea—a bright-blue expanse that makes you wonder if it's the same Adriatic that becomes so murky in Venice. The sight of Slovenia's shadowy hills across the water and the sound of Slavic languages heard in the streets add to the confusion. And then there are the menus, which run the gamut from gnocchi to goulash to strudel. Whose city is this anyway?

The extensive swastika graffiti in Trieste is a disturbing reminder that city has long been a stronghold for neo-fascists and that it was the site of the only Nazi death camp in Italy.

Trieste has been trying to figure out its identity for centuries. It was already an important port in the 2nd century BC when it was absorbed into the Roman empire. It remained independent throughout the Middle Ages, rivaling Venice for control of the seas. In the end Venice kept the upper hand and Trieste fell under the protection of Austria's Emperor Leopold III. Later, under Maria Theresa, Trieste blossomed as Austria's principal Adriatic port. During the next century, much of Trieste was torn down; the uniform, neoclassical buildings that comprise most neighborhoods might lead you to think that the whole city sprang up from sea foam in the mid-19th century. After World War I, Trieste became part of Italy, only to be lost during World War II. The battle for the town lasted until 1954, when it was finally given back to Italy, though everything beyond a thin strip of land that surrounds the city limits belongs to Slovenia.

Trieste's chaotic history has led to tension between Italians and the ethnic Slavic minority, and relations have become increasingly stressful as more and more people flee the former Yugoslavia, pouring into Trieste to look for a safe haven and work. The city's precarious position—about halfway between Venice and Zagreb—makes it a pretty unlikely choice for a vacation spot. Due to Trieste's lack of tourism, it's easy to lose yourself in the city's bustling center or along the craggy white cliffs of **Il Carso** (*see* Near Trieste, *below*), where you might not see a soul for miles.

BASICS The **APT** (tel. 040/420182; open Mon.–Sat. 9–2 and 3–8) in Trieste's train station stocks shelves of brochures and decent city maps. The **main office** (Via San Nicolò 20, tel. 040/369881) is a bit more forthcoming and handles hotel reservations. Trieste is also home to both a **U.S. Consulate** (Via Roma 15, tel. 040/661667) and a **U.K. Consulate** (Vicolo delle Ville 16, tel. 040/302884).

Banca Antoniana (Piazza Borsa 11/A, tel. 040/68401) works a money miracle: great rates and no commission. The **exchange booth** at the train station charges 3% commission and has horrible rates, but it's open daily 6:30 AM–10:10 PM. The **post office** (Piazza della Libertà) is open weekdays 9–1 and 3–7, and the **SIP** office across the piazza is open daily 9–7.

COMING AND GOING **Stazione Centrale** (Piazza della Libertà 8, tel. 040/418207) runs trains to Venice (hourly, 2 hrs, L13,400) and Udine (hourly, 1½ hrs, L7600). From the adjacent bus station, **SAITA** buses (tel. 040/425001) run to Aquileia (1 hr, L5500), Grado (45 min, L5500), Udine (1 hr 15 min, L7800), Sistiana (20 min, L1500), and Duino (20 min,

Trieste's Literati

Trieste was home to some literary giants in the early part of this century, including Rainer Maria Rilke, James Joyce, and native son Italo Svevo. Rilke lived and wrote his "Duino Elegies" near Trieste, inspired by the cliffs along the coast. Joyce taught English at the local Berlitz Institute from 1905 to 1914 and was fast friends with Svevo, with whom he exchanged early drafts of his works.

Trieste

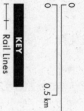

KEY

— Rail Lines

N

0   0.5 miles

0   0.5 km

Gulf of Trieste

Sights ●

Capitoline Hill, **6**
Castello di
San Giusto, **10**
Castello
Miramare, **2**
Museo Civico di
Storia ed Arte, **9**
Museo Revoltella, **8**
Riseria di
San Sabba, **11**
Scala dei Giganti, **7**

Lodging ○

Julia, **4**
Locanda
San Nicolò, **5**
Ostello Tergeste, **1**
Pensione Locanda
Centro, **3**

93

L1500). To reach the center of town from either station, head down Corso Cavour, which runs along the coast until it hits Piazza Unità d'Italia.

For L8500 and an hour of your time, the ferry takes you from Trieste to Grado, where you can catch a bus to Aquileia (*see* Aquileia, *above*). Five daily boats also run to Venice (L28,000). For information and tickets, contact **Agemar Viaggi** (Piazza Duca degli Abruzzi 1/A, tel. 040/363222; open daily 8:30–1 and 3–6).

GETTING AROUND Trieste is on the large and sprawling side, but most sights are in a nucleus that includes **Piazza Unità d'Italia** and the **Colla Capitolina** (Capitoline Hill). Via Ghega leads left from the station to **Via Carducci**, the shop-lined main drag. **Corso Cavour** runs from the stations down the shoreline, changing names several times as it heads south; Piazza Unità d'Italia is on this street. The Capitoline Hill starts at the Scala dei Giganti (Giant's Staircase) off Piazza Goldoni on Corso Italia. **Viale Miramare** runs along the coast north of the train station and hits the youth hostel and Castello Miramare.

Local buses (L1200) run regularly until midnight; call toll-free 167/016675 for bus info, or pick up a free map of all the bus lines at the tourist offices. Bus 36 travels the 7 kilometers up Viale Miramare to the hostel; catch it at the newsstand at the beginning of Viale Miramare.

WHERE TO SLEEP Trieste is not good for cheap lodging; the hostels and campgrounds in Opicina and Sistiana (*see* Near Trieste, *below*) are your best options. If all else fails, take Bus 25 from Piazza Goldoni to the remote **Silva** (Via Marchesetti 56, tel. 040/910749), which has doubles with bath for around L40,000.

Julia. The dank, smelly staircase of the building is disheartening, but the hotel itself has surprisingly clean, airy rooms with well-scrubbed sinks and showers. Doubles are L66,000. *Via XXX Ottobre 5, tel. 040/370045. From stations, walk down Via Ghega to Via Carducci; turn right at Piazza Oberdan to Via XXX Ottobre. 8 rooms.*

Locanda San Nicolò. The L49,000 doubles are dark and dusty, and you have to pay for the showers down the hall (a travesty at L2000). But at least this hotel is central, and the proprietors are sweet people. *Via San Nicolò 2, tel. 040/366532. From stations, walk down Corso Cavour; turn left at Piazza Tommaseo to Via San Nicolò. 11 rooms, none with bath.*

Pensione Locanda Centro. The white walls and institutional beds at this pension are a little sterile, but fresh flowers in every room brighten things up. An affable staff invites you to watch TV in the common room, and everything is "guaranteed clean." Doubles are L70,000. *Via Roma 13, tel. 040/634408. From stations, walk down Corso Cavour; turn left on Via Valdrivio and right on Via Roma. 16 rooms, none with bath.*

➤ **HOSTELS** • **Ostello Tergeste.** Seven kilometers north of the center, this hostel is smack on the sea and has the feel of a beach bungalow. The patio hops with locals on summer nights, when the bar often hosts live bands and the 11:30 PM curfew is extended until 2 or 3 AM. L20,000 gets you a bunk and breakfast. *Viale Miramare 331, tel. 040/224102. Take Bus 36 from stop catercorner to train station (last bus 10 PM). 74 beds. Lockout 10–5.*

FOOD Trieste is known for its buffets—crowded, self-serve affairs where you eat cheap and bump shoulders with locals. One of the most popular is **Buffet Da Pepi** (Via Cassa di Risparmio 3, tel. 040/366858), which charges L13,000 for a meal. Get supermarket vittles from **Standa** (Viale XX Settembre 20). Or take part in transplanted Viennese culture by sitting down for a leisurely coffee at one of the city's many chichi cafés. **Caffè Tergesteo** (Galleria Tergesteo, tel. 040/365812), **Caffè Tommaseo** (Riva III Novembre 5, tel. 040/366765), and **Caffè San Marco** (Via Cesare Battisti 18, tel. 040/371173) are the big three (Tergesteo and Tommaseo stay open until 2 AM). For about L5000 you are served a cappuccino on a silver platter or an espresso with cream, Austrian-style. At **Pasticceria Giorgi** (Via Palestrina 4, tel. 040/635978) locals nosh on fresh, steaming bread and pastries.

Osteria da Libero. Known to literary types as James Joyce's old stomping ground, this place considerably declines to play up its tourist possibilities. At night a mix of hip intellectuals and salty dog sailors stumble in and get drunk on the excellent vat wine. Lunch is more mellow, when you can get a meal of soup, bread, and wine for L5000. Particularly tasty is the Trieste specialty, *polpi alla triestiana* (octopus marinated in paprika and olive oil). *Via Risorta 9. From Colla Capitolina, walk down Via San Giusto, which starts to the right of Castello San Giusto; it intersects Via Risorta down the hill. Open Thurs.–Tues. 8 AM–1 AM.*

Risoteca. This place majors in multitudes of delicious risotto (hence the name), sold at great prices and served in a friendly atmosphere. Risotto with zucchini (L9500) is only one of the many meatless versions. *Via Economo 14, tel. 040/311262. Walk down Corso Cavour to waterfront; turn left on Via Campo Marzio and left on Via Economo. Open Tues.–Sun. 6:30 PM– 10:30 PM.*

Trattoria Tevere. More classy than casual, this place serves excellent seafood. Risotto with scampi, tagliatelle with prawns, and grilled calamari are recommended by the chef, but you're crazy if you don't try the *vongole fritte* (fried clams) first—some locals eat them for breakfast. Expect to pay around L20,000 for a meal. *Via Malcantoro, behind Piazza Unità d'Italia, tel. 040/361506. Open Mon.–Sat. 12:30–2 and 6:30–9:30.*

WORTH SEEING Most of the Trieste's older architecture was smashed by Austrians in the 19th century, when neoclassic architecture was considered the apex of taste. Those who beg to differ won't get a thrill from walking around the streets, especially through the tidy *borgo teresiano* (Theresa's neighborhood), named after landmark-razer Empress Maria Theresa. More interesting art nouveau designs are scattered around the city, like the leafy-green, delicate **Casa Bartoli** in Piazza Borsa and the monumental figures on the columns of the Cinema Eden on Viale XX Settembre.

➤ **CAPITOLINE HILL** • The only evidence that Trieste was ever a Roman settlement sits in shambles on a huge hill overlooking the sea; the view from this site is much more impressive than the few Roman columns that remain here. Also on the hill, the **Basilica di San Giusto** (Piazza Cattedrale; open daily 8–noon and 4–8) is an asymmetrical composite of two smaller churches, filled with stiff Byzantine bas-reliefs. The ivy-covered 15th-century **Castello di San Giusto** offers the all-around best view of Trieste, but skip the dull Museo Civico inside. Walk down Via Cattedrale, the small street starting from the basilica, to the **Museo Civico di Storia ed Arte** (Via Cattedrale 15, tel. 040/310500; admission: L3000) for a more interesting museum experience. The archaeological museum has a small Egyptian collection, including a female mummy, as well as medieval and Roman sculptures. Outside, the **Orto Lapidario** (Lapidary Garden) includes Roman ruins and a temple. *Colla Capitolina. From Piazza Goldoni, walk up Scala dei Giganti and turn right on Via Capitolina at the top.*

➤ **CASTELLO MIRAMARE** • Looming over sunbathers on the shore north of the city is a castle built by Archduke Maximilian, brother of Austrian Emperor Franz Josef. The boxy, pretentious structure is real proof that money can't buy good taste. It is rumored that anyone who sleeps in the castle will die violently, as "proven" by the assassinations of the Duke Amadeo of Aosta, who owned the castle 1931–38, and of Archduke Franz Ferdinand, who stopped here shortly before being offed in Sarajevo. There's no charge to wander through the gardens and woods (open dawn–dusk) surrounding the castle. *Parco di Miramare, tel. 040/224143. Take Bus 36 (L1200) from train station; tell driver to let you off at the castello. Admission: L7000. Open Mon. 9–12:30, Tues.–Sun. 9–1:30 and 2:30–6.*

➤ **MUSEO REVOLTELLA** • The museum's main building, the former palace of 19th-century Baron Revoltella, hasn't changed much since he kicked the bucket; the rooms are still rich and darkly majestic, with bad paintings on the walls. The modern annex, designed by the wacky architect Carlo Scarpa, hits you like cold water thrown in your face. Suddenly the lighting becomes starker and the art becomes much weirder, especially on the top floor. *Via XXIV Maggio 4, tel. 040/361675. From stations, walk down Corso Cavour and turn left at Piazza Venezia; museum is on left edge of square. Admission: L4000. Open Mon., Wed.–Sat. for guided visits at 10:30, 3, 4:30, and 6, Sun. at 10:30 AM.*

➤ **RISIERA DI SAN SABBA** • During World War II, this former rice-husking plant was the site of the only Nazi concentration camp in Italy, where as many as 20,000 people may have been killed. It's now a national monument with a small, chilling museum. *Via Ratto della Pileria 1, San Sabba district, tel. 040/826202. Take Bus 10 from Piazza Unità d'Italia; ask driver to stop at Risiera. Admission free. Open Tues.–Sat. 9–1.*

AFTER DARK Trieste's after-dark scene revolves around the university. Basically the students engage in a "café crawl" hopping from café to café and downing plenty of wine in the interim. To join in the fun, head to **Avant Garde** (Via Matteotti 4, tel. 040/773535) or **Rex** (Galleria Protti, tel. 040/367878).

NEAR TRIESTE

IL CARSO Il Carso refers to the strip of beautiful, jagged limestone cliffs that run up the shoreline north of Trieste and into Slovenia. Take Tram 2 (L2500) from Trieste's Piazza Oberdan up the hill to **Opicina**, just before the Slovenian border. It's a scenic ride, though the driver's claim that it's "just like San Francisco" doesn't quite ring true. In this tiny town, **Camping Obelisco** (Via Nazionale S.S. 58, tel. 040/211655), a pleasant, woodsy, 360-tent site, charges L5000 per person and L10,000 per tent. While in Opicina, look for **osmizze**, open houses that provide the most down-home way to eat in northern Italy. Every summer and fall, farmers open their homes to serve their own fresh prosciutto, cheese, bread, wine, and sometimes soup or dessert, all at half the price of a pizza. Walk along Via Nazionale until you see a bunch of dried flowers and an arrow on a post and follow these markers to the nearest osmizza.

You can find a unique natural wonder right outside of Trieste—the Grotta Gigante (Via Machiavelli 17, tel. 040/327312; open sporadically Tues.–Sun.). Large enough to accommodate a football stadium, it's probably the most enormous cave you'll ever get to walk around in. From Trieste, take Bus 45 (40 min, L1200); entrance to the cave costs L12,000.

The small villages of **Duino** and **Sistiana** lie about 15 kilometers north of Trieste along the sea. They are connected by the **Rilke Trail**, a 2-kilometer cliff-side walk where the poet Rainer Maria Rilke penned his *Duino Elegies*. The trail starts at the Sistiana Bay near the 1,500-site **Camping Marepineta** (Sistiana Monte, S.S. 14, tel. 040/299264; closed Oct.–Apr.), which charges L10,000 per person and L20,000 per tent. **Alle Rose** (Sistiana 27, tel. 040/299457; closed Oct.–Apr.) is cheaper and more basic (L5000 per person, L11,000 per tent). The Rilke Trail ends in Duino, a little fishing town and home to the Duino Castle, still inhabited by the Torre Tasso princes. You can only enter the castle if you're in a group with an appointment, but anyone can climb out to the huge rock known as *La Dama Bianca* (The White Lady). Legend has it that the lord of Duino threw a woman out the castle window when she wore out her welcome; she was turned into stone before she hit the water. **SAITA** buses (tel. 040/425001) run from Trieste's bus station to Sistiana and Duino (20 min) every half hour.

MILAN, LOMBARDY, AND THE LAKES

By Janet Morris

During the Renaissance, palaces, churches, even entire cities were erected as monuments to the egos, libidos, and eccentricities of Lombardy's ruling classes. The most notable of these families were the Visconti, Sforza, and Gonzaga clans, who at various times ruled Mantova (Mantua), Como, Milano (Milan), and Pavia. Until Lombardy was conquered by the Spanish in 1525, these families spent most of their time (and other people's money) obsessively building grand monuments to themselves—which has proved to be a boon for modern-day visitors, especially those who are into art and architecture. Even in the 20th century, the Lombard tradition of self-aggrandizement continues with writer Gabriele D'Annunzio, who built his kitschy, egomaniacal warehouse, Il Vittoriale, along the shores of Lago di Garda.

The *Risorgimento* (the unification of Italy; *see box* The Shot of Espresso Heard 'Round the World, in Chapter 5) also played a major role in Lombardy's cultural milieu—there's hardly a town without a museum dedicated to movement leader Giuseppe Garibaldi, and street names everywhere bear witness to this 19th-century national uprising. Still, despite the historical stress on national unity, Lombards retain a deep sense of regional patriotism and a hatred of domination, be it by foreigners, the European Union, or even the Italian government. During World War II, the revolt in Lombardy against Mussolini and the Germans was better organized and more *Lombardy takes its name from the Longobards, or Lombards, one of the barbarian tribes who in the 6th century invaded and settled the Italian peninsula.* effective than anywhere else in Italy; today, with the creation of the Lega Nord (Northern League), an exclusive union between northern Italy's more prosperous regions, Lombardy is looking to become a semiautonomous power. Many Lombards claim to be of a different nationality than their "lazy" and "criminal" southern cousins who, Lombards complain, sap their region's economic strength. Snobbishness is definitely *not* lacking in Lombardy—so don't expect Lombards to greet haggard backpackers with open arms.

This sense of superiority is deeply rooted in the region's economic history. From the time of the industrial revolution, Lombardy's economy (and standard of living) has been more similar to that of southern Germany or France than Italy's bottom half, and through the years these characteristics have been accentuated rather than erased. Italy's unification, at least at first, only made matters worse; poor southern peasants were taxed, some to the point of starvation, in order to finance the north's industrial development. Today, however, it is the northerners who complain about being taxed to the hilt, only to support an ever "backward" south. (Though it's just as likely that much of the cash is going to line the pockets of corrupt politicians.)

SWITZERLAND

Chiavenna

Locarno
Ascona
Brissago

Cannobio

Mt. Zeda

Intra

Borromeo
Islands

Lago Maggiore

Menaggio
Tremezzo

Lago di Como

Bellano
Varenna

Lugano

Lago di
Lugano

Bellagio

Monttarone
Omegna
Pella

Lago
di
Orta

Orta

Broleto

Arona

Stresa

Laveno

Lago
Varese

Porto
Cerèsio

S340

Asso

Cernobbia
Como

Lecco

Varese

Angera

S233

A8

A8

A9

S35

S342

S36

S342

S36

Bergam

A4

S32

Monza

Novara

Cassano d'Adda

Trevigl

A4

Milan

Adda

Vigevano

A7

Ticino

Certosa

Cre

Lodi

N

Pavia

A7

A1

Po

A21

A7

A21

A26

0   20 miles

0   30 km

KEY

⊢⊣ Rail Lines

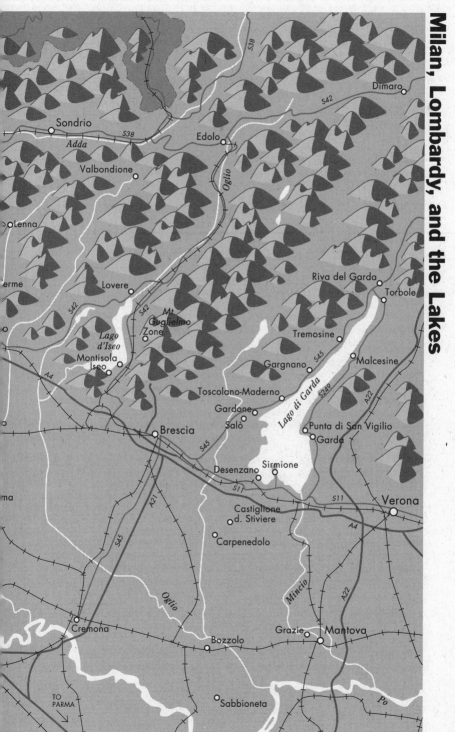

Dimaro

Sondrio

Adda

S38

Edolo

S42

S38

Valbondione

Oglio

Lenna

erme

Lovere

Riva del Garda

Torbole

S42

S42

Mt.
Guglielmo
Zone

Tremosine

*Lago
d'Iseo*

Gargnano

S45

Malcesine

Montisola
Iseo

A4

Toscolano-Maderno

Lago di Garda

S249

A22

Gardone

Salò

Punta di San Vigilio

Brescia

S45

Garda

Desenzano

Sirmione

ma

S11

S11

Verona

Castiglione
d. Stiviere

A4

A21

S45

Carpenedolo

A22

Mincio

Oglio

Cremona

Grazie

Mantova

Bozzolo

TO
PARMA

Sabbioneta

Po

Despite apparent drawbacks—a snotty populace, high prices, and some serious pollution—visitors are still attracted *in droves* to the esthetic beauty of Lombardy's lakelands, to its miles of wooded hiking trails, and to the architecture of Milan. Be prepared to encounter the vacationing masses during the summer: Even if you set out on a solo adventure through Lombardy, you may end up feeling as if you, too, are on a package tour. Worst of all, the influx of well-heeled tourists has driven prices up, making budget travel a real challenge.

Milan

Milan ain't cheap, but the city's dazzling array of restaurants, shops, and hip nightclubs will tempt you to dig a little deeper into your pockets.

In no way will Milan satisfy your yearnings for the laid-back, beautiful, and charmingly disorganized Italy; it's faster, more serious, and annoyingly expensive. It the winter the city is foggy; in the summer it's suffocating. (Most natives flee from the city's scorching temperatures to the mountains or the sea, leaving behind a virtual ghost town mid-July through August.) It also lacks the visual appeal of other Italian cities, thanks to wars in AD 539, 1157, and 1944. Still, Milan does have the cultural buzz and amenities of an international metropolis. It also offers excellent shopping and people-watching, a glitzy nightlife, and one of the few gay scenes in Italy.

The city's history is a tale of foreign domination. From 1277 until 1500, Milan was controlled by the Visconti and, subsequently, the Sforza clan. These aristocratic families ruled the city with an iron fist, which though not terribly humane is largely responsible for Milan's Gothic and Renaissance architecture. Or at least what's left of it: Virtually every invader in European history—Gaul, Roman, Goth, Longobard, and Frank—as well as rulers from France, Spain, and Austria has taken a turn at Milan. As a result, stoic churches share Milan's *centro storico* (historic center) with ultramodern eyesores.

Though Milan is home to some of Italy's finest artistic masterpieces (its Gothic duomo and Leonardo da Vinci's *Last Supper*, to name two), it's not a living museum in the same sense as Venice, Florence, or Rome; rather the city teems with modern-day business and commerce. As the industrial capital of Italy, Milan is responsible for 25% of all of Italy's exports and is home to the nation's largest stock exchange. The city is also a center of fashion and design (Armani, Versace—need we say more?). Unlike many of Italy's cities, Milan is a place to visit not only for what it was in centuries gone by, but more important, for what it is today.

BASICS

AMERICAN EXPRESS The only AmEx office in Lombardy, Piemonte, and Valle d'Aosta provides the usual services for cardholders. *Via Brera 3, 2 blocks behind La Scala, tel. 02/7200–3605, fax 02/8646–3478. For lost or stolen traveler's checks, tel. 167/872000; 24-hour assistance for cardholders, tel. 02/067–2282. Mailing address: Via Brera 3, 20121 Milano. Open weekdays 9–5.*

CHANGING MONEY Change cash and traveler's checks for a 1%–2% fee at the information office in **Stazione Centrale** or at the Malpensa and Linate airports. A number of banks in the city also change cash and traveler's checks; your best bet is **Banca Commerciale** (there's a branch in front of Stazione Centrale), which does not charge commission. Scattered throughout the city are 24-hour exchange machines that change larger bills for a 1% fee.

CONSULATES Australia. *Via Borgogna 2, tel. 02/7601–3330. Open weekdays 9–noon and 2–4. Closed Fri. afternoon.*

Canada. *Via Vittor Pisani 19, tel. 02/67581. Open weekdays 9–noon.*

United Kingdom. *Via San Paolo 7, tel. 02/723001. Open weekdays 9–1 and 2–5.*

United States. *Via P. Amedeo 2/10, tel. 02/290351. Open weekdays 9–noon and 2–4.*

DISCOUNT TRAVEL AGENCIES Agenzia CLUP Viaggi. This organization gives student discounts on airfare, as well as general travel information. *Via Pascoli 55, tel. 02/266–6815. Open weekdays 9:30–1 and 2:30–6:30.*

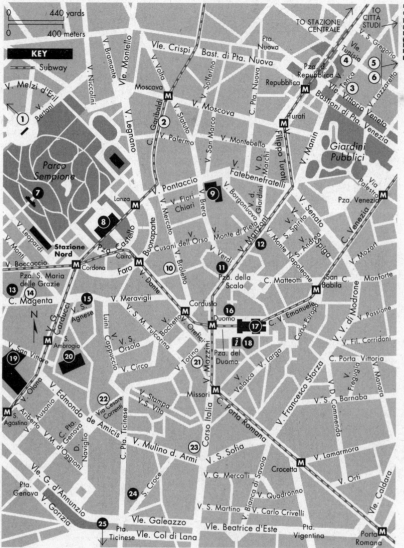

KEY
=·=·= Subway

TO STAZIONE CENTRALE

TO CITTA STUDI

Sights ●

Castello Sforzesco, **8**

Il Duomo, **17**

Galleria Vittorio Emanuele, **16**

Museo Civico Archeologico, **15**

Museo Civico d'Arte Contemporanea, **18**

Museo Nazionale della Scienza e Technica, **19**

Museo Poldi Pezzoli, **12**

Navigli district, **25**

Pinacoteca di Brera, **9**

San Eustorgio, **24**

Sant'Ambrogio, **20**

Santa Maria delle Grazie, **13**

La Scala, **11**

The Triennale, **7**

Lodging ○

ACI SJF, **2**

Hotel Cara Mia, **3**

Hotel Catalani and Madrid, **5**

Hotel Cesare Correnti, **22**

Hotel Kennedy, **4**

Hotel Pedrotti, **10**

Hotel Speronari, **21**

Hotel Ullrich, **23**

Pensione Jolanda, **14**

Pensione Winston, **6**

Piero Rotta Hotel, **1**

CTS (Centro Turistico Studentesco). Tickets for train, plane, and ferry travel can be purchased here, with discounts for students and those under 25. *Two locations: Via S. Antonio 2, tel. 02/5830–4121; and Corso di Porta Ticinese 100, tel. 02/837–8204. Both open weekdays 9:30–6, Sat. 9:30–noon.*

ENGLISH BOOKS The **American Bookstore** (Via Campello 16, tel. 02/878920), conveniently located in Largo Cairoli in front of the Castello Sforzesco, features all kinds of English-language reads. A gay bookstore, **Babele** (Via Sanmartini 21, tel. 02/669–2986), sells literature in both Italian and English and lists current events in the gay community.

MAIL The **main post office** (Piazza Cordusio 4, tel. 02/869–2069), at the Cordusio Metro stop, is open weekdays 8:15–7:40 and Saturday 8:15–5:40. Window 9 sells *francobolli* (stamps). Collect *fermo posta* (held mail) at Window 5. The express-mail service in the same office is called **CAI-POST** and is open weekdays 8:30–7:30, Saturday 8:30–noon. For telegrams, faxes, and telexes within continental Europe and a few other countries around the world (Australia yes, United States no), the **Telegrafo e Telecommunicazioni** office (tel. 02/869–2874), in the same building, is open 24 hours.

MEDICAL AID The **Policlinico** hospital (Piazza Francesco Sforza 35, tel. 02/55031, emergency tel. 02/551–1656) has English-speaking staff and doctors. Stazione Centrale has a 24-hour **pharmacy** (tel. 02/669–0735). Other pharmacies rotate 24-hour service; the Vivere Milano section of *La Repubblica* and the Cronaca di Milano section of *Corriere della Sera* newspapers list the schedule under the heading "*Farmacie.*"

PHONES Make local calls at public phones in bars and booths around the city. You can also make local as well as long-distance collect or cash calls from either of **TELECOM**'s central offices: in the Galleria Vittorio Emanuele (*see* Worth Seeing, *below*) and in Stazione Centrale. Both offices are open daily 8 AM–9:30 PM.

VISITOR INFORMATION The two main APT tourist offices are at **Stazione Centrale** (tel. 02/669–0532; open Mon.–Sat. 9–6, Sun. 9–12:30 and 1:30–6) and in **Palazzo del Turismo** (Via Marconi 1, Piazza del Duomo, tel. 02/809662; open weekdays 8:30–8, Sat. 9–1 and 2–7, Sun. 9–1 and 2–5). Both have hotel info, and though they're not officially supposed to make reservations for you, they just might if you look pitiful enough. Be sure to pick up the indispensable (and free) publications *Youths in Milan* and *Milano Is Milano* for more info on nightlife and cultural events. Another good source of arts information is **Comune di Milano** (Galleria Vittorio Emanuele, at Piazza della Scala, tel. 02/878363; open Mon.–Sat. 8–8).

Resources for women are available by contacting the **Centro Azione Milano Donne** (Via Fleming 15, tel. 02/4000–1960). For handicapped/disabled services, inquire at **Ledha**, Lega Difesa Diritti Handicappati (Viale Monte Santo 7, tel. 02/657–0425). For information on AIDS, call **Centralino Informazioni AIDS** (tel. 1678/61061). Call **Arci Gay** (Via Torisceni 19, tel. 02/5810–0299 or 02/5810–0399) for general info on events in the gay and lesbian community.

COMING AND GOING

BY PLANE **Linate Airport**, about 10 kilometers southeast of Milan, handles domestic and international flights. Car rental agencies that have offices here include Autotravel Italiana, Avis, Company Service, Europcar, Hertz, Italy by Car, Maggiore, and Tirreno. You can store luggage at the airport for L6000 per day. The major airlines serving Linate are **Alitalia** (tel. 02/26853), **British Airways** (tel. 02/809896), **KLM** (tel. 02/7010–0542), **Lufthansa** (tel. 02/583721), and **Olympic Airways** (tel. 02/878692).

Malpensa Airport, 45 kilometers from downtown, also handles domestic and international flights. Malpensa has the same car-rental offices and the same major carriers as Linate, with the addition of **United Airlines** (tel. 02/864831). For general information (English upon request) at both Malpensa and Linate, call 02/74851.

➤ **AIRPORT TRANSIT** • From Linate Airport, **STAM buses** (tel. 02/6698–4509) depart every 20 minutes 7–7 (one also at 5:40 AM) and every half hour 7 PM–11:30 PM. Tickets for the 10-minute trip to Stazione Centrale (L4000) can be purchased on board. To return to the airport, the last bus leaves the train station at 9 PM. Look for signs marked AEROPORTI DI MILANO outside the station to the right. From the city center to Linate, Bus 73 departs every 10 minutes (5:30 AM–12:20 AM) from the southeast corner of Piazza San Babila, at Corso Europa.

From the Malpensa airport, **STAM buses** (tel. 02/4009–9280) leave for Stazione Centrale at least every hour 6:30 AM–11 PM and thereafter in correspondence with flights (1 hr, L12,000). The ticket office is open daily 6:30 AM–11 PM; tickets can be purchased on board when the office is closed. From Stazione Centrale, buses run to Malpensa 5:10 AM–9 PM. STAM buses also connect Malpensa and Linate.

BY TRAIN **Stazione Centrale** (tel. 02/67500), a few kilometers northeast of downtown on Metro lines 2 and 3, handles the bulk of Milan's rail traffic. Destinations from here include Venice (14 daily, 4–5 hrs, L20,800), Turin (18 daily, 1½–2 hrs, L13,600), Florence (8 daily, 3 hrs, L36,200), and Rome (10 daily, 5–7 hrs, L66,200), as well as other major European cities. U.S.-issued credit cards are no longer accepted at the station; to charge a ticket with your card, go to a travel agency (there's a CIT office in the station). Luggage storage is open daily 5 AM–4 AM (L1500 per piece per 24 hrs); currency exchange is available, although not at the best rates.

BY BUS Long-distance buses depart from outside the **Autostradale** office (Piazza Castello, tel. 02/801161; open Mon.–Sat. 6:30 AM–7 PM, Sun. 6:30–4). Buses—painted a hard-to-miss blue—run hourly to Turin (2¼ hrs, L15,700), five times daily to Aosta (2½–3½ hrs, L20,500), and twice daily to Rimini (5 hrs, L48,000). At the nameless travel agency (tel. 02/720013; open weekdays 9–1 and 2–6) next door to Autostrade, you can book international bus, plane, and train trips and buy **Tourbus** tickets to Eastern Europe (cheaper and faster than trains). Buses leave on Thursday and Sunday for Prague (17½ hrs, L90,000).

GETTING AROUND

The city's layout resembles a bull's-eye, with three concentric thoroughfares encircling **Piazza del Duomo**. Milan's main attractions generally lie within the two most central rings. When downtown, orient yourself in relation to Piazza del Duomo and the major streets that lead to it: **Via Torino**, which runs southwest into Corso di Porta Ticinese; **Corso Italia**, which runs south toward Naviglio Canal; and **Via Dante**, which runs northwest to Piazza Castello and Castello Sforzesco. Beyond these rings the city sprawls and sprawls.

Neighborhoods are not clearly marked by streets, but each area has a distinct atmosphere. The district that lies within the center circle, **Cerchia dei Navigli**, boasts the majority of Milan's attractions. Its designer boutiques and exclusive cafés draw packs of tourists as well as leggy supermodels who enjoy posing in Galleria Vittorio Emanuele and around the Accademia di Brera. The outer ring follows the outline of the city's medieval walls, passing by the Giardini Pubblici, Parco Sempione, and around the far side (across the canal) of **Navigli**. The Navigli and **Ticinese** sections are cool and artsy, drawing young hip Milanese to trendy restaurants, bars, and shops. Another happenin' area lies between Corso Garibaldi and Via Brera. All three neighborhoods are fairly expensive places to hang, although not above average by Milan's standards. The main difference between the zones is that the Navigli has a more alternative feel, with jazz clubs and a few boutiques selling 1960s- and 1970s-style garb.

Tickets good for the Metro, buses, and trams cost L1400. Once validated, each ticket is good for 75 minutes of travel on all three means of transport. Ten-ticket packs cost L13,000, or buy *abbonamenti* (passes) for one day (L4800) or two days (L8000) of unlimited travel. Tickets can be purchased at newsstands and automated machines in the subway stations, and above ground in bars and *tabacchi* (tobacco shops). Buy reduced-fare passes at offices marked ABBONAMENTI in the Cadorna, Romolo, San Donato, and Centrale Metro stations. Generally, ticket windows are open Monday–Saturday 7:45–1 and 1:45–7. The **ATM** transportation information offices in the Duomo Metro station (tel. 02/8901–0797) and Stazione Centrale (train level, tel. 02/669–7032) provide maps and info on all public transport within the city, including a list of prices and a general explanation of the bus and Metro systems in English. Both offices are open Monday–Saturday 8–8.

BY METRO The Metro is the fastest and easiest way to get around Milan. Tickets (L1400) can be validated at machines in each station. The Metro's three lines (color- and number-coded) all run 6 AM–midnight. The clean, safe stations are conveniently named for major sights, piazze, or streets, and route maps are posted throughout the system. Final destinations indicate the direction of each train. At transfer points—Cadorna, Duomo, Stazione Centrale, and Loreto stations—passageways are marked by the number of the line to which you are transferring.

BY BUS AND TRAM The Metro will get you to most major attractions, but buses and trams are more convenient for crossing the canal. Buses also run circles around the city—ideal for an overview of central Milan. (From Stazione Centrale, buses marked DESTRA circle the city to the right, buses marked SINISTRA to the left.) Buses and trams run 5 AM–1 AM. For free maps contact an APT office (see Basics, above).

WHERE TO SLEEP

Except for Milan's lone hostel, most "cheap" lodgings are generic hotels that are reasonably clean and tolerable. Città Studi, famed for its thriving community of prostitutes, is not the safest at night, nor is it conveniently located to most sights. If you want to stay near the station, you're better off near the Giardini Pubblici. Your best bet, however, is in the center near the **Duomo** and most museums, as prices are uniformly high in Milan, regardless of location. Milan's hotels are at their fullest March–May, and in September when international trade fairs take over the city, but it's always wise to make reservations a few days in advance.

CITTA STUDI **Hotel Catalani and Madrid.** It's a bit run-down but not as sleazy as most places in the area. The owners are friendly and keep the rooms (L70,000 without bath) reasonably clean. Via Catalani 71, off Via Poppora, tel. 02/284–6361. Metro: Loreto. 17 rooms, 10 with bath. Luggage storage. Reception closed 3 AM–6 AM. Closed Aug. MC, V.

Pensione Winston. Few hookers hang out here, but the place still has a slightly grimy feel, though at L50,000 for a double you may not care. Clean enough rooms almost make up for substandard communal bathrooms. Via Catalani 21, tel. 02/266–4780. Metro: Loreto. 7 rooms.

BETWEEN THE STATION AND GIARDINI PUBBLICI **Hotel Casa Mia.** This second-story hotel has clean, modern rooms (L65,000 doubles without bath) with telephones and comfy furniture. The hotel is undergoing renovation that will result in a new bar downstairs and private baths in all the rooms. Viale Vittorio Veneto 30, off Piazza della Repubblica, tel. 02/657–5249. From Stazione Centrale take Via Vittor Pisani, left on Viale Vittorio Veneto. 15 rooms, 9 with bath. Closed July and Aug. MC, V.

Hotel Kennedy. Catering to mostly American and Japanese tourists, this hotel's rooms are clean and in good condition. Bathless doubles are L70,000, triples L120,000 (with bath); one room for four people is L160,000 (with bath). Ask for discounts on longer stays. Viale Tunisia 6, 5th floor, tel. 02/2940–0934. From the station, take Via Vittor Pisani, left on Viale Tunisia. 12 rooms, 3 with bath. Curfew 2 AM. V.

CITY CENTER **Hotel Cesare Correnti.** The tidy, well-lit Correnti is one of the only hotels in the center that has doubles (L55,000–L65,000) with TVs in each room. The manager (and the kids who help run the place) are accommodating, and the location is ideal—halfway between Piazza del Duomo and San Lorenzo. Via Cesare Correnti 14, 2nd floor, tel. 02/805–7609. 10-min walk from Piazza del Duomo. 10 rooms, none with bath. Checkout 11:30 AM.

Hotel Pedrotti. This place is centrally located and dirt cheap, with doubles at L45,000. Rooms are kinda shabby, but for the price you'd expect much worse. On the down side, the manager usually imposes a three-night minimum stay. Via San Tomaso 6, 3rd floor, tel. 02/864–6971. Off Via Dante, a few blocks from Cordusio and Duomo Metro stops. 8 rooms, none with bath. Reception closed Sun. Closed Aug. Reservations advised.

Hotel Speronari. You couldn't ask for a better location—only one block from the Duomo. To top it off, service is friendly, and the somewhat generic rooms are spotlessly clean. There's a café/bar downstairs, and a lounge with a TV. Doubles run L70,000–75,000 without bath. Via

Speronari 4, tel. 02/8646-1125. Take Via Torino from Piazza del Duomo, left on Via Speronari. Metro: Duomo. 32 rooms, 22 with bath. MC, V.

Hotel Ullrich. In terms of location, quality, and price, this hotel is one of the best. Owned by a relative of the man who runs Cesare Correnti (*see above*), the Ullrich is spotlessly clean and a few blocks from the Duomo. Doubles and triples are L60,000 and L68,000, respectively. *Corso Italia 6, tel. 02/8645-0156. Metro: Duomo. 8 rooms, none with bath. Laundry (L8000).*

Pensione Jolanda. This pension, near Santa Maria delle Grazie (*see* Worth Seeing, *below*), has something most budget lodgings in Milan lack: atmosphere. The rooms (L70,000–L80,000 for a double without bath) are clean and contain antique wooden furniture; even so, the friendly owners are used to putting up scruffy backpackers. There's even a small garden in the back, and a cozy lounge with a TV. *Corso Magenta 78, tel. 02/463317. 10-min walk from Cadorna or Duomo Metro stop. 12 rooms, 5 with bath. Luggage storage. AE.*

HOSTELS **ACI SJF.** This Catholic pension only accepts women under 25. And while it's cheap and sanitary, you'll probably get the third degree from the sisters who run it. Expect to pay L25,000–L28,000 for a bed and shower. *Corso Garibaldi 123, tel. 02/2900-0164. Metro: Moscova. 5–7 beds per room. Curfew 10:15 PM (Thurs.–Sat. 11 PM). Reservations advised.*

Piero Rotta Hostel (HI). Milan's hostel is set in a green and peaceful environment on the outskirts of town—an easy commute on the Metro. The 12:30 AM curfew makes it difficult to carouse, but the price (L20,000 per person) eases the pain. Two other bummers: There's a strict daytime lockout, and an HI card is required, though you can buy one at the hostel (L30,000). *Via Martino Bassi 2, tel. 02/3926-7095. Metro: Lotto. 348 beds. Lockout 9 AM–5 PM. Hot showers (L1000), luggage storage, sheets provided. Closed Dec. 23–Jan. 13.*

FOOD

Milanese food is conspicuously rare among budget choices. If you're looking to sink your teeth into some of the city's traditional dishes, you'll need to keep your eyes peeled for *risotto alla milanese* (rice cooked with stock and saffron), *ossobuco* (marrow-bone stew), *cottoletta alla milanese* (breaded veal cutlet), and *cassöeula* (a pork and vegetable stew traditionally made in the winter). Milan's famous sweet *panettone* (light yellow cake with raisins and/or candied fruit) is one bit of Milanese gastronomy that's easy to find, especially at Christmastime.

Though Milan does not pander to budget-minded diners, there are a few affordable places out there. These are primarily fast-food and self-service chains scattered throughout the city: **Spizzico** is a safe bet for pizza slices and whole pies, **Brek** for pasta dishes and salads. More authentic (and cheaper still) are Milan's *latterie* (milk and cheese stores); those marked TAVOLA CALDA serve simple, hearty local dishes. The cheapest meals are best assembled at a supermarket; try **Esselunga** (Viale Piave 38/40, tel. 02/204-7871), **Standa** (Corso Buenos Aires 37, tel. 02/204-9297), or **La Coloniale** (Via Cesare Correnti 6, tel. 02/7200-0067).

For sweets, bread, or pizza by the kilo, try **Il Forno dei Navigli** (Streda Alzaia Naviglio Pavese 2, tel. 02/832-3372), **Sorelle Pelizzoni** (Via Ponte Vetero 11, in the Brera-Garibaldi area, tel. 02/8646-3804), or **Pizzeria Mimi** (Via Torino 48, btw Duomo and Ticinese areas, tel. 02/7202-1075), which doubles as a *rosticceria* (store selling fresh roasted meat). An **outdoor market** on Piazza XX Maggio in the Navigli is open weekdays 8:30–1 and 4–7:30.

➤ **UNDER L15,000 • Circolo Combattenti.** There isn't a sign in front of this place, within the monument of the Arco della Pace, but this hidden eatery (popular among war veterans) serves simple food that happens to be some of the cheapest in Milan. At lunch a *primo*, *secondo*, and *contorno* (side dish) will cost you only L12,000 (L18,000 at dinner). Call ahead for dinner (by lunchtime of the same day), so Signora Pignatoro knows how much to cook. *Piazzale Sempione 21/A, tel. 02/3310-1578. Metro: Cadorna. Open Mon.–Sat. noon–2 and 8–midnight. Closed last week of July to 2nd or 3rd week of Aug. Wheelchair access.*

Grand'Italia. Hugely popular among the student crowd, this congenial place serves gigantic salads (L9000), pasta (L5000), and homemade desserts (L5500). Highly recommended are the *focacce farcite* (filled pizza bread; L9000) and the *tris di primi* (three types of pasta served together; L12,000). *Via Palermo 5, tel. 02/877759. Metro: Moscova. From Metro station, take Corso Garibaldi and go left on Via Palermo. Open Wed.–Mon. noon–2:30 and 7–1:30 AM. Wheelchair access.*

Latteria Unione. Though the menu is always different at this latteria near the Duomo, the food is dependably good and the service friendly. Vegetarians will appreciate the Unione's large mixed salads. It's pricier than most latterie (L15,000 for pasta, wine, and coffee) but worth it. *Via Unione 6, tel. 02/874401. Metro: Missori. From Piazza Missori, take Via Unione. Open Mon.–Sat. 11:30 AM–3:30 PM.*

L'Osteria del Pallone. Stop at this informal *osteria* (tavern) for a quick sandwich (L4500–L6000) or a big salad (L9000) and finish it off with *tris di grappa* (three types of grappa for L12,000). *Corso Garibaldi 46, in Brera-Garibaldi area, tel. 02/805–1865. Metro: Moscova.*

Pizzeria Popeye. Its location near the Duomo is ideal, and the food is remarkably cheap, considering the prices of most places in this touristy area. Tasty pizza (L6000–L12,000) makes up for the tasteless bright green and yellow decor. Be sure to ask for the 10% student discount. *Via S. Tecla 3, tel. 02/8646–3712. Off Largo Schuster. From Duomo, walk south. Open Fri.–Wed. noon–3 and 7–1 AM.*

➢ **UNDER L25,000 • Al Pont de Ferr.** This osteria in the Navigli–San Lorenzo area has a wide selection of antipasti and cheeses (L5000–L10,000), simple but wholesome main dishes (L6000–L16,000), and homemade desserts (L6000). Wash it all down with a fiery grappa. At dinner expect to spend about L6000 more. *Ripa di Porta Ticinese 55, tel. 02/8940–6277. Metro: Sant'Ambrogio. From Sant'Ambrogio, take Via de Amicis Edmondo and go left on Porta Ticinese. Open Mon.–Sat. 12:30–2:15 and 8:30–1 AM. Closed Aug., last week of Dec., and 1st week of Jan.*

Premiata Pizzeria. Pizzas cost a little more than usual at this popular pizzeria in the Navigli, but you can order food late into the night and dine in the leafy garden. Pizzas go for L7000–L15,000; beer and wine are L4000–L7000. *Via Alzaia Naviglio Grande 2, tel. 02/8940–0648. Open Wed.–Mon. 12:30–2:30 and 7:30–1:30 AM. Closed for lunch in Aug. Wheelchair access. AE, MC, V.*

➢ **UNDER L40,000 • Al Matarel.** This is one of the few moderately priced places in Milan where you can find authentic Lombard cuisine done right. And though you pay for it through the nose, it's definitely worth a one-night splurge. Al Matarel is slightly elegant (don't show up in jeans and a T-shirt), yet it has a warm trattoria feel. Try the cassöeula (L24,000) or the cottoletta (L26,000). Primi are L10,000–L15,000; secondi start at L20,000. *Via Laura Solera Mantegazza 75, at Corso Garibaldi, tel. 02/654204. Metro: Moscova. Open noon–3 and 8–midnight. Closed Tues., Weds. at lunch, and July.*

CAFES AND GELATERIAS Milan's most expensive cafés line the Galleria Vittorio Emanuele, where you can sip an aperitif or espresso and watch the beautiful fashion set and the not-so-beautiful hordes of tourists strut by. If atmosphere is what you're after, try **Portnoy Caffè Letterario** (Via de Amicis at Corso Porta Ticinese, tel. 02/5811–3429) in the Ticinese–San Lorenzo area. This café features rotating art exhibits, evening poetry readings, and lectures several times a month (call for schedules). In the Brera-Garibaldi area, check out the romantic **L'Ecurie** (Via Ponte Vetero 23, near Piazza del Carmen, tel. 02/804403), complete with dim candlelight and air-conditioning. When the weather's nice there's nothing better than **Piazza del Carmine**, also in the Brera-Garibaldi area, for seeing and being seen, although you end up paying dearly for the view (L3000 for an espresso). Milan's best *gelaterie* (ice cream shops) include, the **Alemagna** (Piazza del Duomo, southern portico, no phone), **Gelateria Toldo** (Via Ponte Vetero 9, tel. 02/8646–0863), and **Gelateria Ecologica Artigiana** (Corso di Porta Ticinese 40, tel. 02/5810–1872).

WORTH SEEING

If your goal is to cover the "main" attractions, most of which lie within Milan's two innermost ring roads, you won't get a chance to see much of the rest of the city. For a complete tour, tackle one neighborhood at a time. You won't see much from the Metro, so pick stations central to each district and start your exploring from there. The Duomo Metro station is convenient to the city center, the Moscova and Lanza stations to the Brera area, the Cordusio Cadorna stations to Castello Sforzesco, and the Cadorna station to Santa Maria delle Grazie, where you'll find Leonardo's *Last Supper* fresco. The Porta Genova and Romolo stops will put you in a good position to explore the areas beyond the Navigli canal.

The Visconti family ruled medieval Milan with a cruel hand; on your wanderings look for the family emblem—a viper with its jaws open wide, devouring a child.

CASTELLO SFORZESCO In 1450 Francesco Sforza, a wealthy mercenary soldier who eventually married Bianca Maria Visconti, commissioned the rebuilding of this brawny castle. It stands as a monument to the Sforza and Visconti clans and, ultimately, to their lasting impact on Milan. Under another Sforza, Lodovico ("Il Moro"), the castle became an important venue for Renaissance art. Lodovico hired Bramante to design the castle's *rochetta* (fortress) and Leonardo da Vinci to decorate the interior. The castello now houses a variety of museums. Most memorable is the **Pinacoteca**, which contains Arcimbaldi's *Spring* and works by Bellini, Mantegna, and Foppa; the Egyptian collection in the dungeon is refreshingly different from the usual Italian masterpieces. The castle's **Museo d'Arte** is noteworthy, if only for Michelangelo's haunting, unfinished *Rondanini Pietà*, which the artist worked on until four days before his death at the age of 89. Even if you've had it with museums, Castello Sforzesco is worth a visit just for a romp about the castle grounds and courtyard. *Piazza Castello, tel. 02/62081. Metro: Cairoli. Admission free. All museums open Tues.–Sun. 9:30–5:30.*

IL DUOMO Reigning serenely over the city center, Milan's Gothic duomo is the third-largest—church capacity is said to be 40,000—and one of the most ornate cathedrals in the world. Not surprisingly, it took centuries to complete. Construction began in 1386 under the guidance of Galeazzo Visconti III, the first duke of Milan, and was not finished until 1897 (as late as 1958, workers were still tying up loose ends). The exterior is a complex conglomeration of spires and pinnacles, making the cathedral look like a giant ice-castle. The many artists who worked on the mammoth structure created an odd but mesmerizing mix of Gothic and baroque styles, unified only by the primary building material: marble from the quarries near Lago Maggiore. Outside, atop the highest pinnacle, is the "Madonnina" (little Madonna), a statue of the Virgin Mary covered in 3,900 leaves of gold. Also worth noting on the exterior are the beautiful bronze entrance doors and the prophets perched on the church's 135 marble spires.

The vast interior is softly colored by stained-glass windows; the first six on the right date from the 15th century. Down the right aisle near the southern transept lies the tomb of Gian Giacomo Medici, sculpted in the 1560s by Leone Leoni. Straight ahead is the duomo's most famous sculpture—the very morbid figure of St. Bartolomeo, whose glorious martyrdom consisted of being flayed alive. The central crucifix hangs from a suspension device designed by da Vinci; directly below, under the mosaic floors, is the church **treasury** (admission: L3000; open 9–noon and 2–6), which displays heavily embroidered vestments and bejeweled crowns from the 4th–12th centuries.

For a view of central Milan and a closer look at the duomo's prophet-capped spires, walk outside the left (north) transept and take the stairs (L5000) or the elevator (L7000) to the roof (open 9–5:30). Pollution sometimes detracts from the view, but on a clear day you can see the Alps and a close-up view of the impressive Gothic spires. From 10 to noon and 3 to 6 you can visit the remains of the original Roman basilica (admission free) upon which the duomo was built. Architecture enthusiasts will want to check out the **Museo del Duomo** (Piazza del Duomo 14, across the piazza from the cathedral, tel. 02/860358; admission: L7000, L4000 students), for a detailed account of Il Duomo's construction. The museum is open Tuesday–Sunday 9:30–12:30 and 3–6. *Piazza del Duomo. Metro: Duomo. Admission free. Open daily 7–7.*

GALLERIA VITTORIO EMANUELE Inside this cross-shaped, 19th-century promenade, which is covered by a lofty glass-arched ceiling, you'll find expensive cafés, bookstores, and designer boutiques, plus fast-food chains, the TELECOM phone office, and the Commune di Milano information center. The main reason to visit this Italian-style mall, however, is people-

The Galleria's original architect, Giuseppe Mengoni, accidentally slipped and fell (and died) in here just days before the promenade opened.

watching: The trendy Milanese who parade here certainly are a sight. If the crowd becomes too much to handle, switch to gawking at the huge glass dome. *Btw Piazza del Duomo and Piazza della Scala, no phone. Metro: Duomo.*

PINACOTECA DI BRERA This is Milan's most important museum, known throughout the world. Because of its size you'd be wise to limit your visit to works you're especially interested in, rather than attempting to see it all. The Brera's 38 rooms house such master-pieces as Lorenzetti's *Madonna and Child*, Gentile da Fabriano's polyptych *Valle Romita*, Piero della Francesca's *Urbino Altarpiece*, Raphael's *Marriage of the Virgin*, Mantegna's *Dead Christ*, Giovanni Bellini's *Pietà*, and Caravaggio's *Supper at Emmaus*. While 14th- to 18th-century art is the museum's strong suit, recent donations have enabled the Brera to acquire numerous contemporary works, displayed in the first hall as you enter. The building itself was constructed in the 17th century and was made into a museum during the Napoleonic era. *Via Brera 28, tel. 02/722631. Metro: Lanza. Admission: L8000. Open Tues.–Sat. 9–5:30, Sun. 9–12:30.*

SANTA MARIA DELLE GRAZIE To the left of this church is the former refectory of a Dominican monastery, now basically a shrine to Leonardo da Vinci's **Last Supper**. Since Leonardo's death in 1519, the *Last Supper* has suffered an amazingly cruel fate. First off, Leonardo used an experimental primer, which has peeled and crumbled over time. According to at least one source, well-meaning monks in the 19th century actually whitewashed the fresco. Bad idea. Napoleon's troops used the wall for target practice, and in August 1943 an American bombing raid nearly destroyed the work. Worst of all, attempts at restoration over the centuries have mostly hastened the fresco's deterioration, leaving the *Last Supper* in a some-what sad state today. It still has an odd, transfixing power about it, though. In addition, the piece is a striking example of Renaissance individualism, as each apostle expresses a singular and distinct emotion. Notice the figure of Judas, small and dark, calmly reaching for bread as pandemonium strikes the other apostles. Also notice the repetition of threes in the windows and the groupings. The Lombard Gothic church itself was designed by Guiniforte Solari between 1466 and 1490; Bramante added the Renaissance dome and three apses, as well as the cloister and sacristy. *Piazza Santa Maria delle Grazie, tel. 02/498–7588. Metro: Cadorna. Admission: L12,000. Open Tues.–Sun. 8:15–1:45 PM.*

LA SCALA OPERA HOUSE La Scala, a sacred pilgrimage site for opera buffs and Verdi lovers, was inaugurated on August 3, 1778, with Antonio Salieri's *Europa Riconosciuta.* Today the bill inevitably includes Puccini and Verdi—this is your chance to hear an Italian opera sung by Italians in Italy—as well as Wagner, Mozart, and the usual suspects. The small stalls and horseshoe shape of the auditorium give the interior a feeling of intimate grandeur, as well as incredible acoustics. It's no surprise that La Scala is *the* place to hang out among elite Milanese. (When the opera season begins in September all of the *pellicerie*, or furrier stores,

La Scala was the first theater in the world to use electric lights—on December 26, 1883.

put the best furs of the new season up for sale.) But if you can't find or afford the sought-after tickets, you can always sneak a peek inside by visiting the adjacent museum, the **Museo Teatrale**. On display here are strands of hair from Mozart and Puccini; death masks of Puccini, Wagner, and Verdi; and batons used by Toscanini. Inquire at the museum about discount tickets (as little as L5000) on the day of a performance. *Piazza della Scala, tel. 02/805–3418. From Il Duomo walk through the Galleria to Piazza della Scala. Admission: L5000, L4000 students. Open Mon.–Sat. 9–noon and 2–6, Sun. 9–noon (closed Sun. Nov.–Apr.).*

CHURCHES AND CHAPELS Sant'Ambrogio. St. Ambrose, the patron saint and 4th-cen-tury bishop of Milan, established this basilica and was himself buried here in AD 397. Inside, notice the Byzantine pillar next to the nave, topped with a bronze serpent (symbolizing Aaron's rod), and the pulpit depicting animals in a feeding frenzy. A mosaic of Ambrose, in the church's Capella di San Vittorio in Ciel d'Oro, is famous for its rendering of his slightly deformed face. *Piazza Sant'Ambrogio 15, tel. 02/8645–0895. Metro: Sant'Ambrogio.*

San Eustorgio. Near the canal, this beautiful, simple church is named for Bishop San Eustor-gio, who according to legend was given the relics of the Magi by Emperor Constantine. Of note in the basilica, which was rebuilt in the 9th and 14th centuries, is the Portinari chapel, with 15th-century frescoes by Foppa that depict the life of St. Peter. Also look for the fading frescoes on the many columns and the remains of the Roman basilica near the nave. *Piazza San Eustorgio. Bus 59 from the center.*

MUSEUMS Milan's primary exhibits are held in Castello Sforzesco (*see above*), but there are smaller museums and galleries throughout the city. Stop by the information office (*see* Visitor Information, *above*) in the Galleria Vittorio Emanuele for listings of shows.

Museo Civico Archeologico. Located in a 16th-century Benedictine convent, the Monastero Maggiore, this museum is home to a vast collection of Greek, Roman, and Etruscan pieces. One particularly interesting section is dedicated exclusively to the Roman period in Milan. *Corso Magenta 15, tel. 02/8645–0665. Metro: Cadorna. Admission free. Open Tues.–Sun. 9:30–5:30.*

Museo Civico d'Arte Contemporanea. The central hall of this modern-art museum is dedicated to works by contemporary artists, while the left wing houses "older" pieces by futurists, as well as works by Modigliani and de Chirico. The right wing (which ought to house the futurists) focuses on postwar paintings. *Palazzo Reale, Piazza del Duomo 12, tel. 02/6208–3914. Metro: Duomo. Admission free. Open Tues.–Sun. 9:30–5:30.*

Museo Nazionale della Scienza e Technica. Housed in a former Benedictine monastery, this is one of the world's foremost museums of science and technology. Inside, the **Leonardo Gallery** has a collection of models based on technical designs by the man himself. *Via San Vittore 21, tel. 02/4801–0040. Metro: Sant'Ambrogio. Admission: L10,000. Open Tues.–Sun. 9:30–4:50.*

Museo Poldi Pezzoli. Named after the 19th-century art collector who once lived here, the Pezzoli museum is a private collection that includes furnishings, ceramics, and glassware, as well as paintings by Mantegna, Piero della Francesca, and Botticelli. Highlights include Pollaiolo's *Portrait of a Lady* and Gaudri's *Gray Lagoon.* The museum is worth a visit not only for the works on display but for the house's Liberty-style interior. *Via Manzoni 12, tel. 02/794889. Metro: Duomo or Manzoni. Admission: L10,000. Open Tues.–Sun. 9:30–12:30 and 2:30–6, Sat. until 7:30. Closed Sun. afternoon Apr.–Sept.*

The Triennale. Not exactly a museum in the traditional sense, the Triennale is a constantly changing exhibition officially titled the "International Exhibition of Modern Decorative and Industrial Arts and Modern Architecture." It's been around since the first half of this century, but as the name Triennale suggests, it was to be held only once every three years. As of Fall 1994, however, it has been in operation year-round and is the most important exhibition of its kind in Italy. Themes range from modern architecture to fashion to virtual reality. For information on current showings, inquire at the APT office, check local newspapers, or call the Triennale directly. *Via Alemagna 6, inside Parco Sempione, tel. 02/7243–4241. Metro: Cadorna. Admission: L10,000. Open Tues.–Sun. 10–6, summer until 8.*

SHOPPING

Milan is Italy's fashion and design center, and nearly all major clothing and furniture designers have boutiques here. Even if you can't afford to buy, window-shopping in the posh Duomo district—nicknamed the *Quadrilatero d'Oro* (Golden Quadrilateral)—is still a trip. The epitome of excessiveness can be found on **Via Monte Napoleone**, just northeast of Piazza della Scala. Dozens of don't-touch-anything antiques and clothing stores as well as high-priced jewelers line the street. If you want to actually buy something, the bric-a-brac **market**, held the last Sunday of each month along the Navigli, is probably more up your alley. Also, for **designer seconds**, try the weekly Saturday-morning market on Via Papinaio. Other good options for secondhand clothing are **Surplus** (7 Corso Garibaldi, tel. 02/869–3696); **Mercatino Michela** (8 Corso Venezia, tel. 02/7600–3205); and, for funky 1960s and 1970s styles, **Napoleone** (5 Via Arcimboldi, off Via Union, tel. 02/875223), near the Duomo. Clothing at warehouse prices line the shelves at **Il Salvagente** (16 Via Filli Bronzetti, tel. 02/7611–0328). **Antiques markets** are held the third Saturday of each month (except Aug.) on Via Fiori Chiaria, near Via Brera.

AFTER DARK

Milan's nightlife is hoppin' but costly. Ticket prices for concerts, theater, and even movies tend to be exorbitant. Your best strategy is to either pick judiciously or consider going on a simple evening *passeggiata* (leisurely stroll). The newspapers *Il Corriere della Sera* and *La Repubblica* regularly list cultural events and club schedules. On Wednesday check the *Corriere della Sera* "Vivi Milano" insert. The information office in the Galleria (*see* Visitor Information, *above*) has flyers on current cultural happenings and can book tickets for most of them. Buy tickets for big-name rock concerts at the **Virgin Megastore** (Piazza del Duomo, at Via Marconi, tel. 02/7200–3370). For information on Milan's gay scene, call **Arci Gay** (Via Torisceni 19, tel. 02/5810–0299).

BARS AND CLUBS Even if you get into a club wearing tennis shoes and shorts, you'll wish you had been rejected at the door when you inevitably face the disdainful gazes of the always-elegant Milanese. And it's not enough to simply look like you're loaded with lira—most dance clubs require a cover of L20,000–L60,000. Bars are generally free.

Bar Magenta. This legendary bar is where many Milanese go to drink an *aperitivo* (before-dinner drink), from 6 to 8 PM. Later on, the bar, near Santa Maria delle Grazie, is filled with a livelier crowd and louder music. *Via Carducci 13, at Corso Magenta, tel. 02/805–3808. Open Tues.–Sun. 7 PM–3 AM.*

Coquetel. This very trendy club is *the* place to be. A look at the sidewalk in front, packed with hipsters, proves its popularity. All kinds of cocktails are available, though none of them are cheap. *14 Via Vetere, tel. 02/836–0688. Open Mon.–Sat. 8 PM–2 AM.*

New Parco delle Rose. This dance club has three swimming pools as well as slides and fountains, not to mention several dance floors on which patrons groove to whatever musical style suits them most—mainstream club-scene, Latin, even ballroom dancing (all with separate entrances). The cover (L12,000–L25,000) includes one drink and varies depending on the day of the week. *Via Fabio Massimo 36, tel. 02/569–4755.*

Nuova Idea. This is Italy's largest gay disco. Shake your moneymaker on the main dance floor, or get involved in an intricate polka or tango on the couples' dance floor. Cover is L20,000, which includes one drink. *Via de Castiesa 30, no phone. Open nightly Thurs.–Sun.*

Old Fashion. Amazingly, one of the hottest nightclubs in Milan is reasonably priced. The L15,000 Old Fashion cover includes one drink. *Via Alemagna 6, at Gare Alemagna in Parco Sempione, tel. 02/8056231. Metro: Cadorna.*

Il Patuscino. This joint, which pulls in a young crowd, plays live music ranging from jazz (if you're lucky) to New Age (if you're not). There's no cover, which makes it worth the risk of being subjected to an Italian Bee Gee wanna-be. *Via Madonnina 21, tel. 02/807264.*

Il Resentin. This place dates back to the days when the Brera-Garibaldi area was home to prostitutes and artists. The former owner, Gabriele or *il papà degli artisti* (father of the artists), often housed and fed poor artists who paid him with their paintings, many of which hang on the walls today. The current owner keeps the bar stocked with Trentino wines and 80 different grappas (L7000). *Via Mercato 24, around cnr from Il Patuscino, tel. 02/875923.*

Simposio. This bar, near the Basilica of San Lorenzo, looks like just another place to slam a few brewskis (L5000), but the ice-cream crepes (L3000–L7000), spiked with a touch of liqueur, make it unique. *Corso di Porta Ticinese, tel. 02/837–8508).*

During the Naviglio Festival in June, look for free open-air jazz and classical concerts throughout Milan.

MUSIC Milan's rock scene ain't great, but its jazz clubs are good, and its classical concerts and operas kick butt. Make an effort to see absolutely *anything* at La Scala (*see* Worth Seeing, *above*). Opera season runs from September to July, and even from abroad you can book tickets in advance (fax 02/887–9297). The average seat is definitely not budget, but there are 200 standing-room tickets available for each performance (L5000–L10,000) that go on sale the day of the show, at the door; a line starts forming sometimes as early as 6 AM, so get there as early as possible.

Capolinea (Via Lodovico il Moro 119, tel. 02/8912–2024; closed Mon.) remains the preeminent jazz club in Milan, featuring big-name Italian and international performers. **Scimmie** (Via Ascanio Sforza 49, tel. 02/8940–2874), a small and smoky club, features a different—usually jazz-fusion—band every night except Tuesday. Both clubs are open 8 PM–2 AM, and both require a cover charge, depending on the performance.

CENTRI SOCIALI If your sympathies lie with the left (and we *don't* mean the Democrats), you might enjoy the offerings of a **Centro Sociale**. These are illegal but tolerated organizations run by young communists and anarchists. Stop by the bookstore **Libreria Utopia** (Via Moscova 52, tel. 02/2900–3324) for more information on events and concerts. Or ask for *Piede di Porco* (L1500), a publication with a monthly calendar of activities. You can also try contacting the organizations directly: **Centro Sociale Leoncavallo** (Via Watteau 7, near Stazione Centrale, tel. 02/2614–0287), **Centro Autogestito Garibaldi** (Corso Garibaldi 89/B, tel. 02/2900–02464), **Circolo Anarchico Ponte della Ghisolfa e Info Shop** (Viale Monza 255, no phone).

MOVIE THEATERS A few movie theaters show films in English once a week. Hit the **Anteo** (Via Milazzo 9, tel. 02/659–7732) on Mondays, **Arcobaleno** (Viale Tunisia, tel. 02/2940–6054) on Tuesdays, and **Mexico** (Via Savona 57, tel. 02/4895–1802) on Thursdays. Admission each costs L7000, L5000 for students; a listing of films can be picked up at an APT office.

Lombardy

Traveling on a budget in Lombardy will challenge your imagination, your ability to deal with bland one-star hotels, and your appetite for pizza (the only consistently affordable food). But your efforts will be rewarded by the medieval and Renaissance glory of Mantova, Bergamo, and Cremona, and by the eccentricity of Grazie and Sabbioneta. While all of these towns—and the Po plain on which they sit—are industrialized and heavily touristed, you'll discover the intriguing remnants of many dynasties, from the bullying Longobards and regal Visconti to the superwealthy and utterly kooky Gonzagas.

The average Lombard is part stereotypical Italian and part stereotypical New Yorker; don't expect everyone to be warm and welcoming. On the other hand, it's not unheard of for a tourist to ask for simple directions to the nearest historical monument and get a personal escort. The territory itself is equally diverse, combining fertile plains, rugged mountains, and vacation-land lakes. Like the people, the landscape can sometimes be annoyingly cold and unwelcoming. Other times it will fill you, like a plate of steamy risotto, with feelings of comfort and warmth.

Pavia

Pavia's redbrick architecture and serene, cobblestoned streets belie its bellicose past. This quiet university town sits on the left bank of the Ticino River and, because of its strategic location, came into being as a Roman outpost. Pavia was later fortified by the Goths and Byzantines to ward off the evil Longobards. The city was eventually taken by that bigwig Milanese family, the Visconti, whose legacy is apparent in both Pavia's castle and university, which was founded in

The Crown of Iron

The city of Monza, 15 minutes by train from Milan, is known primarily for its duomo, a jumble of architectural and decorative styles that houses the bejeweled Corona del Ferro (Crown of Iron). Mind you, this is not just any crown of iron—the central ring is made from a nail reputedly taken from Jesus's cross. The relic is kept safe in the Chapel of Queen Teodolinda, the walls of which are covered with frescoes by Zavattari. It costs L1000 to see the crown, but what a small price to pay for a possibly religious experience.

1361. Today, town life centers around the university; during summer, Pavia is endearingly sleepy. Come during the school year for college-town culture and nightlife, but don't expect prices to cater to student budgets. Another reason to visit is strictly practical: From Pavia, you're within a short hop of the stupendous Certosa monastery (*see* Near Pavia, *below*).

BASICS **APT.** This is the place for brochures, maps, and hotel information (they aren't supposed to make reservations). *Via Fabio Filzi 2, tel. 0382/22156. From train and bus stations, turn left up Via Trieste and go right on Via Fabio Filzi. Open Mon.–Sat. 8:30–12:30 and 2–6.*

COMING AND GOING Trains run all day between Milan and Pavia (30 min, L3400). The same trip by bus costs L4200, with buses leaving about every half hour during the day. Buses from Pavia depart from the **Autocorriere Station** (Via Trieste 21, tel. 0382/302020), open Monday–Saturday 6:15 AM–7:50 PM, Sunday 8:15–noon and 4:45–7. Due to Pavia's small size and many pedestrian-only streets, walking is the best way to get around.

WHERE TO SLEEP The only budget choices in Pavia are substellar one-star hotels. The centrally located **Splendid** (Via XX Settembre 11, off Corso Cavour, tel. 0382/24703) has adequate though somewhat neglected doubles (all without bath) for L60,000. If they're full, try the **Stazione** (Via B. de Rossi 8, tel. 0382/35477), off Corso Manzoni (it's not well marked). Noise is a problem because of its location near the train tracks. Doubles, all without bath, are L70,000. Also near the train station but one step up in luxury is the **Aurora** (Viale V. Emanuele 25, tel. 0382/23664). Doubles, all with bath, cost L85,000.

FOOD Food in Pavia isn't cheap, but the budget traveler probably won't mind skipping out on the city's costly culinary specialties, like fried frogs' legs. For cheaper and less challenging eats, try **Pizzeria Toscana** (Via Cardano 6, tel. 0382/26907). Sandwiches (L5000–L6000) and atmosphere abound at the old-style **Bar Bordoni** (Via Bordoni 24, tel. 0382/21652). The artsy **Caffè Teatro** (Corso Strada Nuova 75, across from the theater, tel. 0382/23098) features sandwiches and evening poetry readings Wednesday–Saturday. **Hosteria del Senatore** (Via Menocchio 21, main entrance on Vicolo del Senatore off Corso Cavour, no phone) boasts an open courtyard in summer and a fireplace in winter; primi are L6000, secondi L9000. Typical Lombard cuisine is dished out at **Osteria della Malora** (Via Milazzo 79, tel. 0382/34302). And to satisfy your sweet tooth, indulge in the aptly named *torta paradiso* (paradise cake) at **Pasticceria Vignon** (Strada Nuova 110, tel. 0382/22103). A covered **market** is held Monday–Saturday under Piazza della Vittoria (look for staircases leading underground from the piazza).

WORTH SEEING Dominating the skyline is Pavia's **duomo** (Piazza del Duomo, off Corso Cavour). Begun in 1488, numerous architects, including da Vinci and Bramante, have contributed to its design. Its cupola, the third largest in Italy, wasn't completed until 1885, and its facade was finished under Mussolini in 1933. The cathedral is a good example of the simple redbrick architecture that flourished in Lombardy during the Renaissance. Inside you'll find encased skeletons on display.

The duomo's tower collapsed suddenly on Friday, March 17, 1989—a particularly eerie event when one considers that Friday the 17th is Italy's version of our superstitious Friday the 13th.

Pavia boasts several other historic churches as well. **San Michele** (Corso Garibaldi and Via Diacono), the last of four Pavian churches dedicated to Michael, patron saint of the Longobards, was the church of choice for crowning medieval kings and emperors. It was rebuilt in yellow sandstone and red brick after a 12th-century earthquake destroyed much of the structure. The exterior is home to such stone curiosities as griffins and snake-tailed fish. **San Pietro** in **Ciel d'Oro** (Via Griziotti) dates from the 12th century and is mentioned in Dante's *Divine Comedy*. **Santa Maria del Carmine** (Piazza Carmine, off Via XX Settembre) was begun about 1370 and remains a wonderful specimen of Lombard-Gothic architecture. It contains paintings and frescoes by Foppa, Vidolengo da Marzano, Lenzani, Faruffini, and Moncalvo. All of Pavia's churches are open daily 8–noon and 3–6.

The imposing **Castello Visconti** (Piazza Castello, at end of Strada Nuova; open Tues.–Sat. 9–1:30, Sun. 9–1) houses a museum of Lombard and Romanesque sculptures, as well as a respectable collection of 14th- to 17th-century religious paintings and altarpieces. Look especially for da Messina's *Portrait of a Man*. The most characteristic landmark in Pavia, the **uni-**

versity (Strada Nuova and Corso Goldoni), is one of the oldest in Italy. Of its 12 courtyards, the most visit-worthy is the Sforzesco. Pavia's two other defining features are its medieval towers and bridge. The **Ponte Coperto** (covered bridge) is actually a 1951 reconstruction of a bridge originally built on Roman foundations in the 14th century.

NEAR PAVIA

CERTOSA Even if you'd rather die than tour yet another church, Certosa is absolutely worth a visit. Founded and financed by Galeazzo Visconti III, duke of Milan, in 1396, the **Certosa della Madonna delle Grazie** is an intoxicating swirl of decoration and detail. Only the best marble was used for this church/monastery, transported from the legendary quarries of Carrara, and its sculpted marble facade goes a few steps beyond ornate—"extravagant grandeur" comes closer to the mark. When he commissioned this monastery, the duke envisioned the "most solemn and remarkable" of buildings. More than half a millennium later, Certosa certainly remains one of Italy's most remarkable (though hardly solemn) landmarks.

More than 250 artists and architects have worked in and for Certosa, creating Lombardy's most mishmashed masterpiece. The church's richly decorated red-green-and-white marble facade is covered with all sorts of friezes and statues—from medallions of Roman emperors and Eastern monarchs to a low-relief cycle of the life of Christ. Inside stand the incomplete funerary monument to Lodovico il Moro and Beatrice d'Este, and the old sacristy with its triptych made of hippopotamus teeth. Other interesting artifacts include the presbytery, the most ornate part of the church, and the lavabo, with the marble fountain that's still used for the monks' ritual washing. Check out the refectory, with its Renaissance pulpit, then visit one of the monks' cells, each of which has its own garden and a device for passing meals through the wall without speaking. This is still a functioning monastery, evidenced not only by the wandering robed brothers but also by the continuing production of their famous Chartreuse liqueur, herbal medicines, and perfumes—all for sale or perusal in the adjoining shop. Make your way through Certosa alone, or take a guided tour, in Italian only, with one of the monks. You might want to pack a picnic; nearby there's a shady area with tables (and a few mosquitoes) as well as a bar where you can sample good local brews. *Viale Certosa, tel. 0382/925613. Admission free. Open May–Aug., Tues.–Sun. 9–11:30 and 2:30–6; Nov.–Feb., Tues.–Sun. 9–11:30 and 2:30–4:30; Sept., Oct., Mar., Apr., Tues.–Sun. 9–11:30 and 2:30–5:30.*

➤ **COMING AND GOING** • From Pavia's Autocorriere station, take a **SGEA** bus (every ½ hr, 10 min, L1900) to the Certosa stop along the autostrada; then follow Viale Certosa for 1 kilometer, until it dead-ends into Certosa. Buy your ticket for the return trip from the newsstand by the bus stop.

Cremona

Cremona remains an enchanting, historic town, despite its efforts to sell itself as an enchanting, historic town. With numerous piazze and roomier streets, Cremona feels more airy than most Lombard towns. With its museums and churches, not to mention its original Stradivarius violins and guitars, it also feels more high-cultured than some one-piazza-and-a-fountain towns. The bottom line: Cremona makes a good day trip from Milan and a good base for exploring the surrounding Po plain.

Cremona's musical tradition began in the 16th century, when it was home to composer Claudio Monteverdi and Andrea Amati, founder of the town's first violin workshop. Although Amati's nephew, Nicolò (1596–1684), might still boast an international reputation, it was Amati's star pupil, Antonio Stradivari (1644–1737), whose name became synonymous with the world's finest string instruments. Cremona's international violin school, the Scuola di Liuteria, still trains violin makers, and scattered throughout town are more than 50 craftspeople working by traditional methods in small shops.

BASICS **APT.** *Piazza del Comune 5, opposite the duomo, tel. 0372/23233. Open Mon.–Sat. 9:30–12:30 and 3–6, Sun. 10–noon.*

COMING AND GOING Choose one of 14 daily trains between Milan and Cremona (1 hr, L7200). Cremona's small **train station** (tel. 0372/22237) is on Via Dante. If you're coming from Venice (15 trains daily, 3½ hrs, L19,000), you must change trains twice, at Verona and Mantova. The ticket counter is open daily 6 AM–8:30 PM.

Antonio Stradivari, who learned the finer points of his trade in Cremona, handcrafted upwards of 1,200 violins, guitars, cellos, harps, and mandolins during his 68-year career. More than two centuries later they remain the most coveted string instruments in the world.

Six buses leave Milan for Cremona before 9:30 AM, one leaves at midday, and two leave in the early evening. The one-hour trip to Cremona's **Autostazione** (Via Dante, tel. 0372/29212), next to the train station, costs L6700. The office is open weekdays 7:15–1 and 2:15–6:30, Saturday 7:15–1. After hours, buy tickets at the *pasticceria* (pastry shop) at Via Dante 105. From both the bus and train stations, it's a 10-minute walk down Via Palestro to the city center.

WHERE TO SLEEP Cremona has reasonably priced *and* clean hotels; just remember to book in advance. As the town is small, none of the hotels are far from the center or the train and bus stations. If the places listed below are booked, try the **Brescia** (Via Brescia 7, tel. 0372/434615). It's a little farther from the center, and more expensive—doubles without bath go for L50,000. Otherwise the APT office (*see* Basics, *above*) books private rooms and *agriturismo* (farm-stay) packages.

Ideale. The Ideale is well located (five minutes on foot from both the bus and train stations) but rather unremarkable. The best that can be said is that breakfast is included, as are hot showers. You'll pay L45,000 for a double. *Viale Trento e Trieste 2, at Corso Garibaldi, tel. 0372/38953. 10 rooms, none with bath. Closed Sun. to arrivals without reservations.*

Touring. Stay here if you can afford it: Besides large and clean rooms and bathrooms, downstairs there's a TV room, kitchen, dining area, and bar. Doubles fetch L50,000, L70,000 with bath. Breakfast is available for L2500. *Via Palestro 3, at Corso Garibaldi, tel. 0372/36976. 11 rooms, 3 with bath. Closed Sat. afternoon and Sun. to arrivals without reservations.*

➤ **CAMPING** • **Camping Parco al Po.** You'll find this shady campground along the Po River, just outside the city. It's a family-oriented place with little kiddies and lots of RVs, but easing the pain are a restaurant, bocce ball green, amusement area (slides and swings), and bar (!). Tent sites cost L6000, plus an extra L6000 per person. *Via Lunga Po Europa 12/A, tel. 0372/21268. Bus 1 from train station. Closed Oct.–Mar. Wheelchair access.*

FOOD Pizza is your best deal, unless you buy your own supplies at Cremona's **open market**, held every Wednesday and Saturday morning (about 7 AM–1 PM) on Piazza Mercato. If you can't hold out, **Voglia Pizza** (Corso Garibaldi 38, tel. 0372/413881) serves large, portable pizza squares (L6000). **Nuova Piedigrotta** (Piazza Risorgimento, tel. 0372/22033) is a good bet if you want to sit down in a restaurant to eat your pizza (L8000). **Ristorante Centrale** (Via Pertusio 4, off Via Solferino, tel. 0372/28701) serves first-rate Cremonese cuisine; the local specialty, particularly in winter, is *mostarda* (a piquant fruit served in syrup) spooned over *bollito misto* (a mixture of boiled meats). Even if you can't afford to eat at the Centrale, check out the bar, filled with old men arguing vehemently about soccer. For fresh bread and pizza by the kilo (L1600 for 100 grams), hop on over to **Forno Antico** (Corso Garibaldi 59, tel. 0372/456022).

WORTH SEEING Cremona's museums are not as thrilling as the town's effusive, goofily translated tourist literature claims, but still consider buying an all-in-one museum ticket (L5000) from whichever museum you visit first. Not exactly the Louvre, but certainly unusual, the **Museo della Civiltà Contadina** (Via Castelleone, tel. 0372/21411) tries to explain what life was like for generations of Cremonese peasants (in Italian only). The largely unremarkable **Museo Civico** (Via U. Dati 4, tel. 0372/461885) displays paintings by minor artists and various archaeological artifacts.

Cremona's **Piazza del Comune** is considered one of the loveliest in Italy: The duomo, campanile, baptistery, and town hall harmoniously mix brick, cream-colored marble, terra-cotta, and copper. Like other patchwork monuments in the region, the duomo's exterior successfully blends Gothic, Renaissance, and baroque styles. Climb to the top of the *torrazzo* (tower) for a view of the city (L5000). The **Palazzo del Comune** (Piazza del Comune, tel. 0372/4071–31971), still used as a town hall, displays 17th- to 19th-century furniture and paintings, as well as violins crafted by Andrea and Nicolò Amati, Stradivari, and Guarneri. It's open Tuesday–Saturday 8:30–6, Sunday 9–12:15 and 3–6.

From Piazza del Comune, continue two blocks along Via Solferino to **Piazza Roma**, a leafy square where Stradivari lived and worked. Look for Stradivari's simple grave in the park's center. For more on the master, head to the **Museo Stradivariano** (Via Palestro 17, tel. 0372/461886); its designs, wooden models, and finished violins are great if you're a fan of the stringed instrument. If not, you can breeze through the place. Currently it's open Tuesday–Saturday 8:30–5:45 and Sunday 9:15–12:15 and 3–6, but hours are subject to change.

AFTER DARK Cremona's after-dark scene is, in a word, bleak. During summer, films are sometimes screened outside on **Piazza Roma** (tel. 0372/27501 for movie info); other nights you'll find local youth carousing on said square. From July 5 to 31, the Palazzo del Comune hosts a **dance festival** (tickets L15,000), and from May to June classical music performances (tickets L25,000–L30,000) are held at the **Teatro Ponchielli** (Corso Vittorio Emanuele, at Via Gaetano Cesari). For more information on tickets and other events contact the APT office (*see* Basics, *above*).

Bergamo

Bergamo is a city divided. Charmless Bergamo Bassa (Lower Bergamo) is overshadowed by the majestic Bergamo Alta (Upper Bergamo), set imperially on a hill. Although the city's two halves are connected by a funicular railway, there's almost no reason to leave the compact, vehicle-free upper city and forsake its museums and architecture for the lower city's bland offerings. That is, of course, unless you're on a budget: Bergamo may be a university town, but high lodging prices reflect its popularity with foreign, rental-car-driving culture vultures. Backpackers beware. Also keep in mind that the **Bergamo Jazz** festival, held February–August, brings crowds in and prices up.

BASICS

➤ **CHANGING MONEY** • In Bergamo, exchange houses uniformly charge L8000 or 1% to change money, and most close weekdays around 5:30 and weekends. To draw lire from your AmEx card, there's an ATM at the **Banca Popolare di Milano** (Viale Papa Giovanni XXIII 116, tel. 035/237642).

➤ **VISITOR INFORMATION** • Bergamo has two **APT** tourist offices, one in each half of the city. The lower city office has more information on the province as a whole than on Bergamo itself. The upper city office has hotel, campground, and agriturismo listings as well as city maps and event guides. *Bergamo Bassa: Viale Papa Giovanni XXIII 106, tel. 035/242226. Open weekdays 9–12:30 and 3–6:30. Bergamo Alta: Vicolo Aquila Nera 2, off Piazza Vecchia, tel. 035/232730. Open Apr.–Oct. 10–12:30 and 2:30–7.*

COMING AND GOING There is hourly service between Milan and Bergamo's **train station** (Piazza Marconi, tel. 035/247624); the one-hour trip costs L5000. There is one train on Sunday, at 8:21 AM, from Bergamo to Venice (3½ hrs, L19,000); otherwise change trains in Brescia. Luggage storage is available daily 7 AM–9 PM. Bergamo's bus depot, **Stazione Auto Linee** (tel. 035/248150), is across the parking lot from the train station. Buses leave every half hour for Milan (1 hr, L6700); there are seven buses a day to Brescia (1½ hrs, L6300).

GETTING AROUND West of the bus and train stations is where you'll find most cheap hotels and pizzerias, while uphill and northwest of the station, in the upper city, is where you'll find Bergamo's main attractions. To reach Upper Bergamo take Bus 1 (L1200); it runs along Lower Bergamo's main avenue, Viale Papa Giovanni XXIII (which turns into Viale Vittorio Emanuele II at Porta Nuova). Bus 1 also stops at the funicular (L1200) that climbs uphill to Bergamo Alta. Buy tickets at *giornalai* (newsstands) or at vending machines at the funicular. For more bus and funicular information, contact the **ATB** transportation office (tel. 035/255255).

WHERE TO SLEEP Unfortunately, most budget lodgings are in Lower Bergamo, generally in the area just northwest of the train and bus stations. All of the hotels near the station are of the sanitary (and safe) variety, and most have nighttime lockouts around 1 AM. If every place listed below is full, try **Quarenghi** (Via Quarenghi 35, tel. 035/320331), with doubles for L70,000 without bath. During summer it's best to book ahead.

Agnello d'Oro. The cheapest place in Bergamo Alta has clean and comfortable rooms equipped with TVs, phones, and big bathrooms. It also has a good (but not especially cheap) trattoria on the ground floor, which closes in winter. Doubles are L95,000. *Via Gombito 22, tel. 035/ 249883. 3-min walk from funicular station. 20 rooms with bath. Luggage storage. Reservations advised. Wheelchair access. AE, MC, V.*

S. Giorgio. With newly redone bathrooms, this hotel is a good choice, even with its somewhat inconvenient location. Doubles run L55,000–L70,000. *Via S. Giorgio 10, tel. 035/212043. From train station, take Via G. Bonomelli, right on Via Giacomo and then left on Via S. Giorgio. 36 rooms, 29 with bath. MC, V.*

➢ **HOSTELS** • **Hostel Bergamo.** This newly renovated, three-star hostel in the northeast end of Bergamo Bassa has a restaurant, bar, TV, laundry facilities, and bike rental. Beds go for L17,000, including breakfast (other meals cost L12,000). *Via Galileo Ferraris 1, tel. 035/361724. Bus 14 from Porta Nuova. 60 beds. Curfew midnight, lockout 9 AM–3 PM. HI card required.*

FOOD As with lodging, finding cheap food is a problem in Bergamo, especially in the upper city, where even an orange juice will set you back L7000. If you crave nothing more than focaccia and pastries, try the *birrerie* (beer halls) along the upper city's Via Gombito. But for honestly cheap eats, head straight for Bergamo Bassa. Its self-service **Green House** (Via Verdi 31/F, tel. 035/ 226351; open weekdays noon–2 PM) has a fixed menu for L13,000. Also look for generic pizzerias near the train station on Via Quarenghi, Via Previtali, and Via San Bernardino. For do-it-yourselfers, there's a **Roll Market** (Viale Vittorio Emanuele II 17, tel. 035/234767) supermarket on Bergamo Bassa's main drag. It's open Monday 8:30–1, Tuesday–Saturday 8:30–1 and 4–8.

Antica Hosteria del Vino Buono (Via Donizetti 25, tel. 035/247993), near the Mercato delle Scarpe funicular stop in Upper Bergamo, is a friendly place with excellent regional food. Primi include *casoncelli* (stuffed pasta) for L10,000, and Bergamese polenta with sausage or rabbit for L15,000. **Da Mimmo** (Via Bartolomeo Colleoni 17, tel. 035/218535), in the heart of the upper city, is a busy pizzeria/restaurant with a covered terrace in back (and a menu in four languages). Pizza costs L6000–L12,000; *menu turistica* is L30,000. **Trattoria al Castello** (Via Castello 14, tel. 035/259607), at the base of the castle, offers spectacular views. Primi cost about L8000; main courses, like *bresaola di cavallo con grana* (thinly sliced raw horsemeat with parmesanlike cheese) cost L10,000.

WORTH SEEING Bergamo contains a few major cultural and visual surprises. Its **Piazza Vecchia** is considered one of Italy's loveliest squares—at least according to Bernard Berenson, Le Corbusier, and Frank Lloyd Wright. It marks the heart of the upper city and is a favorite gathering spot for locals and tourists alike—particularly during the evening passeggiata, between 5 and 7 PM. Sights farther afield include **Sant'Agostino** (Piazza Sant'Agostino), with its simple, bold, elegant facade (closed to the public), and the overwhelmingly ornate **Santa Maria Maggiore** (Piazza del Duomo, tel. 035/219955; open 8–noon and 3–6). The latter's polychromatic marble facade, lavishly frescoed interior, and exquisite wooden choir stalls (designed by Lotto) all leave you a bit bleary-eyed.

Accademia Carrara. You'd hardly expect a town like Bergamo to have such an exceptional art museum, but it does, with mostly Italian art from the 12th–18th centuries. Highlights include works by Raphael, Mantegna, Bellini, Tiepolo, Titian, Canaletto, Giorgione, and Guardi, as well as by major Bergamese artists. Across the piazza, the contemporary art museum has temporary exhibitions. *Piazza dell'Accademia, tel. 035/399643. Admission: L3000, Sun. free. Open Wed.–Mon. 9:30–12:30 and 2:30–5:30.*

Capella Colleoni. Considered the most notable edifice on Piazza del Duomo, this small but impressive chapel was commissioned in the late 13th century by Bartolomeo Colleoni as a mausoleum for himself and his daughter, Medea. Designed by Giovanni Antonio Amadeo, the intricate pink-and-white marble facade is equaled by the elaborate interior decoration, complete with an equestrian statue of Colleoni that looks slightly awkward perched atop his sarcophagus. Also worth a quick peek is Bergamo's **duomo** (admission free), dedicated to St. Alessandro, the city's patron saint. Step inside and risk being made queasy by the colors gold, pale green, and pink, all of which give the duomo the appearance of a turn-of-the-century tearoom. *Piazza del Duomo. Admission free. Open Mar.–Oct., Tues.–Sun. 9–noon and 2–6:30; Nov.–Feb., Tues.–Sun. 9–noon and 2:30–4:30.*

Castello. Though there's not much left of Bergamo's ancient castle, the ruins, which sit strategically atop Calle di San Vigilio, provide breathtaking views of the city. If you're tired of frescoes and statues, bring yourself and a loved one, a bottle of wine, and some picnic fixin's around sunset. If you need more excitement, the **Gruppo Speleologico le Nottole** (Bergo 5, Caterina 11/B, tel. 035/241020) arranges tours of the castello's underground passageways a few times a year for free. *Via S. Vigilio. Take funicular (L2000) from bottom of Via S. Vigilio. Admission free. Open Mar.–Oct., daily 9–8; Nov.–Feb., daily 10–4.*

Museo Donizettiano. Dedicated to Bergamo native Gaetano Donizetti, this museum houses a collection of the composer's sheet music, manuscripts, his piano, and other instruments, plus portraits and even the bed in which he died. If you're a fan of Donizetti and his operas, go to the humble house where he grew up, **Casa Nataledi Gaetano Donizetti** (Via Borgo Canale 14, tel. 035/247116), and a local theater that's been dedicated to him, the **Teatro Donizetti** (Piazza Cavour 14, tel. 035/249631). *Via Arena 9, tel. 035/399269. Admission free. Open weekdays 9–noon and 2:30–6.*

Rocca. Perched atop the highest hill in town (Sant'Eufemia), this former arsenal and prison—and the adjacent park—offers some powerful panoramas. Stroll through the memorial park or climb around its towers. *Via Rocca. From upper city funicular, follow well-marked road 50 meters to right. Admission free. Open Apr.–Sept., daily 9–noon and 2–8; Oct. and Mar., weekends 10–noon and 2–6; Nov. and Feb., weekends 10–noon and 2–4.*

Brescia

Brescia ought to be a hopping Lombard town with its university, famous artwork, striking architecture, and prime location on the Milan–Venice train line. Instead Brescia is smug and overpriced. The city is famed for its weapons industry, not its tourist trade; perhaps this explains the lack of concessions to visitors (Brescians don't exactly welcome tourists with open arms). Still, if you can ignore the attitude, Brescia does have two smart-looking duomos, beautiful medieval and Renaissance architecture, a romantic castle on a hill, and perhaps the ugliest piazza in Italy—a Fascist abomination known as Piazza Vittoria.

BASICS **APT.** The office will furnish you with pamphlets on hotels and sights in the area; ask for the brochure "Brescia: Ancient City of Lombardy." *Corso Zanardelli 34, tel. 030/43418. From station, take Viale Stazione to Corso Martiri della Libertà, right on Corso Palestro (which becomes Via Zanardelli). Open weekdays 9–12:30 and 3–6, Sat. 9–12:30.*

COMING AND GOING From Brescia's **train station** (Piazzale Stazione, tel. 030/37961) there are roughly 25 trains daily to Venice (2½ hrs, L15,500) and 30 daily trains to Milan (1 hr, L7200). Luggage storage (L1500) is open 7 AM–8 PM. Brescia's historic center is a short walk from the station, either along Corso Martiri della Libertà or Via Antonio Gramsci.

WHERE TO SLEEP Predictably, budget hotels are concentrated in the area around the station. One that is cheap and fairly clean is **Solferino** (Via Solferino 1, tel. 030/46300), where doubles run L50,000–L60,000 (without bath). From the station take Via Stazione and make the first right onto Via Solferino. If you'd rather be closer to the student area, **Vellia** (Via Calzavellia 5, tel. 030/373–6472), right off Corso Mameli, charges L55,000–L60,000 for doubles. If you're female and don't mind an early curfew (10 PM), two convents in town accept temporary boarders and are clean, safe, and cheap. The first, **Istituto Suore delle Poverelle** (Via Fratelli Bronzetti 17, tel. 030/375–5387), charges L10,000 per person and has laundry and kitchen facilities. At the second, **Paola di Rosa** (Contrada Santa Croce 17, tel. 030/377–2531), you'll pay at least L20,000 for a shared room, L35,000 for your very own. The convent has laundry facilities and—bless your favorite deity—air-conditioning. At either convent it's best to call ahead for reservations, but don't call after 9 PM—nuns are not late-nighters.

FOOD Typical Brescian dishes include *polenta pasticciata* (corn meal with cheese, meat, or vegetables), casoncelli, wild rabbit, and pigeon. Corso Mameli and the streets around it are home to many budget-friendly eateries, including **Caffè Osteria dei Mercantini** (Via Delle Battaglie 2, where Corso Mameli becomes Corso Garibaldi, tel. 030/40258); a two-course lunch with wine is just L15,000. Finish it off with a scoop of amaretto gelato (L1500) at the nearby **Prima Cremeria** (Corso Garibaldi 2, tel. 030/40625). Another nice spot for either lunch, dinner, or just a drink is **Osteria delle Dame** (Via S. Francesco d'Assisi 1/B, tel. 030/377–1868), which serves sandwiches (L5000), salads (L5000–L12,000), and a selection of wines and beers. If you're museum-hopping on Via Musei, stop in **Caligola Caffè** (Via Musei 51/A, next to the Capitolino, tel. 030/42197) for a quick sandwich and a beer. For coffee and pastries in an exotic setting, try the pasticceria **Capuzzi Ai Musei** (Via Piamarta 1, tel. 030/375–5369); it's just off Via Musei, in front of the Santa Giulia church. More cafés are grouped along Corso Palestro and near the duomos. There's a **supermarket** in Standa (Via IV Novembre, btw Piazza della Vittoria and Piazza del Mercato, tel. 030/296461), and **markets** on Piazza Rovetta and Piazza del Mercato are open weekdays 7–2, Saturday 7–1.

WORTH SEEING Every Saturday and Sunday, free museum tours with varying topics are available. Call 030/44327 to make reservations.

Standing at the corner of Piazza del Duomo, it's hard to miss the **Broletto** (Vicolo Sant'Agostino 29, no phone), a typical medieval town hall and still the seat of Brescia's local government. The rooms are closed to the public, but you can see the inner courtyard. The Broletto incorporates the city's oldest tower, the **Torre del Popolo**, which dates from the 11th century, and the church of **Sant'Agostino**, a 15th-century structure with a colorful terra-cotta facade. On Piazza del Duomo itself, the late-Renaissance **Duomo Nuovo**, much too large for its square, overshadows the more simple and elegant **Duomo Vecchio** (also known as the Rotonda) next door. Inside the duomo are the noteworthy crypt and treasury and a collection of paintings by local masters.

One of the most outstanding sights in Brescia is the **Capitolino** (Via Musei 57, tel. 030/46031), a Capitoline temple built by the emperor Vespasian in AD 73. Only its grand stairway, columns, and lintel remain, yet it's still an impressive testament to Brescia's Roman origins. In the adjoining **Museo Romano** is a fine collection of engraved stones, mosaics, glass, porcelain, and bronzes, not to mention *Winged Victory*, the famed 1st-century bronze sculpture. *Via Musei, tel. 030/46031. Admission: L5000. Open Tues.–Fri. 9–12:30 and 3–5 (until 6 PM June–Sept.).*

The churches of **Santa Giulia**, **Santa Maria in Solario**, and **San Salvatore** have been joined together to form a single museum. Respectively dating from the 16th, 7th–9th, and 12th centuries, the three churches form part of the monastery of San Salvatore, where Charlemagne's wife, Ermengarde, spent her last days. *Via Musei 81, tel. 030/44327. Combined admission to all three: L5000. Open weekdays 10–12:30 and 3–6, weekends 10–12:30 and 3–7.*

Brescia's central network of squares and lanes is great for aimless strolls. Along the way you'll inevitably stumble upon the stately Renaissance **loggia** (Piazza Loggia 1, tel. 030/29831), completed in 1574 after being fiddled with by Palladio, Sansovino, and Titian. Facing the Loggia from across the piazza is the **Torre dell'Orologio** (Clock Tower), modeled on the campanile in Venice's Piazza San Marco. The town's **castello** (Piazza Castello, end of Via del Castello), atop Cydean Hill, has ancient origins but largely owes its present structure, including the circular Mirabella Tower, to the 13th-century designs of the Visconti clan. Today the castle houses armor and weaponry from a variety of eras in its **Museum of Arms** (tel. 030/293292; admission: L5000; open Tues.–Fri. 9–12:30 and 3–5).

One of Brescia's best museums, the **Pinacoteca Civica**, is housed in the 16th-century Palazzo Martinengo da Barco. Its collection is composed mostly of works by lesser-knowns and/or locals, but includes a few pieces by bigwigs such as Raphael, Paolo Veneziano, Tintoretto, and Lorenzo Lotto. *Piazza Moretto 4, tel. 030/59120. Admission: L5000. Open Tues.–Fri. 9–12:30 and 3–5.*

AFTER DARK Two bars that have live music (Thurs.–Sun. only) are the colorful **Arancia Meccanica** (Via Rua Soveral 95, no phone), open 2 PM–2 AM, and the **Fahrenheit Club** (Via Inganni 6/C, no phone), open until 6 AM. In July and August, don't miss the open-air concerts held regularly on the Castello's grounds, in addition to open-air movies (also at the Castello) and theater held throughout town. Check with the APT tourist office (*see* Basics, *above*) for details.

Mantova

A city rich in art, history, political intrigue, and that amorphous quality called atmosphere, Mantova (Mantua) alternates between solemn and outrageously decadent. Even its origins are dark and exotic: Some say the town was settled by a witch named Manto who, after years of wandering, settled where the River Mincio becomes a swampy lowland. According to legend, she practiced magic until her death, when loyal followers built this city over her grave and named it Mantova in her honor.

The construction of two dams in the River Mincio in the 13th century partially drained this swampy region and formed three lakes that surround the city today.

While Mantova's documented origins go back to the Etruscan period, the city you see today was essentially created by the Gonzaga family and their preferred artists: Leon Battista Alberti, Andrea Mantegna, and Guilio Romano. The Gonzagas—the Adams family of the Renaissance—ruled the city for three and a half centuries with great skill, seeing to the creation and decoration of everything from Palazzo Ducale, Palazzo Te, and the duomo, to the churches of Sant'Andrea and San Sebastiano. Yet with each successive generation the clan grew more ostentatious, and there is something alarming about this prolific gathering of structures and artworks in Mantova's small center, so out of proportion to the small town itself. Too much wealth and flamboyance in too small a circumference have left the city both enchanted and overwhelmed, which is why Mantova is one of the most fascinating towns in the region, despite its nearby factories and aggressive swarms of mosquitoes (definitely bring repellent).

BASICS

➤ **CHANGING MONEY** • If you're planning to arrive in Mantova after 6 PM or on a Sunday, it's best to change money before you come, because the exchange places will definitely be *chiusi* (closed). Otherwise, the banks scattered around the city generally change money for a 1% fee. The **main post office** (Piazza Martiri di Belfiore 15, tel. 0376/326544) will also change money and American Express traveler's checks for a L2000–L5000 fee.

➤ **VISITOR INFORMATION** • The town's **APT** information office provides bus schedules and the usual maps and pamphlets along with information (mostly in Italian) on nature walks, bike paths, boat trips, and regional festivals in the province of Mantova. *Piazza Mantegna 6, tel. 0376/328253. From station, take Via Bonomi, left on Corso Vittorio Emanuele II (which becomes Corso Umberto I) to Piazza Mantegna. Open Mon.–Sat. 9–noon and 3–6.*

The **Centro Prenotozione Alberghiera** arranges private accommodations in Mantova. *Via Accademia 46, tel. 0376/365401. From station, take Via Bonomi, left on Corso Vittorio Emanuele II (which becomes Corso Umberto I) through Piazza delle Erbe, turn left on Via Accademia. Open weekdays 8:30–12:30 and 2–6.*

COMING AND GOING Mantova's small **train station** (Piazza Don Leoni) has luggage storage 6:05 AM–9 PM (L1500 per piece per 24 hrs). Trains leave nine times daily from Milan (2 hrs, L13,600) and 11 times daily from Verona (45 min, L3400), where you can change for Venice (2 hrs, L13,000). Trains are the cheapest and easiest way to reach larger Italian cities.

Buses are useful to reach nearby small towns such as Grazie and Sabbioneta (*see* Near Mantova, *below*); all buses depart from the **Autostazione**. *Piazzale Mondadori, tel. 0376/327237 From train station, turn right, take first left onto Via S. Bettinelli (becomes Via Mutilati Caduti del Lavoro) to Piazzale. Open daily 7–1:30 and 3–6:30; closed Sat. afternoon.*

GETTING AROUND From the train station the city center is a 10-minute walk east on Via S. Bettinelli. Take the first left on Corso Vittorio Emanuele, which leads to Piazza Cavalotti, where you pick up Corso Umberto to reach the heart of the city—Piazza Mantegna, Piazza delle Erbe, and Piazza Sordello. To reach Palazzo Te from the center take Via Roma to Via Amadeo and continue straight (the street changes names). If walking is not your speed, **La Rigola** (Lungolago dei Gonzaga, at Piazza Arche, tel. 0376/327487) rents bikes both by the hour (Mon.–Sat. L3000, Sun. L4000) and the day (Mon.–Sat. L10,000, Sun. L15,000).

➢ **BY BUS** • **Apam** bus tickets (L1200) are available in bars and newsstands. To reach the center, take any bus leaving from the station near Albergo Apollo. To reach Palazzo Te, take Bus 4 from the station to the Risorgimento or Repubblica stop. Detailed maps and timetables are available at APT (see Visitor Information, above) or at the Apam office (Dosso del Corso 4, tel. 0376/2301).

WHERE TO SLEEP Unless L50,000 a night is your idea of cheap (because that's as cheap as Mantova gets), you should consider making this a day trip from Milan. Otherwise, if every place listed below is full, the three-star **Due Guerrieri** (Piazza Sordello 52, tel. 0376/325596) offers mediocre rooms considering the price-to-quality ratio (singles L85,000, doubles L125,000). Mantova's hostel and campground have closed indefinitely, but you might try calling the APT office to see if they've reopened. Perhaps the most appealing option is agriturismo; get information at the APT.

Albergo Bianchi Stazione. This hotel is housed in what used to be a 16th-century convent. Because of its thin walls, be sure to ask for a room that doesn't face the street. Though the hotel is noisy, the garden and the friendly owners make it worthwhile. Doubles without bath go for L90,000. *Piazza Don Leoni 24, across from train station, tel. 0376/321504. 53 rooms, 48 with bath. Breakfast bar, TV room. AE, MC, V.*

Hotel ABC. This newly renovated hotel is cleaner and in better condition than many of the city's three-star spots. What's more, breakfast is included, all rooms have phones, and most have a TV (if yours doesn't you can request one at no extra charge). Rooms facing the train tracks supposedly have soundproof windows. *Piazza Don Leoni 25, tel. 0376/322329. 31 rooms, all with bath. Curfew 1 AM (flexible). Closed Dec. 24–Jan. 8.*

Maragò. If a bed for a few bucks is all you care about, try this place in the nearby town of Virgiliana. Accommodations here are definitely rudimentary, and the location is somewhat inconvenient, but you might not care with doubles for L38,000, without bath. *Via Villanova De Bellis 2, tel. 0376/370313. From the center, take Apam Bus 2M (15 min) from Piazza Cavalotti to last stop.*

FOOD Mantova is famous for its rich and varied cuisine, such as *tortelli di zucca* (pumpkin-stuffed pasta sweetened with amaretto cookies), *stracotto d'asino* (braised donkey meat and vegetables), and for dessert *la sbriciolona* (named for the crumbs or "briciole" it makes when broken). The regional wine is the sweet and fizzy Lambrusco. For a true culinary splurge, try the slightly upscale **Al Garibaldini** (Via S. Longino 7, off Piazza Mantegna, tel. 0376/328263). A full meal (L22,000–L27,000) will empty your pockets, but you'll definitely get your lira's worth. If affordable is what you're after, join the locals at **Trattoria Quattrotette** (Via Nazione 4, off Piazza Alberti, tel. 0376/369810). The cheapest lunchtime option is **Speedy-Spizza** (Via Grazioli 12, off Via Roma near post office, tel. 0376/224540), where you can get pizza-by-the-slice to go. Right next door, at **Gelateria K2** (Via Grazioli 16, tel. 0376/320548), you'll find the best gelato in town. For groceries, head to **Vivo** (Via Giustiziati 15, behind Palazzo della Ragione, tel. 0376/321244). Mantova's open market operates Thursday morning 7 AM–1 PM in Piazza delle Erbe and Piazza Sordello.

Antica Osteria Ai Ranari. A five-minute walk from Piazza Broletto, this friendly osteria, recommended by many a Mantovan, features a simple rustic decor and tasty traditional specialties. Primi go for L8000, secondi L9000–L12,000. *Via Trieste 11, tel. 0376/328431. From Piazza Broletto, take Via Broletto, go right on Via Accademia and right on Via Pomponazzo (which becomes Via Trieste). Open Tues.–Sun. noon–3 and 7:15–11; closed July 20–Aug. 7, and Dec. 24–Jan. AE, MC, V.*

Antica Osteria Taverna "S. Barbara." The location draws a lot of tourists during the day, but on weekend nights this place teems with Mantovan youths. Prices are reasonable for regional dishes (primi L8000–L9000 and *piadine* [flat-bread sandwiches] L6000); the atmosphere is casual and the setting simply unbeatable. After your meal try a *nocino* (after-dinner liqueur, L4000). *Piazza S. Barbara 19, tel. 0376/329496. From Piazza Sordello, take Via Tazzoli, go left on Via Rubens and follow signs. Open Mon. and Tues. noon–3, Wed.–Sun. noon–3 and 7:30–midnight (Fri. and Sat. until 2 AM). Wheelchair access. MC, V.*

Leoncino Rosso. Come to this neighborhood osteria for *luccio in salsa* (pike in green sauce; L11,000) and a wide selection of roasted meats (L7000–L11,000). More mundane are the sandwiches (L4500). At night this is a good place for low-key carousing (*see* After Dark, *below*). *Via Giustiziati 33, behind Piazza Erbe, tel. 0376/323277. Open Mon.–Sat. noon–2:30 and 7–10. Closed Aug. and 2 weeks in mid-Jan. Wheelchair access.*

Trattoria Due Cavallini. This slightly out-of-the-way place is more expensive and somewhat less atmospheric than other recommended spots, but if you eat here your stomach will thank you for it. Run by the same family for 56 years, Due Cavallini serves up fresh local dishes (primi L7000, secondi L11,000), with specialties highlighted on the menu in red. *Via Salnitro 5, tel. 0376/322084. From Piazza Broletto, take Via Broletto, go right on Via Accademia, right on Via Pomponazzo (which becomes Via Triese and Corso Garibaldi), left on Via Salnitro. Open Wed.–Mon. noon–2 and 7:30–10; closed mid-July–late Aug., and 1st week of Jan.). AE.*

WORTH SEEING Mantova is not a place to bury your nose in a guidebook. Look around and be overwhelmed by architecture ranging from severe and heavy-handed to frothy, eccentric, and over-the-top. Whether you're a fan of Renaissance grace or erotic mannerist kitsch, Mantova will not disappoint.

➤ **CASA DI MANTEGNA** • Make a quick stop on the way to Palazzo Te to visit this house commissioned by Mantegna in the late 15th century. It's unclear whether Mantegna himself is responsible for the design; however, the general structure is quite similar to the ceiling oculus in the Ducal Palace's Camera degli Sposi (*see below*), which the artist frescoed between 1465 and 1474. The house is periodically used as an exhibition site for art shows and cinema. *Via Acerbi 47, tel. 0376/360506. Admission free. Open Mon.–Thurs. 10–12:30 and 2–5 (10–12:30 and 3–6 during exhibits).*

➤ **PALAZZO D'ARCO** • In 1872 Antonio d'Arco bought a large plot of land next to a small Renaissance palace. On said land, Tony built a lovely garden, being careful not to interfere with or diminish the beauty of the adjoining Renaissance buildings that still form the garden's boundary. Giovanna d'Arco, the last member of the family, willed the palace to the city, and today you can visit a number of its rooms, many complete with period furnishings, to get a feel for Mantovan life as it was lived by aristocrats. *Piazza d'Arco 1, tel. 0376/322242. Admission: L5000. Open Nov.–Feb., Sun. 9–noon and 2:30–4; Mar.–Oct., Tues., Wed., Fri. 9–noon, Thurs., Sat., Sun. 9–noon and 3–5.*

➤ **PALAZZO DUCALE** • Actually more of a city within a city, the mammoth and intricate Palazzo Ducale was the 500-room "home" of the Gonzaga family. The palace comprises various structures that were originally built around seven large gardens and eight courtyards. But between the 14th and 17th centuries, the Gonzagas continued to add and renovate, creating a sprawling complex of living quarters, courts, meeting halls, and lots, lots more. In the 18th century all the structures were finally joined by a web of halls and covered passageways. Palazzo Ducale bears the mark of such luminaries as Mantegna, Romano, Pisanello, Fancelli, Titian, Rubens, and Correggio.

Most notable among the palace's rooms are the **Sala del Pisanello**, where Pisanello frescoes depicting chivalric battles were discovered in 1969; the **Sala dello Zodiaco**, covered by frescoes with an astrological theme; and the dining room, also known as the **Salone dei Fiumi**, where Giorgio Anselmi's frescoes of Mantovan rivers are punctuated by actual miniature grottoes through which water once flowed. The **Galleria delle Metamorfosi**, frescoed with Ovidian scenes, once housed a mummified corpse, which the Gonzagas believed was a good-luck charm. Many blamed the fall of the dynasty on the destruction of the mummy by the last Gonzaga duchess. The world's first modern opera, *L'Orfeo,* was conducted by Monteverdi in the palace's music hall and ballroom, the **Galleria degli Specchi** (Hall of Mirrors).

The first floor of **Castello di San Giorgio**, also part of the Palazzo Ducale, contains Isabella d'Este's apartments, which once housed a troupe of court dwarfs. (A peculiarity of Renaissance nobility was their penchant for surrounding themselves with dwarfs, who acted as servants and entertainers.) The castello's most famous room is the **Camera degli Sposi**, lavishly frescoed by Mantegna between 1465 and 1474. Though Mantegna was a court artist here from 1460 until his death in 1506, this room's frescoes are the palace's only surviving example of his work. If you look closely you can see Mantegna himself sternly watching the room from a column just to the right of the door, near the painting *The Meeting. Piazza Sordello, tel. 0376/320283. Admission: L12,000. Open Mon. 9–1, Tues.–Sun. 9–1 and 2:30–6. Hrs subject to change.*

Outside the palazzo, on **Piazza Sordello**, look for the **Torre della Gabbia** (Tower of the Cage), named for the 16th-century cage that Guglielmo Gonzaga had built for his prisoners so they could be gawked at publicly. Opposite is **Palazzo Bianchi**, also called the Bishop's Palace, built between 1756 and 1786. Piazza Sordello is notable as the site of many Gonzaga family events, from executions to joustings to weddings. Call the tourist office for opening hours, as they are constantly changing.

➤ **PALAZZO TE** • Built between 1525 and 1535 for Federico II Gonzaga, Palazzo Te, simply put, was intended as a Renaissance pleasure palace. Built on the island of Tejeto (later called Te), the palace gave Federico the necessary seclusion for his amorous dallyings with mistress Isabella Boschetto. Giulio Romano was commissioned to design and decorate the place, and he let his bent for the fantastic and rhetorical run wild. Palazzo Te is a study in mannerist excess, from the mythological trompe l'oeil frescoes to the puffy moldings and gilded fixtures. Additional motifs are the lizard (whose cold blood symbolically contrasts Federico's hot-blooded passions) and Federico's motto, QUOD HUIC DEEST ME TORQUET: WHAT THE LIZARD LACKS (warm blood) IS THAT WHICH TORTURES ME.

The **Sala dei Cavalli**, a reception area and ballroom, immortalizes Federico's favorite stallions and recalls the island's former use as Lodovico II's stud farm. The **Sala di Psiche** banquet hall is dedicated to the love affair of Federico and Isabella. The **Sala dei Giganti** depicts Jove's revenge on the giants who had dared to conspire against him. The entire room is covered with frescoes, immersing you in the scene of destruction. The palazzo also houses an Egyptian collection (open only to tour groups with previous arrangements) and rotating art shows, but the palace itself is what really grabs you. *Viale Te, tel. 0376/323266. Admission: L12,000. Open Tues.–Sun. 9–6; last tickets sold at 5:15.*

➤ **PIAZZA BROLETTO AND PIAZZA DELLE ERBE** • The **Palazzo del Podestà**, built in 1227 and rebuilt in 1462, divides two of Mantova's better-known piazze—Broletto and delle Erbe, around which there's a gaggle of palaces and lesser piazze. In a niche shooting off from Piazza Broletto stands the **Statue of Virgil**. Sculpted by an unknown artist at the time of the palace's construction, it pays homage to Mantova's greatest writer (Virgil was born here in 70 BC). The nearby Palazzo del Massaro and Palazzo Comunale are connected by a dark, vaulted *arcone* (huge connecting arch). Check out the ceiling—it's speckled with rings once used to hang prisoners by their wrists, after their hands had been bound behind their backs. On a lighter note, both piazze host open-air **markets** on Thursday mornings, selling everything from antiques to fresh pasta.

In enlightened Mantova, death-by-hanging sentences were reduced to "simple flogging" for geriatrics, pregnant women, and hernia sufferers.

➤ **SANT'ANDREA** • In 1470, after Ludovico Gonzaga obtained permission from Pope Sixtus IV to raze this site, Ludovico commissioned Leon Battista Alberti to design Sant'Andrea, his much-imitated, monumental landmark. Even though work on the church was not completed until the 18th century, Sant'Andrea was widely emulated by lesser architectural lights in the Renaissance—which may explain its familiar profile. Inside you'll find Mantegna's tomb and burial chapel and, in the crypt, a reliquary containing the supposed blood of Christ. Legend has it that Longinus brought the blood to Mantova after thrusting his very own spear into Jesus—earning him some seriously bad karma. The golden vases that hold the blood are displayed every March 18, the feast day of San Anselmo (Mantova's patron saint); they're then carried in a procession to the duomo for a special mass. *Piazza Mantegna. Open daily 7:30– noon and 3:30–7.*

AFTER DARK Mantova isn't exactly rocking after dark, but two good places to have a drink are **Leoncino Rosso** (Via Giustiziati 33, tel. 0376/323279), an osteria that becomes a bar between 10 PM and 2 AM, and **Oblo** (Via Arrivabene 50, tel. 0376/360676), which serves light meals and has a big selection of beer and wine.

NEAR MANTOVA

GRAZIE Lying in the marshy plain that surrounds Mantova, Grazie is home to a very strange little church. The **Madonna delle Grazie** (open daily 7–noon and 3–7) was commissioned in 1399 by Francesco Gonzaga after Mantova miraculously survived a bout of plague. Today, people come to thank the Madonna for lesser favors. Inside, prepare yourself for no-longer-ailing body parts made of wood; no-longer-necessary crutches; soccer balls; and a collection of cartoonlike paintings of car, train, and motorcycle accidents. Other objects of veneration include a 15th-century painting in the marble tabernacle and, oddly enough, a stuffed crocodile suspended from the ceiling. (See Ken Russell's movie *The Devils* for more on the mysterious link between stuffed crocodiles and Christianity.) The church lies smack in the center of town, in the piazza next to where the **Asolo**-bound bus from Mantova (10 min, L2100) lets you off. Buses from Mantova depart almost hourly Monday–Saturday, less frequently on Sunday and June 17–September 15.

SABBIONETA Intended as a "New Rome," the town of Sabbioneta became the physical manifestation of Vespasiano Gonzaga's unfathomable ego. From 1577 (when he acquired the town) until 1591 (when he died), Duke Vespasiano built incessantly, transforming this once-rural hamlet into a bejeweled minimetropolis. It's extraordinary how much Gonzaga was able to build in 15 short years, and equally stunning how quickly his dream was shattered. Following his death the town was pretty much forgotten, except by its original agricultural workers. (Vespasiano's son died before he did, leaving no heir to Sabbioneta.) The tourist board began hyping Sabbioneta in the 1950s, yet nearly half a century later it still feels like a Renaissance ghost town. The main inhabitants here are tourist-board people and restoration workers. The feeling of desolation is heightened by the siesta-time arrival of most buses, although on sunny weekends and holidays the sleepy town fills with tourists.

Sabbioneta's buildings—the **Palazzo Ducale** and **Chiesa dell'Incoronata** among them—are interesting enough for a brief visit. You can see the interiors on guided tours only (in English upon request; L10,000) that leave from the **tourist office** (Via Vespasiano Gonzaga 31, tel. 0375/52039). To reach Sabbioneta from Mantova, hop on one of five daily buses (45 min, L5400). There are fewer buses June 17–September 15; on Sundays only one noontime bus will get you to Sabbioneta in time to see the sights.

The Lakes
The lakes of northern Italy denote a vast region spread over the middle third of the borderlands and on into Switzerland. North of Milan, things are uniformly green and watery, and scenic panoramas range from vast stretches of plains to towering mountains blocking your view. To hydrophobes and the uninitiated, water may be an annoyingly recurring theme, but each of the lakes does have a distinct personality: Among them are **Garda**, the so-called party lake; **Como**, the posh where-do-I-park-my-Ferrari? lake; and **Orta**, the serene lake. Unfortunately, one unifying trait is industrial pollution, which is particularly acute in these three larger lakes. Even so, tourists flock to the lakes for their watersports (you're in prime windsurfing territory) and beauty. If you're lucky enough to have a car, the region's small mountain roads definitely rank among the world's most beautiful and challenging.

Lago di Garda

Shared by Lombardy, the Veneto, and Trentino-Alto Adige, Lago di Garda is Italy's largest lake, combining stylish lake life with RV camper culture. Luckily its large size means it's not that hard to find a little peace and quiet. Still, if hordes of well-heeled tourists fray your nerves, you might be happier at calmer Iseo or Orta.

Among the thousands of visitors to this lake, Garda has hosted its fair share of famous people since ancient times. Catullus (a Roman poet) is said to have owned a villa here in the 1st century BC; Irish writer James Joyce and the American poet Ezra Pound are known to have met more than once along this lakefront; and Gabriele d'Annuzio, the ultra-nationalistic Italian poet and chum of Mussolini, built his extravagant home, *Il Vittoriale*, in Gardone. Even Mussolini himself set up his short-lived puppet government, the Republic of Salò, here.

With a "Gardaland" amusement park and countless, limitless, never-ending souvenir stands, tourist junk blankets the area like Alfredo on fettuccine.

Garda's vegetation and topography vary noticeably. In the south it's smooth and shrubby, in the north it's mountainous and leafy. The weather is a lot more constant: mild to warm and breezy, except during winter, when rain and cooler temperatures may dampen your spirit. Throughout the year you can enjoy numerous water sports—from sailing to diving to windsurfing—in lakeshore towns such as Torbole and Riva del Garda (*see below*); excellent mountain hikes start from Riva del Garda, Malcesine, and Gardone (*see below*). Finally, at the end of a long day, indulge in the fine local wines and prepare yourself for meals flavored with two local specialties: olive oil and huge, juicy lemons.

COMING AND GOING The easiest way to reach Lago di Garda's many resorts is from Desenzano, on the lake's southern tip. Desenzano's **train station** (Via Cavour 48, tel. 030/914–1247), on a hill behind the city, serves Milan via Brescia (20 trains daily, 1½ hrs, L10,000) and Venice via Verona (20 trains daily, 2½ hrs, L10,000). Catch long-distance **buses** at Desenzano's APT stop on Via Anelli, right next to the pier on Piazza Matteotti; buy tickets at the bar in the train station. From Desenzano there are hourly buses to both Brescia (50 min, L4600) and Verona (1½ hrs, L4600). To explore the lake itself, hop on a **boat** or **hydrofoil** (operating Easter–Sept. only, with a reduced fare before June) from Desenzano's dock (Piazza Matteotti); for schedules contact Navigazione Lago di Garda (tel. 030/914–1321).

SIRMIONE

Sitting on a spit of land on Lago di Garda's southwestern shore, the village of Sirmione *ought* to be an idyllic place to ponder the rhythms of nature. Unfortunately, its natural beauty has been tainted by the tourist trade—expect steep prices, gaudy souvenir shops, and a zillion snack bars. There's little to do here but lounge in the sun and watch other vacationers turn pink and peel. The old part of town, in the shadow of the fortress **Rocca Scaligera**, is still medieval in appearance and worth a brief tour. The fortress itself, built by the della Scala family in the early 1300s (admission: L8000; open Apr.–Oct., Tues.–Sat. 9–6; Nov.–Mar., Tues.–Sat. 9–1), has sweeping lake views from its tower.

The most impressive sight in Sirmione is the **Villa of Catullus**. Located at the very tip of the peninsula, the villa and bath house (now mere ruins) sit atop a grotto and ancient hot springs. *Admission: L8000. Open Apr.–Sept., Tues.–Sun. 9–6; Oct.–Mar., Tues.–Sun. 9–4.*

COMING AND GOING In the summer there are hourly buses to and from Desenzano (20 min, L2100) until 9 PM, and 12 daily boats (20 min, L4000). The **APT** tourist office (Viale Marconi 2, tel. 030/916114; open Apr.–Oct., daily 9 AM–10 PM; Nov.–Mar., weekdays 9–12:30 and 3–6, Sat. 9–12:30 and 3–8, Sun. 3–8) has plenty of information on lodging, sights, and water sports.

WHERE TO SLEEP AND EAT Try to avoid Sirmione in July and August, when it's seriously crowded and nearly impossible to find a place to stay without making reservations. If you're looking for a crash pad in the historic center, **La Magnolia** (Via Vittorio Emanuele, tel. 030/

916135; open June–Sept.) is the cheapest; doubles with bath are L50,000. A marginally cheaper option is **Lo Zodiaco** (Via XXV Aprile 18, tel. 030/916035), which has doubles without bath for L40,000–L48,000. Next door is the three-star **Miramar** (Via XXV Aprile 22, tel. 030/916239). It's surprisingly economical at L68,000–L90,000 for a double (with bath), but be sure to reserve ahead of time. **Campeggio Sirmione** (Via Sirmioncino 9, tel. 030/910–9045) fills up fast with RVs and gaggles of teens on mopeds, but it's cheap (L10,000–L19,000 per tent site, plus L5000–L9000 per person, depending on the season) and has a beach. Sirmione's historic center is crowded with excellent gelaterias (just pick one, you can't go wrong) and mediocre restaurants. One exception is **La Botte** (Via Antiche Mura 25, tel. 030/916273), which serves up simple food, including homemade pastas such as cheese tortellini (L8000), and desserts.

GARDONE

Gardone, on Lago di Garda's western shore, is a turn-of-the-century resort turned sleepy and faded. As with most lakeside settlements, it occupies a beautiful plot of land and is blessed with lush flora and a mellow climate. Gardone is a congenial place, complete with grand old villas (most of which have been converted into hotels) and restaurants where old men play cards, smoke, and down red wine. Crowds are a problem in summer, but what else is new? Cynics may say that Gardone has little to offer aside from ho-hum "resorting," but that's not entirely true: Il Vittoriale and the Hruska Botanical Gardens are definitely worth checking out.

Set on 22 walled-in acres, **Il Vittoriale**, halfway up the hill near the ancient settlement of Gardone Sopra, is the former home of Gabriele D'Annunzio (1863–1938), one of Italy's greatest modern poets. In 1921 D'Annunzio bought the villa and surrounding grounds for their isolation; in 1938 he died peacefully at his desk. The official line is that D'Annunzio himself bought the house and paid all the taxes, but rumor has it that Mussolini gave it to him to keep his poetic, critical mouth shut. Either way, during his tenure the poet radically altered what he referred to as the estate's priorylike starkness, creating an eccentric's haven, chock-full of Oriental, religious, and wartime oddities (D'Annunzio even dry-docked the warship *Puglia* on the grounds). With the help of architect Gian Carlo Maroni, the poet added porticoes, an open-air theater where performances are still staged, a mausoleum, and myriad rooms (among them an auditorium that displays the biplane D'Annunzio flew in a famous wartime expedition to drop leaflets rather than bombs). The house is worth a visit even if you can't understand a word of Italian. *Piazza Vittoriale, no phone. Admission: L7000 grounds, L15,000 house. Open daily 9–12:30 and 2–6:30.*

Hruska Botanical Gardens was created by naturalist Arturo Hruska during his years in Gardone, from 1940 to 1971. In this 2½-acre area there are more than 2,000 different species of plants and flowers brought from around the world. If you're really into flowers, yee-haw; but beware if you have allergies. *Via Roma, no phone. Admission: L6000. Open Apr.–Sept., daily 9–6:30.*

COMING AND GOING To reach Gardone from Desenzano, take one of six daily buses (40 min, L3400). In Gardone, buy your bus tickets at the Molinari travel agency (Piazza Wimmer 2, tel. 0365/21551). Another travel option from mid-June through September is by boat. There are five daily ferries (1 hr, L9000) from Desenzano to Gardone's pier on Piazza Wimmer; in Gardone, buy tickets at the Navigarda office next to the pier.

WHERE TO SLEEP AND EAT The **tourist office** (Via Repubblica 35, tel. 0365/20347; open daily 9–12:30 and 3–6) has hotel listings as well as city maps and transportation schedules. For a bite to eat in between sights, try **Ristorante Pizzeria Sans Souci** (Vicolo al Lago 12, tel. 0365/21076), where the food is decent and the atmosphere is comfortable and friendly.

RIVA DEL GARDA

This large and prosperous town, on the northern end of Lago di Garda, is the largest and best known of the region's resorts. Beyond the olive and lemon trees that grow on the outskirts, Riva del Garda is a city of medieval palaces and piazze. From the main square, lakeside

Piazza III Novembre, it's hard to miss the **Torre Apponale**, a 12th-century crenellated tower that looms above the houses. It's also hard to miss the dozens of sailboats and windsurfers on the water.

The **tourist office** has maps, hotel and restaurant listings, and flyers outlining Riva del Garda's outdoor activities. The office is right across from a large disco, this being one of the lake resorts with a nightlife. *Giardini di Porta Orientale 8, tel. 0464/554444. Open Apr.–mid-Sept., Mon.–Sat. 9–noon and 3–6:30; Nov.–Mar., weekdays 8:45–noon and 2:15–5:30.*

COMING AND GOING There are five buses daily (2 hrs, L8300) between Desenzano and Riva del Garda's **Stazione Autocorriere** (Viale Trento, tel. 0464/552323), on the northern outskirts of town. Boats (one daily, 4 hrs, L15,000) and hydrofoils (four daily, 2 hrs, L20,200) from Desenzano dock at Riva del Garda's **Porto San Nicolò** (tel. 0464/551258). For more info call **Navigarda** (0464/552625).

WHERE TO SLEEP AND EAT Riva del Garda has more one-star hotels than you can count, but prices are high and reservations highly recommended, especially in July and August. Of the town's many hotels, two of the better ones include **Montanara** (Via Montanara 20, tel. 0464/554857), which charges L52,000 for a double without bath, and the **Vittoria** (Viale Dante 39, tel. 0464/554398), where doubles cost L80,000 (with bath). The **Benacus Youth Hostel** (Piazza Cavour 10, tel. 0464/554911; closed Nov.–Feb.) is cheap—a bed and breakfast from L17,000 for rooms with two to six beds; the hostel is clean, has laundry facilities, and is in a good location. The **Alimar SRL** cafeteria (Piazza Cavour 6, tel. 0464/554911), next door to the hostel, serves full meals for less than L15,000. **Camping Monte Brione** (Via Brione 32, tel. 0464/520885), set amidst olive trees and within a stone's throw of the beach, has 100 tent sites (L15,000 plus L10,000 per person). They also offer tons of services and special discounts, including bike rental (L6000 per hour), discounts to the nearby dance club, pizzerias, and windsurfing school (*see* Outdoor Activities, *below*).

OUTDOOR ACTIVITIES Water sports, especially windsurfing, are a big attraction in Riva del Garda. Work on your sunburn at the large public beach, or learn the basics from the bronzed experts at the **Professional Windsurfing Sailing School** (Viale Rovereto 100, tel. 0464/556077). Rentals—including boards, wet suits, and life jackets—cost about L22,000 per hour, L40,000 per half day, and L60,000 per day in season (Easter–Oct.). If you'd rather stay on land, consider renting a mountain bike (L5000 per hr, L20,000 per day) from **Girelli** (Viale Damiano Chiesa, tel. 0464/556602). For hiking and trail maps, listings of *rifugi* (mountain huts), and all variety of information on the nearby Dolomites, stop by the **Club Alpino Italiano** (Via Fiume 52, in the Porta San Marco). **The Club Ippico S. Giorgio** (S. Giorgio, tel. 0464/556942) has horseback riding for L30,000 per hour.

Riva del Garda is a popular windsurfing spot. Even on otherwise calm days, strong mountain drafts cruise briskly across the water.

AFTER DARK While many nightspots near the lake are difficult to get to without a car, at Riva there are good clubs right in town. One worth mentioning is **Après Club** (Via Monte d'Oro 12, tel. 0464/552187), with a cover charge that ranges from L20,000 to L40,000 depending on the day of the week, and a fairly mainstream crowd.

Lago d'Iseo

Lago d'Iseo lies halfway between Brescia and Bergamo, reflecting the surrounding green hills like an emerald. Iseo is an excellent place for swimming in relatively clean water, hiking in peaceful mountains or on Montisola Island, or just plain snoozing. Iseo's provincial towns exist without the glitz, tourism, and pretensions that burden many lakeside resorts, so even in July and August you shouldn't have to battle crowds. However, there are also fewer hotels here, so still plan on booking ahead during these months. Steady winds make for decent sailing, but the main activity on Lago d'Iseo is fishing. Don't complain: Restaurants in even the tiniest of villages serve fresh fish that's surprisingly affordable (and best accompanied by local Franciacorta wines). The thing to appreciate most here is peace. Como may be more chic, and Garda more lively, but Lago d'Iseo is the place for getting away.

ISEO

Lago d'Iseo's major "city" is a good base for exploring the area. Although the town is not exactly the cultural center of Italy, there are a few sights here to visit if you have the time, namely the **Santa Maria del Mercato** church (Via Mirolte at Vicolo Borni), with its recently discovered and restored 14th-century frescoes, and **Oldofredi Castle** (Via Mirotte 74, tel. 030/980035), which now houses a public library and cultural center. There's also a big, bustling market that takes over the town's medieval center on Friday mornings. Stop by the **tourist office** (Lungolago Marconi 2, tel. 030/980209) for maps and brochures, and info on **Torbiere Sebine**, a protected marshland just outside Iseo. Tell them how you want to spend your day and they'll plan everything, from where to go to what time to take your ferry. **Prehistoric carvings** sound interesting? Ask about the **Naquane National Park** in nearby Valle Camonica. The hugely helpful office also has info on bike rentals, which you can get at the train station in Piovaglio d'Iseo (L8000 per hr, L20,000 per ½ day, L30,000 per day).

COMING AND GOING Trains to Iseo, the lake's primary transport hub, arrive throughout the day until about 7:30 PM from Brescia (40 min, L3500); Iseo's train station is on Via XX Settembre (tel. 030/980061). There's no official bus station here, only a long-distance bus stop at the end of Viale Repubblica, where it meets Via XX Settembre. Buy tickets for Milan, Brescia, and other nearby towns at newsstands in town; for general bus information call 030/980060 or ask at the tourist office. Boats connect Iseo with most lakeside towns. The dock in Iseo is at Porto G. Rosa; buy your tickets at the booth marked BIGLIETTERIA. For ferry information stop by **Gestione Navigazione Lago d'Iseo** (Via Nazionale 16, Costa Volpino, tel. 035/971483; open daily 9–noon), or inquire at the APT.

WHERE TO SLEEP The cheapest hotel in Iseo is the **Cenacolo** (Via Mirolte 13, tel. 030/980136), which charges L40,000 for a double (without bath). The hotel is closed mid-October–Easter, and it's best to phone ahead in July and August. Otherwise, **Campeggio del Sole** (Via Per Rovato 26, tel. 030/980288), open from the end of April to the first week of September, is equipped with everything you could possibly want or need, to the point of being a little obnoxious. We're talking restaurant, bar, bike rental (L10,000 a day), and *paddle-boat* rental. Prices vary from low season to high; a space costs L12,500–L19,000, plus L7500–L9500 per person. Cheaper and more informal are **Campeggio Iseo** (Via Antonioli 53, tel. 030/980213), **Punta d'Oro** (Via Antonioli 51, tel. 030/980084), and **Quai** (Via Roma 65, tel. 030/9821610). All three are on the lake, open April–October, and charge about L13,000–L17,000 for campsites (plus L5500–L7000 per person), depending on the season. Quai also has bungalows (L38,000 for two, L50,000 for four).

FOOD For budget-friendly dining, head over to **All'Incontrario** (Via Campo 25, tel. 030/982–1464; closed Mon.), which serves everything from sandwiches and salads to full meals—and even pizza if you haven't had enough by now. **Promessi Sposi** (Largo Zanardelli 15, tel. 030/980306) is more touristy and slightly pricier, but it has nice outdoor tables and a menu in English. For killer gelato stop at the **Gelateria Leon d'Oro** (Largo Dante 2, tel. 030/980540).

MONTISOLA

Montisola is a sleepy island with picturesque fishing villages strung along its shores. In the hills among the olive groves, vineyards, and chestnut woods, small farming villages seem caught in a medieval time warp, an impression that's fueled by the lack of cars on tiny Montisola, as only service vehicles are allowed on the island (although the place buzzes with the occasional moped). Don't come if you're into nightlife: This quiet oasis is more about beautiful lake views, pensive rambles along the shore, and simple meals with unhurried locals. During the day, your time is best spent lounging on one of the island's beaches—try Sensole or Carzano—or hiking. From the main road (which has no real name; it's the only one that circles the island), follow the marked path through the woods to **Oldofredi-Martinengo** fortress. Its interior is closed to the public, but it's a great spot for a quiet picnic. If you've got the stamina, another good hike is to the 600-meter-high peak of **Madonna della Ceriola** (follow the signs and the main road uphill). You can walk all the way around the island and visit all of the waterfront villages by sticking to the main road. It's about a three-hour walk, even shorter by bike, which you can rent (*see above*) and take with you on the ferry.

WHERE TO SLEEP The island is best used as a day trip, but if you want to crash here, **Paradiso** at (Corzano, tel. 030/98 25 201), with its own separate ferry stop, is the most economical hotel. Doubles with a view of the lake cost L45,000. The hotel's restaurant is also one of the island's most affordable. Also at Corzano, **Campeggio Monte Isola** (Via Croce, tel. 030/982–5221), on the beach, has 45 sites (L14,000 plus L9000 per person), and bungalows for L60,000. About nine boats per day run between Iseo and Montisola (1½ hrs, L3700). Ferries run until about 10 PM, but check with the APT office for the exact times, as the schedule is very irregular.

FOOD Most trattorias on the island serve the same kind of food at the same price, so just pick a pretty spot and park your booty. At Sensole go to the **Vittoria** (no address, tel. 030/988–6222; from the main road turn right from the dock). It's quieter and a bit cheaper than the restaurant at the ferry dock. Make the most of clean waters by trying the fresh fish (L14,000–L16,000).

ZONE

This tiny mountain village located at the northeast end of the lake is, as yet, largely undiscovered by tourists. The only folks who seem to know of green and hilly Zone are ambitious hikers who crave an escape from civilization. Needless to say, it's a beautiful place, with steep cobbled streets and stunning views. Yet the real highlight is the **Piramidi d'Erosione**, a large rock formation that dates back to the time when the Camonica Valley was first eroded by glaciers. Below town, in a deep river basin, these "pyramids" look like a Gaudi-inspired Stonehenge and alone are worth the trip to Zone.

The landscape around Zone is so evocative that Leonardo is said to have used it as the backdrop for his painting "Madonna of the Rocks."

Apart from its rugged scenery, Zone is a good base for those planning an ascent of Mt. Guglielmo, which rises majestically behind the town. Stop by the **tourist office** (Via Mt. Guglielmo 42, tel. 030/988–0116) for hiking and topographic maps; the staff will also ring the **Almici** (tel. 030/987–0990), a lodge on the mountain, to check the availability of its 19 beds, which cost L60,000 for a double with bath. (Plan ahead if you want to stay here, because from late June to late Aug. the place books up months ahead.) The hike from Zone up to the lower elevations of Mt. Guglielmo takes about 2½ hours and is fairly easy. Budget a few more hours to reach the peak (elevation 1,960 meters).

COMING AND GOING To reach Zone you must first get to Marone. Luckily there are 10 daily trains (20 min, L2300) between Iseo and Marone's **train station** (Via Metelli, tel. 030/987447). Buses connect Iseo and Marone 12 times daily (20 min, L2500). From Marone, either hike the scenic but steep 6 kilometers to Zone or, from a stop of sorts on Via Zanardelli (right in front of Marone's train depot), take a **bus** (four to six daily, 25 min, L2400). Tickets for Zone are available on board, but buy your return ticket at **Marcone's tobacco shop** on Via Roma, half a block from Marone's bus stop. Boats for Iseo depart Marone once a day (1 hr, L10,000).

Tired of humdrum Italian Sundays? Want to put a little spring in your step? Team Xtreme Bungee-Jumping (town of Vello, tel. 039/245–0432) offers Sunday jumps from heights of no less than 70 meters (230 feet) for L100,000.

WHERE TO SLEEP AND EAT If you want to stay overnight in Zone, the one-star **Piramidi** (Località Cislano, tel. 030/987–0932) charges L40,000 for doubles (all without bath). It's also a good place to grab a bite to eat. The restaurant downstairs serves good food with a view of the spectacular Piramidi d'Erosione. If you're traveling solo, you can negotiate a lower price for a "single." **Camping Corni Stretti** (Via Valle di Gasso, tel. 030/987–0910) is set on a lush hillside with 35 sites (L18,000 plus L5000 per person) and five bungalows (L40,000).

Lago di Como

Long a favorite escape for artists, jet-setters, and wealthy Italians, Lago di Como remains an alluring spot even for budget travelers. There's no denying that it suffers from pollution and unsightly resort development, yet Lago di Como has managed to remain quiet and unassumingly genteel; it's also encircled by sumptuous villas and peaceful small towns. Water sports and challenging mountain hikes draw younger types, which offsets some of the stuffiness that comes with the summer crowds of luxury-package tourists. Practically speaking, if you're headed to or from Milan or Switzerland, Lago di Como couldn't be more convenient.

COMO

Como, perched on the lake's western tip, is the largest city for miles, which means it's expensive and developed. Because it's a hub for lake-bound trains and buses, Como is hard to avoid—like it or not, you'll inevitably spend at least a little time here if Lago di Como is on your itinerary. But don't be scared away: Despite high prices and summertime crowds, Como is a pretty little city with some impressive churches. First and foremost is the architecturally jumbled **duomo** (Piazza del Duomo), which is hard to miss in the center of town. Also worth a quick look are **Castel Baradello** (Via Castel Baradello, tel. 031/592805), built by Frederick Barbarossa in 1158, and the **Villa Olmo** (Via Cantoni, tel. 031/572910), with its big and beautiful (and free) gardens.

BASICS Como is not a good place to change money—rates are universally poor and commissions high. If you're desperate, the **main post office** (Via Gallio 6, tel. 031/262026) offers slightly better rates; it's open weekdays 8:15–4, Saturday 8:15–noon. For long-distance and international calls, go to the **TELECOM** office (Via Alberti at Piazza Cavour) open Monday–Saturday 9–noon and 2:30–6. The **APT** tourist office offers info on train travel, hotels, and sports. *Piazza Cavour 17, tel. 031/269712. Open Mon.–Sat. 9–12:30 and 2:30–6.*

COMING AND GOING Como has two train stations. The smaller **Stazione F.N.M.** (Largo Leopardi, tel. 031/304800), next to the bus station, serves Milan, Varese, and smaller towns along the way. The main **Stazione S. Giovanni** (Piazzale S. Gottardo, tel. 031/261494), on the Milan–Switzerland–Central Europe rail line, is at the end of Via Gallio, a 15-minute walk from the central Piazza Cavour. From the main station nearly 30 trains run daily to Milan (30–45 min, L7700), with connections to Rome, Naples, Genova, and Venice. Many of these trains require that you buy a supplement—ask when you purchase your ticket. Como has a bus station of sorts, **Stazione Autovie** (Piazza Matteotti, tel. 031/304744), but it offers service only to principal lake villages, the Brianza, and Bergamo (5 daily, 2 hrs, L7600).

WHERE TO SLEEP It sure ain't cheap to sleep in Como's hotels, so if money's tight head for the hostel (or, if you're female, to the convent/pension). Como's handful of budget one-star hotels is on Via Borgo Vico, which intersects the stairs leading to the main station. Of them, the **Grotta Azzura** (Via Borgo Vico 161, tel. 031/572631) is a restaurant with three rooms upstairs; doubles go for L50,000 without bath. If Grotta's full, try **Sociale** (Via Maestri Comancini 8, tel. 031/264042). Located to the right of the duomo, near Piazza Cavour, it has doubles for L55,000 or L75,000 (with bath). As always, reservations are important during summer.

For women who don't mind a 10 PM curfew (11 PM on Sat.), the convent/pension **Protezione della Giovane** (Via Borgo Vico 182, tel. 031/574390) is a great deal, with beds for L11,000. The **Villa Olmo Youth Hostel**, housed in an ancient building close to the lake, charges either sex only L14,000 for breakfast and a bed. The place offers tons of services and discounts for guests, including bike rental (L6000). *Via Bellinzona 2, tel. 031/573800. Curfew 11:30, lockout 10–4. Closed Oct.–Feb.*

FOOD Eating cheaply in Como is not easy, so cruise Via Borgo Vico for the handful of pizzerias and *birrerie* (beer bars) where sandwiches and slices won't deplete your life's savings. Another option is **El Merendero** (Via Crespi 4, tel. 031/304477), a local hangout near the church of St. Antonio, which has large, exotic, but expensive sandwiches (L6000 and up), beer, and a bouncy owner. For tasty seafood, pasta, and pizza at moderate prices, try **Carretiere** (Via Coloniola 18, tel. 031/303478). **Geral's Self Serve** (Via Bianchi Giovini 10, tel. 031/304872) offers the best deals in town but is only open for lunch. **Al Molo** (Lungo Lario Triesto 9, no phone) has the cheapest lakefront coffee in town (only L1500 with table service), in addition to decent ice cream and sandwiches. If you have a sweet tooth, try the local specialty **resca** (a sweet yellow bread with raisins and a stick through it).

OUTDOOR ACTIVITIES If you want to swim or sunbathe, you'll find public beaches on Viale Geno and in front of the Villa Olmo (which also has a swimming pool for L7000) on Via Cantoni. If you're a guest you can rent a bike from the youth hostel (*see* Where to Sleep, *above*) for L6000 per day. Even if you despise physical exertion, take the **funicular** (Piazza Funicolare, tel. 031/303608) from the west side of town to Brunate, known for its stunning view.

TREMEZZO

In spring or early summer it's hard not to be enchanted by the 14-acre gardens of **Villa Carlotta**, a pink-and-white villa that lies a few hundred yards north of Tremezzo, on Lago di Como's western shore. Built in 1690 and later modified, the villa is best known for its splendid flora—from mid-April to mid-May the gardens blaze with the brilliant colors of azaleas and rhododendrons in full bloom, not to mention cacti, orchids, and camellias. There's also a picnic area.

Inside the villa you'll find a collection of marble friezes and statues, along with some period furnishings. Also on display is Antonio Canova's sculpture *Cupid and Psyche,* which depicts poor Psyche waiting eternally for a kiss that will never come. *Villa Carlotta, tel. 0344/40405. 200 meters north of Tremezzo dock; follow only road along lake. Admission: L9000. Open Apr.–Sept., daily 9–6; Mar.–Oct., daily 9–11:30 and 2–4:30.*

COMING AND GOING From Como there are 15 daily buses to Tremezzo (1 hr, L3900). More scenic is the trip by boat (7 daily, 2 hrs, L9500) or hydrofoil (7 daily, 45 min, L14,300). Both dock along the Lungo Lario in front of Piazza Cavour. For ferry information call 031/304060 or stop by the dockside ticket office.

VARENNA

This stoic, ancient fishing village is best appreciated on foot; spend an afternoon wandering through Varenna's quiet streets. Along the way you'll inevitably encounter Varenna's main attraction, **Villa Monastero**, a convent turned nuclear-physics research center in the early 1950s. The original Cistercian convent was dissolved in 1676 by Pope Pius V after it was discovered that the nuns were being "visited" via underground tunnels by the town's priests—and not to pray together. The research center is closed to the public but the gardens are on view. *Via IV Novembre, tel. 0341/830129. Admission: L2000. Open daily 10–12:30 and 2:30–6.*

High above town are the ruins of the ancient and poorly preserved **Castello di Vezio**. The views—and not the ruins—make the uphill hike worthwhile: From up here you get tremendous panoramas of the lake and surrounding countryside. For directions and keys to the building, inquire at Varenna's **APT** information office (Piazza San Giorgio 19, tel. 0341/830367; open Mon.–Sat. 9–noon and 3–6, Sun. 10–12:30 and 3–6), uphill from the town's dock. From Como to Varenna there are five daily boats (2½ hrs, L11,000) and two daily hydrofoils (1 hr, L16,400).

BELLAGIO

Practically in the middle of Lake Como, Bellagio is a popular tourist spot that still succeeds in maintaining its charm and beauty. Iron-balconied homes looking out onto the town's narrow streets make the town center a sight in and of itself. The clear blue waters at its *lido* (beach) also draw visitors. Another plus, its location at the meeting point of Lake Como's southern "legs" makes it easy and cheap to travel via boat or hydrofoil to Tremezzo (10 min, L4500), or Varenna (½ hr, L4500). The **APT** tourist office hands out brochures, maps, and town info. *Piazza della Chiesa, tel. 031/950204. Open daily 9–noon and 3–6.*

Aside from the town itself, Bellagio's main sight is the **Villa Serbelloni** (entrance is visible from Piazza della Chiesa, tel. 031/950204; open mid-Apr.–mid-Oct., Tues.–Sun.). The building, now owned by the Rockefeller Foundation, is closed to the public, but its lush hilltop gardens overlooking the picture-perfect town below can be visited by guided tour (L5000), twice daily at 10:30 AM and 4 PM. If more active entertainment is what you're after, **Crotto del Misto** (Frazione Crotto, in Lezzeno, tel. 031/914541), half an hour from Bellagio, operates a ski school. A 10-minute run costs L26,500; call ahead.

WHERE TO SLEEP AND EAT Cheap rooms abound at **Giardinetto** (Via Boncati 12, tel. 031/950168), which has bathless doubles at L55,000. The hostel, **La Primula** (Via IV Novembre 86, tel. 0344/32356) in nearby Menaggio, will give you a bed and breakfast for L13,000. Their widely acclaimed meals, for only L12,000, are worth the trek even if you aren't staying at the hostel. Boats leave every hour to Menaggio (L4500).

Lago Maggiore

One of the region's most scenic lakes borders relatively flat Piemonte to the west, higher and more mountainous Lombardy to the east, and Switzerland to the north. The water's natural beauty and the idyllic, forested hills that surround Lago Maggiore have inspired musicians such as Wagner and Toscanini, numerous writers—Flaubert, Mann, Hemingway, and Goethe among them—and the Borromeo family, who built palaces on the lake's scattered islands. It may not do the same for you, however. Crowded with lavish hotels and resorts dating back to the turn of the century, it was once a prominent vacation spot for well-to-do tourists. Today, unfortunately, it is merely an overpriced shadow of its once glorious past, a hot spot for senior citizens. The major resorts are on the Piemontese shore, yet whether a resort's architectural style is described as "characteristic fishing village" or "art nouveau," most lakeside towns feel contrived and decidedly well established. Stresa is the place to be if you're rich and famous; otherwise, you'll want to head for a garden-ensconced villa or escape into the mountains for hikes that put you in touch with both nature and reality.

STRESA

Stresa's spotless streets—most are lined with grand hotels, smiling townspeople, and restaurants with menus in three languages—make it easy for visitors to wander in a stupor and spend money foolishly. Some guidebooks describe Stresa as charming, genteel, and pleasantly languorous, but swank and overdeveloped come closer to the mark. Still, it *is* the region's main transport hub, making it convenient for coming and going and for exploring the mountains and nearby Borromee Islands.

BASICS The main **post office** (Via Roma 5/7, tel. 0323/30065; open weekdays 8:15–1:40, Sat. 8:15–11:40) changes money and American Express traveler's checks. Otherwise go to one of the banks along the waterfront. Stresa's **APT** offers the standard maps, brochures, and hotel information, but remember that they don't make reservations. *Via Principe Tomaso 70/72, tel. 0323/30150. Open Mon.–Sat. 8:30–12:30 and 3–6:15, Sun. 9–noon. From station, turn right onto Via Carducci, which becomes Via Gignous, and left onto Via Principe Tomaso.*

COMING AND GOING The town's **train station** (Piazza Stazione, tel. 0323/30472) has trains to Milan (20 daily, 1–1½ hrs, L7200), Genova (at 6:50 AM, 2½ hrs, L15,500), and towns in nearby Switzerland. Boats and buses both depart from the embarcadero at Piazza Marconi, along Corso Umberto I; tickets and schedule information are available at ticket windows here. For boat schedules, contact **Navigazione Sul Lago Maggiore** (Viale F. Baracca 1, tel. 0322/46651), which is based in the southern lakeside town of Arona.

WHERE TO SLEEP Stresa's budget lodging is sort of a joke, with only a meager selection of generic one-star hotels. The cheapest of these is **Orsola** (Via Duchessa di Genova 45, tel. 0323/31087), a two-minute walk downhill from the train station. Its rooms are lean, but many have balconies. The drawback is train noise, though with the shutters closed you should be able to sleep at night. Doubles run L50,000 (without bath). A nicer, quieter, more expensive option is the pink-and-white **Mon Toc** (Via Duchessa di Genova 69, tel. 0323/30282), where doubles are L65,000 (with bath). If you instantly detest Stresa, make the short trek to nearby Isola Superiore (sometimes called Isola dei Pescatori), one of the Isole Borromee, and the clean, quiet **Belvedere** (Via Ugo 54, tel. 0323/30047); double rooms with lake views cost L80,000 (with or without bath).

FOOD For cheap takeout, try **Gastronomia de Piero** (Via A. M. Bolongaro 41/43, tel. 0323/31934) or the small grocery store **Commerciale di Verio** (Via Roma 11, tel. 0323/30075). If you want to eat sitting down, be careful—Stresa is full of overpriced tourist traps with downright bad food. One exception is the pizzeria **Venezia** (Via Duchessa di Genova 49, near the station, tel. 0323/31398). It's nothing spectacular but is good and affordable in comparison to many spots in town, serving reasonably priced pizzas, pastas, main dishes, and assorted large salads. Another plus is the mostly local clientele. If you crave Chinese food, head to **Shan Gril-La** (Via Principe Tomaso 74, tel. 0323/31182), next to the APT office. The best bargain is the lunchtime fixed-price menu: appetizer, rice or pasta, main course, and bottled water and coffee costs L15,000.

OUTDOOR ACTIVITIES Even though it sits on a lake, Stresa's main outdoor activity is hiking—either in the surrounding forested hills, or on Monttarone, the small mountain that doesn't quite loom over town. For info and maps on hiking, visit the APT office (*see* Basics, *above*) and be sure to ask for the "Lago Maggiore Trekking Per Tutti" brochure (with English translation). To reach the trailheads, take the *funivia* (gondola) from Piazzale Lido 8 (tel. 0323/30295). It leaves every 20 minutes 9:15–noon and 1:40–5. Tickets cost L10,000, or L15,000 with your own mountain bike. You may also rent a bike inside the gondola station (L25,000 for ½ day, L30,000 for a full day) and pay L9000 for the gondola ride. In winter, Monttarone has not-so-challenging skiing.

ISOLE BORROMEE

The so-called Crown Jewels of Lago Maggiore are the Isole Borromee (Borromeo Islands), which form a triangle in the water between Stresa, Laveno, and Pallanza. Although a bit tarnished by the burgeoning tourist trade, the islands still shine both architecturally and, don't laugh, horticulturally. The islands take their name from the Borromeo family, which has owned them since the 12th century. These days, however, you don't need an engraved invitation to reach them—only a few thousand lire and a water-worthy stomach. Boats for the islands leave from the dock on Stresa's Piazza Marconi, starting at 9 AM. A boat runs every half hour, with stops at Isola Bella (5 min, L4000), Isola Superiore (10 min, L4000), and Isola Madre (30 min, L5500). If you want to visit all three, buy a day pass for L11,000; the pass is also valid for boats to Laveno and Pallanza. As for food, everything here is so overpriced that it's best to do some grocery shopping before you leave Stresa.

The most well-known island, **Isola Bella**, got its name not only from its natural beauty but also as a play on the name Isabella, wife of Count Carlo III Borromeo, who commissioned the island's baroque **palazzo** and its majestic gardens in 1670. The palace is grand and magnificent, as are the 10 terraced gardens, complete with roaming white peacocks and picture-perfect views of the lake. *Tel. 0323/30556. Admission to gardens and palazzo: L12,000. Open Mar. 27–Oct. 24, daily 9–noon and 1:30–5:30.*

Tiny **Isola Superiore**, less than 100 meters wide, supposedly retains the look and feel of an ancient fishing village, with its winding lanes and sleepy shops. In reality the island is little more than a patch of sand with tacky restaurants and souvenir stands. Fortunately, **Isola Madre** compensates for touristy Superiore: except for one restaurant, the Madre's only development is a vast **botanical garden** and a small **palazzo**. The palace is furnished with ancient mannequins that look shocked to see visitors in their midst. The rambling gardens have a more casual atmosphere than those on Isola Bella and are definitely worth checking out. Two good times to visit are April (for the camellias) and May (for the azaleas and rhododendrons). *Tel. 0323/31261. Admission to palace and gardens: L12,000. Open Mar. 27–Sept., daily 9–noon and 1:30–5:30 (Oct. 1–24 until 5 PM).*

CANNOBIO

Though it's often overrun by tourists (largely German, Swiss, and Italian), Cannobio, the last Italian town before the Swiss border, has more character and more in the way of outdoor activities than Stresa. As far as character goes, Cannobio boasts narrow streets and traditional houses with tall wooden shutters spread along the hillside—a definite Kodak moment. Outdoorswise, strong mountain breezes attract Windsurfer- and sailboat-loving types in summer. For hikers, there's an old network of footpaths and mule tracks that have been developed into a sign-posted system that connects a variety of landscapes and ecosystems. The **tourist office** provides both hotel and campground listings as well as hiking maps for every experience level, from he-man to heavy smoker. Ask for the detailed, multilingual guide "Lago Maggiore Trekking Per Tutti." *Viale Vittorio Veneto 4, tel. 0323/71212. Open daily 9–noon and 4:30–5; closed Sun. afternoon, and Thurs. afternoon in winter.*

If you want to swim and sunbathe, Cannobio has the lake's largest public beach, which means it gets a bit crowded in July and August. For water sports, **Tomaso Sail and Surf** (Lido Cannobio, tel. 0323/72214) rents all sizes and sorts of equipment. They may also help you find a waterskiing boat, but expect to pay L45,000 for a brief 10-minute circuit of the lake.

COMING AND GOING From Stresa to Cannobio there are two daily boats from April to about the third week of September (1 hr 40 min, L11,000) and two hydrofoils (1 hr, L12,000). Otherwise, take a boat to Intra (15 daily, 1 hr, L6500) and catch an **ASPAN** bus to Cannobio (16 daily, 30 min, L3000).

Lago di Orta

Sunk in the green hills of Piemonte, this smallest of the Italian lakes is truly stupendous. Though it's only over the mountain from Lago Maggiore, serene Lago di Orta feels far away from the tourist hordes. Most of its towns are small and scattered, some perched on the shore, others built into a hillside. The most picturesque is **Orta**, on the eastern shore; it's a good base for further exploring, as well as home to the oddly disturbing **Sacro Monte** (Via Sacro Monte, tel. 0322/905642), a church with 20 chapels where quasi-grotesque mannequins act out scenes from the weird life of St. Francis.

Foremost among the lake's attractions are **Isola San Giulio**, Lago di Orta's only island; **Pella**, a small lakefront town with a medieval tower and Romanesque church; and the largish city of **Omegna**, with its medieval city walls and 14th-century church. Understand, though, that these sights aren't why most people come to Orta—relaxation is. Lago di Orta is for strolling, gazing, and perhaps falling in love (just as Nietzsche did here with the Russian poetess Lou Salomé). Orta's **tourist office** has truckloads of information for you. *Via Olina 9/11, tel. 0322/90354. Open Tues.–Sat. 9–noon and 3–5:30, Sun. 10–noon and 3–5.*

COMING AND GOING Orta's **train station** (Via Lunati) is so small that no one save the bartender works here; schedules are posted, and you buy tickets on board. From Orta there are trains to Milan (12 daily, 1 hr 45 min, L9800; change at Navarre) and to Turin (1 hr 15 min, L11,700).

WHERE TO SLEEP AND EAT The cheapest hotel in Orta is the **Taverna Antico Agnello** (Via Olina 18, tel. 0322/90259), which charges L55,000–L65,000 for a double (no bath). **Olina** (Via Olina 40, tel. 0322/905656) has clean doubles with bath starting at L70,000. Both have quality restaurants downstairs, but they're not cheap (primi L10,000). **Cusio** (Via Giovanni Bosco 5, tel. 0322/90290), the closest campground to Orta's center, charges L6000–L7000 per person, L10,500–L12,000 per site. **L'Edera** (Via Bersani 11, tel. 0322/905534) serves sandwiches and simple hot food and is open late. Delicious fresh bread from **Il Fornaio** (Piazza Motta 7, tel. 0322/911713) will fortify you for yet another stroll.

PIEMONTE AND THE 5
VALLE D'AOSTA

By Paul Kottman with Janet Morris

Sequestered in Italy's northwestern corner, Valle d'Aosta is the country's smallest region, while Piemonte (Piedmont) is its second largest, with nearly five million inhabitants. Despite their differences in size, the two regions have a lot of similarities in terms of culture and landscape. Both betray close historical ties to France: Their dialects have French origins, and semiautonomous Valle d'Aosta retains French as its second official language. Even the area's rich cuisine is influenced by its northern neighbor, incorporating mountain cheeses, truffles, game dishes, and creamy desserts. Local wines, especially around Asti, are some of Italy's best.

Both regions border the Alps, and their landscapes are a mix of dramatic mountains and peaceful plains and valleys. Although Piemonte is one of Italy's most industrialized regions, the modern development of **Torino**'s suburbs quickly gives way to small agricultural villages, and the Piemontese share with their Valle d'Aosta neighbors a real appreciation of nature. Northern Piemonte in particular is set up for summer and winter Alpine sports. Though ripe for exploitation, much of the land in the Valle d'Aosta has been carefully preserved, especially in the enormous **Parco Nazionale del Gran Paradiso** (Gran Paradiso National Park), which comprises a hefty chunk of the region's eastern section. Both regions' mountains, forests, and rivers provide excellent opportunities for hiking, skiing, rafting, and mountain biking. Of course, at times the pristine landscape is interrupted—particularly around **Mont Blanc** (Monte Bianco in Italian), where ski resorts encroach on the Alps' natural charms. Nevertheless, the valley is overall remarkably beautiful, a must-see for every nature lover.

According to the Italian Constitution of 1945, Valle d'Aosta maintains administrative and cultural autonomy from the rest of Italy—the kind of freedom about which many in Quebec and Spain's Basque region continue to dream.

Piemonte's abundance of religious monuments illustrates the power and wealth of the Savoy family, whose members commissioned most of them. From 1045 until the reign of Vittorio Emanuele some eight centuries later, the House of Savoy continuously ruled Piemonte and its surroundings—continuously with the exception of Napoléon's pesky intervention, that is. You won't find many historical towns here, but old-time Christianity asserts itself in highly visible ways: Eerie abbeys and *sacre monti* (sacred mounts) dot the Piemontese landscape, especially in Varallo and Orta. Ironically, the region's capital, Torino—as one of Italy's leftist-politics and liberal-culture hot spots—is distinctly secular at heart.

Both regions' general lack of tourism means that budget travelers will find warm, unjaded locals and relatively low prices (though restaurants are still alarmingly expensive in parts of

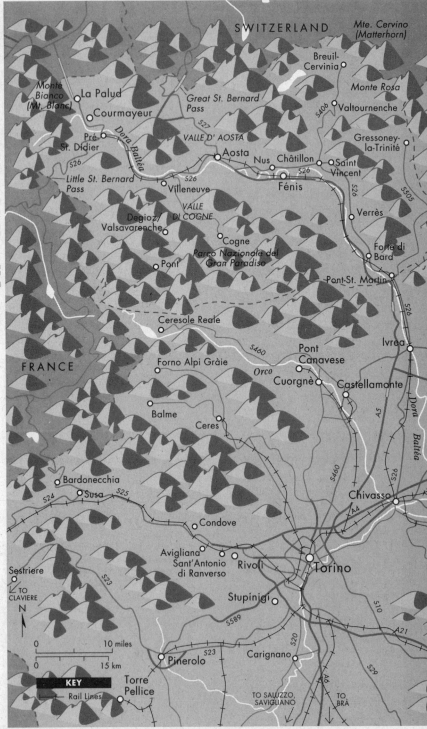

SWITZERLAND

Mte. Cervino
(Matterhorn)

Breuil-
Cervinia

Monte Rosa

*Monte
Bianco
(Mt. Blanc)*   La Palud

Courmayeur

Great St. Bernard
Pass

S27

S406   Valtournenche

Gressoney-
la-Trinité

Pré
St. Didier

Dora Baltéa

VALLE D' AOSTA

S26

Aosta   Nus   Châtillon   Saint
Vincent

Little St. Bernard
Pass

526

Villeneuve

*VALLE
DI COGNE*

Fénis

S26

S26

Verrès

S505

Degioz/
Valsavarenche

Cogne

Forte di
Bard

*Parco Nazionale del
Gran Paradiso*

Pont

Pont-St. Martin

S26

Ceresole Reale

Ivrea

S460

Pont
Canavese

FRANCE

Forno Alpi Gràie

Orco

Cuorgnè

Castellamonte

A5

Dora Baltéa

Balme

Ceres

S460

S26

Bardonecchia

Chivasso

S24   Susa   S25

A4

Condove

Avigliana
Sant'Antonio
di Ranverso

Rivoli

Torino

Sestriere

TO
CLAVIERE

N

S23

Stupinigi

S10

S589

A21

0   10 miles

0   15 km

Pinerolo   S23

Carignano

S20

A6

S29

KEY

Rail Lines

Torre
Pellice

TO SALUZZO,
SAVIGLIANO

TO
BRÀ

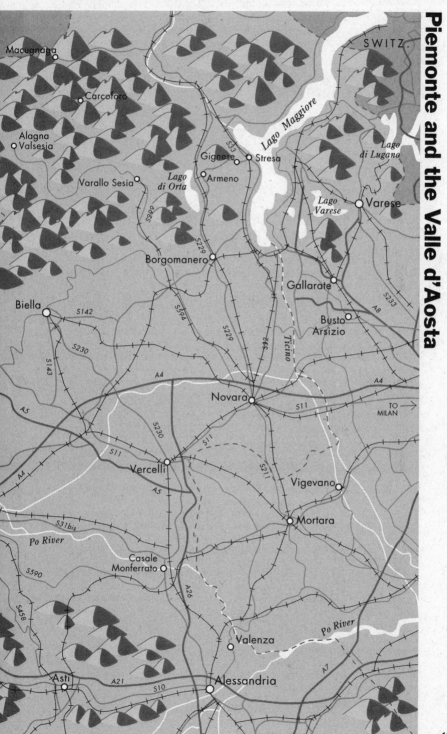

SWITZ.

Macugnaga

Carcoforo

Alagna
Valsesia

Varallo Sesia

Lago
di Orta

Gignese
Armeno

Lago Maggiore

Stresa

Lago
di Lugano

Lago
Varese

Varese

S33

S229

S229

Borgomanero

Gallarate

Busto
Arsizio

A8

S233

Biella

S142

S230

S143

A5

S394

S229

Ticino

A4

A4

TO
MILAN

Novara

S11

S230

S11

Vercelli

A5

S11

A4

S211

Vigevano

S211

S31bis

Mortara

Po River

Casale
Monferrato

A26

S590

S458

Po River

Valenza

A7

Asti

A21

S10

Alessandria

137

Piemonte). Planning ahead will improve your trip greatly, as transportation, especially in the Valle d'Aosta, can be tricky. All things considered, if you veer off the Rome–Florence–Milan–Venice line, you'll be rewarded.

Piemonte

Best known for its industrialized capital, Torino (Turin), Piemonte has more to offer than the executive offices of Olivetti (computer specialists) and acres of Fiat factories, though these two corporations combine to make Piemonte one of the wealthiest regions in Italy. Perhaps as a result of this wealth, Piemonte has become a stronghold of the "Lega Nord," a south-hating organization pushing for northern secession. Ironically, Piemonte—and Torino in particular—is known for its left-wing politics. If your Italian is up to par, look no further than Torino's newspaper, *La Stampa*, for evidence of this liberal agenda.

Torino is a good base for exploring nearby Gothic castles and baroque churches. The towns of **Asti**, **Saluzzo**, and **Savigliano** are filled with time-capsuled medieval buildings, and nearby vineyards and farmlands produce the incredible wines and rich foods for which this region is known.

Torino

Though it holds the dubious title "Car Capital of Italy," Torino is much more than just a factory town. Years of planning have made the city an urban designer's dream, and it possesses a grace that defies its size and modernity. The bordering suburbs are not exactly things of beauty, but the chic shops, elegant cafés, and excellent museums in the city center quickly erase any memories of the monotonous kilometers of housing projects on the outskirts. The Crocietta district is home to Torino's amazing aristocratic residences, and, in the city center, wide arches and graceful colonnades connect spacious piazze.

Torino's position at the confluence of two rivers has long made it desirable as a military stronghold. In the 1st century BC, it came under the rule of Augustus Caesar, who commissioned the easy-to-navigate grid of streets. In the 11th century AD, the city became part of the Savoy dominion. The Savoys transformed Torino into an elegant European capital, bringing in generations of artists and thinkers to enrich the city's culture and skyline. Up through the 20th century, the city's cultured, educated, liberal atmosphere continued to draw such thinking types. Friedrich Nietzsche spent his last productive years living and writing in and around Torino, where his house still stands. He allegedly chose Torino for its relative peace and quiet and its proximity to the Alps. Leftish Italians such as the novelist Natalia Ginzburg and the poet Cesare Pavese also did time here. Torino is home to an excellent university and boasts a large, politically active student population, not to mention quality bookstores on almost every corner.

Torino was key in the Risorgimento (*see box, below*), and it served as the capital of a newly unified Italy in 1861. Expansion slowed when Florence replaced Torino as the capital in 1864, but the beginning of the 20th century saw a surge in both industrialization and worker activism. Industrialist Gianni Agnelli and his clan began an empire that now essentially holds a monopoly on car manufacturing in Italy (Fiat is the best-known of his many car companies), as well as controlling Olivetti and *La Stampa*—all of which has made Agnelli one of Italy's most feared and powerful men. Meanwhile, Antonio Gramsci became a folk hero for organizing occupations of the Fiat factory and later helping to found the Italian Communist Party. Along with a large worker population, Torino boasts a nobility that is still intact (if a little worse for wear) in all its snobby glory. Torino's wealth gets around, however, and though there are still a few clans in charge, the city's prosperity has been felt far and wide.

BASICS

➤ **CHANGING MONEY** • The Porta Susa and Porta Nuova train station exchange booths, both open daily 8 AM–9:30 PM, have decent rates and charge no commission. Porta Nuova also

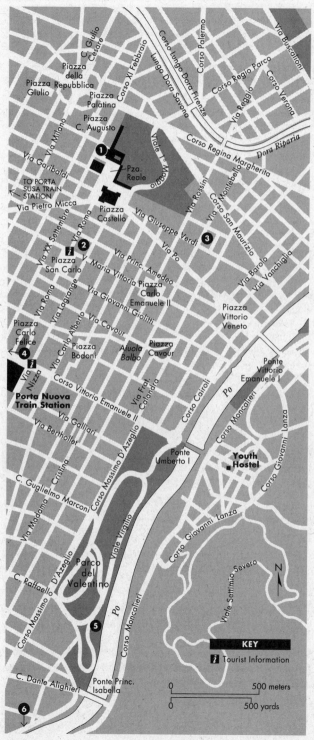

Torino

Castello e Borgo Medioevale, **5**

Duomo di San Giovanni, **1**

Galleria Civica d'Arte Moderna e Contemporanea, **4**

Mole Antonelliana, **3**

Museo dell' Automobile, **6**

Palazzo dell' Accademia delle Scienze, **2**

C. Giulio Cesare

Piazza della Repubblica

Piazza Giulio

Piazza Palatina

Piazza C. Augusto

Corso XI Febbraio

Via Milano

Lungo Dora Savona

Corso Lungo Dora Firenze

Corso Palermo

Corso Regio Parco

Via Buscalioni

Corso Verona

Via Reggio

Via Garibaldi

Pza. Reale

Viale T. Michel

Corso Regina Margherita

Via Rossini

Dora Riparia

TO PORTA SUSA TRAIN STATION

Via Pietro Micca

Piazza Castello

Via Giuseppe Verdi

Via Montebello

Corso San Maurizio

Via XX Settembre

Via Roma

Via Princ. Amedeo

Via Po

Piazza San Carlo

V. Maria Vittoria

Via Barolo

Via Vanchiglia

Via Roma

Via Lagrange

Via Giovanni Giolitti

Piazza Carlo Emanuele II

Piazza Vittorio Veneto

Via Cavour

Piazza Carlo Felice

Via Carlo Alberto

Piazza Bodoni

Aiuola Balbo

Piazza Cavour

Ponte Vittorio Emanuele I

Po

Porta Nuova Train Station

Via Nizza

Corso Vittorio Emanuele II

Via Frat. Calandra

Corso Cairoli

Corso Moncalieri

Corso Giovanni Lanza

Via Galliari

Via Berthollet

Ponte Umberto I

Youth Hostel

Corso Giovanni Lanza

C. Guglielmo Marconi

Via Madama Cristina

Corso Massimo D'Azeglio

Corso Giovanni Lanza

Via Madama Cristina

D'Azeglio

Parco del Valentino

Po

Viale Virgilio

Corso Moncalieri

Viale Settimio Severo

N

C. Raffaello

Corso Massimo

C. Dante Alighieri

Ponte Princ. Isabella

KEY

i Tourist Information

0   500 meters

0   500 yards

139

has a currency exchange machine. The banks on Corso Matteotti just west of Porta Nuova have good rates and charge a fair 1% commission; they are generally open weekdays 8:30–1:30 and 2:30–4:30. ATMs are always open and can be easily found at almost any bank. **Banca Popolare di Milano** (Corso Matteotti 8) has an automated teller that accepts AmEx cards.

➢ **MAIL** • Along with normal postal services, telegram and international fax services are available 24 hours a day in the office to the left of the front door. *Via Alfieri 10, off Piazza San Carlo, tel. 011/562–5240. Open weekdays 8:15–5:30, Sat. 8:15–1.*

➢ **PHONES** • There are several **SIP** offices in Torino, but the most convenient one is on Via Roma between Piazza San Carlo and Piazza Castello. The only operator-assisted phone office is **IRITEL** (tel. 011/534880; open Mon.–Sat. 8–7:45) at the Porta Nuova station.

➢ **VISITOR INFORMATION** • Torino has two **IAT** offices, one at the Porta Nuova train station (tel. 011/531327) and one at Piazza San Carlo (Via Roma 226, tel. 011/535181). Both have maps, museum listings, and hotel info, and both are open Monday–Saturday 9–7. An **API** office (Corso Ferrucci 122/128, tel. 011/335–2440; open weekdays 9–7, Sat. 10–4) handles info on all of Piemonte. The **Centro Informagiovani** (Via Assarotti 2, tel. 011/5765–4976; open Wed.–Sun. 10:30–6:30) is the place for budget travelers and students; pick up their pamphlets "Torino Giovani" and "Informagiovani!" for info on art happenings and nightlife.

COMING AND GOING

➢ **BY TRAIN** • Near the center of town, the **Porta Nuova** train station (Piazza Carlo Felice, tel. 011/561–3333) handles most of Torino's rail traffic. Every day about 14 trains run to Milan (1½–2 hrs, L12,000) and three go to Venice (4 hrs, L32,500). Ten head south for Rome daily (6½ hrs, L52,000), stopping in Pisa, which sets you up with a quick connection to Florence. To reach the center of town, walk 10 minutes down Via Roma to Piazza Castello, or take Bus 61 or 63 or Tram 4 or 15 from in front of the station.

Torino's second station, **Porta Susa** (Piazza XVIII Dicembre, tel. 011/538513), has 13 daily trains to Milan (1½–2 hrs, L12,000) and three to Venice (4 hrs, L32,500). Tram 1 and Bus 52 connect this station to Porta Nuova; Tram 13 and Bus 55 go to Piazza Castello in the center of town.

The Shot of Espresso Heard 'Round the World

"Risorgimento" literally means revival, and in the 1830s café philosophers and radical thinkers decided it was time to oust Italy's foreign rulers and forge an Italian state. Almost 30 years later, King Vittorio Emanuele II of Piemonte and his prime minister, Count Camillo Cavour, began to whip up a nationalist, anti-Austrian frenzy in the north. To get rid of a pesky Bourbon king in Sicily whose presence menaced the country's unification, Vittorio Emanuele and Cavour conspired with trigger-happy Giuseppe Garibaldi. Along with 1,000 volunteer soldiers called the Red Shirts, Garibaldi made an infamous voyage from Genova to Sicily, where he helped the Sicilians oust King Francis II and turned the territory over to Vittorio Emanuele. In 1861, after war with Austria and much political back-stabbing and wheeling and dealing, the Kingdom of Italy was established with Torino as its capital and Vittorio Emanuele as its monarch.

Though almost every street sign in Piemonte proudly commemorates the Risorgimento and the country's subsequent unification, Italy remains a fiercely regional land. Antagonism between northerners and southerners, speakers of diverse dialects, and rival soccer fans shows how many people consider themselves first Milanesi or Siciliani, and then Italiani.

➤ **BY BUS** • Torino's **bus station** (Corso Inghilterra 1, tel. 011/301616), just south of Porta Susa, has only one window (and one long line) for tickets and info. Southern Piemonte towns like Saluzzo (30 min, L5000) are easier to reach by bus than by train. Fourteen daily buses serve Milan (2 hrs, L17,000). Tram 15 runs from the bus station to Porta Nuova and Piazza Castello.

➤ **BY PLANE** • Torino's **Caselle** airport (tel. 011/5778–3612) has regular flights to most major European and Italian cities. **Sadem** buses connect the airport to the bus station (35 min, L6000) and run every 30–45 minutes.

GETTING AROUND Despite the city's size, the city center is easy to navigate on foot. **Piazza Castello** marks the heart of the city; **Via Roma**, Torino's chichi shopping street, runs out of the piazza to the southwest. Along Via Roma the stately **Piazza Carlo Felice** spreads out in front of the Porta Nuova train station. **Via Po** also runs out of Piazza Castello to **Piazza Vittorio Veneto** before opening onto the Po River. Funky stores line **Via Garibaldi**, which heads northwest out of Piazza Castello.

➤ **BY BUS OR TRAM** • Torino has a comprehensive network of buses and trams, so getting around is a snap. In the lobby of Porta Nuova station look for the **Trasporti Torinesi** office (tel. 011/538376), which has info on the system. Buy tickets anywhere the CONSORZIO TRASPORTI TORINESE sign is displayed, including at automatic ticket machines and the Porta Nuova IAT office (*see* Visitor Information, *above*). Tickets cost L1500 and are good on an unlimited number of lines for 70 minutes after validation.

WHERE TO SLEEP Not exactly tourist-oriented, Torino is an outlandishly expensive place to sleep. The cheapest hotels are clustered in the seedy red-light district around Via Nizza, just east of the Porta Nuova train station. Within this neighborhood, **Porta Susa** (Via San Martino 4, tel. 011/542375) has doubles for L60,000; you can expect some sarcasm from the management. For nicer hotels, try those along Corso Vittorio Emanuele II and off Corso Re Umberto I, a block west of the Porta Nuova train station.

Astoria. Easy to find off Piazza Carlo Felice, this hotel has it all. A friendly proprietor, nice rooms—even TVs with satellite connections. Doubles are cheap for Torino at L70,000. *Via XX Settembre 4, tel. 011/562–0653. From Porta Nuova Station, turn left on Vittorio Emanuele II, right on Via XX Settembre. 15 rooms, all with bath.*

Bella Vista. This hotel is much nicer than most others west of the station, and costs more accordingly. Large doubles with TVs go for L90,000. The management is helpful to out-of-towners, so milk them for all they're worth. *Via Galliari 15, tel. 011/669–8139. From Porta Nuova Station, quick right on Via Nizza, left on Via Galliari. Wheelchair access. AE, MC, V.*

Magenta. The Magenta feels intimate even though its rooms, with their high ceilings and huge windows, are large and airy. The turtle-print curtains prove that taste is subjective. Doubles cost L70,000. *Corso Vittorio Emanuele II 67, tel. 011/542649. From Porta Nuova station, walk west (left as you exit) for 5 min. 18 rooms, 10 with bath. AE, MC, V.*

Monte Vecchio. The recently remodeled Monte Vecchio is clean and safe, and is the most decent hotel close to Porta Nuova station. But it's probably not worth the L105,000 unless convenience is your first priority. Ask the friendly staff about weekend specials. *Via Monte Vecchio 13, tel. 011/562–0023. From Porta Nuova station, follow Via Sacchi south 3 blocks to Via Monte Vecchio. 30 rooms, all with bath. AE, MC, V.*

➤ **HOSTELS** • **Ostello Torino.** This modern hostel sports a restaurant/bar, sunrooms, and garden and is Torino's only real budget option. The 11:30 PM curfew means you can't really enjoy the city's nightlife, but beds go for a mere L17,000 with breakfast. Other meals cost L12,000. Only HI members can stay here (but you can buy membership), and it admits only large groups December 22–February 15. *Via Alby 1, at Via Gatti, tel. 011/660–2939. From Porta Nuova station, take Bus 52. 97 beds. Check-in daily 6 PM–11:30 PM.*

FOOD Torino's specialties tend to be heavy and decadent, with lots of butter, oil, cream, truffles, and meat filling out every meal. You can start with an antipasto like *corne all'albese* (slivers of raw veal with oil, lemon, Parmesan, and white truffles), and then go on to *tajarin* *all'albese* (tagliatelle with butter and truffle shavings). A concoction of boiled meats, *bollito misto*, is the most traditional Piemontese main course. Desserts—such as baked peaches stuffed with crushed *amaretti* (almond cookies), cocoa, and sugar—are as divine as they are fattening. On the other end of the spectrum, Torino is also home to a variety of vegetarian, macrobiotic, and international eateries, all rarities in Italy. If you're craving Chinese food, try **Du Cheng** (Via XX Settembre 62, tel. 011/546159), but be warned that everything is toned down to suit local palates. Pick up picnic pickings at the large morning **market** in Piazza della Repubblica. If you really need to save cash in Torino, many bars serve up good panini for L3000–L5000.

➢ **UNDER L20,000** • **Erewhon.** It's not big on atmosphere, but this is one of the few restaurants in Italy where you can choose from a large selection of vegetarian and macrobiotic dishes. You have to be a member of an Italian veggie club called ENDAS to eat here, but they'll sign you up on the spot for a small fee. *Via Frat. Calandra 16, tel. 011/882450. From Porta Nuova station, right on Corso Vittorio Emanuele II to Via Frat. Calandra. Open Mon.–Sat. 12:30–2:30 and 7:30–10.*

La Pergola Rosa. A kindly older couple serve up affordable Spanish and Italian food with subtlety and care. They serve paella every now and then, but even if you just order the daily special, you'll be happy. *Via XX Settembre 18, just NW of Piazzo Carlo Felice, tel. 011/537562. Closed Sun.*

Il Punto Verde. This veggie joint is frequented by young Torinesi. The platters of mixed grilled vegetables with Parmesan cheese and olive oil drizzled on top are particularly yummy; a full meatless meal costs less than L15,000. *Via Belfiore 151/F, tel. 011/650–4514. From Piazza Nizza (south of Porta Nuova station), walk 2 blocks east. Open Tues.–Fri. noon–2:30 and 7:30–10:30, weekends 7:30 PM–10:30 PM.*

➢ **UNDER L35,000** • **Arcardia.** This truly unique place offers both Japanese and Italian menus. You can order authentic sushi and sashimi while your companion goes for the gnocchi and ragù (a combination of the two is not recommended). It's run by a Japanese woman and and an Italian man who manage to please all appetites. *Galleria Subalpina 16, SE cnr of Piazza Castello, tel. 011/561–3898. Closed Sun.*

Dai Saletta. This small, simply furnished trattoria serves traditional Piemontese cuisine. Try one of the homemade pastas flavored with local cheese, and a bottle from the restaurant's good selection of local wines. Call for reservations. *Via Belfiore 37, tel. 011/687867. From Piazza Nizza (south of Porta Nuova station), walk 2 blocks east. Open Mon.–Sat. 12:30–2:30 and 7:30–1. Closed Aug.*

➢ **CAFES** • Torino's café culture reached its peak in the 19th century, when plans for the Risorgimento were hatched over coffee and pastries (*see box* The Shot of Espresso Heard 'Round the World, *above*). Cruise Via Roma between the train station and Piazza Castello for a good selection of gelaterias and coffeehouses whose interiors and customers are elegantly decorated. Torino's most famous café, **Baratti and Milano** (Piazza Castello 29, no phone), is a tony joint complete with bronze bas-reliefs and painted crystal. **Mulassano** (Piazza Castello 9, tel. 011/547990) has a recently reconstructed art-nouveau interior where the hip sip espresso. **Elena** (Piazza Vittorio Veneto 5, tel. 011/817–7332) attracts the university set and is more lively than the staid Piazza Castello spots.

WORTH SEEING If you think the only things to see in industrial Torino are car factories and the controversial Holy Shroud (*see below*), you're in for a surprise. Besides a museum devoted to the automobile and a chapel for the shroud, the city sports architectural jewels and museums housing everything from Egyptian artifacts to contemporary art. Most of these attractions are in the town center and are often linked by Torino's famous porticoes. Boat rides on the Po River are available daily just south of Piazza Vittorio Veneto; considering the view, they don't cost too much (L8000).

➢ **DUOMO DI SAN GIOVANNI AND THE HOLY SHROUD** • The 15th-century duomo is an entirely uninteresting Renaissance building whose adjoining Chapel of the Holy Shroud houses one of the world's most fascinating relics. The **Holy Shroud**, a cloth imprinted with a bearded man's image, enjoys long repute as the shroud in which Jesus's body was wrapped after the crucifixion. Although recent carbon dating sets the cloth's manufacture between 1260 and 1390, debates still rage about how the image was created. While the real shroud is safeguarded in a silver casket, an eerie replica is on display. *Piazza S. Giovanni, tel. 011/4366101. Open daily 7:30–12:30 and 3–7.*

➤ **GALLERIA CIVICA D'ARTE MODERNA E CONTEMPORANEA** • The three floors of this museum house an excellent exhibit tracing modern art's progress from the 19th century to the present. Everything from frenetic futurism to experimental abstractionism is displayed, mostly via French and Italian works. *Via Magenta 31, tel. 011/562–9911. From Stazione Porta Nuova, head west up Corso Vittorio Emanuele II, turn left on Corso Re Umberto, and right on Via Magenta. Admission: L8000. Open Tues.–Sun. 9–7 (shorter hrs in winter).*

➤ **MOLE ANTONELLIANA** • Piercing the skyline like a needle, the Mole—designed as a synagogue by architect Alessandro Antonelli in 1863—looks far more modern than it actually is. Occasional visiting exhibitions notwithstanding, the Mole now sits empty. At 167 meters it's still one of Europe's highest brick buildings, with an elevator (L4000) that grants visitors a magnificent though smog-besmirched view. *Via Montebello 20, tel. 011/817049. Open Tues.–Sun. 9–7.*

If you liked Alessandro Antonelli's Mole, head to the corner of Corso San Maurizio and Via Barolo, where you'll find one of his more curious creations, called the "Fetta di Polenta" (piece of polenta): a 27-meter-high, 27-meter-long building that is less than 1 meter wide at some points.

➤ **MUSEO DELL'AUTOMOBILE** • Any "car capital" would be incomplete without a museum dedicated to the won-derwagon. Torino's car museum naturally stars the Fiat, but many Bentleys, Benzes, and Fords round out the collection. You can also see the beautiful blue Isotta Franchini that bears the golden initials "ND" for its onscreen owner Norma Desmond, Gloria Swanson's character in *Sunset Boulevard. Corso Unità d'Italia 40, tel. 011/677666. From Porta Nuova station, take Bus 34 up Corso Unità d'Italia. Admission: L9000. Open Tues.–Sun. 10–6:30.*

➤ **PALAZZO DELL'ACCADEMIA DELLE SCIENZE** • The palazzo houses two note-worthy collections. The **Museo Egizio** is the first thing a Torinese will tell you to visit in the city. Supposedly one of the world's best Egyptian artifact collections, the Palazzo dell'Accademia boasts 30,000 pieces dating from the 6th century BC to the 7th century AD. Of particular note are findings from the 1400 BC tomb of the royal architect, Kha, including pages from the Book of the Dead. *Via Accademia delle Scienze 6, tel. 011/561–7776. Admission: L12,000. Open Tues.–Sun. 9–7 (shorter hrs in winter).*

The **Galleria Sabaudia**, also in the palazzo, has a large collection of art treasures—with an emphasis on religious subjects and portraiture—that the Savoy princes gathered for their homes. *Above Museo Egizio, tel. 011/547440. Admission: L8000. Open Tues.–Sun. 9–2.*

➤ **PARCO DEL VALENTINO** • Parco del Valentino is home to the **Botanical Garden of the University of Torino** and its 1,700 plant specimens. It occupies a scenic stretch of the Po's western bank, and aside from being a bit untended and overgrown, it's a good place to pass a few hours. Across the park, you can wander around the **Castello e Borgo Medioevale**, a repro-duction of a medieval castle and village built for a world exposition in 1884. (At press time, the castle was closed for restoration.) *Parco del Valentino, tel. 011/669–9372. Village admis-sion free. Open daily 8–8.*

CHEAP THRILLS Every Saturday from 5 AM to 2 PM the streets Via Borgo Dora, Via Lanino, Via Mameli, and Via Andreis come alive with the **Balôn Market**. As well as bric-à-brac and lace, you might even see your future here: The occult has long intrigued the Torinese, so tarot cards are a big deal. If you've ever wanted to try your hand, so to speak, here's the place.

➤ **FESTIVALS** • The two-day **Feast of San Giovanni** (June 23–24) honors Torino's patron saint with parades and a canoe race on the Po, ending with an impressive fireworks display. The subsequent **Vogalonga** festival (June 25–26) honors San Giacomo with a rowing contest, a torchlight boat procession, and more fireworks over the Po. If you're visiting Torino at this time, be sure to book ahead. From September 15 to 25 the festival of **Birra & Dintorni** offers 10 days of music, dancing, food, and beer from around the world. It's held at the Arena Metropolis and on the 47th floor of Torino Expo. Call 011/535529 for more info.

AFTER DARK Torino's after-dark options are largely dictated by the tastes of a young student crowd. Venues are scattered about the city, but if you stick close to Piazza Castello you should find enough places to hang out. Friday's edition of *La Stampa* details upcoming events and has listings of ever-changing club hours and cover charges. Most clubs charge a membership fee, which, along with a cover, you pay at the door. The **Fuori Orario Pass Club** (L15,000) provides access to Portes, Studio 2, Doctor Sax, Roclò, Stilimisti Club, A Biciclette, Akhenathon, Sound Club, and Vicolo Corto. Pick up the pass at the Centro Informagiovani office (*see* Visitor Information, *above*). **Cinema Cuore** (Via Nizza 56, tel. 011/668–7668) shows films in English October–April. From June to September, the city runs **Cinema all'Aperto**, or "Cinema Outdoors," in different garden settings around town. Call 011/650–3203 for info about the films, or look for posters throughout Torino.

Divinia Commedia (Via San Donato 47, tel. 011/488356) has a *birreria* (beer hall) on the ground floor (purgatory), a steaming dance floor in the basement (hell), and a tearoom upstairs (paradise). From the Porta Susa station, take Bus 13 to Piazza Statuto and follow Via San Donato. At the calm, alternative **Folk Club** (Via Perrone 3/B, tel. 011/537636), you can listen to either live music or dance standards spun by a mellow DJ. From Piazza Castello, follow Via Garibaldi and turn left on Via Perrone, just before Piazza Statuto. The perennially hip **Hiroshima Mon Amour** (Via Belfiore 24, tel. 011/650–6287) keeps abreast of the latest music. The occasional performance artist entertains the young trendies who pack the place.

➢ **DISCOS** • **Stardust** (Corso Francia 261, at Via Fabbrichetta, tel. 011/405–6288), just outside the city in Collegno, caters to a mostly lesbian crowd. Medium-size and smoky, it has more character than your standard Europop disco. The **Tuxedo Club** (Via Belfiore 8, near Porta Nuova station, tel. 011/658690) is as unpretentious as it is crowded. Though it's more of a place where young discoers socialize than a hard-core dance spot, you'll feel comfortable here even if you're not dressed in the Italian fashion of the moment. Cover charges depend on the night and the season; it's best to call in the afternoon to find out.

NEAR TORINO

PALAZZINA DI CACCIA DI STUPINIGI Not exactly your average hunting lodge (a large bronze deer caps the cupola), the palazzina is a gilded rococo pleasure palace built for Vittorio Amadeo II by master Piemontese architect Fillipo Juvarra. The richly decorated interior now holds a **Museum of Art and Furnishings** that gives you a glimpse at how loftily the Piemontese nobles lived. The round central room, once used for receptions and balls, is particularly stunning, if a tad bit over the top. A massive crystal chandelier hangs from the heavily frescoed ceiling, spoiling the airy atmosphere Juvarra intended, and gold-leaf sconces—complete with carved deer heads—hang from columns ringing the room. Outside you can see the ornate carriages that once ferried women who wanted to watch or join in as their menfolk slew deer. The only way to see the inside is by guided tour. These start about every half hour (10–11:50 and 2:30–4:20), last about 40 minutes, and are available in English. The ride to the palace from Torino takes about an hour. *Tel. 011/358–1220. From Torino's Porta Nuova station, take Bus 63 or Tram 4 to Piazza Caio Mario, then Bus 41 to palace. Admission: L10,000. Open Tues.– Sun. 9:30–12:30 and 2–6.*

SACRA DI SAN MICHELE The hallucinations caused by thin air and overexertion during the 45-minute uphill hike will have you feeling close to God long before you even arrive at this vast, creepy abbey. Begun in AD 998, it was built on a hill at the mouth of the Susa Valley to protect it from passing marauders. The steep **Scalone dei Morti** (Stairs of the Dead), where loved ones' corpses were once laid out for last respects, now simply provide access to the Gothic-Romanesque complex, but the air of solitude and death somehow lingers. Whimsical frescoes inside the church are overshadowed by views of the valley through the flying buttresses. From Torino's Porta Nuova station, take the train to Condove (25 min, L2700). From Condove, head through Chiusa San Michele (a 10-minute walk) to the rocky path behind the village. From here it's a 45-minute hike to a paved road that leads to the abbey's entrance. *Tel. 011/939130. Admission free. Open Apr.–Sept., Tues.–Sat. 9–12:30 and 3–6, Sun. 9–noon and 3–6; Oct.–Mar., Tues.–Sat. 9–12:30 and 3–5, Sun. 9–noon and 3–5.*

SAVIGLIANO Savigliano's magnificent surrounding countryside and Renaissance palaces made it a popular 19th-century vacation spot for the Savoy clan, but most people today pass through the train station rather than pausing to enjoy the town's extensive artistic and architectural offerings. Savigliano's lack of tourists makes it a dream to explore the cobblestone streets and the churches and piazze that cling to each other in the old center. It's one of Piemonte's few remaining well-preserved historic towns, and it's easy to reach from Torino. The **APT** office (Corso Roma 36, upstairs in Municipal Building, tel. 0172/22322) will roll out the red carpet for you, with info on all of Piemonte.

➤ **COMING AND GOING** • The **train station** (Piazza Sperino) has 20 daily trains to Torino (30 min, L5000), making this the most efficient way of getting in and out. A few buses do run from Savigliano's **bus station** (Via Mutuo Soccorso 13, tel. 0172/33228) to Torino and other Piemonte destinations, but they're pretty scarce and cost more than the train.

➤ **WHERE TO SLEEP AND EAT** • **Hotel Oriente** (Via Cervino 19, tel. 0172/31108) is a steal, with doubles for L50,000 with bath. There's also a good, cheap restaurant downstairs—the whole scene looks a lot like the "Bagdad Café." If Hotel Oriente is full, head to **Hotel Eden** (Via Novellis 43, tel. 0172/712239), which gives you more comfort for more of your money. Doubles go for L90,000, all with bath, TV, and phone. Savigliano's best restaurants are around Piazza Santa Rosa. **Marechiaro** (Corso Roma 101, tel. 0172/31751) makes good pizzas for a school-age crowd at about L12,000 a shot (it's worth it). **Osteria del Teatro** (Via Del Teatro 7, tel. 0172/31088) prepares delicious local specialties. They don't have a menu, but relax; it's all good at about L15,000, and they have a great wine cellar. **Bar Wall Street** on the corner of Via Cervino and Corso Vittorio Veneto is a good breakfast stop.

➤ **WORTH SEEING** • **Piazza Santa Rosa** is a great place to hang out and listen as old-timers cackle away in dialect. A medieval tower, topped by a 17th-century octagonal turret, rises over the square's palazzi and porticoed sidewalks. Pass through the 16th-century **Triumphal Arch**, built in 1585 to celebrate the wedding of Carlo Emanuele I and Caterina of Austria, then head up Via Sant'Andrea to the **Abbey of Sant'Andrea**. Dating back to the 10th century, this is one of the oldest structures in town, with beautiful, fading frescoes. If you turn left on Via Jerusalem, you'll see two of the city's grandest palaces, **Palazzo Taffini d'Acceglio** and **Palazzo Muratori-Cravetta**, both of which have incredibly ornate frescoed interiors. Unfortunately, they're not all that easy to visit; enquire at the tourist office for more info.

SALUZZO Between the feet of the Monviso mountains and an orchard-covered plain is Saluzzo, one of several storybook towns in the valleys south of Torino. The people here claim to be able to cure any Torinese of his or her industrial weariness, and judging by the food, mountain views, and fresh air, they might be right. Just one problem: While it is nice, Saluzzo has zero budget hotels, and is best explored on a day trip for a picnic and stroll. Head to the **APT** office (Via Griselda 6, tel. 0175/46710; open Tues.–Fri. 9–12:30 and 2:30–5:30, Sat. 9–noon) to get started.

➤ **COMING AND GOING** • From Torino, you'll have to change trains in Savigliano (15 daily, 40 min, L5000). Buses also run directly from Torino (6 daily, 30 min, L6000) and Savigliano (15 daily, 15 min, L1500).

➤ **WORTH SEEING** • The **Castello di Manta** hovers above to remind you of Saluzzo's aristocratic past, though the castello is now a prison. In the town's medieval quarter, orient yourself by the 13th-century **Chiesa di San Giovanni**, whose Gothic chapel deserves a minute or two. Just down the street, the **Casa Cavassa** (Via S. Giovanni 5, tel. 0175/41455) houses the Museo Civico, though the building itself, with its porticoed interior courtyard, is more charming than the collection, basically a tribute to local writer Silvio Pellico. In the lower section of town, the **duomo** shadows the newer buildings and is famous for its 14th-century wooden crucifix. Afterwards, you can sample provincial Piemontese food at **La Lanterna** (Via Piave 7, tel. 0175/44491) for around L12,000 per person.

Asti

You've seen cheesy couples clink glasses of the stuff in commercials—now see where the famed Asti Spumante is made. Although it has a history reaching back to the Romans and still retains many of its medieval turrets, the town itself isn't all that exciting—that is, except during its **Palio**, a crazed bareback horse race that takes place on the third Sunday in September, and the **Douja d'Or Wine Festival** and the **Festival of Village Feasts**, both held in the week leading up to the Palio. Budget hotel and restaurant pickings are meager, so it's best to tour Asti's churches and Roman ruins on a day trip from Torino, which is only about one hour away. Only during the festivals is it really worth spending the night.

BASICS The **APT** has a list of lodging and restaurants, as well as transport schedules. *Piazza Alfieri 34, tel. 0141/530357. From train station, head across parking lot to Piazza Marconi and go up steps at far side. Open weekdays 9–12:30 and 3–6, Sat. 9–12:30.*

COMING AND GOING The **train station** (Piazza Marconi 7, tel. 0141/535411) has 40 daily trains from Torino (45 min, L5000). It's too far to walk from the station to town, so take Bus 2 or 4 (until 11 PM) to either Corso Alessandria or Corso Torino in the center of town.

WHERE TO SLEEP Finding a room is no problem, except in September when Asti's festivals pack 'em in. Finding a *decent* room is a problem. The APT office (*see* Basics, *above*) has a very small list of rooms for rent in private homes and a list of nearby *agriturismo* sites (rural homes that rent rooms). **Campground Asti** (Località Valmanera 152, tel. 0141/271238; closed Oct.–Mar.) is 2 kilometers from town, and costs L5000 plus L4000 per person. From the train station, take Bus 1 to Corso Volta and then walk 1½ kilometers.

In town, one-star **Antico Paradiso** (Corso Torino 329, tel. 0141/214385) is the cheapest and nicest in a series of crummy hotels. Its clean, quiet doubles (with bath) go for L50,000. From the station, take Bus 2 or 4 toward Corso Torino, get off at the Via Corridoni stop, and walk 5 minutes. The only thing going for grim, two-star **Cavour** (Piazza Marconi 3, tel. 0141/50222) is its location: right across from the train station. The small, somewhat noisy doubles are L55,000–L70,000.

FOOD Local gastronomic treats are much ballyhooed but don't come cheap. Specialties include *bagna cauda* (garlicky artichoke pâté), polenta, tagliatelle in various sauces, *bollito misto*, and game dishes like potted hare. Typical cheeses include the *tome di Cocconato* and *robiole di Roccoverano*, often served with stuffed peaches. Of course, all of these go very well with local wines, including the reds Barbera d'Asti, Freisa d'Asti, Dolcetto d'Asti, the white Cortese dell'Alto Monferrato, and, of course, Asti Spumante and Mascato.

If you're ready to splurge after weeks of living off hostel breakfasts and pizza, Asti is a great place to try out local wines and culinary delicacies.

If you want to try the excellent local dishes at **Osteria Il Convivio** (Via Giuloni 6, tel. 0141/594188) or **Ristorante-Enoteca Barolo & Co.** (Via Battisti 14, tel. 0141/592059), expect to pay dearly for the privilege. On the other hand, **Ristorante Porta Torino** (Viale Partigiani 144, tel. 0141/216883; closed Sun.) has pasta specialties for under L6000. Otherwise, you're really limited to pizzerias, most of which also serve a few local pastas: **Leon d'Oro** (Via Cavour 95, tel. 0141/530113) and **Monna Laura** (Via Cavour 30, tel. 0141/530113) are two of the best.

WORTH SEEING The **Collegiata di San Secondo** (Piazza San Secondo, tel. 0141/50066; open daily 7–noon and 3:30–7) is dedicated to Asti's patron saint, who got his head lopped off here. His decapitated remains are kept in the church's crypt. Asti's **cathedral** (Piazza Cattedrale) is a mammoth structure with frescoes covering its ceiling and walls, two altarpieces by Gandolfino d'Asti (in the left chapels), and San Giovanni's remains in the crypt downstairs. The brick exterior boasts a stunning 15th-century portal on its southern side. The ruins of the 9th-century **Cripta di Sant'Anastasio** (Via Goltieri 3/A, tel. 0141/54791) were discovered when the baroque church built on top was demolished in 1907. A collection of the recovered capitals and architectural fragments is now housed in the **Museo Lapidario** on the site. Arrange a free, guided visit to the museum—the only way to go—by calling the **Pinacoteca Civica** (Corso Alfieri 357, tel. 0141/54791; open Mon.–Sat. 10–1 and 3–4).

Northern Piemonte

Stretching from the flat Vercelli Plains up to the Alps, the vast valleys and hills of northern Piemonte stand in dramatic contrast to overdeveloped Lombardy, which lies east. The hiking, skiing, kayaking, mountain biking, fishing, and climbing popular here will help you work up enough of an appetite for the region's very rich foods and full-bodied wines. The only thing is, this part of Piemonte is quite remote, and it's really easier to access from the lake region of Lombardy (*see* Chapter 4) unless you have your own wheels. The area's isolation means that both local mountain traditions and nature have been well preserved, giving you two good reasons to make the trek.

VARALLO SESIA

Varallo Sesia is the principal town of the greenest valley in Italy, the Valsesia, thus named because the river Sesia runs through it. The valley is dotted with villages whose residents' lifestyles have hardly changed in the last 100 years; villagers still wear traditional garb for festivals and practice the crafts of lacemaking and woodcarving. Varallo's districts still bear the names of the products— for example, fabric, butter, and wine—that were once produced there. The tiny and picturesque town serves mainly as a base for sports enthusiasts who come to the region to hike, ski, climb, mountain bike, raft, and kayak. For maps of the area's mountains and rivers, go to the **CAI headquarters** (Via C. Durio 14, tel. 0163/51530). Based in the nearby town of Campertongo, **Acqua Vita & Monrosa** (tel. 0163/7737) provides lessons and rents equipment for all types of river sports. One rafting run costs about L70,000, and kayaking goes for about L40,000.

High on a mountain above Varallo in a forested natural reserve, **Sacro Monte** (tel. 0163/53938) is an impressive testament to religious zeal. Almost a city itself, the massive complex comprising a basilica and 45 chapels was founded in 1486 by the Franciscan monk Bernardino Caimi in an attempt to evoke the holy sites of Palestine. In the late 16th century, Saint Carlo Borromeo decided to liven up the original site by adding to the chapels lifelike mannequins enacting scenes from the life of Christ. In many of the Sacro Monte's chapels, popular Valsesian artist Gaudenzio Ferrari painted frescoes that create an overwrought, at times eerie, atmosphere that continues to draw hordes of pilgrims, who make a day of the visit, complete with a family picnic. The serene reserve is free and always open.

> **BASICS** The **APT** office has info on hotels, outdoor activities, and nearby towns. *Corso Roma 38, tel. 0163/51280. Open Mon. 9:30–12:30, Tues.–Fri. 9–noon and 2:30–6:30, weekends 9–12:30 and 2:30–6; closed Sun. Oct.–May.*

> **COMING AND GOING** To reach Varallo, take a bus from Torino (2–4 daily, 2¼ hrs, L11,600) or one of seven daily trains from Novara (1¼ hrs, L5000). Buses to Alagna leave 1–3 times a day (1 hr, L3800). Varallo's **bus depot** is in front of the **train station** (tel. 0163/51309) on Piazza Marconi. To reach Sacro Monte, either walk up the steep grade called Salita Sacro Monte from Piazza Ferrari or catch the bus (7 daily, 15 min, L1300) in front of the train station's café.

> **WHERE TO SLEEP AND EAT** The cheapest lodgings in town are *affitacamere* (private rooms); the easiest to reach is the one above the restaurant **Fra' Dolcino** (Piazza Marconi 3, in front of train station, tel. 0163/51258), where simple doubles go for L45,000. Spacious **Monte Rosa** (Via Regaldi 4, tel. 0163/51100) is much nicer, with views from the balconies and a friendly staff, but a double costs L80,000. Grab some *toma* (a regional cheese) for a picnic on your way up to the Sacro Monte at **La Casera** (Via Camaschella 6, tel. 0163/54181), which stocks the best in town. Next door is a market and a bakery.

ALAGNA VALSESIA

At the foot of Monte Rosa, people visit tiny Alagna Valsesia to participate in Alpine sports. Mountain biking has gained prominence, but skiing, hiking, and free climbing remain tremendously popular. For a dose of culture amidst all this outdoor fun, visit the small **Walser Museum**. The Walser people were Germanic nomads who wound up in northern Piemonte in the 9th century but maintained their northern heritage and traditions; the wood and stone buildings you see in Alagna are remnants of the town's Walser origins. The museum's rooms full of clothing, furniture, and tools used for cooking, farming, and weaving illustrate how this community once lived. *Pedemonte, tel. 0163/91180. Follow Via Centro out of town for 10 min, then follow signs up road to right. Admission free. Open July–Aug., Tues.–Sun. 2–6; Sept.–June, weekends 2–6.*

BASICS **APT** (Piazza degli Alberghi, tel. 0163/92298) gives out listings for hotels and *rifugi* (mountain shelters); it's also home to the **Guide Alpine di Alagna**, which leads guided trips across and around the Alps and provides maps and general info on free climbing and skiing.

COMING AND GOING Getting to Alagna Valsesia is no piece of cake, making it even more of an isolated getaway. Two buses arrive here daily from Varallo (1 hr, L3800) with an additional bus on Monday and Tuesday (but there's only one bus on Sunday). Buses from Milan run twice daily in summer and once daily in winter (3¼ hrs, L8900).

WHERE TO SLEEP AND EAT Ask at the APT office for the shelter best suited to your hiking plans. The rifugio **F. Pastore** (Alpe Pile, tel. 0163/91220; closed Oct.–mid-June), near the entrance to Valsesia's natural reserve and surrounded by waterfalls, has dorm beds for L11,000 (L40,000 with full pension) in a large room or for L22,000 (L50,000 with full pension) in a smaller room. A tent site costs L7000 per person. Not particularly cheap, the centrally located **Mirella** (Bonda 10, tel. 0163/922965) offers woodsy doubles for L80,000. As for eats, you can get your best meals of typical mountain grub at rifugi along the various trails.

OUTDOOR ACTIVITIES Buy ski passes (L45,000 a day) at the *funivia* (funicular) station on Piazza Funivia (tel. 0163/922932). **Monterosa Sport** (Piazza degli Alberi, tel. 0163/922970) rents out skis (L23,000 a day) and snowboards (L20,000) as well as hiking and climbing equipment. You can rent a mountain bike for L35,000 per day from **Maurizio Restelli** at the gas station along the *autostradale* (highway), at the border of Alagna and Riva Valdobbia.

Valle d'Aosta

The mountains and valleys of the Valle d'Aosta fairly cry out to be strolled, climbed, and skied. **Mont Blanc** (Monte Bianco) is the biggest draw, but chairlifts dot every eligible slope. The **Parco Nazionale del Gran Paradiso**'s protected valleys, mountains, and waterfalls are great places to go hiking, kayaking, and off-trail skiing and mountain biking. And an impressive collection of castles is scattered throughout the area, adding a pleasant, unexpected dash of history to otherwise pristine surroundings.

Historically, life has been difficult in the valley and those who live here consider themselves quite apart from the rest of Italy. French is the second official language; and since some of the original inhabitants came from Switzerland, a German-based dialect can be heard around these Alpine summits and the many buildings resembling Swiss chalets. Thus this region is an oddball, enjoying cultural and municipal autonomy as decreed by Italy's post-WWII constitution. All this lends the place an isolated atmosphere, especially notable in the smaller towns; yet the fiercely independent people of the valley are warm and gracious to visitors. In turn, tourists here remain mostly unobtrusive—except during the ski season, when the sheer number of bodies impinges on the serenity.

Aosta

Although it's only 110 kilometers northwest of Torino and 180 kilometers northwest of Milan, Aosta seems worlds apart from both. The Valle d'Aosta's capital and largest city retains a strong sense of independence and is proud of its French heritage. Many of the street names and signs are in French, and the dialect here is sort of an Italianized Provençal.

Aosta's shops are filled with merchandise affirming the area's Alpine traditions: carved wooden and wrought-iron utensils, traditional garb, local wines and liqueurs, and fontina cheese, with which the ever-popular fondue is made. The town was founded as a Roman military settlement in 25 BC, when the locals were sold into slavery and forced to construct the Romans' fort. The old encampment's surviving walls, forum, theater, Arco Romano, Pailleron Tower, and Porta Pretoria are all evidence of Aosta's Roman roots. Other main attractions date from the Middle Ages and bear witness to the town's Christianization. St. Anselm (an Archbishop of Canterbury) and St. Bernard (hospice founder and dog namesake) made Aosta an actively Christian community—note the preponderance of dramatic wooden crucifixes throughout the region. All the sights, plus the warm and open locals, make this small metropolis a natural base for visiting nearby castles and the rest of the green, rugged valley.

Aosta's central square, Piazza Chanoux, is named for a local hero who struggled against Mussolini, among whose Fascist aims included the obliteration of all "nonstandard" Italian. Chanoux was eventually killed by the Nazis.

BASICS

➤ **CHANGING MONEY** • **Banca CRT** (Av. Conseil des Commis 19, tel. 0165/23721) charges no commission for currency exchange, but levies a L4000 fee for traveler's checks; it also has an ATM that takes Visa and MasterCard. If you need to exchange on a Sunday, you'll have to suffer stinky rates at the travel agency **Club Soleil** (Piazza Chanoux 12, tel. 0165/361943), open daily 8:30 AM–12:30 PM.

➤ **MAIL AND PHONES** • The **SIP office** (Viale della Pace 9, tel. 0165/43997) is open weekdays 8:15–12:15 and 2:30–6:30, Sunday 8–3. Aosta's **main post office** (Piazza Narbonne 1/A, tel. 0165/262287) handles regular postal services Monday–Saturday 8:15–7.

➤ **VISITOR INFORMATION** • The **tourist office** (Piazza Chanoux 8, tel. 0165/303725), up Avenue Conseil des Commis from the train station, has a multilingual staff that gets very excited when foreign visitors come; they dole out maps, accommodations lists, and excellent info on local walks, many of which are guided free of charge. The office is open daily 9–1 and 3–8. For info on Gran Paradiso National Park, visit Aosta's **park headquarters** (Via Losanna 5, tel. 0165/44126). From the station, go left on Via Bonifacio, right on Via Gramsci, and left on Via Losanna.

COMING AND GOING Aosta's **train station** (Piazza Manzetti 1, tel. 0165/262057) sends 10 trains daily to Torino (2 hrs, L12,000). The ticket office is open Monday–Saturday 7:30–12:30 and 2:30–7, Sunday 8–noon and 4–7. Unfortunately, there's no luggage storage. The SAVDA **bus station** (Piazza Narbonne 11, tel. 0165/262027) is across from the train station. Buses run to Torino (10 daily, 2 hrs, L12,000), to Milan (7 daily, 3½ hrs, L22,200). SAVDA also sends buses to Cogne (L2000, 30 min) and Courmayeur (45 min, L3500) plus other key valley spots. Check the schedule in front of the station.

GETTING AROUND The city is oriented around **Piazza Chanoux**, which you can reach from the station by taking Viale Stazione. Out of this piazza run the two major streets, **Via de Tillier** and **Via Croix de Ville**. To the west of the piazza is **Via E. Aubert**, the city's main shopping and dining drag.

WHERE TO SLEEP In the heart of the city, small **La Belle Epoque** (Via d'Avise 18, tel. 0165/262276) is the best of Aosta's budget lodgings. It's a comfortable place run by a kind staff, though the rooms (doubles L50,000–L65,000) are of the one-star, spartan variety. From the train station go up Viale Stazione and hang a left on Via de Tillier. **Mancuso** (Via Voison 32, tel. 0165/34526) has smart doubles (L55,000–L60,000) on a quiet street not far from the station. All come with modern, clean bathrooms. Take the *sottopassaggio* (underpass) from the train station to Via Paravera, turn right, then go left on Via Voison. The inexpensive rooms at **Monte Emilius** (Via G. Carrel 9, tel. 0165/35692) are on the seedy side, though the hotel itself is well located on a bustling street. Doubles cost L60,000. From the train station, head east (right) along Via Carrel.

➤ **CAMPING** • The hills just outside Aosta are home to **Mille Luci** (Località Roppoz, tel. 0165/44274 or 0165/42374), a campground that offers hot showers, laundry , a bar, tennis courts, bathrooms, and electricity. You pay L6400 per person plus L13,000 for the site. Take

Bus 6 from the train station or Piazza Chanoux, and ask the driver where to get off. Smaller **Ville d'Aoste** (Località Les Fourches, tel. 0165/32878) has the same facilities but charges only L5000 per person and L10,000 per site. Take Bus 4 from the train station.

FOOD Finding an excellent meal is surprisingly easy in Aosta. Restaurants and pizzerias line main streets including Via E. Aubert and Via Porta Pretoria, and Piazza Chanoux has several pleasant cafés. **Moderno** (Via E. Aubert 21, tel. 0165/33669) is a bustling, friendly joint that serves pizza, pasta (L6500–L8500), and fried calamari. **Ulisse** (Via E. Aubert 58) up the street serves its pastas (L6000–L8000), seafood (L9000–L12,000), and big, tasty salads (L10,000) in a more sedate setting. **Piemonte** (Via Porta Pretoria 13, tel. 0165/40111) serves terrific, somewhat expensive specialties like fondue, *padellina di funghi trifolati* (porcini and vegetables in a savory broth; L13,000), and chamois, as well as a platter of mixed grilled vegetables. A bit out of the way, **Pub Leon d'Oro** (Via M. Vavolan 15, tel. 0165/903157; closed Sun.) serves light evening meals and is a fun place to hoist a few brews. The **Pasticceria** (Via St. Anselm 104) has local sweets that look as good as they taste.

Aosta's annual summer and autumn "Bataille des Reines" (Battle of the Queens) is perhaps the only Italian festival during which cows fiercely duke it out for the honor of being crowned queen of the pasture.

WORTH SEEING Aosta is often referred to as the "Rome of the Alps," and its ancient ruins really are impressive. Dating from the 1st century BC, the **Arco Romano** (Piazza Arco d'Augusto) looms over Aosta's eastern entrance. Built as a monument to the Roman victory over the local Salassi people, this Roman triple arch is a mélange of Doric and Corinthian orders. The **Porta Pretoria**, Aosta's eastern entrance, was built in 25 BC; it and the **Roman bridge** are each a short walk away on opposite sides of the Arco Romano. A few steps down Via Porta Pretoria, the **Sant'Orso complex** (Piazzetta Sant'Orso, tel. 0165/362026) is an architecturally diverse 11th-century assemblage of buildings. When the complex was renovated in the 15th century, artisans spruced up its interiors with frescoes, carved wooden choir stalls, and stained-glass windows. A series of Ottoman frescoes is upstairs in the attic—you'll have to find the guard to let you up. The **Teatro Romano** (Via Baillage, between Sant'Orso and the Porta Pretoria) once took up an entire Roman city block. The area is open to visitors daily 9:30–noon and 2–4:30 in winter and 9–7 in summer. The **cathedral complex** (Piazza Giovanni XXIII), on the site of a Roman forum, is a group of Aosta's earliest episcopal edifices, built in the 4th century when the area was a bishopric. Inside, beautiful mosaics depict the months of the year and ferocious animals surrounded by the Tigris and Euphrates rivers. If you're here at the end of January, check out the **Festa di Sant'Orso**, which offers a taste of Aosta's artistic heritage.

Parco Nazionale del Gran Paradiso

Five heavenly, lake-filled valleys render this national park worthy of its title. Vittorio Emanuele II launched preservation efforts when in 1865 he established a royal hunting ground in the valleys while ironically awarding official endangered-species status to the ibex, a nearly extinct species of mountain goat. Immediately after World War I, Vittorio Emanuele III offered the property (and his shooting rights) to the Italian state, and Gran Paradiso became a national park in 1922.

The stunning mountains and waterfalls make you want to go outside and play—in organized excursions, semiplanned adventures, or day-trip wanderings. Despite a smattering of horseback-riding clubs, hot-air ballooning organizations, and kayaking gangs, the park eschews overdevelopment. Of its five valleys, the Cogne, Valsavarenche, and Rhênes are the best known and the easiest to reach from Aosta. Farther south, the relatively untouched Orco Valley slopes down from the Nivolet Pass where it borders the equally obscure Soana Valley. For maps, brochures, and insight, stop by the tourist offices in Torino or the park headquarters in Aosta (*see above*). There's another office in **Villeneuve** (Località Champagne 18, tel. 0165/236627).

WHEN TO GO Gran Paradiso is characterized by butt-cold winters and mild summers. Summer is the most popular season, with great hiking weather, beautiful vegetation, and—particularly if it snows at higher elevations—the chance of seeing ibex and chamois. (Even though it's usully warm in the summer months, don't get caught without a light jacket.) Winter, though, is actually a better time to see these creatures at lower altitudes (1,000–1,500 meters), when there's also a lot of good skiing. In spring, the animals move down to the valleys, hungry for new grass, and the waterfalls and rivers swell with snowmelt, making for great kayaking and rafting. Fall's striking colors and cool air make hiking and horseback riding that much nicer.

VALLE DI COGNE

The Valle di Cogne is the most highly developed of the park's valleys and the most popular with tourists, though even here the visitors aren't too intrusive. Lodged in the widest part of the valley, the town of **Cogne** offers modern conveniences without being overdeveloped. Cogne's **tourist office** (Piazza Chanoux 34, tel. 0165/74040; open Mon.–Sat. 9–12:30 and 3–6, Sun. 9–12:30) offers the usual accommodations lists as well as maps that outline challenging local hikes. Five daily **buses** run from Aosta to Cogne (30 min, L2000). The sidewalk in front of Cogne's post office serves as the bus station, and you buy tickets on board.

WHERE TO SLEEP Finding a place to sleep here is easy, though it's smart to call ahead during July and August and from October to April. At the tourist office, grab the lodging pamphlet, which has a listing of rooms in private homes. Cozy **Stambecco** (Rue des Clementines 21, tel. 0165/74068) has doubles with bath for L60,000. The campground **Lo Stambecco** (tel. 0165/749178), 1½ kilometers out of town on the road to Valnontey, is a spacious spread of wooded grounds and riverbanks with plumbing and a telephone. The sites are open June–September, but the bus runs in July and August only. The camp costs L7000–L10,000 plus L6000 per person. For winter camping, the small **Al Sole** (tel. 0165/74237) in Lillaz, 1½ kilometers from Cogne, is open year-round. The crowded sites cost L8000–L9300 plus L5500 per person. Farther into the park, the nearest rifugio is hotel-like **Vittorio Sella** (tel. 0165/74310; open Easter–September), a three-hour walk on a marked trail from Valnontey. It costs L25,000 per person, and you should call ahead. Other rifugi lie three to six hours' walk from Valnontey; a full list is available at Cogne's tourist office (*see above*).

FOOD You'll find sandwiches, cold beer, and cute waiters at **Le Bistrot** (Via Mines de Cogne 5, tel. 0165/749310). The **Ristorante Tavola Calda** (Via Bourgeois 30, tel. 0165/74101) serves up inexpensive and hearty (if sometimes bland) pizzas and pasta dishes. Splurge on typical local dishes in a romantic atmosphere at **La Brasserie du Bon Bec** (Via Bourgeois, tel.

The Castle of Fénis

The Castle of Fénis's square towers and graceful round turrets loom over the town that bears its name, 17 kilometers east of Aosta. Commissioned in 1340 by Count Aimone di Challant to protect the iron route between Aosta and Champorcher, the castle has double walls and narrow interior doors that were constructed with military defense in mind. Several saints' images keep watch over the castle, including that of Apollonia, patroness of dentists and their patients; she stands benignly as elephantine pliers dangle eternally from her teeth. Other curiosities are the enormous oven once used for cooking big game and the prison where the charming Challant family used to evade medieval anti-capital-punishment laws by dousing prisoners with water and opening the windows, leaving the prisoners to die "naturally" of pneumonia. Tours of the castle depart every half hour. To get here, take the SAVDA bus from Aosta to Fénis (30 min, L1700). Tel. 0165/764263. Admission: L4000. Open Mar.–Sept., daily 9–7; Oct.–Feb., daily 9–noon and 2–5.

Look out for the chamois and the ibex. Both creatures—the latter a goat and the former a goat-like antelope—have hooked horns and feet well-adapted for climbing. The lucky ibex is treasured for being nearly extinct, but the poor chamois is best known for its flavor and its incredibly soft skin, which is used to make chamois cloth for polishing cars and furniture.

0165/749288). To stock up on food for excursions into the wilderness, a nameless **fruit and vegetable store** (Via Mines de Cogne 11, tel. 0165/749194) and the **Despar Market** (Via Bourgeoise 21, tel. 0165/74019) sell survival necessities.

OUTDOOR ACTIVITIES The tourist office (*see above*) has details on all local sports, and the pamphlet titled "Avec Nous" lists useful addresses and phone numbers. You'll find many of the sporting facilities in the tiny towns flanking Cogne; all are within easy walking distance. You can rent mountain bikes at the **Hotel La Barme** (tel. 0165/749177) in Valnontey for L30,000 per day. If you want to fish, you'll need a license and your own gear—for details, contact the **Pesce Sportiva** offices (tel. 0165/749172) in Lillaz. Ski passes are available at the funivia station (tel. 0165/74008) and cost L30,000 for a full day, L20,000 for a half-day. A simple joyride on the funivia (no skiing) costs about L10,000 round-trip. The adventurous can try bungee-jumping and whitewater rafting through **Rafting Avventure** (Località Chiesa, Fénis, tel. 0165/95082). The **Centro di Turismo Equestre** (tel. 0165/95667) arranges horse rentals out of a school in Rhêmes-Saint-Georges for L25,000 per hour.

VALSAVARENCHE

The largest community in the rugged central valley of Valsavarenche is **Degioz** (sometimes called Valsavarenche). But nearby **Pont** has the best camping and is the best base for hikes into the heart of the park and up the mountain of Gran Paradiso. Valsavarenche is further into the mountains, and therefore more rugged than Cogne, though the flora and fauna here are much like those in the rest of the park and include larch, pine, and spruce trees; Alpine wildflowers; and ibex, chamois, marmots, and eagles. Come to Degioz to get mapped and brochured by the folks at the **Pro Loco Visitor Information Office** (Degioz, tel. 0165/905816; open July–Aug. only), the **Municipo office** (Degioz 70, tel. 0165/905703), or the **Gran Paradiso visitor center** (Degioz 76, 2nd floor, tel. 0615/74147), and then scoot on down the road to Pont. From Aosta, three daily buses stop in Degioz on their way to Pont (1 hr, L3500), 9 kilometers down the road.

WHERE TO SLEEP **Fior di Roccia** (Località Pont 6, tel. 0165/95478) is only open July–September and charges L60,000 per double. Luckily, the camping in Pont is good, and there are four rifugi within a three-hour hike. At the gateway to the heart of the park, **Campground Pont-Breuil** (Località Pont 24, tel. 0165/95458) comes with hot showers, laundry facilities, electricity, a pay phone, a bar, a restaurant, and a market. Prices run L7000 per person plus L8000–L12,000 for the site. One kilometer away (closer to Degioz) is **Campground Gran Paradiso** (Località Plan de la Presse, tel. 0165/95433). Smaller and a little more secluded, it has the same facilities as Pont-Breuil and costs L5500 per person plus L8500–L10,000 per site. Both grounds are only open June–September, and it's wise to call ahead—especially at Campground Gran Paradiso. The nearest rifugio is **Vittorio Emanuele** (Località Moncorvé, tel. 0165/95920), a two-hour hike into the park. It's open April 5–September 20. Call ahead to reserve a bed. In winter, the **Vittorio Emanuele Vecchio** (tel. 0165/95920), a few meters down the path, has more rugged accommodations. Another option is agriturismo—contact Emilia Vittoria Dupont (tel. 0165/905979), who rents out rooms in her quiet house in Bien, a 30-minute walk from Pont, with a minimum stay of two nights.

OUTDOOR ACTIVITIES People come to Valsavarenche primarily to hike and ski. Ski-lift tickets range from L20,000 to L40,000 per day. Half-day tickets are available for slightly less, and various Aosta hotels offer discounts. There are also two-day, five-day, and one-week passes available, which can save you lots of money. The slopes are reached either by foot or by shuttles that run regularly.

The **Società Guide Gran Paradiso** (tel. 0165/95574 or 0165/905734) leads guided excursions and nature walks. For a challenging—but not heart-attack-evoking—Alpine hike complete with a night in a rifugio, contact **Savoia Al Nivolet** (tel. 0165/94141), which sleeps 50 within three hours' hike from Degoiz. From Degoiz you can ascend **Punta Bioula** for a magnificent view of the Central Valley. (The 3,000-meter-plus altitude limits this to a summer hike.) Rent mountain bikes in Pont at either the **Hotel Gran Paradiso** (tel. 0165/95454) or **Hotel Genzianella** (tel. 0165/95393); both charge L45,000–L60,000 per day.

Courmayeur and Mont Blanc

Tucked in the valley's northwest corner at the very foot of Mont Blanc, Courmayeur is a scenic destination on its own as well as a base for exploring the Alpine giant, which sits on the border between Italy and France. Nearby quartz mines facilitated the town's founding; its prime position on a passageway through the Alps ensured that ancient Romans would be frequent visitors. The Savoys set up shop here in 1032 for the same reason. You can follow in their footsteps by taking a funivia from **La Palud** (5 km from Courmayeur) over the summit of Mont Blanc into France. Good skiing and proximity to Mont Blanc attract well-to-do tourists; nevertheless Courmayeur's setting is truly magnificent.

BASICS Visit the **tourist office** (tel. 0165/842060) in Piazzale Monte Bianco, where you get off the bus, and pick up the brochure "Valdigne," which has info on ski passes and rentals.

COMING AND GOING **SAVDA** runs 15 buses daily to and from Aosta (1 hr, L4000) to Courmayeur. Buses run every half hour (L1000) for a three-minute ride to the funivia at La Palud, which takes you over Mont Blanc to skiing and France.

WHERE TO SLEEP AND EAT Courmayeur is overrun by four-star hotels, but you can sleep cheaply right next to La Palud's funivia at **Hotel La Quercia** (tel. 0165/89931), where doubles are L65,000, or down the street at **Hotel Funivia** (0165/89924), which is almost identical in price and quality. Eating out in Courmayeur is not cheap, but you can avoid spending too much by sticking to pizza. The best is **K2** (Villair Ineeriore 8, tel. 842475), which has the usual favorites for L10,000–L13,000. **Snack Bar du Tunnel** (Via Circonvallazione 3, tel. 0162/841705) is the cheapest place in town, period, with panini for L5000.

OUTDOOR ACTIVITIES Two words: Mont Blanc. The tourist office has a complete list of hikes and rifugi, as well as prices and other info on ski lifts and runs. La Palud's funivia crosses over the summit at a very high altitude and it's not for those with vertigo, but floating up the mountainside can be quite a thrill for the rest of us. You can stop at **Rifugio Torino** (L36,000 round-trip) or keep going all the way over (L64,000 round-trip) to enter France, auspiciously, at posh Chamonix. The funivia controller will stop you at 4,500 meters, at which point you can sway, take pictures of the summit, and clutch your stomach. **Noleggio Ulisse** (tel. 0162/842255), in front of the funivia, rents skiing equipment.

THE ITALIAN RIVIERA   6

By Sara Fisher

The Italian Riviera of the flashy '60s postcard—absurdly long yachts and beach goddesses in gold-plated bikinis—is a hazy delusion for people wearing expensive sunglasses. That kind of luxury exists only for those who don't carry their own luggage—the rest of us have to settle for sprays of bougainvillea and honeysuckle flowers, balmy air, hot focaccia, and hostel beds. Genova (Genoa), the fascinating, complex port town in the center of the Ligurian coast, seems an inappropriate hub for the palm-covered landscape of the Riviera di Ponente region to the west and the Riviera di Levante to the east. Ponente beach towns have catered to tourists for the past 100 or so years. As their grandeur has faded, they've become sleepy getaways for the over-40 set, but some towns, like Finale Ligure and San Remo, are still worth a long visit. Unsung mountain villages a few kilometers inland from these hubs are respites from coastal vacationers and the heat. Finally, the Levante coastal towns, particularly Santa Margherita Ligure and Cinque Terre, draw younger crowds of hikers and campers and are more lively than Ponente towns. The Riviera's generally mild climate makes any season a good time to visit, except for the most popular months, July and August, when accommodations and beaches fill up fast.

Genova
The central town of the Italian Riviera is a composite of extremes. Its people seem to mimic the geographic highs and lows of mountains and sea as they vacillate between wild gesticulation and melancholic reserve. Inside Genova's medieval walls (testimonies to centuries of defense) lies a typically rough port town, but the city challenges you to transcend its grime and grasp its multiple personalities. At one turn you might chance upon a hooker in 5-inch heels stumbling over filthy cobblestones, at another you'll glimpse a stunning fountain through a palace portal.

Genova would like to play up the "home of Christopher Columbus" shtick and play down its mean streets reputation. But the streets are mean: The city's serious crime and drug problems are aggravated by inklings of a fascist resurgence, plus there's the often xenophobic (and plain nasty) attitude of the locals. Visibly, Genova has come down in the world since its Renaissance glory days of commerce and conquest. It was once the province of noble rulers like Andrea Doria, who drafted Genova's independent constitution before the town fell under Spanish and later Austrian rule. It was also the launching point of the Risorgimento (*see box* The Shot of Espresso Heard 'Round the World, in Chapter 5) and the home of Giuseppe Mazzini, the brains behind the operation. Though Genova is now hurting from neglect, you don't have to look hard to see its former splendor—artistic spoils procured from the Crusades, the colonial era, and foreign occu-

The Italian Riviera is comprised of the Liguria region, a vulnerable seaside strip of land that has been shaped by the ebb and tide of autonomous naval republics and marauding invaders, creating a region of survivors. Whether it's the weathered fishermen in Camogli or the generally mirthless inhabitants of Genova, Ligurians may never be effusive, but they are proud to share their unique culture and delicious cuisine with those who venture here.

pation are everywhere. The best way to understand the city is to surrender to its mood swings: Get lost in back alleys, feast on regional cooking, and take in the view from high on a hill.

BASICS

CHANGING MONEY The *casse di cambio* (exchange bureaus) in the two major train stations, **Stazione Principe** (tel. 010/284081) and **Stazione Brignole** (tel. 010/562956), offer the best rates and charge no commission. The ground floor of the **post office** (Via Dante 4/R, btw Piazza de Ferrari and Piazza Dante, tel. 010/593516; open Mon.–Sat. 8:10–7:40) deals with money exchange and AmEx traveler's checks, but watch out for big commissions.

MAIL AND PHONES Both train stations have banks of phones, but the main **SIP** office (Via XX Settembre 139; open Mon.–Sat. 8 AM–10 PM) also offers operator-assisted phone calls. The **correspondence division** of the post office (Via d'Annunzia 34, tel. 010/591762; open Mon.–Sat. 8:15–7:40), just off Piazza Dante, is where you can buy *francobolli* (stamps).

VISITOR INFORMATION Ente Provinciale Turismo (EPT). This office is not too useful—you ask a question and the staff hands you a stack of brochures. At the Stazione Principe branch (tel. 010/262633; open Mon.–Sat. 8–8) the staff will call hotels to see if rooms are available, but they cannot make reservations. *Via Roma 11, tel. 010/541541. From either station, take Bus 39, or any bus that stops at Piazza Corvetto, and head SW on Via Roma. Open weekdays 8–1:30 and 2–5, Sat. 8–1:15.*

COMING AND GOING

BY TRAIN Genova has two main train stations: **Stazione Principe** (Piazza Acquaverde, tel. 010/262455) and **Stazione Brignole** (Piazza Verdi, tel. 010/586350). For general train information, call 010/284081. More trains stop in Stazione Principe, but Stazione Brignole is more convenient to the safer lodging area and the hostel. Both stations are on the same line, but sometimes trains scheduled to pass through both will only stop at one, so ask the conductor when you board. The train to Milan (hourly, 1½–2 hrs, L13,600) runs through both stations unless otherwise noted. The train to Rome (every 2–2½ hrs, 6 hrs, L40,500) leaves only from Stazione Brignole. Trains head west to Ventimiglia (every 30 min, 3 hrs, L13,600) from Stazione Principe and east to Cinque Terre (6 daily, 1¾ hrs, L6500) from Brignole. Both Principe and Brignole have post offices, money exchanges, and 24-hour luggage storage.

BY BUS The **Tigullio** bus line (tel. 010/313851) runs frequently from Piazza Vittoria (near Stazione Brignole), linking Genova with the Riviera di Levante. To reach the Riveria di Ponente, you can only take trains, not buses.

BY FERRY Genova is a good jumping-off point for Corsica and Sardinia, but Sicily and Tunisia are better reached via Civitavecchia (*see* Chapter 10). **Vintiadis Shipping & Travel** (Via Ponte Reale 27, tel. 010/205651; open Mon.–Sat. 9–5) has information and conducts reservations. **Tirrenia Navigazione** (Stazione Marittima, Ponte Colombo, tel. 010/258041) has ferries to Sardinia's Porto Torres (July–Sept., 2–3 daily; L38,000) and Olbia (June–Sept., 1–2 daily; Oct.–May, 3 weekly; L38,000), as well as to Palermo (3–4 weekly, L86,000). **Moby Lines** has ferry service to Bastia, Corsica (June–Sept., 8 weekly; Oct.–May, 2–4 weekly; 15 hrs, L36,000), as does **Corsica Ferries** (Ponte Caracciolo, tel. 010/253473).

GETTING AROUND

You'll get lost on foot, but walking is the best way to see this city. Stazione Principe is in the west end of town, Stazione Brignole in the east; in between lies the **centro storico** (historic cen-

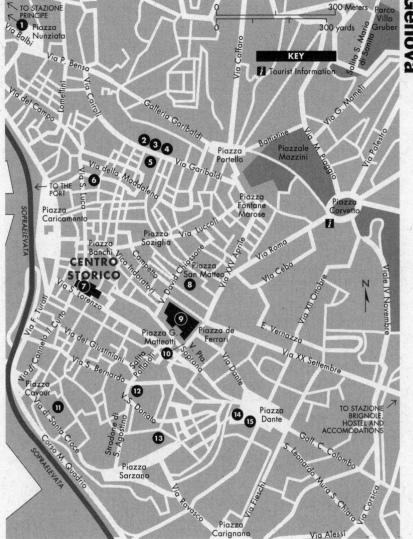

TO STAZIONE PRINCIPE

Parco Villa Gruber

0 — 300 Meters
0 — 300 yards

KEY

i Tourist Information

① Piazza Nunziata

Via Balbi

Via P. Bensa

Lomellini

Via Carroli

Via del Campo

Galleria Garibaldi

Via Caffaro

Salita S. Maria di Santia

Via G. Mameli

Via Palestro

② ③ ④

⑤

Via della Maddalena

Via Garibaldi

Piazza Portello

Battistine

Piazzale Mazzini

Via M. Piaggio

TO THE PORT

Via S. Luca

⑥

Piazza Caricamento

Piazza Banchi

Vico Indoratori

Campetto

Piazza Soziglia

Via Luccoli

Piazza Fontane Marose

Via XX Aprile

Via Roma

Via Ceba

Piazza Corvetto

i

SOPRAELEVATA

CENTRO STORICO

Via S. Lorenzo

⑦

V. David Chiassone

Piazza San Matteo

⑧

N

Viale IV Novembre

Via F. Turati

Via d' Cannelo n Curto

Via dei Giustiniani

Via S. Bernardo

⑨

Piazza G. Matteotti

⑩

Piazza de Ferrari

V. Pta Soprana

Via Dante

E. Vernazza

Via XII Ottobre

Via XX Settembre

Piazza Cavour

Salita Pollaioli

⑪

Via di Santa Croce

Stradone di S. Agostino

V.S. Donato

⑫

⑬

⑭

⑮

Piazza Dante

TO STAZIONE BRIGNOLE, HOSTEL AND ACCOMODATIONS

Corso M. Quadrio

SOPRAELEVATA

Piazza Sarzano

Goll. C. Colombo

S. Leonardo Mura S. Chiara

Via Corsica

Via Ravasco

Via Fieschi

Piazza Carignano

Via Alessi

Casa di Colombo, **15**

Cattedrale San Lorenzo, **7**

Chiesa San Matteo, **8**

Chiesa Sant'Ambrogio (Gesù), **10**

Galleria Nazionale di Palazzo Spinola, **6**

Museo di Sant'Agostino, **13**

Palazzo Bianco, **2**

Palazzo Ducale, **9**

Palazzo Lecari, **3**

Palazzo Podestà, **4**

Palazzo Reale, **1**

Palazzo Rosso, **5**

Porta Soprana, **14**

San Donato, **12**

Santa Maria di Castello, **11**

ter), where most of the interesting sights are. Major landmarks include **San Lorenzo** (the main cathedral) and **Piazza de Ferrari**, an important transportation hub and the dividing point between the old and new towns. **Taxis** cluster in front of the two train stations and Piazza de Ferrari. Their rates are modest but they can't enter the centro storico because of prohibitively narrow streets.

The maze of alleyways in Genova's centro storico leaves travelers searching for the position of the sun as a reference point, or pirouetting and squinting to make out names of worn street signs (many of the streets don't appear on maps anyway).

BY BUS Bus tickets are available at *tabacchi* (smoke shops) and at the train stations. One ticket (L1400 including transfers) is good for 90 minutes on any city bus. Bus 33 travels between the train stations, and from Stazione Principe, Buses 37 and 41 go to the city center and Bus 31 goes to the waterfront.

BY FUNICOLARE AND ASCENSORE A series of *funicolari* (funiculars) and *ascensori* (elevators), traveling at a very steep incline, help truck you up and down the hills. Several funicolari and ascensori in town offer great views (*see box* Two Great Escapes from Genova, *below*). Both use normal city transport tickets (also valid for the buses), which you can buy at local tabacchi for L1400.

WHERE TO SLEEP

The area around Stazione Principe is cheap but uninviting; a better choice for affordable lodging is near Stazione Brignole. Way up high, like a beacon on the hillside, lies the glorious youth hostel, which only accepts HI members but knows no age limit. Don't sleep in the train stations; Genova is not safe at night.

Albergo Carletto. If you can't stand the noise of Vespas whizzing by, come to this hotel in a pedestrian zone. Clean, spacious doubles (L60,000–L75,000) have high ceilings and mosaic floors. *Via Colombo 16/4, tel. 010/561229. Off Piazza Verdi near Stazione Brignole. 24 rooms, most with bath. Call a day in advance. AE, MC, V.*

Albergo Fiume. The proprietor bemoans the fact that his hotel offers "all the services of a three-star hotel but only has one star." His headache, your bargain. Rooms, starting at L65,000 for a double, are clean and charming, and the original mosaic floors are perfectly intact. *Via Fiume 9/R, tel. 010/591691. From west end of Piazza Verdi, take Via Fiume. 20 rooms, some with bath. AE, MC, V.*

Albergo The Garden. This simple, clean albergo and its garden are in a quiet, safe neighborhood between Piazza Corvetto and Piazza Manin. Rooms run L55,000–L65,000. *Via Calatafimi 7, tel 010/812688. From Stazione Brignole, Bus 39, 40, or 18 to Piazza Corvetto, go up Via Palestro to Piazza Marasala, and turn right on Via Calatafimi. 9 rooms, 2 with shower.*

Pension Ricci. This neat, efficient place is a mere five minutes from Stazione Brignole. Rooms facing the street have bigger windows but more noise than those on the inside. Prices vary depending on the season; doubles cost L65,000 in summer. *Piazza Colombo 4–8, tel. 010/ 592746. From Stazione Brignole, take Via Fiume to Via Colombo to Piazza Colombo.*

HOSTELS **Ostello per la Gioventù (HI).** This hostel, high on a hill overlooking the town and the sea, has to be the most efficient establishment in the country aside from the Mafia. Although it's about a 25-minute bus ride away in Genova-Oregina, the hostel is such a relief at the end of the day that it's worth the trip. HI members (only) pay L18,000 for a bunk bed in a dorm-style room with six others, or L23,000 per person for a "family room," with space for four and a bath. The rooms are immaculate and spacious, and breakfast is included. *Via Costanzi 120, tel. 010/242-2457. From Stazione Brignole, Bus 40 to top of hill; or, from Stazione Principe, take Bus 35, switch to Bus 40 at Via Spinola, and get off at Via Costanzi (both buses run until midnight). 204 beds. Midnight curfew, lockout 9–3:30. Laundry, lockers. Wheelchair access.*

CAMPING The best place to camp is **Villa Doria** in Genova-Pegli. At night, the guy who runs the place brings out his guitar and everyone sings. Sites go for L6000 per person, plus L4000 per car and L9000 per tent. You can also stay in a bungalow for L50,000–L100,000 (2–6 people). *Via al Campeggio Villa Doria 15, tel. 010/696–9600. From either station, take local train to Pegli, then transfer to Bus 93.*

FOOD

Genova is the home of pesto, so don't leave town without indulging in some of it over *trennette* (a potato-based pasta) or a pesto-smothered pizza with delicious *stracchino* (a soft cheese). Genova's food is among the cheapest in any big Italian city, and the centro storico (a good place for daytime meals but not dinner), the *lido* (boardwalk), and the hills overlooking the sea all overflow with trattorias and pizzerias. The area by Stazione Brignole and Via San Vicenzo is flooded with bakeries and shops that sell focaccia, a regional specialty. The little flaky snack that residents eat at lunchtime is *torta pasqualina*, a pastry filled with spinach (or sometimes artichoke) and egg. **Mercato Orientale**, near Piazza Colombo, is bursting with stands that sell delicious bread, cheese, and fruit. From Stazione Brignole, cross the piazza and look for signs on the left side.

CENTRO STORICO **Caffè degli Specchi.** This restaurant/crepe shop/tearoom/bar is filled with harried businesspeople grabbing cappuccino on their coffee breaks and refined locals enjoying their teatime rituals. The building dates from the 17th century, and the original decor of tile and leaded-glass *specchi* (mirrors) has been maintained. You can buy hot and cold sandwiches (L4000–L6000) downstairs at the bar; the restaurant is upstairs. A plate of cold house specialties (L11,000) includes *la farinata*, a pie-shaped torte made with garbanzo beans. *Salita Pollaioli 43/R, off Piazza Matteotti, tel. 010/281293. Open Mon.–Sat. 7 AM–8:30 PM; tea and snacks 5 PM–7:30 PM.*

Trattoria da Maria. This place may seem a bit intimidating when you hear the roar of heated Italian "discussions" from half a block away, but come on in and squeeze yourself between toothless seadogs and execs in power suits at communal tables. The pasta is homemade, and plates run about L5000. A full meal, including first and second courses and wine, costs L12,000. *Vico Testadoro 14/R, tel. 010/581080. From Piazza Fontane Marose, take Via XXV Aprile, and 2nd left on Vico Testadoro. Open Mon.–Thurs. and Sun. 10–2:30 and 7–9, Fri. 10–2:30.*

Trattoria Ugo. At this wonderfully authentic restaurant, the proprietor gives you the daily menu verbally and proceeds to order for you. If you're lucky, you'll end up with the delicious *pansotti* (spinach and ricotta ravioli with a walnut cream sauce). A meal runs L5000–L15,000. *Via Giustiniani 86/R, tel. 010/298302. From Piazza Matteotti, take Salita Pollaioli, and turn right onto Via Giustiniani. Open Tues.–Sat. noon–2:30 and 7–9:30. Wheelchair access.*

DINING WITH A VIEW **Bagni Italia.** Overlooking the beach, this is *the* happening place to eat in the summer, with amazing calzone (L8000) and fresh seafood (L12,000 and up). *Corso d'Italia 9, on water south of Stazione Brignole, tel. 010/362–0885. From Stazione Brignole, Bus 31 to Corso d'Italia. Open Mon. noon–3, Tues.–Sun. noon–3 and 7–midnight.*

La Rosa del Parco. When the weather is nice, retreat from the crowded city center to this pizzeria, just a short walk from the hostel (*see* Where to Sleep, *above*). It has a great rural feel—lots of greenery and no traffic—and serves classic trattoria food, including pasta, pizza *al forno* (cooked in a wood-burning oven), meat, and fresh fish. You can eat a hefty meal for L15,000. *Via Costanza 40, tel. 010/242–5375. From Stazione Brignole or Piazza de Ferrari, Bus 40 to end of line; take stairs up behind hostel and turn left. Open May–Sept., Fri.–Wed. 5 PM–midnight; Oct.–Apr., Fri.–Wed. 10–2 and 6–11. Wheelchair access.*

WORTH SEEING

Genova's allure isn't instantly obvious, but it's not hard to imagine the city's former baroque splendor as you walk down palace-packed **Via Garibaldi** to the west of Piazza delle Fontane Marose. Now an office building, **Palazzo Podestà** (Via Garibaldi 7) is worth a peek for its rococo fountain in which male sea creatures of Herculean stature emerge from a mossy, vine-covered

In the 17th, 18th, and 19th centuries, about 900 marble statues, shrines, and paintings of the Madonna were placed on street corners throughout the city, probably to ask for protection from the problems to which the city has always been prone. About 450 remain in place today—a good excuse for a scavenger hunt.

grotto. The fountain is hidden behind a sometimes-open portal—typical of Genova's tendency to shield its beauty under a layer of grime. The statues adorning **Palazzo Lecari** (Via Garibaldi 3) have the curious trait of being noseless and earless. The marble features were chisled off so that art would imitate life—local nobleman Megollo Lecari had the nasty habit of cutting off his enemies' ears and noses when irked. Also on Via Garibaldi, **Palazzo Rosso** (Via Garibaldi 18, tel. 010/282641; admission: L4000) houses outstanding 15th- to 18th-century paintings by Italian and Flemish masters. It's open Tuesday–Sunday 9–1 (Wed. and Sat. until 7).

The **centro storico** is a perfectly preserved medieval web of alleys, down to the authentic squalor. But limit your exploration of the centro to daylight and business hours—it gets eerie even during the afternoon siesta. **Palazzo Ducale** (Piazza de Ferrari/Piazza Matteotti 5, tel. 010/562440) now holds offices, a gelateria, and the music academy, but back in the 14th century it was the palace of the doges. You can get a good view of the city and marvel at the inside of the palace as you wander into its cool hallways with a gelato in hand. Next door, **Chiesa Sant'Ambrogio**, or **Gesù** (Piazza Matteotti, tel. 010/204420), is decorated in blinding baroque gold and silver—perfect for Guido Reni's *Assumption* and Rubens's *Circumcision* inside. Farther south, off Stradone di Sant'Agostino near Piazza Sarzano, the simple **San Donato** (Vico San Donato) is an early-12th-century basilica with an 18th-century tabernacle. The **Porta Soprana**, an entrance to the medieval district off Piazza Dante, leads to a maze of convents and monasteries and to Piazza Sarzano. It stands next to Casa Colombo (in fact, Christopher Columbus's father was the gatekeeper of the Porta Soprana), an ivy-shrouded stone house that you can only view from the outside.

The **Università di Genova**, centered around **Via Balbi**, is primarily housed in a series of stunning palazzi, where historical grandeur meets frenzied student energy. The 17th-century **Palazzo Reale** (Via Balbi 10, tel. 010/247–0640; admission: L8000) was originally built by the prestigious Balbi family, but was taken over by Savoy royalty in the 1800s. The upstairs art gallery has preserved the lifestyle of the rich and royal; the most noteworthy paintings are by Van Dyck. Free guided tours are given every day but Sunday.

CATTEDRALE SAN LORENZO The exterior of this cathedral, built in 1118, is made of the signature Genovese black-and-white striped marble (which is supposed to symbolize Genovan austerity) and features an elaborately carved French-Gothic portal. Inside, a 16th-century Renaissance roof shelters 14th-century frescoes and a World War II bomb that hit the church in 1941 but never exploded. The beautiful **Capello di San Giovanni** (chapel of St. John the Baptist), containing his 13th-century sarcophagus, is on the north side of the cathedral. *Via San Lorenzo, off Piazza Matteotti, tel. 010/296469. Cathedral open daily 8–noon and 4–7.*

GALLERIA NAZIONALE DI PALAZZO SPINOLA As you move through the beautifully preserved 17th- and 18th-century rooms in the Ligurian National Gallery, notice the detailed old maps lining the stairway walls. Also look for Van Dyck's *Madonna in Prayer*, *Portrait of a Young Boy*, and *The Four Evangelists*, all of which master the use of light and luminescent color. *Via Pellicceria 1, tel. 010/294661. From Via Garibaldi, walk south on Via Angeli, turn right onto Via della Maddalena and left onto Via Pellicceria. Admission: L8000. Open Mon. 9–1, Tues.–Sat. 9–7, Sun. 2–7.*

MUSEO DI SANT'AGOSTINO Off Piazza Sarzano, the Gothic church of Sant'Agostino is now a beautiful architecture and sculpture museum. The collection includes stone and marble fragments from Roman pillars and sculptures as well as medieval and Renaissance works, including 15th-century panels that were part of a famous funerary monument by Giovanni Pisano. *Piazza Sarzano 35/R, tel. 010/201661. Admission: L8000, free Sun. Open Tues.–Sat. 9–7, Sun. 9–12:30.*

PALAZZO BIANCO Though it's not so *bianco* (white) anymore, this palace is one of the few that's open to the public. It houses a collection of Ligurian, Dutch, and Flemish masters, with pieces dating from the 13th century (Byzantine school) to the 18th century. Among the works are *San Sebastiano* and *Madonna and Child with Saints* by Filippino Lippi, *Christ and the Tribute Money* by Van Dyck, and *Venus and Mars* by Rubens. *Via Garibaldi 11, tel. 010/291803. From Piazza de Ferrari, walk north on Via XXV Aprile to Piazza Fontane Marose, and turn left onto Via Garibaldi. Admission: L4000. Open Tues.–Sat. 9–7, Sun. 9–noon.*

PIAZZA SAN MATTEO The richly adorned **Doria Apartments** (mansions, really) and the **Chiesa San Matteo** circumscribe Piazza San Matteo, home of the powerful Doria family during the Renaissance. The church was built before the rest of the piazza, and bears the traditional Genovese black-and-white stripes. Summaries of glorious Dorian achievements are ever-so-modestly inscribed on the outside of the church. Though most of the interior dates from the 16th century, the cloister and frescoes by Luca Cambiaso and Bergamasco are from the 14th century. *Admission free. Open daily 8–noon and 4–7.*

SANTA MARIA DI CASTELLO Once a way station for the Crusaders, this Gothic and Romanesque 12th-century basilica still has Roman columns and capitals. Attached is a 15th-century Dominican convent and library. The museum houses works by Barnaba da Modena and Ludovico Brea. *Salita Santa Maria di Castello 15, tel. 010/292986. From Piazza Sarzano, head NW (toward water) and turn right on Salita Santa Maria di Castello. Admission free. Open daily 9–noon and 2:30–6.*

CHEAP THRILLS

Tired of its less-than-hospitable reputation, Genova has started a program called **Genova Si Apre** (Genova is open). During the high seasons in summer and winter, information tents pop up around the city with multilingual workers who will shower you with information on free concerts, guided tours, and other events. **Genova Jazz**, which is held in mid-July, attracts big names like the Joshua Redman Quartet, but maintains its modest prices (tickets around L20,000). Also in July, the city hosts an **International Festival of Poetry**, with readings and seminars presented by poets from around the world. Ask at the tourist office for more details about these festivals.

AFTER DARK

Stay away from the centro storico after dark unless you know exactly where you're going or have local friends who do. Especially avoid Piazza Matteotti and the bus station near Stazione Brignole, which are frequented by prostitutes and drug peddlers at night. Check posters around town for theater and club listings, and look for the publications *Succedere a Genova*, *La Rosa Purpurea del Cairo*, and *Il Secolo XIX*. Big concerts featuring international artists take place at **Teatro Verdi** (Piazza Oriani 1, Genova-Sampierdarena, tel. 010/671263). The **Palazzo Ducale**, in Piazza de Ferrari, hosts concerts in its courtyard.

Two Great Escapes from Genova

- *Take the funicolare (L1400) from Largo della Zecca, near Piazza Nunziata, to Righi, which overlooks the city. From the top of the hill, you can hike to three castles or follow signs for the nearby trattoria, La Bolognese (Passo a Porta Chiappe, tel. 010/272–5490). Between lunch and dinner hours, have a beer on tap and gaze at the water.*

- *From Piazza Nunziata, ride the ascensore (L800) up to Spianata di Castelletto. Have a gelato at Bar G. Guerino (Via Crosa di Veragni, tel. 010/200664) and take in the panoramic view of the city.*

South of Stazione Brignole, get your karaoke fix at **Bla Bla** (Via Casaregis 64/R, at Via Cecchi, no phone), a popular *panificio* (bakery) and sandwich shop in a converted train car. Or head to **Polena** (Vico del Filo 21/R, off Piazza San Lorenzo, tel. 010/207400), where people bring their own instruments and play while Massimo, the owner, supplies them with good English beer on tap. **Antica Vetreria del Molo** (Vico Chinso Gelsa 8/R, tel. 010/293451), on the *sopraelevata* (levee) at Piazza Cavour, is a great place to kick back, have a beer, and listen to music. In the hot summer months when the university is closed, most of the action relocates to the beach-front. **Discotheques** line Corso Italia, but people don't start shaking their stuff until midnight. The various *bagni* (beach clubs) also become outdoor bars and hangouts.

Near Genova

In summer, many of Genova's sweaty inhabitants relocate to **Nervi**, a suburb with a beach boardwalk. Day or night, you can take a stroll, have a leisurely gelato or espresso, and spy on teenage couples. A five-minute train ride from either station or a 20-minute ride on Bus 31 will get you here. **Casella**, a nearby mountain town, is worth a trip if you like mountain biking or if you want a taste of small-town Ligurian life. Rent mountain bikes at **Cicli Cerati** (Casella Via le Europe 5, near train station in Casella, tel. 010/937520) for L10,000 an hour or L30,000 a day. To reach Casella, head to Stazione Principe, take Bus 34 to Piazza Manin, and climb the stairs to the **Stazione per Casella** (Via alla Stazione per Casella 15, tel. 010/839–3285). From here the train takes about an hour.

Riviera di Ponente

In the Riviera di Ponente, which extends from Genova as far west as Ventimiglia, water, mountains, and tourists peacefully coexist. There is no untouched sand in these parts, but the coast is so beautiful that it takes little coaxing to resign yourself to a herd mentality. With the exception of Finale Ligure, the pace is pretty slow here, and you're more likely to see wannabe "Bain de Soleil" types—middle-aged folks from France, Germany and Italy—than backpackers. If you're looking for the "real" Ponente, locals insist you'll have to go at least a kilometer inland from the coast. Excursions into the mountains from coastal Finale Ligure and San Remo reveal dramatic transformations as the Mediterranean meets the Apennines and casinos are replaced by castles. The coastal towns are easily accessed by train along the Genova–Ventimiglia line, but buses are the only means of transportation inland.

Finale Ligure

Finale Ligure is the choice vacation spot for many a German tourist in Birkenstocks with socks. (At least Americans aren't the only ones bludgeoning native sensibilities with unsightly footwear.) Finale Ligure is probably the most happening town on the Riviera di Ponente, with an interesting history, lively local street life, and beautiful hiking and biking terrain in the immediate vicinity. The city is divided into three districts, all of which are easily accessible by foot or by bus. Social life is centered around the beach, and the two nearby districts, **Finalmarina** and **Finalpia**, are filled with shady benches, sprays of flowers, and people of all ages. At night, Finale's over-priced restaurants turn up their music, and the entire town shows up to mingle and compare sunburns.

When sunstroke threatens, check out the walled-in, historic **Finalborgo** district, a 20-minute walk from the beach. The baroque **Basilica di San Biagio** (Piazza San Biagio; open daily 9–noon and 4–7), which was constructed during the Spanish occupation, crouches between an octagonal Gothic belfry and a medieval tower. The plain facade doesn't prepare you for the ornate interior filled with amazing trompe l'oeil frescoes. The Dominican convent **Chiostro Santa Caterina** (Piazza Santa Caterina; open Tues.–Sat. 10–noon and 3–6, Sun. 10–noon) houses a **Museo Archeologico**, with a fascinating display of relics from Finale's grottos, which were once the homes of Paleolithic dwellers. Higher up in Finalborgo on a torturous cobble-

The Italian Riviera

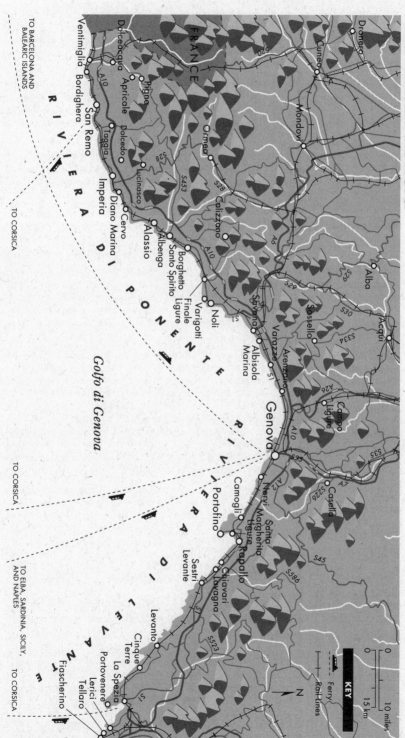

TO BARCELONA AND
BALEARIC ISLANDS

TO CORSICA

TO CORSICA

TO ELBA, SARDINIA, SICILY,
AND NAPLES

TO CORSICA

FRANCE

Dronero
Cuneo
Mondovì
Alba
Acqui

Ventimiglia
Bordighera
San Remo
Taggia
Apricale
Dolceacqua
Pigna
Dolcedo
Ormea
Lucinasco
Imperia
Diano Marina
Cervo
Alassio
Albenga
Santo Spirito
Borghetto
Finale Ligure
Varigotti
Noli
Calizzano
Savona
Varazze
Albisola Marina
Arenzano
Sassello
Campo Ligure
Genova
Casella
Nervi
Camogli
Portofino
Santa Margherita Ligure
Rapallo
Chiavari
Lavagna
Sestri Levante
Levanto
Cinque Terre
Portovenere
La Spezia
Lerici
Tellaro
Fiascherino

RIVIERA DI PONENTE

RIVIERA DI LEVANTE

Golfo di Genova

S20
A10
S28
S453
S28
A6
S29
S29
S30
S334
A26
S1
A10
A12
S45
S35
S226
A7
S586
S523
S1
S1

KEY

Ferry
Rail Lines

N

0   10 miles
0   15 km

163

stone path (reminding you how modern security systems are *so* much more convenient than the old citadel approach), is the **Castel San Giovanni**. The castle's schizophrenic architecture reflects its varied incarnations: It was built by the Spanish in the 1600s, partially destroyed by the Genovese in 1715, then later converted to a women's prison (the castle is now closed to the public).

BASICS **Informazione Accoglienza Turistica (IAT).** This tourist office will get you oriented with maps, hiking information, and promotional brochures for Finale and other Riviera di Ponente towns. *Via San Pietro 14, tel. 019/692581. From station, cross Piazza Vittorio Veneto to Via Saccone, and turn left on Via della Concezione, which becomes Via San Pietro. Open weekdays 9–1 and 4:30–7, weekends 9–12:30.*

SAR. Although they primarily offer bus and train information, the multilingual staff here can help you find a hotel. They also exchange money at decent rates for a small commission. *Via Mazzini 28, tel. 019/692275. Across from train station on the left. Open weekdays 9–1 and 3–6:30, weekends 10–1 and 3–6 (shorter hrs in winter).*

COMING AND GOING Finale is more or less dead center on the Genova–Ventimiglia train line. The **train station** (Piazza Vittorio Veneto, tel. 019/692777) is in Finalmarina. Trains to Torino (2 hrs, L13,600) leave hourly; those to Milan (3 hrs, L17,200) leave less frequently. There is no luggage storage, which is a major headache if you're heading to the hostel.

Two bus lines depart from the piazza in front of the train station. **SAR** (*see* Basics, *above*), a coastal service, runs from Savona through Finale to Andora, its westernmost stop. **ACTS** (office in Savona, tel. 019/220123) offers the same service, but its buses also go up into the hills and all around Finale. Buy tickets for ACTS buses at the *giornalaio* (newsstand) outside the train station. SAR tickets are sold at the SAR office. Buses to nearby Noli (10 min) cost L1700; to San Remo (1½ hrs) L5000.

WHERE TO SLEEP Finale Ligure has yet to achieve the snootiness and inflated prices of a true Riviera tourist town, and the town is generally safe. The only problem is availability, especially in July and August, when you may have to settle for a campsite or a bed in someone's home. Just across the piazza from the train station, the **Associazione Alberghi e Turismo** (Piazza Vittorio Veneto 10, tel. 019/692615 or 019/694252) will help you find a place in high season, but they'll only recommend hotels with which the office is affiliated. The SAR office (*see* Basics, *above*) can also help locate rooms in private homes, which tend to run about L60,000 for doubles. You might regret sleeping on the beach (particularly when the evening tide rolls in, taking your worldly possessions with it), but many an unauthorized budget traveler has crashed a kilometer inland (particularly around Finalborgo).

Hotel Marina. Only two blocks from the beach, this hotel has fresh, pleasant rooms (doubles L64,000) with a distinctly nautical air. The small trattoria downstairs serves up good home cooking. *Via Barrili 22, tel. 019/692561. From station, take Via de Raymondi, which becomes Via Barrili. 9 rooms, most with bath. MC, V.*

Eating on the Riviera

Blessed with a mild climate and a profusion of fruit trees, olive groves, and vineyards, Liguria produces magical and surprisingly affordable cuisine. Fresh seafood abounds (although it can be expensive), mushrooms from the mountains are delectable over pasta or baked into focaccia, and each "trofie al pesto" (a potato-based pasta with pesto sauce) seems better than the next. Wash it all down with the region's wines, including rossesse, pigato, and moscadello de Taggia. The best and cheapest sit-down meals are in the "casalinga" (homestyle) joints, where proprietors give you sound, if unsolicited, nutritional advice, banging both fists on the table for emphasis.

Soggiorno Ferrando. At this friendly hotel, tiny, bright doubles cost only L50,000, and the trattoria downstairs is excellent. *Via Barrili 31, across from Hotel Marina, tel. 019/692355. 9 rooms. Closed 2 weeks in Aug.*

➤ **HOSTELS • Ostello Wuillermin (HI).** Inconveniently perched atop a virtual Mt. Everest, this hostel is terrific if you can survive the 20-minute, 312-step hike. The turreted pseudo-castle welcomes HI members (only) looking for clean sheets at L16,000 a head. It's got a great view and serves dinner (for an extra L12,000); unfortunately, the facilities are slightly run-down. They don't accept reservations, but call before you make the trek. *Via Caviglia 46, tel. 019/690515. From train station, turn left at Via Mazzini, which becomes Via Torino, turn left at Esso gas station and up Gradinata delle Rose, and follow signs. 80 beds. Curfew 11 PM, lockout 9:30–5. Reception open 5 PM–10:30 PM. Closed mid-Oct.–mid-Mar.*

➤ **CAMPING • Eurocamping.** This site is far from the ocean, but it's got more facilities than some third-world countries. Spots are L10,200 and tents cost L8000. *Via Calvisio 37, tel. 019/601240. From station, take bus toward Calvisio and ask driver for stop. Closed Sept.–Easter.*

FOOD Despite the proliferation of touristy trattorias and restaurants with dull fixed-price menus, you can eat cheaply and well in Finale. **Da Carlo** (Via Garibaldi 21, Finalmarina, tel. 019/692776), in the center of town, makes a great spaghetti *alle vongole* (with black clams) for L8000, and it's one of the few places besides the hostel that's open for lunch. **Asterix Pub** (Via Roma 45, no phone) is decorated like its namesake French cartoon strip, but serves savory original pasta dishes. The gnocchi (L8000) and the tortellini (L8000) are both exceptional. **Il Posto** (Via Porro 21, Finalpia, tel. 019/601677) offers a unique, ever-changing menu—the only constant is a giant bowl of excellent carbonara.

"Beware the viper" sounds like something a sadistic camp counselor would say to traumatize preadolescents. But Ligurians allude to this mythical beast whenever they discuss sleeping outside. Some say it's a mere snake, others a carnivorous land shark. Whatever the viper's true nature, anyone who's seen "An American Werewolf in London" knows what happens to foreign backpackers who ignore locals' cryptic warnings.

AFTER DARK Aside from the *birrerie* (beer halls), Finale slows down at night. But after a five-minute bus ride or a leisurely 20-minute stroll to Varigotti, you'll find **Il Covo** (Capo San Donato, tel. 019/601284), an indoor/outdoor bar and discotheque right on the water. At the **Scotch Club** (Via San Pietro, tel. 019/692481), watch people hit on each other or catch someone's eye yourself (you devil).

OUTDOOR ACTIVITIES For info on hiking and rock climbing, inquire at the **IAT** office (*see* Basics, *above*). Biking is great around Finale, and the best deal for wheels is at the youth hostel, where mountain bikes rent for L15,000 a day. You can check out the Roman arches in the **Val Ponci**, behind Finale Ligure, by bike or on foot. The IAT office has maps and details about this day trip.

NEAR FINALE

SASSELLO Tiny, mountainous Sassello is punctuated by three small rivers and the Savonese Apennines. A ski resort in winter and a cool retreat in summer, it becomes covered with a wall-to-wall carpet of mushrooms in fall. Because it's cool and high in the hills, Sassello has a northern feel—a nice contrast to the sun and crowds of coastal towns. Precious few tourists come here, so the locals aren't yet jaded.

Despite its present-day placidity, Sassello had a turbulent past; it fortified the Genovese Republic against rebellious subjects in the 13th century and then rebelled itself in the 16th century. The **Saracen Tower** is all that remains of a former castle in the middle of town. Go to the **AAST** information office (Viale Marconi 3, tel. 019/724020) to pick up a brochure that discusses sights and walks in endearingly bad English. There are only two hotels in the whole village, one of which is **San Giovanni** (Via Avila 4, tel. 019/724025), a family-run albergo/trattoria with clean rooms (doubles L50,000) overlooking rolling, green farm country and the mountains. They make a mean *penne arrabbiata* (penne with hot-pepper tomato sauce), and half the town (literally) eats here for dinner. After a blissful food coma, you'll wake up to a rooster's crow.

➤ **COMING AND GOING** • Sassello is accessible only by car or bus from Savona, which you can reach by train from Finale (20 min, L2700). Near Savona's train station on Piazza Popolo, catch the ACTS bus (9 daily) toward Martina or Urbe and get off at Sassello (1 hr, L2900). You can buy your ticket on board. Ask the driver if he goes to Sassello before you get on, because service is inconsistent and (surprise, surprise) stops are poorly marked. The last bus back to Savona leaves at 6:15 PM.

NOLI About 8 kilometers north of Finale on the coast, Noli is one of the few preserved medieval centers in Liguria. Although it's touristy, the town has nice beaches and plenty of places to stay. The ancient buildings hardly betray the town's impressive autonomous past: Noli was a naval republic with its own statutes from 1196 to 1797. The Romanesque **Chiesa di San Paragorio** (off Via Collegio Cesari, just east of Via Turin) dates from the 11th century and is jammed full of goodies, including a baptismal font and a painting of abloody St. Sebastian. For outdoor buffs, the **Paleolithic grottos** (whose spoils are now in the Museo Archeologico in Finale) are easily accessible, and free-climbing has become popular in the area. Talk to the **tourist office** (Corso Italia 39, tel. 7490101) by the beach for more information. **Albergo-Ristorante Romeo** (Via C. Colombo 83, tel. 019/748973) is a family-run pension with small, cheerful rooms (doubles L75,000). For great food and an old-world feel, try **Da Gigi** (Via Sartono 4, tel. 019/748–5109). Dante's *Divine Comedy* speaks of Noli's inaccessibility, but these days the town can be reached by an ACTS or SAR bus (every 15 min, 10 min, L1700) on the Finale–Savona line.

San Remo

San Remo cannot hide the wear and tear of 100-odd years of international carousing. In the early part of the century, this was the Riviera's high-class vacation spot; now it's a mini-Vegas by the sea. But the town has more to offer in terms of street life and nightlife than other Ponente towns. It's great for people watching—full of the young and the old, the chic and the

San Remo is like Norma Desmond, played by Gloria Swanson in "Sunset Boulevard"—an aging star who's still trying to fit into that tight satin dress and pose for another close-up.

tacky. Elderly men who've been roasting in the sun for millennia drive underage girlfriends around in brand-new Ferrari Testarossas. And look out for the young gangs of jaw-clenching idlers on Vespas (Testarossa testosterone in training). The town also offers miles upon miles of cultivated, sandy beaches. They're mostly private, but if you head east, you'll find some free, rocky areas.

The hilltop **medieval town**, with its churches and tiny artisan shops, is worth a look. Note the **Russian Orthodox Church** (Via Nuvolini, near the train station), whose patrons were rich 19th-century Russian exiles. In the newer part of town you'll find all the stuff that makes San Remo party central: Palm-lined **Corso Matteotti** features chichi shops and is a locus for the town's clubs, casinos, live music, drinking, and general hedonism. The grandiose **Casino Municipale** (Corso Inglese 18, tel. 0184/534001) keeps the spirit of Monte Carlo alive, although it looks more like a courthouse or town hall than a blackjack palace. If you're 18 or older, you can play the slot machines without being subjected to a snooty dress code.

BASICS At the no-nonsense, friendly **Azienda di Promozione Turistica** (Via Nuvolini 1, across from train station, tel. 0184/571571), you can state your price range, and they'll call hotels for you. They can also give you information about hiking in the area.

COMING AND GOING San Remo is on the Ventimiglia–Genova line, and **trains** to Bordighera (10 min, L1500) and Finale Ligure (1½ hrs, L6500) are the most convenient. From San Remo, **RT buses** make a run to the French Riviera, hitting Ventimiglia, Monte Carlo, and Monaco (6 buses daily). RT buses also run from San Remo to Bordighera (20 min, L2000) and Finale Ligure (2 hrs, L5000).

WHERE TO SLEEP AND EAT Try the small, clean **Ginetta** (Via Mameli 18, tel. 0184/570070), where doubles run L50,000, or **Margherita** (Via Pallavicino 25, tel. 0184/506567), with doubles for L45,000. When other places are closed, **Albergo Vittoria** (Via San Francesco 1, tel. 0184/507294) usually has a room that would appeal to your grandmother's decorating sensibilities (doubles L50,000). Along Corso Matteotti, you'll find shops that specialize in ready-made food like *peperoni ripieni* (stuffed peppers) and stuffed zucchini. For scrumptious homemade ravioli in a charming atmosphere, try **Antica Trattoria Piccolo Mondo** (Via Piave 7, tel. 0184/509012).

NEAR SAN REMO

BORDIGHERA One young local described Bordighera in the off-season as a town with *"tre vecchi ed una machina"* (three old people and a car). Once a British colony and now a resort town, Bordighera retains a certain elegance—perhaps at the expense of a pulse. There's not much to draw you here, aside from the sea and some manicured palm gardens (Bordighera is the Vatican's official supplier of palms for Holy Week). The walkable old town, called **Bordighera Alta**, feels like an old-age home with all its elderly residents; the once-grand **Hotel Angst** (Via Manzoni), now boarded up, resembles a haunted house with its Gothic spiked fence and cobwebs.

Bordighera is a good place to hole up and hibernate for a while. Pensions become like home—you sleep and take all your meals in them. Head to the **IAT information office** (Via Roberto 1, tel. 0184/262322) for a list of hotels and more information about the town. For some fresh air, take the steep walk to **Sant'Ampelio** (Via S. Ampelio, in Bordighera Alta), a church with a Romanesque foundation. Sloping down the hill towards the ocean is the **Giardino Esotico Pallanca** (Via Modonna), an exotic garden specializing in transplanted flora from South America. Bordighera's sandy beaches are right in front of the train station, but if you head a bit east you'll find less crowded but rocky promontories.

➤ **COMING AND GOING** • Bordighera's **train station** (Piazza Eroi della Libertà) lies on the Ventimiglia–Genova train line, with trains to Genova (3 hrs 10 min, L11,700), San Remo (15 min, L2000), and Ventimiglia (10 min, L1500). The bus company **Riviera Trasporti** (in Ventimiglia, tel. 0184/351251) serves the surrounding area.

Beach Protocol

So much of Italian socializing occurs outdoors, and the beach is no exception. On the first warm day of summer, trains and highways heading towards the coast become packed all over Italy. On summer weekends and during "ferragosto" (the August holidays), you can count on the beach being filled with families, packs of teenagers happy to have the day off from parents, and persistent towel-to-towel merchants. For middle or lower class families, ferragosto usually entails camping by the beach and renting little cabanas, where the family takes siesta, eats lunch, and plays cards.

Unlike many other resorts in Italy, most of the Riviera's beaches have not been completely monopolized by private clubs. You may not always find smooth-as-silk white sand beaches, but in most towns you can just head towards the blue horizon, find a rock, and spend your day like a turtle in the sun. If you simply cannot find a free beach, don't try to stake out a renegade spot, because security at private beaches is stringent. Private beaches are broken up into blocks of color representing the businesses that own them, and the basic fee for a patch of sand is L8000. This sometimes includes an umbrella and two chairs, and most establishments don't care how many bodies you pack into a spot.

➤ **WHERE TO SLEEP AND EAT** • In the high season (July–Aug.) most places require full (three meals a day) or half (two meals) pension, which inflates prices tremendously. Still, it's worth it if you were planning on eating out anyway. At **Albergo Centrale** (Via Libertà 48, tel. 0184/262630), some of the spotless rooms have delicately hand-painted walls. The food is excellent and served in a charming dining room with a view. Doubles go for L105,000 with half-pension (L45,000 without pension). From the station, cross the piazza to Via Vittorio Emanuele and go right; the street becomes Via Libertà. Just in front of the train station, **Albergo Nagos** (Piazza Stazione 7, tel. 0184/260457) is a family-run pension with decent food and a group of loud regulars chugging their weekly supply of red table wine. Doubles are L55,000 without pension; L115,000 in July and August, when pension is required. The best thing about this place is the flower-covered terrace, which overlooks the sea.

CERVO In the days of ancient Roman rule, Cervo's valley was a pagan sanctuary for Ligurians, dedicated to the worship of the divinity Borman (equivalent to the Greek deity Apollo). Today the town is best known for its 13th-century **Clavesena Castle** and the remains of its Genovese walls. Though Cervo has become a big tourist attraction, the old buildings—Roman and medieval architecture with a little baroque plastic surgery—are still worth a visit. Be sure to see the **Church of St. John the Baptist** (also called Church of the Corals), built in the 16th and 17th centuries. According to popular lore, the church is supposed to protect its congregants from enemy attack. A good time to be here is on June 12, when Cervo (along with other Ligurian towns) is covered in rose petals for the observation of Corpus Dominicus. If you want to stay overnight, try the beachside **Camping Miramare** (Via N. Sauro 12, tel. 0183/400285). From San Remo, it's a half-hour ride to Imperia's Piazza Dante, where you can catch RT Bus 12 (every 20 min, L2500) to Cervo.

VENTIMIGLIA Primarily a transport hub near the Italian-French border, Ventimiglia gets a bad rap. It's certainly not the most beautiful place on earth, but it does have a few attractions besides the train station. There's an 11th-century church, **San Michele** (Piazza Colleta), and a terrific **open market** every Friday morning on Via della Repubblica. RT Bus 1 leaves the Ventimiglia train station hourly for the picturesque **Hanbury of Mortola Botanical Gardens** (on the way to Ponte San Luigi; admission: L8500). Less than a half hour out of town, the enormous gardens feature both wild Mediterranean vegetation and exotic flora from all over the world. The gardens are open mid-June–September, Thursday–Tuesday 9–6 (shorter hours in the off-season). If you're taking the bus to Apricale (*see below*), you'll spy the remains of a **Roman amphitheater** on the eastern outskirts of Ventimiglia before you traverse the Nervia River.

➤ **COMING AND GOING** • Ventimiglia is a transfer hub for both the French and Italian Rivieras. Trains travel from Ventimiglia to Genova (5 daily, 3 hrs 20 min, L13,600), Milan (16 daily, 3¾ hrs, L22,600), and Turin (12 daily, 4 hrs, L15,500). Trains from Ventimiglia to Nice, France (every ½ hr, 45 min, L12,100) run until 11:30 PM. The **RT** bus service (tel. 0184/351251) operates out of Ventimiglia, with Bus 7 heading to the Nervia Valley and its mountain villages. The RT San Remo–Monte Carlo–Monaco line also passes through Ventimiglia (6 buses daily).

➤ **WHERE TO SLEEP** • Accommodations are cheap here: The two-star **Albergo Calypso** (Via Matteotti 8, tel. 0184/351588) and **Villa Franca** (Corso Repubblica 12, tel. 0184/351871) both have doubles starting at L60,000.

DOLCEACQUA The temperature drops dramatically as you enter the labyrinthine alleys of Dolceacqua's old town, on the banks of the Nervia River. The medieval quarter is connected to the main piazza by the frequently photographed **Ponte Vecchio**. The 19th-century impressionist painter Claude Monet no longer hangs out here (the bridge was one of his favorite spots), but Dolceacqua's woodworkers and ceramic artists operate as they have for centuries . . . except that some now accept credit cards. Like many Ligurian towns, Dolceacqua has seen its share of foreign rulers, ever since the days of the Guelphs and Ghibellines to the 18th century when the Austrian wars of succession against France and Spain resulted in the destruction of the **Castello Doria**. The remains of the castle now perch precariously atop a mountain, and every summer a theater and music festival is held on the castle steps. RT Bus 7 makes the trip from Ventimiglia's train station to Dolceacqua (10 daily, 30 min, L2500), continuing on to Apricale.

APRICALE This storybook town on a hill is something of an artists' colony and doesn't see too many tourists. Murals painted in the '60s (which depict locals working the land) cover remarkably large portions of the little town. Several paths wind up the hill and meet at an unbelievable piazza overlooking the valley, home to the Romanesque **Chiesa di Sant'Antonio**. The town makes a good day trip, but you'll find a reasonably priced hotel, **Da Adolfo** (Via Roma 145, tel. 0184/208111), in Isolabona off the main road. Spacious, clean rooms go for L45,000 per double. For outstanding homemade ravioli topped with porcini mushrooms (L10,000), try the trattoria **A Ciassa** (tel. 0184/208280) on the main piazza. Not every RT Bus 7 heading to the Nervia Valley stops in Apricale, so make sure you consult a schedule or the bus driver before getting on. Six buses leave daily from Ventimiglia (1½ hrs, L5000).

Riviera di Levante

While the Ponente's gentrified coastal resorts have gone into decline, the towns in the Riviera di Levante—filled with rich vacationers and young backpackers alike—are still going strong. Even Portofino, the Levante's flashiest town, has a few genuine attractions, including a stunning semicircular port and rustic Monte Portofino in the surrounding hills. Santa Margherita Ligure and Rapallo have nice beaches and a lively nightlife, and Cinque Terre on the eastern end of the Levante welcomes traveling waifs with excellent food, homey accommodations, and the deep blue sea.

Camogli

The name "Camogli," an adaptation of *casa della moglie* (house of wives), refers to a past when toothless, tough women stood in for their seafaring husbands. No longer famous for its merchant ships or its matriarchal culture, this small fishing port has resigned itself to a tranquil resort-town status. Though not as pristine as some other Levante towns, Camogli retains a classic Mediterranean look, intermittently pockmarked by graffiti and disrepair. The town boasts one of the better stretches of pebble beaches in the area, and picturesque hiking trails take you along the cliffs to gorgeous views of the sea. Camogli's already expensive rooms can be difficult to find in summer, but luckily you can see the town and beach on a day trip from Santa Margherita or Genova.

BASICS Across the street and to the right of the train station, you'll find the **IAT tourist office** *Via XX Settembre 33, tel. 0185/771066. Open Mon.–Sat. 8:30–12:30 and 3:30–6, Sun. 8:30–12:30.*

COMING AND GOING Camogli's **train station** (Via XX Settembre, tel. 0185/771137) is on the Genova–La Spezia line. Trains run to Santa Margherita (every 20 min, 10 min, L1500), Genova (8 daily, 35 min, L2000), and Milan (5 daily, 2½ hrs, L13,800). The **Tigullio** bus from Camogli to Santa Margherita (17 daily, 40 min, L2000) isn't as quick as the train, but it offers excellent views of the sea. Buses stop in front of the train station.

If you're traveling through Camogli on the second Sunday in May, you'll witness the Sagra del Pesce (Blessing of the Fish), also a blessing for hungry budget travelers: Fried sardines cooked in vast kettles of oil are on the house.

WHERE TO SLEEP AND EAT Check hotel availability at the tourist office if you happen to fall in love with the town and decide to stay. **Aurelia** (Via Aurelia 249, tel. 0185/770281) is a classic small-town inn perched above Camogli. Doubles (all with bath) run L80,000–L95,000 year-round. To reach Aurelia from the train station, take the bus to Ruta, and head southeast on Via Aurelia just beyond the arch. **La Camogliese** (Via Garibaldi 55, tel. 0185/771402), in front of the train station, has big, spotless rooms for L80,000–L90,000, and the friendly management will give you advice on everything from restaurants to hiking trails. The restaurants in the center of town take advantage of the fact that there isn't much to choose from, but you can find down-home cooking and typical Ligurian fare at the modestly priced **Trattoria del Boschetto** (Via P. Risso 33, tel. 0185/771068). Other than that, your best bet is to pick up a piece of *torta zucchini* (zucchini pie) at **Focacceria Il Magnaio** (Via della Repubblica 148, tel. 0185/770507) or gather provisions at the supermarket to the left of the tourist office.

Trattoria Barache. If the gourmet in you is feeling neglected, the effort of getting to this trattoria is well worth it. From a small, unassuming kitchen, sisters Martola and Luigia produce edible ecstasy. A generous portion of homemade *lasagna al pesto* at L6000 is only the beginning. Don't leave without trying *tortelloni di ortiche*, spinach-stuffed, melt-in-your-mouth homemade tortelloni (L7000). The house specialties also include oven-fresh *focaccia al formaggio* (focaccia with cheese) and fresh seafood (fried calamari is L15,000). Good luck waddling back up to the bus stop after your meal. *Località San Nicolò 6/R, tel. 0185/770184. From station, bus to San Rocco (L2000; change at Ruta), and take footpath behind church toward Punta Chiappa/San Nicolò. Open Thurs.–Tues. 12:30–3:30 and 7:30–10.*

WORTH SEEING The baroque **Chiesa Santa Maria Assunta** (Via Isola, tel. 0185/770130), just off Piazza Colombo in the old town, combines swirling columns and simple Doric capitals. The first altar on the left, after you enter, looks like the tomb of a pirate: It's done entirely with inlaid black and white marble and uses skulls and crossbones as capitals. The church invites you to donate money to "souls burning in hell"—a kind of Western Union cable to the damned. Right around the corner, a fee of L4000 will get you into the **Acquario Tirrenico** (Castel Dragone, tel. 0185/773375; open daily 10–11:45 and 3–5:45), an interesting aquarium housed in the crumbling remains of an old castle.

OUTDOOR ACTIVITIES The tourist information office will give you a map of hiking trails. If you don't have good traction, try the path that runs from San Nicolò to the **Abbey of San Fruttuoso**, a beautiful 10th-century monastery and 13th-century abbey tucked away in a secluded bay. To reach San Nicolò, follow the directions to Trattoria Barache (*see* Where to Sleep and Eat, *above*). Follow the BACA DEI CORRI and PIETRE STRELLE signs for the less difficult trail to the Abbey of San Fruttuoso, or the FORNELLI and M. COMPANO signs for the tough trail. Both of these 1½ hour-long hikes start in a lightly forested terrain and end on cliffs overlooking the water.

Santa Margherita Ligure

For those who had their image of the Italian Riviera crushed by geriatric Bordighera or utilitarian Ventimiglia, your equilibrium will be restored by the sight of Santa Margherita Ligure. In a setting that Captain Steubing would have approved of, the town epitomizes the Riviera with brightly colored flower stands, pastel trompe l'oeil houses, and a proliferation of lapdogs on semi-precious leashes walking their bronzed owners. Easily accessible trains, buses, and bikes make neighboring Portofino, Camogli, and Rapello easy day trips, or just while the day away on Santa Margherita's small but pleasant beach. Between seaside snoozes, investigate the **Basilica di Santa Margherita** (Piazza Caprera), a testament to baroque ornateness with its crystal chandeliers and an abundance of gold leaf.

Santa Margherita is like a perfect dinner-party guest: charming in a group, but not the one-on-one kindred spirit with whom you'd share a cheap bottle of port while contemplating life.

BASICS The **IAT** office (Via XXV Aprile 2/B, tel. 0185/287485) has an eager staff and detailed information on the Riviera di Levante. **Banca Carige Cassa di Risparmio di Genova e Imperia** (Largo Antonio Giusti 17, off Via Caprera, tel. 0185/286034; open weekdays 8:20–1:20 and 2:30–4) has great rates but charges a L3000 commission.

COMING AND GOING Santa Margherita is on the Genova–La Spezia train line. The ticket window and luggage deposit at the **train station** (Piazza Nobili, tel. 0185/286630) are open daily 7 AM–9 PM. Trains to Genova (40 min, L2700) run every 40 minutes and are even more frequent in the evenings. There are also trains to Milan (4 daily, 2–2½ hrs, L24,000) and Rapallo (every 20 min, 6 min, L1600). Local **buses** leave from Piazza Vittorio Veneto (along the Lungomare). Buy bus tickets at the **Tigullio** bus information office (Piazza Vittorio Veneto, tel. 0185/288834; open daily 7:10–7:40 (in winter until 5:40) or from the vending machine just outside the office. Buses leave every 20 minutes for Camogli (35 min, L2000), Portofino (25 min, L1700), and Rapallo (30 min, L1400).

WHERE TO SLEEP The possibility of stumbling upon an unknown little pension in this resort town is slim, but you can follow the trodden path to plenty of one- and two-star hotels. In summer, book ahead if you want reasonable prices. The nearest camping is in Rapallo, just a six-minute train ride or a 30-minute bus ride away.

Albergo Annabella's. This comfortable, quiet hotel with dark green walls and antique furniture offers special bargains for parties of three or four (L30,000 per person). The food, if you decide to take pension, is good. Doubles run L65,000 (L110,000 with half pension). *Via Costasecca 10, tel. 0185/286531. From Piazza Vittorio Veneto, walk north on Via Cavour to Piazza Mazzini, pass church, and follow signs to Via Costasecca. 11 rooms, none with bath. Closed Oct.–Easter.*

Albergo Azalea. If you're exhausted after your journey, this is the place to crash—it's practically across the street from the train station. The seven comfortable rooms all have views of the bay and bathrooms. Doubles start at L70,000. *Via Roma 60, tel. 0185/288160.*

Hotel Nuova Riviera. The proprietors adore their clientele and pride themselves on homemade pasta and fresh-cut flowers. During the high season, the bright doubles run about L80,000 with breakfast. Dinner costs around L15,000. *Via Belvedere 10/2, tel. 0185/287403. From train station, take bus to Piazza San Siro; get off before Piazza Mazzini and follow signs up Via Belvedere. 9 rooms, 1 with bath.*

FOOD Everything by the water is attractive, but head slightly inland if you want to save money. For good food to go, try **Da Renato** (Via Largo Amendola 1, tel. 0185/287038); a great hunk of lasagna is L4000 and fresh seafood salads cost L6000. At **La Paninoteca** (Vico Chiuso Masaniello 5, tel. 0185/289920), communal wooden picnic tables make it easy to meet people, and you can carve your initials into them (the tables, not the people). Delicious sandwiches (L5000) and frosty beers make this the perfect midday escape. At **Trattoria da Pezzi** (Via Cavour 21, tel. 0185/285303), a good, hearty Ligurian meal including drinks can cost as little as L12,000. If you're ready to break down and splurge on seafood, try **Da Alfredo** (Piazza Martiri della Libertà, tel. 0185/288140) by the waterfront. The *spaghetti al capriccioso* (L30,000 for two people) is a blend of garlic and fresh seafood in an oven-baked tin-foil pouch, which the waiter breaks open at your table.

AFTER DARK The decor is reminiscent of Disneyland's Pirates of the Caribbean ride, but **Cutty Sark** (Via Roma 35, tel. 0185/287009) is a good place to hang. It stays open until 3 AM and tap beers start at L4000. The wood-beamed back room, complete with jukebox and tavernesque wooden tables, teems with late-night drinking and snacking locals. For a taste of Old World male bonding, check out **Vanny Bar** (Santa Margherita Vigole 18, tel. 0185/286868), which also stays open until 3 AM. Seventy-two-year-old Vanny, with his pompadour and three gold teeth, indulges his customers with extra-large shots of grappa.

OUTDOOR ACTIVITIES Hiking trails connect Santa Margherita with neighboring coastal and mountain villages; get a map from the tourist office. **Bici a Noleggio** (Via Roma 1, tel. 0185/288542) rents bikes for L5000 an hour (L3500 after 3 PM) and mopeds for L10,000 an hour.

NEAR SANTA MARGHERITA LIGURE

PORTOFINO In the '70s and '80s, Portofino was a prime "champagne wishes and caviar dreams" hotspot. Now the flood of yachts and yacht owners has slowed to a stream of Arab princes and the occasional international rock star. Despite it's decline in popularity, the tiny port is still taken up entirely by boats, so unless you happen to have a yacht handy or have somehow managed to charm the owner of one, swimming is not an option. Instead, get a hiking trail map from the **IAT** tourist information office (Via Roma 35, tel. 0185/269024). The half-hour hike up the well-marked, hilly path past Chiesa di San Giorgio to **Hotel Splendido** (Viale Baratta 13) affords an awe-inspiring view of the sea and a glimpse of the lifestyles of the rich and catatonic, who roast themselves by a swimming pool for L856,000 a night. A slightly more rugged hike up to the ruins of **Castello di Portofino** (Via la Peninsula, tel. 0185/26904) also takes around a half hour. Another good outing is to the **Abbey of San Fruttuoso** (*see* Outdoor Activities, Camogli, *above*), a 1½-hour hike or 15-minute boat ride. If you decide to come to Portofino, don't plan on sleeping here; bring a sack lunch and take the boat from Santa Margherita (10 min; L5000 one-way, L8000 round-trip). Entering the spectacular port, with its tiny, trompe l'oeil houses lining a famous curve in the coast, is one of the few experiences in life that actually lives up to its postcard promise. Buses also run from Santa Margherita every 20 minutes (15 min, L1700).

RAPALLO At first glance, Rapallo seems like just another high-priced, tourist-filled Levante town, but it's actually an appealing place to stay, with several affordable hotels and campgrounds and a more happening nightlife than its neighbors. Hike up to Montallegro, in the hills above Rapallo, to see the striking 16th-century **Sanctuary of Montallegro**, which enshrines a Byzantine icon called the Madonna di Montallegro. The first three days of July, Rapallo celebrates the Madonna with incredible fireworks and general partying in the streets. Or visit the **Antico Castello** (Lungomare Vittorio Veneto, tel. 0185/61859), a guard station designed to protect the town from the Saracens in the 16th century. The castle and its promontory are besieged daily by sunbathers.

Albergo Bandoni (Via Marsala 24, tel. 0185/50423) is a great place to stay, with terraces overlooking the water and antique-filled rooms for L70,000. You'll also find the best campground in the area in Rapallo, **Campeggio Miraflores** (Via Savagna 10, tel. 0185/263000; closed mid-Oct–Mar.). Camping costs L7000 per person, plus L7000 for a small tent. To get here from the train station, take the bus toward San Pietro (every 30 min, L1500). Young and old people in Rapallo stay out until all hours of the night at dance clubs, gelaterias, and piano bars that double as pizzerias. **Lungomare Vittorio Veneto**, along the water, is dotted with piano bars (some with open mikes) where crooners cover songs by Stevie Wonder and Neil Diamond. From Santa Margherita, trains (30 min, L1500) and Tigullio buses (30 min, L1700) run every 20 minutes to Rapallo.

Cinque Terre

The cluster of five tiny villages (Monterosso, Vernazza, Corniglia, Manarola, and Riomaggiore) called Cinque Terre is the Cinderella of the Italian Riviera. In their rugged simplicity, the five old fishing towns seem to mock the caked-on artifice of glitzy neighboring resorts. With a clear blue sea in the foreground, multicolored buildings emerge almost seamlessly from cliffs, and rocky mountains rise precipitously to gravity-defying vineyards and dusty olive groves. The geography here prevents expansion or any real technological advancement, and the small towns can't help but retain their enchanting intimacy. Each town has about one street, with no room for cars. One word of warning: Cinque Terre is the latest backpackers' "discovery" and like all hotspots is slightly overrun by desperados looking for bed and beach space. The towns still merit your attention, but be sure to call ahead if you plan on staying here in summer.

In the small towns of Cinque Terre, couples grow up together, get engaged at the age of 12, marry at 20, and never leave home.

Monterosso is the largest, least attractive, and most expensive of the towns—a good place to take care of business (sending mail and changing money) but a lousy place to find a hotel. It does have the sandiest beaches, however, and offers the 14th-century hillside **Castello Cappuccini** and the unimpressive **Chiesa Cappuccini** (up Via Bastione from the station). The latter, built in 1619, houses a *Crucifixion* by Van Dyck. The towns of Vernazza, Corniglia, and Riomaggiore are more appealing. (The runt of the litter, Manarola, is the kind of place you walk through without realizing it.) In Vernazza, climb the octagonal **bell tower** of the 14th-century church dedicated to Santa Margherita, on a hill overlooking the piazza and the water. From its tiny windows you can see the port and the entire area. Riomaggiore is such a tight-knit community that it shares one alarm clock: Church bells attempt to wake even the dead every morning at seven.

BASICS The **Visitor Associazione Turistica Pro Loco** (Via Fegina 38, tel. 0187/817506; open daily 9–1:30 and 4:30–8, shorter hrs in winter), just outside the Monterosso train station, has snotty employees but lots of info about hotels, boat rides, and hiking trails. The **Cassa di Risparmio della Spezia** (Via Loreto 49, tel. 0187/817509; open weekdays 8–1 and 2:20–3:20) in Monterosso has good rates and only charges a L2500 commission. Monterosso also has a **post office** (Via Roma 73, tel. 0187/818394; open weekdays 8–1:30 and Sat. 8–noon).

COMING AND GOING Train service to Cinque Terre is sketchy at best. You first need to head to La Spezia, which can can be reached via hourly trains from Genova (1½ hrs, L6500). From here you wait around for the hourly train that goes to each town. The towns are 20 minutes apart by this lethally slow local train, and a trip between them costs L1500. By foot, Cinque Terre is less than five hours from one end to the other (*see* Outdoor Activities, *below*).

WHERE TO SLEEP Since this area is so trendy, places to sleep fill up early, especially in the high season, and reservations are strongly recommended. If you get stuck, talk to Ivo at the gelateria in Riomaggiore (Sounds like finding a rave, doesn't it?), and he'll do his best to set you up. Riomaggiore, Vernazza, and Corniglia are the best places to stay, in terms of both price and atmosphere, because hotels in Monterosso are ridiculously overpriced and often insist that you take full pension in the high season. *Affitacamere* (private rooms for rent) abound, especially in tiny Riomaggiore; look for signs posted on houses or ask the first matronly person you encounter. Often, these are not just rooms in people's homes but whole separate apartments, fully equipped with a bathroom, kitchen, terrace, and a spectacular view.

Luciano and Roberto Fazioli. The Fazioli brothers rent out a huge assortment of rooms and apartments around Riomaggiore that range from tiny and immaculate to grandiose and slightly rank—ask to see the place before agreeing to pay the flat fee of L30,000 per person. The cost is the same regardless of whether you get a bath or kitchen, so you might as well go whole hog. Call ahead, and someone will meet you at the train station to escort you to your place. *Tel. 0187/920587 or 0187/920904.*

Margherita Guelfi. The Guelfi family rents beautifully furnished rooms, some with a view. One room is a triple with a kitchen and bath, and others share a bath. Doubles are L55,000. *Via Fieschi 95, Corniglia, tel. 0187/012328. At end of Vernazza–Corniglia trail.*

Pensione Barbara. In Vernazza's main piazza, this pension has pleasant rooms overlooking the port for L65,000 per double. From the nine rooms (which share two bathrooms and one shower), you may hear a sax playing "The Pink Panther" and "Feelings." A good restaurant is downstairs. *Piazza Marconi 23, tel. 0187/812201. Closed Nov.–Jan. MC, V.*

➤ **HOSTELS** • **Ostello Mamma Rosa.** If you love cats, you came to the right place. Cats, cat hair, and cat urine abound. Regardless of Mamma Rosa's popularity, her hostel should have been condemned by the board of health long ago. On the plus side: Mamma Rosa will call around to find a place for you when the hostel is full, trivialities such as lockouts and curfews are cheerfully ignored, and it's the main spot for evening social gatherings. A bed costs L20,000 and no membership is required. *Piazzale Unità 2, Riomaggiore, tel. 0187/920050. From train station, head right and turn right at weathered "Rio Major Sporting Club" sign. 60 beds. Laundry.*

➤ **CAMPING** • The closest campground is in neighboring Levanto. **Acquadolce** (Via Guido Semenza 5, tel. 0187/808465) charges L7000 per person, plus L8000 for a small tent and L12,000 for a large one. Take the Genova–La Spezia train from Cinque Terre to Levanto (almost hourly, L1500).

FOOD Avoid trattorias, ristorantes, and pizzerias (especially in Monterosso) that don't advertise their prices outside, or you may get suckered into paying L35,000 for a tourist menu. **Vecchio Rio** (Via T. Signori 30, Riomaggiore, tel. 0187/ 920173) serves nice, heaping portions. Try spaghetti Vecchio Rio (L10,000), a seafood pasta spiced with curry. **Mister D & G** (Via Columbo 127, Riomaggiore, tel. 0187/920820) produces some of the best pasta sauces in Liguria. The *penne al pesto* (L8000) is amazing, and the unusual *penne all'oliva* (L8000) is a rich creamy dish made with black olives. The tourist menu (L20,000), with pasta, fresh seafood, and a salad, is a bargain. For snacks or bag lunches, locals go to the popular **Focac-**

ceria Il Frantoio (Via Gioberti 1, off of Via Roma, tel. 0187/818333) in Monterosso. Crammed between clothing stalls along Monterosso's waterfront every morning is an **open-air market** with fresh cheeses, fruits, veggies, roasted chickens, and deep-fried seafood.

AFTER DARK There are a few cheesy discos in Monterosso, where tanned *ragazzi* (kids) peacock around. Some cafés stay open until 2 AM, so you can get coffee, alcohol, or something to eat until late at night. **Caffè Cagliari** (Via Roma 13, tel. 0187/817164) evokes images of a San Francisco coffeehouse with Grateful Dead album covers plastered on the walls. It gets packed around midnight.

OUTDOOR ACTIVITIES A visit to Cinque Terre should revolve around the great outdoors. The best places to go swimming are at Monterosso's "sandy" beaches, or off the rocks between Manarola and Riomaggiore. In addition to unbelievably clear blue waters, Cinque Terre is famous for its hiking, which is the best way to see the vineyards, olive groves, and the sea. You can get from one town to the next on foot by a series of well-marked (though steep and narrow) trails. The hardest and longest trail is from Monterosso to Vernazza (1½ hrs), most of which feels uphill. The hike from Vernazza to Corniglia (1½ hrs) is less strenuous. At the end of all the hilly terrain, Corniglia looks like the Emerald City of Oz. Along the way, amid cacti and olive groves, you'll find **Bar Il Gabbiano** (tel. 0187/812192), a pit stop with a view. It specializes in pastries (great *crostatas,* or tarts) baked in a wood-burning oven and *sciacchetrà,* a regional wine. The next leg between Corniglia and Manarola (1 hr) is down by the cliff line, and the last easy stroll from Manarola to Riomaggiore (30 min) is so famous that it has its own name—**Via dell'Amore**. At night, courting couples make sure that the name endures.

BOLOGNA AND EMILIA-ROMAGNA 7

By Laura Altieri

Stretching between the flat northern plains of the Padana, the foothills of the Apennines, and the Adriatic Coast, Emilia-Romagna, known as the heartland of Italy, has something for everyone. In the region of Emilia, the peacefulness of stately Renaissance towns is interrupted only by the cosmopolitan decadence of one of central Italy's most beautiful cities: Bologna. East of Bologna lies the district of Romagna, the last Roman (and later Byzantine) outpost during the Middle Ages, when the rest of central Italy was under Lombard (barbarian) rule. Here you'll find Ravenna, whose collection of mosaics is considered the finest in the western world, and Rimini, a beachfront resort so vast that it's a civilization (or lack thereof) unto itself.

Emilia-Romagna is Italy's most prosperous region, and at the same time, one of the country's most diverse. It's the birthplace of the supersophisticated opera, the testosterone-inspired Ferrari, and the world's first university, which was founded here in 1088. And today, with 240 out of 341 municipalities voting for the Left, the region is the stronghold of the liberal *Partito Democratico della Sinistra* (Democratic Party of the Left). Not only are there more academics

Si Mangia Bene

Much of Italy's quintessential cuisine comes straight from Emilia-Romagna, and it's widely accepted that in this region, the breadbasket of Italy, "si mangia bene" (one eats well). The region's hams and roasted meats are world-famous, particularly Parma's renowned "prosciutto crudo" (ham that's cured rather than cooked). Parma's other claim to fame is "Parmigiano reggiano" (Parmesan cheese), a rich, crumbly cheese that is eaten by the slice as well as grated in mounds over pasta—it's nothing like the American imitation in the green can. Typical Emilian pastas include "tagliatelle" (a flat, wide pasta generally served with a rich meat sauce), "tortellini" (fortune cookie-shape pasta filled with meat), and "tortelloni" and "tortelli" (pasta filled with ricotta and spinach). In Romagna, you'll find the Roman-derived "piadine" (unleavened bread filled with cold cuts, cheeses, veggies, or even Nutella, a chocolate-hazelnut paste) and the affordable and ever-present "crescioni" (flaky pastry pockets filled with cheese and vegetables).

Emilia-Romagna

Ligurian Sea

TO CORSICA

La Spezia

Carrara
Massa

Villafranca in Lunigiana

Bardi
Bedonia
Bore

Salsomaggiore
Cortemaggiore
Piacenza

Cremona

Montechiarugolo
Torrechiara
Ciano d'Enza
Casina

Sant'Agata
Busseto
Roncole

Parma

Mantova

Reggio Emilia

Mirandola
Poggio Rusco

Montecatini
S. Marcello Pist.
Abetone

San Martino di Mugnano
Sestola

Carpi
Modena

Finale
Cento

Ferrara

Rovigo

Pistoia
Prato

Rancobilaccio

Bologna

Rovereto
Copparo
Codigoro

Adria
Chioggia

Dozza
Imola
Brisighella

Argenta
Comacchio

Valli di Comacchio

Predappio
S. Benedetto in Alpe
Bagno di Romagna

Faenza
Forlì

Ravenna
Sant'Apollinare in Classe

Adriatic Sea

San Leo

Cesena
Savignano

Cervia
Cesenatico

SAN MARINO

Rimini

KEY

Rail Lines

30 miles
45 km

N

176

and intellectuals in Emilia-Romagna than anywhere else in the country, but there is also the highest concentration of restaurants. Even proud Italians from Milan and Naples agree: Emilia-Romagna is, deservedly, the food capital of Italy.

Bologna

Are all Italian towns beginning to look alike? If so, Bologna is sure to bedazzle. Renaissance architects went to great lengths to distinguish Bologna from Florence, and the result is one of the most spectacular skylines in Italy, with a sea of red rooftops interrupted only by towers and domes rising skyward. But aside from being particular in appearance, Bologna is particular in spirit: It's crowded, it's cosmopolitan, and with 80,000 students attending its 900-year-old university, it's truly alive. Bologna is also the party capital of the country, with more than 200 *osterie* (pubs or bars), discos, and pizzerias accommodating the hordes of twentysomethings who descend upon the city.

The influx of vivacious students into this city of rich history gives Bologna an appealing paradoxical nature. Harlotry, political radicalism, and Catholicism seem to be bound in unholy wedlock: Prostitutes circumscribe the city's wall, anarchists' headquarters dot the centro storico, and the *duomo* (cathedral), insulated by its position in the city center, turns a blind eye to all that surrounds it. Priests, pundits, poets, Communists, gluttons, lesbians, and nuns pass each other nonchalantly on the street, demonstrating the intrinsically progressive nature of this city.

While wandering through Bologna, be sure to check out the portico at Strada Maggiore 19. Two wooden arrows that were lodged in the ceiling during medieval warfare are still visible today.

BASICS

CHANGING MONEY Though the many banks on Via Rizzoli have decent rates and give credit-card cash advances, the best place to change money is at the **train station**. The ticket office (tel. 051/246490), open daily 7:15–1:15 and 2:15–7:30, doubles as a *cambio* (exchange booth) with great rates and no commission.

DISCOUNT TRAVEL AGENCIES CTS (Centro Turistico Studentesco) offers travel discounts to students under 26 with ID. *Via delle Belle Arti 20/B, tel. 051/228506. From the towers, head down Via Zamboni and turn left on Via delle Belle Arti. Open weekdays 8:30–12:30 and 2–5.*

University Viaggi helps book plane and train tickets. They don't offer many student discounts, but they can tell you about cheap fares and other good deals. *Via Zamboni 16, at Piazza Rossini, tel. 051/236255. Open weekdays 9:30–12:30 and 3–6:30. Closed Aug.*

ENGLISH BOOKS AND NEWSPAPERS Feltrinelli International (Via Zamboni 7/B, tel. 051/268070) has a decent English-language section, including books and tapes for those trying to learn Italian, and a big TV upstairs exclusively showing CNN. Store hours are Monday–Saturday 9–7:30. For English newspapers, check the newsstands on Via Ugo Bassi/Via Rizzoli.

LAUNDRY Lava and Lava charges L6000 to wash eight kilograms of dirty stuff and L6000 to dry it. Lemon-scented soap is an extra L1000. *Via Irnerio 35, no phone. Open daily 8 AM–10 PM.*

MAIL AND PHONES For international phone calls head to **IRITEL** (Piazza Otto Agosto 24, no phone), open daily 7 AM–10:30 PM. The **post office** at Palazzo Comunale (Via Oleari 3, off Via Ugo Bassi, tel. 051/223598) is open weekdays 8:15–6:30 and Saturday 8:15–12:20.

PHARMACIES Most pharmacies in Bologna alternate staying open all night, but **Farmacia Speranza** (Via Ugo Bassi 6, off Piazza Maggiore, tel. 051/232436) is open round the clock. For emergency medical service, call 5555.

VISITOR INFORMATION APT tourist offices are located at the train station, the airport, and Piazza Maggiore (in Palazzo Comunale). The tiny information booths at the train station

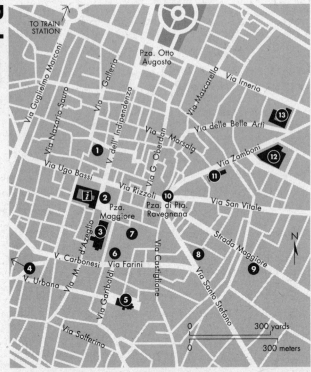

Basilica Santa Maria dei Servi, **9**

Basilica San Petronio (Duomo), **3**

Basilica Santuario della Madona di San Luca, **4**

Fontana del Nettuno, **2**

Museo Civico Archeologico, **7**

Museo Civico Medievale, **1**

Palazzo dell' Archiginnasio, **6**

Pinacoteca Nazionale, **13**

San Domenico, **5**

San Giacomo Maggiore, **11**

Santo Stefano, **8**

Torre degli Asinelli, **10**

University, **12**

(tel. 051/246541) and airport (tel. 051/381732) will book accommodations. Neither is as fully equipped as the Piazza Maggiore office, but they can give you a good street map of Bologna, a hotel map with addresses and phone numbers, and a detailed map to the hostel. For information about tours, sights, and everything else, go to the main office in the Palazzo Comunale. *Piazza Maggiore 6, tel. 051/239660. Open Mon.–Sat. 9–7, Sun. 9–1.*

COMING AND GOING

Bologna's **train station** (Piazza della Medaglia d'Oro, tel. 050/246490) is a major national and international rail hub. Trains depart frequently to Rome (4½ hrs, L35,000), Florence (50 min, L10,400), Milan (1 hr 40 min, L17,200), and Ancona (3 hrs, L20,200). The cranky employees at the information desk provide information daily 8–8. There is also 24-hour luggage storage (L1500 per piece). Once in town, check the official train schedule posted outside the travel agency at Piazza Maggiore for departure and arrival times. For urban and suburban bus information and tickets, head to **ATC** (Piazza XX Settembre 1, tel. 051/248374), open daily 6 AM–8 PM.

GETTING AROUND

Though Bologna is a major Italian city, it still retains the look and feel of an entirely walkable smaller town, and you'll find most of the major attractions within the city walls. These Renaissance structures are punctuated by 12 city *porte* (entrances), usually connected to *vie* (streets) that one way or another lead to Piazza Maggiore, in the middle of the centro storico. **Via Ugo Bassi/Via Rizzoli** runs west–east, and **Via dell'Indipendenza/Via Massimo d'Azeglio** intersects it on a north–south route, dividing the city center into quarters. It's easiest to orient yourself using the leaning medieval towers in Piazza di Porta Ravegnana, visible from just about anywhere.

BY BUS Getting around Bologna is made easy by an efficient system of shiny, orange **ATC** (Azienda Trasporti Consorziali) buses, which crisscross the city. Bus 32 and 33 run around the perimeter of the city walls, starting at the train station and stopping at some of the porte along the way. Offices at the train station and the **bus station** (Piazza XX Settembre 1, tel. 051/ 248374) post schedules and sell tickets daily 6 AM–8 PM. The ticket and information booth on Via Marconi, at Via delle Lame (open 6:45 AM–7:15 PM), is much more convenient. You can also purchase tickets, good for one hour, at tabacchi (L1300). Or buy a *citypass* good for eight separate trips, each lasting up to one hour (L10,000). Most buses run 5:30 AM–12:30 AM, but check posted schedules at bus stops.

WHERE TO SLEEP

Unless you stay at the youth hostel or one of the brand-new campgrounds, accommodations in Bologna are expensive. You won't find a double for less than L75,000, but at least rooms are plentiful and almost all places take credit cards. Be sure to call ahead, especially in August; many places shut down for a few weeks a year. The IAT office at the train station has a list of hotels, and they'll check availability for you.

➤ **UNDER L85,000 • Albergo Apollo.** This hotel, in the middle of the centro storico's shops and markets, is clean and efficient but nothing special. The proprietor is a little suspicious of foreigners at first but warms up quickly. Doubles without bath cost L75,000. *Via Drapperie 5, tel. 051/223955. From train station, Bus 25 to Piazza Maggiore, walk down Via Rizzoli, and turn right on Via Drapperie. Closed Aug. Reservations advised.*

Albergo Centrale. Smack in the center of town, this hotel lives up to its name. The clean, air-conditioned rooms are newly remodeled and not entirely charmless. Doubles without bath go for L80,000. The bar and lounge area is a good place to relax between sightseeing and a night on the town. *Via della Zecca 2, tel. 051/225114. From train station, Bus 25 to Via Ugo Bassi. AE, MC, V.*

Albergo Panorama. With clean, spacious rooms overlooking Bologna's red rooftops, this enchanting establishment (open year-round) is the best bargain in town. Doubles without bath are L80,000. Ask for one of the quieter rooms with a view of the courtyard. *Via Livraghi 1, tel. 051/221802. From train station, Bus 25 to Via Ugo Bassi; Via Livraghi is btw Via Cesare Battisti and Via della Zecca.*

Albergo Perla. The exterior of this small hotel may be dingy, but the medium-size doubles are a bargain at L75,000. As an added bonus, the hotel is across from Bar Bambi and the Vicolo Bolognetti (*see* After Dark, *below*), making it the perfect crash pad for late-night partyers. *Via San Vitale 77, tel. 051/224579. From train station, Bus 33 to Via San Vitale. 10 rooms, none with bath.*

Albergo Rossini. Near Piazza Verdi, the university's main piazza, the Rossini has decent doubles without bath for L80,000 (there's one for L50,000). The friendly, funny proprietor prides himself on his relaxed establishment, open 24 hours a day, 365 days a year. Though not the most tastefully decorated hotel, it's clean and has a lively bar. *Via Bibiena 11, tel. 051/ 237716. From train station, Bus 50 to Piazza Verdi/Teatro Comunale and turn right down Via Bibiena. AE, MC, V.*

Pensione Marconi. This hotel is centrally located and relatively clean, but you'll have to put up with a lot of noise. Plain doubles (L78,000) come with high ceilings and a sink. *Via Marconi 22, tel. 051/262832. From train station, Bus 21, 30, or 38 for 3 or 4 stops; then walk down Via Gramsci through Piazza dei Martiri to Via Marconi.*

Pensione Sant'Orsola. Run by a kind old man, this clean and simple hotel has doubles without bath for L70,000. Most of its guests are folks visiting the nearby Sant'Orsola hospital, which makes for an exceedingly quiet, if not slightly depressing, environment. *Via Palmieri 25, tel. 051/302997. From train station, Bus 36 or 37 to Ospedale Sant'Orsola; walk down Via Giuseppe Bentivogli and head left on Via Palmieri; it's on a cul-de-sac.*

➢ **UNDER L100,000** • **Albergo San Vitale.** Not too far from the medieval towers, San Vitale combines a central location with privacy, quiet, and charm. The 14 rooms, some with bath, are small but attractive. Doubles (L90,000 with bath) are cozy and clean. *Via San Vitale 94, tel. 051/225966.*

Albergo Villa Azzurra. This peaceful and homey villa has 15 bright and newly remodeled rooms (L95,000), all with great, tiled bathrooms, but is inconveniently located on the outskirts of town. Large fields and a placid park separate it from a cluster of skyscrapers. *Viale Felsina 49, tel. 051/535460. From train station, Bus 37 or 25 to the big supermarket on Viale Felsina and follow the signs.*

HOSTELS **Ostello per la Gioventù San Sisto (HI).** This hostel is far from the center of town, but is housed inside a former villa with peaceful grounds and a comfortable bar. Beds cost L16,000 per night, breakfast included. A satellite hostel (Via Viadagola 5, tel. 051/501810), just down the street, is run by the same man and accommodates overflow from this one. *Via Viadagola 14, San Sisto, tel. 051/519202. From train station, walk 1 block to Via dei Mille/Via Irnerio and take Bus 93, 20B, or 301 to Località San Sisto (last bus 8:30 PM). Curfew 11:30 PM, lockout 9–5. Reception open 7–9 and 5–11:30. Closed Dec. 20–Jan. 19.*

CAMPING **Camping Città di Bologna.** This new grassy campground north of the center is equipped with laundry facilities, bar, restaurant, and minimarket. It'll cost you between L9000 (low season) and L12,000 (high season) per person. Spacious, furnished bungalows for two, with TV and refrigerators cost L110,000, plus an additional L15,000 for each extra person (up to four). *Via Romita 12, tel. 051/325016. From train station, Bus 25, 11, or 30; ask driver where to get off, and follow the signs. Hot showers (L500). Wheelchair access.*

FOOD

Bologna's hypnotic porticoes lead the hungry traveler from one eating establishment to the next. If you're vulnerable to food coma, thank God for the siesta: Find a bed or bench, undo your zipper, and try to breathe after a heaping plate of *fettuccine bolognese.* Two good places to window-shop for cheap eats are **Via Pratello**, at the opposite end of Via Ugo Bassi from the towers, and the area near **Via delle Belle Arti**, just north of Via Zamboni. To pick up your own supplies, head to the **Mercato delle Erbe** (Via Ugo Bassi 2; open Mon.–Wed. and Fri. 7:15–1 and 5–7, Sat. 7:15–1) or **Via Pescherie Vecchie**, next to Piazza Maggiore, which is lined with stalls selling everything from fruit to pig heads to swordfish.

➢ **UNDER L10,000** • **Irnerio Mensa.** Though officially restricted to those bearing student IDs, budget travelers can often get in with a quivering lip or a good story. For L6000 you get a tasty full meal, including a primo (usually pasta), secondo (usually red meat), contorno (vegetable), drink, dessert, and bread. *Piazza Vittorio Puntoni 1, tel. 051/246115. From towers, Via Zamboni to Piazza Vittorio Puntoni. Open Tues.–Sun. 11:45 AM–3 PM.*

L'Osteria il Cantinone. Il Cantinone has an aesthetic born of age: You'll sit knee to knee on warped benches and eat off sticky tables stained with years of spilled wine. The food is delicious and inexpensive, with pasta dishes ranging from L5500 to L8000—try *penne Cantinone* (pasta with a unique creamy saffron sauce). The wine comes straight from their own vineyard. *Via del Pratello 56/A, tel. 051/553223. From towers, take Via Rizzoli/Via Ugo Bassi until it ends; veer left on Via del Pratello. Open Thurs.–Tues. 8 AM–1 AM.*

Osteria del Montesino. Noisy and crowded, particularly after 10 PM, this is a great place for a late-night snack and a liter of house Sardinian wine (L7000). Share a table and a mixed *crostini* platter (toasted bread with a variety of toppings; L9000) alongside old bohemians sporting graying ponytails and their younger counterparts. *Via del Pratello 74/B, tel. 051/523426. From towers, follow Via Rizzoli/Via Ugo Bassi until it ends; veer left on Via del Pratello. Open Tues.–Sun. 8 PM–1:30 AM.*

Pizzeria I Cavalieri. The best pizza in town and they'll make it any way you like. Try a pie with *mais e ricotta* (corn and ricotta cheese) for L9000. Save money by getting it *d'asporto* (to go) and eating outside on the adjacent bank steps. *Andrea Costa 2, tel. 051/423575. From train* *station, take Bus 33 or 32 from train station to Porta San Isaia. Open Thurs.–Tues. 8AM–1AM. Closed Aug. MC, V.*

Ustaria da Matusel. This restaurant offers simple fare at a low price. Its lurid past as a brothel is immortalized on the walls, which are decorated with murals and an official letter of condemnation. Go for the company of sociable students and the good *zuppa d'asparaghi* (asparagus soup). Primi run L5000–L7500. *Via Bertoloni 2, tel. 051/231718. From the towers, take Via Zamboni, left on Via del Guasto, right on Via delle Belle Arti, first right on Via Bertoloni. Open Mon.–Sat. 11:45–2:30 and 7–12:45.*

➤ **UNDER L20,000 • Ristorante da Bertino.** This classically unhip trattoria specializes in homemade pasta (L8000–L9000) and excellent meats. Though meatless dishes are served here, vegetarians might be horrified by the house specialty: *bollita mista* (L11,000), an array of boiled meats that comes rolling to your table on a stainless-steel cart. Dessert choices include homemade *tiramisù* (an espresso- and liqueur-drenched pastry). *Via delle Lame 55, tel. 051/52230. From towers, follow Via Rizzoli/Via Ugo Bassi to its end; veer right on Via delle Lame. Open Mon.–Sat. noon–3 and 7–10:30. Closed Aug. AE, V.*

Ristorante Double Face Centro Free Flow Gastronomia. With about as many names as dishes to choose from, this self-service restaurant, unlike most similar places, charges by the dish. The tortelloni and lasagna are both homemade and delicious, and the salad bar is decent. Primi run L4000–L7000 (secondi L5000–L10,000), but fruit is expensive. *Via dell'Indipendenza 45, tel. 051/234216. From towers, take Via Rizzoli and turn right on Via dell'Indipendenza. Open Mon.–Sat. 11:45–3 and 6:30–9:30.*

➤ **UNDER L40,000 • Al Montegrappa da Nello.** If you're going to splurge, this is the place to do it. They specialize in hand-picked mushrooms, wild boar, and homemade wine. The menu changes all the time, but ask the helpful waiters what the house specialty is, or go with truffles over anything. The veal with prosciutto is out of this world. A good-size meal will cost you about L40,000. *Via Montegrappa 2, tel. 051/236331. From towers, head down Via Rizzoli and turn right on Via dell'Indipendenza; the first left is Via Montegrappa. Open Tues.–Sun. noon–3 and 7:30–11:30. Closed Aug.*

GELATERIAS Wherever there are *ragazzi* (student-age folk), there are sure to be gelaterias. Particularly notable is **Gelateria delle Moline** (Via delle Moline 13, no phone), which dishes out the best pistachio gelato around (L2500) Wednesday–Monday. Chocolate lovers should head to the hugely famous and just plain huge **Bar Gianni** (Via Montegrappa 11/D, off Via Indipendenza, tel. 051/233008) for an intriguing "chocolate surprise" (L3000). At **Gelateria Ugo** (Via San Felice 24, tel. 051/263849), you can indulge in a delicious twist on the ice-cream sandwich: gelato stuffed inside warm raisin focaccia and topped with whipped cream (L4000). From the towers, walk five minutes up Via Ugo Bassi to Via San Felice. Ugo is open March–October, Wednesday–Saturday 2:30 PM–11 PM.

WORTH SEEING

Despite Piazza Maggiore's grandiose air, this is a town of subtlety; Bologna doesn't bludgeon you with its attractions. Although it may not boast a *David* or a *Mona Lisa,* the city as a whole is exceptionally beautiful, and, unlike many heavily touristed places, it maintains a genuinely Italian feel. The **university,** in spite of its worldwide acclaim, is without a distinct campus, blending in with the arcaded streets of the historic town. Bologna's museums are generally open from 9 to 7 with a siesta break from 1 or 2 to 3:30 PM. Siesta time is particularly dead in late July and August, when Bologna is hellishly hot.

BASILICA SAN PETRONIO (DUOMO) The plans for this 14th-century basilica were so impressive that, according to one account, its construction was curtailed by papal decree to prevent it from surpassing St. Peter's in size. On either side of the triangular brick facade, the transepts abruptly cut through the windows, allowing you to see the exact point at which the

The meridian line on the floor of the duomo is actually a giant sundial; the sunlight streaming in from the hole in the ceiling indicates the time and date. **181**

duomo grew too large. Also notice that the marble runs out before reaching the top—a good indication that the money ran out as well. Other noteworthy features include the Gothic arches, Parmigianino's *San Rocco,* and the frescoes by Giovanni da Modena. *Piazza Maggiore, tel. 051/225442. Open daily 7–noon and 3:30–7.*

BASILICA SANTA MARIA DEI SERVI If you're sweltering in the heat of summer, the interior of this well-preserved Gothic church provides a cool and restful respite. The church's best feature is Cimabue's *Blessed Virgin;* also noteworthy are Vitale da Bologna's fading 14th-century frescoes. *Strada Maggiore 43, tel. 051/226807.*

BASILICA SANTUARIO DELLA MADONNA DI SAN LUCA This 19th-century tribute to the Virgin Mary is perched high above Bologna, 3 kilometers from the city center. The church can be reached on foot from Via Saragozza by following the city's longest portico, which is sheltered by 666 arches. Thousands of pilgrims make the arduous climb each year during Easter. The basilica's interior is nothing special, but the view makes it well worth the trek. It's also an ideal spot for a picnic. *Via San Luca 36, tel. 051/412460. From train station, Bus 20 or 94 to steps on·Via Saragozza. From towers, head south on Via Castiglione, turn right on Via L. Farini, veer left on Via Collegio di Spagna (which becomes Via Saragozza), follow signs to basilica. Open 7–12:30 and 2:30–7.*

FONTANA DEL NETTUNO Neptune's monumental endowment and the highly erotic cherubim and breast-clenching sirens of this fountain were rejected by the Catholic church for their impropriety, so sculptor Giambologna had to manipulate Neptune's left arm in the interests of modesty. If you enter Piazza Maggiore from Via Rizzoli at Via dell'Indipendenza, veer right up the slope that leads to the memorial wall; look at Neptune's left arm from this angle and decide for yourself if Giambologna suffered any artistic castration. *Piazza Maggiore.*

MUSEO CIVICO ARCHEOLOGICO This museum is known for its collection of art and artifacts dating from prehistoric times to the Villanovan, Greek, Etruscan, and Roman Bronze ages. The impressive Egyptian collection includes some great mummies and text from the *Book of the Dead.* Don't miss the courtyard collage of inscribed stone slabs from various periods. *Via dell'Archiginnasio 2, tel. 051/233849. Admission: L5000. Open Tues.–Fri. 9–2, Sat. 9–1 and 3:30–7, Sun. 3:30–7.*

MUSEO CIVICO MEDIOEVALE This fabulous collection of 13th- to 14th-century sepulchers depicting masters with their sleeping or otherwise distracted students is beautifully displayed in **Palazzo Ghisilardi-Fava**, along with medieval and Renaissance ceramic, glass, and bronze instruments. The palace, while typically Bolognese Renaissance, incorporates the remains of a Roman wall, still visible from the courtyard. *Via Manzoni 4, tel. 051/228912. From towers, take Via Rizzoli, turn right on Via dell'Indipendenza, and left on Via Manzoni. Admission: L5000, L2500 students. Open Mon. and Wed.–Fri. 9–2, weekends 9–1 and 3:30–7.*

PALAZZO DELL'ARCHIGINNASIO This palace, covered with intricate family shields and tributes to Renaissance intellectuals, became the first permanent seat of Bologna's university in 1563, five centuries after its founding. Dante, Petrarch, Copernicus, Marconi, and St. Thomas Beckett are all alumni of the **Università di Bologna**, an institution made avant-garde by its early acceptance of female professors. (Not too avant-garde though: Legend has it, the first women professors had to cover their faces to keep from distracting male students). You'll pass beautifully carved sarcophagi to reach the **Anatomical Theater** and its impressive interior of unique inlaid wood designs by Antonio Levanti. The famous "skinless" statues by Erobe Lelli, like Greek caryatids (human-shaped pillars), hold up the canopy that covers the lecturer's chair. *Piazza Galvani 1, west of the duomo, tel. 051/277643. Admission free. Open weekdays 8:30 AM–1:45 PM, Sat. 8:30 AM–12:45 PM.*

PINACOTECA NAZIONALE This museum has a decent-size collection of paintings in styles ranging from Byzantine to baroque. Huge canvases by Guido Reni include the impressive *Pietà dei Santi Petronio, Domenico, Carlo Borromeo, Francesco d'Assisi, e Procolo,* and the highly dramatic *Crosifissione.* There are more paintings of the martyrdom of St. Sebastian than you can shake a stick or shoot an arrow at. Ludovico Carracci's *Madonna and Child* (1590) combines a rich Venetian palette with Caravaggesque attention to anatomy (notice Mary's bare feet). Art-history students get in free, so do like all other budget travelers and fake it. *Via delle Belle Arti 56, tel. 051/243249. Admission: L8000. Open Tues.–Sat. 9 AM–2 PM and Sun. 9 AM–1 PM.*

SAN DOMENICO This often-forgotten church houses one of Bologna's greatest treasures: the *Arca di San Domenico* (St. Domenico's tomb). In the sixth chapel on the right is the saint's tomb, an intricately carved, collaborative effort by Nicola Pisano, Michelangelo, and others. Notice the resemblance in the stance and gaze of Michelangelo's *San Procolo* to his later *David.* Ask any priest to point you to a man named Carlo Cati, who gives tours of the church in English. In his endearingly dramatic way, he'll detail the life and love of St. Domenico and the subtleties of the tomb constructed in his honor. *Piazza San Domenico 13, tel. 051/237017. Open daily 7 AM–8 PM.*

SAN GIACOMO MAGGIORE Construction on this church began in 1267 in the Romanesque style, but San Giacomo's appearance slowly metamorphosed toward Gothic as the church expanded. Inside are works by Carracci, Tibaldi, and Jacopo della Quercia. Ask the sacristan to let you into the **Oratorio di Santa Cecilia** for a look at some of Lorenzo Costa's frescoes. His real masterpieces, however, are in the attached **Bentivoglio Chapel**, with cycles depicting everything from the *Madonna Enthroned* to the ruling Bentivoglio clan themselves. *Piazza Rossini, tel. 051/ 225970.*

SANTO STEFANO Probably the most interesting architectural attraction in Bologna is this hodgepodge of four adjoining churches (there were originally seven) from the 5th to 13th centuries. The Romanesque **Crucifix Church**, despite various transformations, retains a medieval Lombard style, thanks to recent restoration. The **Holy Sepulchre Church**, containing St. Petronio's remains, is thought to have been a pagan temple in the 1st century AD, before its conversion to a baptistry. The **Chiesa di Santi Vitale e Agricola** is the oldest church in the group, built from bits and pieces of Roman artifacts. Legend has it that St. Agricola was nailed to the metal cross now hanging on the wall. Don't overlook **Pilate's Courtyard**, with its sepulchers and *St. Peter's Cock,* a stone rooster whose presence is a reminder of St. Peter's denial of Christ. The **cloister** influenced Dante's *Inferno;* allegedly, the unsavory laymen leaning and wallowing along the lower tier inspired the famous poet. Inside the fourth church, the **Trinità**, is a thoroughly underwhelming but free museum, containing a 13th-century fresco and later paintings. *Via Santo Stefano 24, tel. 051/223256. Open daily 9–noon and 3:30–6.*

CHEAP THRILLS

For a glimpse of Bologna's red-roofed splendor, climb the city's most conspicuous point of reference, the tower known as **Torre degli Asinelli** (Piazza di Porta Ravegnana). The physically fit can make the long but rewarding climb 9–7 daily for L3000. For a completely different perspective on the city, peek through the little window on Via Piella, off Via Righi. You'll see what remains of the 14th-century canals that once ran beneath Bologna. If you're tired of sightseeing, the sprawling **Giardini Margherita** off Viale Gozadina offers a trampoline (10 min, L1000), merry-go-round, and basketball courts, as well as outdoor concerts and plays (*see* After Dark, *below*). Friday and Saturday 7 AM–6 PM, you'll find everything from hot-pink panties to antique lamps at Bologna's **outdoor market** (Piazza 8 Agosto, off Via Indipendenza). Used bicycles are sold daily in Piazza Verdi, but be careful—at L20,000 they are literally a steal.

Those still waiting for their diplomas should stay away from the Torre degli Asinelli. Urban lore has it that university students who climb the tower won't graduate.

AFTER DARK

As in any other college town, what's hot and what's not in Bologna is in a constant state of flux. Pick up a copy of *Dove* (L2000) at any newsstand for listings of live music, dancing, restaurants, and theater. For information on gay and lesbian entertainment, call *Arci-Gay Nazionale* (tel. 051/644–7054) and ask for an English speaker.

During July and August the city hosts *Bologna Sogna,* a series of free events ranging from classical concerts and live jazz in palace courtyards to DJs spinning dance grooves in parks and on hillsides. Ask at the tourist office for a list of events. Just off Via San Vitale, the bar **Vicolo Bolognetti**, located in the alleyway of the same name, serves up outdoor concerts, watermelon, and beer every night from mid-May to September. Performances vary from reggae to punk to (gasp) country, and they're all free. **Teatro Comunale** (Via Largo Respighi 1, tel. 051/529999) hosts seasonal opera, ballet, symphony, and music festivals, some of which are free, and **Circolo della Musica di Bologna** (Via Galliera 11, tel. 051/227032) has free classical-music concerts throughout the summer. From mid-May to September 10, a variety of (often free) concerts and a disco are held in **Giardini Margherita** from 9:30 PM to 3 AM.

OSTERIE During the school year, Bologna's nightlife is found in the city's many *osterie* (wine bars or taverns where friends meet to drink and snack at long wooden tables). The oldest and most authentic osteria is the charmingly squalid **Osteria del Sole** (Vicolo Ranocchio 2/B, no phone). It's only open 7:45 PM–8:45 PM and there's no signpost, but it's worth finding this hovel for the authentic medieval atmosphere and an incredibly cheap glass of wine (L2500). If food is what you're after, try **Osteria Broccaindosso** (Via Broccaindosso 7/A, off Strada Maggiore, tel. 051/234153), open Monday–Saturday, for yummy mascarpone (L6000) or *strozzapreti con funghi porcini* (rolled dumplings with mushrooms; L8000). A rowdier crowd fills the **Buca delle Campane** (Via Benedetto 4/1, off Via San Vitale, tel. 051/220918), just two blocks from the towers. Listen to sweaty bands covering American and Italian hits from the '70s and '80s. Dance, sing along, or just laugh over a beer (L8000).

BARS AND DISCOS If you're planning on a night of barhopping, head to the concentration of bars on **Via del Pratello**, where Via Ugo Bassi meets Via Marconi.

Irish Times Pub. Tired of things Italian? This large Irish pub serves the queen's Guinness and Harp on tap (L7000). Stop by for happy hour 7 PM–8 PM and mingle with English and Italian students. *Via Paradiso 1, tel. 051/261648. From towers, follow Via Rizzoli (which becomes Via Ugo Bassi), veer left on Via del Pratello and take 3rd right on Via Paradiso. Open Tues.–Sun. 7 PM–2 AM.*

Oassfeo. This dance place caters to a mostly gay crowd, and is always happening, even during the summer when most of the action moves to the hills. Though a *tessera* (prepaid membership) is usually required, bouncers will often make exceptions for tourists. Oassfeo also shows films and hosts theme events. *Piazza di Porta Saragozza 2, tel. 051/433395. From Via Ugo Bassi, take Via Massimo d'Azeglio south to Via Barberia and veer left on Via Saragozza.*

Proloco. This new bar has almost as many board games as Toys 'R' Us; luckily most of them don't require knowledge of Italian. (Connect Four anyone?) A wide assortment of beer (L7000) and cocktails (L8000), along with the charming English-speaking manager, Filippo, make it worth a stop. *Via dell'Unione 2/B, tel. 051/227320. No cover. Open Tues.–Sun. 8 PM–2 AM.*

MOVIE THEATERS Movies in English play nightly at **Adriano d'essai** (Via San Felice 52, tel. 051/555127) for L12,000. **Tiffany** (Porta Saragozza 5, tel. 051/585253) shows English language films weekly, also at L12,000; check newspapers for specific day of the week, as it alternates seasonally. Both theaters close in July and August. For the latest listings, pick up a free copy of *Anteprima* at any newsstand or bar.

Emilia-Romagna

Emilia-Romagna, composed of Emilia to the west and Romagna to the east, is a wealthy, tranquil region where life slowly cruises by, and the residents still stop to smell the proverbial flowers. The cities here date back to the Roman era and have a history of barbarian attacks, endless conquests, and vicious wars throughout the Middle Ages. When the Renaissance dawned in Italy, Emilia-Romagna's towns developed into court cities, glorified by their often eccentric and generally tyrannical dukes and lords: the Farnese in Parma, the Este in Ferrara, the Bentivoglio in Bologna, and the Malatesta in Rimini. In the 16th century, Pope Julius II ousted the ruling families and took control of the two regions, making them pawns of the Papal States. In 1848, during the Risorgimento unification movement, both Emilia and Romagna officially became part of Italy, and in 1860 the two territories were combined—though only in name, as they still retain distinct attitudes, accents, and traditions.

Despite the region's long history of bloodletting, turmoil, and rebellion, the arts have always flourished in Emilia-Romagna. The ruling families financed painters, sculptors, and writers; Dante hung out in Ravenna after being booted out of his native Florence; and the world's first cookbook and opera were written here. More recently, Emilia has been home to film director Federico Fellini and tenor Luciano Pavarotti. The culinary arts have prospered as well, as you'll discover as soon as you sit down to a plate of *zampone* (stuffed pigs' feet) in Modena, or anything flavored with the region's potent, jet-black herb vinegar, *aceto balsamico*.

Modena

Modena appears, at first glance, a much larger city than it actually is, a consequence of the extensive industrial suburbs and the fast-paced metropolitan lifestyle of the modenesi. The centro storico is atmospheric and well preserved, but the outer reaches of town and the surrounding countryside are packed with factories producing everything from pork sausage to race cars. Modena's big-city bustle, though, is tempered by a warm and intimate atmosphere. This paradox is personified by the Via Emilia; buses thunder and mopeds zoom along the main thoroughfare as the old and the young alike sit in the cafés and under shaded porticoes, watching life pass by.

Although Modena was established as the Este duchy at the end of the 16th century, the city's intrigue doesn't lie in its history or its monuments; Modena's appeal is in its hedonistic present. Home of Lambrusco wine, Vignola cherries, Luciano Pavarotti, and the Ferrari, Modena is a wealthy town, fat with fine food, heavenly music, and fast cars. But for a town of plenty, there's surprisingly little to see and do. Like the Este, you'll be best served by making Modena a side trip, not a resting ground.

BASICS For long distance calls, the **SIP** office (Luigi Farini 26, no phone) is open 24 hours. The central **post office** (Via Emilia 86, tel. 059/242030) is open Monday–Saturday 8 AM–7:40 PM. Change money at any of the banks along Via Emilia. The central **tourist office** is stocked with maps, historical pamphlets, and info on travel within the region. *Piazza Grande 5, tel. 059/206580. From train station, Bus 7 to Piazza Grande. Open weekdays 9:30–12:30 and 3:30–6:30, Sat. 9:30–12:30.*

One block east of Piazza Grande, the **Informa Giovane Office** has news on nightlife and the local youth scene. *Via Scudari 8, tel. 059/206583. Open Mon., Tues., and Thurs.–Sat. 10:30–12:30 and 4–7.*

COMING AND GOING Trains shuttle back and forth between Modena and Milan (2 hrs, L14,600) and Modena and Bologna (30 min, L3400) day and night. Modena's **train station** (Piazza Dante Alighieri, tel. 059/223101) lies on the northern edge of the historical center. From station, Bus 7 runs to the **bus station** (Via Bacchini 27, tel. 059/308833), where you can catch a bus to one of the smaller towns surrounding Modena. Pick up a schedule here or at the tourist office (*see* Basics, *above*). Buses to mountain towns, including Sestola (1½ hrs, L7900), run about every two hours.

GETTING AROUND As long as you stay within the centro storico, Modena is a city easily traversed on foot. Via Emilia bisects the town into northern and southern halves. At the center, **Piazza Mazzini**, better known as the **Via Emilia Centro**, is both a transportation hub and gathering place. To reach Via Emilia Centro from the train or bus station, take Bus 7. You can also walk there from the train station by taking Viale Crispi out of Piazza Dante and turning right onto Vittorio Emanuele, which runs smack into the back of the **Palazzo Ducale**. Walk around the palace to Piazza Roma; from here all streets run to Piazza Mazzini. If your boots aren't made for walkin', Modena's intercity buses stop at Via Molza, in front of the bus station.

WHERE TO SLEEP Modena doesn't have a hostel, and its campground is outside town, but with several bargain hotels just off Piazza Grande, the city is well equipped for budget travelers. The **Hotel Astoria** (Via Sant'Eufemia 43, tel. 059/225587) is the best bargain in town; doubles without bath cost L50,000 and showers are L3000 extra. The rooms are bare bones, but the beds and bathrooms are cleaner than most, and the proprietress is extremely kind.

Hotel La Torre (Via Cervetta 5, tel. 059/222615) is a sparkling clean, modern establishment hidden away in an aging building. Doubles with bath cost L85,000, but singles without bath are a good deal at L40,000. The hotel is closed in August. **International Camping Modena** (Via Cave Ramo III, Località Bruciata, tel. 059/332252) is a favorite among European motor homers, who hang around in beer-guzzling circles all night. Evenings in the great outdoors with Gunther, Helga, and a Heineken won't be cheap, either; each site costs L115,000 for a tent plus L6500 per person. To get here, take Bus 19 from the bus station.

FOOD One word: pork. The Modenesi have found 101 ways to prepare it, from traditional cured hams to the more unusual *cotechino* (animal bladders stuffed with pork shank) and *tigella* (fried herbed bacon, lard, and pancetta). Vegetarians and the gastronomically meek will find refuge in the *tortelloni di ricotta e spinaci* (pasta squares stuffed with ricotta and spinach). Finish off dinner with world-famous Vignola cherries, and accompany any meal with Lambrusco, a fizzy, dark-purple wine that aids digestion.

Eating in restaurants is expensive, but *mense* (cafeterias) fill Modena and offer a reprieve from high prices. Head to **Il Chiostro Ristorante Free-Service** (Via San Geminiano 3, tel. 059/230430) or **Mensa Ghirlandina** (Via Vescovo 9, off Via Sant'Eufemia, tel. 059/236255) for a tasty full meal under L12,000. If you'd rather fix lunch yourself, the bustling **covered market-place** (entrances at Via Albinelli 15 and Via Mondatora 18) is overflowing with fruits, vegetables, meats, and cheeses. Go weekdays between 7:15 AM and 1:30 PM. The bread, cookies, pastries, and pizza at **Forno San Giorgo** (Via Taglio 6, just behind Piazza Mazzini, tel. 059/223514) will make your mouth water.

The area around Piazza Mazzini just off Via Emilia Centro is thick with restaurants serving typical Modenese cuisine. **Galleria Mazzini** (Piazza Mazzini 9/C, tel. 059/225369; closed Sun.) has tables right in the center of the piazza and slightly cheaper prices than many of the surrounding restaurants. Primi range from L7000 to L12,000, and the *menu turistico* (tourist menu; a huge meal plus coffee) is a bargain at L20,000. **Trattoria Giardinetto** (Via Levizzani 26, tel. 059/230404), also closed Sunday, is a typical Modenese restaurant that takes a little searching to find: To get here, take Canal Chiaro from Piazza Grande and turn right on Via Levizzani. Once here, you can relax in a small ivy-canopied garden squeezed in among the neighboring buildings and indulge in amazing tortelloni (L8000).

WORTH SEEING Modena doesn't overwhelm you with sights, but what remains of the Este duchy's art and property is definitely impressive. While Via Emilia Centro is the official center of town, **Piazza Grande** is the unofficial center, hosting occasional concerts, speeches, and volleyball tournaments.

➤ **DUOMO OF SAN GEMINIANO** • This masterpiece of Romanesque Lombard architecture was built in 1099, and later transformed by the sculptor Wiligelmo and his apprentices into a bas-relief storyboard. The exterior sculptures you'll see are reproductions, though; the real ones are now in the **Lapidary Museum** (Via Lanfranco 6, tel. 059/216078), open by appointment only. The interior of the duomo is equally magnificent, particularly the long, sculpted panel of the Last Supper, which divides the crypt and the sanctuary. The white tower connected to the duomo, **La Torre Ghirlandina**, shows both Romanesque and Gothic influences. Unfortunately, it's only open to the public a few days each year; inquire at the tourist office for specific days and enter the tilting tower at your own risk. *Corso Duomo, tel. 059/216078). Open daily 7–noon and 3:30–6.*

➤ **PALAZZO DEI MUSEI** • This museum complex extraordinaire houses the city's most famous artworks, a research library, and an enormous collection of ancient, medieval, and modern testaments to everyday life in Emilia. On the top floor, the **Galleria Estense** was established in 1598 in an attempt to save the family treasures when the papacy snatched Ferrara from the Este dukes. The gallery was sacked in a 1992 art heist, and many of its principal attractions probably hang on the wall of a stingy millionaire's mansion. You can still appreciate what the thieves left behind, including Correggio's *Madonna dei Limoni*, Bernini's bust of Francesco I, and Veronese's organ doors from the church of San Geminiano in Venice. Just below the gallery, the **Museo Civico Archeologico** presents a fascinating portrait of Emilian life through the ages. Another story below that is the **Biblioteca Estense**. Borso d'Este's two-volume Bible, created between 1455 and 1461, is the most-decorated book in the world, with over 2,000 miniature paintings in all. Outside the mighty museum complex and around the corner, the **Galleria Civica** hosts changing art and photography exhibits. After paying the general admission fee of L5000, pay an additional L2000 for each separate museum inside the complex. *Piazzale San Agostino. From Via Emilia Centro, walk west for about 10 min, until you near the Viale; the palazzo is on your left. Galleria Estense: tel. 059/222145. Admission: L5000. Open Tues.–Sat. 9–2, Sun. 9–1. Museo Civico Archeologico: tel. 059/223440. Admission: L5000. Open Wed., Fri., and Sat. 9–1; Tues. and Thurs. 9–1 and 3–6; Sun. 10–12:30 and 3–6. Biblioteca Estense: tel. 059/222248. Admission: L5000. Open Mon.–Thurs. 9–7:15, Fri. and Sat. 9–1:40. Galleria Civica: tel. 059/222100. Admission: L5000. Open Thurs.–Sat. 10:30–12:30 and 3:30–6:30.*

➤ **GALLERIA FERRARI** • For all you speed demons dreaming of slick, shiny automobiles, this place will make your heart race. The Ferrari factory, a vast complex employing thousands, is actually in Maranello, a suburb of Modena. You can't get into the factory itself, but the showroom displays trophies, engines, and new and vintage hot rods. *Via Dino Ferrari 43, Maranello, tel. 0536/943204. From the bus station on Via Bacchini, buses leave hourly for Maranello (L1300). Admission: L12,000. Open Tues.–Sun. 9:30–12:30 and 3–6.*

AFTER DARK For a relaxed evening out, head to the bars and gelaterias in Parco Amendola, which borders the southern end of the centro storico. You can boogie down at **Charly** (Via Riccoboni 45, off Viale Vittorio Veneto, tel. 059/214741), the one discothèque open in summer, or ask around for the nearly hidden **Irish Pub** on Via Gallucci. During the summer, the city hosts the **Sipario in Piazza**, a series of concerts and ballets in Piazza Grande. Tickets cost L20,000–L30,000 and can be purchased at the *palazzo comunale*, or town hall (Piazza Grande, tel. 059/206111). You might get lucky and catch a show by native son Luciano Pavarotti.

NEAR MODENA

REGGIO-EMILIA Reggio-Emilia exemplifies the overwhelming contradictions of Emilia-Romagna. This sleepy town has both the highest standard of living in Italy and the most Communists in city offices (over 50% of the city government is Red). It's the birthplace of the national tricolor flag, but it's also home to the most immigrant–Italian marriages in Italy. Even physically, the town is a study in contrast: The outskirts are dotted with modern factories and cellular phone companies, while the centro storico houses Renaissance and medieval palazzi.

Reggio is a town for aimless wandering, and the best place to start is the town's central pair of piazze, each with its own basilica. **Piazza Prampolini** is home to Reggio's sprawling medieval **duomo**, but the baroque **Basilica di San Prospero**, in the neighboring **Piazza San Prospero**, has more appeal, with its six roaring lions of pink Veronese marble and its oddly incongruous tower. Every Tuesday and Friday, Piazza San Prospero is also the site of a large **outdoor market**, where booths selling everything from flowers to fish heads line the covered passage leading to Piazza Prampolini. Nearby lies the proclamation site of the tricolor Italian flag, the **Palazzo del Capitano del Popolo** (Piazza C. Battisti 4, tel. 0522/432944). This palazzo, with its dramatic battlements, is one of the most attractive buildings in town. Also of architectural merit, is the 17th-century baroque **Madonna dell Ghiara** (Corso Garibaldi, tel. 0522/459707), containing frescoes by Guercino. As small and peaceful as it is, sophisticated Reggio draws an astonishing number of performances and exhibits to its six theaters. The palatial **Teatro Municipale Valli** (Piazza Teatro, tel. 0522/458811) often has good art exhibitions, as well as music and ballet performances.

➤ **BASICS** • The **tourist office** (Piazza Prampolini 5, tel. 0522/451152), open weekdays 8:30–5, Saturday 8:30–2:30, can give you information on Reggio. **Bicitta** (Parcheggio di Via Cecati, tel. 0522/456650) can rent you a bike for L8000 per day, Monday–Saturday 7:30–7:30.

➤ **COMING AND GOING** • Reggio Emilia is only a 15-minute train ride from Modena (hourly, L2800). From the **train station** (Piazza Marconi 8, tel. 0522/439650), take Bus 1, 4, or 9 to the center of town. On foot, walk down Viale IV Novembre to Piazza del Tricolore and follow Via Emilia to the right until you hit Piazza C. Battisti; turn left on Via Corridoni and you'll find yourself in Piazza Prampolini.

> **WHERE TO SLEEP AND EAT** • The **HI hostel** (Via dell'Abbadessa 8, tel. 0522/454795), just off Via Emilia, charges L16,000 a night, and there's no curfew or lockout. Staying at the hostel entitles you to a reduced-price meal at the adjacent **mensa** (Via dell'Abbadessa 8, tel. 0522/46207) for L10,000; buy your meal ticket at the hostel. The cafeteria-style **Job's Bar** (Piazza Gioberto 2/E, tel. 0522/452999), open Monday–Saturday noon–2:30 PM, serves cheap and tasty lunches for around L12,000. After a night at the theater, choose from one of the many beers (L4000) available at **Vecchia Reggio** (Vicolo del Clemente 1/C, off Via Angelo Secchi, no phone).

SESTOLA Sestola is a strange combination of antique mountain village and modern ski resort. Spilling over the sides of its hilly perch and surmounted by its craggy *rocca* (fortress), Sestola, at 1,020 meters, is the highest town in the Modenese Apennines. Most people come here for the hiking, mountain biking, horseback riding, and skiing (which, by the way, is not to be scoffed at—Alberto "La Bomba" Tomba trains in Sestola). The town caters to vacationers, but it doesn't succumb to the tackiness of most tourist resorts; its hotels and restaurants have maintained a subdued grace, as has its maze of narrow, shop-lined streets.

> **BASICS** • The **tourist office** supplies town and trail maps, hotel reservations and information, and anything and everything on outdoor activities. *Piazza Passerini 18, tel. 0536/62762. Open Tues., Wed., Fri., and Sat. 9–12:30 and 3–6; Thurs. and Sun. 9–12:30.*

> **COMING AND GOING** • Seven buses leave daily for Sestola (1½ hrs, L7900; transfer at Pavullo or Fondavalle) from Modena's bus station on Via Bacchini. The bus takes you to **Piazza Passerini**, the center of Sestola.

> **WHERE TO SLEEP AND EAT** • Sestola has a number of hotels, but they all require that you take full pension and charge about L70,000 per person; the nearby campground and *rifugio* (mountain hut) are a much better deal. **Camping Sestola** (Via Tintoria, tel. 0536/61208), on the back slope of town, is a tranquil and luxurious place that's packed with motor homes. In July and August you'll pay L15,000 a tent and L9000 a person; the rest of the year, prices drop to L12,000 per tent and L7000 per person. The campground is closed in October. The **rifugio** in Pian del Falco (Viale Europa 34, tel. 0536/61113 or 0544/992343), open June 10–September 30 and December 1–March 30, charges L70,000 for a double with bath. Pian del Falco is a 2-kilometer hike from Sestola, but you can take the ski lift (*see* Outdoor Activities, *below*) during ski season. For typical Emilian mountain specialties, such as *tagliatelle ai porcini* (pasta with mushrooms), try **Il Faggio** (Via Liberta 68, tel. 0536/61566; closed Mon.).

> **OUTDOOR ACTIVITIES** • Of the many **hiking** and **mountain-biking** trails, the most beautiful and popular is Trail 6, leading from Sestola to Monte Cimone. At an elevation of 2,165 meters, Monte Cimone is the highest peak in the area and is topped by snow most of the year. The trail begins at Via delle Ville just off Piazza Passerini. **Ski** season in Sestola and the Monte Cimone area lasts from Christmas to Easter. Cimone, Doccia, Piandelagotti, Piane di Mocogno, and Sant'Anna Pelago are the five major resorts, and one L30,000 ticket entitles you to ski at all of them. Cimone is the biggest and the best, and all except Doccia have cross-country circuits in addition to downhill. Directly beneath the tourist office, **Pool 2000 Sport** (Piazza Passerini 18, tel. 0536/62372) rents sturdy mountain bikes for L25,000 a day, open daily 8–1 and 5–8. They also rent skis for L18,000 a day, boots included. A **ski lift** (Via Statale Ovest, to the right of Piazza Passerini) runs from Sestola to Pian del Falco and is equipped to carry bikes, allowing you to bypass the most excruciating part of the ride. During ski season, a bus will take you from Pian del Falco, where the lift lets you off, to Passo del Lupo, where you can catch lifts farther up the mountain to Pian Cavallaro (L5000 round-trip). At 1,827 meters, Pian Cavallo allows incredible views of Lombardy and the Veneto.

Parma

In spacious Parma, a town of parks, piazze, and Parmesan cheese, flawlessly dressed locals leisurely pedal their bicycles over the cobbled streets, giving the visitor a sense of what Italian life is supposed to be about. The city, an hour west of Bologna, boasts the highest standard of living in Italy and manifests its style in everything it does. Life ambles along at the unhurried pace of the well fed, and many visitors have to drag themselves out of Parma's excellent restaurants in order to get any sightseeing done. It's worth the effort though: Parma is home to the internationally renowned opera house, the Teatro Regio, and a vast collection of artworks by hometown boys Correggio and Parmigianino.

Parma's unparalleled elegance is a product of its past. The outlandishly decadent Renaissance court of the Farnese dukes (who controlled the city from 1545 to 1731) spoiled themselves on the riches of the region while mercilessly oppressing their subjects. Following the Farnese, the home fires were kept burning by Napoleon's widow (Marie-Louise of Austria), then a great patron of the arts. She continued to develop Parma's cultural richness during her 30-year reign, but without the Farnese brand of cruelty. The resulting wealth and prosperity would seem to put Parma beyond the reach of budget travelers, but the youth hostel and campground, plus free summer concerts in the churches and piazze, make almost every aspect of Parma's opulence available.

BASICS The helpful, centrally located **tourist center** hands out maps and festival information in six languages. *Piazza Duomo 5, tel. 0521/234735. From Piazza Pilotta, turn left on Strada Pisacane (which turns into Strada al Duomo), and follow it to Piazza Duomo. Open weekdays 9–12:30 and 3–5, Sat. 9–12:30.*

COMING AND GOING Hourly trains pass through Parma's **train station** (Piazzale C. A. dalla Chiesa, Via Altissimo 11, tel. 0521/771118) on their way to Milan (1½ hrs, L10,500), Bologna (1 hr, L7200), Ancona (5 hrs, L20,400), and Rome (6 hrs, L50,700). Luggage storage (L1500) is open 6:30 AM–7:10 PM. Parma has two **bus stations** right down the road from each other, and all buses leaving the city stop at both. The first (and most useful) is just a booth in front of the train station; the ticket and information window (tel. 0521/273251) is open daily 6 AM–7:20 PM. Beside the river and behind Palazzo della Pilotta is the second bus station (Viale Toschi 2, tel. 0521/285861), popular with commuters; what it lacks in information, it makes up for in parking spaces. Bus tickets are sold at the bar in the station Monday–Saturday 7 AM–8 PM.

GETTING AROUND The **River Parma** bisects the city into east–west halves, and most tourist destinations, sights, and lodgings lie on the eastern side. To reach the city center from the train station, take Bus 9 to Piazza Garibaldi. If you'd rather make the 15-minute walk, follow Via Verdi from the train station until you cross under the arches of the Palazzo della Pilotta and find yourself in the shadow of the hulking fortress. To get to Piazza Garibaldi, turn left down Via Melloni, at Piazza Duomo turn right on Strada Cavour; 4 blocks south is Piazza Garibaldi.

WHERE TO SLEEP Most of Parma's hotels are geared toward people with fat wallets; even the cheaper places reflect the city's high standard of living. You'll find a couple of affordable hotels within spitting distance of the train station and a couple more in the heart of town, near Piazza Garibaldi. The **Albergo Croce di Malta** (Borgo Palmia 8, tel. 0521/235643) offers clean, spacious doubles (L60,000) above a street-level restaurant. You can't beat the location; from Piazza Garibaldi, follow Via Farini for a block and turn right on Borgo Palmia. The hotel is closed Sunday unless you've made previous arrangements. The **Albergo Moderno** (Via A. Cecchi 4, tel. 0521/772647), a couple doors down from the train station, has clean and attractive doubles (L66,300). The expensive **Hotel Astoria** (Via Trento 9) will help you find their hidden satellite hotel, **Hotel Brozzi** (Via Trento 11, off Via Altissimo, tel. 0521/272717). The furniture looks like it came from a flea market, and some of the beds aren't much better than cots, but you'll pay only L50,000 for a double.

From May through September the 16th-century Farnese citadel becomes the **HI Ostello Cittadella**. The six-bed rooms (L15,000 per person) are gritty, and you have to ask the proprietor for toilet paper before using the facilities, but the hot showers are free. And remember, the citadel was originally built as a prison, so don't think you can sneak in after the 11 PM curfew. The hostel also has areas for **camping**, but at L8000 per person and L6500 per tent, a single-tent camper will end up paying only L500 less than for a bed in the hostel. *Via*

Passo Buole, tel. 0521/581546. From station, take Bus 9 for 15 min, follow sign for ostello. Lockout 9:30–5.

FOOD As the production center of parmigiano reggiano and prosciutto, this city screams *mangia!* (eat!). The highest concentration of eateries—pizzerias, trattorias, osterias—is found in the Piazza Garibaldi/Piazza Duomo area, but you'll pay extra for the scenery. For lunch fixings at one-third the price of a ready-made sandwich, head to the **outdoor market** in Piazza Ghiaia, just south of the Palazzo della Pilotta. The fruit and vegetable stalls in the center of the piazza are open all day Monday–Saturday, and the covered market in the corner is open weekdays 7–1, Saturday 1–3. Or stop by Parma's oldest food shop, **Salumeria Specialità di Parma** (Strada Farini 9/C, tel. 0521/233591) and pick up some of the city's finest meat, cheese, and pasta, and a bottle of *malvasia*, a sparkling white wine produced in the region.

Enoteca Fontana. You'll find all the flavors of Parma for reasonable prices in this beautifully simple tavern. Sample the famous prosciutto crudo (L4500), or try Mr. Ed on bread—*pesto di cavallo panino* (mashed horse meat sandwich; L3500). Thirsty? Choose from over 100 wines (only L1400–L2200 per glass) and plop down at one of their long communal tables. *Via Farini 24/A, tel. 0521/286037. From Piazza Garibaldi, walk 2 blocks down Via Farini. Open daily noon–10. AE, MC, V.*

Mensa Università. A full *pasto* (meal) here includes a primo, secondo, contorno, bread, fruit, wine, and dessert for only L9200 (L12,500 without student ID). The atmosphere here is pure cafeteria, but the staff is ultrafriendly, and the food is more than worth the money. Unfortunately, the mensa is open for lunch only from mid-July to mid-September. *Vicolo Grossardi 4, tel. 0523/213638. From Palazzo della Pilotta, cross Ponte Verdi to west side of river, turn left on Via Farnese, then right on Via Tanzi, which turns into Borgo Rodolfo and takes you to the building; the mensa is on the 2nd floor. Open weekdays 11:40–2 and 6:40–8:30, Sat. 11:40–2.*

Ristorante Taverna Galla d'Oro. Sit at a table tucked among casks and crates of wine and enjoy the incredible *tris di tortelli* (three types of tortellini stuffed with pumpkin, potato, and ricotta with spinach; L10,000). Primi go for L8000–L11,000, secondi L10,000–L12,000. A half-liter of the restaurant's own label of Lambrusco is only L6000. *Borgo della Salina 3, tel. 0521/208846. From Piazza Garibaldi, take Strada Farini and turn left on Borgo della Salina almost immediately. Open Mon.–Sat. noon–2:30 and 8–11. AE, MC, V.*

WORTH SEEING For a town this size, Parma is full of important sights, most of which are located within easy walking distance of each other.

➤ **BAPTISTRY** • The only church in Parma that can get away with charging an entrance fee, Parma's medieval pink baptistry is truly unique. The 12th-century, octagonal, marble structure, which bridges the gap between Romanesque and Gothic architecture, contains sculptures symbolizing the seasons (around the upper ledge) and reliefs of animals and mythical beasts (on the exterior) by Benedetto Antelami. A single chamber rises to a beautiful dome, covered with frescoes of the apostles. *Piazza Duomo. Admission: L4000, L1000 students. Open daily 9–12:30 and 3–6.*

➤ **CAMERA DI SAN PAOLO** • The highly decorated frescoes found here were painted as a protest against the ever-growing papal power that threatened this convent's independence. Correggio and Araldi were commissioned for the job by an avant-garde humanist abbess, Giovanna Piacenza. *Via Melloni 3, tel. 0521/233309. From Piazza Pilotta, follow Via Melloni; it's on the left, in a recessed courtyard. Admission free. Open daily 9–7:30.*

➤ **CHURCH OF SAN GIOVANNI EVANGELISTA** • This church, part of the Benedictine monastery next door, is filled with works by Correggio and Parmigianino. Inside is yet another controversial fresco by Correggio that predates the one in the duomo by six years. The cloister houses an ancient **pharmacy** (Borgo Pipa 1, tel. 0521/233309) that produced herbal medicines and cures as early as the 13th century, and still contains recipes and weighing devices. *Piazzale San Giovanni, tel. 0521/235592. From Piazza Pilotta, head toward duomo along Strada Pisacane and continue right of the duomo. Church admission free. Pharmacy admission: L4000. Open daily 6:30–noon and 3:30–8.*

➤ **CHURCH OF SANTA MARIA DELLA STRECCATA** • The ethereal 16th-century Church of Santa Maria della Steccata, built in the shape of a Greek cross, is home to the tombs of the Farnese dukes and a pair of organ doors by Parmigianino. Its cupola was frescoed by Bernardo Gatti in the tradition of Correggio's perspective realism, but Gatti seems to have been more interested in propriety than reality. *Via Garibaldi, between Via Dante and the Piazzale Steccata, tel. 0521/234937. From Piazza Pilotta, follow Via Garibaldi south 3 blocks. Admission free. Open daily 9–noon and 3–6.*

➤ **DUOMO** • Built in the mid-11th century, the duomo is noteworthy for its Romanesque triangular facade and the striking frescos that cover nearly every inch of the interior wall space. One such fresco is Correggio's *Ascension of the Virgin,* famous for its radical and innovative perspective, which leaves the Virgin apparently suspended in space, providing some pretty risqué views up her billowing skirt. The duomo also contains the *Deposition,* the first sculpture by Benedetto Antelami. *Piazza Duomo, tel. 0521/235886. From Piazza Pilotta, follow Strada Pisacane, which turns into Strada al Duomo and leads into Piazza Duomo. Admission free. Open daily 9–noon and 3–7.*

Correggio's "The Martyrdom of Four Saints" in the Galleria Nazionale stands out because of its twisted nature; angels circle overhead like vultures, while saints beam in orgasmic ecstasy as they're slashed, skewered, decapitated, and stabbed.

➤ **PALAZZO DELLA PILOTTA** • A symbol of ducal absolutism, the Palazzo della Pilotta dominates the banks of the Parma River. Jagged remnants of walls that were shelled to oblivion during World War II are visible as you pass under the Pilotta's archways. Inside the palazzo, the **Teatro Farnese**, a lavishly sculpted and frescoed court theater, exemplifies the Farnese penchant for overstatement. The theater is open daily 9–7:30, and admission is L5000. The **Galleria Nazionale** (open daily 9–1:45), entered through the theater, is a showcase for Correggio and Parmigianino. In the back of the museum, Leonardo da Vinci's drawing, *Head of a Young Girl,* unobtrusively faces a wall. The gallery's L10,000 admission price includes a look at the Teatro Farnese. *Palazzo della Pilotta, tel. 0521/233309. From train station, follow Via Verdi 6 blocks.*

➤ **PARCO DUCALE** • Need a dose of nature? Directly across the river from the Palazzo della Pilotta, the ducal park is yet another flourish of Farnese grandeur. With its marble statues, large duck pond, and kiddie playground, it's the best spot in town for a picnic, especially if you buy food at the market in the nearby Piazza Ghiaia (*see Food, above*). *Parco Ducale. Open May–Aug., daily 6 AM–midnight; Sept.–Apr., daily 7–6.*

CHEAP THRILLS In August, Parma celebrates all things cheesy during the annual parmesan festival. Cheesemongers set up cheese and snack booths in the main piazze, and free concerts are held in castles surrounding the city. For more information, pick up a free brochure at the tourist office. If you're really a cheese fanatic, call **Consortio di Parmigiano** (Via Gramsci 26/A, tel. 0521/292700) one week in advance and reserve a space for a free guided tour of the cheese factory and a plate full of samples. If you're more of a ham fan, the **Consortio di Prosciutto** (Via M. Dell'Arpa 8/B, tel. 0521/208187) offers a similar tour—graciously leaving out the unpleasantries of the ham-making process.

NEAR PARMA

TORRECHIARA Torrechiara is the most spectacular of the many castles around Parma. Remodeled in the 15th century, the immense, walled fortress with crenellated towers stands on a hill overlooking the fertile farmlands south of Parma. The structure is composed of vast courtyards, chamber after frescoed chamber, and grassy terraces among turrets and arcaded walks. *Castello di Torrechiara, Langhirano, tel. 0521/355255. Admission: L5000. Open Tues.–Sat. 9–1, Sun. 9–1 and 3–7.*

To reach the castle, take a Langhirano bus from either of Parma's bus stations (40 min, L3600 one-way). These leave almost hourly between 6:30 AM and 5:30 PM. When your stomach starts makin' noise, head for **Taverna del Castello** (Strada al Castello 25, tel. 0521/355121), which is built into the castle's former dungeon and has retained a medieval flavor. Meals are a bit expensive, but you can get a pizza or a primo for L7000–L10,000.

Piacenza

Piacenza may not be as popular a tourist destination as it was 900 years ago, when it was the economic center of the Carolingian empire, but it's still well worth a visit. The tiny city center was built around self-aggrandizing works commissioned by the Farnese dynasty, and today the area fairly bursts with frescoes and belltowers built by the region's most important artists, including Guercino and Alberti. Due to its small size, Piacenza can be explored in a day, but plan which day you visit carefully; Piacentine Thursdays are veritable Italian Sundays (everything closes and the city seems to move at a snail's pace), while Wednesdays the streets teem with market-day merchants. Whatever you do, don't miss the city's eccentricities, such as its citizens' French-influenced accents (a leftover from the Gaul traders) and its strangest museum piece, a bronzed sheep's liver purported to have magical properties.

BASICS A good source of information is the publication, *Tutto Città*, which is full of detailed city maps and up-to-date info on Piacenza's goings-on; you can pick up a free copy at the main **SIP** office (Corso Vittorio Emanuele II 118, tel. 0523/229544), open weekdays 8:30–12:15 and 2:15–4. Piacenza's **tourist information** office is built into the side of Il Gotico, Piazza dei Cavalli's double-decker brick-and-stone palace. *Piazzetta del Mercanti 10, tel. 0523/29324. From Piazza Duomo, take Via XX Settembre to Piazza dei Cavalli; the adjacent Piazzetta is to the left. Open Mon.–Sat. 9–12:30 and 4–6; closed Thurs. afternoon.*

COMING AND GOING From Piacenza, hourly trains run to Milan (40 min, L5900) and Parma (½ hr, L4500). The **train station** (Piazzale Marconi 19, tel. 0523/20637), on the eastern edge of town, has an exchange desk (open daily 7 AM–7:30 PM) and luggage storage (open daily 8 AM–8:20 PM). The walk to the center of town takes about 15 minutes. To reach Piazza dei Cavalli and Piazzetta del Mercanti, the two joined piazze at the heart of the city, cross diagonally through the park opposite Piazzale Marconi (in front of the train station); on the opposite side of the park, follow Via Alberoni to the right and turn left on Via Legnano, which leads into Piazza Duomo; from here Via XX Settembre leads straight to Piazza dei Cavalli.

WHERE TO SLEEP Piacenza's accommodation situation leaves a lot to be desired, but at least the budget hotels are central. The **Hotel Moderno** (Via Tibini 3, tel. 0523/385041) has clean, modern doubles without bath for L45,000. Reception is closed 1 PM–7 PM. The furniture at **Hotel Corona** (Via Roma 141, tel. 0523/320948) is a bit shaky, but the rooms are well kept. Doubles without bath cost L60,000, and there's a trattoria downstairs. Call ahead if you plan to check in on a Wednesday. To reach the Corona, take Viale dei Mille from the station.

FOOD True to the spirit of Emilia-Romagna, eating in Piacenza is considered as much of an art as cooking. The narrow streets south of Piazza dei Cavalli are filled with great restaurants, and if you've ever felt hungry enough to eat a horse, here's your chance. Regional specialties include lasagna, *picola di cavallo* (minced horse meat), and *pisarei* (dumpling pasta with beans and mushrooms), best washed down with the local wine, Colli Piacentino. The friendly signora at **Trattoria da Pino** (Via del Castello 14, tel. 0523/334729) serves the aforementioned delicacies as part of a fixed-price menu for L25,000–L30,000, Monday–Saturday. The restaurant is always packed with locals waiting to taste her latest creation. **Ristorante Balzer** (Piazzetta del Mercanti 1, tel. 0523/331041) also serves regional specialties for similiar prices Friday–Wednesday. Try to get one of the outdoor tables so you can check out the action in ironically named Piazza dei Cavalli (Plaza of the Horses). For a more pious view, grab a pizza (L6000–L10,000) at **Pizzeria da Pasquale** (Piazza Duomo 36, tel. 0523/24669; closed Thurs.), across from the duomo.

WORTH SEEING Most of Piacenza's sights are clustered around **Piazza dei Cavalli**, the social and governmental seat of town; the area is filled with artistic representations of the egotistical Farnese and their attempts to immortalize themselves. The square itself is home to a pair of early 17th-century equestrian statues by Francesco Mochi, likenesses of Alessandro Farnese and his son Ranuccio stoically standing guard in front of **Il Gotico**. The 13th-century Gothic palace is the square's central and most fantastic structure; unfortunately, the elaborate mesh of archways and battlements is not open to the public. The medieval **Church of San Francesco** (Piazza dei Cavalli 70, tel. 0523/21988), a stylistic complement to the great palace, sits to the side of Il Gotico. The Lombard Romanesque **duomo** (Piazza Duomo, tel. 0523/335154), looming over the piazza with three large doors and a rose window, contains a cupola frescoed by Guercino, frescoes by Carracci, a painting of St. Jerome by Guido Reni, and northern Italy's darkest, dankest crypt.

The 16th-century **Palazzo Farnese** houses the **Museo Civico**, with an inordinate number of works glorifying Alessandro Farnese, mercenary turned pope. The museum also houses Botticelli's *Madonna and Child*, but the main attraction is the bizarre *Fegato Etrusco*, an ancient bronzed sheep liver engraved with Etruscan stellar systems and used by priests to predict storms, marriages, deaths, and Elvis sightings. *Piazza Cittadella, tel. 0523/28270. Admission: L5000. Open Tues.–Sat. 9–12:30 (Thurs. afternoon 3:30–5:30), Sun. 9:30–noon and 3:30–6:30.*

One of Italy's finest collections of 19th- to 20th-century Italian art is hidden away in Piacenza's **Galleria Ricci Oddi** (Via San Siro 13, off Corso Vittorio Emanuele II, tel. 0523/320742), including two paintings by Klimt. The gallery is open Tuesday–Sunday 10–noon and 3–8. Not an inch of the interior of the **Church of Santa Maria di Campagna** (Piazzale Crociate 5, off Via Campagna, tel. 0523/490728) remains unfrescoed, and the effect is dizzying. The cupola by Pordenone is particularly spectacular.

FESTIVALS Every Saturday the entire teen population of Piacenza pours into Il Corso and Via 20 Settembre for the 1,000-year-old **vasche**, or fishbowl, so named because of the frenzied and repetitive aspect of this evening walk. The bizarre stampede of gelato-slurping ragazzi (young'uns) heads up one side of the street and back down the other giggling maniacally all the while.

Ferrara

It doesn't take much of an imagination to figure out what Ferrara looked like during its heyday as the court of the Este family; the city fairly glitters with palaces left behind by the ruthless Renaissance dukes. The grand residences, however, present only one face of Ferrara. The dark knot of alleys in the medieval quarter, the labyrinth of arch-covered streets, and the silent churches all evoke a vivid sense of how most of the city's citizens were living while the tyrannical Este dukes built themselves pleasure palaces, threw lavish parties, and patronized the great artists and poets of the age. While Ariosto, Tasso, Cellini, and Copernicus dined and danced in the palace, the peasants were living like sardines, taxed to the heavens to support the extravagance of the Este. This rapacious noble family controlled Ferrara from the early 13th century until 1598, when they found themselves without a legitimate heir. The ever-hungry papacy intervened, and the Este fled to Modena, carrying a great many of their court's treasures with them. Today, the decrepit churches and palazzi, abandoned by their occupants and empty of their riches, offer an atmospheric though somewhat sad glimpse into the city's past.

BASICS You can change money at **Banco Credito Italiano** (Corso Martiri della Libertà 51, tel. 0532/207440) and **Banco Nazionale di Lavoro** (Corso Porta Reno 19, tel. 0532/781674). Both are open 8:30–1:30 and 3:15–4, and charge a L3000 commission. Be sure to stop at the helpful **tourist office** to pick up maps, get information on museums and hotels, or rent a bike. *Corso Giovecca 21, tel. 0532/209370. From station, veer left on Viale Costituzione until it turns into Viale Cavour (which becomes Corso Giovecca). Open Mon.–Sat. 9–1 and 2:30–7, Sun. 9–1.*

COMING AND GOING Ferrara lies on the Bologna–Venice line, about a half hour from Bologna (hourly, L4200) and an hour from Venice (hourly, L9200). Another line connects Ferrara with Ravenna (1 hr, L5700) and Rimini (1½ hrs, L8800), with trains passing through about once every two hours. Ferrara's **train station** (Piazzale Stazione 20–26, tel. 0532/770340) is a 20-minute walk from the center of town and the Castello Estense. Luggage storage (L1500) is open daily 8–8.

GETTING AROUND Ferrara is divided in half by **Viale Cavour**, which becomes **Corso Giovecca** as it passes Castello Estense, the tremendous moated fortress. To the south of Viale

Cavour, with the castle and cathedral, is a chaotic medieval city; the north side was added during the Renaissance and is a carefully planned town filled with stately palazzi and wide avenues. The best way to see the city is by bicycle. Rent one at the tourist office by the hour (L6000) or by the day (L20,000) and save 20% on museum entrance. The rental office is open 9:30–7:30 daily.

Ferrara's train station is on the western edge of town: To reach Castello Estense on foot, take Viale Costituzione to Viale Cavour; Bus 1, 2, or 9 will also get you there. If you stay on Bus 2 a stop or two past the castle, it will drop you off amid the small clump of budget lodgings in the Piazza Cattedrale/Piazza Trento Trieste area. Bus 9 continues down Corso Giovecca to most of the city's sights. To reach the Renaissance addition, take Bus 3 from Corso Porta Reno (just south of Piazza Cattedrale). Most buses run 6 AM–11 PM, and bus tickets (L1100) can be found in any tabacchi.

WHERE TO SLEEP **Albergo Alfonsa.** At press time this small, central motel was undergoing large-scale renovation—when the face-lift is complete, it should be one of the nicest budget alberghi in Ferrara. If you don't cough too loudly, the few rooms open shouldn't collapse. Doubles, all with bath, go for L60,000. *Via Padiglioni 5, tel. 0532/205726. From station, head down Viale Cavour, turn left on Corso Ercole; Via Padiglioni is the first right.*

Albergo Santo Stefano. Two minutes from both the castle and the cathedral on a pleasant, shop-lined street, this hotel is simple, small, and well kept. A double without bath costs L62,000. A bar, just off the lobby, serves hot coffee and fresh pastries in the morning. *Via Santo Stefano 21, tel. 0532/206924. From Piazza Cattedrale, take Via Cortevecchia to Piazza Sant'Etienne and turn left on Via Santo Stefano. Curfew 2 AM. MC, V.*

Albergo Stazione. Directly across from the train station, this hotel is built over two arches that let a trickle of traffic in and out of the small piazza. The large rooms are furnished with heavy oak beds and desks, but the atmosphere stops with the rooms; the lobby is almost nonexistent, and the outside of the building and surrounding area are charmless. Doubles without bath go for L50,000. *Piazza Castellina 1, tel. 0532/56565. From train station, walk straight ahead under archways of Piazza Castellina. Curfew 1 AM.*

Albergo Tre Stelle. Don't be misled by the name; this is a one-star hotel in every sense of the word. It's also the cheapest hotel in Ferrara (L25,000 singles, L38,000 doubles, all without bath), with a great location just five minutes from the castle and cathedral. The rooms are dark, dingy, and a little worn around the edges, but at least they're spacious. *Via Vegri 15, tel. 0532/209748. From Piazza Cattedrale, follow Via Cortevecchia and head right as it becomes Contrada Borgo Ricco and later Cia Mercato; turn left on Via Vegri. Curfew 1 AM. Reservations advised.*

Casa degli Artisti. Light streams through enormous windows into the impeccably clean rooms (L40,000 doubles without bath). Each floor has a kitchenette with refrigerator and stove, the showers are the size of a large bathroom, and you can look out over the tiled roofs of Ferrara from the rooftop patio. *Via Vittoria 66, tel. 0532/761038. From Piazza Trento Trieste, south on Via San Romano, left on Via Ragno, and left again on Via Vittoria.*

➤ **CAMPING** • **Camping Estense.** Neither terribly convenient nor terribly attractive, this campground on the outskirts of town is not much cheaper than the hotels and much harder to reach. It's L8400 per tent (L9200 July and August), plus L5000 per person. The campground itself is a shadeless grass lot at the edge of farmland, and the hike from the nearest bus stop is 20 minutes of hard walking. They rent bikes for only L8000 per day. *Via Gramicia 80, tel. 0532/752396. From station or Corso Giovecca (a little east of castle), Bus 1 to Borgo Punta and ask driver when to get off (last bus 8:20). From here, walk along Via Calzolai to Via Pannonio, turn left, and you'll see signs. Turn right on Via Gramicia; the campground is about ¼ km ahead on right. Curfew 10 PM. Closed Nov.–Apr.*

FOOD The medieval neighborhood abounds with restaurants, as well as markets and shops for putting together your own meal. **Via Cortevecchia**, off Piazza Cattedrale, is stocked with *pasticcerie* (pastry shops), *forni* (bakeries), *salumerie* (delis), cheese shops, fruit and veggie stands, and candy stores. Just down the road, the **Mercato Coperto** (Via Santo Stefano 14/E) has stalls selling all sorts of food and wine Monday–Saturday 7–1:30 (Friday also 4:30–7).

Ferrara's cuisine doesn't stray much from the typical regional dishes, but you will find a couple of distinctly Ferrarese delicacies, including *salama da sugo* (a big sausage ball soaked in wine) and *pampapato* (chocolate-covered fruitcake). Nearly every restaurant in the city serves rich and delicious tagliatelle with ham and peas, a primo that goes nicely with the typical wine, *vino del Bosco Eliceo*. **Mezzaluna Enoteca Gastronomica** (Via Terranuova 60–62, tel. 0532/209151) prides itself on its wine, but the cuisine is anything but unremarkable. Primi usually go for L8000–L11,000, and the ambience surpasses that of all other restaurants in town. **Pizzeria Orsucci** (Via Garibaldi 76, tel. 0532/205391), open Thursday–Tuesday noon–3 and 5–midnight, serves terrific pizzas, typical Ferrarese pastas, and hearty secondi for good prices (L6000–L9000). **Osteria al Brindisi** (Via degli Adelardi 11, next to cathedral, tel. 0532/37015) has been the place for the Ferrarese to get tipsy since 1435. It's earned itself a place in the *Guinness Book of World Records* as the world's oldest wine bar, serving up wine, grappa, whiskey, and port. They also provide sandwiches (L4000–L6000) to give your stomach a fighting chance. **Mensa Universitaria** (Corso Giovecca 154, tel. 0532/206401), in the southeast part of town, serves full meals for L9100, Monday–Saturday noon–2 and 7:15–8:45. Technically, non-University of Ferrara students can't enter, but employees aren't usually too particular.

WORTH SEEING Ferrara's sights are clustered in three main areas: the medieval quarter south of Corso Giovecca, the southeast additions that grew in the 14th and 15th centuries, and the stately Renaissance city of Ercole I d'Este that began stretching the city northward in the late 15th century.

➢ **THE MEDIEVAL QUARTER** • The medieval center of Ferrara preserves a sense of history better than any city in the region: Its web of narrow alleys is twistier, its ancient buildings crumblier. The **Via delle Volte**, with its canopy of arches is an excellent example of a typical medieval thoroughfare.

Castello Estense. It's a testament to the tyrannical policies of the Renaissance rulers that one of the country's most magnificent fortified castles was never meant to protect the city from outside invasion, but rather the dukes from their subjects. Niccolò II d'Este ordered the castle built in 1385 after a citizens' revolt over unjust taxation left the minister of finance dead. At the time of its construction, the castle stood at the extreme northern edge of town; today the massive redbrick fortress surrounded by a moat and drawbridges is the city centerpiece.

Within the fortress, the 16th-century ceiling frescoes in the **Sala dell'Aurora** depict Time in the center, surrounded by Aurora (Dawn), Sunset, and Night. The frescoes in the **Sala dei Giochi** (Game Room) portray muscular nude men and fat cupids playing various games. There's a small Protestant chapel (Duke Ercole II's wife was Protestant) and a throne room to admire, but the most intriguing part of the castle's interior is its dark **dungeon**, reached via a rickety staircase that runs through a trapdoor. Descend into the creepy low-ceilinged corridor and crouch through half-size doorways into the cells where the dungeon's celebrity denizens languished: Nicolò III d'Este's young wife Parisina Malatesta and her lover Ugo d'Este (Niccolò's son) were beheaded for adultery, but not before being imprisoned here, in separate chambers of course. *Tel. 0532/299279. Admission: L10,000. Open Tues.–Sat. 9:30–12:30 and 1:30–6:30, Sun. 10–6.*

Cattedrale di San Giorgio. Ferrara's cathedral is spectacularly unusual in design; its facade is divided into three symmetrical sections and laced with carved illustrations of the Last Judgement. The cathedral was begun in 1135; the campanile, designed by Leon Battista Alberti, was added in 1412 and remains unfinished. Check out the long **Loggia of the Merchants** along the length of the Piazza Trento Trieste side, added in the 18th century. To see the sculptures that were removed to make way for this addition, climb the steps at the cathedral entrance to the **Museo del Duomo.** *Piazza Cattedrale, tel. 0532/207449. Admission free. Cattedrale open daily 7:30–noon and 3–6:30. Museo del Duomo open Mon.–Sat. 10–noon and 3–5.*

➢ **EAST OF THE MEDIEVAL QUARTER** • The amazing cluster of palazzi in this area of town can be squeezed into a morning or afternoon of sightseeing. Bus 1 or 9 will take you from the train station or the castle down Corso Giovecca, a good starting point for seeing this section of the city.

Casa Romei. This villa once belonged to Giovanni Romei, a wealthy banker who married into the Este family, and still looks much like it did when built in 1445. Inside the palazzo you'll find two peaceful courtyards, a lovely loggia, and walls covered with 15th-century frescoes. The villa is now an orphanage for statues and frescoes rescued from decaying churches. *Via Savonarola 30, tel. 0532/40341. From Castello Estense, walk down Corso Giovecca to Via Coramari and turn right; turn left on Via Savonarola. Admission: L5000. Open daily 10–5.*

Palazzina di Marfisa d'Este. With its large rooms, vaulted and frescoed ceilings, and beautiful wood furniture, this palazzina is easier to imagine as a residence than other Este palaces. When you enter the **Loggia degli Aranci**, look up at the vaulted ceiling, painted with an arbor of twisting grapevines. *Corso Giovecca 170, tel. 0532/207450. From Castello Estense, head straight down Corso Giovecca. Admission: L5000, L3000 students. Open daily 9–12:30 and 3–6.*

Palazzo di Ludovico il Moro. The palazzo was closed for restoration at press time, but pass by for a look at the palace's imposing brick exterior and a glimpse of its courtyard. The residence is attributed to Biagio Rossetti, a major architectural player in the city, and now houses the **Museo Archeologico Nazionale** (also closed indefinitely), containing artifacts from the Etruscan city of Spina. *Via XX Settembre 124, no phone. From Corso Giovecca, turn right on Via Ugo Bassi (changes names several times) and left on Via XX Settembre.*

Palazzo Paradiso. Fans of Ariosto won't want to miss the writer's tomb and the **Biblioteca Ariostea** (library), housed in a 14th-century palazzo. The library holds over 150,000 volumes, 3,400 prints, and 2,500 manuscripts written at the Este court. Highlights include a manuscript of *Orlando Furioso* and the illuminated astrological tables of Blanchinius. *Via Scienze 17, tel. 0532/207392. From Castello Ostense, head down Corso Giovecca and turn right on Via Terranuova, which becomes Via Scienze. Admission free. Open weekdays 9–7:30, Sat. 9–1.*

Palazzo Schifanoia. The palace's name, stemming from the Latin for "evade boredom," reveals the palace's function as a house of folly (one of many inhabited by the pleasure-loving Este family). Construction on Schifanoia began in 1385, but its impressive upper story with the magnificent **Sala dei Mesi** (Room of Months) was added by Borso d'Este from 1465 to 1469. Each month is painted in three sections: The upper section depicts mythical rebellion and revelry, the middle is filled with signs of the zodiac, and the large lower section contains scenes from the life of Borso d'Este. *Via Scandiana 23, tel. 0532/64178. From Castello Estense, follow Corso Giovecca, turn right on Via Ugo Bassi, and left on Via Scandiana. Admission: L6000, students free. Open daily 9–7.*

➤ **RENAISSANCE QUARTER** • During the 15th and 16th centuries, Duke Ercole I embarked on a major civic expansion project, employing architect Biagio Rossetti to design the new additions. The result is an extremely orderly and astoundingly symmetrical Renaissance town. Piazza Ariostea (off Corso Porta Mare) is the centerpiece of Rossetti's developments. Take a break from sightseeing and kick back on the piazza's terraced lawn, which is surrounded by grandiose palaces typical of Rossetti's style.

Church of San Cristoforo alla Certosa. Yet another Biagio Rossetti masterpiece, this church has long porticoed wings that sweep out like a pair of welcoming arms encircling the green lawns. The adjoining **Certosa cemetery**, added in 1813, contains rows of manicured grave sites topped with flowers and enclosed by porticoes. Try not to miss this quiet corner of the city. *Via Borso 1, tel. 0532/230161. From Castello Estense, take Corso Ercole I d'Este, turn right on Corso Porta Mare, and left on Via Borso. Open daily 8–8.*

Jewish Cemetery. Hands down the most peaceful spot in town, the old Jewish cemetery is the perfect place for a picnic, unorthodox as the suggestion may be. Here the grass grows wild, the tombstones lean at 45° angles, and the clumps of grave sites seem somewhat haphazard. Climb up on the wall for a view of San Cristoforo from behind. *Via Vigne. From Castello Estense, take Corso Ercole I d'Este, turn right on Corso Porta Mare, and left on Via Vigne. Admission free. Open Apr.–Sept., daily 8–6:30; Oct.–Mar., daily 9–4:30.*

Palazzo dei Diamanti. One look at this palace, covered in thousands of diamond-shaped marble stones, and you'll see why it's considered Rossetti's most outstanding work. Today the building houses the **Pinacoteca Nazionale**, filled with 13th- to 18th-century works by local artists; the lack of pieces from the city's 15th-century artistic heyday is the result of centuries of looting. The most outstanding works in the museum include the massive *Allegory of the Old and New Testament* by Garofalo and paintings by Dosso Dossi and Cosimo Tura. *Corso Ercole I d'Este 21, tel. 0532/205844. From Castello Estense, head straight down Corso Ercole I d'Este. Admission: L8000. Open Tues.–Sat. 9–2, Sun. 9–1.*

Palazzo Massari. Several museums are housed inside this grand residence, but the **Museo Documentario della Metafisica**, on the first floor, is the most compelling. Its highlights include reproductions of strange works by metaphysical painter Giorgio de Chirico and other 20th-century Italian artists. Upstairs, the **Museo Giovanni Boldini** contains works by modern figurative painter Giovanni Boldini, with about 150 of his best works spread throughout the magnificent palace. This exhibit flows into the **Museo Civico d'Arte Moderna**, which houses temporary shows and works of regional painters and sculptors. *Corso Porta Mare 9, tel. 0532/206914. From Castello Estense, follow Corso Ercole I d'Este to Corso Porta Mare and turn right. Admission to all 3 museums: L8000, L5000 students. Open daily 9:30–1 and 3:30–7.*

AFTER DARK Ferrara is home to a small university and, in turn, a good nightlife. Friendly Ferrarese students party on the river at **Birreria Sebastien** (Via Darsena 53/A, tel. 0532/768233), a floating pub. If solid ground is more your scene, you can check out live jazz every Thursday at **Non Sul Collo** (Via Cisterna del Follo 39, tel. 0532/47061; closed Mon.). Cover is L7000. To reach the club, head down Corso Giovecca, turn right on Via Bassi, and continue one block to Via Cisterna.

Ravenna

On the surface, Ravenna is much like other Italian cities, its narrow streets spiraling out from a palazzo-lined central piazza, bell towers poking into the sky. But Ravenna's treasure—what makes this city unique—is its mosaics. Griffins and peacocks, ships sailing for the Crusades, and an arc of midnight decked with stars glimmer on the walls and ceilings of Ravenna's basilicas, baptistries, and tombs. It was Byzantine emperor Justinian and his scandalous wife Theodora who brought the city to its artistic and cultural climax, creating the blend of East and West that gives Ravenna its unique appeal. However, Ravenna's romantic and dramatic aura comes not only from this legacy of artistic achievement, but also from the exiled geniuses who have lived here. Dante Alighieri, the brightest light in Italian literary history, lived in Ravenna while exiled from Florence, and Lord Byron, the brooding genius of romanticism, was hosted by a local noble family here for several years.

BASICS To change money, head to the banks in Piazza del Popolo or the **post office** (Piazza Garibaldi 1, tel. 0544/404270; open Mon.–Sat. 8–7), which charges a L3000 commission. The friendly folks at the main **tourist office** answer questions in English, give out maps, and make hotel reservations. *Via Salara 8, near Piazza del Popolo, tel. 0544/35404. Open Mon.–Sat. 8:45–1:45 and 3–6, Sun. 9–12:40 and 3–6.*

For youth-oriented information, stop by the **Informa Giovane** office. They'll tell you what the Ravennese youth do for fun and can even supply you with computer printouts of all the town's pubs and seaside discothèques. *Via Guido da Polenta 4, tel. 0544/36494. From Piazza del Popolo, cut south through Piazza Garibaldi to Via Alighieri and turn right on Via Guido da Polenta. Open Mon. and Thurs. 9:30–1, Tues., Wed., and Fri. 9:30–1 and 3:30–6, Sat. 10–1.*

COMING AND GOING Trains arrive in Ravenna from Bologna (8 per day, 1 hr 20 min, L7200), Ferrara (12 per day, 1 hr 10 min, L6100), and Rimini (10 per day, 1 hr, L4200). The **train station** (Piazza Farini 13, tel. 0544/36450) has luggage storage (L1500 per piece) open daily 7:20–1 and 1:30–8:10. Most local and some long-distance buses leave from Piazza Farini, next to the train station. The **ATM** office (Piazza Farini, tel. 0544/35288), open daily 6:30 AM–8:30 PM sells bus tickets to Ravenna's beaches (hourly, 20 min, L1700) and the church of Sant'Apollinare in Classe (*see* Worth Seeing, *below;* hourly, 15 min, L1100). For cities outside Ravenna's provinces, buses leave from **Piazza Aldo Moro**, behind the station. The ticket window (Via Magazzini Anteriori 55, tel. 0544/420428), open Monday–Saturday 6:15 AM–9 PM, is in the white building across the piazza. Purchase tickets in advance, because they cost more if you buy them on the bus. Keep in mind though, that trains are faster, cheaper, and come a lot more often.

GETTING AROUND Ravenna's small centro storico spirals out from the main square, Piazza del Popolo; the train and bus stations are a 10-minute walk east. From the train station, walk straight down Via Farini, which becomes Via Diaz before spilling into Piazza del Popolo. Ravenna's sights are spread out, and the best way to explore is by bike; you can rent one to the left of the train station. The rental shop (Piazza Farini, tel. 0544/37031) is open Monday–Saturday 6:15 AM–8 PM, and bikes cost L2000 per hour, L12,000 per day. They also have city maps to get you started. If you're getting around town by bus, line **MB** (minibus) squeezes through the alleys of the city center, stopping near most of Ravenna's attractions. Buses leave every 10 minutes and stop in Piazza del Popolo, Piazza Caduti, and near the duomo. Tickets cost L1100 and are good for one trip.

WHERE TO SLEEP All of Ravenna's budget hotels are a two-minute walk from the train station and a 10-minute walk from the town center. The youth hostel is a little farther off, about a kilometer from the train station. If beaches and discothèques are your thing, the camp-grounds and cheaper hotels at Ravenna's beaches (*see* Near Ravenna, *below*) are your best option; they're only a 20-minute ride away via hourly bus.

Albergo al Giaciglio. The pleasant rooms here are randomly furnished, with footstools as night-stands and small bookshelves substituting for desks. The hall bathrooms are cramped (the sink showers with you), but you can get a well-maintained double without bath for only L43,000. For L25,000 you can have dinner in the great restaurant downstairs. *Via Brancaleone 42, tel. 0544/39403. Follow Via Farini out of Piazza Farini and turn right into Piazza Mameli; Via Brancaleone leads to the right. Midnight curfew. Closed 3 weeks at Christmas. V.*

Albergo Ravenna. Everything here—from the functional bedrooms to the modern hallway bath-rooms—is simply and tastefully decorated and always immaculate. The noise from the traffic in Piazza Farini is the only drawback, but all hotels around here have the same problem. They lock the doors at 12:30 AM, but you can ask for a key. Doubles without bath go for L60,000. *Via Maroncelli 12, tel. 0544/212204. From Piazza Farini, turn right down Via Maroncelli. V.*

Albergo Roma. Every room in this newly remodeled hotel comes with a television, phone, and bathroom. Doubles cost L77,000, and the useful management speaks English. *Via Candiano 26, tel. 0544/421515. From station, exit back way through underpass to Via Darsena, veer left at intersection. Open year-round. MC, V.*

➤ **HOSTELS • Ostello Dante (HI).** Big, noisy, friendly, and grungy, this hostel isn't cheap, but it's still half the price of any hotel in Ravenna: A bed is L16,000 per night (breakfast included). If slimy showers and gritty floors gross you out, splurge for a hotel. You'd also do best to skip the dinner option (L12,000). *Via Aurelio Nicolodi 12, tel. 0544/420405. From train sta-tion, Bus 1 to Via Molinetto, at Via Aurelio Nicolodi. 140 beds. Curfew 11 PM, lockout 9–6.*

FOOD Ravenna's cuisine reveals its Roman ancestry. Typical dishes include piadine and crescioni, both of which go well with the heavy red Sangiovese wine from the hills and the white Trebbiano. Ravenna's **Mercato Coperto** (Piazza Costa) overflows with fresh bread, cheese, fruits, and vegetables Monday–Saturday 7–1:30 and Friday 4:30–7:30. The **Mensa al Duomo** (Via Oberdan 8, off Piazza Duomo, tel. 0544/213688) serves simple but hearty cafeteria fare weekdays 11:45–2:50. The L10,500 buys you a primo, secondo, contorno, fruit, bread, and drinks.

Cà dè Vèn (Via C. Ricci 24, tel. 0544/30163) serves the ultimate in Ravennese cuisine in a beautiful wineshop next to Dante's Tomb. It's the hip spot of the moment, but the prices are still good, piadine costing L1500–L5000 and crescioni L3000–L4500. You can dine here Tuesday–Sunday 11–2 and 6–10:30. **Osteria Al Quattro Gatti** (Via P. Traversari 35, tel. 0544/212091), in the alley behind San Vitale, does its part to preserve local tradition with homemade pasta, carpaccio, and suckling pig that's roasted over a fireplace right in the dining room (Nov.–Mar. only). Directions and hours are complicated: From Piazza del Popolo, follow Via IV Novembre to Piazza Costa; turn left on Corso Cavour, right on Via Salara, left on Via San Vitale, and right on Via P. Traversari. The restaurant is open weekdays 12:30–3 and 7:30–11:30, Sunday 12:30–3, though it's closed Wednesdays September–May. You may have to wrestle a local for a table at **Ristorante la Gardela** (Via Ponte Marino 3, tel. 0544/217147), but it's definitely worth it. Delicious food goes for unbelievably cheap prices: L6000–L7000 for a primo and L8000–L10,000 for a secondo. It's open Friday–Wednesday noon–3 and 7–10.

WORTH SEEING A good way to see Ravenna's monuments is to rent a bike (see Getting Around, above), although walking is feasible. A special L9000 ticket will get you into all of Ravenna's mosaic attractions as well as the relatively uninteresting **Chiesa di Spirito Santo**; tickets are available at the Basilica di San Vitale, Basilica di Sant'Apollinare Nuovo, and the Neonian Baptistry. Although not quite as brilliant as Ravenna's mosaics, the town's unconventional, cylindrical campaniles are also worth a look-see.

➢ **BASILICA DI SANT'APOLLINARE IN CLASSE** • A 6th-century redbrick church a few kilometers outside Ravenna is one of the city's many monuments that has stood, decked out with incredible mosaics, for over a millennium. The lower portion of one mosaic depicts Ravenna's patron saint, St. Apollinare, in a pastoral setting—a symbol of the faithful being shepherded toward Christ. The upper part of the mosaic, in lustrous gold (achieved by applying real gold leaf to glass tesserae), portrays the transfiguration of Christ on Mt. Tabor. The four mythical creatures flying toward Christ in the apse, represent the Evangelists: John, the eagle; Matthew, the angel; Mark, the lion; and Luke, the calf. *Via Romea Sud, Classe, tel. 0544/527004. Bus 4 or 44 from Piazza Farini or Piazza Caduti. Admission free. Open daily 8–noon and 2–6.*

Ravenna's Mosaics

Ravenna's churches sparkle like no others in the Western world; the mosaics covering the walls and ceilings seem to come alive with gleaming lights. The mosaics are the product of highly technical skills that reached their peak in the 4th and 5th centuries. The glittering effect is achieved by carefully placing "tesserae" (bits of glass or calcareous rock) at uneven levels in the plaster base so that different colors catch the light at different angles. Most modern mosaic artists have abandoned this older, more difficult technique, and their works lack the shimmer of the ancient mosaics.

Ravenna's mosaic workshops, however, continue to use the old techniques, and you can watch the artists at work inside the courtyard of Basilica di San Vitale. Studio il Mosaico (Via Fiandrini 14, tel. 0544/36090) makes and sells reproductions of the city's most famous mosaics, as well as original pieces. Coop Mosaicisti Ravenna, next door, does primarily restoration work. You can watch artists at both studios chisel glass and fit it into elaborate designs 8–12:30 and 2:30–6. Call Giorgio La Pira (Via Bixio 1, tel. 0544/33696) for information on mosaic sights and workshops.

If you're so impressed by the mosaics you've seen in Ravenna that you want to pledge your life to the craft—or at least a couple of weeks—CISIM (Centro Internazionale di Studi per l'Insegnamento del Mosaico; Viale Parini 48, Lido Adriano, tel. 0544/494086) gives beginning and advanced courses in the art and charges L450,000–L550,000 for two weeks of instruction, at the end of which your efforts are yours to keep.

➤ **BASILICA DI SANT'APOLLINARE NUOVO** • The apse is bare in this 6th-century church, but the nave is festooned with mosaics. The left side of the church, where women sat during worship services, depicts a procession of virgin female saints offering gifts to the Virgin Mary, enthroned with the Christ child on her lap. All the figures in the procession, as well as in the procession of male saints opposite, are actual historic characters; dates and text give information about their martyrdom. On the men's side of the church, the saints offer crowns to an enthroned Christ. The small scenes along the very top of the nave date to the period of Theodoric and show scenes from the life of Christ. The first scene on the men's side of the church is the earliest-known artistic depiction of the Last Supper. *Via Carducci, tel. 0544/497629. From Piazza del Popolo, take Via Diaz to Via Roma, turn right and continue to cnr of Via Corducci. Admission: L4000. Open Apr.–Sept., daily 9–noon; Oct.–Mar., 9–4:30.*

➤ **BASILICA DI SAN VITALE** • One of the most glorious examples of Byzantine art in the West, this basilica is illuminated by the mind-bogglingly complex mosaics within. Unlike most Christian basilicas built on a cross plan, San Vitale is a hulking octagon, composed of an open central circle rising to a frescoed dome. Constructed in the 6th century, it's said to be where East meets West in Ravennese mosaic art. In the apse, Christ is portrayed young and uncharacteristically beardless, though the somber Christ overhead sports the usual facial hair. To the left, the Byzantine emperor Justinian is flanked by bishop Maximillian, who consecrated the church, and the empress Theodora, dripping with jewels. Note how the use of irregularly shaped tesserae gives them a more lifelike look than figures around them.

Just behind the basilica, a small and unremarkable brick building hides some of the city's— and the world's—most splendid mosaics. **Galla Placidia's mausoleum** (Via Fiandrini) ironically never contained her remains, which reside in Rome. Nevertheless, the mausoleum is a breath-taking spot filled with Roman classical mosaics portraying scenes of Christian salvation. Between the scenes, ribbons, leaves, geometrical designs, flowers, and circular patterns make the walls and ceilings vibrant with color; the vault is a sublime night sky decked with stars, the symbols of the four Evangelists decorating the corners. *Via San Vitale, tel. 0544/34266. From Piazza del Popolo, walk north on Via IV Novembre, turn left through Piazza Costa onto Via Cavour, take a right on Via Salara and a left on Via San Vitale. Admission to basilica and mausoleum: L4000. Open Apr.–Sept., daily 9–7; Oct.–Mar., daily 9–4:30.*

➤ **BATTISTERO DEGLI ARIANI** • The Arian Baptistry was built under Theodoric in the late 5th century, when Arianism was Ravenna's official religion (It was declared heresy 100 years later). The Catholics took over the bapistry in the 6th century, along with the neighboring Church of Spirito Santo. The remaining ceiling mosaic depicts the baptism of Christ in a cartoonlike style. *Piazzetta degli Ariani, no phone. From Piazza Farini, walk up Via Farini past Via Roma and turn right on Via Ariani. Admission free. Open daily 8:30–noon and 2:30– sunset.*

➤ **BATTISTERO NEONIAO** • The cathedral's baptistry is Ravenna's oldest monument. Begun in the 4th century, atop the foundations of an ancient Roman bathhouse, the baptistry was decorated with mosaics in the 5th century under Bishop Neone. Tucked behind the baptistry and the unimpressive duomo lies the **Museo Arcivescovile**, containing the Oratorio di Sant'Andrea, the marvelously decorated private chapel of the bishops. In the vault, four angels uphold the heavens, while above the door, Christ is shown as a warrior. The museum also houses Bishop Maximillian's carved ivory throne and mosaic fragments rescued from a demolished church. *Via Battistero, tel. 0544/33696. From Piazza del Popolo, walk through archway of Palazzo del Commune into Piazza XX Settembre and turn left down Via Rasponi, which ends in Piazza Duomo. Admission to baptistry and museum: L4000. Open Apr.–Sept., 9–7; Oct.–Mar., 9:30–4:30.*

➤ **TOMBA DI DANTE** • The humble proportions of this monument belie the scope of the battle that was waged between the Ravennese and Florentines for the remains of Italy's greatest poet. Dante made Ravenna his home several years after he was exiled from Florence in 1302; he died here in 1321. In the 16th century, the Florentines were given papal permission to take his body home. The monks of the attached **Basilica di San Francesco** (Piazza San Francesco, tel. 0544/33256) spirited it away in the night, and the Florentines never got their hands on it. Three hundred years later the poet was finally given a tranquil place of rest, and now an oil lamp burns perpetually with oil given ceremoniously by the resigned Florentines: a rite that takes place in the basilica every September 10. Inside, don't miss the sunken crypt; it's often flooded, and you can watch goldfish swim around over the mosaic floor. Through the gate, the **Museo Dantesco** (Via Dante Alighieri 4, tel. 0544/33667), open daily 9–noon and 3–6, contains a manuscript of the *Divine Comedy*, Dante memorabilia, and some minor works of art. Admission is L4000. *Via Dante Alighieri. From Piazza del Popolo, walk straight through Piazza Garibaldi and along Via Alighieri. Basilica admission free. Open daily 8–7.*

The inscription on Dante's tomb reads "Here in this corner lies Dante, exiled from his native land, born to Florence, an unloving mother," which pretty much sums up the Ravennese attitude about their rightful claim to Dante's body.

CHEAP THRILLS On the third weekend of every month, Ravenna explodes with antiques and handicrafts fairs throughout the center, and a small market selling organic products sets up shop on Piazza San Francesco. Free classical music concerts and theatrical performances take place outdoors in the central piazze from June 4 to August 30. Check the tourist office for schedules and information.

FESTIVALS From mid-June to the end of July, **Ravenna in Festival** hosts incredible performers such as Luciano Pavarotti, La Scala's orchestra, and the Emilia-Romagna Symphony, as well as ballet and dramatic performances in the town's piazze, theaters, and churches. Tickets can get outrageously expensive, but most shows also sell balcony seats at student prices (L10,000–L30,000). For tickets, call **Teatro Alighieri** (Via Mariani 2, just off Piazza Garibaldi, tel. 0544/32577) or pick up information here between 9 and noon. There are two **Ravenna Jazz Festivals**: April 15–17, and a larger one August 20–27. Both present big-name American artists like B. B. King and Lester "Big Daddy" Kinsey. Tickets run L25,000–L35,000 and can be bought at the **Palazzo Mauro de Andrè** (Viale Europa 1, tel. 0544/423194), quite a ways outside the center, or at **Tatum Dischi** (Via Cavour 107, west from Piazza Costa, tel. 0544/212842). Contact the tourist office for further information.

NEAR RAVENNA

RAVENNA'S BEACHES Ravenna's beaches are close enough (20 min by bus) to use as a base for exploring Ravenna while you take advantage of the seaside budget accommodations and raging nightlife. **Marina di Ravenna** has a little bit of everything: the best campground, some hopping discothèques and pubs, and a beach full of young people surfing (though there are more surfers than waves) and baking in the sun. **Lido Adriano** has a couple discos but is the least attractive of the three areas, and **Punta Marina** has campgrounds and beautiful beaches abutting a pine forest, but no real nightlife. **Visitor information** for the beaches is available at the main tourist office in Ravenna (*see* Basics, *above*).

➤ **COMING AND GOING** • Bus 70 from Ravenna's Piazza Farini hits Punta Marina and Marina di Ravenna twice hourly until 7:20 PM. Bus 71 leaves hourly from Piazza Farini for Punta Marina and Lido Adriano until 7:30 PM. Tickets cost L1700 each way and can be bought in tabacchi on Piazza Farini. Buses drop off and pick up passengers from nearly every *bagno* (beach club) on the *lungomare* (seafront street). The beaches are only separated by a few kilometers, and a good way to get around is to rent a **bike** for about L12,000 a day (in Marina di Ravenna, Viale dei Mille 27, no phone; in Punta Marina, Piazza Saffi 19, tel. 0544/437226; and in Lido Adriano, Viale Marziale 19 and Via Virgilio 6, no phone).

➤ **WHERE TO SLEEP AND EAT** • The tourist office in Ravenna can give you a list of the zillions of hotels in all three towns. **Regina** in Punta Marina (Via Fontana 73, south of Piazza Saffi, tel. 0544/437148) is the queen of budget hotels, with its great location and low prices (L70,000 for a double with bath). In Marina di Ravenna, **Albergo Adriatico** (Viale delle Nazioni 48, near breakwater, tel. 0544/530111) charges a rock-bottom L54,000 for a double with bath. For camping, the huge **Rivaverde** (Viale delle Nazioni 301, tel. 0544/530491; open April 25–Sept. 12), in Marina di Ravenna, sits just across from the beach in a quiet forest, only 10 minutes from pubs, discothèques, and restaurants. In July and August you'll pay L12,000 for a spot and L6000 per person; L8000 and L6000 respectively in other months. In Punta Marina, take Bus 71 to the adjacent **Park Adriano** (Via dei Campeggi 7, tel. 0544/437230) and **Coop 3** (Via dei Campeggi 8, tel. 0544/437353), both noisy, crowded, and squished up against the road. Both campgrounds charge L5000–L7000 per spot and L5000–L10,000 per person. Fortunately for foreign travelers, Italians aren't into "roughing it"—in all three sites, you'll find showers and electricity. Mediocre restaurants abound on Ravenna's beaches; for a truly yummy snack, head to any of the rolling carts along the lungomare, which sell fortifying **piadine** (L3000–L6000).

➢ **AFTER DARK** • Marina di Ravenna is where the action is. Pay the L10,000 cover and check out **Xenos** (Viale delle Nazioni 159, tel. 0544/530514), which rages every night in summer. Another nightly summer spot, **Santa Fe** (Viale delle Nazioni 180, tel. 0544/530740; no cover) is a terrific open-air dance club only 15 meters from the surf. Though slightly less hip, **Hemingway** (Via T. de Revel, at base of 2nd breakwater, tel. 0544/530681) offers a more relaxed atmosphere and food.

BRISIGHELLA Brisighella's trio of craggy peaks lift a castle, a battlemented clock tower, and a church up against the sky while the town stretches though the valleys and vineyards between them. In the Apennine foothills, where the green foliage is brilliant and the brick of ancient buildings glows russet and orange, this medieval village has a beauty like no other in Romagna. Brisighella is said to date back to the days of Galla Placidia, the Roman noblewoman who ruled the empire for years, and its outrageous Medieval Festival (*see below*) affords an authentic taste of Italy's bygone days. Although the incredible scenery is the real reason to come, Brisighella has a fair number of sights for so small a town. Poke your nose into the **Antica Via degli Asini**, the oldest street in town, a raised and covered mule-train path with low beamed ceilings and crescent windows. To find the hidden path, head uphill from Piazza Carducci, the town's main square, turn right on Via Naldi, and follow the signs. The **clock tower**, open Monday and Wednesday–Friday 3–6, Sunday 10–noon and 2–7, has been bonging off the hours since 1290. Inside, the **Museum of Time** is an overdone but funky tourist attraction with clocks, tarot cards, alchemical vials, and arcane devices (including a copy of Foucault's pendulum). Included in the L3000 admission is an astrological reading by the tower's keeper. The museum is open Monday and Wednesday–Friday 3–6, weekends 10–7.

On the town's central peak sits the 14th-century **fortress**, which now holds the **Museum of Country Life** (Admission: L3000). Re-creations of the country kitchens, bedrooms, and workrooms of the Middle Ages fill the castle's towers, and the view from the battlements and catwalks is stunning. The town's third and most distant peak, topped by **Il Santuario del Monticino**, isn't really worth the arduous journey to get there. Fridays, Brisighella abounds with open markets and free *concertini* (small concerts) in its piazze. Brisighella's **tourist office** (Via de Gasperi 6, tel. 0546/81166; open daily 9–noon and 4–6:30), next to the train station, hands out maps and festival info—they'll also book hotel rooms.

➢ **COMING AND GOING** • Brisighella's **train station** (Via de Gasperi 12, tel. 0546/81064) lies on the Florence–Ravenna and Bologna–Rimini train routes. Eight daily trains arrive from Florence (via Faenza, 2 hrs, L8800) and more sporadically from Bologna (via Faenza, 1 hr, L5500); plan train connections accordingly.

Galla's Got Gaul

Galla Placidia, daughter of the Roman emperor Theodosius, gained recognition not because of her bloodlines but because of her scandalous behavior: She was taken hostage when the Goths sacked Rome, but after realizing she couldn't beat 'em, rebellious Galla joined her abductors. She married her captor, ruled alongside him, and accompanied him in battle until his death and her forced marriage to the Roman general Constantius. He soon died, and she gained free reign over the empire on behalf of her son, who fell into power at age six.

Getting around Brisighella's hilltop sights takes some climbing; you'll find the staircases up to the fortress and the clock tower uphill from Piazza Carducci—follow the signs. You can also take Viale Pascoli from the train station to the fortress; a dirt path loops around the local vineyards joining the fortress and the clock tower, providing a splendid view of both.

➢ **WHERE TO SLEEP AND EAT** • Unfortunately, Brisighella doesn't have much in the way of cheap sleeps. Your three options are taking a train back to Ravenna's cheaper hotels, making the shorter trip to Faenza for the night, or splurging on one of Brisighella's beautiful but painfully expensive two-star hotels. In Faenza, the two-star **Albergo Toricelli** (Piazzale Battisti 7, tel. 0546/22287) charges only L45,000 for a double without bath, and it's right next to the train station. In Brisighella, **Albergo Gigiolè** (Piazza Carducci 5, tel. 0546/81209) and **Albergo La Rocca** (Via delle Volte 10, tel. 0546/81180) both charge L80,000 for a double with bath but are outstanding hotels with sensational restaurants. Ask for a room on the top floor to ensure a view of Brisighella's incredible scenery.

Wine and olive oil tasting are offered year-round by the **Cooperativa Agricola** (Piazzetta Porta Gabolo 8, tel. 0546/80131), Monday through Saturday. Sample the pasta specialties made at **Il Pazzo**, such as *strichetti* (a thick, rolled pasta) with porcini mushrooms (L9000), and stringy *garganelli* (L8000). *Via Fossa 39, tel. 0546/80282. Walk down main road from main piazza. Open 12:30–2:30 and 8–11.*

➢ **FESTIVALS** • Brisighella's **Medieval Festival** is a pagan pleasure fair that transforms the village, taking it back to rowdier and more colorful days. Banquet halls serve plebeian meals in the "garden of delights" (off Piazza Carducci), and restaurants serve patrician suppers. You'll find plenty of medieval culinary specialties to eat, drink, and make merry with. The annual festival goes on for roughly two weeks between mid-June and mid-July, but weekends are the best time to come. Each Saturday and Sunday, music, theater, dance, and acrobatics fill the streets and piazze, climaxing between 8 PM and midnight. Admission to the city center (unless you're staying in a local hotel) ranges from L5000 to L15,000 depending on the day of the week. For details call the tourist office. Other festivals, though less famous, present every bit as much gluttony as the above. The **Sagra della Polenta** in October celebrates, guess what, *polenta* (cornmeal); in November, the *tartufo* (truffle) gets the honor, and the olive is in the limelight in December.

Rimini

Rimini, the playground and meat market of Italy, is pillaged and plundered by four million tourists every summer. On the one hand, it's a family resort attracting German grannies, Italian families, and thousands of screaming prepubescents to its 1,500 hotels and endless white-sand beaches. On the other hand, Rimini is a town of drugs, drinks, and dancing—a favorite haunt for Brazilian transvestites, disco barons, and mafioso drug lords.

Beyond the plastic beach culture, exhausting singles scene, and modern coastal development though, Rimini is a city of fascinating history. Its centro storico—never seen by most sun worshipers and nightclub habitués—spreads out between a triumphal arch and a stone bridge, two of the oldest Roman monuments left standing in all Italy. Rimini's Renaissance history reads like a soap opera; the long reign of the Malatesta ("Evil Head") family is colored with murdered wives, deviant sexuality, power conquests, and unparalleled dictatorial narcissism. During WWII, almost all of historic Rimini was destroyed, to be transformed, seemingly overnight, into the sprawling mass of hotels, cafés, and bars you find today. If you're out for a little sleazy, cheesy fun, Rimini is great. But if overpriced strips of touristy shops and polluted waters don't turn you on, bypass this resort, or head straight from the train station to the centro storico for a look at the phenomenal Tempio Malatestiano (*see* Worth Seeing, *below*)—then continue on your way.

BASICS Rimini has two **tourist offices** in key locations. You can barely get out of the train station without bumping into the first one. Both offices have exhaustive information on activities, excursions, and lodgings, but won't make hotel reservations. *Train station office: Piazzale Cesare Battisti 1, tel. 0541/51331. Open June–Sept., daily 8–8; Oct.–May, Mon.–Sat. 8–7.*

In Marina Centro: Piazzale Indipendenza 3, tel. 0541/51101. Open June–Sept., daily 8–8; Oct.– May, Mon.–Sat. 8–2.

One exchange office that doesn't charge commission is **Cambio** (Via Pola 2, tel. 0541/21637), open daily 8 AM–10 PM. The **post office** (Corso Augusto 8, tel. 0541/781687) also changes money, although you'll pay a small commission.

COMING AND GOING Rimini is easily reached from virtually every major Italian city. Trains blow through to Milan (via Bologna, hourly, 4 hrs, L23,700), Ancona (hourly, 1 hr, L7200), Ravenna (12 daily, 1 hr, L3900), and Bologna (35 daily, 1 hr, L8800). Rimini's **train station** (Piazzale Cesare Battisti, tel. 0541/53512) forms the boundary between Rimini-Città and Rimini-Marina, the two completely contradictory city zones. In high season it's an absolute zoo, but helpful hotel-locating services abound at the station. Luggage storage (L1500 per piece) is open 24 hours a day.

You need never lay eyes on the **bus station** (Via Clementini 33, tel. 0541/25474), because all buses pass through the more convenient Piazza Battisti, in front of the train station. The ticket window in Piazza Battisti, open 6 AM–2 AM, sells city bus and tram tickets as well as tickets to nearby towns. In Rimini-Marina, buses also depart from Piazza Tripoli (Tram 11, Stop 14), on the waterfront. The ticket window (Piazza Tripoli 8/B, tel. 0541/391472) is open daily 8:30–noon and 1:30–9. Tickets are sold on the buses; schedules and prices are posted at the train station and on nearby windows at Piazza Tripoli.

GETTING AROUND There are two Riminis: **Rimini-Città**, a centro storico full of beautiful piazze and ancient monuments, and **Rimini-Marina**, a modern beach resort full of topless women and Speedo-clad men. The stretch of beaches extends south of Marina Centro (Rimini's central beach area) to Miramare, Riccione, Cattolica, and Gabicce, and north to Rivabella and Viserba. Rimini operates a tram-bus to tote people up and down the coast. Line 4 leaves frequently from the centro storico's Piazza Tre Martiri (5:30 AM–2:35 AM in high season), stopping at the train station and heading north to Rivabella. Line 11 also leaves from Piazza Tre Martiri and the train station (5:20 AM–2:10 AM in high season) and runs south all the way to Riccione, where you can catch the connecting Line 125 to Cattolica. One-hour tickets cost L1300, a L5000 orange ticket is good for one day, and an L18,000 ticket is good for eight days.

Via Vespucci is the main strip in Marina Centro, but it changes names every few blocks. You don't have to pay much attention to addresses though, because hotels and discos print the number of their tram stop on all business cards and flyers, and you'll soon find yourself speaking in *fermate* (stops). The centro storico is only slightly more complicated: The main street, Corso d'Augusto, cuts across town from the Bridge of Tiberius to the Arch of Augustus, bisecting the two main piazze on the way. To reach Piazza Tre Martiri from the train station, take Minibus 1 or 2, Tram 11, or walk 10 minutes up Via Dante, which changes names to Via IV Novembre. You can rent bicycles (L5000 per hour) and mopeds (L25,000 per hour) at **Noleggio Ambra** (Piazzale Kennedy 6, Stop 12, tel. 0541/375699) May–September, 8 AM–midnight.

WHERE TO SLEEP There are literally hundreds of hotels in Rimini, but they all fill up in August—"reservation" is the magic word. If you're desperate, you can crash on the beach for a couple nights without getting in too much trouble, but it gets surprisingly cold out there. Finding a bed is no problem the rest of the year. The **hotel information** desk at the train station, open June–August, daily 8–8, will help you get reservations as soon as you arrive. Representatives from local hotels will undoubtedly accost you—take advantage, because they'll usually arrange transportation to the hotel. Be sure to establish location and cost ahead of time, though. Prices are generally negotiable, except in August, so play hardball and you won't wake up to find out your neighbors are paying less than you. Most hotels in Rimini are full-pension establishments; it's not a bad deal for all the food you get, but if you plan to snack your way up and down the main drag, look for a half-pension (breakfast only) or *meublé* (room only) establishment, which often serve optional breakfast for around L5000. The hostel and campgrounds are a ways out of the center, but buses can tote you to them efficiently.

Hotel Meublé Lucciola (Viale Derna 25, Tram 11 to Stop 13, tel. 0541/390852), in Marina Centro, is packed with young people during the summer. The beach is only two blocks away and the rooms (L35,000 per person, all with bath) are decent and generally clean. Only one block from the central beach you'll find nearly luxurious rooms with phones and TVs at **Hotel Peru** (Via Pascoli 3, tel. 0541/381677; open year-round) for L37,000 per person. **Hotel Amsterdam** (Viale Regina Elena 9, near Tram 11 Stop 14, tel. 0541/391132) is right on the strip, but it doesn't cater exclusively to a student clientele. This full-pension hotel offers a breakfast-only option, charging L35,000 per person for a slightly upscale room with bath. Like many hotels in Rimini, Amsterdam is closed October–Easter. If for some reason you'd like to stay a whole week in Rimini, you can rent an apartment at **Residence Internazionale** (Viale Elena 37, tel. 0541/390160), just one block from the beach. For groups of three or four people, it's a great deal at L420,000 a week (June 24–July 7; slightly more in Aug.) To get here from the station, take Tram 11 to Stop 14. If all else fails, jump on Bus 9A from the train station to **Ostello Urland** (Via Flaminia 300, tel. 0541/373216), Rimini's HI hostel. This harsh concrete slab of a building, a 20-minute walk from the seaside, is definitely not Italy's best hostel. Beds go for only L15,000 a night (breakfast and hot shower included), but with its 1 AM curfew you'll miss out on Rimini's swinging late-night party scene.

➤ **CAMPING** • **Camping Maximum** (Viale Principe di Piemonte, Tram 11 to Stop 33, tel. 0541/372602), just across from the beach in Miramare, is filled March–September with Italian families and RV inhabitants. The unsightly but well-equipped campground charges L8000–L12,000 for a tent space and L6000–L10,000 per person, depending on the month; August is the costliest. There's a bar, showers, and plenty of electricity. Bathroomless bungalows run about L50,000 (2 people), L90,000 (4 people), and L110,000 (6 people), slightly less in the off-season. Its shady lawns and proximity to Rimini (10 min north on Tram 4) make **Camping Italia** (Via Toscanelli 112, Tram 4 to Stop 14, tel. 0541/732882) slightly more pleasant than Maximum. The ultracommunal campgrounds are packed in summer with RVs, as well as beer-drinking, catcalling young people from everywhere. Prices range from L6000 to L10,500 per person and L12,000 to L19,000 per tent—making a hotel a very attractive option. There are showers, a little store, a bar, and electricity on the grounds. For even more comfort try the bungalows, which cost anywhere from L60,000 to L90,000, depending on the season.

FOOD Rimini's main strip consists of restaurant after generic restaurant, overpriced pizzerias with tables on the sidewalk, and dozens of snack bars selling almost every type of finger food you can imagine. **Pizza al Taglio** (Via Vespucci 12, no phone) serves up the hottest, freshest pizza, piadine, and crescioni on the strip. If it's groceries you're after, the **Standa Supermarket** on the strip (Via Vespucci 133, tel. 0541/391494) is open Monday–Saturday 8:30 AM–11 PM, Sunday 9 AM–11 PM.

Restaurants in the old city are less pointedly aimed at the tourist population, but even so, they're expensive and mediocre compared with those in the rest of the region. **Ristorante La Botte** (Via Vespucci 75/B, tel. 0541/391962) serves tasty pizza, pastas, and secondi ranging from L5000 to L9000. They're open Easter–September, until late at night, so if all that dancing made you hungry, stop by for an ice cream. **Trattoria Pizzeria Aquila d'Oro** (Corso d'Augusto 207, tel. 0541/54172), a modest trattoria in the tranquil city center, serves 45 kinds of pizza (L4000–L7000) Wednesday–Monday noon–3 and 7–1). The pizza topped with truffle oil (L9000) is worth a splurge. **China Town** (Vicolo San Michelino in Foro 9, tel. 0541/25412), open daily noon–3 and 7–midnight, has an extensive menu and good prices. Tantalizing chicken, beef, seafood, and pork dishes cost L5000–L6000, and the cuisine is as authentic as you're gonna get in Italy. For a tasty full meal near the water for L29,000, try **Ristorante da Tonino** (Via Beccadelli 13, tel. 0541/50190), one block from Piazza Fellini.

WORTH SEEING Corso d'Augusto stretches from the arch to the bridge and is bisected by **Piazza Tre Martiri** and **Piazza Cavour**, the centro storico's main piazze. Cavour is much more interesting and is made lively by the ancient **pescheria**, an ancient Roman open-air fish market with a triple-arched entrance, a long marble arcade, and four dolphin fountains in its corners. The **Arco d'Augusto** (Corso d'Augusto, south of Piazza Tre Martiri), the triumphal arch at the southern edge of the centro storico, is the oldest Roman arch left standing (27 BC). The **Chiesa di Sant'Agostino** (Via Cairoli, tel. 0541/781268), an imposing brick church built in 1247, contains an amazing fresco cycle painted by three different Riminese artists. On the right wall of the apse is a scene of particular interest, depicting Dante (in profile in the long gown) and Petrarch in a crowd welcoming St. John home from exile. You can visit the church daily 8–noon and 3:30–6. The **Castel Sismondo** (Piazza Malatesta, no phone) was once a massive moated fortress complete with six towers, four bridges, several dungeons, and a hearty supply of earthworks. Built in 1437 and dismantled in the 19th century, the castle is now home to the **Museo Dinz Rialto** (tel. 0541/785780), open Monday–Saturday 8–1 (Thurs. and Sat. also 4–6 PM). You can see the anthropological and ethnological relics collected by Italian adventurer Delfino Dinz Rialto for L4000. The castle also hosts **summer cinema** from the beginning of July to mid-August, playing American and European films nightly at 9:45 in the courtyard. Admission is L6000. The **Museo della Città** (Via Tonino 1, tel. 0541/21482) is a showplace for centuries of Rimini's painters; the museum's masterpiece is Bellini's *Dead Christ*. The museum is open Monday–Saturday 8–1, Friday and Sunday 4–6.

To see a true testament to the architectural skill of the Romans, head to the **Ponte di Tiberio** (north on Corso d'Augusto from Piazza Cavour). The stone bridge, constructed between AD 14 and 21, is still standing and supporting heavy traffic after nearly 2000 years of wear and tear, and five years of heavy WWII bombing. Immediately beyond the bridge, on the right, lies the

The Republic of San Marino

An excursion into "the world's smallest and oldest republic" feels like nothing so much as a vacation from your cultural vacation. Perched on a mountain looking out over Italy on all sides, the microcountry of San Marino is like an amusement park with its own government, currency, philatelic society, and a dubious history. It claims to have been a free Republic since Martino, a stonecutter, settled here with a small community of Christians, escaping persecution by pagan emperor Diocletian. Today it's impossible to tell whether San Marino has been around as long as it claims, or sprang up yesterday as a tourist trap, with its fairy-tale castles and shameless tourist economy. However, it's worth the 40-minute trip from Rimini for a view of the stunning green countryside that spreads from Mt. Titiano down to the Adriatic on one side and the Apennines on the other.

Follow the yellow brick road to San Marino's Castello della Guaita (tel. 0549/991369), the oldest and largest of its castles, which dates back to the 10th century. Both this and the other castle, Castello della Cesta (tel. 0549/991295), have ramparts for wandering and towers for exploring, as well as fabulous views and sheer drop-offs down cliff faces. Other must-sees around town are the Piazza della Libertà, whose battlemented and clock-topped Palazzo Pubblico is guarded by San Marino's real-life tin soldiers in their green uniforms, and the Ferrari Museum (Maranello Rosso), with an example of every Ferrari made since the 1950s. Via Tre Settembre 3, tel. 059/900824. Admission L10,000. Open Mar.–Oct., daily 9–6; Nov.–Feb., Sun. 9–6.

Fourteen buses (40 min, L3600) leave daily from the bus stop in front of Rimini's train station in Piazza Battisti, also stopping in Piazza Tripoli to pick up passengers. You arrive in San Marino at Piazzale Marino Calcigni and must climb uphill to get to town. The tourist office (Via Contrada del Collegio 40, tel. 0549/882914) can give you unnecessary maps and a pretentious historical brochure or two; the office is open weekdays 8–8, weekends 9–noon and 3–6. San Marino works best as an afternoon stop; the evenings are deathly calm, and the hotel prices are killers, too.

only remnants of Old Rimini. This cute neighborhood of small, brightly painted houses, called **Borgo San Giuliano**, is the spot where Fellini filmed most of his *Amarcord* (dialect for "mi ricordo"—I remember).

It's worth making the trip into the centro storico just to see the **Tempio Malatestiano**, brainchild of Florentine master-architect Leon Battista Alberti. The peculiar church is appropriately referred to as a temple; the pagan connotations of the title are fully justified by the extent to which this is more a temple of love than of piety. The church was begun in 1447 by Sigismondo Malatesta, the military prodigy who at the age of 16 overthrew his brother's government and became the narcissistic lord of Rimini. In only 10 years he managed to transform the humble Romanesque-Gothic Basilica di San Francesco into a monument to his love for himself and his mistress-turned-wife, Isotta degli Atti. Leon Battista Alberti's vision, Agostino di Duccio's sculptures, Giotto's crucifix, and Piero della Francesca's fresco turned this once-ordinary church into a powerhouse of Renaissance art. Look closely at the sculptural detail of the interior: The intertwined "S" and "I" represent the love of Sigismondo and Isotta (she was the lifelong love whom he finally married after his first two wives died of "mysterious causes"). The idolatrous nature of the temple was strictly censured by Pope Pius II, who referred to Sigismondo as an incestuous, adulterous, homosexual tyrant, and had him not only excommunicated but also burned in effigy on the steps of three different churches. *Viale IV Novembre 35, tel. 0541/51130. Open daily 7–noon and 3:30–7.*

AFTER DARK Like a vampire, Rimini lives for the nights, when the strip is packed with pleasure seekers. The *passeggiata* (stroll) begins early in the evening and keeps going until well after midnight, with a few pit stops at pubs along the way. The discos pick up where the passeggiata drops off, and thrive until around 3:30 or 4 AM.

➤ **DISCOS** • The most elaborate and extensive collection of discos in Italy lights up the Adriatic coast around Rimini and will drain your wallet in a heartbeat if you don't go about things the right way. If you're loaded (with money, not mind-altering substances), head to one of Rimini's best discos, sprawling open-air affairs shooting laser beams into the sky. Be forewarned, however, that they're not only hard to reach, but the cover often costs L25,000–L35,000. **Bandiera Gialla** (Via Antiche Fonti Romane 76, Covignano, tel. 0541/752053) operates buses that will deliver you to the disco from the train station; that service is generously included in the L25,000 admission. You're more likely to get discount passes for the discos around Rimini's Marina Centro though. Look for **City Jungle** (Via Vespucci 119, Tram 11 to Stop 14, tel. 0541/390820), which is gratingly techno but happening, and **Chic** (Viale Regina Margherita 83, Marebello, Tram 11 to Stop 25, tel. 0541/374304), which is loud, crowded, and lots of fun. The three-tiered **Carnaby** (Via Brindisi 20, tel. 0541/373204) operates a private bus to pick up carless clients if they call ahead. These less elaborate clubs cost L15,000, but discount passes abound. The life of a disco is an ephemeral thing; to find out the latest, pick up a copy of *Book Instantaneo* at the tourist office, or just ask around.

➤ **PUBS** • The two main pubs frequented by the Riminese locals are the **Bounty Adventure Club** (Via Weber 4, tel. 0541/391900) and **Rock Island** (end of Rimini pier, tel. 0541/50178). Both play live music and go until 5 AM. Tuesday nights at Bounty are outrageous; cover is L10,000 (free other nights), but it's worth it just for the entertainment value of the silly charade: You can write a note to that special somebody across the room and uniformed "mail car-

It's a Small Country After All

Don't have time to see all of Italy? Well, for just L18,000 you can visit all the important sights in one afternoon at "Italia in Miniatura" (Italy in Miniature, Viserba, tel. 0541/732004). See the Colosseum and the Leaning Tower of Pisa at ⅕ their real size, get nauseous on various fun-filled rides, and pay exorbitant prices for lousy food. From the train station, take Bus 8. The park is open July–September 9–8; October–June 9–sunset.

riers" will hand deliver it to them. **The Old Bull and Bush** (Viale Regina Elena 99, tel. 0541/386755), and another Riminese standby, the swingin' **Rose and Crown** (Via Regina Elena 2/A, tel. 0541/391398), are favorite pre-disco stops, serving Guinness on tap (L8000) to a young rowdy crowd.

OUTDOOR ACTIVITIES With over 18 miles of coastline, Rimini's biggest draw is obviously its **beach**. Each divided acre consists of a *bagno* (bath house) governed by a *bagnino* (the guy with the cash register), who rents umbrellas (L6000) and deck chairs (L5000). Bagni numbers 1–50 are the hippest, as they're closest to central Rimini; some even have waterslides. Bagno 12 has free volleyball and basketball courts. If waterslides and wave machines float your boat, you'll be happy as a clam at **Aquafan**, a water park that magically transforms into a pretty happening disco on summer nights. *Autostrada 14, Riccione, tel. 0541/605709. From Marina Centro, take hourly private bus from train station or take Tram 11 to end of Riccione, transfer to Bus 41 or 42. Admission: L10,000. Open 10 AM–6:30 PM and 10 PM–4 AM. AE, MC, V.*

FLORENCE AND TUSCANY

8

By Sara Fisher

Nowhere in Italy does the landscape resemble a Renaissance painting so much as in Tuscany. This should be no surprise, since it was here, particularly in Florence (Firenze) and Siena, that the most important developments in Renaissance art took place. Italy even took its official language from Tuscany's dialect, the language Dante used in place of scholarly Latin in his *Divine Comedy*. What *is* surprising is that so many Tuscan towns have changed so little since their glory days. Though industry thrives in **Pistoia**, **Prato**, and the outer districts of Florence, vine-laden **Chianti**, farm-flanked **Arezzo**, and the resort island of **Elba** rely mostly on either agriculture or tourism to bolster their economies. Hill towns like **San Gimignano** and **Volterra** remain behind their original walls, with populations smaller than in medieval and Renaissance times. And locals in rural Tuscany still tend to be interested in foreigners, usually trying to strike up a conversation even if your Italian vocabulary is limited to about 10 words.

In the heart of Tuscany, Florence stands unparalled in terms of both its appeal for tourist and cultural prominence. Centuries of intercity warfare, a little dirty fighting (Florentine armies supposedly catapulted dead donkeys over Siena's walls in a failed attempt to start a plague), and the rise of a stable merchant class sealed Florence's political and economic dominance. As the Florentine banking industry flourished, the city's prosperity even rivaled the Vatican's. Political power became linked to financial clout and could no longer be identified exclusively with the divine right of kings—as in the case of the Medici family, which rose to power by virtue of its banking wealth. During the Medici's 400-year reign, the arts flourished under their patronage, as artists flocked to the region in search of financial support.

As one might expect of the home of the Leaning Tower of Pisa and Michelangelo's *David*, Tuscany is subject to a year-round tourist invasion, which gathers strength in the summertime. Towns like Siena don't feel so small when you're battling hordes of international tourists on a hot summer day. But if you're in Tuscany during this time, don't try to beat the crowds by avoiding the area—grab your lire and join them.

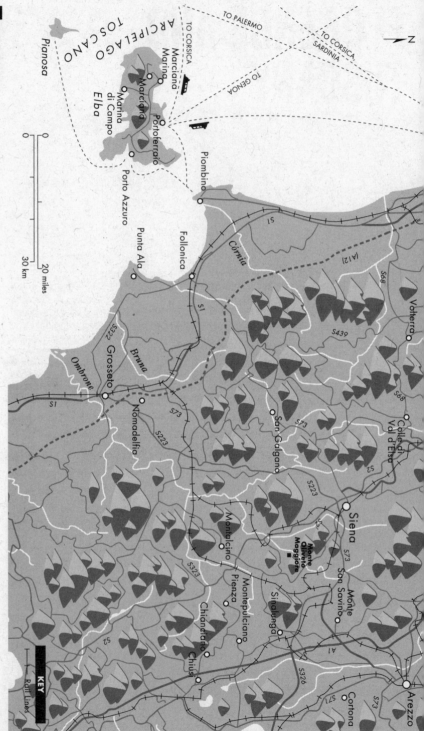

Tuscany

ARCIPELAGO TOSCANO

Pianosa

TO CORSICA

TO PALERMO

TO CORSICA,
SARDINIA

TO GENOA

N

Marciana
Marina

Marciana

Marina
di Campo

Elba

Portoferraio

Porto Azzuro

Punta Ala

Piombino

Follonica

Cornia

S1

0

20 miles

0

30 km

Ombrone

S322

Bruna

Grosseto

S1

S73

Nomadelfia

S223

Volterra

S68

S439

S68

Colle di
Val d'Elsa

San Galgano

S73

S2

S223

Montalcino

S323

Pienza

Montepulciano

Chianciano

Chiusi

S2

Siena

Monte
Oliveto
Maggiore

S73

Sinalunga

Monte
San Savino

A1

S326

S571

Cortona

S73

Arezzo

KEY

Rail Lines

210

TO CORSICA

Ligurian Sea

TO SANSEPOLCRO

La Spezia

A12

A15

S63

Carrara

A L P I

A P U A N E

GARFAGNANA

S45

S324

S12

Abetone

S. Marcello
Pist.

S12

Panaro

Reno

S64

Seravezza
Pietrasanta
Forte dei Marmi

Viareggio

S1

A12

Arno

Pisa

S12

Lucca

S435

Marlia

Montecatini
Terme

Pistoia

S64

Livorno

S206

Cecina

S439

S6

A11

Altopascio

Empoli

Elsa

S429

S2

Prato

A1

S503

S65

S610

S302

CHIANTI

S222

Strada

Greve

Castel di
Uzzano

Florence

Fiesole

S65

Arno

Pontassieve

Sita

S67

S71

To Corsica

Livorno

Page 211

Florence

Michelangelo's *David* and Botticelli's *Primavera* may be the most famous works of art in Florence, but the city's attitude toward visitors is best represented in Donatello's *St. George*. Valiant but cautious, the saint surveys an approaching dragon with a slightly worried eye. Florentines are prepared to meet the city's massive onslaught of tourists, but they don't exactly wait with open arms. True, many of the 400,000 inhabitants make a good living from the tourist industry, and they thrive while the rest of Italy suffers through economic depressions. But the financial prosperity is bittersweet, as they will tell you, complaining about the crowds in flawless English.

Florence is increasingly being called the Los Angeles of Italy. The populace's preoccupation with presenting "una bella figura" (good appearances) has resulted in the highest per-capita number of cellular phones in Europe.

Regardless of the tourist influx, Florence should be high on the list of anyone touring Europe for the first time. The modern city has protected its Renaissance flavor beautifully, farming out industry to distant suburbs or neighboring cities. The streets are relatively clean and safe, major sights lie within a few blocks of each other, and nearby hill cities like Siena and San Gimignano make great day trips.

The best reason to come to Florence, though, is to immerse yourself in a truly astounding collection of Renaissance art and architecture. Florence's Renaissance greats possessed talent difficult to conceive of in contemporary times. Michelangelo succeeded incomparably in painting, sculpture, and architecture, and he's just the tip of the proverbial iceberg in Florentine art. Spend a little time here and you'll get to know architect-sculptor Brunelleschi, painter-architect Giotto, architect-painter-theorist Alberti, and many more. Most of these figures, as well as the key poets and writers of the era, were at one time or another employed by the Medici family, who commissioned the great talents of the day to paint and sculpt their likenesses and build impressive structures in tribute to the family. Cosimo de' Medici (1389–1464), his grandson Lorenzo (1449–1492), and their offspring were responsible for much of the city's massive and overbearing architecture, most notably the Pitti Palace and the Palazzo degli Uffizi, Florence's greatest museum.

In the high season Florence may seem like an international summer camp, but the city is still considered an artistic nucleus and an excellent place to live by people from all over Italy. Florentines are fiercely proud of their cultural heritage and protective of the assets that define their city, as evidenced by the way they rallied to reopen the Uffizi less than a month after it was bombed in May 1993. Even if the city is a little wary of the backpack-toting tourist dragon, you can bet they'll be ready for it when it arrives.

BASICS

AMERICAN EXPRESS Florence's main AmEx office issues traveler's checks, changes money at mediocre rates (no commission on AmEx traveler's checks), has a travel agency, and keeps cardholder mail for 30 days. A second office, just south of the Arno across the Ponte Vecchio (Via Guicciardini 49r, tel. 055/288751; open weekdays 9–5:30), changes money and sells train tickets only. *Via Dante Alighieri 22r, tel. 055/50981. From Duomo, walk south (toward river) on Via de' Calzaiuoli, turn left on Via dei Tavolini (which becomes Via Dante Alighieri). Open weekdays 9–5:30, Sat. 9–12:30.*

CHANGING MONEY Banks have the best rates but often charge a L5000 commission (a drawback if you're changing small amounts), and they only exchange money in the morning. One thing to look out for: Most exchange offices don't post rates for traveler's checks, which are usually lower than for cash; be sure to ask. You can change Thomas Cook or MasterCard checks at decent rates without commission at the **Thomas Cook Office** (Lungarno Acciaioli 6r, tel. 055/289781), half a block west of the Ponte Vecchio's north end; they charge a L4000 commission on all other checks. If you're stuck at the train station with no lire, head to the money exchange at the info counter by Track 5. They don't charge commission but have poor rates.

CONSULATES For emergencies ranging from lost documents to arrests, births, deaths, or military invasions, head to your consulate. The **U.S. Consulate** (Lungarno Vespucci 28, tel. 055/239–8276), open weekdays 8:30–noon and 2–4, is on the north bank of the Arno, about a 15-minute walk west of the Ponte Vecchio (look for the flag). The **U.K. Consulate** (Lungarno Corsini 2, tel. 055/212594), along the same bank of the river, has comfy chairs and English newspapers in the waiting room. It's open weekdays 9:30–12:30 and 2:30–4:30. Canadians, New Zealanders, and Aussies need to contact their consulates in either Rome or Milan.

DISCOUNT TRAVEL AGENCIES The crowded-beyond-belief **Centro Turistico Studentesco (CTS) Giovanile** is where all of Florence's students go for 20%–30% discounts on flights and trains. To be eligible for discounts, you need to purchase a CTS membership (L36,000), and you must be under 26 (though registered students remain eligible up to age 32). The office also sells ISIC cards (L20,000). *Via de' Ginori 25r, tel. 055/289570. From Duomo, walk north (away from river) on Borgo San Lorenzo (which becomes Via de' Ginori). Open weekdays 9–12:45 and 2:30–5:45, Sat. 9–12:45.*

GAY AND LESBIAN RESOURCES **ARCI Gay** (Via del Leone 5r–11r, tel. 055/239–8722) is the local gay resource center, with info on gay clubs and meeting places. It offers HIV tests and consultations (tel. 055/288126) Monday and Wednesday 4–8. At the center, pick up a copy of *Quir* magazine, a monthly Italian/English publication of essays, interviews, and listings of gay and lesbian cultural events, clubs, and discussion groups. You can also find *Quir* at tourist offices or The Paperback Exchange (*see* English Books and Newspapers, *below*).

ENGLISH BOOKS AND NEWSPAPERS Florence is one of the few cities in Italy with a good selection of books in English. The following bookstores both have bulletin boards that list apartments for rent, language-conversation partners, and stuff for sale.

After Dark. Come browse Florence's best selection of English-language books, newspapers, and magazines, from the *L.A. Weekly* to the latest biker tattoo zine. *Via dei Ginori 47r, tel. 055/294203. From Piazza del Duomo, take Borgo San Lorenzo (which becomes Via dei Ginori). Open Mon.–Sat. 10–1:30 and 3–7; closed Sat. afternoon in off-season.*

The Paperback Exchange. They've got the best deals on new and used English-language books and let you trade your books in for used ones. *Via Fiesolana 31r, tel. 055/247–8154. From Piazza Santa Croce, take Via G. Verdi (which becomes Via Fiesolana). Open Mon.–Sat. 9–1 and 3:30–7:30; closed Mon. mid-Nov.–mid-Mar.*

LAUNDRY **Wash & Dry Lavarapido** (Via de' Servi, just south of Piazza Santissima Annunziata) is a coin-op chain with other locations near virtually every hotel area. Ask your pension or hostel proprietor for the closest branch. It costs about L6000 per load, by far the cheapest deal around. **Lavanderia Guelfa** (Via Guelfa 106, near Via Faenza, tel. 055/490628), near the train station, charges you L12,000 for 4 kilograms (L18,000 for 8 kg) to do your wash for you.

MAIL If you're an AmEx member, have your mail sent there (*see* American Express, *above*). Otherwise, mail marked *poste restante* or *ferma posta* (held mail) will be held at the **main post office** for up to a month. The main post office also offers money exchange weekdays 8:15–5, though the rates aren't the greatest. Branch offices around town close at 1:40 PM on weekdays and at noon on Saturdays. The postal code is 50100. *Palazzo delle Poste, Via Pellicceria, tel. 055/213384. Off Piazza della Repubblica. Open weekdays 8:15–7, Sat. 8:15–12:30.*

PHARMACIES In addition to the *farmacia* (pharmacy) in the train station, **Molteni** (Via Calzaivoli 7r, near Piazza della Signoria) is always open and posts a schedule of rotating pharmacies that also remain open 24 hours. For help finding a pharmacy, dial 192 from any phone.

PHONES **SIP** and **TELECOM** offices are scattered throughout the city and usually offer both operator-assisted and phone-card calling. The post office and the office at Via Cavour 21r provide the quietest environments, whereas the train station's phone office (to the right of Track 16) is exceedingly loud. The phones keep a running display as your lire and time tick away. You can buy phone cards from any office or at *tabacchi* (tobacco shops).

Sights ●

Baptistry, **33**

Bargello, **51**

Boboli Gardens, **66**

Campanile, **34**

Cappella Brancacci/
Santa Maria del
Carmine, **59**

Casa Buonarroti, **46**

Duomo, **35**

Forte Belvedere, **67**

Galleria
dell'Accademia, **12**

Mercato
Centrale, **19**

Mercato Nuovo, **48**

Museo
Archeologico, **15**

Museo dell'Opera
del Duomo, **36**

Museo di Storia
della Scienza, **53**

Museo Marino
Marini, **39**

Museo di
San Marco, **10**

Ognissanti, **37**

Orsanmichele, **49**

Palazzo
Medici-Ricardi, **22**

Palazzo Rucellai, **40**

Palazzo Strozzi, **41**

Palazzo Vecchio, **55**

Piazzale
Michelangelo, **69**

Pitti Palace, **65**

Ponte Vecchio, **52**

San Lorenzo, **27**

San Miniato
al Monte, **68**

Sant'Appollonia, **9**

Santa Croce, **56**

Santa Maria
Novella, **26**

Santissima
Annunziata, **14**

Santo Spirito, **63**

Spedale degli
Innocenti, **13**

Synagogue and
Jewish Museum, **24**

Uffizi Gallery, **54**

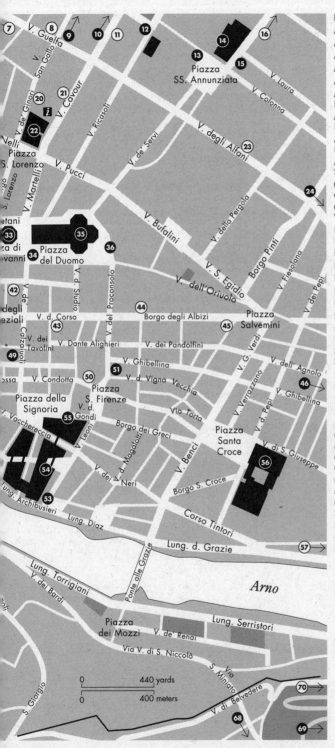

Lodging ○
Albergo Azzi, **2**
Albergo Fiorita, **1**
Albergo Firenze, **43**
Albergo Merlini, **3**
Albergo Mirella, **23**
Albergo
Montreal, **25**
Albergo
Il Perseo, **31**
Albergo
La Romagnola, **17**
Albergo
San Giovanni, **32**
Camping Italiani
e Stranieri, **70**
Camping
Villa Favard, **57**
Hotel
Il Bargellino, **7**
Hotel Boboli, **64**
Hotel Casci, **21**
Hotel Cristina, **50**
Hotel Ginori, **20**
Hotel Globus, **18**
Hotel Monica, **4**
Hotel Pensione
Maxim, **42**
Hotel
San Marco, **11**
Hotel Tina, **8**
Hotel Universo, **28**
Hotel Le Vigne, **29**
Istituto Gould, **61**
Locanda
Orchidea, **45**
Ostello and
Camping Villa
Camerata, **16**
Ostello
Archi Rossi, **5**
Ostello
Santa Monaca, **58**
Pablo House, **38**
Pensionato
Pio X, **60**
Pensione
Bandini, **62**
Pensione
Ferretti, **30**
Pensione
Indipendenza, **6**
Pensione Teti
e Prestige, **47**
Soggiorno
Bavaria, **44**

VISITOR INFORMATION Three well-located offices with helpful, harried, English-speaking staffs dispense maps, historical info, and special-events listings. The best **visitor center** (Via Cavour 1r, tel. 055/276–0382) is right beside the Palazzo Medici-Riccardi, about two blocks north of the Duomo. From June to September, it's open Monday–Saturday 8:15–7:15, Sunday 8:15–1:30; off-season hours are daily 8:15–2. A second office just off Piazza della Signoria (Chiasso Baroncelli 17r, tel. 055/230–2124) is open Monday–Saturday 8:15–1:45; look for the yellow sign beside Giambologna's *Rape of the Sabines*. A third office is beside the train station across from Track 16 (Piazza della Stazione, tel. 055/212245; open Mon.–Sat. 8:15–7:15, Sun. 8:15–2).

COMING AND GOING

If you're looking to get out of town quick, Florence's **Lift Center** (Corso Tintori 39, tel. 055/280621) hooks up passengers with drivers for a variable fee, but there's no screening process for drivers, so approach it with caution. As far as hitchhiking in and out of Florence goes, people are unlikely to pick you up, and it's not recommended if they do.

BY TRAIN Don't get off the train at one of Florence's satellite stations; you'll know you're in the right place when you see the FIRENZE SMN signs and enter the huge **Stazione Santa Maria Novella** (tel. 055/288785). The station, open 24 hours, has nonstop luggage storage (L1500 per bag per day) by Track 16, info counters (open daily 7 AM–8 PM), a reservations desk for international trains and couchettes (open 7 AM–8:30 PM), a 24-hour pharmacy, and an office that books hotel rooms for a small fee (open daily 8:30 AM–9 PM). If you really need to change money, skip the station's bank and go to the info office near Track 5.

Trains to Rome (2½ hrs, L36,200) and Milan (3 hrs, L36,000) leave about every 1½ hours, while trains to Venice (2 hrs, change at Bologna, L31,200) leave about every two hours. A few trains from Rome stop just outside the city at the **Campo di Marte** station. If this happens, just exit the station and take Bus 19 to Santa Maria Novella. Many visitors to Florence fly in and out of Pisa and catch one of the express trains that run hourly between Pisa's airport and Florence's station (1 hr, L6500). Some airlines even allow you to check bags through to your Pisa flight at an air terminal in the Florence train station, near Track 5.

BY BUS The long-distance bus system that serves Florence is messy, but it takes you to the hilly areas where trains don't go. In general, Siena, San Gimignano, and the Chianti region are best reached by bus, while Pistoia, Lucca, and Pisa are easier by train. The most comprehensive service is **SITA** (Via Santa Caterina da Siena 15r, tel. 055/483651 on weekdays or 055/211487 on weekends), with hourly service to Siena (1¼ hrs, L9000) and San Gimignano (1½ hrs, L8100; change at Poggibonsi), and buses to Arezzo (1½ hrs, L10,000) and Greve-in-Chianti (1 hr, L5000) about every two hours. The SITA station is open daily 6 AM–8:30 PM. To reach it from the train station, walk out the doors by Track 5, cross Via Luigi Alamanni and go left, and make a right on Via Santa Caterina da Siena. A few other companies serve Tuscany, such as **Lazzi** (Piazza della Stazione 4r–6r, tel. 055/215154), which runs buses to Pistoia, Lucca, and Pisa. The office is open Monday–Saturday 6:40 AM–7:50 PM, Sunday 7:40–7:30, with a few coffee breaks thrown in for good measure.

BY CAR If you're thinking about exploring the Tuscan countryside after you visit Florence, the easiest way to do so is to rent a car. The best bargain is **Italy By Car** (Borgognissanti 134r, tel. 055/293021), whose cheapest rates are L98,000 per day, L588,000 per week.

GETTING AROUND

Because the city center is a virtual open-air Renaissance museum, many streets are open only to pedestrians. It's usually faster to walk (even to the Oltrarno) than to wait for the bus and plod slowly through traffic. If you're willing to brave Italian roads on two wheels, you can rent a bike (L15,000 per day) or a scooter (L40,000 per day) at **Alinari** (Via Fuelfa 85r, tel. 055/280500). To follow the changing street names, it's essential to arm yourself with a map; the best one is the glossy **APT** map, available at the tourist office and many hotels for free.

Florence is actually quite large, with ever-sprawling suburbs being dubbed "the New Florence." Most of the sights and ambiance are in the **centro storico** (historic center), and this is where you'll spend most of your time. Although navigating the small, convoluted streets can be difficult, there are two main routes traced out by the town's piazze. In the north is the permanently crowded **Piazza del Duomo**, jammed with tourists and Italian pickup artists. The main artery, **Via Calzaiuoli**, runs from the Duomo south to the **Piazza della Signoria**, which is lined with important Medici buildings. Intersecting this north–south path is the other main chain of piazze. Flanking the train station in the west is the **Piazza Santa Maria Novella**. Moving east is the modern and utilitarian **Piazza della Repubblica** and then the **Piazza di Santa Croce**, home to medieval-dress soccer games in summer and amorous local youths in search of privacy year-round. Most major streets in the city center eventually filter into one of these piazze.

You'll be mystified by street addresses in Florence. Each street has two numbering systems: blue numbers for hotels and residences, and red numbers (denoted here by an "r") for businesses. The blue and red numbers—not to mention the numbers on either side of the street—can be wildly out of sync, so be patient.

BY BUS You only need to use the bus to reach Fiesole (a 20-minute ride away), the HI hostel, or the campgrounds. The city bus line, **ATAF** (tel. 055/580528), gives out free route maps from a booth just outside the train station on the Track 16 side, where most major bus lines make a stop. A ticket good for an hour costs L1100 and can be purchased at tabacchi or machines. When you climb aboard, punch your ticket on the time clock to validate it (otherwise you could pay an exorbitant fine). Most buses stop running around midnight or 1 AM.

WHERE TO SLEEP

No one would mistake Florence's budget hotels for charming country villas, and prices climb rapidly every year. Expect to pay around L70,000 for a double and upwards of L40,000 for a single. Luckily, many hotels lower their prices in the low season (July and August and November–February). Reservations are always helpful, but hotels often require a deposit. And while it's best to arrive in Florence early in the morning if you haven't reserved a room, don't panic if you arrive late at night without reservations: Managers at filled hotels will often call around for you. Otherwise, try questioning other frantic-looking backpackers—a group of three may just have turned down the single in the pension behind you.

The area around the station has dozens of small, cheap hotels, and you can store your luggage at the station while you look for rooms. If you need help, the **Consorzio ITA** (tel. 055/282893) in the train station, open daily 8:30 AM–9 PM, books rooms for a small service fee (L3000 minimum, depending on the cost of the room). Should you be lucky enough to get a space, the hostels are good deals; campgrounds are even cheaper but get packed in summer. Crashing in a park or the train station is not safe, and the police will probably hassle you.

SANTA MARIA NOVELLA AND WEST On a map, this neighborhood seems far from the major sights, but the hotels here are generally within a 10-minute walk of the Duomo and a hop, skip, and jump from the train station. The area is filled with budget inns tucked into the top floors of old apartment houses. Make sure you get a look at your room before you pay. One drawback: Piazza Santa Maria Novella becomes the site of some serious drug-dealing late at night, though it's pleasant and safe during the day and early evening. Just don't come home too late if you're alone, and definitely don't rough it here.

➤ **UNDER L70,000** • **Albergo La Romagnola/Soggiorno Gigliola.** A helpful staff brightens this otherwise musty hotel. With over 40 rooms, it's less likely to fill up than other budget lodgings, so it's worth calling if you've come in on a late train. Doubles start at L66,000. *Via della Scala 40, tel. 055/211597. Exit station near Track 16, turn right on Via della Scala. 42 rooms, some with bath. Midnight curfew.*

➤ **UNDER L85,000** • **Albergo Montreal.** The young, mellow managers charge fair prices, and the rooms have much more light than others in the area. Doubles begin at L75,000. *Via della Scala 43, tel. 055/238–2331. 14 rooms, some with bath. Curfew 1:30 AM.*

Pablo House. The feisty proprietor of this signless albergo recently redecorated every room and added private baths. The place is so intimate that it feels like you're staying with an older Italian relative. Doubles cost L70,000. *Via del Porcellana 14, tel. 055/285376. 4 rooms, all with bath. MC, V.*

Pensione Ferretti. Because of the odd shape of the building, each room in this simple, family-run inn has a distinct character. Ferretti lies just beyond the madness of Piazza Santa Maria Novella, so it stays quiet and peaceful. Doubles start at L80,000. *Via delle Belle Donne 17, tel. 055/219288. 21 rooms, some with bath. MC, V.*

➤ **UNDER L115,000** • **Hotel Universo.** Though normally a bit beyond budget range, this upscale hotel drops its rates in the low season, when doubles are only L70,000. Other months, you'll pay L110,000 for doubles. Some of the clean, white rooms offer atmospheric views of the piazza and/or TVs. *Piazza Santa Maria Novella 20, tel. 055/281951. 42 rooms, some with bath. AE, MC, V.*

Hotel Le Vigne. The elegant interior comes as a surprise, since the outside of this building looks decrepit. Dark, sepia-toned rooms have the hushed feel of a library, and you could sleep all day in the cushy beds. Rooms that face the piazza have an awesome view but are fairly noisy at night. Doubles start at L110,000, but prices drop about L20,000 in the low season. *Piazza Santa Maria Novella 24, at Via delle Belle Donne, tel. 055/294449. 19 rooms, some with bath. AE, MC, V.*

EAST OF THE STATION This area has lower prices than the Santa Maria Novella area, and it's the best place to set up camp if you're planning a quick trip to Florence and want to stay close to the train station. Three blocks east of the station on **Via Faenza**, which has 20 or so small alberghi, is the best place to begin a search; most one-star places have doubles in the L70,000–L80,000 range. Hotels on **Via Fiume** (2 blocks east of the station) are generally very quiet, while the places on crowded **Via Nazionale** (heading northeast from Piazza Stazione) are often dingier and noisier.

➤ **UNDER L65,000** • **Albergo Merlini.** Great top-floor views of the hills surrounding Florence and rooms with tasteful decor and comfy beds are the draw at the Merlini, one of the least-hectic hotels near the train station. Doubles start at L60,000. *Via Faenza 56, tel. 055/212848. 10 rooms, some with bath. Curfew 1 AM.*

➤ **UNDER L80,000** • **Albergo Azzi.** The bright young staff, headed by a Frank Zappa fan who plays trombone, knows how to make tired visitors feel welcome. This affordable hotel is especially popular with solo travelers, who can share triples and quads for only L23,000 per night (L28,000 with breakfast), which beats paying L50,000 for a single. Terrific doubles start at L70,000. *Via Faenza 56, tel. 055/213806. 20 rooms, some with bath. Curfew 12:30 AM (after-hour keys available). AE, MC, V.*

Albergo Fiorita. A stellar staff keeps things in the finest shape at this roomy top-floor inn just one block from the train station. Cheerful doubles start at L70,000, breakfast included. *Via Fiume 20, tel. 055/283183. 13 rooms, 6 with bath. MC, V.*

Hotel Il Bargellino. This meticulous place features Mediterranean tile and a gorgeous garden terrace where you can kick back. Ask for a room that opens directly onto the terrace. Doubles start at around L70,000. *Via Guelfa 87, tel. 055/238-2658. Exit train station at Track 16 and turn left, then right on Via Cennini, left on Via Faenza, right on Via Guelfa. 10 rooms, some with bath.*

Hotel Globus. Follow the bordello-red carpets, and you'll find pleasant rooms practically on top of the San Lorenzo church. Ask for a room on the third floor to cut down on the street noise. Doubles average L75,000, breakfast included. *Via San Antonino 24, tel. 055/211062. From train station, head south to Piazza della Unità Italiana, left on Via San Antonino. 23 rooms, some with bath. AE, MC, V.*

Pensione Indipendenza. Located next to Florence's law school and the green Piazza della Indipendenza, this tiny pension feels downright secure. The rooms (doubles L75,000) are typical one-star fare, and prices are the same with or without a private bath. *Piazza Indipendenza 8, tel. 055/496630. 10 rooms, 2 with bath.*

➤ **UNDER L105,000** • **Hotel Monica.** The pastel colors in the lobby and hallways give the Monica a Southern California feel, though the view from the comfortable outdoor terraces will quickly remind you that you're in Italy. Clean, bright doubles cost L100,000. *Via Faenza 66, tel. 055/283804. 15 rooms, some with bath.*

THE CENTER The heart of historic Florence, between the Duomo and Santa Croce, is a bit of a haul from the train station, but it's great for sightseeing. Prices fluctuate wildly, and they're a lot lower during the season. In this neighborhood, unlike others, you should pay attention to the number of stars each hotel displays. A two-star classification definitely means you'll pay more.

➤ **UNDER L65,000** • **Hotel Cristina.** This hotel's location, a block from the Uffizi and the Bargello, is fantastic. The rooms have your typically thin, lumpy mattresses, but at least they're large and very affordable. Doubles run L62,000, and rooms for 4–5 people go for L140,000. *Via Condotta 4, off Via Calzaiuoli before Piazza della Signoria, tel. 055/214484. 9 rooms, some with bath. Curfew 12:30 AM.*

➤ **UNDER L80,000** • **Albergo Firenze.** If you want the security and comfort of an American-style hotel in the heart of Florence, this is the place for you. The rooms vary markedly between the Best Westernesque new wing and the shabbier, though pleasant, old wing. The rooms with private baths (L86,000) are especially nice. Doubles without bath will set you back L74,000, including breakfast. *Piazza Donati 4, off Via del Corso, tel. 055/214203. 50 rooms, some with bath. Wheelchair access.*

Albergo San Giovanni. A high standard of cleanliness and a central location make the San Giovanni a good deal. Big, spartan rooms (doubles begin at L70,000) overlook the Duomo and the baptistry. *Via de' Cerretani 2, tel. 055/213580. 9 rooms, some with bath. AE, MC, V.*

Locanda Orchidea. The rooms are small but comfortable, with enormous windows that open onto pleasantly neglected gardens. The English-speaking proprietors go out of their way to help you. Doubles run L74,000. *Borgo degli Albizi 11, tel. 055/248–0346. 7 rooms, none with bath. Closed 1 week in Aug. MC, V.*

Soggiorno Bavaria. In this recently renovated inn atop an old palazzo, a smooth-talkin' young manager navigates the hallways, cellular phone in hand. The rooms on the top floor verge on enormous; most are very sunny and have great views. The downstairs rooms are smaller and darker. Prices vary dramatically, but the cheapest double is L76,000. *Borgo degli Albizi 26, tel. 055/234–0313. 17 rooms, some with bath.*

➤ **UNDER L90,000** • **Albergo Il Perseo.** Almost every room in this hotel has a stunning view of Florence. It's under new management and goes out of its way to make travelers feel at home, but the church bells that ring at 7 AM could wake the dead. Doubles go for L85,000. *Via de' Cerretani 1, tel. 055/212504. 19 rooms, some with bath. Curfew 1 AM. AE, MC, V with 3% surcharge.*

Hotel Pensione Maxim. Students and young wayfarers flow in and out of the Maxim, which occupies a utilitarian building one block south of the Duomo. The walls are thin, but the rooms and baths are more than adequate. Doubles cost L80,000 (breakfast included), but prices drop nearly 30% in the low season. *Via de' Calzaiuoli 11, tel. 055/217474. 23 rooms, some with bath. Curfew 1 AM. AE, MC, V with 5% surcharge.*

➤ **UNDER L110,000** • **Pensione Teti e Prestige.** Don't be scared away by the fading sign on the street; inside you'll find comfortable beds; sunny and clean top-floor rooms; and a gregarious management that is delighted to help you plan your sightseeing. Request a room with a view. Doubles cost L105,000, breakfast included, and there's a discount in the low season. *Via Porta Rossa 5, tel. 055/239–8435. 18 rooms, some with bath.*

PIAZZA SAN MARCO AND THE UNIVERSITY QUARTER A few blocks beyond the train station and the tourist area, hotels are a bit more scattered, and standards are slightly higher (though prices are surprisingly fair). Prepare yourself for a long walk from the station with your pack, or take Bus 7 to Piazza San Marco. Busy **Via Cavour**, which runs north–south through the piazza, has some good upper-floor inns, while one block west on **Via de' Ginori** and **Via San Gallo** there are a few quieter options. The farther down **Via degli Alfani** (which runs east from Via Cavour one block south of Piazza San Marco) from the station you go, the more student cafés and restaurants pop up.

➤ **UNDER L60,000** • **Albergo Mirella.** Inch for inch, these are the cheapest rooms in Florence: Enormous, pleasant doubles cost L58,000. The energetic young proprietor welcomes anyone and everyone, and the location is perfect for checking out cafés along Via degli Alfani. A 25-minute walk from the train station, the Mirella also tends to fill more slowly than other budget hotels. *Via degli Alfani 36, tel. 055/247–8170. 10 rooms, none with bath.*

➤ **UNDER L75,000** • **Hotel San Marco.** The heavenly smell of pastries from the shop downstairs might just inspire you to get out of bed in the morning. The rooms in this hotel just off Piazza San Marco are a cut above the norm and justify the initial schlepp up the stairs. Doubles begin at L70,000 (but move quickly up to L90,000), breakfast included. *Via Cavour 50, tel. 055/284235. 15 rooms, most with bath. MC, V.*

Hotel Tina. If you're not charmed by the spotless, perfectly maintained rooms, you will be by Piero, the happy-go-lucky manager. He serves up friendly advice and keeps hundreds of magazines for guests to peruse in the breakfast rooms of his welcoming inn. Some rooms have showers in the corner, though none has a toilet. Doubles start at L65,000, breakfast included—a guaranteed price if you're clutching a *Berkeley Guide. Via San Gallo 31, tel. 055/ 483519. 18 rooms. V.*

➤ **UNDER L105,000** • **Hotel Ginori.** The modern, streamlined rooms in this hotel are much more inviting than those in the cheap alberghi that surround it. Immaculate and comfortable, it's deservedly popular with students. Bright doubles with semi-disposable Swedish furniture cost L100,000. *Via de' Ginori 24, tel. 055/218615. 7 rooms, all with bath.*

➤ **UNDER L125,000** • **Hotel Casci.** When you need to take a break from backpacking strain, Hotel Casci is the place to indulge. In a newly renovated 14th-century building, this family-run hotel offers immaculate, comfortable rooms, all with modern bathrooms, TVs, and large continental breakfasts. The atmosphere is so peaceful that you don't realize how close to the bustling *centro* you are. Prices in the low season (July, August, December, and January) start at L90,000 for doubles; in the high season they go up to L120,000. *Via Cavour 13, tel. 055/211686. 25 rooms, all with bath. AE, MC, V.*

THE OLTRARNO If you've struck out at all the hotels in the center of town, head south of the Arno as a last resort. The restaurants in this area offer good deals, but the hotels certainly don't.

Hotel Boboli. The small rooms are very clean and in good shape, and the location beside the Boboli Gardens is one of the most peaceful in the city. But doubles (all with bath) are overpriced at L110,000. *Via Romana 63, tel. 055/229–8645. 22 rooms. MC, V.*

Pensione Sorelle Bandini. In a Renaissance palazzo, the Bandini has sunny rooms that are big enough to host a medium-size rave. More important, you're right on happenin' Piazza Santo Spirito. Doubles run about L90,000 (breakfast included), but the outgoing young manager will usually lower the price for students or those with a *Berkeley Guide. Piazza Santo Spirito 9, tel. 055/215308. 13 rooms, some with bath.*

HOSTELS Florence's hostels are a great bargain, but the smaller ones fill dizzyingly quickly in the high season. If you haven't reserved ahead, you'll have to arrive early and get to know your fellow desperados while waiting in line.

Istituto Gould. Unfortunately, this glorious hostel only has room for 80 people. If you haven't called or written ahead to reserve, you need to show up when the office opens at 9 AM and pray. The thoroughly scrubbed rooms resemble nice university dorms with big windows, and you get a key so you can come in whenever you want. Per person, doubles start at L30,000, triples at L29,000, and quads at L26,000 (solo travelers will be put in a quad with others). The office is closed Saturday afternoon and all day Sunday, but you can prepay and checkout ahead of time. *Via de' Serragli 49, tel. 055/212576. Office open weekdays 9–1 and 3–7, Sat. 9–1.*

Ostello Archi Rossi. They don't take reservations, but it's worth waiting in line for Archi Rossi's excellent location and high level of cleanliness. A staff full of characters (with a tendency to affectionately hassle the patrons) make this hostel even cooler, and a snack shop, patio, and free movies in English are added bonuses. Beds cost L20,000; in a room with bath they're L23,000. *Via Faenza 94r, tel. 055/290804. 86 beds. Curfew 12:30 AM, lockout 11–2:30. Max. stay 1 week. Wheelchair access.*

Ostello Santa Monaca. The bathrooms and dorms (with 8–20 beds) are standard hostel fare at best. You can't reserve ahead and the sexes are strictly segregated—at least they have a deal with a local trattoria that provides slightly reduced-price meals. Beds go for L18,000 per person, sheets and shower included. *Via Santa Monaca 6, off Via de' Serragli, tel. 055/268338. 140 beds. Curfew 12:30 AM, lockout 9:30–2. Reception open 9:30–1. Max. stay 7 nights.*

Ostello Villa Camerata (HI). Florence's megahostel isn't convenient to the city center, but if you make it out here, you'll be glad you did. Yep, it really is a villa, and it's on a mountainside surrounded by green acres (a campground adjoins the hostel). You won't bask in luxury, but the rooms are fine. You can reserve by writing months ahead with a credit card deposit or by faxing several weeks in advance. In addition, the hostel computer is linked with hostels in Rome, Naples, and Venice, and you can reserve a bed as little as 24 hours ahead from one of those hostels. Check-in begins at 2 PM (3 in winter). Beds cost L18,000 with a hostel card, L23,000 without one. Breakfast is included, but dinner costs L12,000. Another plus: English-language movies are shown nightly. *Viale Augusto Righi 4, tel. 055/601451, fax 055/600315. Exit train station at Track 5 and take Bus 17B (17A and 17C take longer routes) for 15 min to hostel gates; it's a 10-min walk from here. 320 beds. Midnight curfew, lockout 9 AM–2 PM (until 3 in winter).*

Pensionato Pio X. You're likely to share a room, there's a 12:30 AM curfew, and crucifixes abound. But don't let any of that scare you away: The rooms are large and clean, and the management is friendly. Beds cost L20,000 per person with a two-night minimum and five-night maximum stay. They don't take reservations, but if you show up between 8 and 10 AM or call ahead from the train station, you'll probably get in. *Via de' Serragli 106, tel. 055/225044. 46 beds.*

CAMPING Campgrounds may be hot and crowded in summer, but they're also the cheapest places to sleep in Florence. The sites themselves are nice, but wall-to-wall people distract from the great outdoors. From July 1 through mid-September, the city opens a free campsite to accommodate the hordes of tourists: **Camping Villa Favard** (Via Rocca Tedalda), basically a covered space to lay out a sleeping bag. It's probably not a good idea to come here alone, but the penniless may want to take their chances. There are bathrooms (without hot water) and security guards. For more info, call the **Comune di Firenze** (tel. 055/284015). The campground closes 10:30 AM–7 PM daily; take Bus 14 from the train station. Don't overlook the campground in Fiesole (*see* Near Florence, *below*) if you don't mind staying a 20-minute bus ride outside the city.

Camping Italiani e Stranieri. Tremendous views of the city redeem this scorching-hot campground just below Piazzale Michelangelo, where you've got to arrive super-early to rumble with 1,000 other campers for a minimally shady site. Still, your chances of finding a place are good, and it's hard to argue with a price of L7000 per person and L7500 per tent. *Viale Michelangelo 80, tel. 055/681–1977. Exit train station at Track 5, and take Bus 13 to stop after Piazzale Michelangelo. Office open 6 AM–midnight, check-in from 10 AM. Closed Nov.–mid-Mar.*

Camping Villa Camerata. Just beside the Villa Camerata hostel (*see above*), in a wooded area northeast of town, this year-round site is cool and calm. You can usually get a spot in the shade, so your tent won't become a sauna at 7 AM. Facilities are basic, but some campers sneak into the hostel in pursuit of nicer bathrooms. It's a good idea to show up before the office opens at 2 PM to scope out sites (L6000 per person, L8000 per tent, L12,000 for larger tents); pay in the hostel if the campsite kiosk is closed. *Viale Augusto Righi 4, tel. 055/601451.*

FOOD

In Florence you can sample some of the best of Tuscan cuisine, which exemplifies simplicity, heartiness, and abundance. Excellent local olive oil is drizzled on everything from the other-

The tourist menus posted everywhere are both a blessing and a curse: They allow you to eat a multiple-course Italian meal without paying the service charge and standard L2000 "coperto" (cover fee), but they often feature the dregs of the menu.

wise flavorless bread to the seasoned *fave* or *fagioli* (Tuscan white beans) that appear in everything from delicious, filling soups to pizzas. Vegetables and fruits are grown right in the countryside and tend to be extremely fresh. The crown of Florentine cuisine is the exquisite if expensive *bistecca alla Fiorentina*, a peppered beefsteak usually served extremely rare and big enough for two. If all you want is a cheap, filling meal, you could do worse than to join the tourist horde on **Via Palazzuolo** and its side streets, near Santa Maria Novella. The best local cuisine, however, is south of the river in the Oltrarno.

The cheapest way to eat in Florence is to stock up on provisions for breakfast and lunch at *alimentari* (general grocery stores) and markets. The nationwide chain **Standa** (Via Pietrapiana 94r, after Via del Corso becomes Via Pietrapiana) is a good budget option, but open-air markets are more interesting. The main one, **Mercato Centrale** (open Mon.–Sat. 7–2), is in an abandoned train station just north of the Church of San Lorenzo. Downstairs you'll find bread, cheese, and butcher shops worthy of a horror movie; upstairs is the produce section. A small market beneath the train station stays open until 8 PM. Walk out by Track 5, go down the steps, and hang a right; the market is hidden behind the flower stands. For a quick, cheap lunch, you can always buy *panini* (sandwiches) at a bar or deli for L3000–L5000.

PIAZZA SANTA MARIA NOVELLA The good news is that you can find a decent sit-down meal in this area for around L20,000. The bad news is that in recent years every tourist and her mother has figured that out, and any claims to authentic local cuisine are fading fast. Prices are low, but it's almost impossible to distinguish one place from the next. One fortunate exception is the incredible, hard-to-find Il Latini, which serves dozens of deliciously prepared local specialties.

➤ **UNDER L25,000 • Il Latini.** If you think your appetite knows no bounds, this is the place to discover your limit. Everything Il Latini serves is excellent, from chopped-liver *crostini* (toasts) to thick and rich soups (about L6000) to savory roast meats (about L15,000). They even make their own house wine. To save money and still eat yourself silly, order the assortment of *primi* (first courses) for L9000 per person. Is the place is packed with locals every night because it's the best restaurant in Florence? Yeah, probably. *Via dei Palchetti 6r, tel. 055/210916. From Piazza Santa Maria Novella, walk down Via de' Fossi, turn left on Via della Spada, right on Via de' Federighi, left on Via dei Palchetti. Open Tues.–Sun. 12:30–3 and 7:30–midnight. Closed mid-July–late Aug. Wheelchair access.*

La Lampara. With a sports bar in the back and a pizzeria in the front, La Lampara serves up top-quality, creative pizzas and is one of Florence's few eateries open on Sundays. Enormous pizzas (around L10,000) are topped with regional specialties like fagioli and *salsiccia* (spicy sausage) or just the traditional fresh tomato sauce and cheese. *Via Nazionale 36r, tel. 055/215164. Open Wed.–Mon noon–3 and 7–midnight.*

Trattoria da Giorgio and **Trattoria Il Contadino.** Just across the street from each other, these places have different names, but they serve similar food at the exact same price (though some contend that Il Contadino presents slightly more interesting dishes). You get pasta, meat, a vegetable, and unlimited bread, water, and wine for L15,000. The menu changes daily, but you won't be surprised by any exotic creations—it's just the basics. *Trattoria da Giorgio: Via Palazzuolo 100r, no phone; open daily 11–3 and 6–10. Trattoria Il Contadino: Via Palazzuolo 69r–71r, tel. 055/238–2673; open Mon.–Sat. 11–3 and 7–midnight. From Piazza Santa Maria Novella, walk down Via de' Fossi, turn right on Via Palazzuolo.*

THE CENTER The city center is home to horrendously expensive tourist traps, terrific little take-out stands, and everything in between. The area around Piazza della Signoria contains no bargains, but near Santa Croce you'll find tantalizing options on **Via dei Neri** and the streets branching off to the north.

➤ **UNDER L10,000 ·** **Antico Noè.** The best panini counter in Florence is little more than a hole in the wall, but it's got the freshest turkey and roast-beef sandwiches (around L3500 each) in town. Mouthwatering accoutrements like spinach or *peperoni* (sautéed bell peppers) are an additional L500. It's the perfect antidote to the never-ending prosciutto panini you see elsewhere, and you can enjoy a glass of wine as you stand and eat. *Volta di San Piero 6r, tel. 055/234–0838. From Duomo, walk east on Via dell'Oriuolo; look for covered passageway (Volta di San Piero) on right just before Piazza Salvemini. Open Sun.–Fri. 10–10. Closed Aug.*

Carlie's Bakery. The original American founders are gone, but the torch has been passed to others who understand the secret of chocolate-chip cookies (L1500) and brownies (L2000). The place has earned such a reputation that it now sells its brownies to Häagen Dazs. An English-language bulletin board lists items for sale, apartments for rent, and people looking for conversation partners. If you're in search of a job, you can post a note here. *Via delle Brache 12r–14r, tel. 055/215137. From Piazza della Signoria, walk down Via dei Neri, left at Via Gia dei Legnaioli, which is Via delle Brache. Open weekdays 10:30–6:30, Sat. 10:30–1. Closed mid-July–Aug. Wheelchair access.*

Il Nilo. This cheap take-out counter, very popular with Florence's sizable population of North African immigrants, serves great veal shawarma and falafel (L3500 each) and has a fine selection of bottled beers (L3000 each). *Volta di San Piero 9r, tel. 055/234–4467. Across from Antico Noè (see above). Open Mon.–Sat. 10–10.*

The Piccadilly. Although its neon decor and location right before the Ponte Vecchio seem too glitzy to be good, this place serves some of the best pizza by the slice in the city. Unusual options range from eggplant to seasoned potatoes, and upon request they'll drizzle fresh olive oil and spices on each slice (L4000). Even better, there's a shaded picnic area where you can sit down in back. *Via S. Felice 43r, no phone. Open Wed.–Mon. 10–10.*

➤ **UNDER L25,000** • **Acqua al 2.** Come here for a good, if expensive, meal with half the Americans in Florence. Original, velvety sauces top the pastas (about L8000 each); you can get a small taste of four pastas by ordering the combination plate (L11,900). The main courses aren't nearly as good, so you may want to skip straight to the homemade *tiramisù*, a creamy, espresso-and-liqueur-soaked dessert. *Via della Vigna Vecchia 40r, near the Bargello, tel. 055/ 284170. Open Tues.–Sun. 8 PM–2 AM. Wheelchair access.*

Trattoria I'Che C'è C'è. The best trattoria in the shadow of the Palazzo Vecchio serves everything from staggeringly large bowls of *ribollita* (thick bean soup; L7000) to the costly local specialty bistecca alla fiorentina (L44,000 per kilo, which feeds multiple people). It may look touristy, but the food is wonderful. *Via de' Magalotti 11r, tel. 055/216589. From Piazza Santa Croce, walk west down Borgo dei Greci and turn left on Via de' Magalotti. Open Tues.–Sun. 12:30–2:30 and 7:30–10:30.*

PIAZZA SAN MARCO AND THE UNIVERSITY QUARTER In the small area around Piazza San Marco and Piazza Santissima Annunziata, neighborhood joints cater to the thin wallets of the university population. Students gather at the cafés on **Via degli Alfani**. Northwest toward Piazza della Indipendenza, along **Via Guelfa** and **Via XXVII Aprile**, narrow side streets offer solid, reasonably priced restaurants. Florence's only whole-food pasticceria, **Troponais** (Via San Gallo 92r, tel. 055/483017), sells sugarless sesame or sunflower brittle as well as more traditional sweets. From San Lorenzo, walk north 10 minutes on Via San Gallo. **Almanacco** (Via delle Ruote 30r, tel. 055/475030) is one of Florence's few all-vegetarian restaurants. You have to pay a L10,000 membership fee to eat here, so unless you're in town for some time, it may not be worth it.

➤ **UNDER L10,000** • **Betty Boop.** The inside looks like Pee Wee's Playhouse: chairs created from spare parts, tables shaped like flowers, and crayons for drawing on the place mats. Surprisingly good salads go for L5000 each, and tasty pastas are about the same price. *Via degli Alfani 26r, just west of Via della Pergola, tel. 055/234786. Open Sept.–June, Mon.–Sat. noon–2:30 and 8–midnight (café/bar open noon–1 AM); July–Aug., Mon.–Sat. noon–2:30 (café/bar open noon–8). Wheelchair access.*

Caffellatte. This dreamy little haven is just a café, but it's a café in the best sense, with six uneven wooden tables that seem to invite meaningful discussions or a long, slow session with a newspaper. Students drop in for a cuppa joe or one of dozens of fresh teas and a piece of homemade cake. It's probably the only place in town to get a bowl of yogurt topped with fresh fruit or muesli (L5000). *Via degli Alfani 39r, just west of Via della Pergola, tel. 055/247–8878. Open Mon.–Sat. 9 AM–8 PM. Wheelchair access.*

Rosticceria. Labeled only with an unassuming *rosticceria* sign, this tiny eatery has delicious Arabic sandwiches and salads (all around L3500). In addition to having lots of vegetarian choices, it's a nice change from pizza. *Via Guelfa 40r, no phone. Open Mon.–Sat. 11–7.*

Rosticceria Alfio e Beppo. Lasagna, ravioli, and tortellini (L4000 per serving) vie for your attention with roasted chickens and rice salads priced by weight. They're all delicious. *Via Cavour 118r, near Piazza San Marco, tel. 055/214108. Open Sept.–June, Sun.–Fri. 8 AM–9 PM; July–Aug., daily 8 AM–9 PM. Wheelchair access.*

➤ **UNDER L20,000 • Trattoria San Zanobi.** Off the beaten tourist track, this authentic Italian trattoria offers rich and filling pastas (around L10,000) in a gleaming brass and linen environment. Homemade desserts ranging from cakes to *Macedonia* (fresh fruit salad, L4000) are worth the investment. *Via San Zanobi 33r, tel. 055/475286. From San Lorenzo, walk north up Via dell'Ariento, turn right on Via Panicale, which becomes Via San Zanobi. Open Mon.–Sat. 7 PM–midnight. Closed for part of Aug. MC, V.*

EAST OF SANTA CROCE Tourists rarely venture beyond Santa Croce, but the colorful neighborhoods to the east feature good, cheap food. Near the church, follow Via dell'Agnolo east to Piazza Ghiberti and you'll hit **Mercato Sant'Ambrogio**, the town's oldest food market. In addition to meat (sold inside) and produce (sold outside), vendors peddle cheap clothes and knickknacks.

➤ **UNDER L25,000 • La Maremmana.** You won't find a bad dish here, and the menu is extensive enough to make that some mean feat. This is a good place to splurge on seafood antipasti, pasta, and roasted-meat secondi. The *scoglio*, a big plate of pasta with seafood for three people (L25,000) is expertly prepared. *Via de' Macci 77r, tel. 055/241226. From Santa Croce, take Via dei Pepi, right on Via Ghibellina, and left on Via de' Macci. Open Mon.–Sat. 11–3 and 7–midnight. Wheelchair access. MC, V.*

Trattoria Il Giova. This small corner establishment is one of the few that offer their daily specials on the tourist menu. The thorough menu (L18,000) includes pasta, meat, a vegetable, bread, water, wine, and fruit. A generous portion of spaghetti with clams is a great way to start your meal. *Borgo la Croce 73r, tel. 055/248–0639. From Piazza Salvemini, walk east on Via*

Frozen Ecstasy

Inevitably, the local gelato shops will suck you in to eat the soft Italian version of ice cream until you suffer from extended brain freeze. The most famous, popular, and expensive gelateria is Vivoli (Via Isola delle Stinche 7, tel. 055/292334). The flavors here are rich beyond belief; the best are hazelnut and the alcoholic flavors (particularly eggnog), which really pack a punch. Skimpy servings all come in cups (L2000 for a tiny cup). To reach Vivoli from Piazza Santa Croce, take Via Torta and turn right on Via Isola delle Stinche. Quantity isn't a problem at L'Angolo del Gelato (Via della Scala 2r, at Piazza Santa Maria Novella, tel. 055/210526), where L2000 gets you a massive cone or cup nearly as heavenly as Vivoli's. To ensure quality and freshness, the young owner, Fabrizio, never has more than 20 flavors at once, and great fruit flavors change with the season. The oldest gelateria in Florence, Perchè No! (Via dei Tavolini 19r, off Via de' Calzaiuoli, tel. 055/239–8969) is one of the few places that has truly mastered a white-chocolate flavor.

Pietrapiana (which becomes Borgo la Croce). Open Mon.–Sat. noon–2:30 and 7–10. Wheelchair access.

THE OLTRARNO You'll have no problem eating well south of the Arno. Just one block away from the river, **Borgo San Jacopo/Via Santo Spirito/Borgo San Frediano** (one long street that changes names) is packed with restaurants. Farther south, cafés line Piazza Santo Spirito, which is a pleasant place to sit outside in the warm months. You can pick up organic food at **Sugar Blues** (Via de' Serragli 57r, tel. 055/268378), right beside the Istituto Gould hostel (see Where to Sleep, above).

➤ **UNDER L15,000 • I Tarocchi.** Tarot cards are the theme here, and your fate is to dine on Florence's best pizza. The menu also includes pastas and daily specials, but it's the thin-crust pizzas, including the *margherita dei Tarocchi* (fresh tomato and mozzarella; L9000) and the *sparagina* (asparagus and shrimp; L11,000), that make the trek worthwhile. *Via de' Renai 12r–14r, tel. 055/234–3912. Cross river at Ponte alle Grazie and make 2nd left on Via de' Renai. Open Tues.–Sat. noon–3 and 7–1. Wheelchair access.*

➤ **UNDER L25,000 • La Corte de' Pazzi.** This basement tavern is only open for dinner, and even then the locals don't come streaming in until after 9. Very original dishes include *galletto alla Diavola* (crispy baked hen; L12,000) and a tantalizing tortellini *all'arrabbiata* (in spicy sauce; L9000). If you have a full meal, with wine and dessert, it may cost more than L25,000, but there's no question you'll be eating well. *Borgo San Frediano 26r, just west of Piazza N. Sauro, tel. 055/238–1569. Open Wed.–Mon. 7 PM–11:30 PM.*

Trattoria La Casalinga. Very large and very crowded, the Casalinga draws a crowd almost as diverse as its menu. Truly memorable pastas go for about L6000, and main dishes are about L8000. Watch for daily specials, including the affordable fried chicken breast (L7800)—a nice change from the typical pork dishes that most trattorias serve day after day. *Via dei Michelozzi 9r, tel. 055/218624. From the steps of Santo Spirito (facing the piazza), turn left. Open weekdays 11–3 and 7–midnight.*

WORTH SEEING

Florence is compact, but it's impossible to see all that's left of the Renaissance—which is a heck of a lot—in one or two days. Zillions of people will join you in the pilgrimage to Donatello and Michelangelo's *Davids* and Brunelleschi's churches, so unless you get to the Uffizi, Pitti Palace, or Accademia the minute they open, expect serious lines during morning hours. You're better off hitting the big museums later in the afternoons, when crowds thin out. Spend mornings in the city's voluminous churches or at smaller museums, which never fill to capacity, even in summer. Museum hours can change drastically from season to season, so pick up a free schedule of the latest opening hours from the tourist office. Keep in mind that most museums are closed on Mondays.

Florentine sights are insanely expensive. Churches are the only places that let you in for free, and even then you may have to pay to enter the cloisters, chapels, towers, or domes. A student ID is pretty much useless in state and city museums, which include most of the major attractions. Only privately owned museums like Casa Buonarroti or the Museo di Storia della Scienza offer even a slight discount.

PIAZZA DEL DUOMO Even the thousandth glimpse of the **Duomo** (officially called Santa Maria del Fiore) makes the jaw drop and the mind boggle. Brunelleschi's fabulous engineering breakthrough, the huge dome, is offset by the rest of the exterior's heavily patterned green, white, and pink marble, following the design of Arnolfo di Cambio and Giotto. The facade wasn't completed until the 19th century, when low quarrying standards allowed inferior marble to be used. The porous stone absorbs pollution, so it's constantly undergoing cleaning.

Construction on the Duomo was fitful in the 14th century because traditional building methods could not support the dome's size. In 1418, after a steady stream of boasts, challenges, and insults, Brunelleschi intimidated the cathedral committee into allowing him to give it a try. His dome is an adaptation of a perfectly hemispherical Roman dome—slightly taller than it is wide. Brunelleschi designed nearly every aspect of this architectural masterpiece, including new types of tools required to build it. The structure consists of an interior and exterior shell linked by an elaborate system of hidden ribs and supports. Bricks were interlaced to create a self-supporting structure, and the beautiful cupola creates a central supporting axis. You can still climb the **cupola** (open summer, Mon.–Sat. 9:30–6; winter, 10–5) for a supreme view of Florence. On the way down have a look at some of Brunelleschi's instruments, which are displayed on the walls. You can also climb Giotto's **campanile** (open Apr.–Oct., daily 8:30–7; Nov.–Mar., daily 9–4:30), which may be more bang for your buck since it has multiple levels of look-out points along the way. Admission to either the dome or the campanile is L8000.

After the dazzling exterior, the Duomo inevitably disappoints inside—the space is too gargantuan to give any sense of intimacy, and it's almost empty, as the best artistic works have been moved to the cathedral museum (*see* Museo dell'Opera del Duomo, *below*). To the left as you enter the cathedral are two monumental frescoes of equestrian figures representing foreign mercenaries hired to protect Florence. In Paolo Uccello's portrait of John Hawkwood (1436), on the right, the horse and rider appear at eye level, yet your perspective is from the pedestal

The Florentine Renaissance

Inspired by the Greeks and Romans whose achievements had been ignored during the Dark Ages, artists flocked to Florence in the late 14th century, embarking on a new era of humanism and individual expression. Leonbattista Alberti, one of the first Renaissance art theorists, commented, "we have dug this art up from under the earth. If it was never written, we have drawn it from heaven," indicating the double nature of this rebirth—both modeled after the ancients and inspired anew.

- *Giotto di Bondone (1277–1337) worked all over Italy, so the most famous works in his hometown are limited to design work on the Duomo, the magnificent Uffizi altarpieces, and a few frescoes. But Giotto is considered to be the father of the Renaissance—and sometimes of the modern era—as the first individual artist since antiquity. He broke new ground with his natural representations of the human experience, played out by three-dimensional figures in dramatic compositions.*

- *Filippo Brunelleschi (1377–1446) went to Rome to study the ancients and eventually came to be considered one of the greatest architects of all time. He is best known for his brave design proposal for the Duomo's dome, but he was also responsible for the Ospedale degli Innocenti, San Lorenzo, and Santo Spirito, among other major Florentine buildings. His work is known for its scientific display of measure and proportion.*

- *The scuptor Donatello's (1386–1466) figures move with intense, subtly drawn and contrasting expressions, conveying the inner life of the subject, as in his bronze David. His major works are displayed in the Bargello and the Museo del Duomo.*

- *Michelangelo Buonarroti (1475–1564) is probably the Renaissance's most prolific, versatile, and transcendent artist. Though he mastered the marble nude statue, as you can see in his monumental David, his crowning achievement is the Sistine Chapel ceiling fresco in the Vatican. He also dabbled in architecture.*

below them. Uccello is said to have changed his mind about how to portray Hawkwood while painting the fresco, and he never got around to unifying the two halves. Uccello also created the clock above the entrance, an intriguing device that moves counterclockwise and counts down the hours from the last sunset until the next one. Downstairs, the **crypt** (open Mon.–Sat. 10–5) holds the remains of several churches dating back to the late-Roman period. The crypt's hardly worth the L3000 admission fee, but if you head down the stairs and turn left, you'll get a free look at Brunelleschi's tomb, discovered during an excavation only 30 years ago. **ARS**, a student organization, gives free guided tours of the cathedral and baptistry for four weeks every summer (usually mid-July–mid-Aug.), about five times daily, in English, Italian, French, German, Spanish, Swedish, and Dutch. Tour info is posted in the crypt. *Piazza del Duomo, tel. 055/294514. Open daily 10–5:30.*

➤ **BAPTISTRY** • Just opposite the Duomo's facade, the baptistry is the city's oldest standing building, originally built in the 6th or 7th century and adorned with distinctive marble patterning in the 11th or 12th century. The Baptistry's **bronze doors**, especially those facing the Duomo (on the east side), are the most famous sculptural panels in Renaissance art. Ghiberti beat out Donatello and Brunelleschi for the chance to redesign the northern doors, but he was limited by the conventions of quatrefoil framing, which forced him to contain his panels in an oddly shaped space. On the eastern doors, he did away with the limiting decorative borders, and the result prompted Michelangelo to call them "The Gates of Paradise." The 10 panels survey the Old Testament from Adam and Eve to Solomon and Sheba with a depth and emotion unprecedented in this medium. Ghiberti included a portrait of his balding self in the middle band (on the left door, right-hand side, fourth head from the top). The panels on the Baptistry doors are copies—some originals are in the Museo dell'Opera del Duomo (*see below*), and some are being restored.

Inside the baptistry, the ceiling is covered in opulent gold medieval mosaics. Above the altar is a depthless Byzantine-looking portrait of Jesus. Marching around the rest of the dome are five levels of biblical allegories; the most arresting one is a lively, macabre depiction of the Apocalypse over the west door. *Piazza del Duomo, tel. 055/230–2885. Admission free. Open Mon.– Sat. 1:30–6, Sun. 9–1.*

➤ **MUSEO DELL'OPERA DEL DUOMO** • Don't make the mistake of passing up the superb museum just opposite the dome end of the cathedral, with works taken from the interior chapels and sculpture from the facade and campanile. It's not nearly as crowded as Florence's other major museums, and it's definitely worth a visit, even if you're only here for a couple of days. There are free guided tours in the summer (Tues. at 4 PM, Thurs. at 11 AM), which meet inside the courtyard.

Michelangelo's *Pietà* dominates the landing between the ground level and second floor. Upstairs, the most impressive room holds Donatello's harrowing and haggard *Mary Magdalene* and several of his paintings of prophets, most notably *Habakkuk*, also known as *Zuccone* (Pumpkinhead) because of his ugly bald head, agonized expression, and rumpled outfit. The room also contains a wonderful celebration of youth, Luca della Robbia's *Choir Stall*. The 10 sculpted panels offer an affectionate depiction of riotous young boys and girls clashing cymbals, banging drums, and dancing in circles. Also upstairs are the first four of Ghiberti's restored panels from the eastern doors of the baptistry. Most amazing is the complex *Adam and Eve* panel, which relates the entire story from the creation of Adam to the expulsion from Eden in its small space. *Piazza del Duomo 9, tel. 055/230–2885. Admission: L8000. Open Mon.–Sat. 9–7:30 (until 5:30 in winter).*

The Pietà was a source of frustration for Michelangelo. He intended it for his own tomb, sculpting the figure of Nicodemus on top as a self-portrait, but the 80-year-old genius hacked off Christ's left arm and leg in a fit of anger over his failure to achieve perfection. A servant stopped him, and a student reattached the arm, but the back leg is still missing.

PIAZZA DELLA SIGNORIA Now a major hangout spot and recognizable from Merchant-Ivory's *A Room With a View*, Florence's principal piazza was designed in part as a celebration of Medici power. The family dominated the piazza: They lived in the Palazzo Vecchio and funded the Palazzo degli Uffizi (now the Uffizi Gallery) and the **Loggia della Signoria**. The last, a covered porch on the square's south side, was originally a platform for political uses, but since the late 1700s has contained Cellini's bronze *Perseus* (carrying Medusa's head) and Giambologna's spiralling *Rape of the Sabines*, both masterpieces of the 16th century. Unfortunately, the loggia is being restored, so you have to admire the sculptures from 20 feet away.

Lining the Palazzo Vecchio are copies of Michelangelo's *David* (the original stood here until 100 years ago), Donatello's *Judith and Holofernes* (the original is inside the palace), and *Marzocco* (in the Bargello), as well as the original ornate *Neptune Fountain*. The piazza is an overhauled version of its former self, having been renovated in 1986 in anticipation of a tourist surge for the 1990 World Cup matches. In the course of the renovation, archaeologists discovered extensive remains of a Roman bath and a 5th-century church, as well as Bronze Age relics, and evidence pointed to the possibility that possibly the entire city center was built over a Roman settlement. What could they do? Rip out magnificent Renaissance buildings so that a pile of ancient rubble could be unearthed? Three years into the dig the city chose to sew it up and complete the piazza's face-lift in the interest of tourism and staying with the times.

A block west of Piazza della Signoria (two blocks north of the Ponte Vecchio), the **Mercato Nuovo** is the place to pick up religious paraphernalia, leather goods, and piggy banks modeled after Michelangelo's *David*. On the west side of the market is the *Porcellino* fountain—a wild boar with a shiny snout that has become a Florentine talisman. Rubbing it supposedly brings good luck.

➢ **UFFIZI GALLERY** • Vasari (artist, architect, historian) was commissioned by the Medici family in 1560 to design offices for the local government, with a top floor reserved for the family's art collection. The last of the Medici, Anna Maria Ludovica, donated the entire collection to the city of Florence in 1737. Anyone with even a passing interest in Renaissance art will be amazed at the number of recognizable works inside, representing just about every breakthrough of the period. A thorough visit merits several hours or lifetimes, but it can be covered in less. Several rooms unfortunately remain closed due to repairs in the aftermath of the bomb (*see box, below*). Before heading up the stairs to the main gallery, have a look at the remains of **San Piero Scheraggio** off the entrance hall. The 11th-century church walls are lined with Andrea del Castagno's fabulous frescoes of famous folks, including Dante, Petrarch, and Boccaccio. The portrait of Pippo Spano (with a curved sword) is probably the artist's best-known work.

The main galleries line the long corridors on the palazzo's top floor. **Room 2** contains the three masterful Madonna altarpieces by Cimabue, Duccio, and Giotto, the earliest artists represented in the museum. In **Room 3**, Simone Martini's *Annunciation* (1333) is the crucial work of Siena's International Gothic movement, while Gentile da Fabriano's *Adoration of the Magi* (**Room 5–6**), in which gold paint is used to great effect, exemplifies the Florentines' contribution to International Gothic. Tiny **Room 7** shows off the most talented artists of mid-15th-century Florence. Piero della Francesca's portraits of Federico da Montefeltro and his wife, Battista Sforza, in face-to-face profiles, show both a cool precision in details (notice the duke's misshapen nose) and a complete mastery of Flemish-style landscape. Paolo Uccello's *Battle of San Romano* (1456) is the center portion of a triptych; the two side panels are now in the Louvre and London's National Gallery. It contains several fascinating perspective effects, most notably in the enormously foreshortened legs of the orange rearing horse on the right side. Room 7 also contains two Fra Angelicos, a *Madonna and Child* by Masolino and Massaccio, and one of Veneziano's few known paintings, *Madonna and Child Enthroned*.

Room 8 is full of fine works by Filippo Lippi and his bastard son, Filippino, but most first-time visitors rush anxiously through it to reach Botticelli's showcase (in **Rooms 10–14**), which contains just about every major easel painting by the artist, including *The Birth of Venus* (concealed behind thick glass), *Primavera, Adoration of the Magi, Pallas and the Centaur*, and the circular *Madonna of the Pomegranate*. This is the Uffizi's most popular room, and one of its best. **Room 15** contains some of Leonardo da Vinci's work: *The Annunciation*, for which the young Leonardo painted the angel (and perhaps more), a *Baptism* by his teacher Verrocchio that includes an angel (far left), and Leonardo's unfinished, mysterious *Adoration of the Magi* (1482).

After being funneled back into the main corridor, traffic flows into the octagonal **Tribuna**, containing sculptures of the Medicis, Rosso Fiorentino's endearing *Angel Playing a Lute*, and several impressive portraits by Bronzino. **Room 19** holds works by Perugino and Signorelli, students of Piero della Francesca. **Room 20** contains works from Northern Europe, including Dürer's *Adam* and *Eve*, which are hung directly across from Cranach's similar (but more subtle) portraits of the two. **Room 23** has works by Mantegna and Correggio, most notably the latter's accomplished *Rest on the Flight to Egypt*.

You're only about halfway done when you reach **Room 25**, which contains Michelangelo's *Doni Madonna*. The richly colored tondo is known for the sculpted figures of the Holy Family, characteristic of Michelangelo's very three-dimensional style of painting. **Room 26** contains treasures by Raphael, including a stunning *Self-Portrait* from 1508, his celebrated *Madonna of the Goldfinch*, and *Leo X with Cardinals*. **Room 28** houses the sexy *Venus of Urbino*, the key work of Titian's career. **Room 41** contains various works by Rubens and Van Dyck, while Caravaggio has several major works in **Room 43**, including a very sick-looking *Young Bacchus*, the unnerving *Medusa*, and *The Sacrifice of Isaac*. Rembrandt's masterly self-portraits, as a young and old man, hang in Room 44.

If you have the chance, try to arrange a visit to the **Corridoio Vasariano**, an extraordinary covered passage designed by Vasari in 1565. In addition to offering astonishing views of the city, the hallway contains scores of self-portraits by Renaissance artists. The corridor, entered by a door to the right of Room 25, continues uninterrupted from the Uffizi to the Pitti Palace, crossing the Ponte Vecchio in the process. To arrange a visit, go to the office on the top floor of the Uffizi Tuesday–Saturday mornings; if you're lucky, you'll be able to hook up with a tour that day, but usually you must schedule a day in advance. You can also call ahead to check when they're showing it next. *Uffizi Gallery: Loggiato degli Uffizi 6, tel. 055/23885. Admission: L12,000. Open Tues.–Sat. 9–7, Sun. 9–2.*

➤ **PALAZZO VECCHIO** • The Palazzo Vecchio, a fortresslike, rusticated brickwork structure at Piazza della Signoria's southeast corner, was the city hall in medieval times and is so again today. The off-center, top-heavy bell tower atop an intimidatingly tall (by medieval standards) building is, along with the Duomo, a recognizable symbol of the city. The original design by Arnolfo di Cambio (who also designed the Duomo) was flawed, and a fair share of Renaissance talents took a swing at fixing it, including Michelozzo (who designed the harmonious courtyard) and Vasari (who redesigned much of the interior for the Medicis when the family moved in briefly in the 1540s).

The first room at the top of the stairs is the **Salone dei Cinquecento**, the meeting room for Italy's Grand Council during Florence's brief tenure as capital of the Italian Republic (1865–1871). Vasari and his assistants painted the frescoes of glorious battle scenes, and Michelan-

Death of Venus?

In the early morning hours of May 27, 1993, a car bomb exploded in an alley just off Piazza della Signoria, causing irreparable damage to the Uffizi Gallery, the world's greatest museum of Renaissance painting. Immediate panic spread through Florence— not just remorse for the five lives lost, but also fear that the city might have lost something that has come to define it. Amidst the rubble, it was discovered that no masterpieces were destroyed, but many lesser paintings were damaged beyond repair. Amazingly, locals rallied to reopen more than half of the museum within a month. Popular sentiment assigns responsibilty to the Mafia, explaining the bombing as an act of revenge prompted by the Italian government's attempts to root out Mafia corruption in its own ranks. No arrests were ever made.

gelo's *Victory* sculpture is along the wall facing the entrance. Off to the side is the interesting **Studiolo di Francesco I**, devoid of windows but covered with art from the Mannerist period by Vasari and Bronzino, as well as statues by Giambologna. Beyond that, some 20 rooms "celebrate" the humanist republic with never-ending gold glitz. *Piazza della Signoria, tel. 055/276-8965. Admission: L8000. Open Mon.-Wed. and Fri. 9-7, weekends 11-8.*

➤ **BARGELLO** • The hierarchy goes like this: The Bargello is Italy's foremost museum of Renaissance sculpture. It's probably Florence's second-best museum after the Uffizi, and it's superior to the much more crowded Accademia. Florence's police headquarters and jail during the Renaissance, the Bargello now houses important works by Donatello, Ghiberti, Giambologna, and Michelangelo. On the ground floor of the museum are some of Michelangelo's early works: a grape-strewn *Bacchus*, a somber bust of *Brutus*, and a *Madonna and Child* tondo. Several of Cellini's small bronze statues of Perseus (studies for the Loggia della Signoria) and a few major works by Giambologna, including the spiral *Florence Defeating Pisa* and the harmonious bronze *Mercury*, are also here. Almost more interesting than these masters' works is the inner courtyard. Now a pleasant shaded area lined with terra-cotta, the walls once held manacled prisoners, and a gallows graced the center of the yard.

The sculptures downstairs hardly prepare you for the amazing works from a century earlier upstairs in the Donatello room. The most famous work in the museum is Donatello's bronze *David*, which with its sly pose, prepubescent physique, and feminine face make Michelangelo's *David* seem like he just walked out of Gold's Gym. This was the first freestanding male nude in Christian sculpture since ancient times. Donatello's earlier and more classical, marble *David* (1408) is also here, as are his *Marzocco*, the heraldic lion symbol of Florence; his guarded, watchful *St. George;* and his colored bust of *Niccolò da Uzzano*. The original bronze panels of *The Sacrifice of Isaac* by both Ghiberti and Brunelleschi line the walls, their entries for the 1402 competition that determined the designer of the baptistry doors (*see* Piazza del Duomo, *above*). The second-floor loggia is home to a series of bronze birds by Giambologna, while the top floor houses della Robbia terra-cottas and, more important, Verrocchio's small, skirted *David*. *Via del Proconsolo 4, tel. 055/210801. Admission: L8000. Open Tues.-Sun. 9-2.*

➤ **MUSEO DI STORIA DELLA SCIENZA** • Science fanatics may want to check out the Museum of the History of Science, which displays the Medici's collection of astrolabes, quadrants, globes, compasses, telescopes, sextants, and barometers, and Galileo's middle finger, an extra-special bonus. Most of the good stuff is on the first floor, but upstairs is a fascinating room of wax and terra-cotta models of the womb, illustrating the stages of childbirth. An English-language book explains all the devices in great detail, though it might make you feel like you're back in physics class. *Piazza dei Giudici 1, tel. 055/293493. Admission: L10,000, L7500 students. Open Mon.-Sat. 9:30-1 (Mon., Wed., Fri. also 2-5).*

➤ **ORSANMICHELE** • A solitary Gothic presence, the Church Orsanmichele stands out against the surrounding Renaissance backdrop of Florence's premier *passeggiata* (social stroll) street, Via de' Calzaiuoli. Some of the earliest and best examples of Renaissance sculpture decorate the facade, including Verrocchio's *St. Thomas* and Ghiberti's *John the Baptist* on the Via de' Calzaiuoli side of the building, and Donatello's worried *St. George* on the north side. (This is a copy; the original stands in the Bargello.) Restoration has claimed many of the statues, most of which will eventually be replaced by copies. Inside, a heavily detailed tabernacle by Andrea Orcagna, complete with pinnacles and colored stone, dominates the altar. *Via de' Calzaiuoli, tel. 055/284715. Admission free. Open daily 9-noon and 4-6.*

PIAZZA SANTA MARIA NOVELLA During the day, this is the best free grassy area in the center of Florence, where sunbathers and picnickers abound. The ambiance changes drastically at night, after the surrounding pubs close down, and the piazza is filled by Florence's homeless immigrant population. Drug deals are common but the police stay away from the scene—it's by no.means a good place to wait for your midnight train.

➤ **SANTA MARIA NOVELLA** • This church is most famous for its complex facade, which you can gaze at for hours as you nurse a beer in one of the piazza's outdoor cafés. The somber Gothic lower level was begun in the 14th century, but Alberti completed the facade with a series of arabesques and other ornamental additions now considered early versions of baroque. The interior features arches seamed with the black-and-white striped marble characteristic of the early Renaissance, and includes a number of significant works. The most important is Massaccio's luminescent fresco, *Trinity* (1428), on the left-hand wall along the nave. The strict compositional and geometric patterning in the painting—the arched ceiling, triangular grouping of the figures, and inverse triangle framed by the crucifix—brought painting forward as much as Brunelleschi's dome advanced architecture. Behind the main altar, you'll see Massaccio's influence in Domenico Ghirlandaio's frescoes, *The Lives of St. John and the Virgin*, which employed the relatively new concept of a single-point perspective. To the right of the altar, Filippino Lippi's melodramatic frescoes decorate the **Strozzi Chapel**, where Filippo Strozzi is buried. *Piazza Santa Maria Novella, tel. 055/210113. Open weekdays 7:15–11:30 and 3:30–5, weekends 3:30–5.*

To the left of the facade is the entrance to the church **cloisters** (tel. 055/282187; open Mon.–Thurs., and Sat. 9–2, Sun. 9–1), which unfortunately have an admission price of L4000. If you haven't yet run out of dough, you can find some excellent Old Testament frescoes that Paolo Uccello and his school whipped out on the right-hand wall beyond the entrance. Most of them have peeled away into nothingness, but the *Flood* (upper right) is still in pretty good shape, and has a fascinating scene. It displays the deep foreshortening and heavy diagonal lines the artist is known for.

➤ **PALAZZO STROZZI AND PALAZZO RUCELLAI** • Florentine architects pioneered a style of civic architecture in their palazzi, which stake their ground with fortresslike authority, while soothing elements from antiquity, like arched windows and carved pilasters, mellow the impact. They followed the wisdom of the ancients concerning proportion, but they usually believed that their innovations were superior (and the improvements normally were at a very grand scale). Palazzo Medici-Riccardi (*see* Piazza San Lorenzo, *below*), is one of the most important, but **Palazzo Rucellai** (Via della Vigna Nuova 16r) was the prototype, designed by Leon Battista Alberti in the mid-15th century. The street that houses Palazzo Rucellai, Via della Vigna Nuova, is lined with Florence's swankest shops. The nearby Via Tornabuoni also reeks of money, thanks to its designer stores and the Renaissance **Palazzo Strozzi** (Piazza Strozzi). The late-15th-century design clearly follows Alberti's lead, but it's more imposing.

➤ **MUSEO MARINO MARINI** • Florence's only full-time modern-art museum contains the work of just one artist, the marvelous but not widely known Marino Marini, from nearby Pistoia, where the Centro di Documentazione Fondazione Marino Marini (*see* Pistoia, Near Florence, *below*) is likewise devoted to his work. The roomy gallery, a former palazzo with fading frescoes on the ceiling, has been converted into a sleek, multilevel exhibition space containing mostly sculpture. Marini's favorite subjects—clowns, acrobats, and horses—are well represented, and his work has a childlike, playful quality. *Piazza San Pangrazio (cnr of Via della Spada and Via de' Federighi), tel. 055/219432. Admission: L5000. Open summer, Wed.–Mon. 10–5., Sun. 10–10.*

➤ **OGNISSANTI** • Originally a 13th-century Romanesque structure, this church got a baroque overhaul in the 17th century when the Franciscans remade the exterior. Inside you'll find Botticelli's *St. Augustine* (to the right of the entrance) and Ghirlandaio's *St. Jerome* (to the left), a matching pair of portraits facing each other across the nave. Continue to the **refectory** off the church cloisters; Ghirlandaio's massive *Last Supper* hangs brightly along the far wall. *Borgo Ognissanti 42, tel. 055/239–8700. Admission free. Open Mon.–Sat. 9–noon and 3:30–7, Sun. 3:30–5:30.*

PIAZZA SAN LORENZO Standing both literally and figuratively in the shadow of the Duomo, San Lorenzo is one of the city's most elaborate churches. The area around the cathedral is congested, but not with churchgoers: Shoppers crowd leather stands near the church, and the premier food market, the Mercato Centrale (*see* Food *above*), is a block away.

➤ **SAN LORENZO** • Since the Medici were so successful in putting their stamp on Florence's 15th- and 16th-century political and cultural movements, they figured they also could do local religion their way. Over the course of two centuries, the family rounded up the usual suspects—Brunelleschi, Donatello, Michelangelo—to attempt a church equal in beauty and prestige to the Duomo. Although the all-star cast had a fun time trying, they fell short of their goal. Because the facade and exterior designed by Michelangelo were never built, San Lorenzo is a lonely, unimpressive building from the outside. The sumptuous interior, however, holds some of the legendary artists' best work.

Brunelleschi's gray-and-white interior is one of the first to have a purely Renaissance design, with monumental pillars and arches forming a strictly measured Latin cross. On both sides of the nave are bronze pulpits by Donatello sculpted in 1460, six years before his death. The sculptor's body rests peacefully in a chapel in the left transept, to the right of Filippo Lippi's *Annunciation*. On the other side of the transept is the **Sagrestia Vecchia**, designed by Brunelleschi, which features more sculpture by Donatello, including bronze doors and polychrome tondi of St. John the Evangelist. *Piazza San Lorenzo, tel. 055/216634. Open daily 7–noon and 3:30–5:30.*

The church cloisters, upstairs off the left aisle, contain Michelangelo's **Biblioteca Medicea Laurenziana** (tel. 055/210760; open Mon.–Sat. 9–1). This is the only place in Florence where you can see for free something that Michelangelo had a hand in designing. The library itself, full of stiff-backed, uncomfortable-looking wooden carrels, is fairly standard for the Renaissance, but not so in the case of the vestibule (the room leading to the library). Michelangelo decided to ignore classical rules by sculpting massive columns that appear to be supported by fluted S-curves recessed into the wall. The artist's famous convex staircase, a pun on the Renaissance exactitude of architects like Brunelleschi, pushes outwards for no other reason than because it looks cool.

Nowhere is Medici ostentation more apparent than in the **Cappelle Medicee**. Although the chapels were originally integral parts of San Lorenzo, visitors today can only enter them from the back end of the church for a fee of L9000. It's worth shelling out the money to see the unbelievably opulent interior of a chapel that was intended for a single family's use: The **Cappella dei Principi** (Princes' Chapel) will either have you on your knees wailing, "I'm not worthy" or thinking it's the gaudiest thing this side of Vegas. The dome of deep green, pink, and black marble soars dizzyingly above. Escape to Michelangelo's much more subtle **Sagrestia Nuova**, containing the sculpted tombs of two members of the Medici clan. The tomb of Lorenzo (to the left of the entrance) has him in a thoughtful pose above the splayed figures of Dusk and Dawn; the tomb of Giuliano (opposite) shows his bounding image towering over Night and Day. The unusual poses of the four stages of day confirm Michelangelo's total mastery of the human form. *Admission: L9000. Open Tues.–Sun. 9–2.*

➢ **PALAZZO MEDICI-RICCARDI** • Michelozzo's original design for Medici headquarters ushered in a new age of Florentine civic architecture with its solemn but unimposing, rusticated brick facade. The building was redone over the years by subsequent owners, and part of it is still used for government offices, but its most famous feature, the second-floor **chapel**, hasn't been touched. Inside is the exquisite *Procession of the Magi* by Benozzo Gozzoli (1460),

Let's Make a Deal

The open street market that springs up every day around the Mercato Centrale offers everything from Florentine paper goods to reasonably priced clothes. Accept the fact that you will get disoriented in the maze and dive in. The listed prices are not engraved in stone, and assume that bargaining is expected when there are no prices printed (especially with leather goods). Don't be shy—when a merchant seems to pull a price out of his head, counter with half and go from there. If there aren't other potential customers distracting the merchant, try the "two-person rush." This maneuver requires an impatient friend to pretend to tug the interested buyer away. The price of that leather jacket may suddenly fall like the Dow Jones.

an example of feel-good Medici propaganda, depicting the savvy patrons as illustrious, well-dressed kings. Unfortunately, the cost to enter the small chapel is L6000, and the frescoes, though delightful, are all you get. *Via Cavour 1, tel. 055/276–0340. Open Mon., Tues., Thurs.–Sat. 9–1 and 3–6, Sun. 9–1.*

PIAZZA SAN MARCO AND PIAZZA SANTISSIMA ANNUNZIATA These two neighboring squares north of the Duomo are hangouts for local students (the university is nearby) and contain a cluster of earnest sights, of which only the Accademia is heavily trafficked. If your nerves need soothing, head for the church and museum of San Marco, where a quiet, monastic cloister provides the perfect complement to Fra Angelico's art.

➤ **GALLERIA DELL'ACCADEMIA** • The L12,000 entrance fee is awfully steep to see essentially one statue, but the huge lines out front should convince you that Michelangelo's *David* is worth it. The master began the work in 1501 at the age of 26, out of a single block of discarded marble. Originally designed to stand outdoors in the Piazza della Signoria and be viewed from a distance, the proportions of David are slightly odd. Most noticeably, the hands are enormous compared to the rest of him, his head is slightly too large for his body, and his calf-to-thigh ratio is askew. Walk completely around the statue and watch his expression change from the famous calmly accepting look to one of extreme trepidation. The statue was moved inside about 100 years ago after his left wrist was broken in a riot.

The gallery that leads to *David* is lined with a series of Michelangelo's *Slaves* from the 1520s. Believing that every slab of marble inherently possessed a figure struggling to emerge, Michelangelo partially "freed" them, allowing the powerful figures to continue to fight for liberation on their own. The museum also contains a distinguished collection of Renaissance painting. *Via Ricasoli 60, tel. 055/214375. Admission: L12,000. Open summer, Tues.–Sat. 9–7, Sun. 9–2; winter, Tues.–Sat. 9–2, Sun. 9–1.*

When a nut case tried to smash David five years ago (claiming that the woman in the adjacent portrait was jealous and had asked him to destroy the statue), he only succeeded in pulverizing a big toe. Good samaritans tackled the culprit, while others scrambled for the marble shards as mementos. Museum guards had to strip search everyone and successfully retrieved all the pieces.

➤ **MUSEO DI SAN MARCO** • This serene museum is one of Florence's best. San Marco was the city's Dominican convent and the home of Savonarola, the hot-headed friar who conducted the Bonfire of the Vanities (*see box* Bonfire of the Vanities, *below*) in 1497. The most devout of Renaissance painters, Fra Angelico, spent years here as a friar, creating some of his best works. To the right of the entrance, a gallery contains his oil paintings and altarpieces, including two *Deposition*s and a *Last Judgment* with a graphic vision of hell on its right side. In the **Sala Capitolare** is his wall-size *Crucifixion*, and at the top of the stairs near the dormitory cells you'll find his most famous work, the *Annunciation*, with sparkling colors projected onto a perfectly geometrical space. On the same floor are 44 monks' cells, each with its own small fresco by Fra Angelico and his students. Cosimo I de' Medici spent some of his old age here, well before Savonarola preached against the family. Michelozzo designed the Brunelleschi-influenced chapel on this floor in the 1430s. The museum also includes the work of Ghirlandaio, among others. *Piazza San Marco 1, tel. 055/210741. Admission: L8000. Open Tues.–Sun. 9–2.*

➤ **MUSEO ARCHEOLOGICO** • This museum houses an extensive collection of ancient finds started by the Medicis (surprise, surprise), mostly local Etruscan and Roman urns and tiny bronze figurines, but also Egyptian mummies and masks. The most notable finds are several spectacularly preserved life-size male bronzes from the Roman period; the *Chimera*, a mythical beast from the 5th century BC; and an astonishing Roman sculpture of a horse's head. The museum provides a nice break from the endless archives of Renaissance art. *Via della Colonna 36, tel. 055/247–8641. Admission: L8000. Open Tues.–Sat. 9–2, Sun. 9–1.*

➤ **PIAZZA SANTISSIMA ANNUNZIATA** • A brigade of moped-revvin' teenagers crowds this wide piazza, one of Florence's most artistically important squares because of the

Spedale degli Innocenti. The orphanage's portico, designed by Brunelleschi, is considered by some the first manifestation of true Renaissance style in architecture. Begun in 1419 by the master, it was completed in 1445 by Francesco della Luna. The hospital's simple columns, topped by perfect half-circle arches, seem standard today, but they mark the beginning of Brunelleschi's infatuation with perfect mathematical equilibrium.

Andrea della Robbia sculpted the 10 tondi of babies between the arches, and about 150 years later a symmetrical loggia was built across the piazza to complement Brunelleschi's porch. Inside the old hospital is the **Galleria dello Spedale degli Innocenti** (Piazza Santissima Annunziata 12, tel. 055/247–7952; open Mon., Tues., Thurs., Fri. 8:30–2, weekends 8:30–1). The undistinguished collection of Renaissance paintings barely justifies the L3000 admission fee—have a look at Ghirlandaio's *Adoration of the Magi* and head elsewhere.

On the north side of the square is **Santissima Annunziata** (tel. 055/239–8034; open daily 7:30–12:30 and 4–6:30), one of the city's busiest Catholic churches. You don't have to interrupt mass to see the lively series of frescoes by Andrea del Sarto, Jacopo Pontormo, and Rosso Fiorentino, which is in the atrium outside the church.

➤ **SANT'APPOLLONIA** • Andrea del Castagno's brilliantly colored *Last Supper* covers a wall of the refectory in this old Dominican monastery. It is a moving, fascinating take on the subject, maybe the best in Florence, and was once attributed to Uccello because of its dazzling, skewed perspective effects. *Via XXVII Aprile 1, tel. 055/287074. Admission free. Open Tues.–Sat. 9–2, Sun. 9–1.*

PIAZZA SANTA CROCE Santa Croce is the southeastern edge of the Florentine tourist triangle; east of here lie narrow neighborhood streets and underpopulated restaurants. The church of Santa Croce is the Westminster Abbey of Italy, providing an eternal resting place to many of Florence's rich and famous.

➤ **SANTA CROCE** • Florence's main Franciscan church, begun in the late 13th century, holds the tombs of an all-star lineup including Michelangelo, Galileo, Ghiberti, and Machiavelli, as well as monuments to Dante, Leonardo da Vinci, and Raphael (the last three are buried elsewhere). As you walk through, it's eerie to stumble over an uneven flagstone and real-

Bonfire of the Vanities

If you thought "Bonfire of the Vanities" was just a Tom Wolfe novel, think again. The original one took place in Florence on Piazza della Signoria on the last day of Carnival in 1497. The radical Dominican monk Girolamo Savonarola, who was ruling Florence for a brief period during the Medici's exile, was convinced the city was going to hell and tried to eliminate everything that led to sinning and sleazing. A pack of devoted henchmen ransacked private homes and collected "licentious" goods. Then they built a pyramid with carnival disguises on the bottom tier, Latin and Italian manuscripts above, and women's ornaments and toiletries, music manuscripts, and games above that. Even Botticelli got caught up in the moment and threw a few of his paintings on top, and Savonarola proceeded to torch the whole affair. The participants supposedly enjoyed the show so much they made for Piazza San Marco for a little dancing and merriment. By the following year, though, the political tide had turned, and the Florentines were tired of Savonarola's puritanical rule. Ironically, he was hanged and burned by the Medicis on Piazza della Signoria, the site of the bonfire. A plaque on the square commemorates the event.

ize you tripped over a worn-down relief portrayal of the grave's occupant. To the right of the entrance is Michelangelo's sculpted tomb, designed by Vasari, although the artist's body is actually under the Buonarroti family medallions carved into the floor to the left of the tomb. (Florence decided to bury him safely under the floor since they were worried that Romans would sneak in and carry his body off as a trophy.) Also on the right-hand side of the nave (just below the organ) is Donatello's gold-plated *Annunciation*, one of the best Florentine sculptures of the familiar scene. Galileo's tomb lies opposite Michelangelo's, near the entrance on the left side. Because he put forward the theory that the sun, rather than the earth, was the center of the solar system, his corpse wasn't allowed in until 100 years after his death, when the Vatican formally conceded that the universe wasn't geocentric after all.

Giotto's fresco cycles of St. Francis (in the **Cappella Bardi**, close to the altar) and St. John the Baptist (in the adjacent **Cappella Peruzzi**) helped prod painting out of stiff medieval conventions and into more imaginative and psychologically complex compositions. The color has faded and huge splotches are missing, but the frescoes remain impressive. The chapel at the far end of the left transept contains Donatello's *Crucifix*, sharply criticized by Brunelleschi, who sculpted his cross in Santa Maria Novella as a lesson to his fellow artist. *Piazza Santa Croce 16, tel. 055/244619. Open summer, Mon.–Sat. 8–6:30, Sun. 8–12:30 and 3–6:30; winter, Mon.–Sat. 8–12:30 and 3–6:30, Sun. 3–6.*

On the right-hand side of the facade is the entrance to the cloisters, containing the church **museum** and Brunelleschi's justly famous **Cappella dei Pazzi**. Brunelleschi's mathematically calibrated, geometrically planned chapel with its squat dome was begun in the 1430s and completed almost 40 years later. Luca della Robbia and friends did the terra-cotta tondi of the apostles, as well as the evangels above the door. The adjacent museum boasts Donatello's massive bronze *San Ludovico d'Angio* (1423) and Cimabue's *Crucifixion*, heavily damaged by Florence's disastrous flood in 1966, as well as work by lesser-known artists. *Museum and Cappella admission: L3000. Open in summer Thurs.–Tues. 10–12:30 and 2:30–6:30 (winter afternoon hours 3–5).*

➤ **CASA BUONARROTI** • Casa Buonarroti, owned but never lived in by Michelangelo, houses the largest collection of his drawings in the world. Upstairs are several impressive sculptures by a very young Michelangelo, including *Madonna of the Steps* and *Battle of the Centaurs*, both unfinished. A wooden crucifix from Santo Spirito dates back to 1492, when the artist was only 17 years old. Downstairs are rotating displays of his sketches. They're generally interesting, but the lack of complete, mature works is somewhat disappointing. *Via Ghibellina 70, tel. 055/241752. Admission: L8000, L6000 students. Open Wed.–Mon. 9:30–1:30.*

➤ **SYNAGOGUE AND JEWISH MUSEUM** • In the mid-19th century, as most of Florence's old synagogues were being demolished to facilitate modernization, the leader of the local Jewish community, David Levi, bequeathed his estate to the founding of a new synagogue. Built in the 1870s in Moorish/Byzantine style, the enormous synagogue is both wonderful and garish, with ornate, hand-painted arabesques covering the walls and Turkish-style domes on the exterior. Upstairs, a small, worthwhile museum depicts the history of Florence's Jews. Orthodox services are held weekly. Next door, **Cuscusso** (Via Farini 2) serves pricey kosher lunches and dinners. *Via Farini 4, tel. 055/ 245252. Admission for both: L5000, L4000 students. Open Sun.–Thurs. 10–1 and 2–5, Fri. 10–1.*

THE OLTRARNO Although Florentines once perceived the other side of the Arno as a world away, most sights (except those up the hill) are really within 10 minutes' walk of the Uffizi. On the way over, cross the **Ponte Vecchio**, the oldest bridge in Florence. Rebuilt in the 14th century from a wooden structure dating to Roman times, the bridge was originally lined with butchers and produce sellers. In the late 16th century, Ferdinando I installed jewelry merchants, and the tradition continues today. The Oltrarno is a pleasant area to explore, especially once you clear crowded **Via Guicciardini** between the Ponte Vecchio and the Pitti Palace. To the east, the

The combination of jewelry hawkers, caricaturists displaying outdated sketches of Ed Asner and John Travolta, and throngs of tourists has inspired some to rename Florence's oldest bridge "Ponte Dreckio."

streets become narrow and twisted as they ascend toward the Belvedere and Piazzale Michelangelo; to the west, beyond Santo Spirito, the tranquil streets are filled with trattorias and local hangouts.

➤ **PITTI PALACE** • Designed as a home for Luca Pitti, a prosperous local businessman, the original building of the palace (the middle section, minus the wings) was begun in the 15th century. Then the Medicis got their hands on the place and had the perennially unsubtle Ammanati make enormous additions. In its expanded state, it's by far the largest building in Florence, nearly twice the size of the Duomo. The palace is just as extravagant today in terms of budget travel—if you don't watch yourself, you could spend more than L20,000 visiting all of the museums and gardens.

The most substantial of the palace's museums is the **Galleria Palatina** (tel. 055/210323; admission: L12,000; open Tues.–Sun. 9–2), with works by Rubens, Caravaggio (look for his tooth-pulling scene in the first room), Tintoretto, and Van Dyck. Titian and Raphael are well represented, the former by *La Concerta* and some moving portraits, the latter by a number of stirring *Madonna and Child* scenes. There's also a **Galleria d'Arte Moderna** (tel. 055/287096), but at press time it was temporarily closed with no projected reopening date.

The other major museum in the palace, the **Museo degli Argenti** (tel. 055/212557), holds Medici capes, urns, chalices, and other such booty. As with the palace's art galleries, there's much more here than you can really take in. The L8000 admission also lets you see the attractive displays in the **Galleria del Costume** (which has a L6000 fee if you don't get the Argenti ticket), and it gets you into the cloying, unimpressive **Museo delle Porcellane** (tel. for both 055/212557). All three museums are open Tuesday–Sunday 9–2.

➤ **BOBOLI GARDENS** • These luxurious, spacious gardens were built by the Medicis as an idyllic (and private) outdoor retreat in the late 16th and early 17th centuries. When the park was transformed into free public space in the last century, just about every Florentine visited regularly. Unfortunately, the city recently imposed a L5000 entrance fee, essentially taking the park away from the masses and returning it to the moneyed. Now most visitors are foreigners, but on weekends Italian families still come for picnics.

A succession of landscapers groomed the grounds for the Medici family, creating an odd blend of classic formal gardens with twisting, shaded bowers. Look for the **Grotta del Buontalenti** beside the park exit on the palace's north side. Inside the dazzlingly ornamented artificial cave are copies of Michelangelo's *Slaves* (the originals are now in the Accademia). Near the grotto, look for the bizarre statue of Cosimo's obese, nude court dwarf riding a turtle. The rest of the garden is wonderful for exploring, with dazzling views of the city (especially at the highest point, near Forte Belvedere) and breezy walks. The most spectacular of the fountains, the **Isolotto**, features a huge pond with a garden island in the center. Look for it toward the park's south end, at the bottom of the hill. *Piazza Pitti, tel. 055/213440. Admission: L5000. Open summer, Tues.–Sun. 9–7:30; winter, Tues.–Sun. 9–1 hr before sunset.*

➤ **SANTO SPIRITO** • You wouldn't guess it from the decaying, unadorned yellow exterior, but the church of Santo Spirito is one of the most ambitious creations to come out of the Renaissance—another one of Brunelleschi's mathematically precise projects. He believed that classical proportion was tantamount to beauty, so he lined the nave with an abundance of arches, columns, and chapels, all lined up nice and symmetrical. The church plan was intended to be perfectly square (a Greek-cross shape), but unfortunately he died in mid-construction and his design was modified to a more traditional style. In the right transept is Filippino Lippi's *Madonna and Child with Saints* (also known as the Nerli Altarpiece), and off the left aisle of the nave sits a harmonious sacristy designed by Giuliano da Sangallo. *Piazza Santo Spirito, tel. 055/210030. Open weekdays 9–6, weekends 9–10:30 and noon–5:30.*

➤ **CAPPELLA BRANCACCI** • Perhaps the most important and moving fresco cycle in Florence is the one in the tiny Cappella Brancacci, behind the church of **Santa Maria del Carmine,** a few blocks west of Santo Spirito. The chapel is known for Massaccio's brilliant, legendary frescoes, *Expulsion from Eden* and *The Tribute Money*. The latter is a dramatic three-part painting taken from the New Testament: In the center, the tax man comes to collect from

Jesus and the apostles; to the left, St. Peter reaches into the river and takes a gold coin from a fish's mouth; and on the right, St. Peter pays the tax man. Massaccio, who died at age 27, painted it in less than a month. The Adam and Eve expulsion scene—the first painting to have only one source of light on its figures—is probably the most wrenching artistic image of the Renaissance. A recent restoration brought back the brilliant color and revealed that the fig leaf covering Adam's privates was added by prudish clerics soon after Massaccio's death. After several centuries of being covered, Adam is once again in all his glory. *Piazza del Carmine, tel. 055/238–2195. Admission: L5000. Open Mon., Wed.–Fri. 10–5, weekends 1–5.*

➤ **OLTRARNO HILLS** • Buses 12 and 13 from the train station head up to **Piazzale Michelangelo**, with a fantastic view of Florence and the church of **San Miniato al Monte**, surveying the city from a cozy perch. The church is one of the city's earliest, dating to the early 11th century; only the Duomo's baptistry (which it intentionally resembles) is older. The patterned green-and-white marble facade is a style specific to Florence, as opposed to the innumerable Tuscan churches with a striped Pisan Romanesque look. Inside, the church is calm and cool, with enchanting floors depicting small animals up the center aisle. Look for some beautiful terra-cotta angels by Luca della Robbia on the ceiling of the chapel, off the left aisle. Throughout the year monks perform chants at special twilight services. *Via Monte alle Croci, tel. 055/233–2731. Open summer, daily 8–noon and 2–7; shorter hours in winter.*

Just beyond the valley west of San Miniato is a peak crowned by the **Forte Belvedere**, which is yet another Medici project, largely designed by Ammanati and Buontalenti. The views, which rival those from San Miniato, are more impressive than the building itself, but the fort is a wonderful place to spend several peaceful hours lolling about. It's usually free, except when sculpture exhibits come to the fort. *Via San Leonardo, tel. 055/234–2425. Open summer, Wed.–Mon. 9–8; winter, Wed.–Mon. 9–5.*

CHEAP THRILLS

To make up for the sky-high admission prices at many of Florence's sights, the city's cultural minister created ***Una Sera al Museo*** (An Evening at the Museum). From mid-June through late September, some of the city's best museums open their doors from 9 PM to 11 PM free of charge. One museum per night participates, but no museum is free more than three or four nights during the summer. The tourist office has a brochure with the complete schedule. The most popular places, notably the Uffizi, Accademia, Bargello, and Pitti Palace, have yet to join, but the Museo dell'Opera del Duomo, Museo San Marco, Cappelle Medici, and Museo Marini all take part. Crowds can be enormous; if you're going to a popular museum, arrive about an hour early. Often, the evenings feature live classical-music accompaniment, making the experience all the more memorable.

If you want to spend some time in the outdoors and kick back, the beautiful public park adjacent to the Fortezza da Basso offers lots of grass, flowers, and a small lake (only ducks, not people, are allowed to swim in it). Head north on Via Faenza to Viale Filippo Strozzi and make a right to reach the park. You can rent a bicycle for about L15,000 for a day and take off to explore the fringes of Florence or the outlying country. Take a picnic and you're set (*see* Getting Around, *above*, for bike rental information).

FESTIVALS Florence's patron-saint celebration, the **Festa di San Giovanni**, is a massive celebration that is held June 24 but has the entire city talking about it year-round. Colorful medieval-dress parades, complex flower arrangements that blanket Piazza della Signoria, and a fireworks show over the Arno make the festival unforgettable. Most amazing, however, is the *calcio storico* competition. The city's four quarters fight it out in a series of medieval soccer matches to assert their neighborhood's dominance. With 34 burly men in medieval costumes on a mud field, the main requirement for making the team seems to be having served hard time. The entire town gets drunk after the finals.

In December, Florence hosts a **film festival** that is starting to attract as much attention as its counterpart in Venice. The city also hosts a music festival called **Maggio Musicale Fiorentino**, which lasts from May to August. The festival features different types of music at various venues throughout the city. Publicity posters are plastered everywhere, but you can get the details at the tourist office, or by calling the **box office** (tel. 055/211158).

AFTER DARK

At night Florentines divide into two camps: those who frequent the standard clubs in the center in the hope of meeting Americans, and those who hang out at the bars on the periphery, in search of locals-only spots. If you want to party with the latter crowd, plan to take a cab or bum a ride home; buses stop running around midnight or 1 (but if you're motivated or drunk enough, it's possible to walk back to the centro from the outlying areas of Piazza San Michelangelo or the Cascine). The Italian-language *Firenze Spettacolo* (L2500), available at local newsstands, lists films, discos, music, and cultural goings-on.

The main evening socializing occurs while taking a *passeggiata*. Hoards of people (young and old alike) grab a gelato and stroll from the Duomo to the Piazza della Signoria and back again. Young *pappogalli* (pick-up artists) line the street scoping out the selection of foreigners, and street performers set up shop in the piazze. Other hot spots to check out are the **Ponte Vecchio** and **Piazza San Michelangelo**, both of which get unbelievably crowded.

BARS AND CAFES If you want to sit down and have a drink, look for signs that say AMERICAN BAR. These generally have indoor seating and a fully stocked bar, whereas traditional Italian "bars" are more like cafés. The **Dublin Pub** (Via Faenza 27r, tel. 055/293049) offers happy hour before 9 PM, when pints of world-class draft beer (like Guinness) cost only L3000. A much better pub, though, is **The Fiddler's Elbow** (Piazza Santa Maria Novella 7r, no phone), which is open nightly in summer. Beer isn't cheap (L6000 a pint), but you can drink it on an outdoor patio or on Piazza Santa Maria Novella itself.

The other square that draws a diverse, sometimes wild, nightly crowd is **Piazza Santo Spirito**. This is where the locals congregate, peacefully coexisting with a few addicts of different sorts. As a foreigner, you may attract less attention here, but you may also feel unwelcome. The piazza feels less safe than the centro, and women should be careful, but once you plop down in one of its hip outdoor cafés, you should be okay. Most locals buy beer at the bar and take it outside (having a drink served to you is frightfully expensive). **Cabiria Café** (Piazza Santo Spirito, tel. 055/215732) is the hippest place in town, hopping all afternoon and evening. In the student area on the other side of town, try the happening **Cardillac Caffè** (Via degli Alfani 57r, tel. 055/234–4455; closed Sun.), which hosts gay and lesbian night every Friday beginning at 10 PM. **Rex Café** (Via Fiesolana 25r; closed Tues.) serves a great *birra rossa* (red beer) which draws raucous crowds of Italians nightly. If you're in search of live music, **Be Bop** (Via dei Servi 76r, no phone) hosts bands every night of the week with special prices for students.

DISCOS Admission to the discos is around L15,000–L20,000, but women often get in free. Also look for discount passes handed out on Piazza del Duomo, Piazza della Repubblica, and Via de' Calzaiuoli. Few places in the center get much business from the locals; two of the better ones are the cavernous **Yab Yum** (Via Sassetti 5r, tel. 055/282018; closed Mon. and summer) and **055** (Via Verdi 57, tel. 055/244004). Both are just as full of Americans as Italians, but the techno/house music brings everyone together, at least rhythmically.

The best local radio station is Contraradio (93.6 FM), which plays punk, funk, and international music in a rotation similar to U.S. college radio. DJs often announce concerts and clubs of note over the air.

Most locals are much more keen on places outside the center, where there's space to dance outdoors. During summer the wildest dancing takes place at **Meccanò** (Viale degli Olmi 1, on the south edge of Cascine Park, tel. 055/331371), which features live music, women dancing in go-go cages, and a general air of carousing. Covers run L25,000–L30,000. You can get there on Bus 17, but the area is sketchy and the bus stops running around midnight. **Central Park** (Via Fosso Macinante 13, tel. 055/322723) is on the other edge of the Cascine and is also difficult to get home from. The cover is L20,000, with huge floors inside and outside that stay packed into the night.

> **GAY AND LESBIAN CLUBS** • Gay discos come and go in Florence, and the scene here is much more accommodating for gay men than for lesbians. **Tabasco** (Piazza Santa Cecilia 3, just off Piazza della Signoria, tel. 055/213000; closed Mon.), for men only, has been a favorite of visitors for a few years. Friday night, **Flamingo** (Via de' Pandolfini 26r, near Piazza Salvemini, tel. 055/234–0210) is the city's lesbian hot spot; other nights it's men only. The club closes in July and August. Call **ARCI Gay** (tel. 055/239–8722) for more info, or look for *Quir*, an Italian/English gay magazine listing local events (*see* Basics, *above*).

MOVIE THEATERS Florence has plenty of cinemas, although nearly all of them close in summer because they lack air-conditioning. The obvious remedy is outdoor screens, and many have popped up in and around Florence. The closest is just outside the walls of Forte Belvedere (*see* Oltrarno Hills, in Worth Seeing, *above;* tel. 055/234–0266). From late June to early September, recent films are shown nightly beginning at 9:30 (admission: L10,000). All English films are dubbed into Italian. To get there, catch Bus 13 or cross the river at Ponte alle Grazia and follow the signs. The hike up the hill takes a little effort but the view is stunning. The only screen in town that shows English-language films full-time is the indoor **Cinema Astro** (Piazza San Simone, no phone). Here you can sit in uncomfortable wooden seats and watch American hits from three months ago, interspersed with inevitable showings of *Room with a View*. Astro closes in mid-July and reopens in mid-August. Don't confuse it with the similarly titled **Cinema Astra** (Via de' Cerretani 54r, tel. 055/294770), which shows English films with Italian subtitles on Mondays and Tuesdays during summer for L12,000. For schedules, check the tourist office and English-language bulletin boards.

Near Florence

FIESOLE

Fiesole, only a 20-minute bus ride (8 kilometers) from downtown Florence, has all the characteristics of the tiny hill towns that dot the Tuscan countryside, and a magnificent view of Florence to boot. Even if you have only two hours to spare, it's definitely worth the (very simple) journey up the hill to get a different angle on the local scene. The most exciting way up is to rent a scooter in Florence for the day (*see* Getting Around, *above*) and explore the country roads on your way. And since most of the sights remain open on Monday when most of Florence's museums close, it's a good way to spend the day.

Fiesole's history predates that of Florence. Etruscans founded the city around 600 BC on the site of a long-dead Bronze Age town, and the Romans constructed one of the region's most sophisticated amphitheaters here around 80 BC. Its ruins and the remnants of Roman bathhouses stand before an unspoiled series of hills north of the city. Today many visitors explore the hillside on mountain bikes; the steep, uncrowded roads around town afford terrific views. During summer the city is home to the spectacular **Estate Fiesolana** festival, a music, dance, theater, and film series that many consider the region's richest cultural event.

COMING AND GOING Fiesole is so close to Florence that it's on the city bus line. Tickets, available at tabacchi, cost L1100, and the ride takes about 20 minutes. Bus 7 leaves every 15 minutes during peak hours from the stop near Santa Maria Novella Station's Track 16. It drops you at Piazza Mino da Fiesole, in the middle of town one block south of the entrance to the Roman ruins. The last bus returns to the city around 12:30 AM. The **tourist office** (Piazza Mino da Fiesole 37, tel. 055/588720) is right beside the stop.

WHERE TO SLEEP AND EAT Unless you plan on camping, head back to Florence for the night, where hotels are cheaper. The lavish **Camping Panoramico Fiesole** (Via Peramonda 1, tel. 055/599069) is about 3 kilometers from Fiesole, but it's a city unto itself, with a market, a restaurant with great views of Florence, and better facilities than most hotels. The price (L8500 per person, L15,000 per tent) is unbelievably low for this area. The campground also has cabin-style bungalows at L55,000 for two people (L10,000 for each additional person). Take Bus 70 from Piazza Mino da Fiesole to the campground stop and follow the signs.

Local food is overpriced and nothing special. Two decent trattorias, **La Romagnola** (Via Gramsci 43, tel. 055/59258) and **Il Lordo** (Piazza Mino da Fiesole, tel. 055/59095), serve typical Italian meals for a slightly steep L20,000 or so. A better idea is to stroll up Via Gramsci, which has a **Coop** supermarket (Via Gramsci 20, tel. 055/59219), a bakery, and a couple of places to buy fruits and vegetables. Head in any direction out of the city center and find a tranquil spot high in the hills, where only wildflowers will witness a picnic.

WORTH SEEING You can purchase a combination ticket to the Museo Bandini, the ruins, the Museo Civico, and the Antiquarium Constantini for L6000. A combination ticket to the last three costs L5000 (L2500 students). All of the churches mentioned below are open Monday–Saturday 7:30 AM–4:30 PM (approximately), but be careful about early morning services when nonworshipping visitors are not very welcome.

The town's well-preserved Roman ruins merit more attention than they get from most visitors. The **Teatro Romano** has been partially restored and holds performances, but the view of the hills beyond the theater is often more impressive than what's on stage. Below the theater are remains of the baths; only one arch still stands to give you a sense of the original architecture. The **Museo Archeologico** (Via Portigiani 1, tel. 055/59477) contains Etruscan and Roman finds from the area. The most prized piece is a barely recognizable bronze copy of Rome's symbol, the Romulus and Remus she-wolf. *Teatro and Museo: Admission: L5000. Open summer, Wed.–Mon. 9–7; winter, 10–6.*

The **Antiquarium Constantini** (Via Portigiani 9, tel. 055/59477) houses a well-maintained, private collection of mostly Greek and Etruscan urns and vases from Sicily and southern Italy. The **Museo Bandini** (Via Duprè 1, tel. 055/59061), an air-conditioned collection of early Renaissance art, including della Robbia terra-cottas. *Antiquarium and Museo admission: L3000, L2000 for students. Open summer, Wed.–Mon. 10–7; winter, 10–6.*

The church of **San Romulus** (Piazza della Cattedrale, tel. 055/599566) has a flattened sandstone facade thanks to messy restoration work, but inside it's a somber take on the Pisan Romanesque style, with several sculptures by local artist Mino da Fiesole. Head up the hill outside the church (on Via di San Francesco), and you'll reach the town's main vista point, just below the two highest churches. The church of **San Francesco** (Via di San Francesco, tel. 055/59175; admission free), at Fiesole's highest point, has probably the best museum in town in its basement. It's filled with both Egyptian finds and dozens of fabulously detailed ivory and alabaster carvings brought from China by missionaries, many of which date to the 1st century BC and are much more sophisticated than Roman sculpture of the period.

A bit out of town is the church of **San Domenico** (Piazza San Domenico 4, tel. 055/598837), where the great Fra Angelico became a priest and created some of his most brilliant paintings. One of his major works, a triptych comprising an *Annunciation*, a *Coronation of Christ*, and a *Maestà*, once hung in the church; of the three panels, only the *Maestà* remains. San Domenico is about 2 kilometers below Fiesole, and Bus 7 stops right in front of the church on its way to and from Florence. Since bus tickets are good for an hour, you can run into the church for a short visit and hop back on the bus without buying another ticket.

FESTIVALS One of Italy's most prestigious cultural festivals, the **Estate Fiesolana**, runs nightly from late June to late August, with most events taking place in the Teatro Romano. Events change nearly every night, and the variety is incredible. Plays are performed in Italian, and films are shown in their original language with subtitles. The dance and music performances attract an eclectic group of performers—primarily Italian, but international acts do appear. Tickets for theater and dance cost L20,000–L25,000, music events run about L20,000 for all seats, and tickets for films cost L8000. You can pick up pamphlets for the festival all over Fiesole and Florence, or call the box office at the Teatro Romano (tel. 055/597277). Events rarely sell out, so just arrive early enough to find a good seat.

PRATO

The city of Prato knows it wouldn't win a beauty contest with its neighbor, Florence. An industrial center, Prato can boast neither a scenic setting nor a blockbuster collection of medieval or Renaissance art (though you can find some works by big names like Uccello and the Lippis in the cathedral). It has been the regional center of cloth and textile production since the days of the Medici. Now the third-largest city in Tuscany, Prato has moved its factories well outside the city walls. The modern city may seem mundane, but the *centro storico* is captivating in its tranquility and its surprisingly attractive piazze. Its major contemporary art museum also provides an interesting contrast to the barrage of Renaissance work that fills Tuscany.

Pick up a city map at the **tourist office** (Via Cairoli 48–52, tel. 0574/24112). To reach the office from the central train station, cross the piazza and the bridge, take Viale Vittorio Veneto across Piazza San Marco onto Viale Piave, and turn right just beyond the fortress on Santa Maria delle Carceri. Opposite the church is the back entrance to the office, marked with a yellow "i." If you're coming from the Porta al Serraglio station, take Via Magnolfi through Piazza del Duomo to Via G. Mazzoni, and go left at Piazza del Comune onto Via Cairoli. The office closes down with the rest of the city from 1 to 4 PM every day.

COMING AND GOING Trains make the 15-minute journey to Prato from Florence (L2000) about three times an hour. They stop first at Prato's **central station** (Piazza della Stazione, tel. 0574/26117), but westbound trains (to Pistoia, Lucca, and Pisa) also stop at a far more convenient second station, **Porta al Serraglio** (Via Cavallotti, tel. 0574/26117), two blocks north of the duomo. Don't bother with the **CAP** buses (L2500), which leave Florence from Stazione Santa Maria Novella hourly and take about twice as long as the train. Prato's two busiest spots are Piazza del Duomo and Piazza Santa Maria delle Carceri. To the east is the enormous Piazza Mercatale, with a park and a number of cafés and restaurants.

WHERE TO SLEEP AND EAT Prato lacks a hostel or campground, so it's a hotel or bust. The city is an easy day trip from Florence, so it's probably not worth it to stay here anyway. If you do, the **Hotel Stella d'Italia** (Piazza del Duomo 8, tel. 0574/27910), with bright rooms that overlook the cathedral, is the best deal in town. The accommodating manager charges L69,000 for a double, but prices drop in August. Another clean, cozy option is the **Albergo Il Giglio** (Piazza San Marco 14, tel. 0574/37049), just off Piazza San Marco toward Piazza Mercatale. It offers doubles for around L74,000 with TVs in most of the rooms.

Chez Le Crouton (Via Carraia 51–53, tel. 0574/35065; closed Sun.), one block west of Piazza del Duomo off Largo Carducci, is a typical Italian trattoria despite its French name, and it's incredibly cheap. Primi like risotto with zucchini go for L4500, and meaty second courses are just L8500. For terrific food to go, drop into **Rosticceria Gigi** (Via del Sirena 11, off Piazza del Duomo, tel. 0574/25227), with lasagna for about L4000 a slice and full roast chickens for about L12,000. Unfortunately, Prato doesn't have many good picnic spots, so you'll probably have to dine on the steps of the duomo.

WORTH SEEING Don't come to Prato on Tuesday, when all the museums are closed. Also be careful about the siesta period, which even the tourist attractions take seriously. The **Centro per l'Arte Contemporanea Luigi Pecci** (Viale della Repubblica 277, tel. 0574/570620; admission: L6000; open Wed.–Mon. 10–7), an enormous gallery and art center complete with a library, presents temporary exhibits by today's most experimental Italian and international artists. Downstairs you'll find Prato's hippest café/bar, serving cocktails until 1 AM in summer. Next to the café is an outdoor amphitheater, which books excellent if infrequent concerts (only two or three biggies per summer). Call the tourist office for a complete schedule. The museum is beyond walking distance from the city center, but Bus 8 takes you right there from Viale Piave, across from the Castello dell'Imperatore on Piazza Santa Maria delle Carceri.

The cathedral of **San Stefano** (Piazza del Duomo, tel. 0574/26234), in the center of town, is a moldering variation on the familiar, striped Pisan Romanesque style. Suspended on the right corner of the facade is Michelozzo's unusual pulpit. Decorated with Donatello friezes (the originals are housed in the museum next door), the **Pulpit of the Sacred Girdle** is atypically located so that the priest could address both the crowd inside the small church and the spill-over outside in the Piazza. The girdle itself, which the Virgin Mary gave to the perpetually doubting Thomas (that time he questioned her Assumption), is carried out onto the pulpit and displayed to a cheering crowd about five times a year. Inside the Duomo is Agnolo Gaddi's illustrative *Legend of the Holy Girdle* fresco cycle, another fresco cycle by Filippo Lippi, and one formerly

In a kinky twist of fate, Filippo Lippi's model for his fresco character Salome, the biblical prostitute, was a real-life nun. She played her part a little too well and bore a child by the artist-monk; the son, Filippino Lippi, also became a highly acclaimed painter (his works are in the cathedral museum and the Museo Civico).

attributed to Paolo Uccello (scholars can no longer identify the artist), and a blue-and-white terra-cotta above the entranceway by the ubiquitous della Robbia clan.

Next door, the **Museo dell'Opera del Duomo** (Piazza del Duomo 49, tel. 0574/29339; open Wed.–Mon. 9–12:30) holds Filippino Lippi's *Santa Lucia*, Uccello's *Jacopone da Todi*, and the original panels from Donatello's pulpit, mostly unexceptional putti carvings. The L5000 admission charge includes admission to the **Museo Civico** (Palazzo Pretorio, Piazza del Comune, tel. 0574/452302), which has several impressive altarpieces by both Lippis, and the **Museo di Pittura Murale** (Piazza San Domenico 8, tel. 0574/29339), which displays murals in various stages, from *sinopias* (the original trace drawings under frescoes) to completed works.

The church of **Santa Maria delle Carceri** (Piazza Santa Maria delle Carceri, tel. 0574/27933) has a squat dome with small windows and a long, blue-and-white terra-cotta frieze by Andrea della Robbia. Next door to the church is the **Castello dell'Imperatore**, a 13th-century fort that recently closed its doors to visitors. The only reason to go now is to see occasional classical music concerts or recent Italian and dubbed American movies, shown nightly in the courtyard during July and August (L8000).

PISTOIA

Nestled in the foothills of the Apennines, in the Tuscan industrial belt west of Florence, Pistoia sustains an intriguing combination of art and industry. An independent city in medieval times, it was annexed by Florence in 1530, just about the time Pistoians perfected the pistol, which took its name from the city. Not nearly as charming as neighboring Lucca, Pistoia does boast an almost completely tourist-free atmosphere, and the town's many churches and surprising variety of cultural activities (including a famous blues festival in late June/early July) make it a worthwhile day trip from Florence. Be sure to stop at the overstocked **tourist office** (Piazza del Duomo, tel. 0573/21622) for maps and information.

COMING AND GOING Reaching Pistoia is a breeze. The **train station** (Piazza Dante Alighieri, tel. 0573/20789), a 10-minute walk from the town center, has hourly trains from Prato (15 min, L2000), Lucca (30 min, L4200), and Florence (35 min, L3500). Buses take longer than the train and are more expensive, but the **CO.PI.T.** office (Piazza Dante Alighieri, across from the station, tel. 0573/21170) sends hourly buses to Florence (L3800) and will store your bags for L1000 per day.

The map supplied by tourist information makes Pistoia appear immense, but as soon as you start walking you realize how compact it is. To reach Piazza del Duomo (the town center) walk straight out of the train station onto Via XX Settembre, which becomes Via Atto Vannucci and later Via Cino; turn right on Via Cavour and left on Via Roma. This main piazza is lined by the cathedral and its baptistry, as well as Pistoia's most important medieval buildings.

WHERE TO SLEEP AND EAT Hotels tend to be three-star in Pistoia, making a visit here best as a day trip. The **Firenze** (Via Curtatone e Montanara 42, tel. 0573/23141) recently renovated its rooms, but it's still the best budget option in town, with doubles for L80,000. Cheap food is much less of a problem in Pistoia. The most popular joint in town is the marvelous **Rosticceria Francesco** (Corso Gramsci 10, just west of Via Atto Vannucci, tel. 0573/22216), where you can get a delicious meal for under L10,000. Take a number and try not to drool as you wait for fresh-from-the-oven pasta (about L5000), pasta salad, or roasted meat. For pizza or spaghetti, **Pizzeria Tonino** (Corso Gramsci 159, tel. 0573/33330) has good grub in a sit-down setting; pizzas go for about L7000. For a more eclectic menu, try **La Sala** (Via Sant'Anastasio 4, across from San Giovanni Fuorcivitas, tel. 0573/367267), a reasonably priced trattoria with pastas like gnocchi with four-cheese sauce (L6800) or *penne alla fume* (penne with smoked cheese; L6000). La Sala is closed Wednesday.

WORTH SEEING Pistoia's main churches date back to the 12th and 13th centuries with familiar black-and-white zebra stripes à la the cathedrals in Pisa and Siena, but on a much smaller scale. The **duomo** (Piazza del Duomo, tel. 0573/25095), bordering the main square, sports a campanile that looks like a fashion coordinator's nightmare. Its three levels are completely mismatched, moving from plain sandstone blocks to busy marble stripes, to ornate red brickwork, and topped off with a copper cupola. On the right-hand side of the interior in the **Cappella di San Jacopo** is a silver altarpiece begun in the 13th century and completed 200 years later. Portraits of saints fill the upper niches, while biblical scenes are depicted below. Numerous artists, including Brunelleschi, contributed to this crowning achievement of Pistoian metalwork. Just opposite the facade is the companion **baptistry**, its octagonal exterior decorated by Giovanni Pisano in the early 14th century.

The facade of the church of **San Giovanni Fuorcivitas** (Via Cavour, btw Via Carducci and Via Crispi, tel. 0573/24784) is hidden away on a side street, and it's so zanily striped that it may cause your eyes to cross. Inside are usually several lesser works by the Pisano clan, a pulpit by Fra Guglielmo da Pisa, and a *Visitation* terra-cotta by Luca della Robbia, but most of these works have been removed while the church undergoes heavy restoration. For a real Pisano fix, check out Giovanni's ornate pulpit uptown at the church of **Sant'Andrea** (Via Sant'Andrea 21, tel. 0583/21912); the busy, deeply carved panels show magnificent detail, particularly in the crucifixion scene. The pulpit is one of the family's best works. Unfortunately the church's facade has eroded so much that the stripes are barely visible.

Pistoia has a more dignified collection of modern art than Renaissance art, thanks to dozens of works by hometown boy Marino Marini (1901–1980), a painter and sculptor obsessed with the properties of color and slender lines. You can see a stunning display of his works, including a bronze head of Igor Stravinsky, free, at the **Centro di Documentazione Fondazione Marino Marini** (Palazzo del Tau, Corso San Fredi 72, tel. 0573/30285), one block south of San Giovanni Fuorcivitas. Marini returned again and again to figures of acrobats and riders on horseback, often portraying them as slivery stick figures. Admission to the center is free, and it's open Tuesday–Friday 9–1 and 3–7, weekends 9–12:30.

AFTER DARK Screaming microbus hordes descend on Pistoia the last weekend of June or first weekend of July for the **Pistoia Blues Festival**, which hosts second-string blues legends in Piazza del Duomo. Shirtless fans set up stands and hawk tie-dye shirts and Rasta caps all over town. Tickets cost L35,000 for one night or up to L100,000 for all three nights. Call or stop by the tourist office (*see above*) for more information.

During July and August, nightly films are screened outdoors at the **Fortezza Santa Barbara** in the southeast corner of town. Tickets for the movies (Italian flicks and dubbed American films) cost L10,000. **Teatro Comunale Manzoni** (Corso Gramsci 125, tel. 0573/27112) stages plays (in Italian, of course), sometimes outdoors on Piazza del Duomo. Tickets go for about L30,000. Information for all events is available at the tourist office.

CHIANTI

France has Bordeaux, America has the Napa Valley, and Italy has Chianti. The wine-making region between Florence and Siena is a long stretch of vineyards and picturesque hill towns. The region's most famous export, the *Chianti classico* evokes images of raucous meals at crowded tables, and along with the region's olive oil, is rumored to promote longevity. As a result, a large community of Northern Europeans and Brits have settled in the area in order to soak up the romantic hillside views, the gentle sunlight, and of course, the vino.

You'll need a car to really see the entire Chianti region, because buses miss most of the out-of-the-way towns. If you're short on time, however, the town of **Greve** is relatively easy to reach by bus, and it's only a short bike ride to many vineyards, country villas, and castles. Plus, its tourist office is loaded with great information. To do Chianti right, you'll want to taste (and probably buy) plenty of wine, and spend a little extra on a meal—in short, an enjoyable visit to the region is a budget buster, but it's definitely worth it.

COMING AND GOING SITA buses from Florence's main station make it to Greve (every 1½ hrs, 1 hr, L4200), but most don't continue farther into the region. Buses drop you off on Via Vittorio Veneto, one block away from the central Piazza Matteotti. Go up Via Vittorio Veneto and make a right on Via Battisti. Cars give you the freedom to explore the area. If you rent one in Florence (see Coming and Going in Florence, *above*, for car rental information) and drive to Greve, you can stop along the way at hilltop vineyards. Considering the challenges of driving on windy Chianti roads, however, you'll need a designated driver if you plan on doing some tasting.

The other increasingly popular way to get around is by mountain bike. Some of the big towns have bike-rental shops; in Greve, try **Marco Ramuzzi** (Via Italo Stecchi 23, tel. 055/853037), which rents nice mountain bikes for L20,000 per day and scooters starting at L40,000. Helmets are included in the price, which is a good thing since you'll have to contend with speeding Fiats and buses that drive down the center of terrifyingly narrow and winding roads. Bike trails are still an alien concept, but it's less than 10 kilometers to some tremendous vineyards.

WHERE TO SLEEP AND EAT Since this is the domain of upscale tourists, luxurious accommodations are the norm, with no camping allowed. The best bet is to stay in an *affita camera* (room in a private home). The **tourist office** in Greve (Via Luca Cino 1, tel. 055/854–5243; open weekdays 9–1 and 4–6) can provide a list of private rooms and will even help make phone calls for you. It also has information on hotels ranging from expensive to very expensive, maps of the whole region, lists of wineries, and a wonderful multilingual staff. The only other option is the comfortable **youth hostel** (tel. 055/851034), with beds around L20,000. Unfortunately it's 15 kilometers out of town, and to reach it you'll have to take the bus from the stop on Via Vittorio Veneto to Lucolena, then follow the hostel signs for the remaining 4 kilometers.

Food is incredibly expensive, so you'll probably want to pick up your own supplies. Luckily, you won't have any problems finding a butcher, baker, or market around Piazza Matteotti in Greve. The piazza holds a great market on Saturdays, with produce, music, leather goods, fresh fish, and everything else but the kitchen sink. In addition there is a **Coop Supermarket** (Viale Vanghetti 2, 1 block east of Piazza Matteotti, tel. 055/853053) that has a deli counter and an enormous selection of wine. For more good food to go, try the town's rosticceria, **La Mia Cucina** (Piazza Matteotti 80, tel. 055/854–4718), which has baked lasagna, great cannelloni, and delicious penne for around L5000–L6000. There's also a good selection of roast meats.

WORTH SEEING From Greve, you can explore Chianti's best attractions by car or bike. The helpful staff at the visitor's center will happily trace out the easiest routes to the various vineyards on a well-detailed map, and an abundance of signs point the way. Everywhere you look you'll see *enoteche* (wine stores), but if you wait until you reach the vineyards to taste wine, you're likely to get free samples. Greve is the rare tourist town that gets better with more visitors. For two weeks in early July, St. Anne's Park hosts the **Festa dell'Unità**, a local festival with live music, films, and many different food stands.

Apparently the cast and crew of Kenneth Branagh's "Much Ado About Nothing," filmed at Vignamaggio, won the hearts of the local populace with their genteel manners. They provided jobs for many residents, set the local record for beer consumption, and left the villa in perfect condition.

Vignamaggio (tel. 055/853559), an unbelievably gorgeous Renaissance villa surrounded by perfect gardens, was one of Chianti's first huge homes. La Giaconda, the subject of Leonardo da Vinci's *Mona Lisa*, was born here. You can arrange garden tours weekdays if you call a day ahead and speak to Sabina Hornung. If she's not too busy, she'll walk you through the gardens, which contain classical statues and big green hedges recognizable from Kenneth Branagh's film *Much Ado About Nothing*, which was shot here. (The baths, small chapel, and large fountain built specifically for the movie are now gone.) Despite the high-profile film, the villa remains quiet, relatively empty of tourists, and still completely enchanting. Tours are free, and afterward you can taste wine in the front office. Sabina even helps budget travelers find cheap rooms (about

L50,000 per person) in private houses nearby if they call well ahead of time. To get here, take Route N222 south from Greve about 3 kilometers, and turn left at the sign for Vignamaggio; from there, follow signs uphill to the villa.

Perhaps even more beautiful is **Castello di Uzzano** (Via Uzzano 5, tel. 055/854032), about 3 kilometers north of Greve and the onetime home of Niccolò da Uzzano—humanist, philanthropist, and patron of the arts. Much of the ivy-covered, austere castle was added on in the 17th and 18th centuries, and the garden is beyond description. You're supposed to pay L4000 per glass to taste wine, but the owner, Marion de Jacobert, lets most people taste for free so long as they aren't obviously greedy about it. Visiting the gardens costs L10,000. For a romantic splurge Chianti-style, Marion will make a picnic lunch for you to enjoy in the garden, with bread, prosciutto, salami, tomatoes, eggs, water, some very good wine, and coffee for about L30,000 per person (including admission to the gardens). To reach the castle from Greve, head north from the town center, go right at the Uzzano turnoff, and follow the signs up the dirt road. Visitors are welcome weekdays from 9 to 7.

Tuscany
Replete with small vineyards, dusty olive groves, and fields of sunflowers stretching out to the horizon, Tuscany's countryside radiates an allure that has attracted wave after wave of artists. In addition to providing the birthplace for Renaissance art, the vibrant and verdant area inspired the Romantic poets. The impressive roll call of those who made pilgrimages to the Tuscan countryside includes Keats and Shelley, who produced some of their best work here. Artists and art students continue to stalk the countryside in pursuit of the ultimate vista, because the vistas haven't really changed. Tuscany has maintained its prosaic agricultural focus: You'll find an industrial presence only in coastal towns like Livorno, a modern commercial and naval port since World War II, and in the mercantile belt northwest of Florence. The production of wine and olive oil is the mainstay of the rest of the local economy, which is (thankfully) reflected in its cuisine.

The best way to explore the rural areas of Tuscany is by bus or car (*see* Coming and Going, in Florence, *above*, for rental information), which allows you the experience of following a sharp turn in the road only to spy a walled town perched precariously on top of a cliff, regally overlooking its farmland. Once you get inside a town's walls, you'll find hidden-away art collections, fantastic views of the countryside, medieval ambiance, and friendly locals. Tuscany's only real downside is that it's one of Italy's most popular areas for tourism, which means you'll occasionally come across crowds and high prices. And though it can be difficult getting around the area, a bus schedule, patience, and good walking shoes will help.

Lucca

The word "unspoiled" comes to mind when thinking about Lucca—secure within its walls, the city has somehow avoided the plagues of modernity, tourism, and traffic (the locals imitate college students and bike). Sights are undemanding and uncrowded, and you can indulge in a big meal as you detox from an overdose of sightseeing in Florence and Pisa. If there were more cheap lodging, Lucca would be ideal.

It wasn't always this peaceful. The remarkably fertile land surrounding Lucca has been in high demand since Roman times. The first city in Tuscany to accept Christianity, Lucca was actually a political powerhouse up through the 14th century. It quickly shook off conquering Pisa, and even kept its voracious neighbor Florence at bay. Lucca preserved its autonomy until Napoléon decided it was a good place to occupy. Fortunately Napoléon's sister was an art fanatic and encouraged Lucca's cultural development and consequent prosperity. Lucca today remains one of the most affluent Tuscan cities, as you'll see from the abundance of luxury stores that grace its streets.

BASICS Lucca's only **tourist office** (Piazzale Verdi, tel. 0583/419689; open daily 9–7) is in a park near the bus station. The office rents bikes (L2500 per hour, L12,000 per day) and has an exchange counter with mediocre rates. The town's **post office** (Via Antonio Vallisneri 2, tel. 0583/47538; open weekdays 8:15–7, Sat. 8:15–noon) is beside the cathedral.

COMING AND GOING Lucca is on the convoluted Florence–Viarreggio line. Trains run hourly to Florence (1½ hrs, L5700) and Pisa (30 min, L2400) from Lucca's **train station** (Piazza Ricasoli, just south of the city walls, tel. 0583/47013). Ticket windows are open Monday–Saturday 5:10 AM–9:10 PM, Sunday 6 AM–9:40 PM; luggage storage is open 8–8. **Lazzi** buses leave from the **bus station** (Piazzale Verdi 2, tel. 0583/584876; open daily 6 AM–8 PM), in a wide-open park just west of the city center. Buses go to Pisa (40 min, L3000) every 30 minutes and to Florence (1 hr 10 min, L8400) hourly.

GETTING AROUND For a walled city, Lucca is positively enormous—the circumference of its walls measures 4 kilometers. Buses don't really help you within the walls, but if you plan to stay at the hostel or outside Lucca, you'll want to catch the orange **CLAP** buses (Piazzale Verdi, tel. 0583/87897) that pass by the train station or stop in Piazza del Giglio, just east of Piazza Napoleone. Buy tickets (L900) at cafés and tabacchi. Bikes are the best way to get around the city center; you can rent them at **Cicli Barbetti** (Via Anfiteatro 23, just off Piazza Anfiteatro, tel. 0583/954444) for L3000 per hour or L15,000 per day. They have a few mountain bikes for L25,000 per day.

Inside the medieval walls, Lucca's gridded layout reflects its Roman origins. To reach the town center from the train station, turn left and then right through the city gates at Piazza Risorgimento, drift to the left one block, and walk up Via Vittorio Veneto, which passes the main squares, **Piazza Napoleone** and **Piazza San Michele**. The bus station and the tourist office are west of these squares; to the east you'll find shops and small businesses.

WHERE TO SLEEP The limited options for cheap lodging make Lucca considerably more attractive as a day trip than as an overnight destination. The hard-to-find **Albergo Cinzia** (Via della Dogana 9, tel. 0583/491323) is the only cheap place inside the city walls. Plain, relatively clean doubles go for L45,000. From Piazza Napoleone, walk east through Piazza del Giglio and through the unmarked alley at the corner on the far right-hand side, which leads to Via della Dogana. **Hotel Ilaria** (Via del Fosso 20, off Via Santa Croce, tel. 0583/47558) is a great place to spend a quiet night just outside the town center, along a green miniature canal. It's more expensive than most budget hotels (L87,000 for a double with bath), but it's also much nicer. The second-floor terrace is a perfect place to drink Cinzano in the evening.

➤ **HOSTELS** • **Ostello Il Serchio (HI).** Lucca's hostel offers blocky, functional architecture, 10 beds per room, and tolerable bathrooms. The staff cooks lunch and dinner nightly (L12,000). Call ahead before you trek out here, and remember that buses stop running at 8 PM. HI members pay L14,000 per person, nonmembers L19,000. *Via del Brennero 673, tel. 0583/341811. From train station, take Bus 1A (Bus 11 from Piazza del Giglio) and ask driver for hostel; then turn left on Via Brennero and walk 300 meters. Midnight curfew, lockout 9– 4:30. Check-in 4:30. Closed Nov.–Feb.*

FOOD You can't swing a cat without hitting a pasticceria, produce market, or some other specialty store in Lucca. Restaurants are very affordable, but you can also put a good meal together yourself at the indoor **produce market** just off Piazza del Carmine. **Cereali Marcucci** (Via Santa Lucia 13, no phone), off Piazza San Michele, sells organic produce and bulk foods.

At **Pizzeria Sbragia** (Via Fillungo 144–146, tel. 0583/492641), **Lucca's** cheapest pizzeria, just about everything is good, from the *margherita* (tomatoes and mozzarella; L5000) to the *funghi* (mushrooms; L6000). It's open until 1 am for late-night munchers (closed Monday). From Piazza San Michele, take Via Roma and turn left on Via Fillungo. The remarkably cheap **Trattoria da Guido** (Via Cesare Battisti 28, tel. 0583/47219) charges about L4500 for primi like spaghetti with pesto and L7000 for second courses, including roast rabbit and veal. From Piazza San Michele, take Via Calderia, which becomes Via d. Asili, turn right on Via San Giorgio, and left on Via C. Battisti. **Trattoria da Leo** (Via Tegrimi 1, tel. 0583/492236), a huge place that rarely has an empty table, serves pastas with very rich sauces for about L6000 and large main dishes, including a terrific fried calamari, for around L10,000. From Piazza San Michele, walk north one block on Via Calderia and look for the restaurant on the left.

Lucca

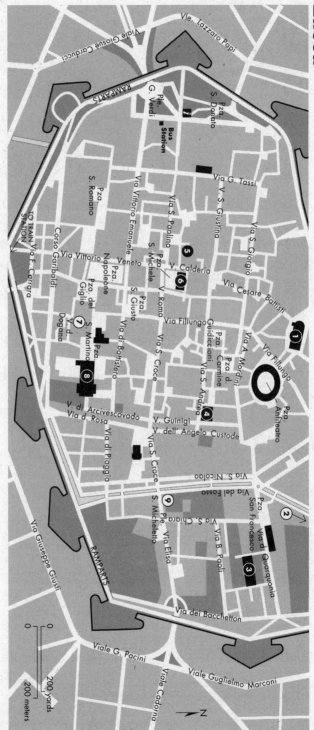

Sights ●

House of Giacomo
Puccini, **5**
Museo Nazionale, **3**
San Frediano, **1**
San Martino, **8**

San Michele
in Foro, **6**
Torre Guinigi, **4**

Lodging ○

Albergo Cinzia, **7**
Hotel Ilaria, **9**
Ostello Il Serchio
(HI), **2**

247

WORTH SEEING One of the best ways to see this city is to rent a bike and cruise through the city's colorful, medieval streets and the rich green fields that surround its walls. Even without a bike, meandering around the city and stumbling upon the various churches and piazze allows you to slip into the city's tranquil attitude. A stroll up **Via Fillungo**, the town's best-preserved street, indicates how locals spend their money—in cafés, hair salons, and leather-goods stores. Just off the street is **Piazza Anfiteatro**, a fascinating, oval piazza built on the site of an ancient Roman amphitheater. In July and August, an open-air cinema screens the latest American and Italian hits. Shows start at 9:30 PM on Piazza Guidiccioni, and tickets are L8000.

The town's principal duomo, **San Martino** (Piazza San Martino, tel. 0583/452218), sits off the main street, on the south end of the town. The facade is more intricate and delicate than standard Romanesque architecture, with each of its columns sculpted in a different style. Inside the church, to the left of the nave, is local sculptor Matteo Civitali's *Tempietto*, an elaborate, Greek-style miniature temple. Also inside the church is Ghirlandaio's *Madonna and Saints*, a typically geometric Renaissance composition that sits in the sacristy alcove right next to the postcard counter, while Tintoretto's superb *Last Supper*, to the right of the nave, still retains its dramatic, velvety colors.

According to legend, the crucifixion figure inside Civitali's Tempietto is said to be an authentic copy of Christ's "true face," mystically transported to Lucca of its own volition (although it was also known to have been aided on an earthly level by a lost bishop and some stubborn farm animals who hauled the statue to the city).

San Michele in Foro (Piazza San Michele, tel. 0583/48459) displays an unusual variation on the Pisan Romanesque style: The facade stands much taller than the church behind it, and the best sculptural work is on a series of columns on the upper levels with human and animal heads leering down. Not far away, the church of **San Frediano** (Piazza San Frediano) has a Byzantine-inspired, gold mosaic from the 13th century on its otherwise unremarkable facade.

For the best view of Lucca, head to the **Torre Guinigi** (Via Sant'Andrea, tel. 0583/47261; admission: L4500), a tower that was once the home of the Guinigi clan, Lucca's most powerful family, and now has trees growing out of its top. Their other home, the Villa Guinigi, today houses the **Museo Nazionale** (Via della Quarquonia, tel. 0583/46033; admission: L4000), with an impressive *Immaculate Conception* by Vasari that features a bizarre serpent with an androgynous human head. Closer to the center of town is the **House of Giacomo Puccini** (Corte San Lorenzo 9, tel. 0583/584028), where Lucca's most famous native (1858–1924) lived. For L3000, you'll see the Steinway, furniture, and mementos of the composer of *Madame Butterfly*, *Tosca*, and *La Bohème*. The small museum is dramatically improved by the strains of Puccini's operas, which play regularly throughout the day.

FESTIVALS Lucca may seem a little sleepy, but the town has several notable festivals that break the rhythm of daily life. In July and August, classical music venues spring up everywhere for the **Estate Musicale Lucchese**. For the more sports-oriented (or bloodthirsty), Lucca hosts the **Palio della Balestra** every July 12. Locals dress up in period costume and see who can outshoot each other on the cross-bow range. Every September 13, the Tempietto's crucifix (the one bearing Christ's "face") is paraded through the town in commemoration of its miraculous journey to Lucca, and lots of pilgrims come to honor the event.

Pisa

Thanks to an engineering mistake, Pisa's name is instantly recognized worldwide. Most visitors stop in the town only long enough to catch a glimpse of the famous Leaning Tower, and maybe peek into the remarkable duomo and baptistry, between connecting trains. Most tourists never get beyond the Campo dei Miracoli (focus of the major sights) to wander along the quiet banks of the Arno, which is lined with well-preserved Renaissance structures. Pisa's secondary sights are mediocre, it's true, but the city does have redeeming qualities. Lodging is much more affordable than in nearby towns like Siena and Florence, and the university gives Pisa a youthful character (when in session). If possible, arrive in the late afternoon when the Campo dei Miracoli quiets down, see the sights, stay in a cheap hotel, and move on.

Pisa's location near the mouth of the Arno made it a natural port for the Romans. After the empire crumbled, the port remained strong enough to form its own republic since it was the region's only developed gateway to the sea. The city's power peaked in the 11th and 12th centuries, a bit earlier than the heydays of nearby rivals Siena and Florence. Work began on the baptistry, cathedral, and campanile (today's Leaning Tower) in the late 12th century. The simultaneous construction gave the three buildings a unique architectural unity, enhanced by the distinctiveness of the Pisan Romanesque style, with its trademark black-and-white-striped marble, its tall, sculptured columns supporting miniature arches, and its long loggias.

This style of architecture is now ubiquitous in Tuscany since all the towns wanted to curry favor with the powerful city, and imitation is effective flattery. By the early 15th century, the city had been defeated at sea by Genova and on land by Florence; its glory days long gone, poor Pisa became just another Medici colony. Since then, the most famous local to emerge has been Galileo Galilei, who conducted his experiments from the Leaning Tower and put forward Copernicus's controversial theory that the planets revolve around the sun.

BASICS

➤ **CHANGING MONEY** • Change money at the Campo dei Miracoli cambio only in a dire emergency. If you're desperate, the train station has fairly good rates without a commission. The office is open 9–noon and 2–7. The best option is one of the banks that line Corso Italia up by the river. **Banca di Roma** on Via Santa Maria is now open on Saturdays in the summer.

➤ **DISCOUNT TRAVEL AGENCIES** • Insanely crowded with university students and run by an over-worked staff, **CTS** has an office that will help with your local, regional, and international travel plans. *Via Santa Maria 45/D, tel. 050/45431. Open weekdays, 9:30 AM–1 PM.*

➤ **MAIL AND PHONES** • The central **post office** is one block north of the station on the left side of Piazza Vittorio Emannuele II (tel. 050/501869; open weekdays 8 AM–7 PM, Sat. 8–noon). There are plenty of **SIP** telephones available at the train station. You can also try the **TELECOM** office (Via Caroucci 15).

➤ **VISITOR INFORMATION** • The office at the **train station** (tel. 050/42291) runs out of maps early in the day but will gladly point you in the right direction. It's open daily 7 AM–10:30 PM in summer; Monday–Saturday 9:30–12:30 and 4–7 in winter. An office with more resources and a multilingual staff is just north of the Leaning Tower on **Piazza del Duomo** (tel. 050/560464). It's open daily 8–2 and 3:30–6:30 in summer, with shorter hours in winter.

COMING AND GOING

The perpetually busy **Pisa Centrale** (Piazza Stazione, tel. 050/41385) is a major stop for trains on the Rome–Genova line, a transfer point for those heading to Florence. Trains to Florence (1 hr, L7700) and Lucca (30 min, L2700) leave hourly, as do trains to Siena (1 hr, change at Empoli, L9800). The station has 24-hour luggage storage.

Buses to and from Pisa aren't nearly as efficient as trains, but if you insist, **Lazzi** (Piazza Vittorio Emanuele IV, tel. 050/46288) sends buses to Lucca hourly (L3000). You can transfer there to a Florence-bound bus (L10,000). Pisa is also home to **Galileo Galilei International Airport** (Piazzale d'Ascanio, tel. 050/500707), 1 kilometer south of the central train station. If you're headed to Florence from a European country, consider flying through here. Only about one train per hour goes from Pisa's central station to the airport (L1700), but Bus 7 leaves for the airport (L1100) from the central station every 20 minutes.

GETTING AROUND

The Arno River splits Pisa into two parts. The area south of the river is dominated by the train station, wide streets, and a luxurious pedestrian-only thoroughfare called **Corso Italia**, lined with banks, chic cafés, and boutiques. North of the Arno lie the **Campo dei Miracoli** and the **Scuola Normale Superiore**, a thriving university centered around Piazza dei Cavalieri. If you want to see the Leaning Tower, you can walk through town (30 min) or jump on one of the city's frequent and efficient buses (L1100). Most buses stop in front of the train station: Bus 1 runs to the duomo, baptistry, and Leaning Tower, Bus 3 to the youth hostel, and Bus 7 to the airport.

WHERE TO SLEEP Hotel prices in Pisa are much more reasonable than in most of Tuscany, and it's usually easy to find a room. Pick up the accommodations booklet from the tourist office for more suggestions on cheap hotels.

Albergo di Stefano. This hotel has some of the best cheap rooms in the whole country, and it's only about three blocks from Piazza dei Cavalieri. Rooms are large, clean, and well lit; some even open onto an outdoor terrace. The nice family that runs the inn and the small bar downstairs charges only L48,000 per double. *Via Sant'Appollonia 35, tel. 050/553559. From Piazza del Duomo, walk east past tower, veer left on Via San Giuseppe, right on Via Sant'Appollonia. 11 rooms, some with bath. Wheelchair access.*

Albergo Gronchi. The four rooms in this ideally located hotel beside the Campo dei Miracoli are big and comfortable, marred ever so slightly by bathrooms that show their age. The tiny hotel emanates an air of fading elegance. Doubles cost L48,000. *Piazza Arcivescovado 1, tel. 050/561823. From Piazza del Duomo, walk east past tower to Piazza Arcivescovado. 4 rooms, some with bath. Reservations advised.*

Leon Bianco. This two-star inn near the river seems a bit upscale, but the price is right (doubles L53,000). Big rooms with big beds are the draw, and some even have TVs. The hotel is midway between the station and the tower, in an interesting, largely untouristed area near the heart of old Pisa. *Piazza del Pozzetto 6, tel. 050/543673. From the train station, take Viale Gramsci through Piazza Vittorio Emanuele II to Corso Italia, cross bridge, turn right at end of Piazza Garibaldi into Piazza del Pozzetto. 17 rooms, some with bath. MC, V.*

➤ **HOSTELS** • **Ostello Madonna dell'Acqua.** The adequate rooms, pretty setting, and very friendly managers at this church-run hostel can't hide the questionable odor emanating from the nearby canal, actually called the Dead River. Three-bed "family rooms" cost L23,000 per person, and the church really means it when they say family—no unmarried couples allowed. The signs at the train station saying it's only a 1-kilometer walk are cruel lies; wait for Bus 3 across the street from the station. *Via Pietrasantina 15, tel. 050/890622. Curfew 11 PM, lockout 9–6. Reception open July and Aug., daily 6 PM–11 PM; Sept.–June, daily 6 PM–9 PM.*

➤ **CAMPING** • **Camping Torre Pendente.** This flat, grassy, well-maintained campground, situated near a factory and busy railroad tracks, is close to town (about 2 kilometers from the station). You'll pay L8000 per person, L5000 per tent, and L5000 per car; reserve ahead in July and August. *Viale delle Cascine 86, tel. 050/561704. Take Bus 4 from train station; ask driver for nearest stop and walk back toward town about 200 m. Reception open daily 8:30– 10:30 and 6–9. Bar, laundry, market. Closed mid-Oct.–Easter.*

FOOD Pisan food is heavily influenced by Tuscan cuisine and by Livornese seafood, but does proudly claim a few original concoctions. Most famous is the *torta di cecina,* a cake made of garbanzo beans (it's more appetizing than it sounds). *Ribollita* (thick, savory stews) and roasted meats are other specialties. The Pisans give the ubiquitous olive oil a rest in favor of more tomato-based sauces. If you have the patience to wander more than a few blocks beyond the Leaning Tower, you'll find traditional fare instead of the "ristorante self-service" places meant for tourists. The best place to find reasonably priced food is around Piazza dei Cavalieri, home of starving students. Numerous *tavole calde* (cafeterias) and trattorie line the nearby streets. For fresh fruits and vegetables, head to the **outdoor market** on Piazza Sant'Omobono, open Monday–Saturday mornings.

Il Cristallo (Corso Italia 34, tel. 050/20031) is great for snacks like homemade ricotta pastries (L1500). They also make panini, gelato, and a strong espresso, which locals quaff on the back patio. Skip the restaurant section at **La Sapienza** (Via San Frediano 21, tel. 050/20503) and go straight to the café for a cheap meal, with primi like lasagna for L5000 and main dishes from L6000. **Trattoria S. Omobono** (Piazza Sant'Omobono 6–7, off Piazza Donati, no phone) serves great Pisan specialties at a fair price. Try the tasty risotto with seafood (L8000), and finish it off with one of the homemade desserts. **Pizzeria da Matteo** (Via l'Arancio 46, right off Via Santa Maria, tel. 050/41057) offers a lunch special of a pizza and cold beer for L5000. For dinner, their large servings of rich primi (L7000) are a delicious alternative to the pizzas.

The best deal in the Piazza di Cavalieri area is the **Mensa Universitaria** (Via Martiri, near Palazzo dei Cavalieri, tel. 050/599395). The food isn't bad, and it's worth stopping by just to check out its bulletin boards, which list local concerts, films, and theater events. Buy tickets at the downstairs office; students (even those without ID) get a full meal for L6000, including two courses, salad, bread, fruit, and water, beer, or wine. The mensa is open mid-September–mid-July, weekdays noon–2:30 and 7–9, weekends noon–2:30.

WORTH SEEING Contrary to popular belief, Pisa isn't just a mundane town with one major sight—it's a mundane town with three major sights. Beyond the Leaning Tower, the cathedral, and the baptistry (all conveniently grouped together in the Campo dei Miracoli), a number of lesser museums with little worth seeing vie for the tourist dollar. You can buy an inclusive ticket for five sights (the duomo, baptistry, Camposanto, Museo del Duomo, and Museo delle Sinopie) for L17,000, four for L15,000, or two for L10,000.

A couple of interesting churches line the river. As you're strolling along, take a minute at the ornately Gothic **Santa Maria della Spina** (Lungarno Gambacorti, no phone), with pinnacles and spires jutting from every surface. It was originally built to showcase a supposed thorn from Christ's crown. When you tire of tromping through the city, you can collapse on a bench in the **Botanical Gardens** (Via L. Ghini, tel. 050/561795; open weekdays 8–1 and 2–5:30, Sat. 8–1), two blocks south of the Leaning Tower.

➤ **CAMPO DEI MIRACOLI AND THE LEANING TOWER** • The tower on Campo dei Miracoli is one of the world's most famous buildings because of its amazing tilt (about a 4-meter discrepancy between top and bottom). Originally intended as the duomo's bell tower, the structure is smaller than most visitors expect; its highest point barely clears the top of the duomo and baptistry. Work began on the tower in 1173, but the soil under the site began to shift by the time the third tier had been built. The original architect, Bonnano Pisano, fled the city fearing for his life, and a slew of frustrated architects attempted to correct the tilting over the next two centuries, with little success. Galileo, a professor at the University of Pisa, utilized the angle and conducted his famous gravitation experiments, as well as a bit of stargazing, from the tower. The six blind arcades are in the same style as the cathedral's facade, and a wondrous belfry by Tomasso di Andrea da Pontedera crowns the tower. The tower has been closed to visitors for the past six years, and it doesn't look like it will ever reopen, especially since the more they do to prevent the tower from falling over, the more it seems to disintegrate. Maintenance crews have constructed a barrier around the base of the tower, so you can't even get within spitting distance of it.

The **duomo**, however, is still gloriously open and deserves a long visit. Each column on the facade's three-tiered arcades is slightly different. The charcoal gray-and-white striping is perhaps the cathedral's most famous and most emulated trait. The richly decorated arcade stretches on into a deep apse, where Cimabue's enormous golden mosaic of an enthroned Christ looks down upon the crowd. The complicated interior seems to go on forever, with a deep apse and a beautiful, gold inlaid ceiling. Have a look at Giovanni Pisano's eight-sided pulpit, which is more technically and artistically complex than his father's in the baptistry. Also in the duomo are several paintings by Ghirlandaio that survived a destructive fire in 1596. *Piazza del Duomo, tel. 050/560547. Admission: L2000. Open daily 7:45–1 and 3–sunset.*

The remarkable circular **baptistry** is externally as elaborate as the duomo, with Gothic fluted spires and detailed scrollwork on the upper levels ornamenting its Romanesque base. It's probably the most famous baptistry in the world, thanks to its perfect acoustics and an irregularly shaped dome that looks as if some big hand squeezed the top. Free guided tours move regularly through the building, with tour guides singing a few notes to demonstrate the amazing acoustics. The interior of the baptistry is stark, except for Nicola Pisano's pulpit, which features different marble in each of the columns. *Piazza del Duomo, tel. 050/560547. Admission: L7000. Open Apr.–Oct., daily 8–7:40; Nov.–Mar., daily 9 AM–sunset.*

The least known of the major buildings on Piazza del Duomo is the **Camposanto**, the long, low, white edifice on the north side of the field. Legend holds that the soil in this cemetery is from the hill where Jesus was crucified (and brought to Pisa by crusading knights). The cloistered tombs inside have been in bad shape since a large fire swept the interior during an Allied bombing raid in 1944. Most of the frescoes were destroyed, but the twisted, 14th-century frescoes depicting *The Triumph of Death* by an unknown artist remain visible. The building looks more promising from the outside than it really is on the inside, so think twice before paying to enter. *Piazza del Duomo, tel. 050/560547. Admission: L5000. Open Apr.–Oct., daily 8–7:40; Nov.–Mar., daily 9–sunset.*

The two museums on the perimeter of the campo, the **Museo dell'Opera del Duomo** and the **Museo delle Sinopie**, are disappointing compared to Pisa's three blockbuster sights. The first displays a hodgepodge of works stripped from the baptistry and duomo; the second shows the *sinopie*, sketches used as guidelines under fresco painting, found in the Camposanto. Admission to each costs L7000.

➤ **PIAZZA DEI CAVALIERI** • Currently the home of both the University of Pisa and a flock of obese pigeons, this piazza was originally Giorgio Vasari's answer to the Medici's request for headquarters for the Cavalieri di Santo Stefano, a group of crusading knights. He constructed the elaborately decorated **Palazzo dei Cavalieri** and the adjacent church of **Santo Stefano** for the Renaissance crusaders. The strange building in the corner with peeling frescoes is the **Palazzo Gherardesca**, adapted by Vasari from several medieval buildings. Here, in 1208, Count Ugolino della Gherardesca ate his children, in a futile attempt to ward off starvation after his imprisonment in the wake of a humiliating naval defeat. Dante condemned the count to eternal hunger in one of the lower rings of hell for his dastardly deeds.

CHEAP THRILLS Throughout the summer, free, evening, classical-music concerts are held on the steps of the duomo for music lovers sprawled out on the lawn. Concerts are also regularly held on **Piazza XX Settembre** (right by the Arno); performances range from classical to tribal rhythm. Check the tourist office for more info. In June, the city breaks out into medieval pagentry for the **Gioco del Ponte**. Each quadrant of the city presents richly costumed parades, then meets for a showdown in the middle of Ponte de Mezzo. Dominance of the quadrant is determined in a bizarre clash reminiscent of tug-of-war. As in all college towns, check the university quarter and mensa for posters advertising upcoming events.

Livorno

Let's be honest: The only compelling reason to come to Livorno is to use the port as a gateway to more exotic island destinations. Tuscany's largest port has all the stretch marks of industrial sprawl. Much of its soulless squalor can be traced to Allied bombing during World War II. The rich Renaissance port was destroyed, and has since been rebuilt in the nondescript style that marks most Italian suburbs but usually steers clear of civic centers. Livorno has an interesting history but is devoid of aesthetic proof of such a past, except perhaps in its cuisine, which centers around some of Italy's freshest and most inexpensive seafood.

Originally a struggling medieval fishing village, Livorno quickly became a pawn in Genova, Pisa, and Florence's quest for maritime power. Not surprisingly, Florence won, and in an effort to create an instantly thriving port town, the Medici family made the city a haven for the traditionally persecuted and outcast. Sephardic Jews, Moors, and retired pirates settled into a calmer lifestyle here. In the early 1920s, the Italian Communist Party was forged here, and since World War II, Livorno has housed an enormous American naval base on the north side of town.

Tortured Romantic poet Percy Shelly drowned off the Livorno coast while on a joyride. Ironically, his body was discovered with a copy of his poem "The Triumph of Life" in his pocket.

If you have time to explore the city, it is worth investigating the moated **Fortezza Nuova**, a crumbling fort surrounded by canals on three sides. Also interesting is the **Acquario Comunale** (Viale Italia, tel. 0586/805504; closed Mon.), which has local aquatic life displayed in a slightly cramped environment. You can also tour the ugly postmodern **synagogue** (Piazza Benamozegh 1, tel. 0586/896290), which replaced a beautiful structure that held 5,000 congregants in Napoléon's time.

BASICS If you're coming into town in the late afternoon and need accommodations listings or ferry schedules, be forewarned that all three tourist offices usually close by 2 PM. Most ferries come to the **Terminal Passeggeri**, where there's a tourist info desk (tel. 0586/210331; open summer, daily 8–2). The **Porto Mediceo** tourist office (tel. 0586/895320) is open Monday–Saturday 8–1:30. The **main office** (Piazza Cavour 6, tel. 0586/899111), open daily 8–2 (Tues. and Thurs. 3–6), is centrally located uptown but very hard to find. Take Bus 2 to Piazza Cavour; it's up two flights of stairs and the sign is hidden. The best place to change money is at one of the many banks that line Via Cairoli, which links Piazza Grande and Piazza Cavour.

COMING AND GOING

➤ **BY TRAIN** • **Livorno Centrale** (Piazza Dante, tel. 0586/401105), on the coastal train line just 20 kilometers south of Pisa, has service all over Italy. Trains run frequently to Pisa (15 min, L2000) and every hour to Florence (1½ hrs, L9000). You don't want to be caught in the huge complex after dark, and it's well out of walking distance of the port and the rest of the town, so plan your travels accordingly.

➤ **BY BUS** • **ATL** (Via Lungo Duomo 2, tel. 0586/899562) handles regional bus service, with a station that is much closer to the port than the rail line. Buses leave regularly to Pisa (30 min, L4000). From there you can transfer to Lazzi buses for other destinations. To reach the bus station from Piazza Cavour, walk straight down Via Cairoli about five blocks.

➤ **BY BOAT** • Chances are if you're in Livorno, you're here to catch a ferry. The city is Tuscany's gateway to Corsica and Sardinia. Ferries leave from the **Terminal Passeggeri** (tel. 0586/210331), the inconvenient northern dock. Prices fluctuate wildly in summer, but generally run about L40,000 for daytime ferries, L65,000 for night voyages (peaking on weekends and at the beginning and end of the month). **Corsica Marittima** (tel. 0586/210515) sends ferries to Bastia, Corsica, Saturday at 3 PM from late June through mid-September, and alternate Saturdays in April and May. More frequent service to Bastia is offered by **Moby Lines** (tel. 0586/890325), which sends at least one ferry daily from mid-June through early September. The morning ferry departs at 8:15, the afternoon ferry at 2. Moby also runs to Olbia, Sardinia, daily in summer at either 10:30 AM or 10:30 PM, or sometimes at both times. **Toremar** (tel. 0586/896113) sends three daily ferries to Elba, but it's better to leave from Piombino (*see* Elba, *below*).

GETTING AROUND A branch of **ATL** (tel. 0586/896111) manages the city bus system, which is easy to use; tickets cost L1100. The buses are well marked, and their routes are clearly posted on most bus stops. From the train station, Bus 1 goes to central **Piazza Grande** and **Piazza della Repubblica**, just south of an area replete with cheap and good restaurants; Bus 2 gets you to **Piazza Cavour**, a good base for lodging, buses, and tourist info; and Bus 18 heads for the docks. Both Bus 1 and 7 go back to the station.

WHERE TO SLEEP Choose your hotel with care: You may spend long evenings there, since most of Livorno is dangerous at night. Two hotels offer fair deals and have big, clean rooms disguised by dilapidated exteriors. The best option near Piazza Cavour is **Albergo Cavour** (Via Adua 10, tel. 0586/899604) with L50,000 doubles. If convenience is paramount, **Albergo Giardino** (Piazza Mazzini 85, tel. 0586/806330) is only a 10-minute walk from the port. Doubles with bath cost L85,000 in the high season, but prices are chopped in half the rest of the year. **Hotel Ariston** (Piazza della Repubblica 11, tel. 0586/880149) is removed from the transit areas, but its pleasant doubles are only L55,000.

FOOD A visit to Livorno is at least partially redeemed by the utterly delicious and surprisingly affordable seafood calling to you from nearly every corner restaurant. Daily catches are unbelievably fresh, and local restaurants create innovative fish sauces for pasta. **Trattoria da Galileo** (Via della Campana 18–22, just north of Piazza della Repubblica, tel. 0586/889009) serves incredible gnocchi in fish sauce (L10,000) and *cacciucco* (fish soup; L20,000), a local specialty. **La Libecciata** (Piazza Guerrazzi 15, tel. 0586/893311) specializes in *frutta di mare* (antipasto of clams, mussels, and squid; L6000). There's also an enormous **Mercato Centrale** (Via Buonatalenti 71), if you want to stock up on provisions for your trip.

San Gimignano

High on a hill surrounded by crumbling towers in silhouette against the blue sky, it's difficult not to slip into the medieval spell of San Gimignano. A dozen towers dot the skyline, though around 70 were originally built in the 12th and 13th century by the feuding Ardinghelli and Salvucci families. Used as tools in their struggle for status (and more practically as warehouses), the towers filled the compact city to the point that it became possible to cross the town by rooftop rather than on the street. The pandemonium of the feud must have weakened San Gimignano's immune system, for when the Black Plague devastated the population in 1348, power and independence faded fast. In a last-ditch effort to salvage the economy, the Ardinghelli family surrendered civic autonomy and struck an alliance with Florence.

Today San Gimignano isn't much more than a gentrified walled city, but it's definitely worth exploring. Unfortunately, tour groups arrive early and clog the wine-tasting rooms (San Gimignano is famous for its light white Vernaccia) and art galleries for the majority of the day, but most sights are open through late afternoon during summer. Escape midday to the uninhabited areas outside the city walls for a hike and a picnic, and return to explore town in the afternoon and evening, when things quiet down and the long shadows cast by the imposing towers take on fascinating shapes.

BASICS   The tourist office is extremely crowded, especially in the afternoon, when it's the only place in town to get good exchange rates. The yellow "i" signs scattered around Piazzale Montemaggio and Porta San Giovanni mark offices that book accommodations. *Piazza Duomo 1, tel. 0577/940008. Open daily 9–1 and 3–7.*

COMING AND GOING   San Gimignano isn't on any major north–south bus or train line, so you have to catch the bus from Poggibonsi (every 1½ hrs, L2400), about 12 kilometers away. Poggibonsi's **train station** (tel. 0577/936462) is on the Florence–Siena line; trains from Florence cost L6500 (1 hr 20 min), from Siena they're L2800 (30 min). The station's luggage storage (open daily 5 AM–8:30 PM) helps if you plan to make San Gimignano a day trip. TRA-IN buses leave Florence and Siena about every 1½ hours for Poggibonsi's **bus station** (Via Trento 33, tel. 0577/937207), from where you switch to the San Gimignano line. The entire trip costs L9100 from Florence, L7600 from Siena.

GETTING AROUND   The city is so small that buses don't travel within the walls, and few cars are allowed. In San Gimignano, buses stop at **Piazzale M. Montemaggio**, outside Porta San Giovanni, the city's southern gate; buses departing the city leave from the opposite side of the square. Schedules to Poggibonsi and the campground in nearby Santa Lucia are posted at the stop, but there's no station, so buy your tickets at bars and tabacchi. Most streets within the city walls point toward the town's two major catercorner piazze, **Piazza della Cisterna** and **Piazza del Duomo**.

WHERE TO SLEEP   Arrive early in the day to look for a place. Hotels are generally expensive here, but the youth hostel is convenient and above average, and the campground has cheap sites. The best lodging deals of all in San Gimignano are the *affittacamere*, some of which are spectacular and cheap. The tourist office at Piazza del Duomo provides a computer printout of the houses with available rooms, as do the private agencies around town with the "i" signs out front. One comfortable place is the **Conforti Totti Dina** (Via Mainardi 6, off Via San Matteo, tel. 0577/940478), which charges L45,000 for a double with use of the kitchen. For L60,000 at **Nencioni Rino** (Via Mainardi 6, tel. 0577/940137), you can get a double with a view and a bath, right above the restaurant Le Vecchie Mura (*see Food, below*).

➤ **HOSTELS** • **San Gimignano Youth Hostel.** The conscientious managers of this way-above-average hostel take real pride in their place. They recycle (a rarity in Italy) and ask guests not to waste water (the town has long drought periods). The hostel is right in the center of the walled city, but it's rarely full. It may also be the best hostel in Italy for hooking up with other travelers. Beds are L18,000 per person, including breakfast. *Via delle Fonti 1, tel. 0577/941991. From bus station, walk through Porta San Giovanni along Via San Giovanni, cross both piazze to Via San Matteo, turn right on Via XX Settembre (which becomes Via Folgore), right on Via delle Fonti. 75 beds. Curfew 11:30 PM, lockout 9:30–5. Closed Nov.–Feb.*

➤ **CAMPING** • If you want to sleep in the great outdoors but like modern conveniences, head to **Campeggio Il Boschetto di Piemma** (Santa Lucia, tel. 0577/940352; closed mid-Oct.–Mar.). Great facilities and an easy bus ride from Piazzale Montemaggio make this an excellent option during mild months. The hillside setting among olive groves and farms is fabulous, though the sites themselves are usually composed of dirt and gravel under shady trees. Sites cost L6500 per adult, L6000 per tent, and L3000 per car.

FOOD If you're up for a picnic, just grab some food to go from a market or take-out counter, exit the city gates, walk about 10 minutes in any direction, and sit down. Look for the **grocery store** at Piazza della Cisterna 31, which is considerate enough to remain open through the afternoon and sells everything you need for a basic meal. Within the city walls are a number of decent trattorie and a ton of gelaterias, especially around the gathering point Piazza della Cisterna. The best is **Gelateria di Piazza** (Piazza della Cisterna 4, tel. 0577/942244), with overwhelming fruit varieties and a delicious flavor called *dolce-amaro* (bittersweet). If you want to taste the local Vernaccia or Chianti, wine stores line every street. They have signs saying "free entry," but that usually doesn't extend to tasting. If you look like you're not going to buy, the workers' snide attitude increases correspondingly. It's best to by-pass the ultra-touristy stores on Via San Giovanni and go for the ones on Via San Matteo.

Antica Latteria di Maurizio e Tiziana. This gourmet deli counter in the center of town serves up salads and panini any way you want them, priced by weight. Try something unusual, like smoked salmon, spinach, and ricotta cheese on a whole-wheat roll (about L4000) or seafood salad (about L5000 for a large serving). *Via San Matteo 19, off Piazza Duomo, tel. 0577/ 941952. Open Mon.–Sat. 8–12:30 and 4–8. Wheelchair access.*

Chiribiri. This is the only trattoria in town that won't blow your budget as soon as you sit down. The kitchen opens at noon and produces good pastas, like lip-smackin' lasagna with pesto (L8000). *Piazzetta della Madonna 1, tel. 0577/941948. From Piazzale Montemaggio, walk through Porta San Giovanni and go left up first set of stairs. Open May–Sept., Thurs.–Tues. noon–11; Oct.–Apr., Thurs.–Tues. noon–9.*

La Vecchie Mura. Tourists keep this restaurant busy year-round, but they haven't lowered the cooks' standards or ruined the atmosphere. Dine in the arched-brick room with a glass of Chianti—it's that sort of place. Avoid the fixed-price menu (L25,000), and instead pick and choose from the pasta dishes (around L7000) and heavier secondi such as roast lamb (L11,000). *Via Piandornella 15, tel. 0577/940270. From Piazzale Montemaggio, walk through Porta San Giovanni, turn right on Via Piandornella. Open Wed.–Mon. noon–3:30 and 6–9.*

WORTH SEEING Like Siena, San Gimignano's most impressive sight is the city itself, rising and falling over hilltops. Its truncated towers compete with one another for prominence while providing shade on nearly every street. For the best free view of the city, head up the hill to **La Rocca**, the town's medieval fortress. Weeds are beginning to cover most of the stones, but you're privy to an exhilarating vista from the fortress's wide open courtyards. Besides the views, San Gimignano offers a variety of museums and civic attractions. If you're intent on seeing most of them, the best deal is to pay L16,000 for an inclusive ticket, giving you access to the Museo Civico, the Torre Grossa, the Museum of Religious and Etruscan Art, the Ornithological Museum, and the Cappella. If you're rushing through town, skip the ticket and just visit the Museo Civico and its tower.

The principal civic building, the Palazzo del Popolo, was built in the late 13th and early 14th centuries, when the city reached its economic peak. Today the palazzo houses the **Museo Civico**, featuring Taddeo di Bartolo's celebratory *Bethroned San Gimignano and His Miracles*. Gimignano, a bishop of Modena, was sainted because he drove hordes of barbarians out of the city in the 10th century. Head to the Sala di Dante to check out the *Maestà* by Lippo Memmi. (Dante visited San Gimignano for only one day in 1300 as a Guelf Ambassador, but it was long enough to get a room named after him.) Across the stairwell, a small room contains Memmo di Filipuccio's frescoes, depicting the courtship, shared bath, and wedding of a young, androgynous-looking couple. Recent scholarship indicates that this may actually be the story of a young man's initiation with a prostitute; either way, it's quite an unusual commission for a public palazzo. The nearby **Torre Grossa** is sadly the only tower you can climb, but at least it's the biggest in town. *Museo Civico and Torre Grossa: Piazza Duomo, tel. 0577/940340. Admission: L7000. Open June–Aug., Sun.–Wed. 9–7:30, Thurs.–Sat. 9–11:30 AM; shorter hrs off-season.*

Museum of Religious and Etruscan Art (Piazza Luigi Pecori, beside the Museo Civico, tel. 0577/940340) contains interesting relics dating from the 7th century BC to the 2nd century AD, all discovered in excavations. Around the corner is the **Ornithological Museum**, not terribly exciting unless you have a deep passion for birds.

One of the Renaissance's more curious complexes, the **Duomo Collegiata** isn't much to look at from the outside, but the interior has a treasure trove of well-preserved frescoes. Bartolo di Fredi's Old Testament scenes, to the left of the entrance, were completed in the 14th century, yet many have a medieval feel, with misshapen bodies, skewed perspectives, and buckets of spurting blood. The New Testament scenes on the opposite wall, mostly done by Barna da Siena, are fairly traditional and not quite as thrilling. Taddeo di Bartolo's otherworldly *Last Judgment*, on the arch just inside the facade, depicts distorted and suffering nudes—avant-garde for such an early work. The biggest name on display is Domenico Ghirlandaio, whose work in the **Cappella di Santa Fina** tells the story of an obscure local saint. Although the duomo is free, admission to the chapel costs L3000. *Piazza Duomo, tel. 0577/940316. Church open Apr.–Sept., daily 9–12:30 and 3–6:30; Oct.–Mar., daily 9–12:30 and 3–6. Cappella open Apr.–Sept., daily 3–6; Oct.–Mar., daily 9–12:30 and 3–6:30.*

If you cringe when you hear the words "rectal," "emasculate," or "impale," steel yourself for the Museo di Criminologica Medievale.

The **Museo di Criminologica Medievale** displays the cutting edge in medieval torture technology. The exhibit showcases each device and provides brief operating instructions and a description of their effects in both Italian and English. The words are unflinching, but with a purpose; the museum's agenda is actually progressive, aimed at explaining the inherent racism and sexism in certain torture devices and how they've been "updated" for current use around the world. After seeing whips, masks, and rectal spikes, you'll be relieved to reach the guillotine. *Via del Castello, off Piazza della Cisterna, tel. 0577/942243. Admission: L9000, L5000 students. Open daily 9–1 and 2–6.*

Volterra

Historically, Volterra has been through the wringer. Established by the Etruscans, it temporarily fell into the hands of the Romans, withered during a short autonomous medieval period, and was reborn in the Renaissance. Like other Tuscan hill towns, Volterra was caught in the triangle of the region's three major city-states: Florence, Siena, and Pisa. Of all the phases the town has passed through, it wears its medieval face most prominently. The fortress, walls, and gates still stand mightily over green Tuscan valleys on one side and **Le Balze**, a stunning series of gullied hills and valleys formed by irregular erosion, on the other. Manmade structures bow before this unrelenting natural process. Medieval and Renaissance buildings have collapsed as the ground crumbles, and an Etruscan burial site was literally unearthed.

The town is at its best in the late afternoon and evening, when the locals take over and the pizzerias start swinging. The general tranquillity of the town, the crumbling remnants of historical greatness, and a great youth hostel all make Volterra worthy of a visit. Stop by the **tourist office** (Via Turazza 2, tel. 0588/86150; open daily 9–12:30 and 3:30–6:30) for info.

COMING AND GOING Getting in and out of Volterra is a tricky business. Buses make the journey from Siena (4 daily, 2 hrs, L7500; change at Colle di Val d'Elsa) and Pisa (10 daily, 2¼ hrs, L8000; change at Pontedera), dumping you off at **Piazza della Libertà** inside the city gates. Tickets are sold at local tabacchi and bars, and schedules are posted in the piazza, the tourist office, and the youth hostel. Call **APT** in Volterra (tel. 0588/67370) or **TRA-IN** in Siena (tel. 0577/204111) for info.

Trains don't make it all the way to Volterra. To get here, take a trian first to Saline from Pisa (1½ hrs, L7900) or Livorno (1½ hrs, L5000); both require switches in Cecina. In Saline, 15 kilometers from Volterra, you'll be dropped at the **Saline di Volterra** (Piazza della Stazione, tel. 0588/443016); from here, APT buses go to Volterra (L2200) every 30 minutes. The main square in Volterra is **Piazza dei Priori**, a focal point for eating out and sightseeing.

WHERE TO SLEEP Hotels in Volterra are all three-star and up; if you're willing to pay for this kind of comfort, contact **Albergo Sale** (tel. 0588/84000), with doubles starting around L70,000. The best deals are the hostel and campground, but you can also ask about *affitta-camere* (rooms for rent in private homes) at the tourist office. **Camping Le Balze** (tel. 0588/87880; closed Oct.–Mar.) has a ton of grassy sites with views for L6500 per person, L6000 per tent. You get free use of a swimming pool, hot water, and electricity. Four- or six-person bungalows (more like hovels) are L50,000 and L60,000, respectively; book well ahead for these. Follow signs from the city toward Le Balze (about 2 kilometers), and you'll reach the campground and a great spot from which to view the town's crumbling hills.

➤ **HOSTELS** • True to the abandoned look of its exterior, the town's **youth hostel** is largely empty, even in July and August. Rooms have four beds and sparkling views, the manager isn't too strict with the 11:30 curfew, and it's plenty quiet. Beds cost L18,000, and no HI membership is required. *Via del Poggetto, across from fortress, tel. 0588/85577. Lockout 10 AM–7 PM. Reception open 8 –10 and 7 –11. Closed Nov.–Mar.*

FOOD Streets branching off Piazza dei Priori have restaurants with four-language menus and flashy signs; the food may actually be good, but you'll pay at least L20,000 for a meal. One of the few tourist spots worth the money is **Il Porcellino** (Vicolo delle Prigioni 16, tel. 0588/86392), which serves up its specialty, a raging slab of *cinghiale* (boar) for L10,500. Under dim lighting, enjoy filling Tuscan dishes like steaming minestrone (L7000) at **Osteria Dei Poeti** (Via Matteotti 55, tel. 0588/86029), a good place to settle in for a slow, intimate dinner. **La Taverna dei Priori** (Via Matteotti 19, tel. 0588/86180), a glorified cafeteria, has good prices; the risotto with zucchini (L4800) and roast beef (L7000) are delectable.

Pizzerie and delis charge a lot in this town, but you can nab an incredibly filling pizza at the local hangout, **Pizzeria da Nanni** (Via delle Prigioni 40, tel. 0588/84087). The vegetarian primavera (L7000) is especially good. The deli counter at **Gastronomia Scali** (Via Guarnicci 3, tel. 0588/86939) has a great selection of picnic goodies like prosciutti, cheeses, spreads, dips, and fillings, but panini can cost as much as L7000.

WORTH SEEING Besides a medieval atmosphere and fabulous views, Volterra can also claim two of Italy's best small-town museums, which share the same ticket (L8000). The first is the **Museo Etrusco Guarnacci** (Via Don Minzoni 11, tel. 0588/86347), which displays hundreds of Etruscan funeral urns found in nearby excavations. On the second floor of the museum, check out the endlessly mysterious *Ombra della Sera* from the 3rd century BC, a 2-foot-high, 1-inch-wide male figurine that is so elongated that it resembles a shadow cast by a setting sun (thus the poetic name). The **Pinacoteca Comunale** (Via dei Sarti 1, tel. 0588/87580) houses a highly acclaimed collection of religious art in a very quiet palazzo just off Piazza dei Priori. Luca Signorelli's *Madonna and Child with Saints* is the best-known painting in the museum, but look directly across from it at Rosso Fiorentino's amazing *Deposizione*, with its writhing, agonized figures sketched with quick but accurate brush strokes. Thanks to a recent restoration, the colors on Signorelli's *Annunciation* are practically psychedelic.

Medieval **Palazzo dei Priori** (Piazza dei Priori) has an impressive facade filled with Florentine medallions and a large five-sided tower that you can't climb. The town's **duomo** (Piazza San Giovanni, tel. 0588/86192) is unfinished and unimpressive from the outside. The back side, facing Piazza dei Priori, has Pisan marble striping, while the interior's most impressive feature is the detailed gold ceiling. To the right of the altar is a pained *Deposizione* from the 13th century, now currently restored in disturbingly bright colors, and to the left is Jacopo della Quercia's terra-cotta *Our Lady of Acolytes*. The church faces a crumbling **baptistry** that you can only see from the outside. Original works from the duomo and baptistry are in the **Museo Diocesano d'Arte Sacra** (Via Roma 13, tel. 0588/86192); admission is L3000, L2000 for students.

Volterra was confident enough in the strength of its medieval **Fortezza Medicea** to turn it into a prison during the 19th century. Right beside this still-functioning facility is the **Parco Arche-**

ologico, complete with enormous grassy knolls, couples making out, and brigades of harmless insects. During summer the park is open 8:30–8 (until 5:30 in winter), and it's a wonderful refuge from the phalanx of tourists elsewhere in town. A few excavated remains are scattered about the park, but they're nowhere near as exciting as those in the extensive **Teatro Romano**—definitely one of the best-preserved Roman remains in Tuscany—just north of the city gates. About half the theater stands, but the adjoining bath complex is skeletal. Even more ancient is the Etruscan **Porta all'Arco** (Via Porta all'Arco), a 3rd-century arch which was built without the aid of cement but is now supported by bricks and, yes, concrete. Local artisans specialize in carving alabaster, and shops filled with their craftsmanship are clustered along Via Porta all'Arco and Via del Mandorlo. To see an artist at work, walk up from the Etruscan arch along the wall to Via Lungo le Mura 27.

Siena

Once a world leader in art, banking, and commerce, Siena stopped growing about 600 years ago, but it never stopped flourishing. Unlike many of the hill towns that surround it, Siena has aged well, retaining its traditional charm while integrating the conveniences of modern life. Fourteenth-century palazzi now house laundromats and pastry shops, and residents still gather in the central piazza. The town's character is very much defined by its 17 medieval *contrade* (neighborhoods). These 'hoods—each with its own church and animal symbol—act out their ancestral rivalry in the centuries-old **Palio**, a biannual free-for-all in which civic pride rests on the outcome of a horse race (*see box* This Ain't No Rodeo, *below*).

In each contrada, streetlights are painted the contrada's colors, plaques above contrada organization buildings display their symbol, and there is a small statue that is supposed to embody the spirit of the contrada. One of the livelier groups, "La Contrada del Drago" (The Contrada of the Dragon), often marches in Piazza Matteotti on Sunday at noon. It's a great show, with Renaissance costumes, child drummers, and flag twirlers.

A privileged hilltop location and strong fortifications helped Siena prosper during the Middle Ages, allowing it to retain autonomy as a city-state when the rest of central Italy was in shambles. Siena began vying for power with Florence, and the resulting battles claimed over half its population in the 13th century alone. The Black Plague struck a century later, decimating the population once again. (Siena still hasn't completely recovered from these demographic misfortunes: Its current population is around 65,000, while the preplague total was closer to 100,000.) Siena and its cosmopolitan neighbor have battled on the cultural as well as the political front. Locals argue that the Renaissance started here, not in Florence—and with early Renaissance masters Duccio, Simone Martini, and the Lorenzetti brothers all being hometown boys, the claim is pretty convincing.

Siena's geographic and social center is the town square, **Il Campo**, a fan-shaped red brick piazza adored by locals and visitors alike. It's easy to fall into the Sienese pace of life. Embark on a passeggiata through hilly, turning medieval streets or engage in a cappuccino-sipping marathon in Il Campo's many cafés, and you'll get the idea. Unfortunately, Siena is growing increasingly expensive, with the dubious distinction of having the most expensive public restrooms (L1000) and the highest coperto charges (up to L4000) in Tuscany. But while Il Campo and Pasticerria Nannini (*see* Food, *below*) may become crowded with camera-laden travelers, the streets and museums rarely become too congested. During the school year, Siena is more than anything a college town. By the evening, tour buses depart and locals emerge to reclaim their home. Take a day or two here to see how different Siena is from its rival cities.

BASICS Siena's **tourist office** (Piazza del Campo 56, tel. 0577/280551) is right on Il Campo. It's open April–September, Monday–Saturday 8:30–7:30; October–March, Monday–Saturday 9–12:30 and 3:30–7. The office has an exchange bureau with pathetic rates, pamphlets that list hotels and places to eat, and a **travel agency** (tel. 0577/283004) that books train tickets for long-distance journeys.

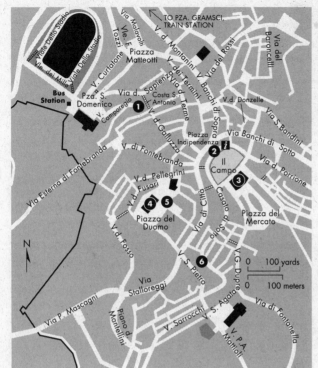

Duomo, **4**
Fonte Gaia, **2**
Sanctuary and
House of
St. Catherine, **1**
Museo dell'Opera
del Duomo, **5**
Palazzo Pubblico, **3**
Pinacoteca
Nazionale, **6**

The crowded main branch of the **post office** (Piazza Matteotti 36–37, between bus station and Piazza Gramsci, tel. 0577/202000) offers decent exchange rates without commission. It's open weekdays 8:15–7. For phone calls, head to the local **Telecom** office (Via dei Termini 36), which is open for assisted calls weekdays 9–1 and 4–7:30, Saturdays 9–1.

COMING AND GOING Siena's **train station** has a tourist information counter, a currency exchange with typically adequate train-station rates, and 24-hour luggage storage. Trains from Florence aren't as frequent as buses, but they're cheaper (12 daily, 1½ hrs, L7800). You may have to transfer at Empoli. Trains to Rome (every 2 hrs, 2½ hrs, L19,900) require a switch at Chiusi. The station is a 30-minute, uphill climb to town, so save your breath and catch Bus 2, 4, or 10 to Piazza Gramsci. Bus 15 goes to the hostel. *Piazza Fratelli Rosselli, tel. 0577/ 280115. Ticket office open daily 6 AM–9:30 PM; information/currency exchange counter open daily 8 AM–1:30 PM and 2:30–6.*

Smooth, efficient, blue **TRA-IN/SITA** buses run hourly to Florence (1½ hrs, L10,000) and San Gimignano (1 hr, change at Poggibonsi, L7600), and once every two hours to Montepulciano (2 hrs, L8000). There are also six daily buses to Arezzo (1½ hrs, L7500). **SENA** buses run regularly to Rome (2½ hrs, L20,000). The *extraurbano* (inter-city) **bus station** (tel. 0577/204245; office open daily 5:50 AM–8:15 PM) is about a 10-minute walk uphill from Il Campo; it's easy to find because the behemoth Church of San Domenico looms next door.

GETTING AROUND It seems like no matter which direction you go in Siena, it's always uphill. Orange city buses move constantly from the outskirts of town, like the train station and hostel, and swirl you into the city center, but beware—Siena's bus system is loopy (literally), as some buses take surprisingly roundabout routes. To avoid this headache, ask the driver if the bus is going to your destination *diretto* or *in giro* (you want the former). Tickets are sold at local tabacchi and at automated machines in major piazze. A ticket rated "A" (L1200) is good for one hour. Buses headed toward the center make their last stop on **Piazza Gramsci**, about one block from the bus station. To get to Il Campo from here, take Via Malavolti through Piazza Matteotti to Via delle Terme.

WHERE TO SLEEP Hotels in Siena charge outrageous prices and get away with it because of the city's popularity. Masquerading under a yellow information sign, the **Cooperativa Siena Hotels Promotion** (Piazza San Domenico, across from bus station, tel. 0577/288084) books rooms in hotels for a fee of L2000. Within the city walls, it's just as cheap to stay near Il Campo as it is to stay on the outskirts, so you might as well be close to the action. The cheapest options are the youth hostel and campground, a bit outside the city but easily accessible by bus. Lodging is sparse and prices skyrocket when the Palio comes to town (July 2 and Aug. 16), so make reservations well in advance during that period.

Alma Domus. Formerly called the Casa del Pellegrino, this convent only goes for clean-cut pilgrims. They don't officially limit their clientele to women, but they certainly prefer them. The nuns' stern looks and 11 PM curfew are almost redeemed by the clean and spacious rooms overlooking the city. Doubles go for L75,000. Prices drop by about L25,000 in the low season. *Via di Camporegio 37, tel. 0577/44177. From bus station, turn right down Via di Camporegio and right down alley (follow signs). 31 rooms, some with bath.*

Bernini. If you have always dreamed of throwing open your bedroom shutters to a postcard panorama of a medieval hillside village, splurge on the Bernini, a bit removed from Il Campo but only one block from the bus station. Sunbathing chairs await you on its spectacular rooftop terrace. Doubles are L80,000 in the high season, but prices drop nearly 50% in the low season. Request a room with a view. *Via della Sapienza 15, tel. 0577/289047. From bus station, take Via della Sapienza. 9 rooms, none with bath. Midnight curfew.*

Locanda Garibaldi. Right behind the Palazzo Pubblico, this comfortable hotel embraces you like one of the family. Small doubles (L65,000) are ameliorated by the tantalizing smells coming from the restaurant below. *Via Giovanni Duprè 18, tel. 0577/284204. Via Giovanni Duprè begins on right-hand side of Palazzo Pubblico. 8 rooms, none with bath. Midnight curfew.*

Tre Donzelle. A never-ending series of staircases leads to sizable rooms overlooking the steep alleys of Siena. The hotel is rough around the edges (the floors show their age), but it's still the best deal in town: Doubles cost L56,000. With the wind at your back, you can walk to Il Campo in about 10 seconds. *Via delle Donzelle 5, tel. 0577/280358. From Il Campo, climb stairs next to tourist office, turn right on Banchi di Sotto, left on Via delle Donzelle. 27 rooms, some with bath. Curfew 12:30 AM.*

➤ **HOSTELS** • **Ostello Guidoriccio.** The staff seems to have studied a Dickens novel for advice on running an establishment, but this hostel provides what it should: a clean place to shower and sleep. The L18,000 charge includes a piece of bread in the morning. Take Bus 15 from the train station or from Piazza Gramsci near the bus station. Evenings and weekends you need to catch Bus 10, which drops you off around the corner, and the last bus is at 11:10 PM. You can also ask the driver on the Florence bus to let you off at the hostel. *Via Fiorentina 89, tel. 0577/52212. 111 beds. Curfew 11:30 PM, lockout weekdays 9–3, weekends 9–4:30. Reception open 7–9 and 3–11:30.*

➤ **CAMPING** • **Camping Colleverde.** If you've come to Siena to meet Germans, look no further. Enjoy with them the super-clean, efficient facilities at this campground about 4 kilometers from the center of town. If you contort your body a little, you can glimpse the towers of Siena through the trees. Sites are L8000 per person, L10,000 if you come by car. It gets crowded during summer, and reservations are advised. *Strada di Scacciapensieri 47, tel. 0577/280044. Take Bus 8 from Piazza Gramsci and ask driver for "il camping." Flush toilets, market, pool (L3000), showers. Closed mid-Nov.–mid-Mar. Wheelchair access.*

FOOD Siena has a neighborhood pasticceria and rosticceria on every corner, so you're never hurting for inexpensive, homemade, take-out food. For good vegetarian pizza and spectacular focaccia (about L2000 per huge slice), come to **Forno Indipendenza** (Piazza Indipendenza 27, tel. 0577/280295), Siena's premier bakery. Have your picnic in the sun on Il Campo's slanted brick floor, two blocks away. Accompany a passeggiata with a fruit sorbet or homemade *granita* (slushy) found at **Gelateria Brivido** (Via dei Pellegrini 1, tel. 0577/

280058), or look in specialty shops for delicious *ricciarelli*, airy almond pastries shaped like a cookie (about L1500 per piece). Of Siena's many great pasticcerie, the oldest and most renowned is **Nannini** (Via Banchi di Sopra 22–24). It offers an assortment of temptations in the form of home-made candies and cookies, but the panforte (L2500 per slice) is what made the place famous.

At a sit-down meal, it's nearly impossible to fill up for under L20,000, except for at the **Mensa Universitaria** (Via Santa Agata 1, tel. 0577/281085). It's a good place to meet local students, but you basically get an Italian version of dorm food—complete with mystery meat—for L11,000. All the restaurants mentioned below (except for Trattoria la Tellina) are wheelchair accessible, with the exception of one step at the entrance.

Every café and market in Siena sells the legendary local specialty, "panforte." Dense enough to double as a lethal weapon, this flourless concoction of nougat, stewed fruits, nuts, and honey defies categorization.

Antica Pizzicheria al Palazzo del Chigiana. This authentic, upscale butcher shop is a great place to pick up food to go, complete with hanging salami and a bespectacled hog's head peering down from the entryway. The butcher also looks the part, with a big mustache and a blood-splattered apron. Panini start at L2500. *Via di Città 93–95, tel. 0577/289164. From NW side of Il Campo, walk up any set of stairs and turn left. Open daily 9–7:30.*

Osteria dell'Artista. This restaurant offers one of the cheapest and best sit-down meals in Siena, with grilled chicken for L8000 and *pappardelle alle crema di noci e porcini* (flat noodles with cream, nuts, and mushrooms) for L10,000. It's out of the tourist crunch, just above the turnoff for the Pinacoteca (*see* Worth Seeing, *below*). *Via Stalloreggi 11, tel. 0577/40064. From Il Campo, walk up any stairs and turn left on Via di Città (which becomes Via Stalloreggi). Open Fri.–Wed. noon–2:30 and 7–9:30.*

Osteria la Chiacchiera. Possibly the only good restaurant in the center of town that doesn't charge a cover, Osteria la Chiacchiera is also quite intimate. Dine at a leisurely pace on dishes like risotto with artichokes (L6000) or roast veal (L10,000) in a dimly lighted tavern. *Costa di Sant'Antonio 4, tel. 0577/280631. From bus station, take Via della Sapienza toward center and turn right on Costa di Sant'Antonio. Open Wed.–Mon. noon–3 and 7–midnight.*

Trattoria la Tellina. Graced with redbrick arches, flowers, and most important, air-conditioning, this bustling trattoria makes its own olive oil and uses it liberally. Exotic risotto dishes (L8000) are delicious vegetarian options, or spot the daily specials on a chalkboard in front. *Via delle Terme 52, off Via di Città, tel. 0577/283133. Open Sat.–Thurs. noon–3 and 7–10.*

WORTH SEEING No motorized form of transportation can handle Siena's streets or hills, so you have to explore the town in all its hilly glory on foot, with amazing views of the duomo and the city's many towers as a reward. If you only have one day in Siena, see the duomo and the Palazzo Pubblico; if you have more time, meander a bit and discover the free **Botanical Gardens** (Via Pier Andrea Mattioli 4, tel. 0577/298874), a lush expanse overlooking the countryside.

➤ **IL CAMPO** • Piazza del Campo, known as Il Campo (The Field), is one of civic architecture's crowning achievements and continues to be the city's heart. Nearly every citizen makes a daily visit to the piazza, either to patronize a favorite café or just to plop down on the red bricks and bake like a pizza. The square was built in the 14th century on a market area unclaimed by any contrada. The bricks of the campo are patterned to demark nine different sections—one for each sector of the medieval "Government of Nine." Its relatively level position and neutral location make it the logical place to hold the Palio (*see box* This Ain't No Rodeo, *below*). On Palio days (July 2 and August 16), Il Campo and all its surrounding buildings are packed with cheering locals and tourists craning their necks to take it all in.

At the top of Il Campo is the **Fonte Gaia**, a monument of civic pride that capped the Sienese Renaissance in 1348, just before the plague struck. Siena's greatest sculptor, Jacopo della Quercia, created the panels that line the fountain. The ones you see are copies; the originals are carelessly strewn about the top-floor porch of the Palazzo Pubblico and slowly decomposing. This is the only body of water in the entire town, and it starts to look amazingly enticing around high noon in summer.

The southeast corner of Il Campo is dominated by the stupendous Gothic facade of the **Palazzo Pubblico**. Built at the height of the city's power in the late 13th and early 14th centuries, the building features the crenelated cornices (the zigzagging line of the rooftop) and three-part arches that define Sienese architecture. Inside, the **Museo Civico** contains frescoes and paintings by Siena's greatest artists. The best room is the **Sala del Mappamondo**, with Simone Martini's great large-scale *Maestà* (1315), a Virgin-and-child scene of tremendous delicacy and balance. On the opposite wall is a famous portrait of Sienese general Guidoriccio da Fogliano on horseback, previously accredited to Simone Martini but now alleged to have been the work of another artist.

In the **Sala della Pace**, where the local government once met, are the famous frescoes *Allegories of Good and Bad Government*, crafted by Ambrogio Lorenzetti from 1337 to 1339. The good government side depicts a utopia, showing first the virtuous ruling council surrounded by angels and scenes of a perfectly running city and countryside. Conversely, the bad government fresco tells a tale straight out of Dante. The evil ruler and his advisors have horns and fondle strange animals, while the town scene depicts the seven mortal sins in action. Interestingly, the bad government fresco is severely damaged, while the good government fresco is in terrific condition. These frescoes are located where the civic council made its governing decisions, so the call to the ruling conscience wasn't very subtle at all. *Piazza del Campo, tel. 0577/ 292263. Admission: L6000, L3000 students. Open Mar.–Oct., Mon.–Sat. 9–7, Sun. 9–1:30; mid-Nov.–Feb., daily 9–1:30.*

The Palazzo Pubblico's most distinctive feature is the famous **Torre del Mangia**, a 102-meter structure built by Minuccio and Francesco Rinaldo in 1334. It offers the greatest possible view of Siena—only fair, since you'll climb more than 400 stairs to get to the top. Once you reach it, prepare yourself for kids ringing the ear-splitting bell repeatedly. *Admission: L5000. Open screwy hours depending on season and mood, generally 10 AM–early evening.*

➤ **IL DUOMO** • When the city council approved the cathedral's color scheme in the late 13th century, they touched off the construction of one of Italy's finest churches. A bizarre com-

This Ain't No Rodeo

Siena's Palio horse race takes place twice a year, on July 2 and August 16, but its spirit lives all year long. Three laps around a makeshift track in Il Campo earn participants the respect or scorn of the other contrade, and the event is so important to the Sienese that almost nothing is too underhanded to be against the rules. Bribery, brutality, and kidnapping of the jockeys are commonplace—sabotaging a horse's reins is the only thing that remains taboo. A horse doesn't even need its rider to be considered a valid winner.

The festivities begin three days prior to the main event, with trial races, banquets lining the streets, and carousing that sometimes stretches until four in the morning. As the Palio approaches, residents don scarves with their contrada's colors and march through city streets in the medieval costumes of their forerunners. Despite the festive atmosphere, many Italians—especially those outside Siena—look down on the Palio. Like the Spanish bullfight, the tradition is criticized for its violence and inhumanity. Horses are repeatedly impaled by the track's wooden guardrails, while jockeys knock the competition off their horses. Television hasn't helped: Super-slow-motion replays of horses spurting blood just make the event gorier. The Palio, however, is too ingrained in the hearts of the Sienese and the pockets of the tourist industry to ever be stopped.

bination of Gothic and Romanesque architecture, Siena's cathedral makes all other Tuscan duomos appear underdecorated. Major artists of the era, like the Pisano family, came to town to leave their mark on the church. Both outside and in, the vivid black-and-white color scheme prevails. In the nooks and crannies of the bottom half of the facade are Giovanni Pisano's statues of great figures from philosophy and religion whose kinetic poses were a major sculptural development. (The originals are housed in the Museo dell'Opera del Duomo.) When you enter the duomo, look up. The enormous vaulted ceilings are painted a rich, midnight blue with scattered golden stars, reflecting the Church's doctrine that this cathedral directly connected to the heavens. When your neck starts to cramp, look down. Over 40 artists created various inlaid marble floorings, depicting assorted biblical stories. About two thirds of the different works are covered at any given time for protection. Don't miss Nicola Pisano's beautifully carved **pulpit**, which depicts the life of Christ. Sadly, the distinctive **campanile** is closed to the public. Also in the cathedral is the **Piccolomini Library**, which contains a taciturn fresco cycle by Pinturicchio in honor of Pope Pius II. *Piazza del Duomo, tel. 0577/283048. Admission to duomo free; to library L2000. Open mid-Mar.–Oct., daily 7:30–7:30; Nov.–mid-Mar., daily 7:30–5. Organ recitals Sun. at noon.*

Right next door is the **Museo dell'Opera del Duomo**, a slightly disorganized but nevertheless enchanting collection of painting, sculpture, and religious trinkets from Siena's golden age. The first floor has lots of unlabeled sculpture, mostly prophet figures by Giovanni Pisano. The museum's best room is the dimly lighted **Sala di Duccio**, which houses Duccio's *Maestà* (1310), one of his most ambitious works. Brave the slippery, worn steps of the museum's **tower** for an amazing vista of the surrounding hills and farms fading into the mist. Also on the top floor is the **treasury**, which contains the vividly displayed skull and bones of St. Clement, a late 15th-century pope. *Piazza del Duomo, tel. 0577/283048. Admission: L5000. Open mid-Mar.–Sept., daily 9–7:30, hrs change on a monthly basis.*

Built underneath the duomo (it provides structural support for the portion of the huge cathedral that sprawls off its hilltop site), the **baptistry** is relatively unremarkable except for its carved baptismal font. Sculpted by four top-notch artists (Donatello, Ghiberti, Jacopo della Quercia, and Giovanni Tierino), the font's significance comes from the comparison of Ghiberti's Gothic style and the Renaissance development of Donatello's work.

➤ **PINACOTECA NAZIONALE** • On the south side of town, the National Picture Gallery houses a memorable collection of Madonna-and-child paintings. You'll see the theme repeated in nearly every work in this expansive gallery, which also features Simone Martini's (unlabeled) *St. Augustine and His Miracles* (1324), depicting the bloody occurrences the magic man's powers reversed. Local artists Domenico Beccafumi, Il Sodoma, and Sano di Pietro get more than enough wall space. *Via San Pietro 29, tel. 0577/283048. Admission: L8000. Open daily 8:30–1:30; free guided tours Tues.–Sat. 2–5.*

➤ **SANCTUARY AND HOUSE OF ST. CATHERINE** • The cell of Catholicism's first beatified woman isn't much more than a small brick altar that's chained shut with a bicycle lock. Through a small window you get to peer at St. Catherine's disintegrating bones. It's worth a brief stop to pay homage to a woman who overcame sexism's glass ceiling as early as the 14th century. In addition to having numerous visions, including one in which she married Jesus, Catherine was a much-respected diplomat, noted for ending the Great Schism by convincing the pope to return to Rome from Avignon. Above her cell are two unspectacular churches; frankly, the legend is more interesting than the sight. *Costa di S. Antonio, tel. 0577/280330. Admission free. Open daily 9–12:30 and 3:30–6.*

FESTIVALS Free entertainment doesn't end with the Palio, because Siena also prides itself on becoming an open-air concert hall in the summer. July 20–26 is the **Settimana Musicale Senese**, which provides a week of classical music with student tickets going for as low as L10,000. Overlapping this event is **Siena Jazz**, a five-day event that starts July 24.

AFTER DARK Siena's nightlife revolves around the passeggiata and hanging out in the central piazza. It will cost you about L10,000 just to sit and have a beer in a café along Il Campo, but it's worth it for the unforgettable ambience. Siena has several nightclubs, but whether they're open is a crapshoot. Walk down Via Pantaneto, the continuation of Via Banchi di Sotto, in search of discos, or hang out in the piazza until you meet some locals who can point you toward the happening spots.

A place that attracts a young, relaxed crowd is the **Blue Eyes Pub** (Via Giovanni Duprè 64, tel. 0577/42650.) Close to the University mensa, it stays open until 2 AM serving local and imported beer (L4000–L7000). **The Gallery** (Via Pantaneto 13, tel. 0577/288378) is the butt-shakin' dancetorium of choice. **Al Cambio** (Via Pantaneto 48, tel. 0577/43183), just down the street, sometimes grooves when The Gallery is closed. The hours for both are unfathomable—they're open something like every 10 days from 10 PM to 3 AM. Only the socially challenged show up before midnight.

NEAR SIENA

`SAN GALGANO` The spectacular ending of Andrei Tarkovsky's film *Nostalgia* depicts a convergence of the medieval and the contemporary: The camera slowly pulls back from a small house, reflected in a pool of water, to reveal that it is encompassed by an enormous roofless cathedral overgrown with grass. **San Galgano**, that cathedral, is not really large enough to contain even a modest house within its walls (Tarkovsky's must have been a dollhouse), but nonetheless it is one of Italy's most memorable sights, absolutely not to be missed if you have a car and are anywhere near Siena.

The abbey was constructed by Sienese Cistercian monks around 1218 to commemorate Galgano, the local saint who, in a renunciation of war, thrust his sword into a stone and prayed to it as to a cross. Relations between Siena and the abbey were good, and the local order quickly flourished. But war with Florence and the plague wiped out much of the abbey's population, and soon both order and church were reduced to ruin. Today San Galgano's impact lies in its atrophy. It's remarkably peaceful to stand among the pointed arches or gaze through the emptiness of the missing rose window out to the open sky.

Up the hill from the abbey is the older but much less spectacular church of **Monte Siepi**, which displays San Galgano's sword in the stone. Look for the spiral designs on the interior of the cupola and crumbling frescoes by Ambrogio Lorenzetti in the side chapel. *Abbey Church and Church of Monte Siepi tel. 0577/751044. Admission free. Open daily 7 AM–9 PM.*

➤ **COMING AND GOING** • Getting to San Galgano requires some ingenuity. Two buses (1 hr, L4200) leave Siena daily at 6 AM and 3:50 PM; the late return bus leaves for Siena at 6:30. Make sure you tell the driver that you're going to San Galgano, or the bus may take a different route that skips the abbey and leaves you an unpleasant 6 kilometers away. The stop for San Galgano is beside a red shed on the main road; from there, go left down the road about 100 meters until you reach the road to the abbey on your right. If you have a car, drive south from Siena toward Massa Marittima on Route 73.

Arezzo

Located in serenely beautiful eastern Tuscany, Arezzo has gracefully accommodated the demands of big-city life while keeping in touch with its rural heritage. The city center spreads out into the more modern outskirts of town, which quickly blend into farmland and forested valleys. Locals seem to have struck a good balance between accommodating tourists and maintaining their municipal identity.

Arezzo passed through the hands of the Etruscans, Romans, and Florentines while producing a steady stream of great talents, such as the critic Giorgio Vasari, Petrarch, and Michelangelo, who came from nearby. More than these native sons, though, it's Piero della Francesca who dominates Arezzo artistically. His frescoes in the Basilica di San Francesco are the town's biggest crowd-pleasers. Solid bus and rail connections make Arezzo an easy trip from Florence, Siena, or Cortona, and amenities like the youth hostel make it worth at least a night's stay.

`BASICS` The town has two well-stocked tourist offices. The most convenient one is directly in front of the train station entrance on Piazzale della Repubblica (tel. 0575/377678; open

June–Sept., daily 8:15–8:00). The year-round office (Piazza Risorgimento 116, tel. 0575/23952), two blocks from the train station, is open weekdays 8–2 and 4–8.

COMING AND GOING   Trains run from Florence hourly (1½ hrs, L7200) and from Rome about six times per day (2½ hrs, L19,000). The **train station** (Piazzale della Repubblica, tel. 0575/22663) has 24-hour luggage storage. The **bus station** (Piazzale della Repubblica, tel. 0575/914520; office open Mon–Sat. 6:25 AM–7:40 PM) is just outside the train station on Viale Piero della Francesca, under the sign that says ATAM POINT. Buses leave about five times daily to Florence (1½ hrs, L8100) and Siena (1¼ hrs, L7500), and hourly to Cortona (1 hr, L4500), and Sansepolcro (45 min, L5300). Local buses, **ATAM** (tel. 0575/984520), cost L1100 per 70-minute ride (buy tickets at tabacchi or bars), and most make a circuit through Piazza Guido Monaco, one block from the train station.

WHERE TO SLEEP   Arezzo's youth hostel is nicer than many alberghi, but if you prefer your own room, the tourist office compiles a complete list of hotels. Book ahead in June and July, and on weekends when the antique fair is held (*see* Festivals, *below*). Outside the city walls, **La Toscana** (Via M. Perenino 56, tel. 0575/21692) is a 15-minute walk from the center of town, but it features some of the best cheap rooms around, with bright white walls and garden views. Doubles cost L55,000. Catch Bus 4 on Via Roma, near Piazza Guido Monaco, and get off on Via M. Perenino after passing three gas stations on the right. For L58,000 doubles, **Albergo Roma** (Via V. Veneto 46, tel. 0575/902494) is also worth a try.

➤ **HOSTELS** • **Ostello Villa Severi.** It's practically worth the trip to Arezzo just to stay in this magnificent hostel. Ensconced in the Tuscan countryside, it's housed in a beautiful, upgraded 16th-century villa. The bathrooms are works of art, with spotless floors and those cool metal trough sinks that you never see anymore. Except for groups of German students, the hostel (and Arezzo) are so far off the beaten track that hardly anyone comes here. It's a pleasant half-hour walk from the train station, and the bus stops right near the hostel (the bus stops running at 10:30 PM). Beds go for L20,000 per person, including breakfast. *Via F. Redi 13, tel. 0575/29047. From train station, take Via Guido Monaco, turn right on Via Cavour (which eventually becomes Via F. Redi), left down long gravel driveway. Or take Bus 4 from right side of Piazza Guido Monaco, exit 2 stops after hospital. 68 beds. Curfew 11:30 PM, lockout 2:30–6. Closed Oct.–May. Wheelchair access.*

FOOD   Arezzo's best food is in the foothills, between the new city and the Piazza Grande. Sit-down meals are expensive, but you'll find plenty of markets where you can make your own sandwiches, especially along Via Mazzini. The best bakery, right in the center, is **Forno Pane e Salute** (Corso Italia 11, tel. 0575/20657). The large, aromatic **Rosticceria Polleria Corrado** (Via della Madonna del Prato 54, tel. 0575/27376; closed Mon.), is a great place to pick up some grub before a long train ride. Whole roast chickens (L15,000) will feed three comfortably, and a sizable chunk of homemade lasagna costs about L5000.

Antica Osteria l'Agania. With bottles on the wall, deep-red paneling, and brick arches, Arezzo's best restaurant by far is the kind of place that American restaurateurs studiously and unsuccessfully try to re-create. No matter how crowded, you'll get a seat, as long as you don't mind sharing a table and a bottle of wine with locals. Go whole hog with the fixed-price menu (L20,000) or order individual dishes like super-thick minestrone (L7000), or roast duck (L10,000). *Via Mazzini 10, tel. 0575/25381. From train station, take Via Guido Monaco, turn right on Via Cavour (which becomes Via Mazzini). Open Tues.–Sun. 11:30–3 and 7–midnight. Wheelchair access. AE, MC, V.*

Ristorante Altro. It looks like an English pub inside, with a wooden bar and Guinness on tap. One of the only restaurants in town to offer vegetarian grub like baked zucchini or eggplant dishes (L8000), the Altro draws a young crowd. *Piazza San Agostino 36, tel. 0575/33990. From train station, take Via Guido Monaco to piazza, turn right on Via Roma, left on Corso Italia, right on Via Garibaldi to Piazza San Agostino. Open Tues.–Sun. noon–3 and 6–11. Wheelchair access.*

WORTH SEEING   Although Arezzo has given birth to a number of important artists, the most enduring works in town are by Piero della Francesca of neighboring Sansepolcro. Check out della Francesca's fresco cycle of biblical themes in the **Basilica di San Francesco** (Piazza San Francesco, tel. 0575/20630), where the Renaissance master painted 12 scenes behind the altar between 1452 and 1466, having been commissioned to spiritually educate the illiterate with heavily symbolic art. Time has badly damaged several frescoes, and restoration has been going on since 1986. The apse contains several of della Francesca's most amazing works, including the *Annunciation* (straight ahead, lower left), *The Dream of Constantine* (straight ahead, lower right), and *The Raising of the True Cross* (left wall, upper panel).

If you want to get a little closer to a della Francesca masterpiece, head up the hill to the cream-colored **cattedrale** (Piazza Duomo, tel. 0575/23991). His mystifying *Mary Magdalene* is just to the left of the bizarre gold coffin of St. Donatus. Nearby, the church of **San Domenico** (Piazza San Domenico, tel. 0575/20620), which features Cimabue's bloated, contorted *Crucifix* from the 13th century, in which Christ's chest is twice the size of his belly and his feet look like tooth-picks. The interior of the church has the black-and-white striped look so fashionable in Pisa.

Along Piazza Grande is the church of **Santa Maria della Piove** (Corso Italia, tel. 0575/22629), the largest Romanesque church in this region. Its two most interesting features are its tower, dubbed "one hundred holes" for its plethora of double-arched windows, and Pietro Lorenzetti's altarpiece, which follows the medieval style of not creating the illusion of depth to the point that it looks like a cut-out. It's displayed on the upper half of an unusual two-tiered apse. Behind the church is the **Piazza Grande**, which is lined by an eclectic assortment of buildings that represent every architectural movement from medieval times to the 16th century. The ruins of a 2,000-year-old **Roman amphitheater** adjoin the town's **Museo Archeologico** (Via Margaritone 10, tel. 0575/20882; admission: L8000), which has collections of Etruscan and Roman bronzes, coins, and lesser trinkets. At the top of town is the **Passeggio del Prato**, a busy park with a Renaissance fortress, sunbathers, and lots of shady benches for picnics.

If you're interested in getting to know one of Arezzo's favorite sons a little better, it's worth checking out **Casa Vasari** (Via XX Settembre 55, tel. 0575/300301). The wizened curator will follow you around to point out Vasari's self-portraits, which adorn every room.

FESTIVALS Medieval Arezzo is remembered the first Sunday every September in the **Giostria del Saracino** (Joust of the Saracen) in Piazza Grande. Costumed knights from the different quarters of the city charge on horseback to tilt at an effigy of a Turk and commemorate the glory days. The medieval buildings in the piazza are decked out with colorful flags, and musicians and jugglers keep the atmosphere festive. The first weekend of every month the city hosts the **Fiera Antiquaria**, an enormous antiques fair that spills out from Piazza Grande onto just about every street of the upper town. Arezzo is also the home of **Arezzo Wave**, the self-proclaimed biggest free rock concert in all of Europe. Acts from around the world come to play for the three-day event, which is usually held on the last weekend of June.

NEAR AREZZO

SANSEPOLCRO Sansepolcro gave birth to Piero della Francesca, one of the most important painters of the quattrocento. If you love art, a trip to this town is a real treat. The **tourist office** (Via della Fonte 5, tel. 0575/730231), which looks like a library, can tell you all you ever needed to know about the city and its most famous citizen. The office is open daily 9–1 and 4–7 May–September, daily 10:30–1 and 4:30–7 in the off-season. This town's big event is the **Palio della Balestra**, a crossbow competition and medieval festival similar to the one held in Lucca, which is held the second Sunday in September.

The **Museo Civico** (Via Aggiunti 65, tel. 0575/732218; admission: L5000) has a collection of crucifixes, papal capes, and della Robbia terra-cottas, as well as one of the great paintings of the Renaissance, della Francesca's magnificent *Resurrection* fresco (1458–1474). The painting, which displays his pioneering use of single-point perspective and unified, symmetrical groupings, was moved into this building, wall intact, from its original location across town. The resurrected Christ stands triumphant above four guards who are either sleeping or reveling in ecstasy at his reemergence—take your pick. The second figure from the left, in brown costume, is probably a self-portrait. The room contains several other terrific works by della Francesca, including the resoundingly humanist fresco portraits of San Giuliano and San Ludovico, and a large altar stand with an unusual *Deposizione* scene.

➤ **COMING AND GOING** • Getting to Sansepolcro from Arezzo is a snap. Buses (1 hr, L5300) leave about every 45 minutes Monday–Saturday, and five buses run on Sunday. The descent into Sansepolcro, situated in a perfectly flat valley, is unforgettable. The bus stops right outside the city walls, and you can buy tickets for the return trip next to the stop at **Bar Autostazione**, one of the town's friendliest cafés. The last bus back to Arezzo leaves around 7:30 PM. For more bus information, check the schedules posted outside the bar or call the local bus company, **SITA** (tel. 0575/742885).

➤ **WHERE TO SLEEP AND EAT** • If you miss the bus back to Arezzo, reasonably priced lodging is available. The first call you make should be to **Albergo Fiorentino** (Via Luca Pacioli 60, tel. 0575/740350), which has doubles for L55,000. The small rooms are tastefully decorated, and the restaurant is Sansepolcro's most romantic spot. A good second choice is the **Orfeo** (Viale A. Diaz 12, tel. 0575/742061), just outside the city gates and half a block from the bus stop. Doubles, all with bath, cost L70,000. Reserve ahead if possible at both hotels, even in the off-season. The hippest spot to grab a bite to eat is **Bar/Gelateria Berghi** (Via G. Bruno 45, tel. 0575/740590), crowded with postadolescents enjoying beer at outdoor tables.

Cortona

From the hilltop town of Cortona, the plains of the perfectly flat Valdichiana valley stretch out like a *New Yorker* map of the world, making the few towns below seem minute and insignificant. Cortona holds the distinction of being the oldest Tuscan hill town; archaeological finds date the city from well before the Etruscans arrived in the 8th century BC and Virgil claimed that it was originally founded by the mythological warrior Dardanus. This battered acropolis passed from Roman to Goth to Arezzian and Florentine hands over the ages, with intermittent periods of affluent autonomy. It's easy to see what made the site appealing. Besides the great panorama, the site was easy to fortify and hard to conquer, with dramatic cliffs dropping to the north and west of the town.

During the Renaissance, artists like Luca Signorelli and Fra Angelico found the mystical setting stimulating, and today the town (almost all of which remains inside the walls) still draws a crowd that hopes to find inspiration in the landscape—or if that fails, to boogie down late at night. Cortona is a haven for the young, who comfortably settle themselves in piazze and parks at all hours or in bars and restaurants, many of which are open until 1 AM. The town is more cosmopolitan than you might expect, due to several international scholarly conferences and a few study-abroad programs held here.

BASICS The staff at Cortona's **tourist office** goes a long way toward making a visit better. They sell rail and bus tickets—which comes in handy considering the random hours of the strange "bus station" half a block away. *Via Nazionale 72, tel. 0575/630353. Open Mon.–Sat. 8–1 and 3–6.*

COMING AND GOING Buses are the best way to reach Cortona, making the trip from Arezzo (1 hr, L4500) frequently and taking you up the hill into Piazza Garibaldi, just outside the city walls. The **bus station** (Via Nazionale 75, across from tourist office, tel. 0575/370687), which sells tickets for LFI buses to major cities, has an exchange bureau and baffling hours. In summer, it's open weekdays 9–1 and 4:30–6:30, but winter hours are severely limited. Otherwise, buy tickets at the tourist office or bars. Schedules are posted outside the bus office, and the last bus returns to Arezzo at 7 PM.

There are two train stations in the Cortona area, but at each you'll wait forever for a bus to scale the hill into town. The station in **Camucia** (Piazza della Libertà, tel. 0575/603018) is closer than the one in **Terontola** (Piazza Nazioni Unite, tel. 0575/67034). Trains to Florence (1 hr, L9800), Siena (1 hr, change at Chiusi, L9800), and Arezzo (30 min, L3700) come about every one and a half hours. The bus into town costs L1800 from Camucia and L2000 from Terontola. The only advantage of taking the train is the luggage storage at the stations.

GETTING AROUND Bring your most comfortable walking shoes to Cortona, because the town is too damn steep for public transportation of any sort. From Piazza Garibaldi, where the bus lets you off, Via Nazionale (with both the tourist and the bus offices) heads north into **Piazza della Repubblica**, the town center. For a few of your shekels, you can rent a bike and explore the city and surrounding countryside from cleverly named **Rent A Bike** (Piazza della Repubblica 12a, tel. 0368/450191). It's a nice coast down, and the country roads are pleasantly flat, but the ride back up can be a killer.

WHERE TO SLEEP The best lodging option in town is the **Ostello San Marco** (Via Maffei 57, tel. 0575/601392), which has a good location, a rathskelleresque dining room, and clean, modern bathrooms. Bed and breakfast cost L14,000 per person and an HI card is required. The hostel is open March–October, and reservations are recommended in August.

The town's two convents, **Betania** (Via G. Severini 50, tel. 0575/62829) and **Istituto Santa Margherita** (Via C. Battisti 15, tel. 0575/630336) both offer immaculately clean rooms (nuns are funny that way) and fair prices. Betania's doubles are around L40,000, Santa Margherita's L25,000. But you've got to play by their rules: a shifting curfew as early as sunset some nights and a strict code of conduct. Don't come knocking after the sun has gone down, and don't come at all if you're in a mixed-sex group or want to enjoy the city's nightlife. You'll pay about L55,000 for a double at the carefree **Italia** (Via Ghibellina 7, tel. 0575/630254), a three-star hotel that seems to have missed the news about price inflation. Nice rooms with TVs make for a relaxing retreat.

FOOD For a cheap picnic, wander through the town's markets, which line Via Nazionale, Piazza della Repubblica, and Via Dardano. If you want a sit-down meal, walk up Via Dardano from Piazza della Repubblica. The street is lined with the town's best trattorie, particularly **Trattoria Etrusca** (Via Dardano 37–39, no phone), which has an outdoor patio and a menu that lets you mix and match pastas and sauces as you like. Primi go for about L8000, heavier stuff is in the L10,000 range, and an inclusive tourist menu is L20,000. Nearby, the hearty **Trattoria Dardano** (Via Dardano 24, tel. 0575/601944) offers traditional specialties at similar prices. Their major perk is a liter of house wine for L6000. Right next to the bus stop on Piazza Garibaldi is the humongous **Ristorante Tonino** (Piazza Garibaldi 1, tel. 0575/630333), with amazing views of the valley below. A full meal with drinks goes for L25,000. Unfortunately, University of Georgia students use it as a cafeteria, which alters the ambience a bit.

WORTH SEEING Cortona's most impressive church, **Santa Maria delle Grazie al Calcinaio** (tel. 0575/663375), lies a couple kilometers outside the city. A hike to the church is an uphill battle all the way, but it provides its fair share of Kodak moments. If you're riding the bus up to Cortona, you can hop off and check out the church; another bus will come in 30 minutes (except Sun.) and your ticket should still be good. The building was designed in the late 15th century by Francesco di Giorgio Martini, who adapted Brunelleschi's geometric style (extenuated dome, interior colonnades and arches). Sometimes the grounds can be disconcertingly desolate, but the wooden door on the western side should open to allow you in. The crisp whitewashed interior, in much better shape than the outside, shows a classical influence. Stroll next door to the ornate cemetery; nearly every grave is covered with fresh flowers and candles, which radiate an otherworldly glow at night.

Within town, start your exploration at **Piazza della Repubblica**. Just behind the **Palazzo Comunale** (the very medieval-looking building with the tower) is Palazzo Casali, a 13th-century Gothic building housing the **Museo dell'Accademia Etrusca** (Piazza Signorelli, tel. 0575/630415; open summer, Tues.–Sun. 10–1 and 4–7, winter, 9–1 and 3–5). The museum gives a rich picture of local life, with surprisingly deep coverage of various periods (it even includes modern art), but the best rooms display finds from the Roman and Etruscan eras. Admission is L5000. More pious is the **Museo Diocesano** (Piazza del Duomo, tel. 0575/62830; open Tues.–Sun. 9–1 and 3–6:30), which houses a collection of Renaissance paintings by Sassetta, Luca Signorelli, and Fra Angelico, whose kneeling *Annunciation* panel is here. The small museum is definitely worth the L5000 admission.

Up the hill, the church of **San Niccolò** (Via San Niccolò) contains Luca Signorelli's interesting double-sided standard; the fresco depicts a *Madonna and Child with Saints* on one side and a

Deposizione (when Jesus is taken down from the cross) on the other. If you've got the stamina, hike up to the Venetian church of **Santa Margherita**, remodeled in the 19th century. Inside the saint's mummified remains rest in peace in a glass coffin. The dirt road on the right-hand side as you exit leads up to the town's **fortress**, which is only open for a brief period during summer. Even when you can't explore the interior, you can bring a bottle of wine and a picnic lunch, and enjoy a panorama of the city below. The **Giardino Pubblico**, just outside the city walls beyond Piazza Garibaldi, offers shady lanes and benches for writing postcards to those you left behind.

Cortona is the one Tuscan hill town that takes nightlife seriously, and much of it goes on outdoors.

AFTER DARK **Piazza della Repubblica** is a hot spot for nightlife. Young and old hang out on the steps of the Palazzo Comunale and on **Piazza Garibaldi**, which has plenty of benches and a few cafés. The town's disco, **Tuchulcha** (Via del Guioco del Pallone, off Piazza Garibaldi, tel. 0575/ 62727), stays open late most nights, and many restaurants keep their bars open until 1 AM or later. For a late-night beer or Campari, try **Trattoria Etrusca** (*see* Food, *above*) or **Pub Fufluns** (Via Ghibellina 3, tel. 0575/604140).

Southern Tuscany

Italy's most vicious red wines are produced in a region so topographically demanding that towns have been unable to expand outside their medieval city walls. The original planners of southern Tuscany sought dramatic cliffs that were easily defensible during the nonstop wars between Florence and Siena. Like the rest of Tuscany, the southern region is incredibly beautiful, and the towns' lingering rural character—the result of an economy based on wine making—makes them even more appealing. It's easiest to tour the region by car, but you can do it by bus if you've got the stamina to decode the schedules.

MONTEPULCIANO

Montepulciano spreads across a hillside at a higher elevation than any other Tuscan town. It was first inhabited by the omnipresent Etruscans, and later its prime location sparked the interest of Florence and Siena. The two towns engaged in an all-out battle for control of the beautiful city, Florence eventually won, and Cosimo de' Medici presumptuously re-created Montepulciano as a Florentine showcase. His influence can be seen in the large-scale, ostentatious palazzi that dominate **Il Corso** (Montepulciano's main drag). Many of of the town's gracious palazzi and interesting churches were designed by Renaissance architect Antonio da Sangallo.

At heart Montepulciano remains a small town. It has barely expanded beyond its medieval walls, welcoming a manageable stream of visitors who come to sip the excellent Nobile wine and to roam the well-preserved streets. The locals are helpful, and tremendous views of the surrounding rustic plains are everywhere. It's only about a two-hour bus ride from Siena, and if you can make it up here on August 29th, you'll catch the **Bravìo**, a contest in which two strapping young lads from each of the town's eight contrade imitate Sisyphus in attempting to roll heavy barrels up the incredibly steep hill of the centro storico.

BASICS Montepulciano has two **tourist offices**. The better one (Via Ricci 9, tel. 0578/ 757442) is just below Piazza Grande and across from the Museo Civico, in the Palazzo Ricci. The other office (Piazza Don G. Miazoni 2, tel. 0578/758687) is much more convenient to the bus station outside the Porta al Prato, the city's northeast gate. It's the best place to call if you need information on local buses. Both offices are open Tuesday–Saturday 10–12:30 and 4– 6:30, Sunday 10:30–12:30 and 4:30–6, although the office near the bus station often closes inexplicably. Even more inexplicable is why the maps distributed by the office contain no street names. Fortunately, the street corners are well labeled.

COMING AND GOING The nearest you can get to Montepulciano by train is the town of **Montepulciano Stazione**. The town's station (Via Stazione, tel. 0578/738070) has an automated ticket machine because there's no staff. Most trains fly right by, but there are fairly frequent trains from Siena (1 hr, L6500). From the station, eight buses daily trek up to Montepulciano (about 10 kilometer). A ticket costs L1600, and you'll probably be stuck waiting awhile for the bus. A better idea is to get off the northbound train from Rome at Chiusi, a very busy station with a 24-hour ticket window and luggage storage. From here, buses make the hour-long trip to Montepulciano hourly (L4200).

Overall, the easiest way to get here is to take a bus from Siena (9 daily, 2 hrs, L8000) straight to Montepulciano. Buses stop at **Piazza del Mercato**, north of the city gates. Schedules are posted on the piazza and at the tourist office on Piazza Don G. Miazoni (*see* Basics, *above*), and you can buy tickets at many cafés. Call **TRA-IN** (tel. 0577/204111) in Siena for more info.

GETTING AROUND   To get into town from Piazza del Mercato, walk up Via Birnabei past the supermarket and turn left on Viale Sangallo. Every 15 minutes, TRA-IN runs a squat orange bus through town, from the bus station to Piazza Grande; one bus every 30 minutes continues to the church of San Biagio (L1100 for either). There's no service on Sunday morning. **Piazza Grande** (from Il Corso, turn right up Via del Teatro) and its neighboring streets contain most major sights and the tourist office.

WHERE TO SLEEP   The tourist office carries a booklet of local inns and private homes that rent rooms. Reserve ahead in summer. **Bellavista** (Via Ricci 25, tel. 0578/716455, across from the tourist office), on a quiet corner in the center of town, is one of Montepulciano's best budget options. Small but clean rooms run L45,000 for a double. **Il Cittino** (Vicolo della Via Nuova 2, tel. 0578/757335), an inn and restaurant run almost single-handedly by super-mom Marcella Trabalzini, offers pleasantly decorated rooms for L55,000 per double. Take Via di Gracciano nel Corso from Porta al Prato, and go left on Via di Voltaia nel Corso and right on Vicolo della Via Nuova. **Mueblé Il Riccio** (Via Talosa 21, tel. 0578/757713) is a bit more expensive, but the comfort level and views of the countryside justify the price. Doubles (with bath) are L70,000.

FOOD   The best places to eat are along Il Corso and its side streets. You can stock up on supplies at **Conad** (Via Birnabei 4a, tel. 0578/716731), which reproduces the American supermarket experience. The breezy, comfortable **Caffè Poliziano** (Via di Voltaia nel Corso 27–29, tel. 0578/758615), open since 1868, features an oak bar, chess sets, recent magazines, and a balcony overlooking the valley with a view you need to see to believe. They serve coffee, drinks, and amazingly, a good selection of entrée-size fresh salads. Thursday nights at 9:30, the talented Flavia offers free tarot-card readings, and Saturdays at 5 the café hosts live classical music. Montepulciano's best pizzas are served on an outdoor patio at **Sconvoltino** (tel. 0578/758229; closed Mon.), right along Il Corso, for around L10,000.

If you're planning to sample Montepulciano's vino, Nobile, famous since AD 790, you'd better put some food in your stomach, or you'll be stumbling around town all night. The dry, heavy red wine is available in every restaurant and store, so you'll have ample opportunity to try it.

Il Cantuccio. Tucked away in a dark, cavelike side street, this trattoria is optimal for those with a little extra money, extra time, and the desire for a satisfying meal. The crowded and atmospheric brick basement serves a wide variety of local specialties like tagliatelle (12,000) and *salsicce alla brace* (charbroiled sausage; L12,000). *Via della Cantine 1, off Il Corso, tel. 0578/738216. Open Tues.–Sun. 12:30–2:30 and 7:30–9:30.*

Il Cittino. Come to Il Cittino and its adjoining inn (*see* Where to Sleep, *above*) if you aren't sure what you're hungry for. A menu is posted by the door, but Marcella usually serves whatever she feels like making, and it's sure to be good. Pasta dishes go for around L8000, main courses for about L10,000, but she'll estimate a price and she won't overcharge. In fact, you'll probably feel guilty when you get out of there for under L15,000 per person. *Vicolo della Via Nuova 2, tel. 0578/757335. Open Thurs.–Tues. noon–2:30 and 7–10.*

WORTH SEEING   **Piazza Grande,** the town square, is flanked by the cathedral, city hall, and the homes of the super-wealthy. The **duomo** (Piazza Grande, tel. 0578/716418) houses Taddeo di Bartolo's memorable *Assumption of the Virgin* behind the altar, its gold paint still shining brightly. The asymmetrical medieval facade was left unfinished by the original architect, Antonio da Sangallo. The adjacent **Palazzo Comunale** (tel. 0578/757442) still houses the municipal government. Florentine architect Michelozzo redesigned the Gothic structure, adding an enormous **tower** (admission free) that provides a great view of the land. Da Sangallo designed most of the remaining palazzi along the piazza, including the **Palazzo de' Nobili-Tarugi**, which faces the cathedral. Just down Via Ricci is the **Palazzo Neri-Orselli**, a brick palace sporting different variations of the arched-window theme on each of its three levels. Inside, the **Museo Civico** (Via Ricci 10, tel. 0578/716935; admission: L6000; closed Mon. and Tues.) contains della Robbia terra-cottas and an authentic portrait of St. Francis.

Il Corso, Montepulciano's major thoroughfare, is dominated by foot traffic and imposing Renaissance buildings. Coming from the Porta Il Prato, at the first turnoff you'll encounter two of da Sangallo's creations, the **Palazzo Cucconi** (Via di Gracciano nel Corso 70) and the **Palazzo Bucelli** (Via di Gracciano nel Corso 73) face one another in imitation of the Florentine civic architecture pioneered by Alberti. A bit farther along is Michelozzo's church of **Sant'Agostino** (Piazza Michelozzo, tel. 0578/716418), a comfortable white-stone building with fake spires carved into the second tier of the facade. Just across the piazza, a small medieval **clock tower** is topped by the rusting iron figure of the Pulcinella, a bell-ringing harlequin statue with a plumed hat and ornate trousers.

Da Sangallo's naveless, harmonious church of **San Biagio** lies just outside the city walls down a very steep street. The Greek-portico facade and elaborate dome owe a lot to such Renaissance masters as Alberti and Bramante. Just beyond the church, da Sangallo's **Canonica** has a lovely split-level loggia. Bring a picnic and join kids from the nearby school for lunch on the church lawn. A bus runs to the church from Il Corso and Piazza Grande. *Via di San Biagio, tel. 0578/716418. From tourist office, take Via Ricci to alley before Piazza San Francesco, go right on Via del Paolino, left on Via de Grassi, through gate, and down hill. Admission free. Open June–Sept., daily 9–7; Oct.–May, Mon.–Sat. 3–6, Sun. 9–7.*

CHEAP THRILLS You can spend the afternoon in Montepulciano strolling from one enoteca to another sipping local concoctions gratis. Some stores like **Fattoria Pulcino** (Via del Corso 94) also provide samples of fresh salami, local pecorino cheese, and dessert breads. But none of the enotecas is as impressive as **Cantina del Redi** (Via di Collazzi 5, tel. 0578/757166; open Mon.–Sat. 9:30–12:30 and 3–8). Beyond its automatic glass doors lie the cool vaults of one of the town's oldest cellars, carved right into the live rock. It's worth a visit to crawl through the caves of a business established in the 14th century, and on a hot day you might want to chill with the bottles a while. Follow the signs from the Via Ricci tourist office.

Just off the piazza on Via Talosa, look for the **Scuolo Italiana Mosaico** (Via Talosa 21, tel. 0578/757272), an artisan's workshop that you can visit for free when it's open (usually weekday mornings and late afternoons). Inside, three men create mosaics from Venetian stone.

FESTIVALS Montepulciano puts a lot of energy into performances during the summer. The town comes alive July 20–August 10 with the **Cantiere Internazionale d'Arte**, a series of musical performances featuring artists from around the world. More exciting is the **Bruscello**, when locals put on lavish amateur productions in front of the Duomo. The plays are presented in August, and tickets cost about L10,000.

PIENZA

Commissioned by Eneo Silvio Piccolimini, the poet and politician who became Pope Pius II, Pienza was designed as a model Renaissance city, with a central piazza surrounded by a cathedral, city hall, and the ruler's palace. After becoming pope in 1458, Pius geared some of the church's tremendous resources toward restructuring the town, formerly called Corsignano. The most fascinating aspect, other than the vanity of it all, is how the town was built within only three years (and promptly rechristened by Pius after his own name). Ironically, Pius died two years after Pienza's completion, ending the town's brief role as a religious center.

Pienza looks and feels like a scale model of more powerful Tuscan towns. The buildings are small, and the town is so clean that it's hard to believe anyone actually lives here. All roads literally lead to **Piazza Pio II**, the main square surrounded by all the key buildings. The **cathedral** (Piazza Pio II, tel. 0578/748546) doesn't seem quite big enough to warrant that name; it's no larger than most small-town churches. The blocky, three-arched facade indicates its Renaissance vintage, but the ambiguous interior is almost entirely made of simple white marble, capped by pointed Gothic rib vaulting. Inside are five panel paintings commissioned for the church; the best is Vecchietta's *Assumption*, in the left rear chapel. More impressive is the **Palazzo Piccolomini** (tel. 0578/748072), also on the main square, which housed Pius II and his descendants all the way through 1962, when the last Piccolomini died. It's obvious why the family wanted to stay here—the back windows have a panoramic view of the area, and the palace has the three biggest assets in real estate: location, location, and location (it's right on the main square). You may have to wait awhile before being allowed into the palace; ring the bell and eventually the manager will let you in for a fee of L5000. The **tourist office** (tel. 0578/748502; open Tues.–Sat. unpredictably) is just across the Piazza in the Palazzo del Comune.

COMING AND GOING Pienza is on the bus line between Siena and Montepulciano; it's much closer to the latter, making it a good stop-off for a couple hours of sightseeing before your arrival in Montepulciano. TRA-IN buses leave from Siena (L5500) or Montepulciano (L1500) about four times per day; when it's time to head out (which will be relatively soon), buy bus tickets at **Bar Il Giardino** (Via della Madonnina 2, tel. 0578/748607). The bus stops in front of the bar for about 10 seconds, so be ready.

WHERE TO EAT AND SLEEP If you insist on staying the night, the best option is **Camere Il Falco** (Piazza Dante Alighieri, just outside the city walls, tel. 0578/748551), which has clean, modern doubles with TVs (and is located above a restaurant) for L65,000. Pienza's main street, Corso Il Rossellino, is lined with shops selling locally made cheeses, jams, and wines. The trattoria **La Buca delle Fate** (Corso Il Rossellino 38/A, tel. 0578/748448) serves pasta dishes for around L7000 and secondi like roast veal for L12,000. The butcher **Laura Bernardini** (Corso Il Rossellino 81) makes excellent panini for L3000.

MONTALCINO

Despite the medieval vineyards covering the hillside, the approach to the walled city of Montalcino seems more Sicilian than Tuscan: The air is a little drier, the grass is a bit yellowed, and the stones look more worn than in other towns in the area. The village's weathered look reflects its history. For nearly 400 years, between 1200 and 1559, an off-again, on-again peace treaty with Siena kept Montalcino busy trying to identify its enemies, and battles were regular occurrences. Today the town seems frozen in time. The streets are always quiet, and new buildings are constructed to look like the old ones, complete with faux brick paneling.

The main industry comes from over 100 vineyards in the hills outside town. Just about every shop in Montalcino—from the ubiquitous enotecas to the produce stands—sells locally made wines. The *Brunello*, a full-bodied red wine, is the town's most famous export. Other regional specialties are honey and dry biscuits called *ossi morti* (dead bones).

Montalcino's four neighborhoods hold two annual, citywide celebrations: the **Archery Tournament** (second Sun. in Aug.), in which the neighborhoods politely battle it out over an archery range, and the **Feast of the Thrush** (last Sun. in Oct.), in which citizens celebrate the hunting season by parading through town clad in 14th-century costume, torches in hand. The uncrowded and unfriendly **tourist office** (Piazza del Popolo, tel. 0577/849321; open Tues.–Sun. 9–1 and 3–7) sells an English-language pamphlet about the city for L1500 and gives out free maps and accommodations listings. In light of the relative high cost of the town and the dearth of activity, Montalcino is best as a day trip from Siena unless you're in search of pure, untarnished Tuscany.

COMING AND GOING You'll either have to get up with the roosters to catch the 7 AM bus from Siena (L5600), wait for the sluggish 10:45 AM bus, which stops at every small town along the way and arrives just in time to see everything close for the midday break, or take one of the hourly afternoon buses. In Montalcino, the bus drops you at Piazza Cavour, a 10-minute walk from the fortress on the opposite end of town. Buy tickets for the bus from the friendly folks at **Bar Prato** (Piazza Cavour 5, tel. 0577/848121).

WHERE TO SLEEP Cheap beds are nearly impossible to come by in Montalcino—it's the rare city that makes Siena look affordable. It will be a coup if you land a room at the **Affita-camere Mariuccia** (Piazza del Popolo 28, tel. 0577/849319), run by one of the sweetest women in town. At L50,000 for a double with bath, the three rooms fill quickly. **Il Giardino** (Piazza Cavour 4, tel. 0577/848257) has small, clean doubles at L70,000, but you may be able to talk the price down to about L60,000 during the off-season.

FOOD One of the few places in town where you can procure a reasonable meal is **Il Grappolo Blu** (Via Scale Moglio 1, tel. 0577/849078), with dishes like spaghetti with clams for around L7000. The town's best pizza joint is **Pizzeria San Giorgio** (Via Saloni 12, tel. 0577/848507), with pizzas for around L7000. Most grocery stores and cafés are along Via Mazzini, the main thoroughfare, and its extensions, Via Matteotti and Via Saloni.

WORTH SEEING You can get a double dose of culture by drinking wine and listening to a brief history lesson at the town's fortress, referred to as the **Rocca**. Built in the 14th century and still standing proudly after repeated assaults, the fortress is empty except for a museum that seems to contain whatever the townies decide to post on the walls, usually an exhibit of recent local paintings. From the fortress walls you get a picture-perfect definition of how the region hasn't grown: Look any direction and all you see are endless green hills, only occasionally interrupted by a flock of sheep or a hilltop villa. *Piazzale Fortezza, tel. 0577/842–9211. Admission to fortress and walls: L3500 each, L1750 students. Open Apr.–Sept., Tues.–Sun. 9–1 and 2–8; Oct.–Mar., Tues.–Sun. 9–1 and 2–6. Follow Via Mazzini, the main strip, to where it turns into Via Matteotti and continue to the top.*

On the main floor of the fortress is Montalcino's classiest enoteca. For L4500 a glass, you can sample Brunello as you sit in the shadow of the fortress and munch on bread and prosciutto. If you want to walk off the heavy wine, continue straight from the fortress steps down (and then up) Via Ricasoli, which becomes **Via Cialdini**. This narrow, steep residential street of well-worn brick is one of Tuscany's loveliest. It will eventually bring you back to Via Mazzini.

If just tasting isn't enough, you can also view rows of bottles representing every wine produced in Montalcino and their brief histories at the **Palazzo Comunale** (Costa del Municipio 1, tel. 0577/849320), a smaller-scale model of Siena's town hall. In the same building, the high-tech office of the **Consortio del Vino Montalcinesco** (tel. 0577/848246) compiles a list of the local wines, their growers, and how to contact the vineyards. The bus from Siena passes many wineries; look for signs along the road and ask the driver to let you off (most vineyards are less than 1 kilometer from the main road).

Elba

Once a highly desirable source of iron ore for the Greeks, Etruscans, and Romans, today the island of Elba is, lira for lira (or given all the German tourists, deutsche mark for deutsche mark), one of the most expensive tourist destinations in Italy. Still, if you're worn-out after breezing from city to city in the Tuscan countryside, Elba, with its 147 kilometers of coastline, crystal-clear water, and all-night discos, may be the best—and most convenient—indulgence this side of the Greek islands. The island's main ferry landing, Portoferraio, is only an hour away from the mainland. If timed correctly, a trip from Florence or Pisa could take as little as three hours. Unfortunately, in July and August finding accommodations can be a nightmare—advance planning is necessary. For the rest of the year, tourists clear out, and the island becomes more affordable and wide open for exploration.

Napoléon was exiled here for a only a year after his disastrous Russian campaign, but he managed to leave his mark everywhere, from his two villas to the omnipresent postcard sellers hawking his image. In any case, most visitors come here less for the history than for the beaches, and the small towns scattered around the island all offer lovely places to relax.

COMING AND GOING To reach Portoferraio, the island's transit hub, take the ferry from the mainland town of **Piombino**. Trains heading south on the coastal route from Pisa to Rome stop at Campiglia Marittima; from here, take a train to the second Piombino station, the port stop.

The station is right next to the docks; call 0565/34263 for info. At the port, you can choose from two ferry lines: **Navarma** (in Piombino, Piazzale Premuda 13, tel. 0565/221212; in Portoferraio, Viale Elba 4, tel. 0565/914133) and **Toremar** (in Piombino, Piazzale Premuda 13–14, tel. 0565/31100; in Portoferraio, Calata Italia 22, tel. 0565/918080). The standard cost is L9000 per person (up to L14,000 on peak weekends) for the pleasant hour-long trip. From early June through mid-September ferries run hourly in both directions; off-season they run less frequently. Toremar also runs ferries from Livorno to Elba—a trip that takes three times as long, and costs three times as much.

GETTING AROUND Mopeds give you the freedom to scout beaches off the bus routes without wasting too much time or exerting too much energy. You can rent one almost anywhere and can often return it somewhere else. Prices vary depending on the month, peaking from mid-June to late August. Mountain bikes are available at most moped-rental places, but make sure you understand the challenge of Elba's hills before committing yourself to one. One of the best rental shops, with branches in Marina di Campo, Lacona, Porto Azzurro, and Marciana Marina, is **Two Wheels Network Motonoleggio** (in Portoferraio next to bus station, tel. 0565/914666). The shop rents mopeds for around L40,000 a day or L126,000 a week and mountain bikes for L20,000 a day or L63,000 a week. If you want to circumnavigate Elba with two arms, they even rent **kayaks** for L35,000 a day or L85,000 for three days. You must have some experience with kayaks, be over 18, and pay a L100,000 deposit (Visa and MasterCard accepted). Costs are reduced in the low season, and 20% discounts are offered to HI members.

➤ **BY BUS** • Buses run from Portoferraio's **bus station** (Via Elba 20, ½ block from port, tel. 0565/914392) all over the island. Fifteen buses go daily to Marina di Campo, seven to Marciana Marina, and 12 to Porto Azzurro; a ticket to any of the three costs L3000, and the trips from town to town average about a half hour. The station offers the island's only luggage storage (L2500), which is open weekdays 7:40–1:20 and 4–6, weekends 9–12:30 and 2–6. Buy bus tickets at the many cafés and bars around the island.

OUTDOOR ACTIVITIES Most tourist offices carry a free booklet called "Trekking all'Elba" (conveniently translated into German), with a map of the island's main roads and walking paths. The best hike leads up to Monte Capanne from Marciana Marina (*see below*). Major resort beaches (particularly Marina di Campo and Porto Azzurro) are centers for water sports, but only during peak months. For windsurfing, snorkeling, or boat rentals, look along any beachfront for signs, or at the tourist office for brochures. If you want to try scuba diving, a good place is in Marina di Campo, called **A M Centro Sub** (Via Pietri 3, tel. 0565/977035).

AFTER DARK The discos in the hills are where things really get going after midnight. Unfortunately, you can't get there by foot (they're well off the beaten path), but if you meet some swingin' locals on the beach, you can probably bum a ride. The two places to aim for are side-by-side on the Portoferraio–Procchio road, in the town of Capannone. **Club 64** (tel. 0565/969988) looks like a palace and has an outdoor dance floor, while **Norman's Club** (tel. 0565/969943) has the same crowd in slightly less swanky surroundings. Both clubs are packed nightly in the summer primarily with locals since the rest of the island shuts down by midnight. In the off-season, call first to find out what nights they may be closed. Both charge a L20,000 cover, but if you're a woman, they might forget the entrance fee. Look for the bronzed and the beautiful handing out complimentary passes to these places (and other fly-by-night ventures) on the beaches.

PORTOFERRAIO

From a distance, Portoferraio looks like a lovely seaside town, with stone houses angling to the sea and dramatic hills rising in all directions. But a closer look reveals an overcommercialized strip of pricey bars and tourist rackets. A little familiarity with Portoferraio may convince you that both impressions are equally valid: Elba's main town is attractive *and* tacky, dramatic *and* overbearing. In any case, you must go through the town if you want to see the rest of the island, since all ferries from Piombino drop anchor here. At least the picturesque centro storico and the two forts overlooking the town are well worth a twilight stroll, and the **museo archeologico civico** (Darsena Medicea, tel. 0565/917338; admission: L4000) is good for a peek into the area's ancient culture. Located in Torre della Linguella, the museum displays Etruscan and Roman archaeological finds from land and sea.

Getting oriented is easy. The town has dozens of offices with tourist information, but their real purpose is to book rooms for commission. The bus station (*see* Getting Around, *above*) has an information desk, and two flights up in the same building is the official **information office** (Calata Italia 26, tel. 0565/914671; open daily 8–8).

Elba is definitely the place to suffer exile in style. Poor Napoléon, sequestered in 1814 after becoming a bit too ambitious, was allowed the luxury of two houses in Elba and rule over the entire island during his penance. One of his houses, **Villa dei Mulini** (Via Villa Mulini, tel. 0565/915846), lies right above Portoferraio in the old part of town. His "country" estate, the **Villa Napoleonica** (tel. 0565/914688) in San Martino, is only about 5 kilometers away. The location in the foothills is exquisite: The break in the surrounding mountains provides a breath-taking view of Portoferraio and the bay from the house's upper level. The interior hardly justi-fies the L8000 admission, although the very short bed is a reassuring sign that he actually did live there. From Portoferraio, take Bus 1 to San Martino; by moped, follow the road to Procchio and turn left at the sign to San Martino. The villa is open weekdays 9–7 and weekends 9–1; ask for a ticket that includes same-day admission to Villa dei Mulini.

WHERE TO SLEEP AND EAT Portoferraio isn't a bad place to use as a base, but hotel prices rise dramatically during summer. If you don't have a room booked when you arrive, go to a reservations office (*see above*). The two best budget hotels in town are **Ape Elbana** (Salita Cosimo de' Medici 2, tel. 0565/914245), located in the heart of the centro storico, where dou-bles with bath start at L50,000 and move on up to L98,000; and **Nobel** (Via Manganaro 72, tel. 0565/915217), which has doubles for around L65,000 in the high season. Food in town is awfully pricey; pick up supplies at **Coop** (Via Teseo Tesei 40, tel. 0565/915180), supermar-ket extraordinare, or at one of numerous smaller markets throughout town. If you want a light meal in a relaxed atmosphere, head to the reasonably priced **Joe's Garage** (Via dell'Amore 48, no phone). This aptly named pub/*tavola calda* (cafeteria) warns away anyone in search of refined elegance. Crostini, small salads, and beer all go for around L4000.

MARINA DI CAMPO

The nearly perfect, sandy beach at Marina di Campo is obviously the town's major draw—the other island cities generally have uncomfortable, rocky shores. Mountains plunge into the sea on all sides of the gorgeous bay, but despite the long stretch of coast, you can barely see the sand under the stretches of greased bodies. The recent proliferation of "American" bars, Benetton shops, and newsstands selling the *Frankfurter Allgemeine Zeitung* indicates that this town knows its economy thrives on the tourist trade. Nonetheless, it's the best place on the island to encamp yourself if all you want to do is collapse on a beach.

WHERE TO SLEEP AND EAT If you want a hotel, the best budget option by far is the **Hotel Lido** (Via Mascagni 29, tel. 0565/976040), which will fit up to five beds in a room if you've got a big group. Doubles cost about L55,000. If you find yourself salivating at all the five-star hotels lining the beach, treat yourself at **Hotel Elba** (Via Mascagni 51, tel. 0565/976224), which, like the Lido, is about a block from the beach. In July and August, doubles go for L85,000; other months you can get a room for about L60,000. Two side-by-side campgrounds are a hellish 25-minute trek from the bus station (follow the yellow signs), but once you get there, you'll want to stay for awhile. **La Foce** (tel. 0565/976456) is the nicer one, but it costs L13,100 per person with tent, L12,500 without, and it's on hard dirt above the beach rather than right on the water. **Del Mare** (tel. 0565/976237; closed Nov. and Dec.) is crowded with motor homes and old folks but has lots of shade and charges L12,250 per person with tent. From early June through September, reserve well ahead of time at these campgrounds.

Food is easy to find along Via Roma, one block up from the beach, and on its extension, Via Marconi. In addition to the numerous markets, several fruit trucks line the street during sum-mer, selling incredibly fresh oranges, peaches, and melons. The best place to pick up prepared pasta dishes is the **Rosticceria e Gastronomia** (Via Roma 19, tel. 0565/977304), which sells large roast chickens stuffed with rosemary for L11,000 or chicken in basil and white wine for about L5500. The only other relatively affordable joint is **Canabis** (Via Roma 41–43, tel. 0565/977555). Aside from the atmosphere, which is reminiscent of Cabo San Lucas, it's pretty good—beer on tap and yummy crepes for L8000. They also host regular tequila blowout shindigs during the summer.

AFTER DARK Locals head west (toward Lacona) to **Marina 2000** (tel. 0565/976332), a heaving discotheque. You can't walk here, but if you're on a moped or in somebody's car, follow the signs posted at regular intervals as you head out of town on Via Mascagni. The L15,000 cover guarantees a lot of loud music and sweating bodies. For a less techno experience, have a cocktail with a view at one of the swinging "American bars" that line Via Marconi and the western edge of the waterfront. They stay open late, but they'll gouge you for a drink.

MARCIANA MARINA

Lots of the activity on Elba hovers around Marciana Marina, a lively and accommodating town. It has a dandy waterfront area and is conveniently located near the region's main attraction, **Monte Capanne** (*see below*). On the way up the mountain is **Poggio**, a town with a lot of cultural and social happenings. If you've planned ahead, you can get a decent room without paying a fortune. Right in the center of town is the **Soggiorno Tagliaferro** (Viale Principe Amedeo 10, tel. 0565/99029), a little villa a block from the beach with doubles at L70,000 in the high season, L50,000 in the low. From the bus stop, make the first right. Pick up fruits and veggies at the stand near the water, **Frutta e Alimentar** (Piazza della Victoria, tel. 0565/99109). From Viale Amedeo walk to the beachfront and turn right. Try affordable pasta dishes at **Rosticceria Il Gastronomo** (Via del Sette 10, from Viale Amedeo turn left on the beach front, tel. 0565/997021), with lasagna for L7000. You can get a good crepe at **Creperie l'Onda** (Viale Principe Amedeo 4), which serves up both the sweet and the savory varieties.

OUTDOOR ACTIVITIES **Monte Capanne**, the island's highest point, is prime hiking territory. From the top, you can look out over the entire island, Sardinia, and the mainland. To walk it, catch a bus from Marciana Marina towards Poggio and ask the driver to let you off near the hiking trail, or take the bus to Marciana, which is at the base of one of the hiking trails. The walk up takes about two hours. The alternative is a steep (in more ways than one) cable car that runs to the mountaintop from just above Marciana, the hillside sister town of Marciana Marina. The ride costs about L13,000 for a round-trip. Take the bus to Marciana and ask the driver to drop you off outside of town by the cable car. At the summit of the Monte is a little church next to a famous font of blessedly cool spring water.

UMBRIA AND MARCHE

9

By Laura Altieri

Central Italy does not begin and end with Tuscany. The pastoral, hilly provinces of Umbria and Marche pick up where the well-traveled route between Florence and Rome leaves off. Extending from the middle of the peninsula all the way to the Adriatic, the area's principal attraction is its landscape. Medieval towns, orchards, vineyards, and olive groves are everywhere, and unlike in Tuscany they aren't interrupted by industry and big business. Umbria, in the exact center of Italy, is close to some of the most popular Italian cities but fails to attract the hordes that flood Florence, Siena, and Rome. Marche, to the east, encompasses the wonderful university town of Urbino as well as mountains and Adriatic beaches. And while the region supports more than its fair share of overcrowded resort towns, it still manages to feel like a serene getaway, proffering sunset-stained villages silhouetted against brilliant skies, and wind-churned fields flecked with golden sunflowers and red poppies.

Umbria

Tuscany's quiet sister, Umbria boasts olive groves and vineyards that swell and dip around a wealth of extraordinary hill towns. Three thousand years of history are rooted in Umbria's fertile soil. The Umbrii, a tribe that settled in central Italy around 1000 BC, left behind few traces. The Etruscans, who dominated during the 6th century BC, left much more evidence for archaeologists, including necropolises and wells. The Romans made their mark later, fighting multiple barbarian and Byzantine invasions over several centuries. But Umbria's towns are most apparently medieval, relics of the late Middle Ages, when the region was torn apart by the Guelph-Ghibelline conflict (between supporters of the papacy and supporters of the Holy Roman Empire). The towns are mazes of dark, twisting alleys lined with somber palazzi amply fortified for battle.

The only hill town with heavy tourist traffic is Assisi, home of the ascetic St. Francis (AD 1181–1226) and an important pilgrimage site since medieval times. Perugia is the provincial capital, a russet-colored university town known for its cultural vivacity and its chocolate. Also worth a visit are Orvieto, built atop a volcanic outcropping; Spoleto, with its international arts festival; and Gubbio, one of Italy's best-preserved medieval cities. Buses are the way to travel in the region, since trains often leave you and your backpack with a long uphill walk to the town center. You have to go through Perugia to get almost anywhere, so take advantage of its hostel and use the city as a base for day trips.

277

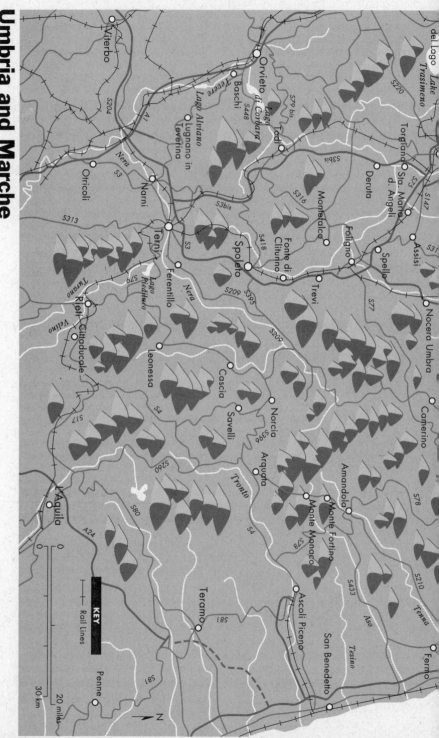

Umbria and Marche

KEY
—|—|— Rail Lines

30 km
20 miles

N

278

Isola
Maggiore×
S75
Passignano sul
Trasimeno
Sansepolcro
S73
Tevere
Umbertide
S3bis
Città di Castello
S3
Gubbio
S298
S3
S76 Fabriano
Pergola
S76 Jesi
Misa
Cesano
Potenza
Macerata
Recanati
Loreto
Numana
Ancona
Senigallia
S424
Marotta
A14
E78
Metauro
Fano
E78
S3
Fossombrone
Fermignano
E78/S73bis
Urbino
S423
Pesaro
S16
S423
San Marino
S72
S258
S71

Adriatic Sea

TO
GREECE

Perugia

In the heart of Umbria, the provincial capital Perugia boasts a dramatic history to match its spectacular views. In addition to enduring the usual barbarian conquests and medieval chaos, the town gave rise to the Flagellants, a sect of masochistic Christians who publicly whipped themselves bloody to atone for the sins of humankind. Today Perugia seems civilized enough, although its ruins hint at past nastiness. The town's large student population and resulting cultural savvy have kept it from languishing like other Umbrian hill towns.

BASICS Perugia's **tourist office** (Piazza IV Novembre 8, tel. 075/572–3327), open weekdays 8:30–1:30 and 4–7, weekends 9–1, hands out a lame map and bus and train schedules galore. To get there from the train station, take Bus 20, 26, 27, 28, or 29 to Piazza Italia and then walk down Corso Vannucci to Piazza IV Novembre.

Pick up a copy of "Perugia What, Where, When" (L1000) from a newsstand as soon as you arrive—its monthly calendar of events, printed in English and Italian, is a gold mine of information.

If you're just passing through, a convenient *albergo diurno* (day hotel) has toilets, showers (L4000), and luggage storage (L1500 per day). It's near Piazza Italia, where buses shuttle to and from the train station, and Piazza dei Partigiani, where buses leave for other cities in the region. *Viale Indipendenza 7. From Piazza Italia take escalator down to Via Bagliona (underground street) and follow signs for ALBERGO DIURNO out a door onto Viale Indipendenza. Open daily 8 AM–8 PM.*

➤ **MAIL AND PHONES** • Perugia's main **post office** handles packages and *fermo posta* (held mail) Monday–Saturday 8:10–7:30. There's also a *cambio* (currency exchange) open 9–5 weekdays and 9 AM–12:30 PM Saturdays, and a **telegraph office** open Monday–Saturday 8:10–7:30 and Sunday 8:10 AM–1 PM. *Piazza Matteotti 1, tel. 075/573–0703. From Corso Vannucci take Via Mazzini or Via Fani to Piazza Matteotti.*

The self-service **SIP** office (Corso Vannucci 76, off Piazza della Repubblica, no phone; open 8 AM–10 PM) has phone-card vending machines and phone books. The town's two **IRITEL** offices allow you to pay after making your call. The one at the train station (Piazza Vittorio Veneto 8) is open Monday–Saturday 8–8, and the one in the town center (Via Mazzini 26, off Corso Vannucci) is open daily 8 AM–midnight.

COMING AND GOING The main **train station** (Piazza Vittorio Veneto, tel. 075/500–1288) is outside the town center, below the city. The cambio at the information desk is open daily 7 AM–8 PM and charges no commission. Trains go to Rome (17 daily, 3 hrs, pass through Foligno, L17,300), Florence (14 daily, 2 hrs, L12,100), Assisi (hourly, ½ hr, L2700), and Spoleto (17 daily, 1 hr, L5000). Six trains leave daily for Castiglione del Lago (1 hr 10 min, L4300), Passignano (1½ hrs, L3200), and Orvieto (2 hrs, L8800). **Luggage storage** is open daily 6:30 AM–8:30 PM and costs L1500 per 24 hours. From the station, Bus 20, 26, 27, 28, or 29 will get you to Piazza Italia, and Buses 33 and 36 go to Piazza Matteotti.

Long-distance buses depart from Piazza dei Partigiani, just beyond Piazza Italia (an escalator leads from Piazza Italia to Via Bagliona, which connects to Piazza dei Partigiani). Buy tickets from the **ASP** booth in the middle of the square (tel. 075/573–1707). Six buses go to Gubbio (1 hr 15 min, L7400) as well as other destinations in Umbria and beyond.

GETTING AROUND Finding your way around Perugia can be tricky. The tourist office's map excludes many streets and gives no indication of how hilly the town is. **Corso Vannucci**, a short street, runs through the center of town between the transit hub **Piazza Italia** and **Piazza IV Novembre**. Most budget lodgings lie within walking distance of Piazza Italia, but **Piazza Matteotti** is closer to the youth hostel. Local buses run frequently between 5:15 AM and 9:30 PM. Buy tickets (L1000) at the train station newsstand.

WHERE TO SLEEP You'll find several budget hotels in the town center, but only the hostel (down the street from the *duomo*) and the campground outside town in Colle della Trinità are dirt cheap.

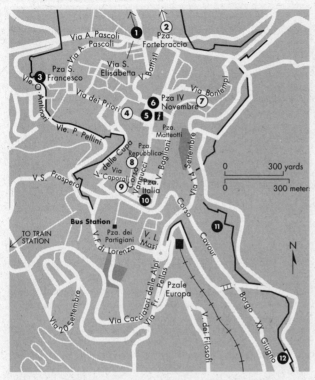

Sights ●
Duomo, 6
Oratorio di
San Bernardino, 3
Palazzo dei Priori, 5
Rocca Paolina, 10
San Domenico/
Museo Archeologico
Nazionale
dell'Umbria, 11
San Pietro, 12
Sant'Angelo, 1

Lodging ○
Convento di
Monteripido, 2
Hostel, 7
Hotel Eden, 9
Pensione Anna, 4
Piccolo Hotel, 8

Convento di Monteripido. If you manage to hike to this Franciscan monastery, you'll feel like you're in a peaceful dream. The second-highest point in Perugia, it offers a stunning view, beautiful courtyards and gardens, a small church, and a library. Friars mill about the tranquil grounds outside the city walls, and students from Perugia's university come and go. Doubles, all with bath, go for L50,000. *Via Monteripido, tel. 075/42240 (ask for Signora Vincenza). Take Bus CS or CD (last bus at 9:20) from train station to Piazza Fortebraccio and walk northwest on Corso Garibaldi. 1 km outside city gate you'll see monastery; head up stairs off Via Monteripido. Midnight curfew.*

Hotel Eden. Doubles (all with bath) cost a high L80,000, but this is one of the cleanest, nicest hotels in the city, with whitewashed corridors and a sunny entryway. The spacious rooms have telephones and TVs (and sometimes balconies). *Via Caporali 9, tel. 075/572–8102. Descend steps on west side of Piazza Italia and turn left; hotel is around corner to the right. Closed for 2 weeks around Christmas.*

Pensione Anna. Well-worn antiques and solicitous proprietors make the Anna feel more like a home than a hotel. You get your own set of building keys, and if there are enough guests, you eat in the dining room around a big table. Rooms (doubles without bath L50,000) have glass doors with curtains, firm beds, and ample towels. *Via dei Priori 48, off Corso Vannucci, tel. 075/573–6304.*

Piccolo Hotel. One block off central Vannucci, this small hotel offers nice, quiet doubles for L60,000—some also have a balcony over the quiet backyard. *Via Bonazzi 25, tel. 075/572–2987. From Piazza Italia, head down Corso Vannucci, left on Via Bonazzi.*

➤ **HOSTELS • Centro Internazionale di Accoglienza per la Gioventù.** In a terrific location minutes from the duomo and Piazza IV Novembre, Perugia's hostel has kitchen facilities, a library, hot showers, and a spectacular view. Big rooms house six sets of bunks, and bathrooms are large. Other bonuses include a TV room, a dining area, and lots of lounging space. Italian lessons are held Friday evenings in the library. Beds cost L14,000 a night; sheets are L1000 extra. There's a three-week maximum stay. *Via Bontempi 13, off Piazza Dante (just north of Piazza IV Novembre), tel. 075/572–2880. 80 beds. Midnight curfew, lockout 9:30–4, reception open 7:30–9:30 and 4–11. Closed Dec. 15–Jan. 15.*

➤ **CAMPING** • **Camping il Rocolo.** This terraced, tree-lined campground has the orderly look of an orchard. Tent campers set up among rows of trees that climb a broad, grassy staircase on the hillside. The trees are skinny and shade is scarce, but the spot is wonderfully peaceful, and the funky, round indoor/outdoor bathrooms have hot water and toilet paper—scarce commodities in many Italian campgrounds. You'll pay L8000 per person and L6500 per tent site July–August, slightly less in the off months. A market and a small bar that serves *tavola fredda* (cafeteria-style fare) serve the site. *Via della Trinità 1, tel. 075/517–8550. Take Bus 36 from station or Piazza Matteotti (Piazza Italia on Sundays) to Colle della Trinità and follow yellow signs uphill about 1 km. 100 spaces. Midnight curfew. Open June 15–Sept. 15. AE.*

FOOD Culinary specialties from all over Umbria flood into Perugia's markets and restaurants. Look for *salume* (cold cuts) like sausage, salami, and ham, and the expensive *tartufo* (truffle), a wild-looking fungus with a cult following. Perugia's wines include the white Torre di Giano, the red rubesco, and vin santo, a sweet dessert wine.

Perugia's claim to fame is the chocolate bacio (kiss), wrapped in paper inscribed with multilingual love messages. The chocolates are produced outside town at the enormous Perugina factory in San Sisto (Viale San Sisto 207, tel. 075/52761; group visits only).

For produce and fresh deli specialties, the **Mercato Coperto** (Piazza Matteotti 18/A) is open weekdays 7–1:30, Saturdays 7–1:30 and 4:30–7:30. For a more generic approach to groceries, try the big **COOP** supermarket (Piazza Vittorio Veneto), open Monday–Saturday 9–7:45. The ultimate place to fill a basket is the gourmet grocery **Le Delizie** (Piazza Matteotti 15, tel. 075/572–2937), with fresh pasta, truffles, olive oil, wine, and sausage. If you don't have cooking facilities, hit Le Delizie's surprisingly affordable deli counter, where you'll find a mouthwatering assortment of meats, cheeses, fresh-baked quiches, stuffed vegetables, and pasta salads. The shop is open Monday–Saturday 9–2 and 4:45–8:15.

Akropolis. Looking for something new and different? Dig into Greek specialties like filling souvlaki (L2800) and chicken kabobs (L3500) at this unpretentious family restaurant. *Via Danzetta 10, off Corso Vannucci, tel. 075/572–6575. Open Mon.–Sat. 11–8.*

Brizi Ristorante. Perhaps the cheapest truffles you'll ever eat can be found atop Brizi's homemade cheese ravioli (L6500). This small restaurant, close to both universities, also has tasty grilled fish (L10,000). *Via Fabretti 75, just down from Piazza Fortebraccio, tel. 075/572–1386. Open Wed.–Mon. 7:30 PM–11 PM.*

Mensa Universitaria. If you have any student ID, you can eat a cheap and substantial three-course meal here. Just how cheap depends largely on the mood of the cashier: Sometimes any student ID will get you a *primo* (first course), *secondo* (main course), and vegetable for L4000; other times you'll pay L7000 if you're not a Perugia student. After you eat, adjourn to the courtyard café, up 100-plus steps through the park, for a quick caffeine fix. *Via A. Pascoli, just past Via Vanvitelli on the right, tel. 075/43670. From Piazza Fortebraccio, go down steps on left side of palace and take Via Santa Elisabetta, which becomes Via A. Pascoli. Open Mon.–Sat. 11:45–2 and 6:30–8:30.*

Pizzeria Medio-Evo. This popular place makes the biggest pizzas in town and serves them in a small, crowded dining room where you're likely to sit at a long table with other guests. Most pizzas cost L5000–L7000; delve into a special creation like the Perugiana, with four cheeses, tomatoes, and ham. *Via Baldo 6, off Piazza della Repubblica, tel. 075/572–0764. Open Thurs.–Tues. noon–2:30 and 7:30–midnight.*

Ristorante Vecchia Perusia. Walk into this pink-tableclothed little restaurant for a three- or four-course splurge. Specialties include tagliatelle *ai tartufi* (with truffles; L15,000), or *agli* *asparagi* (with asparagus; L9000). End your debauchery with the homemade ricotta pie (L4000). *Via Ulisse Rocchi 9, tel. 075/572–5900. Open Wed.–Mon. 7:30 PM–10:30 PM.*

Il Segreto di Pulcinella. One of Umbria's only Neapolitan-style pizzerias, this joint also serves Greek salads (L8000) and hamburgers (L5000). The tasty pizzas range from L6000 to L9000. *Via Largo 8, off Via Vannucci, tel. 075/573–6284. Open Wed.–Mon. noon–2:30 and 7–11.*

WORTH SEEING Perugia's main street, Corso Vannucci, runs from Piazza Italia to Piazza IV Novembre, where two key monuments, the Palazzo dei Priori and the duomo, face each other across the **Fontana Maggiore** (1275). Three nymphs decorate the head of this fountain (currently under restoration), which was designed by Perugian architect Fra Bevignate and sculptors Nicola and Giovanni Pisano. Water spills into a basin ringed by 24 figures; below, panels depict the months, biblical scenes, and philosophical concepts.

South of Corso Vannucci, the **Rocca Paolina**, a fortress destroyed and rebuilt three times, is partially submerged in the city that has grown up around it. The subterranean **Via Bagliona**, dating from the 15th century, runs through the ruins of the fortress; enter it from Via Marzia or by escalator from Piazza Italia—a weird modern ride through ancient architecture. On one side of the fortress lies the **Porta Marzia**, a 3rd-century-BC Etruscan city gate.

Perugia's sprawling, hilly northern sector is home to two universities (the University for Foreigners and an Italian university) and offers some of the city's best views. Take Via Bartolo from the duomo and turn right on Via delle Prome to reach Piazza Scotti. From here, a staircase winds uphill to the picturesque street **Vecchio Acquedotto**, which soars over rooftops and offers views of gardens that are visible only from this elevated walkway. The aqueduct-turned-footpath was built to carry water to the Fontana Maggiore. Nearby Via Rocchi, which leads to Piazza Fortebraccio, dips under the massive **Arco Etrusco d'Augusto**, an Etruscan gate built three centuries before Christ. Farther along, at Corso Garibaldi, the **Porta Sant' Angelo** marks the edge of the *centro storico* (old town). This tall defensive tower was built in 1326.

➤ **DUOMO** • Perugia's duomo, the Cattedrale di San Lorenzo, was constructed between 1345 and 1490. Its exterior was never completed, though the marble design on the lower wall facing the piazza hints at how spectacular it might have looked. The interior houses Federigo Barocci's *Deposition* and the Virgin's wedding ring, a hunk of onyx Mary is supposed to have worn in her earthly marriage to Joseph. It's kept in an elaborate reliquary of 15 locked boxes, one inside the other, and is removed only once a year, on July 30. *Piazza IV Novembre, tel. 075/572–3832. Open daily 7–noon and 3–7.*

➤ **PALAZZO DEI PRIORI** • More than a century's worth of architects, builders, and sculptors worked on this enormous structure of white travertine stone, begun in 1293 and completed in 1443. Inside, the **Galleria Nazionale dell'Umbria** contains works by Fra Angelico, Agostino di Duccio, Taddeo di Bartolo, and Piero della Francesca. Beginning with gleaming medieval polyptychs, the collection quickly segues into Renaissance masterpieces, including a *Pietà* by Piero di Cosimo, a *Madonna with Child* by Raphael, and a multipaneled Pinturicchio altarpiece on which elegant golden columns divide the scenes. After such a beginning, the rest of the gallery is a bit anticlimactic, except for the **Cappella dei Priori**, across the hall from the gallery's main entrance. This recently restored room, frescoed by Benedetto Bonfigli, overwhelms you with 15th century scenes of urban Perugia. *Corso Vannucci 19, tel. 075/572–0316. Admission: L8000. Open Mon.–Sat. 8:45–1:45 and 3–7, Sun. 9–1.*

The palazzo's guildhalls are equally impressive. Upstairs, in the striking **Sala dei Notari** (an old assembly hall for lawyers), arches painted with scenes from the Bible and Aesop's fables cover the ceiling, and the walls are frescoed with coats of arms. Around the corner you'll come to the **Collegio della Mercanzia**, an intricately paneled hall from the 14th century that still serves as the meeting place of Perugia's merchant guild. Farther down Corso Vannucci is the most impressive of the chambers, the **Collegio del Cambio**. Peruse the frescoes—they are Pietro Perugino's best, painted between 1498 and 1500, when Raphael was his apprentice. Some of the work is credited to the young student, including the figure of Fortitude on the right wall; but since Raphael learned to copy his master's style exactly, it's impossible to know for certain if they're really Raphael's. Perugino's self-portrait is on the left wall (he's the one in the red cap). The work in the adjacent chamber was done by another of Perugino's students, Giannicola di Paola. *Notari: Upstairs off Piazza IV Novembre. Admission free. Open Tues.–Sun. 9–1 and 3–7. Mercanzia: Corso Vannucci 15, tel. 075/573–0366. Admission: L5000. Open Mar.–Oct., Mon.–Sat. 9–12:30 and 3–7, Sun. 9–12:30; Nov.–Feb., daily 8–2. Cambio: Corso Vannucci 25, tel. 075/572–8599. Admission: L5000 (L6000 for both Mercanzia and Cambio). Open same hrs as Mercanzia, except 2:30–5:30 instead of 3–7.*

➤ **SAN DOMENICO** • The church of San Domenico, Perugia's largest, has the same layout as the duomo: a nave flanked by two aisles and ceilings that rise to impressive heights throughout. The Gothic exterior gives way to a spartan, remodeled interior in somewhat bad repair. The frescoes are peeling away, but the apse, brightened by one of Italy's largest stained-glass windows (23 meters tall) and surrounded by gilded green organ lofts, is still beautiful. San Domenico's claim to fame is Pope Benedict XI's Gothic tomb, in the first chapel on the right. The **Museo Archeologico Nazionale dell'Umbria**, inside the cloister to the left of the double staircase, displays Etruscan and Roman artifacts, including funerary urns, bones, weapons, and jewelry dating from as far back as the 6th century BC. *Piazza Bruno, off Corso Cavour, tel. 075/573–0750. Museo Archeologico: tel. 075/572–7141. Admission: L4000. Open Mon.–Sat. 9–1:30 and 2:30–6, Sun. 9–1.*

➤ **SAN PIETRO** • The spire of this church pierces Perugia's skyline in the south end of town. Three courtyards with porticoes as elegant as the tower link the various parts of the complex, which was started in the 10th century and finished in the 17th century. The elaborate portal was sculpted in the 16th century by the school of Agostino di Duccio. Take a look at the paintings in the sacristy: There's one of St. Francis, by Caravaggio; one of Jesus and little St. John, by Raphael; and a few small works by Perugino. *Borgo XX Giugno, tel. 075/34770. Follow Corso Cavour through Porta San Pietro. Open daily 7–noon and 4–6:30.*

➤ **ORATORIO DI SAN BERNARDINO** • Beside the large church of San Francesco al Prato, now just an attractive facade, shines the Oratorio di San Bernardino. Its marvelous facade (1461) of pink, gray, and white marble is the work of Florentine sculptor Agostino di Duccio, famous for the Tempio Malatestiano in Rimini. Duccio completed the masterpiece in just 10 years, and spent the rest of his days in Perugia. The sarcophagus that serves as the altar is a 3rd-century Roman work. *Piazza San Francesco, off Via dei Priori, tel. 075/373–3957. Open daily 8–12:30 and 3:30–7.*

➤ **SANT'ANGELO** • The flawlessly manicured lawns in front of this 5th-century church, the oldest in Perugia, are good for lolling about with students who come to sunbathe or sleep. The church is without parishioners (they dispersed when the last priest died), but it's open for visits and worth a look if only for the large, round room inside supported by a collection of mismatched columns taken from the ruins of various pagan structures. *Via del Tempio, off Corso Garibaldi, tel. 075/372–2624. Open Tues.–Sun. 9–noon and 3–5.*

FESTIVALS In the second and third week of July, the whole city hums to the beat of the famous **Umbria Jazz Festival**. Along with traditional jazz, the show includes gospel, marching bands, and sometimes the Neville Brothers. The piazzas, streets, churches, and theaters spill over with people from around the world shelling out L15,000–L35,000 per performance. A few concerts, such as those performed in the Giardini Carducci, are free. For tickets, stop by **Ceccherini Record Store** (Via Boncambi 21, tel. 075/572–1778) or call the festival organizers at 075/572–5007.

AFTER DARK Lots of students mean lots of nightlife, especially near the universities. Popular with foreign students, the **Australian Pub** (Via del Verzaro 39, tel. 075/572–0206) serves beer (L7000) and plays live music Thursday–Tuesday. For a wilder night out, head down the block to **Disco Black Berry** (Via del Naspo 3, no phone); or listen to live jazz at **Caffè Morlacchi** (Piazza Morlacchi 6, tel. 075/572–1760). There's a cover charge for both venues, depending on the night of the week.

Lake Trasimeno

A low ring of mountains dotted with towns and castles surrounds Lake Trasimeno, which spreads out amid the hazy hills of northwestern Umbria. Its green, fish-filled waters and a trio of islands in the center provide hiking, water sports, beaches, and excellent camping. Isola Maggiore is the most accessible island, while Castiglione del Lago and Passignano sul Trasimeno, both easily reached by train, are the two main towns. The town of **Tuoro sul Trasimeno** is not as well fixed for tourism, but it possesses the most colorful history: 16,000 Roman soldiers died here in 217 BC, when the Carthaginian general Hannibal defeated the Roman consul Flaminius. Buses, which stop closer to campgrounds than trains do, are the best way for backpackers to travel into this region. Unfortunately, no buses run between the lake towns, so you have to pay the high price of the ferry.

PASSIGNANO SUL TRASIMENO Passignano makes a good base for exploring the lake—it's easy to reach and offers quick access to Isola Maggiore. The scenery may be better in Castiglione, but Passignano is plenty attractive, and it has a nice public beach. Rent a sailboat (L15,000 per hr) at **Sualzo** (Lungolago L. Giappesi, tel. 0336/599645). The **Pro Loco** office (Via Roma 36, tel. 075/827635) can answer questions about other beach activities; open Monday–Saturday 9–noon and 4–7, Sunday 9–noon.

➤ **COMING AND GOING** • Passignano's **train station** (Piazzale A. Buattini, tel. 075/827-6635 or 075/500-1288) has direct connections from Perugia (10–12 daily, ½ hr, L3200). Five **buses** come from Perugia each day (2 on Sundays, 1 hr, L5000), but you have to change in Magione and the layover can be a couple of hours. The bus stops on the waterfront near the ferry terminal (if you're headed for Isola Maggiore, this is the way to go). **Ferries** depart from the Imbarcadero, at the center of the waterfront off Via Pompili. Twelve ferries leave daily for Isola Maggiore (20 min, L4800) between 8:10 and 7:15. To reach Castiglione by boat you must transfer at Isola Maggiore.

➤ **WHERE TO SLEEP AND EAT** • Passignano's most convenient and affordable hotels are **Albergo Aviazione** (Via Roma 54, across tracks from station, tel. 075/827162) and **Albergo del Pescatore** (Via San Bernardino 5, tel. 075/827165). Doubles without bath cost L60,000–L65,000 at both. On the beach, **Kursaal Campeggio** (Via Europa 41, tel. 075/827182; open April–Sept.) charges L9000 per person and L8500 per tent site; it includes a swimming pool, restaurant, private beach, hot showers, and Windsurfer and pedal-boat rentals. To get there, follow Via Pompili about 800 meters out of town (it becomes Via Europa). The restaurant inside Albergo del Pescatore offers fresh local fish from L10,000 to L16,000. For groceries, hit **Discount Alimentari** (Piazza Trento Trieste 1, at base of castle), open Monday–Saturday 8–1 and 5–8.

CASTIGLIONE DEL LAGO Castiglione, a walled town on a rocky promontory, is the most picturesque of the lakeside towns. The medieval **castle** and the Renaissance church of **Santa Maria Maddalena** create a stunning silhouette on hazy summer days. At night you can groove to techno music at the beachside disco **La Sciaramada** (Lido Arezzo, no phone; closed Mon.). Castiglione's **tourist office** (Piazza Mazzini 10, tel. 075/965–2484), open Monday–Saturday 8–1 and 3–7:30, Sunday 9–1, will help with everything from getting a room in a hotel or private apartment to renting a Windsurfer for the day.

➤ **COMING AND GOING** • To reach Castiglione by train from Perugia (1 hr 10 min, L4300), you must transfer in Terontola. Castiglione's **train station** (Viale della Stazione, tel. 075/965–2484 or 075/500–1288) is outside the town center (there's no bus, so you must walk 25 min down Via Buozzi). **Buses** run directly from Perugia (7 daily, 1 on Sun., L8000), dropping you in Piazza Marconi. Castiglione's **ferry terminal** is beside the *lido comunale* (public beach) on Via Lungolago. Three ferries leave daily between 8:50 AM and 6:40 PM for Isola Maggiore (30 min, L5500), where you can catch connections to other towns. There is also a ferry from Castiglione to the smallest, least-populated island in the group, **Isola Polvese** (every hour, L5500). Here you'll find a peaceful park and one of the few uncrowded beaches around.

➤ **WHERE TO SLEEP AND EAT** • **Albergo Santa Lucia** (Via B. Buozzi 84, tel. 075/965–2492), outside the town center, is the closest thing to a budget hotel Castiglione has to offer. Doubles, all with bath, cost around L80,000. **Camping Listro** (Via Lungolago, Lido Arezzo, tel. 075/951193), a simple campground with a small sandy beach, charges L6000 per person and L5000 per tent. It's a 25-minute walk to the Imbarcadero, where ferries depart for Isola Maggiore. Slide over to **Ristorante L'Acquario** (Via Vittorio Emanuele 69, off Piazza Mazzini, tel. 075/965–2432; closed Wed.) for *chitarrini con anguilla* (homemade spaghetti with eel; L8500). It's open noon–12:30 and 7–10.

ISOLA MAGGIORE Take an island vacation in the heart of landlocked Umbria on Isola Maggiore. The charming, forested island has a tiny "main street" and a large salamander population. The winding footpath that circles the island will take you to the **Castello Guglielmi**, in terrifically poor repair (and closed to the public). This romantic, crumbling structure was once a Franciscan monastery. In the 19th century the Guglielmi family took over and turned it into a faux-ancient castle with battlements, a chapel, a private theater, and a balcony that has great views of Isola Minore and Passignano. Climb to the pinnacle of the island, the Gothic church of **San Michele Arcangelo**, to check out a cemetery and another gorgeous view. On your way, look for the chapel erected on the spot where St. Francis prayed and fasted for 40 days during Lent in 1211.

Isola Maggiore's lone hotel, **Albergo da Sauro** (Via G. Guglielmi 1, tel. 075/826168), has doubles (all with bath) for L75,000. The hotel's restaurant is excellent, but if you want to eat cheaply, plan ahead and bring food from a market on the mainland. For transportation information, *see* Passignano sul Trasimeno *and* Castiglione del Lago, *above.*

Gubbio

Perched beside a mountain, the placid, well-preserved walled city of Gubbio watches over green countryside. Although tourism is on the rise here, Gubbio is not yet the madhouse Assisi has become. At heart it's still a medieval commune whose true wild and wacky spirit unleashes itself on only a couple of days every year, during two festivals (*see below*). Cramped 13th- and 14th-century cobblestone alleys are a major part of Gubbio's charm, but they're a bit overwhelmed by restoration equipment and shops that push the town's major exports: ceramics, truffles, and toy crossbows.

Gubbio is expensive, especially if you enjoy eating out, so the best way to see it may be as a day trip from Perugia. Two tourist offices can help you plan your visit. The privately owned **Easy Gubbio** (Via della Repubblica 11, tel. 075/922006) is open daily 8 AM–10 PM. Or check out the regional **tourist office** (Piazza Oderisi 6, tel. 075/922–0693 or 075/922–0790) for identical maps and brochures. To get to the latter from Piazza Quaranta Martiri, head up Via della Repubblica and turn right on Corso Garibaldi.

COMING AND GOING Gubbio doesn't have a train station; you come and go by Perugia's **ASP buses.** Ten buses daily (four on Sunday) shuttle back and forth between Perugia's Piazza dei Partigiani (1 hr 10 min, L6000) and Gubbio's **Piazza Quaranta Martiri.** Buy tickets in advance at the Easy Gubbio office (*see above*) or at the newsstand in Piazza Quaranta Martiri. This square is the transit hub of the steep hill town, while the vacuous **Piazza della Signoria** (a.k.a Piazza Grande) marks the town center. To get to Piazza della Signoria from Piazza Quaranta Martiri, follow Via della Repubblica uphill; use the white tower as a guide and check out the dramatic view once you get here.

WHERE TO SLEEP The town's two campgrounds, **Villa Ortoguidone** and **Città di Gubbio** (Via Perugina, tel. 075/927–2037), occupy the same complex outside town and are tough to reach without a car. The Gubbio–Perugia bus will drop you a kilometer away (ask the driver), but it doesn't come as frequently as a city bus. The managers of **Trattoria San Martino** (Piazza Bruno 6, tel. 075/927–3251) can arrange a double with bath in a private house for L60,000. The centrally located **Albergo Galletti** (Via Piccardi 3, off Piazza Quaranta Martiri, tel. 075/927–7753) has moderately clean doubles for L58,000 without bath, breakfast included. The restaurant downstairs offers a tourist menu for L18,000. The hotel closes for the month of June and every Friday, but you can stay Friday night if you arrange ahead.

FOOD Because truffles figure into most regional specialties, eating can be very costly—a typical meal costs about L40,000. Your best bet is to buy at *alimentari* (small grocery stores) or the **Conad Market** (Piazza Bosone 1), open 7:30–1 and 5:30–8. To reach Conad from Piazza Quaranta Martiri, follow Via Cavour to Piazza Bosone. A couple places on Via della Repubblica, near Piazza Quaranta Martiri, serve pizza *al taglio* (by the slice). **Pizzeria la Cantina** (Via Piccolti 3, tel. 075/922–0583), open Tuesday–Sunday noon–3 and 7–1, has a sunny courtyard and an indoor dining room with brick arches and stone vaults. Pizzas are L4500–L7500, and the tourist menu costs L22,000 (an extra L4000 if truffles are involved). From Piazza Quaranta Martiri, take Via della Repubblica, turn right on Via Massarelli, and go right on Via Piccolti after three blocks.

Bartolini Produzione Propri di Prodotti Gastronomici. This specialty shop serves *panini* (sandwiches) to go for L3000–L4000; all are stuffed with Umbria's finest cheeses, sausages, and cold cuts. You'll also find a full array of picnic supplies, including wine, honey, mushrooms, truffles, Franciscan liqueurs and sweets, marmalades, and pastas. *Via Mastro Giorgio, tel. 075/927–4322. From Piazza della Signoria, head toward Via XX Settembre funicular, turn right down Mastro Giorgio staircase. Open daily 9–1 and 2:30–8.*

Along with Norcia, Gubbio is the truffle capital of Italy. Truffle markets flourish in October and November, when the pricey fungus is in season. Fans of the 'shroom should scope out the Bartolini truffle laboratory (Via XX Settembre 33, tel. 075/927–7579), open weekdays 9–1 and 2:30–8.

Ristorante Fabiani. Extremely elegant yet accessible to budget travelers, Fabiani has several dining rooms and an outdoor patio with tremendous views of Gubbio. The unusual risotto with basil and pecorino cheese (L12,000) makes use of local specialties. Most primi cost between L8000 and L10,000; truffle dishes are much more. *Piazza Quaranta Martiri 26/A, tel. 075/927–4639. Open Wed.–Fri. and Sun.–Mon. 12:30–2:30 and 8–10.*

Trattoria San Martino. This classy but unpretentious trattoria serves local specialties on an ivy-canopied patio. Primi run L8000–L9000, secondi L10,000–L13,000. Try the *gnocchi ai funghi* (gnocchi with mushrooms) or the house specialty, *lasagna San Martinare;* both are about L9000. The fixed-price tourist menu costs L23,000—truffles not included. *Piazza G. Bruno, tel. 075/927–3251. Walk down Via dei Consoli from Piazza della Signoria until you hit Piazza G. Bruno. Open Wed.–Sun. 12:30–2:45 and 7:30–10.*

WORTH SEEING In the early 14th century the city had to be rearranged to make way for the massive **Palazzo dei Consoli**, or Palace of the Consulate (Piazza della Signoria, tel. 075/927–4298), open Tuesday–Saturday 9–12:30 and 3:30–6, Sunday 9–1, with reduced hours October–May. This symbol of civic power and architectural elegance (admission: L4000, L3000 students) stands guard over the austere Piazza della Signoria (a.k.a Piazza Grande), where outlaws were once hanged. Inside, the **Museo Civico** houses coins, stone fragments from buildings and tombs, and the famous seven bronze Eugubine Tablets, discovered in 1444 outside the city walls. The tablets are a key to the little-understood Umbrii, one of the oldest tribes to populate the Italian peninsula. Apparently the Umbrii were surprisingly civilized: Their complex laws are explained in great detail on these tablets. A long staircase climbs one wall of the museum to the **Loggietta**, with an amazing view of Gubbio, and the **Pinacoteca Comunale**, containing works by local artists.

Head up the steep streets to the top of town to see the recently restored **Palazzo Ducale** (Via Ducale, tel. 075/927–5872; open daily 9–2; admission: L4000). Built in 1470 by Luciano Laurana for Urbino's duke, Federico da Montefeltro, the palace is a smaller version of Laurana's magnificent palace in Urbino. Across the way sits Gubbio's **duomo** (Via Ducale, tel. 075/927–3980), open daily 9–12:30 and 3:30–8:30. The exterior of this 12th-century church is relatively uninteresting, but see inside the small, elaborate dome and apse, frescoed in the design of a night sky and flanked by organ lofts that look like small theaters. You can pay to illuminate the beautiful **Cappella di S.S. Sacramento**, to the right of the nave.

In the 13th century the Spadalonga family, friends of St. Francis of Assisi, lived at the site now occupied by the Romanesque church of **San Francesco** (Piazza Quaranta Martiri, tel. 075/

927–3460). Here they hosted Francis during his exile from his family's home. The outside of the church features a crumbling octagonal tower; the inside holds some of local artist Ottavio Nelli's best frescoes.

The funicular just off Via San Girolamo will take you to the top of **Monte Ingino**, where you can wander around the **Basilica di Sant'Ubaldo** (tel. 075/527–3872) and enjoy a view of the city. From Piazza della Signoria, follow the FUNIVIA signs on Via XX Settembre to reach the lift (L6500 round-trip), which operates July–August, Monday–Saturday 8:30–7:30, Sunday 8:30–8; June and September, daily 9:30–1:15 and 2:30–6:30; and October–May 10–1 and 2:30–5. The basilica, dedicated to Gubbio's patron saint, houses the three huge *ceri* (wooden candles) used in the famous Gubbian festival Corsa dei Ceri (*see below*). Even if the church doesn't thrill you, the ride alone merits a visit.

The fountain in Piazza Bargello (one block from Piazza della Signoria) is known as "the fountain of the mad," the legend being that anyone who circles it three times will go insane.

FESTIVALS Utter insanity seizes the city every May 15 during the **Corsa dei Ceri** (Race of the Candles), which is held in honor of Gubbio's favorite bishop, Sant'Ubaldo. Despite the religious pretext, the festival is purely bacchanalian, shamelessly flaunting its pagan roots. Three teams of Gubbian men lift three huge ceri (topped with icons of the saint) and race from the Piazza della Signoria up to the Basilica di Sant' Ubaldo. Reserve a room ahead if you'll be in town at the time. The **Palio della Balestra** (Crossbow Contest), held each year on the last Sunday in May in Piazza della Signoria, began in the 12th century as a competition between Gubbio and Sansepolcro. The use of the crossbow, the most powerful of all feudal weapons, is still looked on as an art form in Gubbio.

Assisi

The legacy of St. Francis, founder of the Franciscan order of monks, surrounds the rose-colored hill town of Assisi. Each year, thousands of pilgrims make the trek here to pay homage to the man who made God accessible to commoners. St. Francis lived a life of asceticism. He was the first person to receive the stigmata (wounds in his hands, feet, and side, corresponding to the torments of Christ on the cross); and his mystical approach to poverty, along with his appreciation for the beauty of nature, struck a responsive chord in the medieval mind. Today, Franciscan friars in simple brown habits and belts of knotted rope still stroll among the *vicoli* (alleys) that wind from one magnificent church to the next. Even if you're not on a pilgrimage, the pretty little town is still well worth the trek uphill.

BASICS Everything you need to orient yourself is in the long, narrow Piazza del Comune. The **tourist office** (Piazza del Comune 12, tel. 075/812534) is open weekdays 8–2 and 3:30–6:30, Saturdays 9–1 and 3:30–6:30, and Sundays 9–1. The **post office** (Piazza del Comune 23, tel. 075/812355) has a **cambio** that charges no commission; it's open weekdays 8:10–6:20 and Saturday until 5:20. **Agenzia Stoppini** (Corso Mazzini 31, tel. 075/812597) changes money, and unlike the post office it takes Visa traveler's checks. It's open weekdays 9–12:30 and 3:30–7, Saturday 9–12:30.

COMING AND GOING Assisi lies on the Terontola–Foligno rail line. **Trains** run almost hourly between here and Perugia (½ hr, L2700). To get to Florence, transfer at Terontola; for Rome or Ancona, transfer at Foligno. The bus labeled ASSISI–SANTA MARIA DEGLI ANGELI travels back and forth between the station and town, 4 kilometers away. Hop off at the end of the line in Piazza Matteotti; it's a downhill walk from here into the center on Via del Torrione, and you'll pass the duomo on your way. For the hostel and campground, follow Via Eremo delle Carceri uphill about 1½ kilometers.

Buses leave from Piazza Matteotti, Largo Properzio, and Piazza Unità d'Italia for Perugia (6 daily, 55 min, L4200), Florence (1 daily, 2 hrs, L20,000), and Rome (1 daily, 2½ hrs, L23,000). Schedules are posted outside the tourist office and the train station. Buy advance tickets for Perugia at the newsstand on Via Santa Chiara, between Piazza del Comune and the

Assisi

Sights ●

Basilica di San Francisco, **1**
Basilica di San Rufino, **7**
Basilica di Santa Chiara, **12**
Basilica di Santa Maria degli Angeli, **10**

Cattedrale di San Rufino, **7**
Chiesa Nuova, **5**
Eremo delle Carceri, **9**
Rocca Maggiore, **2**

San Damiano, **13**

Lodging ○

Albergo Italia, **6**
Camping/Ostello Fontemaggiore, **8**
Hotel Grotta Antica, **4**
Hotel La Rocca, **3**

Ostelo Lapace, **11**

TO TRAIN STATION

0   0   200 yards
0   0   200 meters

Viale G. Marconi

Piazza Unità d'Italia

Pza. S. Pietro

Borgo S. Pietro

Via Fontebella

Via Melastasio

Via S. Francesco

Via S. Paolo

Pza. di Comune

Via S. Rufino

V. della Rocca

Viale Vittorio Emanuele II

Via A. Cristofani

Via Portica

Corso Mazzini

Via S. Rufino

V. Porta Perlici

Via S. Agnese

Via Santa Chiara

Via Borgo Aretino

Viale Umberto I

Piazza Matteoti

V. Santuario d. Carceri

V. Santuario d. Carceri

Viale Vittorio Emanuele

Porta Nuova

Viale Umberto I

Porta Cappuccini

S 147

S 444

289

Basilica di Santa Chiara. For tickets to Florence and Rome, go to Agenzia Stoppini (*see* Basics, *above*).

GETTING AROUND Getting around Assisi is not complicated, but the hills are exhausting. You can walk almost everywhere, though some major sights, including the Basilica di Santa Maria degli Angeli and the Eremo delle Carceri, are outside town. You have to hike the 4 kilometers uphill to the isolated convent of Eremo, but Santa Maria degli Angeli is accessible by the same bus that takes you from town to the train station. Assisi's main square is **Piazza del Comune**; from here Via Portica runs toward the Basilica di San Francesco, Corso Mazzini leads to the Basilica di Santa Chiara, and the steep Via San Rufino goes to the Cattedrale di San Rufino.

WHERE TO SLEEP Way back when, pilgrims who came to Assisi to worship slept under the simple portico of the Basilica di San Francesco, built for just that purpose. Times have changed, and Assisi's pilgrims now have a huge selection of hotels and religious establishments from which to choose. Unless you come to town on Easter or Palm Sunday, you should be able to find a room easily.

Albergo Italia. Up a flight of stairs from Piazza del Comune, the plain little Italia offers spacious, clean rooms, many with a view of the square. The rooms (doubles without bath L47,000) are decorated with attractive wooden furniture, and the bathrooms are large. *Piazza del Comune, up steps above fountain, tel. 075/812625. Closed Dec. 12–26. MC, V.*

Hotel Grotta Antica. The cheesy stone arches in the halls may not live up to the name "ancient grotto," but the dark, cavelike restaurant downstairs does. Pleasant doubles in this small hotel a few paces from Piazza del Comune go for L60,000 without bath. *Vicolo Macelli Vecchi 1, tel. 075/813467. Exit Piazza del Comune on Via Arco dei Priori and turn right on Vicolo Macelli Vecchi. MC, V.*

Hotel la Rocca. One of the cheapest hotels in town, la Rocca sits austerely on the upper terraces of Assisi among alleys leading to the fortress. Clean, spacious doubles, many with balconies and views of the city, go for L46,000 without bath. La Rocca also lets rooms in nearby private apartments for the same price as rooms in the hotel. *Via Porta Perlici 27, tel. 075/812284 or 075/816467. From Piazza Matteotti, take Via del Comune Vecchio to Via Porta Perlici. MC, V.*

➤ **HOSTELS** • **Ostello Fontemaggio.** A kilometer above Assisi, this hostel is part of a recreational compound that includes a campground, a restaurant, and a hotel. Of the hostel's two buildings, the Domus is the nicer. The other, larger building exemplifies the downside of communal living, with slimy bathrooms and grungy floors. Both buildings have cooking facilities and showers, and there's a market upstairs from the registration office. Beds cost L15,000 a night, breakfast included; private rooms L30,000 per person. *Via Eremo delle Carceri, Fontemaggio, tel. 075/813636. From Piazza Matteotti, exit town through Porta Cappuccini and follow Via Eremo delle Carceri (middle path at fork in the road) 1 km uphill to Fontemaggio turnoff on the right.*

Ostello Lapace (HI). This hostel's location near the train station in Santa Maria degli Angeli is less than ideal, but at least buses shuttle between the station and town twice hourly. Lapace is cleaner and better maintained than the hostel at Fontemaggio, but it lacks the beautiful setting. Beds are 17,000, showers and breakfast included. *Via Valecchi, tel. 075/816767.*

➤ **CAMPING** • **Camping Fontemaggio.** In the same complex as the youth hostel (*see* Hostels, *above*), this campground is a beautiful and tranquil green space on a terraced hillside that overlooks the plains below Assisi. The grounds resound with the noises of young pilgrims sharing clean fun, but you can find a secluded ledge if you try. It's refreshingly inexpensive at L6500 per person and L5000 per tent site, though the public potties are a bit grim and hot showers are unlikely. Fontemaggio also has six bungalows with kitchen and bath at L80,000 for four people. *Via Eremo delle Carceri, Fontemaggio, tel. 075/813636. Follow directions to Ostello Fontemaggio, above.*

FOOD For a rundown on regional goodies, stop at **La Bottega dei Sapori** (Piazza del Comune 34, tel. 075/812294), where proprietor Fabrizio will give you a mouthwatering tour. Assisi's specialties include such expensive delicacies as truffles and porcini mushrooms, as well as *pecorino* (sheep's milk cheese). The regional salami is *capocollo,* and *strangozzi* (a fat spaghetti) is the special pasta. At the neighboring **pasticceria** (Piazza del Comune 31, tel. 075/812814) you can get a hunk of *torta alla Nona* (pastry with cream and chocolate) or *torta Francescana,* a tasty raisin pound cake produced by the monks.

Hostaria Agnese. Grab pizza and beer under a portico at this unpretentious pizzeria, or hang out in the cavelike restaurant inside. In addition to small pizzas (L5500–L7000), they have juicy burgers, fries cooked in olive oil, and a huge selection of wine and spirits. *Piazza del Comune 38, no phone. Open Tues.–Sun. 8 AM–10 PM.*

I Portici. A suit of armor in waiter's garb greets you at the door of this cafeteria/restaurant. Low vaulted ceilings and brick archways create a pleasant ambience. Primi in the self-service bar run about L6000, secondi go for L8000, and a trip to the salad bar is L4000. *Via Portica 29/B, off Piazza del Comune, tel. 075/815126. Open Tues.–Sun. noon–2:30 and 7–9:30.*

Ristorante Spadini. The decor and the delicious cuisine typify Assisi. Primi run L6000–L9500, secondi L9000–L11,000. Try one of the Umbrian specialties such as the very amazing but also very expensive *tagliatelle alla norcino* (tagliatelle in cream sauce with sausage and truffles; L40,000). *Via Sant'Agnese 6, off Corso Mazzini, tel. 075/813005. Open Tues.–Sun. noon–2:30 and 7–9:30.*

Ristorante la Stalla. Even if you're not staying at the hostel or campground in Fontemaggio (*see* Where to Sleep, *above*), this restaurant in the compound is worth the 1-kilometer trek from town. Normally expensive local specialties are reasonably priced because of the way they serve the food: You set the table yourself, with red-checkered tablecloths and baskets of bread you can heap as full as you want. Order your meal at the *cassa* (cash register) and then watch women cook the food in a brick oven under an open portico. Try the *assaggini di torta di testo* (assorted mystery-meat sandwiches; L5500) or *strangozzi,* Assisi's premier pasta (L5500). Homemade wine is L4500 a bottle. *Via Eremo delle Carceri, tel. 075/812317. Follow directions to Ostello Fontemaggio. Open daily 12:15–2:30 and 7–11.*

WORTH SEEING The sloping Piazza del Comune, Assisi's main square, shelters the **Pinacoteca** (Palazzo del Priori, tel. 075/812599), a survey of Umbrian art that you can view daily 9:30–1 and 2:30–6 for L2500. The **Tempio di Minerva** has a classical facade and corrugated columns that support a tympanum, and the **Roman forum** (Via Portica, turn left down small flight of steps) contains a museum of Roman remains under the piazza. Stop by the little **Chiesa Nuova** (tel. 075/812339; take Via Arco dei Priori out of the piazza), atop St. Francis's family home; you can descend an enclosed alley and see the room where Francis's father kept him "prisoner," hoping to rid him of his silly ideas (*see box* Who Was That Hooded Man, *below*).

➤ **BASILICA DI SAN FRANCESCO** • In a city full of churches, the Basilica di San Francesco (tel. 075/813061) is exceptional. This celebration of Italy's patron saint is a double church—a Gothic basilica built atop a Romanesque basilica, each one remarkably beautiful and decorated floor to ceiling with perhaps the finest collection of frescoes in the world. Individuals can't schedule tours of the basilica, but monks lead prescheduled group tours, and you might slyly attach yourself to an English-speaking group.

During Francis's life, the site where the church now stands was called **"Hell Hill"** and served as a burial ground for unconsecrated and shunned prisoners. Francis, true to form, chose this spot for his own burial in order to help the unholy become sanctified. Construction of the basilica began in 1228, two years after the saint's death. In one of the great ironies of Christianity, the Franciscan order, based on asceticism, was honored with this monument of unabashed grandeur. Francis didn't even have time to roll over in his grave—his mortal remains were moved too quickly into a tomb in the lower church.

The older of the two churches, the **lower church** has low vaulted ceilings covered with frescoes that depict biblical stories. The most famous medieval frescoes are those by Cimabue, Giotto, and the Lorenzetti brothers. Cimabue's *Madonna Enthroned Among Angels and St. Francis*, in the right transept, is thought to be the portrait that most accurately portrays the saint's features. In the left transept you'll find the Lorenzetti brothers' famous *Madonna of the Sunset,* which sparkles gold when the sun hits it. Notice Mary's pointing thumb; legend has it that baby Jesus is asking his mother which saint to bless and she is pointing at St. Francis. Simone Martini's frescoes, in the first chapel to the left, depict scenes from the life of St. Martin, the first saint who was not martyred. St. Francis's undecorated tomb is down the steps to the right of the nave.

The **upper church** was built just after the lower in the up-and-coming Gothic style. The pointed arches, discovered to be stronger than round arches, allowed for greater height, and this basilica soars. Its stained-glass windows were the first in Italy, predating even those in Rome (the windows in the lower church were added later). The frescoes in the apse and transepts were painted by Cimabue, who used a daring new technique to achieve the brightest colors; unfortunately, because of the lead in the paint, they have faded to a pastel memory. Giotto's fresco cycle in the nave, the most famous work in the two churches, is still brilliantly colored. The upper register portrays biblical scenes, with the Old Testament on the right and the New Testament on the left. The lower register shows scenes from the life of St. Francis, beginning at the altar with the right wall, working toward the main entrance, and then heading up the left wall of the nave back toward the altar.

➤ **CATTEDRALE DI SAN RUFINO** • The Cattedrale di San Rufino (Piazza San Rufino, tel. 075/812285) has one of the finest Romanesque facades in Umbria, featuring a rose window supported on the shoulders of stone figures. Built in the 12th century on the foundation of a 3rd-century church (fragments of which can be seen in the church museum for L2000), San Rufino is where St. Francis was baptized. Farther uphill, the **Rocca Maggiore**, open 10 AM–8 PM, overlooks the town. The wonderfully preserved 14th-century castle, with breathtaking views of the city and valley, houses a torture and martyr museum (admission: L5000, L3500 students). To get here, take Vicolo San Lorenzo, a staircase/alley off Via Porta Perlici.

➤ **BASILICA DI SANTA CHIARA** • The pink-and-white 13th-century Santa Chiara (Piazza Santa Chiara, tel. 075/812216), supported by buttresses on one side, looks like it could fly away at any moment—the darn thing's got wings. The church's namesake, St. Clare, was inspired by her friend St. Francis to found the order of the Poor Clares, one of the three Franciscan orders. A famous talking crucifix, which supposedly advised Francis, is kept in a chapel to the right of the nave. Check out St. Clare's tomb downstairs, a grandiose copy of the one in San Francesco. Outside town, the convent of **San Damiano** (Via San Damiano, off Viale Vittorio Emanuele, tel. 075/816668) is the church Francis rebuilt when the mysterious crucifix spoke to him. It became the Poor Clares' first home and is where Francis composed *The Canticle of the Creatures*, which states that all living things are worthy of God's love.

➤ **BASILICA DI SANTA MARIA DEGLI ANGELI** • The basilica (tel. 075/804–0511), outside town toward the train station, encloses and completely dwarfs the tiny frescoed chapel **Porziuncola**, first home of the Franciscan order. This is where St. Clare took her vows

Who Was That Hooded Man?

The rebellious young Francis rejected his middle-class father (saying, "From now I shall serve only one father: God"), threw the clothes from his back in a public display of anti-materialism, and took a lifetime vow of poverty. Preaching humbleness and simple devotion, St. Francis became quite a force to reckon with in the 12th century, gaining popularity for sermonizing in the language of the common people (Italian) rather than Latin, and for openly criticizing the all-powerful, all-too-greedy Catholic Church. Admiring the highly decorated splendor of the upper church of the Basilica di San Francesco, it seems ironic to read one of St. Francis's credos inscribed therein: "Carry nothing for the journey, neither purse nor bag nor bread nor money."

and had her hair ceremoniously cut off, and where St. Francis died. To reach the basilica, take the bus marked SANTA MARIA DEGLI ANGELI from Piazza Matteotti.

➤ **EREMO DELLE CARCERI** • The utterly tranquil Eremo delle Carceri, or Hermitage of Prisons (tel. 075/812301) was one of St. Francis's favorite places for meditation. This collection of buildings at the top of a wooded grotto is where the holy man is reputed to have preached to the birds. It's open daily from dawn to dusk; to reach the site, exit Porta Cappuccini on Via Santuario delle Carceri and head uphill 4 kilometers. From the site, you can climb down narrow staircases and through miniature doors to the **Grotta di San Francesco**, a series of strange little chapel-caverns.

Spoleto

You have to wonder how Spoleto has escaped the crowds of tourists that clog Assisi. Sure, it lacks the important homegrown saint that rocketed its neighbor to stardom, but that's about all it lacks. Sprawling over a hillside, capped by the best-preserved castle in the region, and dropping off to a wooded gorge spanned by a monumental bridge, Spoleto has one of the most stunning locations of any Umbrian hill town. For a short time the capital of the Holy Roman Empire, Spoleto was later the seat of the powerful Duchy of Spoleto. Today it's best known for its gourmet food and its cutting-edge Festival dei Due Mondi (*see below*).

BASICS The **tourist office** (Piazza della Libertà 7, tel. 0743/220311) is open weekdays 9– 1 and 4:30–7:30, weekends 10–1 and 4:30–7:30. The office hands out a great city map and will give you a free pamphlet with historical info on all the monuments and festivals. The **post office** (Piazza della Libertà 12, tel. 0743/223198), which has a **cambio**, is open weekdays 8– 5:30 and Saturday 8–1.

COMING AND GOING Spoleto is easily reached by rail from Rome (hourly, 1½ hrs, L14,100), and from Florence (hourly, 3 hrs, L20,300) by way of Perugia (1 hr, L6100) and Assisi (40 min, L4200); some routes require a transfer at Foligno. The **train station** (Piazza Polvani, tel. 0743/48720) lies outside town, but buses shuttle between the station and the town center every half hour. Buy tickets (L1200) at the newsstand in the station. The Navetta line runs to Piazza della Libertà, and the Circolare B and E lines run to Piazza Mentana, near the center.

Intercity buses connect Spoleto to nearby towns and major urban centers. Five buses leave for Perugia every weekday (one on Saturday) from Piazza della Vittoria, which is adjacent to Piazza Garibaldi. Buy tickets (L7500) at nearby newsstands or *tabacchi* (smoke shops). Buses for Rome take off twice daily from the intersection of Via Flaminia and the Monteluco road. Buy tickets on the bus. For more info, call the tourist office (tel. 0743/220311).

WHERE TO SLEEP Most of Spoleto's hotels are either expensive or poorly located. Camping offers sublime views, and the tourist office has a list of rooms for rent in private homes. If you're coming between late June and mid-July, the key word is *reserve*.

Albergo Fracassa (Via Focaroli 15, off Via dei Gesuiti, tel. 0743/221177), in the lower town, is Spoleto's cheapest hotel. It's devoid of amenities, and the proprietress could be more pleasant, but with doubles at L40,000 (none with bath), don't complain. The **Hotel Anfiteatro** (Via Anfiteatro 14, tel. 0743/49853), also in the lower town, is a more attractive option for just a few dollars extra. Large, clean doubles, some with great views, go for L65,000 without bath. **Hotel Panciolle** (Via del Duomo 3, tel. 0743/45598), in the upper town just down the street from the duomo, is centrally located, but you pay for the convenience—L80,000 for a clean, well-kept double. **Camping Monteluco** (Località San Pietro, off Strada di Monteluco, tel. 0743/220358; open April–Sept.), in the Sacred Forest of Monteluco (*see Museo Archeologico, below*), has magnificent views and clean, modern facilities, including hot showers, a golf course, a bar, and a restaurant. The Monteluco bus (8 daily, L2200) runs right by it, but you can easily walk from Piazza della Libertà up Via Matteotti. The campground charges L7000 per person and L6000 per tent.

FOOD Spoleto has the highest concentration of gourmet specialty shops in all of Umbria. The area around **Piazza del Mercato** is particularly well stocked with stores selling truffles, Franciscan liqueurs, cheese, honey, sausage, and wine. Cheaper options in the Piazza del Mercato include the small, informal **market** held Monday–Saturday 8:30–1 and the **Self Service del Mercato** (tel. 0743/221974), open daily 12:30–4 and 7:30–midnight. Here, cheap and tasty meals go for about L12,000. Toward the bridge, at **La Portella** (Via del Ponte, tel. 0743/221574), you can sample standard bar sandwiches (L2000–L5000) while enjoying the best view of the city. Try regional specialties, such as *stringozzi alla spolentina* (dumplings with meat sauce; L8000) or *al tartufo* (with truffles; L20,000), at **Taverna dei Duchi** (Via Saffi 1, tel. 0743/40323; open Thurs.–Tues.). Just down the street, at **Enoteca Provinciale** (Via A. Saffi 7, tel. 0743/220484), you can wash it all down with local vino; they're open evenings Tuesday–Sunday.

WORTH SEEING From the churches in silvery olive groves on the outskirts of town to the stately *rocca* (fortress) atop Spoleto's peak, the city radiates grandeur and hushed charm. The notable sights are concentrated in the upper town, with the exception of a pair of exquisite churches just east of the city. The first one, **San Ponziano** (Via della Basilica di San Salvatore, tel. 0743/40655), open daily 9–12:30 and 3:30–6, is dedicated to the city's patron saint (a painting above the altar depicts his decapitation). If you can find the custodian, ask him to take you down into the crypt and show you the 14th-century frescoes. Farther along the same road, the alluring and deserted 4th-century **San Salvatore** adjoins the magnificent town cemetery. Modeled on a Roman temple, the decrepit columns are its only decoration. It's open daily 7–7 from May to September, with reduced hours October–April.

Put on your walking shoes and make a beeline to the most spectacular sight in Spoleto: the skinny brick Ponte delle Torri (Bridge of Towers), a 13th-century wonder designed by the architect Gattapone. A Roman aqueduct once spanned the same gap.

In the upper town, the Romanesque **duomo** (Piazza del Duomo, tel. 0743/47788) is breathtaking against a backdrop of hill and sky with the castle towering overhead. The facade incorporates a graceful portico (added to the 12th-century structure in the 15th century), eight rose windows, and a tympanum with a gleaming 13th-century mosaic. The campanile was thrown together from stones and fragments stolen from Roman ruins around town. Inside are several precious works of art, including recently restored Filippo Lippi frescoes (in the apse and dome) that depict scenes from the life of Mary. The artist died shortly after completing the frescoes, and Spoleto hung on to Lippi's body instead of shipping it back to his native Florence. He is buried in the cathedral, in a tomb designed by his son, Filippino. The first chapel on the right is Pinturicchio's frescoed **Eroli chapel**, painted for Bishop Eroli in 1497. The nearby 12th-century church of **Sant'Eufemia** (Via Saffi) lacks the duomo's allure, but you may want to check out its "women's balconies"—the first of their kind in Umbria—where women had to sit so that the men could occupy the main area. From the duomo, head west on Via Saffi; it's under the arch to the right.

Spoleto also has some great Roman ruins, including the 1st-century-AD **Arco di Druso**, off Piazza del Mercato. The **Teatro Romano** (Piazza della Libertà; admission: L5000; open Mon.–Sat. 9–1 and 3–7, Sun. 9–1) is flanked by porticoes and buildings, but it still evokes images of toga-wearing consuls strutting about. Through a door in the west portico, the **Museo Archeologico** (tel. 0743/223277), open the same hours as the theater, includes assorted artifacts and the *Lex Spoletina* (Spoleto Law) tablets dating from 315 BC. This ancient legal document prohibits the destruction of the **Sacred Forest**, a pagan prayer site that was later frequented by St. Francis. The **Casa Romana** (Via de Visiale 9, off Via Saffi), a house uncovered only in the last century, dates from the 1st century AD. The L5000 admission fee also gets you into Spoleto's **Pinacoteca** (Palazzo del Municipio, Via Saffi 14, tel. 0743/218270), a small collection of 12th- to 18th-century paintings. Both the Pinacoteca and the Casa are open Tuesday–Sunday 10–1 and 3–6.

FESTIVALS The **Festival dei Due Mondi** (Festival of Two Worlds), from late June to mid-July, includes music, theater, art, dance—and thousands of Italian and foreign tourists. Unfortunately, few performances are free; ticket prices range from L10,000 to L150,000 plus a 15% "selling fee." To get tickets, write to the Associazione Festival dei Due Mondi, Biglietteria Festival dei Due Mondi, Teatro Nuovo, 06049 Spoleto. One hour before each performance, remaining tickets are sold at the respective theaters. Last-minute tickets can be purchased in Spoleto at Teatro Nuovo (tel. 0743/40265 or 0743/44097).

Todi

The fairy-tale village of Todi rests peacefully on a hilltop, high above a valley that once supposedly contained 365 castles (one for each day of the year). While most Umbrian hill towns are high enough to suggest an aerie, only Todi is literally that—at least according to legend. The story goes that an eagle stole a tablecloth from an Umbrian dining table. Unable to eat without it, the Umbrii tracked the eagle down, and they liked its nest so much that they settled here for good. With a handful of exquisite monuments and some fine restaurants, Todi makes a great afternoon trip from Perugia. You could spend a restful night here, but once you've tackled the sights (an hour or two for even the slowest of walkers) there's little to do but stare into the green horizon. For a map and an English-language guide to the city's history, hit up the **tourist office** (Piazza del Popolo 38, tel. 075/894–2526), open Monday–Saturday 9–1 and 4–7:30, Sunday 9:30–12:30 and 4–7:30.

COMING AND GOING Todi lies on one meager rail line that runs between Sansepolcro in Tuscany and Terni in southern Umbria. Trains arrive in Todi's Santa Anna or San Giovanni station from Perugia (12 daily, 1 hr, L5400). When you arrive at the **train station** (Ponte Rio, tel. 075/894–2092), take Bus C to Piazza Jacopone (every ½ hr, L1200). Buy bus tickets from the machine in the station (coins only), from the tourist office, or from newsstands. Schedules are posted in Piazza Jacopone. Seven **intercity buses** also run from Todi to Perugia's Piazza dei Partigiani (Mon.–Sat., 1½ hrs, L9200). Buy tickets at the Mercato Margherita (*see below*).

WHERE TO SLEEP AND EAT To stay in the center, call ahead of time at **Proietti Serenella** (Via del Monte 17, off Piazza del Popolo, tel. 075/894–3231), which lets one double room without bath (L40,000) and one small apartment (L50,000). Otherwise, **Hotel Zodaico** (Via del Crocefisso, tel. 075/894–2625) has doubles without bath for L45,000. Take Bus C from the train station to Porta Romana, or walk (15 min) from town.

You can buy groceries in the **Mercato Margherita** (Piazza Jacopone, tel. 075/894–2201), open most days 7:15–1:30 and 4:40–8 but closed Thursday afternoon and Sunday. If you want to treat yourself to a no-holds-barred Umbrian feast, try **Ristorante Umbria** (Via San Bonaventura 15, tel. 075/894–2390), open Wednesday–Monday. The *polenta con funghi e tartufi* (corn meal with mushrooms and truffles) costs L18,000, but the portions are ample and delicious. For a cheaper, less memorable meal, head to **Pizzeria Ristorante Cavour** (Corso Cavour 23, tel. 075/984–2491), open Thursday–Tuesday noon–2, which serves a full tourist menu (L18,000) and pizzas (L4000–L8000) on their outdoor patio.

WORTH SEEING The **Piazza del Popolo** is a model of spatial harmony, temporarily marred by restoration nets and scaffolding. Luckily, the simple pink facade of the Romanesque-Gothic **duomo** (Piazza del Popolo, tel. 075/894–3041) is no longer undergoing a face-lift. You can enter the church 8:30–12:30 and 2:30–6:30, but portions are still being restored. A staircase in the square leads to the **Palazzo del Popolo**, which dates from 1213 and features Ghibelline battlements, and the **Palazzo del Capitano**, built in 1292 in a similar style. The **Palazzo dei Priori**, added in the 14th century, completes the square, its tower mirroring that of the duomo across the way.

From the Piazza del Popolo, head down Corso Cavour and turn left on Via del Vecchio Mercato to reach the old **Roman forum**, now barely visible among the buildings of the Piazza del Vecchio Mercato. Also in the neighborhood is the Romanesque church of **Sant'Ilario**, not open for visitation, adorned by a minimalist rose window. A little farther down the street, the **Fonti Scarnabecco**, spits water out of a contorted gargoyle face. The church of **Santa Maria della**

Consolazione (Viale della Consolazione, tel. 075/894–8482; open 9:30–12:30 and 3:30–6:30) is outside town, downhill from the **Parco della Rocca** (look for the trail on the right side of the castle). The walk there is pleasant, but the journey back is more arduous. The perfectly symmetrical and wonderfully simple white domed church has been attributed to two different Renaissance masters, Bramante and Sangallo.

Orvieto

Orvieto sits atop a circular plateau of tufa stone that was shoved up from the valley floor by volcanic movements. Its natural defenses eliminated the need for medieval walls, making it something of an anomaly among Umbrian hill towns. The Etruscans were the first to take advantage of Orvieto's defensive position, and excavations are constantly revealing more of their history. A subterranean network of wine caves and wells provides insight into Etruscan civilization, but the medieval city and the ornate duomo are Orvieto's primary attractions. Shops along narrow streets sell the town's famous exports, ceramics and wine. The dry white wine, Orvieto Classico, is known around these parts as "liquid gold." Come to the **tourist office** (Piazza Duomo 24, tel. 0763/41772), open weekdays 8–2 and 4–7, Saturdays 10–1 and 3–8, and Sundays 9–7, to pick up maps and info on sights. Unfortunately, much of Orvieto is currently hidden behind restoration nets and scaffolding.

COMING AND GOING Orvieto lies on the Rome–Florence rail line. Thirteen trains leave daily for Rome (1 hr 20 min, L11,800) and eight for Florence (1½ hrs, L15,600). For Perugia (2 hrs, L8800), you have to switch trains in Terontola. A **funicular** (L1100) carries you between Orvieto's **train station** (Piazza Matteotti 14, tel. 0763/300434) and Piazza Cahen, at the eastern edge of the city plateau. From Piazza Cahen, **buses** run to Piazza Duomo (L1400); the ticket covers both funicular and bus. Piazza Cahen is also the place to catch buses to nearby towns. Every weekday, one bus leaves for Todi (L7700), five head to Terni (L9700), and one goes to Perugia (L10,700) at 5:45 AM. Buy tickets on the bus.

WHERE TO SLEEP You'll find a few budget hotels in **Orvieto Scalo**, the area near the train station. Though the neighborhood is uninteresting, it's easy to reach town on the funicular. The clean, modern **Albergo Picchio** (Via G. Salvatori 17, tel. 0763/90246) has some rooms with balcony views of the fortress overhead. Doubles—all with bath, telephone, and TV—cost L60,000. From Piazza Matteotti in front of the station, head uphill on Via della Pesa, which becomes Via Salvatori. Another good choice is the clean, friendly **Hotel Centrale** (Via Sette Martiri 68, across from station, tel. 0763/93281), just minutes from the funicular. Small doubles with bath go for L60,000.

If you want the atmosphere of the centro storico, you can find a couple of inexpensive hotels in the heart of town, a few minutes' walk from the cathedral. A small flower garden in front, very large rooms (doubles L48,000 without bath), and a top floor with a great view make **Hotel Duomo** (Via di Maurizio 7, down steps from Piazza Duomo, tel. 0763/41887) a definite first choice. The big, high-ceilinged **Hotel Posta** (Via L. Signorelli 18, off Via Duomo, tel. 0763/41909), in an alley between Piazza Duomo and Corso Cavour, is pure medieval quarter, with long, narrow hallways and the bells of the campanile sounding through the walls. The beds are huge, the furnishings antique. Doubles without bath run L55,000. The hotel closes once a year in January or February, so call ahead.

FOOD Order Orvieto Classico (L6000 a bottle) at an *enoteca* (wine shop) or an *osteria* (pub), where pitchers of the dry white wine are common as water. **Enoteca Foresi** (Piazza Duomo 2, tel. 0763/41611) will let you sip or buy bottles for the road, and it sells panini made with fresh local products, such as *cinghiale* (wild boar; L4000). You can also descend into the wine caverns, where hundreds of bottles are stored in moist earth. **La Bottega del Buon Vino** (Via della Cava 26, tel. 0763/42373) has affordable meals (primi L5000–L7000, secondi L7000–L10,000) at outdoor tables with windows in the floor that look down into caves. The restaurant, open Wednesday–Monday 10 AM–midnight, sells ceramics, and you can wander into the Etruscan well and caverns below. From Piazza della Repubblica take Via Filippeschi, which becomes Via della Cava.

More traditional restaurants include **Trattoria dell'Orso** (Via della Misericordia 16–18, off Corso Cavour, tel. 0763/41642), open Wednesday–Monday noon–2 and 7:30–10, with yummy soups for around L8000. The self-service **Ristorante al San Francesco** (Via Cerretti 10, tel. 0763/43302; open 12:30–2:30 and 7:15–10:30) doubles as a pizzeria by night. Three-course meals run about L14,000. For groceries, try **Mercato Buona Spesa** (Via Signorelli 25, off Via Duomo; closed Wed. afternoons).

WORTH SEEING Orvieto's **duomo** (Piazza Duomo, tel. 0763/41167) is the most flamboyant of Umbrian churches, a masterpiece of Romanesque-Gothic architecture built in celebration of the Miracle of Bolsena of 1264. A Bohemian priest on a pilgrimage from Prague to Rome claimed to witness blood dripping from the host onto an altar cloth during a mass in Bolsena. The pope seized the opportunity to proclaim a new religious holiday (the Feast of Corpus Christi), and the duomo was built to house the stained altar cloth. The structure represents three centuries of work by some of Italy's finest builders and artists. Sienese sculptor and architect Lorenzo Maitani, who became involved with the project 10 years after its inception, left the most indelible mark when he reworked the facade on a triple-gabled plan. Magnificent mosaics and intricate stonework adorn the facade, whose central elements are a sublime rose window and a monumental arched portal. The bronze doors are 20th-century additions by Emilio Greco.

The cathedral's exterior and interior are striped with marble. The major works inside are the two chapels in the transepts. To the left is the **Cappella del Corporale**, where the famous altar cloth is kept in an amazing golden reliquary built to resemble the cathedral's facade and inlaid with enamel depictions of the Miracle. The cloth is removed on Easter and Corpus Christi (9th Sunday after Easter) for public viewing. The chapel walls are frescoed with scenes of the Miracle by a trio of local artists. Even more glorious is the **Cappella Nuova** (a.k.a Cappella della Madonna di San Brizio), in the left transept. It contains Luca Signorelli's fresco cycle *Stories of the Antichrist,* among the most precious—and delightfully gruesome—works in Italy. As the damned fall to Hell, demons with green buttocks bite off ears, step on heads, and spirit away young girls. Dante would surely have approved—and he is present in the chapel, his portrait accompanying scenes from his *Purgatorio.* Signorelli and Fra Angelico, who worked on the chapel before him, look out upon the gory scene, dressed in mourning. *Open Nov.–Feb., daily 7–1 and 2:30–5:30; March and Oct., daily 7–1 and 2:30–6:30; Apr.–Sept., daily 7–1 and 2:30–7:30.*

Signorelli was paid for his two years' work on the duomo partly with Orvieto's wine— not called "liquid gold" for nothing.

Next door, the **Museo dell'Opera del Duomo** (tel. 0763/42477), closed for restoration, contains the original and later plans for the cathedral, as well as some painting and sculpture. Across the piazza, the **Museo Claudio Faina** (Palazzo Faina, tel. 0763/41511) holds Etruscan and Roman artifacts; the museum is due to reopen in October 1995. On Piazza Cahen, **Fortezza Albornoz**, built in the mid-14th century, provides an incredible view from the remains of a castle on a cliff. The nearby **Pozzo di San Patrizio**, or Well of Saint Patrick (Viale Sangallo, off Piazza Cahen, tel. 0763/43768), was commissioned by Pope Clement VII in 1527 to ensure a plentiful water supply. Descend into the well (a steep L6000) via a pair of zigzaging mule paths, designed to avoid animal traffic jams.

The Wine Caves of Orvieto

Venture beneath medieval Orvieto, into the ancient Etruscan city below, to view miles and miles of caves that were once used to store food, wine, and other supplies. Stop by the tourist office (see above) at 11 AM or 4 PM any day of the week and join a one-hour guided tour of the caves in English (L10,000, L6000 students).

Marche

Until 1860, Marche served as the Pope's private domain and shield against invading powers (*marca* means "boundary"). The people of this province were sent all over Italy as the Church's tax collectors—resulting in the unfortunate adage *Meglio una morte in casa che un Marchigiano sulla porta* (Better a corpse in the house than a Marchigiano at the door). Nowadays, Marche offers a bit of everything: a long coastline full of resorts, breathtaking mountain scenery, and cities bursting with magnificent art. In summer the beaches are packed—don't bother seeking undiscovered territory. Inland bears no resemblance to the glitzy coast. Here, tiny hilltop villages hide surprising artistic treasures. Urbino is Marche's most spectacular city, and one of Italy's as well. Virtually unknown to Americans, Ascoli Piceno, in the south, offers access to the **Sibillini Mountains**, the most beautiful section of the Apennines.

Urbino

You may never have even heard of it, but Urbino is held by many to be the surviving example of the ideal Renaissance city. The concept of absolute harmony is a local preoccupation, exemplified in the popular obsession with the mysterious *Città Ideal* (Ideal City), which hangs in Urbino's Galleria Nazionale. Not only spatially but historically, artistically, and demographically, lively little Urbino feels almost as perfect as the city in the painting. Isolated in the sharp foothills, south of the Sibillini, this model cobblestone-and-brick city flourishes, with a highly respected university and summer programs that attract students from all over the world.

"Il Cortegiano" set the standard not only for Italian gentlemen but for all of Europe's courtiers: Shakespeare himself modeled two characters, and arguably even Hamlet, after this Urbino code of etiquette.

The benevolent ruler Duke Federico da Montefeltro's court set the standard for nobles of the age. Baldassare Castiglione used Federico as a basis for his book *Il Cortegiano* (The Courtier), the definitive work of noble etiquette. Federico hosted a dazzling group of painters in Urbino; the city's artistic heritage includes works by Piero della Francesca, Paolo Uccello, Titian, and, of course, homeboy Raphael. Besides its fine art, Urbino's **Jazz Festival** draws thousands of visitors each year during the second week of June. The **tourist office** will give you info on this and other festivals and direct you to the most important sights. *Piazza Duca Federico 35, tel. 0722/2441. Open Mon.–Sat. 9–1 and 3–6.*

COMING AND GOING One reaches Urbino from Pesaro (10 daily, 50 min, L3500) or Rimini (2 daily, 1 hr, L5500) by bus—there are no trains or alternate routes. Buses arrive at Urbino's Borgo Mercatale, beneath the Palazzo Ducale. **Bar Europa** in the piazza has a schedule you can look at (buy tickets on board), and there's usually a driver close by who can answer your questions.

WHERE TO SLEEP Although most cheap accommodations are reserved for students or those staying awhile, Urbino has several reasonably priced hotels and pensions for short-term travelers. If you can't find one that suits your needs, the tourist office has a long list of rooms available in private homes.

Albergo Italia (Corso Garibaldi 32, tel. 0722/2701), just off Piazza della Repubblica, has spacious lounges, sitting rooms, and breakfast nooks, as well as panoramic views of Urbino, and the surrounding countryside. Some of the clean rooms (L50,000 doubles without bath) have balconies; breakfast is available in the lobby. The hotel is closed for two weeks in September, depending on the university schedule; call ahead. **Pensione Fosca** (Via Raffaello 67, tel. 0722/2542), a few doors up from the house of painter Raphael, lets doubles for L49,000 (none with bath). You get your own key, and there's even free laundry facilities. During the academic year, **Pensione Feltria** (Via Montefeltro, take Bus 4, tel. 0722/328178) rents to students at Urbino's university, but it usually has some rooms available year-round for short-term visitors. It feels a lot like a dorm, with big modern bathrooms and TV hounds in the common room. Doubles (none with bath) go for L45,000 per night.

The ultra-serene **Camping Pineta**, in the hills overlooking Urbino, has amazing views of the city and countryside below. Facilities are modest, but the forest provides a sense of privacy that most Italian campgrounds lack. There's a small market at the site, and a restaurant serves dinner if you request a day in advance. *Via San Donato, Località Cesana, tel. 0722/4710. From central bus depot, take Bus 4 or 7, ask driver for "Camping Pineta"; a minibus will pick you up if you call ahead. L9500 per person; L10,000 per tent site; L14,500 with car. Showers. Open Easter–Sept. 15.*

FOOD In the tradition of university towns, Urbino has a very cheap student cafeteria, plenty of inexpensive snack joints, and fine medium-range restaurants. A local specialty is the snack *crescioni* (flaky pastry folded and stuffed with cold cuts, vegetables, and cheese). *Strozzapreti* is a thick homemade pasta, a little chewy like a dumpling; it's often served *pasticciata* (with a sauce of tomatoes, cream, and sausage). You can buy fruit in Piazza San Francesco on weekdays, and groceries at **Supermarket Margherita** (Via Raffaello 37, tel. 0722/329771), which is closed Thursday afternoon but otherwise open Monday–Saturday 7:45–12:45 and 5–7:45.

For beer (L5000) and sandwiches (L3000–L6000) try **ARCI Bar Pablo Neruda** (Via Pozzo Nuovo 23, off Via Battisti, tel. 0722/2431), popular with Italian and American students. It has an outdoor patio and pool tables. **Mensa Universitaria** (Colle dei Cappuccini, in university complex, tel. 0722/329251), which serves tasty food in plentiful portions, is the only mensa in Urbino that stays open in summer. Daily from noon to 2 and 7 to 9, students with ID can get a primo, a secondo, a *contorno* (side dish), fruit, bread, and a beverage for L4300. You have to work for it—the hike up here is unbelievable. **Un Punto Macrobiotico** (Via Pozzo Nuovo 4, tel. 0722/329790), open Monday–Saturday 8–10, noon–2:30, and 7:30–9:30, serves vegetarian with a flair; try the gnocchi couscous or the vegetarian ravioli. The L4500 menu includes soup, rice, beans, and salad; the L6000 menu has pasta, beans, and veggies. There's also a **macrobiotic grocery** around the corner (Via Battisti 19, tel. 0722/320193), open daily 8–1 and 4–8. **Gelateria Orchidea** (Corso Garibaldi 70, open 10 AM–2 AM), three doors down from Albergo Italia, is a *gelateria* (ice cream store) specializing in soy-milk delicacies (L2000).

Ristorante al Girarrosto (Piazza San Francesco 3, tel. 0722/4445) sells fabulous take-out food all day (beginning at 9 AM). It's also a full-service restaurant with outdoor tables Saturday–Thursday noon–2:30 and 8–11. Crescioni (L5800–L7500) are the specialty, but if you're in the mood for pasta try the strozzapreti pasticciata (L7500). At **Ristorante Pizzeria Tre Piante** (Via Voltaccia della Vecchia 1, tel. 0722/4863), open 7 PM–11 PM every day except Monday, a student crowd enjoys regional specialties and pizza on a canopied terrace that overlooks the hills. Popular dishes include the local favorite, strozzapreti (L8000), and *gnocchi trepiante* (gnocchi in cream sauce; L8000). Near the bus depot, **Ristorante Pizzeria Europa** (Borgo Mercatale 20, tel. 0722/2826) has an enclosed brick patio with a magnificent view of the palazzo. At the appetizer bar, fill up on stuffed eggplant, tomatoes, onions, and other hors d'oeuvres for L11,000; the pizzas are cheap, too, at L5000–L9000. The restaurant is open Wednesday–Monday noon–3 and 7–midnight; closed all of June.

WORTH SEEING Arch-covered passages knit Urbino together, but the hulking **Palazzo Ducale** is the town's most prominent sight. The sublime Renaissance palace presents a stunning facade composed of two towers linked by a trilevel loggia. The driving force behind the 15th-century palace was the magnificent Duke Federico da Montefeltro; the building was constructed on the foundation of his ancestral home. When you enter, the first thing you see is Luciano Laurana's **courtyard**, a masterpiece of symmetry with a white travertine portico. To the left is the door to Federico's **library**, now devoid of books but famous for the beautiful painted eagle (the family symbol) that stretches across the ceiling. To the right of the courtyard is the entrance to the palace's subterranean chambers, which contain baths, stables, heating and cooling systems, and laundry facilities.

Upstairs, the **Galleria Nazionale** occupies the main portion of the palace. The gallery is filled with works by local painters, including Federico Barocci and Giovanni Santi (Raphael's father). The masterpiece *Città Ideal* has been attributed to Piero della Francesca, Luciano Laurana, and Bramante—no one knows for sure who should get credit. Also look for the bizarre *Flagellation* by Piero della Francesca, Titian's *Resurrection* and *Last Supper,* and Raphael's *La Muta;* and notice the many portraits of Federico with his distinct nose (being blind in one eye, he had the bridge of his nose removed so he could see everything with his good eye). The duke's study is itself an incredible trompe l'oeil, its walls done entirely in wood inlay made to look like cupboards full of books and musical instruments, with doors half open and squirrels perched on window ledges. *Piazza Duca Federico, tel. 0722/2760. Admission L8000. Open daily 9–2.*

Compared to the palace, Urbino's other monuments are humble. The **Oratorio di San Giovanni** (Scala di San Giovanni 31, off Via Mazzini, tel. 0722/320936) and the **Oratorio di San Giuseppe** next door (Via Barocci 42, tel. 0722/320936) are small Renaissance chapels with important works of art inside. San Giovanni, which charges L3000 admission, is known for a 15th-century fresco cycle depicting the life of John the Baptist, painted by regional artists Giacomo and Lorenzo Salimbeni. San Giuseppe (admission: L2000) contains two chapels: one with elaborate tempera paintings and the other with a life-size stucco manger scene. The oratories are open Monday–Saturday 10–noon and 3–7, Sunday 10–12:30.

Raphael's House contains only a couple of the artist's original works, including *Madonna col Bambino*, but the beautiful Renaissance home does look a lot like it did in 1483, when he was born here. Check out the torqued wood ceiling beams and the original kitchen equipment. *Via Raffaello 57, tel. 0722/320105. Admission L5000. Open Mon.–Sat. 9–1 and 3–7, Sun. 9–1.*

The **Fortezza Albernoz** is surrounded by the **Parco della Resistenza**, open daily 8–7. The fortress is currently being restored, but that doesn't interfere with the amazing views of the surrounding countryside. To reach this terrace atop the city, follow the vicoli that wind up from Via Raffaello, turn on Via Margherita, and continue up, up, and up. The walk takes 5–10 minutes.

AFTER DARK Thanks to the students, there's plenty to do here after dark—and you don't have to spend a lot of lire to do it. After 10 PM, head to the rocking disco **Club 83** (Via Nuova 4, tel. 0722/2512; open Mon.–Sat.); there's a L5000 cover. Or try **Osteria Gula** (Via Garibaldi across from Albergo Italia) for a beer (L6000) and some Italian rock tunes.

Pesaro

Most of the action in this town takes place by the water at the *lungomare* (boardwalk), but Pesaro has only been a seaside charmer for the last 100 or so years, since a few impudent pioneers started developing outside the medieval core. These days it's a good place to kick back on the beach, wade through calm waters, or join a pickup game of beach volleyball or soccer. It's said that the pesaresi, with their high standard of living, keep their *nasi in sù* (noses in the air) and are the least hospitable townsfolk in the region. But during the month of August, like it or not, their town is overrun by sunseekers and busloads of music fans in town for the **Rossini Opera Festival** (Aug. 12–25). This is Europe's second-largest musical festival (after Salzburg's), with opera and concerts all over town. Tickets cost L15,000–L30,000 and can be bought through the tourist office.

BASICS Pesaro has several visitor information offices. The most convenient one, open daily 8–8 in summer with reduced hours in winter, is along the main drag near Piazza del Popolo (Via Rossini 41, tel. 0721/69341). The other two are near the water (Piazza della Libertà, tel. 0721/64302) and at the train station (*see below*). All can help you find a hotel and book tickets for the Rossini festival.

COMING AND GOING Trains to Bologna (2 hrs, L11,700) leave twice hourly in the morning and once hourly in the afternoon and evening. Trains to Rimini leave about every half hour (25 min), and nine trains go daily to Rome (6 hrs, L23,700). There's also frequent service to Ancona (50 min, L4300), where you can connect to faraway places. The information office in the **train station** (Viale Risorgimento, tel. 0721/33009) is open 8–noon and 3–5; tickets can be purchased 5:45 AM–9:45 PM. To reach Piazza del Popolo from the station, follow Viale Risorgimento to Piazzale Garibaldi and veer left onto Via Branca.

The **bus station** (Piazza Matteotti, tel. 0721/34768), conveniently located off Via San Francesco near Piazza del Popolo, sends buses to Ancona (5 daily, 1 hr 15 min, L7900). Local buses (L1100) leave from outside the train station and from Piazza Matteotti, but everything in Pesaro is easily accessible on foot. The main drag, Via Rossini (off Piazza del Popolo), changes names beyond the old city to Viale della Repubblica. This tree-lined boulevard ends at the sea, where it spills into Piazza della Libertà.

WHERE TO SLEEP Pesaro's waterfront is dominated by unimpressive high-rises, but a few beautiful villas—turn-of-the-century vacation homes for the rich and eccentric—have been converted into seaside hotels. Be sure to call ahead in the winter, as many establishments close down when the flow of customers drops to a trickle. The old-world **Villa Olga** (Via C. Colombo 9, just north of Piazza della Libertà, tel. 0721/35029), one of the first pensions built in Pesaro, is about as close to the water as you can get. Pleasant doubles without bath run around L50,000. **Albergo Aurora** (Viale Trieste 147, off Viale della Repubblica, tel. 0721/34459) has character and old-time appeal. Clean doubles go for L70,000. The hotel is open May–September.

Halfway between Pesaro and Fano stands the clean 1960s-style **Ostello Ardizio** (Strada Panoramica dell'Ardizio, tel. 0721/55798), open mid-May–mid-September. For L14,000 you get a night's stay and breakfast in this charmless but neat 88-bed hostel; additional meals are L12,000, and there's no lockout. Buses run every half hour until 9 PM between Pesaro's Piazza Matteotti and Fano (L1400), stopping at the hostel. **Camping Panorama** (Località Fiorenzuola, Strada Panoramica, tel. 0721/208145), open May–September, offers great sites amid rolling hills. The grounds offer easy access to the coast and contain a supermarket, a self-service restaurant, and a bar. Prices per person range from L5000 in the winter to L7000 in August. From the bus station in Pesaro, take a bus to Fiorenzuola and ask the driver when to get off.

FOOD Hot *piadine* (Italy's doughier version of the Mexican tortilla) are served everywhere; toppings include cheese, prosciutto, sautéed spinach, and salami. Fresh, reasonably priced seafood also abounds. Several places in town and along the lungomare serve delicious snacks in summer. Try **Ristorante della Rovere** (Strada delle Marche 78, tel. 0721/31740), by the water, for a thick piadina stuffed with spinach and cheese (L5000) or an inexpensive pasta dish. **Pizzeria Dino** (Via Almerici 10, tel. 0721/31241), closed all day Sunday and on Monday morning, is the only place in Pesaro that sells pizza by the slice; a fresh, bricklike slab with mozzarella costs L1500. To get there, take Via Branca three blocks from Piazza del Popolo and turn right on Via Almerici. **Trattoria da Maria** (Via Mazzini 73, off Via Settembre, tel. 0721/68764; open noon–2:30 and 7–10) has a variety of seafood dishes and shouting relatives. Primi run L5000–L7000; seafood and meat start at L10,000. For something different head to **Charbonnade** (Via Mazzini 13, tel. 0721/31911; closed Tues.) for a mound of meat brought and sizzled right on your table, Benihana-style (L25,000 including primo and vegetable).

Nightlife in Pesaro revolves around gelato, especially in summer, when guys and gals clutching Herculean cups capped with whipped cream stroll hand in hand along the lungomare. You'll need both hands to manage the gelato from **Bar Pasticceria Gelateria Germano** (in summer, Piazza della Libertà 9, tel. 0721/61963; year-round, Piazzale Collenuccio 12, tel. 0721/64415).

WORTH SEEING Despite the fact that Gioacchino Rossini, composer of *The Barber of Seville,* donated everything he had to Pesaro, the city is no treasure trove of sights. The **Museo Civico** (Via T. Mosca 29, 0721/31213) contains impressive Renaissance paintings, including Giovanni Bellini's *Pala di Pesaro,* and an interesting ceramic collection, but you might want to save your sightseeing juices for Urbino. Unless you're a real opera buff, skip **Rossini's house** (Via Rossini 34, tel. 0721/387357; admission: L2000) and head to the **Teatro Rossini** (Piazza Lazzarini 29, tel. 0721/33184), a typical example of a grandiose European opera house. You usually can't get in to see the main auditorium at the **Conservatorio di Musica G. Rossini** (Piazza Olivieri 5, no phone), but from the entrance in the café-lined piazza you can hear the muted sound of instruments behind closed doors.

You can't miss the grand **Ducal Palace**, off Pesaro's main square, Piazza del Popolo, especially not at noon on Mondays, when there are free guided tours. The icily elegant, cupid-adorned structure dates from the 15th century. The portico-lined Corso XI Settembre takes you to the church of **Sant'Agostino**, which contains lovely wooden choir stalls with inlaid landscapes. Though the surrounding medieval walls and doors have been taken down, the 15th-century castle, **Rocca Costanza**, off Piazza Matteotti, remains intact.

Ancona

You won't want to spend a lot of time in Ancona. Though founded by Syracusans in the 4th century BC, bombing during World War II destroyed almost all evidence of its past (and an earthquake in the early 1970s leveled much of what the Allies missed). These days, Ancona's main cargo is beach-bound backpackers on their way to Greek islands. Still, despite its role as a transport hub, Ancona doesn't really cater to tourists. The town is especially dead during August, when everyone flees to the beach.

BASICS You can find out everything you need to know at the train station's **APT** booth (tel. 071/41703), open 9–2 and 5–7 June 15–Sept. 15. English-speaking Franca will answer any questions and check hotel availability for you. Off-season, you'll have to trek out to the **main tourist office** (Via Thaon de Revel 4, tel. 071/31966), accessible by Bus 1 from the station. Change money at any of the banks on Corso Stamira; **Banca Nazionale del Lavoro** (Via Stamira 10) has good rates on cash and traveler's checks.

➤ **MAIL AND PHONES** • The main **post office** (Piazza 24 di Maggio, tel. 071/201808) is open Monday–Saturday 8:15–7. Make local and long-distance calls at the **SIP** office (Piazza Rosselli 12, no phone; open daily 8 AM–9:45 PM).

COMING AND GOING Ancona's **train station** (Piazza Rosselli, tel. 071/43933) is a national and international transport hub. Trains depart for Milan (hourly, 4–5½ hrs, L30,000); Bari (6 daily, 5 hrs, L30,000); Rome (8 daily, 3–4 hrs, L20,400); Bologna (hourly, 2½ hrs, L15,400); and Pesaro (frequently, 50 min, L4300). Buses run from the train station to Piazza Cavour in the centro storico. **Bucci** (Piazza Cavour, tel. 071/32401) runs buses three times daily to Pesaro (1 hr 15 min, L7600).

➤ **BY FERRY** • If you're traveling through Ancona in summer, you're probably here to catch a ferry. The English-speaking information office at **Stazione Marittima** (Molo Santa Maria, tel. 071/201183) will assist you; they also provide tips on cheap places to eat, and give you the rundown on sights.

Strintzis and Minoan Joint Service (Stazione Marittima, tel. 071/207–1068) sends ferries to Corfu (24 hrs), Igoumenitsa (24 hrs), and Patras (31 hrs) Monday–Saturday between late June and mid-August (off-months less often). Prices for a deck spot run a hefty L98,000 in low season, L112,000 in high season. **G.A. Ferries** heads to Patras, Corfu, and Igoumenitsa on Monday, Wednesday, Friday, and Saturday. The **Mantacas e Vintladis Agency** (Via XXIX Settembre 10, tel. 071/207–0705) handles G.A.'s reservations and ticketing; you'll pay L118,000 in high season and L95,000 in low season. **Marlines** (tel. 071/202566) also runs to Corfu, Igoumenitsa, and Patras. Their prices are lower (L80,000), but their service is less frequent—generally Wednesday and Saturday, plus an additional Friday trip July–August. Friday ferries also go to remote islands such as Rhodes and Crete for a few extra lire. Buy tickets at the company windows along the harbor or at any travel agency. Boats have discos, bars restaurants, etc.—but they're no bargain. To load up on supplies, go to **Standa** grocery (Via Alcide 2), three blocks from the train station; it's open Monday–Saturday 9–1:30 and 4–7.

WHERE TO SLEEP AND EAT You have three lodging options: the unsavory, the expensive, or some combination of the two. An unusually cheap, dependable, and clean choice is the **Albergo Dorico** (Via Flaminia 8, across from train station, tel. 071/42761), with doubles starting at L40,000. Closer to the center you'll pay L90,000 for a 1920s-style double at **Hotel Viale** (Viale Vittorio 23, tel. 071/201861). The news about food is not good, but the centro storico, not too far from the port, has a few affordable trattorias. **Osteria del Pozzo** (Via Bonda 2, near Palazzo Plebiscito, tel. 071/207–3996), **La Cantineta** (Via Gramsci 1, tel. 071/201107), and **Clarice** (Via del Traffico 6, tel. 071/202926) all serve traditional Italian fare at modest prices. All are closed Sunday and most of August. **Pizza e Spaghetti** (Via XXIX Settembre 6/B, tel. 071/205540), closed Wednesday, is good for a tasty meal while you wait for your ferry.

WORTH SEEING If you have the time, check out what remains of the old city, including the magnificent pink-and-white 11th-century Romanesque/Byzantine **duomo** (Piazzale del Duomo), and the 13th-century **Santa Maria della Piazza** (Piazza Santa Maria), with an intricate facade composed of tiny decorative arches. You'll inevitably stumble upon Piazza del Plebiscito; not too far away lies the **Pinoteca Comunale Francesco Podesti** (Via Pizzecolli 17, tel. 071/204262; open Tues.–Sat. 10–7, Sun. 9–1), a classical museum with works by Titian and Guercino, as well as a small modern-art collection. For L5000 you can visit one of central Italy's best ancient-art exhibits at **Museo Archeologico Nazionale delle Marche** (Via Ferretti 1, above Via Pizzecoli, tel. 0721/207–4829; open Mon.–Sat. 9–1:30, Sun. 2:30–7:30), which showcases a number of vases, bronze pieces, and two Roman ivory beds. If you still have time before your ferry leaves, swing by the church of **St. Domenico** (Piazza del Plebiscito), where Titian's *Annuciation* is housed.

Ascoli Piceno

When you've overdosed on hill towns, head for Ascoli Piceno in southern Marche. Ascoli is a valley town, a rarity in central Italy, where ancient tribes were obsessed with impenetrability. Legend has it that a helpful *picchio* (woodpecker) guided a tribe of shepherds to the valley, which lies at the edge of the Sibillini foothills encircled by the Tronto and Castellano Rivers. Ascoli has some of Italy's best-preserved medieval walls, though its defenses proved generally useless throughout its history. Few travelers come here, but prices are reasonable and the town offers a good museum and easy entrance into the *Sibillini* mountains. The **tourist office** has brochures in English and offers helpful info on trains, buses, entertainment, and lodging. *Piazza del Popolo 17, tel. 0736/255250. Open Mon.–Sat. 9–12:30 and 3–7; Sun. 9–1:30.*

COMING AND GOING The only trains into Ascoli come from the seaside town of San Benedetto del Tronto (10 daily, ½ hr, L3200), which can be reached from Ancona (1 hr, L7200) or Pescara (40 min, L5700). Ascoli's **train station** is in Piazza della Stazione, and Bus 2, 3, or 4 will take you to the town center from here. It's easier to hop a **bus** from San Benedetto (every ½ hr, 50 min, L3100), and this way you get dropped closer to the town center, at Viale Alcide. Two daily buses also run to and from Rome (3½ hrs, L20,000). Buy tickets at the train-station bar in San Benedetto; the bus leaves from in front of the station. In Ascoli, buy tickets at the newsstand on Viale Alcide. Fewer trains and buses run to Ascoli on Sundays, so plan accordingly.

WHERE TO SLEEP AND EAT Ostello de Longobardi (Palazzetto Longobardo, Rua Longobardo 12, tel. 0736/259007) offers salvation from overpriced hotels. Built into a medieval tower, the hostel charges L13,000 a night. Curfew is 11 PM, but the signora has a couple keys to give out, and there's no afternoon lockout. To get to the hostel from Piazza del Popolo, take Via del Trivio past the main entrance of San Francesco and follow it as it becomes Via Cairoli; veer left and it will become Via Soderini. If the hostel is full (which it usually isn't, even in peak tourist

An Auspicious Abode

Call the tourist office in Ancona and sign up for a free trip to the nearby town of Loreto, one of Italy's most important pilgrimage sites and the final resting place of Jesus's family home. Legend has it that the house was transported from Nazareth to Dalmatia by a band of angels; shortly thereafter, angels picked it up again, crossed the Adriatic, and deposited it here in Loreto. Only three walls remain of the original humble structure referred to as the Santa Casa, or Holy House. It now rests inside the huge 16th-century basilica Palazzo Apostolico, designed by Bramante.

You can also make a pilgrimage to Loreto on your own by train from Ancona. Trains leave frequently from Ancona's train station (20 min, L3200), depositing you within easy walking distance of the holy house.

season), ask at the tourist office about rooms for rent in private homes. Another option is **Hotel Piceno** (Via Minucia 10, off Piazza Arringo, tel. 0736/252553), which charges L75,000 for a double with bath.

Eating in Ascoli is so cheap that everyone should have a sit-down meal. Ascoli's oldest pizzeria, **Pizzeria Bella Napoli** (Piazza della Viola, tel. 0736/257030), serves pizzas from a wood-burning oven for L5000–L7000. The outdoor patio is usually filled with a rowdy crowd. The pizzeria is open 6:45 PM–midnight each day except Thursday; take Via Giudea from Piazza del Popolo. **Al Teatro** (Via del Teatro 3, off Via del Trivio, tel. 0736/253549), open Tuesday–Sunday 11–3 and 6:30–midnight, is another good pizzeria with an outdoor patio. Pizzas cost L5000–L7000; pastas are similarly priced. To sample the local specialty *fritto all'Ascolana* (olives pitted and stuffed with meat and Parmesan, then fried), head to **Cantina dell'Arte** (Rua della Lupa 5, tel. 0736/251135).

WORTH SEEING First check out Ascoli's central square, the exquisitely balanced and symmetrical **Piazza del Popolo**. The galleries lining two sides of it were created early in the 16th century, around the same time the **Loggia dei Mercanti** was built against the side of San Francesco. The **Palazzo del Capitani del Popolo**, a medieval palace begun in the 13th century and modified throughout the Middle Ages and the Renaissance, looms over the piazza. Its facade, with a statue of Pope Paul III, was designed by local artist Cola d'Amatrice. The palace underwent restoration as far back as the mid-16th century, when it was nearly destroyed by a fire set by a papal official to purge the place of rioters. It burned for two days during Christmas of 1535, and restoration began immediately thereafter. The church of **San Francesco**, open daily 8–noon and 3–6, was modified from a Romanesque to a Gothic structure. You see its side from the piazza; the simple square facade, graced by a beautiful Gothic portal, is to the left.

Piazza Arringo also holds some interesting buildings. The **Palazzo del Comune**, a late-Renaissance structure that incorporates ancient buildings, houses the **Pinacoteca Civica** (tel. 0736/298213; open Mon.–Sat. 9–1, in summer also 3–7:30, Sun. 4–8; admission: L2500). The collection includes works by painters Cola d'Amatrice, Carlo Crivelli, Titian, Tiepolo, Tintoretto, and Caracci, as well as coins, ceramics, musical instruments, and breathtaking contemporary sculpture such as the bronze *Paolo and Francesca*. In this work by Romolo del Gobbs, the lovers swirl through the air wrapped in one another's bodies. Next door, the medieval **duomo**, open daily 8–noon and 5–7, has a hideously gaudy interior.

One of Ascoli's oldest churches, **San Vincenzo e San Anastasio** (Piazza Ventidio Basso) was built in the 6th or 7th century, redone in the early Renaissance, and given its off-center paneled and frescoed facade in the 15th century. The church is always locked nowadays, but seek out the custodian next door to see the small well in the crypt whose waters were believed to cure the sick. From Piazza del Popolo, follow Via Trivio until it becomes Via Cairoli.

OUTDOOR ACTIVITIES The **Sibilline Mountains** offer hikes through some of the most beautiful scenery in Italy. From Ascoli Piceno, take a bus to **Amandola** (3 daily, 1 hr, L4500), where you'll find the **tourist office** (Piazza Risorgimento, tel. 0736/848037). From here, you can pick up maps and make the trek (11 kilometers) to **Lago di Pilota**. From Montemonaco on the lake, catch a bus to Monte San Martino (4 daily, L6000), a beautiful mountain village in **Lake San Ruffino National Park**. The towns here are truly breathtaking, with medieval stone buildings perched on mountainsides. Camping is an option almost anywhere; to reserve, inquire at the tourist office in Amandola. For less rustic digs, take a hike to the **Rifugio Alpina Città** (tel. 0736/847512), 15 kilometers outside Amandola. It's open June–September.

ROME

10

By Erin Williams

Decadence comes easy in Rome. Locals practically invented the word, lavishly adorning their city with classical columns, medieval monasteries, and baroque basilicas. Excess is everywhere and confusion runs high in the Eternal City: Countless sights threaten sensory overload, the rich food leads you down the path to gluttony, and the traffic forces you into fits of hysteria. In eternally extravagant, eternally disintegrating Rome, confusion and decadence have been the bywords for 3,000 years.

For a thousand years, Rome was the capital of the Roman Republic and then of an empire that stretched from the British Isles to North Africa, from Gibraltar to Constantinople. Even after its magnificent stadiums, temples, and palaces fell into ruin and were carted off by barbarians in the Middle Ages, Rome retained its cultural prominence through its new role as the epicenter of the Christian world. The city became the dominion of the pope, who wielded not only ultimate spiritual authority but also commanded an army, conquered lands to increase his holdings, and spent centuries battling against the emperor for secular power. During this period, medieval churches were constructed on top of ancient temples, and the papacy bankrolled fabulously extravagant Renaissance and baroque additions to existing structures. Pagans, pilgrims, Renaissance men, aristocrats on the Grand Tour—everyone flocked to Rome; for everything, it seemed, started and ended here.

Somewhere along the line, ancient Roman building ingenuity and faultless efficiency were lost on the Italians (enter confusion). In "modern" Rome, restoration projects drag on or never get under way, and the infamous bureaucracy makes even standing in line at the post office an exercise in futility. As the country's capital, Rome exemplifies the many problems plaguing Italy today. In particular, the city has been the scene of sweeping corruption in the form of the *Tangentopoli* (Bribesville) scandals, which decimated the political landscape and landed hundreds of government officals behind bars. Despite these modern-day shortcomings, Romans still don't realize their city isn't the center of the world anymore. Romans are a bit like New Yorkers—intensely proud, with a wary eye and no qualms about speaking their minds. Though they argue vehemently in the streets and cafés, passionate Romans definitely enjoy themselves.

Yes, while Rome is certainly about breakneck sight-seeing (what else can you do in a city that contains the Colosseum, *and* the Pantheon, *and* St. Peter's Basilica, *and* the Trevi Fountain), the city is at heart a place of small-town charm and lazy indulgences. Most summer evenings hues of gold and copper bathe the city's piazze and narrow alleyways, casting shadows over matriarchs and pudgy old gentlemen who've been having the same conversation for the last 25 years. Cafés and restuarants are often frequented by an unmistakably local crowd that gathers for a lazy afternoon meal, only to return around 10 PM for dinner and more gossip. Eating well is of utmost importance here, and not indulging in a sit-down meal borders on the criminal—not that it's difficult to be persuaded. Nor will it take much coaxing to indulge in a little post-lunch nap, or a post-nap gelato, or . . . you get the idea. Getting coaxed into Roman decadence is, after all, one of the main reasons for coming.

Basics

AMERICAN EXPRESS The helpful, English-speaking staff offers tourist info, travel services, and currency exchange, and will cash traveler's checks for no commission. Cardholders can cash personal checks and have their mail held here. Two tours of the city (9:20 AM and 2:20 PM; L50,000) leave daily from outside the office. After hours, call 16/787–2000 for lost or stolen traveler's checks, 16/786–4046 for lost or stolen AmEx cards. *Piazza di Spagna 38, tel. 06/67641. Open weekdays 9–5:30, Sat. 9–12:30.*

CHANGING MONEY Rome has almost as many money-changing outlets as it does museums. For instant gratification go to the sketchy-looking office in **Stazione Termini** (south side of the information office) with the cardboard NO COMMISSION sign in the window. Banks change money weekdays 8:30–1:30 and 2:45–3:45 and usually charge a flat fee of L5000. *Casse di cambio* (currency exchange offices) are a common sight around transportation hubs, on main thoroughfares, and near heavily touristed sites; one of the best is **Cambiavalute Aldo Bettini** (Via Vittorio Veneto 4/A, tel. 06/487–1458; open Mon.–Sat. 8–12:30 and 3:30–7:30). The **main post office** (*see* Mail, *below*) has the best rates around and only charges a 1% commission; money transactions take place at windows 25–28. Another option is **Thomas Cook** (Piazza Barberini, tel. 06/482–8082 and Via della Conciliazione 23, near the Vatican, tel. 06/6830–0435). Their rates aren't great, but they will draw money from your MasterCard or Visa, and they're open seven days a week.

CONSULATES AND EMBASSIES Get the latest scoop on home-front happenings from the embassies' respective periodical collections. Most embassies are clustered between Piazza Barberini and Stazione Termini, off Via Nomentana.

Australia. *Corso Trieste 25/B, tel. 06/852721. Open weekdays 9–noon and 1:30–4.*

Canada. *Via Zara 30, tel. 06/440–3028. Open weekdays 8:30–3.*

New Zealand. *Via Zara 28, tel. 06/440–2928. Open weekdays 8:30–12:45 and 1:45–5.*

United Kingdom. *Via XX Settembre 80/A, 4 blocks NW of Stazione Termini, tel. 06/482–5441. Open weekdays 9:30–12:30 and 2–4.*

United States. *Via Vittorio Veneto 121, tel. 06/46741. Open weekdays 8:30–noon and 2–4.*

DISCOUNT TRAVEL AGENCIES Travel agencies are concentrated around Piazza Barberini and are reachable by Metro Line A or by walking a few blocks west of Piazza della Repubblica. **Transalpino** (Piazza dell'Esquilino, tel. 06/487–0870; open weekdays 9–6:30, Sat. 9–1:30) handles discounted tickets for train, air, and boat travel. **CTS** (Centro Turistico Studentesco) is a student travel office where you can pick up ISIC cards and buy discounted plane, ferry, and

You Gotta Pick A Pocket Or Two

Distrusted and disliked, but tolerated by the Romans, Gypsies are more numerous and more ruthless in Rome than in any other Italian city. Be especially wary near the Colosseum, on Via Fori Imperiali, and in Stazione Termini, where 10-year-olds loiter in large groups, their nimble fingers hiding under sheets of cardboard and newspaper, ready to snatch your purse or wallet.

train tickets. *Corso Vittorio Emanuele II 297, tel. 06/6830–7883. Open weekdays 9–1 and 3:30–7, Sat. 9–1.*

EMERGENCIES The general emergency number for **first aid** or **police** is 113. For **fire** call 115; call the Red Cross 06/5510 for an **ambulance**. If you need assistance and don't speak Italian, check for foreign-language–proficiency badges on the left arms of metropolitan policemen—it'll save you from having to play charades in dire circumstances. If you have to file the all-too-routine theft report, an English speaker is usually on staff at the **main police station** (Via San Vitale 15, just north of Via Nazionale, tel. 06/4686). If all else fails, call the Samaritans' English-language hotline: tel. 06/7045–4444.

ENGLISH BOOKS AND NEWSPAPERS *Metropolitan* (L1500) and *Wanted in Rome* (L1000), available at most newsstands, are biweekly English publications with listings of current events and classifieds (a good place to find long- and short-term housing). *This Week in Rome* (L1000), a newspaper supplement available Friday at most newsstands, has information on all city happenings for the week ahead. Otherwise, bring a photo ID to gain access to the **American Embassy Library** (Via Vittorio Veneto 119/A, tel. 06/4674–2481); the **British Council Library** (Via Quattro Fontane 20, tel. 06/482–6641); or the **American Studies Center** (Via Michelangelo Caetani 32, tel. 06/6880–1613). Many of the larger Italian bookstores carry books in English, and their prices are often lower than at stores that only sell English books; try **Feltrinelli** (Largo di Torre Argentina 5/A, tel. 06/6880–3248), with English books and a large travel section on the second floor, or **Rizzoli** (Largo Chigi 15, tel. 06/679–6641).

Economy Book and Video Center. Economy's location, five blocks from Stazione Termini, has ensured a steady flow of English-starved foreigners for the past 28 years. Besides the large selection of new and used books, they rent English movies and VCRs, and hold various workshops. *136 Via Torino, 1 block south of Via Nazionale, tel. 06/474–6877. Open Mon. 3–7, Tues.–Sat. 9:30–7:30.*

The Lion Bookstore. If you're in need of a new novel, or if you've been inspired to brush up on ancient history, this place near Piazza del Popolo has the largest and best selection of English titles. *Via Babuino 181, tel. 06/322–5837. Open Mon.–Sat. 9:30–1:30 and 3:30–7:30.*

LAUNDRY One of the few self-service *lavanderie* (laundromats) around is **Onda Blu** (Via Milazzo 8/A–B, tel. 06/444–1665; open daily 8 AM–10 PM), two blocks south of Stazione Termini. Each load costs L6,000 to wash and L6,000 to dry. If dry cleaning is unavoidable, **Quelli del Pulito** (Via Ostia 38, tel. 06/372–4199), near the Vatican, charges L3500 per article.

LUGGAGE STORAGE The government-run luggage depots at either end of **Stazione Termini**, near Track 1 and 22, are the most central places to stash your bags. The going rate is L1500 per piece per day. The folks at **Enjoy Rome** (*see* Visitor Information, *below*) say they'll stow bags free of charge, but it's basically a service designed for paying customers.

MAIL Post offices are conveniently positioned all over Rome; they all sell stamps and are open weekdays 8:30–7:30, Saturday 8:30–11:30. The **main post office** (Piazza San Silvestro, tel. 06/65643 or 06/6771), one block east of Via del Corso, handles stamp sales at windows 22–24; currency exchange is at windows 25–28. For a small fee—and a glance at your passport—pick up *poste restante* (held mail) at windows 58–60; articles should be marked Fermo Posta, Palazzo delle Poste, Piazza San Silvestro, Roma 00186.

A Message from Il Papa

Bless your beloved with words mailed from the Vatican Post Office (Piazza San Pietro, left of the museum ticket booth), which is reputed to be more reliable than Italian mail. You can buy stamps and post letters weekdays 8:30–7:15, Saturday 8:30–6. During summer, diluvian levels of personal scripture and packages are collected by vans parked in St. Peter's Square.

MEDICAL AID Two public hospitals with emergency care are **Santo Spirito** (Lungotevere 1, tel. 06/650901) and **Policlinico Umberto I** (Viale del Policlinico 255, tel. 06/49971). Private hospitals usually accept credit cards, and sometimes even Blue Cross or Blue Shield coverage. **Rome American Hospital** (Via Emilio Longoni 69, tel. 06/22551) has English-speaking doctors and dentists on hand.

Rome's many pharmacies are marked with white signs bearing a red cross or an illuminated green cross. All post listings of nearby late-night pharmacies. The 24-hour **Farmacia Piram Omeopatia** (Via Nazionale 228, tel. 06/488–0754) and **Internazionale Piazza Barberini** (Piazza Barberini 49, tel. 06/482–5456) are both centrally located.

PHONES Omnipresent orange **SIP** phones charge L200 for local calls. Since they gulp down metallic morsels like monsters, using a *carta telefonica* (phone card), available in denominations of L5000, L10,000 or L20,000 is more practical for long-distance calling; many phones don't accept any other form of payment. Purchase cards at newsstands or *tabacchi* (smoke shops). Long-distance calls can also be placed at several ASST and SIP phone centers in central Rome and near transport hubs—Fiumicino Airport has one, Stazione Termini two. The main **ASST** office, next to the main post office on Piazza San Silvestro, is open daily 8 AM–11:30 PM; the office on Via Porta Angelica, near St. Peter's Basilica, opens at 8:30 Monday–Saturday and closes weekdays around 9 PM, Saturday at 2 PM. The SIP calling center at the Villa Borghese entrance to the Piazza di Spagna Metro station is open daily 8:30 AM–8:45 PM.

VISITOR INFORMATION EPT tourist offices have a wealth of brochures, maps, event schedules, public transport info, and lists of restaurants, travel agencies, and lodgings. English is spoken and all services are free. You'll probably even be able to coax the diffident staff into providing assistance with lodging. Look for the small branch opposite Track 2 in **Stazione Termini** (tel. 06/487–1270), or trek three blocks northwest of the station to the **main office** (Via Parigi 5, tel. 06/488–3748). Both are open Monday–Saturday 8:30–7.

People at **ENIT**, the national tourist board, speak English and have tons of information. *Via Marghera 2–6, tel. 06/49711. 1½ blocks north of Stazione Termini. Open weekdays 9–1 (also Wed. 4–6).*

Enjoy Rome, 3½ blocks from Stazione Termini, is a good stop for maps, accommodation listings, updated event schedules, and friendly advice in English. They'll book private rooms and rooms in hostels or hotels, as well as bus and walking tours, free of charge. They also organize a walking tour of the city for students and other cheapskates at a low cost—ask for the latest schedule. *Via Varese 39, tel. 06/445–1843. Open weekdays 8:30–1 and 3:30–6, Sat. 8:30–1.*

➤ **WOMEN'S RESOURCES** • If you're in need of assistance, info on cultural events, or just company, try the **American Women's Association** (tel. 06/482–5268), the **United Nations Women's Guild** (tel. 06/5225–6503), or the **Feminist Center** (Via San Francesco di Sales 1/A, off Via della Lunghera, in Trastevere, tel. 06/686–4201).

COMING AND GOING

BY PLANE The international **Leonardo da Vinci Airport** (tel. 06/65951), 30 kilometers outside the city center, is also referred to as **Fiumicino**, for the suburb where it's located. Major carriers with flights into Rome include **American Airlines** (tel. 06/483–579 or 06/474–1447), **United Airlines** (toll free 16/7825181 or 06/259–7272), **Continental Airlines** (tel. 06/484597 or 06/483978), **Delta** (tel. 06/4773), **British Airways** (tel. 06/479991), and **Canadian Airlines** (tel. 06/488–3514 or 06/482–0961). Inside the terminal, there's currency exchange, luggage storage, and an **information office** (tel. 06/601–1255). The entire airport shuts down daily between 11 PM and 5 AM.

➤ **AIRPORT TRANSIT** • Between 6 AM and 10 PM, trains connect Fiumicino airport with Rome's Trastevere (30 min, L7000), Ostiense (40 min, L7000), and Tiburtina stations (40 min, L7000). Trains to Stazione Termini (45 min, L12,000) run hourly 7 AM–9:15 PM. If you arrive after 9:15, take the train to Tiburtina station, and tranfer to Night Bus 42, which runs roughly every hour to Termini.

BY TRAIN Rome's principal rail depot is Stazione Termini, a gargantuan complex right in the thick of things. Other stations in Rome include **Ostiense**, with daily service to Genova, Naples, Palermo, and Nice. To reach Ostiense, take Bus 94 from Piazza Venezia, Bus 57 from Stazione Termini, or Metro Line B from anywhere in the city. Rome's **Trastevere** station is useful only if you're forced to sleep in the suburbs. From Rome's **Tiburtina** station—connected to Stazione Termini via Metro Line B—there are buses to towns in Lazio, including Rieti (every 40 min, 1½ hrs, L5000), as well as bus service to Naples, Palermo, and the Abruzzi.

➤ **STAZIONE TERMINI** • Trains from **Stazione Termini** (Piazza dei Cinquecento, tel. 06/4775) serve major Italian and European cities and many points in between. Budget accommodations and public transportation are right outside. The main lobby has snazzy multilingual computers that list train departures, prices, and durations. A **cassa di cambio** (open daily 7–7) is in the glass-enclosed gallery at the front of the station, near a special window that exclusively serves EurailPass holders. Get city maps from **EPT** (see Visitor Information, above) near Track 2.

Stazione Termini has a multitude of shops and restaurants, and 24-hour luggage storage. Downstairs, an **albergo diurno** (day hotel) charges L10,000 for showers; towels are included, but not soap (L500) and shampoo (L1200). You can make local or long-distance phone calls from the **ASST** office near the ticket windows daily 8 AM–9 PM. The **waiting room** near Track 1 is a safe place to kick back because it's inside the ticketed area.

Sad but true, the hordes of tourists who pass through the station draw a desperate element that's adept at taking advantage of disoriented newcomers. If theft befalls you, go to the 24-hour **police booth** at Track 1. To recover **lost items** that disappeared on a train or in the station, go to the **oggetti rivenuti** office (tel. 06/4730–6449) at Track 22.

Just inside the station is a row of ticket windows. Buy international tickets at window 1 or 2 and make sleeping-car reservations at windows 29–43. Avoid long lines by purchasing domestic train tickets—cash or credit cards only—from the vending machines opposite the ticket windows. You can also buy domestic and international train tickets, as well as local and long-distance bus tickets, from the English-speaking staff of **ACOTRAL**, located downstairs. Also remember that tickets for trips of less than 100 kilometers are sold throughout Rome at tabacchi, newspaper kiosks, and anywhere else you see the "FS" emblem.

BY BUS Rome does not have a central bus terminal. Instead, blue **ACOTRAL** buses leave from different points around town. Get service and sales details from ticket agents and tourist offices, or by calling ACOTRAL directly (tel. 06/57531 or 06/591–5551).

➤ **PRIVATE BUSES** • Between Piazza dei Cinquecento and Piazza della Repubblica, coaches from a dozen different private companies leave for destinations throughout Italy. Most charge more than ACOTRAL, but that's because most offer plush seats and air-conditioning. Buy tickets at **Eurojet Tours**, where you'll also find tickets for pricey sightseeing tours. Piazza della Repubblica 54, tel. 06/481–7455. Open weekdays 8:30–4:45, Sat. 8:30–1:45.

BY CAR When driving in Rome, whiplash is probable, headaches inevitable. The main access routes from the north are the A1 (Autostrada del Sole) from Milan and Florence, and the A12/E20 from Genova. If you're headed south toward Naples, hop on the A2. Conveniently, all highways that intersect Rome connect with the GRA (Grande Raccordo Anulare), a confusing beltway that funnels traffic into the center. To conquer the GRA you'll need a good road map and a healthy dose of patience.

HITCHING As anywhere, hitching in Italy comes with a precautionary warning. However, if you're brave, determined, male, and headed north to Florence, take Bus 379 from Termini to Piazza Vescovio, switch to Bus 135 to Via Salaria and A1. A2 heads south to Naples; catch rides at the Via Tuscolana entrance, reached by taking Metro Line A to its Anagnina terminus.

GETTING AROUND

"All roads lead to Rome," then leave you confused, disoriented, and befuddled. Luckily, Rome has gobs of landmarks to orient yourself by. First and foremost, the **Tiber River** runs

Unless you're a race-car driver or related to Evel Knievel, don't even dream of braving Rome's hellish traffic.

north–south through the city, making a big bend that cradles the *centro storico* (historic center) to the east and the Vatican to the west. **Stazione Termini** lies due east of the bend by way of **Via Nazionale**, which becomes **Corso Vittorio Emanuele II** at **Piazza Venezia**, where the gigantic Vittorio Emanuele II monument stands out like a sore thumb. Behind Piazza Venezia, the ruins of Ancient Rome—including Campidoglio, the Forum, the Colosseum, and Aventine Hill—spread southwest. The two-line Metro system is useful for reaching out-of-the-way spots, and frequent buses fill in the gaps, but Rome really is a walking city: Brown-and-white signs are posted throughout the center, directing pedestrians to major sights. Be forewarned: Rome's charming cobblestone streets can be hard on the feet, the city's speeding mopeds and flying Fiats hazardous to your health.

BY METRO Rome's subway system is sorely limited. It was originally meant to be bigger, but each time workers start digging, some new archaeological site is discovered, and work is stopped. So you'll have to make do with the Metro's two routes. The red **Line A** runs between Ottaviano and Anagnina, hitting most of Rome's major piazze—among them Repubblica, Barberini, and Spagna. The blue **Line B** runs between Laurentina and Rebibbia and is useful for reaching the Colosseum and the Ostiense train station (at the Piramide stop). The only point where the two lines intersect is Stazione Termini.

Buying tickets (L1500) can be a comic event: Machines take exact change only, and only when they feel like it. Once you've got a ticket, validate it as you walk through the gates to the trains, though most people simply cruise through the open gate meant for monthly-pass holders—an offense punishable with a L50,000 fine. It's easiest to buy single tickets or books of five or 10 at tabacchi. You can also buy a day pass known as a *biglietto integrato giornaliero* or BIG (L6000) or a weekly pass called a *carta integrata settimanale* or CIS (L24,000). Both the daily and the weekly passes are good for Metro, bus, and urban trains, and must be validated at the beginning of the first journey, either at the Metro station or on the bus. Month-long passes cost L20,000 and are available at Metro and ATAC ticket booths. Line A operates daily 5:30 AM–11 PM. Line B runs 5:30 AM–9:30 PM on weekdays, until 11:30 PM on weekends.

BY BUS Rome's highly visible orange buses are the most useful form of public transportation. Due to Rome's perpetual traffic jams, however, bus service can also be extremely frustrating. Most buses run from 5:30 AM to midnight, with some nocturnal lines transporting night owls. Stops are marked by yellow or green posts and labeled FERMATA. Most stops list bus numbers, the main destinations along each route, and lines with night service (marked with an "N" or by a black circle). Tickets (L1500) are sold at coffee bars, tabacchi, newspaper kiosks displaying the ATAC emblem, and at the ATAC booth in front of Stazione Termini. If you're caught without a ticket, you'll get stuck with a L50,000 fine.

A few rules to remember: Enter at the front of the bus if you have a pass, at the back if you're a ticket holder. The middle doors are for people getting off. Upon boarding, stick the "1" end of your ticket into the validating machine, giving you 90 minutes of travel.

BY TAXI The meter reads L6400 at flag fall; add L1000 every 2.5 kilometers. Expect to pay L10,000 (including tip) for most rides within the city limits. A nonstandardized supplement is usually charged for baggage and rides after 11 PM; make sure you agree on the extra charges *before* you get in the cab. Taxis are usually found lurking in front of hotels and major tourist sights, or call **La Capitale Radio Taxi** (tel. 06/4994) or **Autoradiotaxi Romana** (tel. 06/39898). **Radio Taxi** (tel. 06/3875 or 06/88177) accepts American Express cards if you let them know in advance.

BY CAR Car rentals cost at least L140,000 per day for the cheapest compact. Rates include insurance but not gas, which can cost up to L80,000 per tank. You'll need a valid credit card, a passport, and (of course) a driver's license. Nerves of steel wouldn't hurt either. And in most cases, you'll need to be 25 or older.

Hertz. Get a considerable discount with AIG or HI membership. *Fiumicino airport, tel. 06/6501–1448; Stazione Termini, tel. 06/474–0389.*

Maggiore. Holders of a *carta giovane* (youth card) get a small discount. For reservations within Rome dial 06/854–1620, or call 1678/67067 toll-free throughout Italy. Maggiore's main offices are at Via Po 8/A (tel. 06/854–8698), Fiumicino airport (tel. 06/6501–15008), and near Track 4 at Stazione Termini (tel. 06/483715).

BY BIKE Although the medieval streets in Rome's center don't make for smooth biking, renting a bike is feasible and inexpensive. **Bici Pincio** (Viale dei Bambini, tel. 06/678–4374; open daily 10–8) rents basic bikes by the hour for L5000, tandems for L12,000, and mountain bikes for L7000; full-day renters get substantial discounts. **I Bike Rome** (Via Vittorio Veneto 156, tel. 06/322–5240) rents for similar fees weekdays 9–1 and 3–7, weekends 9–8. **Bicimania** (Piazza San Sonnino, at Viale di Trastevere, tel. 06/780–7755) has five-speed bikes for L5000 per hour, L16,000 per day. It's open daily 9 AM–12:30 AM (until 8 PM in Oct. and Nov.).

Touring Club Italiano (Via Ovidio 7/A, tel. 06/687–4432 or 06/687–4603) publishes detailed biking maps of Rome and most of Italy; look for them in bookstores and tourist offices. If you want to join an organized cycle tour of Rome, check the "Verde" section of the *La Trova Roma* supplement to *La Repubblica*'s Thursday edition.

BY SCOOTER Rent a scooter and mandatory helmet at **Scoot-a-Long** (Via Cavour 302, tel. 06/678–0206) or **St. Peter's Moto** (Via di Porta Castello 43, tel. 06/687–5714). **I bike Rome** rents mopeds (L30,000 for 4 hrs). The going day rate for all three places, for scooters or mopeds, is about L45,000 a day.

Where to Sleep

If you're not too picky, a clean double in a nononsense pension can be had for L55,000–L70,000. In the L80,000–L100,000 range you'll get ambience, a private bath, and a somewhat central address. Definitely make reservations in August and September, when Rome is swamped with foreign tourists. If you do arrive unprepared, it is possible to find something near Stazione Termini year-round, but don't expect the highest levels of comfort and cleanliness. Tourist offices sometimes book rooms or, at the very least, hand you *Logizia di Roma*, a hefty green booklet that lists everything from five-star hotels to no-star pensions. Be wary of solicitors who hang out at Termini and lure travelers to their establishments: They may or may not be legit and will likely charge twice the going rate.

Stick to the area around **Stazione Termini** if price is more important than setting. Rome's **centro storico** is the most convenient and atmospheric place to sleep, but prices here start in the L80,000 range. Across the river in the **Trastevere** district, Rome's nightlife hub, rooms are expensive and hard to find. The same is true near the **Vatican**, where doubles start around L90,000. If your only option is to rough it, the green expanse of Villa Borghese provides limited opportunities for outdoor sleeping (and then only if you're seriously inconspicuous). To reach Borghese, take Metro Line A to Flaminio; stick to the northern reaches of the park, and away from both the Pincio and the Viale delle Belle Arti, where shady characters may linger in the wee morning hours.

NORTH OF STAZIONE TERMINI

In general, the area north of Stazione Termini is nicer than its southern counterpart: The buildings are cleaner and the streets wider, and you won't have to venture far to find mom-and-pop restaurants and daily outdoor markets (there's one on Piazza Vittorio). The downside of staying here is the obligatory walk through grimy Piazza dei Cinquecento. At night, the streets around Stazione Termini are none too safe, so consider a taxi when possible. To reach the pensions and hotels on **Via Palestro** from Stazione Termini, walk north on Via Marsala, turn right on Via Vicenza, then left on Via Palestro.

➤ **UNDER L60,000** • **Home Michele.** Chinese art and lacquered antiques clutter the living room of this tiny family-run pension. The four quiet and spotless rooms (L55,000 doubles,

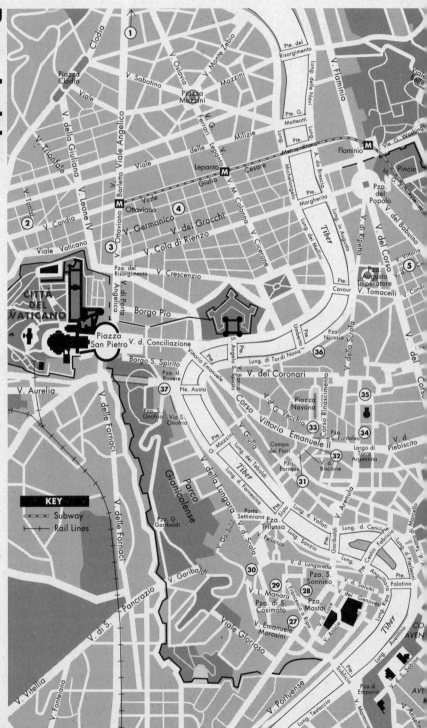

Rome Lodging

KEY
- - - - Subway
+-+-+ Rail Lines

Albergo Abruzzi, **35**
Albergo del Sole, **31**
Albergo
La Rovere, **37**
Albergo Orbis, **23**
Fawlty Towers, **19**
Fraternus
Domus, **36**
Giuggioli Hotel, **4**
Home Michele, **8**
Hotel Akragas, **17**
Hotel Cervia, **11**
Hotel Cisterna, **28**
Hotel Contilla, **23**
Hotel Giuggiù, **17**
Hotel Marini, **8**
Hotel Papa
Germano, **13**
Hotel Pensione
Alimandi, **2**
Hotel Pensione
Cressy, **20**
Hotel Pensione
Manara, **29**
Hotel Pensione
Primavera, **33**
Hotel Pensione
Rosa, **9**
Hotel Pensione
Sandy, **25**
Hotel Pensione
Selene, **16**
Hotel Sweet
Home, **21**
Ostello del Foro
Italico, **1**
Panda, **5**
P. Alessandro, **14**
P. Carmel, **30**
P. Corallo, **10**
P. Esty, **27**
P. Ida, **4**
P. Katty, **7**
P. Lunetta, **32**
P. Mimosa, **34**
P. Ottaviano, **3**
P. Piave, **6**
P. Sameena, **15**
P. Stella Elsa, **23**
P. Terni, **22**
P. Virginia, **12**
P. Eureka and
Arrivederci, **18**
Perugia, **26**
YWCA, **24**

313

L75,000 triples) come with sinks and pictures of the proprietors' children on the walls. *Via Palestro 35, tel. 06/444–1204. 4 rooms, none with bath.*

Hotel Marini. The friendly woman who runs this hotel likes to practice her English on anyone who'll listen. Although meals are not provided, the smells from the kitchen are heavenly. Doubles are L60,000, triples L25,000 per person. *Via Palestro 35, tel. 06/444–0058. 8 rooms, none with bath.*

Hotel Papa Germano. When you reach Papa Germano's place, you'll notice the 23 travel books framed and displayed inside. Papa Germano is listed in all of them, which explains why reservations are a must. The neighborhood is seedy but fairly quiet. Clean, renovated rooms (doubles L55,000) sport twin beds and pastel wallpaper. *Via Calatafimi 14/A, tel. 06/486919. From Stazione Termini, walk north on Via Marsala (it becomes Via Volturno), turn right on Via Calatafimi. 13 rooms, none with bath. MC, V.*

Hotel Pensione Cressy. Cressy won't win any beauty contests, but if you're looking for a place to crash, it's easily reachable from the station. Some of the rooms (doubles L40,000–L70,000, triples L75,000) even have views, though the bathrooms are barely passable. *Via Volturno 27, tel. 06/484917. From Stazione Termini, turn right down Via Volturno. 10 rooms, none with bath.*

Hotel Pensione Rosa. The reception desk sports an espresso machine, tropical plants, and the requisite Jesus memorabilia. Rooms are small but with lots of light and high ceilings, and some even have balconies. Doubles go for L50,000–L80,000. *Via Palestro 87, tel. 06/491065. 7 rooms, 1 with bath. Doors close at midnight.*

Pensione Katty. All 10 rooms at this hotel have high ceilings and mosaic floors, though the "beds" are sometimes merely cots. Vacancies are rare, but the owners will suggest other options in the area. Doubles are L40,000–L70,000; triples L75,000. *Via Palestro 35, tel. 06/444–1216. 9 rooms, 2 with bath.*

Pensione Virginia. This place is a find, with cheap rooms (doubles L45,000–L65,000) pleasantly decorated with faux frescoes. The cheerful proprietress will direct you to her brother's pizzeria downstairs. *Via Montebello 94, tel. 06/488–1786. From Stazione Termini, exit right on Via Volturno, right on Via Montebello. 8 rooms, all with bath.*

➤ **UNDER L80,000 • Hotel Cervia.** These spartan rooms (doubles starting at L75,000) may not be homey, but they're clean and plentiful; 23 rooms means vacancies are common. Helpful *ragazzi* (kids) who look after the joint hang out in the living room watching the tube, and you're welcome to join in. Breakfast—an all-you-can-eat spread including coffee, OJ, and bread with jam—is available for L5,000. *Via Palestro 55, tel. 06/491057. 23 rooms, 6 with bath. Curfew 1 AM in winter, 2 AM in summer. AE, MC, V.*

Pensione Corallo. The rooms in this top-floor pension are simple, but most open onto the terrace encircling the building's interior courtyard. Geraniums abound and the owner sells cold drinks for those who want to lounge *al fresco* (outside). Doubles are L70,000, but ask for the 10% student discount. *Via Palestro 44, tel. 06/445–6340. 9 rooms, 5 with bath. Curfew 2 AM.*

Pensione Piave. It's far enough from the station to be quiet and residential, but close enough to walk to. Sunny doubles with phones and desks start at L70,000; most also have their own blue-tiled bathrooms. The young managers treat you like a grown-up and distribute keys to the street door. *Via Piave 14, tel. 06/474–3447. From Stazione Termini, walk directly across Piazza del Cinquecento to Piazza della Repubblica, continue straight on Via S. Susanna, right on Via XX Settembre, left on Via Piave. Laundry (L5000).*

SOUTH OF STAZIONE TERMINI

Rome's thickest concentration of budget lodgings is in the less-than-desirable neighborhood south of Stazione Termini. Petty theft is a big problem here, and sleeping with your valuables under the pillow is not a bad idea. Via Cavour, Via Manini, and Via Principe Amedeo aren't too sleazy during the day, but when the sun sinks low, lone travelers—especially women—should keep their wits about them. The area's redeeming qualities are its abundance of cheap restaurants and its proximity to the station. To reach the hotels and pensions on **Via Principe Amedeo** from Stazione Termini, walk southwest on Via Cavour and turn left on Via Principe Amedeo. To reach **Via del Viminale** from Stazione Termini, walk northwest through Piazza dei Cinquecento (it's in front of the station) and turn left onto Via del Viminale.

➤ **UNDER L70,000** • **Albergo Orbis.** Rooms here are clean but not nearly as swank as those in Hotel Dina or Pensione Terni (*see below*), all of which are in the same building and owned by the same proprietor. Doubles cost L65,000 with bath, L40,000 without. The front desk is two floors down at Hotel Dina. *Via Principe Amedeo 62, tel. 06/474–5428. 18 rooms, some with bath.*

Hotel Giuggiù. Up a marble staircase from Hotel Akragas, the Giuggiù boasts sunny if scantily furnished rooms (doubles without bath L65,000) big enough to pitch a tent in. The family that runs the place offers breakfast (L8000). *Via del Viminale 8, tel. 06/482–7734. 12 rooms, some with bath. Midnight curfew.*

Hotel Pensione Selene. Guest quarters have high ceilings, competent furnishings, and top-floor views of the neighborhood. The pension is family run, and the long, dark hallways are stumbling grounds for the toddler generation. Doubles run L50,000–L70,000. *Via del Viminale 8, tel. 06/474–4781. 40 rooms, some with bath. Reception open until 12:30 AM.*

Pensione Sameena. This place feels far from the station's hustle; it's on a tiny block on Viminale Hill, one of Rome's ancient seven. The second-floor rooms (doubles L65,000) are all fairly clean and bright. The TV room has fluffy couches for naps and socializing. *Via del Viminale 31, tel. 06/488–1003. 10 rooms, some with bath. AE, MC, V.*

Pensione Stella Elsa. This sunny, third-floor hotel lies behind a courtyard, away from the street and its hookers. A hospitable matriarch makes sure that the rooms (doubles L60,000) are well-kept; all have either a sink (with hot and cold water) or a shower. *Via Principe Amedeo 79/A, tel. 06/731–1513. 5 rooms, none with bath.*

Perugia. Ancient-history buffs will drool over the Perugia's prime location, on an alleyway one block from the Roman Forum and two blocks from the Colosseum. On the downside, the best thing that can be said for the utterly plain rooms (doubles without bath L70,000) is that they all have phones. *Via del Colosseo 7, tel. 06/679–7200. From Stazione Termini, take Metro Line B to Colosseo; or walk ½ km south on Via Cavour, left on Via del Colosseo. 11 rooms, some with bath. AE, MC, V.*

➤ **UNDER L90,000** • **Hotel Akragas.** Healthy green plants oxygenate the common spaces, which include a social room and a large dining area with an espresso bar and TV. Decorative columns remind guests of their proximity to Rome's ruins. Most rooms (doubles L85,000–L105,000) face away from the street and its din. *Via del Viminale 8, tel. 06/487–2536. 16 rooms, some with bath. AE, MC, V.*

Hotel Contilla. The personable, English-speaking owner is proud of his hotel, recently refurbished from top to bottom. Shiny linoleum in the reception and breakfast room looks a bit slick, but the rooms themselves (doubles L80,000–L110,000) are more hospitable. Some have couches, others have desks, and all have TVs and phones. The Contilla is in the same building as Pensione Stella Elsa (*see above*). *Via Principe Amedeo 79/D, tel. 06/446–6942. 14 rooms, most with bath. AE, MC, V.*

Hotel Sweet Home. The word "cute" was made for this place, decorated in lively colors and overrun with floral prints, leaf designs, and bird scenes. Thick doors with gilded molding open onto sunny, immaculate rooms (doubles without bath L80,000), all with TVs and phones. All but two rooms face away from the noisy street. *Via Principe Amedeo 47, tel. 06/488–0954. 15 rooms, 5 with bath. MC, V.*

Pensioni Eureka & Arrivederci. Rooms at these adjoining hotels are a bit frayed, and doubles with showers are a steep L80,000 (breakfast included). On they have views of the Diocletian

Baths from common rooms. *Piazza della Repubblica 47, tel. 06/488–0334 or 06/482–5806. From Stazione Termini, walk north across Piazza dei Cinquecento, veer left onto Via Einaudi, and continue to piazza. 30 rooms, none with bath. Curfew 1 AM.*

➤ **UNDER L100,000** • **Pensione Terni.** Hand-carved wooden doors, tile floors, and Gauguin prints detail the entranceway and halls—the result of a recent renovation. Doubles cost L100,000 and are new, simple, and clean—basically the same as those upstairs at Hotel Dina (*see above*), where you check in. *Via Principe Amedeo 62, tel. 06/474–5428. 17 rooms, all with bath.*

CENTRO STORICO

The centro storico, Rome's heart and soul, is everyone's favorite place to stay, and hotel proprietors know it. Prices here are 30%–50% higher than in the rest of the city. Of course, your money is buying prime location—the centro storico is smack dab in the middle of Rome and within a stone's throw of the "major" sights—but not necessarily more amenities. The bottom line: If you're on a whirlwind tour and really want to savor the flavor of Rome, it's worth the extra cash.

➤ **UNDER L90,000** • **Hotel Pensione Primavera.** Eight large rooms with high ceilings and tiled floors occupy this grand old building with wrought-iron fixtures and a marble staircase. It's far enough away from Corso Vittorio Emanuele II that noise isn't a serious problem. Most rooms (doubles without bath L80,000) open onto an inner courtyard or the small piazza in front. *Piazza San Pantaleo 3, at Corso Vittorio Emanuele II, tel. 06/6880–3109. From Stazione Termini, Bus 64 or 70 to Largo Argentina; proceed on Corso Vittorio Emanuele II.*

Panda. This pension is convenient to public transportation and *passeggiata* (evening stroll) life. Climbing a steep stairwell brings you to clean, functional rooms (doubles L85,000) in this older building undergoing an interminable face-lift. *Via della Croce 35, tel. 06/678–0179. From Stazione Termini, take Metro Line A to Piazza di Spagna; walk 2 blocks south on Via della Croce. 10 rooms, none with bath. AE.*

➤ **UNDER L115,000** • **Albergo Abruzzi.** This hotel's excellent location makes up for its substandard interior. The 25 dreary rooms (doubles L100,000) are ragged around the edges, and there's only one bathroom per floor. Still, the view of the Pantheon from your room makes it all worthwhile. *Piazza della Rotunda 69, tel. 06/679–2021. From Stazione Termini, Bus 64 to Largo Argentina; follow Via Torre Argentina north to Pantheon.*

Albergo del Sole. This is a worthwhile splurge right near Campo dei Fiori and its pubs, eateries, and open-air morning market. Read a book in the antiques-filled common rooms or on the shady garden patio. Doubles fetch L95,000–L140,000, triples L130,000–L190,000. Reservations are a must. *Via del Biscione 76, tel. 06/6880–6873. From Stazione Termini, take Bus 64 (Bus 70 at night) to Largo di Torre Argentina; walk 2 blocks west on Corso Vittorio Emanuele II, left on Largo dei Chiavari, right onto Piazza del Paradiso, left at Via del Biscione. 70 rooms, some with bath.*

Pensione Lunetta. This graying, plain pension around the corner from Campo dei Fiori draws a laid-back crowd of students, musicians, and artist types. Some English is spoken. To get here, *see* the directions to Albergo del Sole *above.* Doubles run L70,000–L100,000. *Piazza del Paradiso 68, tel. 06/686–1080. 35 rooms, 10 with bath.*

Pensione Mimosa. Every few paces something changes—the floor coverings, the wallpaper, the paint. Homely furnishings collected over the decades are equally eclectic and unpredictable from one room to the next. Sleeping quarters (doubles L90,000) range from medium to huge, and if your room doesn't have a private bath it will at least have a sink. Guests are welcome to use two living rooms, the fridge, and any of several tables in the sunny meal room. The Mimosa is across from the heavily guarded parliament building—très secure. *Via Santa Chiara 61, tel. 06/6880–1753. From Stazione Termini, Bus 64, 65, 70, 75, 170, or 492 to Largo di Torre Argentina; walk 3 blocks north on Via di Torre Argentina, turn left on Via Santa Chiara. 11 rooms, some with bath. Continental breakfast (L5000).*

WEST OF THE TIBER

West of the Tiber River, crime and grime are less apparent and things tend to move at a slower pace. Except for the area immediately surrounding the Vatican, this is probably the least tourist-oriented part of Rome. Cheap restaurants are somewhat scarce west of the river, but public transportation—Metro Line A serves Ottaviano and the Vatican area, while a score of buses travel Viale di Trastevere—means you're within easy reach of the main sights.

➤ **UNDER L80,000** • **Albergo La Rovere.** La Rovere occupies a weathered, sienna-stucco building typical of the neighborhood. Antiques-filled rooms (doubles without bath L70,000) add to the Old World feel; many have killer views of the Tiber River. On the reception level there's a coffee bar and an eating area with a big TV. *Vicolo San Onofrio 5, tel. 06/6880–6739. From Stazione Termini, Bus 34, 46, 46B, 98, 808, or 982 to Piazza della Rovere (at Ponte Aosta); walk south along river, turn right on Vicolo San Onofrio. 23 rooms, some with bath. Breakfast (L5000).*

Giuggioli Hotel. The Victorian age meets the 1940s at this first-rate, time-warped place. The same lovely woman has run things for 40 years, and her stately furniture has accumulated in the grand high-ceilinged rooms (doubles L75,000). Her four cats appreciate a good belly scratch. *Via Germanico 198, tel. 06/324–2113. From Lepanto Metro station, walk 1 block west on Via degli Scipioni, turn left on Via Paolo Emilio, right on Via Germanico. 5 rooms, 1 with bath.*

Hotel Pensione Manara. Most rooms have windows that overlook the outdoor market on Piazza di San Cosimato, but overall the Manara is gloomy and unkempt. Still, the plain rooms (bathless doubles L65,000) provide the essentials, and are in demand because of the ideal location. You're welcome to use the couch and TV in the common room. *Via Luciano Manara 25/A, tel. 06/581–4713. From Stazione Termini, Bus 170 to Viale di Trastevere (which becomes Via Luciano Manara). 7 rooms, none with bath. Reservations advised.*

Pensione Carmel. The Carmel is on a mellow, tree-lined street at the edge of Trastevere. The average-size doubles (L65,000–L80,000) have a woody, mountain-lodge flair, some with annoying butterfly designs on the bathroom tiles. *Via Mameli 11, tel. 06/580–9921. 8 rooms, some with bath.*

Pensione Esty. The modern building housing this family-run pension is right on traffic-plagued Viale di Trastevere. Convenient enough, sure, but the street din gets outta hand despite two layers of shutters. Light sleepers should definitely request one of the four rooms facing the parking courtyard out back. Doubles go for L72,000. *Viale di Trastevere 108, tel. 06/589–1201. Just past Viale Aurelio Saffi on Viale di Trastevere; turn up driveway and enter first doorway on left, marked "Scala A." 11 rooms, none with bath.*

Pensione Ida. White walls blend smoothly with the bright and sunny glow of this super-clean pension, in the same building as Giuggioli Hotel (*see above*). The neighborhood is shop- and café-laden and within walking distance of the Vatican. The midnight curfew is the only real bummer. Simple, large, almost sterile doubles run L70,000–L90,000. *Via Germanico 198, tel. 06/324–2164. 8 rooms, none with bath.*

➤ **UNDER L110,000** • **Hotel Cisterna.** Night owls will appreciate this somewhat disheveled pension hidden on a winding street in lively Trastevere, with plenty of nearby espresso bars and bakeries. There's a small rooftop patio plus a courtyard in back with tables and umbrellas. Doubles are L100,000. *Via della Cisterna 7–9, near Piazza San Sonnino, tel. 06/581–7212. From Stazione Termini, Bus 170 to Piazza San Sonnino. 22 rooms, all with bath. MC, V.*

Hotel Pensione Alimandi. Heavy medieval-looking furniture and queer battle accessories are strewn about the TV room, saloon bar, dining room, and entranceway. By comparison, the clean doubles (L100,000–L120,000) seem generic. Head to the rooftop garden for some sun. *Via Tunisi 8, tel. 06/3972–3948. Cnr of Via San Sebastiano Veniero, 1 block from entrance to Vatican museums. 29 rooms, 24 with bath. AE, MC, V.*

HOSTELS

Fawlty Towers. The folks at Enjoy Rome, together with Pensioni Sandy and Ottaviano, created this new hostel steps away from Termini. Common areas include a sunny rooftop terrace and a lounge with satellite TV. Spartan but clean doubles run L60,000–L80,000; a dorm-style bed is L22,000–L25,000, including sheets. Best of all there's no curfew and no lockout. *Via Magenta 39, tel. 06/445–0374. From Stazione Termini, exit right and take Via Maghera north 1 block. 15 rooms, 4 private rooms with bath. Luggage storage.*

Fraternus Domus. This hostel is run by sweeter-than-pie Catholic nuns, which means everything is clean and orderly. The location, between Piazza Navona and the Tiber River, can't be beat. A hearty four-course lunch or dinner is popular with locals (L15,000, wine included). The major drawback is the strictly enforced 11 PM curfew, and the complete lack of double beds; though couples don't have to be married to stay together. The flat rate is L40,000 per person, including bath, towels, and a sparse breakfast. *62 Via Monte Brianzo, tel. 06/654–2727. Metro Line A to Spagna; walk SW on Via Condotti, past Piazza Nicosia. 20 rooms, all with bath.*

Hotel Pensione Sandy. This hostel, close to Stazione Termini and the Santa Maria Maggiore church, is run by the same friendly people who run Pensione Ottaviano (*see below*). Climb four flights of stairs and you'll be rewarded with rudimentary dorm-style rooms, each containing 3–5 cots. Considering Sandy's kickback atmosphere, central location, and its rock-bottom prices (L18,000–L23,000 per person), you shouldn't mind a little filth. *Via Cavour 136, 5 blocks SW of Stazione Termini, tel. 06/488–4585. Luggage storage.*

Ostello del Foro Italico. This hostel's inconvenient location in Rome's northwest corner—and the fact that it's a chunky slab of cold, Fascist architecture—doesn't keep away hordes of international travelers. A flat rate of L20,000 per person includes sheets, hot showers, and breakfast. The sterile, barrack-inspired dorms each hold about a dozen bunk beds, and men and women are channeled into different wings. A basement cafeteria serves bland meals (from L9000) and cheap beer. Hostel cards are required, but can be issued on the spot for L30,000. Don't get too comfy though—there's a three-day maximum stay. *Viale delle Olimpiadi 61, near Stadio Olimpico, tel. 06/323–6267. From Stazione Termini, Bus 32 1 stop past Via Maresciallo Giardino (on the river); walk 1 long block west and turn left on Viale delle Olimpiadi. 334 beds. Midnight curfew, lockout 9 AM–2 PM. Luggage storage (L1500). Wheelchair access.*

Pensione Alessandro. In this privately owned hostel just north of Stazione Termini, L20,000 gets you a red-framed bunk bed (4–6 per room) in a clean and sunny, but not very large room. The atmosphere can get rowdy when guests come home drunk and belligerent, but no one seems to complain. Feel free to use the dining room, TV, fridge, and showers. *Via Vicenza 42, tel. 06/446–1958. From Stazione Termini, walk 3½ blocks NE on Via Vicenza. 45 beds. No curfew, no lockout.*

Pensione Ottaviano. This private hostel is a clean, budget-wise way to crash close to the main sights, only a block from the Vatican and several transport options. Metal cots are stacked three- to six-high per sunny room, some of which have views of St. Peter's dome. Guests may use the fridge and the free, sometimes pressureless, hot showers. Beds run L18,000–L23,000. *Via Ottaviano 6, tel. 06/3973–8138 or 06/3973–7253. Metro Line A to Ottaviano; walk 2½ blocks south on Via Ottaviano. 25 beds.*

YWCA. If you can handle the midnight curfew and segregation of unmarried guests, the YWCA is unbelievably posh. Sexes mix in the TV room, the sitting room, and the peaceful library. The high-ceilinged bedrooms have twin beds, desks, and sinks; many face Via Cesare Balbo, which hosts a morning market. Only one of six floors is set aside for men, but both sexes should make reservations. Eat in the backyard garden or upstairs in the cafeteria (lunch and dinner from L10,000). Doubles are L70,000, triples L90,000, including breakfast. *Via Cesare Balbo 4, tel. 06/488–0460 or 06/488–3917. From Stazione Termini, walk south on Via Cavour, turn right on Via Torino, left on Via Cesare Balbo. Midnight curfew. Reception open 7 AM–11 PM. Luggage storage.*

Food

Romans take their food quite seriously, and it's not unusual to hear them screaming at one another on the street corner over who makes the best spaghetti *alla carbonara* (with cream, peas, and ham). You can't go wrong with all the options available, but if cheap eats are your main concern, keep an eye out for pizza by the slice, called *pizza rustica* or *pizza al taglio*, or head to the nearest *tavola calda* (literally, hot table), where you can choose from a number of cafeteria-style dishes. The main concentrations of inexpensive places are around **Stazione Termini**, **Trevi Fountain**, **Via Del Corso**, and in the **Campo dei Fiori**. If you're staying near the Vatican, head south to Trastevere and its cafés, espresso bars, and trattorias. As a rule, menus are displayed for all to see; if not, suspect high prices. For those on a really tight budget, open-air markets are plentiful around Stazione Termini, Campo dei Fiori, and just west of Piazza Navona. All three are open mornings Monday–Saturday.

Like most Italians, Romans eat a heavy lunch between 1 and 3 and a sizable dinner between 9 and 11. Some restaurants stay open much later, especially on warm summer nights when people linger at crowded sidewalk tables.

Spots with the word *Romanesca* in the name usually specialize in traditional Roman cuisine. Highlights include *saltimbocca* (veal rolls flavored with sage), *abbacchio* (spring lamb), and *filetti di baccalà* (salted cod fillets). *Carciofi* (artichokes) come fried or marinated. Yummy *supplì* (fried rice balls filled with mozzarella) are favored appetizers at restaurants and food stands. When it comes to wine, Frascati, Castelli, and Colli Albani are regional favorites. Expect to pay L8000–L11,000 for a liter, a bit less for *vino della casa* (house wine).

NEAR STAZIONE TERMINI

Stazione Termini is surrounded by cheap trattorias and snack bars. A good place to start looking south of the station is **Via Manin**; north of the station try **Via Milazzo**. There's another cluster of bars and restaurants in the streets surrounding **Piazzale Tiburtino**; to get here from Stazione Termini, exit the station and turn right on Via Marsala, which hits Piazzale Tiburtino.

➤ **UNDER L10,000** • **Formula Uno.** Hectic waiters charge around a large, brightly lit mess of tables, dealing out two-fisted mugs of beer (L4500) and pizza (L6000–L8000) from the wood-burning oven. Don't come for quiet conversation, as most people here are probably drunk and definitely loud. *Via degli Equi 13, tel. 06/445-3866. From Piazzale Tiburtino, take Via Tiburtina to Via degli Equi and turn right. Open Mon.–Sat. 6:30 PM–12:30 AM.*

La Pappardella. In the evening, the promise of a cheap, hearty dinner packs 'em into Pappardella's vine-covered courtyard. Among the myriad pastas try cannelloni stuffed with herbed ricotta (L6000), or the ricotta and spinach ravioli (L6000). Carnivores should consider the very Roman *coratella*—lamb heart, liver, lungs, and windpipe diced with artichokes (L6000). *Via degli Equi 56, tel. 06/446-9349. From Piazzale Tiburtino, follow Via Tiburtina to Via degli Equi and turn right. Open daily 12:30–2:30 and 7:30–midnight (closed Mon. in winter).*

Pizzeria Italia. A short walk from the station will bring you to this heavenly pizza-by-the-slice joint. The lingering crowds munching contendedly outside attest to its popularity among locals and tourists alike. Try pizza with porcini mushrooms, potato pizza, or fresh shrimp for L2000–L3000 per *etto* (⅒ kilo). *Corso d'Italia 103, tel. 4424-9771. From Piazza della Repubblica, take Via Susanna, right on Via XX Settembre, left Via Piave, right on Corso d'Italia. Open weekdays 8 AM–9 PM, Sat. 8 AM–10:30 PM.*

Pizzeria e Paninoteca Andrea. At this pleasant sandwich place, you can eat in or take out fresh sandwiches made to order, either on rolls or focaccia bread (L2500–L5000). They also have pizza by the slice (from L3000). Join the kids watching cartoons on TV while you wait. *Via del Mille 39, tel. 06/446-9980. From Stazione Termini, take Via Milazzo north 2 blocks, right on Via del Mille. Open daily 10 AM–1 AM.*

Quattrocchi Mario. Mario's place is smoke-filled, noisy, and plenty of fun. The dining rooms— each adorned with jaundiced postcards and 15-year-old soccer posters—are massive, so you're usually assured a seat. For under L7000 try the traditional *saltimbocca alla Romana* (veal bundled with prosciutto and sage); for L2800 try *stracciatella alla Romana* (consommé with beaten egg). This is one of the few places where you can custom order an omelet for less than L4000. *Via Flavia 110, tel. 06/481–4420. From Piazza della Repubblica, take Via Susanna, right on Via XX Settembre, left on Via Aureliano, right on Via Flavia. Open daily noon–3 and 7–10:30.*

Ristorante Rossi. Grab your grub to go or pull up a chair at this restaurant, conveniently located near several cheap pensions. Whichever you choose, the eats are tasty and reasonably priced. Try the *bruschetta* (garlic toast with various toppings), especially the one piled high with mushrooms and mozzarella (L3500). Also tasty are pizzas (L5000–L8000), pastas (from L7000), and a wide array of salads (L6000–L9000). *Via Vicenza 23, tel. 06/495–7996. From Stazione Termini, take Via Vicenza north 4 blocks. Open daily 6 AM–11 PM.*

➢ **UNDER L15,000 • Aduliss.** Although billed as a restaurant, Aduliss is more like a social club for Rome's African, Turkish, and Middle Eastern immigrants. Kick back amid colorful wall murals and reggae tunes while Pop Aduliss cooks up piles of Ethiopian food. A gargantuan plate of curried potatoes, lentils, and spiced beef with injera bread goes for L15,000. *Via Milazzo 1/E, 1 block north of Stazione Termini, tel. 06/445–1695. Open Thurs.–Tues. noon–1 AM.*

Trattoria La Suburra. This no-frills trattoria off Via Cavour is *the* place to sample traditional Roman fare. Dig into saltimbocca for L13,000 or *trippa alla romana* (tripe stewed with wine and herbs) for L10,000. You'll annoy the waiter by ordering budget spaghetti and a salad; try instead *bucatini amatriciana* (noodles with bacon, cheese, and tomatoes) or linguine *alla cozze* (with mussels). *69 Via Urbana, next to lower level of Cavour Metro station, no phone. Open Tues.–Sun. noon–2 and 8–10.*

➢ **UNDER L35,000 • Il Guru.** It ain't cheap, but that's because the Indian dishes are first-rate and served in large portions. Il Guru is owned by an ultra-friendly family from southern India who prepares three four-course meals from scratch every day. One centers around fish (L35,000), one around grilled meats (L30,000), and one purely around vegetables (L20,000). *Via Cimarra 4–6, tel. 06/474–4110. From Cavour Metro station, make a left onto Via Urbana and turn right at Via Clemetina. Open Tues.–Sun. 8 PM–midnight.*

CENTRO STORICO

Budget restaurants in the heart of Rome are grouped in three areas: between **Piazza Navona** and the Tiber River, around **Piazza Campo dei Fiori**, and along **Corso Vittorio Emanuele II** between the river and Piazza della Chiesa. Between Piazza Navona and Campo dei Fiori, make a stopover at **Il Fornaio** (Via dei Baullari 5–7, tel. 06/654–3947; open Mon.–Sat. 7 AM–8 PM) for delectable baked goods (there's even bread in the shape of an alligator), or pick up produce at the **open-air market** on Campo dei Fiori. To reach Corso Vittorio Emanuele II and Piazza Navona from Piazza del Risorgimento (near the Vatican), take Bus 81 and alight a few stops after crossing the river.

➢ **UNDER L15,000 • Al Piccolo Arancini.** Even though it's been written up in a dozen guidebooks, this back-alley trattoria continues to balance cheap, tasty meals with an unpretentious atmosphere. Topping the menu are curried noodles with zucchini flowers (L8000) and fettucine with rabbit (L9000). Chicken cordon bleu and veal Marsala both go for L9500. *Vicolo Scanderberg 112, tel. 06/678–6139. From Trevi Fountain, head 2 blocks east on Via Lavatore, turn right on Vicolo Scanderberg. Open Tues.–Sun. 12:30–5 and 7–11:30; closed Aug.*

Da Buffetto. Meals here are simple and damn good. The brief menu features a variety of superthin pizzas (L5000–L9000) and crunchy calzones (L6000–L9000), as well as a couple tasty appetizers. Vie for seating in the street-facing front room, or head to the back for cozy incognito dining. *Via del Governo Vecchio 114, tel. 06/686–1617. From Piazza della Chiesa Nuova, walk west on Corso Vittorio Emanuele II, turn left on Via Soro, right on Via del Governo Vecchio. Open daily 6:30 PM–1 AM.*

Cartoccio d'Abruzzi. In summer this unassuming trattoria sets up outdoor tables on a raised concrete island, complete with fountains and multicolored Christmas lights. Your proximity to

Piazza Navona means first-rate gawking on warm Roman nights. For L8000 chow on generous portions of linguine *alle vongole* (with clams) or spaghetti carbonara. *Via di Tor Sanguigna 4, tel. 06/6880–2427. From Piazza Navona, follow Via di Lorenesi 1 block west to Via di Tor Sanguigna. Open Tues.–Sun. 8 PM–11:30 PM.*

Er Grottino. Meaning "little cave" in the Roman dialect, this is the place to hole up and sample traditional Roman specialties. Budget choices include thin-crust pizzas (L7000–L9000), large bowls of pasta (L8000–L9000), and meat dishes like *piccatina al Marsala* (veal sautéed in Marsala wine; L9000) and *pollo alla diavola* (¼ chicken that's been beaten, abused, marinated, and grilled; L8000). *Via dei Baullari 25/27, tel. 06/688036. From Piazza Campo dei Fiori, walk 2 blocks NE on Via dei Baullari. Open Wed.–Mon. noon–3 and 7–midnight; closed last 2 weeks in Aug.*

Insalata Ricca. If you're craving fare that's as easy on your wallet as it is on your waistline, this is the place. This colorful restaurant offers a dozen meal-size salads (from L7000) and a jovial atmosphere. The *capricciosa* salad (with peppers, corn, olives, and feta cheese; L9000) is especially good, as is the mouthwatering *bruschetta al pomodoro* (garlic bread with tomatoes; L2500). Pastas and main courses are also available. *Largo dei Chiavari 83, tel. 06/6880–3656. Off Corso Vittorio Emanuele II, 2 blocks east of Largo Argentina. Open Thurs.–Tues. 12:30–3:15 and 6:45–11:15.*

La Monte Carlo. This is one of Rome's more affordable wood-oven pizzerias, and a popular hangout for the twentysomething crowd. Tables come equipped with red-checked tablecloths, fake flowers, and potato *crocchette* (croquettes; L1000 each). Super-thin pizzas come in small (L5000), medium (L7500), and large (L9000). There's no real menu, so tell the waiter what toppings you want, or ask for the pizza *della casa* (daily special). *Vicolo Savelli 11A/13, tel. 06/686–1877. From Piazza della Chiesa Nuova, walk 3 blocks east on Corso Vittorio Emanuele II, turn left on Vicolo Savelli. Open daily 6:30 PM–1 AM; closed early Aug. and Mon. in winter.*

La Nuova Shanghai. It ain't great Chinese food, but Italians lap it up like fiends. For a sit-down meal in this neighborhood, you won't find anything cheaper. Skip the soups (thick and bland; L5000) but not the spring rolls (L3000) or steamed dumplings (L3500). Sizzling pork, shrimp, chicken, and beef (L7000 each) are the house specialties. Noodle dishes run a mere L4500, and caramelized pineapple (L3000) makes an exotic finish. The fixed lunch menu (L10,000), including five dishes and drinks, is a virtual banquet. *Via dei Giubbonari 52, off Piazza Campo dei Fiori, tel. 06/654–1636. Open Tues.–Sun. 7 PM–11 PM.*

TRASTEVERE

Trastevere was historically a *zona popolare* (working-class neighborhood), and the food dished out here has always been hearty and serious. You won't find supermarkets—the *trasteverini* insist on buying from the next-door fruit vendor and the trusted butcher down the block. Today, many of Trastevere's restaurants are geared toward the heavy influx of tourists, trading authenticity for high prices. However, there's still an old-style **produce and fish market**, held daily in Piazza San Cosimato 7 AM–1 PM. Be sure to check out one of the city's oldest **bakeries** at Via Politeama 27, near Piazza Trilussa. There is no sign to announce it—only your nose can tell you when you're there. **Biscottificio Artigiano** (Via della Luce 21, tel. 06/580–3926), run by an eccentric husband and wife team, also bakes dozens of sweet delights. Utterly Roman, these two won't hesitate to give you fashion advice or tell you what you should be eating for dinner, all the while shouting through the open door at the passing neighbors.

➢ **UNDER L15,000 • Pizzeria da Ivo.** This is the epitome of a Roman pizzeria, complete with boisterous romani, sidewalk tables, exhaust fumes, and a busy street scene. Beer and pizza are where it's at. Take your pick: individual *pizza normale* (L8000–L12,500), or *pizza gigante* to share (L11,000–L16,000). Also delicious is *rigatoni melanzane* (corkscrew pasta with eggplant; L9500) and mouth-watering desserts. *Via Francesco a Ripa 158, tel. 06/581–7082. From Viale di Trastevere, walk 3 blocks north on Via Francesco a Ripa. Open Wed.–Mon. noon–3 and 7–1.*

Pizzeria Panattoni. Families, ragazzi, and clubbers with the munchies consume huge helpings of beer and fast food in this cafeteria-like space. Wood-oven pizzas (from L8000) and sizzling *filetti di baccalà* (dried salted cod) are popular choices. *Viale di Trastevere 53/59, tel. 06/580-0919. Open Thurs.–Tues. 6 PM–2 AM.*

Popi Popi. A spiffy pizzeria—note the wrought-iron chandeliers and hanging Chianti bottles—with affordable pizzas and calzone (L8000–L12,000), not to mention about a dozen different pastas. Beware the watery house wine. *Via delle Fratte di Trastevere 45, tel. 06/589-5167. From Viale di Trastevere, walk 2 blocks north on Via Francesco a Ripa and turn right. Open Fri.–Wed. 5 PM–2 AM.*

Torrefazione Frontoni. This place is a beauty to behold—an Italian deli *par excellence* with a little of everything your stomach could desire. Choose from pizza (L1300), focaccia sandwiches (from L5000), cold pasta salads, cakes, candy, and coffee beans by the kilo. You'll leave with a smile on your face, whether you came to eat or just to drool. *Viale Trastevere 52, at Via Francesco a Ripa, tel. 06/581-2436. Open daily 9–1:30 and 5—8.*

Il Vicolo. This intimate restaurant, hidden on one of Trastevere's backstreets, offers indoor and outdoor seating. Choose from a dozen variations of inspiring salads (L8000), meat dishes, and pizza, or dig into their pastas, like ravioli stuffed with ricotta cheese and spinach (L8000). *Vicolo dei Cinque 27, near Piazza Trilussa, tel. 06/581-0250. Open daily noon–3 and 6–11.*

➤ **UNDER L20,000 • Il Ciak.** Everything on the menu is traditional peasant and country folk fare; this is the place to sample real Roman "farm food." The cantina atmosphere is cozy, but don't come here if you're the type that flinches at wild boar, mixed birds with polenta, or various innards. The hefty dishes run L12,000–L18,000. *Vicolo dei Cinque 21, off Piazza Trilussa, no phone. Open Tues.–Sun. 8:15 PM–midnight.*

Gianicolo 23. Among the orgasmic pastas here are the creamy *farfalle al radicchio* (bow-tie pasta with cream, tomato, purple lettuce, and bacon) and fettuccine *al Gianicolo* (with mixed mushrooms), each for L8000. If you're feeling meaty, try *straccetti con rughetta* (beef fillet sautéed with arugula, Gorgonzola, and garlic; L14,000). Even with the sizable crowds, there's usually room inside or out front on the tree-lined street. *Via Goffredo Mamelli 23, tel. 06/581-5438. From Viale di Trastevere, take Via Emanuele Morosini north for 2 blocks and turn right on Via Goffredo Mamelli. Open Thurs.–Tues. 5 PM–1 AM.*

Trattoria da Augusto. The menu continually changes at this family-run trattoria, but the food is dependably authentic and without tourist frills. Fresh pastas run L5000–L9000; traditional beef and chicken dishes L6,500–L12,000. On warm nights dine outside on the calm piazza with a liter of Castelli wine (L5000). *Piazza de Renzi 15, tel. 06/580-3798. From Piazza Trilussa, walk 1 block on Via del Moro, turn right on Via de Renzi (it dead-ends at the piazza). Open weekdays noon–3 and 8–11, Sat. noon–3.*

➤ **UNDER L25,000 • Da Corrado.** A one-woman kitchen and no street sign means it's as local as they come. Set meals cost L23,000 and include generous portions of pasta, a savory meat dish, a veggie plate, fresh bread, dessert, and ½ liter of Castelli wine. *Via della Pelliccia 37/39, off Lungotevere Sanzio, tel. 06/580-6004. Open Mon.–Sat. noon–2:30 and 8–10:30.*

NEAR THE VATICAN

Most restaurants anywhere near the Vatican charge exorbitant prices for a meager bowl of yesterday's pasta. Stay away from the schlocky trattorias on **Borgo Pio** and concentrate instead on the small restaurants on and around **Viale Giulio Cesare**, just west of the Ottaviano Metro station. For fresh produce, breads, and cheeses, head to the indoor **market** at Via Caio Mario, between Via dei Gracchi and Via Cola di Rienzo; it's held Monday–Saturday 7–7.

➤ **UNDER L10,000 • Antico Forno.** If you survive the Vatican's five-hour "D Plan" walking tour, trudge a few blocks past the touristy joints on Borgo Pio for some cheap pizza (L1500–L3000). Choose from a long list of toppings: arugula, mozzarella, olive paste, corn, mayonnaise, lettuce, green olives, and even zucchini flowers. Mini-calzone with prosciutto and mozzarella are L2500. *Borgo Pio 8, near Castel Sant'Angelo, tel. 06/6880–5272. Open Mon.–Sat. 7–1 and 5–8.*

Il Bersagliere. This is the place for hefty pizza (L6500–L8500) and frosty tap beer (small L2500, large L4000). It's a little dingy and dim, but filled with jovial locals. Filling antipasto plates cost L6000. *Via Candia 24, tel. 06/3974–2253. From Ottaviano Metro station, walk west along Viale Giulio Cesare, which becomes Via Candia.*

Pizza Rustica al Gracchi. Al Gracchi's prices thankfully do not reflect its convenient location, a short walk from the entrance to the Vatican museums. Get food to go or sit inside contemplating the painting of the restaurant's mascot: a pasty kid stuffing his face with pizza. Slices start at L1500 an etto, calzone L1500–L2500. An entire rotisseried chicken is a bargain at L9000. *Via dei Gracchi 7, tel. 06/372–3733. From Piazza del Risorgimento, walk 1 block north on Via Ottaviano, veer right onto Via dei Gracchi. Open Mon.–Sat. 8 AM–7 PM.*

Cafés

Rome seems to have a café on every corner, so be choosy and find a place that suits your style and budget. If you stand at the bar, an espresso runs L1000–L1500, a cappuccino L1500–L2000, a *cornetto* (croissant) L1000–L1200. However, prices can jump 100%–200% for the simple pleasure of sitting at a table, inside or out, so be sure to check.

Bar San Callisto. This unassuming café, tacked up with old soccer posters, is the familiar haunting ground of local artists and theater people who come to order their morning cornetto and espresso (L1000 each), a bottle of beer (L2500), or some gelato (L1800–L2800). Even though it's steps away from Piazza Santa Maria, there's no extra charge to sit outside. *Piazza San Callisto 3, off Viale di Trastevere, tel. 06/589–5678. Open daily 5:45 AM–1:30 AM.*

Caffè Allemagne. Called Caffè Aragno in the 19th century, this was *the* place for politicians and intellectuals. These days artsy mirrors, and crystal chandeliers are the only features that distinguish it from other Roman cafés. The house specialty, *frulatti* (L3200), a concoction of fruits and "secret" ingredients whipped up into a frothy shake, is killer. *Via del Corso 181, south of Piazza del Popolo, tel. 06/3989–2003. Open daily 7:30 AM–11 PM.*

Caffè dell'Orologio. This is the perfect place to play cards and smoke cigarettes while waiting for a train at Stazione Termini. There's no extra charge for sitting at a table, and the ones outside have good views of Santa Maria Maggiore. Sandwiches—try spinach and mozzarella on whole wheat (L3500)—are fresh and fairly priced. The key to life is fresh grapefruit juice (L3000). *Via Cavour 77, 3 blocks south of Stazione Termini, tel. 06/474–0491. Open daily 7 AM–10 PM.*

Caffè Greco. The Greco is expensive and touristy, but an obligatory stop for anyone interested in literature. The red-velvet chairs and marble tables have hosted the likes of Byron, Shelley, Keats, Goethe, and Stradivari. Sitting down forces a waiter in tails to bring you a L3500 coffee on a silver tray. At the bar it's the regular L1000 for coffee. *Via Condotti 86, 1 block west of Piazza di Spagna, tel. 06/678–2554. Open June–Sept., Tues.–Sun. 8:30 AM–1 AM; Oct.–May, Tues.–Sun 8:30 AM–9 PM.*

Caffè Sant'Eustachio. This classy place, traditionally frequented by Rome's literati, vies with Tazza d'Oro (*see below*), for the city's best coffee. Fork over the extra lire for a *caffè speciale* (sweetened double espresso; L2500). If you want yours without sugar, ask for it *amaro*. *Piazza Sant'Eustachio 82, tel. 06/861309. Open Tues.–Sun. 8:30 AM–1 AM.*

If you're anywhere near Piazza Navona, make an effort to find the Creperie Damiano. Your reward: a juicy crepe stuffed with sweet or savory cheeses.

Creperie Damiano. The crepes here can be sweet, savory, or simply decadent. There's a long list to choose from, or create your own for about L8000. *Via Tor Millina 8, tel. 06/ 686–1091. From Piazza Navona, walk 2 blocks west on Via Tor Millina. Open daily 10 AM–3 AM.*

Tazza d'Oro. The "Gold Cup" is the consistent winner of "Rome's Best Cup of Coffee" contest—not an easy title to come by. Locals and tourists crowd the long bar for espresso (L1000), cappuccino (L1200), and mixed pastries (L1000–L2000). For L15,000 grab a burlap sack stuffed with their own house roast. *Via degli Orfani, off Piazza della Rotonda, tel. 06/679–2768. Open Mon.–Sat. 6:45 AM–8 PM.*

Gelaterias and Pasticcerias

Fiocco de Neve. This low-key place around the corner from Giolitti (*see below*) has a ton of killer flavors (cones L3000, cups L4000). Its outside benches are good for gawking. *Via del Pantheon 51, off NE cnr of Piazza della Rotonda. Open daily 9:30 AM–11 PM.*

Gelateria della Palma. This place is decked out with candy and chocolate in bulk, as well as sixty mind-blowing flavors of gelato. The *frutti di bosco* (a mix of raspberry, blackberry, and blueberry; L2000–L3000) is pure heaven. *Via della Maddalena 20, near the Pantheon, tel. 06/654–0752. Open 8 AM–1 AM.*

Giolitti. It's one of Rome's landmarks, serving the absolute, undisputed best gelato in town. In summer, there are enough delicious varieties to have a different one each day of the month. Wash it all down with coffee (L1000). *Via Uffici del Vicario 42, off Via del Pantheon, tel. 06/699–1243. Open daily 9–8.*

Krechel. This hole-in-the-wall—no tables, just a take-away counter—lurks among the fashionable shops near Piazza di Spagna. Highlights in the L1200–L3000 range include cream puffs, apple strudel, and *Sachertorte* (chocolate cake with raspberry filling). *Via Frattina 134, 1 block west of Piazza di Spagna. Open weekdays 9:30–1:30 and 3–5.*

Exploring Rome

All too often in Rome, the sights are unseeable: either hidden under the scaffolding of interminable restorations, or inexplicably closed due to the whims of the ticket office. Yet despite the logistical frustrations of sight-seeing in the city, the rewards are unbelievable. From the soaring heights of St. Peter's to the grisly depths of the Catacombs, from the ethereal interior of the Pantheon to the sheer mass of the Colosseum, Rome supersaturates the senses. Beyond the list of blockbuster monuments, Rome is also home to a bevy of of tiny neighborhood churches, quirky museums, and long-forgotten treasures. You could spend a month dashing from piazza to palazzo and still not see it all. Of course, just soaking in the view, armed with a bottle of local wine, isn't a bad approach to discovering Rome either.

Those endowed with less time and more money may want to join one of several guided tours, which hit all the major sights in the comfort of air-conditioned coaches. **American Express** (tel. 06/67641), **CIT** (tel. 06/47941) and **Appian Line** (06/488–4151) all offer three-hour bus tours (L40,000–L50,000) with English-speaking guides. American Express tours leave from their office in Piazza di Spagna, CIT tours leave from Piazza della Repubblica, and Appian Line will pick you up from most major hotels.

Gin Slushies on a Hot Afternoon

Usually fruity and sometimes alcoholic, "grattachecca" is a delicious slushy drink sought by Romans on sultry nights. It's often served at street stands in the traditional fashion, with the ice grated by hand. Two stands in particular—Guiliana Tiziano's (Lungotevere Tor di Nona, at Ponte Umberto I) and Lemoncoceo (Piazza Buenos Aires, near Villa Torlonia)—have been around for decades and are the last of a dying breed. See 'em while you can.

A more affordable (and considerably less cheesy) option is a walking or biking tour of Rome given by **Secret Walks** (Via Medaglie d'Oro 127, tel. 06/3972–8728). Choose from a list of intriguing itineraries, such as "In the Footsteps of Caesar," "A Day in the Life of the Pope," "The Eternal Duel: Bernini vs. Borromini," and "The Oldest Wine Bars." Tours last about 2½ hours, are offered mornings and afternoons, and cost L20,000 (L15,000 for students), not including entrance fees to sights. Secret Walks also gives tours for the **physically disabled** on the first Saturday of every month, or upon request. Last minute reservations are usually no problem.

Major Sights

ANCIENT RUINS

Most remnants of Roman antiquity lie south of the chaotic Piazza Venezia—a dense concentration of ruins that once comprised the commercial, political, and religious epicenter of ancient Rome. From 753 BC, when Romulus is said to have founded the city, the Palatine and Aventine hills and the valleys between them were the stage for Rome's imperial glory. In 29 BC, Augustus, Rome's first emperor, is said to have transformed Rome from a city of brick to a city of marble: During his reign, and that of his successors, the city center was laden with monumental displays of opulence and personal glorification. Though little of these marble structures remains today, the ruins still offer an inspiring glimpse into the glory days of old.

Due to frequent sackings and lootings, the ancient city center has suffered serious abuse. Every invading power had to have a souvenir of its Roman conquest, nabbing a piece of a temple here, a column there. Even the Catholic Church scrounged the area freely for building materials. Today very little of the Forum's original grandeur remains, though sights like the Colosseum and the Arch of Constantine continue to impress even the most blasé traveler. You'll need comfortable walking shoes, a good map, and an active imagination to conquer ancient Rome, as well as the ability to overlook the souvenir hawkers, tourist mobs, buses of school-

Emperor Cheat Sheet

- **AUGUSTUS CAESAR (63 BC–AD 14)** was Rome's first emperor, and his rule began a 200-year-long period of peace known as the Pax Romana. Augustus expanded the empire as far as Scotland, Morocco, and Mesopotamia.

- **NERO (AD 54–68)** was known for his violent persecution of Christians. Nero is also famous for killing his mother, wife, and countless others.

- **TRAJAN (AD 98–117)** enlarged the boundries of the Roman empire in the east to include modern-day Romania, Armenia, and Upper Mesopotamia.

- **HADRIAN (AD 117–138)** expanded the empire in Asia and the Middle East. He is best known in Rome for having rebuilt the Pantheon in its present form.

- **MARCUS AURELIUS (AD 169–180)** was considered to be one of the more lenient and humanitarian emperors. Nonetheless, he was devoted to expansion and an aggressive leader of the empire.

- **CONSTANTINE I (AD 280–337)** was the empire's first Christian emperor. His Edict of Milan granted universal religious tolerance and paved the way for the modern Roman Catholic papacy.

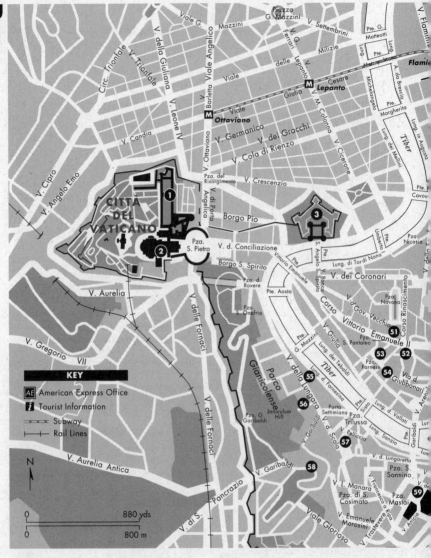

KEY

Ara Pacis, **4**

Arch of
Constantine, **25**

Augusteum, **5**

Basilica San
Marco, **38**

Basilica San Paolo
fuori le mura, **23**

Basilica Santa Maria
in Aracoeli, **36**

Baths of
Caracalla, **22**

Campo dei Fiori, **53**

Castle
Sant'Angelo, **3**

Catacombs, **20**

Il Gesù, **39**

Circus Maximus, **24**

Colosseum, **20**

Column of Marcus
Aurelius, **46**

Forum Boarium, **33**

Galleria
Borghese, **11**

Galleria d'Arte
Moderna, **10**

Galleria Doria, **47**

Galleria
Nazionale, **13**

Galleria Spada, **54**

Isola Tiburnia, **30**

Keats Museum, **8**

Museo Barracco, **51**

Museo
Capitolino, **35**

Museo Ebriaco/
Synagogue, **31**

Museo di Strumenti
Musicali, **18**

Museo Nazionale
Romano, **16**

National Museum
of Pasta, **44**

Palazzo Colonna, **42**

Palazzo dei
Conservatori, **34**

Palazzo Venezia, **40**

Pantheon, **49**

Quirinale, **43**

Roman Forum, **29**

St. Peter's
Basilica, **2**

San Carlo alle
Quattro Fontane, **14**

San Clemente, **27**

Rome

San Giovanni
in Laterno, **21**

San Luigi dei
Francese, **50**

San Michele
a Ripa, **60**

San Pietro in
Montorio, **58**

San Pietro in
Vincoli, **28**

Sant'Andrea
della Valle, **52**

Santa Cecilia
in Trastevere, **59**

Santa Croce in
Gerusalemme, **19**

Santa Maria degli
Angeli, **15**

Santa Maria della
Concezione, **12**

Santa Maria del
Popolo, **6**

Santa Maria in
Trastevere, **7**

Santa Maria
Maggiore, **17**

Santa Maria Sopra
Minerva, **48**

Spanish Steps, **7**

Theater of
Marcellus, **32**

Trajan's Forum, **41**

Trevi Fountain, **45**

Vatican Museums, **1**

Villa Farnesia, **55**

Vittorio Emanuele II
Monument, **37**

Villa Corsini, **56**

children, and very loud mopeds. Be wary of numerous pickpockets and bring plenty of water—there isn't much shade out here and the nearby refreshment stands are a rip-off.

ARCH OF CONSTANTINE Competing with the Colosseum (next-door) in terms of sheer physical presence, is the well-preserved triumphal Arch of Constantine. Erected in AD 312 to commemorate Constantine's victory over rival Maxentius, the arch is decorated with spoils from earlier structures. This frugal approach to ornamentation was partly practical, partly political: Constantine wanted to show the link between Rome's past glories and those of the present. The four sculptures on top were swiped from the Forum of Trajan; the four medallions on the face, portraying hunting and sacrificial scenes, date from the reign of Hadrian (AD 117–138).

BATHS OF CARACALLA Maybe even more than the forums, these gigantic thermal baths provide some sense of the size, scope, and engineering genius of Ancient Rome's civic architecture. The palatial structure once housed three chambers of baths, each one decked out in marble and mosaics: the *calidarium*, with very hot water; the *tepidarium*, kept lukewarm; and the *frigidarium*, for cooling off. The baths were visited by Romans of every class and position, and even the poor could recline in luxury here, enjoying the gardens, libraries, and wine shops. A good English commentary and extensive diagrams provide you with a general layout. *Via Terme di Caracalla. From Piazza Venezia, take Bus 160 directly to the baths; or take Metro Line B to Circo Massimo. Admission: L8000. Open Mon. 9–1 PM., Tues.–Sun. 9–6.*

CIRCUS MAXIMUS The Circus Maximus, once the setting of ancient chariot races, is now a disappointing overgrown field. Nowadays the most exciting thing happening here is a local soccer match, but in its heyday this outdoor stadium could hold 300,000 manic spectators. The obelisk that once stood in the center of Circus Maximus now stands in Piazza del Popolo. *Metro Line B to Circo Massimo; or walk south from Arch of Constantine.*

THE COLOSSEUM The single most evocative symbol of Rome, the Colosseum is equal parts glory and gore: This masterpiece of architectural innovation served as a bloody arena for the mutilation and death of thousands of animals, gladiators, and early Christians. Construction of the theater, originally called the Flavian Amphitheater, began in AD 72. Its inauguration ceremony, just eight years later, consisted of 100 days of slaughter, to the tune of 5,000 animals per day. The elliptical four-story structure held 50,000 people, had a movable canopy to protect spectators from the sun, a safety net with elephant tusks to protect the audience from the beasts, and a vast underground network of tunnels, chambers, and elevators to move creatures, prisoners, and other paraphernalia needed for the events. The name, Colosseum, came from a colossal bronze statue of Nero that once stood nearby. Looted continuously by zealous popes and passing barbarians, the Colosseum has definitely seen better days; but its sheer size alone manages to astound even those with little imaginative powers. You can see what's left from the ground floor for free, or view the upper level (including a reconstruction of the Colosseum in its heyday) for an unjustified L6000. *Piazza del Colosseo, tel. 06/700–4261. Open 9–1 hr before sunset (until 1 PM Wed. and Sun.).*

FORUM BOARIUM The **Piazza della Bocca di Verità** now partially covers what was once the Forum Boarium (Forum of the Cow), originally used as a cattle market. Here you'll find two of Rome's most intact ancient temples, which once formed a part of the Forum Boarium: the rectangular **Temple of Portunus**, built in the 2nd century BC, and the round **Temple of Hercules** (currently undergoing restoration), also called Temple of Vesta because it resembles the one in the Roman Forum. If you can elbow your way through the throngs of tourists outside the medieval church of Santa Maria in Cosmedin (across the street from the temples), take a minute to test your honesty at the **Bocca di Verità** (Mouth of Truth). Stick your hand inside the mouth if you dare—legend has it that those who have recently told a lie will get their hand bitten off.

IMPERIAL FORUMS Lining both sides of the Via dei Fori Imperiali are the **Imperial Fora**, built partly as extensions of the overflowing Roman Forum (which could no longer accommodate all the civic and social functions of the sprawling metropolis of Rome) and partly to fulfill the emperors' desires for self-aggrandizement. Julius Caesar started the trend in 54 BC by paying a whopping 60 million sestertiums for the land behind the Curia. Called—surprise, surprise—**the Forum of Caesar**, the forum included the **Temple of Venus Genetrix**, dedicated to the goddess of love from whom Caesar modestly claimed descent.

On the other side of Via dei Fori Imperiali is the **Forum of Augustus**, completed in 2 BC, and the semicircular **Markets of Trajan** (admission: L4000), open Tuesday–Sunday 9–1:30 (Thurs. and Sat. 9–6). Visually impressive and remarkably intact, these markets featured three levels of wholesale and retail outlets; wandering through the halls you can almost hear the voices of pesky salespeople and toga-clad bargain hunters. North of the market lies the **Forum of Trajan**, built in the 2nd century BC. In the center of the forum stands the incredibly intricate **column of Trajan**, the final resting place of the emperor himself. The 200-meter-long relief, a series of violent battle scenes winding around the column, commemorates the expansion of the Roman Empire in Eastern Europe.

The best view of the Roman Forum is from the southern side of the Campidoglio; the best view of the column of Trajan and the Imperial Forums is from Via Alessandra, which runs parallel to Via dei Fori Imperiali.

PALATINE HILL To reach the Palatine Hill, head uphill from the Arch of Titus through the Roman Forum. At the top, surrounded by the trees and blossoms of the **Farnese gardens**, you'll understand why the Palatine has alway been prime real estate, from the time shepherds first gathered here till Roman emperors made it their official residence. Palatine Hill is where the first traces of Rome (dating from 753 BC) were discovered. Today, the shady lawns and incredible views make for great picnicking, and it's a welcoming place to collapse after a long tramp through the Forum.

Taking advantage of the view, Emperor Augustus constructed his residence, the **Domus Augustana**, here, which has sustained numerous additions over the years. The complex of rooms, halls, temples, and stadiums eventually covered the entire hill and became the **Imperial Palace**. Check out the **Temple of the Magna Mater** (dedicated to the Great Mother Goddess), a shrine brought to Rome from Asia Minor in the 3rd century BC. At the center of the temple is the **Lupercal**, the cave where Romulus and Remus were said to have been suckled by a she-wolf.

THE ROMAN FORUM As far back as the 10th century BC, wandering tribes gathered on Rome's hilltops and made use of the swampy lowland area, the present-day site of the Roman Forum, as a burial ground. In later years, the site's position between the Capitoline, Palatine, and Esquiline hills and its vicinity to the commercial goings-on of the Tiber River made it an ideal spot for a marketplace and civic center. Thus, in the 7th century BC, the swamp was drained by a sophisticated drainage system known as the *Cloaca Maxima*, paved over, and divided in two: Half was to be used as a marketplace and half for political purposes. By the time the Roman Republic emerged in the 6th century BC, this was the core of the city, full of shops and public buildings. The Roman Forum was also the spiritual center of ancient Rome, where priests and priestesses made sacrifices to the capricious gods who determined the fate of the Republic. By the Imperial Age the Forum could no longer accommodate all the structures needed for its numerous functions, and many activities spilled over to the Imperial Forums to the north and east.

To your right as you enter the Forum from Via dei Fori Imperiali stands the **Basilica Emilia**. Built in 179 BC, this purely secular structure served as a money-lending center; there are still traces of ancient coins stuck in the floor tiles. Next door lie the meager remains of the **Curia**, the ancient seat of the Roman Senate. It was here, according to old Willy Shakespeare at least, that Marc Antony gave his "Friends, Romans, countrymen" speech over the body of Julius Caesar. The **Rostra**, the long brick wall that lies perpendicular to the Curia, was a tribune for orators' long-winded debates. In front of the Rostra lies the main square, where merchants hawked their wares, gladiators clashed, and lovers lingered. Between the Curia and the Rostra lies the **Niger Lapis**, a flat black stone that is one of the oldest objects in the Forum (dating from the 8th century BC). Originally a shrine to Vulcan, the stone is said to cover the final resting place of Romulus, mythical founder of Rome.

Towering above the Rostra is the **Arch of Septimus Severus**, constructed by Emperor Severus in AD 203 to celebrate a victory against the Parthians. To the left stand the eight remaining columns of the **Temple of Saturn**, the oldest temple in the Forum. It served as a treasury, and was the site of the Saturnalia, a seven-day feast when slaves and masters sat at the same table, and everyone from children to elders feasted, drank, and exchanged gifts. In front of the Temple of Saturn lies a vast area that was once the site of the **Basilica Giulia**. Named for Julius Caesar, who began the project in 54 BC, the Basilica served as the Tribunal, and was large enough to accommodate four courts at the same time. The pavement stones still display graffiti drawn by impatient spectators.

On the other side of the Basilica Giulia is the **Temple of Castor and Pollux** and the remaining pillars of the small, round **Temple of Vesta**. Here the Vestal Virgins tended the sacred flame to Vesta, goddess of the hearth (*see box, below*). The **Casa dei Vestali** (House of the Vestals), which lies beyond the temple, still encloses a series of sculptures depicting the priestesses of this sacred order. The house was once their resplendent residence, which included bathrooms, central heating, and six secret staterooms.

The **Via Sacra** or Sacred Way, the oldest street in Rome, crosses the entire length of the Forum and leads uphill to the massive **Basilica of Maxentius**. Begun by the Emperor Maxentius in 306 BC and completed by Constantine, this is one of the best preserved structures in the Roman Forum. The three immense barrel vaults that remain hint at the vastness of this once richly decorated structure—Michelangelo used the basilica as a model for the dome of St Peter's. **The Arch of Titus**, at the end of the Via Sacra, is the oldest of Rome's triumphal arches. Check out the reliefs on its interior walls depicting Titus returning to Rome with spoils from Jerusalem.

The **Antiquarium of the Forum**, located in the ancient convent of Santa Francesca Romana (standing between the Basilica of Maxentius and the Arch of Titus), houses the most important archaeological finds from the area. *Entrance to the Roman Forum on Via dei Fori Imperiali. Admission: L12,000, including museum. Open Mon.–Sat. 9–6, Sun. 9–1.*

THEATER OF MARCELLUS Near Piazza Venezia, the Theater of Marcellus (closed to the public) is a prime example of the hybrid results of Rome's multilayered construction. Initiated by Caesar and completed by Augustus in 11 BC, the theater hosted tragedies, comedies, and sporting shows. In the 13th century, the aristocratic Fabi and then Savelli families took over the Roman remains, building their family palace on top of it. Today the hodgepodge of architectural styles is strange and incongruous, but damned interesting; the best views of the building can be had from behind the **Portico d'Ottavia**, or gape at the theater and adjacent **Temple of Apollo** from Via del Teatro di Marcello.

CAMPIDOGLIO

Il Campidoglio (Capitoline Hill) was one of the most important of Rome's original seven hills. Strategically located high above the Tiber River, Campidoglio was Rome's natural bulwark and the center of political and religious activity at the height of the Republic, when it housed a temple to the triad of Jupiter, Juno, and Minerva, as well as the state archives, treasury, and mint. The gubernatorial and municipal offices are still located here in the **Palazzo Senatorio** on

Ain't Misbehavin'

Who ever said that bad girls have all the fun? In ancient Rome, the six prepubescent girls who were chosen as Vestal Virgins (all with no physical imperfections whatsoever) lived a life of luxury in the serene and sumptuous Casa dei Vestali. Priestesses of Vesta and protectors of the family and the Empire, the Virgins' task was to keep the sacred fire of Vesta lit (if it went out, the Empire would supposedly fall). In return the fortunate females were free from paternal authority (unlike other Roman women), got to ride around in special chariots, knew all the goings-on of the imperial house, and acted as ambassadors and judges. The catch: If they ever broke their 30-year vow of chastity, they were thrown in a pit and buried alive.

the majestic **Piazza del Campidoglio**. The adjacent **Palazzo Nuovo** forms another side of the piazza. In 1537 the entire square and bordering palazzi, including the Palazzo Senatorio and Palazzo dei Conservatori, were revamped by Michelangelo, who created what is now hailed as a miracle of Renaissance harmony and balance. The views of Rome and the forums are alone worth the climb. From Palazzo Senatorio's porch, there are also good views of the peculiar symmetrical sidewalks, also designed by Michelangelo.

BASILICA SANTA MARIA IN ARACOELI This plain brick basilica (AD 1348) looks impressive atop its jumbled 126-step staircase, but the interior is dark and undergoing perpetual restoration. Still, its chapel is worth the short hike from Piazza del Campidoglio; inside are colorful 16th-century frescoes—credited to Pinturicchio—that depict scenes from the life of St. Bernard of Siena. Somewhere among the creepy, ragged funerary sculptures is a fading fresco signed by Donatello. *Via del Teatro di Marcello, before steps to the Campidoglio. Admission free. Open daily 7–noon and 4–7.*

MUSEO CAPITOLINO Housed in the **Palazzo Nuovo**, the Capitoline Museum contains one of the most extensive collections of classical sculpture in the world; it also claims to be the first public museum (founded in 1471, opened in 1734). The sculpture collection includes more than 100 busts of emperors, poets, and philosophers, but don't let that scare you away. Less staid pieces include the *Wounded Amazon*, *Laughing and Crying Centaurs*, and the *Capitoline Venus*, as well as the poignant 3rd-century BC sculpture of the *Dying Gaul*. One ticket gets you into both this and the Palazzo dei Conservatori (*see below*). *Piazza del Campidoglio, tel. 06/6710–2071. Admission: L10,000, L5000 students. Open Tues. 9–1:30 and 5–8, Wed.–Fri. 9–1:30, Sat. 9–1:30 and 8–11, Sun. 9–1.*

PALAZZO DEI CONSERVATORI This palazzo's frieze-decorated staircase, rich wallpaper, and gilded ceilings are as pleasing as the hodgepodge works they surround. In the ground-floor courtyard look for the gigantic head and assorted body parts that remain from the mammoth sculpture of Constantine, which once stood in the Basilica of Maxentius—the toenail alone is as big as an adult human hand. On the first floor are several fresco-filled rooms, including the **Salone dei Orazi e Curiazi** with its carved wooden doors and statues by Bernini. Its prize pieces are the 1st-century BC *Spinario*, a boy in bronze pulling a thorn from his foot, and the *Capitoline Wolf*, a 5th-century BC Etruscan bronze work that from time immemorial has been the symbol of Rome. Ironically, the suckling figures of Remus and Romulus were added during the Renaissance to adapt the statue to the legend of Rome's founding. Upstairs in the **Capitoline Picture Gallery**, exhibits range from dark religious icons to portraitures by Rubens and Van Dyck. Admission is free with a ticket to the Museo Capitolino (*see above*), otherwise admission price and open hours are identical. *Piazza del Campidoglio, tel. 06/6710–1244.*

PIAZZA VENEZIA

You'll probably end up in chaotic Piazza Venezia again and again, as it's the hub of Rome's busiest thoroughfares, including **Via del Corso**, **Corso Vittorio Emanuele II**, and **Via Nazionale**. This is also a convergence point for lost visitors, since the piazza's gargantuan Vittorio Emanuele Monument can be spotted from just about anywhere. Numerous bus lines stop at the piazza, but you can also reach it (and the concentration of nearby ruins and sights) by way of the Colosseo Metro stop.

BASILICA SAN MARCO West of Palazzo Venezia, two twin porticoes lead to this small but richly decorated, active parish church—host to weddings, funerals, and baptisms. The basilica dates from the 4th century AD, but was thoroughly renovated in the 15th century by Cardinal Pietro Barbo and again in the 18th century by F. Barigioni (which accounts for its pure baroque interior). The interior can be taken in with a glance, though the wooden, coffered Renaissance ceiling and Byzantine mosaics near the altar deserve two. *Piazza San Marco 48, directly opposite the Vittorio Emanuele II Monument. Admission free. Open daily 9–noon and 4–7.*

PALAZZO VENEZIA You may not notice Palazzo Venezia above the confusion of traffic on Piazza Venezia, but before it was overshadowed by the monument to Vittorio Emanuele II, the structure was an austere and commanding palace. Built in 1455 for Cardinal Pietro Barbo (later Pope Paul II), the palazzo was one of Rome's first purely Renaissance creations. Today it serves as a **museum**, with permanent displays of silver and porcelain works, Flemish, German, and Italian tapestries, and colorful iconic art. Mussolini used some of the rooms as offices, and the balcony over the main portal may be familiar to history buffs as the place where *Il Duce* addressed huge crowds prior to World War II. *Via del Plebiscito 118, tel. 06/679–8865. Admission: L8000, L6000 students. Open Tues.–Sat. 9–2, Sun. 9–1.*

VITTORIO EMANUELE II MONUMENT In 1862 Vittorio Emanuele II became the first king of a unified Italian state. Upon his death in 1878, a contest was held to construct a monument befitting this "Father of Italy." Thirty-three years later, the colossal creation of Giuseppe Sacconi was finally completed to the dismay (read: disgust) of most Romans. Nicknamed the "wedding cake" because of its massive white-marble facade, the monument is commonly thought of as pretentious and overbearing in comparison to the treasured remains of ancient Rome that surround it. Whatever your opinion, it makes an excellent navigational landmark, since you can see its unique outline from a surprising distance. The sprawling central staircase, guarded by uniformed sentinels, leads to the **Tomb of the Unknown Soldier**, commemorating those who died in World War II. The **Museo del Risorgimento** (admission: L6000; open Tues.–Sun. 9–1) houses documents and memorabilia from the Italian unification, as well as the architectural plans for the monument.

PIAZZA DELLA REPUBBLICA AND PIAZZA BARBERINI

Although the area's big boulevards, big buildings, and big price tags are not conducive to wandering, chances are you'll pass through Piazza della Repubblica multiple times on the way from Stazione Termini to the centro storico. The impersonal buildings that encircle the piazza were once home to fashionable hotels and cafés, but these days the square is the domain of porn theaters and bawdy souvenir stands, perhaps inspired by the piazza's turn-of-the-century **Fountain of the Naiads**, featuring busty nymphs wrestling with pumped-up sea monsters. Beyond this, the piazza's highlights are the Museo Nazionale Romano and the church of Santa Maria degli Angeli (*see below*).

Once you've exhausted the museum, head northwest from the square on Via Orlando and veer right onto Via Barberini (also known as "travel agent's row"). This dead-ends at Piazza Barberini, a heavily trafficked square sporting Bernini's graceful **Tritone** (Fountain of the Triton), which depicts a manly sea-god spouting water from a conch shell, designed in 1637 for Pope Urban VIII. From here it's a short walk up Via delle Quattro Fontane to Palazzo Barberini, which houses Rome's excellent Galleria Nazionale.

GALLERIA NAZIONALE This national art gallery inside the 17th-century **Palazzo Barberini** leads you room by room from the 13th to the 18th century with works from Italy's most important schools of painting. Although the collection is by no means vast, you'll recognize the names of Fra Filippo Lippi, Raphael, Perugino, El Greco, and Caravaggio. The palace was originally constructed as a Renaissance villa and once served as the official residence of the Pope's family. Bernini, the ubiquitous baroque master, is responsible for the construction of the central hall and the loggia facing Via delle Quattro Fontane. *Via delle Quattro Fontane 13, tel. 06/481–4591. Metro Line A to Barberini; walk 2 blocks south. Admission: L6000. Open Tues.–Sat. 9–2, Sun. 9–1.*

His Majesty the Pickax

The Via dei Fori Imperiali, linking Piazza Venezia and the Colosseum, was the result of a disastrous urban renewal project undertaken by Mussolini in 1932. Il Duce won himself the nickname of "His Majesty the Pickax" when he leveled a vast medieval quarter and bulldozed an entire hill in order to join, both literally and symbolically, his headquarters on Piazza Venezia with the most definitive symbol of ancient Roman glory.

MUSEO NAZIONALE ROMANO Situated mostly in and around the garden of the monastery of **Santa Maria degli Angeli**, the National Museum of Rome is an "important" but somewhat dull collection of marble statues, busts, funerary monuments, sarcophagi, and gigantic animals. Most of the pieces were found in Lazio and date back to Julius Caesar's time. Highlights of the collection include a colorful mosaic of life on the Nile, complete with wallowing hippos and snorting crocodiles, and an extravagant Greek relief, the *Ludovisi Throne*, depicting the goddess Aphrodite floating on sea foam. *Viale E. de Nicola 79, tel. 06/488–0530. Admission: L3000. Open Tues.–Sat. 9–1, Sun. 9–2.*

SAN CARLO ALLE QUATTRO FONTANE The sumptuous church of the Four Fountains got its name from the four sculptured fountains—each representing a season—that stand on the corners of the intersection. It was designed by Bernini's main rival, Francesco Borromini, and is one of the first experiments in pure baroque style. As such it's somewhat humble in comparison with later baroque works—all of which, ironically, are indebted to Borromini's heavily curved walls and fluted decorations. *Via del Quirinale, at Via delle Quattro Fontane, tel. 06/767–6531. Admission free. Open daily 7–noon and 4–7.*

SANTA MARIA DEGLI ANGELI With its dark austere exterior and crumbly walls, this church looks like a Roman ruin from the outside. Step inside however, and you'll enter a gigantic light-filled space. If Santa Maria doesn't look like most churches, it's because Michelangelo (at the age of 86) designed the basilica within the ruins of the 4th-century Baths of Diocletian. His original design, with its complete lack of decoration, can only be seen in the vaulted ceiling—the rest of the interior has been covered by baroque embellishments. Also of note is the church's art collection, including the *Martyrdom of San Sebastian* by Domenichino and the *Crucifixion of St. Peter* by Ricciolini. *Piazza della Repubblica. Admission free. Open 7:30–12:30 and 4–6:30.*

SANTA MARIA DELLA CONCEZIONE Fluted arches made of collarbones, arabesques of shoulder blades, and spirals of dusty vertebrae—the ornate and gruesome decorations in the crypt of this 17th-century church are definitely worth checking out. The remains of 4,000 priests and monks were used to decorate the five-room crypt in the 18th century, as a means to attract visitors and to inspire piety. Notice the eerie message: "What you are now we once were; what we are now, you will be." *Via Vittorio Veneto 27, tel. 06/462850. Metro Line A to Barberini; walk 1 block north. Donation requested. Open daily 9–noon and 3–6.*

If you've never seen a chandelier made of human remains, Santa Maria della Concezione is a sight to see.

PIAZZA DEL POPOLO

At the end of three of the centro storico's most important streets—Via del Babuino, Via del Corso, and Via di Ripetta—The People's Square, as the name translates, was once the gateway to the city for foreign visitors. Today it's a meeting and mingling place for teenagers on mopeds, grandmothers on park benches, and businessmen on cellular phones. Take in the commotion from the Egyptian obelisk of Ramses II (a mere 3,200 years old) at the center of the piazza, and check out the perfect symmetry of the twin 17th-century churches **Santa Maria dei Miracoli** and **Santa Maria di Montesanto**. For a view of the action from on high, walk up the steps (on the eastern side of the piazza) to the **Pincio**, whose gardens mimic the design of the piazza.

AUGUSTEUM AND ARA PACIS Down Via di Ripetta from Piazza del Popolo, the circular brick Augusteum (closed to the public) once held the glorified remains of Emperor Augustus. Designed in 29 BC by the emperor himself, the monument is now moss covered and sunken into the earth, a testament to the rising ground level of Rome over the last 2000 years. Two huge obelisks once stood at the mausoleum's entrance; they now grace the Piazza del Quirinale and Piazza dell'Esquilino. Adjacent to the mausoleum, housed in a modern glass structure, is the **Ara Pacis** or Peace Altar. Erected by Augustus in 9 BC to exalt his role in ending Rome's civil wars—the altar proved to be both a fine piece of sculpture and a damn good piece of propaganda: Through a series of mythological symbols on the panels, Augustus is given a divine heritage, and the indisputable title of ruler of the Roman Empire.

SANTA MARIA DEL POPOLO Snuggled against the 400-year-old **Porta del Popolo** (Rome's northern city gate) in the northeast corner of the piazza, Santa Maria del Popolo looks oddly plain at first glance. The interior artwork, however, makes up for any decorative deficiency. To the left of the altar are two Caravaggio canvases depicting the martyrdoms of St. Peter (left) and St. Paul (right). Behind the altar—don't be bashful, just make the sign of the cross and head for one of the side doors—is a vaulted room designed by Bramante, with frescoes by Pinturicchio. The biggest splash of color comes from the chapel, designed and decorated with all kinds of bright marble by Fontana. None other than Bernini can take credit for the plump cherubs, ghastly saints, and sweeping angels that hang from the nave's ceiling. *Piazza del Popolo. Admission free. Open daily 8–1:30 and 4:30–7.*

PIAZZA DI SPAGNA

Piazza di Spagna and its famous steps have been the place to "see and be seen" for a few hundred years now. Named for the nearby Spanish embassy, the famous **Spanish Steps** were constructed in 1723 by architect Francesco de Sanctis to link the Church of the **Trinità dei Monti** at the top with **Via Condotti** below. In the 1800s expats and poets like Keats and Goethe made their homes in the neighborhood, and artists once combed the piazza for prospective models. A magnet for international dilettantes, intellectuals, ambassadors, and more recently, Americans seeking the services of American Express and McDonald's, Piazza di Spagna has developed a subculture all its own (unfortunately the atmosphere is somewhat blighted by restoration, which will leave the steps behind glass panels until 1996).

KEATS MUSEUM John Keats (1795–1821) lived out the last months of his life in this cramped flat huddled alongside the Spanish Steps. In the 18th and 19th centuries this was the heart of bohemian Rome, especially popular with American and British writers. For this reason, the cluttered memorial house has an astounding collection of romantic-era relics. Three of the major figures of the time—Keats, Shelley, and Byron—left behind books, letters, pictures, locks of hair, and old furniture. A vine-covered terrace overlooking the steps is a haven in which to examine some of the museum's rare titles. *Piazza di Spagna 26. Admission: L5000. Open weekdays 9–1 and 3–6 (weekdays 9–1 and 2:30–5:30 in winter).*

TREVI FOUNTAIN From the narrow end of Piazza di Spagna, take Via due Macelli past Largo Tritone and turn left at Via in Arcione; follow the sound of crashing water, and there you have it—the utterly famous Trevi Fountain, one of the few in Rome that's actually more absorbing than the people crowding around it. The fantastic baroque arrangement of Neptune atop dolphins, sea creatures, boulders, and cascades flowing into a swimming pool-size basin was conceived by Nicolo Salvi in 1762, years after baroque was thought dead. Its source is a 1st-century BC Roman aqueduct, known as the *Acqua Vergine*, after a virgin who led a group of thirsty soldiers to a spring outside the city. Legend has it that the water made men faithful, and women dragged their hubbies here by the thousands. Ironically, the area around the fountain is now a prime hunting ground for Italian men on the prowl. Brave the lechery long enough to toss a coin over your left shoulder, ensuring your return to the Eternal City.

Recently, supermodel Claudia Schiffer made quite a splash by taking a dip in the Trevi Fountain.

VILLA BORGHESE

Rome's largest park is filled with playful fountains, sculptured gardens, and forests of shady pine trees. Stretches of green and plenty of leafy pathways make this a great place for wandering or biking, but the park's real attractions are Villa Borghese's art museums, especially the magnificent **Galleria Borghese**. The easiest way to reach Villa Borghese is on Metro Line A to Flaminio. From here walk east on the uphill **Viale G. Washington**.

GALLERIA BORGHESE It's a real toss-up which is more magnificent—the villa built for Cardinal Borghese in 1615 or the collection of 17th- and 18th-century sculpture that lies within. Though the exterior of the villa is undergoing extensive restoration, the inside alone could cause sensory overload. The mind-blowing sculpture collection includes Roman sarcophagi, Egyptian figures, and five of Bernini's most celebrated works: *The Rape of Persephone*; *Apollo and Daphne*, in which Daphne is transformed into a laurel tree to avoid being raped by her lusty pursuer; *David*, which Bernini completed at the ripe age of 18; *Aeneas, Anchises, and Ascanius Fleeing Troy*; and *Truth*. The gallery's Raphael, Caravaggio, Titian, and Boticelli paintings are temporarily housed in the church of **San Michele a Ripa** (Via di San Michele 22, tel. 06/581–6732; open weekdays 9:30–1 and 4–8, Sat. 9:30–1:30). To reach San Michele a Ripa from Piazza della Republica, take Bus 57 to Lungotevere Ripa in Trastevere; turn right on Via del Porto, then left on Via San Michele. Hold on to your ticket from Galleria Borghese and get in free. *Galleria Borghese: Piazza Scipione Borghese 5, tel. 06/854–8577. Admission: L4000. Open Tues.–Sat. 9–2, Sun. 9–1.*

GALLERIA NAZIONALE D'ARTE MODERNA Rome's modern-art museum, in an immense neoclassical building on the fringe of Villa Borghese, houses a brilliant collection of Italian impressionist and romantic art. Among the highlights are a series of sculptures by Vincenzo Gemito, and Giuseppe Pellizza's preparatory sketches for *Il Quarto Stato* (The Fourth Estate), his statement about "humanity in the march for progress," inspired by the 1891 industrial revolution in Italy. Also displayed are works by Klimt, Degas, van Gogh, Cézanne, and Zorn. *Viale delle Belle Arti 131, tel. 06/322–4151. Admission: L8000. Open Tues.–Sat. 9–5, Sun. 9–1.*

MUSEO DI VILLA GIULIA The villa of Pope Julius III, on the southwest edge of Villa Borghese, houses one of the world's most important (and exhaustive) collections of Etruscan artifacts. Little is known about the Etruscans, an Italic tribe that inhabited the peninsula before the Romans, but from the looks of things they had a pretty good setup. Inside the villa, you're bombarded with earthenware water jugs, terra-cotta bowls, dozens of small bronze figures, and jewelry. The highlight is the *Sarcofago dei Sposi* (the tomb of the newlyweds), built for an eternally clingy couple. Unless you are a scholar of archaeology or interested in Etruscan culture, think twice before spending L8000 on a ticket. *Piazza di Villa Giulia 9, tel. 06/320–1951. Admission: L8000. Open Tues.–Sun. 9 AM–2 PM (until 7 PM on Wed.).*

CENTRAL ROME

Rome's center—bordered by the Augusteum to the north, Via del Corso to the east, and the Tiber River to the south and west—encompasses the bulk of medieval Rome. It's not where Rome began (that's Capitoline Hill). Yet it is where all the centuries come together—where many of the blockbuster historical sights are concentrated, and where narrow alleyways and outdoor cafés are alive with both locals and tourists. If you only spend one day in Rome, this is the place to do it.

CAMPO DEI FIORI The name of this neighborhood piazza literally means "field of flowers," which seems a bit sardonic considering that it was originally used for public executions. In fact, the central statue commemorates the murdered philosopher Giordano Bruno (1548–1600). After being tried for heresy by the Inquisition, poor Giordi was burned to death on Campo dei Fiori for arguing that the cosmos weren't nearly as ordered as the Church led its flock to believe. The streets around the square have always teemed with artisans and craftsmen, and if you wander Via dei Cappellari in the afternoon you can still see people building furniture and refinishing ornate picture frames. The area was also historically filled with taverns, many of which are still open, making Campo dei Fiori a choice spot for bar-hoppers. Monday through Saturday 9–1, the piazza is home to Rome's oldest outdoor produce and flower market. It's also one of the few church-free piazze in Rome—a reason in itself to visit.

A block toward the river from Campo dei Fiori is the very plain **Piazza Farnese**, watched over by Michelangelo's flamboyant Palazzo Farnese (closed to the public), home of the French Embassy. Be sure to check out the palace's courtyard, the most spectacular part of the complex. Walk another block toward the river and you hit **Via Giulia**, a vine-covered street lined with Renaissance palaces, antiques shops, and art galleries. Pope Julius II wanted the street to be an "imperial road" connecting the harbor with the Vatican, but when the pope died unexpectedly, so did the plans. Continue southeast on Via Giulia and you'll stumble upon the pedestrian-only bridge, **Ponte Sisto**. Cross over the bridge to the Tiber's west bank and you're in Trastevere, Rome's self-styled bohemian quarter.

CHIESA DEL GESU Excluding St. Peter's Basilica, Il Gesù is the most colorful church in Rome—every inch is covered with red, green, gold, and pink marble. The frescoed ceiling, bordered by swirling figures, flows down over the pillars, creating a three-dimensional effect. The silver- and gold-lathered altar to St. Ignatius of Loyola (the founder of the Jesuits) also gets a gasp from the crowd. *Via del Plebiscito, 2 blocks west of Piazza Venezia. Open daily 6–12:30 and 4–7:15.*

GALLERIA DORIA To step inside the gallery you've gotta pay L6000 plus L4000 for a mandatory booklet. But the collection of Ferrara-school works, plus the paintings and sculptures by Raphael, Titian, Bernini, Borromini, and Michelangelo are absolutely outstanding. While it's hard to believe that this is a private collection, remember that family members like Andrea "Liberator of Genova" Doria (1466–1560), Pope Innocent X, and Filippo Andrea V (1818–1876) have been acquiring art since the 15th century. The Doria family still owns the palace, and for an extra L4000 a guide will show you their private apartments, which hold a boggling amount of tapestries, paintings, ancient musical instruments, death masks, and amber oddities from faraway lands. *Piazza Collegio Romano, off Via del Corso. Admission: L6000. Open Tues. and Fri.–Sun. 9–1.*

LARGO DI TORRE ARGENTINA At the crossroads of Via di Torre Argentina and Corso Vittorio Emanuele II, Largo Argentina is perceived more often as a major bus stop than a tourist attraction. But while you're waiting for the bus on this busy square, check out the hole in the ground where archaeologists have unearthed the remains of four temples, each dating back to around the 3rd or 4th century BC—Julius Caesar was supposedly murdered here. More noticeable, perhaps, is the square's huge population of indigent felines, who've recently earned the square the nickname "The Forum of Cats."

The legend of the oculus says that when the Pantheon became a Catholic church, all the evil pagan spirits fled to the top, creating a hole as they burst through the roof.

THE PANTHEON The effect of walking into the Pantheon from the massive front portico is, in a word, breathtaking. This ancient temple-cum-church, the best-preserved ancient Roman structure, was built by Hadrian in 119–128 AD, after the destruction of an earlier version by Agrippa (whose name is still visible on the facade). The dimensions of the interior space—43 meters high and 43 meters wide—were designed with perfection in mind. The immense dome, which seems to hover weightless overhead, was the largest ever built until this century (St. Peter's is a close second). Dedicated to not one, but all of the gods, the Pantheon avoided destruction only because it was converted into a Catholic church in AD 608, thereby protecting it from the looting and neglect suffered by other ancient monuments. Still, much of the roof was stripped of its bronze in 667, and Barbarini Pope Urban VIII snatched what little was left to recycle into the *baldacchino* of St Peter's. *Piazza della Rotunda. Admission free. Open Mon.– Sat. 9–6, Sun. 9–1.*

The Fountain of the Four Rivers in Piazza Navona was carved by Bernini from one enormous rock. The stone statues represent the four corners of the world and, in turn, the world's great rivers: the Nile, the Ganges, the Río de la Plata, and the Danube.

PIAZZA NAVONA If Piazza Navona doesn't enchant you, nothing in Rome will. The queen of all piazze and the crown jewel of the *centro storico*, Navona showcases Bernini's extravagant fountain creations and the church of **Sant'Agnese in Agone**. Emperor Domitian's stadium once stood on this site, hence the piazza's strange oblong shape; always looking to amuse themselves, the ancient Romans flooded the area for naval games and competitions. Today, Navona's attractions are more subdued: Surrounding the piazza are flowered balconies, brilliantly colored palazzi, requisite sidewalk cafés, and every sort of street artist, musician, and pickpocket you can imagine. If you ever pull an all-nighter at Rome's discos, be sure to visit this normally packed piazza at dawn, when only the sound of your footsteps and the squawks of pigeons echo through the vast space.

SAN LUIGI DEI FRANCESI This church, though not spectacular or unique in terms of architecture, is a must-see for all Caravaggio fans. Its chapel dedicated to St. Matthew displays three of the artist's most important works, each depicting the life of St. Matthew: *St. Matthew and the Angel*, *The Calling of St. Matthew*, and *Martyrdom of St. Matthew*. With his characteristically striking use of light and shadow (known as the *chiaroscuro* technique), Caravaggio creates tension, drama, and extraordinary realism on these canvases. *Piazza San Luigi dei Francesi, 1 block east of Pantheon. Admission free. Open daily 8–noon and 4–6.*

SANT'ANDREA DELLA VALLE Because of its imposing size, Sant'Andrea's dome is often mistaken for St. Peter's. Close, but not quite. The large basilica of Sant'Andrea was begun in the late 16th century by della Porta and later altered by Carlo Maderno, who's responsible both for the dome and the baroque **Barberini Chapel**, the first on the left as you enter. The church is richly decorated in frescoes, including the *Glory of Paradise* that covers the dome. *Piazza Sant'Andrea della Valle, off Corso Vittorio Emanuele II. 4 blocks west of Piazza Venezia. Open daily 6–noon and 3:30–8.*

SANTA MARIA SOPRA MINERVA Rome's only Gothic church sports a serene and exquisite interior that's a shock after the usual baroque excesses. The church was built on the site of an ancient temple to Minerva (hence the name) and holds quite a powerhouse of art, including the **Carafa Chapel**, with a brilliant fresco cycle by Filippino Lippi depicting the *Annunciation*, and Michelangelo's sculpture, *The Redeemer*. The elephant supporting the small obelisk in the piazza out front was designed by Bernini for Pope Alexander VII; it is said to signify wisdom supported by strength. *Piazza della Minerva, 1 block south of Pantheon. Admission free. Open daily 7–noon and 4–7.*

VIA DEL CORSO Because of the 20th-century grime, traffic-ridden Via del Corso appears to be nothing more than a major thoroughfare connecting Piazza Venezia and Piazza del Popolo. In fact, between gazing in shop windows and dodging Vespas, it's damn near impossible to realize that the oppressive atmosphere comes from the enormous palaces lining both sides of the street. Most of them were built over the last 300 years by wealthy families who wanted to secure front-row seats for the frantic antics of Carnevale; Goethe, who lived at No. 19, reputedly drew much inspiration from the madness of the festival. Midway down the street is the **Column of Marcus Aurelius**; standing 30 meters above Piazza Colonna, this triumphal column (almost identical to the one in Trajan's forum) commemorates the Roman campaigns of AD 172–173 under Emperor Marcus Aurelius.

JEWISH GHETTO

Rome's Jewish quarter was dubbed a "ghetto" during the Counter-Reformation, when the city's Jews were seriously persecuted for the first time. Prior to this, in 1555, Pope Paul II had decided to "purify" the city by relocating Rome's Jews—about 8,000 at the time—from their homes in Trastevere to five disease-infested acres across the river. Housing here consisted of ramshackle tenements owned by landlords who exacted rent from the community as a whole, based solely on how many rooms a building had. In other words, a landlord could collect rent for an entire five-story building even if only one family was living in it. At the end of the 18th century many Jews took part in the bourgeois revolution that swept the city; they were rewarded by having the ghetto opened to commerce and, in 1849, by having its walls torn down.

In 1986, Pope John Paul II paid a visit to Rabbi Elio Toaff, becoming the first pope ever to pray in a Jewish synagogue; the same synagogue had been bombed in 1982 by anti-Semitic Romans.

When Mussolini was executed by anti-Fascists, German troops occupied Rome. On October 16, 1943, after failing to deliver 110 pounds of gold each, the majority of Rome's Jews were deported to Nazi concentration camps. Today Rome's current Jewish population is 15,000, though only about 1,000 remain in the ghetto. The area, which lies between the Portico d'Ottavia, the Tiber, and Via Arenula, has a neighborhood charm that doesn't readily hint at the horrendous conditions of its past. Among the most interesting sights is the **Fontana delle Tartarughe** (Fountain of the Turtles) on Piazza Mattei, with turtles à la Bernini.

MUSEO EBRAICO The two-room Ebraico Museum contains decorative crowns, prayer books, holy chairs, and tapestries dating from the 17th century, most donated by prominent Jewish families whose ancestors once lived in the ghetto. (It's refreshing to see precious metals and marble crafted into something other than saints and angels.) One of the more haunting displays is a prayer book that literally saved its owner's life during the 1982 attack on the synagogue—bullet holes and bloodstains tell the tale. One ticket grants you entrance to both the museum and adjacent synagogue, but the latter can only be toured with a guide (inquire at the museum). *Lungotevere Cenci, on river near Ponte Fabricio, tel. 06/687–5051. Admission: L3000. Open Mon.–Thurs. 9:30–6, Fri. and Sun. 9:30–12:30.*

The adjacent **synagogue** is a bright, spacious building complete with a rainbow-colored dome gilded in gold and silver. It was built by Catholic designers who, having no first-hand knowledge of synagogue architecture, copied the design from Christian temples in Jerusalem. Arrange guided tours of the synagogue at the museum next door. Men must cover their heads inside; there's a basket of yarmulkes near the synagogue entrance for those who've left theirs at home.

JANICULUM HILL

If you are crowd-weary from the Vatican or feeling boggled by urban chaos, take a walk up the **Gianicolo** (Janiculum Hill) for a shady respite and a chance to view Rome at a safe distance. Rising beyond Trastevere and bordered by the Vatican gardens to the north, the hill offers plenty of good picnicking spots and a hodgepodge of imperial monuments. From Trastevere's Via Lungara, the leaf-lined **Via Garibaldi** winds up the hill to **Piazza Garibaldi** and an exceptional view of the confusion below (that is, if you can see past the many couples jockeying for the choicest make-out spot). The road was the site of a major battle between Garibaldi's troops and the French, commemorated by a single column. If you're approaching the piazza from the north, head up the vine-covered steps of **Via di San Onofrio** from Lungotevere Gianicolense; at its northern point lies **Chiesa di San Onofrio**, the final resting place of the poet Tasso.

Though powerful and ambitious, Giuseppe Garibaldi was a selfless leader and a man of the people. After conquering the southern half of the peninsula in 1862, he handed the reins to Vittorio Emanuele II, who became the first king of Italy.

SAN PIETRO IN MONTORIO Across from the Garibaldi war memorial is the late-15th-century church of **San Pietro in Montorio** (donations requested; open Tues.–Sun. 10–1 and 5–8), and its accompanying convent. Raphael's *Transfiguration* once decorated the space behind the altar but is now on display at the Vatican. In its place is a haunting depiction of St. Peter's upside-down crucifixion. (Humble Peter declared he wasn't worthy to be crucified in the same manner as Christ.) In the adjacent courtyard, look for the celebrated but somewhat decaying *Tempietto* (Little Temple); it's the work of Bramante and supposedly marks the exact spot on which St. Peter was killed. In the front part of the convent, the **Accademia Spagnola** often hosts art and cultural exhibitions, signaled by announcement flyers on L-shaped Piazza di Pietro in Montorio.

San Pietro in Montorio is one of Roman Catholicism's holiest shrines. During recent excavations human bones were found, but because of their age they cannot be dated with any accuracy, let alone attributed to St. Peter himself.

TRASTEVERE

Trastevere is the last of a dying breed: Of all of Rome's *rioni* (neighborhoods), it's the last hanger-on, still struggling to maintain its autonomous identity and traditions. In many ways Trastevere is still a city within a city: The language is cruder here, the food spicier, and the proud natives insist they're the only real Romans left. The area's vibrant character has long drawn devotees of an artistic and bohemian bent, but recently foreigners of all stripes have bought up everything they can get their hands on, driving prices up and authenticity out. Boisterous Trasteverian pride is renewed every July with *La Festa di Noiantri* (which loosely translates as "The Celebration of Us Others), when the streets and alleyways fill with music, crafts, and revelry.

ISOLA TIBERINA This tiny island in the middle of the Tiber connects the Jewish Ghetto with Trastevere by two of the oldest bridges in Rome: Ponte Fabricio, built in 62 BC, and Ponte Cestio, dating to 42 BC. Legend has it that the island was created when the Romans decimated the crops of an Etruscan king and dumped the grain into the river. On this reputed pile of corn meal, a temple was built to Aesculapius, god of medicine, at the behest of the gods. Isola Tiberina has been the dominion of the healing arts ever since: Due to the island's great location for quarantining the fatally contaminated, a hospital was erected here in the Middle Ages, and has been running continuously ever since.

ORTO BOTANICO Beyond the large gates of Villa Corsini (*see below*), 12 acres of the Janiculum Hill serve as the botanical gardens for the University of Rome. Come to see the formal gardens and greenhouses, displaying exotic and medicinal plants as well as palm trees, lily-covered ponds, and pine forests. The **garden for the blind** includes a variety of aromatics and plants unusual to the touch. This island of green is a serene retreat for lounging and sunning. *Largo Cristina di Svezia, opposite Villa Corsini, tel. 06/686–4193. Admission: L4000. Open Mon.– Sat. 9–5:30.*

SANTA CECILIA IN TRASTEVERE Though the church's bright orange facade is unmistakably baroque, the foundations of St. Cecilia are purely ancient. Pass through the flowered courtyard and you'll enter a church that was originally constructed on the site St. Cecilia's house. Brutally assassinated by pagan emperor Marcus Aurelius (she was decapitated by three blows to the neck), St. Cecilia received martyrdom for maintaining the Christian ideals of sanctity and chastity. Her likeness on the altar, sculpted by Stefano Maderno in 1600, reproduces the exact pose of her body—sword marks and all—when found in 1599, completely intact after 1,000 years in the tomb. If Santa Maria seems more like a rococo salon than a 5th-century church, it's because the only ancient remains, still visible today, lie in the crypt beneath (L2000 to enter). *Piazza Santa Cecilia, off Via Anicia, east of Viale Trastevere. Admission free. Open daily 8–noon and 4–6.*

SANTA MARIA DI TRASTEVERE Once you've had enough of sunning and people-watching in Trastevere's most famous piazza, step into the cool and serene interior of the 12th-century Santa Maria in Trastevere. The dazzling series of mosaics surrounding the nave and apse was completed by Pietro Cavallini. Their Byzantine splendor is representative of the eastern influences imported from Constantinople during the Middle Ages. *Piazza Santa Maria in Trastevere. Admission free. Open daily 8–1 and 4–6.*

VILLA CORSINI Ignore the temporary metal facade and head straight inside this flamboyant palace, the home of Sweden's Queen Christina after she abdicated and fled with the royal treasury in 1650. The villa now houses the **National Gallery of Ancient Art** and its collection of works by Caravaggio, Reni, Maratta, Preti, Reubens, and Van Dyck. The entrance to the first-floor gallery is through a hall lined with busts of Greek and Roman statesmen; the hall's butterfly-shaped balcony overlooks a shady, peaceful garden. *Via della Lungara 10, tel. 06/654–2323. Admission: L6000. Open Tues.–Sat. 9–2, Sun. 9–1.*

VILLA FARNESINA Built in 1511 for Agostino "the Magnificent" Chigi, a well-off Roman banker, the two-story Villa Farnesina is a true relic of the High Renaissance. In other words, it's lathered with gaudy decorations that bespeak Chigi's wealth and poor taste. The architect, Baldassare Peruzzi, is responsible for the wall and ceiling frescoes, Raphael for the frescoes in the ground-floor chambers. The villa's main living room (the first room you enter on the second floor) offers sweeping—albeit trompe d'oeil—views over ancient Rome. *Via della Lungara 230, tel. 06/650831 or 06/654–0565. Admission free. Open Mon.–Sat. 9–1.*

VATICAN CITY AND CASTEL SANT'ANGELO

The world's second-smallest nation, the Vatican is Europe's last remaining absolute monarchy, currently ruled over by Pope John Paul II. The Vatican has its own postal system, radio, news-

You're not allowed into St. Peter's or the Vatican in tank tops, short skirts, or shorts— though if you're not afraid of exposing other body parts, you can try pulling your shorts down to cover your knees.

paper, and military force (known as the Swiss Guards), and still exercises a great deal of influence over Italian politics, though you wouldn't know it in a country where abortion, contraception, and divorce are all unquestionably legal. From the river, **Via della Conciliazione** leads to the magnificent **St. Peter's Basilica**, the Vatican's most visible landmark (the building code in Rome states that no structure can be taller than St. Peter's dome, no mean task!). To reach St. Peter's, take Bus 64 from Stazione Termini or Largo Argentina (watch out for the infamous pickpockets on this line); or take Metro Line A to the Ottaviano stop and walk 15 minutes south. A 10-minute walk toward the Tiber will deposit you at the hulking **Castel Sant'Angelo**, which for centuries was used as a fortress to guard the pope and his riches. The entrance to the **Vatican Museums** is a hike to the other side of Vatican City, or a quick ride on one of the Vatican's complimentary shuttles.

CASTEL SANT'ANGELO The round brick fortress that guarded the Vatican for hundreds of years is unlike any other in Rome. It's been added to and rebuilt so many times that even archaeologists can't make heads or tails of it. The original structure was probably built under the orders of Hadrian in AD 135 as a mausoleum for himself and his successors, including Marcus Aurelius and Caracalla. The name change, from Hadrian's Mausoleum to Castel Sant'Angelo, came during the plague of AD 590, when Pope Gregory the Great had a vision of St. Michael (the archangel) on the mausoleum's rampart. Gregory immediately ordered a temple to St. Michael to be built on the site, whereupon the plague magically ended. Eventually the fortress was used to protect the Vatican from attack; underground passages connecting the castle to Piazza San Pietro have allowed popes to escape here in times of upheaval. These days, the only upheaval comes from the clusters of tourists gawking at the frescoed halls, the collection of antique armor, and the views from the rooftop café. One of Rome's more evocative bridges, **Ponte Sant'Angelo**, spans the Tiber directly in front of the castle. *Lungotevere Castello 50, tel. 06/687–5036. Admission: L8000, L6000 students. Open Apr.–Sept., Mon.–Sat. 9–2; Oct.–Mar., Mon. 2–7, Tues.–Sat. 9–1, Sun. 9–noon.*

PIAZZA SAN PIETRO The most common way to approach Vatican City is on **Via della Conciliazione**, which starts near the Tiber River at Castel Sant'Angelo. You'll soon enter the broad, enveloping arms of **Piazza San Pietro** (St. Peter's Square), one of Bernini's unquestioned masterpieces. It took Bernini only 11 years to design and oversee the construction of this massive square, capable of holding 400,000 people within its symmetrical arms (symbolic of St. Peter embracing the people). The balustrade above the quadruple colonnades is topped with over 140 statues of saints and scholars, each one designed by Bernini. Looking toward St. Peter's Basilica, the peaked roof on the right belongs to the Sistine Chapel, out of which smoke billows whenever the cardinals select a new pope.

ST. PETER'S BASILICA Simply put, St. Peter's is the world's largest and most significant Christian church, and an absolute must on any Roman itinerary. In AD 319, Constantine (the first Christian emperor of Rome) decided to bankroll a basilica for the newly legitimized Christian sect. Taking quite literally the passage in the Bible where Jesus tells Peter "You are the rock on which I shall build my church," Constantine ordered the church built directly above the grave of St. Peter, who later became Rome's patron saint. The original church stood for over 1,000 years, undergoing all sorts of restorations and mutilations, until it was on the verge of collapse. Partial reconstruction began in 1452, though little was accomplished until 1506, when Pope Julius II instructed Donato Bramante to raze the site and completely redesign the basilica. Over the next 120 years, Italy's greatest artists and architects—including Bramante, Bernini, Raphael, Perruzi, Sangallo the Younger, and Michelangelo—contributed to the design and decoration, though Bramante deserves the majority of credit for the layout, Michelangelo for the most impressive artworks. Ironically enough, of these artists, only Bernini lived long enough to witness the completion of St. Peter's. (Five days before his own death, Michelangelo inspected his pupils' progress on the dome's mosaics and, feeling the work was going according to his design, announced he could die a happy death.)

Your first tastes of St. Peter's Basilica are the broad steps and carved portico, enhanced by Antonio Filarete's 15th-century bronze doors; they were salvaged from the "old" St. Peter's.

Beyond the doors you enter the temple itself, a vast contemplative space that dwarfs you into submission. Michelangelo's **Pietà**, to the right as you enter and behind lunatic-proof glass (the sculpture was damaged in 1972 when a madman attacked it with a hammer), depicts a very young Mary with the dead Jesus resting peacefully across her lap. To the right of the Pietà is the "Holy Door," opened with a hammer by the Pope on particularly holy years (the next one is AD 2000); the ritual represents "knocking down" the old to make way for the new. Heading toward the altar from the Pietà, look left for the **tomb of Queen Christina**, the only woman buried in St. Peter's. She earned this honor by fleeing her native—and Lutheran—Sweden with the crown jewels in 1650 and thereafter embracing the Roman Catholic papacy.

People born on February 29 will want to pay homage at the **altar of Pope Gregory XIII**, who in 1582 codified the formula for calculating leap years to make up for irregularities in the earth's rotation around the sun. Behind Gregory's unadorned tomb is a bronze **statue of St. Peter**, saved from the original church. Notice the statue's missing toes, worn away by 1,500 years of reverent kisses. At the center of things, where four massive piers support St. Peter's dome, Bernini's *baldacchino* (canopy) stands 44 meters above the main altar; it was made from 20 tons of bronze stripped from the pagan Pantheon by order of Pope Urban VIII. The canopy towers above the crypt, where remnants of the original church, as well as the bones of a few popes, can still be viewed. Below the crypt, under the foundations of the original church, supposedly lie the bones of St. Peter himself. The sacristy hosts a small **museum** (admission: L3000; open daily 9–5:30, until 6:30 in summer) with a hodgepodge of Vatican treasures, among them a 15th-century bronze of Pope Sixtus V by Antonio Pollaiuolo. As you leave St. Peter's, veer left toward the small courtyard and garden. Take the elevator or stairs—a laborious hike—to the top of St. Peter's **dome** (admission: L5000 via elevator, L4000 via stairs; open daily 8–5, until 6 in summer). From here you get glorious and unobstructed views over Vatican City and central Rome. *Via della Conciliazione. Admission free. Open daily 7–6.*

VATICAN MUSEUMS The primary residence of popes since 1377, the Vatican comprises no fewer than nine interlocking buildings with 1,400 chapels, galleries, and private living chambers. The main entrance to the museums, on **Viale Vaticano**, is a long walk from Piazza San Pietro. More convenient are buses (L2000) that shuttle visitors from the piazza to the museums' entrance. Buses run frequently 8:45 AM–12:45 PM except on Wednesday and Sunday (when the piazza is crowded in anticipation of a papal audience). Buy tickets at the Vatican Information Office on Piazza San Pietro. Other options are Bus 49 from Piazza Cavour to the Vatican's front door, Bus 81 to Piazza del Risorgimento and a short walk south, or Metro Line A to Ottaviano and a short walk southeast.

Once inside, four color-coded trails lead through the labyrinthine Vatican, lasting two, three, four, and six hours, respectively. Choose your poison (leaflets at the door describe each in detail) or venture through on your own. Either way, the pre-taped, English-language commentary is definitely worth the L3000 rental fee. General admission to everything covered below is LI3,000, but it's free on the last Sunday of every month.

Unless you make an effort to find the Sistine Chapel straightaway, your first taste will be the **Egyptian Museum** filled with hieroglyphic tablets, jewelry, sculpture, and yes, mummies. The nearby **Pio Clementino museum** holds some of the world's most notable sculptures, among them the *Laocoön*, *Belvedere Torso*, and *Apollo Belvedere*, all works of the 1st century BC. From here the trails lead to the **Etruscan Museum**, of interest only to committed art historians. Another long hall brings you to the superb **Gallery of Tapestries**, hung with dozens of comic, tragic, and purely decorative tapestries designed by Raphael. Farther along is the **Gallery of Maps**, a cartographer's fantasyland with all sorts of charts, maps, strange spheres, drafting tools, you name it. Next are the **Raphael Rooms**, decorated with biblical scenes by the Urbino-born Raphael (1483–1520). One of the rooms, the *Stanza della Segnatura*, contains the artist's *School of Athens* (1511), a painting that typifies the Renaissance ideals of geometric composition balanced by harmonies of color, portraying Plato, Aristotle, and various philosophers and scientists from antiquity; notice the faces of Raphael's contemporaries (Leonardo poses as Plato). The next stop is the cramped **Chapel of Nicholas V**, with frescoes by Fra Angelico (1400–1455), followed by the **Borgia Apartments**, with ceiling mosaics by Bernardino Pinturicchio (1454–1513).

The highlight, of course, is the **Sistine Chapel**, but forget the romantic notion of wandering silently under Michelangelo's masterpiece. The beautiful *cosmati* floor—a term used to describe decorative inlays in colored marble—is *always* packed with neck-craning tourists, and we're not kidding when we say packed. But hey, you *have* to see it, so forget about personal space and dive in. Just about every great Renaissance artist in Rome had a hand in its decoration—Pinturicchio, Signorelli, Botticelli, Cosimo Rosselli—before Michelangelo, much to his dismay, was cajoled by Pope Julius II to paint the ceiling, a barrel-vaulted artist's nightmare. If Michelangelo could have known how famous his ceiling paintings were to become, maybe he would have been more amenable. Instead, he spent four years of his life pissed-off and bitter, firing all of his assistants within the first two weeks and locking the door on the pope whenever he came to check up on things.

Contrary to popular belief, Michelangelo didn't actually work on his back but stood on his tiptoes, and often painted freehand without any guiding lines. The result of Michelangelo's labors, recently restored to (some say excessively) brilliant colors, has been called the most sublime example of artistry in the world. The contortions and muscles of the *ignudi* (male nude figures) show the Renaissance fascination with movement and idealized human form. Biblical stories depicted on the ceiling include the Creation of Light, Creation of the Universe, Creation of Earth, Creation of Adam, Creation of Eve, the Fall from Paradise, the Sacrifice of Noah, the Flood, and the Drunkenness of Noah. Around the sides are Biblical prophets and Greek sibyls in monumental poses that seem to support the ceiling. Twenty years after completing the Sistine Chapel, Michelangelo was commissioned to paint the **Last Judgment** on the wall behind the simple altar. A gruesome and tormented work, it articulates a very different version of the human condition. By this time Renaissance ideals had been shattered, to a great degree, by the upheavals of the Reformation and the Counter-Reformation. Old and ornery, the master of the Renaissance painted his own face on the wrinkled skin of St. Bartholomew's hand; look for St. Bartholomew below and to the right of Jesus. *Viale Vaticano, tel. 06/698–3333. Admission: L13,000, free last Sun. of month. Open Easter week and July–Sept., weekdays 8:45–5 (last admission 4 PM); Oct.–June, Mon.–Sat. 9–2 (last admission 1 PM); also last Sun. of every month 9–2. Closed Jan. 1, Jan. 6, Feb. 11, March 19, Easter Sun. and Mon., May 1, June 29, Aug. 15–16, Nov. 1, Dec. 8, Dec. 25–26.*

VIA APPIA AND THE CATACOMBS

Via Appia (Appian Way) was the first and the most important of all Roman roads. Completed in 312 BC, it was originally known as the "Queen of Roads," connecting the capital with other cities in the empire; amazingly, it still serves its purpose. Via Appia was the major campaign route during the conquest of southern Italy, but today it's best known for the miles and miles of underground cemeteries that lie nearby. Since burial was forbidden within Rome's city limits, residents buried their dead just ouside the walls, digging huge tunnels in the soft tufa rock.

Meet the Pope

You don't have to be Catholic to appreciate the pomp and ceremony of a papal audience. "Private" audiences are held for the masses every Wednesday at 11 AM in the Papal Audience Hall (10 AM if the weather is unbearably hot). Tickets are available Monday and Tuesday 9 AM–1 PM and Wednesday 9 AM–10 AM through the bronze doors on the west side of Piazza San Pietro; look for the Swiss Guards attempting to organize the horrific crowds. For advance tickets write to: Prefettura della Casa Pontifica, 00120 Città del Vaticano, indicating the date you prefer and the language you speak. Another option is to stand with up to 200,000 others on Piazza San Pietro every Sunday at 11 AM, when the pope appears at the window of the Vatican Palace to bless the public.

Most of the remains are long gone, so you'll have to make do with eerie subterranean passageways and lots of Christian graffiti—mainly variations on the Alpha, the Greek symbol for Christ. Although the catacombs themselves stretch for miles, there are only three official entrances. Each charges L6000 and is open 8:30–noon and 2:30–5.

The main entrance to the catacombs, **San Callisto** (Via Appia Antica 110, tel. 06/513–6725; closed Wed.), is named after a 3rd-century pope buried here; it's also the reputed resting place of St. Cecilia, patron saint of music. A friar will guide you through the crypts and galleries. **Domitilla** (Via Appia Antica 190, tel. 06/554–8766; closed Tues.) is where 1st-century jewelry and eating utensils were found in 1985. **San Sebastiano** (Via Appia Antica 136, tel. 06/788–7035; closed Thurs.) is the most famous, most interesting, and consequently the most visited of the catacombs because of its Christ-era mausoleum. There is no need to visit all three unless you have a fascination with caves. To reach the catacombs, take Bus 118 from San Giovanni in Laterano (*see below*) and follow the crowds. Rome's EPT office (*see* Visitor Information, in Basics, *above*) has helpful pamphlets on the catacombs and sometimes organizes cheap guided tours.

Beyond San Callisto is the church **Domine Quo Vadis**, supposedly standing on the spot where St. Peter—who was hightailin' it out of Rome—met Jesus and asked "Where goest thou, Lord?" (Domine Quo Vadis?). Jesus replied, "to be crucified a second time," indicating that Peter, too, should turn back and accept his death and ultimate martyrdom. The church is run by a Polish order that speaks fair English, and only halfheartedly believes in the authenticity of the footprints (supposedly Jesus') in a piece of marble at the church entrance. *Take Bus 118 from San Giovanni in Laterano. Ask the driver to stop at the church.*

Churches and Cathedrals

Besides the "biggie" churches covered in Major Sights, above, Rome contains an almost endless array of religious buildings. The city's major basilicas—Santa Maria Maggiore, San Pietro in Vincoli, San Giovanni in Laterano, and St. Peter's Basilica—compete with scores of smaller neighborhood churches that, despite their often plain exteriors, contain a wealth of art. Women are required to cover their shoulders, and both sexes are rarely allowed entrance in shorts. While devotees expect you to remain quiet, they are totally used to tourists wandering around.

BASILICA SAN PAOLO FUORI LE MURE The dark, ominous basilica of St. Paul Outside the Walls is second in size only to St. Peter's and was supposedly consecrated on the same day: November 18, AD 324. The church was originally just a small affair commemorating Paul's martyrdom. But an influx of funds from the likes of Charlemagne and Leo III caused it to expand into the imposing fortress you see today. The highlights are a candelabra from 1170 that depicts scenes from Christ's life with human-faced monsters; a Gothic tabernacle studded

EUR

Big, intimidating, sterile, cold, and ugly—not a flattering description, but all very fitting for the Esposizione Universale Roma (EUR), a dull, mostly residential neighborhood south of Rome's centro storico on Metro Line B. Built under Mussolini, who intended to hold the World Exposition here in 1942, the fascist-style EUR was brought to a halt during World War II. At the close of the war, building resumed, and huge stadiums, manmade lakes, and apartment buildings covered the once neglected area, creating a new "minicity." In preparation for the 1960 Olympic Games, EUR gained a Palace of Sports and a velodrome. Nowadays the grid plan "city outside the city" is home to a good chunk of Rome's upper-middle class.

with small statues of St. Paul; and a wooden crucifix (in the Chapel of the Sacrament, to the left of the altar) carved in a gruesomely realistic style. The meager light that comes through the dark windows makes it difficult to see the cycle of wall mosaics. If you can stand the crowd that jams the souvenir shop, check out the art on the walls—17th-century religious scenes that tend toward the provocative. *Via Otiense. Metro: S. Paolo. Open daily 9–2 and 4–6.*

SAN CLEMENTE Near the Colosseum, this church contains a number of surprises. First off, the ground-level building is clearly medieval, with its east-facing front courtyard and idealized mosaics. But beneath the surface, literally, lies the remains of an early Christian church (4th century AD). A dank stairway leads underground to the primitive nave and columns and the well-preserved frescoes depicting San Clemente himself. Continue beneath these ruins to an even earlier structure, a 1st-century Roman residence. *Via San Giovanni in Laterano, no phone. 1 block southeast of the Colosseum. Downstairs admission: L1000. Ground floor open Mon.–Sat. 9:30–12:30 and 3:30–6:30, Sun. 10–12:30 and 3:30–6:30. Downstairs open Mon.–Sat. only.*

SAN GIOVANNI IN LATERANO The oldest Christian basilica within the city walls, San Giovanni was for centuries the seat of the papacy and the heart of Christianity. Originally built on land donated by the emperor Constantine to the newly sanctioned sect of Christians, it soon attracted hordes of pilgrims as Christians everywhere wanted a first-hand view of the pope's pad. The church owes its present-day appearance to Borromini, who in 1646 rescued it from decay and successfully incorporated the elements of the ancient structure into a graceful new baroque basilica. The chapels themselves are big and rich enough to be churches; if you linger at each one, plan on spending a few hours here. Under the Gothic tabernacle above the altar, look for the heads (yes, reputedly the actual skulls) of Saints Peter and Paul. To the right of the basilica, **Palazzo Laterano** was once the pope's official residence. *Piazza San Giovanni in Laterano. Metro Line A to San Giovanni; walk 100 meters west to church. Admission free. Open daily 9–noon and 3–6.*

Across the street from the basilica, in the northeast corner of Piazza San Giovanni, is a sight that non-Christians will particularly enjoy: hundreds of worshipers climbing—on their knees, no less—the 28 cold, hard steps of **Santa Scala** (Holy Stairs). These are supposedly the original set imported here from Jerusalem (covered in walnut for protection) that Jesus ascended after his trial by Pontius Pilate. At the end of it all, pilgrims are rewarded with a glimpse of the *Acheropita*, a portrait of Jesus supposedly not painted by the hands of mere mortals. The less devout should take the side stairs.

SAN PIETRO IN VINCOLI Two pieces compete for your attention in this sparsely decorated, nauseatingly overtouristed church: the chains that bound St. Peter during his prison stays in Jerusalem and Rome (you can't miss 'em beneath the altar), and Michelangelo's *Moses*, one of his most powerful sculptures. Anatomically perfect in every sense (even doctors say so), *Moses* was originally intended as part of a funerary monument Michelangelo planned for Pope Julius II. However, the tomb was never finished, so the statue ended up here, to be fawned over by generations of camera-wielding tourists. *Piazza San Pietro in Vincoli, btw Colosseum and Via Cavour. Open daily 7–12:30 and 3:30–6.*

SANTA CROCE IN GERUSALEMME It may date from the 4th century, but this totally baroqued-out church does not deserve the hype it gets. That is, unless you're talking about holy relics, in which case Santa Croce can't be beat. Besides a nail and part of the inscription from the one and true Cross, there are two thorns from Jesus' crown, plus the gangly finger that Thomas poked Christ with, all on permanent display in Santa Croce's "Chapel of the Holy Relics," to the left of the altar. The Rosa d'Oro gift shop in front sells some mean liqueur (distilled by monks) and honey from the Lazio region. Next door, the Museo di Strumenti Musicali (*see* Museums and Galleries, *below*) offers a diversion for the church-weary. *Via Santa Croce in Gerusalemme. Metro Line A to San Giovanni; walk NE on Via Carlo Felice (it dead-ends at Santa Croce). Open daily 7–noon and 4–7:15.*

SANTA MARIA MAGGIORE One of Rome's oldest and most striking cathedrals has a legend behind it. In the 4th century Pope Liberius had a dream in which he was instructed to build a great cathedral to St. Mary on the Esquiline hill. Hesitant to shell out cash because of a sleep-induced fancy, he shelved the project. That is, until St. Mary herself visited Liberius in his sleep, then dumped a bunch of snow (in the middle of August, mind you) on the spot where the church was destined to be built—an event reenacted every August 5 (*see* Festivals, *below*). According to legend, the freaked-out but faithful pope put on his boots and traced the perimeter of the new basilica in the snow. Modern pilgrims can see a re-creation of the scene in a 13th-century exterior mosaic, which costs L3000 to view close-up. The colorful apse mosaics aren't a bad consolation for those who'd rather not pay the extra cash; they depict Mary as a Byzantine Empress being crowned Queen of Heaven by Christ. Either way, don't leave without seeing the vaulted ceiling (gilded with some of the first gold pillaged from the New World), the zany cosmati floors, and the Sistine and Pauline chapels on either side of the altar. *Piazza Santa Maria Maggiore, off Via Cavour. Open daily 9–6:30.*

Museums and Galleries

Many of Rome's "important" paintings belong to the Roman Catholic Church or are in private collections sometimes exhibited in the family palace—you'd need a decade or so to see everything of interest. When the major galleries, with their crowds and overpriced gift shops get you down, check out some of Rome's offbeat collections. Nothing will blow your mind, but there's definitely something to be said for closet-size museums and tacky displays. EPT tourist offices (*see* Visitor Information, in Basics, *above*) have reams of temporary-exhibit schedules, plus listings of private collections displayed at the whim of Italy's modern nobility. Another good bet is **Palazzo delle Esposizioni**, with temporary exhibits from around the world. *Via Nazionale 194, tel. 06/488–5465. Admission: L6000–L12,000, depending on the exhibition. Open Wed.–Mon. 10–9.*

GALLERIA SPADA The majority of the Spada's four-gallery collection is divided between 16th-century portraits and religious scenes, with a few landscapes and still lifes thrown in for good measure. The list of artists, far from earth-shattering, is still impressive: Bologna's Guido Reni (1575–1642), Florence's Pietro Torrigiani (1471–1528), and Naples-born Salvator Rosa (1615–1673) are well represented. The rooms themselves—decorated with Greek and Roman sculpture, Murano glass chandeliers, and, in the Grand Gallery, a pair of 16th-century globes—are dizzyingly elaborate. The palace itself was built in the 1580s and then completely overhauled in 1636 by its namesake, Cardinal Baridino Spada. *Via dei Giubbonari, 1 block SE of Campo dei Fiori, tel. 06/876–1344. Admission: L4000. Open Tues.–Sun. 9–2.*

MUSEO BARRACCO This museum contains a collection of Etruscan, Roman, and Egyptian sculpture—mainly busts and funerary monuments—that date back to 2500 BC. There are also sculptural goodies from Corsica and Asia Minor. Ambitious art students should come here for subjects. *Corso Vittorio Emanuele II, 1 block east of Piazza P. S. Pantaleo, no phone. Admission: L4000. Open Tues.–Thurs. 1–4 and 5–8, Fri.–Sun. 1–4.*

MUSEO DELLA CIVITÀ ROMANA This museum was opened by Mussolini in 1937 to commemorate Augustus's reign as emperor 2000 years earlier. Accordingly, its stark white walls typify Fascist-era architecture. Displays trace all aspects of Roman history, with each room dedicated to a certain emperor, period, or feat of Roman engineering, ranging from bicycles to catapults. Scale models of ancient Rome and the Colosseum show you what Rome *really* looked like in its heyday. You'll also get an up-close view of the reliefs from the column of Trajan in Trajan's Market, presented here in full-scale casts. *Piazza Guglielmo Marconi, tel. 06/544–8993. Metro Line B to EUR Marconi; take Viale Beethoven north, turn right on Viale dell'Astro Nomia. Admission: L5000. Open Mon.–Sat. 9–1:30, Sun. 9–1.*

MUSEO DI STRUMENTI MUSICALI This isn't your average collection of flutes, horns, and drums. First of all, it's housed in an Art Nouveau palace overlooking a shady park, perfect for an afternoon picnic. More to the point, the exhibits include sundry pipes, bells, and string instruments made of jawbones; armadillo-shell guitars; shaman drums; and a dozen bizarre, long-forgotten instruments, the likes of which will never be played again. Rounding things out are 15th-century harps, spinettas, cimbalos, you name it—many elaborately painted, carved, and inlaid with semiprecious stones. *Piazza Santa Croce in Gerusalemme 9, tel. 06/701–4796. Metro Line A to San Giovanni; walk NE on Via Carlo Felice (it dead-ends at Piazza Santa Croce). Admission: L2000. Open Mon.–Sat. 9–1:30.*

THE NATIONAL MUSEUM OF PASTA FOODS Billing itself as the most unique museum in all the world, this place showcases Italy's most famous culinary item. Visit small galleries named "The Wheat Room" or "The Ligurian Room," and learn the compelling saga of pasta and its present-day production. There's even a room where you'll discover the relationship between pasta and art. The museum also holds pasta seminars; because as the brochure says: "This is not just a museum, it's a cultural center for food pastas." *Piazza Scanderberg 117, tel. 06/699–1119. From Trevi Fountain, take Via Lavatore, right on Vicolo Scanderberg to Piazza Scanderberg. Open weekdays 9:30–12:30 and 4–7, Sat. 9:30–12:30.*

PALAZZO COLONNA You have to plan carefully to see Colonna's collection of paintings and sculpture from the 15th to 18th centuries: The palace is only open on Saturday morning and is closed the entire month of August. Your reward: a sumptuous palace displaying masters like Van Dyck, Rosa, Poussin, and Tintoretto. *Piazza dei S.S. Apostoli, 1 block NE of Piazza Venezia, tel. 06/679–4362. Admission: L5000. Open Sat. 10–1; closed Aug.*

Cheap Thrills

Rome's cheapest thrill of all is sitting with friends on a shady piazza, a bottle of cheap Chianti at your feet. People-watching is another prime pastime; grab your guitar, harmonica, tambourine, castanets, or accordion and head for the Spanish Steps, the Pantheon, Piazza Navona, Piazza Santa Maria (in Trastevere), or Piazza Trilussa (in Trastevere opposite the Ponte Sisto footbridge).

PROTESTANT CEMETERY This atmospheric graveyard lies in the residential **Testaccio** district, on the east bank of the Tiber opposite Trastevere. There are plenty of shady picnic spots, though most come to commune with the graves of Keats, Severin, Giacometti, Shelley, Edvard Munch, and Goethe's son. The macabre tone is softened by a huge colony of friendly cats, and by groundskeepers who stay busy carving headstones and helping out visitors. *Via Caio Cestio 6, tel. 06/571900. Metro Line B to Piramide, walk NW across plaza and turn left. Admission free. Open Thurs.–Tues. 8–11:30 and 3:20–4:30 (until 5:30 Mar.–Nov.).*

KNIGHTS OF MALTA At the top of the Aventine Hill lies the residence and headquarters of the Sovereign Knights of Malta, a reclusive sect and a sovereign order. The public is not allowed past the huge wooden doors, but take a look through the keyhole and you'll get an unusual view of St. Peter's dome. The knights intentionally designed the keyhole to afford a view of Rome's three independent states—the Knights of Malta, Italy, and Vatican City. To get here, take Metro Line B to Circo Massimo, take Via Circo Massimo, left on Valle Murcia, (which becomes Via Santa Sabina) to Piazza dei Cavalieri di Malta.

PARCO SAVELLO Many Romans skip town on summer weekends, but those that don't end up at this tree-lined park, also called Giardino degli Aranci (Garden of the Orange Trees). The park stretches across the top of the Aventine Hill (Rome's most exclusive residential quarter), on Via Santa Sabina. The best views are at sunset, when the rooftops of Trastevere are postcard pretty. To reach the park, see the directions to Knight of Malta, above.

Sophia Loren Never Looked So Good

The Museo delle Cere, one of Rome's most obnoxious museums, is full of wax, poor artistry, and cheesy displays. It claims some vague association with Madame Tussaud's Wax Museum in London, but this one is pure Italian kitsch, with popes, kings, emperors, and your favorite Italian movie stars. One plus, depending on your perspective, is that it's open all day, every day—quite an anomaly in the Roman museum scheme. Piazza dei S.S. Apostoli 67, 1 block NE of Piazza Venezia, no phone. Admission: L5000. Open daily 9–8; last admission 7:30 PM.

PASSEGGIATA ROUTES At dusk Romans get together for a stroll through parks and gardens—a ritual known as the passegiatta. **Villa Borghese** is especially popular because of its paths, views, and central location. More chichi routes include **Via dei Condotti** (near Piazza di Spagna), **Via Frattina** (2 blocks south of Via dei Condotti), and **Via del Corso** (it connects Piazza del Popolo with Piazza Colonna). If you want to combine walking with browsing, the streets around **Via dei Coronari**, two blocks north of Piazza Navona, are famed for antiques, with a sprinkling of artsy retail stores and cafés.

PINCIO Right above Piazza del Popolo and Piazza di Spagna, the shady Pincio is an extension of the Villa Borghese's gardens, lined with trees and benches, matrons, old men, and young couples in love. Around 8 PM there's cheesy piano and electric beat-box accompaniment from the restaurant on Viale dell'Obelisco. On weekend afternoons, the scene turns frenetic with bikers and skaters. On summer afternoons, concession stands sell to the crowds gathered for puppet and mime shows.

Festivals

Ask at EPT tourist offices (*see* Visitor Information, in Basics, *above*) for a massive list of Rome's numerous festivals and seasonal events.

JANUARY During Epiphany (Jan. 5–6), Piazza Navona hosts a **Christmas toy fair**, with a wild and rowdy celebration that's meant to encourage the witch Befana to shower nifty toys on good kids and coal-like chunks of candy on rascals. On January 6, hundreds of Italian children recite poems in front of the statue of Santo Bambino, at the church of Santa Maria in Aracoeli atop Campidoglio.

FEBRUARY **Carnevale** is celebrated the Sunday and Tuesday before Lent with disguises and processions throughout Rome. Via del Corso was originally named for the Carnivale processions held along it, and it's still front-row center for the festivities. For Mardi Gras (Fat Tuesday), many restaurants prepare special feasts. Plan on hefty hangovers.

MARCH On March 9 cars are blessed—yes, cars—on Via dei Fori Imperiali, by the church of Santa Francesca Romana. With Rome's gnarly traffic madness, it's no wonder that Italians show up in droves. **Festa di San Guiseppe** (Mar. 19) celebrates Jesus's secular dad, Joseph, with everyone frying up fritters and *bignè* (doughnuts filled with vanilla cream) in streets and piazze north of the Vatican. Take Metro Line A to Ottaviano or Lepanto and follow your nose.

APRIL During Easter the city is mobbed with pilgrims, and the pope is one busy man: Open-air mass in St. Peter's Square on **Palm Sunday**, nighttime mass in the Colosseum on **Good Friday**, and the celebrated **Stations of the Cross** procession on the Palatine Hill, as well as his blessing of the public in St. Peter's Square on **Easter Sunday**. For tickets to papal audiences in April, you must spend all night in line on Piazza San Pietro.

In late April, an **art show** on Via Margutta, between Via del Corso and the southwest edge of Villa Borghese, blankets this old and weathered street with paintings by semi-famous and struggling local artists. There's a repeat engagement in the fall. At the Campidoglio, parades and parties celebrate the traditional date of **Rome's founding** (April 21, 753 BC) with spectacular floral and firework shows.

MAY A month-long **rose show** adds color to Aventine Hill. From mid-May onward, an **antiques fair** on Via dei Coronari (2 blocks north of Piazza Navona) keeps most shops open late; flaming torches line this normally dark and narrow road. The **Italian International Tennis Tournament** draws crowds to the Foro Italico at the end of May. Scan the *La Trova Roma* section in the Thursday edition of *La Repubblica* for ticket information.

JUNE On the first Sunday in June a military parade files down Via dei Fori Imperiali for the **Festa delle Forze Armate** (Armed Forces Day), a low-key affair that would have Mussolini, king of pomp and circumstance, turning in his grave. On June 23 the **Festa di San Giovanni** (Feast of St. John the Baptist) is celebrated most heartily in the neighborhood near the church of San Giovanni, with singing, dancing, games in the streets, and stewed-snail eating (don't ask). The best seats for the fireworks displays are Porta San Giovanni, Aventine Hill, and Campidoglio. On June 29, the **Festa di San Pietro** honors Rome's patron saint in St. Peter's Basilica with candles and song. **Estate Romana**, which runs June–September, has music, dance, theater, and films in venues throughout the city, primarily the Villa Medici, Orto Botanico, and Isola Tiberina. Events are listed in *La Repubblica* in the *La Trova Roma* Thursday supplement.

JULY During the first three weeks of July the **Tevere Expo** invades the banks of the Tiber near Castel Sant'Angelo with product demos, crafts, regional Italian foods, and commotion (admission: L10,000). For **Festa di Noiantri**, held during the last half of July, Romans take to the streets of Trastevere to honor Our Lady of Mount Carmel with religious processions, traditional music, sidewalk fairs, gluttony, and general partying.

AUGUST The **Festa della Madonna della Neve** (Aug. 5) sees white rose petals flurrying about Santa Maria Maggiore, at Via Cavour a few blocks southwest of Stazione Termini. The white petals, thrown from the roof of Santa Maria, are meant to re-create the legendary August snow that marked the spot where the church was destined to be built.

SEPTEMBER A torchlight **handicrafts fair** takes over Via dell'Orso, a few blocks north of Piazza Navona, from September to October. In late September, Via Margutta is crammed with local artwork for the autumn installment of Piazza del Popolo's **art show**.

DECEMBER Romans come to Piazza di Spagna to lay floral garlands atop the statue of the Madonna for **Festa della Concezione Immacolata** (the Feast of the Immaculate Conception). on December 8th. Get a helping of free fish goulash on December 22, during the **Ciotto del Pesce** (Celebration of the Fish); it's held at the Mercato Generale on Via Ostiense. **New Year's Eve** is not only a wild night of champagne and funny hats; here locals play games, wave sparklers, and—mind your head—chuck glasses from windows.

Shopping

Except for a few markets and junk shops, Rome is not a place for cheap shopping. Style is a big deal here, and Romans are willing to pay top lira for leather goods, tailored coats, and that pair of gotta-have-'em shoes. Unless you're traveling on somebody else's credit card, be content with browsing the exclusive shops off Piazza di Spagna, especially those along nearby **Via Frattina** and **Via dei Condotti**. One thing Rome does have is collectables—from priceless Renaissance antiques to modern throwaway baubles. **Via Margutta**, between Piazza di Spagna and Piazza del Popolo, is a mecca of antiques shops, but again, nothing comes cheap. For funky boutiques and used clothing, head toward the Pantheon and Campo dei Fiori; the streets off **Corso Vittorio Emanuele II** are also packed with every sort of boutique and shop. Products of the New Age, from the groovy to the esoteric, abound in shops near Piazza Santa Maria in Trastevere. Religious articles are plentiful near the Vatican and in the centro storico around Piazza della Minerva.

Cheap and cheesy shops—the sort of places with T-shirts, lingerie, ties, posters, and coffee mugs—line the streets south of Stazione Termini. **UPIM** and **La Rinascente** are two of Rome's larger department stores, the former with outlets on Via Nazionale and Piazza Santa Maria Maggiore (3 blocks SW of Stazione Termini), the latter along Via del Corso.

For an earful of Roman subculture, head to San Lorenzo's **Disfunzioni Musicali** (Via degli Etruschi 4, tel. 06/446–1984), which stocks grunge and punk and has flyers advertising the latest shows. For a broader and more traditional selection of CDs and records, try **Ricordi** (Viale Giulio Cesare 88, tel. 06/372–0215), near the Vatican; **Messagerie Musicali** (Via del Corso 122); or **Disco Boom** (Via del Tritone 39).

MARKETS On Sunday from 6 AM to 2 PM, the **Porta Portese flea market** sets up along Via Portuense, on the western bank of the Tiber just south of Trastevere; find your way to the river and walk to Ponte Sublicio, one bridge south of Ponte Palatino. The carnival atmosphere comes from a blend of East Europeans and Africans selling just about anything you can imagine, hippies selling homemade beads and Guatemalan imports, and Italian shopkeepers who come to dump their surplus merchandise. It takes a few hours to cover the entire flea market. Keep a tight grip on your valuables.

After Dark

When Romans go out on the town, they head to the streets and the piazze. These offer an affordable and lively scene, especially on sultry summer nights when someone—and someone always does—takes the obligatory midnight swim in the Trevi Fountain. **Campo dei Fiori** is alive and crowded on weekend nights, and the streets around **Piazza Navona** and the **Pantheon** are lined with pubs and wine bars. **Trastevere** is home to innumerable intimate night spots, and nearby **Testaccio** is for serious grooving. In summer, the majority of discos literally move to the beach, so if you want to shake it to techno, your options are somewhat limited.

Indispensable for anyone with an after-dark agenda is *La Trova Roma*, a supplement published in Thursday's *La Repubblica* newspaper. It's in Italian, yet the lists of clubs, concerts, and raves are easy to decipher. *Wanted in Rome* (L1500) and *Metropolitana* (L1500), are two English-language magazines that also list concerts and clubs.

The big bummer in Rome is the *tessera* (membership fee) charged by many clubs. Memberships last anywhere from a month to a year and cost L10,000–L20,000. Don't worry about two passport-size photos; clubs will take your money and issue a membership card on the spot. Clubs without a tessera inevitably charge twice the price for drinks. If you only want a simple beer and don't care about atmosphere (or about sitting down), head for one of Rome's innumerable cafés, where beer *alla spina* (on tap) or a glass of wine costs L2500–L3500.

BARS Since BAR signs are ubiquitous and usually go hand in hand with what most folks call cafés, head for a pub, *birreria* (beer hall), or *vineria* (wine bar) for more colorful drinking. In Trastevere, check out **Piazza Santa Maria in Trastevere** and **Piazza Trilussa**, where locals and tourists share the scene. The **Borgo** area, north of Trastevere around the Vatican, gets some of the overflow, but Borgo bars and cafés are less exotic, and the neighborhood itself is spread out, making wandering difficult.

Most of Rome's Irish pubs hold happy hour from around 8 to 10 PM, with drinks at half the price.

Guinness Pub. The most appealing of Rome's many Irish pubs, this place has an upscale interior, a laid-back clientele, live music downstairs, a full menu of munchies, and plenty of dark beer on tap (L8000 a glass). *Via Muzio Clementi 12, near Piazza Cavour, tel. 06/321–8424. Cross Ponte Cavour onto Via Vittoria Colonna, right on Via Muzio Clementi. No cover. Open Sun.–Thurs. 7 PM–2 AM, Fri. and Sat. 7 PM–3 AM.*

Johnathan's Angels. The psychedelic fervor of Christmas lights, sunflowers, and kitschy portraits (all with Johnathan's face) mingled with ornate bird cages and faux-marble Venuses, makes this

The Legend of Cheap Leather

Once upon a time it was possible to find quality leather goods for a song at street markets. These days, cheap leather is a Roman fantasy. If you want the good stuff, expect to pay handsomely for it. Browsers should try Fausto Santini, a high-priced but well-stocked outlet on Via Frattina near Piazza di Spagna. If you must buy, the going rates are: shoes L125,000–L160,000, leather skirts L130,000–L175,000, biker jackets L120,000–L160,000, and shoulder bags from L60,000. Caveat emptor: Be sure any leather you buy is stamped "Vero Cuoio," a sign that it's the real thing and not a cheap imitation.

joint truly unique. The bar is usually packed, and crowds often spill onto the street. There's no cover, but drinks are pricey (L12,000–L15,000). *Via della Fossa 16, tel. 06/689–3426. Btw Piazza Navona and Piazza della Chiesa Nuova, off Via della Pace. Open daily 10 PM–3 AM.*

Miscellenia. During lunch and dinner this tavern fills with Italians of all ages who happily wait in line for the generous salads and sandwiches (L4000–L8000). At night it's geared toward a university crowd—and a distinctly American one at that. Beers go for L6000, cocktails L6000, wine L3000, popcorn L2000. *Via delle Paste 110/A, tel. 06/377–2368. From NE cnr of Piazza della Rotonda, take Via del Pastini to Via delle Paste. Open Mon.–Sat. 12:45–3:30 and 4:45–2 AM.*

Night and Day. This smoky watering hole is a rowdy place to do some serious drinking. Frothy beer is served on tap (L6000–L8000 a pint), or choose from their formidable selection of hard alcohol. A favorite with local night owls and other barflies, Night and Day stays open almost till dawn. *Via dell'Oca 50, tel. 06/320–2300. Piazza del Popolo, off Via della Ripetta. No cover. Open daily 9 PM–5 AM.*

Ombre Rosse. This Trastevere hangout is not unlike a San Francisco café, with round marble tables and a tangible intellectual feel. You won't find many foreigners here, just casually clothed Romans downing beers (L5000) and cocktails (L8000) while munching on free popcorn. *Piazza Sant'Egidio 12, no phone. Closed Sun.*

Vineria. This small, low-key wine bar on Campo dei Fiori has only a few benches and wine crates to sit on, and some outdoor tables in summer. From 7 PM it's popular with the after-work crowd, from 10 PM with youthful Romans. Wine starts at L2300 a glass, beer L2300. *Campo de Fiori 15, tel. 06/6880–3268. Closed Sun.*

CLUBS Serious club-goers should truck out to Testaccio (Bus 27 from Stazione Termini) and its main drag, **Via Monte di Testaccio**, off Via Nicola Zabaglia, where you can take your pick of blues, salsa, jazz, or rock from the half-dozen clubs wrapped around the base of Mt. Testaccio. One warning: Testaccio is on the seedy side, and women traveling solo should definitely take a cab (L10,000–L12,000).

➤ **ROCK** • Tickets for big-name shows—be it REM or Green Day—are usually handled by the agencies **Orbis** (Piazza dell'Esquilino 37, tel. 06/482–7403) and **Babilonia** (Via del Corso 185, tel. 06/678–6641).

Angelo Azzurro. Primarily gay clubbers fill this funky, underground disco, awash in black lights and mirrors. Friday is free for women, Sunday is free for all. *Via Cardinal Merry del Val 13, off Viale Trastevere, tel. 06/580–0472. Cover L15,000, including 1 drink. Open Tues.– Sun. 11 PM–3:30 AM.*

Circolo degli Artisti. This warehouse space and bar blasts everything from ragamuffin and hip-hop to electrowave. It's the sort of place where you don't have to worry about offending anyone, no matter what you look like. In summer expect the occasional live band and performance art piece. The tessera is L15,000. *Via Lamarmora 28, tel. 06/446–4968. Metro Line A to Vittorio Emanuele; Via Lamarmora is 1 block south. Open Thurs.–Sat. 11 PM–very late.*

Club Picasso. Live or recorded? Rock, acid, reggae, or funk? The only way to find out what's playing is to call ahead or check the newspapers. Either way, count on frantic dancing in this dank, cavelike club. No hooligans or funky backpackers, but grunge is okay if it looks intentional. Drinks start at L8000. The tessera is L10,000. *Via Monte di Testaccio 63, tel. 06/574– 2975. Open Fri. and Sat. 10 PM–4 AM.*

Folkstudio. Folkstudio's booths and small, intimate tables attract a relatively mellow crowd for Italy—but still no Birkenstocks or tie-dye. Most nights there are live performances by local musicians and poets. Beers cost L4000, wine L9000 per bottle, cocktails L6000. The nightly cover is L10,000. *Via Frangipane 42, tel. 06/487–1063. Open nightly 7 PM–1:30 AM.*

➤ **JAZZ AND LATIN** • At the moment Latin dancing is all the rage in Rome, an infatuation fed by a growing network of clubs. Besides those listed below try **Stellarium** (Via Lida 44, off Piazza Zama, tel. 06/784–8889) and the **Magic Fly** (Via Bassanello 15, tel. 06/ 3326–8956).

Caffè Caruso. Rhumba, mambo, and salsa with a mellow crowd of Italians and Latinos. The music is usually live and always danceable. Fruity cocktails go for L10,000, beer L7000. The one bummer is the L20,000 tessera, valid for nine months. *Via di Monte Testaccio 36, tel. 06/574-5019. Open daily 10:30 PM–3:30 AM.*

Caffè Latino. Burrowed into the foot of Mt. Testaccio, this pottery-lined space—with hunks and shards bulging from the walls—has a complete bar, cocktail area, and dance floor. Live bands range from rock, hip-hop, and funk to soul, jazz, and reggae. The crowd consists mostly of students and twentysomething locals. Nightly cover L10,000. *Via di Monte Testaccio 96, tel. 06/574-4020. Open Tues.–Sun 10:30 PM–3 AM.*

St. Louis. Rome's favorite jazz spot attracts a young, well-dressed crowd with its Casablancaesque setting—not to mention its Latin, Brazilian, swing, and blues shows. Bands start at 10 PM, but by 9:30 things are packed. What we're saying is, the 8–9:30 happy hour is not only a bargain but a good way to ensure getting a seat. *Via del Cardello 13, south of Via Cavour, tel. 06/474-5076. Metro Line B to Colosseo, then walk NW on Via del Colosseo to Via del Cardello. Closed Mon. and Thurs.*

Yes, Brazil. This intimate Trastevere bar bursts with exuberant Brazilian tunes every night of the week. Squeeze in under the palm fronds for tropical cocktails (L12,000) or beer (L8000), or push your table out of the way and join the jumpin' crowd. There's a happy hour daily 8–11 PM with a half-priced menu. *Via San Francesco a Ripa 103, off Viale Trastevere, tel. 06/581-6267. No cover. Open Mon.–Sat. 8 PM–2:30 AM.*

CLASSICAL MUSIC Rome is often criticized for not having a central music hall, but the upshot is that classical concerts are often held in churches—St. Ignacio, off Via del Corso, is a frequent venue—which rate high on the "groovy atmosphere" scale and, better yet, rarely charge admission. Look for posters around town advertising the latest event, or stop by an EPT tourist office (*see* Visitor Information, in Basics, *above*) for current listings.

Rome's main venues are **Accademia di Santa Cecilia** (box office tel. 06/654-1044), **Accademia Filarmonica Romana** (Teatro Olimpico, Via Gentile da Fabriano 17, tel. 06/396-2635 or 06/320-1752), and the **Instituzione Universitaria dei Concerti** (Via Bolzano 38, tel. 06/361-0051). Baroque music fans should check out the **Gonfalone series** (Via del Gonfalone 32, tel. 06/687-5952), one of Europe's best productions of baroque music. Both **Il Tempietto** (tel. 06/481-4800) and **Associazione Musicale Romana** (tel. 06/656-8441) produce concerts throughout the year. Ticket prices run L16,000–L45,000, depending on the location and event. Students with ID get a 10% discount at the Instituzione Universitaria.

OPERA AND BALLET Rome's opera season runs November–May in the **Teatro dell'Opera** (Piazza Beniaminio Gigli 1, tel. 06/6759-5725 for info in English). The box office opens 10–1 and 5–7, two days prior to the performance; tickets run L20,000–L60,000. The **Rome Opera Ballet** also hosts performances in the Teatro dell'Opera; call the box office for schedules.

THEATER Unless you speak Italian or get a kick out of watching others do so, your theater choices here are severely limited. The Teatro Agora sometimes mounts English productions, but don't hold your breath waiting. If you *do* speak Italian, that's another story. Rome's theater season runs October–May; scan the pages of *La Trova Roma*, the supplement to Thursday's *La Repubblica* newspaper, for the latest. Tickets run L15,000–L50,000 (the smaller the theater, the cheaper the ticket) plus an additional L2000 tessera that's good for one year. Don't stress if you've left your best dress at home—casual attire is fine.

Trastevere's **Teatro Agora** (Via della Penitenza 33, off Via della Lungara, tel. 06/687-4167) is a 100-seat playhouse with a mix of classic and modern works. Trastevere's **Teatro Belli** (Piazza S.S. Apollonia 11/A, tel. 06/589-4875) is reminiscent of a Parisian nightclub with its somewhat ribald, light entertainments. **Teatro della Cometa** (Via del Teatro di Marcello 4, off Piazza Venezia, tel. 06/678-4380) is a small stage where people active in drama and the arts come to see little-known works.

MOVIE THEATERS Look for blue-bordered posters that give the current dirt on what's showing when and where at Rome's cinemas, or check *La Trova Roma*, *La Repubblica*'s Thursday entertainment supplement. Expect to pay L7000–L10,000 at most cinemas.

Rome's lone English-only theater is Trastevere's **Pasquino** (Vicolo del Piede 19, tel. 06/580–3622), with daily screenings at 5:30, 8, and 10:30 PM. **Cinema Majestic** (Via S.S. Apostoli 20, off Via del Corso, tel. 06/679–4908) has films in English every Monday. **Greenwich** (Via Bodoni 59, tel. 06/574–5825) shown movies in their original language on Monday and Tuesday; from the Piramide Metro station, walk five blocks toward the Tiber on Via Marmorata and turn left on Via Bodoni. **Labirinto** (Via Pompeo Magno 27, 2 blocks south of Lepanto Metro, tel. 06/321–6283) regularly screens cult classics.

Near Rome

The annual soccer match between the teams from Rome and Lazio is arguably the most hotly contested game in the country. With several million half-crazed devotees of the capital pitted against several million fanatics of the surrounding region, the match is more than a game—it's the physical manifestation of the bad blood between the two rivals. For 3000 years, Rome has squelched everything but Lazio's spirit in order to fuel her own splendor. In ancient times, the Etruscans, Latins, and Sabines who resided in Lazio's hills fought the capital tooth and nail before they were dominated by Rome's military might. In later years, Rome's popes and princes chose Lazio's prime locales as sites for their villas and pleasure palaces, extracting all they could from the fertile plains and the populace and giving little in return. Nowadays, Lazio is still used for weekend getaways, though its hill towns and mountain lakes are less picturesque than those in Tuscany or neighboring Umbria. Still, the region's Etruscan remains and decadent Renaissance villas are worth a day's excursion from the chaotic capital.

If you like Lazio, thank Benito "Il Duce" Mussolini. In 1928 he carried out Julius Caesar's much-delayed plans for draining what was mostly a marshy swampland.

Frascati

Huddled on a steep hillside 40 kilometers southeast of Rome, Frascati is like a balcony to the world, or at least to Rome's rural suburbs. If you need an excuse for a day trip, consider the sweeping views of Rome and the Alban hills—and the Tyrrhenian Sea on exceptionally clear days. Frascati has a distinctively modern air, with few historic sights; the reason for coming here has always been to drink the local wine and to eat yourself immobile. Take your pick from the cafés and trattorias fronting the main piazza, or do like the locals do—buy picnic supplies from the outdoor market on **Piazza del Mercato** (mornings Mon.–Sat.) and bring your own grub to any one of the numerous local *cantine* (homey wine bars). With wooden tables squeezed in between old vats, children's toys, and cans of paint, many cantine have all the elements of a cluttered garage, with the addition of tasty and extremely cheap vino. Try the totally touristy, totally loud, totally fun **Cantina Gomandini** (Via Emanuele Filiberto 1, tel. 06/942–1585; open Tues.–Sun. noon–10), where long picnic tables and big wine vats play well with crowds of tourists. Look for it halfway up the stairs when trekking from the train station to the city center. Or pull up a chair and order a liter (L4000) at **Cantina da Santino** (Via P. Campana; look for the hand-painted sign).

Frascati's 16th-century **Villa Aldobrandini** (Via Catone, tel. 06/455–5743), designed by Giacomo della Porta and adorned with fountains by Bernini, Maderno, and Fontana, was once a weekend getaway house for Roman nobility, but has now fallen into serious disrepair. You can get a pass (L3000) to wander around its rather overgrown gardens from the **AAST** tourist office (Piazza Marconi 1, tel. 06/942–0331; open Mon.–Sat. 9–2 and 3:30–7). AAST also has a detailed map delineating wine-tasting spots in Frascati and nearby villages.

COMING AND GOING Trains from Rome's Stazione Termini (hourly, 50 min, L2400) drop you at Frascati's tiny one-track depot. To reach the center, climb the hillside stairs to Piazza Marconi; Piazza San Pietro is two blocks to the left, and Villa Aldobrandini is straight ahead along Via Catone. **ACOTRAL buses** leave from Rome's Anagnina Metro station (every 20 min, 1 hr, L1500) and drop you in the middle of Piazza Marconi. In Frascati, buy tickets a few doors down from the bus stop at Piazza Marconi 16 (open daily 8–1 and 3:30–8:30).

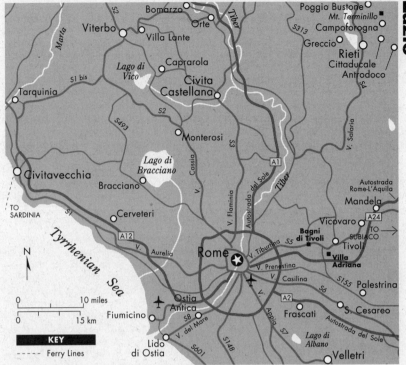

WHERE TO SLEEP Among the 10 or so hotels listed at the tourist office, only two are anywhere near the town center. Above the train station look for **Giadrina** (Via A. Diaz 13, tel. 06/942–0378), where doubles come equipped with TVs, phones, and private baths for L100,000 (including breakfast). The more modest **Panorama** (Piazza Casini, tel. 06/942–1800) has clean, passable doubles from L60,000; head north from Piazza San Pietro along Via Tivoli and turn left on Via Casini.

FOOD There are tons of trattorias and pizzerias near Piazza San Pietro; try **Trattoria del Piave** (Via del Piave 10; closed Tues.) for its oven-fired pizzas (L5000–L9000) and cannelloni e basilico (with tomatoes and basil; L6500). Indulge in homemade pasta at **Trattoria da Giselda** (Piazza Montegrappa 7, tel. 06/942–4161), where a full belt-busting meal will run you about L25,000.

Tivoli

Tivoli has been equated with "getting away" since ancient times, when just about anybody who was anybody had a villa here, including Cassius, Trajan, Hadrian, Horace, and Catullus. In medieval times Tivoli fell into obscurity, until the Renaissance drew popes and cardinals back to the town, where they constructed villas ostentatious enough to rival their extravagant predecessors. Nowadays, Tivoli is a small but vibrant town, with winding streets, views over the surrounding countryside, and easy access to its main attractions, Villa d'Este and Villa Gregoriana. Tivoli's **AAST** tourist office (Largo Garibaldi, tel. 0774/293522; open daily 8–6, shorter hrs off-season) has free maps and listings of the town's food and lodging options. However, Tivoli can and probably should be handled as a day trip from Rome. When hunger strikes, head to **Pizza al Taglio** (Viale Manelli 27, across from bus stop; open daily 7 AM–9 PM) for tasty pizza by the slice starting at L1000 an etto and beer for L2800.

Tivoli has some amazing views of Lazio's rural countryside, encompassing olive groves, vineyards, and long-forgotten ruins. Just don't look south, lest Tivoli's mines and quarries loom into view.

COMING AND GOING Buses are by far your best bet. From Rome's Rebibbia Metro station, ACOTRAL buses run hourly (5 AM–midnight) to Tivoli (45 min, L3000 round-trip). You'll be dropped off on Largo Garibaldi, across from the tourist office.

WORTH SEEING

➤ **VILLA D'ESTE** • Tivoli's best-known and most heavily visited attraction, Villa d'Este was built by Cardinal Ippolito d'Este in the late 16th century. Este, one of the richest and most extravagant men of his time, doled out an astronomical sum to architect Pirro Ligorio to create a mythical garden where water was the artistic center-piece. Inspired by the excavation of Villa Adriana, and a devotee of the Renaissance celebration of human ingenuity over nature, Este wasn't satisfied until over 500 fountains adorned his yard. The fountains cascade, shoot skyward, imitate bird songs, simulate rain—the only thing wrong with this fantastical assortment is that you can't jump in. Bernini's contributions include the *Fontana del Bicchierone* and *Grotto di Diana*. Try to avoid visiting between noon and 2:30 PM, when the water pressure is low. *Tel. 0774/988273. From Largo Garibaldi, take Via Boselli to Piazza Trento; the entrance is right of the church. Admission: L8000. Open daily 9 AM–4 PM (until 7 PM in summer).*

➤ **VILLA GREGORIANA** • This "villa" is really a large overgrown park riddled with trails and shady picnic spots. The lush greenery and cool mists from the nearby Aniene River compensate for the sweaty, steep hike down into the river gorge. The park itself is named after Pope Gregory XVI, who, in 1861, saved Tivoli from chronic river damage by building a tunnel under the Aniene, thereby weakening its flow. An unexpected (but not unappreciated) side effect was the creation of the **Grande Cascata** (Grand Cascades), which shoot streams of spray. After entering the park, follow the footpath to the right; after a short walk, passing clusters of trees and descending some steps, there's a terrace with views of the cascades, plus a terrace from which you can look into the tunnel itself. *Tel. 0774/878563. From ACOTRAL stop on Largo Garibaldi, follow Via Pacifici (it changes names 6 times), veer left on Viale Roma, and turn at Largo Sant'Angelo. Admission: L4000. Open daily 9–4 (until 6 in summer).*

Near the grounds of Villa Gregoriana stand the 10 remaining columns of the round **Temple of Vesta**. Consecrated to the goddess of earth and fire, the temple was similar in appearance to the Temple of Vesta in the Roman Forum. Nearby is the rectangular **Temple of the Sibyl**, which most likely predates the temple of Vesta. The Sibyl was a direct channel to the gods, who could predict the future and reveal divine intentions. Like the Pantheon in Rome, these temples were preserved only because they were transformed into churches in the Middle Ages.

➤ **VILLA ADRIANA** • A short bus ride from Tivoli will deposite you at this expansive structure, which once served as an ancient Roman model for the villas at Tivoli. The complex was commissioned by Roman emperor Trajan himself, and it took the best architects in Rome 13 years to contrive the temples, baths, living quarters, and gardens that made Hadrian's villa the largest ever built by the Romans. (Hadrian even had tunnels burrowed underground so that horse carts could schlepp supplies from end to end.) When the vast complex was completed, the emperor announced: "Finally I can live like a human being." Today signs in English label each section of the still-impressive ruins; don't miss the swimming pool, with resident swans. Also stop by the **Museo Didactico** (open when there's enough personnel to staff it) at the villa's entrance: Its displays put the complex into perspective, as does the miniature model at the nearby snack bar. Before trekking into the unknown, fill up your water bottle at the spring by the entrance. Bus 4 from Piazza Garibaldi in Tivoli departs for Villa Adriana twice hourly between 9:15 AM and 8:45 PM (15 min, L1000). From the bus stop, it's a steep walk uphill to the bulk of the villa's sights. *Admission: L8000. Open daily 9–5 (until 7 PM May–Sept.).*

Subiaco

Perched high above a lush valley, Subiaco's serene vistas have provoked meditation and escapism since the town's inception in the 1st century AD. Founded by Nero with the construction of an opulent villa, Subiaco is better known for its second founding father: In the 6th century, the humble San Bennedetto (Saint Benedict) retreated into a cave in Subiaco's rocky hillside, spending three years in total seclusion before garnering a community of disciples and building 12 monasteries in the area. Today, only two remain—excellent examples of medieval craftsmanship that cannot help but invoke divine inspiration.

The largest of the two monasteries is **Santa Scolastica**, built by St. Benedict and his sister, Scolastica (who continued to distribute Saint Benedict's teachings, even after the jealous local clergy ran her brother out of town). Take a look at the stunning Cosmatesque cloister, with delicately carved spiraling pillars and intricate gold mosaics. The library (closed to the public) contains rare volumes as well as Italy's first printing press, built in 1474. *Tel. 0774/85525. Admission free. Open daily 9–12:30 and 4–7.*

More interesting is nearby **San Benedetto** monastery (follow the footpath that climbs uphill from Santa Scolastica), built over the grotto where St. Benedict lived in seclusion for three years. Here he wrote his *Regola* (rule), which formed the basis of the Benedictine order, a brotherhood of monks who forswore all material possessions. Wait around long enough—the stockpile of monastic homebrew in the souvenir shop eases the pain of waiting—and one of the monks will fetch you for a guided tour; even if you don't speak Italian, it's an authentic and often entertaining way to get a feel of the monastery. You enter by a broad, steep path that passes through a shady wooden veranda, where a Latin inscription reads PEACE TO THOSE WHO ENTER. Inside, every inch of the upper church is covered with brilliant frescoes done by 14th-century Sienese artists. In front of the main altar, a stairway leads to a chapel hewn from the rock, while a second stairway leads to the cave where St. Benedict once lived in blissful seclusion. *Tel. 0774/85039. Admission free. Open daily 9–12:30 and 3–6.*

BASICS Bus 4 leaves hourly (2 hrs, L4800) from Rome's Rebibbia Metro station, stopping at Subiaco's Piazza della Resistenza; it returns to Rome hourly from the piazza. One kilometer southeast along Via Cavour, past Piazza San Andrea, is the **tourist office** (Via Cadorna 59, tel. 0774/822012), open Monday 8–2, Tuesday–Saturday 8–2 and 3:30–7:30, Sunday 9–noon.

Rieti and Monte Terminillo

Rieti proudly claims the title of *umbilico italiano* (the belly button of Italy), as the country's geographical center. Whether or not the calculations are truly valid, Rieti's attractions are many: several ski resorts, four castles, half a dozen lakes, and a number of Franciscan sanctuaries accessible by bus. Rieti itself is a pleasant, well-maintained town, bordered by a daunting medieval wall and centered around the lively Piazza Vittorio Emanuele. Here you'll find the **AAST tourist office** (Piazza Vittorio Emanuele 17, tel. 0746/203220), with loads of information on trails, outdoor activities, and accommodations. Around the corner is Piazza Cesare Battisti and **Palazzo Vicentini**, which offers a peaceful, though unspectacular garden and a view of the entire valley. The Romanesque **Cathedral of Santa Maria Assunta** lies just next door.

Monte Terminillo rises 2,216 meters above the plain of Lazio, making it a popular day trip with skiers and hikers, who clog the highways from Rome. A ski lift (L20,000 for a day pass) reaches the windy summit, which in turn is connected to the surrounding peaks by kilometer upon kilometer of Club Alpino Italiano hiking trails. The towns of **Leonessa**, **Vallomina**, and **Flamignano** also operate ski runs (though they're further away) and the lakes of **Turano**, **Salto**, and **Scandarello** all provide lush and scenic landscapes.

COMING AND GOING From Rome's Tibertina Metro station, ACOTRAL buses travel to Rieti every half hour (5:30 AM–10:45 PM, 1 hr 45 min, L5600). Buses also connect Rieti to Mt. Terminillo (6 daily, L3000).

WHERE TO SLEEP AND EAT Budget accommodations in Rieti mean one of two things: a L70,000 double at the **Albergo Massimo d'Azeglio** (Viale Ludovico Canali 4, near the train station, tel. 0746/274250), half of which is renovated, the other half grimy and thrashed; or else a seriously cheap, seriously run-down room for L20,000 in the unlisted pension (36 Via dei Crispolti, tel. 0746/44784) above the Chinese restaurant. Near Mt. Terminillo lie three more appealing options: the hostel, **Ostello della Neve** (Località Campo Foragna-Anello Panoramico, tel. 0746/261169), with beds for L18,000; the campground **Ski Caravan Club** (tel. 0746/261323), which charges L7000 per person; and the mountaintop **Rifugio Angelo Sebastiani** (tel. 0746/261–184; beds L2500), reachable by bus in winter, or by a spectacular three-hour hike over Mount Terminillo's summit.

Cerveteri

The historic center of Cerveteri is perched atop a small hill, with the modern city encroaching on all sides. This ancient part of Cerveteri, with its narrow streets and alleyways, retains some of its medieval traits, but most people come for the nearby Etruscan necropolis. ACOTRAL buses from Rome's Lepanto Metro station (hourly, 45 min, L3000) will drop you in **Piazza Aldo Moro**, right by a shady park just outside the pedestrian-only centro storico. Take a quick peak, grab a snack from one of a dozen trattorias, then make a beeline for Cerveteri's Etruscan sights.

From the ACOTRAL bus stop on Piazza Aldo Moro it's a 20-minute walk along a narrow road shaded by cypress trees to the **Banditaccia Necropolis**. This Etruscan city, originally called Cere, wielded formidable power over the Mediterranean, and was a center for artistic and cultural activity in the 7th and 6th centuries BC. Having battled successfully against the Greeks, the Etruscans finally succumbed to the superior might of the Romans in the 4th century BC. Many mysteries still shroud the elusive Etruscans; their funerary architecture and elegant sculpture are pretty much the only remaining clues to their sophisticated culture. The Necropolis (burial place) itself, with circular hut-like tombs, was built to imitate the residences of the living. Bring a flashlight to explore the chambers and carved stone beds, and don't miss the **Tomba dei Rilievi**, elaborately decorated in sculptures and reliefs. *Via Mora Castuane, tel. 06/994001. From Piazza Aldo Moro, follow Via Mora Castuane and the yellow signs. Admission: L8000. Open Tues.–Sun. 9–4 (until 7 in summer).*

Cerveteri's **Museo Nazionale** is housed in the impressive Castello Orsini, which towers over the centro storico in full Renaissance splendor. The museum provides explanations of the necropolis through diagrams and reconstructions, displaying Etruscan vases, cups, terra-cotta statues, bronze jewelry, and even some ragged clothing. *Castello Orsini, tel. 06/922342. Admission: L4000. Open Tues.–Sun. 9–3 (until 5 in summer).*

Ostia Antica

Ostia Antica, like Pompeii, is an ancient city preserved in its entirety—only without the volcano and hordes of visitors. Even in summer it's possible to have the place to yourself, and with

The Original Flower Child

Long before anyone cared about rain forests and recycled paper, Francis of Assisi lived as one with nature in the hills above Rieti, where he'd engage in his favorite activities: prayer and long walks. Four "Santanari Francescani" (Franciscan Sanctuaries) near Rieti mark places where St. Francis stayed and performed miracles. Although the religious thing is overdone, the sanctuaries are all set in awesome surroundings, built on or into hillsides riddled with hiking trails. The two sanctuaries nearest Rieti aren't serviced by bus. However, there is regular service to Greccio (30 min, L3000) and Poggio Bustone (25 min, L3000) from Rieti's bus depot. Greccio is a major Christmastime destination for people who want to see the nativity crib built by St. Francis in 1223. If you're headed to the sanctuary at Poggio Bustone, prepare for a steep, kilometer-long hike and, at the top, panoramic views of central Italy.

theaters, apartment buildings, baths, temples, and even ancient pubs to explore (all grown over with ivy and shaded by lofty trees), there's plenty to see. Plus, Ostia Antica's numerous rail and Metro connections make the site Rome's most convenient day trip.

Ostia derives its name from *Ostium* (Latin for river mouth), an appellation that reflects the city's position at the mouth of the Tiber River. Originally, Ostia served as a crucial port connecting Rome to the sea, but today the town is a full 3 kilometers from the ocean; the Tiber changed its course in 1557 and the ocean later receded, leaving the town high and dry. At its height however, Ostia was a bustling port town with a population of 50,000, and boasted a potent middle class of traders, businessmen, and bureaucrats, unionized in efficient *corpora* or corporations. Ostia followed Rome into decline in the 4th and 5th centuries AD, and was completely abandoned by the 9th. Today the ruins still contain a number of murals, mosaics, and sculptures depicting daily life, and it only takes the slightest bit of strain on your imagination to make it come alive. There's no place to get food or drink within the site, so bring provisions (especially water). Down the road from the site, a **grocery** (Piazza Umberto 6; open Mon.–Sat. 8:30–1:30 and 4:30–7) sells snacks and picnic supplies; walk toward the castle on Via Romaguoti and follow the road around the bend.

COMING AND GOING From Rome, take Metro Line B to the Magliana stop and transfer to a Lido train to the Ostia Antica stop. If you're returning to Rome in the same day, a *biglietto integrato giornaliero* (day pass; L6000) costs the same as a round-trip ticket but is valid for unlimited Metro travel. To reach the site from the station, walk across the pedestrian overpass, continue straight, and follow the signs to the left.

THE SITE **Decumano Massimo** is the main street leading through the ancient city. As you enter the site from the ticket booth, proceed down the Decumano; on the right, the **Terme di Nettuno**, the largest of 18 bath complexes that served Ostia's ancient population, is ornately decorated with mosaics depicting the robust Neptune frolicking with all manner of scaly beasts. Next door lies the **theater**, one of Ostia's earliest excavated sights. Beyond the stage is the **Piazzale delle Corporazioni**, once a porticoed gallery that housed the offices of businessmen and merchants. The fascinating series of mosaics encircling the piazzale depicts maritime scenes, Ostian daily life, and declarations of the titles of each office. Within the piazzale is a **temple**, likely dedicated to Ceres, goddess of grain and abundance (and thus trade surpluses), to whom Ostia owed a great deal of thanks. From the Decumano, turn right on Via dei Molini to find an ancient **bakery**, with stone mills and ovens. The nearby **Casa di Diana** is a good example of ancient low-cost housing projects, with five-story apartments and communal toilets. On Via di Diana, you'll see the **thermopolium**, a local dive bar where clients once ate, drank, and made merry. Notice the huge wine vats and the painted menu on the wall.

Continuing away from the Decumano, on Via dei Molini, you'll hit the **Museum of Ostia** (free admission with ticket to archaeological site; open 9:30–1:30), which is definitely worth a gander. The museum contains Ostia's sculptural riches, including remarkable marble reliefs documenting scenes of town life. There are also beautifully preserved sarcophagi and an exquisite altar to the 12 gods of Olympus. Adjacent to the museum is a **bookstore**, with guidebooks, slides, and postcards.

Visible from the museum, on the Decumano, is the **Forum**, which served as the city's civic center. The area is dominated by the imposing **Capitolium**, dedicated to the godly triad of Juno, Jupiter, and Minerva. From the top of the Capitolium's stairs there is a great view of the city and the Forum's other structures, including the **Curia** (headquarters for the town council), the **Basilica** (seat of the tribunal), the **Forum Baths**, and the temple to Rome and Augustus (opposite the Capitolium).

The last street off the Decumano leads to the opulent homes of Ostia's bourgeoisie. Turning right on Cardini degli Aurigni, and left on Vico delle Volte Dipinte, you'll see the entrance to the **Insula delle Muse** (currently under restoration), once a single-family residence. Inside, the extensive but faded wall paintings represent a similar style to that found at Pompeii. The nearby **Domus dei Dioscuri** showcases two striking mosaics dedicated to the divine twins Castor and Pollux, who were well-loved in Ostia as the gods of commerce. Climb to the second-story terraces to catch a bird's-eye view. *Admission: L8000. Open daily 9–6 (entrance closes at 5).*

Civitavecchia

Founded by Emperor Trajan to enhance Rome's Mediterranean trade base, Civitavecchia does have a few Roman relics spread among the modern housing, oil-storage tanks, and port paraphernalia cluttering its shore. But let's be honest: The only reason to visit this bland industrial tragedy is to catch a **ferry to Sardinia**. If you end up trapped here waiting for your boat, as many often are, rest assured that food is cheap and beds are plentiful. And if you're really bored, mosey through the free, peach-colored **Museo Nazionale** (Largo Plebiscito, tel. 0766/23604; open Tues.–Sun. 9–1, shorter hrs off-season), which has a skimpy collection of Etruscan and Roman trinkets. For the usual maps and accommodation listings, stop by **AAST** (Viale Garibaldi 40–42, tel. 0766/25348), on the waterfront between the station and the port. The office is open weekdays 9–1 and 4–7, Saturday 9–12:30.

COMING AND GOING

➤ **BY TRAIN** • Trains leave frequently from Rome's Stazione Termini (1 hr, L7200) for Civitavecchia's waterfront train station (Viale della Repubblica), where you can also catch trains to Pisa, Torino, and Napoli. From the station, it's is a short walk downhill to the port.

➤ **BY BUS** • ACOTRAL (tel. 0766/35961) buses leave every 30 minutes from Viale Giulio Cesare, a few steps from Rome's Lepanto Metro station (90 min, L6000). Buses stop at both Via Cadorna, one block east of the FS ports, and at Piazza Vittorio Emanuele II, two blocks east of the dock for Tirrenia Lines (*see below*).

➤ **BY BOAT** • Civitavecchia is the main Lazio port for ferries to Sardinia. **Tirrenia Lines** (tel. 0766/500580) serves both Olbia and Cagliari with sparkling white ferries that leave from two adjacent docks on Calata Cesare Laurenti, reached directly from Viale Garibaldi. Fares to Cagliari run L60,000–L82,000 (cabin) and L45,000–L64,000 (reclining chair), depending on the season. For Olbia, year-round fares are L50,000 (cabin), L35,000 (reclining chair). **FS** (tel. 0766/23273 or 0766/25850) has service to Olbia only, with fares equivalent to Tirrenia's. All ferries generally leave in the evening between 6 and 11 PM, from the dock at the end of Via Cadorna, where there's a small terminal laden with grimy bathrooms and a not-so-thrilling snack bar. Tickets can be purchased on board, but definitely reserve in advance if you plan to make the crossing in summer.

WHERE TO SLEEP AND EAT

We hope you won't be around long enough to use this section. But if you somehow miss the last ferry, **Albergo Roma Nord** (Via Montegrappa 27, tel. 0766/22770), a few blocks east of the FS dock, has doubles from L35,000. The centrally located **La Palamite** (Via Avrelia Sud 6, tel. 0766/23657) is the cheapest option around, with doubles at L50,000. For cheap fresh sandwiches (L2800) head to **Casa del Gelato** (Largo Plebiscito, at Viale Garibaldi; open daily 6 AM–midnight). For more substantial eats, try **Santa Lucia** (Viale Garibaldi 34, tel. 0766/25235), with wood-oven pizzas from L10,000. **STANDA** (Viale Garibaldi, btw the station and port; closed Thurs. afternoon), is an ideally located market where you can stock up on supplies.

Viterbo

The main attractions in Viterbo, 80 kilometers northwest of Rome, are its 12th-century walls and towers, and its perfectly preserved **Quartiere San Pellegrino**, a medieval labyrinth of enchanting architecture. Coming from Porta del Carmine, cross Ponte Paradiso and step into this eerie 13th-century time capsule, complete with dark, curving roads and a jumble of misshapen houses that tilt gracefully with age. Much of the area is pedestrian-only, which makes it a fine place to plant yourself in a café or piazza with a bottle of cheap wine. If you lean toward the morbid, the **church of Santa Rosa** (Via della Santa Rosa, just inside city walls; open daily 6:45–12:30 and 3:30–5:30) preserves (sort of) the shriveled, 13th-century body of Santa Rosa di Viterbo; look for her in the glass case near the altar.

BASICS

The **EPT** office (Piazza dei Cadotti 16, tel. 0761/346363; open Mon.–Sat. 8–2), in the northern part of the centro storico, has maps and info on accommodations throughout the area. It's also a good source for maps of the Monte Rufeno Wildlife Reserve (*see below*). The same can be said of **AAST** (Piazza Verdi 4/A, tel. 0761/226666; open Mon.–Sat. 8–2), which has the additional charm of an English-speaking staff.

COMING AND GOING

➤ **BY TRAIN** • **Stazione Porta Romana** is in the southwest corner of the city, about three blocks south of the centro storico's Porta Romana entrance. A second station, **Stazione Porta Fiorentina**, is north of the centro storico on Viale Trento, a short walk from the ACOTRAL bus depot. Both stations have a bar, bathrooms, indoor and outdoor waiting areas, and baggage storage for L1500 per piece. For local train information call 0761/327504.

➤ **BY BUS** • ACOTRAL (tel. 0761/308837) buses stop near Via Trieste at the centro storico's northern walls. From 6 AM to 6 PM tickets are sold at **Bar Time Out**, on the corner of Viale Trento and Via Trieste.

WHERE TO SLEEP
Within a block or so of the ACOTRAL bus station and Stazione Porta Fiorentina is the depressing but fairly cheap **Pensione Trieste** (Via Nazario Sauro 32, tel. 0761/341882; doubles L50,000 without bath), which sometimes has additional rooms to let about four blocks west on Viale Trieste. The clean, family-run **Albergo Milano** (Via della Cava 54, tel. 0761/340705; doubles L65,000) is three blocks west of Stazione Porta Fiorentina. **Albergo Roma** (Via della Cava 26, tel. 0761/226487; doubles L75,000), a few doors down from Albergo Milano, has an attractive lobby but only a few clean rooms. Be sure to see yours before handing over the cash, since some rooms are shabby and reek of stale beer.

AFTER DARK
Besides Viterbo's cafés and bars, check out the **Centro Sociale Occupato Autonomo**, a magnet for local anarchists and university students. It's housed in an abandoned building on the outskirts of town, and once you're inside the fence there's plenty of space to thrash and drink with locals (BYOB). Admission is generally free; if there's a band they may ask for a donation. For more info and directions—locals even have trouble finding it—look for notices posted in the bar at Via Garibaldi 47, just inside Porta Romana.

Monte Rufeno Wildlife Reserve

Lazio's little-known nature reserve spans over 2,980 acres of farmland and forest on the scrawny peaks of Monte Rufeno (734 meters). Clusters of pine, juniper, oak, and lush deciduous trees provide shelter for all sorts of critters, including foxes, weasels, deer, porcupines, and wild boar. Depending upon the season you may also spot owls, tortoises, and big brown toads. Hiking trails of varying difficulty crisscross the reserve, providing a measure of seclusion rarely found so close to Rome. Park activities include horseback riding (with a guide), mountain biking, swimming in natural springs, and your basic picnicking in the great outdoors. Pick up scores of maps and detailed trail guides from the **Monte Rufeno Reserve Center** (Piazza Sant' Angelo, Acquapendente, tel. 0763/733642; open daily 9–noon), which also arranges bike

Monster Mash

According to legend, the duke of Orsini commissioned a bunch of gruesome statues in 1552 in an attempt to create something that was uglier than himself. The result is now called Il Parco dei Mostri (Park of the Monsters), with stone ghouls and monsters that even now are gory to behold. From the ticket office it's a kilometer-long hike to the statue-filled gardens. Grim postcards from the adjacent souvenir shop make excellent gifts. Tel. 0761/924029. From Viterbo, catch an ACOTRAL bus from the depot on Viale Trento. Admission: L10,000. Park open daily 8:30 AM–sunset.

and horse rentals. Viterbo's EPT office (*see above*) also has *agriturismo* (farm stays) listings for the entire region.

COMING AND GOING SIRA buses (tel. 06/439-2463 in Rome, 0763/74126 in Acquapendente) depart regularly from Rome's Piazza della Repubblica; **ACOTRAL** (tel. 0763/74814) buses to Acquapendente leave from Viale Giulio Cesare, directly above Rome's Lepanto Metro station. Both lines charge L15,500 for the 1½-hour trip, and will drop you on Highway S2 (Rome–Siena–Florence) on a dirt road that's within easy walking distance to several park entrances. To reach the Monte Rufeno Reserve Center in Acquapendente, ask the driver to drop you by the stadium just west of Acquapendente's centro storico. From here follow Via Porta Sant'Angelo downhill to Piazza Fabricio, turn left and walk to the piazza's end, and turn left again at Piazza Sant'Angelo. The reserve center sometimes arranges shuttles into the park's deepest reaches; definitely ask about it.

WHERE TO SLEEP If you don't have camping gear but still want to spend the day hiking, **Albergo Cacino** (Via Porta Sant'Angelo 1–5, tel. 0763/74086; doubles L60,000) is close to Acquapendente's centro storico, a short walk downhill from the ACOTRAL and SIRA bus stop. Otherwise, three lodges inside the park offer combinations of dorms, semiprivate rooms, and deluxe private digs. In the northern part of the park, **Monaldesca** has five rooms loaded with a total of 18 bunks. The rates are L30,000 per person, L45,000 if you want breakfast and lunch, L60,000 for three square meals. **Tigna**, also in the park's northern perimeter, has the same pricing scheme as Monaldesca. Almost in the center of the park, **Marzapalo** is a basic dorm with beds for L30,000. Each of the lodges requires some hiking to reach; reserve space in advance and then grab trail guides from the reserve center in Acquapendente (*see above*). There are plenty of places to eat inside the park near lodges, but food tends to be expensive. You're better off buying supplies at one of the grocery stores in Acquapendente.

➤ **CAMPING** • The are only 15 official campsites within the park, so book well in advance at the reserve center in Acquapendente. The sites themselves are well into the park in a forest clearing—if you don't have a car, your choices are hiking or hitching. Facilities at the sites are extremely limited; there are no electrical hookups, but there is running water. The going rate is L3000 per person. *Tel. 0763/773642. From Highway S2, take Entrance 3 and follow signs.*

ABRUZZI AND MOLISE

11

By Laura Altieri

In the overlooked center of Italy, mysterious Abruzzi and Molise conjure up an Italy of the past. Here, widows really wear all black (even when it's 100° outside), the *mal'occhio* (evil-eye) is still cast, and 2,000-year-old traditions are upheld fanatically. These regions also provide a variety of outdoor activities, from hiking in the **Gran Sasso** (Italy's highest mountain range) to exploring the wilderness of **Parco Nazionale d'Abruzzo**, to soaking up the sun on the Adriatic coast. Buses will whiz you between the remote hill towns, craggy mountain tops, and wooded ravines that characterize the region's interior, and although prices of lodging and restaurants don't reflect the lack of tourism, camping is an option near most towns. On the downside, Abruzzi and Molise are among Italy's most economically depressed regions, as evidenced by drab cement-block buildings and downtrodden resorts.

Abruzzi
Even with 70 miles of coastline, the real jewels of Abruzzi are found deep inside the rugged interior. Few foreigners bother with the region's isolated mountain villages, and even fewer encounter the still-thriving wildlife in Abruzzi's national park, meaning you'll have it mostly to yourself. Of course, the industrialized coast is another story altogether. Once-pristine beaches are declining every year, partly from pollution and partly from neglect. Some resorts are still worth a gander, but *not* during July and August, when Italian city slickers bring the extended family for an extended vacation.

L'Aquila

With a prime location high in the Gran Sasso Mountains, L'Aquila is a convenient base for exploring Abruzzi's national park. Compared to most Italian cities though, L'Aquila's history, with no known Roman ties, is brief: The city was founded in the 13th century when Frederick II united the 99 surrounding kingdoms under one state and flag (bearing the eagle, or *l'aquila*). Lacking ruins or must-see museums, sightseeing possibilities can be exhausted in an afternoon, though you may want to stay longer to admire brief snippets of beauty: ornate Renaissance architecture, stout medieval churches, and colorful fresh produce at the morning market in Piazza del Doumo. Unfortunately, food and lodging aren't cheap—head to the hills when you're low on lire.

BASICS It's hard to miss the large **post office** (Piazza del Duomo, tel. 0862/6164; open Mon.–Sat. 8:15–7:30), right on the main square. Banks on the piazza change cash at decent

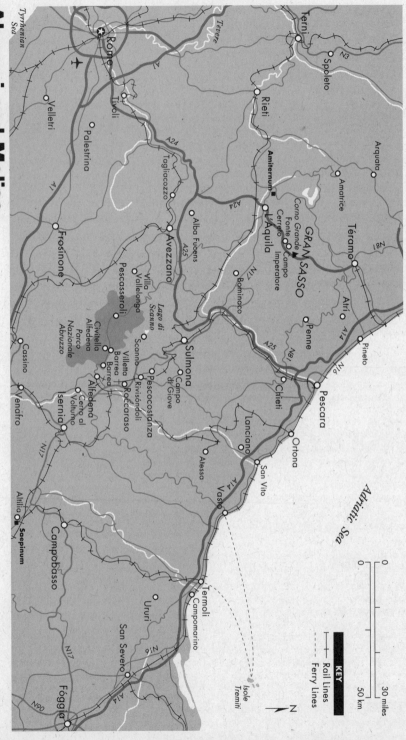

Abruzzi and Molise

Tyrrhenian Sea

Rome

Velletri

Palestrina

Tivoli

Tagliacozzo

Frosinone

A1

A24

A24

Tevere

Terni

Spoleto

N3

Rieti

Arquata

Amatrice

Amiternum

GRAN SASSO

Corno Grande
Fonte
Cerreto
Campo
Imperatore

L'Aquila

Téramo

N81

Atri

A14

Pineto

Penne

N81

Chieti

Pescara

Ortona

N16

Avezzano

A25

Alba Fucens

N17

N17

Bominaco

Sulmona

A25

Campo
di Giove

Pescasseroli

Villa
Vallelonga

Lago di
Scanno

Scanno

Civitella
Alfedena
Parco
Nazionale
Abruzzo

Barrea
Barrea

Villetta
Roccaraso

Rivisondoli
Pescocostanza

Alfedena

Cassino

Venafro

Cerro al
Volturno

Isernia

N17

Atessa

Lanciano

San Vito

Vasto

A14

Adriatic Sea

Altilia
Saepinum

Campobasso

Ururi

San Severo

N17

N16

Termoli
Campomarino

Isole
Tremiti

Fóggia

N90

A14

N

KEY

Rail Lines

Ferry Lines

0 _____ 30 miles

0 _____ 50 km

362

rates and charge no commission for traveler's checks. For operator-assisted calls, head to **SIP** (Via XX Settembre 75, tel. 0862/420142), open daily 9–12:30 and 3:30–6:30. The most central **AAST** tourist office (Corso Vittorio Emanuele 49, tel. 0862/410859), on L'Aquila's main pedestrian strip, is open Monday–Saturday 9–1 and 4–7.

COMING AND GOING Most trains to and from L'Aquila change at Sulmona, an hour away. Upon arrival at L'Aquila's **train station** (Piazza della Stazione, tel. 0862/419290) take Bus 1, 2, 3, or 3/S to reach the city center. The more central **bus station** (Piazza Alpini, tel. 0862/412808) sends hourly ARPA buses to Rome (2 hrs, L14,100), Pescara (1½ hrs, L10,800), and Avezzano (1 hr, L6800). Buy tickets in the small ARPA kiosk on Piazza Alpini.

➤ **RENTAL CARS** • **Ianni Franco** (Via Carlo Franchi 10, tel. 0862/280038) rents small cars for L60,000 a day and large ones for L130,000. **Italy by Car** (Via Croce Rossa 119, tel. 0862/65737) charges a little more, but has a better selection.

WHERE TO SLEEP Excluding the two hotels below, there ain't a double in sight for less than L90,000. So make a beeline for the central **Albergo Aurora** (Via Cimino 21, tel. 0862/22053), which has spacious doubles (L52,000) right off Piazza del Duomo. Another option is **Locanda Orazi** (Via Roma 175, tel. 0862/412889), with doubles for L50,000. It's a hike here from Piazza del Duomo: Follow Corso Vittorio Emanuele to Corso Principe Umberto, turn left, and persevere until the street becomes Via Roma.

FOOD The best place for a cheap meal is **Pizzeria San Marco** (Piazza San Marco 1, tel. 0862/410015), which has scads of freshly baked pizzas priced at L8000–L11,000. In August, the San Marco has outdoor service and live music that alternates between flamenco and Eric Clapton. If you've had enough pizza to last a lifetime, try homemade *strozzapreti* (pasta that translates "choke the priest"; L8000) at **Trattoria da Rino** (Via S. Marciano 2, tel. 0862/25280). Stock up on groceries at **Standa** (Via Indipendenza, at Via Guelfi, tel. 0862/26482), open Monday 4–8, Tuesday–Sunday 9–1 and 4–8. Fresh fruit and vegetables are best at the enormous **outdoor market** on Piazza del Duomo, held Monday–Saturday 6 AM–1 PM.

WORTH SEEING Baroque churches are a dime a dozen and easy to find in L'Aquila, but many of the major sites require more purposeful searching. Walk five minutes east from the train station to reach Piazza San Vito and its famous fountain, **Fontana delle 99 Cannelle**. In the sunken three-sided basin, 93 carved heads drool water into the enormous base, which is understandably popular on hot summer days. Each head represents one of the 99 villages united into a kingdom by Frederick II of Germany in the 13th century (six heads were never carved). Turn back toward the town center to see one of Italy's most peculiar churches: The 13th-century **Santa di Collemaggio** (Piazzale di Collemaggio) is a simple square box—no arching spires, no towering buttresses. Even the interior is almost completely without adornment, save for a mismatched baroque apse, altar, and the so-called Holy Doors, which are opened for 24 hours every August 28 to absolve the sins of those who pass through.

L'Aquila's austere **castello** looms above a dry moat, offering sweeping vistas of the Gran Sasso Mountain range. Inside the castle is the comprehensive but uninspired **Museo Nazionale d'Abruzzo**. The highlight here is the top-floor modern-art gallery; amid the swill are some unusual works by contemporary local artists. *Viale delle Medaglie d'Oro, near bus stop, tel. 0862/63631. Admission: L8000. Open June–mid-Sept., Mon.–Sat. 9–2 and 3–7:30, Sun. 9–1:30 and 3–7:30; mid-Sept.–May, Mon.–Sat. 9–2, Sun. 9–1.*

NEAR L'AQUILA

GRAN SASSO L'Aquila cowers beneath the towering Gran Sasso Mountains, home to one of Italy's tallest peaks, the **Corno Grande** (2,912 meters). For the most part, the unforested Gran Sasso are steep, rocky, and largely untouched by the 20th century—except, sadly, for a nuclear test site and the nearby highway. Bus 6 runs several times daily from L'Aquila to **Fonte Cerreto** (30 min, L1200), at the foot of the Gran Sasso. This hamlet is little more than the sum of its parts—a bar and an overpriced hotel. It's also the base station for the *funivia* (funicular), which leaves every half hour 8:30–5 for Campo Imperatore (10 min, L15,000), where Mussolini was once held prisoner.

Campo Imperatore has trailheads for half-day hikes, and a **lodge** (tel. 0862/411202) with 10 hikes ranging from easy to tough. Anyone planning more than an hour's jaunt should definitely buy the map "Gran Sasso d'Italia: Carta dei Sentieri," which details campgrounds, rifugi, and 22 different hikes. Don't forget to pack something warm, because it gets chilly up here even in summer. In winter, hiking trails become ski runs; full-day lift tickets (which include the funicular to Campo Imperatore) cost L30,000 (L40,000 on weekends). Campo Imperatore also has a **hostel** (Campo Imperatore, tel. 0862/400011; open year-round), which charges L25,000 for dorm-style accommodations and is the last place to find hiking supplies—bring food from L'Aquila if you want more than a sandwich. The hostel also rents skis and boots (L20,000).

Sulmona

Sulmona, with it's majestic mountain setting and excellent rail connections, is an excellent gateway to the Parco Nazionale d'Abruzzo. Although travelers do pass *through* town, Sulmona is trying hard to *retain* visitors by cashing in on its history as a hotbed of Roman and medieval culture. In 1995 the Sulmona city council decided to re-initiate an ancient tradition: a horseback **jousting** competition in Piazza Garibaldi (July 30), followed by a week of theater, music, and art. Another testimony to Sulmona's Roman past dominates Piazza XX Settembre, the town's main plaza: a pensive bronze statue of Sulmona's famous love child, the poet Ovid.

Ever wonder what spurred Ovid to pen his longing love poems? Legend has it that Augustus Caesar's granddaughter was the poet's divine inspiration.

Stick to the main street, Corso Ovidio, and you won't miss the main attractions. Start at **Santissima Annunziata** (Corso Ovidio, at Via dell'Ospedale, tel. 0864/210216), a large baroque church attached to a 15th-century Gothic-Renaissance palazzo. Inside is the forgettable **Museo Civico** (admission free; open Tues.–Sat. 8:30–12:30, Sun. 9:30–12:30). For a view of Sulmona's brown and green mountains, continue past Piazza XX Settembre and numerous confection shops to **Piazza Garibaldi**. This stadium-size square, with arches from a 13th-century aqueduct, is also the site of a daily market.

COMING AND GOING Sulmona has rail service to L'Aquila (11 daily, 1 hr, L5700), Pescara (18 daily, 1 hr, L5700), and Rome (5 daily, 2 hrs, L12,100). Bus A (L1300) runs from the **train station** (Piazza della Stazione, tel. 0864/34293) to the town center every 30 minutes, or you can walk (1½ km) up the tree-lined Viale Stazione. Buses operated by **ARPA** (tel. 0864/210469) stop in a parking lot on Via Japasseri below the old town; to reach the center, walk up Via Japasseri, turn left at the top of the hill, and continue up the zigzaggy stairs. Buy tickets on board for such destinations as L'Aquila (6 daily, 1 hr, L6600), Scanno (8 daily, 50 min, L3500), and Pescasseroli (1½ hrs, L7400; transfer in Castel di Sangro). If you're national park-bound, pick up maps and info at Sulmona's **AAST** tourist office. *Corso Ovidio 208, tel. 0864/53276; open Mon.–Sat. 8–1:30 and 4–7.*

WHERE TO SLEEP AND EAT Judging from the outside, **Hotel Italia** (Piazza Tommasi, off Piazza XX Settembre, tel. 0864/52308) is the most luxurious place in town. From the inside, it's a little less deluxe, but the rooms (doubles L60,000) are neat and spacious. At **Albergo Stella** (Via P. Mazara 15, tel. 0864/52653), L55,000 gets you a spartan double. **Ristorante Italia** (Piazza XX Settembre 26, tel. 0864/33070; closed Mon.) is chock-full of regional specialties. Try the slightly spicy fettuccine *al Nicolò* (a white sauce with sausage; L8000).

NEAR SULMONA

SCANNO The bus ride between Sulmona and Scanno (9 daily, 1 hr, L3500), following a dramatic route along the peaks of **Monte Genzana** (2,170 meters) and **Monte Miglio** (1,712 meters), is as exciting as the town itself. Besieged by tourists in summer, Scanno is still a worthwhile trip year-round for the rich local costume. The most noticeable attire is worn by local women: dark embroidered blouses, cream-colored dresses, and funky drum-shape caps (which supposedly originated in Asia). If the mood strikes, rent your own Scannese costume for L20,000 at **La Violetta** (Via Roma 14, tel. 0864/74473).

Below town lies the incredible **Lago di Scanno**, a cool, shimmering mountain lake. You can camp on its western bank at **I Lupi** (tel. 0864/740100), a friendly, grassy facility that attracts tent campers as well as RVs. Sites cost L7000 plus L7000 per person, and they rent horses (L22,000 per hr) and paddleboats (L4000 per hr). May–September the campground is open daily; November–April it's open weekends only. Hotel options include the central **Belvedere** (Piazza Santa Maria della Valle 3, tel. 0864/74314), where L60,000 doubles come equipped with baths and views. Farther uphill is the well-kept **Albergo Seggiova** (Via D. Tanturri 42, tel. 0864/74371), with doubles at L75,000, all with bath. No matter where you sleep, reservations are a must in July and August. If you're left high and dry, or if you want info on lake activities, head to the **AAST** tourist office (Piazza Santa Maria della Valle 12, tel. 0864/74317), open Monday–Saturday 9–1 and 4:30–6:30, Sunday 10–12:30.

Parco Nazionale d'Abruzzo

The Parco Nazionale d'Abruzzo, central Italy's wild kingdom, combines lakes, streams, castle ruins, wildlife, and rocky terrain with gobs of hiking trails and ski runs. Italians get back to nature here year-round, but for some inexplicable reason foreigners have yet to discover the park. Catering to an Italian sensibility, the park includes a number of stores, hotels, and restaurants—but with just as many hiking trails, it's as easy to get lost in some truly beautiful countryside as it is to find cheap eats and sleeps.

You may want to rent a car (*see* Coming and Going in L'Aquila, *above*), because trains only stop at the fringes of the park, and buses move so slowly it will make you cry.

BASICS Information offices for hiking and camping are marked with UFFICIO DI ZONA signs and the park logo, a dopey bear. Park staffers will recommend the perfect hike but are clueless when asked about campsites. For this reason, it's worth shelling out L10,000 for the "Carta Turistica," an enormous topographical map that lists every trail, campsite, and wildlife refuge. Info offices in **Pescasseroli** (Vico Consultore 1, tel. 0863/910097) and **Civitella Alfedena** (Via Santa Lucia, tel. 0864/890141) are open daily 9–noon and 3–7. In July and August, additional stations are open seven days a week in **Villetta Barrea** (cnr of Barrea and Scanno roads), **Barrea** (Via Roma 7, no phone), and **Camosciara**, on the road to Pescasseroli, 3 kilometers west of Villetta Barrea. The latter office has an English-speaking staff, wildlife displays, and a groovy film about animals that's screened daily in summer at 5 PM. Information on lodging, skiing, and restaurants is handled by the **Azienda Soggiorno** (Via Piave 1; open Mon.–Sat. 9–1 and 4:30–6:30) in Pescasseroli.

COMING AND GOING If you're driving from Rome (2½ hrs) or L'Aquila (1½ hrs), take Autostrada A24 to the A25, get off at the Celano exit, and head south on the N83 toward Pescasseroli. By public transportation, take a train from Sulmona (7 daily, 1 hr, L5000) or Rome (6 daily, 2 hrs, L8800) or a bus from L'Aquila (20 daily, 1 hr, L5800) to **Avezzano**. From Avezzano, 9 buses daily make a slow circuit through the park, stopping along the way in Alfedena (1½ hrs, L3000), and Pescasseroli (2½ hrs, L3600).

WHERE TO SLEEP AND EAT Most regulated campgrounds are well maintained (with bars and showers) and open year-round, although they do charge a pricey L12,000–L16,000 per person. They're all far from public transport, so you'll have to walk, hitch, or take a taxi from the nearest town. The "Carta Turistica" map, available at park information offices, is invaluable for finding the perfect remote campsite.

➤ **BARREA** • If you can stomach the crowds, Barrea has keen views of Lago di Barrea from its hillside perch, not to mention one of the park's two youth hostels, **Ostello le Vicenne** (Via Roma, tel. 0864/88362). Look for the green gate near Bar Il Chioschetto, off Barrea's main drag. Prices—L25,000 for space in a four-bed suite—are steep for a hostel, but the place is clean and vacancies are likely. One kilometer outside of town in the direction of Civitella Alfedena is **Camping La Genziana** (tel. 0864/88101), a quiet site close to hiking trails. The rates here are L6000 per person and L10,000 per tent. As for food, Barrea's **Pizzeria da Francesco** (Via Roma 159, tel. 0864/88144) has first-rate pizza and pasta for less than L8000.

➤ **CIVITELLA ALFEDENA** • The newest and smallest of the park villages, Civitella Alfedena is a gateway to many trails and has two nearby campgrounds. **Camping Wolf** (Via Sotto I Cerri, tel. 0864/890366; closed Nov.–Apr.) comprises a hilly site west of Alfedena and charges L6000 per person and L6000 per tent site. Between June and September, **Campeggio le Quite** (tel. 0864/89141), a shady site near Lago di Barrea, charges identical prices for generally nicer facilities, and more trees. If you're tired of roughing it, the modern **Albergo La Torre** (Via Castello 3, tel. 0864/890121) charges L45,000 per double; tack on an additional L10,000 in summer.

➤ **PESCASSEROLI** • This place is packed with hotels that cater to an upper-crust clientele, so steer clear if you're on a tight budget. In the center of town, the spiffy **Locanda al Castello** (Via G. d'Annunzio 1, tel. 0863/910757) charges L50,000 per double and, sadly, is one of the better deals around. On the budget front are two year-round campgrounds: **Camping La Panoramica** (Vialone della Cabinovia 19B, tel. 0863/910750), spread beneath a sheep-freckled hill south of town, and **Campeggio dell'Orso** (tel. 0863/902334), 2 kilometers south of town on the road to Villetta Barrea, with an attached rifugio. Dell'Orso charges L6000 per site, L6000 per person; sites at La Panoramica cost L3000 more. You can rent horses across from La Panoramica at **Le Foche** (Via Oppieto 1, tel. 0863/912863) for L18,000 per hour. For good regional specialties, cross the bridge from Piazza San Antonio to **Peppe di Sora** (Via Benedetto Croce 1, tel. 0863/91908) for penne *di orapi* (a bitter veggie that grows in these parts; L9800), and other homemade pastas.

EXPLORING PARCO NAZIONALE D'ABRUZZO With more than 150 nature and hiking trails—not to mention ski runs and horseback-riding and mountain-bike trails—there is no excuse to be bored. On the other hand, there's nothing like an official sight here, which means you must create your own fun. Luckily, the "Carta Turistica" map (*see* Basics, *above*) shows every twist and turn of the park's many trails. For carless vagabonds, ARPA buses travel nine times daily (once on Sundays) between Avezzano, Pescasseroli, Barrea, and Alfedena. Even so, buses are unpredictable and unbearably slow. To avoid undo angst, get a photocopy of ARPA's bus schedule from any tourist office.

When speed-crazed Italian drivers get out of their cars, they get on their mountain bikes. One of the most popular areas for this reckless variety of fun is **Altopiano di Macciarvana**, near the town of Opi, off trails C3 and C1; **Monte Tranquillo** is another good spot. To rent a mountain bike (L8000 per hr) or road bike (L4000 per hr) go to **Nolo Bici** (Piazza San Antonio, tel. 0863/912760) in Pescasseroli. **Horses** are for hire at a dozen spots throughout the park—look for CENTRO IPPICO signs near towns and campsites. The going rate is about L20,000 per hour.

➤ **HIKING** • The park's most popular moderate trails are **F1**, which starts near the town of Opi, and **I1**, which begins near Civitella Alfedena. Both meander through forests and valleys before moseying across some rocky hillsides. The only bummer is that you must sign up one day in advance at the *Ufficio di Zona* in Camosciara; between July 15 and August 31 you must also pay L10,000 for the privilege of hiking with the masses on F1 and I1. On the other hand, it doesn't cost a single lira to hike **K6**, although in summer you must get permission first from Barrea's *Ufficio di Zona*. K6 runs through wolf, mountain goat, and lynx breeding grounds, and is best appreciated early in the morning—in the afternoon, they're no longer "in the mood." For a full-day hike from Barrea, try the challenging **K3**, which takes about five hours and ends at photo-worthy Lago Vivo; for a gentler trip down, connect with **K4**. From Pescasseroli, the ambitious can try the steep trek to placid Lago di Scanno (*see* Scanno, *above*) on **D1, A9, A1, A2,** or **Y10**.

➤ **SKIING** • For remarkably little money, you can spend the day tearing down the slopes outside Pescasseroli at the **Società Impianti Funiviari** (tel. 0863/912796) ski lift. There's no public transportation, but it's so close to town you can hitch or call a cab. Ski-lift passes cost L25,000 a day (L18,000 afternoon only); it's L20,000 to rent skis and boots; and lessons are available. The **Orsa Maggiore** chairlift nearby operates year-round (L11,000), whisking you up (and for non-skiers, back down) the steep mountain.

The Abruzzi Coast

Abruzzi does not have the prettiest stretch of coast in the world—while some beaches are sandy and scenic, many are marred by port facilities and heavy industry. Strangely enough, Italian vacationers don't seem to mind a little grime, nor do they seem to care that prices hardly reflect the region's mediocre reputation. Backpackers, however, do care, especially in a town like **Pescara**, Abruzzi's largest and most easily accessible coastal resort. Despite its downtrodden demeanor, every room is booked in July and August, and crafty hotel owners often require guests to pay some portion of their meals whether they want to or not. Stick to smaller towns and avoid the tourists and tourist prices. If you're a bargain hunter, bag the beach and head for **Atri**. There's no swimming or sunbathing to be had, but this picturesque and relatively inexpensive town hovers peacefully above the coast and the hordes.

PESCARA

The largest town on the Abruzzi coast, Pescara draws packs of teenagers in July and August, as well as carloads of extended families. Pescara is also a major transportation hub; if forced to change trains or buses here, give yourself an hour or so to explore the sights—which means heading straight for the brown sand beaches. The main drag, **Corso Umberto I**, accommodates slow-walking beach bums and fast-talking hustlers. At night, squadrons of sunburned Italians walk the corso and the shorefront, or congregate in outdoor cafés on the western end of the corso. For the latest details of Pescara's renowned **jazz festival** (around July 20), contact the **Società del Teatro e della Musica** (Via Liguria 6, tel. 085/422–1463).

BASICS Pescara is a major stop on the Bologna–Bari coastal line and has a modern **train station** (Piazza della Repubblica, tel. 085/378172). Trains run regularly to Rome (3½ hrs, L18,100) and Bologna (5 hrs, L25,200). To reach town, walk out of the station and head straight through the archway to Piazza della Repubblica. On the piazza is Pescara's **bus station** (tel. 085/421–1891), with regular ARPA coaches to Sulmona (5 daily, 1½ hrs, L6600) and Atri (hourly, 1 hr, L2800). To reach the beach from Piazza della Repubblica, continue down the main drag, Corso Umberto I. The sole redeeming feature of Pescara's clueless **tourist information office** (Via Fabrizi 171, tel. 085/421–1707) is that they sell tickets (L10,000–L25,000) to outdoor concerts and plays at **Teatro G. d'Annunzio** (Viale C. Colombo 69, tel. 085/693093).

WHERE TO SLEEP AND EAT **Hotel Centrale** (Via Firenze 283, tel. 085/421–1772) has generic doubles for L50,000; once you see the Centrale's skanky communal bathrooms, the extra L10,000–L15,000 for a private bath will seem like a sound investment. Higher in quality and price is **Albergo Barese** (Via Regina Margherita 39, off Corso Umberto I, tel. 085/27345), with doubles for L80,000. Campers get the best deal in Pescara, since **Camping Internazionale** (tel. 085/65653) is next to Teatro G. d'Annunzio at the crossroads of Lungomare Colombo and Viale La Figlia; take Bus 2 (20 min, L1200) from the train station. Rates are L6500 per person and L6500 per tent. Head to **Ristorante Gaetano** (Via M. Forti 21, Piazza della Repubblica, tel. 085/421–7840) for generous servings of spaghetti *al pescatore* (with seafood; L7000).

PINETO

While Pescara is a chaotic free-for-all, the scene is more sedate 20 kilometers north in Pineto, where the beach is cooler, calmer, and less commercialized. The bummer is that Italian families reserve hotels and campsites literally months in advance, making it difficult for budget types to locate anything under L50,000 in summer. Adding insult to injury, nearly every hotel charges for meals in July and August. Pineto's **train station** (Piazza della Stazione, tel. 085/949–1602) serves only two destinations: Pescara (7 daily, 15 min, L2000) and Ancona (7 daily, 2 hrs, L10,800). ARPA buses don't fare much better, with limited service to Pescara (8 daily, 45 min, L2000) and Atri (6 daily, 30 min, L2000). The bus stop is on Via Gabriele d'Annunzio, north of Via Verona.

WHERE TO SLEEP AND EAT Even the pricey hotels on the waterfront Via Gabriele d'Annunzio, Pineto's main drag, suffer from train noise (the tracks run right along the water). The cheap and friendly **Albergo Pavone** (Via Roma 74, tel. 085/949–1563), only three blocks from the beach, has doubles with bath and balcony for L50,000 (including one meal in summer). The **AAST** tourist office (Via Gabriele d'Annunzio 123, tel. 085/949–1341) lists other options in this price range but will not make reservations.

Camping Helipolis (Via XXV Aprile, tel. 085/949–2720; open Apr.–Sept.) and **Camping Pineto Beach** (Via XXV Aprile, tel. 085/949–2724; open June–Sept.) lie side by side on the beach 2 kilometers north of town. Don't expect peace and quiet, as these megasites have swimming pools, game rooms, laundries, and markets. Sites start at L12,000 plus L8000 per person. To reach the campgrounds, take a taxi from the station or call and ask them to pick you up. Regional cuisine—including six fish pasta dishes (L8000) and wood-oven pizza (L6000–L9000)—is served *al fresco* (outside) at **La Tana** (Via Venezia 30, tel. 085/949–0838). It's open nightly during the summer (closed Wed. the rest of the year).

ATRI

Ten kilometers southwest of Pineto, tiny Atri is a welcome change from beach towns, and is the place to find fresh air and cheap rooms. Olive groves, steep Renaissance streets, Abruzzi's best frescoes, (in the **duomo** on Piazza del Duomo), and ancient Roman baths surrounded by four Renaissance churches (which seem more authentic in their slightly disheveled state) all present beautiful reasons to visit Atri. By bus, Atri is only a short, bumpy ride from Pineto (12 daily, 25 min, L2000) or Pescara (9 daily, 50 min, L3700), so you can be a beach bum in daylight and still spend the evening in laid-back Atri. The ARPA bus stop is outside the town's gates at Porta San Domenico, ½ kilometer downhill from Atri's Piazza del Duomo. Buy tickets at the bar next door.

Punk rock fans should browse The Musical Box (Corso E. Adriano 31), Atri's best—and only—alternative music CD shop.

WHERE TO SLEEP AND EAT Atri's lone *albergo* (inn) is **Hotel San Francesco** (Corso E. Adriano 38, tel. 085/87473), where L60,000 buys an airy double room with breakfast. Conveniently, the hotel bar is one of the town's hippest. Most local restaurants serve up that old standby, pizza, with the crucial exception of **Greentime** (Via Portico 6, off Piazza Minzoni, tel. 085/879–7125), where fresh seafood comes at wholesale prices: A gargantuan plate of spaghetti *al pescatore* (with whatever fish is fresh) costs a reasonable L8000.

Molise

Separated from Abruzzi only 33 years ago, Molise is the least well-known and possibly the oddest province in Italy. Within the region you'll find a large Albanian population, a distinct gastronomic tradition, Europe's oldest human settlement, and a fickle fault line that has regularly wreaked havoc on Molise's landscape. Geography and geology have blessed the province with beaches and mountains, but Molise hasn't managed to turn these assets into a roaring tourist industry. Still, if you're curious about what Italy was like when your great-grandmother lived here (or why she left), Molise merits exploration. For an inside look at this agricultural region, ask the local tourist office about *agriturismo* lodging options, where you can stay in a local farm house and sample tasty regional cuisine.

Isernia

Bloody hell, you're stuck in Isernia, possibly the most unfortunate town in Italy. Part of the problem is the earthquakes that regularly, continually, and perpetually thrash the city. Forced to rebuild from the ground up so many times, it's no wonder that Isernia's old town is now a maze of bricks and scaffolding. Even the old main square, **Piazza San Pietro Celestino**, has been largely abandoned. In the middle of all this rubble and cement lies the sole reason to visit: the **Museo di Santa Maria della Monache** (Corso Marcelli, on Piazza Santa Maria, tel.

0865/415179; open daily 9–1 and 3–7), which showcases Europe's oldest human settlement. Isernian streetlayers discovered the site here in 1979, and the museum's killer display re-creates the painstaking hillside excavation, with the genuine artifacts positioned exactly where they were uncovered. Mysteriously, no bones were found—only weapons, body paint, and animal innards. Computer terminals provide information on the settlement in five languages.

COMING AND GOING The run-down **train station** (Piazza della Repubblica, tel. 0865/50921) serves Rome (4 daily, 3 hrs, L15,800), Naples (2 daily, 2 hrs, L9000), and Campobasso (hourly, 1 hr, L4600). Other rail routes are roundabout, so take a **bus**. These stop in front of the train station (look for the posted schedule) on their way to Naples (6 daily, 3 hrs, L8700) and Campobasso (hourly, 1 hr, L4400), as well as a host of small towns in between. **Cerella** operates most bus routes; call their office in Campobasso (tel. 0874/413675; open 8–8) and be prepared to use your Italian phrase book.

WHERE TO SLEEP AND EAT Visitors take Isernia by surprise, which means slim pickin's for lodgings and restaurants. Only the **Hotel Sayonara** (Via G. Berta 131, tel. 0865/50992) is anywhere near affordable: Spotless doubles are L70,000, and all rooms have baths. To get here, take Via P. Patriarca from the piazza across from the train station and turn right on Via G. Berta. Loads of cheap pizzerias line Corso Marcelli, but for something truly special, indulge in one of Italy's 10 best *pasticcerie* (pastry shops), **D'Agnilli** (Contrada S. Lazaro 10, tel. 0865/416208; closed Tues.). Near Hotel Sayonara is the slightly pricey but good **La Loggetta** (Via XXIV Maggio 8, tel. 0865/414875; closed Tues.), which serves regional specialties like polenta (L9500).

Campobasso

In this dreary embodiment of 1950s depression, nondescript buildings line nondescript streets. The only reason to come is if you're planning to visit the Roman ruins at Saepinum, only an hour's bus ride away. For bus schedules and town info, try the **EPT** office (Piazza della Vittoria 19, tel. 0874/415662; open Mon.–Sat. 8–2 and 4–6).

You won't find concrete buildings, exhaust fumes, and depression at the Roman ruins of **Saepinum**, which doesn't really count as a town anymore, but rather as an extensive collection of arches, walls, and amphitheaters. Ancient Romans founded Saepinum as an administrative center and convenient stopover on the Abruzzi–Puglia road. And because later civilizations found this site neither beautiful nor strategic, Saepinum's ruins were left undisturbed, leaving them in a superbly preserved state. Enter through the **Porta Terravecchia**, one of four doors left standing, and follow the paved path, which will take you past ruined baths, administrative buildings, a marketplace, and the foundations of the temple to Jove. You'll end up at the entrance to two small museums (admission free; open Tues.–Sun. 9–1), which explain how the area was excavated. Admission to the site is also free, but getting here is a real pain in the bum. In Campobasso, buy a bus ticket (L3000) to **Altilia**, a one-café town beside Saepinum's walls. Otherwise, take the more frequent bus (8 daily, ½ hr, L3300) to **Sepino** and either walk back 3 kilometers to the site or plead with the driver to stop on the highway as close to the ruins as possible.

COMING AND GOING Sandwiched between an abandoned stadium and a prison, Campobasso's crowded **bus station** (Via Mons Secondo Bologna) is best avoided at night. **Cerella** (tel. 0874/413675) has an information shed alongside the stadium; but you can buy tickets onboard for Isernia (hourly, 1 hr, L4400), Termoli (every 2 hrs, 1 hr, L4700), and Altilia/Saepinum (2 daily, 1 hr, L3000). The **train station** (Piazza Cuoco, tel. 0874/92785) has hourly trains to Isernia (1 hr, L4300) and Termoli (2 hrs, L6500). Two trains daily make the trek to Naples (3 hrs, L12,100).

WHERE TO SLEEP AND EAT The only cheap solution is to catch any bus from the train station labeled UNO NEGRO in the direction of the *zona industriale* (industrial zone). Be sure to ask the driver to stop at **Albergo Tricolore** (Via San Giovanni in Golfo 10, tel. 0874/63190), where good-size rooms with baths and views cost L30,000 per person. The comparable **Albergo Belvedere** (Via Colle delle Api 32, tel. 0874/62724) lies on the same bus route (and the same road under a different name) and charges L50,000 for doubles, plus L5000 for a private bath. When your stomach starts a growlin', follow the signs to the cavernous **La Pergola** (Corso Bucci 44, tel. 0874/92848). With seating for 200, there's always room to sit and chow on hearty appetizers like gnocchi *al pomodoro* (smothered with fresh tomatoes; L6000).

Termoli

Nothing here will change your life, but if you're heading down the coast and need a day in the sun, Termoli's sandy beaches will do the trick. During July and August, Italians arrive in droves to bake in the sun, driving prices almost beyond the reach of budget-minded folk. Make reservations in advance, or simply make Termoli a day trip on your way to Pescara or Bari. If you already have a third-degree sunburn, explore the town's historic quarter (*Il Borgo Antico*), which dates from the 4th century. Here you'll also find the 12th-century Norman **duomo** and Frederick II's **castello**. For town info, festival dates, and bus schedules, try **AAST**. *Piazza M. Bega, near the bus station, tel. 0875/706754. Open 9–12:30 and 6–8:30.*

Can't make it to Pamplona? The town of Ururi stages a "gladiator revival" each year in early May. Carts pulled by bulls and helmet-wearing horseback riders careen through the streets, as hordes of horrified spectators applaud. A bus leaves Termoli for Ururi twice daily (1 hr, L4600).

COMING AND GOING Termoli's **train station** (Piazza Garibaldi, tel. 0875/706430) dominates the center of town, and the **bus station** (Piazza M. Bega) is hidden one block south. Trains serve Pescara (hourly, 2 hrs, L7100), Bari (5 daily, 2½ hrs, L13,400), and Campobasso (5 daily, 2 hrs, L7800). Major bus destinations include Campobasso (every 2 hrs, 1 hr, L4700) and Pescara (3 daily, 1½ hrs, L10,300). If you're on your way to the **Tremiti Islands** (*see* Vieste, in Chapter 13) a *traghetto* (ferry) departs from Termoli daily (L23,800 boat; L43,000 hydroplane). In August and during weekends in July, there are four daily ferries. Buy ferry tickets at the last booth on Via Del Porto (tel. 0875/705341).

WHERE TO SLEEP AND EAT In July and August, *any* room is hard to come by. The best of the budget bunch, **Villa Ida** (Via M. Milano 27, tel. 0875/706666), is within hearing distance of the ocean and a five-minute walk from the train station. Doubles are L75,000, all with bath. More expensive is the beachfront **Hotel Meridiano** (Lungomare Colombo, tel. 0875/705946), a huge resort-size hotel with comfy doubles –L80,000). One kilometer north of town lies **Campeggio Cala Saracena** (S.S. Europa 2, tel. 0875/52193; open May–Sept.), with tent sites at L12,700 (14,700 high season), plus L6900 per person (L8900 high season). Come dinnertime, the fresh seafood specialties at **Ristorante da Antonio** (Corso Umberto I 59, tel. 0875/705158), to the right of the bus station, cost a reasonable L9000–L12,000.

NAPLES AND CAMPANIA 12

By Paul Kottman

Of the four regions that make up the struggling *Mezzogiorno* (southern Italy), Campania has the most glamorous history. A hedonistic handful of Greeks established the first colonies on the peninsula here, and their successors, the Romans, continued to "civilize" the region by constructing luxury palaces and brothels. In the 17th and 18th centuries Naples was a requisite stop on every noble's Grand Tour of Europe, and by the 19th and 20th centuries, many exiled left-wing intellectuals and artists found refuge and inspiration on the region's islands and small coastal towns. Today Naples is one of the most densely populated cities in Europe, controlled by the *cammorra* (the local organized crime faction), with an unemployment rate hovering at around 30%. In Campania smaller towns suffer from even greater economic hardship, with the exception of coastal resorts buoyed by tourist dollars.

Despite the region's difficulties, more travelers visit Campania than any other region in the south, and it's no wonder. The balmy climate and vistas are enought to cause heart palpitations, and the region's seaside resorts, bougainvillea-draped architecture, and mouth-watering cuisine continue to attract pleasure seekers. You can also visit the famed archaeological sites of Herculaneum (Ercolano) and Pompeii—both with views of menacing Mt. Vesuvius—for a three-dimensional look at life in pagan Italy. In between history lessons, flit from island to island in the Bay of Naples and lie beneath cliffs on the beaches of the Amalfi Coast (Costa Amalfitana). Then, of course, there's Naples, whose bad reputation keeps the tourist crowds away—all the better for those who are willing to discover its innumerable fascinations.

Naples

Naples (Napoli) exasperates both its critics and its defenders. From the moment you arrive at chaotic Piazza Garibaldi, the city blasts you with a confounding mix of beauty, poverty, and a glorious past. The provincial capital of Campania, Naples is also the de facto capital of the Mezzogiorno, by virtue of its size, cultural diversity, and economic strength. Since the 18th century, when Naples was the most prominent city in the Kingdom of the Two Sicilies, it has attracted great musicians, artists, and writers. Yet Naples is at first (and second) look a battered city—crowded, polluted, crime-ridden, and inhospitable to travelers. There's a sense of lawlessness in the streets, exemplified by the multitudinous Vespas, Fiats, and city buses that careen insanely through town, heeding neither traffic light nor hapless pedestrian. In this teeming environment, petty theft—driven by ever-apparent poverty—runs rampant.

Despite the problems, a feeling of community pervades, especially in the neighborhoods of Old Naples. The city has a spirit that makes urban centers of the north look positively comatose.

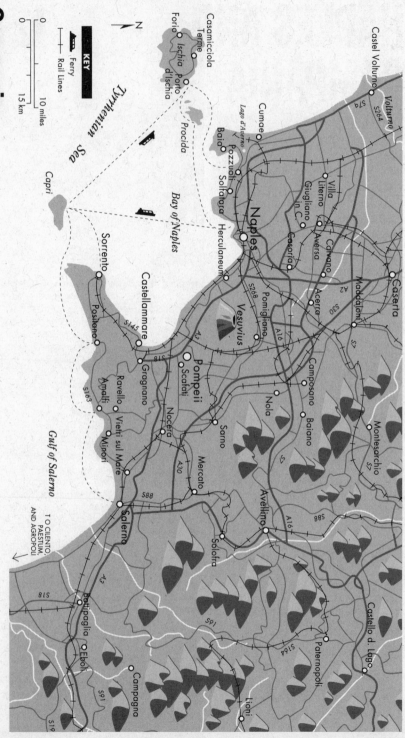

Campania

KEY

Ferry

Rail Lines

N

0   5   10 miles

0   5   10   15 km

Tyrrhenian Sea

Bay of Naples

Gulf of Salerno

Castel Volturno

Volturno

S264

S7a

Casamicciola Terme

Forio d'Ischia

Ischia

Porto d'Ischia

Procida

Capri

Cumae

Lago d'Averno

Baia

Pozzuoli

Solfatara

Herculaneum

Naples

Villa Literno

Giugliano in C.

Aversa

Calvano

Casoria

Acerra

Maddaloni

Caserta

S264

A2

S30

S7

Vesuvius

Pomigliano

S268

A16

A3

Camposano

Baiano

Nola

Montesarchio

S7

Castello d. Lago

Sorrento

Castellammare

Positano

Gragnano

Amalfi

Ravello

Vietri sul Mare

Minori

Scafati

Pompeii

Nocera

Sarno

Mercato

S145

S18

S163

A30

Avellino

A16

S88

Solofra

S7

Paternopoli

S164

Lioni

Salerno

Battipaglia

Eboli

Campagna

S88

A3

S18

S91

S65

S19

TO CILENTO, PAESTUM, AND AGROPOLI

372

Naples is also more picturesque than its reputation might lead you to believe. Situated on the Bay of Naples, it overflows with medieval and baroque buildings: Some of the country's finest churches and museums are here. And whether you try a cappuccino, an expertly crafted pizza, or a plate of spaghetti (pronounced shpa-GET), you won't find such good food for so cheap anywhere else in Italy. So think twice before you shake your head incredulously and pass through toward saner environs. If you can adapt to its ways, Naples may become your favorite city in Italy. After all, who really needs stoplights?

BASICS

Traveler alert: Naples's AmEx office has closed up shop, allegedly because there weren't enough tourists. Sorrento (*see* Bay of Naples, *below*) now has Campania's only **American Express** representative (tel. 081/878–4800).

CHANGING MONEY If you want convenience and aren't changing a big wad, use the **Ufficio di Cambio** inside Stazione Centrale (*see* Coming and Going by Train, *below*); it's open daily 7:15 AM–8 PM. You'll get more for your money in Naples's small financial district around Piazza Municipio, just above the Castel Nuovo. The main branches of several major banks are clustered here, and they offer the most competitive rates in town. The exchange offices around the dock on Via Cristoforo Colombo are open evenings and Saturday mornings.

CONSULATES **United Kingdom.** *Via Francesco Crispi 122, off Piazza Amedeo, tel. 081/663511. Open weekdays 8 or 9–noon.*

United States. *Piazza della Repubblica (a.k.a. Piazza Principedi di Napoli), at west end of Villa Comunale, tel. 081/583–8111. Open weekdays 8–noon and 2–4:30.*

EMERGENCIES For general emergencies call 113; for an **ambulance** call 081/752–0696. To report a medical emergency after 8 PM, call 081/761–3466 and ask for an English-speaking nurse. The main **police station** (Via Medina 75, tel. 081/794–1111) has an *ufficio stranieri* (foreigners' office) that usually has an English speaker on staff. The *farmacia* (pharmacy) on the main floor of Stazione Centrale has a list of pharmacies that are open nights and weekends.

MAIL AND PHONES The best place to make long-distance calls is at **Telecom** (Via A. Depretis 40, between Piazza G. Bovio and Piazza Municipio). The main **post office** (Piazza Matteotti, off Via Diaz, tel. 081/551–1456) is open weekdays 8 AM–7:20 PM and Saturday 8–noon. Branches in Stazione Centrale and Galleria Umberto I have the same hours.

VISITOR INFORMATION A number of tourist offices in Naples make up for the fact that the rest of the city isn't exactly visitor-friendly. There's an **EPT** office (tel. 081/268779; open Mon.–Sat. 8:15–8, Sun. 8–2) in Stazione Centrale, but the main office is in Piazza dei Martiri (tel. 081/405311; open Mon.–Sat. 9–6). There are also two branches at Stazione di Mergellina (tel. 081/761–2102; open Mon.–Sat. 10–6, Sun. 9–noon), and at the airport (tel. 081/780–5761; open daily 10–4). An **AACST** (tel. 081/552–3328; open Mon.–Sat. 9–7 and Sun. 9–2) in Piazza Gesù Nuovo specializes in information on Old Naples. To get here, take Bus 185 toward Piazza Dante and get off at Via Capitelli. Finally, the American consulate has an **American Women's Club** (tel. 081/575–0040) that offers tours and is always a good resource while you're in Campania.

For info on live performances, museum exhibits, and transportation schedules, pick up the free guide "Qui Napoli" at the EPT office.

COMING AND GOING

BY TRAIN **Stazione Centrale** (tel. 081/554–3188) overflows onto Piazza Garibaldi, northeast of Old Naples and the port. Services in this hectic station include a pharmacy, a money exchange office, a 24-hour luggage check, a telephone center, and visitor information offices. Trains leave hourly for Rome (2 hrs 45 min, L17,200) and several times daily for Milan (7 hrs, L59,100) and Brindisi (6½ hrs, L28,600). If you're staying at the youth hostel in Mergellina, many trains stop first at **Stazione di Mergellina** (Corso Vittorio Emanuele 4, tel. 081/680635), which is also right near a hydrofoil port. *See* Getting Around, *below,* for buses and subway trains from either station to other parts of town. If you arrive at night, consider taking a taxi to your hotel. Be sure you and the driver agree on a price ahead of time—Neapolitan taxi drivers like to pretend the meter doesn't work.

Don't take any chances in Naples: It's the sad truth that if you look foreign and are carrying any kind of hanging bag, you will probably get robbed. Carry all cash, traveler's checks, and documents in a money belt, and keep cameras and other large valuables in a backpack with both straps on.

➢ **FERROVIA CIRCUMVESUVIANA** • On the same floor of Stazione Centrale as the Metropolitana (subway), the **Ferrovia Circumvesuviana** line has trains about every 15 minutes to Herculaneum (20 min, L2200), Pompeii (45 min, L2800), and Sorrento (1 hr, L4200). The two train lines have different entrances, so watch the signs. Buy tickets at the *biglietteria* (ticket office) near the platform.

BY BUS Pick up a copy of "Qui Napoli" (*see* Visitor Information, *above*) for a list of major bus routes, departure times, and phone numbers. Trains are usually more frequent and faster to major destinations, but you might need to use buses for more obscure towns. **ACTP** (tel. 081/700–5091) runs buses from Piazza Garibaldi to Caserta every 20 minutes. From dawn until around 10 PM, blue **SITA** buses leave from a depot near Piazza Municipio (Via Pisanelli 3–7, tel. 081/552–2176) for Salerno and intermediate points; you can catch one every half hour Monday–Saturday and every two hours on holidays and Sundays.

BY FERRY Again, you can check out "Qui Napoli" for up-to-date ferry and hydrofoil schedules. **Tirrenia** (Stazione Marittima, tel. 081/761–3688; open weekdays 8:30–1:30 and 2:30–5) handles long-distance ferry service to Sicily, Calabria, Cagliari, and Malta (which has connections to Tunisia and Libya). Boats for Palermo (12 hrs, L66,000) leave daily at 8 PM; boats for Cagliari (13½ hrs, L74,000) leave daily at 7:15 PM; and boats for Malta leave Thursday at 8:30 PM, stopping in Reggio-Calabria (10 hrs), Catania (15 hrs), and Siracusa (19 hrs).

For trips around the Bay of Naples, the main port is **Molo Beverello**, below Castel Nuovo. Both Tirrenia and **Caremar** (Molo Beverello, tel. 081/551–3882) and many other carriers send boats to the islands several times daily (less frequently on holidays and weekends). Major destinations include Capri (hydrofoil 40 min, L17,000; ferry 70 min, L8000–L10,000), Procida (hydrofoil ½ hr, L14,000; ferry 1 hr, L8,500), and Ischia (hydrofoil 40 min, L17,000; ferry 1 hr 20 min, L10,000). There are seven daily hydrofoils to Sorrento (25 min, L22,000), and no ferries, but some ferries to Capri also make stops in Sorrento. Naples's smaller hydrofoil port, **Aliscafi Mergellina** (Via Caracciolo 10, west of Riviera di Chiaia, tel. 761–2348), near the youth hostel and the Stazione Mergellina train station, also has frequent hydrofoil service to Capri (40 min, L17,000), Sorrento (25 min, L10,000), Ischia (40 min, L17,000), and Procida (20 min, L14,000).

BY PLANE **Capodichino Airport** (tel. 081/709–2815) has many domestic and international connections. **Alitalia** (tel. 081/542–5333), **Lufthansa** (tel. 081/551–5440), and **British Airways** (tel. 081/764–5550) all fly from here. Bus 14 runs from Piazza Garibaldi to the airport (20 min) about once an hour between 5:15 AM and 10:05 PM. If you take a taxi from Piazza Garibaldi, expect to pay L25,000–L30,000 (agree on a price beforehand).

GETTING AROUND

Naples stretches along the Bay of Naples with its back to the Vomero Hills. Most visitors arrive at Stazione Centrale, on **Piazza Garibaldi** in eastern Naples. You can bypass this frightening area altogether and save your aching feet by jumping on the Metro (*see below*). If you decide to schlepp it, the most direct route is to take Corso Umberto I from in front of the station to Piazza G. Bovio, and then Via A. Depretis to the harbor and the hubs Piazza Municipio and Piazza del Plebiscito. West of this congested area lie the bayfront districts of **Santa Lucia** and **Mergellina**, and the fashionable **Chiaia** district. The residential **Vomero** district, which looks out over all of Naples, rambles along the hills behind Mergellina.

Starting at Piazza del Plebiscito, **Via Toledo/Via Roma** splits the city in half. West of this lively shopping street is the **Quartiere Spagnoli** (Spanish Quarter), a great place to get your wallet stolen, night or day. Via Roma takes you to the **Spaccanapoli** (literally, "spine" of the medieval quarter), a street which changes names several times on its way through the center of town (it comprises Via Benedetto Croce and Via San Biagio dei Librai, among others). As you head down Spaccanapoli, look for monument-ridden Piazza Gesù Nuovo, in the heart of **Old Naples**. Just north of this area is the café-lined Piazza Dante, in the **university district**. To use the buses, the Metropolitana (subway), or the funicolari, buy a *Giranapoli* (a ticket good for 90 minutes; L1200), or get a day pass for L4000 at most tabacchi or at kiosks inside the funicolare or Metro stations. In addition to the main Metropolitana railway, there is a separate **Cumana** line, which begins at the Montesanto station. It heads north to the ancient settlements of Cuma (1 hr, L4100) and Pozzuoli (30 min, L1200). Buy tickets at kiosks in the station.

BY BUS Remember to secure your valuables aboard the bus, and consider taking a taxi to your hotel after dark. Bus routes are listed at each stop. Important lines include **CD**, from Stazione Centrale to Piazza Dante; **CS**, from Stazione Centrale to the Museo Archeologico Nazionale; and **106** or **150**, from Stazione Centrale through Piazza Municipio and Piazza del Plebiscito to the Mergellina district (Line 150 continues to Bagnoli at the outskirts of the Campi Flegrei).

BY METROPOLITANA The Metro is a limited but efficient subway system that begins at Stazione Centrale's Platform 4, beneath the main floor (the Metro stop is actually called Piazza Garibaldi). Buy tickets at the ticket counters near the entrance. Useful stops include **Piazza Cavour** (just up the street from the Museo Archeologico Nazionale), **Montesanto** (a five-minute walk from Spaccanapoli), **Piazza Amedeo** (in the tony Chiaia district), **Mergellina** (near a hydrofoil port and the youth hostel), and **Pozzuoli** in the Campi Flegrei.

BY FUNICOLARE AND TRAM Several funicolari trek up and down Naples's steep hillsides, and they accept Giranapoli tickets. Funicolare Centrale is closed indefinitely, but you can utilize the **Funicolare di Montesanto**, one block down from the Montesanto Metro stop, which deposits you within walking distance of Castel Sant'Elmo and Certosa di San Martino. The city also has a tram system that runs from Stazione Centrale to the Mergellina district by way of Via Cristoforo Colombo.

WHERE TO SLEEP

Considering how divey the dives can be in Naples, you may want to shell out the extra lire for a little cleanliness and security. In general, the farther you stray from Piazza Garibaldi, the more palatable (and pricey) the accommodations become. When possible reserve ahead and firmly settle on a *final* price over the phone. Many hotels have storage safes, so you can stash your valuables and walk around town worry free.

PIAZZA GARIBALDI If you stay in one of the many hotels around the train station, your perspective on the city will inevitably be skewed. This area is known for prostitution and several of its hotels exist solely to provide mattresses for a few hours. Just remember: All of Naples isn't this tawdry and threatening.

➢ **UNDER L55,000 • Albergo Aurora.** It's a cut above most of the low-end places nearby, but you still have to withstand the noisy piazza, squishy beds, and a sleazy atmosphere. Doubles go for L42,000. *Piazza Garibaldi 60, tel. 081/201920. 2nd block of apartments as you exit the station, above Sayonara Albergo. 10 rooms, 3 with bath.*

Casanova Hotel. This is the best deal near Piazza Garibaldi—just far enough from the square to be relatively quiet and secure, but close enough for you to catch your morning train. Rooms are clean, though the shower in the hall has seen better days. Doubles cost L50,000. *Via Venezia 2, at Corso Garibaldi, tel. 081/268287. Cut diagonally right as you leave the station; hotel is several blocks down Corso Garibaldi on the right. 18 rooms, 12 with bath.*

Hotel Eden. The water is hot, the beds are firm, the TVs work, there's even a restaurant—in Piazza Garibaldi, this *is* Eden. Doubles, all with bath, start at around L50,000 but can go up

Naples

Bay of Naples

Sights ●

Aquarium, **23**
Cappella
Sansevero, **11**
Castel dell'Ovo, **26**
Castel Nuovo, **19**

Castel
Sant'Elmo, **16**
Certosa di
San Martino, **17**
Duomo, **6**
Galleria
Umberto I, **19**

Gesù Nuovo (Trinità
Maggiore), **13**
Museo Archeologico
Nazionale, **3**
Museo e Gallerie
Capodimonte, **1**
Palazzo Reale, **21**

San Domenico
Maggiore, **12**
San Lorenzo
Maggiore, **8**
Santa Chiara, **14**
Teatro San Carlo, **20**

Lodging ○

Albergo Aurora, **5**
Albergo Duomo, **7**
Casanova Hotel, **4**
Europeo Hotel, **15**
Le Fontane al
Mare, **24**

Hotel Eden, **2**
Hotel San Pietro, **9**
Ostello Salita della
Grotta (HI), **22**
Pensione
Teresita, **25**

Il Soggiorno
Imperia, **10**

KEY

+—+—+ Rail Lines
▬▬▬ Metro

0 ⊢——⊣ 300 yards
0 ⊢——⊣ 300 meters

↗ N

Naples

VOMERO

OLD NAPLES

377

to L80,000. Ask for a deal—they're willing to bargain. *Corso Novara 9, tel. 081/285344. Go right from station; Corso Novara is in piazza below highway entrance ramp. 45 rooms. Luggage storage.*

➤ **UNDER L70,000** • **Hotel San Pietro.** What this large, anonymous hotel lacks in character, it makes up for in reliability. The rooms are functional and clean—those without bath include the use of a closetlike shower down the hall (8 AM–5 PM). Doubles are listed at L60,000, but verify the price before accepting anything. *Via San Pietro ad Aram 18, tel. 081/553-5914. 53 rooms, most with bath. Wheelchair access. AE, MC, V.*

OLD NAPLES Old Naples really beats Piazza Garibaldi by virtue of its antiquity, but it has surprisingly few accommodations, budget or otherwise. If you can find a place, you'll have the advantage of being near most of the important sights. All of the hotels below accept reservations.

➤ **UNDER L55,000** • **Europeo Hotel.** This relatively new hotel across from the university is a good deal if space is available. Rooms are clean and orderly, and the location in a small alley helps insulate the place from bone-rattling street noise. Doubles are L50,000, and showers are available on the first floor. *Via Mezzocannone 109, tel. 081/551-7254. From Piazza G. Bovio, take Corso Umberto I and go left on Via Mezzocannone. 10 rooms, 2 with bath.*

Il Soggiorno Imperia. At the top of a *long* flight of stairs, Il Soggiorno provides tidy, secure budget accommodations in a great area near Piazza Dante. The friendly couple who run the place can answer questions about what to do in the city. Doubles are L40,000. *Piazza Miraglia 386, tel. 081/459347. From Piazza Dante, take Via Port'Alba. Cross street to the right of Pizzeria Bellini, go through small piazza, and look for sign. 14 rooms, none with bath. Closed 2 weeks in Aug.*

➤ **UNDER L85,000** • **Albergo Duomo.** This pension offers breezy, immaculate blue- and white-tiled rooms in the heart of Old Naples. The hotel fills up regularly with an international clientele. Right off the entrance to the hotel, there's a small restaurant where Mamma serves traditional Neapolitan dinners (L20,000 and worth it). Comfortable doubles cost L80,000. *Via Duomo 228, south of duomo, tel. 081/265988. 9 rooms, all with bath. Laundry.*

THE WATERFRONT Hotels on the waterfront offer spectacular views and lavish rooms, but their prices will often sink budget travelers. The area is safer than Piazza Garibaldi, and some great seafood restaurants pop up in the streets around the bay.

➤ **UNDER L55,000** • **Pensione Teresita.** These clean rooms by the bay—some with balconies—are almost always full. If you get in, you can kick back in a large, airy TV room with the owners, the maids, and some erotic dancers who lounge here in the afternoon. Doubles are L50,000, including the use of decent showers down the hall. *Via Santa Lucia 90, tel. 081/764-0105. From Stazione Centrale, take Bus 140 east. 13 rooms, none with bath. Luggage storage. Reservations necessary.*

➤ **UNDER L85,000** • **Le Fontane al Mare.** Come here for luxury accommodations at a relatively low price (doubles L82,000). The clean, quiet rooms are cooled at night by an ocean breeze, and you're a short walk from Villa Comunale, a beautiful park on the bay. *Via Niccolò Tommaseo 14, tel. 081/764-3470. Take Bus 140 or 150 from Stazione Centrale. 25 rooms, 7 with bath. Reservations recommended. AE.*

HOSTELS Ostello Salita della Grotta (HI). Naples's only youth hostel may be on the western edge of town, but it also happens to be just below Virgil and Leopardi's tombs (Tombe di Poeti), just above the Mergellina FS and Metro station, and a ten-minute walk from Mergellina's hydrofoil port. Most of the two-, four-, and six-person rooms have their own bath. A three-day maximum stay is enforced during July and August. HI members pay L18,000 per person; nonmembers must fork over L5000 extra a night, which goes towards membership. The cafeteria has full meals for about L10,000. *Salita della Grotta 23, tel. 081/761-2346. From Stazione Centrale, take Metro to Mergellina stop and follow signs. 200 beds. Midnight curfew, checkout 9 AM. Laundry (L4500 per load), luggage storage. Reservations recommended in summer.*

FOOD

Neapolitans like their architecture baroque but their cuisine classic and simple. Take part in Naples's lively street life by shopping in the **open-air food markets** that line Via Tribunali, between Piazza Dante and the duomo, or the narrow streets between Montesanto and Via Roma. Most of the restaurants around Piazza Garibaldi serve mediocre food in a rushed atmosphere: It's definitely worth it to venture into Old Naples or down to the harbor for the real thing. But if you're about to catch a train and you haven't yet had a Neapolitan pizza, head to the esteemed **Trianon da Ciro** (Via P. Colletta 44–46, tel. 081/553–9204), where pizzas range from L9000 to L12,000.

It's no wonder Neapolitan food has won the hearts (and stomachs) of millions: The rich, volcanic soil and fertile waters surrounding the city provide abundant and varied seafood, Vesuvian wines, vine-ripe tomatoes, and luscious fruits.

While usually pricier than pizza joints, Neapolitan trattorias also offer incredible deals. A local specialty is *Mozzarella di bufalo* (made from water buffalo milk), a tangier, juicier version of the cheese we know. Try it fresh in an *Insalata Caprese* (with tomatoes and basil). *Frutta di mare* (seafood, primarily shellfish) mixed into pasta is a staple Neapolitan primo piatto. *Spaghetti alle cozze*, with sweet tomatoes and mussels, and *zuppa di pesce* (fish stew) are other favorites, though these can cost up to L15,000. When you need to be frugal, ask for spaghetti *al pomodoro* (in fresh tomato sauce), which is usually only L4000.

OLD NAPLES AND CHIAIA Competition for student lire has made eating around Piazza Dante and Via dei Tribunali the best deal in Naples. Restaurants are very relaxed, with outdoor seating in a balmy and calm atmosphere—at least at night. Further down Via Toledo in the Chiaia district, you'll find an older crowd in lively, family-run trattorie.

Amici Miei. In this family-run trattoria on a quiet street above Via Chiaia, you'll feel like the somewhat corny name ("My Friends") is heartfelt. The interior is artfully decorated and the ever-changing selection of delicious Neapolitan fare and northern cuisine is seemingly endless, but the prices are incredibly low (L4000–L8000 for pasta). *Via Monte di Dio 78, tel. 081/ 7646–0633. From Piazza del Plebiscito, go down Via Chiaia to arched city gate, ascend stairs inside gate's building (not through the arch), and turn left on Via Monte di Dio. Open Mon.–Sat. noon–3:30 and 8–12:30. Closed Aug.*

Dante e Beatrice. A gas station and car park hamper your view of Piazza Dante until dark, when the cars disappear. The restaurant is a bit more pricey than your typical Neapolitan trattoria, but it's one of the city's favorites. A delicious serving of *maccheroni* with salad and wine goes

Pizza! Pizza!

Pizza, like most Neapolitan cuisine, originated from the demands of poverty and the need to utilize all available resources. A few hundred years ago, some poor Neapolitan discovered that a simple flour dough and a thin spread of tomato sauce and oil makes for a very economical meal. Eventually, the preparation of Neapolitan pizza developed into a real art—today, authentic pizzerias can only use the freshest ingredients and cook the pizza in a wood-fired brick oven. Neapolitan pizzas usually don't have too many toppings: Try a "Margherita," with fresh tomato sauce, basil, and mozzarella, and you'll see how good simplicity can be. "Vera Pizza" signs verify a pizzeria's authenticity—many of these traditional pizzerias have outdoor stands where pizza artisans whip up piping hot pies for only L1500.

for about L15,000. *Piazza Dante 44–46, tel. 081/549–9438. Take Bus 150 from Stazione Centrale. Open Tues.–Sun. noon–4 and 8–midnight.*

Pizzeria Sorbillo. Patronized by university students and folks from the 'hood, this tiny, primarily take-out place has been making delicious brick-oven pizza and calzone since long before you were born (no matter how old you are). Pizzas are cheap (L3000–L8000) and delicious. *Via Tribunali 35, no phone. Open Mon.–Sat. 11:30–3 and 7–11.*

Ristorante Bellini. If you ask any Neapolitan for a restaurant recommendation, they'll probably send you here. It qualifies as a Vera Pizzeria, with lip-smacking pizzas and calzoni (L6000–L8000), but it's also a comfortable sit-down restaurant with an outdoor patio that faces a lively street. Don't miss their pasta dishes, like *vermicelli alle vongole* (thin noodles mixed with razor clams and lava-colored tomatoes; L10,000). *Via Costantinopoli 80, tel. 081/459774. At Via San Pietro, across from Port'Alba. Open Mon.–Sat. noon–2:30 and 7:30–10:30.*

THE WATERFRONT Naturally, restaurants by the water have the best seafood in town. Some are touristy and overpriced, especially around the Castel dell'Ovo, but with luck you can find a good plate of seafood in the L10,000–L15,000 range. If you wander a few blocks inland or further west around Piazza Sannazzaro in Mergellina, you'll find more authentic food and atmosphere.

Ristorante Marino. This ultratypical Neapolitan restaurant is always packed with loud natives getting served by boisterous waiters. Try their pizzas (around L8000), delicious pasta dishes with seafood, like *farfalle al salmone* (butterfly pasta with salmon) or second courses, like fried calamari. *Via Santa Lucia 118, near Castel dell'Ovo, tel. 081/764–0280. From Castel dell'Ovo, turn right on Via Partenope, left on Via Santa Lucia. Open Tues.–Sun. noon–3:30 and 7–1:30.*

Salvatore alla Riveria. Master pizza chefs and their young apprentices press, toss, and stretch some of the best-tasting pizza in Naples (L7000–L12,000) at Salvatore's. They'll even come out and take your order (with their hands covered in flour) if the waiter ignores you. Try the house pizza, with pancetta, mushrooms, olives, and capers, or whatever they feel like. *Riviera di Chiaia 91, tel. 081/680490. From Castel dell'Ovo, walk west on Via Partenope, right on Piazza Vittoria, left on Riviera di Chiaia. Open Wed.–Mon. 1–3:30 and 8–11.*

DESSERT/COFFEEHOUSES Neapolitans do the café scene right, making countless stops throughout the day for coffee, *tè freddo* (iced tea), and delicious pastries. Make it a point to try *sfogliatelle*, a crunchy, flaky triangular pastry filled with vanilla or chocolate cream, or *frolle*, soft, round pastry shells filled with delicately flavored ricotta cheese and candied fruit. Beneath a towering statue of San Domenico, priests and nuns from neighborhood churches gather at **Giovanni Scaturchio** (Piazza San Domenico Maggiore 19) to anticipate what heaven will taste like. The café is open Tuesday–Sunday 6 AM–1 AM. Just as popular, **Gran Bar Riviera** (Riviera di Chiaia 182, across from Villa Comunale; open Tues.–Sun. 6 AM–midnight) overflows with every sweet concoction imaginable and has an open patio.

WORTH SEEING

If you're only in Naples for the day, it's pretty easy to take a walking tour of the main sights on Spaccanapoli and down by the waterfront, but you'll need more time than that to really take in the city's vivacious street culture and excellent museums. If you're overwhelmed by the number of churches and the variety of architecture styles in Naples, head to the tourist office in Piazza Gesù Nuovo. Their free itineraries, which delineate four different tours of medieval, renaissance, baroque, and rococo churches, go a long way in helping you distinguish your apse from your flying buttress.

OLD NAPLES Old Naples centers around the Spaccanapoli neighborhood, where electric-candle shrines pay homage to the Madonna, small shopkeepers supply fresh sausage and bread to the neighborhood, kids play soccer in piazze, and clotheslines crisscross narrow passageways. Most of the Spaccanapoli's residents are poor and religious: The abundant churches are not just museums of religious art but well-attended houses of worship. While you're here, seek out Gothic **San Domenico Maggiore** (Piazza San Domenico Maggiore 8/A, tel. 081/459298), whose airy Renaissance interior was once frequented by St. Thomas Aquinas, and **San Lorenzo Mag-**

giore (Via Tribunali 316, at Piazza San Gaetano, tel. 081/ 454948), a large, tangled complex of altars and chapels that contains newly discovered Greek and Roman remains as well as the Gothic tomb of Catherine of Austria. A foray to the nearby Museo Archeologico Nazionale is a must.

➤ **CAPPELLA SANSEVERO** • Tucked away on a small street near Piazza San Domenico Maggiore, the Sansevero chapel might be the most ghoulish little church you ever set foot in. The mood is set by Mozart's *Requiem*, which drifts over the speakers, and the baroque interior overflows with putti, melancholic Madonna images, and richly colored frescoes. Most spectacular is the centerpiece sculpture, known as the Veiled Christ. Christ's graceful figure lies under what looks like a crepy, transparent cloth, though the whole piece is crafted from a single piece of marble. To add to the macabre atmosphere, two cadavers with (supposedly) preserved cardiovascular systems resembling a tangle of blue and red wires are on display in the basement. *Via Francesco de Sanctis 19, near Piazza San Domenico Maggiore, tel. 081/551–8470. Admission: L6000. Open Tues. and Sun. 10–5:30, Mon. and Wed.–Fri. 10–1:30.*

➤ **DUOMO (CATHEDRAL OF SAN GENNARO)** • The duomo's facade is hidden a bit by neighboring buildings, but its interior makes an impact. Charles II built the cathedral at the end of the 13th century, using more than a hundred ancient granite columns from an earlier pagan temple to line the nave. The duomo's big moment comes each year when it hosts the celebration of San Gennaro, Naples's patron saint (*see box, below*). The cathedral's 17th-century Chapel of San Gennaro contains multicolored marbles and frescoes honoring the popular saint. His blood is kept safe behind the altar, and his crypt is downstairs. *Via Duomo. Open daily 8:30–1 and 5–7:30.*

➤ **MUSEO ARCHEOLOGICO NAZIONALE** • This excellent museum holds one of the most extensive and fascinating collections of Greek and Roman antiquities in the world. The first floor holds hundreds of Greek and Roman sculptures waiting for your identification (labels are

On the hectic shopping street Via Toledo, it's not uncommon to see Vespa scooters serving as the family car: A three-year-old stands on the axel and clutches the handle bars, the father steers, and the mother hangs on to him while holding a second baby sidesaddle.

The Festival of San Gennaro

Neapolitans haven't had it easy, what with earthquakes, volcanic eruptions, cholera epidemics, and their favorite adopted son, soccer great Diego Maradona, turning into a coke fiend and getting booted out of the country. So who can blame them if they turn to their patron saint, Gennaro, for a little help predicting the future?

Twice annually—on the first Saturday in May and on September 19—crowds gather at the duomo to see whether two vials of San Gennaro's blood will liquefy. The blood is withdrawn from the sacristy, and the archbishop (and everyone present) prays over it; if it stays congealed, Naples is in for it. In 1943, for instance, the blood didn't turn, and soon afterward Vesuvius blew its top. In 1973, it again remained congealed, and Naples suffered a severe cholera outbreak. Lest the faithless disbelieve, scientists have put these vials through a series of tests and cannot explain what determines whether or not they liquefy.

If you're in town during the festival, the events surrounding the ceremony are a bloody good time. Neapolitans turn out early (around 7 AM) to rush for the good seats when the cathedral doors open. The entire congregation prays feverishly as the archbishop raises the vials before and (God willing) after the liquefaction.

scarce) as well as the famous Farnese collection, which features a monumental *Hercules* and a violent depiction of the *Farnese Bull*. On the third floor, you could spend hours gazing at the mosaics and wall paintings dislodged from the ruins at Pompeii and Herculaneum. *Piazza Museo Nazionale 19, tel. 081/440166. From Piazza Dante, walk up Via E. Pessina to Piazza Museo. Admission: L12,000. Open mid-Aug.–Oct., Tues.–Sun. 9–7; Nov.–mid-Aug., Tues.–Sat 9–2, Sun. and holidays 9–1.*

➢ **PIAZZA GESU NUOVO** • The piazza has the best tourist information office in town (*see* Basics, *above*) and is surrounded by some of Naples's most important churches. In the middle of the piazza, **Guglia dell'Immacolata**, a prickly looking Spanish spire covered with saints and cherubs, exemplifies the square's baroque style. The spire faces a Jesuit church known formally as Trinità Maggiore, but popularly referred to as the **Gesù Nuovo**. The facade, made up of rows of stones that jut out defensively from the wall, was originally part of a 15th-century palace. In 1601, the palace was turned into a church, with a brilliant baroque interior that contrasts with the grim facade.

➢ **SANTA CHIARA** • Locals come to this huge, lofty church to hear morning mass. Allied bombing in 1943 destroyed the roof and gutted the interior, but restoration work returned the church to its original sparse 14th-century design. It houses an interesting funerary monument to King Robert the Wise and has an exquisite **cloister** in back. The cloister's antique blue tiles and columns, painted with fanciful 18th-century landscapes, are graced by grapevines and a very large family of cats. The cloister is officially open 8:30–12:30 and 4–6, but ask politely and you can see it whenever the church is open. *Via Benedetto Croce, tel. 081/552–6280. Open daily 7–5.*

THE WATERFRONT Right in between the traffic-filled Piazza Municipio and Piazza del Plebiscito near the harbor is the lofty, glass-enclosed **Galleria Umberto I**, which was built in the late 19th century. It was meant to be a grandiose shopping center, but it's now mostly empty. Brides still cross its huge mosaic floor on rainy days to take wedding photos. Farther south, the long walk along the Bay of Naples between the Castel dell'Ovo and the Mergellina district gives you a positive impression of this often harsh city. The bay shimmers, old *pescatori* (fishermen) fly-fish from the rocks, and young Neapolitans bake atop the large, flat stones.

➢ **CASTEL DELL'OVO** • The Castel dell'Ovo (literally "Egg Castle") juts into the Bay of Naples from the Santa Lucia port. Built in the 12th century, this beige monster sits atop the

A Lazy Day in Naples

If negotiating Piazza Garibaldi and Via Toledo has stressed you out, lie in the shade in one of Naples's public parks and relax. Along the bay in the Mergellina district, palm trees and statues are arranged in the style of an English garden, and carnival rides and popcorn stands take you back to your childhood. In the middle of the park, look for the aquarium (tel. 081/583–3263; admission: L3000; open Mon.–Sat. 9–5, Sun. 9–2), one of the oldest in the world. To get here, take Bus 150 or 152 from Stazione Centrale. For a choice view of the Bay of Naples, take Bus 150 (45 min) from Stazione Centrale to overgrown Parco Virgiliano, north of Piazza Sannazzaro in the Mergellina district. Here, amid the hyacinth and the Tombe dei Poeti (where Virgil was buried), Boccaccio was moved to declare himself a poet. A third option is to take the Funicolare di Montesanto to the Vomero district, where you can wander in the gardens of the Villa Floridiana and get views of the villas and pastel-colored apartment buildings that cling to the hillside above the bay. From the funicular station, head up Via Alessandro Scarlatti and turn left on Via Bernini, which will lead you into the park.

remains of a Roman villa. Its eclectic appearance is the result of many different occupants, including the Basilican monks, the Normans, and a few Swabians. Look for a custodian to let you inside, or contact the castle's tourist office (tel. 081/764–5688), open Monday–Saturday 9–3, to arrange a free tour.

➤ **CASTEL NUOVO** • Overlooking the bay, the giant Castel Nuovo in Piazza Municipio was built to protect Naples against sea invasions. Its dark turrets look like something from the Scottish highlands and contrast nicely with the warm Mediterranean in the background. Today the castle houses a museum of eerie 17th-century Neapolitan religious paintings. As you enter the fortress, cross the expansive courtyard to the exhibit room (admission: L6000). Check "Qui Napoli" or posters for information on the castle's summer pop concert series. *Castle open Mon.–Sat. 9–1.*

➤ **PALAZZO REALE** • Huge, grey Palazzo Reale casts a heavy shadow on Piazza del Plebiscito. The facade is flanked by statues of some of the city's conquerors, demonstrating the variety of influences on Naples. Just past the entrance, the space is dominated by a sweeping marble stairway and Aragonese armaments sculpted into the walls. Upstairs, the living apartments stretch endlessly—all gold, mirrors, and family portraits. The **Biblioteca Nazionale**, at the rear of the palazzo, has the oldest copy of Dante's *Divine Comedy* in existence. *Piazza del Plebiscito, tel. 081/413888. Admission: L8000. Open daily 9–1:30.*

➤ **TEATRO SAN CARLO** • Teatro San Carlo, across from Galleria Umberto I, is Italy's largest and acoustically best opera house. Built in a frantic six months, just in time for King Charles's birthday in November 1737, it has since been redone in neoclassical gilded stucco. Tours are given daily, or you can catch a performance October–June (*see* After Dark, *below*). *Via San Carlo 93/F, tel. 081/797–2111. Admission: L5000, free Sun. Open daily 9–noon.*

THE HILLS Naples sprawls, and you'll need to use public transportation to reach the hilly Vomero district to the west or Capodimonte to the north.

➤ **CASTEL SANT'ELMO** • Broad switchback ramparts lead to this castle, which was built under the Bourbon king Robert of Anjou, who chose the site for its strategic vantage point. It was originally designed to look like a six-point star, but later additions have ruined this plan. Ascend to the broad roof and check out the outdoor bar, the new library/archive, and the astounding view. *From Funicolare di Montesanto Vomero station, head back down the hill to the left and around castle grounds until you reach entrance on Via Tito Angelini. Admission free. Open Mon.–Sat. 9–8, Sun. and holidays 9–1.*

➤ **CERTOSA DI SAN MARTINO** • Sharing park space with Castel Sant'Elmo, the 17th-century Certosa di San Martino is a typically ironic piece of Neapolitan architecture—a flowery baroque building designed as a solemn residence for Carthusian monks. Inside, the **Museo Nazionale di San Martino** has some eye-catching landscape paintings, but the church's ornate interior, its peaceful garden, and the views from its upstairs balconies are more thrilling. *Tel. 081/578–1769. Admission: L8000. Open Tues.–Sat. 9–2, Sun. 9–1.*

➤ **MUSEO E GALLERIE CAPODIMONTE** • Set in a large wooded park, the 18th-century Capodimonte was built as a Bourbon homestead. It now houses an important collection of big-name Renaissance paintings. Italian, Spanish, and Dutch works share space with over-the-top furnishings and portraits from the days when flashy Bourbons resided in this 'burb. The museum has been closed for restoration for a few years, but it is scheduled to reopen in the fall of 1995. *Parco di Capodimonte, tel. 081/744–1307. Take Bus 110 or 127 from Stazione Centrale, or Bus 160 or 161 from Piazza Dante, toward Vomero district. At press time, admission prices and opening hours had not yet been determined.*

AFTER DARK

Naples is busy after dark, with outdoor bars in **Piazza Dante** and **Piazza Bellini**, plenty of live music clubs, and nocturnal Neapolitan theatrics on the streets. The American GIs stationed here during World War II introduced jazz and rock and roll to the already lively Neapolitan music scene, and the integration has been smooth. Look in *Qui Napoli* and the local newspaper

Il Mattino for info on free summertime concerts, club events, theater, and movies. Opera productions at **Teatro San Carlo** (*see* Worth Seeing, *above*) run from December to June; economy seats go for L20,000 and L30,000. The box office is open Tuesday–Sunday 10–1 and 4:30–6:30. In sketchy **Piazza Municipio**, near the docks, you can spot the famous *feminelli* (transvestites). They're usually dressed like runway models at a Paris fashion show and surrounded by young Neapolitans on mopeds.

Decorated in '50s Americana, **Le Rock** (Via Bellini 9, next to Piazza Dante) features U.S. rock and blues played by local musicians. The ghost of Elvis is said to haunt the place, and young Italians crowd the floor till closing time. The club is open weekends 9 PM–2 AM, but hours are more sporadic in summer. A student crowd kicks back in outdoor **Club 1799** (Piazza Bellini 71), where it doesn't cost much more for a table on the piazza than for an espresso at the bar. Local musicians demonstrate their jazz skills at **Murat** (Via Bellini 8), an intimate club with a L5000–L10,000 cover (free if you show up very late). It opens Friday–Tuesday at 9 PM and sometimes stays open as late as 3 AM. In Old Naples, **The Riot** (Via San Biagio dei Librai 39, tel. 081/552-3231; closed Aug.) will give you insight into the Neapolitan avant garde. Jazz groups jam throughout the evening in front of young leftist intellectuals. The club is open Tuesday–Sunday 9 PM–2:30 AM. **Tongue** (Via Manzoni 207, tel. 081/769-0800) plays techno and attracts a largely gay crowd. The cover is only L15,000 and it's open weekends 9 PM–3 AM. The nearby **Zeppelin Club** (Via Manzoni 176, tel. 081/640923) has local bands on stage—everything from folk to rock.

The serenade—that plaintive, melancholic, and sometimes corny under-the-moon croon—originated in Naples. Once in a rare while, you'll hear a late-night Romeo with a guitar or harmonica in hand singing a heartfelt song in a lonely alleyway. More often, the crooning will come from a piano bar, often with synthesized (and saccharine) accompaniment.

Near Naples

CASERTA The main reason to go to modern Caserta, 30 kilometers north of Naples, is to visit the **Palazzo Reale**, a bombastic testimony to aristocratic excess. Work began on the palace in 1751 for the Bourbon king Charles II, who commissioned architect Luigi Vanvitelli to design a palace that would match the courts at Versailles and Potsdam. Two kings, more than 30 years, and 1,200 rooms later, the palace was completed in all its baroque grandeur. Hundreds of neoclassical windows peer out at you from enormous, rectangular facades, and archways and interconnecting courtyards abound.

Your visit to the **Historical Apartments** will begin grandly enough: Vanvitelli designed an impressive staircase of marble and inlaid stone that sweeps up to the royal pad. The rest, however, is unremarkable, consisting of gilt-caked rooms with huge chandeliers dangling a few feet from the ground. Take a right at the end of the long entrance hall to reach the royal boudoirs, where Bourbons washed their regal flesh with water from hot and cold taps (a novelty for the time). *Apartment admission: L6000. Open Mon.–Sat. 9–6, Sun. 9–3.*

When you exit the apartments, turn right at the bottom of the staircase to reach the huge **Royal Gardens**, where families come to have picnics. From the entrance, you can walk about 3 kilometers to the **Fountain of Diana**, or hop one of the shuttles (L2000) that stop at various other fountains along the way. The Fountain of Diana depicts Actaeon turning into a deer (he's about to be devoured by his own hounds for spying on the bathing goddess Diana). *Garden admission: L5000. Open daily 9–1 hr before sunset.*

Beyond the famed palazzo, about all there is to do in Caserta is take Bus 11 (hourly, L1500) from the train station or walk about 50 minutes to the mostly abandoned medieval town of **Caserta Vecchia**. Its narrow cobblestone streets, lined with terra-cotta houses, are fun to explore, if a bit spooky. From Naples's Stazione Centrale, trains run to Caserta (45 min, L4500) every 15 minutes starting at 11 AM. Blue SITA buses also leave Naples's Piazza Garibaldi for Caserta (1 hr, L4700), every 20 minutes on weekdays and every hour or so on weekends.

Bay of Naples

The area surrounding Naples has a Greco-Roman history that makes the city look like the new kid on the block. The Greeks set out to Hellenize Italy's boot in the 6th and 7th centuries BC. Later, the Romans used the area as one giant playground, paving the roads from their colonies to numerous pleasure villas along the sea. Both groups left ruins for modern-day explorers to peruse. West of Naples are the ancient settlements of Pozzuoli and Cumae—awash in mythical folklore— and the *Campi Flegrei*, known in classical literature as the Phlegrean fields, which literally means "burning fields" because of all the sulfurous smoke that streams out of them. Mt. Vesuvius looms over the entire bay; in its shadow southeast of Naples are the world-famous archaeological sites of Pompeii and Herculaneum, preserved in mud and lava. Farther south, Sorrento and the islands—huge, volcanic Ischia, popular yet mysterious Capri, and unassuming Procida—suffer from an excess of hotels and restaurants but can still be beautiful, relaxing escapes.

Pozzuoli

Italian cinema's patron saint, Sophia Loren, was born in this ancient seaside city, the biggest in the Campi Flegrei. Most tourists don't come here to pay homage to the pneumatic goddess, but rather to sweat in natural saunas, see the town's Roman ruins, or take a ferry to Ischia or Procida. The city still has the look and feel of a Greek fishing village, though most of its fisherman have been relocated to ugly inland housing projects after an earthquake in 1980 ruined much of the old town. The medieval area is still condemned and looms mysteriously above the port behind tall, barbed-wire fences. The **tourist office** (Via Campi Flegrei 3, tel. 081/526–2419; open weekdays 9–2) provides information on the sights.

The volcanic, sulfuric, and generally smelly Campi Flegrei were alternately condemned by the ancient Greeks as the entrance to Hades and immortalized as the Elysian Fields, a paradise for the righteous dead.

COMING AND GOING The Cumana train line from Naples's Stazione Montesanto will drop you near the port (30 min, L1200). The Metro from Naples's Stazione Centrale (30 min, L1200) leaves you at a station just above the amphitheater. Pozzuoli is also a good jumping-off point for the islands Procida and Ischia, which lie just west of town. There are several ferries per day, most of which stop at Procida before docking in Ischia (1 hr, L6000).

WHERE TO SLEEP If you want to stay overnight, try **Hotel Flegreo** (Via Domiziana 30, 1½ km from tourist office, tel. 081/526–1523), which has doubles with bath for L60,000. Or choose the campground **Vulcano Solfatara** (Via Solfatara 161, tel. 081/526–7413; open Mar.–Oct.) and lay claim to having slept *in* a volcano. You also get free use of the natural saunas nearby. You'll pay L10,500 per person and L6500 per tent, but prices drop in September.

WORTH SEEING From the Metro station, turn right (south) on Via Solfatara and right again on Via dell'Anfiteatro to reach the **Anfiteatro Flavio** (tel. 081/526–6007; admission: L4000), open daily from 9 until two hours before sunset. Built under Emperor Vespasian around AD 70, this amphitheater held more than 40,000 screaming fans, and its subterranean structures remain in near perfect condition. Look for posters advertising concerts and other performances, which are held here in summer. Down near the bay, the columned **Tempio di Serapide** stands in a shallow pool of seawater. Originally thought to be a temple dedicated to the god Serapis, it was actually a bustling Roman market in the 1st century AD. You can visit the giant **Solfatara Crater** by taking a 15-minute walk (or short bus ride on the M1) uphill on Via Solfatara. Here visitors with a good tolerance for the smell of rotten eggs can walk down chalky pumice paths streaked with sulphuric stains, stomp their feet on the hollow ground to hear the echo, and stick their heads in steaming vents. The crater is open daily 8:30–7; admission is L5000.

NEAR POZZUOLI

CUMAE Cumae (Cuma), 8 kilometers west of Pozzuoli, was the ancient Greeks' Plymouth Rock—the settlement on mainland Italy from which they set out to conquer the boot. In addition to some scattered Greek and Roman ruins and views of the sea, it's home to the **Parco Archeologico** (Via Fusaro 35, tel. 081/854–3060; admission: L4000), open daily 9 AM to two hours before sunset. The main attraction in the park is the mysterious *Antro della Sibilla* (Sibyl's Cave): In the 6th or 5th century BC, the Greeks hollowed a tunnel in a triangular pattern from a rock beneath Cumae's acropolis, with vaulted chambers that allow light to stream through intermittently. According to Virgil's *Aeneid*, Aeneas came here to hear oracles from the prophet Sibyl, who sat at the end of the tunnel. You can try out the accoustics, which may have helped Sibyl to eavesdrop on approaching wisdom seekers and prepare her insights. To reach the site, take the "Cuma" bus from the Baia stop of Naples's Cumana railway (1 hr, L4100).

Herculaneum

Named after its mythical founder, the strong man himself, Herculaneum (Ercolano) was a Roman resort town full of posh villas with great bay views. For more than 300 years the town quietly conducted its affairs until AD 79, when pitiless Vesuvius erupted and buried the town under massive lava mud flows. The volcanic mud eventually hardened, protecting and preserving the site better than the burning lava that destroyed a lot of Pompeii before petrifying it. The site was first excavated in earnest in the 18th century when foreigners, mostly British, began to take an interest in it. Herculaneum may be smaller than Pompeii, but it's less crowded and closer to Naples, so it's a wise choice if you want to see Roman houses but you don't have much time.

Herculaneum, a half-day trip from Naples, is best combined with a hike up Mt. Vesuvius (*see* Near Herculaneum, *below*). From Naples's Stazione Centrale, take the Circumvesuviana railway to the Herculaneum stop (1–2 per hr, 20 min, L2200). If you didn't bring a picnic, hit the **open-air market** halfway between the train station and the entrance to the ruins. Pick up a free map of the ruins at the **ticket booth** (Piazza Museo 1; open daily 9–2 hrs before sunset), where you pay the L12,000 admission. For a succinct account of Herculaneum's history, get a copy of Amadeo-Maiuri's masterly guide at the *libreria* (bookstore) just down the street from the entrance.

THE SITE As you enter the site, the **House of Argus** lies directly to your left. Its columns and gardens are the remains of what was once a lavish mansion. Up the street a ways, on the right after the first intersection, lie the **Forum Baths**, a series of intricately painted rooms whose wall

---

One Hell of a Lake

The ancient Greeks believed volcanic Lago d'Averno, in between Cumae and Pozzuoli, was the entrance to Hades. Birds that flew over the lake would pass out from the sulphuric gases and fall in—proof positive of the lake's hellish qualities. Today, as you watch water-skiers glide over the lake's surface without getting sucked in, you may find it less menacing than Homer, Virgil, and Dante reported. The place is still spooky though, and on Sundays you may find an ancient Pozzuolean, for a few thousand of your lire, willing to lead you with torches through clammy tunnels to the underground waterway where boats headed for Hades supposedly disembarked. In 37 BC, Emperor Agrippa dug canals to connect the lake with the sea and Lago Lucrino, but they were partially filled during later volcanic activity, causing the hill above the lake to rise up in 48 hours. Locals figured it was another one of San Gennaro's miracles. To reach the lake, take Bus M1 heading west from Via Sofatra, and ask the driver for Lago D'Averno. For the guided tour, walk around the left side of the lake about 200 meters from where the main road hits the water and look for a vine-covered path off to the left.

and floor mosaics include a mural of Neptune. Note the steam vents ingeniously built into the baths' benches and the small overhead cubbies in which members stashed their clothes. From the baths, the Decumano Inferiore road leads east to the **House of the Wooden Partition**, the **House of the Neptune Mosaic**, and the **House of the Charred Furniture**. In the House of the Neptune Mosaic, a perfectly preserved floor and some carbonized rope and wine bottles are just as they were before the eruption. Pay attention to the street's construction on the way: They were designed to transport waste as well as people and horses—hence the handy stepping stones. Head south down Cardo V to reach the **House of Deer**, whose beautiful interior includes a painting of a deer being attacked by two dogs. It's also the home of the infamous sculpture—seen on postcards everywhere—of a lurching, drunk Hercules grabbing his willy to pee.

NEAR HERCULANEUM

MT. VESUVIUS   The dark, towering Mt. Vesuvius (Monte Vesuvio) looks out over almost the entire Bay of Naples. It beckons to be climbed, but those who answer the call do so at their own risk. Since its first recorded eruption in AD 79, the hot-tempered volcano has blown its top roughly every 50 years, often with catastrophic results (visit the annihilated ancient cities of Herculaneum and Pompeii to see for yourself). The last eruption was on March 19, 1944—more than 50 years ago—so the clock is ticking. Vesuvius is, however, constantly monitored, so nothing should take you by surprise.

Oddly enough, there are no public buses from Naples to Vesuvio, and visiting the mountain has become even more difficult since SESPA buses stopped running from Herculaneum. Getting here is possible though and worth the hassle. You'll have to find people to split the cost of a taxi from Herculaneum (L10,000 each for a group of four), hitch a ride, or hop on a local bus that drops you about a half-hour from Vesuvius's base. Once you reach the base, it's a good 1½-hour hike to the top up gravelly cinder paths. If you're going to make the trek, carry water, wear your best climbing shoes (or rent a pair of reasonably priced boots at the shack at the base), and by all means don't forget your shades. The roads become scorching hot during summer, and you should take serious precautions against sunstroke. Admission sometimes costs L3000, depending on whether you successfully avoid the guides who are supposed to lead you to the summit. Puffs of steam rise up from the core as you walk along the rim, which drops off steeply at each side and lacks guardrails in some places. After you've played queen/king of the mountain, consider hiking back to Herculaneum (2½ hrs); you'll pass interesting vegetation growing out of the lava flows, and there's a volcano-monitoring station partway down the mountain. During the summer months, Vesuvian wine can be bought and tasted at stands scattered around the base. Just be sure and drink it on the way down, not up.

Bring water and your own food (perhaps from Herculaneum's open-air market) to avoid being gouged by snack bars at the summit.

Pompeii

Pompeii, 45 minutes southeast of Naples, is a massive ruin—a classic ghost town where the ancients once lived high. It was a Greek colony before it fell to the Romans in 200 BC, when the city began to really flourish. With more than 20,000 inhabitants, the city had everything: outdoor theaters, banks, bars, working-class and wealthy districts, public baths, health clinics, and brothels. It was a hub of commercial activity in the region, until Mt. Vesuvius destroyed it all in the big bang of AD 79. Luckily, Pompeii had been partially destroyed by an earthquake that preceded the eruption; many citizens fled the town then, leaving only 25% of the original population to be buried in the blast. Today, tourists come in droves to see the incredibly well-preserved buildings, a few pornographic mosaics, and some of the eruption's carbonized victims: Their death screams, flailing arms, and tortured poses are cast permanently in ashen plaster.

The ruins are open daily from 9 AM until one hour before sunset; admission is L15,000. Pick up a free map at the **tourist office** (Via Sacra 1, tel. 081/850-7255) next to the east entrance, or at the smaller office (tel. 081/861-0744) on the west end, near Porta Marina. Don't waste you money on a "guided tour." Since most of the mosaics and frescoes that once decorated

Pompeii's homes—the ones that weren't looted, anyway—have been removed from the site for preservation, visit the Museo Archeologico Nazionale in Naples (*see* Worth Seeing, in Naples, *above*) for a fuller understanding of life in ancient Pompeii. To really see the site itself, you'll need four or five hours. It's best to make it a day trip from Sorrento or Naples, since hotels here are overpriced and there isn't much else to do but visit the site.

COMING AND GOING Take the Circumvesuviana line from Naples to the Pompeii–Villa dei Misteri stop (45 min, L2800), near the west entrance to the site.

THE SITE As you enter the ruins at Porta Marina, make your way to the **Forum**, which served as Pompeii's cultural, political, and religious center. You can still see some of the two stories of columnades that used to line the square. It was here that politicians let rhetoric fly, vendors sold goodies from their reserved spots in the central market, and Jupiter was worshipped in the **Temple of Jupiter**, at the head of the square. Go down Via del Foro and turn left on Via della Fortuna to reach the **House of the Tragic Poet**, believed to be the home of the Latin poet Glaucus. It's more famous for the black and white mosaic of a dog at the entrance, with the message "Cave Canem" (beware of the dog). If you turn around and go east on Via delle Terme, you'll reach the **House of the Faun**, named for the bronzen sculpture of a tiny but wild-looking faun in its central court (the original sculpture is in the Museo Archeologico in Naples). Look for the traces of costly marble which once lined the walls. The **House of the Vettii** across the way boasts a lovely garden and a small room of well-preserved Roman paintings, but most remember it for its depictions of Priapus, who shows off with absurdly swollen pride why he is the god of fertility.

One theory about the bold display of the penis in ancient times was that it was meant to ward off the evil eye and draw in good fortune. Many Neapolitan men still believe firmly in this symbol, wearing chili pepper pendants around their necks—a modern-day phallic symbol.

For more raunchy frescoes, head down Via Stabiana towards the **Lupanare**, ancient Pompeii's red-light district, and make a stop at the two-story brothel **Lupanar Africani et Victoris**. Each prostitute's room, large enough for an uncomfortable-looking stone bed, was decorated with an illustration of the particular sexual position or act promised. Further down Via Stabiana lie the **Stabian Baths**, Pompeii's largest bathhouse, which had a variety of hot and cold baths, steam rooms, a swimming pool, courts for bocce ball, and even boxing rings (without the ropes). The rooms still have intact domed ceilings and traces of decorative mosaics that make you wish there were still water in the pools. Continue along Via Stabian to the **Teatro Grande** and the **Teatro Piccolo**. The Teatro Grande held 5,000 ancient Pompeiians, with box seats for bigwigs. Today, the theater hosts weekend music performances—some by noteworthy classical groups—in the summer and early fall (ask at the tourist office for more info). The covered Teatro Piccolo, used for small concerts, poetry readings, and ballet, held 1,300 people. A block east of the theaters is the luxurious **House of Menander**, which contains a small chapel

Pompeiian Real Estate

You aren't allowed into every house in Pompeii, but even by peeking in from the entryways you'll start to notice patterns in the layout. Life revolved around the atrium (an uncovered inner courtyard surrounded by a columnade), from which the inhabitants received air, sunlight, and rainwater, the latter caught by the Jacuzzi-shaped receptacle under the sloped roof. Opposite the entrance was the living room/dining room; to the left and right were bedrooms and the hearth. Some families built a shop or bar on the street, with living quarters behind it. Try to imagine the interior floors and walls as they once were, covered with colorful marble tiles, mosaics, and frescoes.

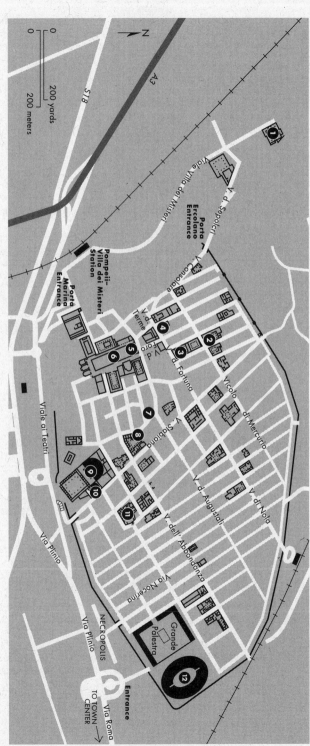

Pompeii

Amphitheater, **12**
House of
Menander, **11**
Forum, **6**
House of Faun, **3**
House of the
Tragic Poet, **4**

House of the
Vettii, **2**
Lupanare Africani
et Victoris, **7**
Stabian Baths, **8**
Teatro Grande, **9**
Teatro Piccolo, **10**

Temple of Jupiter, **5**
Villa dei Misteri, **1**

0
0
200 yards
200 meters

N

A3

S18

Viale Villa dei Misteri

Porta
Ercolano
Entrance

V. d. Sepolcri

Pompeii–
Villa dei Misteri
Station

Porta
Marina
Entrance

V. d. Console

V. d.
Terme

V. d.
Foro

V. d. Fortuna

Vicolo di Mercurio

V. di Nola

V. d. Augustali

V. Stabiana

V. dell' Abbondanza

Viale ai Teatri

Via Plinio

Via Nocerina

Via Plinio

NECROPOLIS

Grande
Palestra

Entrance

Via Roma

TO TOWN
CENTER

389

and wall murals depicting the conquest of Troy. Finally, the large **amphitheater**, near the east entrance to the site, seated 20,000 spectators in its day, and was one of the most raucous (and egalitarian) social spots in town. From here you can meander west on a different route if you'd like to take a look at more of the ruins.

It's a bit out of the way, but the amazingly intact, cryptic murals of the **Villa dei Misteri** (Villa of the Mysteries) are worth the walk. With your ticket in hand (you'll need it if you want to reenter), leave the Porta Ercolano exit and head down Via dei Sepolcri, following the signs. Unearthed in 1909, this villa had over 60 rooms painted deep red and black. One of the rooms features frescoes representing the Dionysian rites of initiation. The process, which is depicted in eight scenes starting from left of the entrance, has plenty of sexual overtones, including flagellation, a symbolic marriage into the cult, a Dionysian dance, and the unveiling of a phallus.

The Islands

The islands in the Bay of Naples offer a scene for everyone. Popular Capri has chichi cafés and Gucci stores, as well as kilometers of pathways running along cactus-covered cliffs, lemon groves, and white-washed Arabian houses. If you've got the lire to spend on a cushy resort, head to Ischia and soak in a mud bath, or just climb its 790-meter-high dormant volcano. Tiny Procida is a good place to escape the crowds and take in island life without shelling out exorbitant sums.

CAPRI

Capri has long been the life of the party in the Bay of Naples, outshining its sister islands in both glamour and scenery. The Greeks and Phonecians partied here, Emperor Augustus had his vacations on Capri, and Tiberius made it a home away from home, littering the island with 12 villas. Later inhabitants included such artists and intellectuals as Maxim Gorky, who headed a school for communist revolutionaries here that was visited by both Lenin and Stalin. In summer a zillion tourists swarm the island, and the towns of Capri and Anacapri (literally "above Capri") and the port feel like ant farms; but the crowds are easily escaped—and it's not difficult to realize that Capri really is a beautiful, mysterious place. You can climb mountains that suddenly drop off into the sea, take in Norman and Arab-influenced architecture surrounded in colorful bougainvillea, wander through Roman ruins, and lie on beautiful public beaches. The only real drawback to Capri is that it's much more expensive than the rest of the region. You can save your money by taking the first hydrofoil and making Capri a day trip, although midnight walks on the islands' deserted pathways, with the smell of jasmine in the warm evening breeze, is pretty unforgettable.

BASICS You'll find an **AAST** information office (tel. 081/837–0634) at the base of the main dock in Marina Grande, as well as one below the campanile in the center of Capri Town (Piazza Umberto I, tel. 081/837–0686) and one off Piazza Vittoria in Anacapri (Via Orlandi 19/A, tel. 081/837–1524). All three offices hand out useful maps of the island's public phones. You can make calls from the **SIP** centers in Capri (Piazza Umberto I, upstairs from the kiosk, tel. 081/837–5550; open daily 9–1 and 3–11) and Anacapri (Piazza Vittoria 5, tel. 081/837–3377). The **main post office** (Via Roma 50, tel. 081/837–7240) is in Capri, off Piazza Umberto I.

COMING AND GOING Alilauro (Agenzia Staiano, tel. 081/837–7577), **Caremar** (tel. 081/837–0700), and **Navigazione Libera del Golfo** (tel. 081/837–0819) are major carriers that serve Capri. Daily hydrofoils run from Marina Grande to Molo Beverollo in Naples (40 min, L17,000–L18,000), Sorrento (20 min, L8000), Amalfi (1 hr, L15,000), Salerno (1 hr 50 min, L17,000), and Ischia (40 min, L15,000). Ferries are less expensive than hydrofoils but take longer. They run daily to Naples (1 hr 15 min, L8000–L10,000) and Sorrento (40 min, L6000), as well as Procida and Ischia. Buy tickets at the windows outside the entrance to Marina Grande (the main port).

GETTING AROUND It's easy to get around by foot on most of the island, but because of the steep terrain, most people use public transportation between the Marina Grande (the main

港), Capri Town, and Anacapri. Buses (L1500) run every 20 minutes between towns and also stop at the two main ports and some major points of interest. A funicular connects Marina Grande with Piazza Umberto I, the center of Capri Town, every 15 minutes (L3000 round-trip). The funicular station in Capri Town has luggage storage for L1500 per piece per day, and you can also pick up a L6000 ticket for rides on both the funicolare and the buses. If you don't have too much luggage, the nicest way to reach Capri Town from Marina Grande is to make the peaceful 20-minute climb on foot (follow the signs to Piazza Umberto I). Boats make trips around the island (L10,000 low season; L15,000–L20,000 high season), affording a glimpse of countless caves and crannies.

WHERE TO SLEEP Even the barest rooms are costly all over swank Capri, but you can try to talk down the price in the off-season, and several private residences offer furnished rooms for decent rates. In Capri Town, **Stella Maris** (Via Roma 16, tel. 081/837–2014), a friendly family-run pension with views of the sea, has doubles for L60,000 right across from the main bus stop. From Piazza Umberto I take a right on Via Roma. **Salvatore Catuongo** (Via Birago 1, Villa Luisa, tel. 081/837–0128) has five doubles near the Giardini di Augusto for L50,000. At **Hotel ABC** (Via Serafina 37, tel. 081/837–0683; open Apr.–Oct.), you can eat in a dining room with the ambience of a tiki hut (Christmas lights notwithstanding). Doubles, many with views of the Marina Grande, start at only L40,000.

There aren't as many accommodations in Anacapri, but you'll compete with fewer people, and prices tend to be lower. Eva and Vincenzo, the owners of **Villa Eva** (Via la Fabbrica 8, tel. 081/837–2040), ask L70,000 for their comfortable doubles, with access to a garden that has tables and a sea view. **Hotel Il Girasole** (Via Linciano 47, tel. 081/837–3620) offers great deals to young budget traveler types, and the owner is incredibly friendly. His cheapest doubles are L20,000–L25,000 per person, but if you spend an extra L10,000–L15,000 each, you get a bath in your room and a view of the sea.

FOOD You'll pay high prices, even for the island's own products: wine, fish, fruits, and vegetables. Buying unprepared foods from bakeries and markets is the best way to eat cheaply. Most restaurants are high on ambience, with patios and views, but they cater to their foreign customers' bad taste. If you explore side streets or head to Anacapri you can find exceptions to this rule. From Capri Town, take Via Matermania toward Arco Naturale to find **Le Grottelle** (Via Arco Naturale 5, tel. 081/837–5719; closed Thurs. in winter). This place has one cave for a kitchen, one for the wood ovens, and another with an outdoor bar and tables overlooking the sea. Fresh pastas average L10,000 and feature homegrown ingredients such as lemon leaves, figs, tomatoes, and cheeses. The owner of **Saracena** (Via Krupp 1, tel. 081/837–0646), on a quiet side street in Anacapri, likes to talk a lot—about his homemade cheeses, pastas, wines, and desserts. It can get pricey if you follow his advice and order them all, but you'll probably want to. Take Via Migliara out of Anacapri to Belvedere Migliara to find **Da Gelsomina** (Via Migliara 72, tel. 081/837–1499), which serves traditional cuisine for about L10,000–L15,000.

WORTH SEEING Sophia Loren made the already super-stylish **Piazza Umberto I** world-famous by getting filmed in its cafés. By spending half your daily budget on a gelato or beer, you're allowed a taste of Capri's glamour world—worth it for the people-watching. Flower-filled **Giardini di Agosto**, at the southern end of Capri Town, has a stupendous view of the Faraglioni rocks and the cliffs to the northwest. It's a great place for photos and illegal picnics, but vertigo sufferers beware—the drop is a doozy.

The Roman emperor Tiberius liked Capri so much, he moved his residence from Rome up to a peak on the island—not the most logical place from which to rule an empire. Much of his enormous palace, **Villa Jovis**, which was once 7,000 square meters and several stories high, has been dismembered since its discovery in the 1930s, but you can still climb around its crumbling walls. Right near the entrance is "Tiberious' Rock," a sheer cliff off of which the manic tyrant supposedly threw unlucky subordinates. Follow the brick path to the baths and the enormous cisterns, a necessity given the difficulty of carrying supplies up the mountain. *To reach Villa Jovis from Piazza Umberto I, head east on Via le Botteghe to Via Tiberio, which leads to ruins (45-min total). Admission: L4000. Open summer, daily 9–1 hr before sunset; winter, daily 9–3:30 (but hours vary).*

In Anacapri, it's definitely worth dealing with the crowds and paying the L5000 admission for a visit to **Villa San Michele** (tel. 081/837–1401). Axel Munthe, a Swedish doctor and humanitarian who came here during a cholera epidemic, built this house in the late 19th century on the foundations of a Roman villa. In addition to period furniture, you get to see his eclectic collection of ancient art, which his servants dug up from the backyard and incorporated into white-washed walls and a shady patio. Stand out on the porch, next an archaic Sphinx statue, and watch boats jet in and out of the Marina Grande. To get here climb the stairs from Piazza Vittoria, turn left on Viale Axel Munthe, and follow signs. The villa is open April–September, daily 9:30–6; October–March, daily 10:30–3:30. Also near Piazza Vittoria is the **Chiesa di San Michele** (Via Orlandi, off Piazza Vittoria; open daily 9–3), an 18th-century octagonal church that has a hand-painted tile floor with a Neapolitan artist's rendition of earthly paradise. To view it from the balcony, pay L1000 and climb the spiral staircase.

Anacapri's most popular sight is the **Grotta Azzurra**. The Romans once used this large cavern to house a temple, but successive earthquakes have transformed it into a partially submerged grotto. Limestone formations are lit by sun shining up through the brilliant blue water, but boatloads of tourists popping flashbulbs detract from the dazzle. Admission is L4000, plus you'll pay L10,000 for a boat from Marina Grande, L15,000 for a second boat that takes you into the grotto, and a L1250 surcharge on weekends and holidays—for a grand total of L30,250. To walk from Anacapri, take Via Tuoro until it becomes Via Grotta Azzurra, or take the walkway that begins west of Chiesa di San Michele. The grotto is open daily from 9 until two hours before sunset, but the hours change depending on the season.

OUTDOOR ACTIVITIES Your best strategy when faced with stampeding tourists is to head for the hills. Part of the fun in visiting **Mt. Solaro** is the 489-meter ascent—a 12-minute ride in a single-seater *segiovia* (chairlift) over vineyards and meadows. But once you get off at the island's highest point, you'll be awestruck by the almost 90° drop and 360° view. A nice outdoor bar and the ruins of a castle take a backseat to it all. The segiovia station (tel. 081/837–1428) is right on Anacapri's Piazza Vittoria; tickets cost L5000 one-way, L7000 round-trip, and the lift runs daily 9:30–7.

➤ **HIKING** • If you've headed up Mt. Solaro, instead of returning on the chairlift you can follow the beaten path opposite the lift through the Cetrella valley. If you want more of a hike, follow the 476-meter path from Mt. Solaro to the peak of Santa Maria Cetrella. Another great hike starts in Capri Town. Follow Via Camerelle/Via Tragara past ritzy hotels and villas to a great southward vista, within spitting distance from the tall Faraglioni rocks. From here continue on Via Pizzolungo and climb the stairs to reach the dramatic cliffs. Along the route, note the red Malaparte Arch on the cliff at Punta Massullo—architecture students come from miles around to marvel at its ingenious design. If you turn right on Via Arco Naturale (at the end of Via Pizzolungo) and climb the hill, you'll reach the Arco Naturale, a large, twisted natural limestone arch that overlooks the sea near plenty of picnickable, shady spots. To return to town, follow Via Arco Naturale to Via Matermania and head down the hill.

➤ **BEACHES** • Despite all the tourists, there are plenty of free beaches in Capri, an island known for its relatively clean and clear waters. To the west of the Marina Grande, along Via Cristobol Colombo, the **Bagno di Tiberio** is a large public beach (accessible by bus) with sand scattered between the rocks. To the east of the private beaches at Marina Piccola you'll find the **Scoglio delle Sirene**, where bathers (some in the buff) perch on rocks above clear blue water. You can access the rocky beach by walking down a series of unmaintained switchbacks that start below Giardini di Agosto at Via Matteoli. If the gate is closed due to "falling rocks," you have to go to Marina Piccola and head west on foot through the private beaches until you reach the Scoglio. For the most remote sun-baking, take a bus from Piazza Vittoria in Anacapri to Faro (every 20 min, 10 min, L1500) and walk out to the **Punta Carena**.

AFTER DARK For many, the most tantalizing after-hours activity is to head for a private lookout point with a bottle of Capri wine, but a passeggiatta and an *aperitivo* (cocktail) in one of **Piazzo Umberto I**'s bars is also a necessary part of the Capri experience. Most of Capri Town's clubs and piano bars are on **Via Camerelle** and **Via Vittorio Emanuele**, in the center. Prepare to spend a bundle on drinks, which cost L10,000–L15,000. Anacapri's night scene isn't as glam, but it can still be fun. Piano bars and small discos have popped up around **Piazza Vittoria**, especially on **Via Orlandi**.

ISCHIA

A stroll along any of the island's yacht-filled harbors might give you the impression that Ischia is not designed for budget travelers, but this huge, volcanic island actually has a lot to offer backpackers and mafiosi alike. Even though much of the island's important natural resources—sand, ancient pine trees, and thermal mud—have been annexed by pricey resorts, there are ways to enjoy them. (Start by asking your hotel proprietor for discount coupons to the spas.) The island's food and lush scenery are wonderful and the island's dormant volcano begs to be climbed—you can be sure won't see many mafiosi on the trail.

Outside of Ischia Porto (the touristy port area), Ischia is divided into six communities—Casamicciola, Lacco Amero, Forio, Sant'Angelo, Serrara Fontana, and Barano. These towns have managed to maintain their identity despite the island's popularity with vacationing Germans.

Just south of Ischia Porto, in mellow Ischia Ponte, a 15th-century bridge stretches to a separate little island, where you'll find the **Castello Aragonese**, open daily 10–5. The castle, which charges L4000 admission, served as a refuge from pirates, plagues, and volcanic eruptions. Nowadays its crumbling, sunbleached tufa walls frame the blue sea and sky. The white-sand cove of **Spiaggia dei Maronti** is Ischia's most picturesque beach, 1 kilometer east of the tiny fishing port of Sant'Angelo on the southern part of the island. The nearby hill town **Serrara Fontana**, where donkeys are still used to carry hay and produce, is the starting point for an amazing climb up to the island's dormant volcano, **Mt. Epomeo**. On the west coast, **Forio** has a stretch of sandy beach (to the north) and the whitewashed chapel of **Santa Maria di Loreto** on a rocky cliff—an incredible sunset spot. Talk to the fisherman on the rocks below about the luck the chapel brings. The **AAST** office (at the hydrofoil dock, tel. 081/991146) gives out info on sights and lodging Monday–Saturday 8–1 and 4–8, Sunday 8–2.

COMING AND GOING Each day, 14 ferries (1½ hrs, L10,000) and 12 hydrofoils (45 min, L17,000) leave Naples's Molo Beverollo for Ischia. The two big carriers are **Caremar** (tel. 081/551–3882) and **Linee Lauro** (tel. 081/552–2838). Buses leave every 20 minutes or so from Ischia's Via Iasolino, between the ferry and hydrofoil docks, for trips around the island (1½ hrs), stopping at every "town" and points in between. Tickets to one destination cost L1200; other tickets are valid for one hour (L1400), half a day (L2200; good 6 AM–2 PM or 2 PM–midnight), or an entire day (L3400).

WHERE TO SLEEP AND EAT Accommodations on Ischia are both plentiful and pricey. For convenience and the best prices, look near Ischia Porto. **Locanda sul Mare** (Via Iasolino 90, 1 block from ferry dock, tel. 081/981470) has big doubles for L50,000, and is rarely full. The owner is an Ischia enthusiast and offers 40% discounts at various thermal resorts. The town of Forio has a few nice waterfront places if you don't mind a bit of isolation. For a splurge, try **Casa del Sole** (Via Giovanni Mazzella 17, tel. 081/997830), with doubles for L74,000–L90,000, depending on the season. Ischia Porto has an open-air market at the port weekdays 11–2. Also on Ischia Porto, **Ristorante da Emiddio** (Via Porto 30, on the docks, tel. 081/992432) offers affordable eating on the waterfront, while **Pizzeria da Scatoletta** (Via Iasolino 64, tel. 081/991389) whips up great pizza and pasta for under L10,000.

PROCIDA

In sharp contrast to its glitzy neighbors, Procida is a small and isolated island that offers a realistic look into Campanian life. It doesn't look a lot different today than it did as the setting for the recent film, *The Postman*, which told the story of Pablo Neruda in exile. The brightly painted fishing boats that crowd the main port still generate the island's primary income, and the old *pescatori* (fishermen) repairing their nets would much rather see a fat morning's catch than a fat tourist. You can cross the 4-kilometer island in about an hour on foot, and the peo-

Procida is a great place to escape for a day trip, but be sure you have a good book and good company if you're staying any longer.

ple you pass on your way will be sure to give you a once-over. The **Porto**, where ferries and hydrofoils dock and buildings sport different stages of fading pastel paint, lies on one end of the island; the small harbor community of **Chiaiolella**, with a few waterfront cafés and bars, occupies the other. Connected by bridge to Chiaiolella is the little island of **Vivano**, with good hiking and bird-watching terrain. Two long, free beaches flank opposite sides of Procida: **Spiaggia Ciraccio** on the north side and the less accessible **Spiaggia Chiaia**, at the foot of huge cliffs, on the south side.

One kilometer south of the port, the town of **Ponte Lingua** has most of the island's historical action, with a 14th-century **castle** (closed to the public) and a 16th-century **basilica** (open daily 11–7) that sits atop the cliffs. The basilica gives you a good sense of the symbolism involved in southern Italian Caltholicism: Skulls adorn the walls and the basement is filled with skeletons. There's a great view from the basilica's library (admission: L2000; students free), which has antique furniture and medieval manuscripts . The **AAST** info office (tel. 081/551–2841; open daily 9:30–1 and 5–9) is down at the port.

COMING AND GOING **Caremar** (Molo Beverello, tel. 081/551–5384), in Naples, runs regular hydrofoils (30 min, L14,000) and ferries (1 hr, L8500) to Procida, as well as to the other islands. Two bus lines, the **C1** and the **C2**, make frequent trips from the port to Chiaiolella and back; buy tickets (L1500 per trip) at the tabacchi by the port.

WHERE TO SLEEP AND EAT The **Riviera** (Via G. da Procida 36, tel. 081/866–7197), near Chiaiolella, has big doubles with bath and kitchen for L50,000. Take Bus C2 from the port, and tell the driver where you're going. **La Rosa dei Venti** (Via Vittorio Rinaldi 32, near the port, tel. 081/896–8385) rents bungalows for 2–6 people for around L35,000 per person per night. Via Roma along the water is lined with restaurants, but **Ipanema** (Via Roma 68, tel. 081/810–1298), with standard Neapolitan fare for around L10,000–L12,000, is recommended by every living soul on the island.

Sorrento

Most of Sorrento stretches across a plateau that ends abruptly at a steep tufa cliff 50 meters above the sea. Along the cliff's edge, aesthetes occupy terraces and benches, soaking in the bay views that inspired artists like Richard Wagner, Maxim Gorky, and Henrik Ibsen when they lived and created here. At the base of the cliff are ports and rocky beaches, where Speedo-clad sunbathers deep-fry in coconut oil. Sorrento's manageable size and secure feel, combined with its location and good transportation connections, make it a fine base for exploring the Amalfi Coast, the islands, and even Naples. Even the abundance of tourists has certain advantages: Credit cards are widely accepted, there are a lot of hotels, cheap food can be found, and there's a decent choice of late-night bars and clubs.

BASICS The **AAST** office (Via Luigi de Maio 35, tel. 081/807–4033) is open Monday–Saturday 8–8 in summer. Follow the yellow signs from the train station. You'll find **currency exchange** offices around Corso Italia and Piazza Tasso. They've conspired with Sorrento's banks to give a consistently poor rate, but at least most exchange commission-free. The only **American Express** representative (Piazza Lauro 12, tel. 081/878–4800) in Campania is an agency called Acampora. They arrange discounted tours of the Amalfi Coast and the islands, as well as cashing personal and travelers' checks weekdays 9–1.

The **post office** (Corso Italia 210/S–V, tel. 081/878–1636) exchanges money weekdays 8:15–5:30 and Saturday 8:15–1. You pay in cash to use the metered phones at the air-conditioned **SIP** office (Piazza Tasso 37, tel. 081/878–2400), open daily 9–1 and 4–10:30. From the station, turn left and walk two blocks on Corso Italia.

COMING AND GOING Sorrento has lots of train and ferry connections to nearby towns and islands. It's also small and relaxed enough that hitching a ride isn't difficult. If you're heading south, try picking up a ride at the southern edge of town on Corso Italia, where it becomes the highway Via del Capo.

➤ **BY TRAIN** • The private trains on the **Circumvesuviana** line (tel. 081/779–2267) make frequent trips between Sorrento and Naples's Stazione Centrale (1 hr, L4200), stopping along the way at Pompeii and Herculaneum. The Sorrento station is a block inland from Corso Italia and two blocks up from Piazza Tasso. The ticket office is at the window on the track level, but you can only buy tickets for the next train (not in advance).

➤ **BY BUS** • **SITA** (tel. 081/552–2176) sends buses to towns on the Amalfi Coast and to Salerno (2 hrs 45 min, change at Amalfi, L5000). These run every half hour and stop at Positano (30 min, L2700) and Amalfi (1 hr 15 min, L3400). Buses pull up in front of the Circumvesuviana station and also make pickups at the small SITA signposts on Corso Italia.

➤ **BY FERRY** • **Alilauro**, a.k.a. **Linee Lauro** (tel. 081/807–3024 or 081/878–1430) sends frequent hydrofoils from Sorrento to Naples (16 daily, 25 min, L22,000), Capri (11 daily, 20 min, L10,000), Ischia (7 daily, 1 hr, L20,000), and Amalfi (daily, 50 min via Capri, L20,000). **Caremar** (tel. 081/807–3077) sends five ferries a day to Capri (50 min, L7000).

GETTING AROUND The city is so small that you can easily orient yourself around **Corso Italia**, Sorrento's main drag, which runs through the length of the town and hits **Piazza Tasso**, the main square, about halfway. For L30,000–L50,000 a day, **Sorrento Rent a Scooter** (Corso Italia 210/A, tel. 081/878–1386) helps you buzz around town. Orange Circumvesuviana buses run the length of town and go down to the port. Buy tickets (L1000) on board. Sorrento's beaches are at the bottom of a steep cliff, but you can reach them via a free elevator carved into the cliff near the main port (on the other side of Peter's Beach). It lifts you to the public gardens near Chiesa di San Francesco daily 8–7 or until dusk in winter. **Marina Piccola**, **Marina San Francesco**, and **Marina Grande** are the most convenient beaches, but they can get crowded. Farther down the coast, below Via Capo, you'll find free beaches mixed in with the private ones; take the bus toward Capo di Sorrento to reach them.

Souvenir shops pack the old quarter, and hawkers try their best to lure you into buying lava-rock ashtrays, inlaid woodwork pictures of "The Last Supper," handcrafted sandals, and other schlocky keepsakes.

WHERE TO SLEEP The cheapest shelter you'll find is the hostel, which closes during the low season and may be losing its lease to a retirement home. A good portion of Sorrento's hotels open only for the high season (mostly July and August); call in advance or you may have a hard time finding a room. If the places below are full, **Hotel Savoia** (Via Fuorimura 46, tel. 081/878–2511) has 25 neat, simple rooms, some with balconies, for L80,000. From the station, go left on Corso Italia and walk two blocks to Piazza Tasso; turn left and walk two more blocks on Via Fuorimura.

Hotel City. The rooms in this small hotel all have a patio or a terrace, but they face busy Corso Italia, which almost never quiets down. Doubles cost L65,000–L90,000, depending on the season. *Corso Italia 221, tel. 081/877–2210. From station, turn left on Corso Italia and walk 1½ blocks. 13 rooms, all with bath. MC, V.*

Hotel del Corso. Past the shabby entranceway, this hotel is comfortable and homey, and it's run by a laid-back family. Sunny doubles decorated with colorful bedspreads and sparse wooden furniture run around L65,000. *Corso Italia 134, tel. 081/878–1299. From station, go left on Corso Italia and walk 2½ blocks. 20 rooms, all with bath. Closed Nov.–Jan. AE.*

Hotel Nice. This is the closest shelter to the station, and though the rooms are cramped and sometimes noisy, the price is right (doubles L65,000–L80,000). *Corso Italia 257, tel. 081/878–1650. From the station, quick right on Corso Italia. 18 rooms, most with bath.*

Pensione Linda. This pension is modern and ugly on the outside, but inside it's decorated with white marble and trimmed in wood. The clean rooms have tile floors and often balconies. Doubles cost L53,000–L60,000, and laundry is L4000 per load. *Via degli Aranci 125, tel. 081/878–2916. From stairs at station, turn left, then left again onto Via Marziale; go left on Via degli Aranci. 14 rooms, 11 with bath.*

➤ **HOSTELS** • **Ostello Surriento.** In high season, the large, single-sex rooms at this hostel fill up with international backpackers and genteel types who've been squeezed out of a room at a multi-star hotel. Beds go for L16,000, and they also serve continental breakfast (L2000) and dinners (L12,000). You might be allowed to stay without an HI membership; otherwise, they issue them for L25,000. *Via Carpasso 5, tel. 081/878–1783. From train station, go right on Corso Italia for 2 blocks and turn left at AGIP station. 130 beds. 11 PM curfew, lockout 10:30–5. Checkout 9:30 AM. Open Mar.–Sept.*

➤ **CAMPING** • **International Camping Nube d'Argento** (Via del Capo 21, tel. 081/878–1344) costs L12,000 per person, L6000 per tent. To get here, take Corso Italia until it becomes Via del Capo. Farther out on Via del Capo, **Villaggio Campeggio Santa Fortunata** (Via Capo 39/A–B, tel. 081/878–2405) has its own beach and costs L8000–L11,000 per person, L8000–L15,000 per site. It's open April–October.

FOOD Much of Sorrento's produce and fresh fish come straight from its own vegetable gardens and off the coast. For cheap nutrition, seek out the delis and produce stands along car-free **Via San Cesario**, toward the bay. A slice of thick pizza with tomato sauce, herbs, and toppings goes for L2000–L3500 around here. Corso Italia is also a locus for cheap pizzerias, offering *pizza sorrentana* (with broccoli, sausage, and mozzarella) or pizza with seafood. A **Standa** supermarket (Corso Italia 221, a block from train station) provides basic food and sundries. Next door, **Bar Rita** has delicious homemade pastries, thick pizza slices, and *arancini* (rice, tomatoes, mushrooms, and meat, with melted mozzarella in the center). The center has some reasonably priced trattorias, but you should avoid eating right on touristy Piazza Tasso. **Gigino** (Via degli Archi 15, off Piazza Tasso), which serves excellent local specialties, has a fixed-price menu at lunch. **La Laterna** (Vico S. Cesareo 23, off Piazza Tasso) offers excellent food and a quiet, elegant atmosphere at a very reasonable price. Dinners range from L8000 to L15,000. Gelaterias are a dime a dozen in Sorrento, but family-run **Homemade Ice Cream** (Via Fouro 19, where Vico S. Cesareo becomes Via Fuoro) is worth a special trip.

WORTH SEEING Most people come to Sorrento to relax, hang at the beach, and take in the view, so they don't care about the town's lack of blockbuster sights. Besides the Museo Correale, about all there is to do is take a peek inside some churches. Step into the 14th-century cloister of the **Chiesa di San Francesco** (between Piazza San Antonio and communal gardens) for a look at its delicate archways and very restful, tropical garden. The small **cathedral** on Corso Italia is known for its modern inlaid woodwork with scenes from Christ's life—a more sophisticated version of the stuff they sell in the souvenir shops.

At the **Museo Correale di Terranova**, Greek, Byzantine, and Roman statues fill the ground floor, and the upper floors feature mostly Italian art, Sorrento inlaid woodwork, and furniture from the 16th century onward. Try to allow enough time to dawdle around the grounds of this former palace before closing time. *Via Correale 48, 2 blocks from Piazza Tasso, tel. 081/878–1846. Admission: L5000. Open Oct.–Mar., Mon. and Wed.–Sat. 9–12:30 and 3–5, Sun. 9–12:30; Apr.–Sept., Mon. and Wed.–Sat. 9–12:30 and 5–7, Sun. 9–12:30.*

AFTER DARK In a town this small, the *passeggiata* (stroll) is an intense activity: During warm months, most clubs dry up around sunset as residents and visitors take to the streets, spilling into Corso Italia, crowding the seaside view spots, and gathering on the main piazze. The youngest crowd collects on **Piazza Achille Lauro** near the train station. British-style pubs are scattered around the center, keeping Sorrento's many English tourists from missing their Guinness. In summer, **classical concerts** take over the cloister of Chiesa di San Francesco at 9 PM, Wednesday through Friday. Those under 27 pay reduced admission (L12,000–L15,000).

The Amalfi Coast

Just below the Bay of Naples, the massive Gulf of Salerno meets the most scenic stretch of waterfront in Italy. Towns sprang up in the most unlikely places on the Amalfi Coast (Costa Amalfitana); stacked between the cliffs and the sea, these tiny communities developing into great sea-faring republics and later vacation empires. In the last few centuries, bigwig politicians, artists, and expatriates, addicted to the region's lemon trees and dramatic Mediterranean vistas, have given it most-favored-holiday-spot status. On the eastern end of the coast, the city of Salerno has grown into an important commercial center, with budget food and lodging; along with the city of Amalfi, it's a logical base for exploring the area. In the regions east and south of Salerno, the golden remains of Paestum's Doric temples stand only a cow-chip's throw away from buffalo pastures, country villas, and farms. You'll also discover the **Cilento** coast—a series of coastal fishing villages turned summer beach resorts.

GETTING AROUND Trains are nonexistent and buses inconvenient along the Amalfi Coast. One bus company employee even recommended hitching over taking the bus. It helps to rent a scooter, but vertigo may strike as you battle Neapolitan drivers for space on narrow, winding roads hundreds of meters above crashing sea and jagged rock.

Amalfi

Amalfi's chalk-colored buildings are stacked high on the rocky base of Mt. Lattari. In its glory days during the Byzantine era, Amalfi was a powerful maritime republic that minted its own money (called *tari*), refined the compass, designed a constitution, and drew up codes for Mediterranean trade practices. Much of the ancient city was destroyed by the sea during an earthquake in 1343 and declined in prominence thereafter, never even becoming an expensive seaside resort. It's stocked with cheap accommodations and food, making it a good base for exploring smaller, more expensive coastal towns.

BASICS The **AAST** office (Via Roma 19–21, tel. 089/871107) is open summer, Monday–Saturday 8–2 and 4:30–7; winter, Monday–Saturday 8–2. From the port, turn right and walk half a block on Via Roma; the office is in the courtyard. You'll get good rates changing money at banks on or around Piazza Duomo: Try **Banco di Napoli** (Piazza Duomo, tel. 089/871005) or **Banca Monte dei Paschi di Siena** (Via Roma 15, tel. 089/871260). Near the port, the **post office** (Via Roma 31–35, tel. 089/871330) is open weekdays 8:15–6 and Saturday 8:15–1. Amalfi doesn't have a regular phone office, but the store **Ceramiche Montefusco** (just past Piazza Duomo on Via Roma; open daily 10–10) has a bunch of pay phones and phone books.

COMING AND GOING Narrow alleys and stairways branch off from Piazza Duomo and the main coastal road, which changes names about seven times (Via Roma, Corso della Repubblica Marinare, etc.) as it cuts through town. By steering clear of this road and the cluttered port area, you can avoid Almalfi's camcorder-wielding visitors. The public beaches north of the main harbor are sandy by Amalfi Coast standards, while beaches to the south are mostly private and charge a fee for use.

➤ **BY BUS** • **SITA** buses (Lungomare dei Cavalieri, tel. 089/871016) leave Piazza Flavio Gioia, by the main port, for Naples (3 daily, 2 hrs, L5500), Sorrento (14 daily, 1½ hrs, L4000), and Salerno (35 daily, 1 hr, L3600). SITA also runs frequent orange buses to Ravello (30 min), Minori (15 min), and Positano (20 min). Buy tickets (L1500) at port-side bars, travel agencies, or tabacchi. Schedules are posted on Piazza Flavio Gioia; service runs from dawn to around midnight.

➤ **BY FERRY** • Several carriers sail throughout the day to Naples, Salerno, the islands, and small coastal towns. Buy tickets from the travel agents by the docks. The big carriers are **Alilauro** (tel. 089/871300) and **Gabbiano** (Via Leone X Papa 10, tel. 089/871483). Check *Il Mattino*, Naples's daily paper (available all along the coast), or the Naples edition of *La Repubblica* for boat schedules.

WHERE TO SLEEP Accommodations are fairly cheap when you consider the city's popularity with vacationers yielding high credit limits. If you can't find a room in the hotels listed below, try **Albergo Sant'Andrea** (Piazza Duomo 26, tel. 089/871023), where guns deck the walls of the reception area, and cell-size doubles (L75,000) are cluttered with proud-to-be-cheesy furniture.

Hotel Fontana. The most convenient sleep in town, this hotel offers large, bright rooms (L90,000 per double) that overlook the marina or Piazza Duomo. *Piazza Duomo, tel. 089/871530. Open Apr.–Oct.*

Hotel Lidomare. The huge, antique-filled rooms here have tile floors, and most are air-conditioned. You can even get a room with a balcony and a view of the marina. Doubles run L58,000–L75,000. *Largo Duchi Piccolomini, tel. 089/871332. From port, cross into town center, go left on Salita Costanza d'Avalos, and follow it to Largo Duchi Piccolomini. 20 rooms, 17 with bath.*

Pensione Proto. A climb up three flights of stairs brings you to the reception area, which is next to an auditorium-size dining room and the patio where breakfast is served. Doubles cost L60,000–L80,000, including breakfast. *Salita dei Curiali 4, off Via Genova, tel. 089/871003. 18 rooms, 9 with bath.*

FOOD In Amalfi, you can feast on some of the freshest, most affordable food in the area. The same people you see out in their yards in the morning picking fruits and vegetables sell their goods in the afternoon around Piazza Duomo. Bar/ristorante **Apicella** (Viale d'Amalfi 27), on the north side of Piazza Duomo, serves fresh, hot baguettes that could be from Paris. If you want a hot meal and service, stay away from the beach, where restaurant prices are high. Instead, venture through the whitewashed staircases and pathways off Piazza Duomo, and you'll find some reasonably priced restaurants with seafood on the menu and outdoor seating.

La Cantinella della Black and White. Nets and fishing gear hang from the dark walls; not surprisingly, seafood is the specialty. Try the *cozze alla marinara* (mussels with light broth and parsley; L5500), or the *risotto alla pescatore* (risotto with mixed seafood; L7000). Pastas are dirt cheap and veggie pizzas run L3000–L5500. A set meal with wine and four courses goes for L20,000. *Via Duca Mastalo II, tel. 089/872296. From Piazza Duomo, take Salita Truglio steps north, and turn right on Via Duca Mastalo II. Open in summer daily for lunch and dinner; closed Mon. in winter.*

The Green Bar. Pop into this small, dark *rosticceria* (a take-out counter specializing in roasted meats) for casual food and an array of international beers. Hunks of pizza, garlic-drenched roasted chicken with potatoes, and obese calzone (L3000) with stuffings such as eggplant, spinach, broccoli, and sausage are whipped up all day long. *Via Pietro Capuano 46, 1 block from Piazza Duomo, tel. 089/871271. Open daily 9 AM–11 PM (Oct.–June, closed Fri).*

Il Teatro Marini. This white-stuccoed place attracts a young crowd. Fish is a bit expensive (L15,000–L20,000), but pizzas (L3500–L8000) and pastas (L8000–L16,000) are affordable and scrumptious. Come on Friday for pizza with a nutty whole-wheat crust. *Via Ercolano Marini 19, tel. 089/872473. From Piazza Duomo, go 1 block on Via Roma, left onto any staircase, and right on Via Ercolano Marini. Open July and Aug. daily 11–3:30 and 7–midnight; Sept.–June, closed Wed.*

WORTH SEEING Earthquakes and other disasters have toppled Amalfi's really ancient stuff, but you can still get a glimpse at some of the city's glorious past. The ornate **duomo** in the center of town has greenish bronze doors from 1066—supposedly the first of their kind. The duomo's colorful facade, on top of a long flight of steps, is a recognizeable image on postcards throughout the region. The 12th-century **Cloistro del Paradiso** (entrance to left of duomo) shares the duomo's Arabic influence, as you'll see from its pointed white arches. Inside are sarcophagi, marble sculptures, and mosaics. The **Museo Civico** (Piazza Municipio, tel. 089/871001), open Monday–Saturday 8–1:30, displays original manuscripts of the Tavoliere Amalfitane, the maritime codes that governed the whole Mediterranean until 1570. Near Amalfi, in the Valle del Mulino, you can watch the famous Amalfitane paper being made in factories surrounding the paper museum, **Museo della Carta** (Via Casamare, tel. 089/872615; open weekdays 10–4). Follow the brown and white signs that direct you inland from the main road (east from Piazza Duomo).

From December 24th until January 6, skin divers make pilgrimages to a submerged ceramic presepe (crèche) at the Grotta della Smeralda.

The **Grotta della Smeralda** (Emerald Cave), Amalfi's most famous attraction, is actually a ways out of town. Take a SITA bus (orange or blue) headed north from Piazza Flavio Gioia and ask to be let off here; then descend the stairs or pay for an elevator ride down the cliff. Guys with boats hang around from dawn to dusk during high season (not as regularly off-season or in bad weather) to whisk you through the limestone caverns for about L10,000 per person. It's a quick little ride—over before you can cock your camera—but the surreal green light coming up through the water creates a chilling beauty.

NEAR AMALFI

POSITANO Climbing up a cove between steep, narrow cliffs, Positano looks more like a toy town or a giant wedding cake than a popular resort. Although boutiques, restaurants, and hotels pamper the gold-card set, Positano has been a favorite destination for artists and expats for 50 years, perhaps because of the glimpse it provides into a perfectly lovely, precariously elegant world. Pleasure boats cruise by its tiny, rocky beaches, which are generously endowed with frying bodies. Check out the **AAST** office (Via Saraceno 2, tel. 089/875067), open Monday–Saturday 8:30–2, for info on sights and accommodations.

➢ **COMING AND GOING** • **Gabbiano** (tel. 089/871483 in Amalfi) runs daily jet boats to Positano from Amalfi (30 min) and Capri (45 min). **SITA** buses run to and from Sorrento (14 daily, 35 min, L2000), Salerno (36 daily, 2 hrs, L4200), and Naples (7 daily, 2 hrs, L5500).

➢ **WHERE TO SLEEP** • It's best to make posh Positano a day trip, but if you're seized by the desire to stay overnight, scramble for one of the six doubles with bath and terrace (L50,000–L70,000) at **Pietro Pane's** place (Via Canovaccio 5, tel. 089/875360), about halfway down the hill from the main road. The manager is incredibly friendly, and it's a great deal for Positano. If they're full, **Villa Verde** (Via Pasitea 338, tel. 089/875506; closed Nov.–Easter) has a peaceful garden and doubles for L85,000. The food situation in Positano is simple. The closer you are to the water, the more you'll pay. For a great meal at a low price, try **Grotta Azzurra**, right where the SITA bus lets off. The pasta is homemade and goes for about L8000 per plate.

RAVELLO You can practically kiss the clear blue sky from this remote city, naturally fortified on a precipitous tower of limestone. Views of the sea and the valley are broken only by citrus, fig, and cypress trees and stucco walls and cottages. A population of less than 3,000 enjoys the silence that comes with a ban on vehicles and Ravello's air of retreat and escape. But unless you have a budget like the town's most famous resident expat, Gore Vidal, Ravello is best as a day trip from Amalfi, Sorrento, or Salerno. For info on sights, stop at the **AAST** office (Piazza Duomo 10, tel. 089/857096), open Monday–Saturday 8–8 in summer, 8–7 in winter. **SITA's** orange buses come from Amalfi (15 daily, 30 min, L1500) and stop on the highway outside the tunnel to Piazza Vescovado/Piazza Duomo.

Ravello's views are its primary draw, though some manmade sights merit your time. On the way into town, take a walk through the 11th-century **duomo**, which has bronze doors and a 13th-century campanile. Inside, look for the elaborate mosaics of the Rufolo family pulpit, supported by spiral columns that rest on the backs of six white-marble lions. A steep walk from Piazza Vescovado/Piazza Duomo brings you to **Villa Cimbrone** (tel. 089/857459), open October–May, daily 9–6:30 and June–September, daily 9–8. The villa itself is a private residence, but for L5000 you can peek into its beautiful Arab-influenced cloister to see decorative tile work and panels that depict the seven deadly sins. The crumbling Sicilian, Arabic, and Norman buildings of **Villa Rufolo** (central piazza, tel. 089/857866) are open daily 9:30–1 and 2–4:30 (July and Aug. daily 9:30–1 and 3–7:30). Built in the 11th century, the villa was chosen by Wagner in 1880 as the setting for his opera *Parsifal*. The coastal panorama from the villa's western edge is the backdrop for pricey Wagner concerts during summer (ask at the AAST office for info). Admission to the villa is L3000 but Thursday is free.

➢ **WHERE TO SLEEP** • Plan to splurge: No hotel here rates less than two stars. The hospitable, family-run **Hotel Villa Amore** (Via dei Fusco, tel. 089/857135) is on the way to Villa Cimbrone from the town center (doubles L83,000–L93,000). **Hotel Garden** (Via Boccaccio 4, tel. 089/857226), open April–October, and **Hotel Toro** (Via Emanuele Filiberto, tel. 089/857211) both have gardens and charge L76,000–L86,000 for a double.

MINORI "Quaint" is a hackneyed adjective, but it accurately describes this town tucked into another one of the coast's nooks and crannies. Stucco buildings cover hills that lead down to a steep and rocky beach, which usually has ample towel space. Prosperous citrus and fishing industries have kept Minori from relying on tourist lire, so you won't pay much for a bed or for fresh fish at the seaside trattorias. On the way into town, stop at the 1st-century ruins of a **Roman villa**, with vaulted, frescoed rooms and displays of paintings, bits of pottery, and building fragments recovered from towns devastated by the eruption of Mt. Vesuvius. Stop at the **Pro Loco** office (Piazza Umberto I, tel. 089/877087), open Monday–Saturday 9–noon and 4–8, for info on other sights. **SITA** buses pass through Minori on frequent runs between Amalfi (15 min, L1500) and Salerno (1 hr, L2800).

Minori's affordable lodgings include the three-star **Hotel Bristol** (Corso Vittorio Emanuele 70, tel. 089/877013) and **Hotel Caporal** (Via Nazionale 22, tel. 089/877408), which is closer to the beach. Both charge L80,000 for a double.

Salerno

Salerno may be a run-down port town, but it's the poor person's best Amalfi Coast depot. In the wake of heavy bombing during World War II and a destructive earthquake in 1954, long rows of architecturally redundant housing units were built around the new town center. The result is more an inexpenisve commercial center than a tourist stop: Hotels offer bare-bones rooms (it's better to make use of the hostel), buses, trains, and hydrofoils blanket the area, and slices of pizza cost as little as L800. Despite the lack of charm, Salerno offers beautiful views of the southern Amalfi coast and a medieval quarter that was home to one of the first universities in Europe.

Salerno's university blossomed into the world's best medical school during the Middle Ages. That's a somewhat dubious distinction considering the unchecked plagues of the time, but the doctors here were able to perform complex surgery.

The 11th-century **Cathedral of St. Matthew**, which dominates a section of the old quarter, boasts a set of bronze doors made in Constantinople. The courtyard, surrounded by marble columns (some heisted from the ruins in Paestum), is more interesting than the church's interior. Just behind the cathedral on Via San Benedetto sits the small **Museo Provinciale** (tel. 089/231135; open daily 9–1), housed in a Benedictine convent and chock-full of archaeological finds. A 15-minute ride on Bus 19 (L1000) takes you to the **Castello di Arechi** (tel. 089/227237), a medieval castle with a spectacular view of the Amalfi Coast. The bus leaves from Teatro Verdi (head on foot toward Amalfi on Villa Comunale). The castle is open daily 9–1 and 3–one hour before sunset.

BASICS The **ENT** office (Piazza Ferrovia, in front of station, tel. 089/231432) dispenses visitor information weekdays 9–1:30 and 3–8, Saturday 9–1:30. If you want to change money near the train station, **Banca di Roma** (Corso Vittorio Emanuele 148) has competitive rates and speedy service and charges a flat L5000 commission. It's open weekdays 8:25–1:35 and 3:10–5:50, like most banks in town. You can make long-distance calls at the **SIP** office (to the left as you leave the train station), open daily 9:15–12:45 and 2:15–5:45. The central **post office** (Corso Garibaldi 203), open weekdays 8:15–5:30 and Saturday 8:15–1, is about 1 kilometer from the train tation.

COMING AND GOING The orange public buses in front of the train station cover the city well, but walking will usually suffice. West of the station, you'll find hotels and fancy stores along Corso Vittorio Emanuele. The street runs directly into Via dei Mercanti and to the narrow corridors of Salerno's medieval quarter, which surrounds the duomo. Three blocks south of the train station, on Via Lungomare Trieste, lies Salerno's port. Here you can begin a prime stroll west along the sea and through a narrow park with palm trees.

➤ **BY TRAIN** • Salerno's train station, in Piazza Veneto, is a stop on the Milan–Reggio di Calabria line. Trains depart regularly until around midnight for Pompeii (45 min, L2800), Naples (1 hr, L4700), and Agropoli (45 min, L4200). Upstairs and behind the station, you'll find 24-hour luggage storage.

➤ **BY BUS** • For long trips, blue **SITA** buses leave from Piazza della Concordia, south of the station near the port; they also stop at the SITA office (Corso Garibaldi 117, tel. 089/

226404) about 1 kilometer west of the station. Buy tickets on the bus or at the office, which is open Monday–Saturday 8–8. Between 6 AM and 10:30 PM, buses leave every 15 minutes for Naples (1 hr, L5000), and every 45 minutes for Amalfi (1 hr, L3600) and Sorrento (2 hrs 45 min, L7000). One bus runs regularly through Praiano to Positano (2 hrs, L4200).

WHERE TO SLEEP Salerno's hotels cluster around Piazza Veneto, in front of the train station. For the best chances in finding a room, try to arrive in town before 4 PM. As always, it's smart to call a week or so in advance in summer. Ask at the tourist office about private residences that let rooms (around L25,000 a person). Just down the street from the train station, **Albergo Santa Rosa** (Corso Vittorio Emanuele 14, tel. 089/225346) offers the nicest budget digs in town, with clean, quiet rooms (L70,000 a double), many with small balconies. The dreary but clean **Albergo Salerno** (Via G. Vicinanza 42, tel. 089/224211) has doubles for L65,000. Via G. Vicinanza is the first left down Corso Vittorio Emanuele from the train station.

➤ **HOSTELS • Ostello per la Gioventù (HI).** Many travelers use this hostel as a cheap base from which to explore the Amalfi Coast and Paestum. You can drop off your bags even during lockout, when the reception is closed (knock loudly). Rooms have 2–8 bunk beds; baths in the hall are cleaned daily but can get a little nasty. You'll pay L15,000 per night, breakfast included. Nonmembers sometimes have to shell out an extra L5000 per night, but they're pretty lax about it and the curfew. *Via Luigi Guercio 112, tel. 089/790251. ½ km from station (follow signs). 60 beds. Curfew 12:30 AM, lockout 10:30–2. Laundry, luggage storage.*

FOOD Salerno's cuisine centers around pasta dishes, *frutte di mare* (seafood), pizza, and the yummy local specialty *baccalà* (dried cod with potatoes and fresh tomatoes). For fast, cheap eats, the pizzerias and *tavole calde* (cafeterias) around the train station are your best bet. A step up in price (L15,000–L20,000 per person) and quality are the small local restaurants off Corso Vittorio Emanuele and Corso Garibaldi, west of the station. Most restaurants by the sea on Via Lungomare aren't worth it (with high prices and a sliding pay scale for foreigners), though they do tend to have nice bay views and stay open late. **La Rosalia** (Via degli Orti 22, tel. 089/229671) is a local favorite, with a beautiful mix of frutte di mare and delicious brick-oven pizzas for L7000–L12,000. **Tavola Calda da Tavola Calda** (Via G. Vicinanza 7, tel. 089/227741) has pizza for L1800 a square, sold at a counter frequented by Salerno's aspiring mafiosi. Tired of pizza? Don't dig shellfish? Try **Fred's Burger** (Piazza Concordia 26), a little seaside tourist trap open until about 1 AM, where pretty decent burgers go for about L3500.

AFTER DARK Salerno's evening passeggiata along Corso Vittorio Emanuele and the lungomare is known throughout the Mezzogiorno as a mondo strolling event. Get out there and see whether you can meander with the best of 'em. After a while, let the wave of walkers lift you onto a comfy bar stool in one of the English-style pubs at the end of the corso.

Paestum

If you grow tired of greased bodies on the beach, a 45-minute bus ride south from Salerno will bring you to a slice of Greece at the archaeological site of Paestum. Once the capital of Magna Grecia (the Greek colonies of southern Italy), Paestum is now a set of Greek and Roman ruins that occupies the countryside just beyond Salerno's industrial tentacles. This part of Campania, at the start of the Cilento region, is quite pretty, especially toward twilight when the last rays of sun bathe the landscape in red and orange light. The site itself consists of a large plain strewn with flowers, the remains of a Roman town, and three stunning Greek temples, supposedly some of the most well-preserved Doric temples in Europe. Paestum's **Cousorzio Iniziative Turistiche**, or **Cointur** (Via Magna Grecia 69, tel. 0828/722520) provides a full list of the area's accommodations and a simple brochure on the site and the museum.

Wandering around the site and munching grass are herds of water buffalo, whose milk is used to make creamy mozzarella buffalo cheese.

COMING AND GOING Four trains leave Naples daily for Paestum on the **FS line** (not the Circumvesuviana, which leaves for Pompeii from downstairs). Tickets for the 1½-hour ride are **401**

L7400; make sure your train from Naples stops in Paestum and not Agropoli. There are no direct trains from Salerno, so take one of the blue **SCAT** buses that leave regularly from the port (45 min, L4000). There are two entrances to the site along Paestum's main road, **Via Magna Grecia**. The bus from Salerno will drop you at either one, but ask to be let off in front of the Basilica of Hera and the Temple of Neptune for easy access. If you arrive by train, walk half a kilometer up the road from the station to reach Via Magna Grecia. You'll probably want to make a day trip out of Paestum, so plan your transportation carefully—it's easy to miss the last bus or train and get stuck.

WHERE TO SLEEP AND EAT Affordable rooms are no problem in Paestum, but most lodging is a bit of a walk from the station. On the corner of Via Magna Grecia and the road from the train station, the threadbare **Pensione delle Rose** (Via Magna Grecia 40, tel. 0828/811070) has fairly clean rooms for L60,000 per double (bargain during the off-season). To stay by the beach, try **Hotel La Bonita** (Via Laura 6, tel. 0828/851312), where doubles with bath cost L45,000. Call ahead during high season.

For an excellent alternative, spend a few days on the fringe of the Campanian countryside. Along with his brother and family, Dr. Nunzio Daniele, a well-regarded author and lecturer on Paestum, has set up **Pensione Arcobaleno** (Via Gaiarda 51, tel. 0828/722178) on farmland just outside the site. He grows his own food, raises livestock, and makes wine (all organically). Immaculate rooms with bath go for L35,000 per person, L40,000 with breakfast, or L75,000 including all meals. Call when you arrive at the train station, and someone will pick you up.

THE SITE Admission to the ruins (including the museum) is L8000. From July to September, the site is open daily 9–6 and the museum daily 9 AM–10 PM. The **Basilica of Hera** is Paestum's oldest temple, dating from the 6th century BC. Its 50 Doric columns were built of heavy circular chunks of stone stacked on top of each other. At the center of the temple, you'll see the three remaining pillars from the inner sanctuary, known as the *cella*. Only the temple priests were allowed in here to perform sacred rituals (which included human sacrifice) in tribute to Hera. Built a century later on the small mound of earth next to the basilica, the magnificent **Temple of Neptune** still displays grand columns only partially pitted and aged. The roof they once supported is now entirely gone, but the columns exemplify the artistic accomplishment and economic power to which the Greeks aspired. Both the Temple of Neptune and Temple of Ceres (*see below*) have been popularly misnamed; the former was actually dedicated to Hera and the latter to Athena.

A walk along Roman roads past the humble remains of the **Roman Forum** and nearby **amphitheater** will bring you to the opposite end of the plain and the lonely **Temple of Ceres**, which was built in 500 BC. In the early Middle Ages, Christians constructed a small village here and converted the temple into a church. Attacks by Saracens forced the Christians to abandon the town, but they left behind several tombs. Across from the site, the **National Archaeological Museum** houses the only known Greek mural, called the *Tomb of the Diver* for its fresco profile of a man diving off of a rock.

NEAR PAESTUM

AGROPOLI Agropoli is one of the highest towns on the Cilento coast, a fact that will be obvious to you after you've climbed the stairs to its old quarter. Up top, you can look down at the marina and the infinite Tyrrhenian Sea and have a *tè freddo* (iced tea) at one of the cafés where fishermen hang out during the day. Amid the narrow passageways of the old quarter is a **castle**, usually open 8–1 and 5–8. Even if it's closed, it's worth the climb to see the neighborhood. From the train station in the new section of town, it's a good 20-minute walk to the town center, where you'll find lodgings, the old quarter, and beach access. You can get your swimming and tanning fix on the rocks in the small harbor by the marina or take the long but very scenic walk along Via Trentova to the **Lido di Trentova**. (If you're lazy, frequent local buses make the run to the farther beach during peak season). Regular trains run between Agropoli and Paestum (10 min, L1500), or you can take a direct train to Salerno and Naples. **SCAT** buses (blue) also make the trip to Paestum (10 min, L1500) from the central piazza.

WHERE TO SLEEP AND EAT **Hotel Carola** (Via C. Pisacane 1, tel. 0974/823005), just above the marina, is Agropoli's best deal. Well-kept rooms with bath go for L65,000 per double in high season; otherwise it's L60,000 per double. For a budget meal with a great view to boot, try **U'Sghiz** (the name means "drop" in local dialect). This place, at the entrance to the old quarter, serves pizza (L3500–L6000) or a tasty plate of *pasta e fagioli* (pasta and beans) with clams. Sometimes you'll sit elbow to elbow with the very fisherman who caught the stuff you're shoveling down.

PUGLIA, BASILICATA, AND CALABRIA

13

By Janet Morris

The Mezzogiorno (southern Italy) is so different from its northern counterpart that it's sometimes hard to believe they belong to the same country. In fact, some northern Italians have even suggested dividing Italy into two nations, making official the schism between the European north and the almost third-world south. The three regions that make up a large part of the Mezzogiorno—Puglia (Apulia), Basilicata, and Calabria—define the Italian backwater. Conquest, climate, and corruption have prevented this region from experiencing anything like the economic and cultural boom of the north. Even at the end of World War II, when the government first came to the region's aid, the economic and social situation of the Mezzogiorno remained stubbornly grim. Welfare programs, housing projects, and newly installed irrigation systems were developed less out of concern for this area's well-being than as a deterrent against the threat of Communism.

Southern Italy's plague of poverty has a long history. Not since the Magna Grecia era (when ancient Greeks settled here in the 8th century BC) have these regions been considered wealthy. Following this relatively brief period of prosperity were a series of foreign invasions lasting until the 1940s. Romans, Goths, Visigoths, Byzantines, Anjous, Aragons, and Bourbons all had a hand in exploiting the unprotected, indefensible residents of southern Italy and their mangled land. Considering the south's tumultuous past, it's no surprise that feudalism lasted until the unification of Italy in the 1860s, longer than anywhere else on the European continent.

Southern Italians fought desperately for a united Italy, mistakenly believing that a new state would improve the standard of living for the average southern "peasant" and that life in the north and the south would even out over time. Sadly, what happened was quite the opposite: Northern politicians, backed by industrialists, heavily taxed the already impoverished in order to finance the modernization of cities such as Turin and Milan. It was during this time that many southern Italians packed their bags and left their problem-ridden homeland, marking the first great wave of emigration from the Italian south, a movement that continues even today. As a result, Calabrian, Basilicatan, and Puglian natives (and their culture) can be found all over the United States, Canada, South America, and Australia.

Women traveling alone will have to deal with plenty of catcalls and stares. It's generally harmless, but stay alert. If you're accompanied by a man, you should have no problem.

Recent reforms have not been enough to turn things around for the south, especially since much of the money slated to develop the region has disappeared into the pockets of corrupt politicians. Fear and skepticism toward the government, aggravated by the presence of organized crime, have prevented badly

405

needed change. The arid climate and the region's geographical isolation from the rest of Europe have also played a tremendous role in limiting the development of the Mezzogiorno, which looks and feels much as it did centuries ago.

But for the Mezzogiorno, the landscape and location are as much friend as foe: All three regions boast spectacular aquamarine seas and perfect beaches; the interior of Basilicata and Calabria is wild and mountainous; and the vast green Sila Massif mountains rank among the few places in Italy where nature wields its power over man and not the other way around. These distinctions have attracted travelers (and their lire) to the region in ever-increasing numbers. Calabria and Basilicata are just beginning to turn tourism into a profitable industry, while Puglia's strategic coastal location put it on vacationers' maps long ago. Puglia's other plus is its extensive railway system, which makes the region a bit more user-friendly than its two neighbors to the west. Buses are the way to go in Basilicata, and in Calabria you'll use a combination of buses and antiquated trains. Still, a visitor to any of the three regions must come equipped with patience and lots of time, since transportation is unbearably slow and unreliable. Not helping matters, transportation officials are exasperatingly apathetic in all three regions. But you'll find the average local to be among the most talkative, most curious, and most genuinely hospitable of all Italians.

Puglia

Puglia forms the heel of the Italian boot, making the region's defining characteristic its long stretch of coastline, which extends for hundreds of kilometers along the Adriatic and Ionian seas. Because of its proximity to Italy's eastern neighbors, Puglia has been the site of much commerce and conquest. The Greeks were among the first to venture over, establishing small colonies and fishing villages up and down the coast from the Gargano Promontory to the Salentina Peninsula at the bottom of the heel. These colonists were followed by the Romans, and then Saracens and Near Easterners who vied with Christian Crusaders and western Europeans for control of Puglia's prime coastal land. Standing above the clash between East and West was Frederick II, king of Sicily and one of the most eccentric personalities of the Middle Ages. His carnivalesque courts—which encouraged religious tolerance, promoted education, and employed panthers as house pets—fused Eastern and Western cultures brilliantly. His legacy endures in the form of castles throughout the province. Other foreign influences, including the Byzantines, Normans, Longobards, Anjous, Bourbons, and Aragons, can also be seen in Puglia's architecture, customs, and cuisine.

Puglia has a hot, semiarid climate that's perfectly suited to its spectacular coastline. Unfortunately many visitors just pass through on their way to Greece without stopping to admire the region's beauty: its beaches, its tiny Mediterranean villages (many of which resemble Greek towns), or its ancient Greek and Roman ruins. For the most scenic stretches, visit the Gargano Promontory, the spur that juts out into the Adriatic in the northern part of the province. Unfortunately, the small cities and towns along this coast are beginning to attract a considerable number of Italian and German tourists; if you are headed for the beach, it pays, of course, to get off the beaten track and to avoid the peak season (late July–Sept.).

But Puglia isn't all beach—in fact, its terrain is quite diverse, both topographically and culturally. Little public transportation penetrates the mountains in the interior of the Gargano Promontory, but with a car the pristine wilderness is absolutely worth exploring. West of the Gargano lies the long, flat Tavoliere region. The name means "chessboard," and the appellation is well chosen: Outside the quiet provincial capital of Foggia, the vast plains stretch for miles, an evocative checkered landscape of golden rows of wheat and fallow fields. Farther south, Puglia's largest and most important city, Bari, has a reputation for crime and congestion, but its big-city bustle, funky old quarter, abundant services for backpackers and budget travelers, and convenient ferry service to Greece make it worth a stop. The interior of this region (known as Le Murge) contains the unusual *trulli*, small homes built of field stones and capped off with whitewashed domes. In Puglia's Salentina Peninsula, the stiletto part of the heel, don't skip Lecce, an important center of baroque architecture, or the small town of Otranto, which feels more like Greece than Italy.

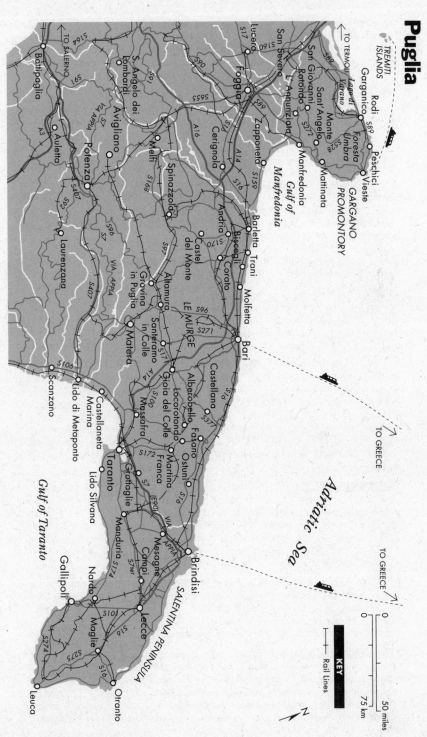

Puglia

TREMITI
ISLANDS

TO TERMOLI

Rodi
Garganico

Peschici

Lago di
Varano

Foresta
Umbra

Vieste

GARGANO
PROMONTORY

TO SALERNO

Barletta

Battipaglia

S164
S160

Lucera

San Severo

S17

Foggia

L'Annunziata

San
Giovanni
Rotondo

Sant' Angelo

Monte
Sant' Angelo

Manfredonia

Mattinata

Gulf of
Manfredonia

S89
S90

S655

S89

S272

S528

S528

Auletta

A3

S91

VIA APPIA

S. Angelo dei
Lombardi

Avigliano

S7

S91

Zapponeta

Cerignola

A16

A14

Potenza

Melfi

S168

S655

Andria

S159

S407

S93

S96

S7

Castel
del Monte

Spinazzola

S170

Biseglie

Trani

Barletta

S581

S407

Gravina
in Puglia

S96

Altamura

S97

LE MURGE

S96

S271

Corato

Molfetta

Bari

Laurenzana

VIA APPIA

Matera

Santeramo
in Colle

S171

A14

S16

Scanzano

S106

Lido di Metaponto

Castellaneta
Marina

Castellaneta

Gioia
del Colle

S100

Massafra

Alberobello

Locorotondo

Fasano

Castellana

S377

S16

TO GREECE

Gulf of Taranto

Lido Silvana

Taranto

Grottaglie

S172

Martina
Franca

Ostuni

S7

(E90)

VIA APPIA

Gallipoli

Nardò

Manduria

S7

S174

Mesagne

Campi

S7ter

Brindisi

Adriatic Sea

TO GREECE

Leuca

S274

Maglie

S101

S16

S275

Otranto

S16

Lecce

SALENTINA PENINSULA

VIA APPIA

KEY

Rail Lines

0   50 miles
0   75 km

N

407

Getting around Puglia can be tricky. Major towns like Foggia, Bari, Brindisi, and Lecce are easily accessible on the main FS train line, but you may run into trouble when you have to travel by bus (in and around the Gargano) or on private train lines (to the small towns of Le Murge and the Salentina Peninsula). But reaching these more isolated areas is worth the time and the effort. Most food and lodging are well within reach of the budget traveler, and you won't be bothered by lots of other tourists.

Foggia

Wheat-covered hillsides brushed with green foliage level to an Ohio flatness as you approach Foggia, the first major stop for trains heading to Puglia from elsewhere in Italy. The city has a history of tragedy, including a massacre of the townspeople in 1528, a serious earthquake in 1731, and extensive Allied bombing during World War II, leaving little of Foggia's *centro storico* (historic center) intact. In more modern times, most of the city has been rebuilt, with wide, clean boulevards and well-shaded parks. There's not much to do here (the city's only real "sight" is the duomo), but the town makes a good base for more interesting treks inland or along the coast. When residents disappear during summer for coastal vacation spots, tourists from Naples and farther north take advantage of Foggia's hospitable atmosphere, its affordable hotels, and its comprehensive train and bus systems, which help to explore the ancient towns of the Gargano Promontory.

BASICS It's hardly worth making the trip from the train station to Foggia's **EPT** office; the place offers little more than a map of the city and some exaggerated brochures about attractions in the Gargano Promontory. *Via Perrone 17, tel. 0881/67681. From train station, Bus MD to Corso Giannone and Via Cirillo; go left onto Via Cirillo (which becomes Viale Bari) to Piazza Puglia and take Via Perrone. Open Mon., Wed.–Fri. 8–2, Tues. 8–2 and 3:30–7.*

You can change money at the **Banca Popolare di Milano** (Piazza Giordano 19, tel. 0881/677021), open weekdays 8:20–1:20 and 2:45–3:30. The ATM machine here gives cash advances against your American Express, MasterCard, or Visa. To reach the bank from the train station, head toward town on Viale XXIV Maggio, pass through Piazza Cavour, and take a right on Via Lanza, which leads to Piazza Giordano. The **post office** (Viale XXIV Maggio 30, 100 meters from train station, tel. 0881/724001) also changes money and is open weekdays 8:15–7:20, and Saturdays 8:15–7:20 (currency exchange until 5:20). For phone calls, try the **TELECOM office** (Via Conte Appiano 14, off Piazza Cavour, tel. 0881/30335), open daily 9–12:45 and 3:50–7:30.

COMING AND GOING Foggia's clean, efficient **train station** (Piazza Vittorio Veneto, tel. 0881/608234) is a central stop on the Naples–Bari and Bologna–Lecce lines. The station is conveniently located near most budget accommodations, and it offers a variety of services, including a helpful train and bus information office (open daily 7 AM–9 PM) and luggage storage (L1500 per piece, per day; open 6 AM–10 PM). Trains head for Naples (6 daily, 3–4½ hrs, L15,500), Bari (1½ hrs, L9800), Lecce (10 daily, 4 hrs, L20,800), Rome (6 daily, 4 hrs, L29,800), and Milan (10 daily, 9 hrs, L54,700).

Blue **SITA buses**, which hang out in the square outside the train station, serve towns around Foggia and on the Gargano Promontory. Buy tickets in the train station at window 6 or at the station's *tabacchi* (smoke shop). Buses leave for Lucera (hourly, ½ hr, L2000), Manfredonia (20 daily, 15 min, L3500), Monte Sant'Angelo (21 daily, 1½ hrs, L6500). Four buses leave for Vieste (2 hrs 45 min, L8500) Monday–Saturday; there's irregular bus service on Sundays.

GETTING AROUND Most of Foggia's sights, cheap eats, and budget accommodations are within easy walking distance of the bus and train stations. **Viale XXIV Maggio** runs from **Piazza Vittorio Veneto**, where both stations are, to **Piazza Cavour**, near the town center, budget lodgings, and affordable restaurants. **Via Lanza**, off Piazza Cavour, will take you to **Piazza Giordano**. It's a short walk from here to the duomo and cathedral in the cobblestoned historic center. If you get an urge to explore the outer limits of the city, local buses (L1200) congregate in front of the train station and at Piazza Cavour.

WHERE TO SLEEP Rooms in Foggia are easy to come by, except during the first week in May when a huge agricultural fair takes place on the outskirts of town, and during August and early September, when tourists invade on their way to the Puglian coast. The neighborhood around the train station is safe and clean, and it's filled with decent restaurants, markets, and trattorias.

Albergo Centrale (Corso Cairoli 5, tel. 0881/671862) is the town's best budget hotel, with immaculate high-ceilinged rooms (doubles L60,000). From the train station, take Viale XXIV Maggio to Piazza Cavour, turn right on Via Lanza, and veer left onto Corso Cairoli. If Centrale is full, try **Venezia** (Via Piave 40, tel. 0881/770903), with doubles for L40,000 (L60,000 with bath). From the station, take Via XXIV Maggio and turn right on Via Piave.

FOOD For an alternative to Italian food, try **Ristorante Chinese Ton Fen** (Via Piave 60, tel. 0881/670212). The portions are small, but tasty fried-rice dishes sell for less than L6000 (other entrées run L6000–L12,000). **Cairoli** (Corso Cairoli 3, tel. 0881/672472) is a great *tavola calda* (cafeteria) beneath Albergo Centrale (*see* Where to Sleep, *above*). A delicious three-course lunch is only L11,000, and there's even a marvelous array of pastries. The menu changes daily, but you can always finish off your meal with coffee and Foggia's delicious dessert specialty, *babà* (a rum-soaked pastry with cream). **Negozi Primavera** (Via Conte Appiano 20, at Via Fiume, tel. 0881/608533) is a well-stocked market that also serves some prepared dishes.

Lucera

Eighteen kilometers (a half hour by bus) northwest of Foggia, Lucera rises above the flatlands of the Tavoliere. Its commanding view of the Puglian plains made it a key strategic outpost for Frederick II, who relocated 20,000 loyal Saracen mercenaries to Lucera in 1224. In what was considered an enlightened gesture for the 13th century, he allowed the Saracens to build mosques in order to practice their faith. When Charles I of Anjou captured the town, however, religious intolerance quickly resurfaced. The Arab community was wiped out, and their mosques were leveled. Alhough today's Lucera retains practically none of its original Arab architecture, some say signs of the Saracen settlement are apparent in the layout of the city. Take an afternoon to wander aimlessly through Lucera's narrow bazaarlike alleyways and lively courtyards, which look like they'd be more at home in Morocco than in Italy. Otherwise, the high points of this unexplored town are the Roman amphitheater and the stunning medieval castle.

BASICS The **tourist office** (Via De Nicastri 36, tel. 0881/546878), open daily 9–noon and 5–8, supplies maps and info, and will help with hotel reservations. **Banca Popolare di Milano** (Via Luigi Zuppetta 34, off Piazza Duomo, tel. 0881/522931) changes money weekdays 8:20–1:20 and 2:45–3:30. The ATM here gives cash advances on American Express, MasterCard, and Visa 24 hours a day.

COMING AND GOING The only way to reach Lucera is to hop on one of the blue **SITA buses** lurking outside Foggia's train station (2 per hr, ½ hr, L2000). You can buy tickets at Foggia's train station; the bus will drop you off in Piazza del Popolo just south of the city center.

WHERE TO SLEEP AND EAT Lucera has only two hotels, but luckily they're both reasonably priced and comfortable (and they both accept credit cards). **Albergo al Passetto** (Piazza del Popolo, just off Via del Popolo, tel. 0881/520821) is in a palazzo in the centro storico, and consequently has more character than its sole competition across the street. Clean, cheap doubles, all with bath, go for L60,000. The restaurant downstairs serves pizzas (L6000–L8000) and full meals (L25,000). The hotel closes for 10 fluctuating days in August or September, so reservations are advised. **Hotel Gioia** (Viale Ferrovia 15, tel. 0881/520988) is a medium-size, well-managed hotel with a decent but overpriced restaurant and clean rooms. Doubles start at L63,000 (with bath). In general, you're better off picking up picnic supplies than eating in Lucera's mediocre restaurants. A sprawling fruit and vegetable **market** takes over Piazza della Repubblica, near the duomo, Monday–Saturday 7–1.

WORTH SEEING After you've explored Lucera's cobblestoned streets and narrow corridors, head for the Byzantine-Gothic **duomo** (open daily 6:45–noon and 4–4:30), or *cattedrale* as the locals call it. The church was built on the site of the town's old Saracen mosque, and remains of the original mosque are visible under the baptistry. To learn more about Lucera's past, head to the **Museo Civico G. Fiorelli** (Via de Nicastri 36), just behind the cathedral. Located in the 17th-century mansion of the Baroness de Nicastri, the museum has a large store of Greek-influenced Puglian handicrafts and pottery. You can check out a wonderful collection of terra-cotta busts, jewelry from the 4th century, and the baroness's elegant furniture. *Admission: L1500. Open May–Aug., Tues.–Fri. 9–1 and 3–6; Sept.–Apr., Tues.–Fri. 9–1 and 5–7.*

Head through the portals in the Roman amphitheater, climb down the steeply inclined brick stairs, and peer into the pits, where many an early Christian became a tasty treat for felines.

From Piazza Duomo follow the yellow AMFITEATRO signs to Lucera's ancient Roman **amphitheater** (admission free; closed Mon.), built in the 1st century BC. Two portals on opposite ends of the theater (which is more than 100 meters long) have been restored. Lucera's most impressive site, however, is its **castle**, built on Mt. Albano, the highest point in town. You can enter the castle Tuesday–Sunday 9–1 (also Tues. and Fri. 3–5), though the place is worth a visit if only to see the exterior. Completed in 1283, under Charles I of Anjou, this is one of the oldest fortresses of its kind in the area, and the second largest in southern Italy. It was constructed around the already existing *Palatium*, a palace built in 1233 under Frederick II. Today only the lowest level of the original palace, called **La Cavalleria**, remains. The perimeter of the castle provides a fantastic view of the Tavoliere—miles and miles of checkerboard fields.

Gargano Promontory

The spur in the Italian boot, the Gargano Promontory juts into the sea three-quarters of the way down the Adriatic coast. Until 20 years ago, the promontory consisted mainly of small fishing towns and an unspoiled woodland interior known as the **Foresta Umbra**. Ever since German and Italian vacationers discovered the region, however, it's been a main stop on summertime travel itineraries. If you approach from Foggia, you can breeze through a whole series of coastal towns, from Manfredonia to Vieste and Peschici. The latter two have the best beaches, and their charming old quarters have hardly been affected by the modernizing influences of tourism. They're also a quick ferry ride away from the Tremiti Islands (*see below*). As for the interior of the Gargano, environmentalists are fighting to have it declared a national park. It's quite beautiful in parts but difficult to visit without a car.

MANFREDONIA

A half hour east of Foggia, the industrialized beach town of Manfredonia is the southern entry point into the Gargano Promontory. Despite its overbuilt residential area and the beginnings of an industrial sprawl that threatens to eclipse the coastline, tourists still come here for the town's long, narrow stretches of sandy beach and clean waters. You can also use Manfredonia as a base for exploring the beautiful pine forests in the interior; several buses run daily to the interior hill town of Monte Sant'Angelo (*see below*).

With the exception of the public beaches, the only "sight" is the large **castle** begun by Frederick II's son, Manfred (hence the town's name). The castle houses a free archaeological museum, **Museo Nazionale di Manfredonia** (tel. 0884/587838; open Tues.–Sun. 8:30–1:30 and 3:30–6:30). You can swim in front of the castle or head to the cleaner beaches in **Siponto**, a quiet little seaside town only a 25-minute walk or a short bus trip from Manfredonia. Beaches here are marginally less crowded than in Manfredonia, and the coastline is considerably more picturesque. After you've fried yourself to a crisp in the Puglian sun, find refuge in the 11th-century Romanesque **Basilica di Santa Maria Maggiore**, which was built atop the ruins of a 5th-century church. A few meters away, take a look at the **archaeological zone**, where workers are currently uncovering more ancient ruins.

During peak season, from the second week of July to early September, it would seem as if someone had shaken the plains of the Tavoliere and spilled all the inland Puglians onto the coast. The Manfredonians rely on these six weeks of heavy tourism to keep them solvent for the rest of the year. If you're traveling through the region during these months, expect lodging and food costs to hit the roof, and don't be surprised if you have to fight for your towel space on the beach. Be sure to call several weeks in advance to reserve a room.

BASICS Manfredonia has an excellent **tourist office** that provides maps of the area, a list of campsites in the Gargano Promontory, and a tourist-oriented, English-language phone directory for all of Puglia. The office also has bus and ferry schedules for the region's interior and coastal towns. *Corso Manfredi 26, off Piazza Marconi, tel. 0884/21998. Open Mon.–Sat. 8:30–1:30.*

COMING AND GOING Trains from Foggia pull into Manfredonia's **train station** (Piazza Libertà, tel. 0884/21025) about eight times daily (½ hr, L3500). Siponto is the stop immediately before Manfredonia. From the Manfredonia station, take a right onto Viale Aldo Moro to reach the town center, around Piazza Marconi. To the left of the station on the strip heading toward Siponto are several inexpensive hotels (*see* Where to Sleep, *below*). **SITA buses** on the Foggia–Vieste and Foggia–Mattinata lines also make frequent stops in Manfredonia (¾ hr, L3500; no Sun. service). The bus takes longer than the train, but it drops you off in Piazza Marconi, close to the restaurants, public beaches, and the tourist office. Buses leave the piazza for Vieste (13 daily, 2 hrs, L5000), Mattinata (18 daily, ½ hr, L1500) and Monte Sant'Angelo (13 daily, 45 min, L3000). Buy tickets at **Bar Impero**, across the piazza from where the buses line up. **Hydrofoils** leave for the Tremiti Islands (7:45 AM, 3 hrs, L30,900). To reach the dock from Piazza Marconi, walk about three minutes toward Siponto; buy tickets at the booth on the dock (open during boat arrivals and departures).

WHERE TO SLEEP AND EAT During June and early July, you can find modestly priced rooms at the nondescript hotels along the strip in front of the train station, about ½ kilometer inland from the beach. Expect to pay around L75,000 for a double with bath (prices rise July–Sept.). A few campsites lie several kilometers south of Manfredonia, but you can't reach them on public transportation. A better bet for campers is to head to Mattinata (*see below*), where sites abound and the beaches are even nicer.

Hotel Azzurro (Viale Giuseppe di Vittorio 56, tel. 0884/581498) is about 250 meters from the train station, less than a kilometer from downtown Manfredonia, and 2 kilometers from Siponto's sandy beaches. Clean doubles with bath run L73,000–L78,000. **Hotel Sipontum** (Viale Giuseppe di Vittorio 229, tel. 0884/542916), about a kilometer up the road from the Hotel Azzurro, is a notch lower in quality, but the desk clerk is friendly and many of the rooms have balconies. Doubles cost L70,000.

You can eat pizza and cheap, thick slabs of focaccia bread with tomatoes at the bakeries on **Via Aldo Moro** and **Viale Giuseppe di Vittorio**. Most keep longer hours than regular pizzerias (7 or 8 AM until midnight is not uncommon), and you can stuff yourself for only L3000–L5000. Fruit stands and supermarkets also line Viale Giuseppe di Vittorio, in case you want to pick up your own supplies and head to the beach. For sit-down meals, check out the restaurants around Piazza Marconi, like **Trattoria Il Barracchio** (Corso Roma 38, tel. 0884/583874), a tasteful little place with delicious pasta and grilled fish. With house wine, dinner will cost L20,000–L30,000.

MONTE SANT'ANGELO

If you've been staying in Manfredonia, you may think the Gargano Promontory is all housing projects and chemical factories. A bus trip to Monte Sant'Angelo, the highest hill town in the Gargano at almost a kilometer above sea level, will expand your horizons. During the Crusades, the faithful made the arduous trek up narrow switchbacks to pray at the town's Sanctuary of San Michele. You can do the inspirational climb more easily today on SITA buses, which depart regularly Monday–Saturday from Manfredonia's Piazza Marconi (45 min, L3000). The bus ride is as impressive as the town itself: The bus lunges into the climb, honking its horn around the sharp, narrow turns, providing you with a view of ashen mountains stitched in at their base by symmetrical rows of olive trees. As you climb, sun-bleached limestone rock gives way to natu-

Up the street from the Sanctuary of San Michele, look for a large, crumbling castle built in the 14th century by Robert Guiscard and finished by Frederick II. It's closed to the public, but make the trip anyway to enjoy a prime view of the Gargano countryside. On your way to the castle, look for the little old lady selling fresh almonds (L1500 a bag) on Via De R. Guiscard.

ral caves and quarries of *carcaro* marble, and you can see how farmers made the most of the inhospitable terrain by building "steps" into the hillsides. If you look carefully you can also spot the tiny stone caves where these farmers once lived.

The SITA bus drops you off in the **Piazza Duca d'Aosta**. You'll be pleasantly surprised by the coolness up here during summer. If you still have an appetite after the bus ride, try local specialties like *capretto alla bracce* (grilled baby goat) or *agnello al forno* (baked lamb) at **La Caravella** (Via Reale Basilica 84, tel. 0884/561444), located just before the sanctuary if you're coming from the bus stop. To reach the **Sanctuary of San Michele** from the stop, walk straight up Corso Vittorio Manuele, following the yellow signs. The church (admission free; open daily 7:30–12:30 and 2:30–6:30) is fronted by a tall, hexagonal tower built by Charles I of Anjou in 1273. To reach the shrine of San Michele, follow the hordes of tourists through the small archway to the left of the tower. As the signs in Italian, German, and English warn, proper attire is required to enter the shrine—no tank tops or miniskirts allowed. Your descent to the grotto upon which the church was founded will inevitably be slowed by throngs of tourists and pilgrims who stop to pray to the archangel Michele, who is said to have appeared here in AD 490. Despite the crush, the dank cave, with pews set before a flashy-looking San Michele, has a mystical atmosphere, reinforced by the fervently praying devotees who dip their hands in basins of holy water at the foot of the saint's shrine.

Before leaving Monte Sant'Angelo, make sure to walk through the old quarter, with neighborhoods of stark white homes stacked on top of each other. Follow signs for the **Museo Tancreai**, with an exhibit of peasant farmers' work tools, wine presses, and a wonderful set of black-and-white photos that capture the townsfolk at the turn of the century. *Piazza San Francesco d'Assisi, no phone. Admission: L3000. Open May–Sept., Mon. 8:30–1:30, Tues.–Sat. 8:30–1:30 and 2:30–7:30, Sun. 10–12:30 and 3–7; Nov.–Apr., Mon.–Sat. 8–2.*

MATTINATA

Five years ago, no foreigners had heard of Mattinata, but word has spread—you can almost hear cries of "The Germans are coming! The Germans are coming!" in the rings of cash registers everywhere. Like Manfredonia, this small beach town is marred by a wave of new construction, but it's worth a visit for its clean waters, terrific pebbled beaches, and natural setting amongst olive groves and pine trees. SITA and ATAF buses (*see below*) drop you off on the main street, Il Corso Matino, where you can find several **pizzerias** that also serve up delicious plates of crayfish at dirt-cheap prices. The beach stretches for uninterrupted miles, as do the campgrounds that line the waterfront. Beachfront **campsites** surrounded by olive groves fill up during high season, but the camps are almost empty the rest of the year, and you'll have the beautiful beaches to yourself. To reach the campsites and beaches, follow the yellow MATTINATA LIDO signs for 1½ kilometers.

COMING AND GOING Since trains don't run this far out on the Gargano Promontory, you'll have to jump on the bus, Gus. **SITA** and **ATAF buses** on the Foggia–Vieste line run regularly Monday–Saturday, fewer on Sundays. Buses from Manfredonia (15 min, L1500), and Foggia (1 hr, L4300) leave frequently May–September. Check with the bus information office in Foggia (*see above*) or on the schedule board in Manfredonia's Piazza Marconi (*see above*). For tickets and a schedule of buses leaving Mattinata for Vieste (8 daily, 1½ hrs, L4000) and Foggia (16 daily, 1 hr, L4300), check at Hotel Alba del Gargano (Corso Mattino 102, tel. 0884/4771), which is open 24 hours.

VIESTE

Vieste, 60 kilometers northeast of Manfredonia, is one of those rare places that, at least in the off-season, actually lives up to the airbrushed photos in its travel brochures: The water is *that* blue and *that* clear; the old Arabic quarter with its whitewashed homes next to the ocean is *that* enticing. The trip from Manfredonia alone is well worth it for its spectacular views of coastline and interior woodland. Do consider taking some Dramamine before you get on the bus, though; you may feel woozy as it lumbers uncomfortably through the steep hills and hairpin turns of the southern corner of the Foresta Umbra, home to Italy's oldest trees.

A small fishing village of less than 15,000 in the off-season, Vieste becomes the favorite resort town on the Puglian coast for Italian and German tourists during July and August. Natives will tell you to show up in late spring or early fall if you want to catch Vieste at its most beautiful, without the glut of out-of-towners, though tourism doesn't even begin to detract from Vieste's charm until mid-July. In fact, it's amazing that more tourists don't come to Vieste considering the spectacular scenery and azure seas. Restaurants serving the catch of the day are plentiful, and the cool, narrow alleyways of the old quarter nicely complement the sizzling, long stretches of stunning beach. Vieste is also the best place to access the Tremiti Islands, to begin a boat tour of the grottoes along the Gargano coast, or to visit the Foresta Umbra.

BASICS For a map of the town, a ton of brochures, and a copy of *Viestestate*, detailing all kinds of events in the city, head to the **tourist office**. *Piazza Kennedy 1, tel. 0884/708806. From bus depot at Piazzale Mazzoni, take Viale XXIV Maggio (which becomes Corso Fazzini); tourist office is on the right as road curves left. Open June 22–Sept. 20, Mon.–Sat. 8:30–1:30 and 4–9, Sun. 8:30–1; Sept. 21–June 21, Mon.–Sat. 8:30–1:30 and 3–8.*

COMING AND GOING SITA and ATAF buses on the Foggia–Vieste line depart regularly from Manfredonia's bus depot (2 hrs, L5000); service is sporadic on Sundays and holidays. Buses drop you off in a parking lot just off Viale XXIV Maggio. If you're approaching Vieste from the north, the **Bologna–Lecce train line** will take you to San Severo, where you can switch to the private train line **Ferrovie del Gargano**; this leaves you at Calanelle, 3 kilometers outside the town of Peschici (*see below*). From here, three or four buses (more in summer) run to Vieste (45 min, L2500). The entire trip takes at least 2½ hours, but the scenery is beautiful.

Motonave Vieste (Corso Fazzini 33, on the dock, tel. 0884/707489) runs ferries from Vieste to San Domino, in the Tremiti Islands, daily at 9:05 AM (2 hrs, L34,000). To reach the port from Piazza Vittorio Emanuele II, head down Viale Italia, and just after it turns into Lungomare Cristoforo Colombo hang a left at Via Ferdinando Magellano, which leads straight to the docks. **Vesta Travel** (Corso Fazzini 37, tel. 0884/701100; open daily 8:30–1 and 4–10) can set you up on the ferry to San Domino or book you on a two-hour tour of the promontory's blue grottoes (L15,000). If the forest you passed through on the way to Vieste caught your interest, their bus tour of the Foresta Umbra (L20,000) leaves at noon and returns by 6 PM.

GETTING AROUND To get from the bus stop to the budget restaurants and lodgings in the centro storico, head up **Viale XXIV Maggio** past the triangular park, Giardini Pubblici Vittorio Veneto, follow it as it becomes **Corso Fazzini**, and continue to **Piazza Vittorio Emanuele II**, the main square. If you're camping or staying outside the centro storico, walk up Viale XXIV Maggio from the bus depot, turn left at the Giardini Pubblici, and make another left on Via Santa Maria di Merino, which becomes the **Lungomare Europa**.

WHERE TO SLEEP Accommodations in Vieste are expensive, especially during high season, but they're still cheaper than in Peschici or the Tremiti Islands. Most hotels close down from the end of September until Easter and are fully booked in late-July and August. **Pensione al Centro Storico** (Via Mafrolla 32, off Via Pola, tel. 0884/707030) is the pick of the hotel litter, with clean and comfortable rooms (doubles with bath L50,000–L85,000, breakfast included) and a central location. Check out the spectacular ocean view at breakfast. If they're full, try **Pensione Giada** (Lungomare Europa 18, 1 km from the bus station, tel. 0884/706593). Doubles, all with bath, go for L55,000–L90,000, though students sometimes get discounts. Also across from the beach, **Hotel Vela Velo** (Lungomare Europa 19, tel. 0884/706303), has clean doubles with bath (L34,000–L55,000) that include use of a bike. Vela Velo also rents Windsurfers and boats and offers all kinds of bike excursions and water sports (*see* Outdoor Activities, *below*). Call them upon arrival and they'll send a shuttle free of charge.

Scores of campgrounds surround Vieste on the northern and southern ends of town. They're difficult to reach on foot, but buses running between Vieste and Peschici make stops nearby. **413**

The tourist office in Vieste has a map of the area's campgrounds; call in advance to reserve a spot. The majority of sites lie along the 10-kilometer stretch of the *lungomare* (boardwalk) between Vieste and Peschici. **Baia degli Aranci** (Lungomare Europa, follow signs from Pensione Giada, tel. 0884/708025) open June–late September, is considerably closer to the station (15–20 min). Like many of the coastal campgrounds, it's shaded by olive trees and has a swimming pool, phones, mailboxes, a market, and modern bathroom facilities. Sites cost L4700–L11,000 per person and L8200–L16,800 per tent, depending on the month.

FOOD Despite the tourist trappings, you can eat very well in Vieste, thanks to the town's proximity to the sea and its long history of traditional cooking. Restaurants and pizzerias have blossomed around Piazza Vittorio Emanuele II in the old quarter and a number of good restaurants cluster around the intersection of Lungomare Amerigo and Lungomare Europa. Monday–Saturday there's an **open market** on Viale XXIV Maggio.

For a sit-down meal, **Trattoria del Fosso** (Via Pola 4, off Piazza Vittorio Emanuele II, tel. 0884/701566; closed Tues.) offers excellent fresh fish at some of the cheapest prices around; their tourist menu is only L15,000. **Il Fornaio** (Corso Fazzini 1, tel. 0884/701895) and **Pizzeria Portofino** (Via Sante 22, 50 meters from Piazza Vittorio Emanuele II, no phone) both have good pizza by the slice (L1500–L2000); the former is known for its calzone-like *panzerotti* (L1500), the latter for its meter-long calzone (L2000 a slice). If you're willing to spend a bit more money for a seriously delicious meal, **Ristorante Box 19** (Via Santa Maria di Merino 19, tel. 0884/705229) is a local favorite, featuring regional dishes like *orecchiette* (pasta, literally "small ears"; L6000), mussels (L8000), and filling fish stew (L24,000). The family-run **Enoteca Vesta** (Via Duomo 14, tel. 0884/706411) features tasty meals and a huge selection of Apulian wines such as *Bollina* and *Cerbinare* (both dry whites), as well as a heavy helping of local hospitality.

WORTH SEEING The call of Vieste's ocean is too strong and its monuments too few to inspire much sightseeing. But before you scamper down to the surf, climb around the **centro storico**, the neighborhood of whitewashed homes and stone archways atop Vieste's southern promontory. The pace and lifestyle here are certainly Old World in contrast to the adjacent modern city, which expands as tourism increases. Signs point the way to the **cathedral** off Via Duomo, with a simple steeple topped by a brass weather vane. The interior is ordinary enough, but it's worth ducking in just to cool off before climbing the stairs to the **castle** (closed to the public) on the summit of the centro storico. It's usually too hot to spend much time here during the day, but if you come toward dusk you can enjoy a great view of the Gargano coast. Before you leave the centro storico, walk back down Via Duomo to Via Cimaglia and check out the **Chianca Amara** (Bitter Stone), where more than 5,000 townsfolk were beheaded when the Turks sacked and pillaged the town in 1554.

OUTDOOR ACTIVITIES For simple beach lounging you can choose between the **Spiaggia di San Lorenzo** and the **Spiaggia del Castello**, both pleasant sandy beaches a short walk from the center. You can rent a bike at **Noleggio Bici** (Via Tre Piccioni 12, tel. 0884/701894) for L5000 per hour, L25,000 per day; or rent a Windsurfer (L20,000 per hr, L40,000 per ½ day) from Hotel Vela Velo (*see* Where To Sleep, *above*). Vela Velo also rents catamarans and sailboats (L30,000 per hr, L60,000 per ½ day), mountain bikes (L10,000 per hr, L30,000 per day), and organizes half-day bike tours of the Foresta Umbra (L50,000).

PESCHICI

Less than an hour northwest of Vieste by bus, the small fishing village of Peschici has some of Italy's best beaches. Locals insist their town is more beautiful than Vieste, but the awesome views of rolling hills and the deep blue sea are Peschici's greatest attributes: The town's centro storico pales in comparison to Vieste's. Although Peschici has lost its off-the-beaten-track charm, it's still an affable place to visit, as long as you arrive during the week and any month but August. What little there is of the old quarter is on a cliff, and long, sun-drenched paths lead down to the crystal-clear water, which you can enter from the beach or from jetties that extend into the ocean. Unfortunately, Peschici no longer has a tourist office.

COMING AND GOING **ATAF buses** leave hourly for Peschici from Vieste (L2000) and drop you off at the Campus Sportivo (a sporting-goods store) parking lot (Via Montesanto 34/40, tel.

0884/964015). From here, it's a short walk (follow the signs) to the centro storico. Buy your return ticket inside the sporting-goods store (open daily 8–1:30 and 4–10:30), where bus schedules and prices are posted. **Trains** approaching the Gargano Promontory from the north stop at Calanelle (*see* Coming and Going, Vieste, *above*). From here a bus heads into Peschici.

WHERE TO SLEEP AND EAT Peschici offers a limited choice of food and accommodations. The city is much quieter than Vieste, although on the whole it's a bit more expensive. Reserve during high season, and haggle over prices during the off-season. **Hotel Locanda Al Castello** (Via Castello 29, follow signs toward castle, tel. 0884/964038), in the old quarter, sits atop cliffs overlooking the ocean. The well-known hotel has a beautiful view, cushy rooms (doubles with bath L75,000), and the best restaurant in town. If it's full, try **Trattoria al Pozzo** (Località Baia di Peschici, tel. 0884/963431), with doubles for L30,000–L40,000 (rooms cost three times as much in July and August). Al Pozzo is also a good place for a meal; try their specialty, spaghetti *alle vongole* (with clams; L12,000). About 50 campgrounds, most with coastal access, line the coast between Vieste and Peschici. From Peschici's city center, hop on the bus headed for the Calanelle train station; it stops on request at hotels and campgrounds along the coast. Buses from Vieste follow the same route. One of the closest campgrounds to Peschici, **Camping Marina Piccola** (Via Marina Piccola, Località Baia di Peschici, tel. 0884/963424), lies along the beach and is open May–September. Tent spaces go for L6000–L7000, plus L6000–L7000 per person, depending on the season.

Food can be costly, and most cheap pizzerias shut down from 2 to 4 PM. You'll find a slew of eateries around Piazza IV Novembre (at the entrance to the old town) and near Piazza Municipio (at the edge of the new town). For excellent pizza, head to **Pizzeria al Castello** (Via Recinto Baronale 1, across from Locanda al Castello, no phone), with pizzas for L7000–L10,000. Otherwise stop at the large **produce market**, open Monday–Saturday 7 AM–1 PM, in Piazza Trieste Trento (off Via Solferino).

Tremiti Islands

From Vieste, a two-hour ferry ride across the high seas takes you to the Tremiti Islands, the most popular day trip from the Gargano Promontory. The main islands are San Domino, Capraia, San Nicola, and Pianosa, but only verdant San Domino and historic San Nicola are inhabited. The largest island, **San Domino**, is the main draw, offering clear water, secluded coves, bright flowers, and paths through pine woods. Day-trippers swarm the beach at **Cala delle Arene**, the small, sandy inlet near the dock. You can head off more or less alone to explore the coves and grottoes to the south or on the western edge of the island, and weekdays (except during August), you'll often have a rocky inlet all to yourself. The swimming here is excellent, but high, steep rocks make getting in and out of the water difficult. If you stay at one of the camps, you'll usually have access to ladders leading down to the water. Scuba diving is very popular on San Domino and can be arranged at the campsites.

According to Homeric legend, the Tremiti Islands were founded by King Diomedes after his victory over Troy. When he died prematurely, the goddess Aphrodite turned his loyal comrades into seagull-like birds called Diomedee. Toward nightfall on the islands, you can hear their rueful cries as they lament their lost leader.

The neighboring island of **San Nicola** has more sights, fewer accessible beaches and pensions, and no camping. From the dock, pass through the archway and follow the path to the church **Santa Maria a Mare**, named after the Virgin Mary visited the island and revealed where King Diomedes's treasure lay. Benedictine monks and Charles II added to the original cathedral, turning it into the fortress monastery that dominates the island today. Wily pirates tricked their way inside the fortress in 1321, slaughtering all but two of the monks and making off with the abbey's treasure. The inside of the church has a masterly mosaic floor, and you can check out the prison, where various political activists were exiled during World War II. Though the islands have no official tourist office, look for a booth at the dock marked CONSOPER (open Mon.–Thurs. 8:30–noon and 3:30–5, Fri.–Sun. 8:30–5). Here you'll find info on lodging, scuba diving, and other activities.

COMING AND GOING It costs L34,000 round-trip to reach the Tremiti Islands by ferry from Vieste; L45,000 from Peschici and L2000 to travel between San Domino and San Nicola. The cheapest ferry company in Vieste is **Motonave Vieste** (Corso Fazzini 33, tel. 0884/707489). Ferries depart at 9:05 AM (show up at 8:30 AM to buy your ticket and board) and arrive at San Domino at 11 AM. You then have the afternoon to spend on either of the islands (or both) before the ferry leaves at 5 PM from San Domino, reaching Vieste at 7:40 PM. For information or to buy your ticket, go to the booth by Vieste's port (Corso Fazzini 33), open daily 7 AM–8 PM. Motonave Vieste also runs ferries between Termoli and the Tremiti Islands (1 daily, 1 hr, L35,000 round-trip). There's also one daily ferry from Termoli (1½ hr, L24,000 round-trip) run by **Navigazione Libera del Golfo** (tel. 0875/704859); buy return tickets at the booth on the dock of San Domino (tel. 0882/663284; open daily 9–noon and 3:30–5).

GETTING AROUND Boats shuttle back and forth every 15 minutes between San Domino and San Nicola for L2000; buy your ticket at the booth on the dock or, for some companies, on board. Don't confuse these boats with the ones that provide tours of the islands, grottoes, and coastline for L13,000–L15,000 (not really worth it). To reach San Domino's small town center, with grocery stores, hotels, bars, and tabacchi, stay to your left as you leave the docks and head up the steeper of the two streets. There are no street signs, but if you go straight for ¾ kilometer you'll reach the main square. Along the same road are countless dirt paths leading to the coast. Ask at the CONSOPER booth (*see above*) to find out which coves have ladders down to the water. Remember not to miss your ferry at 5 PM or else you'll have to spring for a pricey hotel.

WHERE TO SLEEP AND EAT Expect to pay as much as L60,000 per person (L90,000 in July), at the small, well-kept pensions on San Domino, at the end of **Via del Vecchio Forno**, off the town square. **La Nassa** (Via del Vecchio Forno, tel. 0882/663345) is the least expensive of the bunch, with bathroom-equipped doubles for L60,000–L100,000.

The **Villagio Internazionale** campsite (tel. 0882/663405; open May–Sept.) is at the northern tip of San Domino (follow signs along either street from the port). Here you'll find strange but functional aluminum "tents" in the pine woods next to a beautiful cove. A *pensione completa* includes very decent cafeteria-style breakfasts and lunches. Prices are L30,000–L62,000 per person, with access to clean outdoor bathrooms and showers; you'll pay about L5000 more in July and August. If you're just here for the day, it's best to pack a lunch from a market on the mainland; if you came unprepared, **Alimentare Ortofrutta** (Via del Vecchio Forno 3, tel. 0882/663413; open Mon.–Sat. 8:30–1:30 and 3–9), on San Domino, has fresh sandwiches (L4000–L5000.)

OUTDOOR ACTIVITIES On San Domino you can rent a mountain bike for L10,000 an hour at **Gimmy Bike** (Piazzetta San Dominono; open Easter–Sept., daily 9 AM–midnight). Stands along the beach at Cala delle Arene rent kayaks (L15,000 per hr) and small motorboats (L120,000–L150,000 per day). **Tremiti Diving Center** (Villagio San Domino, tel. 0882/663209) charges L95,000 for a two-hour dive, including gear.

Bari

The thriving business and commercial center of Bari has been responsible for shuttling goods and tourists throughout the eastern Mediterranean for centuries. Just about every major European power, including the ancient Greeks, Romans, Ostrogoths, Byzantines, Lombard Dukes, and Saracens, made use of Bari's strategic position, turning the city into one of the most important ports in the Adriatic. Even during World War II, planes and ships left from Bari for attacks on Greece and Yugoslavia, making the city the subject of heavy bombing by both the Allies and the Germans.

The Bari of today has two main sections, the *città vecchia* (old city) and the *città nuova* (new city). The neatly designed new city was built in the early 19th century by the king of Naples, and its grid-like "chessboard" blocks have since been cluttered with designers' shops, a major university, bookstores, and language schools. In complete contrast to the rationally planned new city, the old city is a bewildering array of cobblestoned streets and medieval homes. Although it's unsafe at night, particularly for women and solo travelers, the old city is Bari's

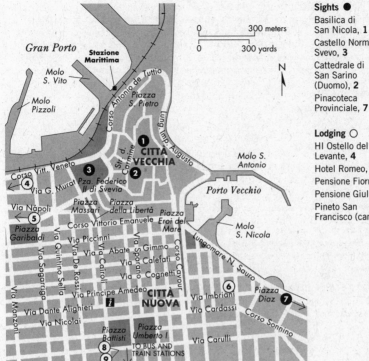

Sights ●

Basilica di
San Nicola, **1**

Castello Normanno-
Svevo, **3**

Cattedrale di
San Sarino
(Duomo), **2**

Pinacoteca
Provinciale, **7**

Lodging ○

HI Ostello del
Levante, **4**

Hotel Romeo, **8**

Pensione Fiorni, **6**

Pensione Giulia, **9**

Pineto San
Francisco (camp), **5**

most interesting sector and holds the greatest appeal for tourists who've come for more than just a boat outta here. The città vecchia also holds the remains of good old St. Nick (*see* Worth Seeing, *below*). Despite a fair amount of grime and crime, Bari is also the best place to base yourself while exploring Puglia, with an extensive transportation network and a central location on the coast.

BASICS

➤ **CHANGING MONEY** • You can cash traveler's checks or use an ATM at major banks in the città nuova. Most are located just past Piazza Umberto I if you come from the train station. The **Automobile Club Italiano (ACI)** in Stazione Marittima changes money, but it's open only when boats are leaving or arriving. For an ATM that provides cash advances on Visa, Master-Card, and American Express, head to **Banca Popolare di Milano** (Via Calefati 46, tel. 080/524–6811), off Corso Cavour.

➤ **EMERGENCIES AND MEDICAL AID** • Unfortunately, this city supports many pro-fessional thieves; contact the **municipal police** (Largo Chiurla 27, tel. 080/521–0344). For your medical needs, try **Lojacono di Berrino** (Corso Cavour 47, tel. 080/521–2615), a conve-niently located pharmacy, open weekdays 8:30–1 and 5–8. From the train station, walk east two blocks to Corso Cavour. There's also a list of all-night pharmacies in the newspaper *La Gazzetta del Mezzogiorno*; look under *farmacie notturne* in the "Bari" section.

➤ **MAIL AND PHONES** • A TELECOM office (Via Marchese di Montroni 123, tel. 080/520–2286; open daily 8 AM–9 PM) has phone books for all of Puglia. The **post office** (tel. 080/521–6426), open weekdays 8:20–8 and Saturday 8:20–1, is on Piazza Battisti.

➤ **VISITOR INFORMATION** • The ubiquitous **Stop-Over in Bari** stands help young bud-get travelers (under age 30). Their "magic bus," open daily 8:30–8:30, outside the main train station, has got all the information you need, including a map of the town, tips on where to stay, and listings of cheap bars and restaurants; they also organize excellent **free excursions** on Sundays. A branch booth in **Stazione Marittima** provides comparable information and help. Stop-Over's **main office** (Via Dante Alighieri 111, off Piazza Umberto I, tel. 080/521–4538), just a short walk from the train station, can set you up at free campgrounds, help you make a reservation, or book you a room in a private apartment. You also get the lowdown on discount train and ferry fares for students. The office is open Monday–Saturday 8:30–8:30, Sunday 8:30–6.

Left your wheels at home? Stop-Over in Bari loans out new mountain bikes and skateboards free for the day.

Much outdone by the Stop-Over program (*see above*), the **EPT** office (Piazza Aldo Moro 33/A, tel. 080/524–2361), diagonally across from the train station, has good maps of Bari and Puglia. The office, open Monday–Saturday 8–1:30, is usually less hectic than the Stop-Over booths, and it's a good place to discuss sightseeing options and day trips in the region.

COMING AND GOING

Coming and going is what Bari is all about. The city offers a plethora of train connections, and it's a better choice than overcrowded Brindisi for ferries to Greece. Unfortunately, ferries from Bari don't accept EurailPasses, which is why most people go to Brindisi instead (where ferries do accept them).

➤ **BY TRAIN** • Bari's many train systems include the **Ferrovie dello Stato (FS)** (tel. 080/521–6801) and three private lines, **Ferrovie del Sud-Est (FSE)** (tel. 080/553–0274), **Ferrovie Bari–Nord (FBN)** (tel. 080/521–3577), and **Ferrovie Apulo–Lucane (FAL)** (tel. 080/572–5229). The FS railway, at the main station in **Piazza Aldo Moro**, handles most traffic, with 10 trains a day to Milan (10 hrs, L65,400), five to Rome (8 hrs, L37,500), and about four to Naples (5 hrs, L24,400). Trains on the FS line also leave regularly for Foggia (1½ hrs, L9800), Lecce (2½ hrs, L11,700), and Taranto (1½–2 hrs, L9800). Luggage storage (L1500 per piece per day) is available 6 AM–midnight. In the same station, but beneath the tracks and through the underpass, is the FSE line, which services points east and south. Its trains head almost hourly to Castellana (1 hr, L3400) and Alberobello (1½ hrs, L5000). Be forewarned: Private lines like this one move slowly, taking long pauses and making frequent stops. Outside the main station to the left, the FBN line has frequent trains north to Bitonto (25 min, L2000) and Barletta (1 hr 15 min, L5700); the FAL line next door runs hourly to Matera in Basilicata (1½ hrs, L4300).

➤ **BY BUS** • Orange local buses and blue **SITA buses** leave from the front of the train station in Piazza Aldo Moro. Buy tickets at the main train station at window 1 (open 8 AM–9 PM). For buses to towns north of Bari, head to the **AMET** depot (Piazza Eroi del Mare, at Corso Cavour, tel. 080/5210171), open 6:15 AM–7:10 PM.

➤ **BY FERRY** • Bari's **Stazione Marittima**, port of choice for the discriminating Adriatic voyager, has cheaper and better ferry connections to Greece and the eastern Mediterranean than Brindisi. On the whole, **Poseidon** (Stazione Marittima Box 11–12, tel. 080/524–1039) has the cheapest fares with ferries to Patras (15–20 hrs; deck L60,000–L75,000, seat L70,000–L95,000), and Igoumenitsa (12 hrs; deck L45,000–L65,000, seat L90,000–L115,000). **Ventouris** (Stazione Marittima Box 9–10, tel. 080/521–8783) is your best bet for Corfu (9 hrs; deck L45,000–L65,000, seat L55,000–L100,000). There's a 10% discount for a round-trip ticket, and a L5000–L20,000 discount for students on some lines. You must show up at least two hours before boarding to have your boarding pass stamped, and you'll have to show your passport and sometimes your visa at the Stazione Marittima police station. Most lines recommend that you show up three hours in advance and will revoke you reservation if you show up less than one hour before departure. Remember, EurailPasses are not accepted.

➤ **BY PLANE** • The **Bari Palese Airport** (tel. 080/531–6220), 8 kilometers east of Bari, has flights to major cities in Italy and throughout Europe (with connections through Rome). **Alitalia** (Via Argiro 56, tel. 080/521–6511) has direct flights to Rome (L176,000), Milan (L292,000), and Florence (L215,000). **Air France** (tel. 080/521–3246), **British Airways** (tel.

080/558–4944), and **Lufthansa** (080/538–1225) also fly into and out of Bari. Bus 16 takes you from the airport to Piazza Massari in town; the 25-minute ride (almost hourly until around 9 PM) costs nothing during summer for tourists under 30 (L1000 otherwise).

GETTING AROUND

Trains and buses drop you in Piazza Aldo Moro. From here, Piazza Umberto I is a block north and the città vecchia is about 10 blocks north. The orange **local buses** that hang out in Piazza Aldo Moro are useful for getting around the city, particularly if you arrive at night; otherwise Bari is very walkable. To reach the ferries from the train station, take Bus 20 (L1000; free during summer for visitors under 30).

WHERE TO SLEEP

You have two choices if you want to spend a night or two in Bari: Use Stop-Over in Bari, or just "flop over and be sorry" in one of the budget dives around the station. The kindly hippie types at Stop-Over have done their best to make Bari desirable by setting up a free (yes, *free*) camp-site at the edge of town, in the large **Pineta San Francesco Park** (take Bus 3, 5, or 19 from the station—there's one about every 15 min until 11 PM). If camping isn't your style, they can set you up in a pension or private apartment with kitchen facilities for only L30,000 for two nights. Call their English-speaking office (tel. 080/521–4538) in advance to arrange home stays. The only hitch to all this is that you have to be under 30, and you must visit between mid-June and mid-September.

If you don't use Stop-Over in Bari, there are a few places within the realm of decency, and within walking distance of the train station. **Hotel Romeo** (Via Crisanzio 12, 1 block north of train station, tel. 080/523–7253) has doubles with bath for L70,000. **Pensione Giulia** (Via Crisanzio 12, tel. 080/521–6630) is a notch up in quality with doubles for L70,000, L80,000 with bath (breakfast included). The cheapest place around is **Pensione Fiorini** (Via Imbriani 69, tel. 080/554–0788), with doubles without bath for L48,000.

When all else fails, there's always the **HI Ostello del Levante** in a tranquil setting just outside of town. The dorm-style bunk beds are nothing special, and the bathrooms scream "shower shoes," but rooms tend to fill up throughout the summer anyway, so call ahead. The cost is L14,000 per person. *Lungomare Nicola Massaro 33, tel. 080/552–0282. Take Bus 1 (every 40 min, L1000) from Piazza Eroi del Mare, off Corso Cavour. Curfew 11, lockout 9–4.*

FOOD

Bari is known for its tasty and reasonably priced seafood, and you'll find some great trattorias around the città vecchia. Grab warm focaccia with tomatoes (L2000) at **Panificio Signorile** (Corso Sonnino 6, tel. 080/554–0895). To satisfy your sweet-tooth stop at **Portoghese** (Strada Palazzo di Città 55, in the città vecchia, tel. 080/524–1890), for *castagnedde* (sweets with almonds, sugar, and a touch of lemon peel). The supermarket **SIDIS Spesa** (Via A. Gimma 144, no phone) gives a 10% discount to those who mention the Stop-Over in Bari program; a conveniently located **open market** is held Monday–Saturday mornings at Piazza Balenzano, near Piazza Moro.

A tradition among Bari's youth is to end an evening out by having a snack of warm *cornetti* (croissants; L2500). There are places all over Bari that turn out these buttery pastries well into the wee hours: **Il Dolcetto** (Via De Rossi 148, off Corso Italia), near the train station, and **Laboratori Artigianali** (Corso Benedetto Croce at Via Toti), conveniently located near the Baronda disco (*see below*). Both bakeries stay open until midnight on weekdays, until 2 AM on Saturdays.

Al Pescatore. This is a great seafood restaurant where everything is fresh and delicious. Try a plate of *risotto alla pescatore* (risotto with seafood; L8000) or *gamberoni* (shrimp; L16,000). You dine in the shadow of the impressive castle. *Piazza Federico II di Svevia 6, across from castle on edge of città vecchia, tel. 080/523–7039. Open Tues.–Sun. noon–4 and 7–midnight.*

419

El Pedro. This highly recommended self-service joint serves complete meals for only L16,000. *Via Piccinni 152, 1 block from città vecchia, tel. 080/521–1294. Open Mon.–Sat. 11:30–3 and 6:30–10:30.*

Osteria delle Travi il Buco. For a piddly L16,000 you can sit in an actual grotto and stuff yourself full of *orecchiette* (little round pasta) in red sauce and the unearthly fish delight *seppia* (grilled cuttlefish). The *menu turistico* (tourist menu) is the best deal, offering several choices, including a *bragiola* (thin slices of veal or horsemeat rolled up, garnished with ham, parsley, garlic, cheese, and tomato sauce). *Largo Chiurlia 12, no phone. Take Via Sparano to end, and turn left through arches into città vecchia. Open Tues.–Sun. noon–3 and 8–11.*

WORTH SEEING

The **città vecchia** hasn't changed much in 500 years—it's still a wonderful maze of crooked cobblestone alleyways, low-hanging arches, and whitewashed dwellings. Working-class folks and poor people live here, and a strong sense of community shows through, as if the neighborhood were a world unto itself. But crime is a serious problem in the città vecchia, and women and solo travelers should avoid coming here at night. It's reasonably safe during the day, but play it safe and leave your stuff at the Stop-Over main office.

The remains of **St. Nicholas**, the patron saint of fishermen, Orthodox Russians, pawnbrokers, and greedy children the world over, were stolen by more than 60 boisterous sailors from their original home in Asia Minor and brought to Bari. The sailors built a wonderful crypt for him, with translucent marble and a colonnade of 28 stone columns. You can visit the crypt in the **Basilica di San Nicola** (Piazza San Nicola, tel. 080/521–1205; open daily 7–1 and 4–7).

Bari's labyrinthine città vecchia was originally designed to thwart foreign invaders, who would be too preoccupied arguing over whether to take a left at the arch back there or a right at the small alleyway up ahead to coordinate their attack on the elusive Baresi.

Smack in the heart of the old city, the basilica is an eclectic mixture of Norman, Saracen, Lombardian, and Byzantine influences. The simple A-frame centerpiece at the front gives the church a sturdy, barnlike look that exemplifies Lombardian and Norman siege-mentality design. To the right is a tower co-opted from an earlier Byzantine fortress; the tower on the left was added for balance. The roof is embroidered with Saracen-inspired arabesques, and the portal is laced with more arabesques and miniature gargoyles.

Bari's duomo, the **Cattedrale di San Sabino** (Piazza Odegitria, tel. 080/521–0605) is open daily 8–12:30 and 4–7:30. It was built at the end of the 12th century for Bari's original patron saint, before the more popular St. Nicholas came along and took the title. The simple but beautiful medieval church houses the *Madonna Odegitria*, a dark-skinned Madonna icon said to have been based on a sketch of her by the apostle St. Luke. Across from the duomo, the seaside **Castello Normanno-Svevo** guards the perimeter of the città vecchia. The Normans built the castle on a Roman fort, and Frederick II, as he often did, rearranged and built on top of the original Norman design, finishing in 1290. Check out the carefully manicured hedge garden in what used to be the castle's moat. If you cross the moat to the large courtyard, you can pay a visit to the gargoyles that hang out in the castle **museum** (admission: L4000; open 9–1:30 and 3:30–7). If you're hungry for still more culture, head down Lungomare N. Sauro to the Palazzo della Provincia, which houses the **Pinacoteca Provinciale** (Via Spalato 19, tel. 080/541–2431), including paintings by Bellini, Tintoretto, and Veronese. At press time the museum was closed for renovation.

AFTER DARK

Although Bari has a good number of swinging dance clubs, they're all hard to reach via public transport. Luckily, the Stop-Over people will arrange transportation to and from **Divanae Follie Disco** (Via Ponte Lama 3, no phone), in the nearby town of Bisceglie. Cover is L25,000. If you'd rather just go out for a drink, **Reiff** (Largo Adua 3, no phone; closed Mon.), is a popular bar featuring local musicians. Behind the train station, disco **Baronda** (Largo Ciaia, tel. 080/524-8382; closed Sun.) is also all the rage, especially since there's no cover.

ALBEROBELLO In the heart of the Murge hills, between Bari and Taranto, Alberobello has a dense concentration of **trulli**, some of the oddest dwellings in all Europe. The one-story abodes of whitewashed rock were built during feudal times by impoverished peasants. The most unusual features of the trulli are their roofs, constructed of stones layered without mortar in near-perfect conical domes that often display Christian or pagan symbols. Feudal overlords demanded that no mortar be used so that the trulli could be immediately leveled should they need to evict their tenants. Those who evaded the landlords passed the tradition down to future generations, many of whom still inhabit the trulli.

Alberobello is a 1½-hour train ride from Bari on the FSE line (L5700) and a 40-minute ride from Castellana (L2700). Take Via Mazzini from the train station and follow signs to the first set of trulli; or continue straight ahead to Via Garibaldi, which will take you to the town center and **Hotel Lanzilotta** (Piazza Ferdinando IV 31, off Piazza del Popolo, tel. 080/721511), with doubles with bath for L65,000. For visitor's info, head to **EcoTurAm** (Viale Aldo Moro 49, tel. 080/932–5137), open Monday–Saturday 8:30–12:30 and 3–6:30, Sunday 8:30–12:30. You can rent a bike (L4000 an hr, L20,000 a day) here and get information on hikes, bike trips, and even week-long cooking classes. To sample typical Puglian dishes like *fave e cicorie* (bean purée with chicory; L7000) or *brasciola alla barese* (rolled up veal or horsemeat with tomato sauce; L9000), head to **Gli Ulivi** (Corso da Popoleto 15, tel. 080/932–3796).

Taranto

The ancient port town of Taranto guards the Gulf of Taranto, where the instep of Italy's boot meets the heel. According to legend, the city was founded by Tiras, son of Neptune, 1,200 years before the discovery of Rome. Those skeptical of the myth suggest that Taranto was a Magna Grecia outpost established by the Spartans in 701 BC, chosen for its strategic position on the Ionian coast. Even more than other towns and cities in the Mezzogiorno, Taranto is feeling the effects of Italy's political crisis and economic contraction. The city's high-tech steel industry seems to have produced more pollution than exportable steel, and the Italian navy, Taranto's other dominant economic force, is being scaled back. Taranto may lack the charm of many other Italian cities, but it's still a good base for exploring nearby beach towns, such as **Lido Silvana**. And if you come during holy week, the week before Easter, you'll be able to witness one of Italy's largest and most spectacular series of pre-Easter processions and parades.

BASICS Taranto's **EPT** office provides maps and information on accommodations. *Corso Umberto 113, tel. 099/453–2392. From station, Bus 8 to 3 stops after bridge in new city; walk 1 block to Corso Umberto. Open Oct.–June, weekdays 9–1 and 4:30–6:30; July–Sept., weekdays 9–1 and 4:30–6:30, Sat. 9:30–12:30 and 5–7.*

For decent rates and an ATM machine that accepts cards on the Plus system, head to **Banca Nazionale del Lavoro** (Via de Cesare 21, on edge of new city, tel. 099/45361), open weekdays

A Cool Escape

A slow, boiling-hot train ride on the FSE line south from Bari (see Coming and Going, above) will take you through walled olive groves and small vineyards to the village of Castellana, home to some of the most spectacular underground caverns in the world. Until recently, the caves were hidden beneath the local garbage dump, and the townsfolk didn't even realize they were living atop such wonders. La Grave, the largest of the caverns, marks the entrance to more than 3 kilometers of elaborate grottoes; just follow signs from the train station.

8:20–1:20 and 2:35–4:05. The main **post office** (Piazza Libertà, tel. 099/453–9510), to the right as you exit the train station, is open weekdays 8:15–7:40, Saturday 8:15–1.

COMING AND GOING Taranto is a main stop on the **FS** and **FSE train lines**. The info office in the station, open weekdays 9–1, hands out train schedules. Trains leave regularly for Brindisi (1¾ hrs, L5700), Bari (1½–2 hrs, L9800), and Metaponto (40 min, L4200). Three trains leave daily for Naples (5 hrs, L24,400), and one to Reggio di Calabria (6½ hrs, L37,000).

Ferrovie Autobus del Sud-Est, in Piazza Castello just before the second bridge to the new city, sends frequent buses to Martina Franca (1 hr, L3400) and Bari (2 hrs, L8500). **SITA** sends buses to Matera (2 hrs, L7500). In July and August, **A.C.TT.** buses go to Lido Silvana (9–12 daily, 35 min, L2500). Purchase tickets at **Bar Poseidon** (Piazza Castello 10, tel. 099/470–6893; open daily 6–2:10 and 4–10); A.C.TT. buses leave from the bar.

GETTING AROUND Getting around town is much less intimidating than it first seems. After picking up a map from the info booth in the train station, travel straight up Viale Duca d'Aosta and cross the bridge to **Piazza Fontana**, at the tip of the old city. The new city is yet another bridge away; head to Corso Vittorio Emanuele (off Piazza Fontana) and hop on a bus toward the castle. The new city consists of a fairly straightforward grid of streets, with most hotels, restaurants, and monuments clustered around the central Via d'Aquino. Local (orange) **AMAT buses** (L1000) shuttle back and forth between the train station and the new city until about 11 PM.

WHERE TO SLEEP **Albergo Pisani.** This hotel on the edge of the new city is a welcome change from the old city's dives. Safely tucked away behind two locked gates, the rooms (doubles without bath L73,000) are cool and immaculate, with paisley bedcovers. *Via Cavour 43, tel. 099/453–4087. From station, take any local bus heading to new city and get off 3 stops after 2nd bridge. Walk up Via d'Aquino; Via Cavour is on your right.*

Rivera. This clean, hospitable pension in the new city is run by a friendly signora. Doubles (all without bath) go for L55,000. *Via Campania 203, tel. 099/735–3274. From station, take Bus 8 and get off at Corso Italia where it intersects Via Campania.*

Sorrentino. This mom-and-pop budget hotel caters primarily to families visiting their sons at Taranto's naval base. The rooms (doubles with bath L50,000) could use some modernizing, but they're passable for a night or two. *Piazza Fontana 7, tel. 099/470–7456. From station, take Viale Duca d'Aosta to Piazza Fontana.*

FOOD Taranto has a few choice finds and a lot of mediocre restaurants offering a *menu militare* to sailors. At the entrance to the old town, **Panificio Due Mari** (Via Matteotti 16, tel. 099/434584; closed Sun.), serves both Neapolitan-style pizza and pizza by-the-slice. The place doubles as a small general market, selling bread and homemade *taralli* (small doughnut-shaped pastries). **Queen** (Via de Cesare 20–22, tel. 099/91011), in the new city, has a decent *tavola calda* (cafeteria) loaded with seafood plates. A plate of *insalata di riso* (rice salad) is L4000; secondi cost around L5000. For delicious fresh seafood at reasonable prices, try **Gesù Cristo** (Piazza Ramellini 8, in new city, tel. 099/452–6466); a full meal runs L30,000.

WORTH SEEING Wander around the crumbling buildings of the **città vecchia** if you want to experience Taranto as it was before industrialization, but be as careful here as you would in the old quarters of Bari or Naples—avoid the area at night. Begin your tour around Piazza Fontana. **Via Cariati**, the one-way street to the left, has a lively fish market filled with old *pescatori* (fishermen) who've been casting their nets in the surrounding Mare Piccola and Mare Grande for years. Also off Piazza Fontana is the **Chiesa di San Domenico Maggiore**, built by Frederick II in 1223. The church's mix of architectural styles is highly original: Note the Gothic portal, the Romanesque window, and the baroque double stairway. Farther up from the church is the **duomo**, with its **Chapel of San Cataldo**, a florid baroque masterpiece created in honor of Taranto's Irish patron saint. If the church happens to be open (usually between 1 and 5), check out the Byzantine frescoes that adorn the crypt. At the far end of the old quarter, the expansive **Aragonese Castle** (closed to the public) was built in 1480 by Ferdinand of Aragon and is used today by the Italian navy.

Cross Italy's only swing bridge to reach the **città nuova**, a much tidier part of town. Taranto's **Museo Archeologico Nazionale**, one of the south's most important museums, boasts an impressive collection of Bronze Age finds, including sculptures, terra-cotta masks, coins, and jewelry. *Corso Umberto I, in Piazza Garibaldi, tel. 099/453–2112. Admission: L8000. Open daily 9–2.*

Brindisi

If you think Brindisi is hot and crowded with backpackers, just wait until you get to that "quaint," "historic" little Greek town you're on your way to visit. But that's another guidebook's tale to tell. As for Brindisi, you can think of it as the backpacker's rite of passage into the big leagues of budget travel. Exchange offices, ticket agents, and café/bars have multiplied like rabbits on the Americanized strip that leads from the train station to the docks, where ferries depart for Albania, Greece, and beyond.

If you've come to Brindisi to cross the Adriatic (and there are few other reasons to come here), a little advance planning will take you far. To avoid lines and crowds, it's best to buy your ferry ticket ahead of time from a travel agency in another Italian city. Do some shopping around as the different companies charge different prices. For last minute tickets, pick up the free publication *Brindisi Agenda* at newsstands; it lists most ferry lines and the travel agencies where you can purchase tickets. There are more than 20 lines, though most agencies only carry three or four. It's also a good idea to buy a warm shirt for the crossing, and a cushion or mat to sit on while you wait . . . and wait, and wait.

Waiting, in fact, is the main experience of Brindisi for the international "ferry set" that converges upon the town during July and August. Needless to say, the transient crowds are prime targets for petty criminals. Thankfully, you can check your bags at both the train station and Stazione Marittima. The latter is a better choice if you're going to stick by the docks, but the walk from the train station to the ferry is where most thefts occur, especially for unwary first-time visitors. Stay alert and travel in a group when possible.

A major port town since Roman times, Brindisi has probably always had its share of visitors playing the waiting game, from Roman soldiers and merchants tapping their sandals on the stone to medieval crusaders warming up their sword arms before heading off to attack the Saracens.

BASICS The **visitor information** office (Lungomare Regina Margherita 12, no phone) has city maps and can help you find a place to sleep. It's open weekdays 8:30–1:30. To change U.S. dollars or Italian lire to Greek drachmas, stop at any of the banks or exchange offices on and around Corso Umberto and Corso Garibaldi on your way to the launch. Banks are usually open 8:30–1 and 2:30–4. The main **post office** (Piazza Vittoria, tel. 0831/517128) also changes money and is open weekdays 8:15–5:30, Saturdays 8:15–1.

COMING AND GOING The **FS** (tel. 0831/521975) and **FSE** (tel. 0831/598111) lines serve the **main station** in Piazza Crispi, about a kilometer from the ferry port. Two trains leave daily for Rome (8–10 hrs, change in Pescara, L47,700), 11 for Milan (10½ hrs, L72,400). Trains leave hourly for Bari (1½ hrs, L9800), and almost hourly for Ostuni (½ hr, L3400). **FSE buses** leave from the main train station for major Puglian towns, and **Marozzi**, a private bus line, sends buses to smaller cities in the region.

➤ **BY FERRY** • Ferry rates vary month to month, company to company, but you can generally expect Greek companies to charge less than Italian ones.

Adriatica (Viale Regina Margherita 13, tel. 0831/523825) and **Hellenic Mediterranean Lines** (Corso Garibaldi 8, tel. 0831/528531) are the companies you'll be doing business with if have a **Eurail** or **InterRail** pass. Deck seats are free with a pass, but the port tax and inside seating are extra. **Fragline** (Corso Garibaldi 88, tel. 0881/568232) offers the cheapest rates, with service to Corfu (7½ hrs), Igoumenits (9½ hrs), and Patras (17½ hrs). *Passaggio ponte* (deck seat) tickets cost anywhere from L30,000 to L100,000; *poltrona* (reclining seat) tickets cost L5000-L20,000 more. There's also a L10,000 port tax. After buying your ticket, head to the

Stazione Marittima police station to show your passport and have your boarding pass stamped. Remember: You must arrive at the terminal at least two hours before departure.

WHERE TO SLEEP AND EAT Missed your ferrry? **Altair** (Via Tunisi 2, tel. 0831/524911) is a decent place to crash, with doubles for L40,000–L50,000. Or take Bus 3 or 4 (L800) from Via C. Colombo to the **ACLI Youth Hostel** (Via Nicola Brandi 2, tel. 0831/413123), which charges L18,000 for bed and breakfast. Stock up on food at either **Supermercato SIDIS** (Piazza Cairoli 30 or Corso Garibaldi 106; both closed Sun.). For pizza to go, head straight for **Pizzeria da Franco** (Via Umbria 36).

WORTH SEEING Since you'll probably have some time on your hands you might as well take a look around; most of the sights are conveniently close to the port. From the train station, follow Corso Umberto and Corso Garibaldi to the docks, and go left on Lungomare Regina Margherita. Just beyond the tourist office on your left is the broad, steeply inclined **Scalinata Virgilina** (Virgilian Stairway), near the house in which Virgil purportedly died. Step over the sun worshipers to see the **Colonne Romane al Terminale della Via Appia**, the end of Rome's Appian Way. A block inland from the columns, you'll pass the 12th-century **duomo** and its small and free **Archaeological Museum**, which houses Roman remains and urns. It's open Tuesday–Sunday 9–1 and Tuesday afternoons 3:30–6:30. If you follow Via Giovanni Tarentini from the duomo and go left on Via San Giovanni, you'll reach the crumbling **San Giovanni al Sepolcro**, built by the crusaders upon their return from the Holy Land. If you stand in front of the facade, it almost looks like a movie prop with 48's holding it up from behind—the construction is that fragile.

NEAR BRINDISI

OSTUNI Known as La Città Bianca (The White City) for the chalk-white facades of its buildings and homes, Ostuni makes a pleasant stop if you have some time to kill before jumping a ferry to Greece. The city spreads over three hills, and the beautiful centro storico crowns the highest of the three, providing commanding views of olive groves. Ostuni, which predates the Roman Empire, was an important Greek outpost, but it most obviously bears signs of medieval times. The 11th-century *borgo antico* (old city center) is the most interesting place for a stroll. Stop at the **tourist office** (Piazza della Libertà, tel. 0831/303775) for suggestions about what to see. It's open September–June, weekdays 9:30–12:30 and 4–7; July–August, Monday–Saturday 9:30–12:30 and 6–9). Two notable sights are the 21-meter **Column of Sant'Oronzo** (1771) at the head of Piazza della Libertà, and the lovely 15th-century **cathedral** at the highest point in town.

Ostuni is only half an hour by train from Brindisi (L3400). Local **Circolare buses** shuttle back and forth between the train station and town every half hour (10 min, L800), dropping you at **Piazza della Libertà**, on the edge of the centro storico. Unfortunately, the old part of town lacks budget accommodations, but the tourist office may be able to track down a private room where you can stay. Otherwise, head to the **Orchidea Nera** (Corso Mazzini 118, off Piazza della Libertà, tel. 0831/301366); which has spartan but clean doubles with bath for L78,000. Ostuni is packed with pizzerias and bars, especially near Piazza della Libertà, but the best eating takes place in the old quarter. Even if you're on a budget, you should splurge for a meal at **Osteria del Tempo Perso** (Via G. Tanzarella Vitale 47, tel. 0831/303320). Try *fave e cicorielle selvatiche* (bean purée and wild chicory; L8000) and creamy *cacio cavallo alla brace* (grilled local cheese; L9000) in an air-conditioned setting.

Lecce

If you've come as far down the peninsula as Bari or Brindisi, you might as well go for "baroque" and continue south to Lecce, the jewel of the Salentina Peninsula. Known as the *Firenze del Mezzogiorno* (the Florence of the south), Lecce is also sometimes called the "baroque capital of the world," thanks to churches and edifices so lavishly carved and ornamented as to overwhelm the senses. *Barocco leccese* (Leccian baroque) is characterized by its fantastical embellishments (verging on gaudy) used to decorate buildings and churches in the 17th and 18th centuries. Despite problems of urban pollution, the buildings in Lecce have been kept spectacularly clean, thus enhancing their brilliance and beauty. An **APT** office (tel. 0832/304443) is due to open in Piazza San Oronzo, but in the meantime, head to their temporary digs (Via Monte San Michele 20, off Piazza Mazzini, tel. 0832/314814; open weekdays 8–2) for maps, brochures, and a list of accommodations.

COMING AND GOING Lecce is on the **FS train line**, which connects the major cities of the Puglian coast. Trains run regularly from the station in Piazza Stazione to Brindisi (½ hr, L3400) and Taranto (2 hrs, L9800). To reach points farther south, you have to take the plodding **FSE line**. Show up early—trains are only two or three cars long and they fill up fast. Several trains leave for Otranto (1 hr, transfer at Maglie, L4200) and Gallipoli (1 hr, L5000). For information on buses, take Bus 7 from the train station to the **Sud-Est** office (Via Torre del Parco, tel. 0832/347634), open weekdays 5:45 AM–8 PM.

GETTING AROUND Lecce's train station is near several budget accommodations and about a kilometer from **Piazza Sant'Oronzo**, in the center of the old quarter. Streets in the old quarter are poorly marked, so it's a good idea to pick up a map at the visitor information office (*see above*) before wandering around. To reach the piazza from the station, follow Via Oronzo Quarta to Via Cairoli, bear left onto Via Paladini, go right on Via degli Ammirati, and go left onto Via Augusto Imperiale.

WHERE TO SLEEP Given the beauty of its old quarter, Lecce is surprisingly short on tourists and, consequently, on budget accommodations. Pensions that rent rooms to college students during the year, like **Luigi Tozzi** (Via Martiri d'Otranto 29, tel. 0832/249817), open up to tourists in July and August with doubles for L60,000, including bath and use of kitchen facilities. **Andreina Goffredo** (Via Taranto 31, tel. 0832/246182) rents doubles (L60,000) year-round; rooms include breakfast and there are two bathrooms for every three rooms.

Hotel Cappello (Via Montegrappa 4, near the station, tel. 0832/308881) has spacious, newly remodeled doubles with bath for L80,000 (most rooms even come with TV). It's a good idea to call ahead, because during the week this place fills up with workers from nearby towns. The **Grand Hotel** (Via Oronzo Quarta 28, tel. 0832/309405), a high-ceilinged, red-carpeted mammoth, is 25 meters from the train station and accepts credit cards. Many of the rooms (doubles with bath and breakfast L120,000) don't live up to the promise of the spiffy entrance, but some have been redone with beautiful furniture and televisions. **Camping Torre Rinalda** (Litorauvea, tel. 0832/652161) is a bit out of town toward San Cataldo, but it's the only camping around and has its own pizzeria and swimming pool. In August you'll pay L9500 per person and L8500–L13,500 per tent. In June, July, and September, rates are L8000 per person and L7000–L11,500 per tent. To get here, take an STP or Baglivi bus toward San Cataldo from the bus stop on Viale Gallipoli (every ½ hr, 20 min, L1500).

FOOD La Capannina (Via Cairoli 13, tel. 0832/304159; open Tues.–Sun. for dinner only), about 1 kilometer from the train station, has a tasty self-service antipasti array (L6000) and great mixed salads (L3000). **Carlo V** (Piazzetta Falconieri 1, tel. 0832/243509; closed Mon.) has outstanding *piatti speciali* (vegetarian dishes) for L8000–L11,000 and elaborate pizzas for L9000–L14,000. For a quick bite, get delicious *arancini di riso* (fried rice balls; L1500) to go at **La Rustica** (Corso Vittorio Emanuele 31, tel. 0832/300544; closed Wed.). There's a **covered market** Monday–Saturday 7 AM–1 PM in Piazzetta Libertini. From Piazza Sant'Oronzo take Via S. Trinchese and turn right at the Teatro Apollo.

WORTH SEEING Begin your tour in **Piazza Sant'Oronzo**, where the ancient, the baroque, and the modern coexist harmoniously. A **Roman amphitheater** (closed to the public), on the south side of the piazza, was completed during Hadrian's rule in the 2nd century AD. The theater seated 20,000 bloodthirsty spectators, all cheering on their favorite gladiators. Nowadays, kids and old-timers hang out by the "bleachers" in front of the **Sedile** (Town Hall), waiting for Godot. The hall was built in the comparatively restrained early baroque style by the Venetian Pier Moceigo in the late 16th century. Across from the Sedile, a wooden, copper-coated statue of Lecce's patron saint, Lorenzo, stands atop the **Colonna di Sant'Oronzo**. In 1686 Giuseppe Zimbalo completed the column's base and the statue on top in typical baroque fashion.

From the piazza, walk up Via Tealori to Via Umberto to see what no postcard can successfully frame, the **Basilica di Santa Croce**. Architect Gabriele Riccardo started work on this bravura display of the baroque in 1532. One and a half centuries later, the church was completed, its raucous basilica designed by Antonio Zimbalo. You'll spend lots of time noting the infinite details of the contorted, flowery facade, but be sure to also look for the statues of St. Benedict and St. Peter standing amid the dazzling architectural flora and fauna and looking a bit troubled. The interior of the cathedral is laid out according to a simple Latin cross plan, but notice how the severe Corinthian columns can't keep from bursting into flames of baroque at their capitals. The comparatively austere **Palazzo del Governo** stretches out beside the basilica. Originally a Celestine convent, the edifice was begun in 1659, the lower half of its facade designed by Zimbalo and the upper half by Cino.

The master architect of the Lecce baroque style was Giuseppe Zimbalo, who must have had a few hallucinatory dreams, judging by his flair for the outrageously ornate. His canvas was the soft, sandstone-like rock tufa, easy to carve but hardy enough to resist decay.

As you head toward Piazza del Duomo on Via Vittorio Emanuele (off Piazza Sant'Oronzo), you'll see the **Church of St. Irene**. The protectress of the city stands atop what looks like a fruit bowl on the Roman baroque church. The large **Piazza del Duomo** was designed for stately affairs, but it makes a great soccer field for young kids. From left to right, you'll see the campanile (closed to the public), the duomo, the seminary, and the Palazzo Vescovile. The **duomo** was built by Giuseppe Zimbalo, the master of Lecce baroque, between 1655 and 1670. The bell tower stands 75 meters tall, with Sant' Oronzo topping off its fifth floor.

The **Museo Provinciale** (Viale Gallipoli 28, tel. 0832/307415), near the train station, is also worth a look. Some great decapitated Roman sculptures and busts lifted from the amphitheater have found their final resting place here. The museum is open weekdays 9–1:30 and 2:30–7:30, Sundays 9–1:30, and admission is free.

NEAR LECCE

OTRANTO Otranto lies deep in southern Italy, an hour south of Lecce by train (7 daily, transfer at Maglie, L4200) in an area that feels as much Greek as Italian. It's a quiet, little backwater town with some interesting history and architecture, great seafood, good campsites, and a surprisingly decent music scene. Like most Puglian coastal towns, Otranto has a long legacy of foreign rule, beginning with its Greek origins. Next the Byzantines came into town, holding sway until Norman rule began in 1070. In 1480 the Turks arrived, hoping to conquer the entire peninsula, but they only stayed long enough to massacre the town's 800 citizens before turning back. A year later, things settled down when Duke Alfonse of Aragon came into power. Today Otranto looks much as it did centuries ago: The water to the east is navy blue, and the terrain to the west is alternately verdant and rocky. It's difficult to get around the scenic countryside without a car, but you get a good taste of the region in Otranto itself.

The **duomo** (alias Cattedrale di Santa Maria Annunziata), off Piazza Basilica in the town center, is Otranto's most important sight, built in Romanesque style by the Normans in 1080. The facade is a typical Puglian mixture of Greco-Byzantine and Arabic influences. Most striking, however, is the interior, with terrific floor mosaics crafted by the monk Pantaleone in the 12th century. The entire length of the nave is covered by the *Albero della Vita* (Tree of Life), and a great cast of characters hangs out in its limbs, including Alexander the Great ascending to heaven, King Arthur fighting the Cat of Losanna (but looking more like a wide-eyed kid waving to the crowd), Noah building his ark, and lots of pagan serpents, mermaids, and signs of the zodiac. Next to the Tree of Life, to the right of the altar, is what could be called the Chapel of Death: A small chapel houses the bones of people killed in a Turk attack.

➣ **BASICS** • Otranto's **Azienda Autonoma di Soggiorno e Turismo** (Via Pantaleone Presbitero 12, tel. 0836/801436) is open July and August, Monday–Saturday 9–1 and 4–8 (shorter hrs off-season).

➣ **COMING AND GOING** • Otranto's **train station** is a good 10 minutes from the center of town (follow signs and bear left at the fork in the road). Trains depart regularly for Lecce (transfer at Maglie, L4200). **Linea Lauro** sends ferries to Corfu (8 hrs) and Igoumenitsa (6 hrs) about four times a week in high season. For a list of times and prices, stop by **Ellade Viaggi** (Via Porto, at the port, tel. 0836/802747). Expect to pay L70,000 for either destination from mid-July to August (L50,000 for those 25 and under). In off-season the trip costs about L45,000.

➤ **GETTING AROUND** • Because most visitors to Otranto (usually Italian or German tourists) come by car, the town has no public transportation. You can rent a bike or a moped (no special license required) at a small shop with no name at Via Facolli 41. You can get a bike for L8000 a day and a *motorino* (small moped) for L20,000. *Open Mon.–Sat. 9–1 and 3–9. From station, take road leading to town, continue straight to the Lungomare, turn right and follow road past gardens to end.*

➤ **WHERE TO SLEEP** • Staying in Otranto can get expensive, but **agriturismo** (shacking up in the countryside) is a good way to save money. Most farmhouses with agriturismo within easy reach of the ocean, and if you pay full board you'll eat very well. **Il Contadino** (Località Frassanito, tel. 0836/85065), one of the more popular farmhouses, charges L10,000 per person to camp or L65,000 for a double room with bath. It's open from Easter to September. Frassanito is 10 kilometers north of Otranto and can be reached by taxi from the station (about L20,000). In town, **Hydrusa** (btw historic center and port, tel. 0836/801255) is a wooded campsite and the cheapest place around. You'll pay L8000 per person, L3500 per tent, and L2000 for electricity. You can also go four to a bungalow for L90,000 (15-day minimum). **Il Gabbiano** (Via Porto Craulo 13, tel. 0836/801251) has rooms in a pleasant setting near the water. Doubles go for L84,000, but try to talk them down in the off-season. Along the lungomare there are countless places serving reasonably priced pizza and sandwiches. Also along the shore you'll find more upscale seafood joints.

➤ **AFTER DARK** • For a town of its size, Otranto is well endowed with night spots. If dancing's your thing, boogie down at **Nike** (Riviera degli Haethey, 2 km north of Otranto, tel. 0836/801196), located in a 16th-century country home with a private beach. Cover is L25,000. If you're staying at Il Contadino, head to the oddly named **Country Club** (Via Allimini, tel. 0836/85221; open nightly 10 PM–3 AM), with mainstream dance music, a swimming pool, and crepes to munch on. Cover is L25,000. If you'd rather have a mellow night out, head over to **Griffin's Pub** (Via Castello 10, near the Cattedrale, tel. 0836/801301).

Basilicata

Basilicata forms the arch in Italy's boot, touching the Ionian Sea to the southeast and a small portion of the Tyrrhenian Sea to the west. Until the end of World War II, the region was characterized by *la miseria,* the misery of extreme poverty. After World War II, however, the Italian government (with American backing) let loose a torrent of welfare lire on the south, out of fear that the desperately poor southern peasants might turn to Communism as a solution to their problems. Sadly, the region still has one of the lowest per capita incomes in Italy, and a tour through the countryside suggests that this province has received less than its fair share of Italy's "economic miracle." Despite the improvements, many Basilicatans express regret over the communities and value systems they left behind, as they struggle to reconcile their traditional agrarian past with the industrial, consumerist society built by lire from the north.

Since the Italian government started to pour welfare funds into Basilicata in the 1950s, peasant families of 10 or more (not including the mule and chickens) were moved from their primitive hut-like homes into equally brutal concrete housing projects.

Still, a trip through Basilicata can be extremely rewarding. The region's hot sun, sloping hillsides, and ocher mountains seem to stretch time, and what the towns and countryside lack in Renaissance art they make up for with the simple charm of their ancient ruins, modest churches, whitewashed farmhouses, and stunning hillsides. Getting around the region is always frustrating without a car, especially when you venture off the coastal route, but buses at least offer more thorough and frequent service than trains.

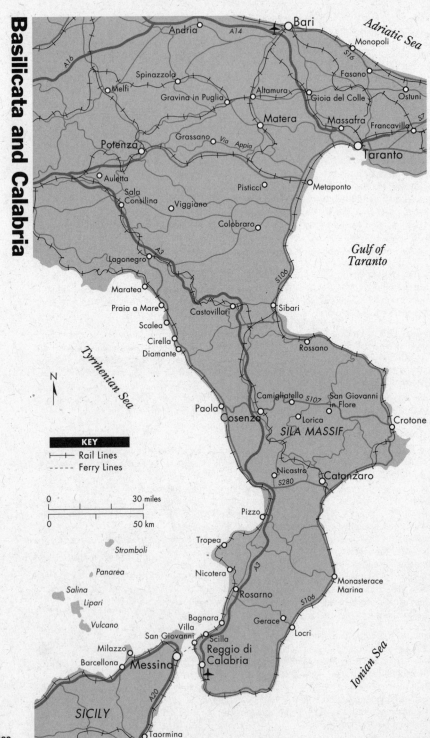

Adriatic Sea

Bari
Andria
A14
Monopoli
S16
Spinazzola
Fasano
Melfi
Altamura
Gioia del Colle
Ostuni
Gravina in Puglia
A16
Massafra
Francavilla
Matera
S7
Potenza
Grassano
Via Appia
Taranto
Auletta
Metaponto
Sala
Consilina
Pisticci
Viggiano
Colobraro
Gulf of
Taranto
Lagonegro
A3
S106
Maratea
Praia a Mare
Castovillari
Sibari
Scalea
Cirella
Diamante
Rossano

Tyrrhenian Sea

N

Camigliatello
S107
San Giovanni
in Flore
Paola
Lorica
Crotone
Cosenza
SILA MASSIF

KEY
Rail Lines
Ferry Lines

Nicastro
Catanzaro
S280

0   30 miles
0   50 km

Pizzo

Tropea
A3

Stromboli
Nicotera
Monasterace
Marina
Panarea
Rosarno
S106
Salina
Lipari
Bagnara
Gerace
Vulcano
Villa
Locri
San Giovanni
Scilla
Milazzo
Reggio di
Calabria
Barcellona
Messina

SICILY
A20

Ionian Sea

Taormina

Avoid Potenza, the region's capital, if you can; repeated earthquakes have depleted what little cultural legacy the town once had. But Matera, home of the famous *sassi* (caves); Metaponto, on the Ionian coast; and Maratea, on the Tyrrhenian coast, are worthwhile stops for those exploring the Mezzogiorno. Plus the relatively undiscovered **Parco Nazionale del Pollino**, in the southwestern corner of Basilicata (extending into Calabria), possesses some of Italy's last virgin forests, though it's difficult to explore without a car.

Matera

Matera, in eastern Basilicata close to the Puglian border, has one of the world's most unique old quarters: It's made entirely of caves known as sassi, the oldest of which date back to the Paleolithic age. Two sassi neighborhoods border a ravine on one side and a new city on the other. Until 1952, when the government ordered the caves vacated (residents were sometimes evacuated by force), many Materans lived in these close-knit but desperately poor districts (we're talking no plumbing). Now, after 20 years in which Materans shook off their poverty and acquired modern comforts (and problems, including widespread drug use), the sassi are experiencing a comeback. Some have been transformed by wealthy artistic types into stylish luxury abodes. Explore the town on foot; you'll find many incomparable vantage points of what is considered by many to be southern Italy's most picturesque town.

BASICS The well-stocked **APT** office (Via de Viti de Marco 9, off Via Roma, tel. 0835/333541) has maps of Matera and information on Basilicata. The friendly English-speaking staff can answer your questions Monday–Saturday 8:30–2. The **Cooperative Amici del Turista** (Vico Solitario, in the sassi, tel. 0835/310113) has fluctuating open hours; call ahead. They can answer any questions you have about the caves, suggest an itinerary for exploration, and offer tours of the sassi (1 hr, L10,000).

The central **Banca di Napoli** (Piazza Vittorio Veneto 48, tel. 0835/371445) is open weekdays 8:20–1:35 and 3:20–4:05, Saturdays 8:20–11. To make long-distance phone calls, head to the **TELECOM** office (Via del Corso 5, tel. 0835/330200; open weekdays 9–12:30 and 2:30–6). Just up the street sits the **post office** (Via del Corso 15, tel. 0835/332591), open weekdays 8:15–5:30, Saturdays 8:15–1.

COMING AND GOING Matera's **train station** is across from Piazza Matteotti. Trains cover the region only sparsely, though there are regular departures for Bari (1½ hrs, L4300). Buses provide the most extensive coverage of Basilicata. The **SITA** office (Piazza Matteotti, tel. 0835/385007) sells tickets to destinations within the region and provides schedule information weekdays 6–8:20, 11:45–2:15, and 4:45–6:50. Buses leave regularly from Piazza Matteotti for Laterza (1½ hrs, L2500), Metaponto (50 min, L5000), and Taranto (1¾ hrs, L7500).

Short and Sassi

The sassi, chiese rupestri (rock churches), and sandstone homes of the ancient city of Matera provide a palimpsest of human history. Peer out from the low-ceilinged caves on the far side of the ravine and you'll see each successive stage in human architectural development: simple, naturally carved niches by the river's edge, inhabited by the first nomadic tribes of the Paleolithic age; churches and apartments that seem to rise up out of rock itself; and elaborate fortress walls and palazzi built during medieval and Renaissance times. Anthropologists have touted Matera as "the most ancient city in the world," but over the next few years the sassi neighborhoods will be buzzing with the sound of construction as workers restore the caves, adding plumbing, electricity, and other modern-day amenities.

FCL buses leave for Bari (1½ hrs, L4400) and other destinations from the front of the train station; schedules are posted next to the train-ticket window. The private **Marozzi** line sends three buses to Rome on weekdays (6¾ hrs, L43,000), and **Marino** sends two buses to Milan (12¾ hrs, L78,000), Torino (14¾ hrs, L90,000), and one to Florence (10:35 AM, 9½ hrs, L73,500). Buy tickets and check schedules at the **Kronos Travel Agency** (Piazza Matteotti 8, next to SITA office, tel. 0835/334653), open weekdays 9–1 and 3:45–8.

GETTING AROUND Local buses (L1000) cover all of Matera except for the sassi neighborhoods, though it's easy to get around on foot. Most buses come and go from Piazza Matteotti, and tickets can be purchased at newsstands and tabacchi. To reach the sassi from Piazza Vittorio Veneto, which divides the old and new parts of town, head down Via delle Becherie to Via Duomo. The street climbs up to the cathedral, spills into Piazza Duomo, and bisects the **Sasso Barisano** and **Sasso Caveoso** neighborhoods.

WHERE TO SLEEP Around festival time (late June and early July), call ahead to reserve a room. **Da Nicola** (Via Nazionale 158, tel. 0835/385111), far from the bus depot but just down the street from the Sasso Barisano, has the best mid- to high-priced rooms in town. The large, bland building is open around the clock, so it's okay to arrive after Matera's bedtime. Doubles (all with bath) cost L99,000 (L125,000 with air-conditioning). From Piazza Matteotti, take Bus 5, 7, 10, or 14 and tell the driver you want to get off at Da Nicola (10 min; last bus 9:30 PM). **Roma Hotel** (Via Roma 62, tel. 0835/333912) has been in business for more than 50 years, and the charming family that runs it keeps the aged rooms and beds immaculate. It's the best deal in town, with doubles at L50,000 without bath. From the bus depot in Piazza Matteotti, take Via Roma.

FOOD Food here is generally fresh, excellent, and cheap, except for the posh but pricey cafés in Piazza Vittorio Veneto. The town has two large fruit markets—the most convenient of which is at Piazza Asconio Persio (open Mon.–Sat. 7 AM–1 PM), and some great cafés that dish out gelato to the over-heated masses. **Gelateria Cardinale** (Via del Corso 102, no phone; open daily 6–1 and 4–11) has incredibly creamy gelato. **Il Terrazino sui Sassi** (Vico San Giuseppe 7, tel. 0835/332503), in one of Matera's famous caves, has great food and an amazing view of the sassi from its terrace. It's open Wednesday–Monday noon–3 and 7:20–midnight. Delicious pizza or homemade pasta plus bread and wine runs about L20,000, including the cover charge. **Trattoria Lucana** (Via Lucana 48, off Via Roma, tel. 0835/336117) also deserves its popularity: Prices are good (usually around L20,000), the food is delicious, and the atmosphere is friendly. *Primi* (first courses) cost L7000–L8000. The *antipasti della casa*, a sampling of appetizers (L15,000), is a meal in itself. Lucana is generally open Monday–Saturday 12:30–3:30 and 8–10, but it closes during the first two weeks of September.

WORTH SEEING Begin your tour of Matera in Piazza Duomo, visible from afar because of its tall 13th-century **duomo**, built in the Puglian Romanesque style out of *tufa* (a soft sandstone). The piazza leads right to Matera's ancient neighborhoods, **Sasso Barisano** and **Sasso Caveoso**. Sasso Barisano, with its tip reaching all the way to Piazza Veneto, is the newer and more complex of the two. Walk down any side street off Via San Biagio and you'll twist and wind through ancient homes built right on top of one another. When you reach the small piazza at the bottom, head toward Via Madonna delle Virtù (alias Strada Panoramica dei Sassi), which winds around the periphery of the neighborhood toward the *chiese rupestri* (rock churches) on the other side of the ravine. There are thought to be as many as 120 rock churches, built between the 6th and 13th centuries. As you make your way along the road, you'll come to the cave monastery, **Convicinio di Sant'Antonio** (admission: L2000), made up of four rock churches built between the 12th and 13th centuries, and later transformed into a residence by Materan peasants, who lived here until the 1950s. The monastery is open July and August 10–10 (winter hours vary). Afterward, grab a drink on the terrace of the mystical **Bar Libreria**, open June–September, daily 9:30 PM–2 AM.

The spiritual heart of Basilicata, Matera embodies the contradictions of a people who have one foot in a farmer's boot and the other in something like a Gucci loafer.

Continuing down Via Madonna delle Virtù, you'll eventually reach the churches of **Santa Maria d'Iris** and **San Pietro Caveoso**, both of which contain Byzantine frescoes dating back to the

12th–16th centuries. Sasso Caveoso, the older of the two ancient quarters, is dotted with rock churches. To reach them, pass behind San Pietro and veer right. Near Piazza di San Pietro Caveoso, take the small car turnoff and hike down the switchbacks to the river's edge. The view from here captures the entire evolution of Matera, from its humble paleolithic origins at the base to a modern skyline above the amazing rock apartments.

Below Via Duomo on Via Corso lies the morbid church **Purgatorio**. The entrance has a fantastically sinister door etched with skulls and crossbones and topped with a figure of a grim reaper. Near the church, the **Museo Nazionale Ridola** (Via Ridola 24, tel. 0835/311239; admission: L4000), a former monastery, houses a collection of prehistoric and early classical art. The museum is open Tuesday–Sunday 9–1 and 4–7.

FESTIVALS During the last week of June and the first week of July, Matera celebrates the **Festa della Madonna della Bruna**, one of the most important religious festivals in the south. The annual event commemorates the return of a dark-skinned Madonna figure stolen by the Turks in the 8th century. Local artists compete to build ornate carriages to transport the Madonna through the streets. After a week of parades, fireworks, and religious ceremonies, the festival comes to a head on July 2, when the whole town turns out at dawn in Piazza Duomo for the **Assalto al Carro** (Assault on the Cart). The main parade has turned into somewhat of a media spectacle in recent years, but it's still amazing to behold. Try to hitch a ride from the square with one of the cars heading to the other side of the ravine. From the mountaintop perch you'll have a great view of the thunderous fireworks display, which lasts well into the evening.

In a Felliniesque juxtaposition, horseback riders in medieval garb lead shiny new Jeeps covered with streamers and filled with priests, as the Madonna is paraded through town.

Metaponto

Founded in the 7th century BC by Greek colonists, Metaponto is home to the region's most important set of Magna Grecia ruins. Though these impressive ancient remains are Metaponto's main attraction, many tourists are content to let dead Greeks lie, heading straight to Metaponto's prime Ionian beaches. The coast here is typical of the Ionian Sea: flat as a board with long stretches of white sandy beach. The city itself is quite unattractive, but if you're willing to walk a bit from the center, you'll be able to find a quiet stretch of sand to call your own.

BASICS Metaponto's small **EPT tourist office** (Viale delle Sirene, near the beach, tel. 0835/741933) hands out information on Metaponto and Basilicata from July to early September, daily 8–8. To change money, head to the **Cassa di Risparmio di Calabria e di Lucania** (Via Eroi della Bonifica, in the center, tel. 0835/745203), open weekdays 8:20–1:20 and 2:35–3:20.

COMING AND GOING Metaponto makes a viable day trip by bus from Matera, with five daily buses (fewer on weekends) traveling the route (50 min, L5000). The bus stops at the train station, at the beach where the hotels are, or in front of the Magna Grecia campground. Metaponto is also a main stop on the Taranto–Reggio di Calabria train line, and trains leave regularly from Taranto (1 hr, L4200) and Reggio (6 hrs, L33,400).

WHERE TO SLEEP AND EAT Several hotels and a ton of campsites in Metaponto are close to, if not right on, the beach. A mere 100 meters away from the water, on the street that connects the train station and town center, **Hotel Kennedy** (Viale Ionio, tel. 0835/741960) offers clean, modern rooms (doubles L60,000–L70,000) in a nondescript building. Grab a tasty dinner or a cup of coffee in the bar/restaurant downstairs. **The Oasi** (Via Olimpia 12, tel. 0835/741930), up the road from the Hotel Kennedy, is indeed an oasis for budget travelers. Plain doubles with bath (L40,000) are hard to come by during July and August, so call ahead.

For a night under the stars, head to **Camping Magna Grecia** (Via Lido 1, tel. 0835/741855; open Easter–Sept.), Metaponto's most happening campground and one of the better spots in Metaponto for summertime nightlife. It has everything, including a swimming pool (L2500 per

½ day), horseback riding (L20,000 an hr), tennis courts (L6000 per hr), a cafeteria, a small market, a restaurant, a discotheque (always free to campers; free to noncampers except in Aug.), telephones, and clean, modern bathrooms. You'll pay L5000–L10,000 per person, L6000–L10,000 per tent site. They also send a bus to and from the train station, and to and from the beach.

You definitely won't confuse Metaponto with any of Italy's culinary capitals. If you're staying at a hotel or campground, your best bet is to eat there. Otherwise, buy picnic food from the vendors that set up regularly in and around Piazzale Nord, or stop at **Mini Market Da Lucia** (Viale Ionico 18/A, no phone). For takeout, head to **Pammarolo** (Viale Ionio, at Strada Nazionale del Lido) for a roast chicken (L10,000), sandwiches (L4000), pizza by the slice (L2000–L4000), and *pattatine* (french fries; L2000). They're open July and August, daily 9 AM–12:30 AM.

WORTH SEEING Metaponto's biggest drawback is its inconvenient layout. The city includes four distinct sections: the area around the train station, the inland section of Metaponto known as **Metaponto Borgo**, the **Archaeological Park** where all the important Greek ruins are located, and the seaside section called **Metaponto Lido**. A bus (L1000) travels hourly between the station and Metaponto Lido in July and August. To reach Metaponto's **ruins** from the station, head up S.S.175 from the train station in the direction of Reggio Calabria. On your left, about 300 meters from the station, you'll see the **Archaeological Museum**, set above a small piazza and housing project. The museum, built a few years ago to display an increasing number of Magna Grecia finds, includes ceramics, costumes, and the skeletal remains of the Sybarites and various Lucanian tribes. Archaeologists have excavated more than 600 tombs from the Basilicatan countryside, discovering relics that date as far back as the 7th century BC. *Tel. 0835/745327. Admission: L4000. Open Sept.–June, daily 9–7; July and Aug., daily 9–1:30 and 5:30–9:30.*

About half a kilometer farther down S.S. 175, take a right and follow signs along the narrow road to Metaponto's **Parco Archeologico**. The remains of the Doric **Temple of Apollo Licius** and the **Greek theater** sit quietly in a field near a farm. The 32 columns that once stood here were cannibalized for other projects throughout the centuries. Back on S.S. 175, continue another kilometer and you'll pass the **Necropoli di Crucinia** (ancient burial grounds). Walk 1 kilometer farther, and turn right at the highway to Taranto (S.S. 106) to reach a beautiful Doric temple, the **Tavole Palatine**. This was the temple of Hera, later turned into a school where the great mathematician-philosopher Pythagoras is supposed to have taught until his death in the late 6th century BC.

Maratea

Maratea, a dazzling 30-kilometer stretch of sheer cliffs and aquamarine ocean, is the only Basilicatan city on the Tyrrhenian coast. The area, presided over by a 25-meter **Statue of the Redeemer** atop a cliff (with arms outstretched to welcome beach-bound vacationers), is notable for its natural beauty more than its religious or cultural artifacts. Aside from the awe-inspiring scenery and postcard-perfect coastline, there are no real sights of interest, though Maratea's centro storico is worth a peek. Be forewarned: Getting around requires a good deal of walking, and accommodations are geared toward lira-laden travelers. If you can't find an affordable room, you can easily make the town a day trip from Calabria's Praia a Mare (*see below*). Make sure you check bus and train schedules ahead of time; transportation in this region is sparse. Stop by the **visitor information office** (Piazza del Gesù, Località Fiumicello, tel. 0973/876908) for brochures on the area, a list of hotels, and a schedule of SITA buses. It's open daily 9–12:30 and 4–7 (shorter hours in winter).

COMING AND GOING Maratea is spread out. Fortunately many regional and long-distance trains stop at **Marina di Maratea**, **Maratea**, and **Acquafredda**, although areas like **Castrocucco** (where the campground is) and **Fiumicello** (home to the tourist info office and many hotels) cannot be reached by train. It's best to get off the train at the Maratea stop since it's centrally located and well served by public transport. From Maratea, trains leave for Salerno (1¾ hrs, L11,700); and there are frequent connections to Maratea from Calabria's Praia a Mare (10 min, L2000). To reach the centro storico, take any bus from the station to Piazza Immacolata (hourly, 15 min, L1000). From the Marina di Maratea station, trains make short hops (5–6 min) to Acquafredda, where you can explore the northernmost part of Maratea's coast.

WHERE TO SLEEP AND EAT Most hotels in Maratea are strictly for the wealthy, but the tourist offices can help you find something within your budget from lists of hotels and private rooms. Modern, white-tiled **Settebello** (Località Fiumicello, head toward cove on Via Santavenere, tel. 0973/877441) sits in a beach cove in one of Maratea's suburbs. Request a room with a balcony on the beach side for a view of the precipitous cliffs that surround the inlet. Doubles run L60,000–L100,000 (prices vary according to season), and all rooms have private baths. **Camping Maratea** (Località Castrocucco, tel. 0973/877580), at the southern end of Castrocucco, is by far the most affordable option in town, despite the fact that you'll pay L11,000–L15,000 for a two-person tent site plus L7,000–L11,000 per person (prices vary depending on the season). What's more, only two buses head out to the site from the train station and both are at night (8:10 PM and 12:20 AM); plan ahead or be prepared to pay around L20,000 for a cab.

Maratea is one of the more expensive towns in southern Italy. To save money, stop at one of the many small food markets. If you've decided to live it up however, this is a great place to splurge on delicious, fresh seafood. At **Trattoria Da Cesare** (Contrada Certusa 52, no phone; closed Thurs. Sept.–June) try spaghetti *al nero di seppia* (with a black sauce of cuttlefish ink; L12,000) and fresh grilled fish for around L35,000. You can still gorge yourself on local pastries without going broke at **L'Antica Pasticceria Iannini Dolci e Rosli** (off Via Rovita 9, in the centro storico, no phone). Try regional desserts flavored with *pasta di mandorle* (almond paste), *cedro* (citron), or *noci* (walnuts).

Calabria

Calabria is the southernmost province on the Italian peninsula, the toe of the boot poised to kick the island of Sicily clear into Africa. This impoverished agrarian region, controlled by the Mafia (known down here as the *'ndrangheta*), displays many of the *Godfather*-like stereotypes foreigners have about southern Italy. The Mafia isn't a threat to travelers, but its effects are certainly visible: As you travel through the region, you'll notice whole towns bereft of young people, who've fled north. What's left are lots of old men, who hang out in piazze and complain about the heat, the corrupt government, and the problems of the south.

Calabria does possess features that should not be missed by anyone with an interest in the Mezzogiorno. Its mountainous regions are Italy's last bastion of unspoiled nature—a rugged expanse of giant mountains, hilltop towns, and forests that quickly drops off to a flat coastline that extends along the crystal blue waters of the Tyrrhenian and Ionian seas. Of the two coasts, the Tyrrhenian claims the lovelier seaside towns, particularly those farther south. The towns along the Ionian coast, to the east, seem designed for travelers to pass right through—most consist of little more than a main street with houses and businesses built up on either side— although the water itself is calm, clean, and oftentimes empty; if you're looking for a beach

Fountain Facts

Fountain water is the lifeblood of the cruelly hot south, and no simple aluminum box with a stainless steel button will serve as a suitable conduit. Southern Italy's fountains, especially those in the old quarters, are comparatively grand affairs: a lion's head, a serpent, a brass faucet in a marble seashell. Everyone, regardless of class or occupation, age or attitude, takes a hit, fills a water bottle, or somehow relies upon their neighborhood fountain. As long as there's no sign that reads IMPOTABILE (undrinkable), go ahead and take a slug for yourself.

with lots of towel space, you'll certainly find it on the Ionian. The town of Cosenza makes a good stop for travelers on their way to exploring the mountains, and the beaches are no more than an hour's drive by car, although public transportation is another story. Reggio disappoints as the region's capital, despite its fantastic archaeological museum, but it does serve as a good transportation hub, especially if you're on your way to Sicily.

Cosenza

The first major Calabrian city you reach from the north, Cosenza holds few apparent charms. In fact, most travelers come here in order to leave: It's the departure point for one of Italy's most spectacular train rides, through the pine-forested mountains of the Sila Massif. Cosenza itself displays the schizophrenic character of many southern towns. The crumbling centro storico will transport you back to medieval times, while the new town hustles and bustles without much of anything interesting going on. The city feels as though it's been evacuated during summer, as residents head for the hills and beaches.

Like so many other Calabrian towns, Cosenza was originally inhabited by ancient Greeks of the Magna Grecia. In 204 BC it was conquered by the Romans and became an important link between Rome, Reggio Calabria, and Sicily. By the 16th century, with the foundation of the Academia Cosentina, it became an important Renaissance city, drawing artists, poets, and thinkers from all over the peninsula. Today, Cosenza is still considered to be one of the region's greatest cultural centers, especially with the fairly recent establishment of the University of Calabria.

BASICS The **APT tourist office** (Corso Mazzini 92, 3rd floor, tel. 0984/27271) is open Monday–Saturday 8–8. The **Banca Nazionale del Lavoro** (Corso Mazzini 86, tel. 0984/6861) is the best place in town to change traveler's checks and the only place with ATM machines on the Plus system. It's open weekdays 8:20–1:30 and 2:45–4. Cosenza's **TELECOM** office (Via dell'Autostazione, above the main bus station) is open weekdays 8:30–1 and 4:30–8, Saturday 8:30–1. The **post office** (Via Vittorio Veneto, at end of Via Piave off Corso Mazzini, tel. 0984/26435) is open Monday–Saturday 9–12:30 and 4:30–5:30.

Leaving town may be the best part of your visit to Cosenza. The train that departs from here, en route to Camagliatello, Lorica, and San Giovanni in Fiore, climbs through some of Italy's most amazing natural scenery— ravines, pine forests, and shimmering lakes—en route to the mountains.

COMING AND GOING

➢ **BY TRAIN** • Cosenza's **train station** (sometimes referred to as Cosenza-Vagliolise or Stazione Nuova) is located in the modern part of town, a short bus ride from the hotels and the centro storico; take Bus 5, which leaves from the station every 20 minutes. **Ferrovie della Calabria (FC)** trains head to San Giovanni in Fiore (5 daily, 2½ hrs, L3500), stopping en route at Camigliatello (1 hr 20 min, L2500). Purchase tickets at the FC booth, open daily 6 AM–8 PM. **Ferrovie dello Stato (FS)** runs frequent train service to Paola (15 min, L2700), a major hub for travel along the Tyrrhenian coast, and Reggio di Calabria (3 hrs, L19,000), the region's capital. FS trains also head for the Ionian coast, running to Sibari (1 hr 10 min, L5700) and Metaponto (3 hrs, L11,700). The station offers luggage storage (L1500 per piece per 24 hours; open daily 6 AM–7:45 PM), and there are info booths that can help with trains and buses throughout the region.

➢ **BY BUS** • Ferrovie della Calabria (tel. 0984/36851) runs frequent buses to the Sila Massif, stopping in Camigliatello (45 min, L2800) and San Giovanni in Fiore (1½ hrs, L4800). Buses leave from the **Piazza Autostazione depot**, off Corso Mazzini, and from the main train station in the center of town. Both have information booths. The ticket booth at the Autostazione is open daily 6 AM–7:30 PM.

GETTING AROUND Cosenza is a sizable city, but for the most part you need only concern yourself with the centro storico, which includes the area around the old train station and a small group of budget lodgings. Orange **ATAC** buses run through town; the most crucial one for visitors is Bus 5, which connects the train station to the city center (where the hotels and sights are) and stops at the Piazza Autostazione bus depot. Buy tickets (L1000) at tabacchi near bus stops. Buses run every 20–25 minutes 6 AM–9 PM and every 40 minutes 9 PM–11:30 PM. Two small bridges lead from Piazza Matteotti into the old quarter. To reach the most historically important part of town, take **Corso Mazzini** from Piazza Ferra, near the Autostazione, to Piazza dei Bruzi just a few blocks before the oldest part of the centro storico.

WHERE TO SLEEP For a city of its size, Cosenza has a disappointingly slim selection in the budget lodging catagory. Your best bet is **Albergo Bruno** (Corso Mazzini 27, 1 block from Viale Trieste, tel. 0984/73889), with cheap, clean, and more pleasant rooms (doubles L55,000, L70,000 with bath) than the small, dilapidated sign in front suggests. The main drawback is the sketchy neighborhood; women might not want to wander around alone at night. Your second choice is **Hotel Centrale** (Via del Tigrai, off Corso Mazzini, tel. 0984/73681), which charges a budget-busting L118,000 for doubles with bath.

FOOD Cosenza doesn't overflow with places to eat, but you can easily live off the cream-filled *cornetti* (croissants) that the townsfolk whip up with a passion. **La Cornetteria** (Piazza dei Bruzi 6, across from police station; open daily 7–noon and 7–1 AMish) serves up cream, amaretto, peach, and chocolate cornetti to a late-night crowd. If your budget is tight, hunt for a slice of pizza and a beer at one of several pizzerias around the main streets of the centro storico. The cheapest option of all is the **open market**, held mornings Monday–Saturday on Via Panubio, between Via Puvocati and Corso Umberto. **Ristorante da Giocondo** (Via Piave 53, off Corso Mazzini, tel. 0984/29810) is a favorite among locals, with traditional fare in a simple but elegant white-tablecloth setting. Primi run about L8000; try one of the delicious grilled fish dishes as a secondo (L9000–L12,000). The restaurant is open Monday–Saturday 7 PM–midnight. Most restaurants close in August, when residents head for the coast.

Next door to the APT office on Corso Mazzini, you'll find a candy store selling one of Cosenza's specialties: decadent and delectable chocolate-covered figs.

WORTH SEEING Cosenza's centro storico is worth a day of exploration. From the newer part of town, take the **Ponte Mario Martire** over the Busento River to the old town's **Piazza Valdesi**. From here, Corso Telesio crosses the heart of the centro storico, running through Piazza del Duomo and passing Cosenza's **Cattedrale** (Piazza del Duomo, tel. 0984/77864; open daily 8–12:30 and 2:30–8:30). Built in the 12th and 13th centuries, the cathedral's construction resembles the Gothic style of Provence, France. The interior was redone in full baroque 600 years later. Behind the Cattedrale in Piazza Giano Parrasio is the **Palazzo dell'Arcivescovado** (Piazza Giano Parrasio 16, tel. 0984/24819), containing a museum of artifacts from Cosenza's varied conquerors. You can also visit the church of **San Francesco d'Assisi** (Via S. Francesco d'Assisi, above Piazza Valdesi, tel. 0984/26063; open daily 7–noon and 4–6:30), with its 13th-century doorway and elegant cloister. A long hike from the city center is the **Norman castle** (admission free) seriously damaged by a series of earthquakes. Though the interior is bare and hardly worth the calories burned, the castle does offer a great view of the countryside. The castle is open daily 9–1 and 3:30–sunset (9–1 only in winter).

Near Cosenza

When the sweltering summer heat descends upon Calabria's coast and warm scirocco winds blowing northward from Africa set your backpack on fire, it might come as something of a shock to know that a cool "Little Switzerland" exists in the heart of the region. The **Sila Massif** is an immense, largely unspoiled swath of pine-wooded mountains, where you'll find the best hiking, fishing, and camping in southern Italy. The massif consists of three sections: the **Sila Greca** to the north, the central **Sila Grande** (the largest of the three zones, including the most accessible and interesting villages and campsites), and the **Sila Piccola** to the south. The alpine countryside teems with tumbling brooks, mountains capped with snow in winter, and every type of flora and fauna imaginable. As the Sila Massif gains recognition for its natural beauty, the villages are becoming increasingly touristed, but you can still spend quality time communing with nature here. The best way to approach the Sila is to take the mountain train from Cosenza to the alpine villages in the Sila Grande, including **Camigliatello**, **Lorica**, and **San Giovanni in Fiore**. Lorica, though difficult to reach, provides one of the best natural settings in the region. San Giovanni is humdrum, but the train ride there and the unusual layout of the town make it a worthwhile day trip. West of Cosenza, the Tyrrhenian coast unapologetically offers surf, sun, and lots of beach towns, and train service makes travel here relatively easy. Much train traffic goes through unappealing **Paola**, a main stop on the FS line with connections to Taranto, Brindisi, Cosenza, and Rome.

CAMIGLIATELLO

The first alpine village that you reach on the train from Cosenza, Camigliatello is the Sila Grande's most touristed (and most expensive) town. It caters to a middle-aged crowd looking to be pampered in the upscale hotels that fill the town center. In spite of this wealthy element, Camigliatello betrays signs of Calabria's impoverished condition, with its worn-around-the-edges look and relative emptiness even in high season. The town offers almost nothing in terms of organized fair-weather sports, and is really hopping only during the winter ski season. Another deterrent to visitors is the fact that very little here is accessible without a car. However, if you're the kind of person who likes to hike aimlessly and enjoy beautiful natural surroundings without the bother of intrusive crowds, Camigliatello is worth a visit. For those less energetic types who appreciate nature's beauty but not its inconveniences, a visit to Camigliatello is advisable only for the breathtaking scenery you'll pass on the train ride here from Cosenza.

Once in town, stop at the *Casa del Forestere* or ranger's station (*see* Basics, *below*) for info and maps, then get out of town and explore the countryside. A 12-kilometer hike on a country road leads away from the train station and town center to Lake Cecita. The reservoir is almost overwhelmed by the towering hills and an abundance of masticating cows. Camping in most of the area is illegal, but the law is not strictly enforced as long as you're discreet. They're mainly concerned about forest fires, since the area gets dry as a bone by summer. Several signposted campsites just off the road to the lake are legal and relatively rustic. If you visit in winter, the **Complesso Monte Curcio** ski resort (Via Tasso, off Via Roma, tel. 0984/578037 or 0984/579400) is right in Camigliatello. A day of skiing on the resort's three runs costs about L25,000; another L20,000–L30,000 extra buys you skis and boots for the day.

The resort town of Camigliatello does double tourist duty: During summer, Italians come to escape the heat, breathe in fresh mountain air, and venture into the pine woods; during winter, they return to ski the 1,700-meter-high Tasso Ski Trail on Monte Curcio.

BASICS The **Pro Loco** office (Via Roma 5, tel. 0984/578091), open daily 9–noon and 3–6, sells phone cards and has phone books from all over Italy. For hotel and campsite listings, plus information on hiking and skiing in the area, try next door at the **Casa del Forestere** (tel. 0984/578243), open July–early September, Monday–Saturday 8–8, Sunday 8:30–1 (reduced hours in winter).

COMING AND GOING The most scenic route to Camigliatello is by train from Cosenza. Four to five trains (1½ hrs, L2500) leave the Cosenza daily, the first between 6:30 and 7 AM and the last around 2 PM. After exploring Camigliatello, you can hop back on the **FS line** and continue on to San Giovanni in Fiore (40 min, L2700). Buses also leave Cosenza regularly for Camigliatello (45 min, L2800) and San Giovanni in Fiore (½ hr, L1700). Camigliatello's bus stop is on **Via Roma**, in front of the town pharmacy, where you can buy tickets (also sold on board). From where the train and the bus both leave you, it's about a 300-meter walk down Via Roma to the small town center.

WHERE TO SLEEP AND EAT Camigliatello has plenty of hotels, but most cater to the wealthy leisure crowd instead of the humble hiker. The cheapest place in town is **Mancuso** (Viale del Turismo, parallel to Via Roma, tel. 0984/578002), with rather forlorn-looking doubles for L36,000–L54,000; in August there's a mandatory full pension, boosting the prices up to L70,000 per person. **Leonetti** (Via Roma 44, tel. 0984/578075) has spick-and-span doubles with bath for L60,000–80,000; ask for one of the newly remodeled rooms.

You can camp legally at a designated campsite or slink off into the woods and sleep (this is illegal, but generally no one will bother you as long as you don't light a fire). The closest campground, **La Fattoria** (Località La Bonia, tel. 0984/578364), is about 5 kilometers outside Camigliatello in the small town of La Bonia. As with most Italian campgrounds, you don't really have to rough it here—amenities include a restaurant, a bar, tennis, minigolf, and even a small bowling alley. Double bungalows with bath go for L70,000 a night, or you can pitch a tent for L4000–L5000 on a wide-open field in front of a mountain range. The bathrooms are clean, the showers are hot, and the place is rarely crowded. From the campground, you can start the 12-kilometer hike to Lake Cecita (ask the management for the most scenic route). To reach the campground, take Via Roma away from town and follow signs through several small villages; if you're not up for a hike, hitch a ride from the top of Via Roma. During the off-season, only one bus runs to the site, leaving at 6:15 AM and returning around 1 PM; doublecheck the times with the Casa del Forestere (*see* Basics, *above*).

If you're staying at a campground or hotel and you are a big eater, consider springing for full board (breakfast, lunch, and dinner) since most restaurants in town are part of a lodging establishment. Otherwise, choose from one of the cafés or pizzerias (they're all pretty much the same) or pick up picnic supplies at one of the small markets on Via Roma. Don't miss the region's specialty, *funghi* (mushrooms) gathered from the nearby hills.

PRAIA A MARE

The touristy hangout of Praia a Mare, on the Tyrrhenian coast just south of Maratea, is perfect if you're nostalgic for an American-inspired scene of water slides, fast food, and crowds serious about fooling around. It's one of the most developed resort towns on the coast, but twilight masks its excesses well, and the town turns quite beautiful as the masses temporarily retreat to their hotels. If noise and congestion are a turnoff though, hop back on the train.

If you do choose to stay, follow signs up the steep set of stairs in back of the town center to the **Grotta del Santuario della Madonna**, open daily 9–1 and 3–6 (later in summer). The view from atop the coastal mountains is astounding. You should also check out the grottoes around the **Isola di Dino**, a squarish hunk of rock about a kilometer down the beach. The island is within swimming distance of shore, but for L10,000 an hour you can rent a little *pattino* (boat) at one of the many stands on the beach and paddle there. Stop into the **Pro Loco** office (Via Crispi 4, tel. 0985/777030), open daily 10–12:30 and 6:30–10, for info on the grottoes. A great way to get around Praia a Mare and the surrounding beaches is by moped or scooter. You can rent scooters (L45,000 an hr), as well as mountain bikes (L8000 an hr), at **Noleggio Praia '90** (Via F. Cilea 24–29, left of train station; open Monday–Saturday 8 AM–11 PM).

COMING AND GOING Praia a Mare's train station, **Praja**, on the main Reggio di Calabria line, handles almost all public transport in and out of Praia. Several trains leave daily for Cosenza (1 hr 10 min, L8000) and Rome (5 hrs, L33,400), and trains to nearby beach towns like Scalea (15 min, L2000) run even more frequently.

WHERE TO SLEEP AND EAT In town and on the beach, you'll find a slew of big, expensive hotels. A better bet is **Pensione La Piedigrotta** (Via Nicola Maiorano, in Piazza Lomonoco, tel. 0985/72192), with bright, clean rooms and a good restaurant. The pension is in a quiet part of town, although not far from the train tracks. Doubles run L40,000–L45,000 (L55,000–L58,000 with bath). Half pension runs L55,000–L65,000 per person in a room without bath. **Hotel Chiaia** (Via Leonardo da Vinci 18, off Viale della Libertà, tel. 0985/72445), right on the beach, has a decent restaurant/pizzeria with outdoor seating. Doubles with bath run L60,000–L90,000, while you can get half pension for L55,000–L75,000 per person, L15,000 more for full pension (mandatory late-July and August).

You can buy fruit and vegetables at the **outdoor market** (Via Leonardo Da Vinci, off Via Turati toward the lungomare), open daily 7 AM–1 PM, or sample refreshing *granita* (an Italian Slurpee; L3000) at **Bar Scarziponna** (Piazza Italia, no phone). Scarziponna is open daily 7:30 AM–11 PM (later in summer). If you're craving fresh-out-of-the-oven, cream-filled croissants late at night, **Il Fornaio** (Via della Libertà) serves them for L1200, 7 PM–7 AM. They also dish out late-night squares of pizza.

There are a number of dance clubs around Praia a Mare, the most happening of which is **Harem** (Località Fiuzzi), a 30-minute walk south along the lungomare. This open-air beachside disco has two dance floors, one techno and one mainstream, and is open Thursday–Sunday 11 PM–4 AM. There's a cover of L15,000–L20,000, depending on the day of the week. Right next door, you can play late-night miniature golf at **Fiuzziland** (Località Fiuzzi), open daily 9 PM–4 AM in summer. In town, spend a mellow evening at **Bix Pub** (Via Turati 79,

Prime Pit Stops

Trains from Cosenza run frequently along the Tyrrhenian coast, which bursts with untouristed beach towns and long stretches of pristine sand. Below are a couple great places to hop off, stretch your legs, and relax until the next train comes along.

- *Pretty Cirella, between Cosenza and Praia a Mare, has been on the wrong side of history one too many times for its architectural health. It was razed when the Romans destroyed Carthage, leveled by the Aragonese, and destroyed during the Napoleonic era. No one has had the heart to rebuild a real town since, but a few choice campsites and a lovely pension lie near the tranquil beach, where you can rent a canoe or begin the 500-meter swim to small Isola Cirella. Il Fortino (tel. 0985/86085), with a small bar/café and a private inlet, has camping for L13,000–L15,000 per person. One of the owners, a lecturer in England during the school year, hangs out at the bar telling visitors all about Cirella's sights and history. The wonderful, air-conditioned Hotel Ducale (Via Vittorio Veneto 254, tel. 0985/86051) was once the garden of Duke Gonzaga Catalano, and its old-world charm remains intact. In low season you'll pay L70,000–L90,000 for a single with bath, L90,000–L110,000 for a double with bath, and L70,000–L140,000 per person for full pension. Prices vary depending on the season but haggling is always a possibility.*

- *On the southern Tyrrhenian coast between Cosenza (1 hr, L9800) and Reggio (1 hr, L8000), appealing Pizzo overlooks 6 kilometers of true-blue water. Get off the train at Pizzo Vibo on the outskirts of town (from here, hourly buses run to town every day but Sunday; buy tickets in the station's bar). Once a humble fishing village, Pizzo is now overrun by vacationing Italians during July and August, but the old quarter retains its charm, and great beaches stretch along both sides of the marina. Pizzo may be best as a day trip, since the hostel—in a castle atop the old quarter—was closed for restoration at press time, and campsites are served only irregularly by bus. The closest campground, Villaggio Europa (tel. 0963/534936), is on the beach 3 kilometers from town. It's open from May to September, and you'll pay L8800 per person and L7000 per tent. Whatever the duration of your stay, pay a visit to the quaint little castle, famous as the site where Joachim Murat, king of Naples, was executed in 1815 after fleeing to Pizzo when Napoléon fell to the Austrians. Supposedly, his last words were "Mirate al petto e salvate il viso" (Aim for the body and save the face). Oh, the vanities of kings.*

tel. 0985/74282), where you can down a few beers (L4000) and snack on *arancini di riso* (fried rice balls) while listening to cool jazz tunes.

ROSSANO

Rossano, with its well-preserved medieval quarter, is one of the most attractive towns on the Ionian coast. If you arrive by train from Cosenza, you'll get off right near the ocean in the new town, **Rossano Scalo**, a bustling place of little cultural interest. From the train station exit in Piazza Leonardo Da Vinci, an orange city bus (hourly, L1000; last bus 8:20 PM) takes you 5 kilometers up the winding hill to the centro storico, which contains several important churches and a museum overflowing with religious icons and treasures. Housed in the **Museo Diocesano d'Arte Sacra** is Rossano's prize cultural artifact—the *Codex Purpureus* (Purple Codex), a mint-condition manuscript of biblical stories dating back to the Byzantine era. The museum is open July and August, Monday–Saturday 10–12:30 and 5–6:30, Sunday 10:30–12:30. The nearby church of **San Marco**, built in the 9th century, is an elegant yet extremely simple example of the Byzantine style. Aside from Rossano's important monuments, the town is a congenial place to spend a day hanging out in a piazza with the old-timers or wandering through winding streets. If you're still around in the evening, try **Trattoria Pizzeria La Bizantina** (in front of the church of San Marco) for reasonably priced regional specialties. Afterwards, make your way back to the new city's bars and discos or content yourself with the more staid goings-on in the main square.

COMING AND GOING Rossano makes a good day trip from Cosenza by train (2 hrs, L8000) or, better yet, by bus (1 hr, L7000). The town is on the **FS train line**, which travels the length of the Ionian coast. The trip to Reggio di Calabria (L26,200) takes six hours. Buy your ticket on the train since the station is entirely unmanned. **SITA buses** drop you off in front of the train station. You'll find a SITA bus schedule at **I.A.S. Scura** (Via Luca De Rasis 9, tel. 0983/511790), open Monday–Saturday 8:30–12:40 and 4–7; buy your ticket on the bus. **SIMET** (Via Luca De Rasis 49, across from train station, tel. 0983/512793) handles northbound buses to cities such as Florence (9 hrs, L71,500). Their office is open weekdays 9–1 and 4:30–8, Saturday 9–1.

Reggio di Calabria

Whether you're traveling through Calabria to Sicily or bumming around the coast at the bottom of the boot, chances are at some point you'll pass through Reggio, Calabria's capital. With the exception of the wonderful Museo Nazionale della Magna Grecia (*see* Worth Seeing, *below*), a few good fish restaurants, and a stupendous pension on the outskirts of town, there aren't many reasons to stick around. The earthquakes that rocked the town at the turn of the century and heavy aerial bombing during World War II leveled most of the historic buildings and destroyed cultural treasures. The city that's left is "modern" in the southern-Italian sense of the word: There are plenty of shops, clothing stores, and traffic, but an exhausted air hangs over the city—a combination of the hot climate, a high unemployment rate, and a Mafia-driven political system.

Reggio is the best place in Calabria to find a decent bottle of wine, the homemade Cirò in most Calabrian small towns being an acquired taste, to put it kindly. Reggio's bars also serve an excellent granita (something between a sorbet and a slushy, usually flavored with lemon or coffee syrup).

BASICS Reggio has more tourist information offices than sights worth seeing. The most convenient branch is at Reggio's main train station, the **Stazione Centrale** (tel. 0965/27120). Also strategically located is the **AAST** booth at Reggio's airport (tel. 0965/643291). Both offices are officially open Monday–Saturday 8–8, though the hours often vary. The **Istituto Bancario San Paolo di Torino** (Viale Zerbi 21, tel. 0965/897474; open weekdays 8:25–1:25 and 2:45–4:10) changes money and traveler's checks and has an ATM that accepts credit cards. It's one block from Stazione Lido (*see* Coming and Going, *below*).

Make phone calls from the **TELECOM** office (Corso Garibaldi 187, tel. 0965/3601), open Monday–Saturday 9–2 and 4–7:30, Sunday 8–3. Reggio's **post office** (Via Miraglia 14, tel. 0965/24606) is between the train stations, off Corso Vittorio Emanuele. It's open weekdays 8–5:30, Saturday 8–1 (closed mid-July–Aug. after 1:30 PM).

COMING AND GOING You can see Sicily across the narrow channel that divides the island from the mainland. **Villa San Giovanni**, a small, unattractive town a short train ride from Reggio, is the best place to catch a ferry to Sicily. The **Ferrovie dello Stato (FS)** runs 30 ferries a day (20 min, L5000) to Messina, 14 on Sundays and holidays. The tourist office at the Stazione Centrale has a copy of the departure schedule, but for the most precise info you can contact the **F.F.S.S. ferry office** (Stazione Marittima, tel. 0965/898123).

➤ **BY TRAIN** • Reggio has two main train stations within several kilometers of each other. All traffic stops at **Stazione Centrale** (Piazza Garibaldi, tel. 0965/898123), a train hub with service to most major Italian cities. Two main lines branch off from Reggio, one heading up the Ionian coast toward Taranto and Brindisi and the other traveling up the Tyrrhenian coast toward Naples and Rome. Trains run regularly to Cosenza (3 hrs, L19,000), Locri (1½ hrs, L8000), and Villa San Giovanni (10 min, L2000), where the ferry departs for Sicily. Frequent trains also run to Lamezia (2½ hrs, L11,700), a major junction for points north, and Paola (4 hrs, L15,500), with connections into the Calabrian interior. Several trains leave daily for the Rome Termini Station (7 hrs, L51,200). Reggio's other train station, **Stazione Lido** (Corso Garibaldi, tel. 0965/898123), a five-minute train ride north of Stazione Centrale, is closer to the sights, restaurants, port, and town center, but serves fewer destinations than Stazione Centrale, with trains leaving for the Tyrrhenian Coast. Both stations have 24-hour luggage storage.

➤ **BY BUS** • It's best to come and go from Reggio by train, but if you want to take the bus to one of the nearby towns, you have a slew of companies to choose from. **Azienda Municipale Autobus** (tel. 0976/620121; open daily 7 AM–11 PM) has frequent bus service to several regional towns. You can also get prices and schedules from the **Simonetta** travel agency (Corso Garibaldi 521, near Stazione Lido, tel. 0965/33145), open Monday–Saturday 9–1 and 4:30–8:30. Reggio's main bus stop, in front of Stazione Centrale in Piazza Garibaldi, has schedules of all bus departures. Frequent local buses run between Stazione Centrale and Stazione Lido along Corso Vittorio Emanuele and Corso Garibaldi. Tickets cost L800 and can be purchased at the newsstand (open Mon.–Sat. 5 AM–9 PM, Sun. 5–noon) in front of Stazione Centrale.

➤ **BY PLANE** • Reggio's **Svincolo Aeroporto**, about 5 kilometers from town, handles both domestic and connecting international flights. Three companies fly here: **Sogas**, which charter planes to Paris, **Aliasiatica**, and **Alitalia** (tel. 0965/643095; ticket booth open daily 6 AM–11 PM). To reach the airport from the train station, catch local Bus 102/5, 113/5, 118, 119, 122, or 125. Buses make the 20-minute trip (L800) from Stazione Centrale every 15–20 minutes from 5 AM to about 10 PM. A taxi from the station to the airport will cost L20,000–L30,000.

WHERE TO SLEEP Not many tourists spend the night here, though you might have to contend with the workers and immigrants who fill the budget hotels near both train stations. These places are simple and drab, but if you're willing to venture to the outskirts of town, you'll find a wonderful pension, the **Albergo Eremo** (Via Eremo Botte 12, tel. 0965/22433). Quiet, immaculate, and affordable, this place is southern Italy at its best. Two kind, older Calabrian women have been running the hotel and tending its jasmine-scented garden since 1962. Doubles go for L55,000 (L65,000 with bath). Take Bus 7 (hourly, L800; last bus 9 PM) from Stazione Centrale.

If the Eremo is full, try **Albergo Noel** (Via Zerbi 13, tel. 0965/330044), located 50 meters from Stazione Lido. It's on a drab, urban street, but it's near the sea and a short walk from the center of town. The rooms are clean, though the brown tile floors might offend your aesthetic sensibilities. Doubles (all with bath) go for L60,000. **Pensione S. Bernadetta** (Corso Garibaldi 585, tel. 0965/894500), on the fifth floor of a building across from Stazione Centrale, has doubles for L40,000, none with bath.

FOOD Reggio has a decent selection of moderately priced restaurants near Stazione Centrale. Standard fare around here consists of an obligatory pasta dish (around L8000), a garden salad with tomatoes (about L5000), a secondo of grilled fish (L9000–L12,000), and a bottle of Cirò, a regional red wine. **Ristorante Ancora** (Piazza Monsolido-Lido Comunale, tel. 0965/876380; follow sign down to beach from Viale Genovese Zerbi) serves incredible *risotto frutti di mare* (seafood risotto; L9000) and *pesce spada alla griglia* (grilled swordfish; L15,000), though the best deal is their L15,000 menu turistico. On the same street as Albergo Eremo (*see* Where to Sleep, *above*) you'll find **Taverna degli Ulivi** (Via Eremo Botte 32, tel. 0965/891461; closed Sun.), dishing out Calabrian fare such as *maccaruni i casa* (homemade pasta with meat sauce; L7000) and *braciolette alla calabrese* (broiled spears of mixed meats; L11,000). They're open for dinner only. For groceries hit the **A&O Supermarket** (closed Sun.) in Piazza Garibaldi, right in front of the Stazione Centrale.

WORTH SEEING Reggio is a relatively easy town to negotiate, since most interesting things transpire between the two train stations. The city's main attraction is the world-famous **Museo Nazionale della Magna Grecia** (Piazza de Nava, tel. 0965/812255; admission: L6000), on Corso Garibaldi near Stazione Lido. The museum is dedicated mainly to archaeological finds from ancient Greek settlements in southern Italy (known as the Magna Grecia). The *Bronzi di Riace*, two bronze statues dating back to the 5th century BC, steal the show. They were discovered in 1972 when a diver off the coast of the small town of Riace caught a glimpse of an arm protruding from the ocean floor. Remarkably, the waters of the Ionian Sea were kind to the statues, preserving them for more than 2,000 years. Other than the museum, about the most interesting thing you'll see in Reggio is old men—unemployed or retired, sometimes as crooked as Don Corleone—who create what little character this city has.

AFTER DARK At night, Reggio is known for its *passeggiata* (stroll). From the main train station, head down to the **lungomare** (parallel to Corso Garibaldi) around twilight to walk with the city folk and catch a great view of the Sicilian coast. Heading in the direction of Stazione Lido, the street ends at **Piazza Independenza** and **Gelateria Cesare**, where they serve a mean *mela verde* (green apple). A good evening hangout is **Metrò** (Via Zecca 3, off Via Giudecca), halfway between Stazione Centrale and Stazione Lido, with beers, sandwiches, and occasional live music until 2 AM.

NEAR REGGIO

The coast near Reggio broils during August, when temperatures climb as high as 105° Fahrenheit. From the capital, trains run up the Ionian coast as far as Taranto, and along the Tyrrhenian coast, passing old fishing villages like **Pizzo**, **Tropea**, and **Scilla** with well-preserved castles and clifftop views.

LOCRI Only 80 kilometers north of Reggio on the Ionian coast, the small town of Locri hugs the water, offering clean beaches and several budget hotels. Locri suffers from (or enjoys, depending on how you look at it) near-Saharan temperatures, which means you can swim in its waters almost any time of year. Quintessentially Calabrian, Locri represents the best and worst of the Ionian coast. The main street can't handle the traffic as residents and vacationers rush toward surrounding beaches, and the town suffers from an excess of concrete housing projects and drab shops. *But* (and it's a big but) the beaches here have been rated as some of the cleanest in all Italy. Only a five-minute walk from the town center, they provide respite from the heat on even the worst days.

At siesta time (noon to 4) in summer, Locri turns into a ghost town from a Wild West movie: You can either sleep in your hotel room with the shades drawn, or put on your cowboy outfit and walk through the sleepy town beneath the blazing sun, acting like Clint Eastwood in a Sergio Leone flick.

While in Locri, you can walk or hitch about 5 kilometers up the main road to a set of rather skimpy **Greek ruins**. The free local museum that fronts the site is open Tuesday–Saturday 9–1 and 3:30–7:30, Sunday 9–1.

Regular trains run to Locri from Reggio (1½ hrs, L7200). You'll find several hotels on and around Viale Matteotti, a few blocks up from Via Garibaldi in front of the train station. **Hotel Teseyon** (Viale Matteotti, tel. 0964/29147) won't wow you with its decor, but it's large, modern, clean, and convenient to both the beach and the town center. Doubles with bath cost L70,000–L90,000.

SICILY

14

By Oliver Schwaner-Albright

Sicily is one big island of contrasts. Salty old farmers, widows in black veils, weathered villages, dry mountains, and clear seas can all be found—in flashback scenes from *The Godfather* or even in your travels. But many cynics, most of them northern Italians, take this stereotype and turn it on its head, believing Sicily to be about nothing but poverty, backwardness, and unemployment, under the all-seeing eye of the Mafia. The truth is that Sicily is all of those things and much more—a varied place with a rich history and an uncertain future.

The roots of Sicily's diversity can be found in its tumultuous past. Over the centuries, the island's handy position, fertile soil, and warm climate encouraged pretty much every great Mediterranean and European civilization to go through the trouble of invading it. The first conquerors to make a name for themselves were the Greeks—both Hellenics from the city-states, and Punics from Troy—in the 8th century BC. These early travelers first colonized the Ionian coast, and one of their initial settlements, Siracusa, quickly rose to become one of the most powerful cities in antiquity. The ambitious Siracusans clashed with the Carthaginians stationed in the western part of the island, and after centuries of beating each other up, Rome crushed them both. By the 3rd century BC Sicily was little more than one big Roman Club Med. The next major change came when the North Africans overran the island in the 9th century, introducing mathematics, couscous, and a third prophet. The island entered its golden period with the 1061 AD invasion of the Norman king Roger I. His son Roger II was crowned the first Norman king of Sicly in 1130, and turned Palermo into Europe's intellectual and cultural center. A later Norman successor, Frederick I, managed to steer the kingdom with a strong system of law and order, building fortresses throughout the island and patronizing the arts. After Frederick's death in 1250, countless European nobilities made loud claims to the island, keeping Sicily in a repressive and backward state of feudalism.

Things got so bad in Sicily in the late 19th century that over a million natives emigrated to America.

The defining moment in Sicly's history came in 1860, when Giusseppe Garibaldi landed with his 1,000 red shirts, sending out Italy's first call for independence from foreign rule in the modern era. But when Garibaldi kicked out the Bourbons, he created a power vacuum that was quickly filled by an instituion of Padrones and their armed families, which we know as the Mafia (*see box, below*). Just as troublesome as the medieval-minded nobles they replaced, the Mafia stifled the island's economic growth and creativity while the rest of Europe was soaring through the last stages of the industrial revolution. Since WWII, the Italian state has tried to modernize the island in spite of the Mafia, but the campaign has been only partially successful, regardless of all the shiny new highways and apartment blocks you'll see.

Sicily

Ustica

TO GENOVA

TO SARDINIA

TO SARDINIA

TO TUNIS

TO SARDINIA

TO TUNIS

TO TUNIS

Tyr

San Vito
lo Capo

*Golfo di
Castellammare*

Mondello

Palermo

Monreale

Bagheria

S113

Erice

Trapani
Levanzo

Favignana

Termini

A19

*EGADI
ISLANDS*

Segesta

TO MARETTIMO

Marsala

S188

A29

Corleone

S121

S115

Castelvetrano

Selinunte

Marinella

S115

S118

TO
PANTELLERIA

Sciacca

S189

Calta

S640

Co

Porto Empèdocle

Agrigento

Mediterranean Sea

S115

Licata

N

KEY
Ferry
Rail Lines

0   20 miles

0   30 km

TO LINOSA

TO NAPLES

TO NAPLES

Stromboli

Panarea

Alicudi
Filicudi

Salina

AEOLIAN ISLANDS
Lipari

Vulcano

onian Sea

Golfo di Gioia

Milazzo

Villa San
Giovanni

Capo d'Orlando
Tindari
Patti

A20

Messina

Reggio

Santo Stefano
di Camastra

A18

Castelbuono

286

S117

Randazzo

Castelmola

Taormina

Bronte

Mt. Etna

Giardini-
Naxos

Adrano

Giarre-Riposto

Regalbuto

Nicolosi

Acireale

Enna

S192

Paterno

Aci Castello

Pergusa

A19

Catania

*Golfo di
Catania*

Casale

Piazza
Armerina

S288

Ionian Sea

Caltagirone

S124

Palazzolo
Acreide

Gela

S114

Castello
Euriclo

Siracusa

Golfo di Gela

Comiso

Ragusa

S124

Noto

Avola

Scicli

Modica

*Golfo
di Noto*

S115

Pozzallo

Pachino

*Capo
Passero*

TO MALTA

In spite of its century-long economic and political instability, or perhaps because of it, much of Sicily retains its Old World flavor. The island's ancient colonies hold some of the best Greek ruins in the world: In addition to spectacular (but touristy) Siracusa and Agrigento, small and obscure Selinute and Segesta to the west have some stunning and relatively under-visited sites. History is equally alive in the capital of Palermo, where you can jump into a quagmire of Norman cathedrals and gardens, medieval alleys, crumbling palazzi, and excellent trattorias. And when you're not improving yourself in archaeological museums, you can enjoy the beaches at resorty destinations like picture-perfect Taormina and the Aeolian Islands, or in countless lesser-known coastal beachtowns. Or grab your hiking boots and head to one of nature's most stunning creations, the volatile Mt. Etna. But it's in the smaller cities—whether baroqued-out Noto or the interior mountain town of Enna—that you'll experience a Sicily almost untouched by tourism. Best of all, after a long day in the sun, you'll have the chance to sample some of Italy's best seafood, prepared with a delicate mix of Arab, Greek, and Spanish spices.

Sicily can be a bizzare, unique, beautiful place, but you'll need more than a few days to do the island justice—just traveling in between coasts is no easy task, as the train service is limited and windy roads slow down buses. When you get to where you're going, you're likely to see an unexpected combination of the clichés and the cynicisms—a crumbling sandstone church next to an Armani store, or decked-out hipsters driving past dry farmlands towards the swank disco of the moment.

Sleeping with the Fishes

Unless you tread on someone's drug-dealing territory, your travels through Sicily probably won't involve the Mafia, an oblique concept that defies succinct explanation. Many scholars believe the term is derived from the Arabic word muafa, which means both "protection" and "perseverance." Whatever the case, the word first began to circulate in Palermo in the mid-19th century, and was used in a positive sense to describe a person of admirably aggressive temperament. Over time it has come to denote the 90 or so "families" based exclusively in Sicily; crime families in Calabria and Naples are respectively called the indrugheta and the camorra. Members of the Sicilian Mafia never refer to the organization as such, preferring "La Cosa Nostra," which literally means "our thing."

The modern-day Mafia is a very influential presence in the daily lives of most Sicilians. Almost all businesses, especially in the larger cities, pay protection to one of the families, who are effectively hidden behind a cloak of omertà, the lifelong pledge of secrecy that its members commit to when first initiated. Until recently, omertà—and the fear of brutal retribution—has kept most Sicilians from even acknowledging the existence of the Mafia. Since the 1960s, the Italian government has periodically cracked down on mob activity, but the primary effect has been to incite violent assassinations of public officials—everyone from prosecutors to liberal politicians. Many people have actually accused the government of intentionally losing the war against the Mafia, claiming that while the government maintains the facade of justice, corrupt officials continue to make illicit deals with mafiosi for huge profits. But when it comes to the longevity of the Mafia, Sicilians will remind you of an insightful local saying: Calati junco 'ca passa la china (the reed lays down until the flood has passed).

WHEN TO GO When planning your trip, keep in mind that the climate here is a more like Tunis's than Rome's. A dry sirocco wind sweeps up from North Africa and the Mediterranean sun glares relentlessly, causing dehydration and serious sunburn. July and August are not the greatest times to visit. June and September are less crowded and not quite so hot, but spring inevitably takes the prize: Wild flowers abound, crowds are minimal, and the weather is so mild that you can comfortably take a dip in the sea.

COMING AND GOING Messina, on the northernmost tip of the Ionian coast, is the main gateway to Sicily and is serviced by frequent trains, hydrofoils, and ferries (*see* Messina, Coming and Going, *below*). It's also possible but expensive to ferry from Genova and Naples to Palermo, and from Reggio di Calabria to Siracusa. If you're traveling on somebody else's credit card, Catania and Palermo have airports served by national carriers.

FOOD Sicily's food is dependably fantastic and incredibly affordable. Prepare yourself for piles of olives and their oil, tons of fresh fish, ripe and luscious produce, homemade pastas, and mouth-watering pastries. Regional specialties you simply *must* taste include *involtini di pesce spada* (swordfish fillets stuffed with spices and bread crumbs); Catania's *pasta alla Norma*, with a sauce of eggplant, fresh tomatoes, basil, and ricotta; pasta *con le sarde*, an excellent Palermo dish with sardines and wild fennel; and Trapani's mind-altering *busiate al pesto trapanese*, handmade squiggly pasta in a pesto of basil, eggplant, olive oil, garlic, and crushed almonds. Dive into huge plates of fresh *tonno* (tuna), *pesce spada* (swordfish), *polpo* (octopus), *aragosta* (lobster), and *gamberetti* (shrimp), particularly on Sicily's fishing-oriented western shore, where you may also find couscous on the menu.

The Ionian Coast

The ancient ruins and natural beauty of Sicily's eastern coast make it the island's most popular destination. After passing through **Messina**'s ferry ports, head south along the coast to the idyllic seaside resort of **Taormina**—expensive and sometimes schlocky but filled with hidden piazze and stunning views of the Mediterranean. **Catania** has a limited amount of urban charm, but it's home to extensive baroque architecture and is a necessary passageway to nearby **Mt. Etna**. The volcano rises in defiance, ready to spread clouds of ash far across the Mediterranean at a moment's notice. **Siracusa**, the southernmost outpost on the Ionian coast, is noteworthy for millennia-old ruins of Greek temples and amphitheaters. Most towns along the coast are well connected by trains and buses, and the roads and tracks often run right above the sea.

Messina

Messina is at its best when seen from across the sea—when you can almost imagine that her squat buildings and sprawling streets still hold the mysteries a 3,000-year-old port should. Once you arrive though, the illusion is broken. Messina has had its share of invasions along with epidemics: Like most of southern Italy and Sicily, the portside town was taken by the Romans, Carthaginians, Arabs, Normans, Angevins, Aragonese, and Bourbons alike. But almost all traces of the town's complicated history disappeared with the 1908 earthquake, when in the course of one day, 91% of Messina was flattened, and the population dropped from 120,000 to 40,000.

Not surprisingly, there isn't much here to distract you from your wait between trains and ferries. If you have time, check out the rebuilt facade of the **duomo**, built by Norman king Roger II in the 12th century (closed for renovation at press time). The adjacent **campanile** sports Europe's second-largest astrological clock, which twirls and dances daily at noon. From the train station, it's a 15-minute ride on Bus 28 to the tiny but interesting **Museo Civico** (Via della Libertà 465, tel. 0942/358605; admission: L2000), which houses fragments of culture salvaged from the earthquake, including Caravaggio's stunning *Resurrection of Lazarus*.

BASICS The main **tourist office** (Piazza della Repubblica, tel. 090/672944) is to the right as you exit the train station. **AST** (Via Calabria 301, tel. 090/674236) is around the corner.

Both offices are open Monday–Saturday 8:30–1:30. An **information desk** (tel. 090/675234; open Mon.–Sat. 6 AM–8 PM) in the train station changes money at mediocre rates, but **Banco di Sicilia** (Via Garibaldi, at Via 1 Settembre, tel. 090/293–1130; open weekdays 8:30–1:30 and 3–5) has excellent exchange rates.

For local and international calls, head two blocks northwest of the station to **Telecom** (Via Giuseppe Natoli 59, off Via Tommaso Cannizzaro), open daily 9–1 and 4–8. Messina's **post office** (Piazza Antonello, 1 block NW of duomo, tel. 090/774437), open Monday–Saturday 8:30–6:30, is probably Italy's only outdoor postal unit.

COMING AND GOING

➤ **BY TRAIN** • From **Messina Centrale** (Piazza della Repubblica, tel. 090/673896) there's frequent service to Palermo (19 daily, 5 hrs, L19,000), Catania (14 daily, 1½ hrs, L10,000), Siracusa (12 daily, 3 hrs, L15,000), and Milazzo (15 daily in summer, 45 min, L4200), as well as Milan (5 daily, 13 hrs, L89,000), Rome (8 daily, 8 hrs, L50,000), and Naples (10 daily, 4 hrs, L37,000).

➤ **BY BUS** • **SAIS** (Piazza della Repubblica 46, left of train station, tel. 090/771914) has an office open daily 6–8 and serves Taormina (12–15 daily, 1½ hrs, L5100), Catania (9 daily, 3 hrs, L9500), and many small towns in between. Western Sicily is better served by **Giuntabus** (Via Terranova 8, tel. 090/673782), which travels to Milazzo 11 times daily in spring and summer (30 min, L3400). Look for its ticket office, open daily 6–8, five blocks west of the train station on the corner of Viale San Martino and Via Terranova.

➤ **BY BOAT** • Messina's ferry terminal, **Messina Marittima** (tel. 090/773811) is an extension of the train station—to get from one to the other, walk on the platforms or Via Calabria. Ferry companies serve the mainland ports of Villa San Giovanni (15 daily, 20 min, L1500) and Reggio di Calabria (10 daily, 35 min, L4000). You might get a funny look if you ask about taking a ferry to the Aeolian Islands from Messina, since you'll save upwards of 50% by departing from Milazzo. Messina's hydrofoil station, **SNAV** (tel. 090/367775), is 1 kilometer north of the train station on Corso Vittorio Emanuele. Hydrofoil service includes Naples (1 daily, 3 hrs, L135,000) and Reggio di Calabria (hourly, 15 min, L5000).

WHERE TO SLEEP The clean and spare **Hotel Touring** (Via N. Scotto 17, tel. 090/2938851) is only two blocks south of the train station, but be wary of the walk at night (doubles L50,000). The only things dustier and creakier than the **Albergo Roma** (Piazza del Duomo 3, tel. 090/675566) are the hotel's three proprietors, but the location can't be beat—most of the rooms have large windows over the piazza (doubles L45,000). The decidedly more upscale **Hotel Monza** (Viale San Martino 63, tel. 090/773755) caters to travelers in need of a little luxury after a long train ride; from the station follow Via Tommaso Cannizzaro downtown and turn right (doubles L53,000). The large **Il Pelitorano** campground (tel. 090/844057; closed Oct.–mid-May), in a beautiful setting about 20 kilometers north of Messina, has clean facilities and hot showers, but bring your own food. Sites cost L5500 per person, and you can rent tents (L6500). From the train station, take Bus 28 to the Rodia stop and follow the signs.

FOOD Inexpensive pizzerias abound around Corso Cavour and Via Cesare Battisti, which lie above and below the duomo, respectively. In the morning, sidewalk fruit stands line Via Tom-

A Rock and a Hard Place

Powerful rail-ferries can whisk you across the swirling Straits of Messina, but the heroes of mythology had no such assistance. Homer wrote that the ship of wayward king Odysseus only narrowly escaped treacherous Scylla (the rock) and Charybdis (the whirlpool) as he fled south past Sicily. Time passes, and modernity conquers all myths: Construction of a Reggio di Calabria–Messina bridge is due to begin in 1997.

maso Canizzaro near the university; from the train station walk down Via Tommaso Canizzaro for 20 minutes. You can get a filling pizza rustica for L7500 at **Pizzeria del Capitano** (Via dei Mille 88, no phone; closed Sun.), and wash it down afterwards with a glass of vino for L1500 from the neighboring wine bar **Fiaccetteria Vini** (Via dei Mille 74, no phone; closed Sun.).

Taormina

Taormina's beauty is a double-edged sword. The city's meandering stairways, bougainvillea-covered palazzi, and dazzling vistas make the prospect of a trip here very appealing, but in July and August you can barely see the sights for all the video cameras. The city had its start in 358 BC when Siracusa's tyrannic ruler Dionysius crushed nearby Naxos, inducing the survivors to flee to the hills and form a new city. You can see the **Teatro Greco** they built, set against an air-brushed panorama of Mt. Etna, on any travel brochure, but it's worth it to visit in person. Obscure parts of the city provide a glimpse of the Taormina that seduced Goethe and D.H. Lawrence, and the scenery really is breathtaking. Even so, consider making Taormini a day trip, as lodging here is a precious commodity and your time and lire may be spent better delving deeper into the island.

BASICS

➢ **CHANGING MONEY** • **Monte dei Paschi di Siena** (Piazza Duomo 5, tel. 0942/626010) has an ATM that will spit money out at your credit card, while **La Duca Viaggi** (Via Don Bosco 39, overlooking Piazza IX Aprile, tel. 0942/625255) runs a full-service AmEx office. You can do worse than settle for the exchange rates at **Sicilcassa** (Corso Umberto I, 2, tel. 0942/23070, across from the ASST), which is open Monday–Friday 8:30–1:30.

➢ **MAIL AND PHONES** • Make calls at **Telecom** (Via S. Pancrazio 6, tel. 0942/24669; open Mon.–Sat. 8–1 and 3–8), in the Avis agency to the right of Porta Messina. The **post office** (Piazza Medaelia d'Oro, at Corso Umberto I, tel. 0942/23010; open weekdays 8–7:30, Sat. 8–7) also changes money.

➢ **VISITOR INFORMATION** • The folks at **ASST** (Corso Umberto I, near Porta Messina, tel. 0942/23243) hand out maps, post train schedules, and help you find lodging Monday–Saturday 8–1 and 5–8.

COMING AND GOING

➢ **BY TRAIN** • **Taormina-Giardini** (tel. 0942/51026; ticket office open daily 5:30–10) serves Catania (20 daily, 45 min, L4200), Siracusa (13 daily, 2 hrs, L13,400), and Messina (29 daily, 1 hr, L4200). It sits uncharitably far below town, so leave your luggage (L1500) and hike 30 minutes uphill or take a taxi (L15,000). Buses make the trek sporadically 5 AM–10:25 PM (Sun. until 7:30 PM); buy tickets (L1500) onboard.

➢ **BY BUS** • The **SAIS** bus terminal—really just a glass booth with some schedules—has service to Messina (12–15 daily, 1½ hrs, L5100), Catania (15 daily, 1 hr 45 min, L5100), and Giardini-Naxos (26 daily, 20 min, L1500). To reach town, take a left out of the terminal on Via Pirandello, which leads to Porta Messina.

GETTING AROUND Taormina's streets cling to the rocky hillside in a crescent shape. Corso Umberto I is at the center of it all, passing east to west through Porta Messina, Piazza Vittorio Emanuele II, Piazza Duomo, and Porta Catania. Downhill from Corso Umberto I is a tangle of stepped paths that all somehow end at Via Roma or Via Bagnoli Croce, the lowest border of the city. To reach the Bay of Mazzarò and its ever-congested beach, take the Funivia (L2000 one-way before 7:45 PM, then L2500 until 10 PM) from its station on Via Pirandello for the five-minute, mass-transit-meets-Disneyland ride. From the lower Funivia station follow the signs to the pebbly shore. If you want to cruise like the natives, **California Motonoleggio** (Via Bagnoli Croce 86, across from Giardini Pubblici, tel. 0942/23769) rents Vespas (L20,000 a day) daily 7–12:30 and 3:30–8 with a credit card deposit.

WHERE TO SLEEP There are plenty of places to stay in Taormina, but few of them are cheap. Most places won't give you a room for less than two nights, and you must reserve ahead of time, although pensions are more likely to take cash-in-hand over a promise made over the phone. If you're in a pinch, try the musty **Hotel Moderno** (tel. 0942/51017; doubles L40,000) across the street from the train station, or head to Giardini-Naxos (*see* Near Taormina, *below*).

Casa Diana. If you're looking for the best deal in Taormina, the septuagenarian Signora Diana rents out homey rooms just a heartbeat from Piazza Vittorio Emanuele II. Some doubles (L40,000) have obscured views of the sea over the city's rooftops. *Via di Giovanni 6, tel. 0942/ 23898. From Piazza V. Emanuele II, walk downhill until the street becomes Via di Giovanni. 4 rooms, all with bath.*

Il Leone. Affable owner Salvatore Arrigo rents tiny and drafty but functional rooms atop his restaurant (doubles L50,000). If your room is without a view, seek out the stunning rooftop terrace. *Via Bagnoli Croci 126/A, tel. 0942/23878. 19 rooms, 10 with bath.*

Pensione Grazia. This small, spotless hotel on a narrow lane close to the town center was completely remodeled a few years ago. The rooms (doubles L50,000) aren't large, but they have big windows that let in cool sea breezes. *Via Iallia Bassa 20, tel. 0942/24776. Down the block from steps near entrance to Greek Theater. 5 rooms, 3 with bath. Open June–Sept., and Easter and Christmas weeks only.*

Villa Pompeii. Directly across from the Giardini Pubblici, this popular pension offers views of Mt. Etna and the sea from its grand patio. The place is well-kept, and the aging signore who run it may fuss over you. Look for the street number because there's no sign. Doubles cost L50,000. *Via Bagnoli Croce 88, tel. 0942/23812. 5 rooms, 2 with bath.*

➤ **CAMPING** • **Camping San Leo.** Sites here fill up fast in summer because of the setting on the bay, but the thundering traffic of Via Nazionale is never far away. Expect to pay L7000 per person to camp; tent and sleeping bag rentals are about the same. *Tel. 0942/24658. Take any bus btw train station and town, and ask driver to drop you halfway at "il camping." 156 sites. Reception closes at 9 PM.*

FOOD Dining in Taormina isn't as expensive as you might imagine; what stings more is its mediocrity. If you prefer to fend for yourself, avoid the gourmet markets on Corso Umberto I and head downtown to the fruit carts on the side streets leading to Via Roma. The salumeria **Bottega di Laganà** (Via Di Giovanni 47, near Corso Umberto I, tel. 0942/23040) won't rip you off, and the panificio **Managò** (Via Giardinazzo 55, tel. 0942/24365) serves little pizzas (L3000). Don't miss Taormina's confectionary contribution, the **Torrone Bianco**, a flat, almond-filled nougat cake topped with candied fruit. They're in every pastry shop window on Corso Umberto I, and they cost about L4000 each.

What the restaurants lack in taste they make up for in ambience—almost all have pleasant outdoor terraces. Scrappy old Salvatore boasts of his *pennette alla vecchia Taormina* (pasta with pesto, cream, mushrooms, and garlic) at the restaurant under his hotel, **Il Leone** (*see* Where to Sleep, *above*). The best out of dozens of similar eateries, **La Botte** (Piazza Santa Domenica, tel. 0942/24198; closed Sun.) serves up eggplant parmigiana pizza on its lantern-lit patio for L8000. From Corso Umberto I, walk down Via di Giovanni until you reach the piazza.

WORTH SEEING Although Taormina is chock full of sights, half the fun is just wandering around. Before you go strolling, pick up a free English guide to the architecture of the city at the AAST, which itself is housed in the **Palazzo Corvaia**, former meeting place of the Sicilian parliament. Behind the tourist office, the comparatively uneventful 1st-century BC **Odeon Romano** (free, open daily 9—one hour before sunset) sits partially excavated, while the Hellenistic-era **Gymnasium** (or Naumachiae) is still standing two streets downhill from Corso Umberto I, half-way between Porta Messina and Porta di Mezzo. The buildings on Corso Umberto I between the **Porta di Mezzo** and **Porta Catania** date to the middle ages, though almost all have been rebuilt since WWII. The 13th-century **duomo** sits opposite the baroque **fountain**, topped by a two-footed dual-tone female centaur, an odd rendition of the town's normal symbol (a conventional four-footed male centaur). Good spots to hang out during the empty siesta hours or the passeggiata are **Piazza IX Aprile**, with its unrivaled view of Mt. Etna and the coast below, and the **Giardini Pubblici** (open daily 6—one hour before sunset), whose shady paths and manicured hedges were pieced together by an eccentric British ornithologist.

First built in the 3rd-century BC, the **Teatro Greco** (tel. 0942/23220; open daily 9–6:30) is the second-largest amphitheater in Sicily. To suit the needs of ever-popular bloodsports, the Romans added holding pens (for animals and warriors) and drainage gutters (for what was inside the animals and warriors). What you see today is a 19th-century reconstruction, which fortunately retains a stunningly perfect view. Admission to the theater is L2000. The theater hosts an arts festival June–August; call **Taormina Arte** (tel. 0942/21142) or AAST for information and tickets, which run L8000–L50,000. Perched above the city on Monte Tauro, **Castello di Taormina** (open daily 9 AM–1 hr before sunset; admission free) was once a proud fortress, but is now a jumble of ruinous walls and wildflowers. Even after the gates close, you can hop the wall to enjoy the best views in town. It's a 30-minute climb from Via Circonvallazione up a stepped path to the castle.

AFTER DARK Taormina is no New York City, but there are a few places to go after the restaurants close. Head downhill to Giardini-Naxos (*see below*) for a more happening dance club scene. Sumptuous **Marrakech** (Piazzetta Garibaldi 12; closed Wed.) serves cocktails (from L5000) on couches and cushions and that are supposed to conjure up images of . . . Marrakech. To reach Marrakech from Corso Umberto I, head downhill on Via S. Domenico de Guzman to the piazzetta. The disco of the moment is **Septimo** (Via San Pancrazio 50, tel. 0942/625522), where L10,000 gets you fake marble columns, mirrors, and strobe lights.

NEAR TAORMINA

GIARDINI-NAXOS Taormina makes the beach town of Giardini-Naxos ("Giardini" for short) look like an ugly stepsister. Giardini may be a 2-kilometer mess of concrete apartment blocks and garish waterfront eateries, but it rivals Taormina as a place to stay with its abundance of cheap hotels, good (or better) restaurants, and dance clubs. When night falls, lose yourself in the discos along Via Stracina (across from the Zona Archeologica). Both **Lady Godiva** (tel. 0942/53306) and **Mirabù** (tel. 0942/54076) charge L15,000 to be graced by mega-bass sound.

This tacky tourism obscures the town's historical significance. In the 5th century BC, a few Greek ships landed here and established Naxos, the first Greek colony in Sicily. Though the colony never amounted to much, it was a crucial first step to Hellenizing the island. All that's left of it—temple foundations, the harbor, and the city walls—is contained in the **Zona Archeologica** (open daily 9–6; admission free). The ruins aren't much to look at, but the site, with its eucalyptus trees and orange groves, is a pleasant place to spend an afternoon. The goods dug up from the site are displayed in the **Museo Archeologico** (Via Schisò 38, tel. 0942/51001; open Mon.-Sat. 9–2). To reach the Zona Archeologica from Taormina, take the Giardini-Naxos bus (26 daily, 20 min, L1500) to the Recanti stop.

A Dip in the Gole dell'Alacantra

If you're tired of fighting the crowd for a glimpse of the water, head to the fascinating Gole dell'Alcantara (Alcantara Gorge) for a swim 18 kilometers inland from Giardini-Naxos. Carved by the "Torrent of Alcantara," the canyon's 20-meter-high walls are striped with colorful sediment, and in some places the gorge narrows to a mere 3 meters, giving the impression of a cavernous, water-bound abyss (the water is great for swimming but VERY cold). There's only one bus from Taormina to the gorge (9:05 AM, 45 min, L4400), and return buses either take you to Taormina or the inconvenient train station. Since public transport isn't a piece of cake, consider renting a Vespa for the day (L20,000) from California Motonoleggio (see Getting Around in Taormini, above). After an afternoon in the gorge, put on your Armani specs, jump on your scooter, and head to the beach—you're ready to blend in with the locals.

➤ **WHERE TO SLEEP AND EAT** • The **AAST** (Via Tysandros 54, tel. 0942/51010), open weekdays 8:30–2 and 4–7, Saturday 8:30–2, can help you find lodging. Lodging may be easier to find in Giardini than Taormina in summer, but be careful: Many pensions charge 1½ times more than listed when demand is high. **Il Pescatore** (Via Naxos 96, tel. 0942/51247), near the center of town, has doubles for L48,000. Both **Hotel Otello** (Via Naxos 25, tel. 0942/51458) and **Hotel Costa Azzura** (Via Naxos 35, tel. 0942/51458) have doubles for about L60,000, and most rooms have showers and balconies. The campground **Campeggio Maretna** (Località Cretazzi, tel. 0942/52794), near the intersection of Via Pietralunga and Via San Giusto, charges L5000 per person. To get here, ask the bus driver to stop at "il camping" on the way to Giardini from Taormina's train station. The place to eat is **Fratelli Marano** (Via Naxos 181, tel. 0942/52316), where you can plunge into a serve-yourself antipasti bar (L8000) before trying the house specialty, spaghetti heaped with fresh seafood.

SAVOCA The languid town of Savoca is little more than a handful of churches and stone houses clinging to the hillside above Santa Teresa di Riva, about 30 minutes north of Taormina. Across from the piazza is the town's one and only café, **Bar Vitelli**, where they shot the breakfast scene from *The Godfather* (there's a picture of Don Brando on the wall to prove it). Annoyingly, they don't serve wine, but you can sip a bitter Messina beer out on the terrace, and let an orange roll out of your hand. After returning to the real world, follow the signs to the **Cappuccini Monastery** (open Apr.–Sept., daily 9–1 and 4–7; Oct.–Mar., Tues.–Sun. 9–noon and 3–5) and its catacombs, containing what could be some of the Godfather's ancestors, mummified in 200-year-old outfits. To reach Savoca, take a Messina-bound bus from Taormina to Santa Teresa di Riva (L2200), where you can either try to catch one of four daily buses up the hill (L1500) or make the 4-kilometer, one-hour hike yourself.

Catania

With all the disasters that tend to plague eastern and southern Sicily, it's no surprise that Catania has had a hard time of it. But this city has its own built-in disadvantage—it sits within explosion range of Mt. Etna. For 122 days in 1669, hot lava so inundated the town that the harbor hissed with steam for two days. Only 24 years later, an earthquake leveled everything left standing. With a stubbornness usually reserved for mules and university registrars, Catania set out to rebuild itself, entrusting the design of a new, grander city to architect Giovanni Vaccarini. The baroque master tried to make the most out of Catania's situation by using gray lava stone in every building, and the result is more than a little glum.

Catania's boutiques and café-lined boulevards may point to a certain sophistication, but the murky, twisting side streets are a part of a second city, an unknowable place of muffled conversations and children who stop playing to watch you pass by. Mysterious and estranged from itself, Catania is great for those who get their kicks from contradiction. It's also reputed to be Italy's most crime-ridden city. The two reasons you might come here: to make a pilgrimage to composer Vincenzo Bellini's birthplace, or to make a connection to Mt. Etna (*see* Coming and Going, *below*).

In Homer's "Odyssey," the cannibal-infested Laestrygonian Fields surrounded Catania. Today, beware of modern-day cannibals (pickpockets and con artists) near the train station and bus depot.

BASICS The **AAPIT** runs two helpful offices that give out information both on Catania and Mt. Etna, the first of which is on Track 1 of the train station (tel. 095/531802; open weekdays 8:30–7:30, Sat. 8:30–6:30). The **central office** (Largo Paisselo 5, 2nd floor, tel. 095/317720), one street west of Via Etnea and one street south of Villa Bellini, is open weekdays 9–1 and 4–6, Saturdays 9–1. For local and international calls, head to **Telecom** (Corso Sicilia 67; open Mon. 4–7:30, Tues.–Sat. 9–1 and 4–7:30).

La Duca Viaggi is the AmEx representative (Via Etnea 65, tel. 095/316155 or 095/316317; open weekdays 9–1 and 4–7:30, Sat. 9–noon). Elegant banks line Corso Sicilia, including **Banca Nazionale di Lavoro** (Corso Sicilia 30; open weekdays 8:20–1:20 and 2:35–4). Pick up a classic from **English Book Vaults** (Via Umberto I 36, tel. 095/325385; closed Sat.–Tues.); a paperback costs around L15,000.

COMING AND GOING Most trains and out-of-town buses depart from the unsavory Piazza Giovanni XXIII. If you arrive after nightfall, you'll probably want to take a cab downtown (L10,000). Trains from the south and inland may stop first at Catania Acquicella, but don't get off until Catania Centrale.

➤ **BY TRAIN** • Catania's **Stazione Centrale** (Piazza Giovanni XXIII, tel. 095/531625) is the place to catch hourly trains to Siracusa (1½ hrs, L7200), Taormina-Giardini (1 hr 15 min, L4100), and Messina (2 hrs, L8100), as well as trains to Palermo (5 daily, 4 hrs, L17,500) and Enna (7 daily, 1½ hrs, L7200). You can store your luggage 6 AM–10 PM for L1500. If you want to circumnavigate Mt. Etna by train (see Mt. Etna, below), head to the privately run **Ferrovia Circumetnea** depot (Via Caronda 352, tel. 095/374042 or 095/541251) on the corner of Viale Vittorio Veneto and Corso Italia. The FCE ticket office is open weekdays 6:55–2:10 and 3:30–8, Saturdays 6:55–12:05 and 4:20–4:40.

➤ **BY BUS** • Long-distance **SAIS** buses (Via d'Amico 181, tel. 095/536168; open 24 hrs) leave for Messina (9 daily, 3 hrs 15 min, L9500), Taormina (15 daily, 1 hr 45 min, L5100), Siracusa (12 daily, 1 hr 15 min, L6100), and Enna (8 daily, 1½ hrs, L8000). Though the depot is located on Piazza Giovanni XXIII, the waiting room is clean and safe.

➤ **BY PLANE** • Catania's airport lies 5 kilometers to the south of town and is a popular entry point for cheap flights into Sicily. To get into the city, take AMT's **Alibus**, which stops at Via Etnea on the way to the train station every 20 minutes, 5 AM–midnight; buy your L1300 ticket from the tabacchi in the airport. A **taxi** to the airport should cost L15,000.

GETTING AROUND Vaccarini's broad, straight thoroughfares cut through the twisty old town streets, making Catania an easy enough place to navigate. Don't stray from the main thoroughfares at night (maybe not even in daylight), especially if you're a woman or alone—you'll find yourself in a mess of narrow alleys and dead-end streets that invite exploration but carry the smell of danger. Via Etnea, the main drag, slices north–south through most of the major piazze and streets, as well as many sights, lodgings, and restaurants, culminating at **Piazza del Duomo** in the south, near the port. To reach Stazione Centrale from Piazza del Duomo, take Via Antonio di Sangiuliano. Buses run daily 5 AM–10 PM, and a 90-minute ticket costs L1500 at any tabacchi. Buses 33, 48, and 49 all go along Via Etnea (Bus 48 continues along Via Umberto I), Bus 28 runs past the Ferrovia Circumventa depot, and Bus 27 goes to the campgrounds and beaches south of the city.

WHERE TO SLEEP It's wisest to stay in one of the hotels around Via Etnea—those around the station and port may be cheaper, but they are *sketchy*. Hotels can fill up in the summer season, so reserve ahead. If the hotels below are booked, **Pensione Ferrara** (Via Umberto 66, tel. 095/316000) is a little pricey (doubles L60,000), but has comfortable rooms and kind owners. It's three blocks east of Via Etnea near the main entrance to the Villa Bellini gardens. If you're set on camping, **La Plaja** (Viale Kennedy 47, tel. 095/340880; open June–Sept.) is on the beach 5 kilometers south of Catania, not far from the highway. From the train station, take Bus 27 or D (summer only) to the Miramare Hotel stop.

Locanda Hollanda. Possibly the best deal in Catania, this funky hotel is run by an English-speaking Dutchman (hence the name). It's in a dodgy neighborhood, but the showers are hearty, a lot of the ceilings are frescoed, and it's *cheap* (doubles L50,000). Their phone number is rumored to change, so if you can't get through, contact the tourist office (see Basics, above). *Via Vittorio Emanuele 8, tel. 095/317489. From train station walk SW on Via VI Aprile to Via Vittorio Emanuele.*

Pensione Royale. If Catania's harsh atmosphere makes you want to coddle yourself a bit, try out elegant Royale, where L90,000 gets you a double with bath, TV, and frescoed ceilings (if you're lucky), plus a downstairs bar and a terrace. *Salita San Giuliano 337, tel. 095/312108. 3 blocks west of Via Etnea on the pedestrian extension of Via San Giuliano.*

Rubens. This hotel looks like your grandparents decorated it, but it's in the middle of the action on Via Etnea. Everything in the hotel—beds, showers, proprietors—is a bit creaky, but they all work just fine. Doubles 50,000. *Via Etnea 196, tel. 095/317073. 7 rooms.*

FOOD It's not difficult to eat well in Catania, especially if you appreciate fresh seafood. Don't bypass the market (*see box, below*), a great place to pick up a picnic *and* check out local culture. The pasta specialty is spaghetti *alla Norma*, with fresh basil, salted ricotta cheese, and eggplant. It's named after the opera by native son Vincenzo Bellini (what the romantic difficulties of a druid priestess have to do with eggplant is better left unexplored). For a taste of Catania's café scene, stop by the entirely unstylish **Savia** (Cnr of Via Etnea and Via Umberto), a local institution that has been serving cappucinos and brioches since 1897.

Trattoria de Fiore. A local crowd comes here for lovingly prepared, huge dinners. The spaghetti alla Norma (L7000) is second only to Da Nino's, and the roast chicken (L11,000) is divine. *Via Coddola 24, tel. 095/316283. 2 blocks east of Trattoria da Nino and 1 block north of Via Sangiuliano. Closed Mon. AE, MC, V.*

Trattoria da Nino. The menu for this lunch spot (rattled off at a furious pace by Nino himself) changes daily and the kitchen is practically at your elbow, but that only adds to the appeal. Crowds gather for the best spaghetti alla Norma in town (L8000), as well as for grilled calamari (L10,000). *Via Biondi, no phone. From Piazza dell'Università, walk 2 blocks east on Via Antonio di Sangiuliano. Open weekdays 12:30 –whenever the food runs out (about 3 PM).*

Trattoria da Santo. This quiet, family-run restaurant is a favorite with actors and audiences from nearby Teatro Metropolitan. The ambience is mellow, the food basic but tasty. Try the hearty gnocchi *al pomodoro picante* (in spicy tomato sauce) for L7000. *Via Sant'Euplio 116, tel. 095/325472. Across from Villa Bellini gardens main entrance, one block south of Viale Regina Margherita. Open daily noon–3 and 7 –midnight.*

WORTH SEEING Catania is the grayest city this side of Pittsburgh, and Mt. Etna is to blame. Vaccarini ensured that everything was lava-tinted and subsequent generations of Cantanesi have expanded on this aesthetic, touching up buildings with ashen stucco and gray paint, but within this monochromatic cityscape are some fascinating bits of architecture. A stroll on Via Etnea and into the side streets to the east of Piazza Università will get you in touch with most of Catania's sights. Sicily's largest church, the imposing **San Nicolò**, remains closed to the public.

If you want to put faces to the names, pull out a L5000 bill— the mug on the front is Bellini's, the broad on the back is Norma.

➤ **MUSEO BELLINIANO** • Home to an interesting collection of death-masks, posters, period instruments, and original manuscripts, this museum is housed in the apartment where Vincenzo Bellini was born in 1801. The composer layered frill upon frill in his popular operas, and came to define the Neopolitan style before dying at the young age of 34. *Piazza San Francesco d'Assisi 3, tel. 095/715–0535. From Piazza del Duomo, follow Via Vittorio Emanuele II 2 blocks uphill. Admission free. Open daily 9–1:30.*

➤ **PIAZZA DEL DUOMO** • This piazza, centered around the **Fontana dell'Elefante** (Elephant Fountain), epitomizes Vaccarini's 18th-century vision of a spacious municipal square. The fountain's friendly pachyderm carries an Egyptian obelisk depicting hieroglyphs of the cult of Isis, and his already elephantine testicles are exaggerated to celebrate Catanesi virility. Of the impressive baroque structures that line the piazza, the **Cattedrale di Sant'Agata** dominates the space with its ornate, towering facade. Inside on the right is **Bellini's tomb**.

➤ **TEATRO ROMEO ED ODEON** • Built in the 2nd century AD on the site of an earlier Greek stage, all that remains of this Roman theater are dirty, cracked lava blocks. It's all a little gloomy, but the view of the city from the theater seats is possibly Catania's most interesting. Afterwards, be sure to gather enough courage to burrow through the theater's dark, underground passageways. *Via Vittorio Emanuele II 266. Admission free. Open daily 9–1 hr before sunset.*

➤ **VILLA BELLINI** • When you need a break from Catania's grimy urban sprawl, head to the peaceful Villa Bellini gardens. Check out the park's unique feature near the swan pond at the main entrance: the date spelled out in shrubs and flowers on the hillside (it's changed by a troop of gardeners every day at dawn). The garden also hosts free contemporary and classical music performances (June–Sept.) in the **Catania Musica Estate** festival; check with the tourist office or on posters around town for schedules. *Main Entrance: Via Pacini, at Viale Regina Margherita, just off Via Etnea. Admission free. Open daily dawn–1 hr before sunset.*

AFTER DARK If you decide to wander at night in search of goings-on, stay out of the port area, where there's nothing to do but get mugged. Instead, check out the handful of bars (open until 11 PM) on Via Umberto, near Piazza Vittorio Emanuele II, or the student hangouts clustered in the streets east of Piazza Università.

Teatro Massimo Bellini opened in 1890 with a performance of Bellini's *Norma*. Now operas are staged January through April, with classical music from the end of April to mid-June. Tickets can be had for as little as L5000; contact the box office or tourist office for details. *Piazza Bellini, tel. 095/312020 or 095/715–0921. 2 blocks north of Via Vittorio Emanuele II. Box office open Mon.–Sat. 9–12:30 and 5–7.*

NEAR CATANIA

ENNA Perched on a ridge in the center of Sicily, the small town of Enna has been mellowed by centuries of economic stagnation. Unable to compete with port towns for international trade, Enna has accepted its role as a humble agricultural center. You'll step off the bus at sand-colored Piazza Vittorio Emanuele, where men mark the passage of time by following the sun as it changes the hue of the beautiful weathered church of **San Francesco**. From the piazza, Via Roma runs through several piazze, each with an accompanying church and café. The street continues past the looming 14th-century **duomo**, whose basalt columns are decorated with sharply delineated Norman carvings. Via Roma ends at the 14th-century **Castello di Lombardia** (tel. 0935/500962; open daily 8–6), one of the most important military buildings of Norman Sicily. You can climb to the top of its reconstructed **Torre Pisana** for a commanding view of the valley. One of the castle's courtyards always has a pickup soccer game, while the other has open-air concerts in summer; contact the tourist office for details.

➤ **BASICS** • The local **AAPIT** (Via Roma 413, tel. 0935/500544; open Mon.–Sat. 9–1) has maps and information on surrounding towns. You can change money at the **post office** (Via Volta, behind Municipo on Piazza Garibaldi, tel. 0935/500950), which is open weekdays 8:10–5:30, Saturdays 8:10–1:20.

➤ **COMING AND GOING** • Getting to Enna can be a pain, but it's more accessible than other parts of Sicily's interior, and can be a good jumping-off point. The **train station** (0935/500910; open daily 6 AM–9 PM) sits at the foot of a hill, so that getting to town requires either an impossible one-hour hike or a 15-minute bus ride (12 daily, L1500; last up 9:10 PM,

---

Roly-Poly Fish Heads

An incredible array of open-air food markets and wholesalers, not to mention upscale boutiques, make Catania one of Italy's most exhaustive market towns. The streets fanning out to the east of the duomo are packed with bulk retailers who group together according to their wares—one block has only undies, another caskets, a third tuxedoes. You might even find such exotic delicacies as Betty Crocker Brownie Mix. Every morning, La Fiera fills Piazza Carlo Alberto with fruit stands. Head across town for La Pescheria, an open-air market held every morning (except Sunday) on Piazza di Benedetto, a short walk southwest of Piazza del Duomo, whose sights and odors are something you won't soon forget. There are piles of fruits, olives, meats, cheeses, useless trinkets, and, of course, buckets of squirming fish, squirting clams, and bloody swordfish heads. By 1 PM both markets are just a bad-smelling memory.

last down 9:30 PM). The station's waiting room is open 24 hours, so if you miss a connection you can rough it here—just have some sort of ticket to flash at the watchful police. Direct trains run to Catania (7 daily, 1½ hrs, L7200), Palermo (2 daily, 2 hrs 15 min, L10,800), and you can reach Agrigento and the east via Caltanissetta (9 daily, 45 min, L3500).

Enna's **SAIS** bus station (tel. 0935/500902; ticket office open Mon.–Sat. 6–2 and 3:30–7) is a 10-minute walk down Via Vittorio Emanuele from Via Roma, though most buses swing by the fountain on the northeast corner of Piazza Vittorio Emanuele. Buses travel to Catania (9 daily, 1½ hrs, L8000), Palermo (3 daily, 2 hrs 15 min, L11,000), Piazza Armerina (6 daily, 45 min, L3700), Pergusa (6 daily, 20 min, L600). For connections to Ragusa and the south, head to Caltagirone (1 daily, 1 hr 40 min, L9200); for Agrigento and the west, go to Caltanissetta (5 daily, 55 min, L4100). AST Bus 4 makes eight additional daily trips to Pergusa (last bus 10:30 PM) from Piazza Vittorio Emanuele.

> **WHERE TO SLEEP AND EAT** • Unless you're willing to spend L100,000 for a room at Enna's only hotel, the **Grande Albergo Sicilia** (Piazza Colaianni 5, tel. 0935/500850), catch the next bus to Pergusa (*see below*). Accommodations in Enna may be sparse—hell, non-existent—but good eats are easy to find just off Via Roma. **Hostaria Impero** (Via Reepentite 17, off Piazza Umberto, tel. 0935/26018) serves Enna's contribution to the culinary world, *pasta 'ncasciata* (lasagna with meat sauce, prosciutto, peas, cheese, and tomatoes). A three-course meal with mineral water costs around L14,000. Popular **Picadilly** (Via Lombardia 12, near Castello; closed Mon.) is a hoppin' bar that serves super cheap pizza (L4000) until 2 AM.

PERGUSA Pergusa may be only a hair more than two blocks long, but the town boasts of amenities nearby Enna can't—more than one hotel, and a Formula One racetrack. Life in the town revolves around this asphalt ribbon, which encircles the waters of **Lago di Pergusa**, site of Persephone's mythical abduction by Pluto into the underworld. Getting to Pergusa from Enna is easy (*see* Coming and Going in Enna, *above*). From Pergusa you can catch buses to Piazza Armerina (6 daily, 30 min, L2400) and Caltagirone (1 daily, 1 hr 20 min, L8800).

Pergusa's hotels are always filled during race time, so call ahead. A 10-minute walk towards Enna, the **Miralago** (tel. 0953/541272) has sparkling doubles with showers for L55,000. A five-minute walk in the opposite direction, **La Pergola** (tel. 0953/541733) charges a little less for similar rooms, but it will be closed for renovations through early 1996. The bar/pizzeria **Da Carlo** (tel. 0953/541194; open daily) is hilarious—everybody from soldiers to racing pilgrims pack in for tasty pizzas such as the Da Carlo, with sausage and bell pepper (L6500). The guy at the espresso machine claims to make the worst cappuccino in Italy. He's right.

PIAZZA ARMERINA AND VILLA ROMANA DEL CASALE Enna founded the Norman town of Piazza Armerina to extend its influence over the mountains, and you'll find the two have everything from creamy sandstone palazzi to a tranquil pace in common. Piazza Armerina's winding spiral of streets ends at the 15th-century **duomo**, whose dome towers over the dull modern buildings on the lower slopes of the valley. The rough, warm-hued 17th-century facade contrasts brilliantly with the cool, whitewashed interior. To reach the **AAST** office (Via Cavour 15, tel. 0935/680201), open Monday–Saturday 8–2 and 4:30–7:30, follow Via Garibaldi into town from Piazza Europa and turn right at Piazza Garibaldi onto Via Cavour.

From Piazza Armerina you're within striking distance of **Casale**, home to Sicily's most stunning Roman ruins. The **Villa Romana** (open daily 9–1 hr before sunset; admission: L2000) was built in the early 3rd century AD and occupied by various people until it was covered by a landslide in the 12th century. It wasn't until the 1950s that local scholars discovered the location of the villa from ancient writings. Little is left of the superstructure (the steel columns and fiberglass roof approximate the dimensions of the original building), but there are plenty of mosaics. Some 3,500 square meters of brilliantly colored, delicately placed tiles depict tense Circus Maximus races, athletic women wearing what souvenir hawkers call "bikinis," gory African hunts, and all the breasts and buttocks you'd expect from hedonistic Imperial Rome. You view the mosaics from suspended walkways, which are easily clogged by tour groups.

> **COMING AND GOING** • From Piazza Europa, buses head south to Enna (via Pergusa, 6 daily, 45 min, L3700) and Caltagirone (3 daily, 1 hr, L7200); stop by the AAST office for

schedules. AAST runs shuttles to Casale (6 daily, 15 min, L1500) May–October. In the off-season you have three options: (1) hitchhike; (2) take a Caltanissetta bus and get off at the Casale turnoff (about 1 km from Casale); or (3) make the relatively flat, 5-kilometer hike yourself—just follow the yellow signs south out of town.

➤ **WHERE TO SLEEP AND EAT** • Given the difficulty of getting around Sicily's interior, it's worth spending a night or two in beautiful Piazza Armerina. **Hotel Villa Roma** (Via Alcide dei Gasperi 18, tel. 0935/682911 or 0935/682912) must have been a swank place in 1972, but today its a little rough around the edges. Clean doubles cost L60,000. Further afield, the tidy **Hotel Mosaici** (Contrada Paratore II, tel. 0935/685453) was built over a popular restaurant on the turnoff to Casale—five minutes from the Villa Romana (L60,000 with bath). Just around the corner, **La Routa** (at the turnoff, tel. 0935/680542) operates a small campground (open June–Sept.; L5000 per person) next to their pizzeria. *Paninotecas* (sandwich shops) cluster around Piazza Europa, or you can find a more serious meal at **Pepito** (Via Roma 10, across from Hotel Villa Roma, tel. 0935/685737), where pizzas go for about L7,000.

Mt. Etna

With soft ridges and gradual slopes, snowcapped Mt. Etna (Monte Etna) only pretends to be sleeping. A temperamental lout that has exploded more than 140 times in recorded history, Etna is the highest (3,432 meters), most active volcano in Europe. Etna's craters continuously belch lava, and on a clear night these flows can be seen glowing from a distance of 250 kilometers. In 1979, six people died when an unexpected tremor flung them into the crater's bubbling cauldron. In the most recent eruption (summer 1992), several houses in Randazzo, at the northern foot of Etna, were totally engulfed by lava. The flip side of these dangerous eruptions is the mountain's fertile volcanic soil, which makes for a lush, green landscape.

Dangerous as it is, Mt. Etna can be conquered by anyone who dares. Along with a few hardy mountaineers, Etna is attacked daily by everyone from perambulating babies carried on their parents' shoulders to unsure-footed grannies. Their tour buses and garish orange warm-up suits won't spoil the fun, but you should be prepared to share the volcano.

Nothing compares to gazing into the infernal abyss of Etna after a long day's hike, but for those short on time and phobic about eruptions, the privately owned **Ferrovia Circumetnea** (FCE) runs a 114-kilometer circuit around the base of the mountain. From the train, you'll be treated to views of the crater, rugged lava fields bearing prickly pear cactus, vineyards, olive and lemon groves, and clay-tiled cottages. If you've got the time, jump ship and check out some small towns along the way. Especially noteworthy are medieval **Randazzo**, built almost entirely of volcanic rock; **Adrano**, home to one of the first archaeological museums in Sicily, the Museo Archeologico Etneo; and **Paterno**, with its 13th-century Norman castle. Since the FCE is a private company, rail passes are *not* accepted. The train makes a four-hour circuit between Catania and **Giarre-Riposto**, and you can start from either point. To reach the depot in Catania (Via Caronda 352, cnr of Viale Vittorio Veneto and Corso Italia, tel. 095/374042 or 095/541251), take Bus 28 from Piazza Giovanni XXIII to Corso Italia.

In the classical myths, Zeus imprisoned the rebellious Giants under Mt. Etna, and the Cyclops hammered out the god's characteristic thunderbolts inside the caldera as if it were an enormous smithy.

BASICS Getting atop Mt. Etna is a confusing process. Ask for guidance at the tourist offices in Catania (*see above*), at the semi-helpful **COOP Pegaso** (Piazza Vittorio Emanuele 4, tel. 095/914488; open Mon.–Sat. 9–1) in Nicolosi, or the usually deserted **AAST** (Via Etnea 32, tel. 095/911505; open Tues. and Thurs.–Sat. 9–noon). There's also a **SITAS** office (tel. 095/914142) in Nicolosi Nord, which posts information on the most expensive routes to the top.

COMING AND GOING From Catania, a single bus leaves every morning (*see* By Bus, *below*) for **Nicolosi Nord**. From here, you can reach the **Rifugio Montagnola** (2500 meters) by foot, jeep, or cable car; the **Torre Del Filosofo** (Tower of Philosophy; 2920 meters), by foot or jeep; or the **Caldera** (cauldron; 3332 meters), which you can only reach on foot. If you'd rather just enjoy the scenery, the **Ferrovia Circumetnea** (*see* By Train, *below*) will take you around the perimeter of the mountain in about four hours. One final option is to take a **ski lift** from Nicolosi Nord to the funivia. It may not compare to Colorado, but Mt. Etna probably has the best skiing in all of southern Italy. The lifts run December–March, and an all-day pass costs L35,000. Contact SITAS for more information on skiing.

➢ **BY BUS** • A single blue **AST** bus (1 hr, L4400) leaves every morning at 8:05 AM from in front of Catania's train station, making a single return trip at 4:30 PM. The bus pauses at the pleasant mountain village of **Nicolosi** before stopping at **Nicolosi Nord**, where you can purchase a lava carving of Mary done up in blue glitter. Twelve additional AST buses leave Catania daily, only going as far as Nicolosi (30 min, L2000), so you could go to Nicolosi later in the day, stay overnight, and then catch the regular bus up the volcano the next morning. Buy your ticket on the bus.

➢ **BY FUNIVIA** • The quickest way to reach Refugio Montagnola from Nicolosi Nord is to hop on an efficient orange cable car, which will whisk you up in a few minutes. To soften the blow of the L15,000 one-way fare, they let you use your credit card.

➢ **BY JEEP** • Clunky Fiat 4x4's, fondly called "Jeeps," will bring you to the Torre del Filosofo from either the SITAS office (45 min, L17,000) or Refugio Montagnola (15 min, L9500). The first option isn't posted at the SITAS office, so you must ask for it and pay there. The jeep is driven by a mandatory "guide" whose services (including walking you up towards the caldera) cost an additional L5500 per person.

➢ **BY FOOT** • Trudging up the mountain is the most honorable course to take—after all, you can't tell somebody you've climbed Mt. Etna unless you actually climbed it. Though possible, it is laborious and the little lava rocks on the path will kill the soles of your feet no matter how tough your boots are. From Nicolosi Nord it's two hours to Refugio Montagnola, then one hour to Torre del Filosofo, and then one more hour to the caldera. The easiest path follows the jeep roads or ski-lift trails, both of which start behind the SITAS building. While the folks back home may think you half mountain goat, half god, the actual trip doesn't get you away from civilization, what with the cable cars looming overhead.

It will be cold no matter when you make it up the volcano. If you only packed Birkenstocks and tank tops, Refugio Montagnola will rent you a puffy down jacket and uncomfortable rubber boots (L2000 each per day).

If you reach the Torre del Filosofo by jeep, your guide will take you to a rope stretched some 250 unsatisfying meters below the caldera and tell you it's not safe to venture further. To tempt fate, shrug off the crowd and head back down the jeep track to the first curve, where you will see a rough footpath going off to the south. This trail is poorly marked—a pole here, a red rock there—but there are plenty of footprints. After an hour climb, you can step over the gaping cracks in the soil and peer into the steamy crater, pondering mortality, mythology, geology, and the long hike back down.

WHERE TO SLEEP AND EAT Its title "refuge" was earned when a 1983 flow of lava stopped at its back wall (you can see the mark), but the **Rifugio Sapienza** (Nicolosi Nord, tel. 095/911062; open year-round) is more like a Quality Inn with a great view. Doubles (L74,000) are plain and modern, but for some reason, getting two singles (L32,000) is actually cheaper. Down in Nicolosi, tiny **Albergo Monti Rosi** (Via Etnea 179, tel. 095/911000) charges L60,000 for a double, though the ancient guy who runs the place can be difficult to reach by phone. **Camping Etna** (tel. 095/914309; open Apr.–Oct.) charges L7000 per person and L8000 per tent. The campsite is on the road from Nicolosi to Etna, 3 kilometers from Piazza Vittorio Emanuele in Nicolosi. It's a good idea to stock up on food in Catania before setting out. During the pit stop at Nicolosi you can scramble for fruit at the stalls on Piazza Vittorio Emanuele and have a panino (L3500) made quickly for you at **Scevola Enrico** (Via Etnea 53, tel. 095/914321). Food further up is expensive and tasteless, with the dubious exception of the Etna Burger (L6000) at Rifugio Sapienza's restaurant.

Siracusa

During the glorious millenium of Greco-Roman domination, Siracusa (Syracuse) rivaled Athens as one the most powerful and influential cities in the western world. Some temples and amphitheaters built during this ancient age of splendor have survived, as have later baroque masterworks. This combination of living history, beautiful architecture, and temperate seaside climate draw the inevitable hordes of archaeology buffs and shutterbugs, but even the crowds can't completely diminish the allure of Siracusa, which still has the feel of the Greek cities that are its distant cousins.

Siracusa got its humble start when Corinth, eager to keep up with the Joneses, packed up a group of Greek colonists and sent them to establish a colony in Italy. Siracusa quickly flourished as a center of art and culture under the rule of Heron, who brought the poet Pindar and the playwright Aeschylus to his court. The later ruler Dionysius, though brutal and unpopular, turned Siracusa into the pre-eminent city of Magna Grecia. Dionysius invited Plato to be his teacher, but he soon found the chattering philosopher tiresome and threw him in prison until his buddies back in Athens could post bail. Siracusa's reign continued until 215 BC when, having entangled itself in regional politicking, it was crushed by Roman forces despite the valiant efforts of Archimedes (*see box, below*).

After Rome's pillagery, precious little happened until about 1960, when Siracusa came into its own as a manufacturing center and provincial capital. Today most of the population lives in bulky concrete apartment blocks, but cross the bridge to the island of Ortygia and you'll find an interesting web of alleyways lined with Arab, Norman, baroque, and 19th-century buildings. These structures—and the Greco-Roman site—are the main reasons to visit.

BASICS The friendly staff at the **AAST** (Via Maestranza 33, 1½ blocks east of Piazza Archimede, tel. 0931/464256) doles out excellent city maps and transport schedules. They're open March–December, Monday–Saturday 8:30–2 and 4:30–7:30. You can also get information on the mainland from **AAPIT** (tel. 0931/60510; open Mon.–Sat. 9:30–1) by the Parco Archeologico entrance, or at **APT** (Via San Sebastiano 45, tel. 0931/67710; open weekdays 8–2 and 3–5), across the street from the Basilica di San Giovanni and the Catacombe.

You'll find **Telecom** (Via Teracati 46, tel. 0931/700111; open Mon.–Sat. 8 AM–10 PM) across the street from Via Augusto, which leads to the Parco Archeologico. The **post office** (Piazza delle Poste, tel. 0931/66995), open weekdays 8:30–5:30 and Saturday 8:30–1, looms over the bus station to the left of the causeway as you enter Ortygia. **Monte del Paschi di Siena** (Piazza Pancali 12, next to bus depot, tel. 0931/691–0494), open Monday–Saturday 8:20–1:20, has a handly ATM on Ortygia, as does the **Banca Nazionale di Lavoro** (Corso Umberto 29, tel. 0931/726294), which is open Monday–Saturday 8:35–1:35 and 3–4.

COMING AND GOING

➤ **BY TRAIN** • All trains to Siracusa arrive at **Stazione Centrale**, northwest of the mainland. Luggage storage is available 6 AM–10 PM, and all tracks have wheelchair lifts. Rail service

---

You Sank My Battleship

The Romans invaded Siracusa in 215 BC, yet it took nearly three years to subdue the city because of one man: Archimedes, physicist and inventor. One of his ideas was to use giant mirrors to make the Siracusan fleet look larger; an additional bonus was the mirrors' ability to ignite enemy sails like paper under a looking glass. The inventor was equally ingenious on land: Castello Eurialo endured a two-year Roman siege thanks largely to kilometers of underground passageways and massive water cisterns designed by Archimedes.

includes: Messina (11 daily, 3 hrs, L15,500), Catania (14 daily, 1½ hrs, L7200), Taormina (10 daily, 2 hrs 15 min, L11,700), Palermo (daily at 6:40 AM, 5 hrs, L24,400), Ragusa (4 daily, 2½ hrs, L9800), Noto (10 daily, 45 min, L3400), Scicli (8 daily, 1 hr 40 min, L7,100), and Modica (8 daily, 2 hrs, L8000).

➤ **BY BUS** • **AST** (Piazza delle Poste 13, tel. 0931/462711) buses generally make short trips to towns like Noto (13 daily, 45 min, L3700), Modica (10 daily, 1½ hrs, L6800), Ragusa (6 daily, 2 hrs, L7500), and Catania (14 daily, 1½ hrs, L6100). **SAIS** buses (Via Trieste 28, tel. 0931/66710) leave one block behind Piazza delle Poste, serving Palermo (5 daily, 4 hrs, L25,700) and Noto (13 daily, 1 hr, L3900).

➤ **BY BOAT** • All ferries to and from Siracusa dock at **Molo Zanagora** (Corso Vittorio Emanuele II), five minutes southwest of Ponte Nuovo. Boats make the run to the island repulic of Malta from mid-June to early September; ferries (6 weekly, 5 hrs) cost L130,000 one-way and L180,000 round-trip (L100,000 one-way, L120,000 round-trip students), hydrofoils (every Wednesday, 2½ hrs) cost L160,000 one-way and L210,000 round-trip (L130,000 one-way, L150,000 round-trip students). You can buy all tickets from **Giovanni Boccadifuoco** (Via Mazzini 8, just above docks, tel. 0931/463866).

GETTING AROUND Siracusa is comprised of two main areas connected by the causeway **Ponte Nuovo**: the old town on the island of Ortygia, and the modern city on the mainland, the site of the major archaeological finds. The city is small, but making the trek between sights can be exhausting. All **AST** city buses (L600) operate until 9 PM, and most run along Corso Umberto on their way to and from Piazza delle Poste on Ortygia. Bus 2 goes from the train station to Ortygia and takes a round-about route back, so take Bus 1 in the opposite direction. To make the 20-minute walk from the station to Ortygia, take a left on Via Francesco Crispi, which merges into Corso Umberto and leads to Ponte Nuovo.

WHERE TO SLEEP The least expensive hotel on Ortygia is **Hotel Gran Bretagna** (Via Savoia 21, 2 blocks south of Piazza XXV Luglio, tel. 0931/68765), where you can pay in plastic for cutesy doubles (L78,000). The mainland atmosphere certainly isn't as idyllic, but there are a bunch of decent, cheap beds near the train station. Campers and hostel devotees have to ride plenty of buses to get to the major sights from their lodgings outside the city limits. Regardless of where you stay, reservations are a must June through September.

Ben Sit. It's like staying with friends-of-friends-of-the family—the owner's kids are always watching TV, and you usually have to step over a toy truck to get out the door. Located in the heart of the mainland city, this hotel gives you an insider's view of local life. Doubles cost L40,000. *Via Oglio 5, tel. 0931/60245. Cross train tracks at Via Catania and follow Corso Gelone 3 blocks, left on Via Tirso (look for hotel sign on lamppost), right on Via Oglio. 11 rooms, some with bath.*

Hotel Centrale. This is the consummate budget hotel: cheap, close to the station, and with rooms that bear more than a passing resemblance to a monk's cell. If you're female, the kind woman who runs the place may give you special treatment, like allotting you a room with a window. Doubles L40,000. *Corso Umberto 141, tel. 0931/60528. Walk straight out of station and head left on Corso Umberto. 14 rooms, none with bath.*

Hotel Milano. This hotel right near Ponte Nuovo has weird karma and wide open views of Corso Umberto. The rooms are big and sparse, and most have refrigerators (doubles L50,000). No other mainland hotel is closer to Ortygia. *Corso Umberto 10, tel. 0931/66981. 18 rooms, some with bath.*

➤ **HOSTELS** • **Ostello della Gioventù.** This private, dorm-style hostel isn't terribly convenient—it's 10 kilometers from Siracusa, in Belvedere—but the friendly proprietors can offer suggestions about what to do in the area. Castello Eurialo is nearby, as is an excellent pizzeria. Beds cost L20,000, including breakfast and a sleep sheet. *Via Epipoli 45, Belvedere, tel. 0931/711118. 20-min ride from Corso Umberto on Bus 9 or 11. 52 beds. Curfew 11 PM.*

➤ **CAMPING** • **Camping Fontane Bianche.** It's 18 kilometers from town, but a popular beach nearby helps ease the pain. During summer, call ahead before hopping on Bus 21 or 23 west from Corso Umberto. Sites cost L6500 per person, tents rent for L10,000, and sleeping bags go for L5000. *Via Mazzarò 1, tel. 0931/790333. 300 sites. Closed Oct.–May.*

FOOD Corso Umberto sports a handful of take-away pizza joints that are better and cheaper than any you'll find on Ortygia. Every day until 10:30 PM, the salumeria **Cassia Ionario** (SE cnr of Piazzale Marconi) does a boisterous job of making sandwiches. The best gelateria in town is **Voglia Matta** (Corso Umberto 34, tel. 0931/67118; closed Thurs.), with a rocking amaretto.

La Cantinaccia. This spacious restaurant on Ortygia isn't out to rip you off (for a change). Large dishes of pasta (L6000–L8000) are good to the last slurp. Pizzas cost L5000–L9000. *Via XX Settembre 13, tel. 0931/65945. From Ponte Nuovo, take 2nd right and go 1 block past ruins. Closed Mon.*

La Foglia. This cozy Mediterranean restaurant would have a line out the door if it were in LA. Specialties include seasonal soups (L7000) and stuffed pastas like spinach ravioli the size of small frisbees. A full meal may run you up to L30,000, but local hipsters and *The New York Times* think it's worth it. *Via Capodieci 29, tel. 0931/66233. Across from Museo Nazionale di Palazzo Bellomo. Closed Tues. AE, MC, V.*

Spaghetteria do Scogghiu. Friendly, chaotic, and authentic (despite a lack of Italian-speakers), this is *the* place to go in Ortygia. The robust Russo brothers really know their spaghetti: Choose from 20 varieties, each only L6000. Don't miss the delicious pasta *puttanesca*, with hot peppers, black olives, tomatoes, and bacon, or the *tutto mare*, with shrimp, squid, and mussels. *Via Gemmellaro Scina 11, no phone. Downhill from Piazza Archimede in the center of the island. Open Tues.–Sat. noon–2:30 and 7:30–11, Sun. noon–2:30.*

Trattoria Paolina. The food and decor are both pretty bad, but the portions are manly and the prices rock-bottom. *Spaghetti alla carrettiera* (with cayenne pepper, garlic, and local olive oil) costs a mere L5000. The incessantly squawking bird caged in the corner isn't on the menu, no matter how much you offer. *Via Francesco Crispi 14, at Piazzale Marconi, tel. 0931/702321. Open Mon.–Sat. noon–3:30 and 6–10.*

WORTH SEEING The bulk of Greek Siracusa's ruins are hidden among the towering apartment blocks of the mainland. On Ortygia, in addition to the **duomo** (*see below*), the **Largo Aretusa** (the mythical origin of Siracusa) attracts a crowd of gawkers who don't seem too impressed with the fishpond before them, and back by the causeway, columns of the **Temple of Apollo** pop out of the **Piazza Pancali.**

➤ **ORTYGIA ISLAND • Museo Nazionale di Palazzo Bellomo.** Although filled with the usual hodgepodge of Madonnas and period costumes, this museum is the unlikely home of two masterpieces. Antonello da Messina's 15th-century *Annunciation* still has enough Flemmish-Mannerist bits left to let you think about why he's regarded as Sicily's greatest painter. A world away is Caravaggio's 17th-century *Limento di Santa Lucia*, a later work where he cuts through the crap and attacks chiaroscuro full-on. Most of the huge canvas is as dark as night and the figures are jumbled on top of themselves—you almost want to ask them to move a little so you can see what's going on. *Via Capodieci 16, tel. 0931/69511. From Piazza Duomo, walk down Via Santa Lucia to Via Conciliazione, first left on Via Capodieci. Admission: L2000. Open Mon.–Sat. 9–2, Sun. 9–1.*

Piazza del Duomo. Ortygia's oblong central piazza sports several fine baroque palazzi, including the 17th-century **Palazzo Senatorio** (now the city hall), and the 18th-century **Palazzo Beneventano del Bosco,** with an inviting courtyard and elegant winding staircase. You can't go into either of these, so give them a sideways glance on your way to the duomo, an opulent concoction of Norman and baroque buildings on the site of a 5th-century BC temple to Athena. You can see some of the original Doric columns, now imprisoned within the church's walls. *Piazza del Duomo. From Ponte Nuovo, take Corso Matteotti to Piazza Archimede; turn right on Via Amalfitania, left on Via Cavour.*

➤ **THE MAINLAND • Castello Eurialo.** Running along several kilometers of seafront hills outside of town are the ruins of a masterpiece of military architecture. Built by Dionysius the Elder in the 5th century BC, the 22-kilometer circuit of walls and towers stood impregnable until the tireless Romans breached it in 212 BC. The official entrance is by the castle proper, but a more interesting approach is to get off the bus as soon as you see the large white walls and walk north through the flower-infested ruins—bring a picnic and feast amongst the crumbling stones. *Via Epipoli, near Belvedere, 7 km NW of Siracusa. Take Bus 9 or 11 from Corso Gelone and ask to be let off at "il castello." Admission free.*

Catacombe di San Giovanni. The earthquake of 1693 cracked open the nave of Siracusa's first cathedral and now flowers grow where early Christians once accepted communion. Still standing are three Norman walls, a Byzantine apse, and several Greek columns. Below ground, the damp **Cripta di San Marziano** contains a few faint frescoes. From the apse you can descend into the 5th-century **catacombs**, where thousands of niches once held the remains of thousands of Christians. *Via San Giovanni, tel. 0931/67955. 1 block east of Museo Archeologico and north of Santuario della Madonnina. Admission: L2000. Open daily 9–6.*

Museo Archeologico. Sicily's newest museum was opened in 1988 to hold the majority of the island's Hellenic and pre-Hellenic artifacts—major and obscure archaeological sites are documented in painstaking detail. Yet the museum isn't wholly academic, with enough freakish gorgons to keep the TV generation entertained. Don't miss the landmark piece—a 1st-century AD Roman statue of Venus. Ask yourself if she is modestly covering herself with her hand or doing something else. *Viale Teocrito 66, tel. 0931/464022. Admission: L2000. Open Apr.–Sept., Tues.–Sun. 9–1 (Wed. and Thurs. also 3:30–6:30); Oct.–Mar., Tues.–Sun. 9–1.*

Parco Archeologico. This site is the only swatch of the ancient city left uninhabited since Roman times, and even after centuries of looting, there are still enough petrified wheel ruts and blocky temple foundations to make for a good couple of hours of exploring. But you will never have the ruins to yourself—every package tourist in Sicily has an innate desire to snap pictures of the blinding white ruins against the shadows of neighboring cypress groves. The most famous ruin is the **Ear of Dionysius**, a cave named for its lobe-shaped entrance; the tyrant used to stand at the mouth of the cave and eavesdrop, thanks to acoustics, on the conversations of his enemies incarcerated inside. Hold on to your ticket while exploring the site and use the stub to gain entrance to the adjacent **Anfiteatro Romano**, a 2nd-century arena built to satisfy the Roman need to see blood flow. The arena is carved almost entirely out of rock, including the rooms that held the gladiators and beasties before they were disemboweled in front of the seething crowd. *Near intersection of Via Cavallari and Via E. Romagnoli. From Corso Gelone or Corso Umberto, Bus 1, 4, 5, 8, or 10 west to park entrance. Admission: L2500. Open daily 9 AM–1 hr before sunset.*

Santuario della Madonnina. In August of 1953, a 2-foot tall plaster bust of the Virgin Mary started crying. Old Ianusto (the guy who owned the Madonnina) ran out to tell the world, and the bishop of Palermo had the alleged teardrops tested. He declared a miracle, and Ianusto's small village was soon overrun with pilgrims. A massive sanctuary—an upside-down 80-meter ice cream cone which can be seen from any point in the city—was constructed in Siracusa to hold the Madonnina. Please remember to be decorous in the sanctuary—this is a very special place for many people. *Tel. 0931/64077. Across Viale Teocrito from Archaeological Museum. Admission free. Open daily 6–12:30 and 4–7:30.*

AFTER DARK Nightlife in Siracusa centers around the *passeggiata* (social stroll) on Corso Celone and Piazza Repubblica or on Piazza Duomo in Ortygia. Most bars on Piazza Duomo are lively but expensive, so head downhill to the **Soup and Beer Pub** (Via delle Vergini 16, no phone; closed Tues.) for an excellent selection of international beers in what could be a pizza joint in Collegetown, USA. There are plenty of discos in Siracusa, but **Malibu** (Via Elorina 172; cover L15,000) is *the* late-night hot spot in summer, sometimes packing as many as 1,000 people onto its flashing dance floor. To get here, you'll have to take a taxi (L20,000).

Southern Sicily

The rugged south of Sicily hides many surprises: quiet baroque towns in the southeast and, further west, the well-preserved Greek ruins at **Agrigento**. In between are hillside farms whose fields (thankfully) have yet to be overrun by tourists. If you're coming from the packed Ionian resorts, you'll find relief in southern Sicily's tranquil beauty. Getting around in the south takes a bit more stamina, however: The trains are tiny and painfully slow, while the bus service is fragmented and disorganized. For this reason, the less-adventurous skip this part of the island altogether—which is excellent news for the rest of us.

Sicily's entire southeastern corner suffered terrible damage from a massive earthquake in 1693. This tragedy paved the way for a talented crew of architects (among them the renowned Rosario Gagliardi) to rebuild in the flamboyant baroque style—a profound contrast to Sicily's dry, stony landscape. **Noto** is the most spectacular of these 17th-century time capsules, while the less photogenic **Ragusa** is a convenient base for day trips. Tiny **Scicli** and **Modica** are good short stops on your way to someplace else. If you have come to Italy to eat, do not miss the pastry shops of Noto and Modica, alone worth a trip to the south.

Noto

Noto is a strange little place that manages to be both luminescent and gloomy at the same time. Not only was the town entirely rebuilt after the 1693 earthquake as a pinnacle of Enlightenment-era architecture, but it was constructed out of a local beeswax-colored sandstone that glows as if lit from within. Though beautiful, Noto feels abandoned—many buildings are vacant or propped up by aging wood braces in case another earthquake comes to town.

The rebuilding of Noto came at an interesting point in the history of architecture, when they realized that cities could be formally planned but nobody knew yet what worked best. Noto's solution is a little awkward—the narrow **Corso Vittorio Emanuele III** transverses the town starting at **Porto Reale**, the ancient city border, but the buildings on it are so big and the street so little that you feel the need for a little perspective. One of these buildings is the 18th-century **duomo**, whose twin bell towers and mammoth triple-tiered staircase seem to exude a glow well beyond dusk. Further down the corso is one of Gagliardi's masterworks, the **Chiesa di San Domenico**, on the same square as the **APT** office (Piazza XVI Maggio, tel. 0931/836744; open Mon.–Sat. 8–2 and 3–5). There are no less than 18 other churches in this town of 20,000 people, each of which is strange and beautiful. If there is any place where it's possible to swim in baroque, it is Noto.

COMING AND GOING Buses are usually the best way to reach Noto. From Siracusa, **AST** buses (13 daily, 45 min, L3700) and **SAIS** buses (12 daily, 1 hr, L3900) drop passengers at the Giardini Pubblici. Nine buses continue to Ragusa (1½ hrs, L5100). Buy tickets on board or at **Bar Efirmedio** (Viale di Piemonte 6, just downhill from Giardini Pubblici), where they also have schedules. Noto's small **train station** (open daily 8:30–noon and 1–6) offers service to Siracusa (4 daily, 1 hr, L3400) and Ragusa (8 daily, 1½ hrs, L5000). While there's no official luggage storage, the guy in the office will stash your bag for free if he's around. Getting into

Beach Bumming

When churches and piazze start blending and the word "art" becomes a synonym for "headache," hop on a bus from Noto's Giardini Pubblici to the beach at Noto Marina, 7 kilometers east. Wide and sandy, the beaches here are clean and perfect for swimming—watch for the tiny fish that flock around your toes. Four buses run Monday–Saturday, and the last returns to Noto about 6 PM.

town from the station requires either a 20-minute walk up Via Principe di Piemonte or taking the lone bus (L600).

WHERE TO SLEEP AND EAT Noto's only hotel, **Albergo Stella** (Via F. Maiore 44, tel. 0931/835695), is run by a talkative world-traveler. The clean rooms are rather dull despite their trapezoidal shapes (doubles L60,000). From Giardini Pubblici walk one block down Via Napoli. Be sure to call ahead during summer. Whatever you do in Noto, *do not* miss a visit to **Pasticcieria Mandolfiore** (Via Ducezio 2, tel. 0931/836615), one of the greatest gastronomic experiences in Italy. The cannoli (L1500) are exquisite, and neighborhood folk like to munch on L500 *ravioli* (sweet ricotta cheese-stuffed pastries) while drinking cappuccino in the small café. **Trattoria del Carmine** (Via Ducezio 9, tel. 0931/83705; closed Wed.), two blocks east of the Chiesa del Carmine, serves outstanding home-style food at fair prices.

Ragusa

Ragusa is not going to make any overt attempts to entertain you. The town sports few postcard sights, and unless you're wearing a T-shirt with "Kiss me, I'm from Kansas" on it, folks will probably assume you're a businessperson interested in the nearby asphalt works. Depending on your mood, this makes Ragusa one of the island's most or least interesting places; either way, the city offers a complete slice of provincial Sicilian life.

As evening falls, pre-teens horse around in the doorways of San Giovanni, teenagers rev their Vespas on Via Vittorio Veneto, twentysomethings gather on Piazza Liberto, older folks stroll along Via Roma, and everybody passes over the Ponte Nuovo at least once.

Like the rest of the region, Ragusa was devastated by the 1693 earthquake. Some decided to rebuild on the rubble of the old town, called **Ragusa Ilba**, while the nouveau riche migrated uphill and built a larger, grander district. The competition between the two was so intense that Ragusa Ilba willingly waited over 15 years for the construction of the more impressive **Duomo di San Giorgio** (1783). In this time Gagliardi created one of the most outstanding pieces of Sicilian baroque architecture, with its three-tiered facade, enormous dome, and galloping horsemen statues. Today, Ragusa Ilba is a walkable, quiet place, while the rest of Ragusa is an interesting bustle of locals. The city is strung across three hill tops, and you'll end up climbing a lot of stairs and crossing many gorge-spanning footbridges. When trying to get around, ignore the directional signs to the tourist office and duomo—they often lead you on major detours.

COMING AND GOING AST (tel. 0932/621249) has the most frequent bus connections to Palermo (3 daily, 5½ hrs, L27,300), Siracusa (6 daily, 2 hrs, L7500), and Modica (17 daily, 20 min, L3000). All buses depart from Piazza Gramsci in front of the train station; schedules are posted and you buy your tickets on board. The **train station** (Piazza del Popolo, tel. 0932/621239) serves Palermo (1 daily, 5½ hrs, L24,400), Siracusa (4 daily, 2½ hrs, L9,800), and Modica (8 daily, 20 min, L2,800); for Agrigento (3 daily, 3½ hrs, L15,500), change trains in Canicattì. Save your legs the 40-minute walk to Ragusa Ilba and take orange AST Bus 1 or 3 (L600) from the station to San Giorgio (Piazza del Duomo).

WHERE TO SLEEP The **AAPIT** (Via Capitano Bocchieri 33, in Palazzo Rocca, tel. 0932/621421) makes lodging recommendations Monday–Saturday 9–1. You could do a lot worse than staying at the quiet **Hotel San Giovanni** (Via Transpontino 3, tel. 0932/621013), which charges L60,000 for a double. From the train station, take Via Leonardo da Vinci down and to the left, turn left on Via I. Migliorisi (which becomes Via Schinina), and continue through Piazza Cappuccini to Via Transpontino.

FOOD If you're in Ragusa Ilba and want to treat yourself, **Ristorante U Saracinu** (Via del Convento 9, tel. 0932/246976; closed Wed.), at the lower end of Piazza Duomo, has great atmosphere, friendly service, and top-notch food. Try the penne *al Turiddu* (with olives, capers, basil, tomato, and a hint of anchovies; L6,000). If all else fails, the **UPIM/SMA** supermarket (Via Sicilia 14) will keep you alive. From the train station, walk down and to the right on Viale Sicilia.

MODICA Relaxed, provincial Modica is home to two extraordinary churches and one magnificent pastry shop, all of which draw in a light trickle of travelers in summer. First and foremost is Gagliardi's 18th-century **Chiesa di San Giorgio**, which sits in the upper town atop a grand, 182-step staircase (brochures say 250 steps—count 'em yourself). Equally imposing is the lower town's 18th-century **Cattedrale di San Pietro**, a towering, baroque structure featuring a staircase adorned with superhero-size statues of the apostles. Modica's baroque heritage is fine and all, but the most salient aspect of this town is the wondrous **Antica Dolceria Bonaiuto** (Corso Umberto I 159, tel. 0932/941225; closed Mon.), a 115-year old confectionery institution which draws pilgrims from all over. They produce possibly the best cannolo (L1300) in all of Sicily, and this isn't a claim to be made lightly. Eight daily trains travel to Modica from Noto (1 hr, L3400) or Ragusa (20 min, L2800). The station (tel. 0932/941791) has no luggage storage, but they'll stash your bag if you ask nicely.

SCICLI Even ignoring its architecture, Scicli is worth a look for the scenery alone. The town is set in a wide valley at the base of a sheer cliff, and it's surrounded on all sides by postcard-perfect hills. Since Scicli is on the Noto–Ragusa train line, pack a lunch, hop on the train, and spend the afternoon hiking in the hills before leaving for Ragusa at dusk. If you haven't had enough 18th-century architecture yet, there's Scicli's majestic **Chiesa di San Bartolomeo**, which boasts intricate interior stuccowork and a 16th-century wooden nativity scene.

Agrigento

It is not too difficult to see how beautiful Agrigento must have been at one time. Built on a broad open field which slopes gently to the sunbaked Mediterranean, the ancient city of Akragas was a showpiece of temples erected to flaunt a victory over Carthage. Despite a later sack by Carthage, mishandling by the Romans, and neglect by the Christians and Muslims, the eight or so monuments in the **Valle dei Tempi** are considered to be, along with the Acropolis in Athens, the finest Greek ruins in all the world. The medieval center, which makes up the focal point of modern Agrigento, is nice to wander in, with plenty of winding alleys. The views of the sunset over the Mediterranean are amazing, and the city is visitor-friendly, but what Greek poet Pindar called "The most beautiful city among mortals" was Akragas, not Agrigento. Factory smokestacks down by the beach are sometimes easier to pick out than the temples, tourists swarm the ruins, and a nearby highway ensures that you never leave the cacophony of civilization behind. A trip to Agrigento is certainly worth the time and effort, but be prepared to see what the industrial age does to ancient Greek cities.

BASICS The most helpful **AAST** office (Via Pirandello 15, tel. 0922/20454; open Mon.–Sat. 8:30–1 and 4:30–6:30) is in the center of town. The fascist-built **post office** (Piazza Vittorio Emanuele II; open Mon.–Sat. 8–1) actually has decent exchange rates, but the **Banco di Sicilia** (Piazza A. Moro I, tel. 0922/481111) across from train station has even better rates.

COMING AND GOING Whether you go by bus or train, getting in and out of Agrigento is slow at best, agonizing at worst. To venture further west, you must take a bus.

➤ **BY TRAIN** • Oddly grandiose, Agrigento's **Stazione Centrale** (Piazza Marconi, tel. 0922/29007) sits just downhill from Via Atenea. Trains head to Palermo (7 daily, 2 hrs, L11,700), Enna (via Caltanisetta; 9 daily, 2 hrs, L10,700), and Ragusa (via Canicattì; 3 daily, 3½ hrs, L15,500). A luggage-storage office (open daily 6 AM –10 PM) will guard your stuff for L1500 per day.

➤ **BY BUS** • Agrigento's long-distance **bus station** (Piazza Fratelli Rosselli) is just east of Piazza Vittorio Emanuele II. A confusing variety of bus companies depart from here, and the only agency with a nearby ticket office is **SAIS** (Via Ragazzi del '99 12, tel. 0922/595620), which offers sparse service to Catania (via Canicattì; 6 daily, 2½ hrs, L6000) and Caltanissetta. **Salvatore Lumia** (tel. 0922/20414) runs four daily buses to Trapani (via Marsala; 3½ hrs, L17,600), Selinunte (2 hrs 15 min, L9600), and Sciacca (via Castelverano; 1 hr 15 min, L6400). **SRL** (tel. 0922/471886) runs three daily buses to Palermo (2 hrs, L13,000). For other companies and routes check the schedules posted in Agrigento's **Bar Sprint** (Via Ragazzi del '99 2) or around the bus lot.

GETTING AROUND From Stazione Centrale, **Via Atenea**—Agrigento's main street—is reached by climbing the stairs to the left, and then making another left halfway through a sorry little public park. From the bus station, follow the huge post office building along Via Imera, then head right through the park for Via Atenea. The main drag winds westward through the city, intersected by Via Bac-Bac almost at its end. The Valle dei Templi, which you can see from the train station, can be reached either by an easy 40-minute walk (start below the train station on Via Crispi, then follow the signs and your nose) or via **TUN** Bus 2, 3, or 11 (L1000).

WHERE TO SLEEP Agrigento gets positively packed during summer—you *must* call ahead for a room.

Hotel Bella Napoli. French novelist Alexandre Dumas may have slept at this hotel smack in Agrigento's medieval center, but he'd hardly stop by today. The few lovely rooms are of the L75,000 with bath variety. The L60,000 without bath kind are barely passable, and the communal bathrooms are outright disgusting. Unfortunately, with only three budget hotels in town, you might just get stuck here. If you do, be sure to confirm the price of a room *firmly* beforehand. *Piazza Lena 6, tel. 0922/20435. Walk up Via Bac-Bac from western end of Via Atenea. 50 rooms, 30 with bath. AE, MC, V.*

Hotel Belvedere. Comfy double beds, clean bathrooms, and vintage furniture await you at this modern-looking hotel. The manager is friendly and proud of his struggling, though lovely, garden, where you can drink a beer as evening rolls into dinnertime. Doubles are L55,000 (breakfast L3500). *Via San Vito 20, tel. 0922/20051. From NE cnr of Piazza Vittorio Emanuele II, follow Via Cicerone to Via San Vito and turn right. 34 rooms, 10 with bath.*

Hotel Concordia. This is the closest hotel to the train station, and while small, the rooms are clean and comfortable with upscale dorm furniture. Rooms without bath (doubles L60,000) are annoying, since the single, tiny communal bathroom has no shower. *Piazza San Francesco 11, tel. 0922/596266. Take Via Pirandello from Piazzale Aldo Moro. 25 rooms, 22 with bath.*

➤ **CAMPING** • **Camping Internazionale San Leone** (Via Lacco Ameno 4, tel. 0922/416121; open Apr.–Oct.) is the cleaner and better-situated of Agrigento's two campgrounds. Sites cost L7000 per person, with tent and bag rentals for L8000 and L5000, respectively. **Camping Nettuno** (Contrada Dune, tel. 0922/416268) isn't as pretty, but it's cheaper and open year-round. You'll pay L7000 per person plus L6000 per tent. Both campgrounds are about 6 kilometers from town and adjacent to San Leone's beaches. From Piazza Marconi, in front of the train station, take Bus 10 (or any labeled SAN LEONE); tell the driver which campground you want, and he'll drop you at the closest stop.

FOOD Most of the restaurants in the center of town cater to tourists, so your best bet may be the well-stocked, affordable grocery stores and food stalls on the side streets below Via Atenea.

Trattoria Black Horse. Though you probably won't be the only foreigner in here, the food is excellent and the service polite. Sit at a quiet outdoor table and try an immense platter of *calamari fritti* (fried calamari) for L12,000. *Via Celauro 8, tel. 0922/23223. Take Via Atenea from Piazzale Aldo Moro. Open Mon.–Sat. noon–3 and 7–10:30, Sun. noon–3.*

Trattoria Concordia. You'll dine with jolly Germans and pale Brits, but the food is simple and reasonably priced—tortellini for L6000, a seafood fritto misto for L12,000. Those who are claustrophobic (there are low ceilings) and impatient (there's usually a short line) should reconsider. *Via Porcello 8, tel. 0922/22668. From public park, straight down Via Atenea, right on Via Porcello.*

Trattoria La Forchetta. One son is in the kitchen, the other serves the wine, and Mamma Guiseppa sits in front and runs the whole operation. The menu changes according to what's fresh, and there's always bound to be penne-with-something-good. Double-check the bill—mine was mysteriously rounded up by a few thousand lire. *Piazza San Francesco, tel. 0922/596266 (they share a phone with Hotel Concordia next door). Open Mon.–Sat. 12:30–3 and 6:30–10:30.*

WORTH SEEING The best reason to come to Agrigento may be to meander through the Valle dei Temple, but that doesn't mean that the town is an uninteresting place to poke around. The 13th-century **Chiesa Santa Maria dei Greci**, which was built by the Normans on the site of a 5th-century BC Doric temple, has some original columns as well as partially preserved, 14th-century frescoes. Enter the underground tunnel from the courtyard to check out the stereobate (ground floor) and column remnants that form the church's foundation. To enter the tunnel, ring the bell, or tip one of the omnipresent neighborhood kids to find the guardian. Further up the hill, the perpetually closed **Duomo San Geriando** looms over the city with its huge sandstone belfry.

➤ **MUSEO NAZIONALE ARCHEOLOGICO** • If you're heading to the Valle dei Templi by bus, get off at the the Archaeological Museum first for a good overview of the site. Ignore the dull introductory exhibits and make a beeline for the displays of objects culled from the temples themselves—among them a group of sculpted lion heads (once waterspouts) and a reassembled *telamone*—a 7½-meter-high figure that was usually used as a decorative column on the sides of buildings. *Contrada San Nicola, tel. 0922/49726. Admission free. Open Tues.–Sat. 9–1:30 and 3–5, Sun. 9–12:30.*

Across the road from the museum is the **Quartiere Ellenistico-Romano** (Greco-Roman Quarter), more than 10,000 square meters of ruined houses, shops, and taverns that date from the 3rd century BC. Some excavated structures still sport mosaic floors, and the complex system of sidewalks and gutters is easy to make out—reminding you that the ancient world wasn't all temples and togas. It's open daily 9–dusk and admission is free.

➤ **VALLE DEI TEMPLI** • Though getting to, from, and around the dusty ruins of the Valle dei Templi is no great hassle, you'll want to give yourself a full day to give this huge archaeological zone its due. The ruins officially close at sunset, but the guards may let you linger depending on the kind of day they've had. Stock up on snacks and water, since the

Although the last bus returns to town around 8 PM, anyone who makes an evening trek down Via dei Templi (with a bottle of wine, preferably) will be well-rewarded.

handful of bars around the site make Tokyo look cheap. Perhaps in atonement, admission to the sites is free. The site is divided into western and eastern sections. For instant aesthetic gratification, walk through the eastern zone; for a more comprehensive tour, start way out at the western end and work your way back uphill—the route decribed below.

Two of the original 34 columns are all that's standing of the **Tempio di Vulcano** (Temple of Vulcan), the last major Akragas project to be built in 430 BC. The **Tempio di Castore e Polluce** (Temple of Castor and Pollux) is a troublesome reconstruction of a 5th-century BC temple, pieced together by some enthusiastic, if misguided, 19th-century romantics. What they came up with is one of the postcard images of Sicily—but the Greeks probably wouldn't know what the hell it is if they wandered by today. Very little remains of the **Tempio di Giove** (Temple of Jove), which was once, appropriately, the biggest of the Akragas temples and one of the largest temples in the Greek world. Only the stereobate and one of the telamones were left behind, and it is now in the museum (the telamone you see here is a reproduction).

Through the gate and across the modern road you notice wheel ruts marking the ancient road to the temples. At the westernmost point overlooking the modern road is the poorly named **Tomba di Terone** (Tomb of Theron)—the stout, squared building was more likely to have been a monument to Romans who died in the Punic Wars. Back up on the acropolis, the 6th-century BC **Tempio di Ercole** (Temple of Hercules), the oldest structure in the valley, was dedicated to the favorite god of the often-warring citizens of Akragas. Further up Via Sacra past the visible cubicles of the necropolis is the 5th-century BC **Tempio di Concordia** (Temple of Concord), thought to be the most well-preserved Greek temple around. Everything but the roof and treasury are still standing, thanks largely to the efforts of San Gregorio delle Rape (St. George of the Turnips), Agrigento's 6th-century bishop who consecrated the pagan temple. For preservation, this temple is blocked off to the public. The final and easternmost structure is the **Tempio di Giunone** (Temple of Juno), a 5th-century BC cleric temple. From here you can see all along the ruins, over the olive groves, and to the sea.

➤ **CASA DI PIRANDELLO** • Aficionados of modern Italian literature inevitably visit the birthplace of innovative playwright Luigi Pirandello (1867–1936), who won the 1934 Nobel Prize for literature and is best known for his plays *Six Characters in Search of an Author* and *Enrico IV*. His house (just west of the temples) is now a small museum that contains his study, murals he painted, and random memorabilia. Pirandello—or at least his ashes—can be found beneath a lonely pine tree outside. *Tel. 0922/48326. Bus 11 from Piazza Marconi. Open daily 9–1 and 3–7 (until 5 in winter).*

NEAR AGRIGENTO

SCIACCA Sciacca is a prosperous fishing port and one of the southern coast's most all-around pleasant towns—and it's only a little more than an hour from Agrigento. In times long past, Sciacca was a thermal spa center (the name comes from the Arabic word *xacca*, meaning "from the water"). Nowadays you can visit the steamy caves of **Monte San Calogero**, 8 kilometers inland, to reap the benefits of soothing vapors and sulfurous waters. The caves are free and always open. Take Bus 5 (every 1½ hrs, L1500) from Villa Comunale, a public garden at the east end of Sciacca's Corso Vittorio Emanuele II. Nearby is Sciacca's **duomo** (Piazza Duomo at Corso Vittorio Emanuele II), which was built by Normans in the 12th century and later given a bright baroque facade. You can find sandy beaches 4 kilometers west of town, the most popular being **San Giorgio**, **Stazzone**, and **Foggia**. Hourly buses run from the Villa Comunale.

Sciacca is not served by train, but there are hourly buses to and from Agrigento (1 hr 15 min, L6400) that will drop you at the Villa Comunale gardens. To reach the town center, walk down from the gardens along Corso Vittorio Emanuele II and, at the fork, veer right onto Via Giuseppe Licata. Be advised that Sunday bus service is scaled way back. Buy all bus tickets at **Bar Lorenz** (Viale della Vittoria 7), across Piazza Friscia from Villa Comunale. The **AAST** tourist office (Corso Vittorio Emanuele II 84, tel. 0925/22744) can help with transportation schedules and lodgings. The office is open Mon.–Sat. 8–1:30 and 3–7:30.

Western Sicily

The western half of Sicily has always been poorer and less visited than the east. And though the west's social and economic situation has improved significantly over the past 50 years, there remains a large, visible disparity of wealth. Beyond those who eke out a living by fishing or farming, and those who claim some allegiance to the Mafia, you'll see very little resembling a middle class. On the bright side, swank tourist resorts are equally few and far between. The region's lack of development, not to mention its sun-beaten landscape, make it one of the last strongholds of a more traditional Sicily left anywhere near the coast.

Facing North Africa, the western coast has been strongly influenced by Arab traders and invaders. Their traces can be found in the white-washed buildings surrounded by palms and in culinary treasures such as couscous *con pesce in brodo* (with fish in broth), which is big in seaside **Trapani**. Towns like **Marsala** and Trapani have their own charms, but they're mostly springboards for treks to remote Mediterranean islands and the many beaches and fishing villages that cling to the rocky shoreline. If beach bumming for days on end isn't your thing, medieval, mysterious **Erice** or the ancient ruins at **Selunite** and **Segesta** are definitely worth a gander.

Marsala

Marsala is a clean, breezy, port town where little happens. This wasn't always the case—in its ancient days, it was Carthage's main Sicilian stronghold, and the port (which now houses a handful of fiberglass yachts) was for 2,000 years one of the most important stops between Europe and North Africa. Arab influences are stronger here than in any other Sicilian town, from the ground chickpea sandwiches in the marketplace to the narrow streets and white-washed buildings. Marsala's 15 minutes of fame came in 1860, when Giuseppe Garibaldi launched his "1,000 Red Shirts" (a band of revolutionaries) and somehow managed to wrench control of the island from the ruling Bourbons. Despite its historical anecdotes and pleasant atmosphere, Marsala is more a place to pass through than to stay and visit, but do allow time for a casual stroll downtown and a taste of the sweet Marsala wine.

BASICS The local **Pro Loco** tourist office has maps, bus and train schedules, and lodging information. *Via Garibaldi 45, SW of Piazza Repubblica, tel. 0923/714097. Open Mon.–Sat. 9–2:30 and 3–7.*

COMING AND GOING Marsala's **train station** (Via Fazio 9, tel. 0923/711252) has frequent connections to Palermo and Trapani. Check your bags (L1500) Monday–Saturday 6 AM–8:15 PM. Piazza del Popolo is the main bus depot: **AST** serves Castelverano (4 daily, 40 min, L4200), Palermo (13 daily, 2½ hrs, L13,600), and Trapani (18 daily, 30 min, L3400) and **Salvatore Lumia** serves Agrigento (4 daily, 3 hrs, L15,200).

WHERE TO SLEEP AND EAT The only affordable hotel in town, **Hotel Garden** (Via Gambini 36, tel. 0923/982320), charges L60,000 for a clean, comfortable double without bath; from the train station, head straight on Viale Fazio, hang a right on Corso Calatafimi, then a quick right on Via Cave, which dead-ends at Via Gambini. For seafood priced under L10,000, locals heartily recommend **Trattoria de Marco** (Via Vaccari 6, tel. 0923/956718), right off Piazza Repubblica and up the tiny lane across from the duomo's front door. Vegetarians and carnivores alike will appreciate the inexpensive *panini con pannelle* (chickpea sandwiches), available from stands in the **market**, held every morning next to Porta Garibaldi.

WORTH SEEING Museo degli Arazzi Fiamminghi. This tiny museum behind the duomo has only one display: an impressive eight-part panel of 16th-century tapestries. The tapestries were fashioned in Brussels and later given to Marsala-born Antonio Lombardo, who served as the archbishop of Messina and ambassador to Spain. The museum's gold-painted walls and white slip-covered chairs look like something out of a trendy club. *Via Garraffa 57, off Via Garibaldi. Admission: L1000. Open Mon.–Sat. 9–1 and 4–6.*

Museo Archeologico Baglio Anselmi. In an old wine-making factory, this museum is home to the *Nave Punica*, one of the few ancient ships ever recovered intact and the only surviving example of a Carthaginian warship. The *Punica* met its demise off the nearby Stagnone Islands, probably in 241 BC, during the First Punic War. The Phoenician inscriptions on some parts of the planking were put there by the original shipbuilders in Carthage. Display cases hold objects dredged from the ship, including some *Cannabis sativa* (i.e., ganja) supposedly used to keep the 68 oars-

Drinking Marsala

Marsala is known throughout Italy for the sweet dessert wine that bears its name. Sometimes flavored with berries or almonds, Marsala (the wine) is traditionally made from the remnants of table wine pressings, and most vintages are still mixed and aged on the outskirts of Marsala. The oldest and most distinguished of the distilleries is Florio (Lungomare Florio 1, tel. 0932/781111), open Monday–Thursday and Saturday 8:15–1:30. Call ahead for a free tour and to sample two or so glasses. From the train station, head left on Via Mario Gandolfo for three long blocks, then turn right onto Via Lipari and continue one block to the sea—it's on your left. You can also explore a variety of brands and flavors at the local wine shops. Enoteca Luminario (Via Lungomare Boeo 36, next to Museo Archeologico, tel. 0923/713150) pours you five free glasses and always has an open package of biscotti. They're open daily 8:30–8 (Jun.–Aug. until 11 PM). Although buying a bottle isn't obligatory at either of these places, there aren't many better ways to blow L6000 in Marsala.

men "awake." The museum is 20 minutes west of downtown. *Lungomare Boeo. From Piazza Repubblica, take Via XI Maggio to Piazza della Vittoria, then follow Viale Sauro to Lungomare Boeo and turn right. Admission free. Open daily 9–2:30 (Wed., Sat., and Sun. also 4–7).*

NEAR MARSALA

SELINUNTE AND MARINELLA As a Greek colony, Selinunte was too close to Carthagian territories to ever enjoy lasting peace, but now it's just remote enough to discourage most modern invaders. Stranded in the southwestern corner of Sicily, Selinunte is one of the most beautiful spots in all of Sicily, because the re-erected Greek columns and tumbled pediments are scattered across sea cliffs and wildflower fields. The temples were built mostly during the 6th and 5th centuries BC, and what wasn't ruined in Carthaginian invasions was toppled by a medieval earthquake. So little is known about the temples that they are referred to by letters rather than by the names of gods. Of these, **Temple G** is incomplete, though it would have been one of the largest buildings of the ancient world. The most evocative of the three temples, **Temple E**, was probably built around the middle of the 5th century BC. All of its columns and some of the cella of have been restructured. Admission to the ruins is L2000, and the site is open daily 9 AM to 1 hour before sunset.

Wrapping around the entrance to the site is the fishing-village-turned-middle-class-summer-resort **Marinella**. Ferry connections to Marinella tend to be in the early morning and early afternoon, making it pretty impossible to turn the ruins into a day trip, unless you're a master of timing. On the waterfront, the useless ASPIT office in **Bar Penguino** (tel. 0924/46888; open Mon.–Sat. 7:45–9:15, Sun. 10–9), is little more than a table of brochures, but they can help you out with accommodations and bus schedules. **Pensione Costa d'Averio** (Via Stazione 10, tel. 0924/46207) charges L55,000 for doubles and is a stone's throw from the ruins. **Camping il Maggionlino** (tel. 0924/46044) is on a beautiful site, but is rather far from the coast. It costs L6000 for a tent and L4000 per person. Food in Marinella isn't cheap, but of the many pizza joints, **Pizzeria Africa di Bruno** (Via Alceste, tel. 0924/46456) is the best deal in town—tell Bruno where you heard of his restaurant and he may invite you for a glass of Marsala wine. The dim but well-stocked **Curiale Salatrice** supermarket (Via SD N. 5, tel. 0924/46238) is just around the corner.

➤ **COMING AND GOING** • To reach Selinunte and Marinella, you must first travel to Castelverano by train from Marsala (4 daily, 40 min, L4200) or by bus from Marsala (4 daily, 40 min, L4800) or Agrigento (4 daily, 2 hrs 15 min, L9600). If you arrive by train, walk to Piazza Regina Marcherita—from here you can take one of six daily buses (20 min, L2000) to Marinella; if you arrive by bus, ask to be let off at **Bar Selinus** (Via Marinella 13), where you can catch one of the Marinella-bound buses en route.

In the Middle Ages, Trapani was a safe harbor where ships traveling between Europe and North Africa could stock up on salted tuna and fresh vegetables. In the 20th century, scads of spaghetti westerns were filmed in the surrounding hills.

Trapani

Several kilometers long but only a few hundred meters across at its widest, Trapani is a spindly finger of a city that points westward into the sea. This relative isolation has kept the tourist flow to the city to a trickle, and as a result, its buildings house weathered fishermen and bare barber shops instead of hotels, discos, and obnoxious cafés. But this is far from a backwater town—one turn of the evening passeggiata along Corso Vittorio Emanuele will give you an eyeful of fashion that'll make you think twice about packing "practical" clothes on your next trip to Italy. This incongruous worldliness is due to the numerous Mafia bosses who call the city home—which may explain the preponderance of well-dressed men with cellular phones.

While Trapani is a fairly interesting, wanderable place, there are two main reasons to make the trek out here: 1) to visit the Egadi Islands, and 2) Easter. Trapani takes the cake for intense Easter traditions with elaborate processions, masses, statues, crowds, bonfires, hooded pallbearers—you name it. If you somehow manage to get a reservation during Easter week, you will be witness to something you may never be able to forget, or really understand.

BASICS Pick up brochures and lodging lists from the **APT** (Piazzetta Saturno 1/A, off Piazza Sant'Agostino, tel. 0923/29000), open Monday–Saturday 8–2 and 2:30–8, Sunday 9–noon. **Monte dei Paschi di Siena** (Via XXX Gennaio 80) has an ATM. The **post office** (Piazza Vittorio Veneto; open weekdays 8:30–5, Sat. 8:30–1) exchanges money at good rates.

COMING AND GOING To reach the port or old town from the train station or bus depot (a 20-minute walk), cross the small park west of the stations, go south one block, make a right on Via Osorio, turn left when it dead-ends at Via XXX Gennaio, then turn right on Corso Italia and continue straight for eight blocks to Piazza Sant'Agostino.

➤ **BY TRAIN** • Trapani's **train station** (Piazza Stazione, tel. 0923/28071) is where the attractive old town fades into the modern city. From Trapani there are trains to Palermo (19 daily, 2 hrs, L11,700) and Segesta (daily, 30 min, L3600). Luggage storage (L1500 per bag) is open daily 7–9:30.

➤ **BY BUS** • The main **bus station** (Piazza Montalto, tel. 0923/21021) is off Via Osorio, immediately south of the train station. From here **AST** serves Erice (10 daily, 1 hr, L2500), Marsala (4 daily, 30 min, L3700), and San Vito lo Capo (6 daily, 45 min, L4400). Buy tickets at the station or on board. Catch **Autolinee Segesta** buses to Palermo (15 daily, 2 hrs, L11,000) either from the bus station or from the Egatour office (Via Ammiraglio Staiti 13, tel. 0923/21956). **Tarantola** buses run to Segesta (4 daily, 30 min, L4000) from Piazza Garibaldi.

➤ **BY BOAT** • All ferries arrive and depart from **Molo di Sanità**, Trapani's main docks, which extend seaward from Piazza Garibaldi between the seaside roads of Via Regina Elena and Via Ammiraglio Staiti. The latter is where boats depart for the Egadi Islands (*see below*).

From Trapani, two companies offer weekly ferries to Tunisia (Tunis). **Tirrenia** (Via Ammiraglio Staiti 55, tel. 0923/21896) sends ferries (L78,500) every Monday at 9 PM, arriving in Tunis 11 hours later. The return boat leaves Tunis Thursday at 9 PM. **Siremar** (Via Ammiraglio Staiti 63, tel. 0932/540515) runs *traghetti* (ferries) to Favignana (4 daily, 20 min, L4600), Levanzo (4 daily, 15 min, L4400), and Marettimo (3 daily, 1 hr, L11,200). **Alilauro** (Via Ammiraglio Staiti, on waterfront next to hydrofoil docks, tel. 0923/24073) runs *aliscafi* (hydrofoils) to Favignana (4 daily, 20 min, L8000) and Levanzo (4 daily, 20 min, L7800).

WHERE TO SLEEP Reservations are imperative around Easter, when even APT (*see* Basics, *above*) has trouble arranging private rooms. If you want to visit during the trippy Easter processions, reserve one month in advance for a front row seat at the **Nuovo Albergo Russo** (Via Tintori 4, tel. 0923/22166), a comfortable two-star hotel where a L70,000 double with bath will get you a balcony overlooking the crowded, festive Corso Vittorio Emanuele. One word of warning: the OSTELLO DELLA GIOVENTU sign near the train station might as well be pointing the way to Moscow (the youth hostel is actually some 40 minutes away), so ignore it unless you have your own transport. The hostel is also irritatingly expensive, making it worthwhile staying in the hotels listed below, which are almost the same price and much more convenient.

Albergo Moderno. Half of this small hotel has been recently refurbished, while the other half has saggy beds, barely functional bathrooms, and dirty floors. The less immaculate doubles cost L50,000. *Via T. Genovese 20, tel. 0923/21247. Heading away from the port on Via Torrearsa, take 2nd left past Corso Vittorio Emanuele.*

Pensione Messina. The Messina occupies an 18th-century apartment block perched high above a noisy courtyard. Despite the din, the rooms are airy and the common baths clean. Doubles cost L45,000. For a nominal fee, the proprietors do laundry. *Corso Vittorio Emanuele 71, tel. 0923/21198.*

FOOD It's worth staying an extra day in Trapani for a few extra meals. If you're ready to splurge, sample scrumptious Trapanese specialties like couscous *con pesce in brodo* (with fish in broth) and *busiate al pesto trapanese* (squiggly pasta in a sauce of crushed almonds, tomatoes, and garlic) at the excellent **Ristorante Da Peppe** (Via Spalti 50). The interior, framed by colorful stained-glass windows, is filled with interesting turn-of-the-century art.

Pizzeria Calvino. Late on a scorching afternoon, sag over to this popular pizzeria. It's always crowded, even the little rooms in back, which have narrow peephole windows left over from the days when Calvino was a brothel. Appease your less carnal hungers with a generously sized pizza. The toppings on the *capricciosa* (capricious) are at the whim of the chef. *Via N. Nasi 79, near Via Giglio, tel. 0932/21464. Closed Mon.*

Trattoria La Botte. A good place to sample Trapanese specialties like couscous with fish (L5000). A simple three-course dinner with fruit will set you back L15,000. *Corso Vittorio Emanuele 191, tel. 0932/871150. Closed Tues. AE, MC, V.*

WORTH SEEING All but two of Trapani's historical attractions are located on the narrow peninsula west of the train and bus depots. This part of Trapani was meant for aimless wandering; the goal is to get as lost as possible in the maze of narrow lanes and alleys.

Starting at 2 PM on Good Friday, Trapani commemorates the Passion and Crucifixion of Christ with a chaotic, emotional, 18-hour Easter procession, a blend of Catholic and pagan rituals. The streets of the old town are awash with painted icons, hooded figures, and weeping onlookers.

➤ **CHIESA DEL PURGATORIO** • If you can't make it to Trapani for Easter, stop by this 17th-century baroque church to see *I Misteri*, the colorful, life-sized wooden statues that depict scenes from the Passion of Christ. Each group is cared for by a trade organization (such as the carpenters or fishermen) that's also responsible for carrying the icons during the procession. *Via Giglio, 2 blocks south of Corso V. Emanuele. Admission free. Open Tues. and Sun. 8–noon, Fri. 8–noon and 4–7.*

➤ **SANTUARIO DELL'ANNUNZIATA** • It's worth delving into the blandly urban section of Trapani to gaze at this joint church and museum. The structure dates from 1315, but because of renovations in 1760, only the spectacular rose window and Gothic portal are original. Inside, check out the **Cappella della Madonna** (Chapel of the Madonna), which houses a statue of the Virgin and Christ sculpted in the 1300s by Nino Pisano. The highlight, though, is the **Museo Nazionale Pepoli** (admission: L2000), entered through the Villa Pepoli gardens next door. Displays in this small museum include beautiful coral work, medieval art, ancient coins, and a huge guillotine built in 1789. Especially poignant is the basket for you-know-what beneath the blade. *Via Conte A. Pepoli 198/200. Take SAU Bus 1, 10, or 11 (L1100) from Piazza Matteotti or Piazza Vittorio Emanuele. Church open daily 7–noon and 4–7; museum open Mon.–Sat. 9–1:30 (Tues. and Thurs. also 3–6:30).*

NEAR TRAPANI

SEGESTA Little is known about Segesta's origins except that the colony was probably founded by travelers from the eastern Agean (perhaps fleeing Trojans). Today all that is left of

Cheap Thrills in Trapani

Most summer evenings there's a pickup soccer game in front of the Liceo Leonardo Ximenes on Corso Vittorio Emanuele, near Palazzo Senatorio. You'll get some stiff competition from a raucous bunch of preteens who know how to throw elbows. Gentlemen who like looking sharp should visit Vito Manzo (Via Garibaldi 38), barber extraordinaire. In his small shop, portly men sit and listen to the radio while Vito sharpens a straight-edge razor. Shave and a haircut: L20,000. Every night until 8 PM, funky old Adamo makes hard candy at his stall next to Porto Saturno—smooching couples line up for a handful (seven for L1000).

the colony is two ruins—some of the most beautiful in all the world. The **temple** and **theater** are not only stunning in their own right (all the temple's unfluted columns are still standing and the theater's acoustics are perfect), but this is one of the few places where the land surrounding the ruins has been left practically intact. The pine trees, rocky gorge, hills smothered in wild daisies, distant vineyards, and herds of grazing sheep make this the most satisfying archaeological stop in Sicily.

Try to visit Segesta during the first two weeks of July in any odd-numbered year, when the **Teatro Classico Segesta** performs classical drama in the hilltop theater. Contact APT in Trapani (*see* Basics, *above*) for advance tickets and information about special buses for theatergoers. In even-numbered years, drown your disappointment with a bottle of local wine at the bar near the theater.

➤ **COMING AND GOING** • There is only one daily train to the Segesta-Tempio station from both Palermo (1½ hrs, L8400) and Trapani (30 min, L3600), but there are four daily Autoservizi Tarantola buses from Trapani's Piazza Garibaldi (30 min, L4000) to Segesta. From Segesta's train station it's a beautiful but lonely 20-minute walk uphill to the temple.

ERICE Founded by the Phoenicians and later dedicated to Aphrodite by the Greeks, Erice is the ultimate medieval fortress. The ol' Goddess of Love attracted countless invaders throughout Erice's long history, despite its inconvenient location, perched on a mountaintop above Trapani and the coast. The mountain is still isolated and remote, with horizon-wide views of the Mediterranean, not to mention a gaggle of brawny fortifications connected by cobbled lanes. It's hard not to be struck by the medieval architecture and mysterious, almost spooky atmosphere, unless of course you arrive on a summer weekend, when Erice is packed to the gills with *turisti* (tourists). Your best strategy then is to start exploring around dusk, when the crowds melt away, and the narrow streets become worthy of a stage setting for *Hamlet*. Check out the fortified 14th-century bell tower, the 15th-century cathedral, and the Norman castle that clings to the cliffside in the southeast corner of town. Then move on to the **Museo Comunale Cordici** (Piazza Umberto I; admission: L2000, open Mon.–Sat. 8:30–1:30), home to a fine *Annunciation* by Antonello Gagini. The most enjoyable sightseeing, however, is among the narrow alleys and durable-looking stone houses—especially intriguing in the old Spanish quarter on the northern side of town, near the ancient city walls.

From Trapani's Piazza Montalto, buses to Erice (12 daily, 1 hr, L2500) will drop you just outside Porta Trapani. Erice's main drag, Via Vittorio Emanuele, is straight ahead and will lead you to Piazza Umberto I. The helpful **AAST** tourist office (Viale Conte Pepoli 11, tel. 0923/869388) is a bit to the right (east) and has an excellent brochure and map of the town. As for lodgings, the **Ostello della Gioventù CSI** (Viale delle Pinete, tel. 0923/869144; open late June–Aug.) charges L15,000 a night. Even though it's a bit northwest of town, the hostel fills up with youth groups, so call ahead. In a pinch, **Affittacamere Italia** (Via A. Palma 7, tel. 0923/869185) arranges private rooms for about L25,000 per person.

SAN VITO LO CAPO The mellow resort town of San Vito lo Capo sits at the tip of a narrow peninsula on the edge of Golfo di Castellammare. Its out-of-the-way location (arrivals are by bus only) means backpackers can afford to linger, contemplating the surrounding expanse of reddish mountains and sparkling sea. Weird rock outcroppings along the coast—not to mention one of Sicily's largest sand beaches—attract Italian tourists during summer, but within a few kilometers of San Vito, there's enough open space to lose yourself in. Walk or bike 6 kilometers east to the abandoned *tonnara* (tuna fishery), where there's good swimming along the rough shore. Rock climbers who find themselves eyeing the sharp peaks that encircle San Vito should contact the **Club Alpino Italiano** in Palermo (c/o Signore Nazzareno Rovella, Via Agrigento 30, tel. 091/625–4352) for information on the best routes up—some of the rock in this area is not secure. Maps, lodging reservations, and bus schedules are available inside San Vito's **police station** (Via Savoia 88, tel. 0923/972160; open Mon.–Sat. 9–noon and 4–7).

➤ **COMING AND GOING** • Unless you have a car, public buses are the only way to reach San Vito lo Capo. AST has nine buses daily to and from Trapani's Piazza Montalto (1½ hrs, L5100). **Autoservizi Russo** (Corso Garibaldi 55, Palermo, tel. 0924/31364) runs three buses a day to and from Palermo's Piazza Marina (3 hrs, L11,400). Buses arrive and depart from the upper stretch of **Via Mattarella**, near its intersection with Via Foritano.

> ➤ **WHERE TO SLEEP AND EAT** • There are two pensions in the same building near the beach: **Sabbia d'Oro** (Via Santuario 49, tel. 0923/972508) and **Pensione Ocean View** (tel. 0923/972613), which both charge L70,000 for a double. Private rooms at the homey **Affitta-camere Eden** are only L45,000 (Via Mulino 62, tel. 0923/972460). **Camping Soleado** (Via del Secco 13, tel. 0923/972166; closed Oct.–May), on the east side of town near the beach, charges L8500 per person and L7000 for a small tent. For ocean views and excellent busiate al pesto Trapanese (L7000), try **Trattoria/Pizzeria Riviera** (Via Lungomare, tel. 0923/972480), on the eastern end of San Vito's beachfront road. Like all respectable Italian beach towns, San Vito has a hoppin' summer disco scene, and the open-air dance floor at **Discoteca Stardust** is packed with frenzied, vacationing Sicilians. Thanks to machismo, women get in free. The Stardust is east of town, about 15 minutes by foot along the coast road. In summer it's jammed Tuesday–Sunday from around 10:30 PM until 1 or 2 in the morning.

Egadi Islands

The wild, barren Egadi Islands (Isole Egadi) loom large off Sicily's western coast. Three principal islands—Favignana, Levanzo, and Marettimo—offer you the chance to swim, beach bum, and hike in an nontouristy environment, though if you spend more than a few nights you may be daunted by the high price of lodging and food on the islands. You can stretch your lire by inquiring about rooms in private homes (L15,000–L20,000 per person) immediately upon arrival.

Using Trapani as a base, you can tackle up to two islands per day and still make it back to the mainland by nightfall—that is, if you're adept at studying ferry timetables. A more relaxed strategy is to spend a day or two hopping between Favignana and rural Levanzo, the most convenient islands from Trapani. Only a trickle of hardy backpackers make it to mellow Marettimo, the farthest island from the mainland (1 hr by hydrofoil, 3 hrs by ferry). Buy tickets in Trapani at Siremar (*see* Coming and Going, in Trapani, *above*). Hydrofoils and ferries both depart from Trapani's waterfront, about one block east of Piazza Garibaldi and the Molo di Sanità.

FAVIGNANA

The largest and most populated Egadi island is also the most touristed. If you're planning nothing more adventurous than a day trip, make a beeline for the sandy **Lido Burrone**, a quiet beach 3 kilometers from the port. Continue south along the rocky coast for Punta Panfalo and Cala Azzurra, headlands that overlook the calm Mediterranean. Farther along the coast is **Cala Rossa** (Red Cove), which has interesting tufa-rock formations and is another good swimming spot. In May or June, Favignana hosts its annual **Mattanza**, when schools of giant tuna are corralled by boats and then harpooned and heaved on deck by local fishermen. The yearly tuna run is bloody and more than a little gruesome. Animal lovers may not enjoy the Old World spectacle too much, but anthropologists should bring their notebooks.

Biking is the best way to get around the island, and several rental joints scattered over the three blocks from the port to the center charge L5000–L10,000 per day. Ask around at the docks or in bars near Piazza Madrice, the port's main square, for private rooms. Or ask the staff at **Pro Loco** (Piazza Madrice 7, tel. 0923/921647; open Mon.–Sat. 9–noon and 2–5) to arrange one for you.

LEVANZO

The biggest debate in Levanzo is how many people live on the island—most agree that the population hovers around 120, though some (usually stubborn, elderly buggers) insist it is closer to 100. As you can imagine, there are limits to what can be done with a cast of 100 (or even 120) characters, though the quiet beauty of the steeply sloped island and the sugar-cube houses can be a source of inexhaustible, if mellowed, pleasure. In addition to three restaurants, two cafés, one market, and one bakery, Levanzo is home to the **Grotta del Genovese**, a cave decorated with 6,000-year-old Paleolithic animals and abstract designs, as well as Neolithic human representations. The grotta is only accessible by contacting its official guardian, **Signore Giuseppe Castiglione** (Via Calvario 11, above the dock, tel. 0923/921704), who usually meets arriving ferries and hydrofoils. He charges L10,000–L15,000 per person for a guided, several-hour journey by car and foot to the cave.

MARETTIMO

Hardly any tourists visit Marettimo, which lies in the middle of nothin', some 40 kilometers west of Trapani. This is bad news for overnight visitors (inquire at the docks for private rooms) but good news for isolationists and rugged hikers. The island's rocky terrain and coastline are ideal for solitary exploring, and several trails wind across the isle into its most secluded reaches. From the port, head south for an hour to **Cala Sarde**, a popular swimming spot. Another hour west, near Punta Libeccio, is **Cala Nera**, which is so isolated that you can skinny-dip undisturbed. For a long hike (3 hrs each way), follow the northeastern coast from the port for about 15 minutes, then turn inland for 15 meters to hook up with a major path that stretches along the entire shoreline. You'll eventually end up at some cement steps that lead to a hidden beach just below the ruins of **Castello di Punta Troia**, which the Spanish used as a prison in the 17th century.

Palermo

Natives of Palermo like to say that their city has two faces: *la bella e la brutta* (the beautiful and the ugly). Crowded, crumbling, impoverished, and unwieldy, Palermo has been undergoing a steady decline since the 14th century, but historical and artistic attractions showcase the exotic influence of its Arab and Norman conquerors. Don't expect Palermo to charm you at first glance. Sicily's capital is a *city* in all senses of the word, and with every stride you take on the traffic- and people-infested streets, you push further into a seemingly untamed metropolis of 800,000. That said, its rich heritage makes it too intriguing to ignore, and its winding medieval streets, with dilapidated but beautiful baroque palaces, are fascinating to explore.

Perched on a crescent-shaped bay at the foot of Monte Pellegrino, Palermo was first colonized in the 6th century BC, during Carthage's control of northwestern Sicily. After the Romans enjoyed a few centuries of dominance, Moorish princes from Spain conquered the city around the turn of the millennium. Over the next 700 years they refashioned Palermo in the image of Cairo and Córdoba, with mosques, minarets, and palm trees. But the city's heyday really began in 1130 AD, when the Norman king Frederick II named it the capital of his empire. One of the great intellectual leaders of the Middle Ages, Frederick II transformed Palermo into the most cosmopolitan, vibrant center of learning in all of Europe—many of the city's greatest monuments date from this period. For the next seven centuries, Palermo and Naples were in competition for domination of lower Italy, though almost all of the innovative spirit of the 12th century had been lost.

After Sicily merged into the embryonic Italian state, a strange institution began to gain influence in Palermo—the Mafia. Today, Palermo is known throughout the world as the home of Italy's most powerful dons. The images you've come to expect from movies—burly men kissing each other and exchanging suitcases, armor-plated Alfa-Romeos, and police-turned-hit-men—are mostly based on reality, but you probably won't see any of it. What you may experience is adept pickpockets and Vespa-riding bag snatchers. The petty crime shouldn't discourage you from a visit, but you should understand that Palermo is more than what you've seen on the silver screen or read in a history book—it's a real live city.

BASICS

AMERICAN EXPRESS AmEx cardholders can cash personal checks, replace lost or stolen cards, and pick up mail (Palermo's postal code is 90139). The rest of us can exchange money and replace lost or stolen traveler's checks. *G. Ruggieri e Figli, Via Emerico Amari 40, tel.*

Palermo

Sights ●

Catacombe dei Cappuccini, 19
Il Duomo, 11
Galleria Nazionale di Sicilia, 10
La Martorana, 13
Mercato della Vucciria, 7
Museo Archeologico Regionale, 3
Museo Internazionale delle Marionette, 8
Palazzo Chiaramonte, 9
Palazzo dei Normanni, 18
Piazza Castelnuovo, 2
San Giovanni degli Eremiti, 17
Teatro Massimo, 1

Lodging ○

Albergo Concordia, 15
Albergo Luigi, 12
Albergo Orientale, 16
Albergo Paradiso, 14
Hotel Ariston, 4
Hotel Joli, 6
Hotel Petit, 5

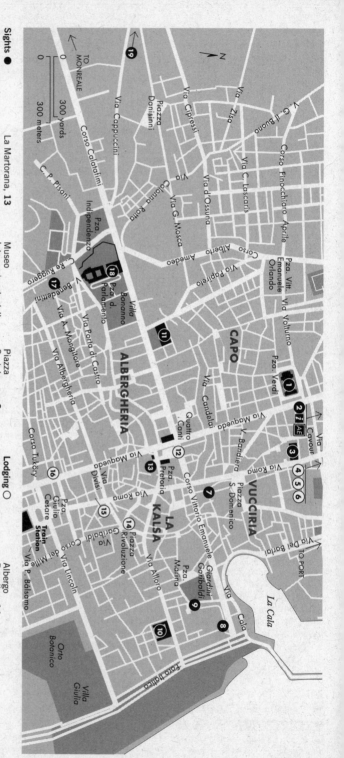

091/587144. *From Stazione Centrale, Bus 101 or 107 to Piazza Castelnuovo, then follow Via Emerico Amari toward port. Open weekdays 9–1 and 4–7, Sat. 9–1.*

CHANGING MONEY In addition to the train info office, the post office, and countless banks along Via Roma, **Banca Nazionale di Lavoro** (Via Roma 291, tel. 091/602411; open weekdays 8:25–1:30 and 2:50–4) has an outdoor ATM that accepts cards on the Plus system, with three additional machines inside.

ENGLISH BOOKS AND NEWSPAPERS Travelers can find British and American newspapers at Stazione Centrale, in the bigger newsstands along Via Roma, and at the newsstands around Teatro Massimo on Piazza Verdi. For more substantial reading material, **Feltrinelli** (Via Maqueda 457, tel. 091/587785; open weekdays 9–1 and 4–8, Sat. 9–1), on Piazza Verdi opposite Teatro Massimo, has an excellent selection of classics and modern fiction.

MEDICAL AID Pharmacies open 24 hours include **Farmacia lo Cascio** (Via Roma 5, across Piazza Giulio Cesare from train station, tel. 091/587785) and **Farmacia Inglese** (Via Mariano Stabile 175, tel. 091/334482), to the port side of where Via Marino Stabile intersects Via Maqueda.

MAIL AND PHONES The best place to make an international call is one of **SIP**'s two locations: Piazza Ungheria 22 (across Via Cavour to the north of Teatro Massimo; open Mon.–Sat. 8–8) or on Via Lincoln across the street from the train station (open daily 8 AM–9:30 PM). **Posta Centrale** (Via Roma 322, tel. 091/160 or 091/186) is open Monday–Saturday 8:10–7:30.

VISITOR INFORMATION EPT, on the opposite side of town from the train station, has maps and a sometimes gracious, sometimes outright rude English-speaking staff. Other EPT offices around town—at the train station, the docks, and Piazza Pretoria—are semi-indefinitely closed. *Piazza Castelnuovo 34, opposite Teatro Politeama Garibaldi, tel. 091/658–3847. From Stazione Centrale, take Bus 101 or 107 to Piazza. Open weekdays 8–8, Sat. 8–2.*

COMING AND GOING

BY TRAIN **Stazione Centrale** (Via Roma at Piazza Giulio Cesare) is at the southern end of Via Roma near Palermo's medieval districts. This station is the hub for all rail traffic in and out of Palermo, with trains to Agrigento (7 daily, 2 hrs, L11,700), Catania (6 daily, 4 hrs, L19,000), Bagheria (17 daily, 10 min, L2400), Cefalù (14 daily, 1 hr, L5700), Enna (6 daily, 2½ hrs, L13,600), Messina (16 daily, 3½ hrs, L19,000), Milazzo (5 daily, 3 hrs, L15,500), and Marsala (9 daily, 2½ hrs, L13,600). Palermo also has direct routes to Rome (7 daily, 13 hrs, L68,900) and Milan (3 daily, 19 hrs, L81,000). Inside the station, the **railway information office** (tel. 091/616–1806; open daily 7:20 AM–9:10 PM) exchanges money at mediocre rates and can answer questions about timetables. **Luggage storage** (L1500; open daily 6 AM–10 PM) is on the far right side of the tracks.

BY BUS Since there is no central bus station, Palermo's 18 privately-owned companies usually make two stops before leaving town: one in front of their office, and one at the train station. Guess which is easier to find. The best thing to do is ask the bus drivers themselves when you should be at the stop, preferably a day in advance, as the company offices tend to be of little help. **AST** (091/688–2783 or 091/688–2906) goes to Ragusa (4 daily, 3½ hrs, L17,900); **Cuffaro** (tel. 091/616–1510) travels to Agrigento (3 daily, 2 hrs, L13,000); **Russo** (tel. 091/31364) goes to San Vito lo Capo (3 daily, 3 hrs, L11,400); **SAIS** (091/616–6028) goes to Catania (10 daily, 2 hrs 45 min, L10,800), Messina (15 daily, 5 hrs, L24,500), and Siracusa (5 daily, 4 hrs, L25,700); **Salemi** (tel. 091/617–5411) runs to Marsala (13 daily, 2½ hrs, L14,600) and Trapani (15 daily, 2 hrs, L11,000); and **Stassi** (tel. 091/617–5348) goes to Erice (4 daily, 1½ hrs, L8300).

BY BOAT All ferries and hydrofoils dock at **Stazione Marittima** (Via Francesco Crispi 118). During high season, make reservations a few days in advance, especially if you want a cabin. The following agencies are usually open Saturday mornings as well as during normal weekday hours. **Tirrenia** (Via Emerico Amari, tel. 091/602–1230) has daily service to Naples (7 hrs, L65,000) and thrice-weekly service to Genova (23 hrs, L102,000). **Siremar** (Via Francesco

Crispi 120, tel. 091/582403) sails Monday–Saturday to Ustica by ferry (daily, 2 hrs 20 min, L15,400) and hydrofoil (2 daily, 1¼ hrs, L28,000).

GETTING AROUND

Stazione Centrale lies at the southern edge of the city at the foot of Palermo's two main drags: **Via Roma** and **Via Maqueda**. The equally busy **Corso Vittorio Emanuele** runs perpendicular to these two thoroughfares. The intersection of Corso Vittorio Emanuele and Via Maqueda at Piazza Vigliena is known as **Quattro Canti** (Four Corners) and is the axis of the old town's four traditional neighborhoods: Capo to the northwest, Vucciria to the northeast, La Kalsa to the southeast, and Albergheria to the southwest. Most of the major monuments and sights are scattered around these medieval quarters, which are characterized by a web of winding, narrow streets and alleys.

BY BUS Palermo's extensive **AMAT** bus system was just recently revamped and smoothed out. Some major routes are 101 and 107, which run from the train station along Via Roma to Piazza Castelnuovo (Bus 101 continues north along Via Libertà). Bus 109 goes from the train station to Piazza Indipendenza, which is at the western end of Corso Vittorio Emanuele—transfer here for the 389 to the outlying district of Monreale. Bus 118 takes you to the port.

WHERE TO SLEEP

Palermo's cheapest hotels are squashed between Via Maqueda, Via Roma, Corso Vittorio Emanuele, and Stazione Centrale. Hotels often share the same building, and the prices go down as the stairs go up. Traffic near the train station can be deafening, but things mellow out after 10 PM. If you're exceptionally worried about crime, head to the modern part of Palermo near Piazza Castelnuovo—take Bus 101 or 107 from Stazione Centrale—and keep out of La Kalsa district. All of the places below will store your luggage. Beds fill up fast during Palermo's Festival of Santa Rosalia, July 11–15 (*see* Cheap Thrills, *below*).

NEAR STAZIONE CENTRALE **Albergo Concordia.** You'd expect more for the price (doubles L50,000), even though the elevator is straight outta *Angel Heart*. Spartan, tile-floored rooms have high ceilings and balconies, and the bathtubs are almost big enough for two. *Via Roma 72, 4th floor, tel. 091/617–1514. 14 rooms, 2 with bath.*

Albergo Orientale. Housed in a decaying, 18th-century palace with a wide central courtyard, this hotel tops the list for bizarre management. Some rooms are quite large, and all are a little dusty. The highlight of any stay is walking up the vast, grand, and chipped pink marble steps. Doubles are around L40,000; haggle if you plan to stay more than three nights. *Via Maqueda 26, tel. 091/616–5727. 24 rooms, 4 with bath.*

Albergo Paradiso. Hardly "paradise," it's still the best of the worst in La Kalsa. You make the call—bad neighborhood, cheap price (doubles L45,000). The beds and rooms are small and the noise level is high. On the plus side, everything is clean and some rooms overlook the piazza. *Via Schiavuzzo 65, tel. 091/617–2825. From train station, take 5th right off Via Roma (Via Divisi) to Piazza della Rivoluzione. 10 rooms, none with bath.*

NEAR QUATTRO CANTI **Albergo Luigi.** Clean if slightly seedy rooms (note the red-satin bedspreads) matter less than the excellent location. The two rooms with views of Piazza Pretoria are a real score. Doubles start at L50,000. *Salita Santa Caterina 1, tel. 091/585085. Off Corso Vittorio Emanuele just east of Quattro Canti. 9 rooms, 5 with bath.*

NEAR PIAZZA CASTELNUOVO **Hotel Ariston.** Rooms at the Ariston are boring but exceptionally clean (doubles L42,000). The manager is a friendly fellow who might let you use his washing machine for a small fee. *Via Mariano Stabile 139, tel. 091/332434. 2 blocks off Via Roma towards Via Ruggero Settimo. 5 rooms, 2 with bath.*

Hotel Joli. A baby-step up from your average budget hotel, Joli has doubles (L85,000) with wide, comfortable beds, TVs, and commodious bathrooms with hot showers. It's in the safe but dull Castelnuovo district, but within a few blocks from the rambling streets of old Palermo.

Many rooms overlook the quiet and grassy Piazza Florio. *Via Michele Amari 11, tel. 091/ 611765 or 091/611–1766. From Piazza Verdi, walk east on Via Cavour, north on Via Roma for 5 blocks, and right on Via Granatelli.*

Hotel Petit. This hotel is in the most congenial part of Palermo, on a pedestrian-only thoroughfare that has a few good bars. The bathrooms sparkle, and many of the comfortable rooms have balconies. For comfort, quiet, and safety, it's worth the L60,000 for doubles. *Via Principe di Belmonte 84, tel. 091/323616. Off Via Roma near Piazza Castelnuovo. 7 rooms, 6 with bath. Reservations advised. AE.*

CAMPING **Camping Trinacria.** Way out on the northern outskirts of the city, this is a semirustic, fairly luxurious (hot showers, market) year-round campground. A site costs L5500 per person; a tent is an additional L5500. *Località Sferracavallo, Via Barcarello, tel. 091/530590. From Stazione Centrale, Bus 101 for 20 min to Stadio stop; transfer to Bus 128 to Via Barcarello (ask driver for "Camping Trinacria").*

FOOD

Seafood fans should try *pesce spada* (swordfish) and *polpo* (octopus), which is more appetizing than it sounds. Vegetarians should look for *capunata di melanzane* (a sweet-and-sour eggplant relish), olives, and stuffed artichokes from the city's antipasti tables—reputed to be the best on the island. At the cheap end of the spectrum are markets like **Vucciria market** (*see* Worth Seeing, *below*) and **STANDA** (Via Roma 59, near Stazione Centrale). Top off any meal with delectable pastries and marzipan from one of the city's pasticcerie.

NEAR STAZIONE CENTRALE **Hostaria Da Ciccio.** Come for some of the best home-cooked food in Palermo. Try fried shrimp (L9000), the excellent antipasti plate (L6000), and a variety of omelets (L5000). On warm summer evenings, linger over dinner at an outdoor table. *Via Firenze 6, tel. 091/329143. Off Via Roma, just before Corso Vittorio Emanuele.*

NEAR QUATTRO CANTI **Osteria al Ferro di Cavallo.** The atmosphere at this blue-collar lunch spot is hectic and lively. There's no menu, but the polpo and sarde dishes are dependable. A full lunch consists of salad, pasta, bread, meat or fish, and beer or wine, all for L7000–L12,000. *Via Venezia 20, tel. 091/331835. Off Via Roma, 1 block north of Corso Vittorio Emanuele. Open Mon.–Sat. noon–3:15.*

Ristorante/Pizzeria Ca' d'Oro. This unassuming restaurant in the center of town is an excellent place to sample pasta (L3000–L6000) or pizza (L4500–L10,000) at balcony tables overlooking a lively street. *Corso Vittorio Emanuele 254, near Via Roma, tel. 091/329911. Open Mon.–Sat. noon–3 and 6–midnight. AE, MC, V.*

Trattoria Primavera. Primavera has received excellent reviews from *The New York Times* and several Italian publications, so it's downright shocking that the prices are still affordable. The food here lives up to its reputation, especially the squid-ink spaghetti (L7000). It's best to make reservations about two days in advance, but it's worth it to try your luck and stop by if foresight isn't your thing. *Piazza Bologni 4, tel. 091/329408. From Quattro Canti, walk west down Corso Vittorio Emanuele. Open Wed.–Mon. 12:30–3:30 and 7:30–midnight.*

Trattoria Stella. In the courtyard of a seemingly abandoned palatial hotel, this is one of the best places to eat cheaply and well in the old district of Palermo. Spaghetti with seafood (L8000) is more than a full meal, but if you're hungry enough, try the delicious *antipasto della casa* or *involtini di spada*. Reservations are imperative, especially if you want a courtyard table in summer. *Via Alloro 104, tel. 091/314806. From Via Roma, walk east on Via Divisi through Piazza Rivoluzione, turn right onto Via Alloro. Closed Sun.*

NEAR PIAZZA CASTELNUOVO **La Gondola–Da Pippo.** A thoroughly funky restaurant, with photographs of Bruce Lee and Telly Savalis on the wall, fresh fish in the cooler by the door, and a serve yourself antipasti bar (L3000 per plate) on a bookcase in back. Pippo broods around the register looking like Humphrey Bogart (who's also on the wall), while Mamma Pippo runs the kitchen and turns out dishes like spinach- and ricotta-stuffed ravioli (L7000) and succulent grilled squid (L12,000). *Via di Scordia 144, tel. 091/320488. From Piazza Castelnuovo, walk towards the port on Via Emerico Amari, right on Via di Scordia. Closed Sun. AE, MC, V.*

Hosteria al Duar 2. Sample Tunisian delicacies (complete meal L15,000) or try the Italian side of the menu at this popular spot with small sidewalk tables. *Via Emerico Amari 92, near Via Roma, no phone. Open Mon.–Sat. noon–3 and 7–11.*

Osteria Fratelli lo Bianco. This local joint has been going strong for more than 90 years, largely due to its "secret" recipes for simple, delicious Palermitan dishes. A small menu is posted near the entrance, but the brusque waiters will tell you what's on for the day in rapid-fire Italian. A variety of pastas (from L4500) are always available. The desserts are luscious (L2500) and the local wine potent (L5000 per liter). *Via Emerico Amari 104, tel. 091/585816. Walk toward port from Piazza Castelnuovo. Open Mon.–Sat. noon–3 and 7–10.*

Ristorante/Pizzeria Italia. It's considered the best pizzeria in Palermo, which explains the long lines of drooling locals. Sit outside in a shady alleyway and choose from 25 different kinds of pizza (L5000–L8000). The *Greca*—with fresh tomatoes, mushrooms, onions, eggplant, and Parmesan—is one of the best. *Via dell'Orologio 54, tel. 091/589885. From Quattro Canti, take Via Maqueda north and turn right just before Teatro Massimo. Open Tues.–Sun. 12:30–3 and 7–midnight. Closed mid-Aug.–early Sept. AE.*

WORTH SEEING

Palermo's attractions are scattered among the labyrinthine streets and alleyways of its four medieval quarters. While neighborhood identity is no longer as strong as in days past, the poorer La Kalsa and Vucciria quarters are associated with rubble and grime because of the still-unrepaired damage wrought during World War II. Many of these sooty tenement houses, some without running water, are actually crumbling villas of an earlier wealthy class once based in the area. Traces of the buildings' original glamour comes in snatches—a neo-classical window touched up with brown stucco, a baroque pink staircase standing alone in a deserted courtyard. The four medieval quarters are notorious for pickpockets and purse snatchers. During the day, however, it's quite safe to wander the narrow, mainly pedestrian streets of central Palermo.

Factionalism between the Albergheria, Capo, Vucciria, and La Kalsa districts was once so strong that each had a distinct dialect. Back then, few natives married across neighborhood divides.

LA KALSA **Galleria Nazionale di Sicilia.** Housed in the 15th-century Palazzo Abatellis, this spectacular art gallery contains paintings and sculpture from the 11th–17th centuries. The most striking piece is the massive, pock-marked 16th-century fresco *Trionfo della Morte,* in which the angel of

Palermo, a City of Rich Dentists

The gastronomic world is forever indebted to Palermo for the invention of gelato, but other than its historical appeal, the gelato you'll find here is pretty similar to what you'll find all over Italy. Pastries are another matter—Palermo is known as having the nation's greatest sweet shops. Of these, two stand out. Alba (Piazza Don Bosco 7, tel. 091/309016; closed Mon.) is the undisputed god of pastry shops, and though they are way off the beaten track in upper-middle class suburban Palermo, it's worth the trek to sample their babà (cake soaked in sweet rum) for L1800 or assorted semifreddi (mousses) for L4000. Closer to the center and still excellent, Gran Café Nobel (Via della Libertà 35, tel. 0931/611–0750) has an elegant tearoom and specializes in seasonal fruit tarts (L2400) and cannoli (L2500).

death gallops through a crowd of wealthy folks and turns them stiff and blue with his arrows. *Via Alloro 4, near the waterfront. Admission: L2000. Open Mon.–Sat. 9–2 (Tues., Thurs., and Fri. also 3–8), Sun. and holidays 9–1.*

La Martorana. Originally founded in 1143 by the Norman admiral George of Antioch, this chapel later became part of a convent established by a Spanish noblewoman, Eloisa Martorana. The baroque exterior was refurbished in 1588, but the interior still houses some 12th-century Byzantine mosaics. The political meets the spiritual in two mosaics near the entrance. One shows the admiral offering the church to the Madonna, and the other has Christ crowning King Roger de Hauteville, who conquered Palermo in 1061. *Piazza Bellini 3, off Via Maqueda near Quattro Canti. Admission free. Open Mon.–Sat. 9:30–1 and 3:30–5:30, Sun. 8:30–1.*

Museo Internazionale delle Marionette. Palermo has succeeded in the difficult task of taking an almost-lost tradition and making it spooky and vibrant in what is usually the driest of places—a museum. It's hard to overstate the cultural importance of puppets in Sicily: The lengthy and often brutal history of the island was handed down through generations by the dolls' violent and comical antics. The displays (illuminated by eerie, undulating lights) feature the local hero Orlando and his arch-enemy Saladino, but they aren't limited to Sicilian puppets—it's like "It's a Small World" without the inane singing. *Via Butera 1, tel. 091/328060. Admission: L5000, L3000 students. Open weekdays 9–1 and 4–7, Sat. 9–1.*

Palazzo Chiaramonte. This imposing Arabic-Norman structure, built in 1307 by the influential Chiaramonte family, is the second-largest palace in Palermo. More to the point, in the late 17th and 18th centuries it served as the seat of the Inquisition in Sicily. Unfortunately, the palazzo is open only during temporary exhibitions (which are usually quite good). *Piazza Marina 61, near Giardini Garibaldi. Admission and opening hours vary.*

ALBERGHERIA **Palazzo dei Normanni.** Situated on a slight hill above the gardens of the palm-filled Villa Bonanno, this former Saracen castle was transformed into a royal palace by Sicily's 11th-century Norman king, Roger de Hauteville. During the next century, in the reign of Roger II, it became famous throughout medieval Europe as a center of culture and the arts. Today it houses the Sicilian Parliament and is closed to the public (thanks to a spate of political bombings in 1992). Fortunately, the **Cappella Palatina** remains open. The French writer Guy de Maupassant called the chapel "the finest religious jewel dreamt of by human thought," and it's hard to disagree. Constructed between 1130 and 1143, every inch of the chapel's interior is covered with brilliant Byzantine mosaics, except for its honeycomb wooden ceiling, which is itself ornate. Upstairs are the royal apartments, including **Sala di Ruggero** (King Roger's Hall), which has some outstanding mosaics of hunters and their prey. At press time, they were closed to the public for restoration. *Piazza Indipendenza. Admission free. Open weekdays 9–noon and 3–5, Sat. 9–noon, Sun. and holidays 9–10 and noon–1.*

Death by Vinegar

In the early 18th century, a woman known as "La Vecchia dell'Aceto" (The Old Lady of the Vinegar) sold different types of vinegar from her stall in the Vucciria market. She had red vinegars, balsamic vinegars, fruit-scented vinegars, and even medicinal vinegars. One tasteless, odorless, and toxic blend was combed through the hair to kill lice. It was also used by young matrons of Palermo to kill bothersome pests of a different kind: their husbands. This went on for several years, until somebody ratted and La Vecchia was arrested. At her trial, she claimed to have indirectly rid the world of over 350 husbands, a quantity that so infuriated the local (male) authorities that they skinned her alive and had her drawn and quartered in Piazza Marina.

San Giovanni degli Eremiti. This 12th-century church, topped with five pink domes, was designed by Norman-employed Arab architects and built on the foundations of a mosque. The real attraction, however, isn't the exotic architecture. It's the ruined 13th-century cloisters and peaceful gardens—wild masses of flowering vines, roses, and drooping palms—that surround the building. *Via dei Benedettini 3. Across from Palazzo dei Normanni, to right of royal palace entrance. Admission free. Open daily 9–1 (Tues., Wed., and Fri. also 3–5).*

CAPO **Il Duomo.** This imposing 12th-century cathedral is a grab bag of architectural styles. Of the original church, only the twin towers, gigantic cupola, and triple apse remain, appearing as if they were transplanted from a completely different structure. Inside the often-renovated and subsequently uninteresting interior, notice the numerous saint sculptures, the 15th-century portal, and the royal tombs, including those of Roger II and Frederick II. The **treasury** (admission: L1000), to the right of the altar, displays the gold tiara of Constance of Aragon, intricately detailed liturgical vestments, and an assortment of fine jewelry. *Corso Vittorio Emanuele. Open Mon.–Sat. 7–noon and 4–7, Sun. 8–1:30 and 4–7.*

Teatro Massimo. This neoclassical theater was the second largest opera house in the world (only Paris's was bigger) when it was built at the turn of the century. Recently, its lion-flanked staircase was the backdrop for one of the cinema's worst-delivered lines: Sophia Coppola's "Dad?," from the death-scene in *The Godfather III*. Godfather or no Godfather, the theater is undergoing restoration—it should be open sometime early in the next millennium. *Piazza Verdi, at intersection of Via Maqueda and Via Cavour.*

VUCCIRIA **Mercato della Vucciria.** Palermo's Vucciria market is known throughout Sicily for its animated merchants and congested alleyways. Everywhere you turn there's some boisterous thug holding aloft a head of lettuce, a slab of meat, or the bloody head of a freshly butchered swordfish. Come in the morning—after lunch things really die down—and snack on olives while you shop for contraband cigarettes. Watch your wallet *very carefully* lest it fall into the hands of resident thieves. After a morning of hectic shopping, you can sample market-bought fish and vegetables in one of the restaurants on nearby Vicolo Mezzani. *Off Via Roma, btw Corso Vittorio Emanuele and Piazza San Domenico. Open Mon.–Sat. early morning–early afternoon.*

Museo Archeologico Regionale. A 16th-century convent houses this vast archaeological museum. Artifacts dredged from the Mediterranean—including Roman and Phoenician anchors—are on display in the cloisters, while in an adjacent hall you'll see 5th-century BC lion-headed drip stones from Himera (the gaping mouths and curved tongues were used to drain water from rooftops). The most famous exhibits are in the **Salone di Selinunte**, which has blocky but beautiful 5th- and 6th-century BC metopes from Selinunte. The friezes displayed here (also taken from the temples) illustrate the Greek myths. *Piazza Olivella 4, off Via Roma behind main post office. From Stazione Centrale, Bus 15, 34, or 37. Admission: L2000. Open Mon.–Sat. 9–2 (Tues. and Fri. also 3–6), Sun. and holidays 9–1.*

CHEAP THRILLS

CATACOMBE DEI CAPPUCCINI Entombed within the Catacombe dei Cappuccini (Capuchin Catacombs) are over 8,000 ghostly mummies, most displayed behind flimsy mesh screens. From the early 16th century to the late 19th century, the Capuchin monks dried and embalmed cadavers, which were then dressed attractively and inserted upright into individual wall niches. At first this practice was reserved for their deceased religious brethren, but it became popular among Palermo's upper class, who would come to visit their dearly departed and even change the corpse's outfits and comb its hair.

The Capuchins take their job pretty seriously, and have divided the mummies into well-marked sections according to their earthly occupation, gender, and social class. It's not revolting to your olfactories, but you do need a strong stomach—especially for the glass-encased, mummified remains of babies and small children. Although admission is free, the monks encourage donations of L1000. *Via Cappuccini. Take Bus 614 from Corso Vittorio Emanuele and ask to be let off at Via Pindemonte; from here it's a short signposted walk. Open daily 9–1 and 4–6.*

FESTINO DI SANTA ROSALIA Palermo honors its patron saint during the **Festino di Santa Rosalia** (Festival of St. Rosalia), which begins every July 11 with a raucous parade down Corso Vittorio Emanuele. The parade highlight, no doubt, is the 21-meter-long, 24-meter-high, flower- and musician-bedecked float of St. Rosalia. On the final day, July 15, the saint's relics are carried through the city, after which there's a massive fireworks display. In between, Palermo goes on a five-day eating and drinking binge.

AFTER DARK

BARS Palermo's bars tend to be fashionable spots for socializing rather than venues for unabashed boozing. **Via Principe di Belmonte** (off Via Ruggero Settimo), an upscale pedestrian mall, is lined with pricey bars, trattorias, and outdoor tables where you can gawk at beautiful people. The best choice here is **Bar Fiore** (Via Principe di Belmonte 84, tel. 091/332539), which has fine gelato, a wide selection of fairly priced beers and liquors, and tasty appetizers. It's run by a friendly family headed by patriarch Frank, who digs Americans. **Liberty Pub** (Via N. Cozzo 20, tel. 091/329385; closed Wed.), off Via Maqueda just past Teatro Massimo, is a cool place to grab a cheeseburger (that's right) and a beer while contemplating the latest Italian disco hits. On warm summer nights, all of Palermo heads out to drink and stroll along the strand at Mondello, a dirty little beach to the north of the city. To get here, hop on Bus 327 from the train station.

LIVE MUSIC While Palermo doesn't have any jazz clubs, the Associazione Siciliana Musica Insieme (ASMI) hosts jazz shows every Tuesday and Thursday in June and July at **Villa Virginia Giardino** (Via San Lorenzo 40, near Parco della Favorita); take Bus 4 from Piazza Castelnuovo. Palermo's classical-music season runs November–May and tickets start at L25,000. Concerts are held at the Teatro Politeama Garibaldi (*see below*) and **Teatro Golden** (Via Terrasanta 60, tel. 091/305217), four blocks west of the Giardino Inglese; take Bus 18 from Via Roma. Ask at the EPT tourist office (*see* Basics, *above*) for more details.

OPERA AND BALLET Palermo's opera and ballet season runs January–June. The primary venue is the massive, fresco-smothered **Teatro Politeama Garibaldi** (Piazza Ruggero Settimo), where tickets start at L35,000. Contact the box office (tel. 091/605–3315; open Tues.–Sat. 10–1 and 5–7) for info.

THEATER You've missed the point if you're in Palermo and don't check out a puppet performance. Most are held at the Museo Internazionale delle Marionette (*see* Worth Seeing, *above*); the **Teatro dei Pupi** (Via Bara all'Olivella 95), across from the Museo Archeologico Regionale; the **Teatro Marionette Ippogrifo** (Vicolo Ragusi 6), off Corso Vittorio Emanuele just past Quattro Canti heading west; or the very reputable **Compagnia Bradamante di Anna Cuticchio** (Via Lombardia 25), past the Giardino Inglese off Via della Libertà. Tickets start at L10,000 and peak at L30,000.

NEAR PALERMO

MONTE PELLEGRINO Rising 600 meters above Palermo, Monte Pellegrino is a famous city landmark and the place to come for panoramic views of the coast. Bus 106 (L1100) from Piazza Castelnuovo climbs the winding road up the mountain to **Santuario di Santa Rosalia** (open daily 7–7), a limestone cave in which Palermo's patron saint, St. Rosalia, is said to have once lived in hermetic seclusion. Today the grotto houses a chapel where ailing pilgrims come to pray and cleanse their sins with the waters of the "miraculous" underground spring.

MONREALE If you have time for only one day trip from Palermo, head 9 kilometers southwest to Monreale, a small medieval town with some first-rate architecture. First and foremost is Monreale's **cattedrale**. The cathedral's original facade—comprised of blind arches and an 18th-century portico—pales in comparison to what lies behind the large 12th-century bronze doors: mosaics that rank among the most beautiful in the world. These were composed between 1174 and 1176 by Islamic artisans commissioned by the Norman king William II. All told there are 130 panels covering some 6,000 square yards. The most striking mosaic is reserved for the Messiah—a huge and gorgeous Christ Pantocrator figure whose right hand alone is two meters tall. *Tel. 091/640–4413. Take Bus 389 from Piazza Della Independenza. Admission free. Open winter, daily 8:30–12:30 and 3:30–6; summer, daily 9–7.*

BAGHERIA During the 17th and 18th centuries, tiny Bagheria became a summer hideaway for Palermo's noblest families, who subsequently endowed the town and the surrounding countryside with grand baroque villas. Right in the center of town, the most famous villa, **Villa Palagonia**, is decorated with a bizarre array of grotesque statues commissioned by the crippled prince of Palagonia; the statues, it seems, are caricatures of his wife's many lovers. From Palermo there are several rail connections (17 daily, 10 min, L2400) to Bagheria. *Villa Palagonia, Piazza Garibaldi, 10 min from station along Corso Umberto I. Admission: L1000. Open daily 9–12:30 and 4:30–7.*

USTICA Although it's only 60 kilometers north of Palermo, this volcanic island feels a million miles away from the hurly-burly of the capital. A day trip to remote Ustica is possible if you time the ferry or hydrofoil schedules just right—but you'll need a few days to get to know Ustica's fertile, scenic landscape and its underwater snorkeling spots, reputed to be the best in the Mediterranean. Ferries and hydrofoils from Palermo (*see* Coming and Going, *above*) dock near **Piazza Capitano Vito Longo**, the port's main plaza, with a bank and visitor information center that arranges accommodations. In Palermo, **Siremar** (Via Francesco Crispi 120, tel. 091/582403) serves Ustica by ferry (daily Mon.–Sat., 2 hrs 20 min, L15,400) and hydrofoil (2 daily, 1 hr 15 min, L28,000).

During World War II, Marxist theorist Antonio Gramsci of "The Prison Notebooks" was exiled in Ustica.

To reach Ustica's snorkeling spots, consider hiring a fisherman who knows his way around the island's submerged grottoes. Expect to pay around L80,000 for a party of four. There aren't any sand beaches on Ustica, but some excellent swimming spots are scattered along the western coast, across the island from the port. Mopeds are available for rent in town, and there's a minibus that circles the island hourly.

The Tyrrhenian Coast

The Tyrrhenian coast stretches between Palermo and Milazzo, encompassing rocky coves, sandy beaches, ancient ruins, and—sorry to say—upscale resort communities. A train runs the entire coast, making it easy to jump off at less-touristed nooks. At the other end of the spectrum, **Cefalù**, the best-known and most crowded seaside town, is worth a few days if only to see its photogenic jumble of medieval streets. Beach bums and anyone tired of crowds should head for **Capo d'Orlando** and its mellow beaches. And while a port town is nothing to get overly excited about, **Milazzo** is the place to catch ferries to the **Aeolian Islands**, a volcanically active archipelago that offers curative mud baths, pristine snorkeling waters, and hikes to fiery cauldrons of lava. Throughout the region, lodging is difficult to find only in July and August, when throngs from mainland Italy and France drive prices up and availability down.

Cefalù

This fishing village-turned-resort is the Tyrrhenian coast's main attraction, not the least because it's only an hour by train from Palermo. (And because there's a Club Med resort within 3 kilometers.) Cefalù's cheesy beachfront is easily forgotten amidst the well-tended decay of the old town—a labyrinth of medieval streets pressed between the sea and an immense granite cliff, which locals call **La Rocca**. Number one on the to-do list is a sunset hike up La Rocca, followed by a drink or ice cream on **Piazza Duomo**. The highlight of the busy plaza is Cefalù's **duomo** (open daily 9–noon and 4–6; no shorts allowed), founded in 1131 by Roger II, ostensibly in thanks for having survived a nasty shipwreck. Roger didn't skimp on decorations, and inside you'll find some of the finest mosaics in Sicily, in a Byzantine tradition similar to Monreale's, with a Christ Pantocrator in the center.

BASICS The main tourist office, **Azienda Autonoma Soggiorno e Turismo** (Corso Ruggero 77, tel. 0921/21458; open weekdays 8–2 and 4–7, Sat. 9–1), is equipped with good maps and lists of accommodations. If you don't speak Italian or French, though, be prepared to struggle. The **post office** (Via Vazzana 2; open weekdays 8:30–2:30 and 4–6) is between the train station and the beach in the new part of town.

COMING AND GOING **Stazione Ferroviaria** (Piazza Stazione, tel. 0921/21169) doubles as the railway and bus terminal and is within walking distance of both the old and new parts of town. Hourly trains run to Milazzo (2 hrs, L10,500) via Palermo (1 hr, L5700). Buses connect Cefalù with Castelbuono (5 daily, 1 hr, L6100).

GETTING AROUND Few streets have signs in Cefalù, and if you spend your time pouring over a map, there's a good chance you'll get run down by a scooter. Just remember that when you're facing the ocean (north), the new part of town is to the left (west), and the old part of town and La Rocca are to the right (east). One street you may encounter is **Viale Lungomare**, which runs along the water before becoming **Via Vittorio Emanuele** when it enters the old town. Via Matteotti runs in front of the train station, Via Umberto behind it; they meet at **Piazza Garibaldi** and continue east under the name **Corso Ruggero**, the old town's main drag.

WHERE TO SLEEP Cefalù's Club Med status means that three- and four-star hotels abound. Skip 'em and head for **La Giara** (Via Veterani 40, north of Corso Ruggero, tel. 0921/21562), with big, clean rooms, all with private baths. Doubles are L55,000–L73,000 with breakfast, and plastic (MC, V) is accepted. **Locanda Cangelosi** (Via Umberto 26, tel. 0921/21591), the cheapest place in town, is on a second story overlooking busy Via Umberto. Large doubles and triples—plus a douse in the communal bathroom's strong, hot water—cost L40,000–L55,000.

➤ **CAMPING** • Cefalù's two campgrounds are actually 3 kilometers to the west in Località Ogliastrillo. Fortunately, it's an easy hitch or bus ride: Take any bus labeled LASCARI from Stazione Ferroviaria. If Costa Ponente is full, the adjacent **Camping Sanfilippo** (tel. 0921/20184; L6000 per tent, L5500 per person) has beach access but is shabbier.

Camping Costa Ponente. Camp on a cliff overlooking the sea, in a citrus grove that keeps things cool. Amenities include a pizzeria, a swimming pool, almost-clean bathrooms, and beach access. The rates are L6000 per person and L7000 per tent; prices increase by L1000 from June 15 to August 15. *Tel. 0921/20085. Closed Oct.–Apr. MC, V.*

FOOD There are plenty of markets along Corso Ruggero, and the fruit stand at the east end of Viale Lungomare has reasonably priced produce. **Arkade Grill** (Via Vanni 9, off Corso Ruggero, tel. 0921/921950; closed Thurs.) is a worthwhile splurge for North African dishes like couscous (with fish or meat) and skewers of grilled beef. A full meal costs around L20,000. **Ristorante da Nino** (Viale Lungomare 11, tel. 0921/21543; closed Mon.) is among the cheapest spots on Viale Lungomare. Pizza and pasta start at L5500, the antipasti buffet at L8000.

NEAR CEFALÙ

CASTELBUONO The winding streets of Castelbuono, 25 kilometers south of Cefalù, are spread on a steep hill under the watch of the town's weather-beaten castle. Castelbuono's relaxed, mountainous atmosphere makes a fine change from the resort mentality on the coast, and there are plenty of hiking trails to tackle in the surrounding Monti Madonie mountains—at least for those equipped with more than just sandals. Copies of a topographic map are available from **Ufficio Tecnico** (open weekdays 8:30–1:30 and 4:30–7:30), in the town hall. A favorite hike is the five-hour climb to Piano Battaglia and **Rifugio Marini** (tel. 0921/49994), where dorm beds fetch L15,000 a night. Less strenuous is the two-hour climb from Castelbuono to **Rifugio Francesco Crispi** (tel. 0921/72279), where beds cost L20,000. They serve meals (pasta L7000) or you can buy expensive supplies from their store and use the guest kitchen. Catch buses to Castelbuono (5 daily, 1 hr, L6100) from Cefalù's train station.

CAPO D'ORLANDO If you have time for only one stop between Palermo and Milazzo, Capo d'Orlando is a wise choice. With tree-lined streets, lively piazze, and uncrowded pebble beaches, it's the perfect place to relax and rub elbows with Italians, even if the atmosphere is very un-Sicilian—you could just as well be in southern California or the south of France. And, for once, you won't be overwhelmed by loud-mouthed tourists or cheesy souvenir stands. The **tourist office** (Via Pave 71, at Via Crispi, tel. 0941/912784; open weekdays 9–1 and 5:30–7:30) tries to bill Capo d'Orlando as a "city of history and culture," and glossy brochures tout the town's 3,000-year history. But Capo d'Orlando is a beach town first and foremost. It's also an alternative gateway to the Aeolian Islands; hydrofoils make daily trips (1 hr, L9000) to Vulcano and Lipari from mid-June to September.

Capo d'Orlando hosts two annual religious festivals that are worth checking out. August 15 is the **Feast of Maria Santissima di Porto Salvo**, the protectress of fishermen whose shrine caps the town's eastern hillside. At the end of October, the **Madonna of Capo d'Orlando** is celebrated with a weeklong party. During these festivals, book in advance at the newly spruced-up **Nuovo Hotel Faro** (Via Libertà 7, east end of Lungomare, tel. 0941/902466), the town's only affordable hotel, with doubles for L45,000. The beachside **Camping Santa Rosa** (tel. 0941/901723), 3 kilometers west of town, charges L7500 per tent and L6000 per person.

Milazzo

With all the great spots along the Tyrrhenian Coast, Milazzo should not top your list. It's little more than the most convenient jumping-off point for the Aeolian Islands (*see below*), though you could do far worse than sleep here for a night before moving on. As for the beaches and the town's 13th-century castle (which doubles as an open-air theater in summer), both are overshadowed by Milazzo's massive oil refinery and gloomy industrial port.

BASICS The well-stocked **tourist office** (Piazza Duilio 20, north of port, tel. 090/922–2865) is open Tuesday–Saturday 8–2 and 4:30–7:30, and has information about the surrounding archaeological sites as well as timetables for Aeolian-bound ferries and hydrofoils. The **post office** (Piazza Duilio 2; open weekdays 8:30–5:30, Sat. 8:30–1), a stone's throw from the tourist office, exchanges American Express traveler's checks.

COMING AND GOING Milazzo's **train station**, 5 kilometers southeast of town, has hourly service to Messina (18 daily, 45 min, L3600), Cefalù (13 daily, 1 hr, L5200), and Palermo (14 daily, 3½ hrs, L15,500). **Giuntabus** runs hourly to Messina (45 min, L3400). City buses run every 30 minutes or so from the train station to the center of town; L600 tickets and the exact schedule are available at the station's bar.

➤ **BY BOAT** • Trying to make sense of Milazzo's various *traghetto* (ferry) and *aliscafo* (hydrofoil) schedules can be maddening. Departure times change every two weeks, so try to keep your schedule flexible. The main routes are Milazzo–Lipari and Milazzo–Vulcano. For other islands, you must change in Lipari or Salina. Boats run every 40 minutes between 6 AM and 9 PM in summer; the frequency drops to every two hours in winter. Numerous traghetto and aliscafo lines serve the islands, and the only noticeable differences between them are departure times. For aliscafi to the islands, try **Catalano Viaggi** (Via Luciano Rizzo 9, tel. 090/928–7728), **SNAV** (Via Luciano Rizzo 14, tel. 090/928–4509), or **Siremar** (Via dei Mille 33, tel. 090/928–3242), which also runs a few traghetti. **Navigazione Generale Italiana** (Via dei Mille 26, tel. 090/928–4091) runs three daily traghetti that stop at all of the islands.

Aliscafi run to Vulcano (14 daily, 1 hr, L15,700), Stromboli (daily, 1½ hrs, L45,600), Lipari (14 daily, 1 hr, L16,300), Salina (3 daily, 1½ hrs, L31,000), Panarea (2 daily, 2 hrs, L42,800), and Filicudi (2 daily, 2 hrs, L44,600). **Traghetti** prices and times are about half as much and twice as long: Vulcano (8 daily, 1½ hrs, L8100), Stromboli (2 daily, 7 hrs, L34,000), Lipari (8 daily, 2 hrs, L9800), Salina (2 daily, 3½ hrs, L17,600), Panarea (2 daily, 5 hrs, L23,200), and Filicudi (2 daily, 5 hrs, L24,200).

WHERE TO SLEEP Prepare for a barrage of HOTEL signs near the ferry docks. The good news is that with so many choices, you shouldn't have to pay more than L50,000 for a double. If you want *any* peace and quiet, ask for a room off the street. There's plenty of room at the **Hotel California** (Via del Sole 9, 3 blocks north of ferry dock, tel. 090/922–1389), where clean, simple doubles go for L50,000. If you're not an Eagles fan, cross the street to **Hotel Central** (Via del

Sole 8, tel. 090/928–1043), a smaller, cheaper—but no less respectable—hotel. Doubles without bath cost L55,000. **Hotel Cosenz** (Via E. Cosenz, 1 block west of Via Umberto I, tel. 090/928–2996) has a handful of rooms away from the madness of the port area yet still within walking distance of Milazzo's bars and restaurants.

Aeolian Islands

The seven Aeolian Islands (Isole Eolie) have been inhabited continuously for more than 3,000 years, and Aeolian natives have understandably developed a fearful reverence for their temperamental, volcanic homeland. Ancient legends speak of the islands as the "mouths of hell," the home of fire-breathing gods and goddesses who guarded the gateway to a fiery netherworld. No doubt these tales grew in recognition of the smoldering volcanoes that even today belch steam and ash over the Mediterranean. Then as now, the islands and their inhabitants face the constant threat of extermination—be it from a raging lava flow or a violent volcanic quake.

Of course, this hasn't stemmed the flood of tourists, nor has it hindered the development of resorts and exclusive health spas, which are the islands' economic mainstays. To some, it seems, the Aeolian Islands conjure little more than radioactive mud baths and package tours. Yet seen from afar, the islands seem to float above the water, oblivious to the needs of tourists. In winter, a thick haze envelops the chain, adding to their mystery. In summer, the intense Mediterranean sun brings things to a halt, brightening the white houses against a blue sea that glitters as if with sequins.

With its health resorts and hoppin' nightlife, **Vulcano** is a fun but expensive island—a definite day trip unless you're loaded with cash. **Lipari** is a lot cheaper but also more crowded, so you may have to fight for bed space in summer. There's not much to do on **Salina**, **Filicudi**, or **Alicudi** except bask on the beach—good news if you hate crowds, bad news if you're looking for something resembling a nightlife. Of all the Aeolian Islands, **Panarea** is the most Grecian, with whitewashed houses, kick-back locals, and smooth black-sand beaches. **Stromboli** is the place for hiking to the calderas of active volcanoes.

BASICS Each island has its own tourist office, but only AAST on Lipari (*see below*) stocks the free, superhelpful booklet *Ospitalità in Blu* ("Hospitality in Blue"), which lists the addresses, phone numbers, and prices of hotels, restaurants, banks, tourist agencies, doctors, and most anything else you can think of.

COMING AND GOING Transportation between and to the Aeolian Islands is efficient and easy, so go wild. Most island life revolves around the ferry ports, so you're usually near lodging, food, and tourist info upon arrival. You can buy boat tickets at travel agencies and at the dockside ticket kiosks in Milazzo, the most convenient jumping-off point in Sicily (*see* Coming and Going, in Milazzo, *above*). Inter-island traghetto trips are generally an hour long and cost L6000–L10,000. Aliscafi take about half as long and cost twice as much.

VULCANO

Closest to the Sicilian "mainland," Vulcano is named for the god of fire and metallurgy who supposedly keeps his smithy in the depths of the island's volcano. Although he hasn't reared his head in the past century—the last eruption was in 1890—the onerous sulfur clouds that billow from the *gran cratere* (large crater) suggest he's still in residence. Even so, the Easter-basket-gone-bad smell doesn't keep Vulcano from being the most exclusive Aeolian destination, a paradise where Europeans soak in mud baths and get pink on black-sand beaches. The only problem is that Vulcano's main town combines resort status with exorbitant prices, so stick to day trips.

Vulcano's mud may not cure your aches, but the sight of grown people smearing ash-colored goop all over themselves can definitely mend your sense of humor.

Besides laying in mud or on sand, the prime island activity is hiking. The hour-long climb to the crater of the island's volcano is a definite highlight; along the way there are awesome views into the mountain's murky depths as well as sweeping views of the Mediterranean. The path starts ¾ kilometer southwest of the ferry dock and is accessed via the only road leading from town. Although hiking boots aren't necessary, the sharp stones are murder on sandals.

Vulcanello, a once-distinct island that merged with Vulcano after an eruption in the 1st century AD, also has easy-to-explore hiking trails. On the western side of the spit that joins the two, there's a first-rate beach with fine black sand and placid emerald water. Near the beach, Vulcano's *fanghi* (mud baths) are warmed by sulfuric springs and can supposedly cure rheumatism, arthritis, and skin ailments. Four caveats: (1) Don't step where the scalding-hot gas comes bubbling up, (2) don't get your clothes near the stuff, unless what you're wearing is expendable, (3) don't wear jewelry unless you'd like it permanently discolored, and (4) rinse off in the warm sea (also heated by natural springs) next to the mud pool. If you decide to spend the night, many guest houses will be happy to accommodate you, but they often *start* at L75,000 for a double. The only cheap alternative is camping at dirty, cramped **Togo-Togo** (tel. 090/985203; open June–Oct.), which charges L10,000 per person and L10,000 per tent—follow the signs to the right when you get off the boat.

LIPARI

Lipari is the largest and most visited of the Aeolian Islands and the chain's economic focal point: The large-scale pumice industry on Lipari's north shore assures that it remains the richest and most influential of the islands. And because of Lipari's many tourist facilities—including cheap lodgings and restaurants—it makes a good base for exploring the Aeolian chain. The port's pastel-colored houses and San Calogero's mud baths are enchanting, but if you're looking for isolation and untrammeled countryside, head someplace else.

Local buses circle Lipari and give good views of Sicily and of a 17th-century cliff-top **castle**, Lipari's grand attraction south of the ferry docks and just north of the hydrofoil port. Inside the castle is Lipari's lone youth hostel (*see below*) and the surprisingly entertaining **Museo Eoliano** (tel. 090/981–1031; admission free, open Mon.–Sat. 9–2), which houses archaeological finds from various sites in the archipelago. (As this particular site was occupied continuously from Neolithic times to the Roman Age, archaeologists have been able to use the layers of artifacts as a time line to date other Mediterranean finds.) Besides the museum, your best sightseeing option involves renting a moped and driving the well-surfaced road that circles the island. Scooters, Vespas, and other small motorized numbers are available from **Roberto Foti** (Via F. Crispi 31, 50 meters north of ferry port; open daily 8–1 and 2–6). Full-day rentals cost L35,000 and up, plus a L100,000 deposit on a credit card (MC, V) and your passport.

BASICS All your tourist needs can be met on Via Vittorio Emanuele, the port's main drag. **Banca del Sud** (Via Vittorio Emanuele 241; open weekdays 8:30–1:30) has the best exchange rate and handles Visa cash advances, while **Menalda Tours** (Via Vittorio Emanuele 237; open daily 9–1 and 3–9) is the place to change money after hours. The **post office** (Via Vittorio Emanuele 251; open weekdays 8:30–5:30) also exchanges money.

AAST provides info on all the islands with their ever-so-handy brochure, "Ospitalità in Blu." *Via Vittorio Emanuele 233, tel. 090/988–0095. Open June–Oct., Mon.–Sat. 8–2 and 4–10, Sun. 8–2; Sept.–May, Mon.–Sat. 9–2.*

WHERE TO SLEEP **Locanda Salina** (Via Garibaldi 18, just north of hydrofoil dock, tel. 090/981–2332) has big, comfy rooms in the heart of town. Doubles go for L50,000–L60,000. **Augustus** (Via Ausonia 16, off north end of Via Vittorio Emanuele, tel. 090/981–1232) is a steal in the off-season, when doubles—all with baths and TVs—are L75,000. From May to September, though, prices jump to L150,000. The town of Canneto, 3 kilometers north of Lipari's port, has long pebble beaches, a host of waterfront bars and restaurants, and the island's only campground, **Campeggio Baia Unci** (tel. 090/981–1909; open Mar.–Nov.). Sites are L10,000, plus L10,000 per person.

Ostello della Gioventù. The setting for the archipelago's only hostel couldn't be better; it's in the castle above Lipari's port, with sweeping views of the sea. The well-kept dorms are run by an audacious ex-opera singer with a beautiful baritone voice. Beds cost L11,000 per night (sheets and cold shower included). Breakfast costs L4000, but you can use the kitchen for L500 per person. *Castle grounds, tel. 090/981–1540 or 090/981–2527. Midnight curfew, lockout 9–5. Reception open daily 7–9 and noon–midnight. Hot showers (L1500).*

FOOD On restaurant-lined Via Vittorio Emanuele, you'll find the best bargains at the fruit vendors, the well-stocked market **Upim Supermercato** (Via Vittorio Emanuele 202; closed Sun.), and the handful of pizzerias that sell slices by the kilogram. The best proper restaurant is **Ristorante Pizzeria Pescecane** (Via Vittorio Emanuele 223, 090/981–2706; closed Thurs.), where an eggplant-parmigiano pizza costs L8000 (that's cheap for this town).

SALINA

The second-largest Aeolian island is also the most fertile: Fields of capers and Malvasia grapes (used to make strong, sweet Malvasia wine) are a welcome change from the barren volcanic hills of Salina's neighbors. Five communities lie along the mountainous roads that straddle **Monte Fossa delle Felci** (962 meters), the highest mountain in the Aeolian chain. An 8-kilometer trail runs around the mountain's base, joining the port, **Santa Marina**, with the small village of Santuario Madonna del Terzito. A less strenuous way to see Salina is by bus; a L1500 ticket covers the entire island.

Besides Santa Marina, check out **Lingua**, 3 kilometers south. It has a seaside boardwalk, a saltwater lagoon, and several trattorias with great views. **Malfa**, 8 kilometers northwest of Santa Marina, sits among grape and caper fields, high above a sandy beach. **Leni** is a small mountain town with several baroque churches that are worth a peek. Salina's secondary traghetto and aliscafo port, **Rinella**, lies on the southwest side of the island. Definitely hop off the bus and check out Rinella's black-sand beach, which snuggles up against old fishermen's houses at the base of Monte Fossa.

WHERE TO SLEEP Santa Marina is the most convenient place to crash. Try **Iacono Giovanni** (Via Francesco Crispi, uphill and right from the port, tel. 090/984–3096), with doubles from L55,000. During the off-season, Santa Marina's **Punta Barone** (Via Lungomare Notar Giuffrè, north end of town, tel. 090/984–3172) has oceanfront doubles with bath for L60,000 (high season L85,000). In Rinella, there's a terraced campsite, **Campeggio Tre Pini** (tel. 090/980–9155), with tent spots for L8000 plus L8000 per person. Also in Rinella, **L'Ariana** (Via Rotabile 11, up the hill from dock, tel. 090/980–9075) charges L45,000 for off-season doubles, L105,000 otherwise.

PANAREA

It's fitting that archaeological digs on Panarea have turned up links between the archipelago's Bronze Age culture and the Minoans of Crete. Desert hues and bright bougainvillea cover this tiny island, the smallest in the Aeolian chain, and blue-trimmed, whitewashed houses tumble down to the sea in as close an approximation of Greece as you'll find in Italy. **San Pietro**, where the ferries and hydrofoils land, is Panarea's major town, with a bank, a post office, markets, and plenty of exotic boutiques. But the best action on Panarea lies underwater: The surrounding islets offer incredible snorkeling possibilities. Head 3 kilometers south of town via the villa-lined road (go to the back of town and turn left) and look for a black-sand beach that curves to meet a steep switchback trail. This leads to the **Punta Milazzese** headlands; the western side is prime snorkeling territory.

Unfortunately, lodging, food, and boat rentals—an integral part of any lengthy stay on Panarea—can cost a pretty penny. The locals are friendly, but they know how to milk those willing to pay through the nose to escape the chain's more-touristed islands. As for lodging, one money saver is **Da Francesco** (Via S. Pietro, just north of the dock, tel. 090/983023), where off-season doubles are L60,000 (L85,000 May–Aug.). Da Francesco also serves hearty pasta dishes for under L10,000. Boat rentals are arranged informally near the ferry-hydrofoil landing. You ask how much, they size you up, and then the bartering begins. Typically you'll pay L10,000 per day plus L25,000 for gas.

STROMBOLI

It's hard to imagine how locals get any sleep living at the base of an active volcano. Yet they ramble around their flat, whitewashed homes with seeming unconcern for the nightly displays of spurting lava and gaseous belches. Perhaps they're soothed by profit: The port survives on tourists who come to tackle the relentlessly steep trail to the crater. Although plenty of signs warn you not to climb without an authorized guide, the path is well-marked and manageable on your own. That said, the volcano is in a constant state of flux, and you should check in advance with the tourist office to be sure that the trail is indeed open. Guides charge L20,000; ask at the various stands set up near the ferry-hydrofoil dock, or contact the **Club Alpino Italiano** (tel. 090/986093). If you decide to go it alone, head

Stromboli sits on the cone of an active volcano. At night, fiery lava streams continuously into the sea, which in turn releases hissing plumes of steam into the clear, starry sky.

north through town to **Piscità**, Stromboli's finest black-sand beach. From here the road climbs through tall grass and up the side of the mountain (follow the red-and-white markers). The ascent to the caldera takes about three hours; hiking boots (or sturdy tennis shoes) and lots of water are essential. To experience the volcano in all its lava-belching glory, you'll want to remain at the caldera after dark—in which case camping gear and a flashlight are absolute necessities. If you do remain up top, do not—repeat: *do not*—hike up or down in the dark. The path is way too tricky, and the red-and-white markers are hard to find. Another option is to tour Stromboli by boat (L15,000–L20,000), which gives the best views of **Sciara del Fuoco** (Slope of Fire), where the lava flows into the sea. The man who operates the charter greets all arriving ferries and hydrofoils.

Markets along Stromboli's impossible-to-miss main street, north of the dock, sell food and such hiking provisions as flashlights and canteens. **La Lampara** (open daily noon–midnight) is a good spot for a post-hike beer and pizza (L8500–L12,000). Locals with rooms to spare meet incoming ferries, or try **Locanda Stella** (Via F. Filzi 14, tel. 090/986020), 1 kilometer north of the dock, past the church. Its breezy doubles with bath start at L55,000. Bathless doubles are L45,000, but the communal toilet is a pit.

FILICUDI AND ALICUDI

Off in their own little world, Filicudi and Alicudi are the wildest and least-touristed islands. Their small villages depend more on fishing than tourism, because neither island has any beaches to speak of. All the activity on Filicudi, the larger of the two, takes place in **Peccorino**, the main port. If you decide to spend the night, **La Canna** (Via Rosa 43, tel. 090/988–9956) has L65,000 doubles with views of Salina, Panarea, and Stromboli; from the port, follow the path that starts to the left of Hotel Phenicusa. The hike up to **Fossa Felci**, the island's highest peak, provides good views of the rock terrace that keeps Filicudi's hillsides from becoming an unwanted part of somebody's living room. If you have an extra L15,000 to rent a boat from **Filicudi SNC** (at the port, tel. 090/988–9984), circle the rugged coastline for a firsthand look at the numerous grottoes, cliffs, and rock formations.

Alicudi can be easily summed up: one place to sleep, one place to eat, and two things to do (exploring the steep slopes and caves at the water's edge, or climbing past a crumbly old castle to the island's highest point). In the springtime, purple heather colors Alicudi's volcanic cone, which explains the island's ancient name, Ericusa (roughly translated as "heather colored"). Nowadays the name refers to the island's lone hotel, **Ericusa** (Via Regina Elena, tel. 090/988–9902), which is located just above the port and has L92,000 doubles. In summer, locals offering private accommodations sometimes meet arriving ferries and hydrofoils.

SARDINIA 15

By Erin Williams

After leaving Sardinia (Sardegna), many people suffer from *mal di Sardegna* (Sardinia sickness), a painful longing akin to the pangs felt by parting lovers. Or maybe it's more like a passion that thrives on the impossibility of ever being quenched: Seduced by the island's dramatic coastline, dusty olive groves, and Mediterranean hospitality, visitors leave with a strong sense that they can never conquer, but only be conquered by Sardinia. Although the island has a history of foreign domination, defeat by the Phoenicians, Romans, Pisans, Genovese, and Aragonese strengthened rather than destroyed Sardinia's identity. Those who come to explore the land and culture will alternately experience ingenuous warmth and wariness on the part of a people who have always been on their guard against invading powers.

Sardinia's tumultuous history reaches back to the Neolithic Age, with extant prehistoric remains dating from as early as 6000 BC. The rugged interior of the island is dotted with more than 7,000 towering *nuraghi*, volcanic stone structures that were used as defense towers and fortified villages during the Bronze Age (1800–500 BC). The architectural ingenuity of the nuraghi, as well as numerous sacred wells, giants' tombs, and enigmatic *necropoli* (burial places), attests to the sophisticated culture of Sardinia's original inhabitants.

Due to the island's strategic position in the central Mediterranean, as well as the vast agricultural riches produced in its volcanic soil, control of Sardinia was sought by every major sea power since the beginning of time. With each successive wave of invaders, new languages, customs, and architectural styles washed up on Sardinia's shores. The resulting unique character of the island remains distinct from mainland Italy even today. Even in the face of extensive development on the northern coast, the Sardinians have held steadfastly to their unique culture, maintaining a largely agricultural way of life—rich in folklore, crafts, and traditions. While this proud heritage, combined with the island's archaeological riches and stunning natural beauty, make Sardinia an ideal destination, keep in mind that an authentic experience on the island often comes at the expense of tourist conveniences. Be prepared to get stuck in no-name towns waiting for a snail-paced bus and expect to do plenty of camping. To really see Sardinia, sometimes you have to take a flying leap into the unknown. Your risk taking, however, is rewarded by the possibility of experiencing rural hospitality, painfully blue waters, and a variety of gastronomic treats.

BASICS

WHEN TO GO Sardinia swells in the summer months, when boatloads of Italian vacationers flee their overheated, landlocked homes. The downside to this is packed hotels, higher prices

491

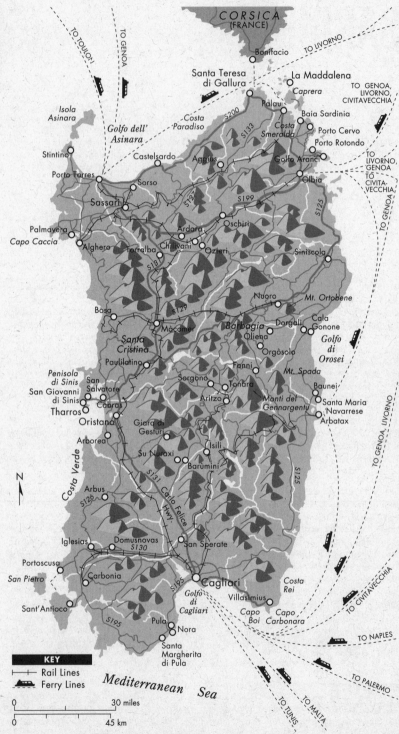

Sardinia

CORSICA
(FRANCE)

TO TOULON
TO GENOA
TO LIVORNO

Bonifacio

Santa Teresa
di Gallura

La Maddalena

Caprera

Palau

TO GENOA,
LIVORNO,
CIVITAVECCHIA

Isola
Asinara

Golfo dell'
Asinara

Costa
Paradiso

S200

Baia Sardinia

Costa
Smeralda

Porto Cervo
Porto Rotondo

TO LIVORNO,
GENOA

Stintino

Castelsardo

S133

Aggius

Golfo Aranci

TO CIVITA-
VECCHIA

Porto Torres

Sorso

S127

S199

Olbia

S125

Sassari

Ardara

Oschiri

TO GENOA

Palmavera

Capo Caccia

Alghero

Torralba

Chilivani

Ozieri

S18

Siniscola

S129

Bosa

Macomer

Nuoro

Mt. Ortobene

Santa
Cristina

Barbagia

Dorgali

Cala
Gonone

Paulilatino

Oliena

Golfo
di
Orosei

Penisola
di Sinis

San
Salvatore

Orgòsolo

San Giovanni
di Sinis

Cabras

Sorgono

Fonni

Mt. Spada

Tharros

Oristano

Giara di
Gesturi

Aritzo

Tonara

Monti del
Gennargentu

Baunei

Santa Maria
Navarrese

Arborea

Isili

Arbatax

S126

Su Nuraxi

Barùmini

S125

Arbus

S131

Carlo Felice Hwy.

Iglesias

Domusnovas

S130

San Sperate

Portoscusa

San Pietro

Carbonia

Costa Verde

Costa
Rei

Cagliari

Villasimius

S195

Golfo
di
Cagliari

TO CIVITAVECCHIA

Sant'Antioco

S195

Pula

Nora

Capo
Boi

Capo
Carbonara

TO NAPLES

TO PALERMO

Santa
Margherita
di Pula

N

KEY

Rail Lines

Ferry Lines

Mediterranean   Sea

0 ———— 30 miles

0 ———— 45 km

TO TUNIS

TO MALTA

for food and lodging, and body-to-body beaches, especially on the northern coast. The upside is a swinging nightlife reminiscent of spring break in Ft. Lauderdale. If none of this appeals to you, Sardinia is peaceful and cheap in the winter months, though many hotels, campgrounds, and restaurants may be closed.

COMING AND GOING

➤ **BY FERRY** • Sardinia is connected by *traghetto* (ferry) to Genova, Civitavecchia, Naples, Palermo, and Trapani. The cheapest option, *posta ponte* (deck class), will either get you an uncomfortable, not-meant-for-sleeping chair in the bar (if you can scrounge one) or else an even less comfortable snooze on deck. Considering most ferry trips are eight- to 20-hour journeys, you should probably spring for a *poltrona* (reclining seat), even though it costs about 50% more. Though there are snack bars and a restaurant on board, you'll save money by bringing your own eats. Solo women travelers should get a reclining seat and stick to it, to avoid being harrassed. Ferry prices vary according to the time of year, time of day, and any other reason the reservation agents can think of, but you should expect to pay about L40,000–L60,000 for a trip from Civitavecchia or Naples, L60,000–L90,000 for a trip from Genova. High season (meaning higher ferry prices) runs June–September.

Tirrenia is the largest ferry line, with offices in Cagliari (Via Campidano 1, tel. 070/666065), Olbia (Corso Umberto 17/19, tel. 0789/24691 or 0789/24692), and Porto Torres (Stazione Marittima, tel. 079/514107 or 079/514108) on Sardinia. **Corsica Elba Sardinia Ferries** links Livorno (Nuova Stazione Marittima Calata Carrara, tel. 0586/898979) with Golfo Aranci (tel. 0789/46780). **Moby Lines** has service between Livorno and Olbia and between Santa Teresa di Gallura and Bonifacio (on the island of Corsica). The major Moby Lines reservation centers are in Olbia (Corso Umberto 187, tel. 0789/27927), Cagliari (Piazza Deffenu 9, tel. 070/655359), Livorno (Via V. Veneto 24, tel. 0586/890325), and Santa Teresa di Gallura (Porto di Santa Teresa di Gallura, tel. 0789/755260).

➤ **BY PLANE** • **Alitalia** flies between mainland cities like Rome, Milan, Genova, and Naples, and the airports in Alghero and Cagliari; **Meridiana** flies from Rome and Milan to Olbia and Cagliari. Flights take about an hour, but since they usually cost well over L100,000, most travelers opt for the ferries (for flight specifics, *see* Cagliari, *below*).

GETTING AROUND Even if you have a car, Sardinia is not an easy place to get around. There are only two *superstrade* (highways); the rest of the streets are unpaved roads, crossed by the occasional flock of sheep. Trains are slow-moving and almost completely useless. Buses are no joy ride either, but at least they'll get you where you want to go. Fortunately, car rental is available in bigger towns, though prices are a steep L130,000–L200,000 per day. Most companies offer considerable discounts for long-term rentals.

WHERE TO SLEEP Like everything else in the summer, hotels are often prohibitively expensive in Sardinia: In coastal towns expect to pay L50,000–L80,000 for a double. Campsites, however, are reasonably-priced, plentiful, and often right on the beach. Another option is **agriturismo**, a program in which owners of private homes and farms rent rooms and serve meals featuring local produce. The out-of-town aspect can be problematic for budget travelers without wheels, but if you can get out to one of these homes, it's usually worth the effort. Rooms run L20,000–L50,000 (including 1–3 meals a day), and should be booked a few days in advance. Most tourist information offices will enlighten you with brochures or phone numbers and will often check availability. You can also call the following participating organizations directly: **Agriturist** (Viale Trieste, Cagliari, tel. 070/668330), **Cooperativa Allevartici Sarde** (Piazza Cattedrale 107, Località Santa Lucia Zeddiani, tel. 0783/418066, in summer, 0783/73954), **Turismo Verde** (Via Libeccio 31, Cagliari, tel. 070/373733), **Cooperativa Agriturismo Gallurese** (Calangiànus, Sassari, tel. 0789/50880), **Cooperativa Agrituristica Matteu** (Teulada, Cagliari, tel. 070/922003).

FOOD Although pizza and pasta with tomato sauce can be found almost anywhere in Sardinia, regional specialties are worth trying. Food here is a mixture of Spanish, Italian, North African, and uniquely Sardo influences. Seafood is particularly enticing when prepared in spaghetti *alle vongole veraci* (with clams) and *all'arselle* (with mussels). Also look for *malloreddus* (a little dumpling), often served with meat sauce.

LANGUAGE Although the influx of foreign and Italian tourists means you probably won't have much trouble making yourself understood using English and broken Italian, there is actually another language spoken on Sardinia—one that only faintly resembles mainland Italian. Sardo sounds like no other language on earth, though inhabitants claim the dialect has Spanish roots. Much of the vocabulary and grammar, however, come directly from Latin. The word for house, for example, is not *casa* but *domus*.

Cagliari

Originally called *Karalis* (rocky place) by the Phoenicians in the 9th century BC, Cagliari struggles to strike a balance between the conservation of its natural and historic splendor and the development of modern amenities: The medieval castle on the hill competes with the freighter-frequented port for the traveler's attention. Sardinia's capital city has always been a center for commerce and export. During the Middle Ages, Cagliari became one of the Mediterranean's most important trading ports for cheese, minerals, and wool. When Pisa gained control of the city in 1326, construction began on the castle, towers, walls, palaces, and churches that now constitute the looming *centro storico* (historic center). Today the Castello (Castle) district is in disrepair, but the city itself keeps thriving. It's one of the few places on the island where you can get back in touch with semimodern, urban reality, and it makes a convenient base for visiting local ruins and beaches.

BASICS

CHANGING MONEY The best place to change money is at the **currency exchange/information booth** in the main train station (Piazza Matteotti, tel. 070/656293; open Mon.–Sat. 7:30–7:25).

MAIL AND PHONES The main **post office** (Piazza del Carmine, tel. 070/663356) provides the usual services, including *fermo posta* (held mail) for L300 a letter at Window 2 (postal code: 09100). For long-distance calls, go to the **IRITEL** office (Via Angiou 4, off Piazza Matteotti, tel. 070/659780; open daily 8 AM–11:30 PM) or the **SIP** phone center (Via Cima 9, no phone; open daily 8 AM–9:30 PM).

MEDICAL AID **Farmacia Schlich** (Via Francesco Crispi 12, tel. 070/658761; open Mon.–Sat. 9–1 and 4:30–7:50) is convenient to both the train and bus stations. Outside is a list of pharmacies that rotate 24-hour service.

VISITOR INFORMATION It looks like a *Star Trek* set plunked in the middle of Piazza Matteotti, but the **Aziende Turistica** has a helpful English-speaking staff that will recommend hotels and give you loads of pamphlets. *Piazza Matteotti, in front of Comune di Cagliari, tel. 070/669255. Open June–Sept. Mon.–Sat. 8–8; Oct.–May, weekdays 8–2.*

COMING AND GOING

BY TRAIN Train service is inefficient but the people at the info booth (open Mon.–Sat. 7:30–7:25) in the train station (Piazza Matteotti, tel. 070/656293) are helpful. Trains run regularly to Oristano (1½ hrs, L8000), Sassari (3 hrs, L20,800), and Olbia (4 hrs, L22,600). Luggage storage (L1500) is available 6 AM–9 PM.

BY BUS **ARST** (Piazza Matteotti, next to train station, tel. 070/657236) is the most reliable means of transportation to other towns on the island. Two daily buses leave Piazza Matteotti for Nuoro (3 hrs, L17,500), Oristano (2 hrs, L10,800), and Barùmini (1½ hrs, L7400); buses also travel to Santa Maria Navarrese (3 daily, 3½ hrs, L14,100). **PANI** (Calata Darsena 4, tel. 070/652326), a private bus service with unpredictable hours, runs buses to many of the same places for similar prices.

BY FERRY **Tirrenia** (Via Campidano 1, tel. 070/666065) has a virtual monopoly on ferry travel. You can purchase ferry tickets at literally hundreds of travel agencies along the *lungomare* (sea-front street) or you can go directly to **Stazione Marittima** (Via Roma, tel. 070/663328); plan to arrive at least half an hour before departure. Ferries from Cagliari to Civitavecchia (13½ hrs, L50,700) leave daily at 6:30 PM year-round. Ferries travel to and from

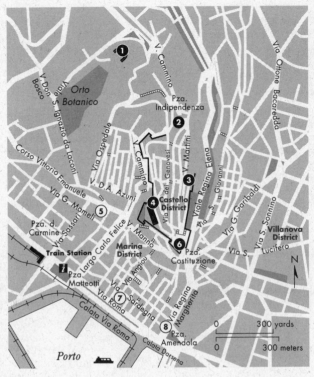

Sights ●

Anfiteatro
Romano, **1**

Bastione di
San Remy, **6**

Cattedrale di
Santa Maria, **3**

Citadella dei
Musei/Museo
Archeologico
Nazionale, **2**

Torre
dell'Elefante, **4**

Lodging ○

Albergo Londra, **8**

Allogio Firenze, **5**

Pensione Vittoria, **7**

Genova mid-July–mid-September only (Tues. and Thurs., 23 hrs, L94,000). Ferries leave for Naples Thursday at 5:30 PM (16 hrs, L46,000); from mid-July to mid-September they also leave on Saturday (L65,000). A ferry goes to Palermo (14½ hrs, L45,000–L60,000) every Saturday at 7 PM and continues on to Tunis, Tunisia (21½ hrs, L107,000).

BY PLANE Aeroporto Elmas (Località Elmas, tel. 070/240111), served primarily by **Alitalia** (Via Caprera 11, tel. 070/6010), handles domestic and some European flights. Many of the major car rental companies (Hertz, Avis, Europe-Car, Maggiore) have offices here. Buses (15 min, L1100) leave the airport hourly for the ARST station.

GETTING AROUND

Cagliari's three main districts are best explored on foot: The Marina district is between Via Roma (the central lungomare) and Corso Vittorio Emanuele; the Castello district is west of Viale Regina Elena and Piazza Costituzione; and the Villanova district, a newer section of town, is east of Piazza Costituzione. If you need to ride the local orange buses, the **ACT** office (tel. 070/20081; open daily 7:15–6:30), across from the ARST station (*see* Coming and Going, *above*), gives out information and sells tickets. Buses run until 10 PM or midnight. For day-tripping or increased mobility, **Hertz** car rental has an office next to the ARST station on Piazza Matteotti (tel. 070/240037 or 070/240855), and another location at Aeroporto Elmas (where you'll also find Avis, Europe-Car, and Maggiore). Cost for rental is L170,000–L200,000 per day plus tax (discounts for rental of two days or more).

WHERE TO SLEEP

You should call at least a day in advance to get a room in one of Cagliari's few inexpensive places, which are concentrated in the charmless Marina district. If you want to spend more money, **Ulivi e Palmi** (Via Bembo 25, tel. 070/485861) has stylish doubles for L70,000.

Albergo Londra. Just up from Via Roma, the "London Hotel" has clean doubles with high ceilings and big windows for L55,000 with bath. *Via Regina Margherita 16, off Via Roma, tel. 070/669083. 9 rooms, 3 with bath. Curfew 1 AM.*

Allogio Firenze. This tiny hotel rents large, quiet, sunny rooms (L42,000–L56,000) that feel like someone's apartment. Comfy couches in the common area plus friendly proprietors add to the homey feel. *Corso Vittorio Emanuele 50, tel. 070/655222 or 070/653678. Bus 1 from Piazza Matteotti, get off at 2nd block of Corso Vittorio Emanuele. 5 rooms, none with bath.*

Pensione Vittoria. Immaculate antique-filled doubles (L65,000–L90,000) in this classic pension overlook the water. The large windows mean it's loud at night, but the mosaic floors and wooden bed frames more than make up for the noise. *Via Roma 75, tel. 070/657970. Across from Stazione Marittima. 14 rooms, 10 with bath.*

FOOD

Restaurants here stay open late, and great, inexpensive meals abound; even midnight snackers can find pizza by the slice or even fresh fish. Most menus in Cagliari are similar, featuring local specialties like spaghetti *all'arselle* (with mussels), malloreddus, and the catch of the day. Though the after-dinner social scene is not particularly wild, there are a few good bars along **Corso Vittorio Emanuele** and **Via Dante** (take Via San Lucifero east to the Chiesa di Santo Saturno). For basic food supplies, go to **Econo Market** (Via Angiou 56, near Piazza Matteotti). To sample Sardinian specialties, try the deli **Pisu Gastronomia** (Via L. Baylle 39; open 8–1:30 and 4–7); if you bring them bread from the bakery across the street, they'll make you an unforgettable sandwich.

Solo Pizza. Like the name says, this place only serves pizza—but boy do they do it right. They've got over 30 varieties of thick-crust pies to choose from, from simple tomato and mozzarella (L4000) to extravagant smoked salmon (L10,000), and the beer is cheap and cold (L2500–L4000). *Corso Vittorio Emanuele 174, tel. 070/663459. Open Thurs.–Tues. 7 PM–midnight.*

Trattoria Deidda. This hopping local hangout specializes in seafood. Start with spaghetti with mussels in a delicious garlic sauce (L6000). Rustic and intimate, Deidda is a great place to introduce yourself to strangers and share food. *Via Sardegna 100, tel. 070/663668. Open Mon.–Sat. 1–3:30 and 8:15–11:30.*

Trattoria Gennargentù. Tucked away in a tiny back room, this elegant but reasonably priced restaurant serves a heap of spaghetti all'arselle with *bottorga* (a salty fish-egg specialty) for L8000. *Secondi* (main dishes) run L8000–L12,000. The *vitello* (veal) is particularly delicious. *Via Sardegna 60/C, tel. 070/658247. Open Mon.–Sat. noon–3 and 8–11.*

WORTH SEEING

In the late Middle Ages, Pisan administrators set up shop in what is now the **Castello district** to regulate port trade and commerce down below. The Genoese, however, were constantly trying to take control of Cagliari, so the Pisans constructed the white **stone walls** that encircle the Castello district and descend all the way to the Marina district below. Despite such military fortifications, the Pisans couldn't hold off the Aragonese, who invaded from mainland Spain in the 14th century. It was under the iron-fisted Aragonese rule that the people of Cagliari were kicked out of the Castello district to make room for foreign nobles. A bastion of Spanish rules and customs, this district was virtually off-limits to non-Spaniards. Though Jews were tolerated for their financial expertise and could live, worship, and set up shop here, Sardinians had to leave at the sound of a warning trumpet every evening at sunset or be thrown off the walls. It was only at the end of the 18th century that the area finally became accessible to the city's indigenous population.

The buildings of the Castello district alternate between being renovated and being run-down, emitting either the aroma of freshly baked bread or that of *"Casteddaius piscia arrenconis"* ("Castellani who piss in the corner"). In Piazza Costituzione, stop for a quick drink (L2000–L3000) at the historic **Caffè Genovese** and proceed across the street to the monumental **Bas-**

tione di San Remy, whose stairs act as an entrance to the whole castle district. Reach the 14th-century **Torre dell'Elefante** by heading left on Via Università from the top of the Bastione di San Remy stairs. Looking up from under the tower, you'll see a small marble elephant (a symbol of strength). The tower was used by the Spanish as a prison, and you can still see the iron gates where Spaniards hung the heads of executed prisoners.

A few blocks to the north, beyond Piazza Palazzo, **Piazza Indipendenza** leads directly to the **Citadella dei Musei**. This newly renovated museum complex includes the **Museo Archeologico Nazionale** (tel. 070/65237; admission: L4000; open Tues.–Sun. 8:30–1:30 and 2:30–7:30), which documents Sardinia's prehistoric civilizations. To see 15th-century Catalan art, check out the **National Art Gallery**, just across the way from the archaeological museum (same hours and admission).

Perched atop the hill above the Castello district are the remains of Cagliari's Roman civilization (238 BC–AD 450), the ruins of the **Anfiteatro Romano**. South of the amphitheater, through the botanic garden, explore the **Casa di Tigellio** (Via Tigellio), the remains of a 2nd-century Imperial Roman housing project. *To reach both sights, follow Viale Buon Camino from Piazza Indipendenza. Always open.*

Though constructed by Pisans in the 13th and 14th centuries, **Cattedrale di Santa Maria** bears the signature of ensuing foreign rulers with its Romanesque style, Gothic influences, and baroque embellishments. Of particular interest are two pulpits on either side of the main door, displaying scenes by the Pisan master Guglielmo, and the Gothic-Catalan Chapel of Sacra Spina. The crypt, with 292 funerary niches and bas-reliefs, holds two Romanesque sarcophagi bearing the remains of early Christian martyrs: Saints Saturno, Bonifacio, and Claudio. *Piazza Duomo, tel. 070/663481. Open daily 9:30–12:30 and 3:30–7.*

NEAR CAGLIARI

NORA Founded by the Phoenicians in the 7th and 8th centuries BC, Nora is the oldest city on the island. Although the narrow peninsula was inhabited for 16 centuries and was once home to 5,000 people, the city is now in ruins and partially submerged in water due to rising sea levels. What remains is the city center, mostly the work of Imperial Roman artists and architects from the 2nd to 4th centuries AD. You can still see mosaic floors, remains of roads and pillars, and baths complete with ancient heating systems. Looking at the small, semicircular theater you can see ancient versions of box seats. If the sea is calm, look under the water along the shore to see more ruins. Adjacent to the archaeological zone, there's a crescent-shaped beach with white sand, clear water, and good swimming. You may want to bring food along, though there is a snack bar on the beach and plenty of cheap eats in nearby Pula. *Tel. 070/921470 for information. Ruins open May–Sept., daily 9–8; Oct.–Apr., daily 9–12:30 and 2–5.*

To reach Nora, take the **ARST** bus (hourly, 45 min, L3500) from Piazza Matteotti in Cagliari to Pula. From Pula, take local Bus 1 (7 daily), which runs to Nora, the beach, and the entrance to the archaeological zone. Otherwise the 30-minute walk through eucalyptus trees to Nora from Pula is not so bad. Hitching is also easy; many families drive from Pula to the beach at Nora. Near Pula, the beachside campground **Cala d'Ostia** (Località Cala d'Ostia, tel. 070/921470) charges L6500 per person and L7000 for a tent in high season. To get here from Pula, follow the CALA D'OSTIA or HOTEL FLAMMINGO signs from the intersection.

BARUMINI One of the best-preserved nuraghi complexes on the island is just outside the small town of Barùmini, north of Cagliari. Before you head straight for the nuraghi, though, spend a little time in Barùmini itself, a charmingly lazy town situated amidst golden fields and rolling hills. Follow the signs to **Parrocchiale della Beata Vergine Immacolata**, a pretty 15th-century church with a late-Gothic interior and a 17th-century bell tower and cupola. Or just wander past the low stone houses with tiny windows and doors that characterize this rustic, well-preserved little town.

The remains of tower-like nuraghi, built by Sardinian folk way back around 1800–500 BC, are scattered across inland Sardinia. Originally built as fortified villages, these clunky rock piles were engineered to hold together without any cement or mortar.

To reach the **Su Nuraxi** nuraghi complex from the bus stop in Barùmini, go left where the signs indicate Thili and nuraghi, and continue for about 10 minutes. The complex provides a fascinating look into a Mediterranean culture that predates the Greeks and the Romans by a good stretch. The initial building (1400 BC) was expanded by the addition of concentric walls and towers, giving its inhabitants room to store grain and livestock. You could spend all afternoon exploring this unusual stone structure, with dark chambers and passageways that once comprised living quarters. The deep well in the interior courtyard and the peaked domes—carved out of volcanic rock using no mortar—show the level of ingenuity used here. The smaller dwellings that made up the surrounding village contain the remains of grinding stones, ovens for baking bread, and altars for water purification rites. (Water was scarce as well as sacred around here). Entrance to the site is free, though a small, sedentary man will motion for you to sign a guest book. In winter, be sure to check bus schedules before trying to trek out to the site. *From Cagliari's Piazza Matteotti, 2 PM bus to Barùmini (1½ hrs, L7000). To return, take 6 PM bus to San Luri; change to 7 PM bus to Cagliari (2½ hrs, L8000). Open June–Sept., daily 8 AM–sunset; Oct.–May, daily 9–4.*

The West Coast

Along the rural west coast, rare species of wildlife share the rocky uplands with sturdy medieval churches and mysterious nuraghi. Unlike resort towns in the north, which lure visitors with their fun-in-the-sun pleasure packages, west coast towns like Oristano attract those looking for a taste of the indomitable Sardinian spirit. If you've got to be on the beach, the endless sandy stretches around Alghero are prime spots for sun and sand, while the city itself offers a distinct Spanish culture and historical attractions. Keep in mind though, because tourism is in its beginning stages, transportation and accommodations are sorely lacking.

Centuries ago, inhabitants of the west coast were driven into the hinterland in order to flee the malaria-ridden coastline. Even today, locals manage to avoid the modern-day coastal plague of tourism, living an essentially agricultural existence.

Oristano

After the Phoenecians living at Tharros on the tip of the Sinis Peninsula (*see* Near Oristano, *below*) suffered one too many Saracen invasions, people started packing up and moving inland to Oristano, a more strategically sound location. An old folk song recalls how the stones of Tharros were brought inland, and Oristano was built from the former town's hand-me-downs. Between the 13th and 15th centuries, Oristano became capital of the local Arborea kingdom; the town jockeyed with Pisa and

Italy's Baddest Pre-Oriana Fallaci Feminist

Oristano's history of independence is bound to Eleanora d'Arborea, a 14th-century civic leader who inherited the difficult task of defending the duchy's freedom against the superior military might of the Aragonese. Although the duchy eventually succumbed to Aragonese rule, Eleanora made a lasting contribution to Sardinian history by implementing the Carta de Logu, a civil code including progressive laws concerning women's rights. This avant-garde doctrine, which guaranteed common property rights within marriage, a woman's choice of a husband, and the ability to redress an act of rape, remained in effect until 1847. Monuments honoring Eleanora pop up all over Oristano.

Genova for control of the island and boasted a substantial centro storico. Though slightly less vital today, Oristano is a good base for excursions to nearby nuraghi and Roman ruins.

BASICS **EPT.** The friendly staff will load you down with maps, brochures, and glossy pamphlets of Oristano and the surrounding area. They also provide listings of hotels and campsites, and will direct you to the **Consorzio Agriturismo di Sardegna** (Via Duomo 17, tel. 0783/73454) for farm-stay info. *Via Cagliari 276, across from ARST station, tel. 0783/74191. Open weekdays 8–2 (Tues. and Wed. also 4–8).*

COMING AND GOING About a 15-minute walk from the town center, the **train station** (Piazza Ungheria, tel. 0783/72270) is down Via Veneto from Piazza del Popolo. Roughly 20 trains leave daily for Cagliari (1 hr 20 min, L8000), four for Sassari (3 hrs, L13,600), and three for Olbia (4 hrs, L15,500). The ticket office, open 6:30 AM–8:30 PM, offers luggage storage (L1500). For longer hauls, **PANI** (Via Lombardia 30, in the Blu Bar, tel. 0783/212268), north of Piazza Roma, is more expensive but more reliable. PANI buses leave for Cagliari (5 daily, 1½ hrs, L10,800), Sassari (4 daily, 2 hrs 15 min, L13,200), and Nuoro (4 daily, 4½ hrs, L10,800). **ARST** (Via Cagliari, tel. 0783/78001) has buses to Cagliari at 7:10 AM and 2:10 PM (2 hrs 15 min, L10,500), to San Giovanni (7 daily, 20 min, L2500), and to Arbus (1 daily, 2 hrs, L6000). The ticket booth is open 6 AM–8 PM.

GETTING AROUND Though Oristano sprawls over a vast area, most of its sights are concentrated around the major piazze: Piazza Roma to the north, Piazza Mannu (close to the ARST station), and Piazza Eleanora d'Arborea in the center. Local orange buses (marked Torre Grande) depart from the ARST station every half-hour for the beach and marina at Torre Grande. In the opposite direction, buses for Arborea will let you off at Santa Giusta. Buy tickets (L1100) at the ARST station or at *tabacchi* (tobacco shops).

WHERE TO SLEEP For some ungodly reason you can't get anything cheaper than an L80,000 double in this town. The **Piccolo Hotel** (Via Martignano 19, tel. 0783/71500) has small, somewhat run-down doubles for L80,000; all have private bath, and some have terraces and views of the old town. From Piazza Mannu, take Via Crispi toward the center and make a right on Via Martignano. The expensive **Hotel CA.MA.** (Via Vittorio Veneto 119, tel. 0783/74374) is relatively luxurious. The 54 brand-new rooms (doubles L98,000) have phones and TVs. From the train station, Vittorio Veneto leads past Piazza Popolo to Piazza Mariano.

➤ **CAMPING** • Campgrounds on the Torre Grande promontory are the most convenient to Oristano, but they're next door to a rather smelly petrochemical plant. Stick to the campgrounds in Cùglieri and Is Arenas. **Camping Is Arenas** (Località Narbolia, Is Arenas, tel. 0783/52284), set in white sand beneath eucalyptus trees, is equipped with a pizzeria, market, and hot showers. Tent sites cost L13,500, plus L7000 per person. Take the ARST bus from the station to Is Arenas at 8, noon, 2, or 6:20, and ask the driver to let you off at the campground. In Cùglieri, the **Europa** campground (Località Cùglieri, Torre del Pozzo, tel. 0785/38058) offers a restaurant, and market, along with a tennis court, swimming pool, and cinema (L15,000 a campsite, plus L8000 per person).

FOOD Restaurants and trattorias are generally on the expensive side, but Via Mazzini and the area around Piazza Roma have some good, inexpensive *rosticcerie* (rotisseries) and pizza-by-the-slice places. The **Civico** open-air market happens every day 7 AM–1 PM at Via Mazzini, or head to the **Europa Europa Supermarket** (Via Veneto 117, near train station; open Mon.–Sat. 7:30–1:30 and 4:30–8:30), which has everything you need to feed.

Trattoria da Gino (Via Tirso 13, tel. 0783/71428; closed Sun.), off Piazza Roma, is a tiny, unpretentious trattoria. Traditional primi such as *ravioli sardi* (with butter and sage) are in the L6500–L8500 range; secondi cost L9000 and up. Fresh calamari is L12,000. **Ristorante-Pizzeria La Torre** (Piazza Roma 52, tel. 0783/70784; closed Mon.) is a friendly place with classic white tablecloths, great pizza (L5000–L10,000), and simple primi, like the savory *risotto ai funghi* (rice with mushrooms; L9000)

WORTH SEEING Particularly when it's hot, you might want to visit the centro storico in the morning; the entire town seems to plummet into a deep coma in the afternoon. The **Cattedrale** (Piazza Duomo) is notable for its double cupola and the adjacent, multicolor, onion-shaped dome atop its 14th-century octagonal bell tower. Glitzed over in an 18th-century baroque frenzy, the cathedral has only a few remaining Romanesque-Gothic traces: the bas-relief balustrade, the bronze doors, and the Cappella del Rimedio. Note the delicate handling of the angels leading to the high altar and Nino Pisano's wooden statue of the Annunciation.

From the cathedral, Via Vittorio Emanuele and Via Eleanora lead to the town's center, **Piazza Eleanora d'Arborea**. Here the town heroine is immortalized in a stone statue surrounded by atmospheric cafés and palaces. The nearby **Pinacoteca l'Antiguarium Arborense** houses an interesting collection of Roman and Punic artifacts from Thorros and Sinis. *Via Parpaglia, at Via Lama Mura, tel. 0783/7911. Open weekdays 9–noon and 4–6, Sat. 9–noon.*

FESTIVALS Introduced in 1350 by Arborean king Mariano II to commemorate his daughter's marriage, **La Sartiglia** is a festival that blends Christian chivalric traditions and pagan purification rituals. The highlight of the festival is the cavalry men in androgynous dress who use swords to try to skewer tiny stars on the ground while zooming by at a full gallop. The festival is notorious for its suggestive gender bending, and the women cross-dress as well. It takes place the last Sunday of Carnival and the following Tuesday, some time in late February or early March, depending on the date of Easter.

NEAR ORISTANO

LA PENISOLA DI SINIS A lone finger dipping into the Gulf of Oristano, the Peninsula of Sinis is home to rare species of birds such as pink flamingoes and pilgrim falcons, as well as several ancient temples and tombs. The peninsula's **San Giovanni di Sinis** is a one-church town with one great church—Chiesa San Giovanni di Sinis. Parts of it date back to the 5th century, and the simple earnestness of the barrel-vaulted sanctuary is enough to turn almost anyone into a believer. In summer, it's open 9–6 daily; off-season, when buses arrive less frequently, you'll have to find a key-bearing nun to let you in. Also take note of the town's archaic fishermen's huts, called *barralas de crucuris*, made of wood and straw.

Established by Phoenicians in 800 BC, **Tharros** is an intriguing ancient ruin at the tip of the peninsula. Protected by the San Marco promontory, it was fortified in the Byzantine era and deserted in the 8th and 9th centuries. Tours of the Punic and Roman dwellings, Roman aqueduct vats, and Punic temples are conducted in Italian only. The site is open daily 9–7, but call L'Area Archeologica di Tharros (tel. 0783/370019) before coming out during the off-season. *Admission free. Tours June–Sept., daily 9–1 and 3–6; Oct.–May, daily 9–1 and 3–5.*

To the right of Tharros's entrance, a path leads up to the **Torre di San Giovanni**. Built by Filippo II during the Saracen invasions, the tower provides an amazing view of the sea and ruins. You can also follow a path down to one of the beautiful (but crowded) beaches. A good, sandy stretch is at **Marina di Torre Grande**, where nightlife hops along its pizzeria-lined lungomare. If you get stranded out here, **Hotel Casas** (San Giovanni di Sinis, tel. 0783/370071) has pleasant doubles for L65,000.

➤ **COMING AND GOING** • Unfortunately, buses only run here in July and August; the rest of the year you'll have to hitch a ride. From Oristano, buses run to San Giovanni's ARST station (tel. 0783/270019) eight times daily (20 min, L2500). Buses from Oristano also run to Tharros (30 min, L2500). To reach Tharros from San Giovanni, you can walk or take a bus (every half-hour, 10 min, L1100) from San Giovanni's station.

SANTA CRISTINA Santa Cristina's archaeological zone has the highest concentration of nuraghic architecture on the island. The **Bronze Age towers** (18th–10th century BC) are a major attraction, but the most remarkable site is the **well temple**, which was used for sacred water rituals. On the other side of Santa Cristina's information office/bar are the remains of a nuraghic village reused by the Carthaginians and the Romans. You can climb up the single-towered structure, dating from 1500–1200 BC, and look out over the sacred olive groves. Two buses leave daily from Oristano's ARST station for Paulilatino (11:45 AM and 2:05 PM, L3000), a few kilometers from the archaeological sites. Ask the driver to let you off at the archaeological zone before you reach Paulilatino, or you'll have to walk from town. Returning to Oristano is tricky: Trains leave Paulilatino for Oristano at 12:53, 2:46, or 5:46 PM (no buses), and the station is several kilometers outside of town. Try begging for a ride from another visitor or from the amiable co-op staff. *Complesso Nuragico Santa Cristina, Località Paulilatino, tel. 0336/ 811756. Admission: L1100. Open daily 8:30 AM–10:30 PM.*

Alghero

Irresistible Alghero caters to travelers with taste and integrity, managing to strike the perfect balance between modern conveniences (such as dependable public transportation, for starters) and the preservation of a pristine medieval core. More than any other town on the island, Alghero maintains a distinctively Spanish air, and years under Catalan dominion have earned it the nickname "Little Barcelona." With endless sandy beaches, the famous Grotto of Neptune, and a number of nuraghi, Alghero makes the perfect base for daily excursions. Though the efficient buses will get you to and from neighboring towns, the best way to do it all is by moped or bike (*see* Getting Around, *below*). At the end of the day, back in town, the piano bar-lined lungomare looks like an international bazaar, with people of all nationalities selling handmade arts and crafts.

Alghero proudly touts its Aragonese-Catalan heritage; Spanish street signs still cling to the medieval town walls, and Spanish-inflected Italian rings between open windows.

BASICS AAST gives out bus schedules, glossy brochures, and maps galore, but can't help with hotel or agriturismo reservations. *Piazza Porta Terra 9, tel. 079/979054. Open June–Sept., Mon.–Sat. 8–8; Oct.–May, Mon.–Sat. 8–2.*

COMING AND GOING

➢ **BY TRAIN** • To reach the **train station** (Via Don Monzoni, tel. 079/950785), walk from the town center along the port on Via Garibaldi or ride on an AP or AF city bus. A 50-minute train ride takes you to Sassari (L3200), where you can catch other trains, including one to Oristano. Four trains leave daily for Cagliari (4½ hrs, L21,900).

➢ **BY BUS** • A booth on the Via Catalogna side of the *giardini pubblici* (public gardens) sells tickets and provides information for **ARST/PANI** and **FDS bus lines.** Buses connect Alghero to Sassari (16 daily, 1 hr, L4500), Màcomer (4:50 AM and 2 PM, 1 hr, L9000), and Bosa (4 daily, 1 hr 15 min, L5300). You have to connect with buses in Sassari (*see below*), a bigger transport hub, to reach Cagliari and other destinations.

➢ **BY CAR** • **Avis** (Via P. Nedda N. 16/A, tel. 079/260648) will make your life a lot easier if you're determined to reach the most secluded beaches. Prices are painful however—at least L125,000 a day, not including gas. You'll find comparable rates at **Nolauto Alghero** (Via Vittorio Veneto 11, tel. 079/953047), **Auto Express** (Via Sebastiano Satta N. 48, tel. 079/ 951505), and **Maggiore** (tel. 1678–67067).

GETTING AROUND All major streets converge at the centro storico, which juts out at the westernmost point of Alghero. The Giardini Pubblici are flanked by the tourist information office to the west and the bus terminal and port to the north. The **lungomare** runs south from the southern entrance of the centro storico, and changes names from Dante to Valencia as it winds toward Bosa, 16 kilometers to the south. Orange local buses are marked by initials according to their destination: **AF** (Alghero Fertilia), **AP** (Alghero Pertraia Maria Pia), and **AO** (Alghero Ospedale Marino). Tickets (L1500) must be purchased beforehand from tobacco shops or newspaper stands.

Cicloexpress rents bikes (L12,000 a day), mountain bikes (L18,000 a day), mopeds (L25,000 a day), and scooters (L50,000 a day). Their main booth is at the port. *Via Garibaldi Porto and Via La Marmora 39, tel. 079/986950. Open Mon.–Sat. 9–1 and 4–8:30.*

WHERE TO SLEEP With the overwhelming demand for cheap sleeps during high season, agriturismo (*see* Chapter Basics, *above*) becomes an increasingly attractive option. The chance to experience (and *taste*) Sardo farm life is worth the minor inconvenience of having to commute in and out of town. For agriturismo stays near Alghero, contact **Cooperativa Agrituristica Dulcalmara** (07040 Santa Maria La Palma, Alghero province, tel. 079/999197), which offers a variety of room and pension plans ranging from L25,000 to L65,000 per person plus a L10,000 booking fee. If the places listed below are full, try **Hotel San Giuan** (Via Angioy 2, off Via Garibaldi, tel. 079/951222), a super-efficient, modern affair with doubles for L80,000–L100,000.

Agriturismo Da Zia Maria. Whatever you do, don't call up asking for a double. The proprietress will quickly inform you of the ways of country hospitality: You pay for a bed and food, not privacy. Maria offers clean, simple rooms (10 beds), plus breakfast and dinner—an unforgettable selection of antipasti and *casalinga* (home-style) dishes prepared with farm-fresh products and loving care—for L60,000 per person. *Strada dei Due Mare, Località Malai, tel. 079/951844. Take AP Bus to end and follow yellow signs 2 km. 5 rooms, none with bath.*

Hotel Normandie. This family-run place is the cheapest hotel around. Small, clean doubles run L50,000 and fill up quickly during July and August. *Via Enrico Mattei 6, tel. 079/975302. From giardini pubblici, take Via Cagliari (which becomes Viale Giovanni XXIII) away from port and bus station; turn right on Via Enrico Mattei. 9 rooms, 3 with bath. Reservations advised.*

➤ **HOSTELS** • **Ostello della Gioventù "Dei Giuliani" (HI).** Located in Fertilia, a short bus ride from Alghero, this is one of only two hostels in all of Sardinia. The friendly staff will point you in the direction of nearby beaches and pizzerias, though they cook up a delicious three-course dinner with wine for L15,000. Beds are L14,000, including breakfast. *Via Zara 1, Località Fertilia, tel. 079/930353. Take orange Bus AF to Fertilia; from Fertilia's Piazza Giulia, take Via Parenzo, right on Via Zara. 70 beds. Hot showers (L1500). Closed Oct. 15–Apr. 15.*

➤ **CAMPING** • Seaside **Camping Calik** (Località Fertilia, tel. 079/930111; closed Sept. 30–June 1) is expensive (L12,500 per person), but it's shaded by eucalyptus trees and equipped with a bar, self-service restaurant, and market. Take Bus AF towards Fertilia and ask the driver when to get off. **Camping La Mariposa** (Via Lido 22, tel. 079/950360; closed Nov.–May) charges a hefty L15,000 per person, but it's just 2 kilometers from the center of town. It has the same amenities as Calik plus bungalows. Tents sites cost L5000. From the train station, take Via Minzoni right, left on Via Malta, right on Via Lido, or take bus AP.

FOOD Nothing in Alghero is untapped by tourism, so don't be daunted by TOURIST MENU signs and credit-card stickers spackled to the windows. For mouthwatering made-to-order sandwiches (L3000–L5000), head to **El Bocadillo** (Via Kennedy 12, tel. 079/982443), open daily 9:30 AM until "as long as there are people around."

Pizzeria La Lanterna. Though popular for its pizza, La Lanterna also offers delicious specialties in an elegant indoor/outdoor setting. Thick, delicious pizzas cooked in a wood-burning stove start at L6000. Traditional primi run L8000–L12,000, and meat and seafood secondi start at about L9000. *Via Giovanni XXIII 82/A, tel. 079/978556. From Giardini Pubblici, head south on Via Cagliari, which becomes Via Giovanni XXIII. Open daily 12:30–3 and 8–midnight.*

Ristorante Dieci Metri. Situated under an alley archway, this colorful place has outdoor tables that are incorporated into the stone structure. The spaghetti alle vongole veraci (L8000) is cooked to garlicky perfection. A large meal that includes spaghetti, fried calamari, and a drink is L23,000. *Vicolo Adami 47, tel. 079/979023. From Torre di Porta Terra, walk down Via Roma, left on Carrer del Barceloneta and right on Vicolo Adami. Open daily noon–4:30 and 7–midnight; closed Wed. in winter.*

WORTH SEEING Alghero's graceful medieval center is glutted with goldsmith workshops and jewelry stores specializing in every shade of coral, and stocky medieval and Renaissance towers spring up in spots along the old town's circular, fortified wall.

On Via Carlo Alverto at Vicolo Teatro, the **Chiesa di San Francesco**'s soberly majestic 14th-century stone facade constitutes one side of a small, triangular piazza. Take a close look at the church's beautiful, carved wood doors. The severe vaulted ceiling is juxtaposed with delicate ornamentation on the capitals and gold-inlaid baroque altars and sculptures. From a higher vantage point you can see San Francesco's famous multicolor, cupola-topped tower—a signature image of Alghero. From the church, turn left (north) on Via Carlo Alberto to **Cattedrale di Santa Maria** (Via Manno). The cathedral's best feature is its late-Gothic octagonal bell tower (currently under restoration).

AFTER DARK Summer nightlife happens along the lungomare, where artists and artisans compete for attention with piano-bar musicians playing covers of cheesy American soft rock. All the while, scantily dressed nymphs and Luke Perry look-alikes show off their tans, old couples stroll arm in arm, and small children toddle by with dripping ice cream cones. Piano bar **Caval Mari'** (Lungomare Dante 1, tel. 079/981570) is a good place to watch all the action, as is piano bar **Opera** (Via Con Minzoni, tel. 079/977633), on the other side of town close to the port. The popular discos **Il Ruscello** (Strada Alghero–Sassari, tel. 079/953168) and **La Siesta** (Strada Alghero–Vilanova) are only accessible by car. Check the daily newspaper *La Nuova* for other club listings.

OUTDOOR ACTIVITIES The charm of Alghero's old town is still intact, but the nearby beaches are where it's really at. The closest sandy stretches lie along the **Lido di Alghero**, an umbrella-lined arc leading from the marina to Fertilia. Boat, Jet-ski, and kayak rentals are available along its **Spiaggia di San Giovanni** and **Maria Pià**. Further away from the screaming toddlers and prowling lifeguards, **La Spiaggia delle Bombarde** is a white, sandy beach bordered by pine trees and the insanely beautiful sea. The neighboring **Spiaggia del Lazzaretto** is protected by an 18th-century tower and is characterized by a swift current and cold waters. Both are accessible by taking the bus from the Giardini Pubblici toward Porto Conte (11 daily in summer, 30 min, L1600). **Porto Conte** itself is said to be the Mediterranean's largest natural harbor; with very calm waters, it's great for swimming and snorkeling. Certified divers interested in exploring the area's coral reefs and grottoes should contact **Centro Sub** (tel. 079/979229). A three-hour excursion including equipment costs L75,000; reserve one day in advance. Inland, you can explore the rocky terrain on **horseback** for L25,000 an hour by contacting **Il Grifone** (Centro d'Equitazione, tel. 079/986294).

NEAR ALGHERO

NEPTUNE'S GROTTO Heading north from Alghero, the promontory culminates at Capo Caccia, a uniquely wild, rocky natural reserve where a motley crew of birds resides and a crop of rosemary, asparagus, and fennel grows. Here the curious can walk down 656 steps into the semisubmerged Neptune's Grotto, a mysterious den where monk seals used to hang out until they were driven away by the noise of boat traffic. Nowadays groups are led through the cave along a roped-off path that winds through compartments called *sale*, or rooms. Spectacular stalagmites look like gigantic drip castles, and Sala delle Rovine and Sala Smith, with their famous "grand organ"-shaped rock formations, will inspire jaw-dropping awe. Three FDS buses leave daily from the Alghero bus terminal for Capo Caccia (50 min, L3000), and three return. Otherwise, you can go by boat to avoid the treacherous hike up from the grotto. Two boat companies run excursions, but be warned that the fare does not include admission to the grotto. **Compagnia Navisarda** (at the marina, tel. 079/975599) charges L14,000 for a 2½-hour excursion; boats leave four times daily (9, 10, 3, and 4) in April, May, and October and hourly 9–5 in summer. In Porto Conte, **Società Purita del Dentul** (at Cala Dragunara, tel. 079/946642) runs 1½-hour trips for the same price in April, May, and October; hourly 9–6:30 in summer. *Località Capo Caccia, tel. 079/946540. Admission: L10,000. Open Sept.–July, daily 9–6; Aug., daily 9–7.*

On the way to Capo Caccia, yet another stony structure, **Nuraghi Palmavera** (admission free; open Apr.–Oct., daily 9–1 and 4–8), is worth a quick look. The main tower and "palace" complex, dating from 1100 BC, is surrounded by 50 circular huts that made up the living quarters of the village. **Cooperative Silt** (tel. 079/980033) offers guided tours (in English by request) for L3500 per person (L2500 per person for groups). To get here, catch the bus to Capo Caccia and ask the bus driver to drop you off at the Nuraghi Palmavera. To return, jump on any bus from Porto Conte or Capo Caccia for Alghero.

The Northern Coast

An incredible coastline leads from Olbia to Sassari. Of the drop-dead-gorgeous coastal towns, cast your sights on Santa Teresa di Gallura and ignore the astronomically expensive Costa Smeralda, developed by billionaire Aga Khan as a playground for the yacht-owning jet set. The islands of Caprera and La Maddalena are equally beautiful, but prepare for the shock of encountering flocks of corn-fed gringos in red-and-white-striped tube socks who reside at the U.S. naval base on La Maddalena.

Sassari

The intrepid Sassarese spirit, characterized by feistiness and independence, dates back to 1236, when local rebels killed foreign tyrant Barrione III, who foolishly tried to control the city's commercial activity. Though reminders of Genovese and Pisan occupation remain here, the Sardo dialect determinedly persists—as does an air of self-sufficiency that borders on the antisocial. Sassari is primarily a transportation hub, not a place to spend more than a day or two, but the town does offer a few excellent ways to spend an afternoon: Enjoy a stroll through the old town with its tiny medieval living quarters that open onto grand, neoclassical piazzas, or have a cappuccino at one of the old porticoed bars off Piazza Italia.

During the Renaissance, inland Sassari served as a haven for malaria- and plague-fleeing coastal dwellers.

VISITOR INFORMATION **AAST.** The staff provides hotel and agriturismo listings and will even help you make a reservation if you're desperate. *Viale Umberto 72, tel. 079/231331. Open weekdays 8–2 and 4–6, Sat. 8–noon.*

COMING AND GOING The **train station** at the northeast end of town has eight daily trains to Olbia (2 hrs, L8000), five to Oristano (3 hrs, L12,100), five to Cagliari (4 hrs, L18,700), five to Porto Torres (20 min, L1600), and 10 to Alghero (1 hr, L3200). *Piazza Stazione 12–15, tel. 079/260362. Ticket/information office open daily 5:30 AM–8:30 PM.*

Pani (Via Bellieni 25, off Via Roma, tel. 079/236983 or 079/234782), the long-distance bus carrier, offers three nonstop daily buses to Cagliari at 6 AM, 2:15, and 6 PM (3 hrs 15 min, L26,000). The Cagliari bus passes through Màcomer (1½ hrs, L8000) and Oristano (2 hrs 20 min, L13,200). Six buses leave daily for Nuoro (2 hrs 25 min, L12,400), and three go to Porto Torres (30 min, L2000). The **ARST** station (Emilio Garibaldi 23, tel. 079/260006; open daily 6 AM–10 PM), off Corso Margherita in the center of town, has 11 daily buses to Alghero (1 hr, L3200), 13 to Ardo (1 hr, L3500), and five to Santa Teresa di Gallura (2 hrs, L11,500). Tickets can usually be bought on board the bus, but cost 10%–20% extra.

GETTING AROUND The city center extends southeast and uphill from the train station. The main drag, **Corso Vittorio Emanuele**, runs northwest–southeast through **Piazza Castello** and **Piazza Italia**, after which it becomes **Via Roma**. Orange APT buses stop frequently in front of the train station and at the public gardens. Bus 8 runs from the station to the southern end of town, passing through Piazza Castello and Piazza Italia. Buses start running at approximately 6 AM and head for the barn around 8 PM–10 PM.

WHERE TO SLEEP Accommodations in Sassari are less than inspiring and fill up fast in the high season, even though it may seem like no one's around. Agriturismo is popular on the outskirts of town; **Azienda Agrituristica Terrosa Giuseppa** (Località Agliado, tel. 079/310070) has listings for the area.

Hotel Giusy. If you get a room on the piazza/street side, you'll think screaming teenagers on Vespas are driving across your bed. Charmless but clean, all rooms (L65,000 for a double including breakfast) have a bathroom, phone, and '60s furniture. *Piazza Sant'Antonio 21, tel. 079/233327. From train station, turn left and make a right at Piazza Sant'Antonio. 26 rooms, all with bath. Closed for a week around Christmas. AE, MC, V.*

Hotel Marini Due. Though more expensive than the others, this hotel is a big leap into the realm of quasi-luxury. The newly remodeled rooms (doubles with bath L90,000, including breakfast) have TVs, phones, air-conditioning, and bathrooms. *Via Pietro Nenni 2, tel. 079/277282. From train station, take Bus 5 or 7 and ask driver when to get off. 70 rooms, all with bath. Wheelchair access. AE, MC, V.*

Pensione Famiglia. The cheapest, simplest hotel in town is a little rough and run-down: The rooms (doubles for L30,000) are clean, but that's more than can be said for the rather grimy showers. The location—around the corner from Piazza Italia—can't be beat, but the traffic noise can be a serious downer. *Viale Umberto 65, tel. 079/239543. From train station, turn left on Corso Vico, pass Piazza Sant'Antonio, and turn right on Corso Trinità (which becomes Viale Umberto). 19 rooms, none with bath. Midnight curfew.*

FOOD Though Sassari is big on excellent restaurants, most are out of the budget traveler's reach. Still, even in the more expensive places, you can always find a big bowl of Sardo-style *gnochetti* (little potato dumplings) cooked with sausage, basil, and tomato for L7000–L9000. **L'Antica Hostario** (Via Mazzini 27, tel. 079/200066) is famous for *lumache* (snails), *trifolate* (pasta cooked in oil, garlic, and parsley), lamb roasted on an open spit with a spicy sauce, and fresh fava beans in a milk sauce. You can buy produce at the Piazza Tola **outdoor market** weekdays 7:30–1:30, or head to the **University Mensa** (Via Padre Manzella 2, tel. 079/219111), which serves cheap meals (L7000) to students with IDs and even to impostors without. Most restaurants in Sassari, including both of the following, are closed on Sunday.

Ristorante Marini (Piazza Italia 10, tel. 079/234250), smack in the center of town, is a local favorite for a big bowl of gnochetti (L7000). Secondi run L7500–L13,000. **Trattoria Gesuino** (Via Alghero 36, tel. 079/273392) is a semielegant, family-run trattoria where locals meet for a late lunch. The house special is tricolor gnochetti (spinach, squash, and potato) with a cheesy sausage, tomato, and basil sauce (L10,000). From the museum (*see below*), continue up Via Roma and make a right on Via Alghero.

WORTH SEEING Between **Piazza Italia**, Sassari's heart, and the train station lies the tangle of streets that makes up the centro storico, home to Sassari's main sights. A walk through the centro storico in the shade of the medieval Pisan walls along **Corso Trinità** will allow you to see some of the best parts of the city. Though many of the town's historic structures have fallen into irreparable decay, it's still filled with little shops and the smell of fresh fish and garlic. Under the porticoes off Piazza Italia, Sassari's oldest cafés, like **Café Florian** on Via Roma or **Café Rau** on Via Crispo, are still popular hangouts. These are fun places to sit and have an espresso, even on Sunday, when everything else in town seems dead. The next piazza down from Italia, Piazza Castello, has not survived the modern era's aesthetic decline unscathed; the towering '60s Banco di Sardinia eclipses the disheveled though lovely 16th-century **Chiesa della Madonna del Rosario** (Piazza del Rosario). Looking up at the top of the church's bell tower, notice the bright glazed-pottery cupola and the iron, trumpet-tooting angel whose feet cling to a delicate Greek cross. Via Turritana, running northeast from behind Chiesa della Madonna del Rosario, takes you to the **duomo** (closed for restoration). The only traces of its original Romanesque design are the bottom part of the campanile and the facade. Closer to the train station is the **Chiesa Extra-Muros di Santa Maria di Betlem** (Piazza Santa Maria, at intersection of Via XXV Aprile and Viale Copino). The 16th- and 17th-century renovations have spoiled much of its original beauty, though, and today it is most famous for the *Festa dei Candelieri* (Festival of the Candlesticks; *see* Festivals, *below*).

The display labels at the **Museo Archeologico Etnografico G.A. Sanna** are written in Italian, but the museum is well organized and arranged chronologically, so it's easy to understand, and definitely worth a visit for those who want to get a handle on Sardinia's complex history. The exhibit includes fragments, utensils, jewels, and coins from the Paleolithic, pre-nuraghic, Bronze, and Roman eras. The nuraghic reconstructions are particularly fascinating. A small *pinacoteca* (picture gallery) contains Sardo paintings from the 14th to early 20th centuries. *Via Roma 64, tel. 079/272203. From Piazza Italia, follow Via Roma 4 blocks. Admission: L4000. Open Mon.–Sat. 9–2, Sun. 9–1.*

FESTIVALS La Farrada de li Candeleri (in Sardo) or **Festa dei Candelieri** (in Italian) takes place every August 14. Local guilds design huge, stunning candlesticks (actually, large columns) in honor of the Madonna, and parade through town dressed in extravagant traditional costumes. Each sculpted column is decorated according to an individual guild's insignia and is carried by eight men through the centro storico, Piazza Castello, and Corso Vittorio Emanuele, ending up at Santa Maria di Betlem. With origins dating back to the Middle Ages, the festival has been celebrated annually since a devastating plague ended here on the eve of Assumption Day in 1582.

NEAR SASSARI

CASTELSARDO Precariously perched above the Mediterranean, the medieval town of Castelsardo was an impenetrable fortress and stronghold of the Genoese Republic in the 12th century. Its fortified wall is completely intergrated with the town's naturally protective setting of rocks and hills—a harmonious union that is only interrupted by the subtle beauty of the campanile's cupola. You can skip the hotel- and restaurant-lined boardwalk, but a trip to the town and its eponymous castle is essential.

Though Castelsardo thrives on tourism, a walk through the old town reveals unexpected authenticity: The artisan workshops, jewelry shops, and reasonable boutiques that line the alleyways leading up to the castle are appealing rather than tacky. The **castle** itself now houses a small museum of Sardo handicrafts, **Museo dell'Intreccio** (open daily 9–1 and 2:30–midnight). The woven baskets aren't thrilling, but the L3000 admission is justified just for the rooftop view of the town and surrounding hillside. For another astounding view, follow the signs to the spectacular 16th-century **Cattedrale Sant'Antonio Abate**, one side of which faces onto the sea and the reefs.

➢ **COMING AND GOING** • Buy bus tickets at the tabacchi just past the *pescheria* (fish shop) on your left as you head up Via Roma from the lungomare; or at the *giornalaio* (newsstand) in the town's sole piazza. From Sassari, **ARST** runs 13 daily buses (1 hr, L3500) to Castelsardo. If you are taking a day trip, get off at the town's second stop, in the piazza just below the *borgo* (old town). Otherwise, if you're headed for a hotel, get off at the first stop along the lungomare when you see the castle in the distance.

➢ **WHERE TO SLEEP AND EAT** • Unfortunately, the old town has no hotels, but you'll find plently of accommodations a couple minutes' walk away along the lungomare. Doubles without bath go for L68,000 at the cozy, family-run **Pensione Pinna** (Lungomare Anglona 7, tel. 079/470168), or try **Hotel Cinsia** (Via Colledi Frigiano, tel. 079/470134), which offers pleasant, very quiet rooms (L80,000 for a double with bath) with terraces and views. Breakfast is included. **La Aragona** (Via Manganella, tel. 079/470488) is a great place for sandwiches (L4000), savory specialties like eggplant Parmesan (L8000), or simply a cold one and a view of the sunset from their large patio overlooking the sea. From the main piazza, take the stairs on Via Trieste, turn right on Via Piave, and head to the top.

NURAGHI SANTA ANTINE An hour south of Sassari lies the **Valley of the Nuraghi**, a rural area with a high concentration of nuraghic complexes dating from Sardinia's Bronze Age (1800 BC–500 BC). Unfortunately, many of these crumbling stone towers have not been excavated, but lie neglected along the rocky hilltops or amidst wheat fields overgrown with olive trees. However, the most sophisticated of the nuraghic villages, the excavated Nuraghi Santa Antine, outside the village of **Torralba**, offers a look at one of the most advanced and well-preserved of these fascinating structures. The main tower, three stories high, is nearly 4,000 years old; it's surrounded by bastions, staircases, internal corridors, and chambers, all constructed out of enormous blocks of volcanic rock using no mortar. A number of bronze figurines representing hunters, mothers with infants, and suppliants with votive offerings were found at the site (they now reside in museums in Cagliari and Sassari). In Torralba, the **Museo della Valle dei Nuraghi** displays reconstructions of the nuraghi, remains of pottery and jewelry, and depictions of Sardinian culture. To reach the nuraghi, take an ARST bus from Sassari (1 hr, L4300) and ask the driver to let you off after the town of Torralba; it's a short walk to the site. Returning to town, either hitch a ride or walk the 35 minutes back to Torralba. *Nuraghi Santa Antine. Admission:*

L5000. Open daily 8–8 in summer; until sundown in winter. Museum open Apr.–Sept., daily 9–1 and 4–8; Oct.–Mar., daily 8–2.

Santa Teresa di Gallura

Don't bother asking people for directions in Santa Teresa di Gallura; nobody actually lives here, and summer never ends in this tourist-packed village by the sea. But comfortable Santa Teresa, which practically plays footsie with Corsica, just across the Strait of Bonifacio, is blessed with one awesome panorama after the next. The closest beach, **Spiaggia Rena Bianca**, is a bun-to-bun rotisserie of scantily clad, tanner-than-thou sunseekers who lounge on the sands and splash around in a ceaseless, shallow stretch of turquoise Mediterranean sea. Though not the place to get a real dose of Sardo culture, this town has an undeniable allure that is surpassed only by the nearby beach (Spiaggia di Rena Maiore), the breathtaking Capo Testa promontory, and Isola Monica (*see* Cheap Thrills, *below*)—all accessible on foot with a little motivation. With a youthful spirit, affordable accommodations, and four campgrounds in the vicinity, Santa Teresa may be the only place on the gorgeous but prohibitively expensive Emerald Coast that's ideal for the budget crowd.

Postcard manufacturers bring in the bucks by photographing the strangely suggestive rock formations found along Sardinia's northern coast and delineating the shapes of female nudes, phalluses, and copulating humans in the rock's form.

BASICS The **tourist office** will hand you scads of listings and brochures. *Piazza Vittorio Emanuele 24, tel. 0789/754127. Open 8:30–1 and 3:30–6.*

COMING AND GOING All buses leave from Via Eleanora d'Arborea off Via Nazionale. Eight **ARST** buses leave daily for Olbia (1 hr 45 min, L6500), passing through Palau (40 min, L3000); and five go to Sassari (2 hrs, L11,500). Get tickets and information at **Bar Black and White** (Via Nazionale, no phone; open daily 7 AM–midnight) near Via del Porto, around the corner from the bus stop. Copies of the bus schedule are available at the tourist information office (*see above*).

WHERE TO SLEEP The few budget hotels, mostly near the port, fill up fast during July and August, but they generally maintain high standards. Agriturismo (*see* Chapter Basics, above) is practically unheard of here, and requires that you have a car. Inquire at the tourist information office about **Agriturismo Saltara** (Località Saltara, tel. 0789/755597).

Albergo Miramare. This *dipendenza* (annex), near the Torre di Longosardo, is simpler and smaller than its three-star affiliate upstairs. Small, airy doubles (L60,000–L70,000) with common bathrooms have a view of the sea. *Piazza della Libertà 6, tel. 0789/754103. From Piazza Vittorio Emanuele, take Via XX Settembre to Piazza Libertà. 4 rooms, none with bath. Closed Sept. 15–July. MC, V.*

Hotel Moderno. This hotel has comfortable and immaculate rooms, all with bathrooms. Quiet doubles (L60,000) are filled with light as well as heavenly scents from the restaurant downstairs. *Via Umberto 39, tel. 0789/754233. 20 rooms, all with bath. MC, V.*

Pensione Scano. This friendly, clean, family-run pension is housed in a cozy old building that was redone in the '60s. Small doubles without bath run L60,000; pension is available. Some rooms have a view of the ocean. *Via Lazio 4, tel. 0789/754447. Walk toward water on Via Nazionale, turn left on Via Capo Testa, and left on Via Lazio. 19 rooms, 5 with bath. MC, V.*

➤ CAMPING • Campeggio La Liccia (Strada per Castelsardo Km. 66, tel. 0789/755190; open June–Sept.) offers numerous amenities including beach access and a restaurant, and is reachable by bus to Castelsardo (30 min). They charge L14,500 per person. **Camping Gallura Village** (Località di Luccianeddi, tel. 0789/755580) runs a free shuttle service to and from Santa Teresa 3–4 times daily, mid-May through mid-October; sites cost L16,000 per person.

Campeggio Arcobaleno. This campground on the water has every amenity you can imagine; it can accommodate as many as 680 people at L13,500 per person in the high season (L9200 in the low season), including tent and electricity. *Località Porto Pozzo, tel. 0789/752044. Take bus toward Olbia and ask driver to let you off at campsite (20 min). Open June–Sept.*

FOOD Good, authentic Sardo cuisine can be very expensive, and you'll spend L20,000–L40,000 for meals that are merely adequate. If you are willing to pay a little more, try **Canne al Vento** (Via Nazionale 23, tel. 0789/754219), reputed to be the best joint in town for homestyle seafood dishes (L35,000–L50,000 for a full meal). At **Pizzeria-Rosticceria Sale e Pepe** (Via Carlo Alberto, no phone; open daily 10–2 and 4–11), a satisfying meal of baked lasagna costs L5000.

Ristorante Pizzeria Il Rosmarino. Though a ways from town, this dimly lit restaurant serves great pizzas and fish specialties. The covered outdoor terrace looks onto trees and the huge wood-burning pizza stove. The fixed-price menu is L25,000; pizzas cost L6000. *Via Nazionale, tel. 0789/755899. Take Via Nazionale away from town all the way to gas station; restaurant is next door. Open daily noon–midnight.*

CHEAP THRILLS From Spiaggia Rena Bianca, trails heading west into the hills will take you to **Isola Monica**, an isolated grass clearing surrounded by large rock formations—a kind of psychedelic Stonehenge. Trails aren't marked, but the footpaths are visible. From the hilltop overlooking both the sea and Santa Teresa, head one hour west (the ocean is north) to **Capo Testa**, a weather-beaten promontory with striking panoramic views.

AFTER DARK There's no difficulty finding action after sundown in Santa Teresa. Piazza Vittorio Emanuele fills with tourists of all ages showing off tans and clutching gelatos, and slick guys with slick hair hand out passes to the latest and greatest clubs. Unfortunately, many hot spots, including the new **Estasi's Disco** (100 Buoncammino, tel. 0789/755570), are outside of town and require a car to reach. A great alternative for all-night music and munchies is the hopping **Poldo's Pub** (Via Garibaldi, near Piazza San Vittorio, no phone; open daily 6 PM–8 AM), where *panini* (sandwiches; L4000), hamburgers (L4000), and beer (L2500–L5000) are served up by a crew of jovial bartenders. **Groove Café**, right on Piazza Vittorio Emanuele, is a kickback place to drink and listen to live music.

OUTDOOR ACTIVITIES Several boat excursions leave daily from the port at the eastern side of town. One of the private companies, **Nardino**, runs boat tours to **Budelli (Spiaggia Rossa)**, **Spargi**, **Cala Corsara**, and **Cala Azzurra** from 9:15 AM to 5 PM. The boats stop for swimming breaks at each of these isolated bays, with their pink coral beaches and breathtaking water, as well as stopping at each and every vaguely phallic rock formation so you can send a photo home to Mom. The L40,000 fare includes a spaghetti lunch. For more information, take Via del Porto from Via Nazionale to the booth at the port (Via Pascoli 45, tel. 0789/754773).

Gulp (Via Nazionale 58, tel. 0789/755689; open daily 9–12:30 and 4–7) rents mountain bikes for L25,000 a day (10% less in June and September, 20% less October–May) and scooters for L50,000 a day with the same discounts. Make a beeline for **Spiaggia di Rena Maiore**, the best beach. If you're without transportation, hop on a bus toward Sassari or Tempio

The Costa Smeralda

You wouldn't know it from looking at it, but the drop-dead beautiful Costa Smeralda (Emerald Coast), stretching along Sardinia's east coast south of Porto Cervo, has only been developed over the last 30 years or so. Legend has it that the very rich Aga Khan stepped off his yacht, was dumbstruck by the coast's beauty, and immediately offered a passing Sardo farmer $2 million for it. Since then, with the help of foreign investors, the area has undergone a major face-lift, and the little fishing villages have all been turned into ritzy resorts. The region goes to show you that money can buy a lot, but it can't buy back the original rustic beauty of these towns.

(L1800) and ask the driver to let you off at the beach. Getting back means begging a ride or a rather disparaging 6-kilometer trek homewards.

NEAR SANTA TERESA DI GALLURA

Though the port town of Palau and the nearby islands of La Maddalena and Caprera have suffered from hasty development in recent years, they at least offer campgrounds, relatively affordable accommodations, and access to perfect beaches.

PALAU While Palau is no great beauty, it's the most convenient place to pick up ferries to several islands just off the coast. **Patagus** (at the port, tel. 0789/708080) runs a daily boat tour from 10:30 AM to 5 PM that will enable you to swim and explore the pink sand beaches and hidden coves of the small, pristine, and otherwise unreachable archipelago islands. The cost is L40,000, plus an extra L10,000 if you want lunch; purchase tickets the day before you want to go. Ticket and information booths are right along the port and are open mid-May through September, daily 8:30–10 and 5–11.

➢ **COMING AND GOING** • Purchase tickets from **Stazione Marittima** (Piazza del Molo, no phone) at the Palau port for the **trenino** (*see box below*) that leaves from behind the station. Two trains run daily from Palau to Sassari (4 hrs, L10,500) and stop in all the small towns in between. **ARST** buses leave from in front of Stazione Marittima for Olbia (16 daily, 1 hr 15 min, L4200) and Santa Teresa di Gallura (16 daily, 45 min, L3200).

➢ **WHERE TO SLEEP AND EAT** • If you're stuck in charmless Palau, try **Hotel Serra** (Via Nazionale 17, tel. 0789/709519), where neat doubles run L65,000–L70,000. For one of two simple, clean rooms in a private home, call **Chiara** (tel. 0789/709613); she speaks a smidgen of English and charges L50,000 for a double. The beachfront campground **Capo d'Orso** (Località Le Saline, tel. 0789/702007; open June–Sept.), with lots of trees, a bar, a market, a restaurant, and opportunities for water sports and tennis, isn't a bad alternative at L11,000 per person during the high season.

You have to pay a little extra for a good meal in Palau, but if you don't mind splurging, try **Trattoria del Sub** (Via Capo d'Orso, tel. 0789/709870), an unpretentious restaurant that's famous for its delicious shellfish soup. Cheaper eats can be found at **Pizzeria Zio Nicola** (Riva dei Listrigoni, along the lungomare, tel. 0789/708520), east of the Stazione Marittima. You can get any kind of pizza to go for L6000–L10,000.

LA MADDALENA AND CAPRERA The islands of Caprera (home to Risorgimento hero Giuseppe Garibaldi) and adjacent La Maddalena form part of a stunning archipelago that hovers

I Think I Can

The train that D.H. Lawrence wrote about in "The Sea and Sardegna" hasn't changed at all since he rode it. The trenino, which looks like a slightly run-down Disneyland choo-choo, is still the best way to see the real Sardegna and the humble attractions of tiny farm towns. The Cagliari–Sorgono line (4 hrs 15 min) takes you from Cagliari directly to Parco del Gennargentu, the largest national park in Sardegna. The Sorso–Sassari line takes you to Galluresi mountain towns, which are typified by 16th- and 17th-century granite houses; particularly cool is Aggius, a free-climbing, bird-watching, hiking paradise that thrives on cork production and sheep farming. Check out nearby Valle della Luna, the most provocative of the Galluresi granite formations. For trenino information, call Gestione Governativa Ferrovie della Sardegna in Cagliari (tel. 070/306221 or 070/498628). The most you'll spend on a ticket is L10,800.

off the coast of Palau. La Maddalena remains alluring despite having sold its peaceful soul to the U.S. navy and a number of boys in blue. Some of the best beaches and rocky ruins on Sardinia are here, but you have to share them with a host of enthusiastic beach bums in the high season.

Even if you're depending on the buses, you can still reach some spectacular beaches. **Cherchi** runs hourly buses from the port around the island of La Maddalena; just get off when the pull of the turquoise water gets too much for you or else ask to be let off at **Monti da Rena** or **Baia Trinità**, both unmistakably awesome. A second bus runs from La Maddalena's port across the bridge to Caprera; ask the driver to let you off near the postcard-perfect beach, **Cala Coticcio**, also known as Tahiti.

Caprera, La Maddalena's smaller and less-inhabited neighbor, is lined with countless clearwater coves that beg to be explored; unfortunately you won't be the only explorer—the nearby Club Med ensures omnipresent flocks of errant beachcombers. If you've had enough of the surf and the sand, head to **Casa Garibaldi**, the humble, red-roofed home of Italy's Risorgimento hero Giuseppe Garibaldi (*see box* The Shot of Espresso Heard 'Round the World, in Chapter 5). Personal objects, locks of hair, portraits, crutches, clothes, tombs, and furniture are well displayed. Guided tours are in Italian only, but you're not missing much if you don't understand the language. *Località Caprera, tel. 0789/727162. Take Cherchi bus from Maddalena port; the bus lets you off ½ km from museum. Admission: L4000. Open Tues.–Sat. 9–1:30.*

➤ **COMING AND GOING** • Ferries run to La Maddalena from Palau every 20 minutes (30 min, L13,800). For information and tickets in Palau, head to Stazione Marittima's bar/tabacchi (Piazza del Molo, tel. 0789/709689), open daily 5 AM–11:45 PM. Once you reach La Maddalena, you might want to rent a *motorino* (moped) for L35,000 a day to check out some of the island's spectacular beaches. The rental shop **Nicol Sport** (Via Amendola 18, tel. 0789/753–5400; open daily 9–1 and 3–8) is right on the lungomare. The bus company **Cherchi** (La Maddalena Port, tel. 0789/737392) runs frequent buses from La Maddalena to Caprera (15–20 min, L1100) and to La Maddalena's beaches (15–30 min, L1100).

➤ **WHERE TO SLEEP** • La Maddalena's many campgrounds are cheap but packed. **Campeggio L'Abbatoggia** (Località Abbatoggia, tel. 0789/739173) is the only one on the water, but it has little shade and is not necessarily the best. However it does have a great restaurant with delicious seafood like *cozze alla marinara* (mussels; L12,000), as well as a bar, a market, and hot showers (L1000). Camping costs L11,000 per person in the high season. Take the Panoramic bus from the port and ask to be let off at Abbatoggia; the campground is a short walk down a dirt road. **Campeggio il Sole** (Via Indipendenza, tel. 0789/727727) is inland, with modest facilities, including a bar and restaurant, and modest prices to match (L8500). From La Maddalena, take the bus to Caprera and ask to be let off at the campground.

➤ **FOOD** • Restaurants and outdoor cafés are concentrated around La Maddalena's port and the nearby streets, Via Garibaldi and Via XX Settembre. For cheap and tasty sandwiches, stop by **Angelo's** (Piazza Umberto 4, on the water, no phone) open from 9 AM until the wee morning hours. Or grab Yankee grub—pizza, burgers, and fries—at **Pizzeria Banana** (Via Vittorio Emanuele 26, no phone; open daily 9 AM–12:30 AM). Pick up supplies for a beach picnic at **Market Ginetto** (Via Amendola 6, on the waterfront, tel. 0789/737541); open Mon.–Sat. 8:30–1:30 and 4:30–8:30.

The East Coast

The harsh, mountainous terrain south of Nuoro has been a notoriously impenetrable region since ancient times. Not surprisingly, in Roman times it took on the name of *La Barbagia* (land of the barbarians), as it was the only region that managed to resist Roman occupation. Ironically, this part of Sardinia was populated long before anywhere else on the island (6000 BC), when resourceful nuraghic civilizations found refuge in mountain grottoes. These days, La Barbagia is proud of its title, remaining stubbornly indomitable and secluded. People here are still bound to the old ways of farming, shepherding, and even folk dancing; sustained by thin Sardo bread called *carta da musica* (sheet music) and deep red wine, these natives won't miss an opportunity to share their bounty and to offer their hospitality.

Olbia

Though the nearby Golfo Aranci beaches are beautiful, Olbia itself is an unattractive port town with meager and expensive hotel and restaurant offerings. Since Olbia is a major ferry hub, it's likely you'll pass through here, but don't waste your time sticking around. As soon as you arrive, head for the **tourist information office** (Via Catello Piro 1, off Corso Umberto, tel. 0789/21453), where the efficient employees will load you up with maps and glossy brochures and then advise you to take the next unpredictable train or bus out of town. The office is open Monday–Saturday 8–1 and 4–6.

COMING AND GOING

➤ **BY FERRY** • All the ferry lines have representatives at the new and very efficient **Olbia Marittima Port**, where you can get ferry info for all of Sardinia. **Tirrenia** (Corso Umberto 17/19, tel. 0789/24691) runs a boat between Olbia and Livorno (13 hrs, L56,500) three times a week January–May, daily in early June, and twice a day from late June to early September. The Civitavecchia–Olbia ferry (7 hrs, L35,000 year-round) is the most frequent, with daily trips even in the lowest of seasons and as many as four daily trips from mid-June to early September. **Moby Lines** (Corso Umberto 187, tel. 0789/27933) chugs between Olbia and Livorno (10 hrs; L33,000–L75,000, depending on the season) about twice a day during the summer, daily during April and May, and twice a week November through January.

➤ **BY TRAIN** • The **train station** (Via Pala, tel. 0789/23462) is off Corso Umberto in the town center. Arriving trains coincide with departing ferries. Eleven daily trains run to Golfo Aranci (20 min, L2400), and 10 to Chilivani (1½ hrs, L5700), where you catch connecting trains to Sassari, Oristano, and Cagliari. Two daily trains head to Cagliari (4 hrs, L20,400), one at 7:15 AM and the other at 3:45 PM.

➤ **BY BUS** • The blue **ARST** buses are scheduled to take arriving boat passengers from just outside Olbia Marittima (the ferry station) to the ARST station (Corso Umberto, tel. 0789/24979) in town. Buses to Nuoro (7 daily, 2 hrs) cost L12,000–L14,000, depending on whether or not they're direct. Two buses leave for Sassari (2–3 hrs, L10,500) every day, one at 8 AM and the other at 9:35 PM. Buy tickets at the bar next to the station.

WHERE TO SLEEP AND EAT

Budget accommodations are scarce in Olbia, but **Albergo Terranova** (Via Garibaldi 3, tel. 0789/22395) offers decent, very cheap doubles without bath for L60,000. Otherwise the clean, cheap doubles at **Hotel Minerva** (Via Mazzini 6, tel. 0789/21190) are L65,000. The most convenient campgrounds are 30 minutes out of town by bus: From the ARST station, take the bus headed for Siniscola (8 daily, L6500) and ask the driver to let you off at the campground **San Teodoro** (Via del Tirreno, tel. 0784/865777), where camping costs L9500–L10,500 per person, plus L9000 for the tent site. Or get off at **Cala d'Ambra** (Località Cala d'Ambra, tel. 0784/865650), which charges L8500–L9500 per person plus L12,000 for the site.

Most restaurants have tourist menus that start at about L30,000. Your best bet is one of the pizza-by-the-slice places or *paninoteche* (sandwich shops) along Corso Umberto, or try **Il Golosone** (Corso Umberto 41, tel. 0789/26475) for delicious crepes (L5000). Beyond the railroad tracks, past the Esso station, **Trattoria Compai Giuanni** (Via dei Lidi 15, tel. 0789/58584) cooks simple, delicious pastas (L5000) and seafood specials.

Nuoro

Nuoro's location amid monochromatic mountains was ideal for keeping it safe from Saracen attacks in the late Middle Ages but couldn't help it withstand aesthetic attacks by 20th-century architects. Although Nuoro was once cluttered with traditional rural stone houses, postwar construction has destroyed much of its harmony with the rocky landscape. The only portion of the original town still extant is the tiny centro storico, around San Pietro. Despite the modern eyesores, Nuoro attracts travelers with its two unique museums and its proximity to several amazing villages and sights. Unfortunately, public transportation to neighboring towns is minimal; the best way to get around is to rent a car or to hitchhike during the day.

Despite Nuoro's modern guise, it feels the most Sardo, the most most insular, the most xenophobic of the island's towns. Don't turn a blind eye to tourist etiquette and discretion, lest a mysterious female figure dressed in black smite you about the head and neck with the quick blink of an eye, launching the malocchio (evil eye) in your direction.

BASICS **ENTE.** Hotel listings and info on mountain excursions are available here. *Piazza Italia 9, tel. 0784/30083. From train station, walk east on La Marmora, turn left on Via IV Novembre to Piazza Italia. Open weekdays 9:30–1 and 4–7.*

COMING AND GOING Nuoro's **train station** (Piazza della Stazione, tel. 0784/30115) is almost useless. You can reach most destinations only through Màcomer (9 daily, 1½ hrs, L4300), though direct trains do go to Cagliari (8 daily, L17,100). **Buses** are a better way of getting around. The people working at the **ARST** bus ticket counter (tel. 0784/32201) in the train station are helpful, but they keep irregular hours; when the counter is abandoned, buy tickets at the snack bar in the station. At press time, buses stopped across the street from the train station, but ask at the ticket counter for the most recent information. Two buses a day leave for Cagliari (6 hrs, L17,500), five for Dorgali (40 min, L3700), six for Olbia (2½ hrs, L11,600), 10 for Orgòsola (30 min, L2500), two for Sassari (3 hrs, L14,500), and eight for Siniscola (1 hr, L5800). Otherwise your only option is to rent a car at **Maggiore rent-a-car** (Via Convento 32, tel. 0784/30461), where they charge a steep L100,000 a day.

WHERE TO SLEEP Accommodations here are generally expensive. If you've got gear, **Camping Cala Gonone** (Via Collodi 1, tel. 0784/93165) is nearby in Cala Gonone, a kickback seaside town connected to Nuoro by frequent buses (1 hr, L4500). It's a four-star, excellently equipped campground (L21,000 per person in the high season) with a bar, restaurant, tennis courts, hot showers, and laundry. In the center of Nuoro, **Il Portico** (Via Mannu, tel. 0784/37535) offers the nicest and most affordable doubles (L70,000), all with bath. The three-star **Fratelli Sacchi** (Monte Ortobene, tel. 0784/31200), atop Monte Ortobene, has a garden and luxurious doubles for L80,000 without bath.

FOOD Affordable food is scarce in Nuoro, though some hotels have good restaurants, and fast-food pizza joints are always a backup. **Il Portico** (Via. M. Bua, tel. 0784/33159), between Piazze San Giovanni and Vittorio Emanuele, serves excellent pizzas (L5500–L8000) and meats (L9000 and up). **Trattoria il Gabbiano** (Via Mughina 11, tel. 0784/32919) is a local hangout on the way out of town, serving up serve delicious fish and homemade ravioli (L6000). From the station, follow Via La Marmora to Piazza della Grazie, and turn right on Via Manzoni; it's across from Piazza Mameli, to the right of the Agip gas station on Via Mughina.

WORTH SEEING The building housing the **Museo della Vita delle Tradizioni Populari Sardì** (Museum of Sardinian Life and Traditions) is itself an example of traditional Sardinian architecture, with wooden balconies and black stone portals. Each room is dedicated to a different aspect of Sardinian culture, such as traditional clothing and accessories (like the intricate turquoise buttons used to fasten shirts). Also check out the phallic *munifica*, a pendant used to cast the evil eye. *Via Mereu 56, tel. 0784/31426. From Piazza Vittorio Emanuele, head downhill and follow signs. Admission free. Open Mon.–Sat. 9–1 and 3–7.*

Casa di Grazia Deledda, the former house of Nobel Prize–winning writer Grazia Deledda, contains a rough manuscript copy of her novel *Malocchio*, displayed along with her pen and glasses, as well as foreign newspaper clippings and criticism. Like Nuoro's other museum, this simple wood-and-stone house attracts visitors with a tactile quality lacking in most museums. *Via G. Deledda 42, tel. 0784/34571. Admission free. Open Mon.–Sat. 9–1 and 3–7.*

NEAR NUORO

If you're looking for a little adventure and isolation, the mountains surrounding Nuoro offer plenty of hiking and spelunking opportunities amidst water-filled grottoes and rocky heights. You'll also find some of the oldest archaeological finds on the island here, as well as some of the best beaches. Down the coast from the places mentioned below, **Santa Maria Navarrese** is a fabulous hub for taking boat trips and seeing the area. Two buses traveling to Arbatax from

Nuoro stop in Santa Maria Navarrese at 8:05 AM and 2:30 PM (3 hrs, L18,500). One stop before Santa Maria Navarrese on the Nuoro–Arbatax bus is **Baunei**, where footpaths connect mountainous goat turf to the sea. Here parched mountain terrain punctuated by ghost-town churches opens onto spectacular turquoise bays that are only accessible by unmarked paths or by boat. Seek navigational help at the **Cooperativa Turistica il Golgo** (08040 Baunei, tel. 0782/610774), run by a group of friends in their thirties who lead excursions and have a fantastically authentic (albeit fantastically remote) restaurant.

DORGALI Perched on the cliffs above Cala Gonone, Dorgali is a touristy but excellent shopping town, with handcrafted pottery, leather, and local wine. Though essentially a one-street village, Dorgali is a good pit stop on your way to Cala Gonone, if only to sample *il pistidu* (a dessert made with cooked wine) at one of the many pastry shops, or to take advantage of the town's very efficient tourist office. The information goddess at **Pro Loco** (Via Lamarmora 1, tel. 0784/96243; open daily 9–1 or 4–6:30) will give you a map and explicit directions in English to nearby caves, nuraghi, and tombs. The area is rich in scattered nuraghic remains, including the **Giants' Tomb**, a mysterious burial ground covered by massive monolithic rocks. Also worth a visit are the nuraghic villages of **Serra Orrios** and **Su Casteddu**; unfortunately most sites in the area are only accessible by car. Pro Loco also conducts guided tours of the **Grotto di Ispinigoli**, a chasm—thought to be the site of ancient Phoenician sacrifice rituals—that includes the tallest stalagmite in the world (38 meters). If you want to stay the night in Dorgali, a L62,000 double at **San Pietro** (Via Lamarmora 20, tel. 0784/96142) is the cheapest in town. Five **ARST** buses travel daily from Nuoro to Dorgali (35 min, L3500).

CALA GONONE The big attraction at cheerful Cala Gonone, a touristy, seaside village, is the boat excursion to the **Grotto Bue Marino**, the spectacular monk seal caves. Formed by an underground spring, this extensive grotto includes 15 kilometers of extraordinary stalactite and stalagmite formations, though only the first kilometer is accessible to the public. Five boat excursions (2 hrs, L15,000) leave daily from the marina in Cala Gonone and include a guided walking tour of the grotto. For L10,000 extra you can also see the beautiful beach of **Cala Luna**. Other day-long excursions run along the cave-riddled coast, stopping at some truly unbelievable beaches accessible only by boat. **Cala Mariolu** is one beach that will leave you *con bocca aperta* (with mouth agape); strewn with white polished boulders, its cliffs and caves end in dreamlike turquoise depths. To reach Cala Gonone, take one of the hourly buses (1 hr, L4500) from the ARST station in Nuoro.

Plenty of hotels and campgrounds make Cala Gonone a good place to settle in for a while. **Camping Cala Gonone** (Via Collidi 1, tel. 0784/93165; open Easter–Oct. 8) is a four-star set up in the middle of town with free hot showers and laundry, as well as a bar, restaurant, BBQ, and sports facilities. Though they charge a hefty L21,000 from mid-July through August, it's still the cheapest sleep in the area. Otherwise **The Bue Marino** (Via Vespucci 31, tel. 0784/93130) has bright doubles without bath for L50,000. If you're hungry, Cala Gonone's numerous beachside trattorias provide scenic spots in which to indulge in pastas and seafood. Or save some bucks and eat just as well at **Snoopy** (Lungomare Palmavera, at Via Caio Duilio; open daily 9–2 and 5–11), where you can pick and choose from a variety of prepared dishes, such as roasted vegetables, seafood salads, chicken, and homemade breads.

OLIENA Nuoro's southern grape- and olive-cultivating neighbor, Oliena is situated amongst volcanic mountains that have eroded over thousands of years, producing a network of extraordinary grottoes flushed by underground rivers and lakes. Cooperativa Enis (*see below*) organizes group and individual excursions through the caves, mountain trails, forests, and natural springs surrounding Oliena. An afternoon excursion begins with a moderately strenuous hike to the nuraghic village of **Tiscali**, with its magnificent view over the valley. The village is only accessible through a passageway in the rock about as wide as your shoulders. Once you reach Tiscali, situated on the top of a mountain, hike back down the same path and explore the cavernous **Grotto su Oche**, and the sacred well of **Carros**. Quench your thirst at the incredibly cold, incredibly deep, and incredibly pure springs of **Su Gologone**. The price for the entire excursion is L10,000–L20,000 per person, depending on the number of people per group. ARST buses from Nuoro run to Oliena hourly 6 AM–8 PM (20 min, L1500).

➤ **WHERE TO SLEEP, EAT, AND BE MERRY** • Signs in the center of Oliena direct travelers up the hill to a hotel/campground co-op. Idyllic **Cooperativa Enis** (Località Monte Maccione/Via Aspromonico, tel. 0784/288363), surrounded by leccio trees, was founded in 1980 by a group of friends who grew up together in Oliena. At night, sit under the stars, sing, and drink mirto (a sweet apertif made from a sort of holly called leccio) with these young philosophers. Spotless doubles, many with a view of endless mountains and trees, go for L65,000. The indoor/outdoor restaurant with a view serves good regional specialties. People who decide to camp (L5000) have access to the bar, restaurant, and bathroom facilities, and can rock climb in the back. Public transportation isn't going to help you with the 4-kilometer climb from Oliena's center, so hitch or call the friendly co-op members for suggestions on getting up here.

ORGOSOLO Nearby Orgòsolo is famous for its provocative murals depicting scenes of political and social protest. A history of repeated invasions has apparently inspired Orgòsolo's artists to develop solidarity with oppressed peoples everywhere, from the peasants of the French Revolution to the students in Tiananmen Square. Nonetheless, the only women on the street are usually draped in black shawls, walking to church, while the men hang out in front of frescoed feminist pleas for emancipation.

If the atmosphere of Orgòsolo seems oppressive, signs point the way up to the mountains and the Montes Forest, which is filled with vegetation and lowing cows. For a rustic retreat, try **Aimonti del Gennargentu** (Località Montes, tel. 0784/402374). Doubles with bath run L55,000, and the regional food served in its restaurant is delicious. To reach Aimonti del Gennargentu, follow signs from the bus stop in Orgòsolo. Ten buses leave daily from Nuoro to Orgòsolo (40 min, L2500).

Italian Glossary

PRONUNCIATION

Lucky for you, Italian is pronounced almost exactly as it is written. If you learn just a few rules, you'll be able to pronounce most Italian words, even if you can't always understand what you're saying. Best of all, Italians, unlike many of their neighbors to the north, will generally be impressed by your efforts to speak their language.

VOWELS A is always pronounced **ah** (as in pasta), **i** sounds like **ee** (as in police), and **u** is always pronounced **oo** (as in blue). **E** sometimes sounds like **eh** (as in memory), sometimes like **ay** (as in weigh). **O** can sound like **oh** (as in most), or like **ah** (as in cost). Happily, you're likely to be understood even if you screw up your e's and o's a little bit—even the Italians themselves don't always agree. When you see two vowels right next to each other, pronounce each one individually. For example, *paura* (fear) is pronounced pa-OO-ra. To accomplish this, you may have to stretch your mouth in directions it's never gone before, but if you didn't make a few faces, you wouldn't be speaking Italian.

CONSONANTS Most consonants are pronounced the same way in Italian as they are in English. Of course, there are a few exceptions just to make life interesting. In Italian **ch** is always pronounced like a **k**, so *chiesa* (church) is pronounced kee-AY-za. A **c** followed by an **i** or an **e** is pronounced like the English **ch**, so *città* (city) is pronounced chee-TAH. A **c** followed by anything else sounds like a **k**; *cambio* (change) is pronounced KAHM-bee-oh. Both **g** and **gg** are pronounced as **j** when followed by **i** or **e**, so Luigi sounds like Loo-EE-jee. Always roll your **r's** if your Yankee tongue has the capacity. **Qu** always sounds like kw, so *qui* (here) is pronounced KWEE. The letter **s** sounds like a **z** when it appears between two vowels, so casa is pronounced KAH-za. Otherwise, the **s** sounds the same as it does in English.

The sound that is most likely to trip up English speakers is the **gl**, which is pronounced sort of like **ly**, much like the sound in million. Gli, the masculine plural for the word "the" is thus pronounced LYEE; try to resist the temptation to say GLEE. Similarly, **gn** is pronounced like **ny**. If you know how to pronounce gnocchi (NYO-kee), you've got it made. Finally, **double consonants** are pronounced differently than single ones, so *fato* (fate) is pronounced differently than *fatto* (made). When saying a word that has a double consonant you should produce a glottal stop, a tiny interruption in your breath stream. To put this into effect, try pronouncing the double letter twice, once at the end of the first syllable and once at the beginning of the second. Fatto is thus prounounced FAHT-to, unlike fato (FAH-to).

BASICS

English	Italian
Getting By	
Yes/no	Sì/no
Okay	Va bene
Please	Per favore/per piacere
Thank you	Grazie
You're welcome	Prego
Excuse me	Scusi
I'm sorry	Mi dispiace
Good morning/afternoon	Buon giorno
Good evening	Buona sera
Goodbye	Arrivederci/ciao

Mr. (sir)	Signore
Mrs. (ma'am)	Signora
Miss	Signorina
Young people	Ragazzi
How are you?	Come sta?
Fine, thank you	Bene, grazie
And you?	E Lei?
Do you speak English?	Parla inglese?
I don't speak Italian	Non parlo italiano
I don't understand	Non capisco
Can you please repeat?	Può ripetere?
Slowly	Piano, piano
How do you say . . .?	Come si dice . . .?
I don't know	Non lo so
What's your name?	Come si chiama?
My name is . . .	Mi chiamo . . .
Where is . . .?	Dov'è . . .?
What time is it?	Che ore sono?
Yesterday	Ieri
Today	Oggi
Tomorrow	Domani
This morning	Stamattina
This afternoon	Oggi pomeriggio
Tonight	Stasera
How?	Come?
When?	Quando?
What?	Che cosa?
What is it?	Che cos'è?
Why?	Perchè?
Who?	Chi?
Where is the bathroom?	Dov'è il bagno?
This	Questo
That	Quello

Changing Money

Where can I change money?	Dove si può cambiare i soldi?
Is there a bank nearby?	C'è una banca qui vicino?
An exchange bureau	Una cassa di cambio
Is there a charge?	C'è una tariffa?
Is it free?	E gratis?
Can I use my credit card?	Posso usare la carta di credito?

Emergencies

I am sick	Sto male
Hospital	L'ospedale
First aid	Il pronto soccorso
Call a doctor.	Chiami un medico.
Help!	Aiuto!
Fire!	Fuoco!
Call the police!	Telefoni la polizia!

Numbers

One	Uno
Two	Due
Three	Tre
Four	Quattro
Five	Cinque

Six	Sei
Seven	Sette
Eight	Otto
Nine	Nove
Ten	Dieci
Eleven	Undici
Twelve	Dodici
Thirteen	Tredici
Fourteen	Quattordici
Fifteen	Quindici
Sixteen	Seidici
Seventeen	Diciasette
Eighteen	Diciotto
Nineteen	Dicianove
Twenty	Venti
Thirty	Trenta
Forty	Quaranta
Fifty	Cinquanta
Sixty	Sessanta
Seventy	Settanta
Eighty	Ottanta
Ninety	Novanta
One hundred	Cento
One thousand	Mille
Ten thousand	Diecimila
One hundred thousand	Centomila

Days of the Week

Sunday	Domenica
Monday	Lunedì
Tuesday	Martedì
Wednesday	Mercoledì
Thursday	Giovedì
Friday	Venerdì
Saturday	Sabato

Months

January	Gennaio
February	Febbraio
March	Marzo
April	Aprile
May	Maggio
June	Giugno
July	Luglio
August	Agosto
September	Settembre
October	Ottobre
November	Novembre
December	Dicembre

Phones and Mail

Hello (over the phone)	Pronto
A telephone	Un telefono
A phone token	Un gettone
A phone card	Una carta telefonica
Post office	La posta
Stamps	Francobolli

517

Envelopes	Le buste
Writing paper	La carta da lettere
A postcard	Una cartolina
I would like to send a letter.	Vorrei spedire una lettera.
Poste restante	Fermo posta

COMING AND GOING

The train station	La stazione/Ferrovia
A ticket	Un biglietto
One-way	Andata
Round-trip	Andata e ritorno
Arrival	Arrivo
Departure	Partenza
Platform	Il binario
A sleeping car	Una cuccetta
First/second class	Prima/seconda classe
Bus (long-distance)	Pullman
City bus	L'autobus
Bus stop	La fermata dell'autobus/dello pullman
Car	Una macchina/automobile
To rent	Noleggiare
Gas	Il petrolio
Kilometers	Chilometri
To hitchhike	Fare l'autostop

GETTING AROUND

A guidebook	Una guida turistica
A city map	Una pianta della città
A country map	Una carta geografica
Here/there	Qui/là
Left/right	A sinistra/destra
Straight ahead	Avanti diritto
Is it far?	E lontano?
Is it near?	E vicino?

WHERE TO SLEEP

Where can I find a cheap hotel?	Dove potrei trovare un albergo a buon prezzo?
Pension	Un pensione
Hostel	Un ostello
A room	Una camera
I would like to make a reservation.	Vorrei fare una prenotazione.
I'm looking for a room for one/two night(s).	Cerco una camera per una/due notte.
Is there a private bathroom?	C'è un bagno privato?
For one person/two people	Per una persona/due persone
A shower	Una doccia
Sheets	Lenzuoli
A key	Un chiave
Campground	Campeggio
Can I leave my bags here?	Posso lasciare qui i miei bagagli?

FOOD

| Breakfast | La prima colazione |
| Lunch | Il pranzo |

Dinner	La cena
Waiter/waitress	Cameriere/a
Please give me . . .	Mi dia . . .
Menu	Il menù
A bottle of . . .	Una bottiglia di . . .
A cup of . . .	Una tazza di . . .
A glass of . . .	Un bicchiere di . . .
Wine	Vino
Bread	Il pane
A napkin	Un tovagliolo
A fork	Una forchetta
A spoon	Un cucchiaio
A knife	Un coltello
Pepper	Il pepe
Salt	Il sale
Sugar	Lo zucchero
An ashtray	Una portacenere
The bill/check	Il conto
I'd like to order . . .	Vorrei ordinare . . .
Cheers!	Cin cin!
Bon appetit	Buon appetito
I am a diabetic.	Ho il diabete.
I am a vegetarian.	Sono vegetariano/a.
I'm hungry/thirsty.	Ho fame/sete.
It's good/bad.	E buono/schifoso.
It's hot/cold.	E caldo/freddo.

WORTH SEEING

The museum	Il museo/la galleria
The church	La chiesa
The cathedral	Il cattedrale/duomo
The park	Il parco
The fountain	La fontana
The statue	La statua
The painting	La pittura

AFTER DARK

Bar/club	Bar/club
Bar crawl	Fare un giro dei bar
A drink	Una bibita
I'm plastered.	Sono ubriaco/a.
Let's go dancing.	Andiamo a ballare.
Cover charge	Coperto
Movie theater	La cinema
Original version (not dubbed)	Versione originale
Will you walk me home?	Mi accompagni a casa?
Do you have a cigarette?	Ha una cigaretta?
A light?	D'accendere?

SHOPPING

To go shopping	Fare lo shopping
To buy groceries	Fare la spesa
Store	Il negozio
Grocery store	Alimentari
Market	Mercato
Bakery	Panificio

Pastry shop	Pasticceria
Dairy	Latteria
Deli	Salumeria
I'd like to buy . . .	Vorrei comprare . . .
A newspaper	Un giornale
A magazine	Una rivista
Cigarettes	Delle sigarette
Matches	Dei fiammiferi
Tampons/pads	Tamponi/assorbente
Film	Il film
How much is it?	Quanto costa?
It's expensive.	E caro/costoso.
Cheap	Buon prezzo
Little/lot	Poco/tanto
More/less	Più/meno
That's all/enough.	Basta/abbastanza.
Too much	Troppo

MORE USEFUL PHRASES

Leave me alone.	Lasciami in pace.
Go away!	Va via!
Asshole!	Stronzo!
Miserable swine!	Porca miseria!
Fuck off!	Va fan culo!
I already have a boyfriend/girlfriend	Ho già un ragazzo/una ragazza
Do you have a condom?	Hai un preservativo?
Let's make love/have sex	Facciamo l'amore/il sesso
I love you.	Ti amo.

Architectural Primer

Temple of Venus and Rome in Rome

You can't avoid cultural overload on a trip through Italy, and the only way to ease the pain—excluding a bottle of cheap red wine—is to get a grasp on some of the ideas that have given form to its streets, museums, and cathedrals. This primer is just to get you started.

ROMAN ARCHITECTURE

From about the 2nd century BC to the 6th century AD, the Romans were busy rampaging through western Europe and northern Africa, establishing colonial settlements all along the way. One of Rome's first major victories came in 241 BC against Carthage, which secured Rome's bridgehead in northern Africa. On other fronts, Roman armies conquered Spain in 133 BC, Athens in 86 BC, Egypt in 30 BC, Britain in AD 43, sections of Germany in AD 90, and much of Arabia and Syria in AD 106.

Needless to say, the Romans needed an efficient method of communicating with and defending their far-flung colonies. Rome's fleets were mighty, but traveling by sea was not sufficient to maintain control over so vast an empire. This prompted the Romans to develop a complex system of **roads.** While it's an exaggeration to say that all roads led to Rome, it's true that the Roman network spanned from England and Africa to Turkey and the Middle East. The Via Appia, which ran from Rome south to Campania, was the road most admired, made of smooth blocks cushioned by crushed gravel. Government officials—particularly the *cursus publicus,* the ancient version of a UPS driver—traveled by horse and could cover up to 120 miles a day. The less fortunate had to plod along by horse-drawn wagon or on foot; according to the poet Horace, even the strongest walkers could cover no more than 20 miles before collapsing at a roadside inn.

To Romans, beauty was a product of utility and order, not necessarily of decoration. Roman architects considered a structure beautiful only if it presented an elegant solution to a practical problem.

Another of the Romans' engineering feats was the **aqueduct,** which was used to transport water from distant sources to large towns. The earliest aqueducts were underground tunnels dug by slaves. Yet water didn't flow through these aqueducts at enough of an angle; they could only carry water short distances and were unable to supply large cities such as Rome, which had an estimated population of 1.2 million in

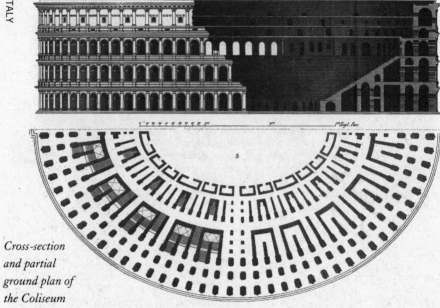

Cross-section and partial ground plan of the Coliseum

Trajan's column in Rome

45 BC. These problems were solved by above-ground aqueducts: The water flowed down a gentle gradient through a channel that was carved along the tops of interconnected arches. An aqueduct had to have a slight slope—no matter what the terrain—so Roman engineers often constructed multitiered aqueducts to span valleys and steep slopes. According to Frontinius, an ancient engineer, Rome in the 1st century AD was supplied with more than 250 million gallons of water every day.

The Roman **baths** were as important as the forum to a city's social life. According to a 3rd-century AD survey, Rome had an estimated 800 public bathhouses. Admission was cheap, and men and women bathed in the nude at different times to ensure at least some decorum. Construction of the baths, however, presented a few technical problems. Owing to the heat and humidity of the *caldaria* (steam rooms) and the *laconica* (sweating rooms), architects used concrete instead of wood (which has a tendency to rot when exposed to moisture). Roman advances in the use of concrete—laboriously made from pulverized earth mixed with limestone—set the foundation, so to speak, for architectural innovations throughout Western Europe.

Another of the Romans' important architectural developments was the **round arch,** which allowed engineers to build bigger and more varied buildings than the Greeks, who generally stuck to cylindrical columns and rectangular floor plans. Round arches were especially handy when building elliptically shaped **amphitheaters,** which were used as arenas for spectacles like gladiator combat and the slaughter of Christians (c.f., *Spartacus*, starring the inimitable Kirk Douglas). Occasionally, amphitheaters were flooded for "sea combat," with dozens of ships and hundreds of sailors battling for supremacy in crocodile-infested waters. (Thousands of these exotic beasts were imported from the colonies to satisfy the morbid fancies of Rome's aristocracy.) Needless to say, amphitheaters were on the architectural cutting edge in their day, with rows of round arches on the exterior and tiers of seats—which often accommodated as many as 50,000 spectators—inside.

The **triumphal arch** and **column** are other uniquely Roman monuments, usually masterminded by some megalomaniacal conqueror who wanted to ensure that his accomplishments were properly commemorated. Trajan's Column in Rome is a fine example. Triumphal arches and columns were decorated with all sorts of bas-relief sculpture; horse-drawn chariots were among the most popular motifs.

BYZANTINE ARCHITECTURE

Constantine I moved the capital of the Roman Empire to Byzantium in AD 330, ultimately inciting an east–west split between Rome and what would later be called both Constantinople and—since 1930—Istanbul, in modern Turkey. Comprising the Balkan Peninsula, Greece and its islands, and most of Asia Minor, Constantine's Byzantine Empire was a unique blend of Hellenic and Roman culture transfigured through the lens of Christianity (Constantine legalized Christianity in the AD 313 Edict of Milan). The Byzantine influence, however, was not limited to the east: Venice, Ravenna, and Sicily all displayed heavy touches of the Byzantine aesthetic, particularly after the fall of the western Roman Empire in AD 476.

Church of San Vitale in Ravenna

Byzantine architecture is heavily indebted to the designs and technical achievements of Rome, which explains why Christian churches in Turkey are built on a north–south axis with a central nave and transept. The primary example of this is Hagia Sophia, in Istanbul, built by Justinian between AD 532 and AD 537.

Another Byzantine development was the eight-sided church; the textbook example is Ravenna's 6th-century San Vitale, which features a Pantocrator (an Eastern Orthodox depiction of an "all ruling" Jesus) and scads of colorful mosaics. Other examples of Byzantine design are Basilica di San Marco, in Venice, which preserves dozens of intricate Byzantine mosaics.

Basilica di San Marco in Venice

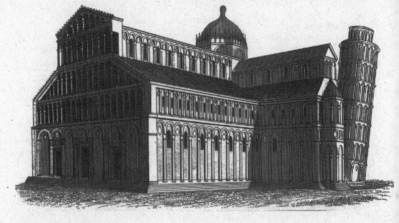

*Cathedral
and tower
of Pisa*

ROMANESQUE ARCHITECTURE

Working primarily during the 11th and 12th centuries, Romanesque architects employed many Roman architectural forms—particularly round arches and the basilica layout. Almost without exception, a church or cathedral was the largest and most important building in any community during the Middle Ages; it symbolized solidity and permanence, as well as the promise of a glorious afterlife, to people who spent most of their days trudging knee-deep in manure. During times of upheaval—which the Middle Ages had aplenty—the massive, blocky Romanesque churches were transformed into well-defended refuges. As a result, your first impression of a Romanesque cathedral is likely to be that of a heavy, solid, somber place—one that's firmly rooted to the ground.

Many Romanesque churches have a **basilica floor plan;** that is, they're shaped like Roman basilicas, with the addition of a perpendicular **transept.** This layout is known

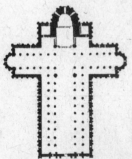

as "cruciform" because of its likeness to a cross, and there's hardly a medieval church in Italy that doesn't employ such a plan. A major aspect of cruciform churches is the central **nave,** the vast open space where worshippers stand during services. The **aisles** on either side allow people to move throughout the church without disrupting services. The **altar**—at the intersection of the nave and transept—stands over the **crypt,** in which the sacred bones of a saint are often buried. (Some churches will display the preserved bones, fingers, and shriveled hearts of saints, not to mention pieces of The One True Cross and maybe even a thorn from Christ's crown.)

*Floor
plan of
Pisa's
cathedral*

The entrance to a Romanesque church is usually at the west end and is often flanked by two towers. Sometimes a number of smaller recessed apses, each with its own altar dedicated to a saint, protrude from the east end of the church, which gets the lion's share of morning sunlight and explains why there are colorful stained-glass panels above many altars.

Perhaps the most characteristic features of Romanesque architecture are barrel vaults and groin vaults, both of which were adopted from the Romans (who adopted them from the Etruscans). A vault is essentially a curved ceiling built of brick or stone that's shaped to form a tight, compact arch over a rectangular space. Earlier Romanesque churches, in particular, used the simple barrel vault—which is named for its straightforward half-barrel shape—to create a heightened sense of space (though, by today's standards, barrel vaults look austere and blocky). A later Romanesque feature is the groin vault, a complicated way of describing the intersection of two barrel vaults at right angles. However, both of these vaulting methods exert an enormous amount of pressure both outward and downward; to avoid collapse they had be hedged in with heavy stone walls. As a result, architects could incorporate only a few small windows into their designs, lest the walls crumble under the intense pressure.

Other than thick walls and round arches, Romanesque churches had few common characteristics, largely because of regional differences in taste. Many Romanesque interiors are austere, but that's because Romanesque architects were typically commissioned by church leaders who felt that decoration was frivolous and blasphemous. Other interiors, however, are richly decorated, according to the principle that art should be employed simultaneously for the glory of God and for the edification of the church's largely illiterate masses. When you ponder the brilliant Byzantine frescoes of Siena and Ravenna, it seems that medieval art was nothing if not didactic: Scenes of gargoyles tormenting lost souls, of hellish monsters devouring the wicked, of the blessed gathered by Christ's side abound.

GOTHIC ARCHITECTURE

When Abbot Suger, an adviser to Louis VI, decided in AD 1140 to build a cathedral in St-Denis, near Paris, he set out to create a towering structure full of heavenly light—an unfettered monument that would reach to the heavens and encourage worshippers to do likewise. In the 12th century, however, building a church with voluminous interior spaces and wide decorative windows wasn't a simple thing. Massive stone walls were required to support the traditional barrel vaults used in Romanesque churches. However, certain Gothic innovations changed all that, particularly **pointed arches**, **rib vaults**, and **flying buttresses**. (The pointed arch and rib vault were generally known to Romanesque architects, but were employed to a much greater degree and in more daring ways starting in the 12th century.)

Basilica of San Saba in Rome

Speaking in Tongues

Here's a handy list of architectural terms to consider before passing through the next church portal (front door):

• **Chancel:** The space around the altar that is off-limits to everyone but the clergy. It's usually at the east end of the church and is often blocked off by a rail.

• **Choir:** The section of the church set off to seat the choir. It's either in the chancel or in a loft in another part of the church.

• **Clerestory:** The upper part of the church walls, typically lined with windows (often of the stained-glass variety) to bathe the nave with light.

• **Crypt:** An underground chamber usually used as a burial site and often found directly below a church's nave.

• **Narthex:** An hall or small room leading from the main entrance to the nave.

• **Nave:** The main section of the church that stretches from the chancel to the narthex. This is where worshippers sit during services.

• **Transept:** The part of the church that extends outward at a right angle from the main body, creating a cruciform (i.e., cross-shaped) plan.

• **Tympanum:** A recessed triangular or semicircular space above the portal, often decorated with sculpture.

Details of Gothic windows

Rib vaults are essentially groin vaults with X-shaped arches exposed on the under-side—an innovation that, via the crisscrossing ribs, distributed the weight of the roof outward instead of downward. This freed up space between the ribs for all sorts of masonry and decorative design. More important, the outward thrust produced by groin vaulting could be counterbalanced by a complex system of buttresses and flying but-tresses—essentially, external stone supports that absorbed the thrust of the nave wall.

Gothic architecture got its name from Renaissance snobs who thought Gothic cathedrals looked awkward and unstable; the name itself comes from the barbarian Goths, who sacked Rome in the 5th century AD.

Buttresses allowed architects to reduce the thickness of walls and to place windows of different shapes and sizes into walls that were no longer solely responsible for the sta-bility of the overall structure. The upshot is that Gothic cathedrals are uniformly bright and voluminous, with arching ceilings and tall towers that command attention for miles. Even the interior vaulting directs the eye upward instead of around and down, an effect that embodies the ideal of Gothic architecture.

Flying Buttress

RENAISSANCE ARCHITECTURE

The Renaissance, or "rebirth," was not based on a newfound set of aesthetics or artis-tic skills, but rather on a re-evaluation of classical ideals. Renaissance architects stud-ied the works of ancient Rome and attempted to recapture the solid, earthly, and sym-metrical tendencies that had been abandoned in the Gothic extravagances of the Mid-dle Ages. Artists studied the proportions of ancient temples, anatomists carved open and catalogued the human body, and engineers and scientists set out to discover and manipulate the complex laws of nature. Art and architecture were no longer myopic fields, but rather poignant aspects of interrelated disciplines—among them poetry, philosophy, anatomy, engineering, and astronomy—that promised a new understand-ing of the universe.

In the 15th century, Florence was the cradle of Renaissance architecture. After spend-ing several years studying in Rome, **Filippo Brunelleschi** (1377–1446) returned to his native Florence in 1420 and began work on the dome for the city's massive duomo. Brunelleschi's octagonal dome wowed the Florentines (who were skeptical that such a thing could be built) and paved the way for a revolution in architectural design. Though it made use of vaulting techniques developed by Gothic architects, Brunelleschi's dome was of a scale and technical design previously unseen, and after its completion it became the standard for countless Renaissance architects. Brunelleschi's other major works include the churches of San Lorenzo and Santo Spirito, in Florence.

Duomo di Santa Maria del
Fiore in Florence

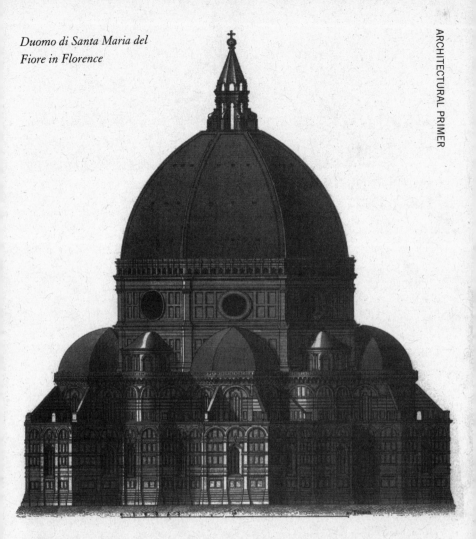

Leone Battista Alberti (1404–1472) was the Renaissance's other architectural lumi-
nary. Author of the first architectural treatise since Roman times, the *De re Aedificato-
ria* (1452), Alberti argued that architecture should imitate nature and incorporate the
ideals of symmetry and order. He felt that buildings, much like music, should conform
to certain harmonic proportions and embody specific ratios.

Outside of Florence, Renaissance ideals were slowly but surely embraced in
Urbino, Mantua, Milan, and Naples. In other parts of Italy, particularly Sicily
and Tuscany, architects abandoned the Romanesque cruciform floor plan in
favor of the **Greek cross plan.** The essential characteristics of the Greek
cross were the polygonal central chamber (as opposed to a rectangular nave)
abutted by four arms of equal length, a nod to the Renaissance obsession
with symmetry. The finest examples of this style are **Donato Bramante's**
(1444–1514) Tempietto in Rome and his original design for St. Peter's in
Vatican City.

Bramante's
plan of
St. Peter's
in Rome

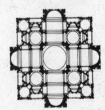

527

Church of St. Ignatius in Rome

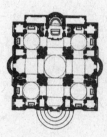

Floor plan for church of the Assumption in Genoa

Church of San Carlo alle Quattro Fontane in Rome

BAROQUE ARCHITECTURE

During the High Renaissance, in the late 16th century, architecture tastes reverted to a heavy decorative style. Although the symmetry and solidity remained, architects began dressing up their staid Renaissance buildings with all sorts of ornaments, curlicues, and lavish paintings. Interiors were well-lighted—either by candles or the sun—so that worshippers could ponder the wealth of expensive marble and gold leaf used to cover every nook and cranny. The architect became a conductor of emotional intensity and used swirling lines and light to give the buildings' interiors a sense of movement intended to engulf the viewer.

While order is the foremost feature in Renaissance buildings, willful confusion is the primary characteristic of Baroque architecture. The reason for this shift can be traced to changing religious ideals. Theologians began to argue that trying to come closer to God through the exercise of the intellect was futile, and that faith was a far superior attribute. Chaotic and confusing church architecture was supposed to encourage worshippers to abandon their reason in favor of raw emotional response. This effect was achieved through complex, massive floor plans, through unfamiliar undulating facades adorned with puffs of sculpted plaster and marble, and through the novel use of vivid, contrasting colors. The two big names to remember in this context are **Francesco Borromini** (1599–1677), who designed the church of San Carlo alle Quattro Fontane in Rome and **Gianlorenzo Bernini** (1598–1681), the Naples-born architect who's best known for the sculptures *David* and *Apollo and Daphne,* and for his design of St. Peter's in Rome.

Index

A

Abbey of San Fruttuoso, *170, 172*
Abbey of Sant'Andrea, *145*
Abruzzi, *361–368*
Accademia Carrara, *116*
Acquario Communale, *252*
Acquario Tirrenico, *170*
Adrano, *457*
Aeolian Islands, *487–490*
Affitacamera, *27*
Aggius, *509*
Agrigento, *465–467*
Agriturismo, *27*
Agropoli, *402–403*
Alagna Valsesia, *147–148*
Alberobello, *420*
Alghero, *501–503*
Alicudi, *490*
Amalfi, *397–399*
Amalfi coast, *396–403*
American Express, *11, 12*
Ancona, *302–303*
Anfiteatro Flavio, *385*
Annunzio, Gabriele d', *125*
Antica Dolceria Bonaiuto, *465*
Antico Castello, *172*
Antiquarium Constantini, *240*
Aosta, *148–150*
Appian Way, *342–343, 424*
Apricale, *169*
Aquila Tower, *81*
Aquilea, *91*
Aragonese Castle, *422*
Ara Pacis, *333*
Arche di Scaglieri, *71*
Archery Tournament, *272*
Arch of Constantine, *328*
Arch of Septimius Severus, *329*
Arco d'Augusto, *205*
Arco Romano, *150*
Arena, *71, 72*
Arezzo, *264–266*
Arquà Petrarca, *65*
Arsenale, *55*

Art galleries and museums

Abruzzi, *363*
Bologna, *182–183*
Emilia-Romagna, *186–187, 191, 193, 196, 197, 206*
Florence, *227, 228–230, 231, 233, 235, 236*
Florence area, *240, 241, 243*
Friuli-Venezia Guilia, *90, 95*
Genova, *160*
Lombardy, *112, 114, 116, 118*
Marche, *299–300, 301, 303, 304*
Matera, *431*
Milan, *107, 108, 109*
Naples, *383*
Palermo, *480–481*
Piemonte, *144*
Rome, *331, 332, 333, 334–335, 336, 339, 341–342, 345, 346*
Sardinia, *497*
Sicily, *461, 473*
Torino, *143*
Tuscany, *248, 255, 256, 262, 263, 266–267, 268, 271*
Umbria, *283, 287, 291, 294*
the Veneto, *64, 67, 74, 75, 76*
Venice, *50–51, 53, 59*
Ascoli Piceno, *303–304*
Asolo, *74*
Assalto al Carro, *431*
Assisi, *288–293*
Asti, *146*
ATMs, *12, 14*
Atri, *368*
Augusteum, *333*

B

Bagheria, *484*
Ballet, *351, 483*
Banditaccia Necropolis, *356*

Baptistry

Florence, *227*
Parma, *190*
Bargello, *230*
Bari, *416–420*
Barrea, *365–366*
Barùmini, *497–498*
Basilica del Santo, *63*
Basilica di San Biagio, *162*
Basilica di San Francesco
Arezzo, *266*
Assisi, *291–292*
Ravenna, *201*
Basilica di San Giusto, *95*
Basilica di San Marco, *48–49*
Basilica di San Nicola, *420*
Basilica di San Prospero, *187*
Basilica di Santa Chiara, *292*
Basilica di Santa Croce, *425–426*
Basilica di Santa Margherita, *170*
Basilica di Santa Maria degli Angeli, *292*
Basilica di Santa Maria Maggiore, *410*
Basilica di Sant'Apollinare in Classe, *199*
Basilica di Sant'Apollinare Nuovo, *200*
Basilica di Sant'Ubaldo, *288*
Basilica di San Vitale, *200*
Basilica of Hera, *402*
Basilica Paleocristiana, *81*
Basilica Palladiana, *67*
Basilica Patriarcale, *91*
Basilica San Marco, *331*
Basilica San Paolo Fuori le Mura, *343–344*
Basilica San Petronio, *181–182*
Basilica Santa Maria dei Servi, *182*
Basilica Santa Maria in Aracoeli, *331*
Basilica Santuario della Madonna di San Luca, *182*

INDEX

Basilicata, *427–433*
Bassano del Grappa, *72–74*
Baths of Caracalla, *328*
Battistero degli Ariani, *200*
Battistero Neoniao, *200*
Bay of Naples, *385–396*
Beaches
Basilicata, *431*
Bay of Naples, *392, 393, 394, 395*
Calabria, *438*
Elba, *275*
Lakes region, *130, 133*
Puglia, *410, 412, 414, 415*
Ravenna area, *201–202*
Rimini, *208*
Riviera di Levante, *169, 170, 174*
Riviera di Ponente, *162, 166, 167*
Sardinia, *503, 507, 510, 511, 513*
Sicily, *463, 468, 473, 474*
Termoli, *370*
Bedding, *14*
Bellagio, *130–131*
Bellini, Vincenzo, *454*
Benedict, St., *355*
Bergamo, *115–117*
Biblioteca Ariostea, *196*
Biblioteca Estense, *186–187*
Biblioteca Laurenziana, *232*
Biblioteca Nazionale, *383*
Bicycling, *24*
Elba, *274, 275*
Emilia-Romagna, *188*
Lakes region, *126, 130, 132*
Piemonte, *148*
Puglia, *414, 416*
Riviera di Ponente, *165*
Rome, *311*
Sardinia, *508*
shipping a bike, *22*
Sicily, *474*
Trentino-Alto Adige, *80, 83*
Valle d'Aosta, *152, 153*
Biennale di Venezia, *56*
Birra & Dintorni Festival, *144*
Boboli Gardens, *236*
Boccaccio, *382*
Bologna, *177–184*
Bolzano, *84–86*
Bordighera, *167–168*
Botanical Garden of the University of Torino, *143*
Brescia, *117–119*
Bressanone, *86–87*

Brindisi, *423–424*
Brisighella, *202–203*
Brixen, *86–87*
Bucket shops, *5, 20–21*
Bungee jumping, *152*
Burano, *59*
Business hours, *25*
Bus travel, *23*

C

Ca' d'Oro, *51–52*
Caffe Pedrocchi, *63*
Cagliari, *6, 494–497*
Calabria, *433–441*
Cala delle Arene, *415*
Cala Gonone, *513*
Ca' Marcello, *65*
Camera di San Paolo, *190*
Cameras and film, *14–15*
Camigliatello, *436–437*
Camogli, *169–170*
Campania, *29, 31, 37*
Campanile di San Marco, *50*
Campgrounds, *26*
Campobasso, *369–370*
Camposanto, *251–252*
Campo dei Fiori, *335–336*
Cannobio, *133*
Canova, Antonio, *75*
Capella Colleoni, *116–117*
Capella degli Scrovegni, *64*
Capella di San Giovanni, *86*
Capitoline Hill, *95*
Capitolino, *118*
Capitolo dei Dominicani, *76*
Capo d'Orlando, *485–486*
Cappella Brancacci, *236–237*
Cappella degli Innocenti, *76*
Cappella Palatina, *481*
Cappella Sansevero, *381*
Cappelle Medicee, *232*
Caprera, *509–510*
Capri, *390–393*
Cappuccini Monastery, *452*
Ca'Rezzonico, *53*
Carnivale, *56, 347*
Car travel, *24*
Casa Buonarroti, *235*
Casa Cavassa, *145*
Casa di Giulietta, *71*
Casa di Mantegna, *121*
Casa di Tigellio, *497*
Casale, *456*
Casa Nataledi Gaetano Donizetti, *117*

Casa Romei, *196*
Casa Vasari, *266*
Casella, *162*
Caserta, *384*
Cash machines, *12, 14*
Casinos, *166*
Castel Baradello, *129*
Castelbuono, *485*
Castel dell'Ovo, *382–383*
Castellana, *421*
Castello Aragonese, *393*
Castello Cappuccini, *172*
Castello Cornaro, *74*
Castello di Arechi, *400*
Castello de Buonconsiglio, *81–82*
Castello di Lombardia, *455*
Castello di Manta, *145*
Castello di San Giusto, *95*
Castello di Uzzano, *245*
Castello di Vezio, *130*
Castello Doria, *168*
Castello e Borgo Medioevale, *143*
Castello Estense, *195*
Castello Eurialo, *459, 461–462*
Castello Guglielmi, *286*
Castello Miramare, *95*
Castello Normanno-Svevo, *420*
Castello Sforzesco, *107*
Castello Visconti, *112*
Castel Nuovo, *383*
Castel San Giovanni, *164*
Castel Sant'Angelo, *340*
Castel Sant'Elmo, *383*
Castelsardo, *506*
Castel Sismondo, *206*
Castelvecchio, *71*
Castiglione del Lago, *285–286*
Castle of Fénis, *151*
Catacombe dei Cappuccini, *482*
Catacombe di San Giovanni, *462*
Catacombs, *90, 342–343, 462, 482*
Catania, *452–455*
Cathedral of St. Matthew, *400*
Cathedral of San Gennaro, *381*
Cathedral of Santa Maria Assunta, *355*
Catherine, St., *263*

Cattedrale di San Giorgio, *195*

Cattedrale di San Lorenzo, *283*

Cattedrale di San Pietro, *465*

Cattedrale di San Sabino, *420*

Cattedrale di Santa Chiara, *292*

Cattedrale di Sant'Agata, *454*

Cattedrale di Santa Maria
Alghero, *502*
Cagliari, *497*

Cattedrale di Torcello, *59*

Cattedrale San Lorenzo, *160*

Cattedrale Sant'Antonio Abate, *505*

Caverns, *297, 392, 398–399, 421, 429, 468, 474–475*

Cefalù, *484–485*

Cemeteries, *60, 74, 196, 251–252, 346, 356*

Centri Sociali, *111*

Centro di Fondazione Marino Marini, *243*

Centro per l'Arte Contemporanea Luigi Pecci, *241*

Centro Terme, *87*

Certosa, *113*

Certosa della Madonna delle Grazie church, *113*

Certosa di San Martino, *383*

Cerveteri, *356*

Cervo, *168*

Chair of Attila, *59*

Chapel of San Cataldo, *422*

Chianca Amara, *414*

Chianti, *243–245*

Chiesa Cappuccini, *172*

Chiesa degli Eremitani, *64*

Chiesa dei Domenicani, *86*

Chiesa della Madonna, *52*

Chiesa della Madonna del Rosario, *505*

Chiesa del Purgatorio, *472*

Chiesa de Sant'Agostino, *205–206*

Chiesa di San Bartolomeo, *465*

Chiesa di San Domenico, *463*

Chiesa di San Domenico Maggiore, *422*

Chiesa di San Francesco
Alghero, *502*
Sorrento, *396*

Chiesa di San Giorgio, *465*

Chiesa di San Giovanni, *145*

Chiesa di San Michele, *392*

Chiesa di San Paragorio, *166*

Chiesa di Santa Caterina, *76*

Chiesa di Sant'Antonio, *169*

Chiesa Extra-Muros di Santa Maria, *505*

Chiesa Nuova, *291*

Chiesa Parrocchiale di Gries, *86*

Chiesa San Giorgio, *65*

Chiesa San Giovanni di Sinis, *500*

Chiesa San Matteo, *161*

Chiesa Santa Maria Assunta, *170*

Chiesa Santa Maria dei Greci, *467*

Chiesa Sant'Ambrogio, *160*

Chiostro Santa Caterina, *162*

Christmas events, *348*

Churches
Abruzzi, *363*
Amalfi coast, *398, 399, 400*
Bay of Naples, *392, 393, 394, 396*
Bologna, *181, 183*
Calabria, *435, 439*
Emilia-Romagna, *186, 187, 190, 191, 192–193, 195, 196, 199, 200, 205, 207*
Florence, *225–227, 230, 231–232, 234–235, 236, 237*
Florence area, *240, 241, 242, 243*
Friuli-Venezia Guilia, *90, 91, 95*
Genova, *160, 161*
Lakes region, *127, 133*
Lombardy, *111, 112, 113, 116–117, 118, 122–123*
Marche, *300, 301, 302, 303, 304*
Matera, *430–431*
Milan, *107, 108–109*
Molise, *370*
Naples, *380–381, 382, 383*
Piemonte, *142–143, 145, 146, 147*
Puglia, *410, 412, 414, 415, 420, 422, 424, 425–426*
Riviera di Levante, *170, 172*
Riviera di Ponente, *162, 166, 168, 169*

Rome, *331, 333, 334, 336, 337, 338, 339, 340–341, 343, 344*
Rome area, *355, 358*
Sardinia, *497, 499–500, 502, 505, 506*
Sicily, *447, 450, 454, 455, 461, 463, 464, 465, 467, 468, 481, 482, 483–484*
Trentino-Alto Adige, *81, 86*
Tuscany, *248, 251, 252, 256, 257, 262–263, 264, 268, 269, 270, 271, 272*
Umbria, *283, 284, 285, 286, 287, 288, 291–293, 294, 295, 297*
Valle d'Aosta, *150*
the Veneto, *63, 64, 65, 67, 71, 72, 75*
Venice, *48–49, 52, 53, 54, 55, 59, 60*

Church of St. Irene, *426*

Church of St. John, *168*

Church of Santa Maria, *91*

Cimitero Ebraico, *60*

Cinque Terre, *172–174*

Ciotto del Pesce, *348*

Circus Maximus, *328*

Cirella, *438*

Cividale del Friuli, *90–91*

Civitavecchia, *358*

Civitella Alfedena, *366*

Clare, St., *292*

Clavesena Castle, *168*

Cloistro del Paradiso, *398*

Clothing, *14*

Coffee, *29*

Cogne, *151*

Colleges and universities, *64, 112–113, 143, 160, 182*

Collezione Peggy Guggenheim, *50–51*

Colosseum, *328*

Column of Marcus Aurelius, *337*

Column of Trajan, *329*

Como, *129–130*

Contraceptives, *17*

Convents, lodging in, *27*

Convicinio di Sant'Antonio, *430*

Corona del Ferro, *111*

Correggio, *190, 191*

Corso dei Ceri, *288*

Cortona, *267–269*

Cosenza, *434–435*

Costs, *5–6*
Council of Trent, *79*
Council Travel offices, *3*
Courier flights, *21–22*
Courmayer, *153*
Credit cards, *12, 14*
Cremona, *113–115*
Crypto di Sant'Anastasio, *146*
Cumae, *385–386*
Curia, *329*
Customs, *15–16*

D
Dante, *200–201*
David (Donatello), *230*
David (Michelangelo), *233*
Degioz, *152*
Deledda, Grazia, *512*
Disabilities, hints for
   travelers with, *18–19*
Dolceacqua, *168*
Dolomites, *28*
Domine Quo Vadis church,
   343
Donatello, *226, 230*
Donizetti, Gaetano, *117*
Dorgali, *513*
Douja d'Or festival, *146*
Drugs
   illicit, *15*
   prescription, *17*
Ducal Palace, *301*
Duino, *96*
Duomo
   Florence, *225–227*
   Milan, *107*
   Naples, *381*
   Palermo, *482*
   Parma, *191*
   Perugia, *283*
   Siena, *262–263*
   Verona, *71*
Duomo Collegiata, *256*
Duomo di San Giorgio, *464*
Duomo di San Giovanni,
   142–143
Duomo of San Geminiano,
   186
Duties, *15–16*

E
Easter events, *348*
Egadi Islands, *474–476*
Elba, *273–274*
Eleanora d'Arborea, *498*
Embassies and consulates
   Florence, *213*

Milan, *100*
Naples, *373*
Rome, *306*
Venice, *35*
Emergencies, *16–17*
Bari, *417*
financial, *12*
Milan, *102*
Naples, *373*
Rome, *307*
Emilia-Romagna, *175–208*
Enna, *455–456*
Eremo delle Carceri, *293*
Erice, *473*
Estate Fiesolana, *240*
Estate Romana, *348*
Etruscan burial mounds, *356*
Excavations crypt, *91*
Exchanging money, *11*

F
Farrada de li Candeleri, *505*
Favignana, *474*
Feast of Maria Santissima di
   Porto Salvo, *486*
Feast of San Giovanni, *143*
Feast of the Thrush, *272*
Ferrara, *193–197*
Ferrari factory, *187*
Ferry service, *24*
Festa della Concezione
   Immacolata, *348*
Festa della Madonna della
   Bruna, *431*
Festa della Madonna della
   Neve, *348*
Festa dell'Unità, *57*
Festa del Redentore, *56*
Festa de l'Unità, *244*
Festa di Noantri, *338–339*
Festa di San Giovanni, *237,
   347–348*
Festa di San Guiseppe, *347*
Festa di San Pietro, *348*
Festino di Santa Rosalia, *483*
Festival dei Due Mondi,
   294–295
Festival of Village Feasts,
   146
Festivals, *6–7*
Abruzzi, *367*
Camogli, *169*
Emilia-Romagna, *193, 201,
   203*
Florence, *237–238*
Florence area, *240, 243,
   244*

Genova, *161*
Matera, *431*
Milan, *110*
Naples, *381*
Piemonte, *143–144, 146*
Riviera di Levante, *169*
Rome, *347–348*
Sardinia, *500, 506*
Sicily, *474, 483, 486*
Tuscany, *248, 262, 263,
   266, 271, 272*
Umbria, *284, 288,
   294–295*
Valle d'Aosta, *150*
Venice, *56–57*
Fiesole, *239–240*
Filicudi, *490*
Film, *56, 57, 111, 239,
   351*
Finale Ligure, *162,
   164–165*
First-aid kits, *16*
Fishing, *152*
Florence, *6, 213*
   campgrounds, *221*
   consulates, *213*
   excursions, *239–245*
   gelaterias, *224*
   hostels, *220–221*
   hotels, *217–220*
   nightlife, *238–239*
   Oltrarno area, *235–237*
   Piazza del Duomo, *225–227*
   Piazza della Signoria,
      227–228
   Piazza San Lorenzo,
      231–233
   Piazza San Marco, *233–234*
   Piazza Santa Croce,
      234–235
   Piazza Santa Maria Novella,
      230–231
   Piazza Santissima
      Annunziata, *233–234*
   restaurants, *221–225*
   shopping, *232*
   sightseeing, *225–237*
   transportation, *216–217*
Foggia, *408–409*
Fontana dell'Elefante, *454*
Fontana delle 99 Cannelle,
   363
Fontana delle Tartarughe,
   337
Fontana del Nettuno, *182*
Fontana Maggiore, *283*
Fonte Cereto, *363*

Fonte Gala, *261*
Food, *27–29*
Foresta Umbra, *410*
Forio, *393*
Forte Belvedere, *237*
Fortezza Albernoz
Orvieto, *297*
Urbino, *300*
Fortezza Nuova, *252*
Fortuny, Mariano, *54*
Forum Boarium, *328*
Forum of Augustus, *329*
Forum of Caesar, *328*
Forum of Trajan, *329*
Fountain of Diana, *384*
Fountain of the Naiads, *332*
Fountains
Bologna, *182*
Caserta, *384*
L'Aquila, *363*
Rome, *332, 334, 337*
Sicily, *450, 454*
Siena, *261*
Southern Italy, *433*
Tivoli, *354*
Umbria, *283*
Francis of Assisi, St., *288, 291–293, 356*
Frascati, *352–353*
Friuli-Venezia Giulia, *89–96*

G
Galla Placidia, *200, 202*
Galleria Borghese, *334–335*
Galleria Civica d'Arte Moderna, *143*
Galleria dell'Accademia, *233*
Galleria Doria, *336*
Galleria Ferrari, *187*
Galleria Nazionale
Parma, *191*
Rome, *332*
Urbino, *299–300*
Galleria Nazionale d'Art Moderna, *335*
Galleria Nazionale dell'Umbria, *283*
Galleria Nazionale di Palazzo Spinola, *160*
Galleria Nazionale di Sicilia, *480–481*
Galleria Ricci Oddi, *193*
Galleria Sabaudia, *143*
Galleria Spada, *345*
Galleria Vittorio Emanuele, *107–108*
Gallerie dell'Accademia, *50*

Gardens
Capri, *391*
Caserta, *384*
Florence, *236*
Lakes region, *125, 129, 130, 132*
Pisa, *251*
Riviera di Ponente, *168*
Rome, *339, 346–347*
Sicily, *450*
Siena, *261*
Torino, *143*
Gardone, *125*
Gargano, *410–415*
Garibaldi, Giuseppe, *443, 510*
Gay and lesbian travelers, resources for, *17–18*
Genova, *6, 155*
Gesù Nuovo church, *382*
Ghetto Ebreo, *52*
Giardini Arcella, *64*
Giardini-Naxos, *451–452*
Giardino di Agosto, *391*
Gipsoteca Canova, *75*
Giudecca, *53–54*
Gole dell'Alcantara, *451*
Government tourist offices, *1*
Grado, *91*
Gran Sasso, *363–364*
Grattachecca, *324*
Grazie, *123*
Greek artifacts, *381–382, 385–386, 402, 432, 441, 449, 451, 461–462, 467, 470, 473*
Greve, *243*
Grotta Azzurra, *392*
Grotta del Buontalenti, *236*
Grotta del Genovese, *474–475*
Grotta della Smeralda, *398–399*
Grotta del Santuario della Madonna, *437*
Grotto Bue Marino, *513*
Grotto di Ispingoli, *513*
Gubbio, *286–288*
Guglia dell'Immacolata, *382*

H
Hanbury of Mortola Botanical Gardens, *168*
Herculaneum, *386–387*
Hiking
Abruzzi, *364, 366*
Bay of Naples, *392, 393*

Calabria, *436*
Elba, *274, 276*
Emilia-Romagna, *188*
Lakes region, *126, 132*
Marche, *304*
Riviera di Levante, *170, 172, 174*
Riviera di Ponente, *165*
Sicily, *487–488*
Trentino-Alto Adige, *79, 82, 83, 86, 87, 88–89*
Valle d'Aosta, *152–153*
History, *30*
Hitchhiking, *24*
Holidays, *6*
Holy Week, *347*
Horseback riding, *152*
Hostels, *4–5, 26.* See also specific regions
Host families, *27*
Hotels, *26.* See also specific regions
House of the Vestals, *330*
Hruska Botanical Gardens, *125*

I
I Frari church, *53*
Il Carso, *96*
Il Gesù church, *336*
Il Gotico, *192*
Il Vittoriale, *125*
Imperial Fora, *328–329*
Insurance, *16–17*
Ionian Coast, *447–462*
Ipogeo Celtico, *90*
Ischia, *393*
Iseo, *126*
Isernia, *368–369*
Isola Bella, *132*
Isola di Dino, *437*
Isola Madre, *132*
Isola Maggiore, *286*
Isola San Giulio, *133*
Isola Superiore, *132*
Isola Tibernia, *339*
Isole Borromee, *132*

J
Jewish Cemetery, *60, 196*
Jewish Ghetto, *52*
Jewish Museum, *235*
Joyce, James, *92*

K
Keats Museum, *334*
Knights of Malta, *346*

L

La Donna nel Tempo, *87*
Lago d'Averno, *386*
Lago di Como, *129–131*
Lago di Garda, *124–126*
Lago di Orta, *133*
Lago di Scanno, *365*
Lago d'Iseo, *126–128*
Lago Maggiore, *131–133*
Lakes region, *97–100, 123–133*
Lake Trasimeno, *285–286*
La Maddalena, *509–510*
La Martorana chapel, *481*
Language, *26*
La Penisola di Sinis, *500*
L'Aquila, *361, 363*
Largo di Torre Argentina, *336*
La Sartiglia, *500*
La Scala, *108*
Last Supper (Leonardo), *108*
Laundry, *14*
Lazio, *29, 31, 352–360*
Leaning Tower (Pisa), *251*
Lecce, *424–426*
Leni, *489*
Leonardo da Vinci, *108, 109*
Levanzo, *474–475*
Libraries, *186, 196, 232, 263, 383*
the Lido, *60*
Lido Adriano, *201–202*
Lido di Jesolo, *60*
Lido Silvano, *421*
Lingua, *489*
Lipari, *488–489*
Litorale di Cavallino, *60*
Livorno, *252–253*
Locri, *441*
Loggia del Capitaniato, *67*
Lombardy, *28, 97–100, 111–123*
Loreto, *303*
Lorica, *436*
Lucca, *245–248*
Lucera, *409–410*
Luggage, *22*

M

Madonna delle Grazie church, *123*
Madonna di Campiglio, *83*
Mafia, *443, 446*
Mail service, *25*
Malfa, *489*
Manfredonia, *410–411*
Mantova, *119–123*

Maratea, *432–433*
Marche, *29, 277, 298–304*
Marciana Marina, *276*
Marettimo, *475*
Marina di Campo, *275–276*
Marina di Ravenna, *201–202*
Marinella, *470*
Marini, Marino, *243*
Marsala, *468–470*
Matera, *429–431*
Mattinata, *412*
Medical assistance. *See* Emergencies
Merano, *87–88*
Messina, *447–449*
Metaponto, *431–432*
Michelangelo, *227, 232, 233, 235, 341, 342, 344*
Milan, *97, 100–102*
cafés, *106*
consulates, *100*
emergencies, *102*
hostels, *105*
hotels, *104–105*
nightlife, *110*
restaurants, *105–106*
shopping, *109*
sightseeing, *106–109*
transportation, *102–104*
weather, *6*
Milazzo, *486–487*
Minori, *399–400*
Modena, *185–187*
Modena, Tomaso da, *76*
Modica, *465*
Mole Antonelliana, *143*
Molise, *361, 368–370*
Molveno, *82–83*
Monasteries
Brescia, *118*
Certosa, *113*
Emilia-Romagna, *190*
Florence, *234*
lodging in, *27*
Matera, *430*
Piemonte, *144–145, 147*
Puglia, *415*
Sicily, *452*
Subiaco, *355*
Tuscany, *264*
Umbria, *293*
Money, *11–12, 14*
Monreale, *483–484*
Monsèlice, *65*
Montagnana, *65–66*
Montalcino, *272–273*

Mont Blanc, *153*
Monte Bondone, *82*
Monte Paganella, *83*
Monte Pellegrino, *483*
Montepulciano, *269–271*
Monte Rufeno Wildlife Reserve, *359–360*
Monte San Calogero, *468*
Monte Sant'Angelo, *411–412*
Monte Siepi church, *264*
Monte Terminillo, *355–356*
Montisola, *126–127*
Monza, *111*
Mopeds, *24*
Moses (Michelangelo), *344*
Mountain huts, *27*
Mt. Epomeo, *393*
Mt. Etna, *457–458*
Mt. Solaro, *392*
Mt. Vesuvius, *387*
Murano, *59*
Museo Archeologico
Arezzo, *266*
Elba, *274–275*
Fiesole, *240*
Florence, *233*
Friuli-Venezia-Giulia, *90, 91*
Giardini-Naxos, *451*
Siracusa, *462*
Spoleto, *294*
Verona, *71*
Museo Archeologico Baglio Auselmi, *469–470*
Museo Archeologico Etnografico G.A. Sanna, *505*
Museo Archeologico Nazionale
Cagliari, *497*
Ferrara, *196*
Marche, *303*
Naples, *381–382*
Perugia, *284*
Taranto, *423*
Museo Archeologico Regionale, *482*
Museo Arcivescoville, *200*
Museo Bandini, *240*
Museo Barraco, *345*
Museo Belliniano, *454*
Museo Capitolino, *331*
Museo Civico
Amalfi, *398*
Bassano, *74*
Cremona, *114*
Gubbio, *287*

Messina, *447*
Pesaro, *301*
Prato, *242*
San Gimignano, *255*
Sansepolcro, *266–267*
Siena, *262*
Sulmona, *364*
Treviso, *76*
Udine, *90*
Vicenza, *67*
Museo Civico Archeologico
Bologna, *182*
Milan, *109*
Museo Civico Correr, *49*
Museo Civico d'Arte
Contemporanea, *109*
Museo Civico d'Arte
Moderna, *197*
Museo Civico di Storia ed
Arte, *95*
Museo Civico G. Fiorelli, *410*
Museo Civico Medioevale,
182
Museo Claudio Faina, *297*
Museo Comunale Cordici,
473
Museo Correale di Terranova,
396
Museo Cristiano, *90*
Museo Dantesco, *201*
Museo d'Arte, *107*
Museo d'Arte Moderna, *90*
Museo degli Arazzi
Fiamminghi, *469*
Museo del Arte Medievale e
Moderna, *64*
Museo del Duomo, *107*
Museo della Carta, *398*
Museo dell'Accademia
Etrusca, *268*
Museo della Città, *206*
Museo della Civilazione
Romana, *345*
Museo della Civiltà
Contadina, *114*
Museo dell'Automobile, *143*
Museo della Valle dei
Nuraghi, *506*
Museo della Vita delle
Tradizioni Sardi, *512*
Museo delle Cere, *346*
Museo delle Sinopie, *252*
Museo dell'Estuario, *60*
Museo dell'Intreccio, *506*
Museo dell'Opera del Duomo
Florence, *227*
Pisa, *252*

Prato, *242*
Siena, *263*
Museo del Risorgimento
Rome, *332*
Trento, *82*
Museo di Criminologica
Medievale, *256*
Museo Didactico, *354*
Museo Dinz Rialto, *206*
Museo Diocesano, *268*
Museo Diocesano d'Arte
Sacra, *439*
Museo di Pittura Murale, *242*
Museo di San Marco, *233*
Museo di Sant'Agostino, *160*
Museo di Santa Maria della
Monache, *368–369*
Museo di Storia della
Scienza, *230*
Museo di Strumenti
Musicali, *345*
Museo di Villa Giulia, *335*
Museo Documentario della
Metafisia, *197*
Museo Donizettiano, *117*
Museo Ebraico, *338*
Museo e Gallerie
Capodimonte, *383*
Museo Egizio, *143*
Museo Eoliano, *488*
Museo Etrusco Guarnacci,
257
Museo Giovanni Boldini, *197*
Museo Internazionale delle
Marionette, *481*
Museo Marino Marini, *231*
Museo Nazionale
Cerveteri, *356*
Civitavecchia, *358*
Lucca, *248*
Museo Nazionale
Archeologico, *467*
Museo Nazionale d'Abruzzi,
363
Museo Nazionale della
Magna Grecia, *441*
Museo Nazionale della
Scienza e Technica, *109*
Museo Nazionale di
Manfredonia, *410*
Museo Nazionale di Palazzo
Bellomo, *461*
Museo Nazionale Pepoli,
472
Museo Nazionale Ridola, *431*
Museo Nazionale Romano,
333

Museo Paleocristiano, *91*
Museo Poldi Pezzoli, *109*
Museo Provinciale
Lecce, *426*
Salerno, *400*
Museo Revoltella, *95*
Museo San Marco, *233*
Museo Storico Navale, *55*
Museo Stradivariano, *115*
Museo Tancreai, *412*
Museo Teatrale, *108*
Museo Vetrario Antica, *59*
Museum of Arms, *118*
Museum of Country Life, *202*
Museum of Ostia, *357*
Museum of Religious and
Etruscan Art, *256*
Museum of Time, *202*
Museums. *See also* Art
galleries and museums
Abruzzi, *363, 364*
Amalfi coast, *398, 400, 402*
Basilicata, *431, 432*
Bologna, *182*
Calabria, *439, 441*
Emilia-Romagna, *186–187,*
196, 200, 201, 202, 206
Florence, *227, 228–230,*
231, 233, 235
Florence area, *240, 242*
Friuli-Venezia Guilia, *90, 91,*
95
Genova, *160*
Isernia, *368–369*
Lombardy, *112, 114, 115,*
116, 117, 118
Marche, *299–300, 301,*
303, 304
Milan, *107, 108, 109*
Naples, *381–382, 383*
Palermo, *480, 481, 482*
Piemonte, *143, 146,*
147–148
Puglia, *410, 412, 420, 423,*
424, 426
Riviera di Ponente, *162*
Rome, *331, 332, 333, 334,*
335, 336, 338, 339,
341–342, 345–346
Rome area, *354, 356, 357,*
358
Sardinia, *497, 500, 505,*
506, 512
Sicily, *447, 454, 461, 462,*
467, 469, 472, 473, 488
Sorrento, *396*
Trentino-Alto Adige, *82, 87*

Tuscany, *248, 255, 256, 257, 262, 263, 266, 268, 271*
Umbria, *283, 287, 291, 294*
the Veneto, *64, 67, 72, 74, 75, 76*
Venice, *49, 50–51, 52, 53, 55, 59–60*

N
Naples, *6, 371, 373*
consulates, *373*
emergencies, *373*
excursions, *384*
hostels, *378*
hotels, *375, 378*
nightlife, *383–384*
restaurants, *379–380*
sightseeing, *380–383*
transportation, *373–375*
Napoléon, *273, 275*
Naquane National Park, *127*
National Archaeological Museum, *402*
National Art Gallery, *497*
National Gallery of Ancient Art, *339*
National Museum of Pasta Foods, *346*
Naviglio Festival, *110*
Neptune's Grotto, *503*
Nervi, *162*
New Year's Eve, *348*
Nicholas, St., *420*
Noli, *166*
Nora, *497*
Noto, *463–464*
Nuoro, *511–512*
Nuraghi Palmavera, *503*
Nuraghi Santa Antine, *506–507*

O
Ognissanti church, *231*
Olbia, *511*
Oldofredi Castle, *127*
Oliena, *513–514*
Omegna, *133*
Opera, *72, 108, 351, 383, 483*
Opicina, *96*
Oratorio di San Bernardino, *284*
Oratorio di San Giovanni, *300*
Oratorio di San Giuseppe, *300*

Orgòsola, *514*
Oristano, *498–500*
Ornithological Museum, *256*
Orsanmichele church, *230*
Orta, *133*
Orta Botanical, *339*
Ortles Mountains, *80*
Orto Lapidario, *95*
Ortygia Island, *461*
Orvieto, *295–296*
Ostia Antica, *356–357*
Ostuni, *424*
Otranto, *426–427*

P
Padova, *60, 62–65*
Paestum, *401–402*
Palaces and castles
Abruzzi, *363*
Amalfi coast, *399, 400, 402*
Bay of Naples, *391, 393, 394*
Bologna, *182*
Bressanone, *86–87*
Calabria, *435*
Caserta, *384*
Chianti, *245*
Emilia-Romagna, *187, 191, 193, 195, 196, 197, 206*
Florence, *229–230, 231, 232–233, 236*
Friuli-Venezia-Giulia, *90, 95*
Genova, *159, 160*
Gubbio, *287*
Lakes region, *124, 127, 129, 130, 132*
Lake Trasimeno, *285, 286*
Lombardy, *112, 115, 117, 118, 121–122*
Marche, *299, 301, 304*
Milan, *107*
Molise, *370*
Naples, *382–383*
Palermo, *481*
Piemonte, *143, 145*
Puglia, *410, 414, 420, 422, 426*
Rapallo, *172*
Riviera di Ponente, *164, 168*
Rome, *331, 340, 346*
Sicily, *455, 461, 481, 488*
Todi, *295*
Trentino-Alto Adige, *81–82*
Trieste, *92–96*
Tuscany, *252, 257, 262, 271, 272*

Valle d'Aosta, *151*
the Veneto, *64, 65, 67, 71, 74*
Venice, *49, 54*
Pala d'Oro, *49*
Palatine Hill, *329*
Palau, *509*
Palazzina di Caccia di Stupinigi, *143*
Palazzina di Marfisa d'Este, *196*
Palazzo Arcivescovile, *90*
Palazzo Beneventano del Bosco, *461*
Palazzo Bianco, *160–161*
Palazzo Bò, *64*
Palazzo Chiaramonte, *481*
Palazzo Colonna, *346*
Palazzo d'Arco, *121*
Palazzo dei Cavalieri, *252*
Palazzo dei Conservatori, *331*
Palazzo dei Consoli, *287*
Palazzo dei Diamanti, *197*
Palazzo dei Musei, *186–187*
Palazzo dei Normanni, *481*
Palazzo dei Priori
Perugia, *283–284*
Todi, *295*
Volterra, *257*
Palazzo del Capitani del Popolo, *304*
Palazzo del Capitano del Popolo, *187*
Palazzo del Comune, *115*
Palazzo del Governo, *426*
Palazzo dell'Accademia delle Scienze, *143*
Palazzo della Pilotta, *191*
Palazzo della Ragione, *64*
Palazzo dell'Archiginnasio, *182*
Palazzo dell'Arcivescovado, *435*
Palazzo de'Nobili-Tarugi, *271*
Palazzo di Ludovico il Moro, *196*
Palazzo Ducale
Genova, *160*
Gubbio, *287*
Mantova, *121–122*
Urbino, *299–300*
Venice, *49*
Palazzo Farnese, *193*
Palazzo Fortuny, *54*

Palazzo Gherardesca, *252*
Palazzo Ghisilardi-Fava, *182*
Palazzo Grassi, *54*
Palazzo Massari, *197*
Palazzo Medici-Riccardi,
  232–233
Palazzo Muratori-Cravetta,
  145
Palazzo Neri-Orselli, *271*
Palazzo Paradiso, *196*
Palazzo Piccolomini, *272*
Palazzo Podestà, *159–160*
Palazzo Pubblico, *262*
Palazzo Reale
Caserta, *384*
Genova, *160*
Naples, *383*
Palazzo Rosso, *160*
Palazzo Rucellai, *231*
Palazzo Schifanoia, *196*
Palazzo Spinola, *160*
Palazzo Strozzi, *231*
Palazzo Taffini, *145*
Palazzo Te, *122*
Palazzo Vecchio, *229–230*
Palazzo Venezia, *331–332*
Palazzo Vescovile, *86–87*
Palermo, *475–483*
Palio della Balestra, *288*
Palio horse race, *262*
Palladio, Andrea, *67*
Panarea, *489*
Pantheon, *336*
Parco Archeologico
Cumae, *386*
Siracusa, *462*
Volterra, *257*
Parco dei Mostri, *359*
Parco della Resistanza, *300*
Parco del Valentino, *143*
Parco Ducale, *191*
Parco Naturale Paneveggio,
  83
Parco Nazionale d'Abruzzi,
  365–366
Parco Nazionale del Gran
  Paradiso, *150–151*
Parco Nazionale dello
  Stelvio, *88*
Parco Nazionale di Tessa,
  88–89
Parco Savello, *347*
Parma, *188–191*
Parrocchiale della Beata
  Vergine Immacolata, *497*
Passegio del Prato, *266*
Passignano, *285*

Passports, *7–8*
Paterno, *457*
Pavia, *111–113*
Peccorino, *490*
Pella, *133*
Pergusa, *456*
Perugia, *280–284*
Pesaro, *300–301*
Pescara, *367*
Pescasseroli, *366*
Peschici, *414–415*
Peter, St., *338*
Petrarch, *65*
Piacenza, *192–193*
Piazza Armerina, *456*
Piccolomini Library, *263*
Piemonte, *31, 135–148*
Pienza, *271–272*
Piero della Francesca,
  266–267
Pietà (Michelangelo), *227,
  341*
Pinocateca
Assissi, *291*
Spoleto, *294*
Pinacoteca Civica
Ascoli Piceno, *304*
Asti, *146*
Brescia, *118*
Pinacoteca Comunale
Gubbio, *287*
Volterra, *257*
Pinocateca Communale
  Francesco Podesti, *303*
Pinacoteca di Brera, *108*
Pinacoteca l'Antiguarium
  Arborense, *500*
Pinacoteca Nazionale
Bologna, *182–183*
Ferrara, *197*
Siena, *263*
Pinacoteca Provinciale, *420*
Pineto, *367–368*
Piramidi d'Erosione, *128*
Pirandello, Luigi, *468*
Pisa, *6, 248–252*
Pistoia, *242–243*
Pitti Palace, *236*
Pizzo, *438*
Plane travel, *20–22, 23*
Poggio, *276*
Pompeii, *387–390*
Pont, *152*
Ponte Coperto, *113*
Ponte degli Alpini, *73*
Ponte di Rialto, *51*
Ponte di Tiberio, *206–207*

Ponte Vecchio
Dolceacqua, *168*
Florence, *235*
Pope, audience with, *342*
Porta all'Arco, *258*
Porta Pretoria, *150*
Portoferraio, *274–275*
Portofino, *171–172*
Positano, *399*
Possagno, *75*
Pozzo di San Patrizio, *297*
Pozzuoli, *385*
Praia a Mare, *437–439*
Prato, *240–242*
Procida, *393–394*
Puccini, Giacomo, *248*
Puglia, *31, 405–427*
Punta Marina, *201–202*
Purgatorio church, *431*

R
Ragusa, *464*
Randazzo, *457*
Rapallo, *172*
Raphael Rooms, *341*
Raphael's House, *300*
Ravello, *399*
Ravenna, *197–201*
Regatta Storica, *56–57*
Reggio di Calabria, *439–441*
Reggio Emilia, *187–188*
Ride sharing, *24*
Rieti, *355–356*
Rifugi, *27*
Rilke, Rainer Maria, *92, 96*
Rimini, *203–208*
Rinella, *489*
Risiera di San Sabba, *95*
Riva del Garda, *125–126*
Riviera di Levante, *169–174*
Riviera di Ponente, *162–169*
Roman artifacts
Amalfi coast, *400, 402*
Aosta, *150*
Bay of Naples, *386–391*
Campobasso, *369*
Fiesole, *240*
Friuli-Venezia Giulia, *91, 95*
Lakes region, *124*
Lombardy, *118*
Naples, *381–382*
Puglia, *410, 424, 425*
Rimini, *205, 206–207*
Riviera di Ponente, *168*
Rome, *325, 328–330, 333,
  336, 345*
Rome area, *354, 356–357*

Sardinia, *497, 500*
Sicily, *450, 454, 456, 462, 467*
Tuscany, *258, 266*
Umbria, *291, 294*
Verona, *71, 72*
Roman Forum, *329–330*
Rome, *6, 305–308*
ancient Rome, *325, 328–330*
cafés, *323–324*
Campidoglio, *330–331*
Centro Storico, *335–337*
embassies, *306*
emergencies, *307*
excursions, *352–360*
festivals, *347–348*
gelaterias, *324*
hostels, *318*
hotels, *311–317*
Janiculum Hill, *338*
Jewish Ghetto, *337–338*
nightlife, *349–352*
Piazza Barberini, *332–333*
Piazza della Repubblica, *332–333*
Piazza del Popolo, *333–334*
Piazza di Spagna, *334*
Piazza Venezia, *331–332*
restaurants, *319–323*
shopping, *348–349*
sightseeing, *324–347*
transportation, *308–311*
Trastevere, *338–339*
Villa Borghese, *334–335*
weather, *6*
Room rentals, *27*
Rossano, *439*
Rossini, Gioacchino, *301*
Royal Gardens, *384*
Russian Orthodox Church, *166*

S
Sabbioneta, *123*
Sacra di San Michele, *144–145*
Sacro Monte basilica, *147*
Sacro Monte church, *133*
Saepinum, *369*
Safe sex, *17*
Sagra del Pesce festival, *169*
Sagrestia Nuova, *232*
St. Peter's Basilica, *340–341*
Salerno, *400–401*
Salina, *489*
Salute, *57*

Saluzzo, *145*
San Benedetto monastery, *355*
San Biagio church, *271*
San Carlo alle Quattro Fontane church, *333*
San Clemente church, *344*
San Cristoforo alla Certosa church, *196*
Sanctuary and House of St. Catherine, *263*
Sanctuary of Montallegro, *172*
Sanctuary of San Michele, *412*
San Damiano convent, *292*
San Domenico church
Ancona, *303*
Arezzo, *266*
Bologna, *183*
Fiesole, *240*
Perugia, *284*
San Domenico Maggiore church, *380*
San Domino, *415*
San Donato church, *160*
San Eustorgio church, *108–109*
San Francesco church
Enna, *455*
Fiesole, *240*
Gubbio, *287–288*
Piacenza, *192–193*
San Francesco d'Assisi church, *435*
San Frediano church, *248*
San Galgano, *264*
San Gennaro festival, *381*
San Giacomo Maggiore church, *183*
San Gimignano, *254–256*
San Giorgio Maggiore church, *54*
San Giovanni al Sepocoro church, *424*
San Giovanni degli Eremiti church, *482*
San Giovanni di Sinis, *500*
San Giovanni e Paolo church, *55*
San Giovanni Evangelista church, *190*
San Giovanni Fuorcivitas church, *243*
San Giovanni in Fiore, *436*
San Giovanni in Laterano church, *344*

San Lorenzo church, *231–232*
San Lorenzo Maggiore church, *380–381*
San Luisi dei Francesi, *337*
San Marco church, *439*
San Marino, *206*
San Martino church, *248*
San Martino di Castrozza, *83*
San Michele, *60*
San Michele Arcangelo church, *286*
San Michele church, *112*
San Michele in Foro church, *248*
San Michele in Isola church, *60*
San Michele in Ventimiglia church, *168*
San Miniato al Monte church, *237*
San Niccolò church, *268–269*
San Nicola, *415*
San Pietro, *489*
San Pietro Caveoso church, *430–431*
San Pietro church, *284*
San Pietro in Ceil d'Oro church, *112*
San Pietro in Montorio church, *338*
San Pietro in Vincoli church, *344*
San Ponziano church, *294*
San Remo, *166–167*
San Romulus church, *240*
San Salvatore church, *294*
San Secondo church, *146*
Sansepolcro, *266–267*
San Stefano church, *241*
Santa Cecilia in Trastavere church, *339*
Santa Chiara church, *382*
Santa Cristina, *500–501*
Santa Croce church, *234–235*
Santa Croce in Gerusalemme church, *344*
Santa di Collemaggio church, *363*
Sant'Agnese in Agone, *336*
Sant'Agostino church
Bergamo, *116*
Brescia, *118*
Montepulciano, *271*
Pesaro, *301*

Santa Margherita church, 269

Santa Margherita Ligure, 170–171

Santa Maria a Mare church, 415

Santa Maria degli Angeli church, 333

Santa Maria dei Miracoli church
Rome, 333
Venice, 52

Santa Maria del Carmine church, 112

Santa Maria della Concezione church, 333

Santa Maria della Consolazione church, 295–296

Santa Maria della Piazza church, 302–303

Santa Maria della Pieve church, 266

Santa Maria della Salute church, 54

Santa Maria della Spina, 251

Santa Maria della Steccata church, 191

Santa Maria delle Carceri church, 242

Santa Maria delle Grazie church, 108

Santa Maria delle Grazie al Calcinaio, 268

Santa Maria del Mercato church, 127

Santa Maria del Popolo church, 334

Santa Maria di Campagna church, 193

Santa Maria di Castello church, 161

Santa Maria di Montesanto church, 333

Santa Maria di Loreto, 393

Santa Maria d'Iris church, 430–431

Santa Maria in Trastevere church, 339

Santa Maria Maddalena church, 285

Santa Maria Maggiore church
Bergamo, 116
Rome, 344–345

Santa Maria Navarrese, 512–513

Santa Maria Novella church, 230–231

Santa Maria Sopra Minerva church, 337

Santa Marina, 489

Sant'Ambrogio church, 108

Sant'Anastasia church, 71

Sant'Andrea church
Mantova, 122–123
Pistoia, 243

Sant'Andrea della Valle church, 337

Sant'Angelo church, 284

Sant'Appollonia monastery, 234

Santa Rosa church, 358

Santa Scala, 344

Santa Scolastica monastery, 355

Santa Teresa di Gallura, 507–509

Sant'Eufemia church, 294

Sant'Ilario church, 295

Santi Maria e Donato church, 59

Santissima Annunziata church
Florence, 234
Sulmona, 364

Santo Spirito church, 236

Santo Stefano church, 183
Bologna, 183
Pisa, 252

Santuario della Madonnina, 462

Santuario dell'Annunziata, 472

Santuario di Santa Rosalia, 483

San Vincenzo e San Anastasio church, 304

San Vito, 74

San Vito lo Capo, 473–474

San Zeno Maggiore church, 71

Saracen Tower, 165

Sardagna, 82

Sardinia, 491–514

Sassari, 504–506

Sassello, 165–166

Savigliano, 145

Savoca, 452

Savonarola, Girolamo, 234

Scanno, 364–365

Sciacca, 468

Scicli, 465

Scuola di Merletti di Burano, 59

Scuola di San Giorgio degli Schiavoni, 55

Scuola Grande di San Rocco, 51

Segesta, 472–473

Selinunte, 470

Serrara Fontana, 393

Servas, 27

Sestola, 188

Shroud of Turin, 142–143

Sicily, 29, 31, 443–490

Siena, 6–7, 258–264

Sila Massif, 435–436

Siponto, 410

Siracusa, 459–462

Sirmione, 124–125

Sistiana, 96

Sistine Chapel, 342

Skiing, 79, 82, 87, 148, 152, 153, 188, 366

Solfatara Crater, 385

Sorrento, 394–396

Spanish Steps, 334

Spedale degli Innocenti, 234

Spoleto, 293–295

STA offices, 4

Statue of the Redeemer, 432

Stradivari, Antonio, 113, 115

Stresa, 131–132

Stromboli, 490

Student and teacher ID cards, 5

Student travel organizations, 1, 3

Studying in Italy, 19–20

Subiaco, 354–355

Sulmona, 364

Su Nuraxi, 498

Svevo, Italo, 92

Synagogues, 235, 252, 338

T

Taormina, 449–451

Taranto, 421–423

Tavole Palatine, 432

Teatro Classico Segesta, 473

Teatro Donizetti, 117

Teatro Farnese, 191

Teatro Greco, 449, 451

Teatro la Fenice, 54–55

Teatro Massimo, 482

Teatro Olimpico, 67

Teatro Romano
Aosta, 150
Fiesole, 240

Spoleto, *294*
Verona, *72*
Volterra, *258*
Teatro Romeo ed Odeon, *454*
Teatro Rossini, *301*
Teatro San Carlo, *383*
Telephone service, *24–25*
Tempietto Longobardo, *90*
Tempio church, *75*
Tempio di Serapide, *385*
Tempio Malatestiano, *207*
Temple of Apollo Licius, *432*
Temple of Ceres, *402*
Temple of Neptune, *402*
Terme di Nettuno, *357*
Termoli, *370*
Tevere Expo, *348*
Tharros, *500*
Theater, *351–352, 473, 483*
Theater buildings, *54–55, 67, 108, 301, 383, 482*
Theater of Marcellus, *330*
Tipping, *15*
Tivoli, *353–354*
Todi, *295–296*
Toiletries, *14*
Tomba di Dante, *200–201*
Tombe Brioni, *74*
Tomb of the Unknown Soldier, *332*
Torbiere Sebine, *127*
Torcello, *59–60*
Torino, *138–144*
Torralba, *506*
Torre Apponale, *126*
Torrechiara, *191*
Torre del Mangia, *262*
Torre del Popolo, *118*
Torre di San Giovanni, *500*
Torre Guinigi, *248*
Train travel, *18, 23*
passes, *8, 10–11*
Trapani, *470–472*
Traveler's checks, *11–12*
Tremezzo, *130*
Tremiti Islands, *415–416*
Trentino-Alto Adige, *29, 31, 77–89*
Trento, *79–82*
Trevi Fountain, *334*
Treviso, *75–76*
Triennale, the, *109*
Trieste, *92–96*

Trinitá dei Monti, *334*
Tritone, *332*
Trulli, *421*
Tuoro sui Trasimeno, *285*
Tuscany, *29, 31, 209, 245–276*
Tyrrhenian Coast, *484–490*

U
Udine, *89–90*
Uffizi Gallery, *228–229*
Umbria, *29, 31, 277–297*
Università di Bologna, *181*
University of Padova, *64*
Urbino, *298–300*
Ustica, *484*

V
Valle d'Aosta, *28, 135–138, 148–153*
Valle di Cogne, *151–152*
Valley of the Temples, *467*
Valsavarenche, *152–153*
Valuables, protecting, *15*
Vaneze, *82*
Varallo, *147*
Varenna, *130*
Vason, *82*
Vatican City, *339–342*
Veneto, the, *28–29, 60–75*
Venice, *7, 33–36*
campgrounds, *44*
Cannaregio, *51–52*
Castello, *55*
consulates, *35*
discount card, *36*
Dorsoduro, *53–54*
emergencies, *35, 36*
excursions, *59–60*
festivals, *56–57*
hostels, *43–44*
hotels, *41–43*
nightlife, *57–59*
Piazza San Marco, *47–50*
restaurants, *44–47*
San Marco, *54–55*
San Polo, *53*
Santa Croce, *52*
shopping, *57*
sightseeing, *47–56*
transportation, *37, 40–41*
weather, *6*
Ventimiglia, *168*
Verona, *68–72*

Vicenza, *66–67*
Vieste, *412–414*
Vignamaggio, *244–245*
Villa Adriana, *354*
Villa Aldobrandini, *352*
Villa Barbaro, *74*
Villa Bellini, *454–455*
Villa Carlotta, *130*
Villa of Catullus, *124*
Villa Corsini, *339*
Villa Cimbrone, *399*
Villa dei Mulini, *275*
Villa d'Este, *354*
Villa Farnesia, *339*
Villa Gregoriana, *354*
Villa Jovis, *391*
Villa Monastero, *130*
Villa Napoleonica, *275*
Villa Olmo, *129*
Villa Palagonia, *484*
Villa Romana, *456*
Villa Rotonda, *67*
Villa Rufolo, *399*
Villa San Michele, *391*
Villa Valmarana, *67*
Violin-making, *113*
Virgil, *122, 382, 424*
Visas, *7–8*
Viterbo, *358–359*
Vittorio Emanuele II monument, *332*
Vivano, *394*
Vogalonga festival, *143*
Volcanoes, *386, 387, 457–458, 487–488, 490*
Volgalonga, *56*
Volterra, *256–258*
Vulcano, *487–488*

W
Walser Museum, *147–148*
Weather, *6*
Well temple, *500*
Western Union, *12*
Wildlife preserves, *359–360*
Windsurfing, *126*
Wine, *29, 31*
Wineries, *273, 469*
Women travelers, *17*
Working in Italy, *19*
World War II sites, *95*

Z
Zone, *128*